About the author

Respected wine critic and vigneron James Halliday AM has a career that spans over forty years, but he is most widely known for his witty and informative writing about wine. As one of the founders of Brokenwood in the Lower Hunter Valley, New South Wales, and thereafter of Coldstream Hills in the Yarra Valley, Victoria, James is an unmatched authority on every aspect of the wine industry, from the planting and pruning of vines through to the creation and marketing of the finished product. His winemaking has led him to sojourns in Bordeaux and Burgundy, and he has had a long career as a wine judge in Australia and overseas. In 1995 he received the wine industry's ultimate accolade, the Maurice O'Shea Award. In 2010 James was made a Member of the Order of Australia.

James has written or contributed to more than 65 books on wine since he began writing in 1979. His books have been translated into Japanese, French, German, Danish, Icelandic and Polish, and have been published in the UK and the US, as well as in Australia. He is the author of *James Halliday's Wine Atlas of Australia* and *The Australian Wine Encyclopedia*.

ONE YEAR
WEBSITE AND MAGAZINE MEMBERSHIP
ONLY $39
(AUSTRALIAN RESIDENTS ONLY)

visit www.winecompanion.com.au/become-a-member

Enter unique code wcb2014 at checkout before 30th November 2013 to redeem this offer.

www.winecompanion.com.au

JAMES HALLIDAY AUSTRALIAN WINE COMPANION

2014 Edition

The bestselling and definitive
guide to Australian wine

hardie grant books

MELBOURNE · LONDON

Wine zones and regions of Australia

NEW SOUTH WALES			
WINE ZONE		WINE REGION	
Big Rivers	(A)	Murray Darling	1
		Perricoota	2
		Riverina	3
		Swan Hill	4
Central Ranges	(B)	Cowra	5
		Mudgee	6
		Orange	7
Hunter Valley	(C)	Hunter	8
		Upper Hunter	9
Northern Rivers	(D)	Hastings River	10
Northern Slopes	(E)	New England	11
South Coast	(F)	Shoalhaven Coast	12
		Southern Highlands	13
Southern New South Wales	(G)	Canberra District	14
		Gundagai	15
		Hilltops	16
		Tumbarumba	17
Western Plains	(H)		

SOUTH AUSTRALIA			
WINE ZONE		WINE REGION	
Adelaide Super Zone includes Mount Lofty Ranges, Fleurieu and Barossa wine regions			
Barossa		Barossa Valley	18
		Eden Valley	19
Fleurieu	(J)	Currency Creek	20
		Kangaroo Island	21
		Langhorne Creek	22
		McLaren Vale	23
		Southern Fleurieu	24
Mount Lofty Ranges		Adelaide Hills	25
		Adelaide Plains	26
		Clare Valley	27
Far North	(K)	Southern Flinders Ranges	28
Limestone Coast	(L)	Coonawarra	29
		Mount Benson	30
		Mount Gambier	31
		Padthaway	32
		Robe	33
		Wrattonbully	34
Lower Murray	(M)	Riverland	35
The Peninsulas	(N)	Southern Eyre Peninsula*	36

VICTORIA			
WINE ZONE		WINE REGION	
Central Victoria	(P)	Bendigo	37
		Goulburn Valley	38
		Heathcote	39
		Strathbogie Ranges	40
Gippsland	(Q)	Upper Goulburn	41
		Alpine Valleys	42
North East Victoria	(R)	Beechworth	43
		Glenrowan	44
		King Valley	45
		Rutherglen	46
North West Victoria	(S)	Murray Darling	47
		Swan Hill	48
Port Phillip	(T)	Geelong	49
		Macedon Ranges	50
		Mornington Peninsula	51
		Sunbury	52
		Yarra Valley	53
Western Victoria	(U)	Ballarat*	54
		Grampians	55
		Henty	56
		Pyrenees	57

* For more information see page 52.

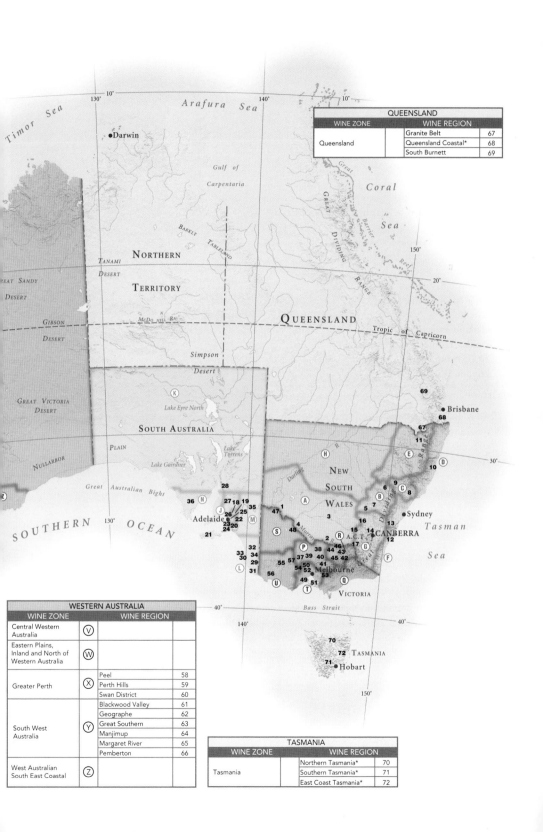

QUEENSLAND		
WINE ZONE	WINE REGION	
Queensland	Granite Belt	67
	Queensland Coastal*	68
	South Burnett	69

WESTERN AUSTRALIA		
WINE ZONE	WINE REGION	
Central Western Australia	Ⓥ	
Eastern Plains, Inland and North of Western Australia	Ⓦ	
Greater Perth	Ⓧ	Peel	58
		Perth Hills	59
		Swan District	60
South West Australia	Ⓨ	Blackwood Valley	61
		Geographe	62
		Great Southern	63
		Manjimup	64
		Margaret River	65
		Pemberton	66
West Australian South East Coastal	Ⓩ	

TASMANIA		
WINE ZONE	WINE REGION	
Tasmania	Northern Tasmania*	70
	Southern Tasmania*	71
	East Coast Tasmania*	72

Published in 2013 by Hardie Grant Books

Hardie Grant Books (Australia)
Ground Floor, Building 1
658 Church Street
Richmond, Victoria 3121
www.hardiegrant.com.au

Hardie Grant Books (UK)
Dudley House, North Suite
34–35 Southampton Street
London WC2E 7HF
www.hardiegrant.co.uk

The *Australian Wine Companion* is a joint venture between James Halliday and Explore Australia Pty Ltd.

ISBN 978 1 74270 539 2

Typeset by Megan Ellis
Cover design by Nada Backovic
Printed and bound in Australia by Ligare Book Printers

Contents

Introduction

The wine industry finds itself buffeted by stormy winds coming from within and without Australia, remarkable as much for their diversity as their strength.

On the domestic front, the two-speed economy has been discussed at great length by economists and politicians, but nothing explains to winemakers, wine retailers and/or restaurateurs why conditions should be so obstinately tough. Except, it must be said, unless it's Penfolds' best red wines, Hill of Grace and one or two others.

Of far greater concern is the barrage of misinformation and/or what seems to be highly suspect scientific pronouncements by those who see any form of alcohol consumption in any circumstances by any person as the source of all evil. Abuse of alcohol cannot be condoned, but how to control it is another matter.

The wine industry has historically taken the view that it was better to be part of a uniform group of beer, spirits and wine producers. The reasons were the risk of divide and (be) conquered, and the far greater financial resources of beer and spirit producers to fund lobbying and (the rapidly diminishing opportunity for) advertising.

It still hesitates to overtly disassociate itself from the beer/spirits group, but I believe it must do so. The first issue is binge drinking. Unfortunately for the neo-prohibitionists, cask wine is the preferred alcohol for 1.4% of 14–19-year-old binge drinkers, compared to 23% for beer and 44% for RTDs, the remainder spirits.

The next hot button is the utterly intimidating suggestion to pregnant women that the consumption of even a little wine may harm the health of their unborn child. Putting aside 500 years of consumption of wine across Europe with no statistically relevant harm to mothers with a healthy diet and lifestyle, there are two recent studies that should cause intelligent people to question the 'may harm' weasel language.

First, three academics at Oxford University's National Perinatal Epidemiology Unit reviewed 3543 papers published between 1970 and 2005, funded by the UK Department of Health. Their conclusion was, 'This systematic review found no convincing evidence of adverse effects of prenatal exposure at low–moderate levels of exposure.'

The second paper, from the International Journal of Obstetrics and Gynaecology, assessed whether light drinking – one glass per week – in pregnancy was linked to unfavourable developmental outcomes in seven-year-old children. The sample was made up of mothers who never drank, those who did drink but gave up during pregnancy, light drinkers, and those who drank more during pregnancy than otherwise. In all, 10 000 children were assessed. Those born to light-drinking mothers were found to have lower behavioural difficulty scores than those born to abstainers, and were also found to have more favourable cognitive test scores compared to children born to non-drinkers – especially in the case of reading and spatial skills in boys.

The external winds are the high Australian dollar, which has caused Australia's exports to collapse from the dizzy heights of $2.992 million for 12 months to June 2007 to $1.847 million for 12 months to March 2013.

In those days Australia's commercial wines were of better quality than, and were significantly cheaper than equivalent wines from the south of France, South Africa and Italy. That period also coincided with a weak Australian dollar, not far short of half its present value. Quite apart from currency issues, the quality of our competitors' wines has markedly improved thanks in no small measure to the lessons taught by Australian Flying Winemakers in northern hemisphere countries.

This has led to (an arguably delayed) recognition that Australia should refocus its export efforts on its best wines, not its next best. This in turn led to the 'Regional Heroes' and 'Australia Plus' promotions by Wine Australia. Southcorp/Wolf Blass/ Foster's/Treasury Wine Estates (as the corporate succession plan for the group evolved) was the first to fully embrace the value of regional brands, followed by Hardys/ Constellation/Accolade, Orlando/Jacob's Creek the last to move, Lion Nathan's brand portfolio largely region-based at the time each producer was acquired.

Wither now? Clearly, a healthy industry depends on export growth at margins that deliver profits sufficient to provide working capital to sustain growth. The UK is beset with broad-based economic problems, automatic indexed duty increases fixed at 2% in excess of the CPI, and the death grip the supermarket chains have on prices and margins. Niche opportunities exist, but finding them is another matter.

The US is likewise no bed of roses; while duty increases and supermarket power are not issues, it is a very competitive market, and the image of Australian wine is largely cast in the image of the (until recently) extraordinary success of yellowtail.

All of which leaves China (PRC) as the very large elephant in the room. There is no question some of the runaway success stories of today will end in tears as there is not enough detailed knowledge of the end use of Australian wine. But Australia has been an active player in the market for over five years, and if one only looked at the volume of overall trade ties between the two countries you would have no doubt about the long-term viability of the wine trade. Factor in the rapid growth of the number of seriously wealthy Chinese and the rapidly increasing inbound tourism to Australia of Chinese nationals, and the future looks even more secure.

The statistics are imposing. For the 12 months ending March 2013, PRC imported three times as much as the UK, and 1.8 times as much as the US, of bottled white and red wines priced at $5 a litre or more. If you look only at $10 or more per litre of bottled wine, the figures are even more stark: PRC imports 30% of the total, the US 9.75% and the UK 5.6%. At the other end of the scale, PRC is the ninth-largest destination for bulk wine, ranking behind minnows such as Denmark, The Netherlands and Belgium, and the leader of the pack, the UK. Put another way, PRC accounts for 1.4% of Australia's bulk wine exports.

Finally, the average price per litre of all wine imported by PRC from Australia is $6.52, twice as much as the US ($3.26). Hong Kong weighs in with a staggering $10.36 per litre, thanks largely to Penfolds. The tendency is to talk about the potential of the PRC/Hong Kong markets (they are Siamese twins); I am as guilty as anyone in the use of the term, but if you combine the share of those two destinations, they are already in clear second place with a fraction under $300 million, fast closing the gap behind market leader, the US, with $387 million.

How to use this book

Wineries

Penfolds   ★★★★★

Tanunda Road, Nuriootpa, SA 5355 **Region** Barossa Valley
T (08) 8568 9408 **www.**penfolds.com **Open** 7 days 10-5
Winemaker Peter Gago **Est.** 1844 **Dozens** NFP

Penfolds is the star in the crown of Treasury Wine Estates (TWE), but its history predates the formation of TWE by close on 170 years. Over that period its shape has changed both in terms of its vineyards, its management, its passing parade of great winemakers, and its wines. There is no other single winery brand in the new, or the old, world with the depth and breadth of Penfolds. In 2013 the retail prices ranged from $18 to $785 for Grange, which is the cornerstone produced every year, albeit with the volume determined by the quality of the vintage, not by cash flow. There is now a range of regional wines with single varieties, and the so-called Bin Range of wines that include both regional blends and (in some instances) varietal blends. It may sound complicated, but given the size of the business, and the long-term history of the Bins (the oldest dating back to the early 1960s) it is not as difficult as one might imagine to understand the winemaking and commercial rationale. Despite the very successful Yattarna and Reserve Bin A Chardonnays, and some impressive Rieslings, this remains a red wine producer at heart. Exports to all major markets.

Winery name Penfolds

Although it might seem that stating the winery name is straightforward, this is not necessarily so. To avoid confusion, wherever possible I use the name that appears most prominently on the front label of the wine.

Winery rating ★★★★★

The effort to come up with a fair winery rating system continues. As last year, I looked at the ratings for this and the previous two years; if the wines tasted this year justified a higher rating than last year, that higher rating has been given. If, on the other hand, the wines are of lesser quality, I took into account the track record over the past two years (or longer where the winery is well known) and made a judgement call on whether it should retain its ranking, or be given a lesser one. Where no wines were submitted by a well-rated winery which had a track record of providing samples, I used my discretion to roll over last year's rating.

While there are (only) 1396 wineries profiled in this edition there are more than 2760 wineries to be found on www.winecompanion.com.au.

The precise meanings attached to the winery star rating follows hereunder. Three caveats: first, I retain a discretionary right to depart from the normal criteria. Second, the basis of the rating will best be understood on the website, where all wine ratings appear. Third a special factor for this edition was the rain-sodden 2011 vintage that so affected Victoria and South Australia; I have not downgraded any winery that either didn't make wines in that vintage, or released red wines that were below the normal standard of the winery in question.

★★★★★   Outstanding winery regularly producing wines of exemplary quality and typicity. Will have at least two wines rated at 94 points or above, and had a five-star rating for the previous two years.
Where the winery name itself is printed in red, it is a winery generally acknowledged to have a long track record of excellence – truly the best of the best.

★★★★★   Outstanding winery capable of producing wines of very high quality, and did so this year. Also will usually have at least two wines rated at 94 points or above.

★★★★☆   Excellent winery able to produce wines of high to very high quality, knocking on the door of a 5-star rating. Will normally have one wine rated at 94 points or above, and two (or more) at 90 or above, others 87–89.

★★★★   Very good producer of wines with class and character. Will have two (or more) wines rated at 90 points or above (or possibly one at 94 and above).

★★★☆   A solid, usually reliable, maker of good, sometimes very good wines. Will have one wine at 90 points and above, others 87–89.

★★★   A typically good winery, but often has a few lesser wines. Will have wines at 87–89 points.

NR   The NR rating mainly appears on www.winecompanion.com.au. The rating is given in a range of circumstances: where there have been no tastings in the 12-month period; where there have been tastings, but with no wines scoring more than 86 points; or where the tastings have, for one reason or another, proved not to fairly reflect the reputation of a winery with a track record of success. NR wineries in the book are generally new wineries with no wine entries.

Contact Details Tanunda Road, Nuriootpa, SA 5355 **T** (08) 8568 9408

The details are usually those of the winery and cellar door, but in a few instances may simply be a postal address; this occurs when the wine is made at another winery or wineries, and is sold only through the website and/or retail.

Region Barossa Valley

A full list of Zones, Regions and Subregions appears on pages 52 to 55. Occasionally you will see 'Various' as the region. This means the wine is made from purchased grapes, from a number of regions, often a winery without a vineyard of its own.

www.penfolds.com

An important reference point, often containing material not found (for space reasons) in this book.

Open 7 days 10–5

Although a winery might be listed as not open or only open on weekends, some may in fact be prepared to open by appointment. Many will, some won't; a telephone call will establish whether it is possible or not.

Winemaker Peter Gago

In all but the smallest producers, the winemaker is simply the head of a team; there may be many executive winemakers actually responsible for specific wines in the medium to large companies (80 000 dozens and upwards)

Est. 1844

Keep in mind that some makers consider the year in which they purchased the land to be the year of establishment, others the year in which they first planted grapes, others the year they first made wine, and so on. There may also be minor complications where there has been a change of ownership or break in production.

Vyds

Shows the hectares of vineyard/s owned by the winery.

Dozens NFP

This figure (representing the number of 9-litre (12-bottle) cases produced each year) is merely an indication of the size of the operation. Some winery entries do not feature a production figure: this is either because the winery (principally, but not exclusively, the large companies) regards this information as confidential.

Summary Penfolds is the star in the crown of Treasury Wine Estates (TWE), but its history predates the formation of TWE by close to 170 years. Over that period its shape has changed both in terms of its vineyards, its management ...

My summary of the winery. Little needs to be said, except that I have tried to vary the subjects I discuss in this part of the winery entry.

New wineries

 The vine leaf symbol indicates the 94 wineries that are new entries in this year's *Wine Companion*.

Tasting notes

The overall meanings to the points and the glass symbols remain the same as in previous years, and appear below. However, space constraints in this edition have forced what may appear to be some arbitrary decisions. Despite protracted attempts to come up with identical criteria for all wineries' tasting notes and scores vying for inclusion, the combination of the possible glass rating groups and the number of wines falling within each rating group, has made it impossible to create an algorithm to govern the inclusion or exclusion of each and every wine. However, tasting notes for all wines receiving 84 points or above do appear on www.winecompanion.com.au.

Ratings		
94–100	♟♟♟♟♟	**Outstanding.** Wines of the highest quality, often with a distinguished pedigree.
90–93	♟♟♟♟♟	**Highly recommended.** Wines of great quality, style and character, worthy of a place in any cellar.
87–89	♟♟♟♟	**Recommended.** Wines of above-average quality, fault-free, and with clear varietal expression.
87–97	✪	**Special value.** Wines considered to offer special value for money.
84–86	♟♟♟♟	**Acceptable.** Wines of fair commercial quality, free of any significant fault.
80–83	♟♟♟	**Over to you.** Everyday wines, usually cheap and with little or no future, needing more character and flavour.
75–79	♟♟♟	**Not recommended.** Wines with one or more significant winemaking faults.

♟♟♟♟♟ Grange 2008 The wine contains 98/2% shiraz and cabernet sauvignon, and spent 19 months in new American oak hogsheads in which it finished its fermentation. Densely coloured, it has an ultra-complex bouquet, with black fruits/anise/licorice, easily dealing with the oak; a remarkable wine in every way. The balance, texture and structure are faultless, so much so that the wine achieves elegance now, many years before you would expect that quality to be commented on. Cork. 14.3% alc. **Rating** 98 **To** 2060 $785

The tasting note opens with the vintage of the wine tasted. This tasting note will have been made within the 12 months prior to publication. Even that is a long time, and during the life of this book the wine will almost certainly change. More than this, remember the tasting is a highly subjective and imperfect art. The price of the wine is listed where information is available. Tasting notes for wines 94 points and over are printed in red.

Where the initials BE or TS appear at the end of a tasting note, this signifies that Ben Edwards or Tyson Stelzer tasted the wine and provided the tasting note and rating.

To 2060

Rather than give a span of drinking years, I have simply provided a (conservative) 'drink to' date. Modern winemaking is such that, even if a wine has 10 or 20 years' future during which it will gain greater complexity, it can be enjoyed at any time over the intervening months and years.

Cork

This is the closure used for this particular wine. The closures in use for the wines tasted are (in descending order): screwcap 91% (last year 87%), one-piece natural cork 4.8% (last year 7%), Diam 3.2% (last year 5%). The remaining 1.1% (in approximate order of importance) are ProCork, Twin Top, Crown Seal, Zork and Vino-Lok. I believe the percentage of screwcap-closed wines will continue to rise for red wines; 96.2% of white wines tasted are screwcapped, leaving little room for any further increase.

14.3% alc

As with closures, I have endeavoured to always include this piece of information, which is in one sense self-explanatory. What is less obvious is the increasing concern of many Australian winemakers about the rise in levels of alcohol, and much research and practical experiment (picking earlier, higher fermentation temperatures in open fermenters, etc) is occurring. Reverse osmosis and yeast selection are two of the options available to decrease higher than desirable alcohol levels. Recent changes to domestic and export labelling mean the stated alcohol will be within a maximum of 0.5% of that obtained by analysis.

$785

I use the price provided by the winery (rounded up to the nearest dollar). It should be regarded as a guide, particularly if purchased retail.

LANGTON'S

FINE WINES SINCE 1988

AUCTION **BROKERAGE** **WINE STORE**

langtons.com.au

Australian vintage 2013: a snapshot

As every year, there is much conjecture about the size of the crush, but official figures are not available at the time of going to print. By the time the book is published, winecompanion.com.au will have the information, but at this stage it seems the engine rooms of the Riverina and Murray Darling will counterbalance the reduced tonnages in many of the eastern states' fine wine regions. This reduction was due to poor weather (stormy) during flowering, followed by a hot, dry summer. This summer weather meant there was very little disease, and many very good wines will be made.

SOUTH AUSTRALIA

The repeating refrain was the vines' demand for water following a dry winter; as one winemaker said, 'If you waited for the spring rains (which didn't arrive) it was already too late to irrigate.' It had to commence in winter (as they do in the Hunter Valley) failing which the yield was significantly reduced. Another maker tersely said, 'I irrigated like never before' and was one of the very few to enjoy above-average yields. The cool **Adelaide Hills** was no exception; by mid-September rainfall had virtually ceased, and from this point on daytime temperatures were higher than normal, tempered by cool nights. Two brief heat spikes prior to the beginning of March compressed the vintage, with all varieties ripening hot on the heels of each other. Vine and fruit condition was nonetheless excellent – one description was 'best ever' fruit composition. The hot **Adelaide Plains** did not dodge the bullet of very low rainfall and a generally hot growing season; yields were down by up to 30%, but the small berries and bunches produced above-average shiraz, merlot and sangiovese. The **Barossa Valley** had the driest November since 1967, but ideal temperatures throughout January and February (plus low yields) promoted berry flavour development and even ripening. Grenache and shiraz were the standouts for adequately watered vineyards; in others, the berries were so small the crop was not harvested. **Coonawarra**'s growing season rainfall was 25% of long term average which impacted adversely, as did the hotter than average temperatures. Cabernet sauvignon, merlot, cabernet franc and petit verdot have all been nominated as particularly successful in the context of medium body, plenty of tannins and excellent colour. The **Eden Valley** provided more of the same, with one pun mistress referring to winter, spring and summer as the 'dryfecta'. Irrigation was a godsend for those who had it, marking the difference between a below-average crop and none at all. The irony was that January and February had very good growing conditions, with only a few hot spikes. Riesling and shiraz will both be very good at least, and maybe better still. **Kangaroo Island** hit the winter jackpot with heavy winter rains (350mm) filling tanks and dams, but then it disappeared. The dry and hot weather that followed meant there was no disease pressure at all; standout varieties were semillon, viognier and grenache. **Langhorne Creek** had good winter and early spring rains. January was warm and dry, but cool nights helped retention of acidity. February saw warmer nights, and picking began on February 7. While all the red varieties are good to very good, they looked like blend components rather than stand-alones as in 2012. **McLaren Vale**, too, had above-average winter and early spring rains. Short periods of heat alternating with cooler days and nights led to a stop-start-stop pattern, with irrigation an important tool; grenache and cabernet sauvignon fared best, with deep colour, and a certain restraint and elegance. Overall yields were down 10% to 20%. **Mount Benson** and **Robe** had slightly above average winter rainfall, grading to average in spring. The dry summer meant no disease problems, but to find sauvignon blanc was the standout variety was unexpected; the red wines are deeply coloured, and quite robust, though not having the elegance of '12. **Padthaway**'s growing season was no different, chardonnay and shiraz the best of the best. **Southern Fleurieu** saw the rain disappear in October, making irrigation imperative. For those with adequate water the heat spikes of the first three months caused little damage, and the best quantity and quality vintage for both white and red wines since '09 was the outcome. **Wrattonbully** had a near-magical vintage, with good winter rainfall, grading to half normal in spring and drier still in summer. In a year that will rank as close to the best in Wrattonbully's brief history, sauvignon blanc and pinot gris were the best whites, cabernet sauvignon and shiraz the standout reds, just in front of the ever-excellent tempranillo and merlot.

VICTORIA

The east coast pattern of a wet winter and/or spring and a dry, warm-to-hot summer prevailed across most of Victoria. A dry winter in the **Alpine Valleys** led into mild conditions and then 10 days above 35°C in early January. Provided adequate water was available and used, vintage was largely completed before Easter, with perfectly ripened shiraz and merlot the standouts. Fortuitously, for **Beechworth**, dams were full by spring, because only 110mm of rain fell between October '12 and March '13, and temperatures over summer were high, absence of disease the good news. Even better is the overall excellence of both white and red wines. For **Bendigo** it was more of the same, with irrigation essential. Shiraz and cabernet sauvignon seemed to have done best, but some elevated alcohol levels may take the gloss off. **Glenrowan** provides a near-identical story, with no rain after October, the days hot, the evenings warm. Standout varieties are shiraz and muscat. The **Grampians** did not break ranks, with a growing season that from veraison onwards simply got hotter and hotter until the last week of March. However, the absence of disease led to an outcome better than '12, with shiraz having excellent acid/fruit ripeness balance. **Heathcote** fared well, even though spring rainfall was only one-third of the long-term average. The summer was dry, warm but not extreme; red wines clearly lead the field, with extremely good colours, high natural acidity and bright flavours. Shiraz yielded very well without diminishing its quality. The **Mornington Peninsula** had good winter rains, and the mild January and early February conditions, followed by a warm spell in mid-February, accelerated ripening and the heatwave in March led to a very compressed vintage. Chardonnay has very good flavours, while pinot noir has great colour, flavour and balance. Shiraz, too, promises to be excellent. The hot and dry conditions in the **Murray Darling** placed maximum reliance on efficient and effective irrigation, and made the difference between good and not so good grapes.

The extreme heat meant a red wine vintage, and even though shiraz was somewhat disappointing, cabernet sauvignon and merlot fared very well, tempranillo and malbec close behind. **Nagambie Lakes** did especially well with rainfall which continued through to December. Dry and warm to hot weather resulted in an early vintage, but marsanne (and even riesling) stood up well, shiraz and cabernet sauvignon good to excellent. The **Pyrenees** saw more of the same, dry and warm to hot weather leading to accelerated ripening. For some, flavour ripeness lagged behind sugar accumulation, with elevated alcohol for fully flavoured ripe shiraz and cabernet sauvignon a consequence. In the **Strathbogie Ranges**, some started irrigating two months early in October, and one reporter used 'a new clay-based vine sunscreen' for the foliage, with excellent results. The star of the vintage is shiraz, described as 'varying degrees of outstanding'. The weather pattern in **Sunbury** was identical to other regions around Melbourne, the outcome good for early-picked whites, and better still for red wines with good pH/acid/baume balance, excellent colour the result. The **Yarra Valley** had sufficient winter and spring rainfall to fill most dams, and the growing season warmth through December, January and February was close to ideal, with a few heat spikes that did not persist. However, there was virtually no rain over January and February, and March arrived with a near-unprecedented period of temperatures over 30°C. The only explanation for the exceptionally good outcome for heat-intolerant varieties such as pinot noir is that there was little wind to accompany the heat, and the nights were not particularly warm. Yields are down, but it will be an excellent to outstanding year for pinot noir, shiraz, merlot and cabernet sauvignon, all deeply coloured. The only question mark hangs over the chardonnay, but – at the very least – it will be good.

NEW SOUTH WALES

There was little consistency in the growing season weather conditions, some regions reporting a great vintage, but most called upon to deal with alternating periods of extreme heat and heavy rainfall. Success or failure was determined in the vineyard, those that were well managed paying big dividends. The **Hunter Valley** had a dry winter and even drier spring, continuing through to the early part of January, leading to lighter canopies to go with the smaller crop. The dry, hot weather intensified through January, culminating in a record temperature of 45.7°C in Sydney. Most of the semillon was picked before 150mm of rain fell on Australia Day, the quality outstanding. A week of dry weather saw the shiraz harvest completed by February 17. Excellent colour, tannin and sugar levels were recorded, low yields the only concern. **Canberra District** had good late winter/spring rain, but Hunter Valley-like alternating heat and rain caused anxiety until vintage started in February/early March with perfect cool nights and dry, warm days. Riesling has been the standout white variety; the red wines are excellent with rich flavours and excellent colour. In the **Hilltops**, good winter and spring rainfall filled the soil profile and dams. But it stopped by mid-October; thereafter warm daytime temperatures, cool nights and no rainfall laid the base for an extremely good vintage, with great balance of flavour, sugar and phenolic ripeness. The standout varieties were riesling, semillon, shiraz and cabernet sauvignon. **Tumbarumba** proceeded in lockstep with Hilltops, chardonnay the standout variety. For **Orange**, it was a case of the glass half full or the glass half empty. The winter and spring rainfall was 30% to 40% lower than average. Thereafter warm to hot spells alternated between significant rain events, the impact depending on altitude, crop levels, and vineyard management; downy mildew and botrytis affected some vineyards. Others produced excellent grapes. Chardonnay and shiraz were the best varieties for most, others singling out riesling and cabernet sauvignon. The '13 growing season in the **Southern Highlands** started with typical winter and spring rainfall, some snow in spring decidedly unusual. Overall, the growing season was warmer than usual; the Australia Day rainfall of 150mm fell while the grapes were still immature and high in acid; subsequent short periods of rain were offset by generally warm and dry conditions. Chardonnay and pinot noir dedicated for sparkling wine were superb, and those two varieties (and sauvignon blanc) for table wine will be very good. The **Shoalhaven Coast** shared the east coast weather pattern. The best varieties were semillon, chardonnay and tempranillo, the volumes much-reduced than normal. The **Riverina** followed established patterns, with a dry winter and early spring. Unrelenting heat through January (five days over 40°C) slowed ripening by about a week. The star varieties are shiraz and durif, chardonnay and (surprisingly) sauvignon blanc proving to be the best white varieties. Finally, **New England** was a case of the glass totally empty, with no less than four well known vineyards electing not to pick any of their fruit, following alternating periods of rain and heat. For those who managed to dodge the bullet, barbera, tannat, tempranillo and nebbiolo are the picks.

WESTERN AUSTRALIA

As ever, the weather across the state presented few challenges to vignerons, resulting in excellent white and red wines. Winter/spring rainfall in the **Margaret River** was less than average, the biggest downpour of around 250mm in June. A significant weather event in late October/early November brought 100km winds and hail, which affected flowering, followed by more wild weather in early December, cumulatively resulting in significant crop losses (up to 40% down). January and February were hot and dry until the middle of March, the white varieties already long-harvested; the red vintage started in March, but light, drizzly rain delayed the completion for some growers. Chardonnay is regarded by all as outstanding, sauvignon blanc and semillon also very good; the biggest success was cabernet sauvignon picked before the rain. Conditions prevailed across the Great Southern, **Denmark**, **Porongurup**, **Mount Barker** and **Frankland**, had winter rainfall well below average, and November rain and wind disrupted flowering and fruit-set, resulting in much-reduced yields. A hot week in early January was followed by mild and dry conditions through to early March. These resulted in excellent whites (riesling and chardonnay outstanding) but then overcast and significant rain across all of the regions delayed ripening of the red varieties, but the ever-reliable, thick-skinned cabernet sauvignon will be very good. The growing season for **Geographe** had many similarities, except for a fairly dry winter, followed by good rains during spring. Then it was more of the same, with storms and hail at flowering significantly reducing yields. Summer was hot and dry, resulting in rapid ripening of the white wines with baume levels elevated above ideal. The mild March which followed resulted in outstanding shiraz and cabernet sauvignon, and, overall, it was a red wine vintage. The rainfall pattern of **Manjimup** was the same as that of Geographe, but continuing rain events were beneficial. Early intake was compressed due to consistent mild to hot weather through to mid March, whereafter ripening slowed down dramatically. The standout varieties were sauvignon blanc, semillon, chardonnay and pinot noir, the late-ripening reds also good. The dry winter/wet spring pattern continued in **Pemberton**, warmer than average temperatures prevailing through December, January and February, but the dry conditions resulted in full-flavoured, disease-free riesling, sauvignon blanc and pinot noir. **Peel** avoided the extreme heat of Perth, with a milder start to the growing season than for the preceding three or four years, contributing to the development of flavour. The harvest period itself was warm to hot, but not extreme. Shiraz, cabernet sauvignon and verdelho were all excellent, the fruit disease-free, clean, uniform and fully-ripened. Good winter and spring rainfall in the **Perth Hills** proved crucial with the arrival of the hottest summer on record, the earliest vintage on record, and dry growing conditions. Standout varieties were petit verdot, viognier and shiraz.

TASMANIA

Winter/spring rainfall in **Northern Tasmania** was well below average, and two-thirds of it fell early in spring. The result was a warmer and drier than average summer, beneficial from a disease control point of view, and a little rain just prior to vintage slowed the start to harvest. Overall, it was a vintage with a return to normality, with the largest crop since 2008. There is abundant flavour, and the warmer weather resulted in a perfect acid/baume ratio for the region. The most successful varieties are gewurztraminer, pinot noir, pinot gris and sauvignon blanc. In **Southern Tasmania** winter started with rainfall and climate conditions close to average, but as the season progressed, increasingly warm and dry weather culminated in all-time record high temperatures in early January and accompanying bushfires in many of the state's grapegrowing regions. Fortunately, the timing, with most grapes yet to soften, meant that no areas appear to have suffered the destructive effects of smoke taint. The warm spring conditions encouraged good fruit-set and above-average yields. Thus, despite ongoing above average temperatures through February and March, the start to vintage was not especially early and harvest proceeded steadily, with little disease pressure. Indications are of a good quality year, but with lower levels of natural acidity than are typical for Tasmania.

QUEENSLAND

The **Granite Belt** had the perfect start to vintage with a dryish winter and spring. Spring and summer were warm and dry until late January when heavy rain fell, delaying vintage, and February and early March remained wet, cool and cloudy. Those who were able to control disease then benefited from dry weather throughout the second half of March. Barbera, cabernet sauvignon, merlot and tannat were the most successful red wines, white wine quality even across all varieties. **South Burnett** had two vintages, the first a hot and dry summer leading to all white grapes being picked in perfect condition before 300mm of rain fell on Australia Day, the rain continuing as winemakers struggled to pick red varieties in acceptable condition.

The Perfect Storage Companions

Love entertaining? When it comes to storing wine and beverages Liebherr offers the perfect storage companions for every entertainment area.

The dual zone wine cellar has two independently controlled zones that can each be adjusted to a precise temperature between +5°C and +20°C, meaning red & white wines can be stored in the same appliance both at their ideal serving temperature. The single zone beverage centre can be set as low as +2°C to chill beer, soft drink and juices. Interior lighting also makes it easy to locate your drink of choice.

Email www.premiumapp.com.au or call 1800 685 899 now for more information and your nearest stockist.

www.premiumapp.com.au

LIEBHERR

Quality, Design and Innovation

Winery of the year

Penfolds

Penfolds is Australia's foremost winemaker, with an unbroken line dating back to its establishment in 1844 when medical practitioner Dr Christopher Rawson Penfold and wife Mary purchased 'the delightfully situated and truly valuable of Mackgill … Comprising 500 acres (202 hectares) of the choicest land'. Here they built the house that still stands today, and within a few years had begun the winery and cellar on the site of today's buildings at Magill Estate.

Mary took charge of winemaking, initially producing grenache prescribed by her husband as a tonic for anaemic patients. By 1870 she, son-in-law Thomas Hyland and cellar manager/winemaker Joseph Gillard had formed Penfolds & Co. With markets in South Australia, Victoria and New South Wales, their wine production was over one-third of South Australia's total.

Growth continued unabated, and in 1945 Penfolds acquired the jewel of the Magill Vineyard, at that time the largest vineyard in South Australia. It now has 2100 hectares of vineyards, the largest share of Australia's total. Two men came together in the 1950s to lay the foundation of Penfolds today: winemaker Max Schubert, and research chemist Ray Beckwith (who died shortly after his 100th birthday in 2012); indeed, their contribution transcended Penfolds to the entire Australian wine industry.

The architecture for the Penfolds wine portfolio of the twenty-first century was established in the 1960s, half a century ago. There has been growth, both in the range of labels and their price points, but it has been cleverly – indeed sensitively – managed; demand-driven growth has been achieved without any quality compromise whatsoever.

There is no possibility that the pre-eminence of Penfolds will ever be challenged by any other Australian wine business. Equally certain is that the Penfolds brand value will continue to gain ground on the world stage of all consumable products. If proof be needed, the overall quality of the wines in this *Wine Companion* is the best Penfolds has ever presented to the markets of the globe.

Previous wineries obtaining 'Winery of the Year' are Paringa Estate (2007), Balnaves of Coonawarra (2008), Brookland Valley (2009), Tyrrell's (2010), Larry Cherubino Wines (2011), Port Phillip Estate/Kooyong (2012) and Kilikanoon (2013).

Wine of the year

Bass Phillip Reserve Pinot Noir 2010

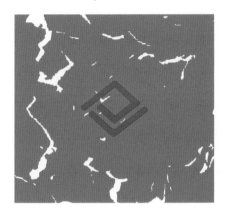

The first Bass Phillip pinot noir was made in 1984, but it was not until 1989 that Phillip Jones put in place a three-tiered structure with Reserve at the top, then Premium, and Estate as the basic release – one which most pinot noir makers in Australia would love to have as their top wine.

The three-tier structure was based on multiple small plot fermentation trials over the 1984 to 1989 vintages, and is thus terroir-based. But even here it is vintage dependent: since 1989, Reserve was not made in 1990, 1992, 2002, 2006 and 2011.

The soil is free-draining, deep and mineral rich, promoting vigorous growth, which gives rise to challenging management issues exacerbated by the ultra close spacing of 9000 vines per hectare (compared to the average of 2000 in Australia). The high rainfall and humidity (similar to Burgundy) increases fungal disease pressure during the peak of the growing season, alleviated by the usually sunny and balmy conditions of late summer and early autumn.

Thanks to inter-vine competition, a naturally balanced cropping level of 2.5–3.2 tonnes per hectare, or a third of a kilo of grapes per vine from a handful of small bunches. Management is biodynamic, an approach that demands ceaseless attention to detail, and vine-by-vine management with leaf and shoot thinning.

The pinot noirs are destemmed, open fermented, and hand plunged, with pumping kept to a bare minimum. The whole approach in the winery is non-interventionist; fining agents are never used, nor are acid or tannins added, and the fermentation temperatures are allowed to run their natural course. The oak is 100% new (only one or two barriques are required each year) and is lightly toasted, very tight grain Allier oak made by Francois Frere. Finally, the wines are not filtered.

They are, however, made to cellar well, with a minimum of six years (and up to 20 years) in which to spread their wings – or, in Burgundian terms, their peacock's tails. As at 2013 Phillip Jones says the '85, '88 and '89 are currently magnificent.

The unique quality of the Reserve wines is strictly a reflection of the minute piece of vineyard that they come from, and a strict regime of hygiene in the winery. Even in the blessed '10 vintage only 50 dozen bottles were made (the maximum volume) from the single small plot; as little as 25 dozen are made in some years.

Best of the best wines

I make my usual disclaimer: while there are two periods of intense tasting activity in the 12 months during which the tasting notes for this edition were made, and while some wines are tasted more than once, an over-arching comparative tasting of all the best wines is simply not possible, however desirable it might be.

So the points for each individual wine scoring stand uncorrected by the wisdom of hindsight. Nonetheless, the link between variety and region (or, if you prefer, between variety and terroir) is in most instances strikingly evident. It is for this reason that I have shown the region for each of the best wines. Medium- and longer-term prosperity will depend on a sense of place, of regional identity. It is also the reason for the overview of the varietal/regional mosaic (page 56).

Best of the best by variety

Riesling

Riesling has undergone the most dramatic change in the geographic origin of any varietal group in the history of the *Wine Companion*; 16 of the wines come from the Great Southern, only nine from the Clare and Eden Valleys. (I have used Great Southern as the region of origin, rather than one or more of its subregions.) I'm not sure whether the utterly unexpected – and overwhelming – dominance of Great Southern will be repeated in the years ahead, but it will give indigestion to the great names in the Clare and Eden Valleys in the short term.

RATING	WINE	REGION
97	2012 Grosset Polish Hill	Clare Valley
97	2011 Castle Rock Estate A&W Reserve	Great Southern
97	2012 Cherubino Porongurup	Great Southern
96	2012 Mt Lofty Ranges Lenswood	Adelaide Hills
96	2012 Petaluma Hanlin Hill	Clare Valley
96	2012 Sons of Eden Freya	Eden Valley
96	2012 Clonakilla	Canberra District
96	2012 Helm Premium	Canberra District
96	2012 Atlas 172° Watervale	Clare Valley
96	2012 Knappstein Hand Picked	Clare Valley
96	2008 Leasingham Classic Clare	Clare Valley
96	2012 Pikes The Merle	Clare Valley
96	2012 Taylors St Andrews Single Vineyard Release	Clare Valley
96	2012 Radford Bio-Dynamically Grown	Eden Valley
96	2012 Castle Rock Estate	Great Southern
96	2012 Cherubino Laissez Faire	Great Southern
96	2012 Duke's Vineyard Magpie Hill Reserve	Great Southern
96	2012 Duke's Vineyard Single Vineyard Porongurup	Great Southern
96	2012 Forest Hill Vineyard Block 1 Mount Barker	Great Southern
96	2012 Frankland Estate Isolation Ridge Vineyard	Great Southern
96	2012 Harewood Estate Reserve	Great Southern
96	2012 Howard Park	Great Southern
96	2012 Howard Park Porongurup	Great Southern
96	2012 Kerrigan + Berry Mt Barker	Great Southern
96	2012 Lamont's Hand Picked Frankland	Great Southern
96	2012 Plantagenet Mount Barker	Great Southern
96	2012 Trevelen Farm	Great Southern
96	2012 West Cape Howe Mount Barker	Great Southern
96	2012 Pooley Coal River	Tasmania

Chardonnay

Chardonnay is a marvelously flexible variety, performing well almost everywhere it is grown. But two regions stand apart: Margaret River with its 15 wines with 96 points and above and the lion's share of the 97–point wines, and the Yarra Valley with 12 such wines. Three regions (Geelong, Mornington Peninsula and Tasmania) contributed five wines each. It is now beyond doubt that modern Australian Chardonnay is our best varietal wine.

RATING	WINE	REGION
98	2011 Giaconda	Beechworth
97	2010 Bannockburn	Geelong
97	2010 Cullen Kevin John	Margaret River
97	2009 Devil's Lair 9th Chamber	Margaret River
97	2009 Leeuwin Estate Art Series	Margaret River
97	2010 Vasse Felix Heytesbury	Margaret River
97	2010 Xanadu Reserve	Margaret River
97	2009 Penfolds Yattarna	Tasmania/ Adelaide Hills
97	2011 Toolangi Vineyards Block F	Yarra Valley
97	2010 Toolangi Vineyards Reserve	Yarra Valley

96 points

Adelaide Hills: 2010 Geoff Weaver Lenswood, 2010 Grosset Piccadilly, 2010 Penfolds Reserve Bin A, 2012 Shaw + Smith M3. **Beechworth:** 2011 Brokenwood Indigo Vineyard, 2010 Golden Ball là-bas. **Eden Valley:** 2011 Mountadam High Eden Estate. **Geelong:** 2010 Bannockburn Vineyards S.R.H., 2009 Bannockburn Vineyards S.R.H., 2011 By Farr Geelong, 2011 Leura Park Estate Limited Release Block 1 Reserve. **Gippsland:** 2011 Bass Phillip Premium, 2010 Bass Phillip Premium. **Great Southern:** 2010 Castle Rock Estate Diletti, 2011 Marchand & Burch Porongurup, 2011 Singlefile Family Reserve Denmark. **Macedon Ranges:** 2011 Bindi Composition. **Margaret River:** 2012 Fraser Gallop Estate Parterre Wilyabrup, 2011 Pierro, 2010 Robert Oatley Finisterre, 2010 Robert Oatley The Pennant, 2010 Streicker Ironstone Block Old Vine, 2011 Vasse Felix Heytesbury, 2010 Victory Point, 2010 Voyager Estate, 2009 Voyager Estate Project 95, 2011 Xanadu Reserve. **Mornington Peninsula:** 2011 Crittenden Estate The Zumma, 2011 Dexter, 2011 Kooyong Estate, 2011 Main Ridge Estate, 2011 Ten Minutes by Tractor Wallis. **Pemberton:** 2012 Castelli Estate. **Tasmania:** 2010 Dawson & James, 2011 Dawson & James, 2010 Frogmore Creek, 2011 Frogmore Creek. **Tasmania/Adelaide Hills:** 2010 Penfolds Yattarna. **Yarra Valley:** 2011 Coldstream Hills Deer Farm Vineyard, 2011 Coldstream Hills Reserve, 2011 De Bortoli Reserve Release, 2012 Domaine Chandon Barrel Selection, 2011 Dominique Portet, 2011 Innocent Bystander Giant Steps Sexton Vineyard, 2011 Mount Mary, 2011 Punt Road Chemin, 2011 Serrat, 2011 Toolangi Vineyards Pauls Lane, 2011 YarraLoch.

Semillon

Little needs to be said, except to repeat Bruce Tyrrell's comment on the impact of screwcaps: 'Hunter Valley is entering a golden age.' These wines are all screwcapped, and span 2002 (the first vintage) to 2013. I strongly suspect they will easily see out 20 years, the best 50 years. As with riesling, sauvignon blanc and sauvignon blanc semillon, I have not differentiated subregions, particularly irrelevant in this (semillon) case.

RATING	WINE	REGION
98	2007 Brokenwood ILR Reserve	Hunter Valley
97	2006 Tyrrell's Vat 1	Hunter Valley
96	2007 Peter Lehmann Margaret	Barossa Valley
96	2008 Peter Lehmann Margaret	Barossa Valley
96	2012 Audrey Wilkinson The Ridge	Hunter Valley
96	2007 Brokenwood Maxwell Vineyard	Hunter Valley
96	2007 Chateau Francois Pokolbin	Hunter Valley
96	2009 McLeish Estate	Hunter Valley
96	2007 McWilliam's Mount Pleasant Lovedale	Hunter Valley
96	2007 Meerea Park Alexander Munro	Hunter Valley
96	2009 Pepper Tree Single Vineyard Reserve Alluvius	Hunter Valley
96	2007 Thomas Cellar Reserve Braemore	Hunter Valley
96	2012 Tyrrell's Johnno's Basket Pressed	Hunter Valley
96	2011 Writer's Block Old Vine Single Estate	Hunter Valley
95	2012 Bimbadgen Signature Mistletoe Lane Vineyard	Hunter Valley
95	2006 Brokenwood Maxwell Vineyard	Hunter Valley
95	2007 Brokenwood Stanleigh Park	Hunter Valley
95	2012 De Iuliis Sunshine Vineyard	Hunter Valley
95	2008 Hungerford Hill Collection Majors Lane Vineyard	Hunter Valley
95	2012 Keith Tulloch Field of Mars Block 2A	Hunter Valley
95	2006 Keith Tulloch Museum Release	Hunter Valley
95	2010 Leogate Estate Reserve	Hunter Valley
95	2009 Pepper Tree Single Vineyard Limited Release	Hunter Valley
95	2012 Pepper Tree Single Vineyard Reserve Alluvius	Hunter Valley
95	2012 Thomas Braemore Individual Vineyard	Hunter Valley
95	2008 Tyrrell's Single Vineyard Stevens	Hunter Valley
95	2012 Tyrrell's Vat 1	Hunter Valley
95	2007 Coolangatta Estate Aged Release Estate Grown	Shoalhaven Coast

Sauvignon Blanc

Sauvignon blanc has held its ground as the waves of Marlborough Sauvignon Blanc continue to flood the market. Happily, Australia has stuck to its knitting, producing wines that have structure, and do not seek to emulate the Marlborough style. This variety is not going to go away anytime soon; Adelaide Hills leads the pack.

RATING	WINE	REGION
96	2012 Alta Vineyards	Adelaide Hills
96	2012 Shaw + Smith	Adelaide Hills
96	2011 Scotchmans Hill Cornelius	Geelong
96	2010 Domaine A Lady A	Tasmania
96	2012 Terre à Terre Down to Earth	Wrattonbully
95	2012 Geoff Weaver Lenswood	Adelaide Hills
95	2012 SC Pannell	Adelaide Hills
95	2012 Wirra Wirra Hiding Champion	Adelaide Hills
95	2012 Oakdene Jessica	Geelong
95	2012 Oranje Tractor Fat Tyre Broke Spoke Albany	Great Southern
95	2012 Willow Creek	Mornington Peninsula
95	2012 Ross Hill Pinnacle Series	Orange
95	2012 Houghton Wisdom	Pemberton
95	2012 Cherubino	Pemberton
95	2012 Terre à Terre	Wrattonbully
95	2012 Out of Step Lusatia Park Vineyard	Yarra Valley

Sauvignon Semillon Blends

This is a distinctly Australian blend to which New Zealand sauvignon blanc has no answer. As in prior years, Margaret River dominates the field. The maritime climate replicates that of Bordeaux, the old world home of the blend (the percentage of muscadelle is rapidly decreasing in Bordeaux).

RATING	WINE	REGION
96	2012 Grosset Semillon Sauvignon Blanc	Clare Valley/ Adelaide Hills
96	2012 Fraser Gallop Estate Parterre Semillon Sauvignon Blanc	Margaret River
96	2012 Hay Shed Hill Block 1 Semillon Sauvignon Blanc	Margaret River
95	2012 The Lake House Premium Reserve Single Vineyard Denmark Semillon Sauvignon Blanc	Great Southern
95	2012 Cape Mentelle Sauvignon Blanc Semillon	Margaret River
95	2010 Cullen Vineyard Sauvignon Blanc Semillon	Margaret River
95	2012 Lenton Brae Semillon Sauvignon Blanc	Margaret River
95	2012 The Alchemists Reserve Elixir Semillon Sauvignon Blanc	Margaret River
95	2007 Vasse Felix Margaret River Classic Dry White	Margaret River
94	2010 Alkoomi White Label Frankland River Semillon Sauvignon Blanc	Great Southern

94	2012 Harewood Estate Reserve Semillon Sauvignon Blanc	Great Southern
94	2012 The Lake House Premium Block Selection Denmark Semillon Sauvignon Blanc	Great Southern
94	2012 Thomas Two of a Kind Semillon Sauvignon Blanc	Hunter Valley
94	2012 Brygon Reserve Birds of a Feather Humming Bird Series Semillon Sauvignon Blanc	Margaret River
94	2011 Brygon Reserve Bin 828 Semillon Sauvignon Blanc	Margaret River
94	2012 Celestial Bay Semillon Sauvignon Blanc	Margaret River
94	2012 Celestial Bay White Zenith	Margaret River
94	2012 Lamont's Semillon Sauvignon Blanc	Margaret River
94	2012 Pierro L.T.C.	Margaret River
94	2012 Windows Estate Single Vineyard Semillon Sauvignon Blanc	Margaret River
94	2012 Woody Nook Kelly's Farewell Semillon Sauvignon Blanc	Margaret River
94	2012 Capel Vale Regional Series Semillon Sauvignon Blanc	Pemberton
94	2011 Merum Estate Semillon Sauvignon Blanc	Pemberton
94	2011 Mount Mary Triolet	Yarra Valley

Other White Wines and Blends

This group of wines shows that the 'alternative' varieties' Charge of the Light Brigade is yet to inflict many casualties on viognier, pinot gris, marsanne and gewurztraminer. The cause of the newer alternatives was not helped by the embarrassing discovery that the CSIRO-supplied albarino is in fact savagnin, a gewurztraminer clone grown in the Jura region of France. However, it is true that the 49 wines that received 94 points do take in a much broader range of varieties.

RATING	WINE	REGION
96	2012 Clonakilla Viognier	Canberra District
96	2009 Yalumba The Virgilius Viognier	Eden Valley
96	2012 Brown Brothers Limited Release Pinot Grigio	King Valley
96	2003 Tahbilk 1927 Vines Marsanne	Nagambie Lakes
96	2012 Delatite Dead Man's Hill Gewurztraminer	Upper Goulburn
95	2011 Arete The Chameleon Pinot Gris	Adelaide Hills
95	2011 Casa Freschi La Signorina	Langhorne Creek
95	2011 Ducks in a Row Fiano	McLaren Vale
95	2011 Ducks in a Row Pandora's Amphora	McLaren Vale
95	2011 Lethbridge Pinot Gris	Geelong
95	2012 Scorpo Pinot Gris	Mornington Peninsula
95	2009 Mount Mary Triolet	Yarra Valley

Sparkling

The best sparkling wines are now predominantly sourced from Tasmania, the remainder come from the coolest sites in the southern parts of the mainland, with altitude playing a major role. They are all fermented in the bottle, and the best have had extended lees contact prior to disgorgement, giving them great complexity.

White and Rose

RATING	WINE	REGION
97	2004 Arras Blanc de Blanc	Tasmania
97	2000 Arras EJ Carr Late Disgorged	Tasmania
96	2001 Freycinet Radenti Chardonnay Pinot Noir	Tasmania
96	NV Bindi 3 Cuvee	Macedon Ranges
96	2004 Mount William Pinot Noir Chardonnay	Macedon Ranges
96	2001 Arras EJ Carr Late Disgorged	Tasmania
96	2004 Arras Rose	Tasmania
96	2005 Arras Rose	Tasmania
96	2004 House of Arras Grand Vintage	Tasmania
96	2008 Jansz Tasmania Premium Vintage Rose	Tasmania
96	2004 Yarrabank Late Disgorged	Yarra Valley
95	2010 Ashton Hills Salmon Brut Piccadilly Valley Pinot Noir	Adelaide Hills
95	NV Henschke Lenswood Blanc de Noir	Adelaide Hills
95	2002 Yellowglen XV Piccadilly Exceptional Vintage	Adelaide Hills
95	2004 Bochara Arcadia Brut Cuvee Blanc de Noir	Henty
95	2006 Brown Brothers Patricia Pinot Noir Chardonnay Brut	King Valley
95	2003 Mount William Jorja-Alexis Pinot Rose	Macedon Ranges
95	NV Centennial Vineyards Blanc de Blancs	Southern Highlands
95	2009 Barringwood Jessica Classic Cuvee	Tasmania
95	NV Bay of Fires Tasmanian Cuvee Pinot Noir Chardonnay	Tasmania
95	NV Bay of Fires Tasmanian Cuvee Pinot Noir Chardonnay Rose	Tasmania
95	2007 Bream Creek Cuvee Traditionelle	Tasmania
95	2008 Clover Hill Cuvee Exceptionnelle Blanc de Blancs	Tasmania
95	2008 Heemskerk Coal River Valley Chardonnay Pinot Noir	Tasmania
95	2007 Jansz Tasmania Premium Vintage Cuvee	Tasmania
95	2005 Josef Chromy Vintage	Tasmania
95	2006 Pipers Brook Vineyard Kreglinger Vintage Brut	Tasmania
95	2004 Winstead Ensnared Sparkling Pinot Noir	Tasmania
95	2004 Domaine Chandon Prestige Cuvee	Yarra Valley
95	2008 Domaine Chandon Vintage Collection Cuvee 500	Yarra Valley
95	2008 Domaine Chandon Vintage Cuvee	Yarra Valley
95	2009 Oakridge Local Vineyard Series Chardonnay Pinot Noir	Yarra Valley
95	2008 Yarrabank Cuvee	Yarra Valley

Sparkling Red

A tiny group of wines, eagerly sought by the small percentage of wine drinkers who understand the peculiarities of the style and who, better still, are prepared to cellar them for a year or more – the longer the better.

RATING	WINE	REGION
96	2006 Ashton Hills Sparkling Shiraz	Adelaide Hills
96	NV Rockford Black Shiraz	Barossa Valley
95	NV Turkey Flat Sparkling Shiraz	Barossa Valley
95	2005 Leasingham Classic Clare Sparkling Shiraz	Clare Valley
94	2008 Peter Lehmann Black Queen Sparkling Shiraz	Barossa Valley
94	2009 Capital The Black Rod	Canberra District
94	2009 Grampians Estate Rutherford Sparkling Shiraz	Grampians
94	NV Blue Pyrenees Estate Sparkling Shiraz	Pyrenees
94	NV Centennial Vineyards Sparkling Shiraz	Southern Highlands

Sweet

Two classes of riesling have continued to evolve, and cannot be grouped together: off-dry (in Mosel Kabinett style) and fully sweet (Auslese in German terminology).

Off-dry Riesling

RATING	WINE	REGION
96	2012 Grosset Alea Off-dry	Clare Valley
96	2011 Pewsey Vale Prima 24GR	Eden Valley
96	2012 Pewsey Vale Prima 24GR	Eden Valley
96	2012 Frankland Estate Smith Cullam Frankland River	Great Southern
95	2012 David Hook Reserve	Central Ranges
95	2012 Centennial Vineyards Reserve Single Vineyard 924	Southern Highlands

Sweet Riesling

RATING	WINE	REGION
96	2010 Pressing Matters R139 Riesling	Tasmania
96	2012 Oakridge Local Vineyard Series Yarrawood Vineyard Botrytis Riesling	Yarra Valley
95	2012 Lark Hill Canberra District Auslese Riesling	Canberra District
95	2012 Heggies Vineyard Eden Valley Botrytis Riesling	Eden Valley
95	2012 Bellarmine Pemberton Riesling Select	Pemberton
95	2011 Frogmore Creek Iced Riesling	Tasmania
95	2012 Pooley Late Harvest Riesling	Tasmania

Semillon and others

It makes no sense to put these and the rieslings into the same group. Altogether different dynamics are in play with the, which largely come from the Riverland; these are barrel-fermented, highly botrytised wines with vanilla bean, peaches and cream, crème brulee, apricot or cumquat flavours – take your pick.

RATING	WINE	REGION
96	NV Charles Melton Sotto di Ferro	Barossa Valley
96	2012 Mistletoe Noble Viognier	Hunter Valley
96	2009 De Bortoli Noble One Botrytis Semillon	Riverina
96	2012 Yalumba FSW8B Botrytis Viognier	Wrattonbully
95	2011 Tomich Hill Ice-Block E Riesling Gewurztraminer	Adelaide Hills
95	2010 McWilliam's Morning Light Botrytis Semillon	Riverina

Rose

The number of Roses on the market may be approaching saturation point. There are no rules: they can be bone-dry, slightly sweet, or very sweet. They can be and are made from almost any red variety, red blends or red and white blends. They may be a convenient way of concentrating the red wine left after the Rose is run off (bleeding or saignee) from the fermenter shortly after the grapes are crushed, or made from the ground up using grapes and techniques specifically chosen for the purpose. The vast majority fall in the former camp; those listed mainly come from the latter.

RATING	WINE	REGION
96	2012 gilbert by Simon Gilbert Saignee	Mudgee/Orange
95	2012 Charles Melton Rose of Virginia	Barossa Valley
95	2012 Golden Ball Cherish a la provencale	Beechworth
94	2012 Honey Moon Fancy Rose	Adelaide Hills
94	2012 Scott La Prova Aglianico Rosato	Adelaide Hills
94	2012 Tomich Hill Vin Gris of Pinot Noir	Adelaide Hills
94	2008 David Franz Cellar Release Survivor Vine	Barossa Valley
94	2012 Turkey Flat	Barossa Valley
94	2012 Farr Rising Saignee	Geelong
94	2012 Willow Bridge Estate Dragonfly	Geographe
94	2011 Vinea Marson	Heathcote
94	2011 Mistletoe	Hunter Valley
94	2012 Dandelion Vineyards Fairytale of the Barossa	Barossa Valley
94	2012 SC Pannell Arido	McLaren Vale
94	2012 Massey Grenache Shiraz Mourvedre	McLaren Vale
94	2012 Port Phillip Estate Salasso	Mornington Peninsula
94	2012 Michael Hall Sang de Pigeon Shiraz Saignee	Barossa
94	2012 Robert Stein Saignee	Mudgee
94	2011 Tarrawarra Estate Pinot Noir Rose	Yarra Valley

Pinot Noir

The three regions that produce most of Australia's best Pinot Noirs are (in alpha order) the Mornington Peninsula, Tasmania and Yarra Valley. The most conspicuous exceptions are Gippsland and Geelong thanks to the contributions of Bass Phillip and by Farr. The Macedon Ranges is also in the fore-front.

RATING	WINE	REGION
99	2010 Bass Phillip Reserve	Gippsland
98	2010 Bass Phillip Premium	Gippsland
97	2011 Farrside by Farr	Geelong
97	2011 Sangreal by Farr	Geelong
97	2012 Clyde Park Vineyard Block D	Geelong
97	2010 Curly Flat The Curly	Macedon Ranges
97	2009 Paringa Estate The Paringa Single Vineyard	Mornington Peninsula
97	2010 Tuck's Ridge Buckle	Mornington Peninsula
97	2010 Yabby Lake Single Block Release Block 6	Mornington Peninsula
97	2010 Hillcrest Vineyard Premium	Yarra Valley
97	2010 Mount Mary	Yarra Valley
96	2010 Romney Park	Adelaide Hills
96	2010 Tout Pres by Farr	Geelong
96	2010 Bass Phillip Issan	Gippsland
96	2011 Castle Rock Estate	Great Southern
96	2010 Bindi Block 5	Macedon Ranges
96	2009 Paramoor Joan Picton	Macedon Ranges
96	2010 Kooyong Single Vineyard Selection Haven	Mornington Peninsula
96	2010 Moorooduc Estate The Moorooduc McIntyre	Mornington Peninsula
96	2010 Paringa Estate	Mornington Peninsula
96	2010 Paringa Estate The Paringa Single Vineyard	Mornington Peninsula
96	2012 Onannon	Port Phillip Zone
96	2012 Chatto	Tasmania
96	2010 Dawson & James	Tasmania
96	2011 Dawson & James	Tasmania
96	2010 Freycinet	Tasmania
96	2009 Glaetzer-Dixon Reveur	Tasmania
96	2010 Glaetzer-Dixon Reveur	Tasmania
96	2010 Heemskerk Derwent Valley	Tasmania
96	2010 Home Hill Kelly's Reserve	Tasmania
96	2010 Moorilla Estate Muse	Tasmania
96	2007 Diamond Valley Reserve	Yarra Valley
96	2012 Domaine Chandon Barrel Selection	Yarra Valley
96	2010 Yeringberg	Yarra Valley

Shiraz

The number of wines that received 96 points or more (a total of 101) may seem extreme, but in fact expressed as a percentage of the total number of wines tasted is on a par with chardonnay. Moreover, there is tremendous diversity of style from the resurgent Hunter Valley, through the whole of Victoria, most of South Australia and to the southwest of Western Australia. Finally, the 2010 vintage was exceptional in almost all regions, '11 simply outstanding in the Hunter Valley, and a tsunami of top wines from '12 will appear in the next *Wine Companion*.

RATING	WINE	REGION
98	2008 Henschke Hill Of Grace	Eden Valley
98	2008 Penfolds Grange	SA blend
97	2012 Ochota Barrels The Shellac Vineyard Syrah	Adelaide Hills
97	2010 Charles Melton Grains of Paradise	Barossa Valley
97	2010 Kaesler Alte Reben	Barossa Valley
97	2009 Penfolds RWT	Barossa Valley
97	2010 Thorn-Clarke William Randell	Barossa Valley
97	2010 Turkey Flat	Barossa Valley
97	2010 Westlake Vineyards Eleazar	Barossa Valley
97	2010 Jim Barry The Armagh	Clare Valley
97	2010 Kilikanoon Attunga 1865	Clare Valley
97	2010 Henschke Mount Edelstone	Eden Valley
97	2011 Cherubino Laissez Faire Syrah	Great Southern
97	2011 Graillot Heathcote	Heathcote
97	2010 Moppity Vineyards Reserve	Hilltops
97	2011 Brokenwood Graveyard Vineyard	Hunter Valley
97	2011 Brokenwood Mistress Block Vineyard	Hunter Valley
97	2011 Leogate Estate Western Slopes Reserve	Hunter Valley
97	2010 McWilliam's Mount Pleasant OP&OH	Hunter Valley
97	2011 Pepper Tree Single Vineyard Reserve Coquun	Hunter Valley
97	2011 Tyrrell's Vat 9 Hunter	Hunter Valley
97	2010 Clarendon Hills Astralis	McLaren Vale
97	2010 BK Mazi Blewitt Springs Syrah	McLaren Vale
97	2007 Tahbilk 1860 Vines	Nagambie Lakes
97	2010 Yeringberg	Yarra Valley

Shiraz Viognier

In best Australian Tall Poppy Syndrome style it has already become fashionable in some quarters to challenge the remarkable synergy obtained by co-fermenting around 5% of viognier with shiraz. When used in cool to temperate regions, the enhancement of colour, aroma and flavour is remarkable, as is the softening and smoothing of texture. It is not a panacea for lesser quality grapes, and yes, it is and should remain a subtext to the thrust of shiraz's flavour. Nonetheless, the wines in this group offer pleasure second to none, even on the face of the 2011 vintage.

RATING	WINE	REGION
95	2010 Spinifex La Maline	Barossa Valley
95	2010 Torbreck Descendant	Barossa Valley
95	2011 Clonakilla	Canberra District
95	2010 Yalumba	Eden Valley
95	2009 Dandelion Vineyards Lion's Tooth Shiraz Riesling	McLaren Vale
95	2010 Pirramimma	McLaren Vale
94	2011 Head The Blonde Stonewell	Barossa Valley
94	2012 Ravensworth Murrumbateman	Canberra District
94	2010 Sirromet Wild	Granite Belt
94	2011 Keith Tulloch	Hunter Valley
94	2010 Willunga 100	McLaren Vale
94	2011 Salomon Syrah V	Southern Fleurieu
94	2011 Centennial Vineyards Reserve Single Vineyard	Southern Highlands
94	2011 Yering Station Yarra Valley	Yarra Valley

Cabernet Sauvignon

The affinity of cabernet sauvignon with a maritime climate is put beyond doubt by its home in Bordeaux's Medoc region. So it comes as no surprise to find that most (but not all) of Australia's top-quality cabernets come from regions with climates similar to Bordeaux (conspicuously Coonawarra and Margaret River) and/or which are within 50km of the sea with no intervening mountains. The far greater number of Margaret River cabernet sauvignons is partly due to four excellent vintages from 2008 to '11 inclusive (and '12 to follow in the same vein when ready). Coonawarra has not had the same fortune.

RATING	WINE	REGION
98	2010 Penfolds Bin 169	Coonawarra
97	2010 Poonawatta Estate Bob's Block	Eden Valley
97	2010 Houghton Gladstones	Margaret River
96	2010 Kilikanoon Reserve	Clare Valley
96	2009 Wendouree	Clare Valley
96	2009 Brand's Laira One Seven One	Coonawarra
96	2010 Majella	Coonawarra
96	2008 Penfolds Cellar Reserve	Coonawarra

96	2010 Punters Corner Sovereign Reserve	Coonawarra
96	2010 Flaxman Shhh	Eden Valley
96	2009 Henschke Cyril Henschke	Eden Valley
96	2010 Poonawatta Estate Wayne's Block	Eden Valley
96	2011 Castelli Estate Frankland River	Great Southern
96	2011 Larry Cherubino The Yard Riversdale Vineyard Frankland River	Great Southern
96	2011 Staniford Wine Co Reserve	Great Southern
96	2009 Aravina Estate	Margaret River
96	2011 Brookland Valley Reserve	Margaret River
96	2010 Cape Mentelle	Margaret River
96	2010 Evans & Tate Redbrook	Margaret River
96	2011 Flametree S.R.S.	Margaret River
96	2011 Harvey River Bridge Estate Joseph River Estate Reserve	Margaret River
96	2010 Hay Shed Hill Block 2	Margaret River
96	2008 Heydon Estate W.G. Grace	Margaret River
96	2010 Laurance Cabernet	Margaret River
96	2010 Night Harvest John George Reserve	Margaret River
96	2009 Robert Oatley Finisterre	Margaret River
96	2010 Umamu Estate	Margaret River
96	2010 Woodlands	Margaret River
96	2010 Wirra Wirra The Angelus	McLaren Vale
96	2008 Reynella Basket Pressed	McLaren Vale
96	2010 Reynella Basket Pressed	McLaren Vale
96	2010 Belgravia	Orange
96	2009 Penfolds Bin 707	South Australia
96	2010 Penfolds Bin 707	South Australia
96	2010 Hillcrest Vineyard Premium	Yarra Valley
96	2010 Yering Station	Yarra Valley

Cabernet and Family

This group revolves around the grapes of Bordeaux, and primarily blends thereof, but with some single varieties, most notably merlot. The majority are from moderately cool regions, Margaret River once again the leader of the band thanks to its succession of top vintages. Also included are the classic Australian cabernet and shiraz (or vice versa) blends.

RATING	WINE	REGION
97	2009 Voyager Estate Cabernet Sauvignon Merlot	Margaret River
96	2000 Geoff Weaver Lenswood Cabernet Merlot	Adelaide Hills
96	2010 Dutschke St Jakobi Vineyard 78 & 95 Blocks Lyndoch Cabernet Shiraz	Barossa Valley
96	2011 A. Rodda Cuvee de Chez	Beechworth

96	2010 Katnook Estate The Caledonian Cabernet Shiraz	Coonawarra
96	2010 Lindemans Pyrus Cabernet Sauvignon Merlot Cabernet Franc	Coonawarra
96	2010 Majella The Malleea	Coonawarra
96	2010 Parker Coonawarra Estate First Growth	Coonawarra
96	2011 Lake's Folly Cabernets	Hunter Valley
96	2010 Cullen Diana Madeline	Margaret River
96	2011 Evans & Tate Metricup Road Cabernet Merlot	Margaret River
96	2011 Moss Brothers Moses Rock Estate 3857 Caves Road The Wilyabrup	Margaret River
96	2010 Sirromet LM Private Collection Cabernet Sauvignon Petit Verdot Merlot	Granite Belt
96	2009 Vasse Felix Heytesbury	Margaret River
96	2010 Vasse Felix Heytesbury	Margaret River
96	2010 Penfolds Bin 389 Cabernet Shiraz	SA blend
96	2011 Yarra Yering Dry Red No. 1	Yarra Valley
96	2010 Yeringberg	Yarra Valley

Shiraz and Family

This is a South Australian stronghold, mostly with some or all of shiraz, grenache and mourvedre.

RATING	WINE	REGION
96	2009 The Lane Vineyard John Crighton Shiraz Cabernet	Adelaide Hills
96	2010 Hewitson Private Cellar Shiraz Mourvedre	Barossa Valley
96	2010 Jacob's Creek St Hugo Grenache Shiraz Mataro	Barossa Valley
96	2010 Lou Miranda Angel's Vineyard Shiraz Mourvedre	Barossa Valley
96	2010 Murray Street Vineyard Benno	Barossa Valley
96	2009 Ferngrove The Stirlings Shiraz Cabernet Sauvignon	Frankland River
96	2010 SC Pannell Grenache Shiraz	McLaren Vale
96	2009 Angove Warboys Vineyard Shiraz Grenache	McLaren Vale
95	2012 Chateau Tanunda The Whole Dam Family	Barossa Valley
95	2009 Grant Burge Abednego	Barossa Valley
95	2010 Hemera Estate ROSS Limited Release GSM	Barossa Valley
95	2012 Purple Hands Mataro Shiraz Grenache	Barossa Valley
95	2010 Jim Barry PB Shiraz Cabernet Sauvignon	Clare Valley
95	2010 Lindemans Limestone Ridge Vineyard	Coonawarra
95	2012 Henschke Johann's Garden	Eden Valley
95	2010 Frankland Estate Smith Cullam Shiraz Cabernet	Great Southern
95	2008 Brown Brothers Shiraz Mondeuse & Cabernet	King Valley
95	2010 Warrenmang Bazzani Shiraz Cabernet	Pyrenees

Other Reds

A wonderfully diverse range of wines, grenache contributing more than any other variety, but leaving room for a Joseph's coat of other single varieties and blends. It is entirely logical that McLaren Vale should contribute most of the wines, with the Barossa Valley not far behind.

RATING	WINE	REGION
97	2011 Best's Old Vine Great Western Pinot Meunier	Grampians
97	2010 Hewitson Old Garden Mourvedre	Barossa Valley
97	2010 SC Pannell Grenache	McLaren Vale
96	2010 Bird in Hand Nest Egg Merlot	Adelaide Hills
96	2008 Hemera Estate Tier 1	Barossa Valley
96	2010 Penfolds Cellar Reserve Mataro	Barossa Valley
96	2012 Purple Hands Old Vine Grenache	Barossa Valley
96	2010 Quattro Mano La Gracia	Barossa Valley
96	2010 The Alchemists Merlot	Margaret River
96	2010 Clarendon Hills Blewitt Springs Grenache	McLaren Vale
96	2011 Ducks in a Row Tempranillo Graciano Mataro	McLaren Vale
96	2010 Rudderless Sellicks Hill Grenache	McLaren Vale
96	2011 SC Pannell Grenache	McLaren Vale
96	2008 Tapanappa Whalebone Vineyard Merlot Cabernet Franc	Wrattonbully
95	2010 Quattro Mano La Reto Tempranillo	Barossa Valley
95	2010 Spinifex Esprit	Barossa Valley
95	2010 Yelland & Papps Divine Grenache	Barossa Valley
95	2010 Balnaves The Blend	Coonawarra
95	2011 Willow Bridge Solana Geographe Tempranillo	Geographe
95	2011 Golden Grove Durif	Granite Belt
95	2011 Golden Grove Mourvedre	Granite Belt
95	2010 Frankland Estate Frankland River Olmo's Reward	Great Southern
95	2006 The Islander Estate The Investigator Cabernet Franc	Kangaroo Island
95	2011 Woodlands Reserve de la Cave Cabernet Franc	Margaret River
95	2010 Clarendon Hills Liandra Clarendon Mourvedre	McLaren Vale
95	2010 Clarendon Hills Onkaparinga Grenache	McLaren Vale
95	2009 Clarendon Hills Romas Clarendon Grenache	McLaren Vale
95	2010 Olivers Taranga Small Batch Cadenzia Grenache	McLaren Vale
95	2010 The Old Faithful Northern Exposure Grenache	McLaren Vale
95	2010 Yarra Yering Dry Red No. 3	Yarra Valley
95	2011 Yarra Yering Dry Red No. 3	Yarra Valley

Fortified Wines

A relatively small but absolutely sensational group of magnificent wines, as quintessentially Australian as a Driza-Bone, and of unique style. It hardly needs to be said that Rutherglen utterly dominates the field; the Seppeltsfield 100 Year Old Para Liqueur from another vinous world.

RATING	WINE	REGION
100	1913 Seppeltsfield 100 Year Old Para Liqueur	Barossa Valley
98	NV Baileys Winemaker's Selection Old Muscat	Glenrowan
98	NV All Saints Estate Rare Muscat	Rutherglen
98	NV All Saints Estate Rare Muscat Museum Release	Rutherglen
98	NV Campbells Isabella Rare Topaque	Rutherglen
98	NV Chambers Rosewood Rare Muscadelle	Rutherglen
98	NV Chambers Rosewood Rare Muscat	Rutherglen
98	NV Morris Old Premium Rare Liqueur Muscat	Rutherglen
98	NV Pfeiffer Rare Muscat	Rutherglen
97	NV Penfolds Grandfather Fine Old Liqueur Tawny	Barossa Valley
97	NV Penfolds Great Grandfather Rare Tawny	Barossa Valley
97	NV Baileys Winemaker's Selection Rare Old Topaque	Glenrowan
97	NV All Saints Estate Rare Topaque	Rutherglen
97	NV Campbells Merchant Prince Rare Muscat	Rutherglen
97	NV Morris Old Premium Grand Muscat	Rutherglen
97	NV Pfeiffer Grand Muscat	Rutherglen
97	NV Pfeiffer Rare Topaque	Rutherglen
97	NV Stanton & Killeen Rare Muscat	Rutherglen
97	NV Stanton & Killeen Rare Topaque	Rutherglen

Best wineries of the regions

The nomination of the best wineries of the regions has evolved into a three-level classification (further explained on page 10). At the very top are the wineries with their names and stars printed in red, these have been generally recognised for having a long track record of excellence – truly the best of the best. Next are wineries with their stars (but not their names) printed in red, and which have had a consistent record of excellence for at least the last three years. Those wineries with black stars have achieved excellence this year (and sometimes longer).

ADELAIDE HILLS
Altamont Wine Studio ★★★★★
Anvers ★★★★★
Arete Wines ★★★★★
Ashton Hills ★★★★★
Barratt ★★★★★
Bird in Hand ★★★★★
Birdwood Estate ★★★★★
BK Wines ★★★★★
Chain of Ponds ★★★★★
Geoff Weaver ★★★★★
Hahndorf Hill Winery ★★★★★
Honey Moon Vineyard ★★★★★
Lobethal Road Wines ★★★★★
Mayhem & Co ★★★★★
Mt Lofty Ranges Vineyard ★★★★★
Mount Torrens Vineyards ★★★★★
Murdoch Hill ★★★★★
Nepenthe ★★★★★
Ochota Barrels ★★★★★
Petaluma ★★★★★
Pike & Joyce ★★★★★
Riposte ★★★★★
Romney Park Wines ★★★★★
Scott ★★★★★
Setanta Wines ★★★★★
Shaw + Smith ★★★★★
The Lane Vineyard ★★★★★
Tomich Wines ★★★★★
Warwick Billings ★★★★★

ADELAIDE ZONE
Heirloom Vineyards ★★★★★
Hewitson ★★★★★
Patritti Wines ★★★★★
Penfolds Magill Estate ★★★★★

ALBANY
Montgomery's Hill ★★★★★
Oranje Tractor ★★★★★

ALPINE VALLEYS
Boynton's Feathertop ★★★★★

BALLARAT
Eastern Peake ★★★★★
Tomboy Hill ★★★★★

BAROSSA VALLEY
Caillard Wine ★★★★★
Charles Cimicky ★★★★★
Charles Melton ★★★★★
Chateau Tanunda ★★★★★
David Franz ★★★★★
Deisen ★★★★★
Dorrien Estate ★★★★★
Dutschke Wines ★★★★★
Elderton ★★★★★
Eperosa ★★★★★
First Drop Wines ★★★★★
Fox Gordon ★★★★★
Gibson Barossavale ★★★★★
Glaetzer Wines ★★★★★
Grant Burge ★★★★★
Groom ★★★★★

Hare's Chase ★★★★★
Hart of the Barossa ★★★★★
Head Wines ★★★★★
Hemera Estate ★★★★★
Hentley Farm Wines ★★★★★
Hobbs of Barossa Ranges ★★★★★
Jacob's Creek ★★★★★
John Duval Wines ★★★★★
Kaesler Wines ★★★★★
Kalleske ★★★★★
Kellermeister ★★★★★
Landhaus Estate ★★★★★
Langmeil Winery ★★★★★
Laughing Jack ★★★★★
Lou Miranda Estate ★★★★★
McGuigan Wines ★★★★★
Magpie Estate ★★★★★
Massena Vineyards ★★★★★
Maverick Wines ★★★★★
Mt Toolleen ★★★★★
Murray Street Vineyard ★★★★★
Naked Run Wines ★★★★★
Orlando ★★★★★
Penfolds ★★★★★
Peter Lehmann ★★★★★
Purple Hands Wines ★★★★★
Quattro Mano ★★★★★
Red Art – Rojomoma ★★★★★
Rockford ★★★★★
Rolf Binder Veritas Winery ★★★★★
Rosenvale Wines ★★★★★
St Hallett ★★★★★
Saltram ★★★★★
Schubert Estate ★★★★★
Schwarz Wine Company ★★★★★
Seabrook Wines ★★★★★
Seppeltsfield ★★★★★
Smallfry Wines ★★★★★
Sons of Eden ★★★★★
Spinifex ★★★★★
Teusner ★★★★★
Thorn-Clarke Wines ★★★★★
Tim Smith Wines ★★★★★
Torbreck Vintners ★★★★★
Trevor Jones Fine Wines ★★★★★
Turkey Flat ★★★★★

Two Hands Wines ★★★★★
Westlake Vineyards ★★★★★
Wolf Blass ★★★★★
Yelland & Papps ★★★★★

BEECHWORTH
A. Rodda Wines ★★★★★
Giaconda ★★★★★
Golden Ball ★★★★★
Indigo Wine Company ★★★★★

BENDIGO
Ansted & Co. ★★★★★
BlackJack Vineyards ★★★★★
Bress ★★★★★
Killiecrankie Wines ★★★★★
Pondalowie Vineyards ★★★★★
Turner's Crossing Vineyard ★★★★★

BLACKWOOD VALLEY
Nannup Ridge Estate ★★★★★

CANBERRA DISTRICT
Capital Wines ★★★★★
Clonakilla ★★★★★
Collector Wines ★★★★★
Eden Road Wines ★★★★★
Four Winds Vineyard ★★★★★
Helm ★★★★★
Lark Hill ★★★★★
Lerida Estate ★★★★★
Mount Majura Vineyard ★★★★★
Nick O'Leary Wines ★★★★★
Ravensworth ★★★★★

CENTRAL VICTORIA ZONE
Mt Terrible ★★★★★

CLARE VALLEY
Annie's Lane ★★★★★
Atlas Wines ★★★★★
Clos Clare ★★★★★
Crabtree Watervale Wines ★★★★★
Eldredge ★★★★★
Grosset ★★★★★
Jim Barry Wines ★★★★★
Kilikanoon ★★★★★
Knappstein ★★★★★
Koonowla Wines ★★★★★
Leasingham ★★★★★

Mitchell ★★★★★
Mount Horrocks ★★★★★
Neagles Rock Wines ★★★★★
O'Leary Walker Wines ★★★★★
Paulett ★★★★★
Pikes ★★★★★
Rhythm Stick Wines ★★★★★
Sevenhill Cellars ★★★★★
Skillogalee ★★★★★
Taylors ★★★★★
Tim Adams ★★★★★
Wendouree ★★★★★
Wilson Vineyard ★★★★★
Wines by KT ★★★★★

COONAWARRA
Balnaves of Coonawarra ★★★★★
Bellwether ★★★★★
Bowen Estate ★★★★★
Brand's Laira Coonawarra ★★★★★
Bundalong ★★★★★
Katnook Estate ★★★★★
Koonara ★★★★★
Leconfield ★★★★★
Lindemans ★★★★★
Majella ★★★★★
Parker Coonawarra Estate ★★★★★
Patrick of Coonawarra ★★★★★
Penley Estate ★★★★★
Punters Corner ★★★★★
Rymill Coonawarra ★★★★★
Wynns Coonawarra Estate ★★★★★
Zema Estate ★★★★★

CURRENCY CREEK
ShowBlock Estate ★★★★★

DENMARK
Harewood Estate ★★★★★
Moombaki Wines ★★★★★
Rockcliffe ★★★★★
Singlefile Wines ★★★★★
The Lake House Denmark ★★★★★

EASTERN PLAINS, INLAND AND NORTH OF WESTERN AUSTRALIA
Across the Lake ★★★★★

EDEN VALLEY
Brockenchack ★★★★★
Chris Ringland ★★★★★
Eden Hall ★★★★★
Flaxman Wines ★★★★★
Heggies Vineyard ★★★★★
Henschke ★★★★★
Leo Buring ★★★★★
Pewsey Vale ★★★★★
Poonawatta Estate ★★★★★
Radford Wines ★★★★★
Rileys of Eden Valley ★★★★★
Yalumba ★★★★★

FRANKLAND RIVER
Alkoomi ★★★★★
Ferngrove ★★★★★
Frankland Estate ★★★★★

GEELONG
Austin's Wines ★★★★★
Bannockburn Vineyards ★★★★★
Barrgowan Vineyard ★★★★★
By Farr/Farr Rising ★★★★★
Clyde Park Vineyard ★★★★★
Lethbridge Wines ★★★★★
Leura Park Estate ★★★★★
Oakdene ★★★★★
Paradise IV ★★★★★
Provenance Wines ★★★★★
Scotchmans Hill ★★★★★
Shadowfax ★★★★★
WH Sweetland ★★★★★
Wirruna ★★★★★

GEOGRAPHE
Capel Vale ★★★★★
Willow Bridge Estate ★★★★★

GIPPSLAND
Bass Phillip ★★★★★
Bellvale Wine ★★★★★
Caledonia Australis/Mount Macleod ★★★★★
Dirty Three ★★★★★
Narkoojee ★★★★★
Tambo Estate ★★★★★

GLENROWAN
Baileys of Glenrowan ★★★★★

GRAMPIANS
A.T. Richardson Wines ★★★★★
Best's Wines ★★★★★
Clayfield Wines ★★★★★
Grampians Estate ★★★★★
Kimbarra Wines ★★★★★
Mount Langi Ghiran Vineyards
  ★★★★★
Seppelt ★★★★★
The Story Wines ★★★★★

GRANITE BELT
Boireann ★★★★★
Golden Grove Estate ★★★★★
Symphony Hill Wines ★★★★★

GREAT SOUTHERN
Castelli Estate ★★★★★
Forest Hill Vineyard ★★★★★
Marchand & Burch ★★★★★
Staniford Wine Co ★★★★★
Trevelen Farm ★★★★★
Willoughby Park ★★★★★

HEATHCOTE
Buckshot Vineyard ★★★★★
Domaine Asmara ★★★★★
Downing Estate Vineyard ★★★★★
Flynns Wines ★★★★★
Foster e Rocco ★★★★★
Graillot ★★★★★
Greenstone Vineyard ★★★★★
Heathcote Estate ★★★★★
Jasper Hill ★★★★★
Margaret Hill Vineyard ★★★★★
Noble Red ★★★★★
Paul Osicka ★★★★★
Sanguine Estate ★★★★★
Shelmerdine Vineyards ★★★★★
Stefani Estate ★★★★★
Tellurian ★★★★★
Vinea Marson ★★★★★

HENTY
Bochara Wines ★★★★★
Crawford River Wines ★★★★★
Henty Estate ★★★★★

HILLTOPS
Barwang ★★★★★
Chalkers Crossing ★★★★★
Freeman Vineyards ★★★★★
Moppity Vineyards ★★★★★

HUNTER VALLEY
Audrey Wilkinson Vineyard ★★★★★
Bimbadgen ★★★★★
Briar Ridge Vineyard ★★★★★
Brokenwood ★★★★★
Chateau Francois ★★★★★
Chateau Pâto ★★★★★
David Hook Wines ★★★★★
De Iuliis ★★★★★
First Creek Wines ★★★★★
Gartelmann Hunter Estate ★★★★★
Glenguin Estate ★★★★★
Gundog Estate ★★★★★
Hungerford Hill ★★★★★
Keith Tulloch Wine ★★★★★
Lake's Folly ★★★★★
Leogate Estate Wines ★★★★★
McLeish Estate ★★★★★
McWilliam's Mount Pleasant
  ★★★★★
Margan Family ★★★★★
Meerea Park ★★★★★
Mistletoe Wines ★★★★★
Mount View Estate ★★★★★
Pepper Tree Wines ★★★★★
Pokolbin Estate ★★★★★
Saddler's Creek ★★★★★
Tallavera Grove/Carillion ★★★★★
Tamburlaine ★★★★★
Thomas Wines ★★★★★
Tinklers Vineyard ★★★★★
Tintilla Wines ★★★★★
Tower Estate ★★★★★
Tulloch ★★★★★
Tyrrell's ★★★★★
Wandin Hunter Valley ★★★★★

KANGAROO ISLAND

The Islander Estate Vineyards
★★★★★

KING VALLEY

Brown Brothers ★★★★★
Pizzini ★★★★★

LANGHORNE CREEK

Angas Plains Estate ★★★★★
Bleasdale Vineyards ★★★★★
Bremerton Wines ★★★★★
John's Blend ★★★★★
Lake Breeze Wines ★★★★★

MACEDON RANGES

Bindi Wine Growers ★★★★★
Cobaw Ridge ★★★★★
Curly Flat ★★★★★
Granite Hills ★★★★★
Hanging Rock Winery ★★★★★
Kyneton Ridge Estate ★★★★★
Macedon Ridge Wines ★★★★★
Mount William Winery ★★★★★
Paramoor Wines ★★★★★

MCLAREN VALE

Battle of Bosworth ★★★★★
Bekkers ★★★★★
Brash Higgins ★★★★★
Cape Barren Wines ★★★★★
Chalk Hill ★★★★★
Chapel Hill ★★★★★
Clarendon Hills ★★★★★
Coates Wines ★★★★★
Coriole ★★★★★
d'Arenberg ★★★★★
Dandelion Vineyards ★★★★★
Di Fabio Estate ★★★★★
Doc Adams ★★★★★
Ducks in a Row Winemakers
  ★★★★★
Fox Creek Wines ★★★★★
Gemtree Vineyards ★★★★★
Geoff Merrill Wines ★★★★★
Hardys ★★★★★
Kangarilla Road Vineyard ★★★★★
Kay Brothers Amery Vineyards
  ★★★★★

Lloyd Brothers ★★★★★
Marius Wines ★★★★★
Maxwell Wines ★★★★★
Mr Riggs Wine Company ★★★★★
Mitolo Wines ★★★★★
Nashwauk ★★★★★
Olivers Taranga Vineyards ★★★★★
Paxton ★★★★★
Penny's Hill ★★★★★
Pirramimma ★★★★★
Primo Estate ★★★★★
Reynella ★★★★★
Richard Hamilton ★★★★★
Rosemount Estate ★★★★★
Rudderless ★★★★★
Rusty Mutt ★★★★★
Samuel's Gorge ★★★★★
SC Pannell ★★★★★
Serafino Wines ★★★★★
Shingleback ★★★★★
Shottesbrooke ★★★★★
Tatachilla ★★★★★
The Old Faithful Estate ★★★★★
Tilly Devine ★★★★★
Ulithorne ★★★★★
Walter Clappis Wine Co ★★★★★
WayWood Wines ★★★★★
Willunga 100 Wines ★★★★★
Wirra Wirra ★★★★★
Woodstock ★★★★★
Yangarra Estate Vineyard ★★★★★
Zonte's Footstep ★★★★★

MARGARET RIVER

Amelia Park Wines ★★★★★
Aravina Estate ★★★★★
Ashbrook Estate ★★★★★
Brookland Valley ★★★★★
Brygon Reserve ★★★★★
Burch Family Wines ★★★★★
Cape Mentelle ★★★★★
Cape Naturaliste Vineyard ★★★★★
Celestial Bay ★★★★★
Chapman Grove Wines ★★★★★
Cowaramup Wines ★★★★★
Cullen Wines ★★★★★
Deep Woods Estate ★★★★★

Devil's Lair ★★★★★
Evans & Tate ★★★★★
Evoi Wines ★★★★★
Flametree ★★★★★
Forester Estate ★★★★★
Fraser Gallop Estate ★★★★★
Happs ★★★★★
Hay Shed Hill Wines ★★★★★
Heydon Estate ★★★★★
Higher Plane ★★★★★
Juniper Estate ★★★★★
Knee Deep Wines ★★★★★
Laurance of Margaret River ★★★★★
Leeuwin Estate ★★★★★
Lenton Brae Wines ★★★★★
McHenry Hohnen Vintners ★★★★★
Marq Wines ★★★★★
Marri Wood Park ★★★★★
Moss Brothers ★★★★★
Moss Wood ★★★★★
Night Harvest ★★★★★
Palmer Wines ★★★★★
Pedestal Vineyard Wines ★★★★★
Pierro ★★★★★
Redgate ★★★★★
Rosabrook Margaret River Wine
    ★★★★★
Rosily Vineyard ★★★★★
Sandalford ★★★★★
Saracen Estates ★★★★★
Stella Bella Wines ★★★★★
Streicker ★★★★★
Swings & Roundabouts ★★★★★
The Alchemists ★★★★★
Thompson Estate ★★★★★
Umamu Estate ★★★★★
Vasse Felix ★★★★★
Victory Point Wines ★★★★★
Voyager Estate ★★★★★
Warner Glen Estate ★★★★★
Watershed Premium Wines ★★★★★
Wills Domain ★★★★★
Windows Estate ★★★★★
Wise Wine ★★★★★
Woodlands ★★★★★
Woodside Valley Estate ★★★★★

Woody Nook ★★★★★
Xanadu Wines ★★★★★

MORNINGTON PENINSULA
Crittenden Estate ★★★★★
Dexter Wines ★★★★★
Eldridge Estate of Red Hill
    ★★★★★
Elgee Park ★★★★★
Foxeys Hangout ★★★★★
Garagiste ★★★★★
Hurley Vineyard ★★★★★
Jones Road ★★★★★
Kooyong ★★★★★
Lindenderry at Red Hill ★★★★★
Main Ridge Estate ★★★★★
Merricks Creek Wines ★★★★★
Merricks Estate ★★★★★
Montalto ★★★★★
Moorooduc Estate ★★★★★
Paradigm Hill ★★★★★
Paringa Estate ★★★★★
Port Phillip Estate ★★★★★
Prancing Horse Estate ★★★★★
Red Hill Estate ★★★★★
Scorpo Wines ★★★★★
Stonier Wines ★★★★★
Stumpy Gully ★★★★★
Ten Minutes by Tractor ★★★★★
Tuck's Ridge ★★★★★
Willow Creek Vineyard ★★★★★
Yabby Lake Vineyard ★★★★★

MOUNT BARKER
Plantagenet ★★★★★
Poacher's Ridge Vineyard ★★★★★
3 Drops ★★★★★
West Cape Howe Wines ★★★★★
Xabregas ★★★★★

MOUNT BENSON
Cape Jaffa Wines ★★★★★

MOUNT LOFTY RANGES ZONE
Michael Hall Wines ★★★★★

MUDGEE
Bunnamagoo Estate ★★★★★
Huntington Estate ★★★★★

Robert Oatley Vineyards ★★★★★
Robert Stein Vineyard ★★★★★

NAGAMBIE LAKES
Mitchelton ★★★★★
Tahbilk ★★★★★

NORTH EAST VICTORIA ZONE
Eldorado Road ★★★★★

ORANGE
Belgravia Wines ★★★★★
Bloodwood ★★★★★
Philip Shaw Wines ★★★★★
Printhie Wines ★★★★★
Ross Hill Wines ★★★★★

PEMBERTON
Bellarmine Wines ★★★★★
Merum Estate ★★★★★

PORONGURUP
Castle Rock Estate ★★★★★
Duke's Vineyard ★★★★★
Mount Trio Vineyard ★★★★★

PORT PHILLIP ZONE
Onannon ★★★★★

PYRENEES
Blue Pyrenees Estate ★★★★★
Dalwhinnie ★★★★★
DogRock Winery ★★★★★
M. Chapoutier Australia ★★★★★
Mitchell Harris Wines ★★★★★
Mount Avoca ★★★★★
Pyren Vineyard ★★★★★
Pyrenees Ridge Winery ★★★★★
Summerfield ★★★★★
Warrenmang Vineyard & Resort
   ★★★★★

QUEENSLAND COASTAL
Sirromet Wines ★★★★★
Witches Falls Winery ★★★★★

RIVERINA
De Bortoli ★★★★★
McWilliam's ★★★★★
Nugan Estate ★★★★★

RUTHERGLEN
All Saints Estate ★★★★★
Campbells ★★★★★
Chambers Rosewood ★★★★★
Morris ★★★★★
Pfeiffer Wines ★★★★★
Stanton & Killeen Wines ★★★★★
Warrabilla ★★★★★

SHOALHAVEN COAST
Coolangatta Estate ★★★★★

SOUTH AUSTRALIA
Angove Family Winemakers ★★★★★
Hand Crafted by Geoff Hardy
   ★★★★★
Tapanappa ★★★★★
Woods Crampton ★★★★★

SOUTH WEST AUSTRALIA ZONE
Kerrigan + Berry ★★★★★
Snake + Herring ★★★★★

SOUTHERN FLEURIEU
Mt Billy ★★★★★
Salomon Estate ★★★★★

SOUTHERN HIGHLANDS
Centennial Vineyards ★★★★★
Tertini Wines ★★★★★

SUNBURY
Craiglee ★★★★★
Galli Estate ★★★★★

SWAN VALLEY
Houghton ★★★★★
Lamont's Winery ★★★★★
Sittella Wines ★★★★★

UPPER GOULBURN
Delatite ★★★★★
Mount Cathedral Vineyards ★★★★★
Rocky Passes Estate ★★★★★
Ros Ritchie Wines ★★★★★

TASMANIA
Barringwood ★★★★★
Bay of Fires/House of Arras ★★★★★
Bream Creek ★★★★★
Chatto ★★★★★
Clarence House Wines ★★★★★

Clemens Hill ★★★★★
Clover Hill ★★★★★
Coal Valley Vineyard ★★★★★
Craigow ★★★★★
Dalrymple Vineyards ★★★★★
Dawson & James ★★★★★
Domaine A ★★★★★
Freycinet ★★★★★
Frogmore Creek ★★★★★
Glaetzer-Dixon Family Winemakers
    ★★★★★
Heemskerk ★★★★★
Holm Oak ★★★★★
Home Hill ★★★★★
Jansz Tasmania ★★★★★
Josef Chromy Wines ★★★★★
Milton Vineyard ★★★★★
Moorilla Estate ★★★★★
Pipers Brook Vineyard ★★★★★
Pooley Wines ★★★★★
Pressing Matters ★★★★★
Riversdale Estate ★★★★★
Stefano Lubiana ★★★★★
Stoney Rise ★★★★★
Tamar Ridge/Pirie ★★★★★

VARIOUS
Accolade Wines ★★★★★
Echelon ★★★★★
Palmarium ★★★★★
Treasury Wine Estates ★★★★★
Twofold ★★★★★

WESTERN AUSTRALIA
Larry Cherubino Wines ★★★★★

WESTERN VICTORIA ZONE
Norton Estate ★★★★★

WRATTONBULLY
Terre à Terre ★★★★★

YARRA VALLEY
Bird on a Wire Wines ★★★★★
Carlei Estate & Carlei Green Vineyards
    ★★★★★
Coldstream Hills ★★★★★
De Bortoli ★★★★★
Denton Viewhill Vineyard ★★★★★

Diamond Valley Vineyards ★★★★★
Domaine Chandon ★★★★★
Dominique Portet ★★★★★
Elmswood Estate ★★★★★
Gembrook Hill ★★★★★
Helen's Hill Estate ★★★★★
Hillcrest Vineyard ★★★★★
Hoddles Creek Estate ★★★★★
Innocent Bystander ★★★★★
Jamsheed ★★★★★
Mandala ★★★★★
Mayer ★★★★★
Medhurst ★★★★★
Mount Mary ★★★★★
Oakridge Wines ★★★★★
Out of Step ★★★★★
Payne's Rise ★★★★★
PHI ★★★★★
Pimpernel Vineyards ★★★★★
Punch ★★★★★
Punt Road ★★★★★
Rob Dolan Wines ★★★★★
Rochford Wines ★★★★★
St Huberts ★★★★★
Salo Wines ★★★★★
Santolin Wines ★★★★★
Serrat ★★★★★
Seville Estate ★★★★★
Steels Creek Estate ★★★★★
Sticks Yarra Valley ★★★★★
Sutherland Estate ★★★★★
Tarrawarra Estate ★★★★★
The Wanderer ★★★★★
Thick as Thieves Wines ★★★★★
Thousand Candles ★★★★★
Toolangi Vineyards ★★★★★
Trellis ★★★★★
Wantirna Estate ★★★★★
Warramate ★★★★★
Wedgetail Estate ★★★★★
Yarra Yarra ★★★★★
Yarra Yering ★★★★★
Yarrabank ★★★★★
YarraLoch ★★★★★
Yering Station ★★★★★
Yeringberg ★★★★★

Ten of the best new wineries

Each one of these wineries making its debut in the *Wine Companion* has earned a five-star rating. They are thus the leaders of the 94 new wineries in this edition, although a number of other first-up wineries also achieved five stars. The ultimate selection criteria included the number of wines earning 94 points or above, and also value for money.

ALTAMONT WINE STUDIO Adelaide Hills, SA / **PAGE 72**
Altamont is a partnership of winemaker Brendon Keys, Brian Gilbert, Steve Harris, Michael Sawyer and Matthew Morrissy. It uses small parcels of high-quality fruit from the Adelaide Hills, but the associated label, Seven Deadly Vins, goes to the Barossa Valley for its grapes, with Michael Sawyer as winemaker. All four wines are line-priced at $25, three of them at 94 points, offering excellent value.

ARAVINA ESTATE Margaret River, WA / **PAGE 82**
When Accolade sold Amberley Estate winery (but retained the brand), Steve Tobin and family acquired the basic infrastructure for what will become a multifaceted business, with sculptured gardens, wedding facilities and a generally expanded cellar door. But it's not just a pretty face; Aravina's three best wines are emblematic of Margaret River at its best, and there are also alternative varietal wines.

DENTON VIEWHILL VINEYARD Yarra Valley, Vic / **PAGE 220**
Leading Melbourne, and indeed Australian, architect John Denton joined forces with son Simon in 1996 to begin the establishment of a 32ha vineyard on an outstanding site. The focus is on supplying high-quality grapes to leading Yarra Valley wineries. The Denton family has built a striking house, but has no winery. Small parcels of estate-grown grapes are made for the Denton Viewhill label by an eclectic group of young winemakers. The DM (dead mouse) label may be a flight of fancy, but this is a serious and successful enterprise.

ELDORADO ROAD North East Victoria Zone / **PAGE 248**
This is a busman's holiday for Bailey's winemaker Paul Dahlenburg (nicknamed Bear); in a win-win scenario, he has leased a paddock with 2ha of shiraz planted in the 1890s. The owners were not able to look after the vines, and were happy that Paul and family would do so. Four years of rehabilitating the old vines has paid an appropriate dividend, and the family has also planted a small area of nero d'Avola and durif. In the meantime they are purchasing small quantities of nero d'Avola and durif.

HART OF THE BAROSSA Barossa Valley, SA / PAGE 312

The ancestors of Michael and Alisa Hart arrived in South Australia in 1845, the parents and seven children initially setting up home in a hollow tree on the banks of the North Para River. 168 years later, Michael and Alisa tend a 6.5ha vineyard, which has a patch of 110-year-old shiraz, and is the oldest certified organic vineyard in the Barossa Valley. Wonderful Shiraz and very good Cabernet is the result.

RED ART – ROJOMOMA Barossa Valley, SA / PAGE 539

Artist/photographer Bernadette Kaeding acquired the 5.4ha property in 1996, at which time it had 1.49ha of eight-year-old dry-grown grenache, now joined by 3.95ha of shiraz, cabernet sauvignon, petit verdot and tempranillo. Until 2004 the grapes were sold to a stellar clientele, but Bernadette now vinifies part of the production, selling the remainder to Spinifex and David Franz. 'My business is small,' she says, and she intends to keep it that way.

ROB DOLAN WINES Yarra Valley, Vic / PAGE 550

Rob Dolan has had a 20+ year career as a winemaker in the Yarra Valley. In 2011 he was able to purchase the Yarra Burn winery from Accolade at an enticing price. It is large and well equipped, giving him the opportunity to build on an extensive contract winemaking business, and, of course, make the wines under his own label. The quality and price of the wines on offer, should guarantee long-term success.

SHOWBLOCK ESTATE Currency Creek, SA / PAGE 596

In 2008 John and Sarae Adamopoulos were able to acquire 12ha of shiraz, cabernet sauvignon and merlot that had been planted in 1997. In a prior life John was an engineer and engineering teacher. His father and uncles have grown grapes in McLaren Vale since migrating to Australia from Greece 60 years ago, so winemaking is in his blood. The wines are not only well made, but very well priced.

THE ALCHEMISTS Margaret River, WA / PAGE 645

Former metallurgists Brad and Sarah Mitchell purchased their 13.6ha vineyard in 2007, then already 11 years old. The prior owners were simply grapegrowers, but The Alchemists have begun converting grapes into wine. They have reshaped the vineyard, removing vines on unsuitable soil, and grafting others to more appropriate varieties, and appointed Dave Johnson (Credaro Family Winery) as their contract winemaker. They have got off to a flying start with significant show success for their wines.

WOODS CRAMPTON South Australia / PAGE 724

Wine marketer and consultant Nicholas Crampton is not by training a grapegrower or a winemaker, but has a very good palate, and a keen understanding of the workings of the wine market at every level. He and winemaking friend Aaron Woods have formed this partnership, making the wines at Sons of Eden winery with yet further advice from winemaker Igor Kucic.

Ten dark horses

There was a large number of contenders for this recognition, and in part to reduce that number to a more manageable level, I have followed last year's pre-qualification that the winery in question has not previously achieved a five-star rating, although many have been knocking on the door of five stars over the years.

CAPE JAFFA WINES Mount Benson, SA / PAGE 153
Cape Jaffa was the Mount Benson pioneer, and has a substantial contract winemaking business as well as producing the excellent wines from its own 22.86ha vineyard. It became a fully certified biodynamic producer in 2008, and has received two Advantage SA Regional Awards for sustainable initiatives in the Limestone Coast, setting the scene early by building the winery from local rock.

COATES WINES McLaren Vale, SA / PAGE 187
Duane Coates has a string of degrees to his name, including a Master of Oenology from Adelaide University. He has made wine in many parts of the world, and has the practical and academic knowledge to sustain a near-natural winemaking regime (no additives or fining agents), a low level of new oak, and the use of organically grown grapes wherever possible.

ELDREDGE Clare Valley, SA / PAGE 249
Leigh and Karen Eldredge established their 21ha vineyard and winery 20 years ago in the Sevenhill Ranges at an altitude of 500m above Watervale. Over the years they have had conspicuous success with one or two wines, but have now produced a suite of lovely wines from the 2010 and '12 vintages, all keenly priced.

GOLDEN BALL Beechworth, Vic / PAGE 292
Planting of the 4ha vineyard began in 1996, and now has an eclectic range of varieties. James and Janine McLaurin have been content to fly under the radar, and have had little difficulty in selling the wines direct to a Who's Who of Melbourne's best restaurants and a handful of specialist wine stores.

GOLDEN GROVE ESTATE Granite Belt, Qld / PAGE 292
The Costanzo family began growing stone fruits and table grapes in 1946; the first wine grape (shiraz) followed in '72, but it was not until '85 when son Sam and wife Grace became the owners that the focus changed to wine. The 1.24ha estate vineyards have gradually taken shape, with an exotic array of varieties, the wines made with great skill thanks to third-generation Ray Costanzo's degree in oenology.

INDIGO WINE COMPANY Beechworth, Vic / **PAGE 342**

By one of those odd quirks, this is the second winery from Beechworth to make this year's selection. This is the largest vineyard in the Beechworth region, with over 46ha, and no less than 11 varieties planted. A substantial amount of the production goes to Brokenwood, which also contract-makes the 2000 dozens of Indigo wines.

MOUNT CATHEDRAL VINEYARDS Upper Goulburn, Vic / **PAGE 455**

The Rosa and Arena families began planting the 5ha estate vineyards on the north face of Mt Cathedral in 1995, completing the planting the following year. No pesticides or systemic chemicals are used in the vineyard, and winemaker Oscar Rosa has a Bachelor of Wine Science degree from CSU, coupled with practical experience working at Yering Station in the late '90s. The 2010 red wines are quite remarkable.

MOUNT TRIO VINEYARD Porongurup, WA / **PAGE 461**

Winemaker and co-owner Gavin Berry (with wife Gill Graham) came to the Great Southern region in 1988 to take up the role of chief winemaker at Plantagenet, but (with the approval of Plantagenet) also founded the estate-based Mount Trio Vineyard, slowly planting the vineyards with riesling, sauvignon blanc, pinot noir and shiraz. Gavin is also one of the partners (and winemakers) of the much larger West Cape Howe, but treasures Mount Trio Vineyard and its now mature vineyards.

SINGLEFILE WINES Denmark, WA / **PAGE 600**

Geologist Phil and Viv Snowden moved from South Africa to Perth in 1986, setting up a very successful multinational mining and resource services company that they sold in 2004, allowing them to fulfil their long-held desire to make and enjoy fine wine. In '07 they purchased an 18-year-old vineyard on a beautiful site, and with Larry Cherubino as consultant, reworked the vineyard and set up long-term grape purchase agreements across the whole of southwest Australia, venturing even further afield for a Barossa Valley Shiraz in '10. All of the wines are immaculately made.

WOODY NOOK Margaret River, WA / **PAGE 725**

Given the quality, and deserved wine show success, of the wines, Woody Nook has always had a low profile in the Margaret River region. Now over 30 years old, it was purchased by Peter and Jane Bailey in 2000, who built a new winery, a gallery tasting room for larger groups, and an al fresco dining area by the pond. Long-term winemaker Neil Gallagher continues to produce truly excellent wines.

Australia's geographical indications

The process of formally mapping Australia's wine regions is all but complete, although will never come to a complete halt – for one thing, climate change is lurking in the wings. The division into States, Zones, Regions and Subregions follows; those Regions or Subregions marked with an asterisk are not yet registered, and may never be, but are in common usage. The bizarre Hunter Valley GI map now has Hunter Valley as a Zone, Hunter as the Region and the sprawling Upper Hunter as a Subregion along with Pokolbin (small and disputed by some locals). Another recent official change has been the registration of Mount Gambier as a Region in the Limestone Coast Zone.

I am still in front of the game with Tasmania, dividing it into Northern, Southern and East Coast, and, to a lesser degree, have anticipated that the Darling Downs (four wineries) and coastal hinterland region of Queensland will seek recognition under this or some similar name. In similar vein, I have included Ballarat (with 17 wineries); and the Southern Eyre Peninsula (three wineries).

State/Zone	Region	Subregion
AUSTRALIA		
Australia Australian South Eastern Australia ★	★The South Eastern Australia Zone incorporates the whole of the states of NSW, Vic and Tasmania and only part of Qld and SA.	
NEW SOUTH WALES		
Big Rivers	Murray Darling Perricoota Riverina Swan Hill	
Central Ranges	Cowra Mudgee Orange	
Hunter Valley	Hunter	
		Broke Fordwich Pokolbin Upper Hunter Valley

State/Zone	Region	Subregion
Northern Rivers	Hastings River	
Northern Slopes	New England (Australia)	
South Coast	Shoalhaven Coast Southern Highlands	
Southern New South Wales	Canberra District Gundagai Hilltops Tumbarumba	
Western Plains		

SOUTH AUSTRALIA

Adelaide (Super Zone, includes Mount Lofty Ranges, Fleurieu and Barossa)

Barossa	Barossa Valley Eden Valley	High Eden
Far North	Southern Flinders Ranges	
Fleurieu	Currency Creek Kangaroo Island Langhorne Creek McLaren Vale Southern Fleurieu	
Limestone Coast	Coonawarra Mount Benson Mount Gambier Padthaway Robe Wrattonbully	
Lower Murray	Riverland	
Mount Lofty Ranges	Adelaide Hills Adelaide Plains Clare Valley	Lenswood Piccadilly Valley Polish Hill River★ Watervale★
The Peninsulas	Southern Eyre Peninsula★	

State/Zone	Region	Subregion
VICTORIA		
Central Victoria	Bendigo	
	Goulburn Valley	Nagambie Lakes
	Heathcote	
	Strathbogie Ranges	
	Upper Goulburn	
Gippsland		
North East Victoria	Alpine Valleys	
	Beechworth	
	Glenrowan	
	King Valley	
	Rutherglen	
North West Victoria	Murray Darling	
	Swan Hill	
Port Phillip	Geelong	
	Macedon Ranges	
	Mornington Peninsula	
	Sunbury	
	Yarra Valley	
Western Victoria	Ballarat★	
	Grampians	Great Western
	Henty	
	Pyrenees	
WESTERN AUSTRALIA		
Central Western Australia		
Eastern Plains, Inland and North of Western Australia		
Greater Perth	Peel	
	Perth Hills	
	Swan District	Swan Valley

State/Zone	Region	Subregion
South West Australia	Blackwood Valley	
	Geographe	
	Great Southern	Albany
		Denmark
		Frankland River
		Mount Barker
		Porongurup
	Manjimup	
	Margaret River	
	Pemberton	
West Australian South East Coastal		

QUEENSLAND

Queensland	Granite Belt	
	Queensland Coastal★	
	South Burnett	
	Darling Downs★	

TASMANIA

Tasmania	Northern Tasmania★	
	Southern Tasmania★	
	East Coast Tasmania★	

AUSTRALIAN CAPITAL TERRITORY

NORTHERN TERRITORY

Varietal wine styles and regions

For better or worse, there simply has to be concerted action to highlight the link between regions, varieties and wine styles. It's not a question of creating the links: they are already there, and have been in existence for periods as short as 20 years or as long as 150 years. So here is an abbreviated summary of those regional styles (in turn reflected in the Best of the Best lists commencing on page 25).

Riesling

The link with the **Eden Valley** dates back at least to when Joseph Gilbert planted his Pewsey Vale vineyard, and quickly made its way to the nearby **Clare Valley**. These two regions stood above all others for well over 100 years, producing wines that shared many flavour and texture characteristics: lime (a little more obvious in the Eden Valley), apple, talc and mineral, lightly browned toasty notes emerging with five to 10 years bottle age. Within the last 20 or so years, the subregions of the **Great Southern** of Western Australia have established a deserved reputation for finely structured, elegant wines with wonderful length, sometimes shy when young, bursting into song after five years. The subregions are (in alpha order) **Albany**, **Denmark**, **Frankland River**, **Mount Barker** and **Porongurup**. **Tasmania**, too, produces high class rieslings, notable for their purity and intensity courtesy of their high natural acidity. Finally, there is the small and very cool region of **Henty** (once referred to as Drumborg) with exceptional riesling sharing many things in common with Tasmania.

Semillon

There is a Siamese-twin relationship between semillon and the **Hunter Valley**, producing a wine style like no other in the world for well over 100 years. The humid and very warm climate (best coupled with sandy soils not common in the region) results in wines that have a median alcohol level of 10.5% and no residual sugar, cold-fermented in stainless steel and bottled within three months of vintage. They are devoid of colour and have only the barest hints of grass, herb and mineral wrapped around a core of acidity. Over the next five to 10 years they develop a glowing green-gold colour, a suite of grass and citrus fruit surrounded by buttered toast and honey notes. Like rieslings, screwcaps have added decades to their cellaring life. The **Adelaide Hills** and **Margaret River** produce entirely different semillon, more structured and weighty, its alcohol 13% to 14%, and as often as not blended with sauvignon blanc, barrel fermentation of part or all common. Finally, there is a cuckoo in the nest: Peter Lehmann in the **Barossa/Eden Valley** has adapted Hunter Valley practices, picking early, fermenting in steel, bottling early, and holding the top wine for five years before release – and succeeding brilliantly.

Chardonnay

This infinitely flexible grape is grown and vinified in all 63 regions, and accounts for half of Australia's white wine grapes and wine. Incredibly, before 1970 it was all but unknown, hiding its promise here and there (**Mudgee** was one such place) under a cloak of anonymity. It was there and in the **Hunter Valley** that the first wines labelled chardonnay were made in 1971 (by Craigmoor and Tyrrell's). Its bold yellow colour, peaches and cream flavour and vanilla oak was unlike anything that had gone before and was accepted by domestic and export markets with equal enthusiasm. When exports took off into the stratosphere between 1985 and 1995, one half of Brand Australia was cheerful and cheap oak-chipped chardonnay grown in the **Riverina** and **Riverland**. By coincidence, over the same period chardonnay from the emerging cool climate regions was starting to appear in limited quantities, its flavour and structure radically different to the warm-grown, high-cropped wine. Another 10 years on, and by 2005/06 the wine surplus was starting to build rapidly, with demand for chardonnay much less than its production. As attention swung from chardonnay to sauvignon blanc, the situation became dire. Lost in the heat of battle were supremely elegant wines from most cool regions, **Margaret River** and **Yarra Valley** the leaders of the large band. Constant refinement of the style, and the adoption of the screwcap, puts these wines at the forefront of the gradually succeeding battle to re-engage consumers here and abroad with what are world-class wines.

Sauvignon Blanc

Two regions, the **Adelaide Hills** and **Margaret River** stood in front of all others until recently joined by **Orange**; these three produce Australia's best sauvignon blanc, wines with real structure and authority. It is a matter of record that Marlborough sauvignon blanc accounts for one-third of Australia's white wine sales; all one can say (accurately) is that the basic Marlborough style is very different, and look back at what happened with Australian chardonnay. Margaret River also offers complex blends of sauvignon blanc and semillon in widely varying proportions, and varying degrees of oak fermentation.

Shiraz

Shiraz, like chardonnay, is by far the most important red variety and, again like chardonnay, is tremendously flexible in its ability to adapt to virtually any combination of climate and soil/terroir. Unlike chardonnay, a recent arrival, shiraz was the most important red variety throughout the 19th and 20th centuries. Its ancestral homes were the **Barossa Valley**, the **Clare Valley**, **McLaren Vale** and the **Hunter Valley**, and it still leads in those regions. With the exception of the Hunter Valley, it was as important in making fortified wine as table wine over the period 1850 to 1950, aided and abetted by grenache and mourvedre (mataro). In New South Wales the **Hilltops** and **Canberra District** are producing elegant, cool grown wines that usually conceal their power (especially when co-fermented with viognier) but not their silky length. Further north, but at a higher altitude, **Orange** is also producing fine, fragrant and spicy wines. All the other New South Wales regions are capable of producing good shiraz of seriously good character and quality; shiraz ripens comfortably, but quite late in the season. Polished, sophisticated wines are the result. Victoria has a cornucopia of regions at the cooler end of the spectrum; the coolest (though not too cool for comfort) are the **Yarra Valley**, **Mornington Peninsula**, **Sumbury** and **Geelong**, all producing fragrant, spicy medium-bodied wines. **Bendigo**, **Heathcote**, **Grampians** and **Pyrenees**, more or less running east-west across the centre of Victoria are producing some of the most exciting medium-bodied shirazs in Australia, each with its own terroir stamp, but all combing generosity and elegance. In Western Australia, **Great Southern** and three of its five subregions, **Frankland River**, **Mount Barker** and **Porongurup**, are making magical shirazs, fragrant and spicy, fleshy yet strongly structured. **Margaret River** has been a relatively late mover, but it, too, is producing wines with exemplary varietal definition and finesse.

Cabernet Sauvignon

The tough-skinned cabernet sauvignon can be, and is, grown in all regions, but it struggles in the coolest (notably **Tasmania**) and loses desirable varietal definition in the warmer regions, especially in warmer vintages. Shiraz can cope with alcohol levels in excess of 14.5%, cabernet can't. In South Australia, **Coonawarra** stands supreme, its climate (though not its soil) strikingly similar to that of Bordeaux, the main difference lower rainfall. Perfectly detailed cabernets are the result, with no need of shiraz or merlot to fill in the mid-palate, although some excellent blends are made. **Langhorne Creek** (a little warmer) and **McLaren Vale** (warmer still) have similar maritime climates, doubtless the reason why McLaren Vale manages to deal with the warmth of its summer/autumn weather. The **Eden Valley** is the most reliable of the inner regions, the other principal regions dependent on a cool summer. From South Australia to Western Australia, and **Margaret River**, with its extreme maritime climate shaped by the warm Indian Ocean, stands tall. It is also Australia's foremost producer of cabernet merlot et al in the Bordeaux mix. The texture and structure of both the straight varietal and the blend is regal, often to the point of austerity when the wines are young, but the sheer power of this underlying fruit provides the balance and guarantees the future development of the wines over a conservative 20 years, especially if screwcapped. The **Great Southern** subregions of **Frankland River** and **Mount Barker** share a continental climate that is somewhat cooler than Margaret River, and has a greater diurnal temperature range. Here cabernet has an incisive, dark berry character and firm but usually fine tannins – not demanding merlot, though a touch of it and/or malbec can be beneficial. It is grown successfully through the centre and south of Victoria, but is often overshadowed by shiraz. In the last 20 years it has ceased to be a problem child and become a favourite son of the **Yarra Valley**; the forward move of vintage dates has been the key to the change.

Pinot Noir

The promiscuity of shiraz (particularly) and cabernet sauvignon is in sharp contrast to the puritanical rectitude of pinot noir. One sin of omission or commission, and the door slams shut, leaving the bewildered winemaker on the outside. **Tasmania** is the El Dorado for the variety, and the best is still to come with better clones, older vines and greater exploration of the multitude of mesoclimates that Tasmania has to offer. While it is north of Central Otago (New Zealand), its vineyards are all air conditioned by the Southern Ocean and Tasman Sea, and it stands toe-to-toe with Central Otago in its ability to make deeply-coloured, profound pinot with all the length one could ask for. Once on the mainland, Victoria's Port Phillip Zone, encompassing the **Geelong**, **Macedon Ranges**, **Sunbury**, **Mornington Peninsula** and **Yarra Valley** is the epicentre of Australian pinot noir, **Henty** a small outpost. The sheer number of high quality, elegant wines produced by dozens of makers in those regions put the **Adelaide Hills** and **Porongurup** (also capable of producing quality pinot) into the shade.

Other Red Varieties

There are many other red varieties in the Wine Companion database, and there is little rhyme or reason for the distribution of the plantings.

Sparkling Wines

The patter is eerily similar to that of pinot noir, **Tasmania** now and in the future the keeper of the Holy Grail, the **Port Phillip Zone** the centre of activity on the mainland.

Fortified Wines

Rutherglen and **Glenrowan** are the two (and only) regions that produce immensely complex, long-barrel-aged muscat and muscadelle, the latter called tokay for over a century, now renamed topaque. These wines have no equal in the world, Spain's Malaga nearest in terms of lusciousness, but nowhere near as complex. The other producer of a wine without parallel is Seppeltsfield in the **Barossa Valley**, which each year releases an explosively rich and intense tawny liqueur style that is 100% 100 years old.

Australian vintage charts

Each number represents a mark out of 10 for the quality of vintages in each region.

red wine   white wine

2009	2010	2011	2012

NSW

Hunter Valley

7	7	10	2
10	9	7	7

Mudgee

8	6	6	5
9	8	8	7

Cowra

7	7	4	7
8	6	6	8

Orange

8	9	6	7
9	9	7	8

Riverina/Griffith

7	7	6	8
6	8	7	9

Canberra District

9	8	8	7
9	9	9	8

Southern Highlands

6	7	6	4
9	7	7	7

Hilltops

8	8	7	7
8	-	6	7

Tumbarumba

8	-	6	-
8	-	7	7

Shoalhaven

8	5	7	6
8	7	8	8

2009	2010	2011	2012

VIC

Yarra Valley

2	9	6	10
7	9	9	9

Mornington Peninsula

9	10	5	9
9	9	6	9

Geelong

9	9	6	10
9	9	7	8

Macedon Ranges

7	8	7	8
8	7	8	7

Sunbury

9	-	6	8
8	-	7	8

Grampians

8	9	7	8
9	8	8	8

Pyrenees

7	8	5	8
7	7	8	7

Henty

9	8	9	8
8	8	8	8

Bendigo

8	4	8	6
8	7	9	6

Heathcote

8	9	8	9
8	8	9	9

2009	2010	2011	2012

Goulburn Valley

7	8	6	7
8	8	8	8

Upper Goulburn

6	9	5	8
8	8	9	7

Strathbogie Ranges

6	8	2	7
7	9	6	7

Glenrowan & Rutherglen

-	8	4	8
-	7	6	8

King Valley

8	8	5	7
7	7	7	8

Alpine Valleys

8	8	4	7
8	8	6	9

Beechworth

2	8	6	8
7	10	8	9

Gippsland

6	10	6	9
8	9	8	8

Murray Darling

8	7	1	9
8	7	4	9

	2009	2010	2011	2012
SA				
Barossa Valley	7	9	5	9
	7	8	7	8
Eden Valley	9	8	5	8
	8	9	7	9
Clare Valley	9	8	5	8
	8	9	7	10
Adelaide Hills	9	9	3	9
	9	9	6	9
Adelaide Plains	-	9	5	8
	-	7	6	6
Coonawarra	7	9	6	8
	8	8	8	8
Padthaway	6	-	6	8
	8	-	8	8
Mount Benson & Robe	7	-	5	9
	8	-	7	9
Wrattonbully	6	9	5	9
	7	8	7	8
McLaren Vale	8	8	7	9
	7	7	8	9

	2009	2010	2011	2012
Southern Fleurieu	7	8	7	9
	7	8	8	8
Langhorne Creek	-	10	7	9
	-	9	8	8
Kangaroo Island	9	8	6	10
	10	9	8	10
Riverland	6	-	5	9
	7	-	5	7
WA				
Margaret River	9	9	9	10
	9	8	8	8
Great Southern	8	8	9	8
	9	8	8	8
Manjimup	7	-	8	7
	8	-	8	7
Pemberton	8	8	8	8
	9	7	8	8
Geographe	8	-	9	9
	8	-	8	7
Swan District	10	8	8	9
	10	8	7	7

	2009	2010	2011	2012
Peel	8	8	-	8
	7	7	-	8
Perth Hills	10	8	-	8
	8	8	-	7
QLD				
Granite Belt	-	7	5	8
	-	7	4	7
South Burnett	-	9	5	8
	-	8	8	7
TAS				
Northern Tasmania	8	8	7	8
	8	9	8	9
Southern Tasmania	8	9	8	9
	8	8	9	8

HARDIE GRANT IS PLEASED TO ANNOUNCE THE INAUGURAL

JAMES
HALLIDAY

AUSTRALIAN
WINE
COMPANION
AWARDS

AWCA

WINE OF THE YEAR

WINERY OF THE YEAR

BEST NEW WINERY

BEST DARK HORSE WINERY

hardie grant books

Acknowledgements

It is, I suppose, inevitable that the production of a book such as this should involve many people in a long chain of events, some seemingly trivial, others of fundamental importance.

The starting point is the making of the thousands of bottles of wine Ben Edwards and I taste each year (Tyson Stelzer a recent contributor), and the end point is the appearance of the book on retailers' shelves across Australia on 1 August 2013. Well prior to that date, many hundreds of tasting notes for the 2015 edition will have been made, and details of yet more new wineries will have been entered.

My foremost thanks must go to the winemakers for sending the wines to me at their cost, and in particular those who treat submission dates as serious deadlines rather than an approximate wish-list on my part. Those who ignored the deadlines are increasingly likely to fall on their own sword as the competition for space in the book intensifies.

Next are those responsible for getting the wine to me, whether by the excellent parcel delivery service of Australia Post, by courier or by hand delivery. I am reliant on the goodwill and tolerance of many people involved in what may seem as a warped version of trivial pursuits as the wines arrive, are placed in bins, in due course fork-lifted up one story and removed from those bins, unpacked, listed, entered into the database, with precise names cross-checked, alcohol, price, and closure type recorded, tasting sheets printed for the day's tasting of 120 wines, initially arranged by producer, but then re-sorted by variety, moved onto a long tasting bench, opened, poured at the same pace I taste, the Riedel glasses returned to washing racks, washed, rinsed and dried, the tasting notes typed, the database now returning the notes to a winery-by-winery sequence, proof-checked by me (and at least three others at subsequent stages before going to print).

In the meantime, my office team of Paula Grey and Beth Anthony (also chief steward, unpacker and enterer of wines into the database), has been busy chasing up new, missing or inconsistent details regarding the winery and the wines. To those who remember to provide the price (and if available, the alcohol) my special thanks. I only wish I could extend those thanks more often.

Then there is the ever-patient, but deadline-conscious, team at Hardie Grant, working on cover design (surely brilliant), page design, paper type, two-colour printing, which give rise to the galley pages for proof-reading again and again.

To my team of Paula Grey and Beth Anthony; Ben Edwards and Tyson Stelzer; Coldstream Post Office (Barry, Trevor and Val); Pam Holmes (and others at Coldstream Hills); John Cook (Programmer); and the Hardie Grant team led by believer-in-chief Sandy Grant, Sarah Shrubb and Hannah Koelmeyer (Editors), Megan Ellis (Typesetter) and Nada Backovic (cover design). This is as much their book as it is mine.

Halliday in your pocket

The James Halliday Australian Wine Companion App

9000 new tasting notes available for download each year.
Access over 80 000 tasting notes, spanning more than 10 years of tastings.
Get 100 new tasting notes every month with each update.
Read over 2800 reviews of Australia's leading wineries.
Create lists of your own favourite wines. Use it as your cellar!

hardie grant books

Australian wineries
and wines

A. Retief

PO Box 2503, Strawberry Hills, NSW 2012 **Region** Southern New South Wales Zone
T 0400 650 530 **www**.aretief.com.au **Open** Not
Winemaker Alex Retief **Est.** 2008 **Dozens** 5000

Owner and winemaker Alex Retief's wine career was prompted by his parents planting a
vineyard near Ladysmith, in the Gundagai region, in 1997. He enrolled in the wine science
course at CSU, and in 2001 was accepted as the trainee winemaker at the university's winery
under Greg Gallagher. In mid '02 he went to California's Sonoma Valley, working at Fetzer
Vineyards, returning to the Hunter Valley for the '03 vintage with Andrew Margan. He
was winemaker there for two and a half years, punctuated by a harvest in Languedoc in '04,
before heading back to France in '05 for a two-year appointment as winemaker at Chateau de
Lagarde in Bordeaux. Since then he has started his own boutique wine distribution company.
Its portfolio includes A. Retief, imported and local wines. The A. Retief wines are made from
contract-grown grapes in the Tumbarumba/Canberra District/Hilltops/Gundagai regions.

ΨΨΨΨΨ **Shiraz 2010** Good bright colour; the grapes come from the biodynamic
Winbirra Vineyard in Gundagai, extremely confusing given there is also a Winbirra
Vineyard in the Mornington Peninsula – and also given the strong, spicy, black
cherry aromas and flavours of this wine, with its cool-climate style. Screwcap.
13.5% alc. **Rating** 93 **To** 2030 $28

Rose 2012 Pale salmon-pink, made from cabernet sauvignon grown in Gundagai.
The deliberate retention of a fine film of tannins has given rise to very good
texture and mouthfeel; the flavours are entirely in red berry territory, and the
whole assemblage works very well. Screwcap. 13% alc. **Rating** 92 **To** 2014 $28

The Cabernets 2010 A Hilltops-grown 55/30/10/5% blend of cabernet
sauvignon, petit verdot, malbec and merlot, the colour deep and bright. There is
a leafy/minty edge in the forest of red and black fruits (plus 18 months in French
barriques). I may be misinterpreting a more simple need for time. Screwcap.
14% alc. **Rating** 92 **To** 2020 $28

A. Rodda Wines

PO Box 589, Beechworth, Vic 3747 **Region** Beechworth
T 0400 350 135 **www**.aroddawines.com.au **Open** Not
Winemaker Adrian Rodda **Est.** 2010 **Dozens** 800 **Vyds** 2ha

Adrian Rodda has been winemaking since 1998, almost entirely working with David Bicknell
at Oakridge. He was involved in the development of the superb Oakridge 864 Chardonnay,
his final contribution to 864 coming in 2009. At the start of 2010 he and his wife Christie, a
doctor, and their growing family, decided to move to Beechworth, home of long-term friend
and viticulturist Mark Walpole. The Smith Vineyard and winery were available for lease; he
now shares it with Mark, who makes his Beechworth wines there. Even more fortunate was
the availability of Smith Vineyard chardonnay, planted in 1974, and thus the release of the
first A. Rodda wine. This was followed by a Yarra Chardonnay, a single vineyard Tempranillo,
and a Bordeaux blend sourced predominantly from the old plantings on the Smith Vineyard.

ΨΨΨΨΨ **Cuvee de Chez 2011** A 59/16/13/12% Bordeaux blend of cabernet sauvignon,
petit verdot, malbec and merlot made with very considerable skill; the components
were hand-picked and fermented separately; the colour is a gloriously clear
crimson-purple, the bouquet fragrant, the medium-bodied palate with superb
line, length and balance to its red and black fruits, the tannins seamless. Enough to
seduce the palate of an elderly lover of pinot noir, and an absolute triumph for '11.
Screwcap. 13% alc. **Rating** 96 **To** 2041 $36

Murrammong Vineyard Yarra Valley Chardonnay 2011 The grapes were
pressed direct to barrels (puncheons) with no SO_2 added until the conclusion of
wild yeast fermentation; the wine is intensely tangy, grapefruit to the fore, but with
some white peach fruit also present; the oak is subtle, and the wine will flower
over the next few years. Screwcap. 13% alc. **Rating** 94 **To** 2019 $36

ΨΨΨΨΨ **Aquila Audax Vineyard Tempranillo 2011 Rating** 93 **To** 2018 $32

A.T. Richardson Wines

94 Hard Hill Road, Armstrong, Vic 3377 **Region** Grampians
www.atrichardsonwines.com **Open** Not
Winemaker Adam Richardson **Est.** 2005 **Dozens** 1800 **Vyds** 7ha
Perth-born Adam Richardson began his winemaking career in 1995, along the way working for Normans, d'Arenberg and Oakridge Estate. Since then he has been appointed Director of Global Winemaking for the international premium wines division of The Wine Group, the third-largest producer in the US. He is responsible for an annual production of more than five million dozen from Argentina, Australia, Austria, California, Chile, France, Germany, Italy, NZ, Oregon, Spain, South Africa and Washington. In 2005 he put down small roots in the Grampians region, acquiring a vineyard with shiraz from old clones from the 19th century, and riesling. They are exceptionally good wines, and given his experience and the quality of the vineyard, that should not come as a surprise.

Chockstone Grampians Chardonnay 2012 Pale straw-green; has the focus, structure and intensity to prove its best years are still in front of it; the oak is totally integrated into the long palate, which reflects its early picking in its grapefruit/mineral flavour profile. Screwcap. 12.5% alc. **Rating** 93 **To** 2020 $25

Chockstone Grampians Shiraz 2011 Full purple-crimson; ripe, round spiced plum and licorice aromas and flavours are bolstered by obvious oak and good tannins; a vintage get out of jail free card courtesy of vigilance in the vineyard and winery alike. Screwcap. 14.1% alc. **Rating** 91 **To** 2017 $25

Chockstone Grampians Riesling 2012 Rating 89 **To** 2016 $20

Abbey Creek Vineyard

2388 Porongurup Road, Porongurup, WA 6324 **Region** Porongurup
T (08) 9853 1044 **Open** By appt
Winemaker Castle Rock Estate (Robert Diletti) **Est.** 1990 **Dozens** 800 **Vyds** 1.6ha
This is the family business of Mike and Mary Dilworth, the name coming from a winter creek that runs alongside the vineyard and a view of The Abbey in the Stirling Range. The vineyard is split between pinot noir, riesling and sauvignon blanc. The Rieslings have had significant show success for a number of years.

Porongurup Riesling 2012 Light straw-green; the fragrant bouquet suggests the wine will be full of lime citrus fruit, but when it is tasted the initial minerally impression on the fore-palate is contrary to that expectation; however, as the wine reaches the back-palate it surges into life with all the citrus and mineral you could ever wish for. Screwcap. 12% alc. **Rating** 94 **To** 2022 $25

Porongurup Pinot Noir 2010 Rating 92 **To** 2016 $30
Porongurup Sauvignon Blanc 2012 Rating 90 **To** 2014 $24
Porongurup Pinot Noir 2011 Rating 90 **To** 2016 $30

Accolade Wines

Reynell Road, Reynella, SA 5161 **Region** Various
T (08) 8392 2300 **www**.accolade-wines.com **Open** Not
Winemaker Various **Est.** 2011 **Dozens** NFP
Accolade Wines came into being in 2011 when a private equity group (CHAMP) acquired the business from Constellation Wines of the US. The principal Australian brands owned by Accolade are Amberley, Banrock Station, Bay of Fires/House of Arras, Brookland Valley, Goundrey, Hardys, Houghton, Leasingham, Moondah Brook, Reynella, Tintara and Yarra Burn. Exports to all major markets.

Across the Lake

White Dam Road, Lake Grace, WA 6353 **Region** Eastern Plains, Inland and North of Western Australia Zone
T 0409 685 373 **Open** By appt
Winemaker Rockliffe (Coby Ladwig) **Est.** 1999 **Dozens** 300 **Vyds** 2ha
The Taylor family has been farming (wheat and sheep) for over 40 years at Lake Grace; a small diversification into grapegrowing started as a hobby, but has developed into more than that with 2ha of shiraz. They were motivated to support their friend Bill (WJ) Walker, who had started growing shiraz three years previously, and has since produced a gold medal-winning wine. Having learnt which soils are suitable, the Taylors intend to increase their plantings.

ΨΨΨΨΨ **Shiraz 2010** Reappears after a lengthy absence. Has excellent colour, and is
✪ flooded with superb shiraz fruit, luscious but vibrant, ranging through black cherry, plum and blackberry flavours; the tannins are in perfect balance, the oak likewise. Exceptional bargain. Screwcap. 13.8% alc. **Rating** 94 **To** 2030 $15

✪ **Shiraz 2007** Utterly remarkable colour, still crimson-purple; likewise, the bouquet and palate are still fresh and vibrant, with a blend of plum and blackberry fruit, spice and licorice. I was Chairman of the Qantas Wine Show of WA in '08, and vividly remember the wine and the excitement it caused. Now a bargain of monumental proportions. Screwcap. 13.9% alc. **Rating** 94 **To** 2020 $20

Adelaide Winemakers

281 Tatachilla Road, McLaren Vale, SA 5171 **Region** Adelaide Zone
T (08) 8323 6100 **www**.adelaidewinemakers.com.au **Open** 7 days 11–4
Winemaker Nick Haselgrove, Scott Rawlinson **Est.** 2010 **Dozens** 25 000 **Vyds** 418ha
As a result of various sales, amalgamations and disposals of particular brands, Adelaide Winemakers is now owned (equally) by Nick Haselgrove, David Watkins and Warren Randall. It either owns, part-owns or is in the process of absorbing some of the external part-ownerships of some of the brands (The Old Faithful – see separate entry – Quorum, Blackbilly, James Haselgrove, The Old Gentlemen, Clarence Hill, Ace High and Martins Road). Adelaide Winemakers works with World Wine Headquarters (with old friend John Larchet) for the Wishing Tree, Hill of Content and Tir na N'og brands. Adelaide Winemakers has over 400ha of vines across Adelaide Hills (5ha), McLaren Vale (27ha), Langhorne Creek (216ha) and Currency Creek (170ha), giving the interconnected businesses a great deal of flexibility. Exports to the US and other major markets.

ΨΨΨΨΨ **Blackbilly McLaren Vale Tempranillo 2011** Deeply coloured, with blackberry, cola, thyme and mocha oak on display; the palate is medium-bodied, lively with tangy acid and long with ample fleshy black fruits; uncomplicated and ready for early consumption. Screwcap. 13% alc. **Rating** 90 **To** 2016 $22 BE

ΨΨΨΨ **James Haselgrove Futures Shiraz 2010** **Rating** 89 **To** 2025 $35
Clarence Hill Adelaide Shiraz 2011 **Rating** 87 **To** 2016 $14 BE

Adelina Wines

PO Box 75, Sevenhill, SA 5453 **Region** Clare Valley
T (08) 8842 1549 **www**.adelina.com.au **Open** Not
Winemaker Colin McBryde, Jennie Gardner **Est.** 2000 **Dozens** 400
When the Gardner family acquired Spring Farm Estate, it had 0.5ha of shiraz and 0.3ha of grenache planted around 1910, and a further 0.3ha of cabernet sauvignon and pinot noir planted in '70. In 2000 they ceased selling the grapes and established Adelina Wines. Winemakers Jennie Gardner and Colin McBryde have a broad background, from winemaking and cellar experience to medical research and hospitality, both having worked in numerous regions in New and Old World wineries over the past 10 years. Both are currently completing their doctorates in oenological science at the Adelaide University, studying yeast metabolism.

♥♥♥♥♥ **Clare Valley Shiraz 2010** Around 200 dozen bottles made, and the striking label is full of shades of black. Getting past that, this is a remarkably elegant wine, with a juicy cascade of red fruits, finely tempered French oak, and silky tannins. Screwcap. 13.9% alc. **Rating** 94 **To** 2025 $45

♥♥♥♥ **Clare Valley Grenache 2010 Rating** 89 **To** 2016 $45

After Hours

455 North Jindong Road, Margaret River, WA 6285 **Region** Margaret River
T 0438 737 587 **www**.afterhourswine.com.au **Open** By appt
Winemaker Phil Potter **Est.** 2006 **Dozens** 1500 **Vyds** 8.6ha
In 2005 Warwick and Cherylyn Mathews acquired the long-established Hopelands Vineyard, planted to cabernet sauvignon (2.6ha), shiraz (1.6ha), merlot, semillon, sauvignon blanc and chardonnay (1.1ha each). The first wine was made in '06, after which they decided to completely rework the vineyard. The vines were retrained, with a consequent reduction in yield and rise in wine quality. Exceptional value for money across the board.

♥♥♥♥♀ ✪ **Margaret River Chardonnay 2011** Pale, bright straw-green; the fragrant and expressive fruit-driven bouquet leads into a fresh, lively palate with white and yellow stone fruit supported by subtle French oak and perfectly judged acidity. Screwcap. 13.5% alc. **Rating** 93 **To** 2016 $19

✪ **9 to 5 Margaret River Semillon Sauvignon Blanc 2012** Pale quartz; the wine nonchalantly over-delivers for its price, opening with fleeting herb/grass/nettle nuances before moving decisively to citrus/guava/passionfruit; the finish is crisp and clear. Screwcap. 13% alc. **Rating** 92 **To** 2013 $14

✪ **Margaret River Sauvignon Blanc Semillon 2012** Pale straw-green; crammed with tropical lychee and passionfruit, with an overall sweetness balanced by good acidity; a no-frills style, ready now. Screwcap. 12.5% alc. **Rating** 90 **To** 2014 $18

✪ **Oliver Margaret River Shiraz 2010** Good red-purple colour; a well-constructed medium-bodied wine made from estate-grown grapes and matured for 18 months in predominantly used French and American oak; there are some spicy notes to the plum and black cherry fruit, and the tannins are well balanced and ripe. Screwcap. 14% alc. **Rating** 90 **To** 2018 $18

Alkoomi

Wingebellup Road, Frankland River, WA 6396 **Region** Frankland River
T (08) 9855 2229 **www**.alkoomiwines.com.au **Open** 7 days 10–5
Winemaker Andrew Cherry **Est.** 1971 **Dozens** 70 000 **Vyds** 104.58ha
For those who see the wineries of WA as suffering from the tyranny of distance, this most remote of all wineries shows there is no tyranny after all. It is a story of unqualified success due to sheer hard work, and no doubt to founders Merv and Judy Lange's aversion to borrowing a single dollar from the bank. The substantial production is entirely drawn from the estate vineyards. Wine quality across the range is impeccable, always with precisely defined varietal character. Sandy Hallet, Merv and Judy's daughter, assumed full ownership of Alkoomi in 2010, having been an integral part of the business for many years. She and husband Rod, together with daughters Laura, Emily and Molly, represent the second and third generations to be involved in this remarkably successful family business. Exports to all major markets.

♥♥♥♥♥ ✪ **White Label Frankland River Semillon Sauvignon Blanc 2010** Straw-green; a compelling argument for the ability of this blend to age without losing the charm it has as a young wine. This wine has filled out, with very good mouthfeel engendered by tropical fruit, citrus and grass nuances, but the balanced acidity holds the wine together. Screwcap. 11.5% alc. **Rating** 94 **To** 2015 $20

✪ **Black Label Frankland River Chardonnay 2011** Pale, bright green-quartz; barrel fermentation in French oak and lees stirring has built up a richly textured, creamy mid-palate, followed by a cleansing fruit and acid finish. Great value. Screwcap. 13.5% alc. **Rating** 94 **To** 2018 $22

Jarrah Frankland River Shiraz 2009 Medium crimson-purple; a fragrant spice, red berry and briar bouquet leads into a medium-bodied palate introducing black fruits, licorice, powdery tannins and quality oak to join the characters of the bouquet. Screwcap. 13.5% alc. **Rating** 94 **To** 2024 $45

✪ Black Label Frankland River Cabernet Sauvignon 2010 Medium crimson-purple; a very attractive medium-bodied Cabernet; it has juicy and lively cassis and redcurrant fruit, polished tannins and integrated oak on the long, well-balanced medium-bodied palate. Screwcap. 14.5% alc. **Rating** 94 **To** 2025 $22

♟♟♟♟♟ Black Label Frankland River Riesling 2011 An elegant wine, with the line,
✪ length and balance the region always confers on its wines; has begun what will be a long journey to full maturity, giving pleasure along the way, toasty notes ultimately joining the citrus of today. Screwcap. 12.5% alc. **Rating** 93 **To** 2021 $20

✪ Frankland River Semillon 2012 Estate-grown, 50/50% fermented in stainless steel and new French oak, with continued lees contact post fermentation. The approach has totally succeeded, the lemongrass and citrus fruit having absorbed the oak flavours, but benefited from the additional mouthfeel and length. Exceptional value. Screwcap. 13.8% alc. **Rating** 93 **To** 2017 $18

✪ Black Label Frankland River Shiraz Viognier 2010 Light, bright, crimson-purple; the spicy, red berry bouquet leads into a juicy, medium-bodied palate, with red and black cherry fruit, touches of pepper and cedary oak imparted by 16 months in French barrels. Screwcap. 14.5% alc. **Rating** 93 **To** 2020 $20

✪ Frankland River Cabernets 2011 Bright hue; a 44/26/21/8/1% blend of cabernet sauvignon, cabernet franc, petit verdot, malbec and merlot separately fermented. Has a long life ahead as the red and black fruits, plentiful tannins and cedary oak all come together, and will richly reward patience. Screwcap. 13.5% alc. **Rating** 93 **To** 2026 $18

✪ Frankland River Semillon Sauvignon Blanc 2012 A small portion of the semillon was barrel-fermented in French oak; estate-grown from the oldest blocks, it has impressive intensity, balance and complexity for a wine at its price. Ripe lemon zest and lemon curd flavours mingle with guava, lychee and gooseberry fruit. Screwcap. 13% alc. **Rating** 92 **To** 2014 $18

♟♟♟♟ White Label Frankland River Sauvignon Blanc 2012 From estate-grown
✪ vines on various blocks up to 25 years old. Quartz-white, the aromas and flavours are in a citrus/herb/snow pea/mineral spectrum. Classic summer seafood style, and very well priced. Screwcap. 13.3% alc. **Rating** 89 **To** 2013 $16

All Saints Estate   ★★★★★

All Saints Road, Wahgunyah, Vic 3687 **Region** Rutherglen
T 1800 021 621 **www**.allsaintswine.com.au **Open** Mon–Sat 9–5.30, Sun 10–5.30
Winemaker Dan Crane, Nick Brown **Est.** 1864 **Dozens** 25 000 **Vyds** 33.46ha
The winery rating reflects the fortified wines, but the table wines are also in the top drawer. The Terrace restaurant makes this a most enjoyable stop for any visitor to Northeast Victoria. The faux castle, modelled on a Scottish castle beloved by the founder, is classified by the Historic Buildings Council. All Saints and St Leonards are owned and managed by fourth-generation Brown family members Eliza, Angela and Nicholas. Eliza is an energetic and highly intelligent leader, wise beyond her years, and highly regarded by the wine industry. Dan Crane's winemaking skills across the whole portfolio are very impressive. Exports to the UK, the US, Singapore and China.

♟♟♟♟♟ Rare Rutherglen Muscat NV A highly aromatic perfumed bouquet, then a palate that, while holding firm to the raisin aromas and flavours expected of muscat, dares to introduce the idea of elegance into this level of intensity. Remarkable wine, marching to the tune of its own drum. 375ml. Vino-Lok. 18% alc. **Rating** 98 **To** 2014 $115

Rare Rutherglen Muscat Museum Release NV The ultimate in complexity and concentration; from a solera started in 1920, and only 250 litres are released in 500 square bottles of 500ml each year, the presentation doing full justice. It is a deep olive-brown, and pours reluctantly from the bottle so viscous is it. While its great age is obvious in the liqueur raisin fruit and Christmas pudding flavours running along the length of the impossibly long palate, the finish is a mix of satin, silk and velvet all at the one time, with none of the volatile acidity that can sharpen these very old wines. Glass stopper. 18% alc. **Rating** 98 **To** 2014 $1000

Rare Rutherglen Topaque NV Burnt umber grading to olive on the rim; apart from a highly perfumed/scented array of spices on the bouquet, it is the sheer intensity and complexity of the wine that tells of its very long time in wood, and the consequent development of rancio; the final magic of the wine is its semi-dry finish. 375ml. Vino-Lok. 18% alc. **Rating** 97 **To** 2014 $115

All Saints Grand Rutherglen Tawny NV Tawny colour; a blend of grenache and shiraz that is traditional in the Barossa Valley, less common in Rutherglen. Has very spicy Christmas cake, butterscotch aromas and flavours; terrific length, balance and a gently drying aftertaste from the rancio. Vino-Lok. 18% alc. **Rating** 96 **To** 2014 $35

Grand Rutherglen Topaque NV Grades to near olive on the rim; has a high-quality array of tea leaf, malt, Christmas cake, butterscotch aromas and flavours; terrific length, balance and a gently drying aftertaste from the rancio. Vino-Lok. 18% alc. **Rating** 96 **To** 2014 $70

Grand Rutherglen Muscat NV Slightly more russet hue to the middle of the glass, and less olive on the rim; gloriously luscious raisin fruit with nuances of spice, treacle and caramelised ginger, the palate long and perfectly balanced. Vino-Lok. 18% alc. **Rating** 95 **To** 2014 $70

Family Cellar Shiraz 2010 Rating 94 To 2025 $50

Estate Merlot 2011 Rating 94 To 2021 $28

Pierre 2010 Rating 94 To 2030 $30

ҭҭҭҭҭ **Durif 2011** Rating 93 To 2016 $28

✪ **Rutherglen Muscat NV** Amber-brown; full-on potent raisin flavours, the spirit, treacle and butterscotch also adding to the weight and concentration of the flavour. 375ml. Vino-Lok. 17% alc. **Rating** 93 **To** 2014 $22

Riesling 2012 Rating 92 To 2018 $22

Alias II 2010 Rating 92 To 2020 $35

✪ **Rutherglen Tokay NV** Light gold-amber; has strong varietal character, with a mix of honey, singed toffee and tea leaf; overall, has greater weight and complexity than many in this bottom-of-the-range classification. 375ml. Vino-Lok. 17% alc. **Rating** 92 **To** 2014 $22

Rosa 2012 Rating 90 To 2014 $18

Shiraz 2010 Rating 90 To 2020 $28

Allies Wines

15 Hume Road, Somers, Vic 3927 (postal) **Region** Mornington Peninsula
T 0412 111 587 **www.**allies.com.au **Open** Not
Winemaker David Chapman **Est.** 2003 **Dozens** 800
Founders Barney Flanders and David Chapman have had an amicable business separation. David will be making the wines under the Allies brand, Barney taking on the Garagiste label. Henceforth, David will concentrate on wines from the Mornington Peninsula and, in particular, Pinot Noir. He has begun to release a range of Pinot Noirs reflecting the diverse sites (climate and soil) of the Peninsula. The wines are line-priced: in other words, the aim is to highlight differing site characters, rather than differing wine quality.

ҭҭҭҭҭ **Main Ridge Mornington Peninsula Pinot Noir 2011** Light garnet, bright; vibrant red cherry aromas and fine Asian spices on the bouquet; the palate with taut acidity and fine-grained tannins framing the fruit with distinction; long, poised and linear to conclude. Screwcap. 13% alc. **Rating** 93 **To** 2018 $31 BE

Merricks Mornington Peninsula Pinot Noir 2011 Mid garnet; with dark cherry and savoury bracken notes on the bouquet; the palate is light to medium-bodied with forceful, almost chewy tannins a feature on the long finish; should evolve gracefully over time. An excellent effort in a challenging vintage. Screwcap. 13% alc. **Rating** 93 **To** 2018 $31 BE

Alta Vineyards ★★★★☆

102 Main Street, Hahndorf, SA 5245 **Region** Adelaide Hills
T (08) 8388 7155 **www**.altavineyards.com.au **Open** 7 days 10.30–5
Winemaker Sarah Fletcher **Est.** 2003 **Dozens** 10 000 **Vyds** 23ha
Sarah Fletcher came to Alta with an impressive winemaking background: a degree from Roseworthy, and thereafter seven years working for Orlando Wyndham. There she came face to face with grapes from all over Australia, and developed a particular regard for those from the Adelaide Hills. So she joined Alta, which had already established a reputation for its Sauvignon Blanc. The portfolio has been progressively extended with varieties suited to the cool climate of the Adelaide Hills. Exports to the UK, Canada and Hong Kong.

🍷🍷🍷🍷🍷 **Adelaide Hills Sauvignon Blanc 2012** Wow. Separate blocks were picked at
✪   different baume levels; part was fermented on skins, part in large French oak casks; part was given extended lees contact post-fermentation; and several specifically chosen yeast strains were used; lime, grapefruit and gooseberry fruit flavours soar through the palate, finish and aftertaste. A triumph of winemaking. Screwcap. 12.5% alc. **Rating** 96 **To** 2014 $20

🍷🍷🍷🍷🍷 **for Elsie Pinot Noir Rose 2012** Very much à la mode winemaking, with
✪   some of the juice fermented in oak, part in stainless steel, then blended and taken through mlf. The result is a wine with tactile mouthfeel, yet retaining strawberry as the dominant flavour. Screwcap. 12% alc. **Rating** 92 **To** 2014 $20
Adelaide Hills Pinot Grigio 2012 Rating 90 **To** 2013 $22

🌿 Altamont Wine Studio ★★★★★

49 Peacock's Road, Lenswood, SA 5240 **Region** Adelaide Hills
T (08) 8327 4188 **www**.altamontwinestudio.com **Open** By appt
Winemaker Brendon Keys **Est.** 2012 **Dozens** 2000
Winemaker Brendon Keys was the inspiration for the establishment of Altamont Wine Studio, but has formed a partnership with Brian Gilbert, Steve Harris, Michael Sawyer and Matthew Morrissy to bring Altamont (and its associated label, Seven Deadly Vins, with Michael Sawyer the winemaker) to fruition. The aim of the business is simple: to secure small but very high-quality batches of Adelaide Hills fruit, thus making each wine in relatively small amounts. All of the wines are priced at $25, and the initial releases are exceptionally good.

🍷🍷🍷🍷🍷 **Single Vineyard Adelaide Hills Sauvignon Blanc 2012** Light straw-green;
✪   a Sauvignon Blanc that is full of life and energy, with delicately poised tropical fruits explosively expanding into a green apple, citrus and mineral finish. Excellent balance and length. Screwcap. 12.8% alc. **Rating** 94 **To** 2014 $25
✪   **Single Vineyard Adelaide Hills Pinot Noir 2012** The vivid, retro label will absolutely polarise opinion – once seen, never forgotten. Excellent purple-crimson colour, the bouquet and palate with a plush array of red and black cherry, supple tannins and integrated oak. It has the balance to develop very well over the next 5 years. Screwcap. 13.5% alc. **Rating** 94 **To** 2021 $25
✪   **Seven Deadly Vins Barossa Shiraz Grenache Mataro 2009** Another label not easily forgotten. Strikingly bright, clear crimson-purple, has far more juicy elegance to its red cherry and raspberry fruit than most such blends of Barossa origin. Ready now. Screwcap. 14.5% alc. **Rating** 94 **To** 2016 $25

🍷🍷🍷🍷🍷 **Single Vineyard Adelaide Hills Chardonnay 2012 Rating** 93 **To** 2019 $25

Amadio Wines ★★★★☆

461 Payneham Road, Felixstow, SA 5070 **Region** Adelaide Hills
T (08) 8337 5144 **www**.amadiowines.com **Open** Wed–Sat 10–5.30
Winemaker Danniel Amadio **Est.** 2004 **Dozens** 75 000 **Vyds** 250ha
Danniel Amadio says he has followed in the footsteps of his Italian grandfather, selling wine from his cellar (cantina) direct to the consumer, cutting out wholesale and distribution. He also draws upon the business of his parents, built not in Italy, but in Australia. Amadio Wines has substantial vineyards, primarily in the Adelaide Hills, and also buys small parcels of contract-grown grapes from Clare Valley, McLaren Vale and Langhorne Creek, covering just about every variety imaginable, and – naturally – with a very strong representation of Italian varieties. Exports to the UK, the US, Canada, Russia, South Korea, Singapore, Hong Kong and China.

ΨΨΨΨΨ **Adelaide Hills Shiraz 2010** Deep purple-crimson; matured in new American
❂ (and a small amount of French) oak for a limited period of time. This is an immensely intense and concentrated shiraz, with layer upon layer of black fruits that have all but eaten up the oak and the solid, ripe tannins. Will live for decades. Screwcap. 14.5% alc. **Rating** 94 To 2040 $25

ΨΨΨΨΨ **Adelaide Hills Pinot Grigio 2012** Has a faint pink-bronze hue; the bouquet
❂ is far more expressive than most, with unmistakable nashi pear aromas, which are married with hints of fresh ginger and incipient honey on the palate. Well up the pinot grigio totem pole of quality, and very good value. Screwcap. 13% alc. **Rating** 93 To 2014 $22
Adelaide Hills Cabernet Sauvignon 2010 Rating 91 To 2030 $25
❂ **Rosso Quattro 2011** A blend of merlot, sangiovese, barbera and grenache, 80% from Amadio's Kersbrook vineyard. A curious blend, but united by the various red fruits that all four varieties possess, and which come together well on the supple, medium-bodied palate. Screwcap. 13.5% alc. **Rating** 90 To 2015 $17

Amberley ★★★★

10460 Vasse Highway, Nannup, WA 6275 **Region** Margaret River
T 1800 088 711 **www**.amberley-estate.com.au **Open** Not
Winemaker Lance Parkin **Est.** 1986 **Dozens** NFP
Initial growth was based on the ultra-commercial, fairly sweet Chenin Blanc, which continues to provide the volume for the brand. However, the quality of all the other wines has risen markedly over recent years as the estate plantings have fully matured. Became part of CWA (now Accolade Wines) following Constellation Wines' acquisition of Canadian winemaker Vincor, which had in turn acquired Amberley Estate in early 2004. Accolade sold the vineyard, cellar and restaurant facility to family interests associated with Stephen Tobin, a Perth-based businessman, in '10, but retained the brand; the wines are now made elsewhere. Exports to the UK, the US and Pacific Islands.

ΨΨΨΨΨ **Secret Lane Margaret River Semillon Sauvignon Blanc 2012** Pale quartz;
❂ all the focus is on varietal fruit, the winemaking task purely that of quality control; the result is a seamless blend of flavours of grapefruit, passionfruit and gooseberry, covering all the bases. Screwcap. 13% alc. **Rating** 91 To 2014 $20
❂ **Secret Lane Margaret River Sauvignon Blanc 2012** The fragrant bouquet has a seductive display of passionfruit and lychee, the well-balanced palate with a similar positive display of varietal character; no frills, but enjoyable, and good value. Screwcap. 13% alc. **Rating** 90 To 2014 $20
❂ **Secret Lane Margaret River Cabernet Merlot 2012** Medium crimson-purple; the price of this wine is enticing, for it has a bright display of cassis, raspberry, redcurrant and blood plum on the bouquet and medium-bodied palate; tannins and an infusion of oak are well balanced and integrated. Screwcap. 13.5% alc. **Rating** 90 To 2017 $20

ΨΨΨΨ **Shiraz 2011 Rating** 89 To 2015 $19
Merlot 2011 Rating 89 To 2016 $19
Chenin Blanc 2012 Rating 87 To 2014 $19

Amelia Park Wines   ★★★★★

PO Box 749, Dunsborough, WA 6281 **Region** Margaret River
T (08) 9756 7007 **www.**ameliaparkwines.com.au **Open** Not
Winemaker Jeremy Gordon **Est.** 2009 **Dozens** 20 000
This brings together Jeremy Gordon, wife Daniela and business partner Peter Walsh. Jeremy
had a winemaking career starting with Evans & Tate and thereafter Houghton, before moving
to the eastern states to broaden his winemaking experience. After several years, he returned to
the west to co-found Flametree Wines in 2007. In its first year, Flametree was awarded six
trophies and over 30 medals. Amelia Park has no vineyards of its own, but that has not stopped
its rapid growth. Exports to the UK, the US, Russia, Hong Kong, Singapore, Thailand, South
Korea, Macau, Indonesia, Japan, China and NZ.

ΨΨΨΨΨ **Reserve Frankland River Shiraz 2011** Deep crimson-purple; while the
majority of the aromas and flavours are similar to its sibling, this is unequivocally
full-bodied, the black fruits with some savoury nuances, the tannins – while
balanced – more powerful. Screwcap. 14.5% alc. **Rating** 95 **To** 2036 $50
Frankland River Shiraz 2011 Bright, full crimson-purple; notwithstanding
12 months in barrel, this is all about fruit, and Frankland River fruit in particular.
Black cherry, blackberry and plum are all threaded through by spice and pepper,
the tannins on the medium-bodied palate very fine, but persistent. Screwcap.
14.5% alc. **Rating** 94 **To** 2026 $29
Margaret River Cabernet Merlot 2011 Good crimson-purple; cassis,
redcurrant fruit are set within a framework of gently savoury, but lingering,
tannins. The balance will underwrite the development for at least another 10 years.
Screwcap. 14.5% alc. **Rating** 94 **To** 2025 $29
Reserve Margaret River Cabernet Sauvignon 2011 A rich and complex
full-bodied Cabernet with multiple layers of blackcurrant, redcurrant and black
olive fruit, the tannins ripe and appropriately persistent, the cedary French oak
adding a further dimension. Screwcap. 14.5% alc. **Rating** 94 **To** 2031 $50

ΨΨΨΨΨ **Margaret River Sauvignon Blanc Semillon 2012** The percentages of the
✪   varieties are not stated, but sauvignon blanc is the major player, with flavours
ranging from cut grass and green pea through to apple and citrus, and finally
guava. Screwcap. 12% alc. **Rating** 93 **To** 2016 $22
Margaret River Chardonnay 2011 **Rating** 93 **To** 2018 $29

Amherst Winery   ★★★★☆

285 Talbot-Avoca Road, Amherst, Vic 3371 **Region** Pyrenees
T (03) 5463 2105 **www.**amherstwinery.com **Open** W'ends & public hols 10–5
Winemaker Luke Jones, Andrew Koerner (Consultant) **Est.** 1989 **Dozens** 3000 **Vyds** 4.5ha
In 1989 Norman and Elizabeth Jones planted vines on a property with an extraordinarily rich
history, which is commemorated in the name Dunn's Paddock Shiraz. Samuel Knowles was
a convict who arrived in Van Diemen's Land in 1838. He endured continuous punishment
before fleeing to SA in 1846 and changing his name to Dunn. At the end of 1851 he married
18-year-old Mary Taaffe in Adelaide and they walked from Adelaide to Amherst pushing a
wheelbarrow carrying their belongings, arriving just before gold was discovered. The title of
the property shows that Amherst Winery is sited on land once owned by Samuel Dunn. In
January 2013 son Luke and wife Rachel Jones acquired the Amherst Winery business, but
not the real estate, thus the grape supply remains unchanged. Luke has had a lengthy lead-up
training, becoming a wine sales representative in 2000, completing a wine marketing diploma
at NMIT, then, having moved into full-time marketing for Amherst, completed a four-year
diploma in Wine Technology at Goulburn Ovens TAFE in '13. Exports to China.

ΨΨΨΨΨ **Rachel's Pyrenees Rose 2012** Pale pink; a blend of Pinot Noir, Shiraz and
Cabernet Sauvignon, all made separately; the Shiraz and Cabernet were whole
bunch-pressed and wild yeast-fermented; it has good texture, with a mix of red
berry/spicy/savoury flavours and a pleasingly dry finish. Serious rose designed for
food. Screwcap. 12% alc. **Rating** 90 **To** 2014 $20

Pyrenees Shiraz 2011 The colour is good, in no way anaemic, and the wine has real presence and structure. Yes, there are earthy/savoury characters upfront, but there are red and black fruits on the mid-palate before fine, persistent tannins return on the finish. Screwcap. 13.6% alc. **Rating** 90 **To** 2020 $28

✪　**Daisy Creek Pyrenees Cabernet Shiraz 2011** Light red-purple; a 70/30% blend, with a savoury/spicy overlay to the bedrock of blackcurrant and blackberry fruit on the medium-bodied palate; a very good outcome for the vintage, and a good wine, period. Very good value. Screwcap. 13.2% alc. **Rating** 90 **To** 2018 $16

♟♟♟♟　**Daisy Creek Pyrenees Sauvignon Blanc 2012** A no-frills sauvignon blanc
✪　with a perfumed, tropical bouquet and a light, fresh palate with passionfruit and lime-accented acidity on the finish. Screwcap. 13% alc. **Rating** 89 **To** 2014 $16
Daisy Creek Pyrenees Chardonnay 2012 Rating 87 **To** 2014 $16

Amphora Wine Group　★★★☆

Stonyfell Winery, Stonyfell Road, Stonyfell, SA 5066 **Region** Adelaide Hills
T (08) 8331 8459 www.amphorawines.com.au **Open** Mon–Fri 9–5, w'ends by appt
Winemaker Karl Gumpl, Dwayne Cunningham **Est.** 2001 **Dozens** 40 000
This is a large-scale negociant business which, in 2001, established its cellar door at the historic Stonyfell Winery and changed its name from Montego Estate Wines to Amphora Wine Group. Winemaker Karl Gumpl followed in the footsteps of previous chief winemaker Michael Sawyer, the two working alongside each other for some years. Karl received his Bachelor of Oenology degree from Adelaide University in '07, and has had extensive experience in Australia and overseas, and, for good measure, spent time working with Dan Murphy. He is responsible for selecting bulk wines, blending and overseeing their development in oak before bottling. Exports to the US, Nigeria, Taiwan, South Korea, Singapore, Fiji and NZ.

♟♟♟♟♟　**Cartel Adelaide Hills Sauvignon Blanc 2012** Pale quartz; has abundant
✪　varietal fruit, the aromas and flavours extending from citrus through to tropical; its intensity and length make it compelling value. Screwcap. 13% alc. **Rating** 90 **To** 2014 $15

♟♟♟♟　**Cabal McLaren Vale Shiraz 2010 Rating** 87 **To** 2015 $26
Barossa Valley Shiraz 2010 Rating 87 **To** 2015 $38
Cartel Coonawarra Shiraz 2010 Rating 87 **To** 2016 $15

Anderson　★★★★☆

Lot 13 Chiltern Road, Rutherglen, Vic 3685 **Region** Rutherglen
T (02) 6032 8111 www.andersonwinery.com.au **Open** 7 days 10–5
Winemaker Howard and Christobelle Anderson **Est.** 1992 **Dozens** 1500 **Vyds** 8.8ha
Having notched up a winemaking career spanning over 50 years, including a stint at Seppelt (Great Western), Howard Anderson and family started their own winery, initially with a particular focus on sparkling wine but now extending across all table wine styles. The original estate plantings of shiraz, durif and petit verdot (6ha) were expanded in 2007–08 with tempranillo, saperavi, brown muscat, chenin blanc and viognier.

♟♟♟♟♟　**Verrier Basket Press Durif Shiraz 2007** It is a 60/40% blend, and is still a vibrant but inky purple-crimson; matured for 12 months in French oak, it is full of black, sombre fruits, tannins still with softening to do – which will happen well before the fruit tires. Screwcap. 14.8% alc. **Rating** 94 **To** 2037 $33

♟♟♟♟♟　**Melanie 2006 Rating** 93 **To** 2036 $25
Methode Traditionelle Sparkling Shiraz 2005 Rating 91 **To** 2015 $29
Classic Tawny NV Rating 91 **To** 2014 $25
Basket Press Shiraz 2008 Rating 90 **To** 2016 $19

Andrew Peace Wines

Murray Valley Highway, Piangil, Vic 3597 **Region** Swan Hill
T (03) 5030 5291 **www**.apwines.com **Open** Mon–Fri 8–5, Sat 12–4, Sun by appt
Winemaker Andrew Peace, Nina Viergutz **Est.** 1995 **Dozens** 460 000 **Vyds** 100ha
The Peace family has been a major Swan Hill grapegrower since 1980, moving into winemaking with the opening of a $3 million winery in '96. The modestly priced wines are aimed at supermarket-type outlets in Australia and exported to all major markets.

Winemakers Choice Langhorne Creek Shiraz 2010 Good hue; an attractive wine from start to finish, exploiting the inherent softness of Langhorne Creek fruit on the mid-palate; here red and black cherry fruit has fine tannins and a whisper of oak, leaving that fruit in command of the palate. Screwcap. 14% alc. **Rating** 90 **To** 2016 $18

Tall Poppy Reserve Shiraz 2010 Bright, clear purple-crimson; has the soft, juicy, rounded mouthfeel of Langhorne Creek, characters identified by and responsible for the empire of Wolf Blass. This wine bypasses the Blass oak, making it ready now, and freeing the red and black fruits to express themselves, with no static in the background. Screwcap. 14% alc. **Rating** 89 **To** 2015 $15
Estate Shiraz Malbec 2009 Rating 89 **To** 2015 $18
Winemakers Choice Barossa Shiraz 2011 Rating 88 **To** 2015 $18
Winemakers Choice Cabernet Sauvignon 2010 Rating 88 **To** 2015 $18
Estate Malbec 2006 Rating 88 **To** 2014 $18
Winemakers Choice Clare Valley Riesling 2009 Rating 87 **To** 2015 $18
Masterpeace Semillon Sauvignon Blanc 2012 Rating 87 **To** 2014 $13
Tall Poppy Select Shiraz 2012 Light, bright hue; light-bodied, for sure, but the soft berry fruits have a delicate infusion of oak ex planks and/or chips, and a wisp of citrus (acidity) on the finish. Clear value, but don't dilly dally in drinking it. Screwcap. 14% alc. **Rating** 87 **To** 2014 $9
Murphy's Block Merlot 2012 Bright, light crimson; yes, it's light-bodied and ready for immediate drinking, but the rush of red fruits, spice, savoury olives and a splash of mint deliver a wine with clear-cut varietal fruit expression. Screwcap. 14% alc. **Rating** 87 **To** 2014 $11
Masterpeace Cabernet Sauvignon Merlot 2012 Rating 87 **To** 2014 $13
Tall Poppy Reserve Cabernet Sauvignon 2010 Rating 87 **To** 2014 $15
Winemakers Choice Cabernet Sauvignon 2010 Rating 87 **To** 2015 $18
Kentish Lane Tempranillo 2012 Rating 87 **To** 2013 $13
Australia Felix Swan Hill Sagrantino 2008 Rating 87 **To** 2014 $45

Angas Plains Estate

317 Angas Plains Road, Langhorne Creek, SA 5255 **Region** Langhorne Creek
T (08) 8537 3159 **www**.angasplainswines.com.au **Open** 7 days 11–5
Winemaker Peter Douglas **Est.** 1994 **Dozens** 5000 **Vyds** 15.2ha
In 1994 Phillip and Judy Cross began planting a vineyard on their 40ha property, situated on the old flood plains of the Angas River, which only flows after heavy rains in its catchment of the Adelaide Hills. With the assistance of son Jason they manage the property to minimise water use and maximise the accumulation of organic matter. Skilled contract winemaking has resulted in some excellent wines from the estate-grown shiraz (14ha), cabernet sauvignon (10ha) and chardonnay (1.2ha). Exports to China.

PJ's Special Langhorne Creek Shiraz 2010 Medium red-purple; a rich and supple palate reflecting the region, and great freshness reflecting the decision to pick early, bringing red fruits into play. The points hinge on its overall elegance. Diam. 12.8% alc. **Rating** 94 **To** 2025 $30
PJ's Special Reserve Langhorne Creek Shiraz 2009 Dense purple-crimson; very different from the '10, with black fruits in the driver's seat on the bouquet and palate alike; it also verges on full-bodied until the finesse of the finish comes into play; here the tannins and overall extract counterintuitively extend the finish and aftertaste. Screwcap. 13% alc. **Rating** 94 **To** 2030 $40

PJ's Langhorne Creek Cabernet Sauvignon 2010 Medium purple-red; a well-made, medium-bodied Cabernet with a strong sense of place to its cassis, redcurrant and mocha aromas and flavours, dark chocolate hiding below the surface; 18 months in French oak has ensured that the tannins are soft and unobtrusive. Diam. 13.5% alc. **Rating** 94 **To** 2020 $25

♀♀♀♀♀ PJ's Special Cabernet Sauvignon 2009 **Rating** 93 **To** 2024 $30

♀♀♀♀ Brick Red Langhorne Creek Cabernet Sauvignon 2010 Medium red-
✪   purple; has that crossover into McLaren Vale dark chocolate in spades; also shows 12 months in (old) French oak; add back blackcurrant fruit and you have a nifty wine at the price. Diam. 13% alc. **Rating** 89 **To** 2017 $18

Angelicus ★★★★
Lot 9 Catalano Road, Burekup, WA 6227 **Region** Geographe
T 0429 481 425 **www**.angelicus.com.au **Open** W'ends & public hols 11–4, or by appt
Winemaker John Ward, Sue Ward **Est.** 1997 **Dozens** 450 **Vyds** 1.6ha
Dr John and Sue Ward moved from Sydney to WA with the aim of establishing a vineyard and winery, settling first on a property in the Middlesex Valley of Pemberton. Despite the success of that venture, they decided to move to the Geographe region, and have purchased a 51ha block of granite-strewn rocky hillside at Burekup, 200m above sea level, looking towards the Indian Ocean. In 2009 they began the planting of their vines, the lion's share to grenache (bush vines, managed biodynamically), five clones of tempranillo, and verdelho. In the interim, they are purchasing grenache, mourvedre and shiraz from growers in the region.

♀♀♀♀♀ Rosa 2012 Light, vivid puce; from hand-picked grenache, not common in
✪   Geographe; the scented rose petal and spice bouquet introduces a fresh, very well balanced palate with strawberry fruit and lemony acidity; pleasingly dry and vibrant. Screwcap. 13.5% alc. **Rating** 91 **To** 2014 $18
    Garnacha and Shiraz 2011 The percentages are not specified, but the blend works well, particularly with its modest alcohol, doubtless partly under the duress of the vintage. The juicy red fruit flavours are delicious, and there are no green characters. A lovely drink-now style. Screwcap. 13% alc. **Rating** 91 **To** 2014 $24

♀♀♀♀ Sauvignon Blanc 2012 **Rating** 89 **To** 2013 $18

Angove Family Winemakers ★★★★★
Bookmark Avenue, Renmark, SA 5341 **Region** South Australia
T (08) 8580 3100 **www**.angove.com.au **Open** Mon–Fri 9–5, Sat 10–4, Sun & pub hols 10–3
Winemaker Tony Ingle, Paul Kernich, Ben Horley **Est.** 1886 **Dozens** 1 million
Vyds 480ha
Exemplifies the economies of scale achievable in the Riverland without compromising quality. Very good technology provides wines that are never poor and sometimes exceed their theoretical station in life. The vast Nanya Vineyard is currently being redeveloped with changes in the varietal mix, row orientation and a partial move to organic growing. Angove's expansion into Padthaway (chardonnay), Watervale (riesling) and Coonawarra (cabernet sauvignon) via long-term contracts, and the purchase of the Warboys Vineyard in McLaren Vale in 2008, have resulted in outstanding premium wines. In 2011 Angove celebrated its 125th anniversary, with the opening of a large, modern cellar door and café on the Warboys Vineyard at the corner of Chalk Hill and Olivers roads, McLaren Vale, open 10–5 daily. Exports to all major markets.

♀♀♀♀♀ Warboys Vineyard McLaren Vale Shiraz 2010 Deep purple-crimson; the bouquet exudes sultry black fruits, spice and dark chocolate, the luscious multilayered palate has exceptional mouthfeel, the fruit on a soft swans-down pillow of tannins, and a lingering finish. Has fined down marginally since first tasted in April '12. An exceptional marriage of value and quality. Screwcap. 14% alc. **Rating** 96 **To** 2030 $35

Warboys Vineyard McLaren Vale Shiraz Grenache 2009 Excellent colour and clarity; a 60/40% blend from two sections of the vineyard, each suited to the variety in question. This is a role model for those seeking elegance to accompany intense varietal flavours of the red fruits of the grenache and the black of the shiraz. Screwcap. 14% alc. **Rating** 96 **To** 2029 $35

Rare Tawny Average Age 15 Years NV A lusciously rich yet nimble mix of fruitcake, mocha, toffee, bitter chocolate and brandy snap. Another major surprise, winning the top gold medal in the small volume, aged fortified tawny class in the National Wine Show '11, causing the judges to comment 'a classic example of the style'. 500ml. Screwcap. 19.8% alc. **Rating** 96 **To** 2014 $45

The Medhyk Old Vine McLaren Vale Shiraz 2010 Deep garnet, red; the savoury bouquet reveals black and red fruits, licorice, and a strong mocha oak presence; the medium-bodied palate is supple and shows plenty of complexity and fine-grained tannin texture; while the oak is a dominant force, the concentration of fruit will go the distance. Screwcap. 14% alc. **Rating** 94 **To** 2022 $65 BE

ϓϓϓϓϓ **McLaren Vale Grenache Shiraz Mourvedre 2012** Pure blackberry, raspberry
✪ and mocha notes intertwine on the bouquet; the palate is fleshy, concentrated and light on its feet, offering a savoury dried herb complexity on the finish. Screwcap. 14.5% alc. **Rating** 91 **To** 2018 $22 BE

Grand Tawny Average Age 10 Years NV Rating 91 **To** 2014 $25

✪ **Kissing Booth Margaret River Manjimup Sauvignon Blanc Semillon 2012** The first time Angove has ventured so far afield, but the bold move has paid off. The wine is zesty, fresh and crisp, with a lingering undertone of tropical fruit and lemony acidity. Screwcap. 12% alc. **Rating** 90 **To** 2014 $16

✪ **Whiz Bang Barossa Shiraz 2012** Full crimson-purple; at the top end of $15 (effectively under $15) quality given its richness of flavour and texture; masses of black fruits, and no lack of tannins. A great informal/barbecue wine at a bargain price. Screwcap. 14.5% alc. **Rating** 90 **To** 2020 $15

✪ **Vineyard Select McLaren Vale Shiraz 2012** Deep crimson; the rich plum and dark berry bouquet leads into a palate stacked with flavour and extract; remarkable for a full-bodied wine at this price, but it does need time to smooth out its feathers. That said, great value. Screwcap. 14.5% alc. **Rating** 90 **To** 2022 $18

Alternatus McLaren Vale Tempranillo 2012 Rating 90 **To** 2016 $25

ϓϓϓϓ **Long Row Riesling 2012** Pale straw-green; well made, with more minerally
✪ structure than normal from a Riverland Riesling; Granny Smith apple and citrus are the drivers of the bouquet and palate; its dry finish takes it into the heartland of food matching. Screwcap. 9.5% alc. **Rating** 89 **To** 2015 $9

✪ **Long Row Shiraz 2010** This is a seriously good wine that will retail for less than $10 a bottle, its light- to medium-bodied palate with juicy black fruits making it ready for immediate consumption. Screwcap. 14% alc. **Rating** 89 **To** 2015 $10

✪ **Long Row Cabernet Sauvignon 2010** Has retained good colour; a testament to the quality of the '10 vintage from top to bottom; there is a startling degree of flavour and texture, dark chocolate and mocha surrounding the blackcurrant fruit, and a platform of soft tannins. Screwcap. 13.5% alc. **Rating** 89 **To** 2015 $9

✪ **Long Row Sauvignon Blanc 2012** Pale straw-green; pleasant tropical aromas and flavours provide as much as one could wish for at a price far higher than that of this wine; well balanced, and not propped up by residual sugar. Screwcap. 11.5% alc. **Rating** 88 **To** 2013 $9

✪ **Long Row Chardonnay 2012** Pale straw-green; as with all the Long Row wines, has that little bit extra; the yellow peach and melon fruit has a waft of oak that mainly contributes to the texture; a wine that needs no excuses nor high levels of residual sugar. Screwcap. 13.5% alc. **Rating** 88 **To** 2014 $10

✪ **Butterfly Ridge Cabernet Merlot 2012** Good colour; if there is a problem with this wine, it is too much varietal character, astonishing at this price; the cassis-accented fruit has support from the oak (ex chips or staves) that is balanced, as are the tannins. Screwcap. 14% alc. **Rating** 87 **To** 2014 $7

✪   **Long Row Cabernet Sauvignon 2011** Bright colour with plenty of depth; an astonishing achievement for '11, it has clear cabernet sauvignon varietal character with a cool-climate flourish to its mix of redcurrant and herbaceous flavours; the tannins are not obvious, but do their job. Ludicrously good value, and masterful winemaking. Don't dream of cellaring it. Screwcap. 13.5% alc. **Rating** 87 **To** 2014 $10

Angullong Wines   ★★★★☆

Victoria Street, Millthorpe, NSW 2798 **Region** Orange
T (02) 6366 4300 **www**.angullong.com.au **Open** W'ends & public hols 11–5
Winemaker Jon Reynolds **Est.** 1998 **Dozens** 16000 **Vyds** 216.7ha
The Crossing family (Bill and Hatty, and third generation James and Ben) has owned a 2000ha sheep and cattle station for over half a century. Located 40km south of Orange, overlooking the Belubula Valley, more than 200ha of vines have been planted since 1998. In all, there are 15 varieties, with shiraz, cabernet sauvignon and merlot leading the way. Most of the production is sold to Hunter Valley wineries.

♟♟♟♟♟   **The Pretender Central Ranges Savagnin 2012** The savagnin vines are young
✪   (as with all producers in Australia), so there is a way to go before final judgements can be made, but this particular wine adds to the pattern with its citrus pith/stone fruit/spice/pepper flavours and good texture. Screwcap. 13.5% alc. **Rating** 92 **To** 2014 $22

✪   **Orange Sauvignon Blanc 2012** Pale straw-green; confirms the reputation of Orange and of Angullong for stylish sauvignon blanc, even in a year such as the rainy '12; full of varietal expression on the gently tropical and gooseberry bouquet, with touches of additional stone fruit and grapefruit on the supple palate and lingering finish. Screwcap. 13% alc. **Rating** 91 **To** 2013 $17

    Fossil Hill Central Ranges Orange Tempranillo 2011 The ultimate GI confusion, the label 'Central Ranges, Orange'. Bright crimson-purple colour heralds a serious tempranillo, flooded with red and black cherry fruits on the bouquet and palate; the only question comes with the unexpected (from this vintage) tannins on the finish. I wonder where they came from. Screwcap. 13.5% alc. **Rating** 90 **To** 2018 $22

♟♟♟♟   **Orange Cabernet Merlot 2010 Rating** 89 **To** 2016 $17
    The Castle Central Ranges Chardonnay 2011 Rating 88 **To** 2014 $22
    Orange Pinot Grigio 2012 Rating 88 **To** 2013 $17
    Orange Shiraz 2011 Rating 88 **To** 2015 $17

Angus the Bull

PO Box 611, Manly, NSW 1655 **Region** Central Victoria Zone
T (02) 8966 9020 **www**.angusthebull.com **Open** Not
Winemaker Hamish MacGowan **Est.** 2002 **Dozens** 20000
Hamish MacGowan has taken the virtual winery idea to its ultimate conclusion, with a single wine (Cabernet Sauvignon) designed to be drunk with premium red meat, or, more particularly, a perfectly cooked steak. Parcels of grapes are selected from regions across Victoria and SA each year, the multiregional blend approach designed to minimise vintage variation. Exports to the UK, Canada, the Philippines, Singapore, Thailand and NZ.

♟♟♟♟   **Cabernet Sauvignon 2011** If it ain't broke, don't fix it. This is the 10th vintage of Angus the Bull, and even in this most challenging of vintages, its blackcurrant fruit does what is needed. Screwcap. 14% alc. **Rating** 89 **To** 2017 $22

Annie's Lane

Quelltaler Road, Watervale, SA 5452 **Region** Clare Valley
T (08) 8843 2320 **www**.annieslane.com.au **Open** Mon–Fri 9–5, w'ends & public hols 10–4
Winemaker Alex MacKenzie **Est.** 1851 **Dozens** NFP

The Clare Valley brand of TWE, the name coming from Annie Weyman, a turn-of-the-century local identity. The brand consistently offers wines that over-deliver against their price points, with both wine show success and critical acclaim. Copper Trail is the flagship release, and there are some very worthy cellar door and on-premise wines. Exports to the UK, the US and Europe.

ΨΨΨΨΨ **Copper Trail Clare Valley Shiraz 2010** Deep purple-crimson; part of the wine was kept on skins in small open-fermenters, part finished its fermentation in barrel. It is a full-bodied celebration of the black fruits that Clare Valley Shiraz can display, complexed by licorice and toasty oak, lengthened by positive tannins. Screwcap. 14.5% alc. **Rating** 95 **To** 2020 $70

ΨΨΨΨΨ **Clare Valley Shiraz 2010** Dense, deep, almost impenetrable purple; for those
✪ searching for a red wine for their recently born child's 21st birthday, and one that will almost certainly be discounted below $20, this is the answer. It is full-bodied, but the blackberry, licorice and tar flavours are not extractive, and the tannins are ripe and balanced. Screwcap. 14.5% alc. **Rating** 93 **To** 2031 $21
Quelltaler Watervale Sparkling Shiraz NV Rating 93 **To** 2018 $27
Clare Valley Riesling 2012 Rating 91 **To** 2016 $21
Quelltaler Watervale Riesling 2012 Rating 90 **To** 2017 $27 BE
Clare Valley Semillon Sauvignon Blanc 2012 Rating 90 **To** 2013 $21

Ansted & Co.   ★★★★★
11 Flood Street, Bendigo, Vic 3550 (postal) **Region** Bendigo
T 0409 665 005 **www.anstedandco.com.au Open** Not
Winemaker Tobias Ansted **Est.** 2003 **Dozens** 550
Ansted & Co. was started as a busman's holiday by Tobias Ansted – then and now winemaker at Balgownie Estate – in 2003. Pressure of work and family commitments led to the sale of the vineyard in '06, but with an agreement to buy back the grapes, and to manage the vineyard. While syrah was the initial planting, marsanne, roussanne and viognier followed. Exports to China.

ΨΨΨΨΨ **One Hundred Acres Marsanne Viognier 2012** Half a tonne of each variety was picked and, after pressing, the juices were combined in a single, new, light toast puncheon for fermentation and 6 months' maturation; it has excellent texture, and (the power of suggestion?) there are flavours of honeysuckle, apricot and spice. Screwcap. 14% alc. **Rating** 94 **To** 2015 $25
North Harcourt Vineyard Syrah 2010 Purple-crimson colour signals a medium- to full-bodied wine with very good mouthfeel to its blackberry and plum fruit, the tannins fine and not diminishing the almost juicy finish. 250 dozen made. Screwcap. 14% alc. **Rating** 94 **To** 2030 $35

ΨΨΨΨΨ **Variation No. 1 Syrah 2010** This wine was made from three vats, one with
✪ 20% whole bunches, one with 100% whole bunches, and the third with viognier skins added; the three were combined along with other components, and the result is a more fragrant and juicy red and black fruit-accented wine, different in structure from its '10 brother, and not of the style Tobias aims to achieve. Self-criticism gives rise to a bargain. Screwcap. 14% alc. **Rating** 92 **To** 2020 $20

Anvers   ★★★★★
633 Razorback Road, Kangarilla, SA 5157 **Region** Adelaide Hills
T (08) 8374 1787 **www.anvers.com.au Open** Not
Winemaker Kym Milne MW **Est.** 1998 **Dozens** 10 000 **Vyds** 24.5ha
Myriam and Wayne Keoghan established Anvers with the emphasis on quality rather than quantity. The principal vineyard is in the Adelaide Hills at Kangarilla (16ha of cabernet sauvignon, shiraz, chardonnay, sauvignon blanc and viognier), the second (96-year-old) vineyard at McLaren Vale (shiraz, grenache and cabernet sauvignon). Winemaker Kym Milne has experience gained across many of the wine-producing countries in both the northern and southern hemispheres. Exports to the UK and other major markets.

ŶŶŶŶŶ The Warrior Adelaide Hills Langhorne Creek Shiraz 2010 Deep and dense
in colour, it is full-bodied, but the black fruits are round and supple in the mouth,
the tannins fine. The quality of the corks does not inspire one to think the wine
will reach its full potential. 14.5% alc. **Rating** 94 **To** 2025 $55

The Giant McLaren Vale Shiraz Cabernet Sauvignon 2009 This deluxe
bottle and packaging pays homage to Myriam Keoghan's Belgian ancestry, not the
dimensions of the wine, which will, however, only be produced two or three times
a decade. The black fruits, dark chocolate and licorice have ripe tannins and a very
generous helping of oak – some (not all) may think a little too generous. Cork.
14.5% alc. **Rating** 94 **To** 2029 $160

ŶŶŶŶŶ Langhorne Creek Cabernet Sauvignon 2010 **Rating** 92 **To** 2025 $28
✪ Razorback Road Adelaide Hills Shiraz Cabernet Sauvignon 2010 Bright
crimson-purple; an attractive array of red and black fruits are neatly supported
by fine tannins (and oak). If only the screwcap was used on its more expensive
siblings, and this sacrificed to cork. 14.5% alc. **Rating** 91 **To** 2018 $22

Adelaide Hills Sauvignon Blanc 2012 **Rating** 90 **To** 2013 $20
Adelaide Hills Chardonnay 2011 **Rating** 90 **To** 2016 $28
McLaren Vale Shiraz 2010 **Rating** 90 **To** 2020 $28

Appellation Ballarat ★★★

67 Pickfords Road, Coghills Creek, Vic 3364 **Region** Ballarat
T 0408 059 454 www.appellationballarat.com **Open** By appt
Winemaker Owen Latta **Est.** 2007 **Dozens** 500 **Vyds** 3.6ha

The striking name and label design is the work of Owen Latta, whose family planted Eastern
Peake in 1983. Owen was born during the first growing season of that vineyard and has always
been involved in Eastern Peake. Indeed, aged 15, and while still at school, he took control of
the winemaking when his father suffered concussion after a fall in the winery that vintage.
Since then he has travelled widely, making wine in Burgundy, the Yarra Valley, Geelong and
the Pyrenees, experience that has led to contract and consulting work. His aim is to have a
Pinot Noir that is affordable, yet distinctive. He has contracted to purchase pinot noir from
three vineyards in the region, planted in 1994 and '95.

Aramis Vineyards ★★★★☆

29 Sir Donald Bradman Drive, Mile End South, SA 5031 **Region** McLaren Vale
T (08) 8352 2900 www.aramisvineyards.com **Open** Mon–Fri 11–5, or by appt
Winemaker Scott Rawlinson **Est.** 1998 **Dozens** 15 000 **Vyds** 26ha

Aramis Vineyards was founded in 1998 by Lee Flourentzou. Located barely 2km from the Gulf
of St Vincent, the estate is one of the coolest sites in the McLaren Vale, and is planted to shiraz
and cabernet sauvignon, the two varieties best suited to the site. This philosophy leads Aramis
to source grapes from other regions that best represent each variety, including sauvignon blanc
and chardonnay from the Adelaide Hills and riesling from the Eden Valley. After a lengthy
sabbatical overseas, head winemaker Scott Rawlinson has returned. The city-based cellar
door also features wines from other boutique producers. Exports to the UK, the US, Canada,
Singapore, Malaysia, Thailand, Vietnam, Japan and Hong Kong.

ŶŶŶŶŶ The Governor McLaren Vale Syrah 2009 A potent, full-bodied wine as far
removed from syrah style as it is possible to conceive; dense blackberry, plum and
bitter chocolate are bound together by ripe tannins and well-integrated oak. It has
every chance of outliving the cork. 14% alc. **Rating** 94 **To** 2035

ŶŶŶŶŶ White Label McLaren Vale Shiraz 2010 Vibrant purple; blackberry, spiced
✪ plum and fruitcake are exhibited on the bouquet. The medium-bodied palate is
warm, fleshy and generous, finishing with spicy oak and gravelly tannins; good
value drinking. Screwcap. 14.5% alc. **Rating** 90 **To** 2017 $19 BE

Black Label Botrytis Semillon 2009 **Rating** 90 **To** 2018 $25 BE

🍇 Aravina Estate   ★★★★★

61 Thornton Road, Yallingup, WA 6282 **Region** Margaret River
T (08) 9750 1111 **www.**aravinaestate.com **Open** 7 days 10.30–4
Winemaker Jodie Opie **Est.** 2010 **Dozens** 4000 **Vyds** 26.17ha
In 2010 seventh-generation Western Australian Steve Tobin and family acquired the
winery and vineyard of Amberley Estate from Accolade, which retained the Amberley
brand. Steve has big plans for turning the property into a multifaceted resource; as a first
step, internationally renowned designer Paul Bangay has been commissioned to design the
estate's gardens. Unsurprisingly, wedding ceremony areas will also be created, along with
a host of other attractions. The vineyard dates back to 1986, and all the major varieties are
encompassed.

🍷🍷🍷🍷🍷 **Margaret River Cabernet Sauvignon 2009** The back labels of Aravina Estate
give no information on any of the wines, but the bold front label of this wine (and
its price) tells you this would have a Reserve or similar tag from most producers.
The colour is deep, and the imposing varietal expression is notable for its purity,
line, length and intensity; oak and tannins no more than props. This is special.
Screwcap. 14% alc. **Rating** 96 **To** 2034 $36
Margaret River Semillon 2011 The bright straw-green colour and complex
palate suggest the use of some oak, although this is largely textural, the herb and
sweet lemon citrus fruit showing clear varietal character; all in all, a very attractive
wine, ready now or later. Screwcap. 12.8% alc. **Rating** 94 **To** 2015 $29
Margaret River Chardonnay 2011 Bright, light straw-green; this is not a
showy style, but everything that should be there is there in synergistic/symbiotic
balance: white peach, subtle French oak, perfume and fruit flavours in sync, and
perfectly balanced acidity. Those interested should note the alcohol. Screwcap.
12.4% alc. **Rating** 94 **To** 2019 $29

🍷🍷🍷🍷🍷 **Geographe Shiraz 2011** Dense purple-crimson; has a great deal to offer at
✪   this price, with notes of dark cherry, coconut, vanilla and spice on the bouquet,
moving to blackberry and black cherry on the spicy, lively medium-bodied palate,
finishing with fine cedary tannins. Screwcap. 14.5% alc. **Rating** 93 **To** 2020 $19
Margaret River Vermentino 2011 Rating 91 **To** 2014 $26
Margaret River Cabernet Merlot 2010 Rating 91 **To** 2020 $26

Arete Wines   ★★★★★

1 Banyan Court, Greenwith, SA 5125 **Region** Adelaide Hills/Barossa Valley
T 0437 658 185 **www.**aretewines.com.au **Open** By appt
Winemaker Richard Bate **Est.** 2008 **Dozens** 500
The name chosen by owner Richard Bate comes from Greek mythology, describing the
aggregate of the qualities of valour, virtue and excellence that make up good character. Having
graduated with a Bachelor of Science (wine science major) from CSU, Richard worked at
Barossa Valley Estate, then Saltram, Wolf Blass and Penfolds. His next move was to work for the
Burgundian cooper François Frères, distributing barrels within Australia, before venturing into
the challenging world of the small winemaker. His intention is to make single vineyard wines
wherever possible, with small quantities of each wine part of the strategy.

🍷🍷🍷🍷🍷 **The Chameleon Adelaide Hills Pinot Gris 2011** Hand-picked, whole bunch-
pressed, wild-fermented in used French oak, weekly battonage/stirring and partial
mlf – an exceptional approach to pinot gris; has great length to its juicy fruit
flavours, and served chilled it could as easily be picked as cool-climate chardonnay
or sauvignon blanc as pinot gris. Totally impressive. Screwcap. 12.5% alc. **Rating** 95
To 2015 $24
Ethos Marananga Barossa Valley Shiraz 2010 Deep, dense crimson-purple;
the wine has almost absorbed the oak from 24 months in François Frères barrels
(35% new); it has exceptional depth and cries out for a minimum of 10 years to
lose its puppy fat; the late Jack Mann would have described it as 'resplendent in its
generosity'. Screwcap. 14.5% alc. **Rating** 95 **To** 2040 $55

☙☙☙☙☙ The Alchemist Barossa Valley Tempranillo 2011 Rating 93 To 2018 $24
The Road Less Travelled Sauvignon Blanc 2011 Rating 92 To 2013 $24
The Chatterbox Barossa Valley Shiraz 2011 Rating 92 To 2021 $24

🌿 Argyle Forest Estate ★★★

101 Ormond Esplanade, Elwood, Vic 3184 (postal) **Region** Heathcote
T (03) 9531 5370 **www.facebook.com/ArgyleForestEstate Open** Not
Winemaker Mark Matthews **Est.** 1995 **Dozens** 350 **Vyds** 4ha
In 2009 Jenny, Tony and Alice Aitkenhead acquired an 8ha property situated in the middle of the lightly wooded Argyle Forest. It had (and has) 4ha of clone PT23 shiraz, which had been planted in the mid 1990s. Both Jenny and Tony have a diploma in viticulture and winemaking, and Alice undertook a number of wine units during her biomedicine degree at the University of Melbourne. They are content that the low-yielding vines should produce less than 2.5 tonnes per hectare (1 tonne per acre) and hand-prune the vines accordingly. The one vintage so far tasted has been well made, but was lighter-bodied than the low yields would suggest. In '10 the region was still coming out of the shadow of a long drought.

☙☙☙☙ **Rowbothams Track Heathcote Shiraz 2010** Light, although bright, colour; a light- to medium-bodied wine with pretty red fruits, matured in used French oak, a correct choice. Made to be enjoyed when young. Screwcap. 13.1% alc. **Rating** 87 **To** 2015 $28

Arimia Margaret River ★★★★

242 Quininup Road, Yallingup, WA 6280 **Region** Margaret River
T (08) 9755 2605 **www.arimia.com.au Open** 7 days 10–5
Winemaker Mark Warren **Est.** 1998 **Dozens** 3685 **Vyds** 5.9ha
Anne Spencer and Malcolm Washbourne purchased their 55ha property overlooking the Indian Ocean in 1997; its northern boundaries are marked by the Cape Naturaliste National Park. Quininup Creek meanders through the property, providing the water source for its blue-green dam. The name is a combination of daughters Ariann and Mia. They have planted a Joseph's coat array of varieties, including semillon, sauvignon blanc, verdelho, chardonnay, cabernet sauvignon, merlot, petit verdot, shiraz, grenache, mourvedre and zinfandel.

☙☙☙☙☙ ✪ **Chardonnay 2010** Pale straw-green; wild yeast barrel fermentation has produced a well-balanced wine, fruit and oak both contributing positively to the peach and grapefruit flavours; there is also a distinct toasty/buttery note from the oak. Screwcap. 13.7% alc. **Rating** 93 **To** 2016 $22

✪ **Semillon Sauvignon Blanc 2011** Light straw-green; the semillon gives the wine structure as well as a shaft of citrus and green pea to accompany the sauvignon blanc tropical fruits of the bouquet and palate alike. Screwcap. 13.2% alc. **Rating** 90 **To** 2014 $17

Petit Verdot 2009 Bright red-purple; while a generous medium- to full-bodied wine, the fruit and tannins are in balance, allowing the multi-flavours of petit verdot to express themselves, with a blend of cassis, raspberry and plum balanced by a spicy/savoury undertone. Screwcap. 14.7% alc. **Rating** 90 **To** 2020 $26

☙☙☙☙ **Rose 2011 Rating** 89 **To** 2014 $17

Arlewood Estate ★★★★☆

Cnr Bussell Highway/Calgardup Road, Forest Grove, WA 6286 **Region** Margaret River
T (08) 9755 6676 **www.arlewood.com.au Open** Sat 11–5, or by appt
Winemaker Bill Crappsley **Est.** 1988 **Dozens** 5000 **Vyds** 9.7ha
A series of events in 2007 led to major changes in the Arlewood Estate structure. The Gosatti family sold the Harmans Road vineyard to Vasse Felix, but retained ownership of the brand and all stock. In mid '08 Arlewood acquired the former Hesperos Estate vineyard, 10km south of Margaret River, and Bill Crappsley, already a partner with the Gosattis in Plan B (see separate entry), became full-time winemaker for Arlewood and Plan B. Exports to the

UK, the US, Canada, Switzerland, Singapore, Malaysia, Hong Kong, the Philippines and China.

🍷🍷🍷🍷🍷 **Margaret River Chardonnay 2012** The early picking has guaranteed the vibrancy, but not robbed the wine of varietal expression. A little too far? Perhaps. This game has some time to run; grapefruit, apple, white peach and honeydew melon are all in the frame, the barrel ferment oak inputs restrained. Screwcap. 12.2% alc. **Rating** 93 **To** 2019 $35

Armstead Estate

366 Moorabbee Road, Knowsley, Vic 3523 **Region** Heathcote
T (03) 5439 1363 www.armsteadestate.com.au **Open** W'ends & public hols 11–5
Winemaker Peter Armstead **Est.** 2003 **Dozens** 500 **Vyds** 0.6ha
Peter Armstead had been a lifelong wine collector and consumer when he was caught up in the Ansett collapse; he had been an aircraft engineer and technical instructor. While he and partner Sharon Egan have full-time day jobs, they were able to purchase a property on the shores of Lake Eppalock, beautiful even when the lake was empty. Now it is full, and they have a very attractive cellar door. They were determined to have a small vineyard, and proceeded to sequentially plant shiraz, marsanne and cabernet sauvignon, deliberately keeping the size of the plantings manageable. Within months of arriving in 2003, the first planting stage had been completed, Peter had joined the Heathcote Winegrowers Association and, before he knew it, had become secretary. He has used all of his numerous local contacts to learn as much as possible about viticulture and winemaking, and has also been able to buy grapes from well-known vineyards in the region. In '09 he took the plunge and took over winemaking: he says, 'still with a little help from my friends'.

🍷🍷🍷🍷🍷 **Roxy's Paddock Heathcote Shiraz 2010** Deep colour; a rich bouquet and plush, medium- to full-bodied palate are built on densely sweet blackberry, plum and licorice fruit; ripe tannins and controlled oak complete the picture. Screwcap. 14.9% alc. **Rating** 91 **To** 2020 $28

🍷🍷🍷🍷 **Heathcote Cabernet Sauvignon 2010** **Rating** 89 **To** 2018 $25

ArtWine

72 Bird in Hand Road, Woodside, SA 5244 **Region** Adelaide Hills/Clare Valley
T 0411 422 450 www.artwine.com.au **Open** Thurs–Mon 10–5
Winemaker Joanne Irvine **Est.** 1997 **Dozens** 2000 **Vyds** 25ha
This may be a relative newcomer on the winemaking front, but it has substantial vineyards dating back to 1997. It is the venture of Glen Kelly, owner of Harrison Research, who previously had senior roles with the Commonwealth Bank. It has two vineyards, one on Springfarm Road, Clare, the other on Sawmill Road, Sevenhill. The Springfarm Road vineyard has a most interesting portfolio of grapes, the largest planting being 3.64ha of tempranillo, followed by (in descending order of size) riesling, pinot gris, cabernet sauvignon, grenache, cabernet franc, fiano, viognier and graciano. A further 2ha of fiano and 1.75ha of graciano were planted in the spring of 2011, replacing part of the cabernet block and the contoured section of the riesling block. The remainder of the cabernet sauvignon and riesling (plus cabernet franc) will be replanted over the next few years, the varieties yet to be decided. This is a lateral approach by any standards. A second cellar door opened in '12 in the Adelaide Hills (Bird in Hand Road, Woodside). Exports to Singapore.

🍷🍷🍷🍷🍷 **Clare Valley Fiano 2012** Light straw-green; this is very well suited to warm/warmer regions, its natural acidity giving it trajectory across and along the palate, with spicy nuances (like pepper in gruner veltliner) to accompany the honeysuckle and citrus fruit. Screwcap. 13% alc. **Rating** 91 **To** 2014 $25

🍷🍷🍷🍷 **Clare Valley Pinot Grigio 2012** **Rating** 87 **To** 2013 $22

Ashbrook Estate   ★★★★★

379 Tom Cullity Drive, Wilyabrup via Cowaramup, WA 6284 **Region** Margaret River
T (08) 9755 6262 **www**.ashbrookwines.com.au **Open** 7 days 10–5
Winemaker Catherine Edwards, Tony and Brian Devitt **Est.** 1975 **Dozens** 14000
Vyds 17.4ha
This fastidious producer of consistently excellent estate-grown table wines shuns publicity and the wine show system alike, and is less well known than is deserved, selling much of its wine through the cellar door and to an understandably very loyal mailing list clientele. The white wines are of high quality, year in, year out. Exports to the UK, Canada, Germany, Indonesia, Japan, Singapore, Hong Kong, Taiwan and China.

🍷🍷🍷🍷🍷 Margaret River Chardonnay 2011 Gleaming pale green-gold colour leads into a largely fruit-driven bouquet and palate with white peach, melon and grapefruit all on display. It has excellent drive and depth, oak evident throughout, but held well in check by the fruit. Screwcap. 14.5% alc. **Rating** 94 **To** 2019 $30
Margaret River Cabernet Merlot 2008 A cabernet-dominant blend, with merlot, cabernet franc and petit verdot included in diminishing amounts. Some colour development is totally consistent with the age of the wine, but the very fragrant cassis-filled bouquet paints a different picture; the medium-bodied palate picks up the fruit of the bouquet seamlessly, adding cedary/spicy nuances on the long, effortless palate; there are ample tannins, but they are very fine. Screwcap. 14.5% alc. **Rating** 94 **To** 2023 $27

🍷🍷🍷🍷🍷 Gold Label Riesling 2012 **Rating** 93 **To** 2020 $22
Margaret River Cabernet Merlot 2009 **Rating** 92 **To** 2018 $27 BE
Margaret River Verdelho 2012 **Rating** 91 **To** 2017 $22
Margaret River Semillon 2012 **Rating** 90 **To** 2022 $22

Ashton Hills   ★★★★★

Tregarthen Road, Ashton, SA 5137 **Region** Adelaide Hills
T (08) 8390 1243 **Open** W'ends & most public hols 11–5.30
Winemaker Stephen George **Est.** 1982 **Dozens** 1500 **Vyds** 3ha
Stephen George wears two winemaker hats: one for Ashton Hills, drawing upon an estate vineyard high in the Adelaide Hills, and one for Wendouree. It would be hard to imagine two wineries with more diverse styles, from the elegance and finesse of Ashton Hills to the awesome power of Wendouree. After years of selecting the best pinot noir vines to provide grafting material, in the spring of 2011 all of the white vines (other than riesling) were grafted to pinot noir. The outcome is that Ashton Hills now has 2.65ha of pinot noir, and 0.35ha of riesling.

🍷🍷🍷🍷🍷 Sparkling Shiraz 2006 The grapes come from Wendouree, 50% from the 1919 plantings, 50% from the '97. Open-fermented, hand-plunged, and held for 4 years in an aged 2250-litre cask; bottled '09 and disgorged May '12; 50% disgorged one more time. Blueberries, crushed ants, licorice and dark chocolate are laced together with very fine tannins, rich fortified shiraz, and refreshingly low alcohol. Well-toned power. Cork. 13% alc. **Rating** 96 **To** 2021 $44 TS
Salmon Brut Piccadilly Valley Pinot Noir 2010 The first of two disgorgements, this from Apr '12. Bright pale pink, without any salmon evident; 6% pinot noir table wine was added to the base partly for colour and also to bolster the red cherry and strawberry of this alluring bottle-fermented wine. Cork. 13% alc. **Rating** 95 **To** 2015 $39
Estate Adelaide Hills Pinot Noir 2011 This received the grapes usually taken for the Reserve, and the step up from the 2011 Piccadilly Valley is very considerable, with more depth to the red and black cherry and strawberry fruit; this is in turn accompanied by some high-quality French oak and ripe, but fine, tannins. Screwcap. 13.5% alc. **Rating** 94 **To** 2018 $44

Adelaide Hills Blanc de Blancs 2010 The grapes are whole bunch-pressed and the juice is fermented in used French barrels with considerable tartrate deposit; partial mlf, and over 2 years on yeast lees. A very attractive wine, with ripe citrus/white peach fruit wound through creamy/yeasty notes; good length and balance. Cork. 13% alc. **Rating** 94 To 2016 $41

ŸŸŸŸŸ **Piccadilly Valley Pinot Noir 2011 Rating** 92 To 2016 $33
Adelaide Hills Riesling 2012 Rating 90 To 2015 $33

Atlas Wines   ★★★★★

PO Box 458, Clare, SA 5453 **Region** Clare Valley
T 0419 847 491 **www**.atlaswines.com.au **Open** Not
Winemaker Adam Barton **Est.** 2008 **Dozens** 2000 **Vyds** 8ha
Owner and winemaker Adam Barton had an extensive winemaking career before establishing Atlas Wines. It took him from Scarpantoni Estate in McLaren Vale to Rolf Binder Wines in the Barossa Valley, Wynns Coonawarra Estate and the iconic Bonnydoon Vineyard in California. Most recently he has been winemaker at Reillys Wines in the Clare Valley, and continues in that role while working on Atlas Wines. He has 6ha of shiraz and 2ha of cabernet sauvignon grown on a stony ridge on the eastern slopes of the region, and also sources small batches from other distinguished sites in the Clare and Barossa valleys; all the riesling is purchased. Exports to Canada, Singapore and China.

ŸŸŸŸŸ **172° Watervale Riesling 2012** A floral bouquet of blossom and spices, then a beautifully precise and focused palate, with lime juice, mineral and crisp acidity lingering long after the wine leaves the mouth. A great vintage given full expression in the winery. Screwcap. 12% alc. **Rating** 96 To 2027 $27
429° Clare Valley Shiraz 2010 Deep crimson-purple; the bouquet is profound, but does not prepare you for the multiple layers of the full-bodied palate; blackberry, anise, bitter chocolate and cedary oak are among the flavours. The most unexpected feature is the freshness and elegance of the finish; this is masterful winemaking. Screwcap. 14.5% alc. **Rating** 96 To 2035 $35
Section 32 Clare Valley Shiraz 2011 Astonishingly deep purple-crimson; made in small batches, and then a barrel selection. The richness of the black fruits on the medium- to full-bodied palate is exceptional. It has spicy/savoury characters, speaking of a cool vintage, layers of black fruits, and a long and even palate, the tannins firm but ripe. Screwcap. 14.5% alc. **Rating** 95 To 2026 $25

ŸŸŸŸŸ **Barossa Valley Shiraz 2011** Very good purple-crimson. Another exceptional
✪   performance in the vineyard and winery alike, with an expressive black fruit bouquet and a supple, medium-bodied palate that has excellent balance and integration of fruit, oak and tannins. Screwcap. 14.5% alc. **Rating** 93 To 2026 $25
Section 32 Clare Valley Cabernet Malbec 2011 Rating 93 To 2021 $25
360° Reserve Watervale Riesling 2012 Rating 91 To 2022 $39 BE

Atze's Corner Wines   ★★★★

PO Box 81, Nuriootpa, SA 5355 **Region** Barossa Valley
T 0407 621 989 **www**.atzescornerwines.com.au **Open** By appt
Winemaker Contract, Andrew Kalleske **Est.** 2005 **Dozens** 600 **Vyds** 30ha
The seemingly numerous members of the Kalleske family have widespread involvement in grapegrowing and winemaking in the Barossa Valley. This particular venture is that of Andrew Kalleske, son of John and Barb Kalleske. In 1975 they purchased the Atze Vineyard, which included a small block of shiraz planted in '12, but with additional plantings along the way, including more shiraz in '51. Andrew purchases some grapes from the family vineyard. It has 20ha of shiraz, with small amounts of mataro, petit verdot, grenache, cabernet sauvignon, tempranillo, viognier, petite sirah, graciano, montepulciano, vermentino and aglianico. Local boutique winemakers provide the physical facilities for the winemaking, with Andrew involved.

ŶŶŶŶŶ **The Bachelor Barossa Valley Shiraz 2010** Impenetrable colour, and loaded with aromas of blackberry, prune and licorice, plus vine sap complexity; while the voluminous nature of the wine can't be denied, the palate draws the fruit back from the precipice with fresh acidity and gravelly tannins lingering evenly on the long, warm and generous finish. Screwcap. 14.8% alc. **Rating** 91 **To** 2020 $26 BE
The Renegade Barossa Valley Mataro Grenache Graciano 2012 Mid garnet; a bright and exuberant blend of red fruits, bramble and spice notes; the palate is medium-bodied, fresh and supple, with vibrant acidity a cleansing feature of the harmonious finish. Screwcap. 14.7% alc. **Rating** 91 **To** 2018 $23 BE
Forgotten Hero 1951 Survivor Vineyard Barossa Valley Shiraz 2010 One single French oak barrel makes up this concentrated wine, displaying vanilla bean, prune, mocha and licorice on the bouquet; the palate is dark and luscious, with fruitcake spice, fine-grained tannins; at 15.5% alc/vol, is pushing the ripeness envelope, a style that many still enjoy. Cork. **Rating** 90 **To** 2018 $100 BE

ŶŶŶŶ **Secret Drop Moppa Creek Vineyard Barossa Valley Cabernet Sauvignon 2010 Rating** 87 **To** 2016 $30 BE

Audrey Wilkinson Vineyard ★★★★★

Oakdale, De Beyers Road, Pokolbin, NSW 2320 **Region** Hunter Valley
T (02) 4998 7411 **www.**audreywilkinson.com.au **Open** Mon–Fri 9–5, w'ends & public hols 9.30–5
Winemaker Jeff Byrne **Est.** 1866 **Dozens** 30 000 **Vyds** 35.33ha
One of the most historic properties in the Hunter Valley, set in a particularly beautiful location and with a very attractive cellar door, this vineyard has been owned by Brian Agnew and family since 2004. The wines are made from estate-grown grapes, the lion's share to shiraz, the remainder (in descending order) to semillon, malbec, verdelho, tempranillo, merlot, cabernet sauvignon, muscat and traminer; the vines were planted between the 1970s and the '90s. More recently, a small McLaren Vale vineyard of 3.45ha, planted to merlot and shiraz, was acquired. Exports to Canada, China and NZ.

ŶŶŶŶŶ **The Ridge Semillon 2012** A restrained and classic young Hunter Semillon, with straw, lemon rind and a touch of bath talc on the bouquet; the palate is tightly wound, and while the acidity is prominent, the concentration of fruit, and the extraordinary length and balance will see this wine continue on its merry way for many years to come. Screwcap. 10% alc. **Rating** 96 **To** 2030 $35 BE
The Lake Shiraz 2011 Deep crimson with a purple hue; the bouquet is an essay in mulberry, spice and fresh leather complexity; the palate reveals the entire story, with a depth of fruit pushing past the normal medium-bodied expression of Hunter shiraz, as there is power, weight and depth in abundance. Long, luscious and beautifully poised. Screwcap. 13.5% alc. **Rating** 96 **To** 2030 $65 BE
Winemakers Selection Hunter Valley Gewurztraminer 2012 A highly expressive wine showing fragrant lychee and musk on the bouquet; the palate is surprisingly taut and racy for the variety, with fresh herbs and a wonderfully refreshing finish; lots of fun, and offers plenty of range for food and wine matching with Asian flavours. Screwcap. 11.5% alc. **Rating** 94 **To** 2015 $23 BE
Reserve Chardonnay 2011 A racy example of Hunter Chardonnay, showing nectarine, grapefruit, hazelnut and savoury oak; the palate is taut, energetic and lacy, with zesty acidity a prominent feature; long and harmonious to conclude. Screwcap. 13% alc. **Rating** 94 **To** 2020 $35 BE
Winemakers Selection Hunter Valley Shiraz 2011 Bright colour, and with an ebullient bouquet of red fruits, clove spice, toasty oak and a fragrant floral note; the palate is lively and beautifully proportioned as a medium-bodied and fleshy offering, with the finish being incredibly long and harmonious. Screwcap. 13.5% alc. **Rating** 94 **To** 2025 $35 BE

ŢŢŢŢŢ **Winemakers Selection Hunter Valley Semillon 2012** A well-balanced
✪   combination of fresh-cut grass, lemon oil and straw are offered on the bouquet;
         the palate is taut and edgy, with just enough generosity of fruit to consider it
         as a young Semillon proposition, while showing the depth of fruit to also last a
         considerable distance. Screwcap. 10.5% alc. **Rating** 93 **To** 2025 $23 BE
         Winemakers Selection Great Western Shiraz 2011 Rating 92 **To** 2023
         $35 BE

✪   **Hunter Valley Semillon 2012** The very essence of nettle and lemon sherbet on
         the bouquet, with a taut, dry and racy palate; the acidity in this as a young wine is
         challenging without food, yet the freshness and vibrancy are undeniable; a wine to
         polarise opinion. Screwcap. 11% alc. **Rating** 91 **To** 2025 $20 BE

✪   **Hunter Valley Chardonnay 2011** A bright and fresh bouquet of peach, melon
         and harmonious oak-derived spices, cinnamon and clove; the palate is medium-
         bodied and fresh on entry, with enough complexity and length to engage the
         senses; a lovely modern take on Hunter Chardonnay. Screwcap. 13% alc. **Rating** 91
         To 2018 $20 BE

Austin's Wines   ★★★★★

870 Steiglitz Road, Sutherlands Creek, Vic 3331 **Region** Geelong
T (03) 5281 1799 **www**.austinswines.com.au **Open** 1st Sun each month by appt
Winemaker Scott Ireland **Est.** 1982 **Dozens** 20 000 **Vyds** 61.5ha
Pamela and Richard Austin have quietly built their business from a tiny base, and it has
flourished. The vineyard has been progressively extended to over 60ha. Scott Ireland is full-
time resident winemaker in the capacious onsite winery, and the quality of the wines is
admirable. Exports to the UK, Canada, Hong Kong, Japan and China.

ŢŢŢŢŢ **Riesling 2012** Pale quartz-white; a fragrant lemon blossom bouquet leads into a
         fresh, juicy lime, lemon and spice palate, the finish clean and very well balanced;
         the overall elegance is a feature. Screwcap. 11.5% alc. **Rating** 94 **To** 2022 $25

ŢŢŢŢŢ **Sauvignon Blanc 2012** Early picking was a winemaker decision, not precipitated
✪   by the weather, and has resulted in a granny smith, citrus and herb-flavoured wine;
         it has a most attractive mouthfeel, and good length. Screwcap. 11% alc. **Rating** 91
         To 2014 $20

✪   **Six Foot Six Pinot Noir 2011** Bright, clear crimson-purple; all in all, a very
         impressive wine given its price and vintage; gently spicy red and black fruits run
         through the long and well-balanced palate, and the varietal expression is not in
         doubt. Screwcap. 13% alc. **Rating** 91 **To** 2019 $20

✪   **Six Foot Six Shiraz 2010** The colour is not especially deep, but the hue is good;
         the light- to medium-bodied palate offers black cherry, plum and a twist of spice;
         tannins and oak are in measured support. Well priced, and already drinks well.
         Screwcap. 14% alc. **Rating** 90 **To** 2017 $20

Avani   ★★★★☆

98 Stanleys Road, Red Hill South, Vic 3937 **Region** Mornington Peninsula
T (03) 5989 2646 **www**.avanisyrah.com.au **Open** By appt
Winemaker Shashi Singh **Est.** 1987 **Dozens** 500 **Vyds** 4ha
Avani is the venture of Shashi and Devendra Singh, who have owned and operated restaurants
on the Mornington Peninsula for 25 years. This inevitably led to an interest in wine, but
there was nothing inevitable about taking the plunge in 1998, and purchasing an established
vineyard, Wildcroft Estate. Shashi, with a background in chemistry, enrolled in viticulture at
CSU, but after coming into contact with Phillip Jones of Bass Phillip in 2000, she moved
across to the wine science degree course. Phillip began making the Avani wines in '00, and
in '04 Shashi began working part-time at Bass Phillip (full-time during vintage), her role in
the winery steadily increasing. While all of this was happening, a substantial reworking of the
vineyard began, increasing the planting density threefold to 4000 vines per hectare, reducing
the cropping level to a little over 1 tonne per acre, moving to organic in '05, and thereafter

to a number of key biodynamic practices in the vineyard. Even more radical was the decision to convert the existing plantings (predominantly pinot noir and chardonnay) to 100% shiraz. Shashi took total control of making the Avani wines at Phillip's Leongatha winery in '09, and in '12 they established their small onsite winery, of which they can be truly proud.

ŸŸŸŸŸ Mornington Peninsula Syrah 2010 Deep, vivid crimson-purple; despite this protracted extraction and ageing, the wine is not the least bit heavy, the dark fruit flavours enhanced by soft tannins, oak a vehicle more for texture than flavour. ProCork. 12.9% alc. **Rating** 94 **To** 2030

ŸŸŸŸŸ Mornington Peninsula Syrah 2009 **Rating** 92 **To** 2019 $55
Mornington Peninsula Syrah 2011 **Rating** 91 **To** 2020 $55

B3 Wines ★★★★

Light Pass Road (via Basedow Road), Tanunda, SA 5352 **Region** Barossa Valley
T (08) 8363 2211 **www**.b3wines.com.au **Open** By appt
Winemaker Richard Basedow, Rob Gibson (Consultant) **Est.** 2001 **Dozens** NA
Peter, Michael and Richard Basedow are the three Brothers Basedow (as they call themselves), fifth-generation Barossans with distinguished forefathers. Grandfather Oscar Basedow established the Basedow winery (no longer in family ownership) in 1896, while Martin Basedow established the Roseworthy Agricultural College. Their father, John Oscar Basedow, died in the 1970s, having won the 1970 Jimmy Watson Trophy for his '69 Cabernet Sauvignon, a high point for the family. As well as retaining consultant winemaker Rob Gibson, the brothers constructed a winery in the old Vine Vale Primary School property in 2008, using the schoolrooms as a cellar door. Exports to the US, Canada, Sweden, Denmark, India, South Korea, Taiwan, Hong Kong, Singapore, Thailand, Japan and China.

ŸŸŸŸŸ John Oscar Barossa Shiraz 2010 A ripe bouquet chock full of dark berry fruits, fruitcake spice, smoky oak and prune; the palate is full-bodied and full throttle, with plush black fruits, ample tannins and fresh acidity providing contrast on the big-boned finish. Cork. 15% alc. **Rating** 93 **To** 2025 $60 BE
Barossa Shiraz 2010 Deeply fruited with blackberry, licorice and fruitcake spice on display; medium-bodied, fleshy and approachable, with a warm and sanguine personality. Screwcap. 14.5% alc. **Rating** 90 **To** 2020 $22 BE

ŸŸŸŸ Pauline Barossa Cabernet Shiraz 2010 **Rating** 88 **To** 2019 $40 BE
Barossa Grenache Shiraz Mourvedre 2010 **Rating** 87 **To** 2015 $25 BE

BackVintage Wines ★★★★☆

2/177 Sailors Bay Road, Northbridge, NSW 2063 **Region** Various
T (02) 9967 9880 **www**.backvintage.com.au **Open** Mon–Fri 9–5
Winemaker Nick Bulleid MW, Rob Moody (Contract) **Est.** 2003 **Dozens** 10 000
BackVintage Wines is a virtual winery with a difference; not only does it not own vineyards, nor a winery, but also it sells only through its website, or by fax or phone. The team of Julian Todd, Nick Bulleid MW and Rob Moody sources parcels of bulk wines that they consider represent excellent quality and value for money. They are then responsible for the final steps before the wine goes to bottle. The value for money offered by these wines is self-evident, and quite remarkable.

ŸŸŸŸŸ Reserve Barossa Valley Shiraz 2010 Shows the excellent vintage to full
✪   advantage, with a particular freshness to the core of the blackberry/dark plum fruit; oak and tannins also make positive contributions to the complexity and length of the wine. Screwcap. 14.5% alc. **Rating** 93 **To** 2020 $20
✪   Mt Barker Riesling 2011 Straw-green; the aromatic, floral bouquet leads into a particularly harmonious palate, which has generous lemon/lemon butter flavours waiting for the toasty notes that will appear in another year or two. Drinkable now, or in 5 years. Screwcap. 11.5% alc. **Rating** 92 **To** 2017 $13

✪   **Margaret River Chardonnay 2011** The wine was predominantly fermented in French oak, with a small portion fermented in tank to add freshness; it says much about the crowded market that a wine of this quality from a region of this stature should be available at this price; it has a fresh, juicy quality to its white stone fruit, apple and citrus flavours, the finish sustained by lingering acidity. Screwcap. 13.5% alc. **Rating** 92 **To** 2016 $13

✪   **McLaren Vale Shiraz 2010** Medium red-purple; while medium- to full-bodied, the overall mouthfeel is soft, and the wine is not burdened by excess alcohol; plum fruit and a dash of dark chocolate provide well above average flavour. Screwcap. 14% alc. **Rating** 91 **To** 2016 $13

✪   **Margaret River Shiraz 2009** Cedary oak plays a role on the bouquet, medium-bodied palate and finish alike, but does not overly suppress the red and black fruits; moreover, the ripe, soft tannins help bolster the finish. An outstanding bargain, ready to drink. Screwcap. 14.5% alc. **Rating** 90 **To** 2016 $13

♈♈♈♈   **Margaret River Cabernet Sauvignon 2010** Rating 89 To 2014 $13
Chardonnay Pinot Cuvee Brut NV Rating 89 To 2013 $13
Adelaide Hills Pinot Gris 2011 Rating 88 To 2013 $13
Margaret River Sauvignon Blanc Semillon 2011 Rating 87 To 2013 $13

Baddaginnie Run   ★★★★

PO Box 579, North Melbourne, Vic 3051 **Region** Strathbogie Ranges
T (03) 9348 9310 **www**.baddaginnierun.net.au **Open** Not
Winemaker Fowles Wine (Lyndsay Brown) **Est.** 1996 **Dozens** 2000 **Vyds** 24ha
Winsome McCaughey and Professor Snow Barlow (Professor of Horticulture and Viticulture at the University of Melbourne) spend part of their week in the Strathbogie Ranges, and part in Melbourne. The business name, Seven Sisters Vineyard, reflects the seven generations of the McCaughey family associated with the land since 1870; Baddaginnie is the nearby township. The vineyard is one element in a restored valley landscape, 100 000 indigenous trees having been planted. Exports to Canada and China.

♈♈♈♈♀   **Strathbogie Ranges Merlot 2011** A little unexpectedly, the merlot has relished the cool season, even if it was wet. Cassis and black olive flavours run through the lively, medium-bodied palate, the finish extended by gently savoury tannins. A major success. Screwcap. 13% alc. **Rating** 92 **To** 2019 $24

♈♈♈♈   **Strathbogie Ranges Rose 2012** Rating 89 To 2013 $18
Strathbogie Ranges Verdelho 2012 Rating 87 To 2013 $18

Badger's Brook   ★★★★

874 Maroondah Highway, Coldstream, Vic 3770 **Region** Yarra Valley
T (03) 5962 4130 **www**.badgersbrook.com.au **Open** Wed–Sun 11–5
Winemaker Michael Warren, Gary Baldwin (Consultant) **Est.** 1993 **Dozens** 2500
Vyds 4.8ha
Situated next door to the well-known Rochford, the vineyard is planted to chardonnay, sauvignon blanc, pinot noir, shiraz (1ha each), cabernet sauvignon (0.35ha), merlot, viognier (0.2ha each), with a few rows each of roussanne, marsanne and tempranillo. The Badger's Brook wines, made onsite since 2012, are 100% estate-grown; the second Storm Ridge label has used only Yarra Valley grapes since '09. Also houses the smart brasserie restaurant/bakery/cooking school Bella Vedere, with well-known chef Gary Cooper in charge. Exports to Asia.

♈♈♈♈♀   **Yarra Valley Sauvignon Blanc 2012** Light straw-green; the fragrant bouquet is
✪   largely in a passionfruit/kiwifruit spectrum, underwritten by a slice of citrus, and the intense palate takes up the message with enthusiasm; the no-frills winemaking approach has put all the focus on the varietal fruit expression. Excellent value. Screwcap. 12.5% alc. **Rating** 93 **To** 2014 $18

✪ **Yarra Valley Chardonnay 2011** Pale green-straw; reinforces the overall outcome for Yarra Valley chardonnay in '11: if disease was kept at bay, the wines have excellent length and intensity, as is the case here; lovely varietal fruit (white peach and citrus) courses through the long palate, finish and aftertaste. Screwcap. 13.5% alc. **Rating** 93 **To** 2018 $22

✪ **Yarra Valley Pinot Gris 2012** Has more texture and structure than is normal for a tank-fermented pinot gris; lees contact and stirring was a very good substitute, as was picking over several days. Kiwi and tropical fruits sit alongside pear and apple, and there is no reason not to drink the wine right now. Screwcap. 12.5% alc. **Rating** 91 **To** 2014 $18

✪ **Storm Ridge Yarra Valley Pinot Noir 2012** Bright purple-crimson; the fragrant bouquet has the red and black cherry and plum plum fruits that also drive the palate; not particularly complex, but has good varietal character and balance, and will gain complexity over the next few years. Keenly priced for Yarra Valley Pinot Noir. Screwcap. 13.5% alc. **Rating** 90 **To** 2017 $18

♟♟♟♟ **Storm Ridge Yarra Valley Chardonnay 2012** Rating 89 To 2014 $18
Storm Ridge Yarra Valley Cabernet Merlot 2010 Rating 89 To 2015 $18

Baileys of Glenrowan   ★★★★★

779 Taminick Gap Road, Glenrowan, Vic 3675 **Region** Glenrowan
T (03) 5766 1600 **www.**baileysofglenrowan.com.au **Open** 7 days 10–5
Winemaker Paul Dahlenburg **Est.** 1870 **Dozens** 15 000 **Vyds** 143ha
Just when it seemed that Baileys would remain one of the forgotten outposts of the TWE group, the reverse has occurred. Since 1998, Paul Dahlenburg has been in charge of Baileys and has overseen an expansion in the vineyard and the construction of a 2000-tonne capacity winery. The cellar door has a museum, winery viewing deck, contemporary art gallery and landscaped grounds, preserving much of the heritage value. Baileys has also picked up the pace with its Muscat and Tokay, reintroducing the Winemaker's Selection at the top of the tree, while continuing the larger-volume Founder series. Paul is utterly committed to both the table and fortified wines made under his watch.

♟♟♟♟♟ Winemaker's Selection Old Muscat NV Dark mahogany; essence of raisins, with a flavour and texture complexity even beyond that of the Topaque; all the spices in Arabia, Christmas pudding, and cognac-soaked plums; despite all this, has the essential freshness to cleanse the gloriously long finish. 375ml. Cork. 17.5% alc. Rating 98 To 2014 $75

Winemaker's Selection Rare Old Topaque NV The extreme age is obvious from the colour, with its olive rim; it is incredibly luscious and complex, with multi-spice, mandarin zest, tea leaf, and Callard & Bowser butterscotch flavours; the palate is like velvet, the rancio and spirit there but not obvious. Cork. 17.5% alc. Rating 97 To 2014 $75

1920s Block Shiraz 2010 Deep crimson-purple; in regal Glenrowan style, wonderfully rich, yet supple, with multiple layers of black fruits, licorice and perfectly controlled tannins. Sold out at the winery, but may still be available at fine wine retailers. Screwcap. 13.5% alc. Rating 95 To 2040 $40

Shiraz 2010 Bright crimson-purple; the synergy between the black fruit flavours and the quality oak is undeniable – indeed I wondered whether it was French; the tannins that add texture have been expertly handled, the finish long and satisfying. Screwcap. 14% alc. Rating 94 To 2030 $25

Petite Sirah 2010 Deep colour; the full winemaker's bag of tricks was employed, with pre-fermentation cold soak, some whole bunches, wild yeast fermentation and French oak (29% new). All of this has paid dividends for a richly fruited medium- to full-bodied wine neatly tied up with ripe tannins. Screwcap. 14.5% alc. Rating 94 To 2022 $25

Durif 2010 Opaque crimson-purple; a full-bodied wine matured predominantly in American oak; it has good mouthfeel and balance given its weight of dark berry and licorice fruit, the tannin support very well judged. Screwcap. 15.5% alc. Rating 94 To 2025 $25

ŢŢŢŢ̧ **Founder Series Classic Muscat NV** The colour has developed past any hint of
✪ red; a good example of the more elegant style that Paul Dahlenburg is seeking to
make, with a perfumed bouquet, and without sacrificing fruit intensity or flavour.
Cork. 17% alc. **Rating** 93 **To** 2014 $30

✪ **Founder Series Classic Topaque NV** Amber with a slight grading to light
olive on the rim; abundant flavour, with Christmas cake, singed toffee and
abundant spice; the long finish is well balanced, although the sweetness continues
to the very end. Cork. 17% alc. **Rating** 92 **To** 2014 $30

ŢŢŢŢ **Fronti 2012** Has come into its own on the back of the moscato craze, which this
✪ wine preceded by a number of years. A neatly balanced mix of small red fruits and
lemony acidity. Serve with ice blocks on a hot day. Screwcap. 10% alc. **Rating** 89
To 2014 $20

Baillieu Vineyard ★★★★

32 Tubbarubba Road, Merricks North, Vic 3926 **Region** Mornington Peninsula
T (03) 5989 7622 **www.**baillieuvineyard.com.au **Open** At Merricks General Store
Winemaker Kathleen Quealy **Est.** 1999 **Dozens** 2500 **Vyds** 9.1ha
Charlie and Samantha Baillieu have re-established the former Foxwood Vineyard, growing
chardonnay, viognier, pinot gris, pinot noir and shiraz. The north-facing vineyard is part of the
64ha Bulldog Run property owned by the Baillieus, and is immaculately maintained without
financial constraints.

ŢŢŢŢ̧ **Mornington Peninsula Chardonnay 2011** Bright green-straw; a crisp, fresh
and elegant wine reflecting the cool vintage; grapefruit and stone fruit flavours in
the driver's seat, any oak incidental. Screwcap. 12.5% alc. **Rating** 90 **To** 2015 $25
Mornington Peninsula Viognier 2011 Light straw-green; there are nuances
of apricot, fresh ginger and citrus to this crisp, lively viognier; needs more depth
for higher points, but has been well made. Screwcap. 12.5% alc. **Rating** 90
To 2014 $20

Balgownie Estate ★★★★☆

Hermitage Road, Maiden Gully, Vic 3551 **Region** Bendigo
T (03) 5449 6222 **www.**balgownieestate.com.au **Open** 7 days 10–5
Winemaker Tony Winspear **Est.** 1969 **Dozens** 21 000 **Vyds** 29.45ha
Balgownie Estate continues to grow in the wake of its acquisition by the Forrester family, and
celebrated its 40th vintage at Maiden Gully in 2012. A $3 million winery upgrade coincided
with a doubling of the size of the vineyard, and Balgownie Estate also has a cellar door in
the Yarra Valley (Yarra Glen). The Yarra Valley operation of Balgownie Estate neatly fits in
with the Bendigo wines, each supporting the other. Balgownie has the largest vineyard-
based resort in the Yarra Valley, with over 65 rooms and a limited number of spa suites. It
specialises in catering for conferences and functions, and Rae's Restaurant is open seven days
for breakfast and lunch. Exports to the UK, the US, Canada, The Netherlands, Fiji, Hong
Kong, Singapore and NZ.

ŢŢŢŢŢ **Bendigo Chardonnay 2011** Pale straw-green; yet another example of the
quality of the cool '11 vintage for white wines; here an intense yet elegant and
harmonious Chardonnay has bell-clear varietal expression, and great balance, line
and length. Screwcap. 13% alc. **Rating** 95 **To** 2018 $45

ŢŢŢŢ̧ **Black Label Yarra Valley Sauvignon Blanc 2012** **Rating** 91 **To** 2014 $24
Black Label Yarra Valley Chardonnay 2011 **Rating** 90 **To** 2016 $24
Black Label Yarra Valley Pinot Noir 2012 **Rating** 90 **To** 2016 $24

Ballabourneen ★★★★☆

2347 Broke Road, Pokolbin, NSW 2320 **Region** Hunter Valley
T (02) 4998 6505 **www.**ballabourneen.com.au **Open** 7 days 10–5
Winemaker Daniel Binet **Est.** 2008 **Dozens** 5000

In December 2008, young gun Daniel Binet, until that time winemaker at Capercaillie, formed a partnership with Alex Stuart OAM. The formerly low profile of Ballabourneen has lifted, the cellar door having been established in that of the former Evans Family Wines on what is known locally as 'The Golden Mile' of the Broke Road. Exports to China.

ŸŸŸŸŸ **The Stuart Chardonnay 2011** A very impressive Hunter Valley Chardonnay, its barrel ferment and 10 months on lees in French oak subordinate to its white peach, melon and grapefruit flavours on the long, elegant palate. It will live for many years, but I would tend to drink it sooner rather than later, while its freshness is in full flower. Screwcap. 13% alc. Rating 94 To 2017 $30

ŸŸŸŸŸ **Majors Lane Semillon 2012** Rating 93 To 2027 $25
Shiraz 2011 Rating 92 To 2016 $32
The Three Amigos 2011 Rating 92 To 2031 $35
Alexander the Great Shiraz 2011 Rating 90 To 2018 $50

Ballandean Estate Wines ★★★★

Sundown Road, Ballandean, Qld 4382 **Region** Granite Belt
T (07) 4684 1226 **www**.ballandeanestate.com **Open** 7 days 9–5
Winemaker Dylan Rhymer, Angelo Puglisi **Est.** 1970 **Dozens** 12000 **Vyds** 34.2ha
A rock of ages in the Granite Belt, owned by the ever-cheerful and charming Angelo Puglisi and wife Mary. Mary has introduced a gourmet food gallery at the cellar door, featuring foods produced by local food artisans as well as Greedy Me gourmet products made by Mary herself. 2009 saw Ballandean wines appearing on the wine lists of Vue de Monde in Melbourne and Aria in Brisbane. One of the specialties of the winery has always been Sylvaner. A devastating fire in December '11 destroyed a large part of the bottled wine stock, but did not affect the winery, and hence the wine in barrel, and there are sufficient bottles of the current releases for the business to continue daily operation as usual. Exports to Taiwan.

ŸŸŸŸ **S.S.B. 2012** A fragrant bouquet of tropical fruits and fresh cut grass; the palate is juicy, fresh, simple and direct. Screwcap. 11.6% alc. Rating 87 To 2014 $18 BE
Viognier 2012 Vivid colour, the bouquet is lightly perfumed with apricot and bath talc; the palate is soft on entry, with fresh acidity providing line and interest. Screwcap. 13.5% alc. Rating 87 To 2014 $18 BE
Messing About Fiano 2012 Pale straw-green; restrained aromatics of straw and citrus are on display; the palate is light, fresh and offers a savoury conclusion; should be consumed soon. Screwcap. 12.6% alc. Rating 87 To 2014 $20 BE
Messing About Malbec Jacquez 2011 Deep crimson, purple; exuberant on the bouquet with blue fruits, violets and a little barnyard complexity; the palate is juicy on entry, with fresh acidity prominent, then making way for a dry, almost rustic, finish. ProCork. 13% alc. Rating 87 To 2016 $28 BE
Late Harvest Sylvaner 2012 Showing poached spiced pear and quince aromas, the palate is sweet and fresh, simple and straightforward. 375ml. Screwcap. 9.9% alc. Rating 87 To 2017 $18 BE

Ballast Stone Estate Wines ★★★★

Myrtle Grove Road, Currency Creek, SA 5214 **Region** Currency Creek/McLaren Vale
T (08) 8555 4215 **www**.ballaststonewines.com **Open** 7 days 10.30–5
Winemaker John Loxton **Est.** 2001 **Dozens** 100000 **Vyds** 461ha
Richard and Marie Shaw ventured into the wine industry by planting shiraz in the early 1970s at McLaren Flat. They still have the original vineyards and during the Vine Pull Scheme of the 1980s saved several neighbours' valuable old shiraz and grenache. Their three sons are also involved in the family business. Extensive vineyards are now held in McLaren Vale (60ha) and Currency Creek (350ha), with a modern winery in Currency Creek. The family produces around 100000 dozen under the Ballast Stone Estate label as well as supplying others. The wine portfolio impressively over-delivers on value, with significantly upgraded packaging in 2012. RMS is the flagship release, named in honour of Ballast Stone Estate founder, Richard

Morton Shaw. Ballast Stone has a second cellar door and café at Signal Point, Goolwa. Exports to the UK, the US, Canada, Fiji and NZ.

🍷🍷🍷🍷🍷 RMS McLaren Vale Cabernet Sauvignon 2009 Made from 65-year-old vines, and spent 2 years in French oak hogsheads. A distinguished full-bodied wine, with blackcurrant and a dash of choc-mint, the tannins ripe. Cork. 15% alc. Rating 94 To 2029 $50

🍷🍷🍷🍷 **Stonemason Currency Creek Sauvignon Blanc 2012** Light straw-green; the aromas and flavours are as much in the herbal/grass/snow pea spectrum as in the tropical end; either way, exceptional value for a wine with good balance and authentic varietal character. Screwcap. 13% alc. **Rating** 89 **To** 2014 $12

Emetior McLaren Vale Shiraz 2010 Rating 89 **To** 2020 $50

Stonemason Currency Creek Cabernet Sauvignon 2012 Bright, youthful hue; the only way to get it onto the market at this price was to bottle it before it was ready; there is a great depth of cabernet varietal fruit, and, with it, cabernet tannins. It was these tannins that needed more manipulation. There are two solutions: give it a couple of years in bottle; or find a friendly T-bone steak to drink it with. Either way, it's a bargain. Screwcap. 14% alc. **Rating** 89 **To** 2018 $12

Currency Creek Chardonnay 2011 Rating 88 **To** 2015 $17

Stonemason Currency Creek Rose 2012 A bright pink blend of sangiovese and grenache, it has a raspberry-driven fragrant bouquet and palate; it is slightly off-dry, but balanced acidity prevents it cloying. Undoubted value for casual summer drinking. Screwcap. 12.5% alc. **Rating** 88 **To** 2013 $12

Moonraker McLaren Vale Merlot 2011 Rating 88 **To** 2014 $17

Monster Pitch Cabernet Sauvignon 2011 Rating 88 **To** 2016 $17

Stonemason Moscato 2012 Rating 87 **To** 2013 $12

Balnaves of Coonawarra ★★★★★

Main Road, Coonawarra, SA 5263 **Region** Coonawarra
T (08) 8737 2946 **www**.balnaves.com.au **Open** Mon–Fri 9–5, w'ends 12–5
Winemaker Pete Bissell **Est.** 1975 **Dozens** 10 000 **Vyds** 53.7ha

Grapegrower, viticultural consultant and vigneron, Doug Balnaves has over 50ha of high-quality estate vineyards. The wines are invariably excellent, often outstanding, notable for their supple mouthfeel, varietal integrity, balance and length; the tannins are always fine and ripe, the oak subtle and perfectly integrated. Coonawarra at its best. Exports to the UK, Denmark, Canada, Vietnam, Japan, Indonesia, Hong Kong and China.

🍷🍷🍷🍷🍷 The Blend 2010 Travels with the Majella Musician in providing exceptional value for money, replete with blackcurrant, redcurrant and mulberry fruit on the bouquet and medium-bodied palate alike; while oak and tannins provide texture and structure, they do not endeavour to assert primacy over the central core of cabernet family fruit (53/37/10% merlot, cabernet sauvignon and cabernet franc). Screwcap. 14.5% alc. Rating 95 To 2015 $19

Chardonnay 2011 Mid gold, vibrant green hue; fresh grapefruit and white peach aromas with spicy oak and grilled nuts; the palate is generously textured, yet light on its feet, as the vibrant acidity provides a fine counterpoint to the fruit on offer. Screwcap. 12% alc. Rating 94 To 2016 $30

🍷🍷🍷🍷 **Cabernet Sauvignon 2011 Rating** 92 **To** 2022 $39 BE

Cabernet Merlot 2011 Rating 90 **To** 2020 $26 BE

Balthazar of the Barossa ★★★★☆

PO Box 675, Nuriootpa, SA 5355 **Region** Barossa Valley
T (08) 8562 2949 **www**.balthazarbarossa.com **Open** At the Small Winemakers Centre, Chateau Tanunda
Winemaker Anita Bowen **Est.** 1999 **Dozens** 6000 **Vyds** 24.93ha

Anita Bowen announced her occupation as 'a 40-something sex therapist with a 17-year involvement in the wine industry'. Anita undertook her first vintage at Mudgee, then McLaren Vale, and ultimately the Barossa; she worked at St Hallet while studying at Roseworthy College. A versatile lady, indeed. As to her wine, she says,'Anyway, prepare a feast, pour yourself a glass (no chalices, please) of Balthazar and share it with your concubines. Who knows? It may help to lubricate thoughts, firm up ideas and get the creative juices flowing!' Exports to the UK, Canada and Singapore.

ŶŶŶŶŶ Marananga Shiraz 2009 Dense purple-crimson; from the 24.93ha estate vineyard in the highly regarded Marananga subregion, and spent 25 months in predominantly French oak hogsheads; it has power and focus to the cascade of black fruits on the medium- to full-bodied palate, yet retains balance and a certain elegance. Screwcap. 14.5% alc. **Rating** 95 **To** 2030 $49

Banks Road

600 Banks Road, Marcus Hill, Vic 3222 **Region** Geelong
T (03) 5258 3777 **www.**banksroad.com.au **Open** Fri–Sun 11–5
Winemaker Peter Kimber, William Derham **Est.** 2001 **Dozens** 2000 **Vyds** 6ha
Banks Road, owned and operated by William Derham, has two vineyards: the first (2.5ha) is on the Bellarine Peninsula at Marcus Hill, planted to pinot noir, chardonnay, pinot gris, shiraz and sauvignon blanc; the second is at Harcourt in the Bendigo region, planted to shiraz and cabernet sauvignon.

ŶŶŶŶŶ Geelong Sauvignon Blanc 2012 Straw-green colour, with some development; a complex bouquet is followed by a rich palate, with tropical overtones throughout; hesitates on the finish. Screwcap. 12.6% alc. **Rating** 90 **To** 2013 $22

ŶŶŶŶ Geelong Pinot Gris 2012 Rating 89 **To** 2013 $28
Geelong Pinot Noir 2011 Rating 87 **To** 2014 $30

Bannockburn Vineyards

Midland Highway, Bannockburn, Vic 3331 (postal) **Region** Geelong
T (03) 5281 1363 **www.**bannockburnvineyards.com **Open** By appt
Winemaker Michael Glover **Est.** 1974 **Dozens** 5000 **Vyds** 30ha
With the qualified exception of the Douglas, which can be a little leafy and gamey, Bannockburn produces outstanding wines across the range, all with individuality, style, great complexity and depth of flavour. The low-yielding estate vineyards play their role. Winemaker Michael Glover is determined to enhance the reputation of Bannockburn. Exports to Canada, China, Singapore and Hong Kong.

ŶŶŶŶŶ Geelong Chardonnay 2010 Whole bunch-pressed direct to a mix of French barriques, puncheons and stainless steel, wild yeast-fermented and left on lees for 2 years. A wonderfully textured wine, powerful and rich, but so seamless there is no semblance of weight; stone fruit, oak and acidity are perfectly balanced. Screwcap. 13% alc. **Rating** 97 **To** 2025 $59
S.R.H. 2010 Spent almost 3 years in barrique/puncheon/stainless steel tank maturation, bottled Jan '13. It is, of course, very complex, with grapefruit and stone fruit wrapped up in a fine web of oak, but has retained remarkable freshness and length. Screwcap. 13% alc. **Rating** 96 **To** 2020 $75
S.R.H. 2009 Bright straw-green, it has retained an exceptional amount of varietal fruit at the heart of a complex web of toasty/nutty oak. A Chardonnay of rare distinction. 100 dozen made. Screwcap. 13% alc. **Rating** 96 **To** 2025 $75
Geelong Chardonnay 2011 Whole bunch-pressed, and taken direct (without settling) to a mix of barriques, puncheons and tank for wild fermentation; it was left on lees for 2 years to gain complexity, texture and natural stability. It has achieved all these things without any loss of freshness; complexity to its savoury fruits is the big winner. 1000 dozen made. Screwcap. 13% alc. **Rating** 95 **To** 2021 $57

Serre 2010 The Serre Vineyard is dry-grown, planted in the '80s at a density of 9000 vines per hectare. The ferment was 100% whole bunches, and the wine spent 1 year in barriques (33% new) followed by 6 months in 4-year-old barriques. It is a supremely fragrant Pinot Noir, and has a light, but silky and long, palate with its red cherry/wild strawberry fruit crosscut with savoury/stemmy complexities. 100 dozen made. Cork. 13% alc. **Rating** 95 **To** 2023 $95

De La Roche Shiraz 2011 Fully destemmed and wild yeast-fermented, it spent 1 year in puncheons (one-third new) and a second year in 5-year-old French barriques. With bright colour of medium depth, it has a vibrant display of black and red cherry fruit; the medium-bodied palate is supple and long, the finish speaking of fine tannins and quality oak. Screwcap. 13.5% alc. **Rating** 95 **To** 2031 $60

Geelong Shiraz 2009 The drought reduced the yield of this wine by two-thirds, resulting in a very concentrated wine; a 100% whole bunch fermentation was followed by 2 years' maturation in new and used French puncheons and barriques; the colour is developed, but the bouquet and medium-bodied palate are full of spicy notes woven through the black cherry and plum fruit, with oak very evident, but balanced. Cork. 13.5% alc. **Rating** 95 **To** 2025 $45

Geelong Riesling 2012 Rating 94 **To** 2020 $27
Geelong Sauvignon Blanc 2012 Rating 94 **To** 2017 $30
De La Terre 2010 Rating 94 **To** 2017 $70
Geelong Pinot Noir 2010 Rating 94 **To** 2020 $57
Stuart Geelong Pinot 2010 Rating 94 **To** 2021 $70

Stuart Geelong Pinot 2011 Rating 93 **To** 2016 $70
De La Terre 2011 Rating 92 **To** 2018 $70
Douglas 2009 Rating 92 **To** 2020 $27

Banrock Station   ★★★

Holmes Road (off Sturt Highway), Kingston-on-Murray, SA 5331 **Region** Riverland
T (08) 8583 0299 **www**.banrockstation.com.au **Open** Mon–Fri 9–4, w'ends & public hols 9–5
Winemaker Paul Burnett **Est.** 1994 **Dozens** NFP **Vyds** 240ha
The eco-friendly $1 million visitor centre at Banrock Station is a major tourist destination. Owned by Accolade, the Banrock Station property covers over 1700ha, with 240ha of vineyard and the remainder being a major wildlife and wetland preservation area. Recycling of all waste water and use of solar energy add to the conservation image. Each bottle of Banrock Station wine sold generates funds that are donated to environmental projects around the world. The wines have consistently offered good value, even the more expensive alternative variety releases that have recently come onto the market. Exports to all major markets.

Bantry Grove   ★★★★☆

519 Three Brothers Road, Newbridge, NSW 2795 **Region** Orange
T (02) 6368 1036 **www**.bantrygrove.com.au **Open** Fri–Sun & Mon public hols 10.30–5
Winemaker Richard Parker, Tony Hatch **Est.** 1990 **Dozens** 1200 **Vyds** 12.3ha
Terrey and Barbie Johnson (and family) raise beef cattle on a property at the southern end of Orange. Seeking to diversify, and to lessen the impact of drought through the establishment of an irrigated perennial crop, the Johnsons have planted a vineyard at an elevation of 960m, making it one of the coolest in the region. The plantings began in 1990 with chardonnay and cabernet sauvignon, the latter now grafted or removed because the climate is simply too cool. Most of the 80–85-tonne production is sold to various producers making Orange-designated wines. A steadily increasing portion of the grapes is retained for the Bantry Grove label. The wines are sold through membership of Bantry Grove's Inner Circle Wine Club and local outlets, with some Sydney distribution. A cellar door in Millthorpe is planned.

Orange Chardonnay 2011 Full straw-green; a tightly folded wine wrapped up in a sheath of minerality; it is finely structured, with only some of the grapefruit zest and pith flavours escaping. Despite this, could shine with the right seafood/Chinese dishes. Screwcap. 13.5% alc. **Rating** 91 **To** 2018 $24

Orange Sauvignon Blanc 2012 Pale colour, vibrant hue; the bouquet is pungent, offering gooseberry, nettle and subtle tropical fruit notes; fresh, lively and focused, with good concentration and energy to conclude. Screwcap. 13.5% alc. **Rating** 90 **To** 2015 $20 BE

Orange Pinot Grigio 2012 **Rating** 89 **To** 2014 $20

Barangaroo Boutique Wines ★★★

928 Plush-Hannans Road, Lower Norton, Vic 3401 **Region** Western Victoria Zone
T 0400 570 673 **www**.barangaroowines.com.au **Open** Thurs–Sun & public hols 10–5
Winemaker Welshmans Reef Vineyard (Ron Snep) **Est.** 2005 **Dozens** 600 **Vyds** 2.29ha
Chris and Sheila McClure have established their vineyard on a ridge running north–south, which allows for morning sun, free drainage and frost protection. It is situated just 10mins southwest of Horsham, the soils buckshot gravel loam. Plantings began in 2005, with the first vintage in '10, and although the largest planting (just under 1ha) is of shiraz, the 0.5ha of vermentino provides the signature wine.

Vermentino 2012 Light straw-green; has the citrus-tinged drive and urgency of the variety, the finish clean and fresh. Suited to the climate. Screwcap. 11% alc. **Rating** 89 **To** 2014 $18

Barnadown Run ★★★★

390 Cornella Road, Toolleen, Vic 3551 **Region** Heathcote
T (03) 5433 6376 **www**.barnadownrun.com.au **Open** 7 days 10–5
Winemaker Andrew Millis **Est.** 1995 **Dozens** 1500 **Vyds** 5ha
Named after the original pastoral lease of which the vineyard forms part, established on the rich terra rossa soil for which Heathcote is famous. Owner Andrew Millis carries out both the viticulture and winemaking at the vineyard, which is planted to cabernet sauvignon, merlot, shiraz and viognier. Exports to Canada, Norway, Hong Kong, Singapore and China.

Henry Bennett's Voluptuary 2007 A 60/25/7.5/7.5% blend of shiraz, cabernet sauvignon, malbec and merlot. Its youthful crimson-purple borders on the extraordinary, as does the sheer power of the ultra full-bodied palate, black fruits and potent tannins in full cry. Diam. 14.5% alc. **Rating** 93 **To** 2037 $45

White Lanyard Heathcote Cabernet Sauvignon 2009 **Rating** 89 **To** 2016 $29
Cascabel Heathcote Shiraz 2009 **Rating** 87 **To** 2015 $45

Barokes Wines ★★★

111 Cecil Street, South Melbourne, Vic 3205 (postal) **Region** Various
T (03) 9675 4349 **www**.wineinacan.com **Open** Not
Winemaker Steve Barics **Est.** 2003 **Dozens** 700 000 (cans)
Barokes packages its wines in aluminium cans. The filling process is patented, and the wine has been in commercial production since 2003. The wines show normal maturation and none of the cans used since start-up shows signs of corrosion. Wines are supplied in bulk by large wineries in South Eastern Australia, with Peter Scudamore-Smith acting as blending consultant. Year after year, my tastings give rise to tasting notes with no mention of reduction or any other fault. The technology has now been licensed by global packaging company Ball Packaging Europe, which will see more producers selling wines in cans in Europe; in Australia Barokes is offering customised canning for Australian companies. Exports to all major markets with increasing success, Japan and China the biggest markets, with production rising to 350 000 cases (24 × 250ml cans per case).

Bin 241 Chardonnay Semillon NV Generously flavoured, albeit with some sweetness; no hint of reduction. Convenience personified when you want a single glass with Red Rooster or fish and chips. Can. 13% alc. **Rating** 87 **To** 2013 $5

Barratt

Uley Vineyard, Cornish Road, Summertown, SA 5141 **Region** Adelaide Hills
T (08) 8390 1788 **www**.barrattwines.com.au **Open** W'ends & most public hols 11.30–5 (closed Jun–Jul)
Winemaker Lindsay Barratt **Est.** 1993 **Dozens** 2000 **Vyds** 8.7ha
This is the venture of former physician Lindsay Barratt. Lindsay has always been responsible for viticulture and, following his retirement in 2001, has taken full, hands-on responsibility for winemaking (receiving a graduate diploma in oenology from the University of Adelaide in '02). The quality of the wines is beyond reproach. Limited quantities are exported to the UK, Malaysia and Singapore.

ŦŦŦŦŦ **Piccadilly Valley Chardonnay 2011** Produced from 28-year-old estate vines, wild yeast-fermented in new and used French barriques; an intense but elegant palate, the fruit poised between citrus and stone fruit, oak an incidental extra, acidity prominent. Screwcap. 13% alc. **Rating** 94 **To** 2017 $30

ŦŦŦŦŦ **Piccadilly Valley Sauvignon Blanc 2012** No-frills winemaking has served to
✪ throw all the emphasis onto the perfumed bouquet and palate, in each case with an ever-changing display of citrus and tropical fruits, freshness being the key word. Screwcap. 13.5% alc. **Rating** 93 **To** 2014 $23

ŦŦŦŦ **The Reserve Piccadilly Valley Pinot Noir 2011 Rating** 89 **To** 2014 $49

Barrgowan Vineyard

30 Pax Parade, Curlewis, Vic 3222 **Region** Geelong
T (03) 5250 3861 **www**.barrgowanvineyard.com.au **Open** By appt
Winemaker Dick Simonsen **Est.** 1998 **Dozens** 150 **Vyds** 0.5ha
Dick and Dib (Elizabeth) Simonsen began planting their shiraz (with five clones) in 1994, intending to make wine for their own consumption. With all five clones in full production, the Simonsens have a maximum production of 200 dozen, and accordingly release only small quantities of Shiraz, which sell out quickly. The vines are hand-pruned, the grapes hand-picked, the must basket-pressed, and all wine movements are by gravity. The quality is exemplary. No wines received for the *2014 Wine Companion*, but a five-star rating has been maintained.

Barringwood ★★★★★

60 Gillams Road, Lower Barrington, Tas 7306 **Region** Northern Tasmania
T (03) 6492 3140 **www**.barringwood.com.au **Open** Wed–Sun & public hols 10–5
Winemaker Josef Chromy Wines (Jeremy Dineen) **Est.** 1993 **Dozens** 1700 **Vyds** 5ha
Judy and Ian Robinson operate a sawmill at Lower Barrington, 15mins south of Devonport on the main tourist trail to Cradle Mountain, and when they planted 500 vines in 1993 the aim was to do a bit of home winemaking. In a thoroughly familiar story, the urge to expand the vineyard and make wine on a commercial scale soon occurred, and they embarked on a six-year plan, planting 1ha per year in the first four years and building the cellar and tasting rooms during the following two years. The recent sale of Barringwood to Neville and Vanessa Bagot should not cause any significant changes to the business.

ŦŦŦŦŦ **Jessica Classic Cuvee 2009** A blend of chardonnay, pinot noir and pinot meunier disgorged Jun '12. A rich, nigh-on opulent, wine with brioche/toast characters balanced by ripe citrus and stone fruit flavours running through to the well-balanced finish. Diam. 12.5% alc. **Rating** 95 **To** 2016 $39

Pinot Noir 2011 Bright, clear crimson-purple; it will not be released until the end of '13, and will relish the extra time in bottle. It is typical Barringwood Park style, very intense, very complex, with dark cherry/plum fruit leavened with savoury dried herb tannins, and will be long-lived. Screwcap. 12.8% alc. **Rating** 94 **To** 2021 $35

ŸŸŸŸ♀ Pinot Gris 2012 Rating 90 To 2014 $32
✪ Rose 2012 Pale, bright pink; although no varietal information appears on the front or back label, almost certainly early-picked pinot noir; it is light-bodied, but has a savoury underlay to the red fruit and spice flavours; good line and length. Screwcap. 12.2% alc. Rating 90 To 2014 $20

Barristers Block   ★★★☆

141 Onkaparinga Valley Road, Woodside, SA 5244 Region Adelaide Hills
T (08) 8389 7706 www.barristersblock.com.au Open 7 days 10.30–5
Winemaker Simon Greenleaf Est. 2004 Dozens 7500 Vyds 18.5ha
Owner Jan Siemelink-Allen has over 20 years in the industry, and spent five years in SA's Supreme Court in a successful battle to reclaim ownership of 10ha of cabernet sauvignon and shiraz in Wrattonbully after a joint venture collapsed; it is not hard to imagine the origin of the name. In 2006 she and her family purchased an 8ha vineyard planted to sauvignon blanc and pinot noir near Woodside in the Adelaide Hills, adjoining Shaw + Smith's vineyard. Exports to the UK, Germany, Vietnam, Malaysia, Korea, Hong Kong, Singapore and China.

ŸŸŸŸ♀ The Bully Barossa Wrattonbully Shiraz 2010 Bright, deep crimson-purple; a medium- to full-bodied wine, filled to the brim with dark berry fruits, integrated but evident oak, and soft tannins. The overall balance points to a long future. Screwcap. 14.5% alc. Rating 93 To 2030 $30

ŸŸŸŸ Bully Single Vineyard Cabernet Sauvignon 2010 Rating 89 To 2016 $30

Barton Estate   ★★★☆

2307 Barton Highway, Murrumbateman, NSW 2582 Region Canberra District
T (02) 6230 9553 www.bartonestate.com.au Open W'ends by appt
Winemaker Capital Wines, Canberra Winemakers Est. 1997 Dozens 500 Vyds 7.7ha
Bob Furbank and wife Julie Chitty are both CSIRO plant biologists: he is a biochemist (physiologist) and she is a specialist in plant tissue culture. In 1997 they acquired the 120ha property forming part of historic Jeir Station, and have since planted 15 grape varieties. The most significant plantings are to cabernet sauvignon, shiraz, merlot, riesling and chardonnay, the Joseph's coat completed with micro quantities of other varieties.

ŸŸŸŸ♀ Riley's Canberra Riesling 2012 A lemon and apple blossom bouquet leads into a light, crisp palate lengthened by acidity that has a tactile quality I can only describe as squeaky or rubbery (nothing to do with flavour) as my tongue moves around my mouth at the finish of the wine. Screwcap. 11.5% alc. Rating 91 To 2018 $18
✪ Canberra Blue Rose 2012 A blend of cabernet franc and malbec, it has a vivid crimson-purple colour and a lively, crisp red cherry/raspberry palate, the finish dry and fresh. Striking wine. Screwcap. 12.3% alc. Rating 90 To 2014 $18

ŸŸŸŸ Canberra Sauvignon Blanc 2012 Rating 87 To 2014 $18

Barton Jones Wines   ★★★★

39 Upper Capel Road, Donnybrook, WA 6239 Region Geographe
T (08) 9731 2233 www.bartonjoneswines.com.au Open Fri–Mon 10.30–4.30
Winemaker Contract Est. 1978 Dozens 2500 Vyds 3ha
The 22ha property on which Blackboy Ridge Estate is established was partly cleared and planted to 2.5ha of semillon, chenin blanc, shiraz and cabernet sauvignon in 1978. When current owners Adrian Jones and Jackie Barton purchased the property in 2000 the vines were already some of the oldest in the region. The vineyard and the owners' house are on gentle north-facing slopes, with extensive views over the Donnybrook area. A straw-bale cellar door was completed in 2010.

ŸŸŸŸ♀ The Shilly-Shally Chenin Blanc 2011 As Australian chenin blancs go, this is a pretty attractive wine; oak maturation has seemingly helped focus the fruit flavours in a citrus spectrum, and tighten and freshen the finish. Should develop well in the short term. Screwcap. 13% alc. Rating 90 To 2015 $22

The Bigwig Shiraz 2010 An attractive medium to full-bodied Shiraz, with layers of dark fruits and oak on the bouquet, multi-spice flavours joining the black cherry and plum of the palate, and pushing the oak into the background; there are adequate tannins. Screwcap. 14.3% alc. **Rating** 90 **To** 2020 $25

The Top Drawer Cabernet Sauvignon 2010 Light to medium red–purple, bright and clear; the wine in fact contains 13% shiraz, and was matured in predominantly French oak (new and used); it is light-bodied, with redcurrant and cassis fruit backed by fine tannins, the oak obvious but integrated. Trophy, Geographe Wine Show '12. Screwcap. 13.5% alc. **Rating** 90 **To** 2018 $25

Barwang ★★★★★

Barwang Road, Young, NSW 2594 (postal) **Region** Hilltops
T (02) 9722 1299 **www.**mcwilliams.com.au **Open** Not
Winemaker Andrew Higgins **Est.** 1969 **Dozens** NFP **Vyds** 100ha

Peter Robertson pioneered viticulture in the Young area when he planted his first vines in '69 as part of a diversification program for his 400ha grazing property. When McWilliam's acquired Barwang in '89, the vineyard amounted to 13ha; today the plantings are 100ha. Wine quality has been exemplary from the word go, value for money no less so. The Barwang label also takes in 100% Tumbarumba wines, as well as Hilltops/Tumbarumba blends. Exports to Asia.

ŸŸŸŸŸ **Granite Track Tumbarumba Riesling 2010** Bright straw-green; Tumbarumba is better known for chardonnay than riesling; successfully made in a Kabinett style, flooded with juicy passionfruit and lime juice, crisp acidity giving balance and length. Screwcap. 10.5% alc. **Rating** 95 **To** 2025 $25

Hilltops Cabernet Sauvignon 2010 Crimson-red; a fragrant bouquet of redcurrant, cassis and violets; the palate is elegantly constructed, with fine-grained tannins, very well-balanced and integrated cedary oak, fresh acidity and fine persistence on the finish. Screwcap. 14% alc. **Rating** 94 **To** 2020 $20

ŸŸŸŸŸ **Granite Track Tumbarumba Riesling 2012** **Rating** 92 **To** 2020 $25 BE
✪ **Tumbarumba Chardonnay 2012** At the top end of unwooded Chardonnay, with both depth and length to the potent mix of white peach and grapefruit; will soften and grow in the bottle if that is what you want. Screwcap. 13% alc. **Rating** 91 **To** 2016 $21

Barwick Wines ★★★★

283 Yelverton North Road, Yelverton, WA 6281 **Region** Margaret River
T (08) 9417 5633 **www.**barwickwines.com **Open** By appt
Winemaker Nigel Ludlow **Est.** 1997 **Dozens** 100 000 **Vyds** 188ha

The production gives some guide to the size of the three estate vineyards. The first is the Dwalganup Vineyard in the Blackwood Valley region; the second is St John's Brook Vineyard in Margaret River; and the third is the Treenbrook Vineyard in Pemberton. Taken together, the three holdings place Barwick in the top 10 wine producers in WA. The wines are released under three labels, The Collectables at the top, from small parcels of estate-grown grapes. Exports to the UK, the US and other major markets.

ŸŸŸŸŸ **Margaret River Cabernet Merlot 2011** Bright red-purple; an attractive medium-bodied blend, but with one unusual attribute: close your eyes, and you might think you were in the McLaren Vale, for the wine has a distinct line of dark chocolate to go with the savoury cassis fruit and French oak. Screwcap. 14.5% alc. **Rating** 91 **To** 2021 $25

✪ **Sauvignon Blanc Semillon 2012** Light straw-green; a particularly rich blend, with a barrel ferment component adding to the impact; the result is akin to a freshly vitamised lemon sherbet plus a touch of cream. Screwcap. 13.7% alc. **Rating** 90 **To** 2013 $17

Margaret River Chardonnay 2011 Bright straw-green; a fleshy Chardonnay, the aromas and flavours focused on white and yellow peach, melon and some creamy notes from French oak. Screwcap. 13.5% alc. **Rating** 90 **To** 2016 $25

✪ **Pemberton Pinot Noir 2011** Light red-purple; here is a wine that supports the proposition that some parts of Pemberton are suited to pinot noir (others aren't). It has a distinct overlay of savoury/spicy/foresty characters to the core of dark cherry fruit. Particularly good value Screwcap. 13.5% alc. **Rating** 90 **To** 2015 $17

🍷🍷🍷🍷 ✪ **Crush Cabernet Merlot 2010** Light, bright crimson-purple; a juicy, red fruit-filled wine with remarkable purity and freshness, tannin and oak more notable for their absence than their presence. May have never seen oak, but either way is exceptional value. Screwcap. 14.5% alc. **Rating** 89 **To** 2015 $12
The Collectables Pemberton Pinot Noir 2009 **Rating** 88 **To** 2014 $35

Barwite Vineyards ★★★☆

1974 Long Lane, Mansfield, Vic 3724 **Region** Upper Goulburn
T (03) 5776 9800 **www**.barwitevineyards.com.au **Open** Not
Winemaker Ros Ritchie **Est.** 1998 **Dozens** 4000 **Vyds** 45ha

Barwite's substantial vineyard was planted in 1998 on a slope facing the mouth of the Broken River and thereon to Mt Stirling. Pinot noir (23ha) and chardonnay (13ha) were planted for Orlando, to be used in sparkling wine. Given the reputation of the region for the production of aromatic white wines, 6ha of riesling were also planted, the intention being to sell the grapes. However, since 2009 some of the best parcels have been kept aside for the Barwite label. Most of the attention over the next few years is likely to focus on Pinot Noir.

🍷🍷🍷🍷½ **Friday's Child Riesling 2012** Light straw-green; has a generous, indeed abundant, array of ripe citrus (lime and grapefruit) on the bouquet and palate alike, neatly trimmed by bright acidity on the finish. Screwcap. 12% alc. **Rating** 92 **To** 2019 $22

🍷🍷🍷🍷 **Friday's Child Chardonnay 2012** **Rating** 88 **To** 2015 $30

Bass Fine Wines ★★★★

16 Goodman Court, Invermay, Launceston, Tas 7250 **Region** Northern Tasmania
T (03) 6326 8778 **Open** Mon–Fri 9–5
Winemaker Guy Wagner **Est.** 1999 **Dozens** 3000

Guy Wagner built the scope of his business over a period of 10 years, the greater expansion starting in 2007–08. He makes wines for 17 small vineyards in Northern Tasmania in addition to his own wines. At the end of '08 his partnership in the Rosevears winery ended, and a new winery was constructed prior to the '09 vintage at Invermay, well inside the city of Launceston. The cellar door at this location has glass walls, allowing visitors to observe the workings of a small winery. Retail distribution in Tas, Vic, NSW and ACT. Exports to the US.

🍷🍷🍷🍷½ **Strait Pinot Noir 2011** Bright, clear purple-crimson; there are some interesting spicy/smoky characters in this wine that have developed with an extra year's bottle age, but without taking away from the plummy fruit. Gold medal Hobart Wine Show '12. Very attractive wine. Screwcap. 13.5% alc. **Rating** 93 **To** 2018 $19

Bass Phillip ★★★★★

Tosch's Road, Leongatha South, Vic 3953 **Region** Gippsland
T (03) 5664 3341 **Open** By appt
Winemaker Phillip Jones **Est.** 1979 **Dozens** 1500

Phillip Jones handcrafts tiny quantities of superlative Pinot Noir which, at its best, has no equal in Australia. Painstaking site selection, ultra-close vine spacing and the very, very cool climate of South Gippsland are the keys to the magic of Bass Phillip and its eerily Burgundian Pinots.

🍷🍷🍷🍷🍷 **Reserve Pinot Noir 2010** The colour is no deeper than that of the Premium, but has more purple mixed in with the crimson, and is sparkling bright and clear. The perfumed bouquet of cherries and wild strawberry is but foreplay for the palate; here there is a wine of astonishing purity and elegant harmony, and I simply couldn't bring myself to spit more than a tiny amount out. Over the years Phillip Jones has toyed with true greatness – here he has achieved it to an awesome degree. ProCork. 12.7% alc. **Rating** 99 **To** 2030 $420

Premium Pinot Noir 2010 Bright purple-crimson; the class, the breed, the quality of this wine take a millisecond to express themselves as you take this wine into your mouth to confirm what the bouquet has semaphored. It has superb length, balance and harmony, red fruits, spices, fine tannins and oak (you know it has to be there) all in a seamless weaving of silk and satin. ProCork. 12.8% alc. **Rating** 98 **To** 2025 $150

Premium Chardonnay 2011 From 32-year-old vines; French oak barrel-fermented and matured. Excellent intensity and equally impressive balance and freshness; the varietal fruit expression spans nectarine, white peach, green apple and grapefruit; the oak is subtle. The one snake in the Garden of Eden is the ProCork, which should prevent taint, but has no 10-year-plus track record of combating random oxidation. ProCork. 12.4% alc. **Rating** 96 **To** 2021 $79

Premium Chardonnay 2010 Pale straw-green; the varietal fruit expression here is less confronting that that of the '11, with more dimensions and a greater range of ripe flavours; while the bedrock of those flavours is similar to that of the '11, the palate is a little more supple and fleshier, inviting consumption at any time up to the end of this decade. ProCork. 12.5% alc. **Rating** 96 **To** 2020 $83

Issan Pinot Noir 2010 By far the deepest colour of the five Bass Phillip pinots; the bouquet and palate are much as one would guess from the colour, rich and dark-fruited, but this is nothing to do with alcohol ripeness. It is a vineyard expression, the wine velvety yet fine and supple, the tannins ripe and thoroughly integrated. ProCork. 12.8% alc. **Rating** 96 **To** 2025 $83

The Estate Chardonnay 2011 Pale straw-green; here the intensity is positively piercing, the length prodigious; while peach and grapefruit are compressed into a single stream of pure flavours, oak is simply a vehicle for the fermentation. ProCork. 12.2% alc. **Rating** 95 **To** 2022 $62

Four Vineyards Pinot Noir 2010 25th. Similar depth to the colour of Crown Prince, but less purple; slightly more complex and robust, but there is plenty of dark fruit to carry the earthy/savoury nuances; the wine has very good length, and a first-class finish. ProCork. 12.6% alc. **Rating** 95 **To** 2020 $55

Crown Prince Pinot Noir 2010 Clear purple-red; an immediately attractive cherry and plum bouquet, then a positively silky palate, with the delicious fruit of the bouquet, the tannins superfine, the finish long and harmonious. ProCork. 12.6% alc. **Rating** 95 **To** 2020 $55

Gewurztraminer 2011 **Rating** 94 **To** 2018 $29
Premium Pinot Noir 2011 **Rating** 94 **To** 2019 $129

ΨΨΨΨΩ **The Estate Pinot Noir 2011** **Rating** 93 **To** 2019 $70
Crown Prince Pinot Noir 2011 **Rating** 92 **To** 2017 $50

Bass River Winery   ★★★

1835 Dalyston Glen Forbes Road, Glen Forbes, Vic 3990 **Region** Gippsland
T (03) 5678 8252 **www**.bassriverwinery.com **Open** Thurs–Tues 9–5
Winemaker Pasquale Butera, Frank Butera **Est.** 1999 **Dozens** 1500 **Vyds** 4ha
The Butera family has established 1ha each of pinot noir and chardonnay and 2ha split equally between riesling, sauvignon blanc, pinot gris and merlot, with both the winemaking and viticulture handled by the father and son team of Pasquale and Frank. The small production is principally sold through the cellar door plus to some retailers and restaurants in the South Gippsland area. Exports to Singapore and China.

ΨΨΨΨ **Gippsland Merlot 2010** Good hue; the fragrant red berry bouquet leads into a medium-bodied, gently spicy palate, with flavours of cassis, plum and mocha; not bottled until Dec '12, suggesting an extended stay in tank somewhere along the way. Screwcap. 12.5% alc. **Rating** 89 **To** 2015 $22

battely wines

1375 Beechworth-Wangaratta Road, Beechworth, Vic 3747 **Region** Beechworth
T 0412 180 671 **www.**battelywines.com.au **Open** By appt
Winemaker Russell Bourne **Est.** 1998 **Dozens** 500 **Vyds** 5ha
Dr Russell Bourne is an anaesthetist and former GP at Mt Beauty who has always loved the
food, wine and skiing of Northeast Victoria. He completed his oenology degree at CSU in
2002 following his 1998 acquisition of the former Brown Brothers Everton Hills Vineyard.
He has since planted 1.6ha of shiraz and viognier, more recently adding counoise, the first
planting of this variety in Australia. All wines are estate-grown. Exports to the UK, the US
and Hong Kong.

ŸŸŸŸŸ **Beechworth Syrah 2011** Deep purple-crimson; painstaking work in the
vineyard, and a perfectly timed decision to pick, have produced a very good Shiraz,
with black fruits, spice and licorice interwoven on the bouquet and medium- to
full-bodied palate alike, quality oak also making a contribution. A triumph for the
vintage. Cork. 14% alc. **Rating** 94 **To** 2025 $58

ŸŸŸŸŸ **Beechworth Durif 2011 Rating** 93 **To** 2030 $44

Battle of Bosworth

Gaffney Road, Willunga, SA 5172 **Region** McLaren Vale
T (08) 8556 2441 **www.**battleofbosworth.com.au **Open** Fri–Mon 11–5
Winemaker Joch Bosworth **Est.** 1996 **Dozens** 10 000 **Vyds** 80ha
Battle of Bosworth is owned and run by Joch Bosworth (viticulture and winemaking) and
partner Louise Hemsley-Smith (sales and marketing). The wines take their name from the
battle which ended the War of the Roses, fought on Bosworth Field, Leicestershire in 1485.
The vineyards were established in the early 1970s by parents Peter and Anthea Bosworth,
in the foothills of the Mt Lofty Ranges in McLaren Vale. Conversion to organic viticulture
began in 1995, with vines now fully certified A-grade organic by ACO. Shiraz, cabernet
sauvignon and chardonnay account for 75% of the plantings, with 10 more varieties making
up the numbers. The Spring Seeds Wine Co. wines are made from estate vineyards. Exports
to the UK, the US, Canada, the Czech Republic, Hong Kong, Singapore and NZ.

ŸŸŸŸŸ **Chanticleer McLaren Vale Shiraz 2010** Intense, deep purple-crimson; only
one hogshead (300 litres) was made of this quintessential McLaren Vale shiraz, with
multiple layers of luscious plum and blackberry fruit, dark chocolate and supple
tannins – a powerful affirmation of the value of organic viticulture. Screwcap.
14.5% alc. **Rating** 96 **To** 2035 $45
Best of Vintage 2010 A blend of cabernet sauvignon, shiraz and petit verdot;
the colour is excellent, and the aromas and flavours are quite striking in their
intensity and persistence; the black fruits have a convincing savoury substrate, the
tannins adding the final dimension. Screwcap. 14.5% alc. **Rating** 94 **To** 2030 $50

ŸŸŸŸŸ **White Boar 2010 Rating** 93 **To** 2025 $45

Bay of Fires/House of Arras

40 Baxters Road, Pipers River, Tas 7252 **Region** Northern Tasmania
T (03) 6382 7622 **www.**bayoffireswines.com.au **Open** 7 days 10–5
Winemaker Peter Dredge, Ed Carr **Est.** 2001 **Dozens** NFP
Hardys purchased its first grapes from Tasmania in 1994 with the aim of further developing
and refining its sparkling wines, a process that quickly gave birth to Arras. The next stage was
the inclusion of various parcels of chardonnay from Tasmania in the 1998 Eileen Hardy, then
the development in 2001 of the Bay of Fires brand, offering wines sourced from various parts
of Tasmania. The winery was originally that of Rochecombe, then Ninth Island, and now, of
course, Bay of Fires. Its potential has now been fully realised in the most impressive imaginable
fashion – Bay of Fires table wines and its successive multi-trophy-winning vintages of Pinot
Noir in particular, have an exalted reputation; the House of Arras traditional method sparkling

wines made by Ed Carr are, if anything, of even greater quality and renown. Exports to all major markets.

ŶŶŶŶŶ **Arras Blanc de Blanc 2004** The grapes come from the Pipers River and Upper Derwent districts, and the wine is not released until it has spent a minimum of 8 years on lees. Pale quartz-green; white flower and brioche aromas; very intense and very long; lovely citrus/white peach fruit; dazzling purity. Cork. 12.4% alc. **Rating** 97 **To** 2017 $80

Arras EJ Carr Late Disgorged 2000 This is the ultimate Australian sparkling wine, and although its price may seem daunting, I believe it's worth it: there are Australian red wines of younger age at higher prices (and no shortage of champagnes). Pale green-gold; 10 years on yeast lees and 100% mlf has invested the wine with all the complexity expected, yet there is an innate elegance to its gently creamy/toasty/spicy flavours; has an exceptional degree of balance and length. Cork. 12.5% alc. **Rating** 97 **To** 2016 $136

House of Arras Grand Vintage 2004 Pale straw-green; bottle-fermented, with 7 years on tirage (per neck label, six per back label); a very complex wine with some attractive funky notes on the bouquet, generosity and richness the key notes of the palate with biscuit, brioche, dried fruits and citrus all on display. Cork. 12.5% alc. **Rating** 96 **To** 2015 $73

Arras EJ Carr Late Disgorged 2001 Made from chardonnay and pinot noir sourced from the Pipers River, Upper and Lower Derwent Valley, not released until it has spent at least 10 years on lees. Glowing green-gold, fine mousse; a rich, complex and toasty bouquet; the palate has all of the foregoing, plus delicacy and perfect balance. Cork. 12.5% alc. **Rating** 96 **To** 2016 $150

Arras Rose 2005 A blend of pinot noir (dominant) and chardonnay sourced from the Lower and Upper Derwent and Huon Valley districts. Here the wine spends at least 7 years on lees. Pale salmon-pink; some spicy forest fruit aromas; the complex palate picks up all of the red fruit characters. A delicious wine, ready now. Cork. 12.6% alc. **Rating** 96 **To** 2015 $80

Arras Rose 2004 Very pale salmon-pink; a blend of pinot noir and chardonnay that spent 7 years on yeast lees; it is vibrantly fresh, and has the fine spider web of tannins that sparkling winemakers seek to build in their best wines, giving the wine a certain reticence and finesse. Cork. 12.5% alc. **Rating** 96 **To** 2014 $80

Bay of Fires Tasmanian Cuvee Pinot Noir Chardonnay NV Bright, pale straw-green; showing little development from its 3 years on lees; the bouquet is complex, with toast/brioche/honey aromas leading into a beautifully balanced palate, with fresh stone fruit to the fore, creamy brioche coming again on the finish. Cork. 12.5% alc. **Rating** 95 **To** 2014 $37

Bay of Fires Tasmanian Cuvee Pinot Noir Chardonnay Rose NV Pale, bright pink; despite spending not less than 3 years on yeast lees, the wine has excellent freshness to its display of strawberry, red cherry and citrus fruit, the dosage judged to perfection. Cork. 12.5% alc. **Rating** 95 **To** 2014 $37

Bay of Fires Riesling 2012 Rating 94 **To** 2022 $32
Bay of Fires Sauvignon Blanc 2012 Rating 94 **To** 2015 $32
Bay of Fires Pinot Gris 2012 Rating 94 **To** 2013 $32
Bay of Fires Pinot Noir 2011 Rating 94 **To** 2017 $38
Arras Brut Elite NV Cuvee No. 501 Rating 94 **To** 2016 $45

ŶŶŶŶŶ
✪ **Bay of Fires Tigress Pinot Noir Chardonnay NV** Light straw hue, with the faintest touch of pink; a lively, indeed punchy, wine with citrus, toast and brioche duelling for a place; there are also strawberry and lychee nuances to the palate. Good value. 100% Tasmanian fruit. Cork. 12.5% alc. **Rating** 92 **To** 2014 $23

Bay of Shoals   ★★★☆

Cordes Road, Kingscote, Kangaroo Island, SA 5223 **Region** Kangaroo Island
T (08) 8553 0289 **www**.bayofshoalswines.com.au **Open** 7 days 11–5
Winemaker Jonothan Ketley **Est.** 1994 **Dozens** 2400 **Vyds** 10ha

John Willoughby's vineyard overlooks the Bay of Shoals, which is the northern boundary of Kingscote, Kangaroo Island's main town. Planting of the vineyard began in 1994 and it now comprises riesling, chardonnay, sauvignon blanc, cabernet sauvignon and shiraz. In addition, 460 olive trees have been planted to produce table olives.

ΨΨΨΨΨ **Kangaroo Island Shiraz 2010** Deep colour, and offering saturated black fruit aromas of blackberry, liqueur-soaked plums, clove and a touch of leather; the palate is medium-bodied and lively, with fresh acidity and fine-grained tannins in balance with the essency fruit on offer. Screwcap. 15.3% alc. **Rating** 90 **To** 2018 $22 BE

ΨΨΨΨ **Kangaroo Island Riesling 2012** Bright pale straw; a fragrant bouquet of ripe lemon and orange blossom is followed by a fresh, forward and accessible palate, with tangy acidity providing line on the even conclusion. Screwcap. 13.6% alc. **Rating** 89 **To** 2016 $18 BE
Kangaroo Island Sauvignon Blanc 2012 **Rating** 88 **To** 2014 $20 BE
Kangaroo Island Rose 2012 **Rating** 88 **To** 2014 $18 BE

Beach Road   ★★★★☆
PO Box 1106, McLaren Flat, SA 5171 **Region** Langhorne Creek/McLaren Vale
T (08) 8327 4547 **www.**beachroadwines.com.au **Open** Not
Winemaker Briony Hoare **Est.** 2007 **Dozens** 1500
This is the thoroughly impressive venture of winemaker Briony Hoare and viticulturist Tony Hoare, who began their life partnership after meeting while studying wine science at Roseworthy. Their involvement in the industry dates back to the early 1990s, Briony working around Australia with many of the flagship wines of (then) Southcorp, Tony gaining extensive experience in Mildura, the Hunter Valley and McLaren Vale (in McLaren Vale he spent five years as viticulturist for Wirra Wirra). In 2005 the pair decided to go it alone, setting up a wine consultancy, and in '07 launching Beach Road. The early focus on Italian varieties stems from Briony's vintage in Piedmont, where she worked with barbera, nebbiolo, gavi and moscato. Along the way they both had a lot of exposure to grenache, shiraz and mourvedre.

ΨΨΨΨΨ **Primitivo 2009** The bright, clear purple-crimson colour and fragrant bouquet are a compelling start, introducing a luscious palate of dark berry fruits interleaved with mocha and fruitcake. Screwcap. 14.5% alc. **Rating** 91 **To** 2020 $25
Nero d'Avola 2010 A robust, full-flavoured wine with spicy/savoury overtones to the blackberry fruit; the tannins are ripe, reflecting the late picking and alcohol-driven warmth of the palate. A southern Italian variety usually encountered in warm to hot Australian regions. Screwcap. 15% alc. **Rating** 90 **To** 2020 $45

ΨΨΨΨ **Aglianico 2010** **Rating** 89 **To** 2016 $25

Beckingham Wines   ★★★
7/477 Warrigal Road, Moorabbin, Vic 3189 **Region** Mornington Peninsula
T 0400 192 264 **www.**beckinghamwines.com.au **Open** W'ends 10–5
Winemaker Peter Beckingham **Est.** 1998 **Dozens** 2400
Peter Beckingham is a chemical engineer who has turned a hobby into a business, moving operations from the driveway of his house to a warehouse in Moorabbin. The situation of the winery may not be romantic, but it is eminently practical, and more than a few winemakers in California have adopted the same solution. His friends grow the grapes, and he makes the wine, both for himself and as a contract maker for others.

ΨΨΨΨ **Pas de Deux Chardonnay Pinot Noir 2006** Sourced from the Mornington Peninsula, Strathbogie Ranges and Sunbury; some of the base wine was matured in new French oak; the dosage is so low the wine is transparent and brisk. Good value. Cork. 11.5% alc. **Rating** 89 **To** 2014 $18

⚘ Beechworth Wine Estates ★★★★

PO Box 514, Beechworth, Vic 3477 **Region** Beechworth
T (03) 5728 3340 **www.**beechworthwe.com.au **Open** Not
Winemaker Glenn Eberbach **Est.** 2003 **Dozens** 1260 **Vyds** 8ha

John and Joanne Iwanuch and John Allen (Joanne's brother) began the planting of the vineyard in 2003. They say Beechworth Wine Estates is a family-run and owned business, with Jo and John's four children participating in all aspects of vineyard life. It is situated on the Rail Trail, 4km from Beechworth, and they have planted sauvignon blanc, pinot gris, chardonnay, shiraz, cabernet sauvignon, merlot, tempranillo and sangiovese. Exports to Germany.

🍷🍷🍷🍷⚲
✪ **Hazelbank Shiraz 2009** Excellent retention of colour and hue; the fragrant bouquet of black cherry/berry, spice and cracked pepper leads into an elegant and supple, light- to medium-bodied, palate. Will live for years, but does not require patience. Screwcap. 13.3% alc. **Rating** 92 **To** 2020 $20

✪ **Hazelbank Chardonnay 2010** Barrel-fermented and matured on lees for 9 months. This is a very well-balanced, generous Chardonnay that manages to maintain elegance, and a silky mouthfeel; the oak also introduces some toasty notes. Screwcap. 13.3% alc. **Rating** 91 **To** 2016 $19

🍷🍷🍷🍷
✪ **Hazelbank Sauvignon Blanc 2012** Quartz-white; fermentation in old French oak has not imparted any colour or flavour, but has introduced a measure of texture to the restrained citrus fruit. Exceptional value for those who don't want sauvignon blanc shoved in their face. Screwcap. 12.8% alc. **Rating** 89 **To** 2014 $14

✪ **Hazelbank Pinot Grigio 2012** Quartz-white; bell-clear pear and citrus fruit on the bouquet and juicy palate; has no need for elaboration. Screwcap. 12.2% alc. **Rating** 89 **To** 2014 $16

Hazelbank Cabernet Merlot 2008 **Rating** 87 **To** 2015 $22

Beelgara ★★★★☆

576 Rossetto Road, Beelbangera, NSW 2680 **Region** Riverina
T (02) 6966 0200 **www.**beelgara.com.au **Open** Mon–Fri 10–3
Winemaker Rod Hooper, Danny Toaldo **Est.** 1930 **Dozens** 600 000

Beelgara Estate was formed in 2001 after the purchase of the 60-year-old Rossetto family winery by a group of shareholders, mostly the Toohey family. The emphasis has changed significantly, with a concerted effort to go to the right region for each variety, while still maintaining very good value for money. Exports to most major markets.

🍷🍷🍷🍷🍷 **Regional Reserve Watervale Riesling 2012** Light straw-green; a powerful, lime-laden, bouquet and palate reflect the quality of the grapes (and the consequent price). Excellent minerally acidity balances the wine and lengthens the finish. Screwcap. 12% alc. **Rating** 94 **To** 2017 $25

🍷🍷🍷🍷⚲
✪ **Springview Clare Valley Shiraz 2010** **Rating** 93 **To** 2030 $40

✪ . **Black Label Adelaide Hills Sauvignon Blanc 2012** I strongly disapprove of the two apparent silver medals on the front label which, on closer inspection, are nothing of the kind. Worse still is one using the five-star rating in the *2012 Wine Companion.* This is an impressive Adelaide Hills sauvignon blanc with a focused, linear citrus and herb palate running through to a fresh and lively finish. Screwcap. 12% alc. **Rating** 92 **To** 2014 $18

✪ **Black Label Clare Valley Cabernet Sauvignon 2010** Excellent crimson-purple, the cassis-laden bouquet accurately tells of the juicy fruits of the palate, again led by cassis; oak is part of the picture, as are fine tannins, but this is a fruit-driven wine with very good balance, and a prosperous future. Screwcap. 14% alc. **Rating** 92 **To** 2020 $18

✪ **Black Label Clare Valley Shiraz 2010** Very good crimson hue and depth; this is a pretty delicious wine, with abundant ripe plum and black cherry fruit on its medium-bodied palate; its charm comes from its sinuous, fluid mouthfeel and fresh, airy finish. Screwcap. 14% alc. **Rating** 91 **To** 2017 $18

⚙   **Regional Reserve Riverina Botrytis Semillon 2009** Rating 91 To 2015 $25
Black Label Clare Valley Grenache Rose 2012 Light, bright puce; mounts a case for all Clare Valley grenache to be turned into rose, but – of course – that won't happen. Fragrant raspberry and red cherry fruit on the bouquet and palate provide plenty of flavour without the use of residual sugar. Screwcap. 13.5% alc. **Rating** 90 **To** 2014 $18

⚙   **Black Label Clare Valley Merlot 2011** Light, bright red-purple; a surprise with its clear varietal fruit profile on both the bouquet and palate; vigilance in the vineyard and skill in the winery have made the most of the cool vintage, with cassis fruit and the barest touch of savoury/black olive on the finish. Screwcap. 14% alc. **Rating** 90 **To** 2015 $18

♟♟♟♟   **Estate Range Pinot Grigio 2012** Pale straw-green; this wine over-delivers at
⚙   this price point, with a nice drizzle of lemon over its core of pear fruit, the finish fresh and bright. Screwcap. 11.5% alc. **Rating** 87 **To** 2014 $10

⚙   **Estate Range Shiraz 2012** Light, bright crimson-purple; has juicy red fruit aromas and flavours, the French oak presumably from staves and/or chips (no dishonour at this price); the faintest touch of sweetness has been to the benefit of the wine. Great value. Screwcap. 12.5% alc. **Rating** 87 **To** 2014 $10

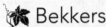 Bekkers   ★★★★★

PO Box 1409, Aldinga Beach, SA 5173 **Region** McLaren Vale
T 0408 807 568 **www**.bekkerswine.com **Open** Not
Winemaker Emmanuelle and Toby Bekkers **Est.** 2010 **Dozens** 150 **Vyds** 5.5ha
This brings together two high-performance, highly experienced and highly credentialled business and life partners. Husband Toby Bekkers graduated with an honours degree in applied science in agriculture from the University of Adelaide, and over the ensuing 15 years has had broad-ranging responsibility as general manager of Paxton Wines in McLaren Vale, and as a leading exponent of organic and biodynamic viticulture. Wife Emmanuelle was born in Bandol in the south of France, gaining university degrees in biochemistry and oenology before working for the Hardys in the south of France, which led her to Australia and a wide-ranging career, including an ongoing role as winemaker at Chalk Hill. Production can be expected to expand significantly in the years ahead.

♟♟♟♟♟   **McLaren Vale Syrah 2011** An exceptional achievement for the vintage, with dark chocolate and black fruits on the bouquet morphing into a complex, decidedly savoury (in the best sense) palate, still with dark fruits, but giving impressive mouthfeel. Admirable balance and length. Screwcap. 14% alc. **Rating** 96 **To** 2041 $110

Belgravia Wines   ★★★★★

Mitchell Highway, Molong, NSW 2866 **Region** Orange
T (02) 6360 0495 **www**.belgravia.com.au **Open** 7 days 10–4
Winemaker Phil Kerney (Contract) **Est.** 2001 **Dozens** 12 000 **Vyds** 104ha
Belgravia is an 1800ha mixed farming property (sheep, cattle and vines) 20km north of Orange, established and owned by the Hattersley family. There are now over 100ha of vineyard, with 38.2ha of chardonnay, 32.7ha of shiraz, 20.8ha of merlot, and smaller plantings of riesling, gewurztraminer, pinot gris and sangiovese. In 2013 Belgravia moved its cellar door from the former Union Bank building in Orange to the heritage-listed railway station in Molong. Exports to Germany, Hong Kong and China.

♟♟♟♟♟   **Orange Cabernet Sauvignon 2010** Bright hue; hand-picked, wild yeast-
⚙   fermented, and matured for 18 months in new French oak; the fruit has dealt with that oak without the slightest demur, gloriously juicy cassis and redcurrant supported by fine and supple tannins. Cool-grown cabernet at its elegant best. Splendid, unbeatable value. Screwcap. 13.5% alc. **Rating** 96 **To** 2030 $24

✪   **Orange Gewurztraminer 2012** Light straw-green; has exemplary varietal character on the bouquet and palate alike; there are rose petal, musk, ginger and Turkish Delight aromas and flavours, yet the wine avoids heavy phenolic notes. Screwcap. 13.5% alc. **Rating** 94 **To** 2020 $22

♟♟♟♟♟   **Orange Riesling 2012 Rating** 93 **To** 2020 $22
Orange Syrah 2010 Rating 91 **To** 2020 $24

♟♟♟♟   **Union Bank Chardonnay 2011** The colour when 2 years old has barely
✪   changed in this unoaked Chardonnay, likely due to low pH and its corresponding crisp acidity. The flavours are not intense, but are clear, with grapefruit and stone fruit doing the work. Good value for a cool-grown chardonnay. Screwcap. 12.5% alc. **Rating** 89 **To** 2014 $15

Bellarine Estate ★★★★☆

2270 Portarlington Road, Bellarine, Vic 3222 **Region** Geelong
T (03) 5259 3310 **www**.bellarineestate.com.au **Open** 7 days 11–4
Winemaker Anthony Brain **Est.** 1995 **Dozens** 4500 **Vyds** 12ha
Anthony Brain, with multiple vintages under his belt at Bellarine Estate's onsite winery, is now a district veteran. With the Bellarine Brewing company (which makes the only micro-brewed beer on the Bellarine Peninsula) also situated in the winery, and the extended operating hours of Julian's Restaurant, it is a popular meeting place. The vineyard is planted to chardonnay, pinot noir, shiraz, merlot, viognier and sauvignon blanc. Exports to the US.

♟♟♟♟♟   **Phil's Fetish Geelong Pinot Noir 2010** Bright crimson; the bouquet is a complex offering of berry fruit, spice and savoury/foresty components, possibly due to whole-bunch inclusion in the ferment; the palate is also complex, long and well balanced, although the 'mystical pinot character' claimed on the back label is indeed mystical. Screwcap. 13.2% alc. **Rating** 94 **To** 2017 $32

♟♟♟♟♟   **Two Wives Geelong Shiraz 2010 Rating** 92 **To** 2020 $32

Bellarmine Wines ★★★★★

1 Balyan Retreat, Pemberton, WA 6258 **Region** Pemberton
T (08) 9776 0667 **www**.bellarmine.com.au **Open** By appt
Winemaker Dr Diane Miller **Est.** 2000 **Dozens** 6000 **Vyds** 20.2ha
This vineyard is owned by German residents Dr Willi and Gudrun Schumacher. Long-term wine lovers, the Schumachers decided to establish a vineyard and winery of their own, using Australia partly because of its stable political climate. The vineyard is planted to merlot, pinot noir, chardonnay, shiraz, riesling, sauvignon blanc and petit verdot. Following the departure of long-term winemaker Mike Bewsher, Diane Miller, previously head of the Vintage Wineworx contract winemaking facility, was appointed winemaker and operations manager. Exports to the UK, Germany and China.

♟♟♟♟♟   **Pemberton Riesling Dry 2012** Light straw-green; the flowery, aromatic bouquet of lemon and lime blossom leads into a seductively juicy palate, with the first hints of the honey that will appear in a few years' time, ultimately followed by toast. Screwcap. 13% alc. **Rating** 95 **To** 2022 $22
Pemberton Pinot Noir 2012 A pinot with its whole life in front of it, thanks to its storehouse of red and black cherry fruit, balanced and integrated French oak, and perfectly weighted tannins. Will steadily gain complexity over the next 7+ years. Screwcap. 14% alc. **Rating** 95 **To** 2020 $25
Pemberton Riesling Select 2012 Light straw-green; here the fermentation has been stopped with the equivalent of 2.5% alcohol remaining as residual sugar; there is still sufficient fresh acidity to make this a delicious aperitif style, or to accompany the major part of Asian cuisine, and I prefer its positive nature to the Half Dry. Lime juice personified. Screwcap. 9.5% alc. **Rating** 95 **To** 2022 $22

Pemberton Riesling Half Dry 2012 The grapes are picked at the same time as those for Riesling Dry, but the fermentation is arrested with the equivalent of 1% alcohol retained as sugar; the wine is distinctly sweeter, but balanced by crisp acidity, and will develop very well over time. Screwcap. 12% alc. **Rating** 94 To 2022 $22

ŶŶŶŶŶ **Pemberton Sauvignon Blanc 2012** Pale quartz; a typically elegant Sauvignon
✪ Blanc with grass, kiwifruit, guava and citrus seamlessly fused, the acidity bright and balanced. Screwcap. 12% alc. **Rating** 93 To 2014 $18

Bellvale Wine ★★★★★

95 Forresters Lane, Berrys Creek, Vic 3953 **Region** Gippsland
T (03) 5668 8230 **www**.bellvalewine.com.au **Open** By appt
Winemaker John Ellis **Est.** 1998 **Dozens** 4000 **Vyds** 18ha
John Ellis is the third under this name to be actively involved in the wine industry. His background as a former 747 pilot, and the knowledge he gained of Burgundy over many visits, sets him apart from the others. He has established pinot noir (10ha), chardonnay (5ha) and pinot gris (3ha) on the red soils of a north-facing slope. He chose a density of 7150 vines per hectare, following as far as possible the precepts of Burgundy, but limited by tractor size, which precludes narrower row spacing and even higher plant density. Exports to the UK, the US, Denmark, Germany, Singapore and Japan.

ŶŶŶŶŶ **Athena's Vineyard Gippsland Chardonnay 2011** Light straw-green; classic cool-climate style, with a strong core of minerality acting as a framework more than the barrel-ferment inputs; the flavours, too, are citrus-accented, all adding up to a Chablis style, the line, length and balance all good. Screwcap. 13% alc. **Rating** 94 To 2018 $35

ŶŶŶŶŶ **Gippsland Pinot Grigio 2012** One of the good things about pinot gris/grigio
✪ is that it is far easier to make and more profitable than pinot noir – although I'm not accusing vigneron John Ellis of mercenary greed. This is, in fact, an altogether superior grigio, made on a cool windy site that enhances the aroma and gives crispness to the nashi pear palate. Screwcap. 12.5% alc. **Rating** 93 To 2014 $22

Bellwether ★★★★★

PO Box 344, Coonawarra, SA 5263 **Region** Coonawarra
T 0417 080 945 **www**.bellwetherwines.com.au **Open** Not
Winemaker Sue Bell **Est.** 2009 **Dozens** 1000
Sometimes good things come from bad. When Constellation decided to sell (or mothball) its large Padthaway winery, built by Hardys little more than 10 years previously at a cost of $20 million, chief winemaker Sue Bell was summarily retrenched. In quick succession she received a $46,000 wine industry scholarship from the Grape and Wine Research Development Council to study the wine industry in relation to other rural industries in Australia and overseas, and became Dux of the Len Evans Tutorial, her prize an extended trip through Bordeaux and Burgundy. She had decided to stay and live in Coonawarra, and the next stroke of good fortune was that a beautiful old shearing shed at Glenroy came on the market, and will be her winery and cellar door. No wines received for the *2014 Wine Companion*, but a five-star rating has been maintained.

Ben Haines Wine Co

7/211 Gold Street, Clifton Hill, Vic 3068 (postal) **Region** Various
T 0417 083 645 **www**.benhaineswine.com **Open** Not
Winemaker Ben Haines **Est.** 2010 **Dozens** 750
Ben Haines graduated from the University of Adelaide in 1999 with a degree in viticulture, waiting a couple of years (immersing himself in music) before focusing on his career. An early interest in terroir led to a deliberate choice of diverse regions, including the Yarra Valley, McLaren Vale, Adelaide Hills, Langhorne Creek, Tasmania and Central Victoria, as did time in

the US and France. Most recently, he worked at Mitchelton as senior winemaker, and in 2008 won The Wine Society Young Winemaker of the Year Award. Exports to the US.

🍷🍷🍷🍷🍷 **Central Victoria Syrah 2009** Deep crimson-purple; a rich, spicy plum and blackberry bouquet flows into a very well-balanced medium- to full-bodied palate; there is abundant fruit, and the oak fits well; the tannins are in balance. Screwcap. 14.4% alc. **Rating** 94 **To** 2025 $58

🍷🍷🍷🍷🍷 **Warramunda Vineyard Yarra Valley Marsanne 2011 Rating** 93 **To** 2026 $28
B Minor Shiraz Marsanne 2012 Rating 92 **To** 2018 $26

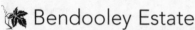 Bendooley Estate ★★★★

3020 Old Hume Highway, Berrima, NSW 2577 **Region** Southern Highlands
T (02) 4877 2235 **www**.bendooleyestate.com.au **Open** Wed–Sun 10–5
Winemaker Jonathan Holgate **Est.** 2008 **Dozens** NFP **Vyds** 1.5ha
Paul Berkelouw is a sixth-generation antiquarian book dealer, with a name known to just about everyone in Australia who has any interest in such things. He and his wife, Katja, live and work at the historic Bendooley Estate with their three young children. Here they make wine, sell books, host weddings and events, and offer accommodation. The website is one of those rare things, up to date, full of information, and handsomely presented, for the full story is a long one.

🍷🍷🍷🍷🍷 **Hand Picked Southern Highlands Chardonnay 2011** Light straw-green; while not particularly complex, the wine has good line, length and focus to the mix of stone fruit, melon and citrus; oak is very much a minor contributor, giving the varietal expression free play. Screwcap. 12.6% alc. **Rating** 90 **To** 2016 $28
Southern Highlands Shiraz Cabernet 2012 Good colour; fresh and lively red fruits, spice and pepper on the bouquet flow through to the medium-bodied palate, with finely tuned tannins and cedary oak adding to the flavour profile. Screwcap. 13.8% alc. **Rating** 90 **To** 2018 $28

🍷🍷🍷🍷 **Southern Highlands Rose 2012 Rating** 88 **To** 2013 $20
Southern Highlands Riesling 2012 Rating 87 **To** 2015 $22

Berton Vineyard ★★★★

55 Mirrool Avenue, Yenda, NSW 2681 **Region** Riverina
T (02) 6968 1600 **www**.bertonvineyards.com.au **Open** Mon–Fri 10–4, Sat 11–4
Winemaker James Ceccato, Sam Trimboli **Est.** 2001 **Dozens** 1 million **Vyds** 12.14ha
The Berton Vineyard partners – Bob and Cherie Berton, Paul Bartholomaeus, James Ceccato and Jamie Bennett – have almost 100 years' combined experience in winemaking, viticulture, finance, production and marketing. 1996 saw the acquisition of a 30ha property in the Eden Valley and the planting of the first vines. It took two years for the dam to fill, and the vines struggled on the white rock soil. This is only a small part of the business, which sources bulk wine from regions across South Eastern Australia. Wines are released under the FoundStone, Head Over Heels and Berton Vineyard (varietals, Soldier Farms and Reserve) labels. Exports to the UK, the US and other major markets.

🍷🍷🍷🍷🍷 **Reserve Eden Valley Chardonnay 2012** Bright straw-green; well made, with the bouquet and palate moving in a peach and honeydew melon spectrum; oak is evident, but not aggressive, and the wine has some cellaring capacity. Screwcap. 13% alc. **Rating** 90 **To** 2015 $17

🍷🍷🍷🍷 ✪ **The Vermentino 2012** Even when cropped with high yields, vermentino manages to capture attention in the same way as petite syrah/durif; there is a burst of citrus blossom and fruit that persists through to the finish. Screwcap. 12% alc. **Rating** 89 **To** 2013 $12

✪ **Reserve Barossa Shiraz 2010** Bright, full crimson-purple; a significant step up from the Black Label Shiraz, with much more emphasis on structure, and the savoury/spicy tail to the core of black cherry and plum fruit; the oak and tannins have been well managed. Screwcap. 14.5% alc. **Rating** 89 **To** 2017 $17

✪ **Head over Heels Semillon Sauvignon Blanc 2012** Good though the value of FoundStone SSB is, this is worth the extra $3; the bouquet is more expressive, the palate with more focus on the bright array of green pea and contrasting tropical fruits; not sweet, and has good acidity. Screwcap. 13% alc. **Rating** 88 **To** 2014 $11

✪ **The Black Shiraz 2011** Deep, vivid crimson-purple; some winery wizardry has been used to produce a wine with amazing colour and structure; there is a dip in the mid-palate, but no one should look this gift horse in the mouth. Screwcap. 14% alc. **Rating** 88 **To** 2016 $12

✪ **Cabernet Sauvignon 2011** Strong colour for the vintage, and above-average varietal fruit flavour and structure; once again, sophisticated winemaking at work. Screwcap. 13.5% alc. **Rating** 88 **To** 2014 $12

Sauvignon Blanc 2012 Rating 87 **To** 2013 $12

✪ **Foundstone Unoaked Chardonnay 2012** Bright straw-green; surely the best value unoaked Chardonnay on the market; it has bell-clear stone fruit and grapefruit on the bouquet and palate, and finishes with grainy acidity and no (apparent) sweetness. Screwcap. 13% alc. **Rating** 87 **To** 2014 $8

The Black Shiraz 2012 Rating 87 **To** 2015 $12

✪ **Foundstone Shiraz 2012** Full crimson-purple; particularly good value at this price; the fruit has good varietal expression via plum and blackberry, plus an oak infusion (ex staves and/or chips) that has not been overdone, and the trace of sweetness is in balance. Screwcap. 14% alc. **Rating** 87 **To** 2014 $8

Best's Wines   ★★★★★

111 Best's Road, Great Western, Vic 3377 **Region** Grampians
T (03) 5356 2250 **www.bestswines.com Open** Mon–Sat 10–5, Sun 11–4
Winemaker Justin Purser **Est.** 1866 **Dozens** 20 000 **Vyds** 34ha
Best's winery and vineyards are among Australia's best-kept secrets. Indeed the vineyards, with vines dating back to 1868, have secrets that may never be revealed: for example, one of the vines planted in the Nursery Block has defied identification and is thought to exist nowhere else in the world. Part of the cellars, too, go back to the same era, constructed by butcher-turned-winemaker Henry Best and his family. The Thomson family has owned the property since 1920, with Ben, the fifth generation, having taken over management from father Viv. Best's consistently produces elegant, supple wines; the Bin No. 0 is a classic, the Thomson Family Shiraz (from vines planted in 1868) magnificent. Very occasionally a Pinot Noir (with 15% Pinot Meunier) is made solely from the 1868 plantings of those two varieties; there is no other pinot of this vine age made anywhere else in the world. In 2012 Justin Purser was appointed winemaker to succeed Adam Wadewitz; he brings with him a remarkable CV with extensive experience in Australia, NZ and (most recently) Burgundy at Domaine de Montille. Exports to the UK, Ireland, Canada, Sweden Singapore, Hong Kong and China.

🍷🍷🍷🍷🍷 **Old Vine Great Western Pinot Meunier 2011** Made entirely from the 1868 plantings. While the colour is light, it is a privilege to taste what is, without the slightest doubt, unique in the world of wine, coming from by far the oldest pinot meunier vines in existence. It has more savoury/spicy characters than the 'young vine', with distinct violet and rose petal nuances. Rated for its history as much as its quality. Screwcap. 12.5% alc. **Rating** 97 **To** 2030 $60

✪ **Bin No. 1 Great Western Shiraz 2011** Full, deep crimson-purple; this richly robed Shiraz, flooded with blackberry, licorice and ripe plum, reflects the 6 vintages winemaker Justin Purser spent in France, Italy and NZ dealing with wet growing seasons. He has built a wine with excellent texture and structure making light of the weather. All in all, winning three trophies at the Melbourne Wine Show '12 was a just outcome. Screwcap. 14% alc. **Rating** 96 **To** 2026 $25

Trevor Mast Tribute Great Western Riesling 2012 Light straw-green; the blossom-filled bouquet and elegant but succulent lime and tropical fruits finish with perfect acidity. All proceeds of sale go to the Lovell Foundation for research into the early onset of dementia. Screwcap. 13% alc. **Rating** 94 **To** 2020 $34

Great Western Chardonnay 2012 Light straw-green; a beautifully made wine, the epitome of elegance, white peach effortlessly spanning the long palate, French oak a near-invisible network. There is little left to say. Screwcap. 12.5% alc. Rating 94 To 2018 $25

ΨΨΨΨΨ **Young Vine Great Western Pinot Meunier 2012** Very light but bright
✪   crimson-purple hue; 'young vines' now over 40 years old (planted in 1971 with cuttings from the 1868 vines, the latter the oldest in the world). Has bright cherry/raspberry fruit, and no hint of any green or minty characters. I would drink it now, slightly chilled in summer, and enjoy the hell out of it. Screwcap. 13.5% alc. **Rating** 93 To 2015 $25
     Great Western Riesling 2012 Rating 91 To 2015 $25
     Great Western Pinot Noir 2011 Rating 90 To 2016 $60

Bethany Wines

Bethany Road, Tanunda, SA 5352 **Region** Barossa
T (08) 8563 2086 www.bethany.com.au **Open** Mon–Sat 10–5, Sun 1–5
Winemaker Geoff and Robert Schrapel **Est.** 1981 **Dozens** 25 000 **Vyds** 38ha
The Schrapel family has been growing grapes in the Barossa Valley for over 140 years, but the winery has only been in operation since 1981. Nestled high on a hillside on the site of an old bluestone quarry, Geoff and Rob Schrapel produce a range of consistently well-made and attractively packaged wines. Bethany has vineyards in the Barossa and Eden Valleys. Exports to the UK, Europe and Asia.

ΨΨΨΨΨ **Reserve Shiraz 2004** Prolonged barrel ageing has left a strong vanilla/mocha mark on the rich fruit; if this style appeals, you will thoroughly enjoy this wine; the fruit has good balance and length. Cork. 14% alc. **Rating** 94 To 2024 $85

ΨΨΨΨΨ **Reserve Eden Valley Riesling 2012** Rating 92 To 2017 $32
✪   **Eden Valley Riesling 2012** Quartz-white a year after vintage; the bouquet accurately forecasts the lime, apple, talc and mineral of the light-bodied, fresh palate; still to show what it can do. Screwcap. 13% alc. **Rating** 91 To 2018 $18

Bidgeebong Wines

352 Byrnes Road, Wagga Wagga, NSW 2650 **Region** Gundagai
T (02) 6931 9955 www.bidgeebong.com.au **Open** Mon–Fri 9–4
Winemaker Andrew Birks **Est.** 2000 **Dozens** 20 000
Encompasses what the founders refer to as the Bidgeebong triangle – between Young, Wagga Wagga, Tumbarumba and Gundagai – which provides grapes for the Bidgeebong brand. The onsite winery will eventually handle 2000 tonnes of grapes for Bidgeebong's own needs, and those of other local growers and larger producers who purchase grapes from the region. Exports to Canada, Singapore and China.

ΨΨΨΨΨ **Birk's Chip Dry Very Dry Fino NV** Pale gold; a very good flor fino with its distinctive almond and apple skin aromas, then a fresh finish, and without any bitterness. Serve chilled. Hides its alcohol, but might be better still if it hadn't needed to do so. 375ml. Screwcap. 18.5% alc. **Rating** 90 To 2013 $25

Bilgavia Wines ★★★☆

PO Box 246, Singleton, NSW 2330 **Region** Hunter Valley
T (02) 6574 5314 **Open** Not
Winemaker Michael McManus **Est.** 2003 **Dozens** NFP **Vyds** 17.87ha
Leona and Phil Gunter purchased Parsons Creek Farm in 2011. Developed by the late Jack Horseman and wife Lucy, it covers 200ha of prime alluvial and loam land, but also enough terra rossa red soil for the shiraz, chardonnay, semillon and verdelho plantings. The farm has a magnificent homestead, meticulously kept vineyard, and an outstanding thoroughbred horse facility. The grapes are sold commercially, with sufficient quantity retained for the Bilgavia

label. They say 'It has always been Leona's dream to one day own a vineyard and produce her own wine', a dream which became a reality in '12.

🍷🍷🍷🍷 **Hunter Valley Verdelho 2012** Relatively early picking has invested the wine with freshness, citrus and lemon notes figuring large in the fruit salad flavours; consequently, has good length. Screwcap. 12.5% alc. **Rating** 90 **To** 2014 $26

🍷🍷🍷 **Hunter Valley Chardonnay 2012 Rating** 87 **To** 2014 $30

Bimbadgen ★★★★★

790 McDonalds Road, Pokolbin, NSW 2320 **Region** Hunter Valley
T (02) 4998 4600 www.bimbadgen.com.au **Open** Fri–Sat 10–7, Sun–Thurs 10–5
Winemaker Sarah Crowe, Mike De Garis (Consultant) **Est.** 1968 **Dozens** 40 000 **Vyds** 27ha
Established as McPherson Wines, then successively Tamalee, Sobels, Parker Wines and now Bimbadgen, this substantial winery has had what might be politely termed a turbulent history. It has vineyards in McDonalds Road and Palmers Lane, Pokolbin, and these produce the Bimbadgen Signature range at the top of the tree. Next comes the Regions range of a diverse selection of varietals from regions known for their ability to produce high-quality wines of a given variety or varieties. The Bimbadgen Ridge range is for wines in the lower price tier. The winemaking team of Sarah Crowe and Mike de Garis is proving to be a potent one. Exports to Switzerland, Taiwan, the Philippines, Hong Kong, China, Japan and NZ.

🍷🍷🍷🍷🍷 **Signature Mistletoe Lane Vineyard Semillon 2012** Pale, bright straw-green; the quality and potential of this semillon establish their mark from the first whiff through to the end of the long palate; everything is there, from citrus blossom on the bouquet, to lemon/lemongrass/lemon curd running a continuous stream across the mouth. Screwcap. 10.5% alc. **Rating** 95 **To** 2025 $40
Signature McDonalds Road Vineyard Shiraz 2011 Good colour; a very well made wine with a strong sense of place while retaining its varietal signature, and certain to develop with grace; plum, blackberry and a touch of Asian spice inhabit the medium-bodied, perfectly balanced, palate; oak and tannins provide the frame for the picture-perfect fruit. Screwcap. 13.5% alc. **Rating** 95 **To** 2040 $50
Signature Chardonnay 2012 Light green-straw; the fragrant, gently perfumed bouquet and palate are at the very heart of modern Hunter Valley style; white peach, nectarine and a hint of creamy cashew are interwoven all the way through to the finish of a supremely elegant wine. Screwcap. 13% alc. **Rating** 94 **To** 2019 $40
Regions Tasmania Pinot Noir 2011 Very good colour; it has exemplary varietal character and structure; plum and dark cherry contribute the fruit aroma and flavour, supported on the supple palate by fine, silky tannins and integrated French oak. Screwcap. 13.5% alc. **Rating** 94 **To** 2018 $39

🍷🍷🍷🍷🍷 **Regions Orange Gewurztraminer 2012** Light straw-green; while the varietal
✪ character is not overt, it is certainly recognisable on the palate in particular, with its blend of lychee, orange zest, ginger and citrus acidity flowing across the tongue and into the aftertaste, building on the wafts of rose petal of the bouquet. Screwcap. 13.5% alc. **Rating** 93 **To** 2017 $23
Estate Hunter Valley Shiraz 2011 Rating 93 **To** 2018 $25 BE
Signature Hunter Valley Shiraz 2010 Rating 91 **To** 2025 $50
Art Series Riesling 2012 Rating 90 **To** 2019 $26
Estate Hunter Valley Shiraz Viognier 2011 Rating 90 **To** 2018 $26 BE
Regions Hilltops Cabernet Sauvignon Merlot 2011 Rating 90 **To** 2017 $26

binbilla ★★★★☆

Good Friday Gully Road, Maimuru, NSW 2594 (postal) **Region** Hilltops
T (02) 6383 3305 www.binbillawines.com **Open** Not
Winemaker Nick O'Leary (Contract) **Est.** 2001 **Dozens** 1000 **Vyds** 6ha
Gerard and Berenice Hines planted their vineyard in 2001, with 4ha of cabernet sauvignon (since grafted over to viognier), 2ha of shiraz and 1ha of riesling, which produced the first

wines in '04. The more recent grafting of some vines to viognier has seen the release of a Shiraz Viognier. The only wine that is not estate-grown is the Chardonnay, which is sourced from a nearby Hilltops vineyard. The quantity made is unlikely to exceed 1000 dozen a year, with limited retail and restaurant listings in Melbourne, Sydney and Brisbane.

ΥΥΥΥΥ Hilltops Riesling 2012 Pale quartz; manages to marry generous, ripe, lime/citrus fruit with finesse and elegance; acidity and fruit run seamlessly along the length of the palate and the lingering finish. Fully deserved gold medal Winewise '12. Screwcap. 12% alc. **Rating** 95 **To** 2022 $20

Bindi Wine Growers

343 Melton Road, Gisborne, Vic 3437 (postal) **Region** Macedon Ranges
T (03) 5428 2564 **Open** Not
Winemaker Michael Dhillon, Stuart Anderson (Consultant) **Est.** 1988 **Dozens** 2000
One of the icons of Macedon. The Chardonnay is top-shelf, the Pinot Noir as remarkable (albeit in a very different idiom) as Bass Phillip, Giaconda or any of the other tiny-production, icon wines. The addition of Heathcote-sourced Shiraz under the Pyrette label confirms Bindi as one of the greatest small producers in Australia. Notwithstanding the tiny production, the wines are exported (in small quantities, of course) to the UK, the US and other major markets.

ΥΥΥΥΥ Composition Chardonnay 2011 Pale straw-green; while the wine has received the full winemaking options, its intensity, power, length and purity swamp all attempts to unpick the bundle, unless it be simply to point to its grapefruit and mineral composition. Screwcap. 13% alc. **Rating** 96 **To** 2021 $50
Block 5 Pinot Noir 2010 Light crystal-clear crimson; there is a spicy background to both bouquet and palate, but it is the intense fruit that provides the heart of an outstanding Block 5; impossible not to think of Burgundy with its texture and superb length. Diam. 14% alc. **Rating** 96 **To** 2020 $100
3 Cuvee NV A monumental Australian sparkling wine, resonating with all the complexity of 13 years on lees in barrel. A blend of half '97 and half '93 through '96, it's layered with great complexity of hazelnuts and butter. Early harvesting and low dosage maintain a wonderfully taut finish and honed freshness. Cork. 12.5% alc. **Rating** 96 **To** 2017 $80 TS
Quartz Chardonnay 2010 Light straw-green; in the typically tight, restrained, slow-developing style of Bindi, needing some years yet to start revealing all its secrets; the way the slatey acidity is built into the grapefruit flavours of the palate is virtually unique to Bindi, the oak eaten by the fermenting wine. Screwcap. 14% alc. **Rating** 95 **To** 2023 $80
Original Vineyard Pinot Noir 2010 Delicious plum and black and red cherry flavours fill the mouth with a caress of sweetly rounded fruit; a very different proposition from Block 5, ready whenever the mood takes you, but will not disappoint as it ages. Diam. 14% alc. **Rating** 95 **To** 2015 $80
Quartz Chardonnay 2011 **Rating** 94 **To** 2019 $80

ΥΥΥΥΥ Original Vineyard Pinot Noir 2011 **Rating** 92 **To** 2017 $80
Composition Pinot Noir 2011 **Rating** 90 **To** 2015 $55
Block 5 Pinot Noir 2011 **Rating** 90 **To** 2015 $100
Pyrette Heathcote Shiraz 2011 **Rating** 90 **To** 2017 $40

Bird in Hand

Bird in Hand Road, Woodside, SA 5244 **Region** Adelaide Hills
T (08) 8389 9488 **www**.birdinhand.com.au **Open** 7 days 11–5
Winemaker Andrew Nugent, Kym Milne (MW), Peter Ruchs **Est.** 1997 **Dozens** 60 000
Vyds 29ha
This very successful business took its name from a 19th-century gold mine. It is the venture of the Nugent family, headed by Dr Michael Nugent; son Andrew is a Roseworthy graduate. The family also has a vineyard in the Clare Valley, the latter providing both riesling and shiraz. A state-of-the-art winery and a straw and mud barrel cellar were completed in 2007.

The estate plantings (merlot, pinot noir, cabernet sauvignon, sauvignon blanc, riesling and shiraz) provide only part of the annual crush, the remainder coming from contract growers. In late 2010, a replica Bird in Hand cellar door was opened in Dalian, in China's northeastern Laioning province, a second following in Yingkou. Exports to all major markets.

ΥΥΥΥΥ **Nest Egg Adelaide Hills Shiraz 2010** Deep crimson-purple; a medium- to full-bodied, very rich and complex wine, with scrumptious black fruits and spices in super-abundance supported by high-quality oak and fine, ripe tannins. A long and distinguished life ahead. Major UK trophy successes. Screwcap. 14.5% alc. **Rating** 96 **To** 2035 $95

Nest Egg Adelaide Hills Merlot 2010 Substantial colour; this is a distinguished Merlot, with excellent varietal definition; cassis, black olive, a hint of earth, fine tannins and good oak are all contributors; the juicy fruit flourish on the finish ties the package in fine style. Bottle no. 614 of 4174. High-quality Australian Merlot is a rare bird. Screwcap. 14.5% alc. **Rating** 96 **To** 2025 $95

Nest Egg Adelaide Hills Chardonnay 2012 Bottle no. 7314 of 8300. Like its sibling, uses whole bunch pressing and French oak fermentation, and has the same alcohol, yet this is a far finer and more intense wine, with precision and focus to its white peach and grapefruit flavours which are drawn out on the finish by lingering acidity. Screwcap. 13% alc. **Rating** 95 **To** 2020 $85

Nest Egg Adelaide Hills Cabernet Sauvignon 2010 Deep, saturated colour; a potent, full-bodied cabernet with exemplary flavour and structure; blackcurrant fruit with hints of briar and leather drives the long, intense, evenly balanced palate. Top-class grapegrowing and winemaking. Bottle no. 5328 of 9696. Screwcap. 14.5% alc. **Rating** 95 **To** 2035 $95

Adelaide Hills Cabernet Sauvignon 2011 More depth to the colour than most of its peers; the palate is equally impressive, with fully ripe, although not over the top, blackcurrant/cassis fruit and fine, ripe tannins. An exceptional outcome for the vintage. One wonders whether 10–15% '12 wine may have (perfectly legally) been blended in. Screwcap. 14.5% alc. **Rating** 94 **To** 2021 $40

ΥΥΥΥ **Clare Valley Riesling 2012 Rating** 93 **To** 2020 $25
Adelaide Hills Chardonnay 2012 Rating 93 **To** 2017 $40
Honeysuckle Clare Valley Riesling 2012 Rating 93 **To** 2019 $25
Adelaide Hills Sauvignon Blanc 2012 Rating 91 **To** 2013 $25

✪ **Two in the Bush Adelaide Hills Semillon Sauvignon Blanc 2012** Pale quartz-straw; has an appealing blend of passionfruit, gooseberry, kiwifruit and lemony acidity, the finish and aftertaste bright and breezy. Screwcap. 12.5% alc. **Rating** 90 **To** 2014 $22
Mt Lofty Ranges Shiraz 2011 Rating 90 **To** 2018 $35 BE
Adelaide Hills Merlot 2011 Rating 90 **To** 2015 $40

Bird on a Wire Wines ★★★★★

51 Symons Street, Healesville, Vic 3777 (postal) **Region** Yarra Valley
T 0439 045 000 **www.**birdonawirewines.com.au **Open** By appt
Winemaker Caroline Mooney **Est.** 2008 **Dozens** 500
This is now the full-time business of winemaker Caroline Mooney, who grew up in the Yarra Valley and who has had (other full-time) winemaking jobs in the valley for over 10 years. The focus is on small, single vineyard sites owned by growers committed to producing outstanding grapes. Having worked at the legendary Domaine Jean-Louis Chave in the 2006 vintage, she has a special interest in shiraz and marsanne, both grown on distinct sites on a single vineyard in the Yarra Glen area. There is also a Chardonnay from the upper Yarra Valley, now generally accepted as a perfect environment for the finest of chardonnay styles. Exports to the UK.

ΥΥΥΥΥ **Chardonnay 2011** Bright straw-green; an elegant, highly focused and linear wine with juicy white flesh stone fruit and grapefruit providing 90% of the impact and character, oak and minerally acidity the remainder on a long, lingering palate. Screwcap. 13% alc. **Rating** 95 **To** 2019 $42

Marsanne 2011 Light straw-green; has come through with flying colours, the vibrant white-flower bouquet leading into a supple palate with hints of pear, a wisp of honey and soft acidity, if there is such a thing. Should easily see out 10 years. Screwcap. 14% alc. **Rating** 94 **To** 2021 $35

Birdwood Estate   ★★★★★

Mannum Road, Birdwood, SA 5234 (postal) **Region** Adelaide Hills
T (08) 8263 0986 **Open** Not
Winemaker Oli Cucchiarelli **Est.** 1990 **Dozens** 1000 **Vyds** 7.5ha
Birdwood Estate draws upon estate vineyards progressively established since 1990 (pinot noir, riesling and sauvignon blanc). The quality of the white wines has generally been good. The tiny production is principally sold through retail in Adelaide and a small amount is exported to Canada. No wine was made in 2011 due to mildew caused by incessant rain.

BK Wines   ★★★★★

Burdetts Road, Basket Range, SA 5138 **Region** Adelaide Hills
T 0410 124 674 **www.bkwines.com.au** **Open** By appt
Winemaker Brendon Keys **Est.** 2007 **Dozens** 3000
BK Wines is owned by NZ-born Brendon and wife Kirsty. Brendon has packed a great deal of high and low living into the past decade, driving tractors in the UK, then managing a chalet in Val d'Isere (in the French Alps) for eight months. Along the way, he bounced backwards and forwards between Australia and NZ before working a vintage in California with the well-known Paul Hobbs, then helping Paul set up a winery in Argentina. Brendon's tagline is 'wines made with love, not money' and he has not hesitated to confound the normal rules of engagement in winemaking (such as leaving pinot noir to macerate on skins post-fermentation for 100 days), and if he isn't remembered for this, the labels for his wines should do the trick. Exports to the US and Singapore.

¶¶¶¶¶ **Mazi Whole Bunch Blewitt Springs McLaren Vale Syrah 2010** Full purple-crimson; Brendon Keys' artistry shows brightly in this harmonious, elegant, medium-bodied wine. Red and black fruits, touches of dark chocolate and oak float across the palate, given shape and texture by the fine-grained tannins. The whole bunch fermentation has been expertly managed, and if this is natural winemaking, bring it on. Diam. 14% alc. **Rating** 97 **To** 2025 $85
Swaby Single Vineyard Piccadilly Valley Adelaide Hills Chardonnay 2011 Gleaming green-yellow; whole bunch-pressed to 30% new French puncheons, the balance to 2–3-year-old barriques; 9 months stirring, 12 months in oak; no acid adjustment, yet 100% mlf. This is too good a wine to be sealed with cork, unless it is to be totally consumed within four years. 13% alc. **Rating** 94 **To** 2016 $55

¶¶¶¶¶ **Single Barrel Adelaide Hills Chardonnay 2010 Rating** 93 **To** 2015 $85
One Ball Adelaide Hills Chardonnay 2011 Rating 92 **To** 2015 $27
Inox Lenswood Adelaide Hills Pinot Grigio 2012 Rating 91 **To** 2014 $21

Black Estate Vineyard   ★★★

Patons Road, Axe Creek, Vic 3551 **Region** Bendigo
T (03) 5442 8048 **www.blackestate.com.au** **Open** By appt
Winemaker Greg Dedman (Contract) **Est.** 1999 **Dozens** 240 **Vyds** 1.5ha
Robert and Leanne Black purchased their 8ha property in 1997, part of a larger block that in the latter part of the 19th century was home to the then-renowned 14ha Hercynia Vineyard. After a trial planting of 100 shiraz cuttings in 1998, they completed planting of their vineyard in the spring of '99. Future plantings of cabernet sauvignon and possibly riesling or verdelho will depend on water availability.

¶¶¶¶ **Shiraz 2010** Medium red-purple; hand-picked from low-yielding estate vines still affected by the drought, matured in French and American oak for 15 months; the black fruits of the bouquet and palate do show some oak impact, but not excessively so; the same applies to the tannins, which are evident but not dry or harsh. Well priced. Screwcap. 13.8% alc. **Rating** 89 **To** 2018 $20

BlackJack Vineyards   ★★★★★

Cnr Blackjack Road/Calder Highway, Harcourt, Vic 3453 **Region** Bendigo
T (03) 5474 2355 **www**.blackjackwines.com.au **Open** W'ends & most public hols 11–5
Winemaker Ian McKenzie, Ken Pollock **Est.** 1987 **Dozens** 4000 **Vyds** 6ha
Established by the McKenzie and Pollock families on the site of an old apple and pear orchard
in the Harcourt Valley, Blackjack is best known for some very good Shirazs. Ian McKenzie,
incidentally, is not to be confused with Ian McKenzie formerly of Seppelt (Great Western).
Despite some tough vintage conditions, BlackJack has managed to continue to produce
supremely honest, full-flavoured and powerful wines, all with a redeeming edge of elegance.
Exports to Canada and China.

♟♟♟♟♟ Bendigo Shiraz 2010 Bright, clear crimson-purple; the bouquet has fragrant
blackberry and plum fruit that signals the beautifully weighted and textured
palate, flooded with berry fruits; like Block 6, is medium-bodied, presenting its
flavours without effort. Impossible to split the two on quality. Screwcap. 14% alc.
Rating 95 To 2030 $38
Block 6 Bendigo Shiraz 2010 Bright crimson; a slightly firmer and darker-
berried version of the Bendigo Shiraz, both estate-grown; the spice and black
fruits break free on the back-palate and finish with a lovely, juicy burst; oak and
tannins play a pure support role. Screwcap. 13.5% alc. Rating 95 To 2032 $38

♟♟♟♟♟ Bendigo Cabernet Merlot 2010 Rating 90 To 2016 $28

Bleasdale Vineyards   ★★★★★

Wellington Road, Langhorne Creek, SA 5255 **Region** Langhorne Creek
T (08) 8537 3001 **www**.bleasdale.com.au **Open** Mon–Sun 10–5
Winemaker Paul Hotker, Ben Potts, Matt Laube **Est.** 1850 **Dozens** 100 000 **Vyds** 47ha
This is one of the most historic wineries in Australia, in 2010 celebrating 160 years of
continuous winemaking by the direct descendants of the founding Potts family. Not so long
prior to arrival of the 21st century, its vineyards were flooded every winter by diversion of
the Bremer River, which provided moisture throughout the dry, cool growing season. In
the new millennium, every drop of water was counted. Bleasdale has taken the opportunity
presented by these challenges and removed under-performing vineyard blocks. The
vineyards have been significantly upgraded and refocused with shiraz accounting for 45%
of plantings, supported by seven other proven varieties. Bleasdale has completely revamped
its labels and packaging, and has headed to the Adelaide Hills for sauvignon blanc, pinot
gris and chardonnay. The future of the business has been greatly strengthened by the arrival
of two investors in May 2013, SA family-owned pastoralist business AJ & PA McBride
purchased 38%, and Bleasdale's long-term Asian distributor Monita 10%. Exports to all
major markets.

♟♟♟♟♟ The Iron Duke Langhorne Creek Cabernet Sauvignon 2010 Purple-
crimson; has excellent varietal character and purity; it is only medium-bodied, yet
also has an infusion of French oak and lingering tannins, neither of which throws
the palate out of balance. Screwcap. 13.9% alc. Rating 95 To 2025 $65
Generations Langhorne Creek Shiraz 2010 Medium to full red-purple; an
attractive medium- to full-bodied palate follows on logically from the expressive
bouquet, both showing plum, blackberry, chocolate and vanilla oak; the tannins
are well integrated and fine, and patience is not required. Screwcap. 14.5% alc.
Rating 94 To 2021 $39
✪ Frank Potts 2010 A complex 65/15/11/5/4% blend of cabernet sauvignon,
malbec, petit verdot, merlot and cabernet franc; it is a finely structured and elegant
wine, with its complex array of red and black fruits neatly framed by 15 months
in French oak; the tannins are fine and persistent, lengthening the finish. Screwcap.
13.9% alc. Rating 94 To 2025 $29

ᵠᵠᵠᵠᵠ **Adelaide Hills Chardonnay 2012** Bright, fresh colour; an attractive wine,
✪   well made, with good varietal character and mouthfeel to its white peach and
grapefruit; the barrel ferment and lees contact elements have been well controlled.
Screwcap. 13% alc. **Rating** 92 **To** 2014 $20

✪   **Uncle Dick's Cabernet Malbec Petit Verdot 2008** This blend is traditional
enough in parts of Bordeaux, but less common in Australia; the wine spent 18
months in French oak, and the end result is very good; the colour is still fresh,
the black and red berry, plum and cedar flavours neatly supported by fine tannins.
Great value. Diam. 14% alc. **Rating** 92 **To** 2023 $17

Double Take Langhorne Creek Malbec 2010 **Rating** 92 **To** 2020 $80

✪   **Adelaide Hills Sauvignon Blanc 2012** Light straw-green; has a tropical fruit
bowl providing both the bouquet and palate of an uncomplicated and easily
enjoyed wine; quite why it should have won a gold medal at the Cowra Wine
Show, I am not sure. Screwcap. 12.5% alc. **Rating** 90 **To** 2013 $18

✪   **Adelaide Hills Pinot Gris 2012** Whole bunch pressing and part fermentation in
used French oak puncheons has invested the wine with varietal purity, and textural
interest. Screwcap. 13% alc. **Rating** 90 **To** 2014 $18

Petrel Reserve Langhorne Creek Shiraz Cabernet Malbec 2010
Rating 90 **To** 2020 $29

✪   **The Wise One Wood Matured Tawny NV** Has many merits, though the
colour is too reddish. That said, it has lovely, lacy mouthfeel and texture, and a
spicy, rancio finish. Exceptional value. Screwcap. 18% alc. **Rating** 90 **To** 2014 $17

ᵠᵠᵠᵠ **Uncle Dick's Malbec 2010** Malbec does not have a great reputation in Australia
✪   because of its straggly, unreliable berry set, and also its lack of structure as a wine.
Presumably its reputation has led to its price, but if you would like a light- to
medium-bodied wine with bright fruit flavours and touches of briar (ex tannins)
on the finish, this is a bargain. Screwcap. 13.5% alc. **Rating** 88 **To** 2015 $9

Bloodwood   ★★★★★

231 Griffin Road, Orange, NSW 2800 **Region** Orange
T (02) 6362 5631 **www**.bloodwood.biz **Open** By appt
Winemaker Stephen Doyle **Est.** 1983 **Dozens** 4000 **Vyds** 8.43ha
Rhonda and Stephen Doyle are two of the pioneers of the Orange district, 2013 marking
Bloodwood's 30th anniversary. The estate vineyards (chardonnay, riesling, merlot, cabernet
sauvignon, shiraz, cabernet franc and malbec) are planted at an elevation of 810–860m, which
provides a reliably cool climate. The wines are sold mainly through the cellar door and by an
energetic, humorous and informatively run mailing list (see, for example, the tasting note for
Big Men in Tights). Has an impressive track record across the full gamut of varietal (and other)
wine styles, especially Riesling, in a variety of styles; all of the wines have a particular elegance
and grace. Very much part of the high-quality reputation of Orange.

ᵠᵠᵠᵠᵠ **Chardonnay 2012** Light straw-green; a wantonly, explosively juicy palate is filled
✪   to overflowing with grapefruit and white peach fruit which has contemptuously
swallowed the French oak in which it was fermented and matured. Sheer
hedonistic pleasure. Screwcap. 12.5% alc. **Rating** 95 **To** 2019 $25

Schubert 2011 The quality of the estate-grown chardonnay has responded
with alacrity, providing a very complex, slightly savoury, and very long palate.
In radically different style from the '12 varietal, but of similar quality. Screwcap.
12.5% alc. **Rating** 95 **To** 2022 $30

✪   **Riesling 2012** Pale quartz-green; the vibrant citrus and green apple flavours are
strung along a core of high-tensile minerality, the finish drawing saliva from the
mouth. Will age superbly. Screwcap. 11.5% alc. **Rating** 94 **To** 2027 $20

Shiraz 2009 Good colour for a wine rising 4 years of age; integrated French
oak (from Burgundian coopers) has been woven through the spicy red and black
cherry fruit of the bouquet, and the supple, medium-bodied palate. Its balance and
length may deceive you into treating this as a drink-now style, which in a sense it
is, but it will also cellar well. Screwcap. 13.5% alc. **Rating** 94 **To** 2024 $28

ρρρρ͡ **Big Men in Tights 2012** A genuinely hilarious back label, inter alia disclosing
✪ a minute percentage of cabernet franc with the usual malbec; light, bright pink, it
has vibrant strawberry and plum fruit, balanced by crisp acidity on the dry finish.
Lives up to its track record. Screwcap. 13% alc. **Rating** 93 **To** 2014 $18
Maurice 2008 Rating 93 **To** 2028 $33

Blue Gables   NR

100 Lanigan Road, Maffra West Upper, Vic 3859 **Region** Gippsland
T (03) 5148 0372 **www**.bluegables.com.au **Open** By appt
Winemaker Mal Stewart **Est.** 2004 **Dozens** NA **Vyds** 2.8ha
This small vineyard, nestled high above the Macalister Irrigation District in east Gippsland,
was established in 2004 with the planting of the first vines, and continued in '05, with 0.8ha
each of sauvignon blanc, pinot gris and shiraz and 0.4ha of chardonnay. It is the culmination
of a long-held dream for chemical engineer Alistair and journalist wife Catherine Hicks;
they purchased 8ha of a north-facing hillside slope (unsuited for irrigation) from Catherine's
father's dairy farm, and built a two-storey gabled roof farmhouse, hence the name. The wines
are made by industry veteran Mal Stewart, and have had significant success in the Gippsland
Wine Show and Victorian Wines Show.

Blue Pyrenees Estate   ★★★★★

Vinoca Road, Avoca, Vic 3467 **Region** Pyrenees
T (03) 5465 1111 **www**.bluepyrenees.com.au **Open** Mon–Fri 10–4.30, w'ends &
public hols 10–5
Winemaker Andrew Koerner, Chris Smales **Est.** 1963 **Dozens** 60 000 **Vyds** 149ha
Forty years after Remy Cointreau established Blue Pyrenees Estate (then known as Chateau
Remy), the business was sold to a small group of Sydney businessmen. Former Rosemount
senior winemaker Andrew Koerner heads the winery team. The core of the business is the
very large estate plantings, most decades old, but with newer arrivals including viognier.
Blue Pyrenees has a number of programs designed to protect the environment and reduce
its carbon footprint: all wines are 100% estate-grown and made, including onsite bottling.
Exports to Asia, primarily China.

ρρρρρ **Reserve Shiraz 2008** A small percentage of viognier has been incorporated,
adding to the focus and intensity of the predominantly black cherry/blackberry
fruit aromas and flavours; the structure and mouthfeel are admirable, fine savoury
tannins in perfect balance. Screwcap. 14% alc. **Rating** 94 **To** 2028 $32
Sparkling Shiraz NV The wine spends 2 years in small and large oak vats
before being taken to bottle for the secondary fermentation, when it has another
1-2 years on yeast lees. This results in an elegant, spicy, complex wine with a
most attractive savoury finish, not the sweetness that dogs many sparkling shirazs.
Blue-gold Sydney International Wine Challenge '13. Diam. 14% alc. **Rating** 94
To 2016 $31

ρρρρ͡ **The Richardson Series Shiraz 2009 Rating** 93 **To** 2025 $53 BE
Midnight Cuvee Chardonnay 2008 Rating 93 **To** 2015 $29
The Richardson Series Cabernet Merlot 2009 Rating 90 **To** 2020 $53 BE
Cabernet Sauvignon 2011 Rating 90 **To** 2017 $20

Blue Range Estate   NR

155 Gardens Road, Rosebud, Vic 3939 **Region** Mornington Peninsula
T (03) 5986 6560 **www**.bluerangestatewines.com.au **Open** W'ends & public hols 11–4
Winemaker Maurizio Mazzocchi, Cosi Melone **Est.** 1987 **Dozens** 5000 **Vyds** 10ha
Established by the De Cicco family in 1987, present owners Cosi and Joe Melone now
have 4ha each of chardonnay and pinot grigio, a little over 1ha of shiraz, and pinot noir and
merlot making up the remainder. The wines are made onsite by Maurizio Mazzochi and Cosi
Melone, and the Blanc de Blanc won the sparkling wine trophy at Les Concours des Vins du
Victoria '10. A feature of the the cellar door is the older vintages that are available.

Blue Rock Wines ★★★★

PO Box 692, Williamstown, SA 5351 **Region** Eden Valley
T 0419 817 017 **www**.bluerockwines.com.au **Open** Not
Winemaker Zissis Zachopoulos **Est.** 2005 **Dozens** 4000 **Vyds** 58ha
This is the venture of the brothers Zachopoulos: Nicholas, Michael and Zissis, the last with a double degree – viticulture and wine science – from CSU gained in 2009. Michael and Nicholas manage the 104ha property, which is situated in the Eden Valley at an elevation between 415m and 475m. The majority of the blocks have a north-facing aspect. The slopes provide good frost protection with natural air drainage, the soils likewise rich and free-draining. Fifty hectares of vineyards have been planted so far to mainstream varieties, with an ongoing planting program extending to 8ha of tempranillo, pinot gris, pinot noir, grenache and mataro. By far the major proportion of the 450–500-tonne grape production is the subject of a sales agreement with Grant Burge up to and including the 2013 vintage. So far 75 tonnes has been retained each year to make the Blue Rock wines.

🍷🍷🍷🍷🍷 **Barossa Ranges Vineyards Eden Valley Shiraz Viognier 2010** Vibrant colour, showing dark berry fruits, smoky/spicy oak on the bouquet; the palate is taut and full of charry oak, graphite tannins and black and red fruits on the finish. Screwcap. 13.5% alc. **Rating** 90 **To** 2018 $20 BE

Boat O'Craigo ★★★★

458 Maroondah Highway, Healesville, Vic 3777 **Region** Yarra Valley
T (03) 5962 6899 **www**.boatocraigo.com.au **Open** Fri–Mon 10.30–5.30
Winemaker Al Fencaros, Rob Dolan (Contract) **Est.** 1998 **Dozens** 3300 **Vyds** 21.63ha
Steve Graham purchased the property, which is now known as Boat O'Craigo (a tiny place in a Scottish valley where his ancestors lived), in 2003. It has two quite separate vineyards: a hillside planting on one of the highest sites in the Yarra Valley, and one at Kangaroo Ground on the opposite side of the valley. Exports to Finland, China and Hong Kong.

🍷🍷🍷🍷🍷 ✪ **Black Spur Yarra Valley Gewurztraminer 2012** Mid straw, bright; ripe and attractive aromas of nectarine, lime zest and musk are evident on the bouquet; the palate is fleshy in accordance with the varietal expression, yet offers almost racy acidity and a fine chalky finish; flamboyance without the fat. Screwcap. 12.5% alc. **Rating** 91 **To** 2016 $20 BE

Black Spur Yarra Valley Chardonnay 2011 Mid gold, bright; a highly expressive bouquet of pear, straw, fig and cashew; the palate reveals high levels of tangy acidity, signing off with a dry, chalky and distinctly nutty conclusion. Screwcap. 12% alc. **Rating** 90 **To** 2017 $25 BE

Dundee SGV Yarra Valley Shiraz Grenache Viognier 2010 A distinctly savoury bouquet, with earthy, undergrowth aromas sitting alongside fragrant red fruit and Asian spices; the palate is refreshing and fragrant, with fine-grained tannins and a linear finish. Screwcap. 13.6% alc. **Rating** 90 **To** 2018 $28 BE

Bobar ★★★☆

253 Gulf Road, Yarra Glen, Vic 3775 **Region** Yarra Valley
T (03) 9730 2668 **Open** By appt
Winemaker Tom and Sally Belford **Est.** 2010 **Dozens** 250 **Vyds** 0.3ha
Tom and Sally Belford have worked full-time for vineyards and wineries in the cooler hilly parts of NSW, the Macedon Ranges and Heathcote, and more recently in the Yarra Valley, where Tom is a winemaker at Sticks. They also managed to spend 15 months in France, dividing their time between Champagne, Beaujolais, Provence, Cahors and Sauternes. In 2010 they decided to 'make a little wine for the hell of it', and purchased shiraz from the Yarraland Vineyard at Chirnside Park. It comes as close to natural wine as is possible, with whole bunches in an open fermenter, no crushing or destemming, no pigeage or pumping over, and no yeast. It is sold by mail list via tomeb@iprimus.com.au and in a few bottle shops and restaurants in the Yarra Valley and Melbourne. Exports to the UK and Norway.

????? **Yarra Valley Syrah 2012** Light, but bright, crimson–purple; shows its early picking, with slightly elevated levels of mint and spice, but there are also attractive whole bunch nuances to the supple red and black cherry fruit; neither fined nor filtered. Screwcap. 12.5% alc. **Rating** 92 **To** 2022 $29

Bochara Wines ★★★★★

1099 Glenelg Highway, Hamilton, Vic 3300 **Region** Henty
T (03) 5571 9309 **www**.bocharawines.com.au **Open** Fri–Sun 11–5, or by appt
Winemaker Martin Slocombe **Est.** 1998 **Dozens** 900 **Vyds** 2.2ha
This is the small business of experienced winemaker Martin Slocombe and former Yalumba viticulturist Kylie McIntyre. They have established 1ha each of pinot noir and sauvignon blanc and 0.2ha of gewurztraminer, supplemented by grapes purchased from local growers. The modestly priced but well-made wines are principally sold through the cellar door on the property, a decrepit weatherboard shanty with one cold tap that has been transformed into a fully functional two-room tasting area, and through a number of local restaurants and bottle shops. The label design, incidentally, comes from a 1901 poster advertising the subdivision of the original Bochara property into smaller farms.

????? **Arcadia Brut Cuvee Blanc de Noir 2004** This is the fifth disgorgement
✪ (Dec '12) of this wine, with 7½ years on yeast lees, made from estate-grown pinot noir. It is still pale in colour, and has excellent mousse; its creamy, yet fine, texture is remarkable, making it a great ageing style, most unusual for a Blanc de Noir. A quite exceptional bargain. Diam. 12% alc. **Rating** 95 **To** 2016 $29

✪ **Pinot Noir 2012** Superb, full crimson–purple; in pinot terms it is medium- to full-bodied, with layers of red and black cherry and plum fruit supported by fine tannins and a touch of oak. Outstanding bargain. Screwcap. 14.3% alc. **Rating** 94 **To** 2017 $20

????? **Sauvignon Blanc 2012** Quartz-white; from a single block of hand-pruned,
✪ hand-picked vines; it has an exceptional depth of flavour, almost all in a green pea/herbal/capsicum spectrum, with just a little tropical fruit peeping through. Very good value. Screwcap. 13.9% alc. **Rating** 90 **To** 2014 $16

Boireann ★★★★★

26 Donnellys Castle Road, The Summit, Qld 4377 **Region** Granite Belt
T (07) 4683 2194 **www**.boireannwinery.com.au **Open** Fri–Sun 10–4
Winemaker Peter Stark **Est.** 1998 **Dozens** 800 **Vyds** 1.6ha
Peter and Therese Stark have a 10ha property set among the great granite boulders and trees that are so much a part of the Granite Belt. They have planted no fewer than 11 varieties, including four that go to make the Lurnea, a Bordeaux blend; shiraz and viognier; grenache and mourvedre providing a Rhône blend, and a straight merlot. Tannat, pinot noir (French) and sangiovese, barbera and nebbiolo (Italian) make up the viticultural League of Nations. Peter is a winemaker of exceptional talent, producing cameo amounts of quite beautifully made red wines that are of a quality equal to Australia's best. The rating has been retained due to the exceptionally difficult 2011 vintage conditions.

????? **Granite Belt Tannat 2011** Medium purple–crimson; ended up being the most successful of the Boireann wines from '11, its tannins ameliorated, yet its fruit not diminished; poached black cherry fruit comes through clearly on a long, fresh finish. Screwcap. 13.5% alc. **Rating** 93 **To** 2018 $35

Granite Belt Shiraz Viognier 2011 Light crimson–purple; more light-bodied and more savoury/spicy than usual, simply due to the wet vintage; there are no mint/green/bitter notes whatsoever, and enough red fruits to make an attractive drink soon-ish style. Screwcap. 13% alc. **Rating** 92 **To** 2017 $35

Granite Belt Pinot Noir 2011 Estate-grown pinot noir was news to me, and it had the ill fortune to make its debut in a rain-sodden vintage. Full judgement must await a more normal vintage, but it has most of the markers of pinot noir, with a supple red fruit palate, and a gently savoury finish. Screwcap. 12.5% alc. **Rating** 90 **To** 2014 $22

Granite Belt Merlot 2011 Light, clear crimson-purple; in typical fashion, Peter Stark manages to get that bit extra which eludes others; while light-bodied, this fragrant wine has the plum and cassis fruit at the heart of varietal merlot. If drunk soon, it will be at its most enjoyable. Screwcap. 13% alc. **Rating** 90 **To** 2014 $22
La Cima Granite Belt Barbera 2011 Light crimson-purple; bright, crisp and fresh polished cherry fruit; the absence of tannin structure is a plus, allowing the fruit to come through without inhibition, making this a drink-now proposition. Screwcap. 13.5% alc. **Rating** 90 **To** 2014 $25

ᵀᵀᵀᵀ Granite Belt Shiraz Mourvedre 2011 **Rating** 89 **To** 2017 $30

Bonking Frog

7 Dardanup West Road, North Boyanup, WA 6237 **Region** Geographe
T 0408 930 332 www.bonkingfrog.com.au **Open** Fri–Sun 12–5
Winemaker Naturaliste Vintners (Bruce Dukes) **Est.** 1996 **Dozens** 2000 **Vyds** 3ha
Julie and Phil Hutton put their money where their hearts are, electing to plant a merlot-only vineyard in 1996. Presumably knowing the unpredictable habits of merlot when planted on its own roots, they began by planting 3500 Swartzman rootstock vines, and then 12 months later field-grafting the merlot scion material. I don't doubt for a millisecond the sincerity of their enthusiasm for the variety when they say, 'Fruity, plummy, smooth and velvety. Hints of chocolate too. If you're new to wine and all things merlot, this is a wonderful variety to explore. A classic red, known for its go-anywhere, please-everyone style, it makes a welcome place for itself at any table.' And the frogs? Well, apparently they bonk – loudly.

ᵀᵀᵀᵀᵀ Foreigner Margaret River Semillon Sauvignon Blanc 2012 Pale quartz-green; a lively and fragrant bouquet, and crisp lemon sherbet palate; the lemony characters are balanced by gooseberry on the finish, the acidity spot on. Screwcap. 12.5% alc. **Rating** 92 **To** 2014 $20
Paterson Reserve Geographe Merlot 2011 Deep crimson-purple; won't be released until '14, but part of its personality is already apparent: a rich, fleshy, dark-fruited wine, with spicy elements obvious, as is the oak. There will be plenty on offer, the only query the question of varietal expression. Screwcap. 14.9% alc. **Rating** 90 **To** 2021

ᵀᵀᵀᵀ Winter Geographe Merlot 2010 **Rating** 89 **To** 2014 $22
Summer Geographe Merlot Rose 2012 **Rating** 88 **To** 2014 $18

Borambola Wines

1734 Sturt Highway, Wagga Wagga, NSW 2650 **Region** Gundagai
T (02) 6928 4210 www.borambola.com **Open** 7 days 11–4 by appt
Winemaker Richard Parker **Est.** 1995 **Dozens** 4000 **Vyds** 8.79ha
Borambola Homestead was built in the 1880s, and in the latter part of that century was the centre of a pastoral empire of 1.4 million hectares, ownership of which passed to the McMullen family in 1992. It is situated in rolling foothills 25km east of Wagga Wagga in the Gundagai region. The vineyards surround the homestead and include shiraz (4.43ha), cabernet sauvignon (3.16ha) and chardonnay (1.2ha). Exports to the US, Norway, Denmark, Vietnam, Thailand, Singapore and China.

ᵀᵀᵀᵀ Hiraji's Spell Gundagai Shiraz 2011 Good depth to the red-purple hue; a generously proportioned and rich Shiraz, with blackberry fruit to the fore, blood plum also making an appearance. Needs an edge to gain even higher points, but will cellar well. Screwcap. 13% alc. **Rating** 89 **To** 2016 $24
Bunya Bunya Gundagai Chardonnay 2012 Light straw-green; has abundant varietal fruit in a stone fruit/fig spectrum; if any oak has been used, it is not obvious, and the wine is ready now. Screwcap. 13% alc. **Rating** 87 **To** 2014 $18

Borrodell Vineyard

Lake Canobolas Road, Orange, NSW 2800 **Region** Orange
T (02) 6365 3425 **www**.borrodell.com.au **Open** 7 days 11–5.30
Winemaker Simon Gilbert **Est.** 1964 **Dozens** 9000 **Vyds** 7ha
Borry Gartrell and Gaye Stuart-Nairne have planted pinot noir, sauvignon blanc, pinot meunier, gewurztraminer and chardonnay adjacent to a cherry, plum and heritage apple orchard and truffiere. It is a 10min drive from Orange, and adjacent to Lake Canobolas, at an altitude of 1000m. The wines have been consistent medal winners at regional and small winemaker shows. Exports to China.

🍷🍷🍷🍷🍷 Wine Maker's Daughter Orange Gewurztraminer 2012 Pale straw-green; a wine that, over the years, has sometimes had strong varietal expression; here it has intense fruit on the bouquet and palate, roughly half in a riesling spectrum, half in gewurztraminer. Accepting that at face value, it is a really attractive wine with very good balance and length. Screwcap. 12% alc. **Rating** 94 **To** 2022 $30

🍷🍷🍷🍷🍷 Orange Chardonnay 2011 **Rating** 91 **To** 2019 $27

Botobolar

89 Botobolar Road, Mudgee, NSW 2850 **Region** Mudgee
T (02) 6373 3840 **www**.botobolar.com **Open** Mon–Sat 10–5, Sun 10–3
Winemaker Kevin Karstrom **Est.** 1971 **Dozens** 2500 **Vyds** 19.4ha
One of the first (possibly the first) fully organic vineyards in Australia, with present owner Kevin Karstrom continuing the practices established by founder (the late) Gil Wahlquist. Preservative-free reds and low-preservative whites extend the organic practice of the vineyard to the winery. Dry Red is consistently the best wine to appear under the Botobolar label, with gold-medal success at the Mudgee Wine Show. Its preservative-free red wines are in the top echelon of this class. A solar generator has been installed on the hill behind the winery in the first step towards lowering their carbon footprint. Exports to Denmark and Japan.

🍷🍷🍷🍷 Preservative Free Mudgee Shiraz 2012 Deep purple-crimson; a little more berry fruit on the mid-palate, and less acidity on the finish would have resulted in a seriously good wine, but vintage rain dictated otherwise. Screwcap. 11.5% alc. **Rating** 87 **To** 2014 $20

Bowen Estate

Riddoch Highway, Coonawarra, SA 5263 **Region** Coonawarra
T (08) 8737 2229 **www**.bowenestate.com.au **Open** 7 days 10–5
Winemaker Emma Bowen **Est.** 1972 **Dozens** 12000 **Vyds** 33ha
Bluff-faced regional veteran Doug Bowen, now with daughter Emma at his side in the winery, presides over one of Coonawarra's landmarks. Doug has now handed over full winemaking responsibility to Emma, 'retiring' to the position of viticulturist. After a number of disappointing vintages, Bowen estate produced excellent wines in 2009, and has followed the lead of that vintage with its terrific '10 wines. Exports to Indonesia, the Maldives, Singapore, China, Japan and NZ.

🍷🍷🍷🍷🍷 Coonawarra Shiraz 2010 Deep purple-crimson; a rich and medium- to full-bodied palate fills every corner of the mouth with blackberry and dark plum flavours, the tannins ripe and adding another dimension. The best Bowen Shiraz for many years. Bravo. Cork. 14.5% alc. **Rating** 94 **To** 2025 $30
Coonawarra Cabernet Sauvignon 2010 Light to medium red-purple; another wine of distinction from Bowen Estate, with pristine varietal expression courtesy of cassis/blackcurrant flavours and fine-grained tannins, good oak the icing on the cake. Cork. 14.5% alc. **Rating** 94 **To** 2025 $30

🍷🍷🍷🍷🍷 Coonawarra Shiraz 2011 **Rating** 93 **To** 2021 $30
Coonawarra Cabernet Sauvignon 2011 **Rating** 90 **To** 2016 $30

Box Grove Vineyard

PO Box 86, Avenel, Vic 3664 **Region** Nagambie Lakes
T (03) 5796 2626 **www.**boxgrovevineyard.com.au **Open** Not
Winemaker Sarah Gough **Est.** 1995 **Dozens** 2000 **Vyds** 25ha
This is the venture of the Gough family, with industry veteran (and daughter) Sarah Gough managing the vineyard, winemaking and marketing. In 1995, having worked for Brown Brothers' marketing department for 10 years, Sarah told Ross Brown she was leaving to get married and establish a family-owned farm near Tabilk. He immediately offered a 10-year contract to buy the grapes from 10ha each of shiraz and cabernet sauvignon; nervous about the long-term future, Sarah also planted 2.8ha of roussanne, promptly becoming the largest grower of the variety in the state. In 2007 Sarah decided to take a pre-emptive step of having five tonnes each of roussanne and shiraz roussanne made at Plunkett from the '08 vintage. Prior to the '09 vintage the supply agreement with Brown Brothers was not renewed (no surprise), leaving Sarah with a number of difficult decisions. The solution was to graft over 6ha of cabernet to 2ha of prosecco and 1ha each of viognier, vermentino, savagnin and primitivo, and manage Box Grove Vineyard as a fully fledged wine and verjus producer. Exports to Singapore and China.

 Vermentino 2012 Bright colour, and vivacious in personality, with ripe lemon fruit and straw on display; the palate is textured, with a bit of grip on the finish, and the slight salty tang is mouth-watering and refreshing. Screwcap. 12.7% alc. **Rating** 90 **To** 2014 $22 BE
Shiraz Roussanne 2010 Deep crimson colour; a spicy and sweet-fruited offering with red and black fruits, game and earthy notes and a touch of spice; the palate delivers the full Rhône varietal expression of sweet fruit in a medium-bodied package with a sappy conclusion offset by fresh acidity and gravelly tannins. Screwcap. 13.7% alc. **Rating** 90 **To** 2018 $25 BE

♟♟♟♟ **Sparkling Roussanne 2010 Rating** 87 **To** 2014 $28 BE

Box Stallion

64 Turrarubba Road, Merricks North, Vic 3926 **Region** Mornington Peninsula
T (03) 5989 7444 **www.**boxstallion.com.au **Open** 7 days 11–5
Winemaker Alex White **Est.** 2001 **Dozens** 9500 **Vyds** 16ha
Box Stallion is now solely owned by Garry Zerbe. The Bittern and Merricks North vineyards remain part of the venture, with 16ha of vines planted between 1997 and 2003. What was once a thoroughbred stud has now become a vineyard, with the Red Barn 'now home to a stable of fine wines'. Exports to the US, Canada, Japan and China.

♟♟♟♟♟ **Blaze Mornington Peninsula Rose 2012** Mid salmon colour, the bouquet offering a savoury blend of wild strawberry, fennel and bramble; the palate is lively and fresh, with a saline tang to the finish. Screwcap. 13.7% alc. **Rating** 90 **To** 2014 $20 BE

♟♟♟♟ **Mornington Peninsula Gewurztraminer 2011 Rating** 88 **To** 2015 $25 BE
The Enclosure Chardonnay 2008 Rating 88 **To** 2016 $25 BE

Boynton's Feathertop

Great Alpine Road, Porepunkah, Vic 3741 **Region** Alpine Valleys
T (03) 5756 2356 **www.**boynton.com.au **Open** 7 days 10–5
Winemaker Kel Boynton, Jo Marsh **Est.** 1987 **Dozens** 12 500 **Vyds** 14ha
Kel Boynton has a beautiful vineyard, framed by Mt Feathertop rising above it. Overall, the red wines have always outshone the whites. The initial very strong American oak input has been softened in more recent vintages to give a better fruit–oak balance. The wines are released under the Boynton Reserve and Feathertop labels. Kel has planted a spectacular array of varieties, headed by shiraz and pinot gris, merlot, savagnin, sauvignon blanc and nebbiolo and sangiovese, with smaller plantings of tempranillo, pinot noir, pinot meunier, vermentino,

chardonnay, riesling, friulano, fiano, prosecco and semillon. The appointment of Jo Marsh as winemaker is almost certain to see a permanent lift to top-tier status for Boyton's; her skill and commitment are beyond question. Exports to Austria.

ΨΨΨΨΨ **Alpine Valleys Riesling 2012** Pale quartz; hand-picked, whole bunch-pressed and cold-fermented clear juice; a floral citrus blossom bouquet leads into a beautifully articulated palate with citrus, apple and acidity all woven together on the very long palate. Screwcap. 11% alc. **Rating** 94 To 2027 $20

✪ **Alpine Valleys Savagnin 2012** Light straw-green; the bouquet seems to hover between blossom and citrus, but the palate is electrifying in its intensity, length, and lingering aftertaste of citrus, Jonathan apple and fruit spice. Multiple pickings were part of an inspired approach to the variety, particularly given this was the first time Jo Marsh has made Savagnin. Screwcap. 12% alc. **Rating** 94 To 2015 $20

Alluvium Reserve Alpine Valleys Cabernet Blend 2006 An estate-grown blend of cabernet sauvignon, merlot and petit verdot, only made in the best vintages; this '06 was the only release in its decade. The colour is still bright, the bouquet with cassis, spice and licorice, the palate with lush black fruits and ripe, balanced, tannins. Screwcap. 13.5% alc. **Rating** 94 To 2020 $70

ΨΨΨΨΨ **Alpine Valleys Shiraz 2010 Rating** 93 To 2020 $25
Prosecco 2010 Rating 91 To 2014 $30

✪ **Alpine Valleys Vermentino 2012** Quartz-white; gentle flowery, blossom aromas on the bouquet gain focus and intensity on the long, clean palate with its array of tropical fruits offset by lively acidity and low pH. Screwcap. 11.5% alc. **Rating** 90 To 2014 $20

✪ **Alpine Valleys Durif Rose 2012** Hand-picked at very low baume to retain crisp acidity, then basket-pressed with a few hours of skin contact prior to cold fermentation in stainless steel; an unusual base for rose, but it has worked well. There are delicate strawberry flavours, and the mouthfeel/balance is very good. Screwcap. 9% alc. **Rating** 90 To 2013 $20

Tawny NV Rating 90 To 2014 $25

Brand's Laira Coonawarra

Riddoch Highway, Coonawarra, SA 5263 **Region** Coonawarra
T (08) 8736 3260 **www**.mcwilliamswinegroup.com **Open** Mon–Fri 9–4.30, w'ends & public hols 10–4
Winemaker Peter Weinberg **Est.** 1966 **Dozens** NFP **Vyds** 278ha
Part of a substantial investment in Coonawarra by McWilliam's, which first acquired a 50% interest from the Brand family, then increased that to 100%, and followed this with the purchase of 100ha of additional vineyard land. Significantly increased production of the smooth wines for which Brand's is known has followed. The estate plantings include the 100-year-old Stentiford block. Exports to select markets.

ΨΨΨΨΨ **One Seven One Cabernet Sauvignon 2009** Seven trophies and 12 gold medals! Its name comes from the cabernet block planted by Eric Brand in 1971. Intense blackcurrant fruit, black olive notes, and quality oak; the tannins need a year or two to loosen their grip. Screwcap. 14.8% alc. **Rating** 96 To 2040 $65

Tall Vines Shiraz 2010 Excellent colour; the wine is laden with dark berry, spices and cedary oak; the tannins are ripe and generous, the only cloud on the horizon the alcohol warmth on the finish. Screwcap. 14.9% alc. **Rating** 94 To 2025 $28

ΨΨΨΨΨ **Blockers Cabernet Sauvignon 2010 Rating** 93 To 2030 $28
August Tide Dry Red 2010 Rating 93 To 2025 $28

ΨΨΨΨ **Two Row Merlot 2009 Rating** 89 To 2019 $29
Stentiford's Shiraz 2008 Rating 87 To 2015 $65

Brandy Creek Wines ★★★★☆

570 Buln Buln Road, Drouin East, Vic 3818 **Region** Gippsland
T (03) 5625 4498 **www**.brandycreekwines.com.au **Open** Thurs–Sun & public hols 11–5,
Thurs–Sat nights
Winemaker Peter Beckingham (Contract) **Est.** 2005 **Dozens** 2000 **Vyds** 3ha
Marie McDonald and Rick Stockdale purchased the property on which they have since
established their vineyard, cellar door and restaurant in 1997. Pinot gris and tempranillo have
been progressively planted, with other varieties purchased from local growers. The restaurant
(and surrounding vineyard) is situated on a northeast-facing slope with spectacular views out
to the Baw Baw Ranges.

ŶŶŶŶŶ **Sauvignon Blanc 2012** Mid straw; the bouquet offers guava, fennel and bath
talc; the palate is fresh and fragrant, finishing bone dry and with an attractive
smoky gun flint and guava note. Screwcap. 12% alc. **Rating** 90 **To** 2014 $25 BE

ŶŶŶŶ **Bairnsdale Vineyard Shiraz 2011 Rating** 88 **To** 2017 $28 BE
Bairnsdale Vineyard Shiraz 2010 Rating 87 **To** 2017 $25 BE

Brangayne of Orange ★★★★☆

837 Pinnacle Road, Orange, NSW 2800 **Region** Orange
T (02) 6365 3229 **www**.brangayne.com **Open** Mon–Fri 11–1, 2–4, Sat 11–5, Sun 11–4
Winemaker Simon Gilbert **Est.** 1994 **Dozens** 3000 **Vyds** 25.7ha
The Hoskins family (formerly orchardists) decided to move into grapegrowing in 1994 and
have progressively established high-quality vineyards. Right from the outset, Brangayne has
produced excellent wines across all mainstream varieties, remarkably ranging from Pinot
Noir to Cabernet Sauvignon. Son David has been managing the business since 2005; it sells a
substantial part of its crop to other winemakers. Exports to the UK, Canada and Spain.

ŶŶŶŶŶ **Cabernet Sauvignon 2010** The vivid hue leads to an expressive bouquet
redolent of red and black fruits, tar and toasted oak spices; medium- to full-
bodied with ample tannins and a high level of fresh acidity to conclude. Screwcap.
13.5% alc. **Rating** 94 **To** 2020 $32 BE

ŶŶŶŶŶ **Pinot Grigio 2012** Pale straw, green hue; fresh-cut pear with straw and a little
✪ spice; the palate is juicy and generous, the acidity is thrilling and fresh. Screwcap.
12.5% alc. **Rating** 93 **To** 2015 $20 BE
Shiraz 2010 Rating 92 **To** 2020 $32 BE
✪ **Isolde Reserve Chardonnay 2011** The vivid green hue leads to a bouquet of
nectarine, melon and spicy oak, with a hint of charcuterie; the palate is fleshy and
fresh, with taut acidity providing a lemony ride to the moderately long conclusion.
Screwcap. 13% alc. **Rating** 91 **To** 2018 $20 BE
Riesling 2012 Rating 90 **To** 2016 $22 BE

Brash Higgins ★★★★★

242 California Road, McLaren Vale, SA 5171 **Region** McLaren Vale
T (08) 8556 4237 **www**.brashhiggins.com **Open** By appt
Winemaker Brad Hickey, Tim Geddes **Est.** 2010 **Dozens** 700 **Vyds** 7ha
Move over Treasury Estate's 'vintrepreneurs', for Brad Hickey has come up with 'creator'
and 'vinitor' to cover his role (together with partner Nicole Thorpe) in establishing Brash
Higgins. The one thing rather less clearly explained is how you move from Brad Hickey,
bypass vintrepeneur, and come up with vinitor. His varied background, including 10 years as
head sommelier at some of the best New York restaurants, then a further 10 years of baking,
brewing and travelling to the best-known wine regions of the world, may provide some clue.
More tangibly, he planted 4ha of shiraz, 2ha of cabernet sauvignon, and recently grafted 1ha
of shiraz to nero d'Avola on his Omensetter Vineyard looking over the Willunga Escarpment
and on to the Gulf of St Vincent. He has used his New York experience to set up distribution
of the wine in the US.

ŸŸŸŸŸ SHZ McLaren Vale Shiraz 2010 Dense purple-crimson; a no-holds-barred full-bodied Shiraz full of brooding black fruits, bitter chocolate and tarry tannins, licorice fighting to get a word in. Patience demanded, but will be rewarded. Screwcap. 14.5% alc. **Rating** 94 **To** 2040 $37

NDV Amphora Project McLaren Vale Nero d'Avola 2012 Kept on skins for 7 months in beeswax-lined clay amphoras made from local soils. It has a gloriously bright and clear colour and excellent fruit; the only consequence of the ancient winemaking process is the level of dryish tannins, and there was no way Brash Higgins was about to fine them. The points are for bravery. Screwcap. 13.5% alc. **Rating** 94 **To** 2020 $42

Brave Goose Vineyard

PO Box 633, Seymour, Vic 3660 **Region** Central Victoria Zone
T (03) 5799 1229 **www**.bravegoosevineyard.com.au **Open** By appt
Winemaker John and Nina Stocker **Est.** 1988 **Dozens** 250
Dr John Stocker and wife Joanne must be among the most highly qualified boutique vineyard and winery operators in Australia. John is the former chief executive of CSIRO and was chairman of the Grape and Wine Research & Development Corporation for seven years, while daughter Nina has completed the Roseworthy postgraduate oenology course. Moreover, they established their first vineyard (while living in Switzerland) on the French/Swiss border in the village of Flueh. On returning to Australia in 1987 they found a property on the inside of the Great Dividing Range with north-facing slopes and shallow, weathered ironstone soils. Here they have established 2.5ha each of shiraz and cabernet sauvignon, and 0.5ha each of merlot and gamay, selling the majority of grapes from the 20-year-old vines, but making small quantities of Cabernet Merlot, Merlot and Gamay. The brave goose in question was the sole survivor of a flock put into the vineyard to repel cockatoos and foxes.

ŸŸŸŸ Viognier 2012 Light straw-green; has been well made, but with a few notable exceptions, the best use for the variety is as a co-ferment component with shiraz. Screwcap. 12.5% alc. **Rating** 87 **To** 2014 $25

Braydun Hill Vineyard

38–40 Hepenstal Road, Hackham. SA 5163 **Region** McLaren Vale
T (08) 8382 3023 **www**.braydunhill.com.au **Open** Thurs–Sun & public hols 11–4
Winemaker Rebecca Kennedy **Est.** 2001 **Dozens** 2000 **Vyds** 4.5ha
It is hard to imagine there would be such an interesting (and inspiring) story behind a vineyard planted between 1998 and 1999 by the husband and wife team of Tony Dunn and Carol Bradley, wishing to get out of growing angora goats and into grapegrowing. The extension of the business into winemaking was totally unplanned, forced on them by the liquidation of Normans in late 2001. With humour, courage and perseverance, they have met obstacles and setbacks that would have caused many to give up, and have produced wines since 2001 which leave no doubt that this is a distinguished site capable of producing Shiraz of consistently high quality. Exports to China, Taiwan and Singapore.

ŸŸŸŸŸ Cellar Reserve Shimply McLaren Vale Shiraz 2008 Healthy colour, still crimson-purple; proclaims its region of origin from the rafters with dark chocolate fruit to the fore, black fruits and licorice bringing up the rear, and classy tannins in support. A disparate string of awards, its moment of glory a gold from the Great Australian Shiraz Challenge. Screwcap. 14.5% alc. **Rating** 92 **To** 2020 $25

ŸŸŸŸ Shimply McLaren Vale Shiraz 2008 Slightly less colour than the Cellar
✪ Reserve Shimply; has a similarly pronounced sense of place, black fruits and dark chocolate woven together in an unpretentious fashion. Screwcap. 14.5% alc. **Rating** 89 **To** 2016 $20

Bream Creek ★★★★★

Marion Bay Road, Bream Creek, Tas 7175 **Region** Southern Tasmania
T (03) 6231 4646 **www**.breamcreekvineyard.com.au **Open** At Dunalley Waterfront Cafe
Winemaker Winemaking Tasmania (Julian Alcorso) **Est.** 1973 **Dozens** 7000 **Vyds** 7.6ha
Until 1990 the Bream Creek fruit was sold to Moorilla Estate, but since then the winery has
been independently owned and managed by Fred Peacock, legendary for the care he bestows
on the vines under his direction. Fred's skills have seen both an increase in production and also
outstanding wine quality across the range, headed by the Pinot Noir. The list of trophies and
gold, silver and bronze medals won extends for nine neatly typed A4 pages. The Tamar Valley
vineyard has been sold, allowing Fred to concentrate on the southern vineyards, where he is
still a consultant/manager of non-estate plantings.

ᵀᵀᵀᵀᵀ **Cuvee Traditionelle 2007** A blend of pinot noir and chardonnay disgorged
Jan '12. Bright, pale quartz, good mousse; its strong point is its mouthfeel, and the
juicy/citrus/berry fruits. Very good wine. Diam. 12.5% alc. **Rating** 95 **To** 2016 $42

ᵀᵀᵀᵀᵀ **VGR Riesling 2012 Rating** 92 **To** 2027 $26
Sauvignon Blanc 2012 Rating 90 **To** 2014 $26
Chardonnay 2011 Rating 90 **To** 2016 $28
Pinot Rose 2012 Rating 90 **To** 2014 $24
Pinot Noir 2011 Rating 90 **To** 2017 $36

Bremerton Wines ★★★★★

Strathalbyn Road, Langhorne Creek, SA 5255 **Region** Langhorne Creek
T (08) 8537 3093 **www**.bremerton.com.au **Open** 7 days 10–5
Winemaker Rebecca Willson **Est.** 1988 **Dozens** 35 000 **Vyds** 101.5ha
The Willsons have been grapegrowers in the Langhorne Creek region for some considerable
time, but their dual business as grapegrowers and winemakers has expanded significantly. Their
vineyards have more than doubled (predominantly cabernet sauvignon and shiraz), as has
their production of wine. In 2004 sisters Rebecca and Lucy (marketing) took control of the
business, marking the event with (guess what) revamped label designs. Can fairly claim to be
the best producer in Langhorne Creek. No wines received for the *2014 Wine Companion*, but
a five-star rating has been maintained. Exports to all major markets.

Bress ★★★★★

3894 Calder Highway, Harcourt, Vic 3453 **Region** Bendigo
T (03) 5474 2262 **www**.bress.com.au **Open** W'ends & public hols 11–5 or by chance
Winemaker Adam Marks **Est.** 2001 **Dozens** 5000 **Vyds** 23ha
Adam Marks has made wine in all parts of the world since 1991, and made the brave decision
(during his honeymoon in 2000) to start his own business. Having initially scoured various
regions of Australia for the varieties best suited to those regions, the focus has switched to
three Central Victorian vineyards, in Bendigo, Macedon Ranges and Heathcote. The Harcourt
vineyard in Bendigo is planted to riesling (2ha), shiraz (1ha) and 3ha of cabernet sauvignon
and cabernet franc; the Macedon vineyard to chardonnay (6ha) and pinot noir (3ha); and the
Heathcote vineyard to shiraz (2ha). Exports to Hong Kong and China.

ᵀᵀᵀᵀᵀ **Gold Chook Macedon Chardonnay 2012** Pale gold, green hue; cool citrus
blossom and fennel aromas emanate from glass, with bath talc also a feature; the
palate reveals a taut and racy framework of citrus fruit and lemony acidity, with
the finish providing a long tail of grilled hazelnut from well-handled use of fine
French oak. Screwcap. 13.5% alc. **Rating** 94 **To** 2018 $35 BE
Gold Chook Macedon Chardonnay 2011 This beautifully elegant
Chardonnay is evidence that Adam Marks' reflective winemaking approach flatters
not only pinot noir and shiraz. Retaining the majority of tense malic acidity in the
cool '11 season was a daring decision, but it is tactically offset by controlled white
peach and grapefruit expression and an undercurrent of mouthfilling mineral
texture. Cork. 12.5% alc. **Rating** 94 **To** 2016 $30 TS

🍷🍷🍷🍷🍷 Harcourt Valley Riesling 2012 Rating 93 To 2018 $30 BE
Silver Chook Pinot Noir 2012 Rating 92 To 2018 $25 BE

✪ **Silver Chook Yarra Valley Macedon Pinot Noir 2011** A Pinot Noir that completely belies both 40% new oak and a (counterintuitively and bravely) very high proportion of two-thirds whole bunches in a vintage as cool as '11. Its fruit is given voice to speak articulately, in elegant tones of red cherry and wild strawberry. The exotic lift of whole bunch spice and the tannin support of new oak build complexity and structure without dominating. Brilliant value. Screwcap. 12.5% alc. Rating 92 To 2016 $20 TS

✪ **Silver Chook Heathcote Bendigo Shiraz 2011** A clever take on the cool '11 season, built more around texture than fruit, benefiting from a chalky, grainy mouthfeel amplified by ageing on lees. A touch of whole bunch brings an understated exoticism and lingering dried herb and dried flower complexity to layers of plum liqueur, high cocoa dark chocolate and mixed spice. Screwcap. 13% alc. Rating 92 To 2015 $20 TS
Macedon Fume Blanc 2012 Rating 90 To 2015 $35 BE
La Gallina Tempranillo Garnacha Syrah 2011 Rating 90 To 2016 $25 BE

Brian Barry Wines   ★★★★☆

PO Box 128, Stepney, SA 5069 **Region** Clare Valley
T (08) 8363 6211 **www**.brianbarrywines.com **Open** Not
Winemaker Brian Barry, Judson Barry **Est.** 1977 **Dozens** 1500 **Vyds** 25.5ha
Brian Barry is an industry veteran – he turned 86 in February 2013 – with a wealth of winemaking and show judging experience, and is still in good health. His is a vineyard-only operation (16ha of riesling, 4ha of cabernet sauvignon, 2ha of shiraz, and lesser amounts of merlot and cabernet franc), with a significant part of the output sold as grapes to other wineries. The wines are made under contract at various wineries under Brian's supervision. As one would expect, the quality is reliably good. Exports to the UK and the US.

🍷🍷🍷🍷🍷 Clare Valley Shiraz 2012 Deep purple-crimson; has a rich blackberry, plum and licorice bouquet and palate, reflecting the vintage; quality oak and ripe tannins also make a positive contribution on the medium-bodied, perfectly balanced palate. Screwcap. 14.5% alc. Rating 94 To 2027 $35

🍷🍷🍷🍷🍷 Jud's Hill Clare Valley Riesling 2012 Rating 93 To 2017 $32

Briar Ridge Vineyard   ★★★★★

Mount View Road, Mount View, NSW 2325 **Region** Hunter Valley
T (02) 4990 3670 **www**.briarridge.com.au **Open** 7 days 10–5
Winemaker Scott Comyns, Karl Stockhausen **Est.** 1972 **Dozens** 15 000 **Vyds** 39ha
Semillon and Shiraz have been the most consistent performers, underlying the suitability of these varieties to the Hunter Valley. The Semillon, in particular, invariably shows intense fruit and cellars well. Briar Ridge has been a model of stability, and has the comfort of substantial estate vineyards from which it is able to select the best grapes. It also has not hesitated to venture into other regions, notably Orange. Since his appointment as winemaker at sister company Pepper Tree, Scott Comyns will continue to oversee winemaking at Briar Ridge for the foreseeable future. Scott has an extraordinary record as a Flying Winemaker in many parts of the world, as well as Australia, working in Tasmania and the Hunter Valley, returning there in '06 to work at Tempus Two. He has a wonderfully gregarious personality, and has many friends in the Hunter Valley. In '10 he was a finalist for The Wine Society prestigious Winemaker of the Year Award, and in '11 was awarded the Alasdair Sutherland Scholarship in the Hunter Valley. Exports to Canada.

🍷🍷🍷🍷🍷 Dairy Hill Single Vineyard Hunter Valley Semillon 2009 The colour is still to show any sign of development; a beautifully and precisely detailed wine when first tasted in May '09, when it had just been bottled, and has barely changed; the lemony fruit is a little more obvious, the acidity a little less so. Sit back and enjoy a long ride. Screwcap. 11.2% alc. Rating 94 To 2024 $50

Dairy Hill Single Vineyard Hunter Valley Shiraz 2011 Good hue, although not particularly deep; has excellent mouthfeel to its mix of red and black cherry fruit, the tannins and oak well balanced and integrated, the length impeccable. Screwcap. 13.1% alc. **Rating** 94 **To** 2026 $55

ŸŸŸŸŸ Karl Stockhausen Semillon 2012 **Rating** 93 **To** 2022 $26
Cellar Reserve Hunter Valley Merlot 2011 **Rating** 90 **To** 2020 $26

Briarose Estate ★★★★

13245 Bussell Highway, Augusta, WA 6290 **Region** Margaret River
T (08) 9758 4160 **www**.briarose.com.au **Open** 7 days 10–4.30
Winemaker Stella Bella Wines (Stuart Pym), Bill Crappsley (Consultant) **Est.** 1998
Dozens 7000 **Vyds** 13.56ha
Brian and Rosemary Webster began developing the estate plantings in 1998. They now comprise sauvignon blanc (2.33ha), semillon (1.33ha), cabernet sauvignon (6.6ha), merlot (2.2ha) and cabernet franc (1.1ha). The winery is situated at the southern end of the Margaret River region, where the climate is distinctly cooler than that of northern Margaret River.

ŸŸŸŸŸ Margaret River Sauvignon Blanc 2012 Bright straw-green; offers the full array of sauvignon blanc in Margaret River style: green pea and capsicum on the bouquet yield to kiwifruit, passionfruit and guava on the mid-palate, then lemony acidity to conclude. Screwcap. 13.5% alc. **Rating** 93 **To** 2014 $20
Margaret River Cabernet Merlot 2011 A lively, fresh, medium-bodied blend with red fruits to the fore first up, then a savoury flourish of blackcurrant on the back-palate and finish. Screwcap. 14% alc. **Rating** 90 **To** 2018 $24
Reserve Margaret River Cabernet Sauvignon 2011 Medium red-purple; the perfumed red berry bouquet leads into a fresh, lively palate with fine, dusty tannins woven through its fruit; it is just over the cusp of ripeness, and some may baulk at the lack of flesh. Screwcap. 14% alc. **Rating** 90 **To** 2019 $30

ŸŸŸŸ Margaret River Semillon Sauvignon Blanc 2012 **Rating** 89 **To** 2014 $20
Reserve Margaret River Merlot 2011 **Rating** 88 **To** 2016 $25

Brick Kiln ★★★★

21 Greer St, Hyde Park, SA 5061 **Region** McLaren Vale
T (08) 8357 2561 **www**.brickiln.com.au **Open** At Red Poles Restaurant
Winemaker Linda Domas, Phil Christiansen **Est.** 2001 **Dozens** 1500 **Vyds** 8ha
This is the venture of Malcolm and Alison Mackinnon, Garry and Nancy Watson, and Ian and Pene Davey. They purchased the Nine Gums Vineyard, which had been planted to shiraz in 1995–96, in 2001. The majority of the grapes are sold, with a lesser portion contract-made for the partners under the Brick Kiln label, which takes its name from the Brick Kiln Bridge adjacent to the vineyard. Exports to the UK, Canada, China, Hong Kong and Singapore.

ŸŸŸŸŸ The Grove McLaren Vale Shiraz 2010 Full purple-red; this is an intense and complex full-bodied wine with layers of blackberry and plum fruit framed firstly by oak, and secondly by firm, ripe tannins. It is only a baby, needing a minimum of 5 years, and with a life span of at least 30 years. Screwcap. 14.6% alc. **Rating** 93 **To** 2040 $40
McLaren Vale Shiraz 2011 This single vineyard wine spent 21 months in American and French oak. Deep purple-crimson, it has remarkably complex flavours for an '11 wine, but no sign of body building on the medium-bodied palate; instead there is an array of blackberry fruit, dark chocolate and licorice-accented flavours, tannins and oak neatly judged. Screwcap. 14.5% alc. **Rating** 92 **To** 2026 $25

Brindabella Hills ★★★★☆

156 Woodgrove Close, Wallaroo, ACT 2618 **Region** Canberra District
T (02) 6230 2583 **www**.brindabellahills.com.au **Open** W'ends, public hols 10–5
Winemaker Dr Roger Harris, Brian Sinclair **Est.** 1986 **Dozens** 1500 **Vyds** 5ha

Distinguished research scientist Dr Roger Harris presides over Brindabella Hills, which increasingly relies on estate-produced grapes,with small plantings of riesling, shiraz, chardonnay, sauvignon blanc, merlot, sangiovese, cabernet sauvignon, cabernet franc and viognier. Wine quality has been consistently impressive, although the problems the region poses for red wines mean the focus has switched for the time being to whites. Much of the 2012 vintage crop fell victim to heavy rainfall.

🍷🍷🍷🍷🍷 Wallaroo Vineyard Canberra District Riesling 2011 There is a Germanic air to the bouquet of this wine as it is loaded with green apple, fragrant bath talc and citrus blossom aromas; the palate is fleshy and generous, with taut acidity providing a thrilling ride from start to finish, and while not bone dry, gives the impression of being exactly that; long and harmonious to conclude. Screwcap. 11.4% alc. **Rating** 94 **To** 2020 $25 BE

🍷🍷🍷🍷 Canberra District Riesling 2012 **Rating** 90 **To** 2018 $25 BE

Brockenchack ★★★★★

13/102 Burnett Street, Buderim, Qld 4556 (postal) **Region** Eden Valley
T (07) 5458 7710 **www**.brockenchack.com.au **Open** Not
Winemaker Shawn Kalleske **Est.** 2007 **Dozens** 3400 **Vyds** 16ha

Trevor (and wife Marilyn) Harch have long been involved in liquor distribution in Qld, owning one of Australia's leading independent liquor wholesalers, servicing licensed premises throughout Qld. Over the years, he became a regular visitor to the Barossa/Eden Valley region, and in 1999 purchased the historic Tanunda Cellars Wine Store. This encouraged him to purchase a wine store at Maleny, renamed Purple Palate, which has spawned four other Purple Palate retail bottle shops across Brisbane and the Sunshine Coast, plus the premier wine bar in Brisbane city, known as Bar Barossa. But that is only part of the story: in 2007, Trevor and Marilyn purchased a 16ha vineyard in the Eden Valley and retained friend Shawn Kalleske as winemaker. The vineyard has 8ha of shiraz, 2ha each of riesling and cabernet sauvignon, and 1.3ha each of pinot noir, pinot gris and chardonnay. The name of the business is appropriately Delphic. While every wine so far released, and those planned for the future, are labelled in honour of one or other of the March family, Brockenchack comes from the Christian names of the four grandchildren: Bronte, Mackenzie, Charli and Jack.

🍷🍷🍷🍷🍷 Mackenzie William 1896 Single Vineyard Eden Valley Riesling 2012 Pale quartz-green; an elegant wine made from vines planted two centuries ago; the bouquet is still to fully evolve, but the finely structured palate points the way, with its beautifully balanced display of sweet riesling fruit framed by minerally acidity. Screwcap. 11% alc. **Rating** 94 **To** 2027 $20

Jack Harrison Single Vineyard Eden Valley Shiraz 2010 Deep purple-crimson; the bouquet immediately expresses black fruits, allspice and a hint of oak, all of which gain volume on the medium- to full-bodied palate; it is positively rich and voluptuous on the mid-palate, but the back-palate and finish have an open weave, and confer an overall spicy/cedary elegance. Screwcap. 14.5% alc. **Rating** 94 **To** 2030 $59

William Frederick Single Vineyard Eden Valley Shiraz 2009 Identical colour to the Jack Harrison Single Vineyard Shiraz; the overall style is also similar, but this wine has even greater intensity. Both wines are to be approached with caution, and will repay a decade or two in the cellar. The price is courageous for a new kid on the block. Screwcap. 14.5% alc. **Rating** 94 **To** 2039 $170

🍷🍷🍷🍷 ✪ Tru-Su Single Vineyard Rose 2012 Bright, light crimson-purple; estate-grown shiraz brings life and energy to the fresh and poached red cherry fruit flavours; the overall balance is very good. Screwcap. 13% alc. **Rating** 92 **To** 2014 $17

Zip Line Single Vineyard Shiraz 2011 **Rating** 90 **To** 2018 $26

Broken Gate Wines

57 Rokeby Street, Collingwood, Vic 3066 **Region** South Eastern Australia
T (03) 9417 5757 **www**.brokengate.com.au **Open** Mon–Fri 8–5
Winemaker Josef Orbach **Est.** 2001 **Dozens** 50 000

Broken Gate is a Melbourne-based multiregional producer, specialising in cool-climate reds and whites. Founder Josef Orbach lived and worked in the Clare Valley from 1994 to '98 at Leasingham Wines, and is currently studying wine technology and viticulture at the University of Melbourne. His is a classic negociant business, buying grapes and/or wines from various regions; the wines may be either purchased in bulk, then blended and bottled by Orbach, or purchased as cleanskins. The wine glut has been a great boon for his business. Exports to Canada, Thailand, Singapore and China.

Josef Orbach Clare Valley Shiraz 2010 The use of the cheapest cork (twin top) on the market is a strange choice for a wine at this price; on the other side of the fence, the wine has attractive blackberry and licorice flavours on the medium-bodied, supple, palate, enhanced by the judicious use of some new French oak, with the tannins soft on the finish. Twin top. 14.5% alc. **Rating** 91 **To** 2020 $50

Side Gate Geelong Pinot Noir 2010 Good colour, clear purple-crimson, exceptional for a 3-year-old wine; this is a pretty smart pinot for its price; very attractive red cherry/plum fruit comes through on entry to the palate before a slightly stalky/green nuance comes on the back-palate; it needed to be a little riper, if so, it would have been a match winner. Screwcap. 12.5% alc. **Rating** 90 **To** 2015 $20

Side Gate Clare Valley Riesling 2012 Pale quartz-green; a fresh and lively bouquet and palate, with lemon citrus flavours backed by zesty acidity; has good length, its only shortcoming a slightly thin mid-palate. Good value. Screwcap. 12.5% alc. **Rating** 89 **To** 2016 $15

Side Gate Adelaide Hills Sauvignon Blanc 2012 This is the vineyard (and vintage) speaking, not the winery; the aromas and flavours are poised between citrus/grass and tropical nuances, the overall effect pleasing, and with plenty of all-up flavour. Well priced. Screwcap. 12.5% alc. **Rating** 89 **To** 2014 $17

Adelaide Hills Pinot Grigio 2012 Has above-average intensity and focus, with a mix of pear, green apple and citrus, crisp acidity lengthening the finish. In true grigio style. Screwcap. 12% alc. **Rating** 89 **To** 2014 $17

Clare Valley Shiraz 2010 Rating 89 **To** 2018 $25

Side Gate Coonawarra Cabernet Sauvignon 2010 Bright, although light, crimson; a fresh, well-made, medium-bodied wine with blackcurrant, mint and mulberry fruit supported by subtle French oak and fine tannins. Screwcap. 14.5% alc. **Rating** 89 **To** 2015 $15

Brokenwood

401–427 McDonalds Road, Pokolbin, NSW 2321 **Region** Hunter Valley
T (02) 4998 7559 **www**.brokenwood.com.au **Open** 7 days 9.30–5
Winemaker Iain Riggs, Simon Steele **Est.** 1970 **Dozens** 100 000 **Vyds** 64ha

This deservedly fashionable winery, producing consistently excellent wines, has kept Graveyard Shiraz as its ultimate flagship wine, while extending its reach through many of the best eastern regions for its broad selection of varietal wine styles. Its big-selling Hunter Semillon provides the volume to balance the limited quantities of the flagships ILR Semillon and Graveyard Shiraz. Next there is a range of wines coming from regions including Beechworth (a major resource being the associated Indigo Vineyard), Orange, Central Ranges, McLaren Vale, Cowra and elsewhere. The two-storey Albert Room tasting facility is named in honour of the late Tony Albert, one of the founders. In 2012 Iain Riggs celebrated his 30th vintage at the helm of Brokenwood, offering his unique mix of winemaking skills, management of a diverse business, and unerring ability to keep Brokenwood's high profile fresh and newsworthy and oversee the exemplary consistency of its large range of top-quality wines. Knocking at the door for Winery of the Year mantle. Exports to all major markets.

ΨΨΨΨΨ **ILR Reserve Hunter Valley Semillon 2007** Incredibly pale, although bright, straw-green; this is the best ILR so far made; while delicate and elegant, the citrus, lemongrass and mineral components are utterly seamless, the palate of perfect balance and length. Arguably its Achilles heel is the pleasure it gives now, as too few will experience the increased complexity of further age. Screwcap. 11.5% alc. **Rating** 98 **To** 2027 $60

Graveyard Vineyard Hunter Valley Shiraz 2011 Full but clear purple-crimson; as ever, an imperious wine, its power so relaxed you might walk by without stopping to gawk; blackberry, licorice and leather are sheathed in quality oak, the tannins exceptionally fine, but perfectly balanced; '11 was a very good Hunter Valley vintage. Screwcap. 13.5% alc. **Rating** 97 **To** 2040 $150

Mistress Block Vineyard Hunter Valley Shiraz 2011 Excellent crimson-purple; the grapes for this beautifully crafted wine come from the 143-year-old hillside, red soil vineyard of Rod and Deeta McGeoch; there is absolute symbiosis between the dark fruits, tannins and oak of the medium-bodied palate, with the finish long and faultless. Screwcap. 13% alc. **Rating** 97 **To** 2041 $75

Maxwell Vineyard Hunter Valley Semillon 2007 Pale straw-green when 6 years old – extraordinary; a wine of exceptional finesse, line, length and balance. There is no thought of the wine becoming frozen in time; it will continue to develop, becoming more complex as honey, toast and lemon curd flavours intensify. Screwcap. 11.5% alc. **Rating** 96 **To** 2027 $50

Indigo Vineyard Beechworth Chardonnay 2011 Light, gleaming straw-green; this may not be the most complex Burgundian chardonnay from the Indigo Vineyard, but in my view it's one of the very best; barrel-fermented, but has absorbed the one-third new oak, the flavours dominated by white peach, the perfectly citrussy acidity and pH enhancing the mouthfeel and length of the palate. Screwcap. 12.5% alc. **Rating** 96 **To** 2018 $32

Quail McLaren Vale Hunter Valley Shiraz 2010 A blend of Graveyard Vineyard (Quail Block) and McLaren Vale shiraz matured for 2 years in French oak; while there is an abundance of chocolate and dark berry fruit (plus oak), there is also a savoury/earthy regional overtone; synergy at its best. Screwcap. 14% alc. **Rating** 96 **To** 2040 $95

Mistress Block Vineyard Hunter Valley Shiraz 2010 Light, clear crimson-purple; from a 42-year-old vineyard on a steep slope; very well made, with savoury/earthy regional fruit characters offset by sweet vanillin oak and ripe tannins. Indefinite life ahead. Screwcap. 13.5% alc. **Rating** 96 **To** 2040 $69

Stanleigh Park Hunter Valley Semillon 2007 Still light, very bright green; the bouquet has elements of beeswax and lanolin along with the feather bed of citrus, and sets the scene for the elegant, fresh and light palate. This is still a baby, but it is a healthy one. Screwcap. 10.5% alc. **Rating** 95 **To** 2032 $45

Maxwell Vineyard Hunter Valley Semillon 2006 Has an extra tang and cut to the citrus fruit at its core, encircled by some of the spice and toast characters that will slowly become more evident as the wine continues its development through to 2020 and beyond. Screwcap. 11% alc. **Rating** 95 **To** 2026 $45

Verona Vineyard Hunter Valley Shiraz 2011 **Rating** 94 **To** 2031 $50
McLaren Vale Beechworth Hunter Valley Shiraz 2010 **Rating** 94 **To** 2035 $35
Indigo Vineyard Beechworth Shiraz 2010 **Rating** 94 **To** 2030 $50

ΨΨΨΨΨ **Hunter Valley Shiraz 2010** **Rating** 93 **To** 2030 $45
Hunter Valley Semillon 2012 **Rating** 92 **To** 2017 $25
Indigo Vineyard Beechworth Pinot Noir 2010 **Rating** 92 **To** 2017 $45
Beechworth Nebbiolo 2012 **Rating** 92 **To** 2017 $40
Wade Block 2 Vineyard McLaren Vale Shiraz 2008 **Rating** 91 **To** 2020 $50
Beechworth Pinot Gris 2012 **Rating** 90 **To** 2014 $28

Bromley Wines

★★★★☆

PO Box 571, Drysdale, Vic 3222 **Region** Geelong
T 0487 505 367 **www.**bromleywines.com.au **Open** Not
Winemaker Darren Burke **Est.** 2010 **Dozens** 300

In his previous life, Darren Burke worked as an intensive care nurse around Australia and in the UK, but at the age of 30 he fell to the allure of wine and enrolled in the Bachelor of Applied Science (Oenology) at Adelaide University. Thereafter he successively became graduate winemaker at Orlando, then Alkoomi Wines (he had done a vintage there during his undergraduate studies), fitting in a vintage in Chianti. With successful vintages in 2005 and '06 completed, and the impending birth of their first child, he and wife Tammy decided to move back to the east coast. There he worked at several wineries on the Bellarine Peninsula before taking up his full-time winemaking post at Leura Park Estate. Says Darren, 'The essence of Bromley is is family. All our wines carry names drawn from our family history. Family is about flesh and blood, sweat and tears, love and laughter. It is all of these things that we bring to the table when we make our wines.'

🍷🍷🍷🍷🍷 **Enigma 2012** Some interesting soft porn is appearing on back labels with
✪ increasing frequency, here ultimately disclosing seduction by semillon. The wine itself has been very well made, the flavours and structure looking to the Adelaide Hills for support; its ripe lemon curd/lemongrass flavours are most impressive. Screwcap. 11% alc. **Rating** 93 **To** 2020 $19

Ryan Geelong Pinot Noir 2011 Light red-purple; has been very well made, with warm spices threaded through the fragrant bouquet, joined by poached cherries on the palate; has considerable length notwithstanding its light body. Screwcap. 13% alc. **Rating** 92 **To** 2018 $30

Brookland Valley

Caves Road, Wilyabrup, WA 6280 **Region** Margaret River
T (08) 9755 6042 **www.**brooklandvalley.com.au **Open** 7 days 10–5
Winemaker Courtney Treacher **Est.** 1984 **Dozens** NFP

Brookland Valley has an idyllic setting, plus its café and Gallery of Wine Arts, which houses an eclectic collection of wine, food-related art and wine accessories. After acquiring a 50% share of Brookland Valley in 1997, Hardys moved to full ownership in 2004; it is now part of Accolade Wines. The quality, and consistency, of the wines has been exemplary. Exports to Hong Kong and Pacific Islands.

🍷🍷🍷🍷🍷 **Reserve Margaret River Cabernet Sauvignon 2011** Deep magenta, bright;
fruit purity is the essence of the bouquet, with cassis, redcurrant, cedar, olive and violet all on display; the palate is poised, polished, pristine and pure, offering a racy subtext of ample fine-grained tannins; layered and long, patient cellaring will be well rewarded, but there will be plenty of enjoyment if you don't have the time to wait. Screwcap. 13.5% alc. **Rating** 96 **To** 2030 $71 BE

Margaret River Chardonnay 2012 Light straw-green; in the typically elegant yet very complex Barossa Valley style, with intense white peach and grapefruit counterbalanced on the bouquet and palate; French oak is little more than a vehicle for what will be a long-lived wine. Screwcap. 13.5% alc. **Rating** 95 **To** 2020 $40

Reserve Margaret River Chardonnay 2012 Light straw-green; a wine of extreme finesse and elegance; it has great length and line, early-picked grapes providing natural acidity and low pH to soak up the oak from barrel fermentation, yet in no danger of crossing into Sauvignon Blanc territory; stone fruits remain the key driver. The points are for today; in another 5 years they may well be higher. Screwcap. 14% alc. **Rating** 95 **To** 2022 $71

Margaret River Cabernet Sauvignon Merlot 2011 Bright, relatively light, crimson-purple; a very attractive example of the blend, something which comes easily in Margaret River; cassis, redcurrant and a dab of oak flow through the medium-bodied palate, tannins simply pointing the way to the finish. Lets terroir and variety speak. Screwcap. 13.5% alc. **Rating** 94 **To** 2026 $47

ŸŸŸŸ♀ Verse 1 Margaret River Cabernet Merlot 2011 Rating 93 To 2016 $20

✪ Unison Cabernet Sauvignon 2011 An elegant Cabernet with a fragrant, cassis-accented bouquet and a medium-bodied, fresh palate with a continuation of the cassis and redcurrant fruit theme of the bouquet, tannins and oak minor players. Screwcap. 13.5% alc. Rating 92 To 2021 $22

Unison Sauvignon Blanc Semillon 2012 Rating 90 To 2014 $22

Unison Chardonnay 2012 Rating 90 To 2016 $22

✪ Verse 1 Margaret River Shiraz 2011 Deep crimson, bright; lifted and fragrant showing redcurrant, blackberry and juniper on the bouquet; medium-bodied and vibrant, full of luscious fruits on entry, and then the firm, ripe tannins lead to a surprisingly long, savoury and even finish. Screwcap. 13.5% alc. Rating 90 To 2018 $15 BE

ŸŸŸŸ Verse 1 Margaret River Semillon Sauvignon Blanc 2012 Pale colour; the
✪ lemon-accented aromas and flavours pay tribute to the semillon, the fleeting touch of passionfruit to the sauvignon blanc. Good value at its price. Screwcap. 12.5% alc. Rating 88 To 2014 $15

Broomstick Estate

4 Frances Street, Mount Lawley, WA 6050 (postal) **Region** Margaret River
T (08) 9271 9594 **www.broomstick.com.au Open** Not
Winemaker Happs (Mark Warren) **Est.** 1997 **Dozens** 500 **Vyds** 16.6ha

The property that Robert Holloway and family purchased in 1993 on which the vineyard is now established was an operating dairy farm. In 1997, 5.5ha of shiraz was planted. Over the following years 3.8ha of merlot and then (in 2004) 5.3ha of chardonnay and 2ha of sauvignon blanc were added. The Holloways see themselves as grapegrowers first and foremost, but make a small amount of wine under the Broomstick Estate label. The name of the business derives from the vineyard's proximity to the town of Witchcliffe, or 'Witchy' as the locals call it. The label design reflects the association of witches with broomsticks and ravens.

ŸŸŸŸ♀ Margaret River Chardonnay 2009 Bright gleaming straw-green; given 90 points in March '10, and earns an extra point for the effortless way it has developed. Best of all, the wine is still available. Screwcap. 12.9% alc. Rating 91 To 2015 $25

Baba Yaga 2009 A 66/22/12% blend of merlot, cabernet franc and cabernet sauvignon; as expected, is showing some bottle development, with cedary/savoury notes prominent on both the bouquet and the medium-bodied palate; the small red berry fruits are alive and well, so the wine will cruise through at least another 3–5 years. Screwcap. 13.2% alc. Rating 90 To 2018 $25

Brothers in Arms

Lake Plains Road, Langhorne Creek, SA 5255 **Region** Langhorne Creek
T (08) 8537 3182 **www.brothersinarms.com.au Open** By appt
Winemaker Jim Urlwin **Est.** 1998 **Dozens** 25 000 **Vyds** 85ha

The Adams family has been growing grapes at Langhorne Creek since 1891, when the first vines at the famed Metala vineyards were planted. Guy Adams is the fifth generation to own and work the vineyard, and over the past 20 years has both improved the viticulture and expanded the plantings. It was not until 1998 that they decided to hold back a small proportion of the production for vinification under the Brothers in Arms label, and now they dedicate 85ha to the Brothers in Arms wines (shiraz, cabernet sauvignon, malbec and petit verdot); the grapes from the remaining 200ha are sold. Exports to the UK, Canada, Germany, Sweden, Denmark, Singapore, Hong Kong and China.

ŸŸŸŸŸ Langhorne Creek Shiraz 2009 Full, deep colour; a more complex, fuller bodied Shiraz than the '10 6th Generation; the flavours are of black fruits, licorice and a touch of dark chocolate, the tannins, while substantial, are soft, and the oak has been well handled. Screwcap. 14.8% alc. Rating 94 To 2029 $48

ŸŸŸŸŸ · 6th Generation Shiraz 2010 Rating 93 To 2025 $30
No. 6 Langhorne Creek Shiraz 2009 Rating 91 To 2024 $24
No. 6 Langhorne Creek Shiraz Cabernet 2008 Rating 90 To 2020 $24
Formby & Adams Leading Horse Langhorne Creek Cabernet
Sauvignon 2009 Rating 90 To 2024 $19

Brown Brothers   ★★★★★

Milawa-Bobinawarrah Road, Milawa, Vic 3678 **Region** King Valley
T (03) 5720 5500 **www.**brownbrothers.com.au **Open** 7 days 9–5
Winemaker Wendy Cameron, Joel Tilbrook, Cate Looney **Est.** 1885 **Dozens** 1 million
Vyds 662ha

Draws upon a considerable number of vineyards spread throughout a range of site climates,
ranging from very warm to very cool. A relatively recent expansion into Heathcote has added
significantly to its armoury. It is known for the diversity of varieties with which it works,
and the wines represent good value for money. Deservedly one of the most successful family
wineries – its cellar door receives the greatest number of visitors in Australia. In 2010 Brown
Brothers took a momentous step, acquiring Tasmania's Tamar Ridge for $32.5 million. It is
intended that there will be no changes to Tamar Ridge until all of the opportunities and
possible synergies have been carefully considered. An onsite airstrip is an (unusual) extra.
Exports to all major markets.

ŸŸŸŸŸ Limited Release Single Vineyard King Valley Pinot Grigio 2012 A grigio
made in the vineyard, coming from the ultra-cool Whitlands Vineyard, with the
yield restricted, the grapes hand-picked and whole bunch-pressed, then cold-
fermented. It is a wine with startling intensity and purity of varietal flavour, which
must surely set the bar for grigio. Screwcap. 13.5% alc. Rating 96 To 2014 $32
Cellar Door Release Single Vineyard King Valley Shiraz Mondeuse &
Cabernet 2008 Very good retention of hue, still purple; a blast from the past
(back to Everton Hills' wines), with a complex array of red and black fruits, multi-
spice and anise; the lively, fine tannins and quality oak add another layer. Screwcap.
15% alc. Rating 95 To 2028 $42
Patricia Pinot Noir Chardonnay Brut 2006 A 79/21% blend made using the
traditional method, it is still vibrantly alive and beautifully balanced; so good is the
balance that it is easy to overlook the complexity of the wine, and the creamy/
yeasty characters held within the fruit. Cork. 12.5% alc. Rating 95 To 2014 $45
Cellar Door Release Single Vineyard King Valley Riesling 2012 Devoid of
colour Mar '13; the single vineyard is in fact Whitlands, at 800m, which explains
the tightly wound nature of the wine, and its unsweetened lemon sherbet flavours
on the prodigiously long palate. Will richly repay extended cellaring. Screwcap.
12% alc. Rating 94 To 2027 $27
Patricia Shiraz 2009 Good retention of hue; a solid, traditional style with depth
to the seamless black fruit, oak and tannins on the full-bodied palate. Destined
for a long life, and with improvement certain. Screwcap. 14.6% alc. Rating 94
To 2029 $56
Patricia Noble Riesling 2009 Full gold; there is the same difference between
this and the Tamar Ridge Botrytis Riesling '11 as there is between a Sauterne
and a Mosel Valley trockenbeerenauslese – so comparison is very difficult. This
wine has become the number one trophy winner in mainland wine shows over
recent years; abundant honey, toast, butter and citrus flavours. Screwcap. 9.6% alc.
Rating 94 To 2016 $35

ŸŸŸŸŸ Patricia Chardonnay 2010 Rating 93 To 2018 $40
Patricia Cabernet Sauvignon 2009 Rating 93 To 2029 $56
✪ Pinot Noir Chardonnay Pinot Meunier Cuvee NV Predominantly sourced
from Brown Brothers' Whitlands vineyard, from other cool vineyards in the King
Valley and elsewhere in Vic. Light straw-green, good mousse; this is a complex
wine with toasty/yeast characters adding to both flavour and texture, yet there
is also plenty of fresh fruit and minerality. Excellent value. Cork. 12.9% alc.
Rating 93 To 2015 $24

Cellar Door Release Single Vineyard King Valley Half Dry Riesling 2012
Rating 93 To 2025 $27

Limited Release Victoria Vermentino 2012 Supercharged with CO_2, manifesting itself with persistent mousse in the glass and bottle, although not so obvious in the mouth. The back label says 'A multitude of winemaking techniques were used on different parcels of fruit' to build the luscious flavour the wine undoubtedly has. Screwcap. 11.5% alc. Rating 91 To 2014 $18

Limited Release King Valley Prosecco 2012 Rating 90 To 2013 $24 TS

Pinot Meunier Sparkling Rose 2010 Rating 90 To 2014 $35

Victoria Tarrango 2012 A CSIRO hybrid grown by Brown Brothers for several decades. The winemakers have resisted the temptation to leave some sweetness, instead relying on the bright, fresh cherry and raspberry fruit. Like any rose worthy of the name, serve slightly chilled, especially in summer. Screwcap. 12.5% alc. Rating 88 To 2014 $15

Brown Hill Estate
★★★★☆

Cnr Rosa Brook Road/Barrett Road, Rosa Brook, WA 6285 **Region** Margaret River
T (08) 9757 4003 **www**.brownhillestate.com.au **Open** 7 days 10–5
Winemaker Nathan Bailey, Sean Ambrose **Est.** 1995 **Dozens** 3000 **Vyds** 22ha
The Bailey family is involved in all stages of wine production, with minimum outside help. Their stated aim is to produce top-quality wines at affordable prices, via uncompromising viticultural practices emphasising low yields. They have shiraz and cabernet sauvignon (8ha each), semillon, sauvignon blanc and merlot (2ha each). By the standards of Margaret River, the prices are indeed affordable.

Bill Bailey Margaret River Shiraz Cabernet 2011 Deep crimson-purple; picked 6 weeks later than normal; a lush, full-bodied blend with the full spectrum of black fruits supported by velvety tannins and quality oak. I don't agree with the back label description of the wine as 'thick', but that's only a semantic quibble. Screwcap. 14.8% alc. Rating 94 To 2026 $50

Perseverance Cabernet Merlot 2011 Rating 93 To 2030 $50
Fimiston Reserve Margaret River Shiraz 2011 Rating 92 To 2021 $30
Ivanhoe Reserve Cabernet Sauvignon 2011 Rating 92 To 2026 $30
Croesus Reserve Margaret River Merlot 2011 Rating 91 To 2026 $35
Golden Horseshoe Chardonnay 2012 Rating 90 To 2018 $30 BE

Brown Magpie Wines
★★★★☆

125 Larcombes Road, Modewarre, Vic 3240 **Region** Geelong
T (03) 5266 2147 **www**.brownmagpiewines.com **Open** 7 days Jan 11–4, w'ends 11–4 Nov–Apr
Winemaker Loretta and Shane Breheny, Chris Sargeant **Est.** 2000 **Dozens** 3500 **Vyds** 9ha
Shane and Loretta Breheny's 20ha property is situated predominantly on a gentle, north-facing slope, with cypress trees on the western and southern borders providing protection against the wind. Vines were planted over 2001–02, with pinot noir (4ha) taking the lion's share, followed by pinot gris and shiraz (2.4ha each) and 0.1ha each of chardonnay and sauvignon blanc. Viticulture is Loretta's love; winemaking (and wine) is Shane's.

Paraparap Single Vineyard Reserve Pinot Noir 2010 Full, bright crimson-purple; the bouquet is very spicy, bordering on clove or star anise, neither over the top, just unusual; the palate is primarily driven by red and black cherry and plum; the spice impact is much diminished. A very good Pinot Noir with a long (pinot) life and great value. Screwcap. 13% alc. Rating 94 To 2020 $27

Single Vineyard Geelong Pinot Noir 2011 Rating 91 To 2017 $25 BE
Single Vineyard Geelong Pinot Grigio 2012 Rating 90 To 2015 $25 BE
Single Vineyard Geelong Pinot Gris 2012 Rating 90 To 2016 $25 BE

Paraparap Single Vineyard Reserve Pinot Noir 2011 Rating 90 To 2016
$35 BE

✪ **Late Harvest Single Vineyard Geelong Botrytis Pinot Gris 2011** Vibrant
colour, with good levels of botrytis and plenty of lift; the palate is unctuous and
sweet, and the conditions of the vintage have provided a sweet wine of character
and distinction. 375ml. Screwcap. 12% alc. **Rating** 90 To 2017 $15 BE

Browns of Padthaway ★★★

Riddoch Highway, Padthaway, SA 5271 **Region** Padthaway
T (08) 8765 6040 **www**.brownsofpadthaway.com.au **Open** By appt
Winemaker O'Leary Walker Wines **Est.** 1993 **Dozens** 20 000 **Vyds** 150ha
The Brown family has for many years been the largest independent grapegrower in
Padthaway, a district in which most of the vineyards were established and owned by Wynns,
Seppelt, Lindemans and Hardys, respectively. Browns has produced excellent wines and wine
production has increased accordingly. The major part of the grape production is sold, and
distribution of the wines in Australia has been sporadic. It seems likely that significant amounts
are being exported. Exports to the UK, the US, Germany and NZ.

🍷🍷🍷🍷 **Ernest Family Reserve Shiraz 2005** A full-bodied shiraz, with black fruits,
earth, dark chocolate and plum cake; the tannins are fully resolved, the wine ready.
Cork. 15% alc. **Rating** 89 To 2017 $24
T-Trellis Shiraz 2010 Medium red-purple; a solid, slightly chunky wine with
black fruits plus touches of earth and dark chocolate; won't fall over soon, and is
well priced. Screwcap. 15% alc. **Rating** 88 To 2016 $18
Glendon Park Vignerons Reserve Sauvignon Blanc 2010 Bright green-
straw, with some development; a fleshy wine with tropical fruits on the bouquet
and palate, but lacking the drive and focus of the best wines. Screwcap. 12.5% alc.
Rating 87 To 2014 $18

Brygon Reserve ★★★★★

Lot 5 Harmans Mill Road, Wilyabrup, WA 6280 **Region** Margaret River
T 1800 754 517 **www**.brygonreservewines.com.au **Open** 7 days 10.30–5
Winemaker David Longden **Est.** 2009 **Dozens** NFP
Brygon Reserve is founded and owned by Robert and Laurie Fraser-Scott. The other
brands are Third Wheel, Birds of a Feather and Winston Lake Estate. Each has numerous
labels, some as subsets (thus Birds of a Feather has seven Reserve varietal wines and eight
Humming Bird wines). In April 2013 there were 23 wine ranges available on their website.
Extraordinary show success continues. The remarkable price range of $18 to $60 continues,
and the business has opened an office in China. Exports to the US, Vietnam, Macau, Taiwan,
Thailand, Hong Kong, Singapore and China.

🍷🍷🍷🍷🍷 **Brygon Reserve Small Batch Oak Aged Margaret River Chardonnay
2010** Bright green-yellow; a rich, full-bodied Chardonnay of the kind unique to
Margaret River, where depth rather than length that defines its quality; stone fruit,
grapefruit and oak are in harmony, and there is good acidity to provide length,
balance and a lingering aftertaste. Screwcap. 12.5% alc. **Rating** 95 To 2019 $60
Nostalgia Wines Flying High Margaret River Shiraz 2009 Deep colour,
much more so than that of the Birds of a Feather Hummingbird; the palate, too,
has fresher, richer and deeper, flesh with spicy plum and blackberry fruit backed
by good oak and ripe tannins. Will well and truly outlive the Birds of a Feather
Hummingbird. Screwcap. 13% alc. **Rating** 95 To 2019 $18

✪ **Westley Manor Margaret River Cabernet Merlot 2010** Medium crimson-
purple; bypassing the incomprehensible story of Westley Manor on the front label,
this is a gloriously juicy blend of redcurrant, blackcurrant on the supple medium-
bodied palate, oak and tannins pushed well off centre stage, but there nonetheless.
Screwcap. 13.5% alc. **Rating** 95 To 2025 $25

Brygon Reserve Small Batch Oak Aged Margaret River Cabernet Sauvignon 2010 Full crimson-purple; a very elegant medium-bodied wine with exemplary varietal character and supple texture; it has an array of cassis, mulberry and redcurrant fruit framed by well-integrated French oak and perfectly weighted tannins. Screwcap. 14% alc. **Rating** 95 **To** 2030 $60

Brygon Reserve Epitome Renaissance Series Margaret River Cabernet Shiraz Merlot 2010 An unusual blend outside Coonawarra, and not even common there. The crimson-purple colour is good, and the palate is better still, with a rich, supple, cascade of blackcurrant, blackberry, plum and licorice fruit; the tannins are soft and ripe, the oak well integrated. Good value. Screwcap. 14.4% alc. **Rating** 95 **To** 2030 $30

✪ **Third Wheel Reserve Margaret River Cabernet Shiraz Merlot 2009** In the 18 months since first being tasted, it has matured to a degree, gaining complexity, but not losing its freshness or the balance of berry fruit, oak and ripe, fine tannins. Screwcap. 13.5% alc. **Rating** 95 **To** 2019 $20

✪ **Birds of a Feather Humming Bird Series Margaret River Semillon Sauvignon Blanc 2012** Pale, bright straw-green; while the percentage of sauvignon blanc is less than that of the semillon, the guava, lychee and gooseberry flavours of the sauvignon blanc drive the bouquet and palate aromas and flavours; the lemon/lemongrass of the semillon is more important for the structure, but does add flavour to a very attractive wine. Screwcap. 12.5% alc. **Rating** 94 **To** 2015 $20

✪ **Bin 828 Semillon Sauvignon Blanc 2011** Putting aside the incoherent babble on the back label, this wine has travelled very well since winning the trophy for Best Semillon Sauvignon Blanc Margaret River Wine Show '11, besting a star-studded field. The structure and texture are particularly good, underpinning the mainstream tropical fruit core, in turn neatly trimmed and balanced by crisp acidity. Screwcap. 12.5% alc. **Rating** 94 **To** 2014 $18

Private Bin Block 3 Chardonnay 2009 Rating 94 **To** 2017 $50
Private Bin Block 9 Shiraz 2010 Rating 94 **To** 2025 $50
Birds of a Feather Hummingbird Shiraz 2009 Rating 94 **To** 2020 $20
Private Bin Block 9 Shiraz 2009 Rating 94 **To** 2025 $50
Small Batch Shiraz 2009 Rating 94 **To** 2020 $60
Private Bin Block 8 Cabernet Sauvignon 2009 Rating 94 **To** 2020 $50

🍷🍷🍷🍷🍷 **Nostalgia Wines Harlequin Margaret River Shiraz 2010** Excellent colour
✪ and clarity; spicy plum and cherry aromas on the bouquet are mirrored on the fresh, medium-bodied palate; oak is well balanced and integrated, the tannins quite firm, but not dry or rough. Has a bright future. Screwcap. 13.5% alc. **Rating** 93 **To** 2022 $18

✪ **Nostalgia Wines Flying High Margaret River Semillon Sauvignon Blanc 2012** Semillon the dominant partner in both aroma/flavour and structure, with its herb and cut grass characters; that said, there is a substantial contribution of guava and melon fruit. Screwcap. 12.7% alc. **Rating** 91 **To** 2015 $18

✪ **Nostalgia Wines Flying High Margaret River Chardonnay 2011** Pale straw-green; a vivid example of how intense varietal fruit flavours can come from early-picked grapes if there has been care taken in the vineyard. The wine is defined by its pink grapefruit flavours, stone fruit and oak in the background on a long, clean finish. Screwcap. 12.5% alc. **Rating** 91 **To** 2017 $18

✪ **Nostalgia Wines Harlequin Margaret River Chardonnay 2011** Very similar to the Reserve Flying High, perhaps with a little more grainy/minerally acidity underpinning the fruit, and a hint of stone fruit and apple on the finish. Screwcap. 12.5% alc. **Rating** 91 **To** 2016 $18

✪ **Brygon Reserve Pilot's Watch Margaret River Shiraz 2011** Bright crimson-purple; the lively berry and spice bouquet is followed by a light- to medium-bodied palate, again with spicy/earthy nuances to its predominantly dark, savoury flavours. Freshness is a particular feature. Good value. Screwcap. 14.5% alc. **Rating** 91 **To** 2018 $18

✪   **Birds of a Feather Humming Bird Series Margaret River Cabernet Sauvignon 2010** Good retention of crimson-purple hue; has typical Margaret River cabernet structure and flavour, with the blackcurrant/cassis fruit sustained by firm, slightly earthy, but not at all bitter, tannins. Screwcap. 13.5% alc. **Rating** 91 To 2020 $20

✪   **Pilots Watch Margaret River Sauvignon Blanc 2012** Pale straw-green; a well-made Sauvignon Blanc with gooseberry and lychee flavours built around grainy acidity, the finish dry and refreshing. Screwcap. 12.5% alc. **Rating** 90 To 2013 $18

✪   **Pilots Watch Margaret River Semillon Sauvignon Blanc 2012** Light straw-green; despite the dominance of semillon, and the modest alcohol, there is an overall richness and sweetness to the palate that will satisfy many consumers; tropical fruits and preserved lemon lead the flavours. Screwcap. 12.5% alc. **Rating** 90 To 2014 $18

✪   **Nostalgia Wines Flying High Margaret River Cabernet Merlot 2009** Good depth to the crimson-purple colour; an easily accessed style, both the bouquet and medium-bodied berry and plum palate framed by oak and relatively light tannins. Screwcap. 13% alc. **Rating** 90 To 2017 $18

✪   **Brygon Reserve The Bruce Margaret River Cabernet Sauvignon 2011** The modest red-purple colour announces a medium-bodied cabernet with a mix of cassis, earth and briary/savoury characters, all of which are varietal, and well within price expectations; has good length and balance. Screwcap. 14% alc. **Rating** 90 To 2018 $20

✪   **Nostalgia Wines Harlequin Margaret River Cabernet Sauvignon 2010** Medium red-purple; the bouquet and palate are both complex, albeit assisted by a generous amount of oak that contributes both flavour and texture; there is also attractive cassis fruit and soft tannins. Attractive wine for early drinking. Screwcap. 13.5% alc. **Rating** 90 To 2018 $18

Buckley's Run Vineyard ★★★

50 Stony Creek Road, Red Hill, Vic 3937 (postal) **Region** Mornington Peninsula
T (03) 5989 3112 **Open** Not
Winemaker Foxeys Hangout (Tony Lee) **Est.** 2000 **Dozens** 110 **Vyds** 3ha
In 1998 Gabrielle Johnston purchased the 17ha property; 3ha of pinot gris had been established; the property also has 165 olive trees and an established Arabian horse stud. Most of the grapes have been sold over the years, but with small amounts made under the Buckley's Run label by a passing parade of winemakers.

🍷🍷🍷🍷 **Pinot Gris 2012** Has an attractive mix of pear, lemon zest and a hint of beeswax/
✪   honeycomb, although the finish is dry. Well priced. Screwcap. 14% alc. **Rating** 88 To 2014 $16

Buckshot Vineyard ★★★★★

PO Box 119, Coldstream, Vic 3770 **Region** Heathcote
T 0417 349 785 **www**.buckshotvineyard.com.au **Open** Not
Winemaker Rob Peebles **Est.** 1999 **Dozens** 600 **Vyds** 2ha
This is the venture of Meegan and Rob Peebles, which comes on the back of Rob's more than 15-years' involvement in the wine industry, including six vintages in Rutherglen, starting in 1993, followed by 10 years at Domaine Chandon, and squeezing in weekend work at Coldstream Hills' cellar door in '93. It is the soils of Heathcote, and a long-time friendship with John and Jenny Davies, that sees the flagship Shiraz, and a smaller amount of Zinfandel (with some shiraz) coming from a small block, part of a 40ha vineyard owned by the Davies' just southwest of Colbinabbin. Rob makes the wines at Domaine Chandon. Exports to the US.

🍷🍷🍷🍷🍷 **Heathcote Shiraz 2010** Cold-soaked for 3 days in small open fermenters, pressed after an additional 7-day fermentation, and spending 19 months in French hogsheads (30% new). The crimson-purple colour is excellent, and both the fragrant bouquet and medium-bodied palate have delicious plum and black cherry fruit, the tannins supple, the oak integrated. Screwcap. 13.9% alc. **Rating** 94 To 2030 $31

Buller (Swan Hill)

1374 Murray Valley Highway, Beverford, Vic 3590 **Region** Swan Hill
T (03) 5037 6305 **www**.bullerwines.com.au **Open** Mon–Fri 9–5, Sat 10–4, Sun 10–4
(school & public hols only)
Winemaker Richard Buller **Est.** 1951 **Dozens** 250000 **Vyds** 22ha
Controlled by Richard and Susan Buller, along with their children Richard Jr, Angela and
Kate, Buller offers traditional wines that in the final analysis reflect both their Riverland origin
and a fairly low-key approach to style in the winery. The estate vineyard is planted to a wide
variety of grapes, and additional grapes are purchased from growers in the region. Brands
include the value-for-money Beverford range, Caspia, Black Dog Creek from the King Valley
and Fine Old fortifieds. In 2012 the company was placed in receivership, and at the time of
going to print its future was not known. Exports to the UK, the US, China and NZ.

King Valley Chardonnay 2011 From a single vineyard, 50% fermented in
new French oak puncheons, 50% tank-fermented with wild yeast; 8 months'
maturation with occasional stirring. The relatively rich stone fruit flavours are
dominant, not oak; there may be a touch of residual sugar, but either way, it has a
generous mouthfeel and finish. Screwcap. 13.5% alc. **Rating** 88 **To** 2014 $23
Beverford Shiraz 2010 Has abundant fruit, oak and tannins, and just a hint
of sweetness for broad appeal. Ready now for casual consumption. Screwcap.
13.5% alc. **Rating** 87 **To** 2014 $15

Bullock Creek Vineyard

111 Belvoir Park Road, Ravenswood North, Vic 3453 **Region** Bendigo
T (03) 5435 3207 **Open** W'ends & public hols 11–6, or by appt
Winemaker Bob Beischer **Est.** 1978 **Dozens** 200 **Vyds** 2ha
Bob and Margit Beischer purchased the well-established vineyard (and surrounding land) in
1998, initially selling the grapes to Bendigo TAFE, where Bob was undertaking viticultural
and winemaking studies, and seeing their grapes vinified. The long-term plan was to build
their own winery, and this was completed for the 2006 vintage. The estate-grown wines are
released under the Bullock Creek Vineyard label; the Bullock Creek Wines label is for those
made incorporating some locally grown grapes.

Single Vineyard Bendigo Shiraz 2010 Deep, dense, purple-crimson; quite
how such depth of colour and flavour could be achieved at this alcohol level I
don't know; I suspect it might be higher. It has absorbed the French and American
oak in which it was matured, and more than a few will enjoy its old-fashioned
style. Diam. 12% alc. **Rating** 90 **To** 2020 $30

Marong Shiraz 2008 Rating 87 **To** 2015 $25

Bulong Estate

70 Summerhill Road, Yarra Junction, Vic 3797 (postal) **Region** Yarra Valley
T (03) 5967 1358 **www**.bulongestate.com.au **Open** 7 days 11–4
Winemaker Matt Carter **Est.** 1994 **Dozens** 2000 **Vyds** 31ha
Judy and Howard Carter's beautifully situated 45ha property looks down into the valley
below and across to the nearby ranges, with Mt Donna Buang at their peak. Most of the
grapes from the immaculately tended vineyard are sold, with limited quantities made onsite
for the Bulong Estate label. The Bulong Estate restaurant, sharing the views, is open Fri–Sun.
Exports to China.

Yarra Valley Chardonnay 2011 Light straw-green; whereas the Sauvignon
Blanc lacked intensity, this Chardonnay is at the opposite end of the spectrum; the
French (Dijon) clones have given excellent results in the Yarra Valley, and this is a
good example. The varietal fruit has absorbed the barrel ferment in French oak,
the white peach and citrus fruits thus given free play on the long and pure palate.
Screwcap. 12% alc. **Rating** 94 **To** 2018 $26

Yarra Valley Cabernet Sauvignon 2010 Rating 93 **To** 2022 $24

Bundaleer Wines

PO Box 41, Hove, SA 5048 **Region** Southern Flinders Ranges
T (08) 8294 7011 **www**.bundaleerwines.com.au **Open** At North Star Hotel, Melrose
and Little Red Grape, Sevenhill
Winemaker Angela Meaney **Est.** 1998 **Dozens** 3500 **Vyds** 7ha
Bundaleer is a joint venture between the Meaney and Spurling families, situated in an area
known as Bundaleer Gardens, on the edge of the Bundaleer Forest, 200km north of Adelaide.
The red wines are produced from estate plantings (equal quantities of shiraz and cabernet
sauvignon are planted), the white wines from purchased grapes from the Clare Valley. Exports
to Taiwan, China and Hong Kong.

Stony Place Clare Valley Riesling 2012 Has the crystal clear varietal
expression expected from the very good vintage, with delicious lime juice and
lemon zest built around a framework of crisp, bright acidity. Great value. WAK
screwcap. 12% alc. **Rating** 93 **To** 2020 $18

Golden Spike Clare Valley Pinot Gris 2012 Rating 87 To 2014 $18
North Star Southern Flinders Ranges Rose 2012 Rating 87 To 2014 $18

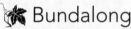 Bundalong

1 Pembroke Street, College Park, SA 5069 **Region** Coonawarra
T 0419 815 925 **www**.bundalongcoonawarra.com.au **Open** Not
Winemaker Andrew Hardy, Peter Bissell **Est.** 1990 **Dozens** 1000 **Vyds** 65ha
The Porter family, headed by James Porter, has been the owner of the Bundalong property for
many years. In the second half of the 1980s, encouraged by an old shallow limestone quarry
on the property, James sought opinions from local grapegrowers about the suitability of the
soil for grapegrowing. Not surprisingly, the answer was yes, and so in '89 the first plantings of
cabernet sauvignon were made, followed some years later by shiraz. The primary purpose of
the 65ha vineyard was to supply grapes to major companies, and Southcorp and its successors
(now TWE) have been long-term purchasers. Trial vintages were made in 1994 and '96,
followed by the first serious vintage in 2008, with both Cabernet Sauvignon and Shiraz made
by Andrew Hardy, Petaluma's chief winemaker. The strategy has been only to make wine in
the very best vintages in Coonawarra, with the '08 the current vintage, and the next in line
to come from '12.

Coonawarra Shiraz 2008 Still has a dense purple-crimson colour; a supple and
rich medium- to full-bodied Shiraz, its black fruits embellished by 18 months in
French oak and perfectly ripened tannins. Enjoyable now or in 10–20 years' time.
Screwcap. 14.5% alc. **Rating** 94 **To** 2030 $25
Coonawarra Cabernet Sauvignon 2008 Densely coloured; a plush, velvety,
multilayered and rich wine, with black fruits, a dash of dark chocolate, quality
oak and ripe, almost fleshy, tannins – echoes of Wynns John Riddoch. Screwcap.
14.5% alc. **Rating** 94 **To** 2038 $25

Bunkers Margaret River Wines

1142 Kaloorup Road, Kaloorup, WA 6280 **Region** Margaret River
T (08) 9368 4555 **www**.bunkerswines.com.au **Open** Not
Winemaker Brian Fletcher **Est.** 1997 **Dozens** 3500 **Vyds** 34ha
Over the past 20+ years, Mike Calneggia has had his fingers in innumerable Margaret River
viticultural pies. He has watched some ventures succeed, others fail, and while Bunkers Wines
(owned by Mike and Sally Calneggia) is only a small part of his viticultural undertakings, it
has been carefully targeted from the word go. It has the five mainstream varieties (cabernet,
semillon, merlot, chardonnay and shiraz), joined by one rising star, tempranillo, in the warm
and relatively fertile northern part of the Margaret River. He has secured the services of the
immensely experienced Brian Fletcher as winemaker, and Murray Edmonds as viticulturist
(both formerly at Evans & Tate). Mike and daughter Amy are responsible for sales and
marketing. They say, 'The world of wine is full of serious people making serious wines for an

ever-decreasing serious market … Bunkers wines have been created to put the "F" word back into wine: "FUN", that is.' Exports to Canada and Hong Kong.

ŢŢŢŢŢ **Lefthanders Sauvignon Blanc Semillon 2012** Pale quartz-green; a well-balanced and well-made wine, with a harmonious mix of citrus/lemon and fresh-cut grass; good length and finish. Screwcap. 13% alc. **Rating** 91 **To** 2015 $20
Guillotines Shiraz 2011 Striking purple-crimson; there's a lot of wine at this price, with plum, black cherry, oak and tannins all having an equal say on the medium-bodied palate. Does need time to settle down. Screwcap. 14.5% alc. **Rating** 90 **To** 2018 $20
The Box Tempranillo 2011 Good hue; a very savoury, earthy, dark-visioned interpretation of tempranillo, and quite different from most eastern states' tempranillos, with the tannins on the finish a reprise of the bouquet and fore-palate. Screwcap. 14.5% alc. **Rating** 90 **To** 2017 $20

ŢŢŢŢ **Windmills Shiraz Tempranillo Rose 2012** **Rating** 89 **To** 2014 $22

Bunnamagoo Estate ★★★★★

603 Henry Lawson Drive, Mudgee, NSW 2850 **Region** Mudgee
T 1300 304 707 **www**.bunnamagoowines.com.au **Open** 7 days 10–4
Winemaker Robert Black **Est.** 1995 **Dozens** 50 000 **Vyds** 108ha
Bunnamagoo Estate (on one of the first land grants in the region) is situated near the historic town of Rockley. Here a 6ha vineyard planted to chardonnay, merlot and cabernet sauvignon has been established by Paspaley Pearls, a famous name in the WA pearl industry. The winery and cellar door are located at the much larger (and warmer) Eurunderee vineyard (102ha) at Mudgee. Exports to the US and China.

ŢŢŢŢŢ **Semillon 2011** The tactic of fermenting the wine in a mix of used French
✪ barriques and hogsheads, followed by 3 months on lees, has succeeded brilliantly, leaving the focus on the lemon/citrus fruit, but adding a subliminal inflexion to the palate and lingering finish. Screwcap. 11% alc. **Rating** 94 **To** 2025 $22
1827 Handpicked Cabernet Sauvignon 2010 1827 was the year in which Paspaley's Rockley property was settled, and it (1827) will only be used for exceptional wines. This is a blend of grapes from the Mudgee and Rockley vineyards; it spent 20 months in new and used French oak, but it is the juicy cassis/blackcurrant fruit that does the talking; the tannins are firm, but no more, the oak likewise balanced. Diam. 13.5% alc. **Rating** 94 **To** 2030 $50

ŢŢŢŢŢ **Sauvignon Blanc Semillon 2012** Pale straw-green; a very attractive blend
✪ sourced from the Central Ranges Zone, which hides a multitude of sins (a time-honoured figure of speech), neatly encompassing a melange of citrus, stone fruit and tropical fruits, with a crisp and lively finish. Top value. Screwcap. 12% alc. **Rating** 93 **To** 2015 $22
✪ **Cabernet Sauvignon 2011** Deep purple-crimson; the destemmed (not crushed) fruit was stainless steel-fermented, then matured for 15 months in new and used French oak; this has worked well. The medium-bodied blackcurrant and earth fruit of the palate has firm tannins, and the oak has done its part well. Will cellar well. Screwcap. 13.5% alc. **Rating** 91 **To** 2025 $24

Burch Family Wines ★★★★★

Miamup Road, Cowaramup, WA 6284 **Region** Margaret River/Denmark
T (08) 9756 5200 **www**.burchfamilywines.com.au **Open** 7 days 10–5
Winemaker Janice McDonald, Mark Bailey **Est.** 1986 **Dozens** NFP **Vyds** 163.5ha
This is the renamed Howard Park, which has two vineyards: Leston in the Margaret River, and Mt Barrow in Mount Barker; it also manages three vineyards, taking the grapes from these. It practises mainly organic viticulture in its owned and managed vineyards, Mt Barrow with a pinot noir block established and operated using biodynamic practices. The Margaret River winery incorporates feng shui principles, and can welcome large groups for concerts, speaking

events, film evenings and private parties. Burch Family Wines also operates a cellar door at Scotsdale Road, Denmark (7 days 10–4). The Margaret River flagships are the Leston Shiraz and Leston Cabernet Sauvignon, but the Margaret River vineyards routinely contribute to all the wines in the range, from multi-region MadFish at the bottom, to the iconic Cabernet Sauvignon Merlot at the top. MadFish is a second label, itself with three price tiers: MadFish Gold Turtle, Sideways and (the original) MadFish. Exports to all major markets.

ŶŶŶŶŶ **Howard Park Porongurup Riesling 2012** Some development evident in the straw-green colour, but this is a positive virtue given the intensity and complexity of the power of the lime and lemon palate, power amplified by the lingering acidity. Slightly atypical for Porongurup, offering much now. Screwcap. 12% alc. **Rating** 96 To 2022 $30

Howard Park Great Southern Riesling 2012 Bright, gleaming straw-green; filled with juicy lime fruit and crisp, crunchy acidity, the length a given; the aftertaste lingers, and echoes the flavours of the mid-palate. Lovely wine. Screwcap. 12% alc. **Rating** 96 To 2027 $30

Howard Park Chardonnay 2011 Light straw-green; an extremely elegant Chardonnay, wild yeast-fermented in French oak; the grapes were picked at precisely the right moment to allow the full range of varietal flavours to express themselves, and the new oak was also judged to perfection. Modern chardonnay style at its best. Screwcap. 13% alc. **Rating** 95 To 2023 $50

Howard Park Scotsdale Great Southern Shiraz 2011 Light to medium purple-red; a fragrant and lively wine that plays a symphony of red fruits, spice and a counterpoint of licorice; the tannins are fine, and line, length and balance are all impeccable. Screwcap. 14% alc. **Rating** 95 To 2026 $45

✪ **Howard Park Flint Rock Great Southern Shiraz 2010** Deep but bright purple-crimson; sourced from vineyards in the Frankland River and Mount Barker subregions of Great Southern; this is an intense and full-bodied shiraz with great balance to its panoply of black fruits, spice, licorice and oak flavours; the texture and balance guarantee a long life. Screwcap. 14% alc. **Rating** 95 To 2030 $27

✪ **MadFish Grandstand Great Southern Riesling 2012** Pale, bright hue; a seductive bouquet and palate offering sweet lime, apple and a touch of bath talc make for a palate providing as much pleasure today as it will in 5–10 years time. Comprehensively over-delivers. Screwcap. 12% alc. **Rating** 94 To 2022 $20

Howard Park Miamup Margaret River Sauvignon Blanc Semillon 2012 **Rating** 94 To 2018 $27

ŶŶŶŶŶ **Howard Park Sauvignon Blanc 2012** **Rating** 93 To 2014 $29

✪ **MadFish Sideways Margaret River Sauvignon Blanc Semillon 2012** Pale quartz; the expressive bouquet opens the curtains on an even more expressive palate with intense green pea, citrus peel, kiwifruit and passionfruit, finishing with good acidity. Screwcap. 13% alc. **Rating** 93 To 2014 $22

MadFish Gold Turtle Margaret River Semillon Sauvignon Blanc 2012 **Rating** 93 To 2016 $25

✪ **MadFish Sideways Margaret River Chardonnay 2012** Whether oak has or has not played a role in shaping this wine doesn't matter, for its fruit-driven bouquet and palate have energy and length; grapefruit leads the way, white peach next in line, the finish long and satisfying. Screwcap. 13% alc. **Rating** 93 To 2016 $22

MadFish Gold Turtle Chardonnay 2012 **Rating** 93 To 2019 $25

Howard Park Miamup Margaret River Chardonnay 2011 **Rating** 93 To 2018 $27

Howard Park Leston Margaret River Shiraz 2011 **Rating** 93 To 2026 $45

✪ **MadFish Sideways Margaret River Shiraz 2010** Good colour; stacked with flavour contributed more or less equally by fruit, oak and tannins, so much so you have to wonder whether the over-delivery against its price (with discounting down to $20) isn't over the top. A quaint proposition, I realise. Screwcap. 14% alc. **Rating** 92 To 2025 $22

MadFish Sideways Margaret River Cabernet Sauvignon Merlot 2010
Rating 92 To 2020 $22

MadFish Gold Turtle Margaret River Shiraz 2011 Rating 91 To 2020 $25

✪ **MadFish Grandstand Shiraz 2010** Strong purple-crimson; a lot on display for a wine at this price, with black fruits, morello cherry, spice and robust tannins all contributing. Screwcap. 14% alc. Rating 91 To 2020 $20

Howard Park Miamup Margaret River Cabernet Sauvignon 2010
Rating 91 To 2016 $27

✪ **MadFish Sauvignon Blanc Semillon 2012** Bright green-straw; has the full package of tropical fruits (guava, kiwifruit and passionfruit among many); fills the palate with its generosity. Screwcap. 13% alc. Rating 90 To 2014 $18

Howard Park Flint Rock Great Southern Pinot Noir 2011 Rating 90 To 2014 $27

✪ **MadFish Grandstand Great Southern Pinot Noir 2011** Light red; marks another stage in the development of pinot noir in the Great Southern; red and black cherry fruit has clear varietal character, and is supported by fine, but persistent, tannins. Great value. Screwcap. 13.5% alc. Rating 90 To 2016 $20

MadFish Vera's Cuvee Methode Traditionnelle NV Rating 90 To 2015 $25

Burk Salter Wines

72 Paisley Road, Blanchetown, SA 5357 **Region** Riverland
T (08) 8540 5023 **www.**burksalterwines.com.au **Open** W'ends & public hols 11–4.30
Winemaker Peter Gajewski, Eric and Jenny Semmler **Est.** 2002 **Dozens** 3000 **Vyds** 20.4ha
The husband-and-wife team of Gregory Burk Salter and Jane Vivienne Salter is the third generation of the Salter family to grow grapes at their Blanchetown property. They have a little over 20ha of chardonnay, semillon, colombard, ruby cabernet, shiraz, merlot, cabernet sauvignon and muscat gordo blanco; 450 tonnes are sold each year, the remaining 50 tonnes contract-made at various small Barossa Valley wineries. The cellar door and a self-contained B&B adjoin the vineyard, which has Murray River frontage.

♀♀♀♀♀ **Cabernet Sauvignon 2010** Medium to full purple-crimson; an enthusiastic
✪ helping of vanillin oak invests the flavours with a sweetness of plum and fruitcake, belied by its modest alcohol. Cassis does make a comeback on the finish, and this wine will have plenty of admirers at its price. Screwcap. 13% alc. Rating 90 To 2015 $16

♀♀♀♀ **Shiraz 2010** A very pleasant wine, with cherry, red berry, vanilla and coconut
✪ flavours plus a dab of oak, the tannins fine but sufficient. Ready for immediate consumption on casual occasions. Screwcap. 12.8% alc. Rating 88 To 2014 $16

Merlot 2010 Rating 88 To 2016 $16

Sparkling Red 2010 Rating 88 To 2014 $15

Muscat Gordo Blanco 2012 Rating 87 To 2013 $12

Burke & Wills Winery

3155 Burke & Wills Track, Mia Mia, Vic 3444 **Region** Heathcote
T (03) 5425 5400 **www.**wineandmusic.net **Open** By appt
Winemaker Andrew Pattison, Robert Ellis **Est.** 2003 **Dozens** 1500 **Vyds** 3.4ha
After 18 years at Lancefield Winery in the Macedon Ranges, Andrew Pattison moved his operation a few miles north in 2004 to set up Burke & Wills Winery at the southern edge of Heathcote, continuing to produce wines from both regions. With vineyards at Mia Mia and Redesdale, he now has 2ha of shiraz, 1ha of cabernet sauvignon and Bordeaux varieties and 0.4ha of gewurztraminer. He still sources a small amount of Macedon Ranges fruit from his former Malmsbury vineyard; additional grapes are contract-grown in Heathcote.

♀♀♀♀♀ **Mia Mia Heathcote Gewurztraminer 2012** Pale quartz; has rose petal and spice varietal aromas in greater abundance than most Australian examples, and good length into the bargain. Screwcap. 13% alc. Rating 93 To 2018 $25

Vat 1 French Oak Heathcote Shiraz 2010 Has retained good hue; estate-grown, hand-picked, open-fermented, basket-pressed and matured in new and used French oak for 20 months; the red-berried bouquet leads into a supple, medium-bodied palate with black cherry and plum sewn through fine, gently savoury tannins. Controlled winemaking with attention to detail. Screwcap. 13.5% alc. **Rating** 90 **To** 2020 $32

♀♀♀♀   **The Aristocrat Heathcote Cabernet Merlot 2009** **Rating** 89 **To** 2015 $35

Burnbrae   ★★★☆

548 Hill End Road, Mudgee, NSW 2850 **Region** Mudgee
T (02) 6373 3504 **www**.burnbraewines.com.au **Open** Mon–Sat 9–5, Sun 9–4
Winemaker Frank Newman **Est.** 1968 **Dozens** 4500 **Vyds** 16ha
Tony and Jill Bryant were broadacre farmers who had a long-held dream of having a vineyard and winery. Following the sale of the family farm in the 1990s Tony studied viticulture and marketing, and went on to manage wineries in the Mudgee area before starting his own viticultural consultancy business. In 2004 he and Jill were able to take the final step by purchasing Burnbrae, and acquiring the services of industry veteran Frank Newman as winemaker. Burnbrae also provides contract winemaking services for others, and Tony is currently president of the Mudgee Wine and Grape Growers Association. Exports to Singapore.

♀♀♀♀♀   **Mudgee Chardonnay 2011** Deep colour, showing ripe fig, grapefruit and wood spice aromas on the bouquet; the palate is rich on entry, yet light on its feet as the concentrated fruit and fine chalky acidity provide freshness and elongation of flavour on the finish. Screwcap. 12.8% alc. **Rating** 91 **To** 2017 $20 BE

♀♀♀♀   **Mudgee Shiraz Viognier 2011** **Rating** 88 **To** 2018 $25 BE
Mudgee Sangiovese 2011 **Rating** 87 **To** 2015 $20 BE

By Farr/Farr Rising   ★★★★★

27 Maddens Road, Bannockburn, Vic 3331 **Region** Geelong
T (03) 5281 1733 **www**.byfarr.com.au **Open** Not
Winemaker Nick Farr **Est.** 1994 **Dozens** 5500 **Vyds** 13.8ha
By Farr, and Farr Rising, continue to be separate brands from separate vineyards, the one major change from previous years being that Nick Farr has assumed total responsibility for both labels, leaving father Gary free to pursue the finer things in life without interruption. This has in no way resulted in any diminution in the quality of the Pinot Noir, Chardonnay, Shiraz and Viognier made by Nick. Exports to the UK, Canada, Denmark, Sweden, Hong Kong, Singapore, Taiwan, the Maldives, China and Japan.

♀♀♀♀♀   **Farrside by Farr Geelong Pinot Noir 2011** The colour has a touch more purple in the hue than Farr Rising, although is no deeper; here black/dark fruits make their presence felt on the bouquet and double that impact on the palate, the flavours reverberating continuously through to the aftertaste. This is the most powerful of the three '11 Farr pinots. For release Jul/Aug '13. Cork. 13.5% alc. **Rating** 97 **To** 2021 $68
Sangreal by Farr Geelong Pinot Noir 2011 Similar hue and depth to Farrside; while perfumed, this is a deceptive wine, its power and intensity held in a silky sleeve, the fruit with both red and black flavours coursing along the palate; this is the most elegant of the three wines, each one of which is a triumph in any context, let alone that of '11. For release Jul/Aug '13. Cork. 13% alc. **Rating** 97 **To** 2021 $75
By Farr Geelong Chardonnay 2011 Pale straw-green; this is an object lesson for those making chardonnay in a vintage like '11, or any vintage for that matter; there is a beautiful harmony to the stone fruit, melon and fig fruit flavours, the quality French oak, and the mouthfeel. However, as the makers of the greatest white Burgundies have discovered to their cost, and Brian Croser with Tiers Chardonnay, using cork with chardonnay is Russian roulette. 13% alc. **Rating** 96 **To** 2015 $68

Tout Pres by Farr Pinot Noir 2010 Exceptionally deep colour, still in its primary phase; this is an impressively rich and complex wine, with every sort of plum imaginable crammed into its palate. If it had a screwcap, or even a Diam, I would give it an even longer cellaring future. Cork. 13.5% alc. **Rating** 96 To 2025 $110

By Farr Geelong Shiraz 2010 Light to medium purple-crimson, only marginally deeper than the '11; a more conventional cool-grown shiraz, but of the highest quality; spice, pepper, licorice, plum and cherry fruit fill the mouth, the flavours constantly changing places with each other, both tannins and oak in their due place. Cork. 13.5% alc. **Rating** 96 To 2030 $55

Farr Rising Geelong Chardonnay 2011 Rating 94 To 2015 $39
Farr Rising Geelong Saignee 2012 Rating 94 To 2015 $25
Farr Rising Geelong Pinot Noir 2011 Rating 94 To 2020 $42
Farr Rising Geelong Shiraz 2011 Rating 94 To 2025 $37

By Jingo! ★★★

Barker Road, Mount Barker, SA 5251 **Region** Various
T 0400 693 812 **www**.byjingowines.com **Open** By appt
Winemaker John Gilbert **Est.** 2011 **Dozens** 2000 **Vyds** 6.5ha

John Gilbert's interest in wine began while working in the pay TV industry; tasting a bottle of 1996 Kangarilla Road Old Vine Zinfandel in '97 led directly to purchasing a small block (1.5ha) overlooking Mount Barker township and partly planting it with zinfandel and shiraz. At the same time he studied at the University of Adelaide, Roseworthy Campus, graduating in 2000. With remarkable alacrity he left for vintages in Sicily and Alto Adige in '01; this fanned the flames, and he instigated the importation of grillo, and planted it and montepulciano, nero d'Avola and negro amaro on the Mount Barker plot. With equal alacrity he created a number of brands, including Jardim do Bomfim, with a production of 20000 dozen, and was able to sell this in early 2011 to concentrate on his alternative varieties, offered at attention-getting prices.

ᵽᵽᵽᵽ Murray Darling Grillo 2012 The justification for the price for the wine, made from 8-year-old vines, is the quantity made (65 dozen), and (apparently) the importation of the variety from Sicily. All barbs aside, the wine does have attractive grainy acidity and a savoury flavour. Screwcap. 13% alc. **Rating** 89 To 2014 $39

Dolce Dolce Adelaide Hills Fortified Shiraz 2007 How John Gilbert expects to sell what is a good vintage port-style Shiraz in this ridiculous bottle (a towering, thin 500ml bottle) and ridiculous label at this price I have not the slightest idea. Cork. 18.9% alc. **Rating** 89 To 2014 $40

Byrne Vineyards ★★★

PO Box 15, Kent Town BC, SA 5071 **Region** South Australia
T (08) 8132 0022 **www**.byrnevneyards.com.au **Open** Not
Winemaker Peter Gajewski, Phil Reedman **Est.** 1999 **Dozens** NFP **Vyds** 508.79ha

Byrne Vineyards is a family-owned wine business. The Byrne family has been involved in the SA wine industry for three generations, with vineyards spanning over 500ha in SA's prime wine-producing regions, including Clare Valley, Eden Valley, Adelaide Plains and Riverland. The vines vary from 20 to over 40 years of age. The portfolio includes Thomson Estate, Scotts Creek, Devlin's Mount, Boutique Wildflower and Karoola Ridge. Exports to the UK, Canada, Germany, Denmark, Sweden, Thailand, the Philippines, Singapore and China.

ᵽᵽᵽᵽ Criminal Minds Clyde Shiraz 2012 Deep garnet; a fresh and spicy bouquet, revealing blackberry, clove and saltbush; the palate is juicy, forward and uncomplicated. Screwcap. 14% alc. **Rating** 88 To 2016 $18 BE

Thomson Estate Back Blocks Clare Valley Cabernet Sauvignon 2009
A combination of red fruits and cool herbal notes, with geranium also evident on the bouquet; medium-bodied and savoury on the palate, with fine tannins and a moderately long finish. Screwcap. 14% alc. **Rating** 88 To 2016 $25 BE

Caillard Wine

5 Annesley Street, Leichhardt, NSW 2040 (postal) **Region** Barossa Valley
T 0433 272 912 **www.**caillardwine.com **Open** Not
Winemaker Dr Chris Taylor, Andrew Caillard MW **Est.** 2008 **Dozens** 400
Andrew Caillard MW has had a long and varied career in wine, including vintage work at
Brokenwood and elsewhere, but has only just taken the final step of making his own wine,
with the support of wife Bobby. Andrew says the inspiration to make Mataro came while
writing the background for the various editions of the Penfolds' The Rewards of Patience
tastings. Apart from anything else, he learnt that both Max Schubert and John Davoren had
experimented with the variety, and that the original releases of Penfolds St Henri included
a fair percentage of mataro. For good measure, Andrew's great (times four) grandfather, John
Reynell, planted one of Australia's first vineyards: at Reynella, around 1838.

Mataro 2011 Tasted in conjunction with the '08, '09 and '10 vintage wines, and
very much in the Caillard Mataro family. The wine is most attractive, more so than
the three older vintages were at this stage. This makes it as much a drink-now as
drink-later proposition, its bevy of red fruits cosseted by silky tannins and subtle
oak. Screwcap. 14% alc. **Rating** 94 **To** 2017 $45
Mataro 2010 Youthful, light crimson-purple; the promise of the colour is
delivered on the juicy, red-berried flavours of the palate, that of the reputation
of the variety in the savoury tannins on the finish – tannins that have exemplary
balance. Screwcap. 13.6% alc. **Rating** 94 **To** 2018 $45

Calais Estate ★★★

Palmers Lane, Pokolbin, NSW 2321 **Region** Hunter Valley
T (02) 4998 7654 **www.**calaiswines.com.au **Open** 7 days 9–5
Winemaker Adrian Sheridan **Est.** 1987 **Dozens** 12 000 **Vyds** 30ha
Richard and Susan Bradley purchased the substantial Calais Estate in 2000. Long-serving
winemaker Adrian Sheridan continues his role, and the estate offers a wide range of facilities
for visitors, ranging from private function rooms to picnic spots, to an undercover outdoor
entertaining area. The winery specialises in the sale of back vintages. Exports to China
and NZ.

Reserve Cabernet Sauvignon 2009 Some colour development is as it should
be; the wine has the earthy, leathery characters of traditional Hunter Valley red
wines of bygone decades, and which are far from unpleasant. Likewise, the soft,
persistent tannins are well integrated, but add to that feeling of déjà vu. Screwcap.
13% alc. **Rating** 89 **To** 2019 $55
Hunter Valley Petit Verdot 2008 The inherent power and tannin strength of
petit verdot makes it a warrior in many places and climates – as here. Its colour
is still good, and the black fruits at its heart are keeping pace with the tannins.
Screwcap. 14% alc. **Rating** 89 **To** 2015 $29

Caledonia Australis/Mount Macleod

PO Box 626, North Melbourne, Vic 3051 **Region** Gippsland
T (03) 9329 5372 **www.**caledoniaaustralis.com **Open** Not
Winemaker Mark Matthews **Est.** 1995 **Dozens** 4500 **Vyds** 16.18ha
In November 2009 Mark and Marianna Matthews acquired Caledonia Australis, but there has
been no change in the pre-existing management arrangements, notwithstanding the skills the
Matthews bring to the table. Mark is a winemaker with vintages in numerous wine regions
around the world; he works as a winemaking teacher at NMIT, and also runs a contract
winemaking business specialising in small high-quality batches. Marianna has extensive
experience with major fast-moving consumer goods brands globally. The Matthews have
converted the main chardonnay block to certified organic, and are rehabilitating around 8ha
of wetlands with the local catchment authority. Exports to Canada and Japan.

ỹỹỹỹỹ Caledonia Australis Gippsland Chardonnay 2010 Green-straw; wild yeast barrel-fermented in French oak, followed by lees ageing for 18 month; an elegant, beautifully balanced and very long palate; a mix of white peach, melon and some citrus easily accounts for the oak. Screwcap. 12.8% alc. **Rating** 94 **To** 2016 $30
Caledonia Australis Gippsland Pinot Noir 2010 Light to medium red-purple, bright and clear; whole berry (destemmed) fruit was cold-soaked for 7 days, then wild yeast fermented for 2 weeks. The approach worked well, as the wine has very attractive plum, cherry and spice fruit that is 100% ripe; the palate is long and well balanced. Screwcap. 12.6% alc. **Rating** 94 **To** 2017 $30

ỹỹỹỹỹ Caledonia Australis Gippsland Pinot Noir 2009 **Rating** 90 **To** 2017 $32

ỹỹỹỹ
✪ Mount Macleod Pinot Noir 2012 Strong red-purple; borders on full-bodied 'dry red' territory; certainly powerful and deep, with black cherry fruit, saved on the finish by an injection of juicy fruit and fine tannins. Will develop, possibly very well. Screwcap. 12.5% alc. **Rating** 89 **To** 2016 $20

🍇 Calico Town Wines   NR

The Wicked Virgin, 165 Hopetoun Road, Rutherglen, Vic 3685 **Region** Rutherglen
T 0438 404 512 **www**.thewickedvirgin.com.au **Open** Thurs–Mon 10–5
Winemaker Andrew Briedis, John Nowacki **Est.** 1999 **Dozens** 500 **Vyds** 4ha
The small vineyard, with the titillating name The Wicked Virgin, has been established by John and Laurel Nowacki. The 3ha of shiraz and 1ha of durif are accompanied by an olive grove. Calico Town is a reference to the goldrush days when numerous miners lived in canvas tents – the property still has mine shafts and a poppet head that stands guard over the cellar door and olive grove.

Camp Road Estate   ★★★

165 Camp Road, Greta, NSW 2334 **Region** Hunter Valley
T (02) 4938 6272 **www**.camproadestate.com.au **Open** Not
Winemaker David Hook, Adrian Sheridan **Est.** 1998 **Dozens** NFP **Vyds** 2.5ha
Duncan and Libby Thomson, cardiac surgeon and cardiac scrub nurse, respectively, say Heartland Vineyard is the result of a seachange that got a little out of hand. 'After looking one weekend at some property in the Hunter Valley to escape the Sydney rat-race, we stumbled upon the beautiful 90 acres that has become our vineyard.' They have built a rammed-earth house on the property, and the vineyard is now a little over 5ha, with shiraz, semillon, merlot, barbera, verdelho and viognier.

ỹỹỹỹ
✪ Anodyne Vineyard Sparkling Shiraz 2009 The base fruit in the wine was clearly good, and had it been left on lees for longer (minimum 2 years) could have made a high-quality sparkling Shiraz. As it is, time on cork has allowed it to flesh out, and will continue to do so for the few who have been canny enough to buy it (the dosage was well judged). Crown seal. 13.5% alc. **Rating** 89 **To** 2019 $17
Anodyne Vineyard Shiraz Viognier 2011 A pleasant light- to medium-bodied wine with soft fruit flavours; I suspect the 'small addition' of viognier was a post-fermentation blend, and 'small' must mean at least 5%. Screwcap. 13% alc. **Rating** 87 **To** 2014 $15
Anodyne Vineyard Merlot 2011 Light colour, though good hue; the Hunter Valley is a hostile environment for merlot, but apart from a hint of sweetness on the finish, this is a good response with its pleasant red fruits. Screwcap. 14.5% alc. **Rating** 87 **To** 2014 $14
Anodyne Vineyard Barbera 2011 Light red-purple; despite its alcohol, a light-bodied red with cherry and spice fruit; its varietal parentage is arguably the most interesting part of a competently made wine, and, like all of the Camp Road wines, fairly priced. Screwcap. 14.3% alc. **Rating** 87 **To** 2014 $15

Campbells ★★★★★

Murray Valley Highway, Rutherglen, Vic 3685 **Region** Rutherglen
T (02) 6033 6000 **www**.campbellswines.com.au **Open** Mon–Sat 9–5, Sun 10–5
Winemaker Colin Campbell, Tim Gniel **Est.** 1870 **Dozens** 36 000 **Vyds** 72ha

Campbells has a long and rich history, with five generations of the family making wine over 140 years. There were difficult times: phylloxera's arrival in the Bobbie Burns Vineyard in 1898 and the Depression of the 1930s. But the Scottish blood of founder John Campbell has ensured that the business has not only survived, but quietly flourished. Indeed, there have been spectacular successes in unexpected quarters (white table wines, especially Riesling) and expected success with Muscat and Topaque. 99-point scores from Robert Parker and a 100-point score from Harvey Steiman (*Wine Spectator*) put Campbells in a special position, dramatically underlined by its Merchant Prince Rare Muscat receiving trophies in 2008 and '10 from the Rutherglen Wine Show as Best Australian Fortified Wine and Best Australian Muscat. It is fair to say that the nigh-on half-century fourth-generation stewardship of Malcolm and Colin Campbell has been the most important in the history of the winery, but the five members of the fifth generation all working in various capacities in the business are well equipped to move up the ladder when Colin and/or Malcolm decide to retire. Exports to the UK, the US and other major markets.

🍷🍷🍷🍷🍷 **Isabella Rare Topaque NV** Deep burnt amber and olive on the rim; exceptionally luscious, intense and rich, its density more like very old Seppelt Paras, but with the unique topaque suite of flavours. Impossible to resist; espresso coffee and walnuts would be a great match. 375ml. Screwcap. 18% alc. **Rating** 98 To 2014 $135

Merchant Prince Rare Muscat NV As with the Isabella Topaque, is more viscous and more luscious than its peers, with the most complex array of flavours adding to the usual raisin, burnt toffee and hints of tar. 375ml. Cork. 18% alc. **Rating** 97 To 2014 $135

Grand Rutherglen Topaque NV Deep olive-brown, especially on the rim; gloriously intense and complex, yet satin smooth; burnt honey/toffee carries the spice and Christmas cake mid-palate, followed by a lovely drying, nutty, aftertaste. 375ml. Cork. 17.5% alc. **Rating** 96 To 2014 $65

Grand Rutherglen Muscat NV Mahogany-brown; high-toned aromas of raisin, multi-spice, the palate very complex, with spice, rancio and sheer richness competing with each other; great balance and length. 375ml. Cork. 17.5% alc. **Rating** 95 To 2014 $65

Liquid Gold Classic Rutherglen Topaque NV Obvious age – all the red/brown colours of youth have gone; the flavours and bouquet are classic butterscotch, tea leaf and Christmas cake. The mouthfeel, too, is rich and luscious. Screwcap. 17.5% alc. **Rating** 94 To 2014 $42

🍷🍷🍷🍷♀ ✪ **Rutherglen Topaque NV** An outstanding wine at this bottom-of-the-range category; bright, light amber; it has great detail to its mix of honey, tea leaf, toffee and cake on the back-palate and a very lively finish. The only problem is a half-bottle won't be big enough. 375ml. Screwcap. 17.5% alc. **Rating** 93 To 2014 $19

Classic Rutherglen Muscat NV Rating 93 To 2014 $42
Limited Release Rutherglen Roussanne 2012 Rating 92 To 2027 $25
Bobbie Burns Rutherglen Shiraz 2011 Rating 92 To 2020 $22
The Barkly Rutherglen Durif 2010 Rating 92 To 2035 $54
Limited Release Rutherglen Durif 2010 Rating 92 To 2035 $28

✪ **Rutherglen Muscat NV** Light, vibrant colour; the palate is crammed with a mix of raisins, burnt toffee and glacé fruits, the finish long and harmonious. Screwcap. 17.5% alc. **Rating** 92 To 2014 $19

The Sixties Block 2011 Rating 90 To 2018 $28
Rutherglen Sparkling Shiraz NV Rating 90 To 2016 $30

Cannibal Creek Vineyard ★★★★

260 Tynong North Road, Tynong North, Vic 3813 **Region** Gippsland
T (03) 5942 8380 **www**.cannibalcreek.com.au **Open** 7 days 11–5
Winemaker Patrick Hardiker **Est.** 1997 **Dozens** 3000 **Vyds** 5ha

Patrick and Kirsten Hardiker moved to Tynong North in 1988, initially grazing beef cattle, but aware of the viticultural potential of their sandy clay loam and bleached subsurface soils, weathered from the granite foothills of the Black Snake Ranges. Plantings began in 1997, using organically based cultivation methods; varieties include pinot noir, chardonnay, sauvignon blanc, merlot and cabernet sauvignon. The family decided to make its own wine, and established the winery in an old farm barn built in the early 1900s by the Weatherhead family, with timber from Weatherhead Hill (visible from the vineyard). It also houses the cellar door. Exports to Hong Kong.

🍷🍷🍷🍷🍷 **Pinot Noir 2010** Mid crimson and bright; the bouquet offers an exotic array of game, dark fruits, spices and a hint of charry oak; the palate is fleshy and deep, full of character and fine-grained tannins, and vibrancy is the key both for today and the future. Screwcap. 13.4% alc. **Rating** 93 **To** 2017 $30 BE

Sauvignon Blanc 2012 A vibrant and fresh bouquet of cut grass and gooseberry, offset by exotic guava notes and chalky complexity; the palate is textured, revealing layers of flavour and some clever winemaking; this style of Sauvignon should be a welcome alternative to more conventional examples of the variety. Screwcap. 12% alc. **Rating** 92 **To** 2016 $28 BE

Merlot 2010 Deep garnet, bright; the bouquet offers dark cherry, plum and cedar; the palate is medium-bodied, and reveals fine-grained tannins and lively acidity; youthful now and should remain so for a few years. Screwcap. 13.5% alc. **Rating** 90 **To** 2018 $28 BE

🍷🍷🍷🍷 **Chardonnay 2010** **Rating** 89 **To** 2016 $28 BE

Capanno ★★★★

PO Box 1310, Double Bay, NSW 1360 **Region** Southern Highlands
T 0417 569 544 **www**.capanno.com.au **Open** Not
Winemaker Eden Road Wines (Nick Spencer) **Est.** 2004 **Dozens** 230 **Vyds** 1.2ha

This is the weekend and holiday retreat of Cameron Jones and Jody Williams. Capanno is the Italian word for 'shed', and is an allusion to the series of architect-designed (almost industrial) pavilions that together make up the house. The vineyard was planted close to and around the house, a foreground to the mountains beyond which, in their words, 'provide a fantastic backdrop for afternoon drinks around the bocce court with great friends'. The vineyard gives equal space to pinot gris and pinot noir clones 115 and 777. The wines are contract-made by one of the best young winemakers around, and grown with the help of an expert viticulturist. Notwithstanding the small production, the wines are sold to restaurants and wine bars in Sydney, Melbourne and Canberra.

🍷🍷🍷🍷🍷 **Single Vineyard Pinot Noir 2011** Light red, early colour development; a fragrant red cherry and strawberry bouquet leads into a light-bodied, but well-balanced palate with gentle red berry and spice flavours, and just enough depth to satisfy. Drink soon. Screwcap. 12.2% alc. **Rating** 90 **To** 2015 $35

Cape Barren Wines ★★★★★

PO Box 738, North Adelaide, SA 5006 **Region** McLaren Vale
T (08) 8267 3292 **www**.capebarrenwines.com **Open** By appt
Winemaker Rob Dundon **Est.** 1999 **Dozens** 8500

Cape Barren was founded by Peter Matthews, who worked tirelessly to create wines of distinction from some of the oldest vineyards in McLaren Vale. Peter sold the business in late 2009 to Rob Dundon and Tom Adams, who together have amassed in excess of 50 years' experience in winemaking, viticulture and international sales. Wines are sourced from 3ha of 80–85-year-old grenache at Blewitt Springs, 4.5ha of 120-year-old unirrigated shiraz at McLaren Flat, and 4ha of chardonnay plus 3ha of sauvignon blanc in the Adelaide Hills. Exports to Canada, Switzerland, Vietnam, the Philippines, Taiwan, Hong Kong, Thailand, Japan and China.

ŦŦŦŦŦ **Old Vine Reserve Release McLaren Vale Shiraz 2010** Finer and more elegant than Native Goose, with a surge of juicy fruit flavours coursing through the mid-palate, tannins and oak perfectly balanced. Screwcap. 14.5% alc. **Rating** 96 To 2035 $40

ŦŦŦŦŦ **Silly Goose Adelaide Hills Sauvignon Blanc 2012 Rating** 90 To 2014 $17 BE
Native Goose Adelaide Hills Chardonnay 2011 Rating 90 To 2015 $23

Cape Bernier Vineyard ★★★★

230 Bream Creek Road, Bream Creek, Tas 7175 **Region** Southern Tasmania
T (03) 6253 5443 **www**.capebernier.com.au **Open** By appt
Winemaker Winemaking Tasmania (Julian Alcorso) **Est.** 1999 **Dozens** 1800 **Vyds** 4ha
Alastair Christie and family have established 2ha of pinot noir (including three Dijon clones), 1.4ha of chardonnay and 0.6ha of pinot gris on a north-facing slope overlooking historic Marion Bay. The property is not far from the Bream Creek vineyard, and is one of several developments in the region changing the land use from dairy and beef cattle to wine production and tourism. In 2010 Cape Bernier won the title 'Tasmanian Vineyard of the Year', an award conducted by the Royal Agricultural Society of Tasmania in association with the State Government and Wine Industry Tasmania. Exports to Singapore.

ŦŦŦŦŦ **Chardonnay 2011** Deep gold, green hue; the bouquet is full of meyer lemon, biscuit dough and grilled hazelnuts; the palate reveals taut acidity and a saline minerality that sits neatly alongside the moderately long grilled nut conclusion. Screwcap. 13% alc. **Rating** 90 To 2017 $34 BE
Pinot Noir 2011 Deep colour; the bouquet offers dark fruits, spiced plum and charry roasted meat aromas; the palate is big-boned and hefty, certainly at the big end of the pinot spectrum, and muscular to conclude. Needs time. Screwcap. 13.5% alc. **Rating** 90 To 2018 $34 BE

ŦŦŦŦ **Pinot Rose 2012 Rating** 89 To 2014 $30 BE
Pinot Gris 2012 Rating 88 To 2015 $30 BE

Cape Grace ★★★★☆

281 Fifty One Road, Cowaramup, WA 6284 **Region** Margaret River
T (08) 9755 5669 **www**.capegracewines.com.au **Open** 7 days 10–5
Winemaker Mark Messenger (Consultant) **Est.** 1996 **Dozens** 2000 **Vyds** 6.25ha
Cape Grace can trace its history back to 1875, when timber baron MC Davies settled at Karridale, building the Leeuwin lighthouse and founding the township of Margaret River; 120 years later, Robert and Karen Karri-Davies planted the vineyard to chardonnay, shiraz and cabernet sauvignon, with smaller amounts of merlot, semillon and chenin blanc. Robert is a self-taught viticulturist; Karen has over 15 years of international sales and marketing experience in the hospitality industry. Winemaking is carried out on the property; consultant Mark Messenger is a veteran of the Margaret River region. Exports to Singapore.

ŦŦŦŦŦ **Margaret River Cabernet Sauvignon 2010** Good colour; it has a mix of cassis fruit trimmed by notes of black olive, the medium-bodied palate long, restrained and balanced by fine, savoury tannins. Classy wine. 450 dozen made. Screwcap. 14% alc. **Rating** 94 To 2025 $48

ŦŦŦŦŦ **Margaret River Cabernet Franc 2011 Rating** 93 To 2021 $40

Cape Horn Vineyard

Stewarts Bridge Road, Echuca, Vic 3564 **Region** Goulburn Valley
T (03) 5480 6013 **www**.capehornvineyard.com.au **Open** 7 days 11–5
Winemaker Ian Harrison, John Ellis (Contract) **Est.** 1993 **Dozens** 3500 **Vyds** 11ha
The unusual name comes from a bend in the Murray River considered by riverboat owners of
the 19th century to resemble Cape Horn, which is depicted on the wine label. The property
was acquired by Echuca GP Dr Sue Harrison and her schoolteacher husband Ian in 1993.
Ian has progressively planted their vineyard to chardonnay (3ha), shiraz, cabernet sauvignon
(2ha each), durif, marsanne (1.5ha each) and zinfandel (1ha).

ΨΨΨΨΨ **Echuca Goulburn Valley Durif 2010** Durif has an amazing ability to produce
deep, vibrantly coloured wine when grown in the Riverland, together with a
well of luscious black fruits, and a soft but complete finish. Screwcap. 14.5% alc.
Rating 91 **To** 2018 $26

ΨΨΨΨ **Echuca Goulburn Valley Cabernet Sauvignon 2010 Rating** 89 **To** 2016 $22
Echuca Goulburn Valley Shiraz 2010 Rating 88 **To** 2015 $22
Goulburn Valley Primitivo 2010 Rating 87 **To** 2015 $26

Cape Jaffa Wines

459 Limestone Coast Road, Mount Benson via Robe, SA 5276 **Region** Mount Benson
T (08) 8768 5053 **www**.capejaffawines.com.au **Open** 7 days 10–5
Winemaker Anna and Derek Hooper **Est.** 1993 **Dozens** 12 000 **Vyds** 22.86ha
Cape Jaffa was the first of the Mount Benson wineries, and all of the production now comes
from the estate plantings, which include three major Bordeaux red varieties, plus shiraz,
chardonnay, sauvignon blanc, semillon and pinot gris. The winery, built from local rock,
crushes between 800 and 1000 tonnes a year, with a significant proportion used for contract
winemaking. In 2008 Cape Jaffa became a fully certified biodynamic vineyard; it has installed
solar panels to partly offset electricity usage. It received the Advantage SA Regional Award for
its sustainable initiatives in the Limestone Coast in both '09 and '10. It has also discontinued
the use of heavy glass bottles. Exports to the UK, Canada, Thailand, Cambodia, the Philippines,
Hong Kong and Singapore.

ΨΨΨΨΨ **La Lune Mount Benson Chardonnay 2012** Bright gleaming colour; it has
intense drive to its grapefruit, white peach and nectarine fruit. I do hope the cork
does not destroy the wine down the track, however 'natural' it may be. 13.5% alc.
Rating 94 **To** 2017 $38
La Lune Mount Benson Shiraz 2010 Purple-crimson; full-on biodynamic
practices, cloth labels and lunar-controlled picking are part and parcel of a rich,
medium- to full-bodied wine with plenty of oak in support; the overall texture and
structure is soft, making it accessible right now. 15% alc. **Rating** 94 **To** 2018 $45

ΨΨΨΨΨ **Epic Drop Limestone Coast Shiraz 2010 Rating** 93 **To** 2025 $35
Cabernet Sauvignon 2010 Rating 93 **To** 2020 $26
La Lune Mount Benson Semillon 2010 Rating 92 **To** 2016 $30 BE
La Lune Mount Benson Chardonnay 2011 Rating 91 **To** 2015 $35

ΨΨΨΨ
✪ **Waxed Lyrical Marsanne 2012** It is not complex, but does have some drive
to the mix of sweet citrus, honeysuckle and peach fruit; good acidity help its
definition and structure. Could be a major surprise for the few who will see what
happens with a few years in bottle. Screwcap. 13% alc. **Rating** 89 **To** 2016 $15

Cape Lodge Wines

Caves Road, Yallingup, WA 6282 (postal) **Region** Margaret River
T (08) 9755 6311 **www**.capelodge.com.au **Open** Not
Winemaker Liz Dawson **Est.** 1998 **Dozens** 1000 **Vyds** 3ha
Cape Lodge has evolved from a protea farm in the early 1980s, through a small luxury B&B
operation in '93 into a boutique hotel, via a multi-million dollar investment. This has resulted

in a plethora of awards since 2005; most recently, being voted one of the World's Best of Best Hotels '11, Best Boutique Hotel in Australia, and among the World's Top 20 Vineyard Hotels '10 and Condé Nast Traveller Gold List 'Best for Food' '11.

ŦŦŦŦŦ **Margaret River Sauvignon Blanc 2012** Light straw-green; made by the skilled and highly experienced Cliff Royle; he has focused all the attention on the delicious combination of citrus and passionfruit that fill the long, finely balanced palate. Screwcap. 12% alc. **Rating** 94 **To** 2015 $28

ŦŦŦŦŦ **Margaret River Shiraz 2010 Rating** 91 **To** 2025 $38

Cape Mentelle   ★★★★★
Wallcliffe Road, Margaret River, WA 6285 **Region** Margaret River
T (08) 9757 0888 **www.**capementelle.com.au **Open** 7 days 10–4.30
Winemaker Robert Mann, Paul Callaghan, Evan Thompson **Est.** 1970 **Dozens** 105 000
Vyds 166ha
Part of the LVMH (Louis Vuitton Möet Hennessy) group. Cape Mentelle is firing on all cylinders, with the winemaking team fully capitalising on the extensive and largely mature vineyards, which obviate the need for contract-grown fruit. It is hard to say which of the wines is best; the ranking, such as it is, varies from year to year. That said, Sauvignon Blanc Semillon, Chardonnay, Shiraz and Cabernet Sauvignon lead the portfolio, and Cape Mentelle is one of those knocking on the door of the Winery of the Year Award. Exports to all major markets.

ŦŦŦŦŦ **Wallcliffe 2010** Bright straw-green; fragrant tropical fruits, nettle, fine oak and a tightly wound palate that is both complex and refreshing; long, layered and impeccable There is a strong streak of juicy fruit that adds further to the appeal of a high-quality wine, with some savoury nuances to provide contrast. Sauvignon Blanc/Semillon. Screwcap. 13% alc. **Rating** 96 **To** 2022 $45
Margaret River Shiraz 2010 Deep but clear purple-crimson; the bouquet calmly announces its cool-grown southern Margaret River origins, with fragrant, almost flowery, red fruits and spices; the medium-bodied palate is supple and smooth, building impressively on the finely structured finish thanks to exactly poised tannins. Will be very long-lived. Screwcap. 13.5% alc. **Rating** 96 **To** 2030 $40
Margaret River Cabernet Sauvignon 2010 Bright crimson-purple; an elegant and vibrant wine, the purity of its varietal fruit expression quite exceptional, as is the handling of the French oak and tannins; the finish is very long and totally harmonious. Screwcap. 13.5% alc. **Rating** 96 **To** 2030 $89
Margaret River Sauvignon Blanc Semillon 2012 Quartz-white; a 54/46% blend of 40 individually vinified parcels of grapes; the bouquet is particularly expressive, with flowery, scented aromas, the palate with an almost pinot noir-like peacock's tail expansion on the finish, and the aftertaste with a gamut of citrus and tropical flavours. Screwcap. 12.5% alc. **Rating** 95 **To** 2014 $27
Margaret River Chardonnay 2012 Pale straw-green; grapefruit/citrus fruit is the outer layer of the wine; inside are white peach/stone fruit flavours, and largely inside these two layers are the oak and some nutty touches associated with that oak. Since all the layers are translucent, the net result is a fruit-driven Chardonnay of considerable elegance. Screwcap. 13% alc. **Rating** 95 **To** 2020 $41
Margaret River Shiraz 2011 Full crimson-purple; the fragrant, almost flowery bouquet is followed by an intense, long and complex medium- to full-bodied palate, reflecting an extended maturation in predominantly used French oak; the plum and blackberry fruits have a generous sprinkling of spice and pepper coupled with fine, savoury tannins. Screwcap. 13.5% alc. **Rating** 95 **To** 2031 $39
Wallcliffe 2011 Rating 94 **To** 2020 $45
✪ **Marmaduke Margaret River Shiraz 2011** Great reds are in store from Margaret River's magnificent '11 season, and Marmaduke is one of the first indications. Intricate craftsmanship rarely witnessed at this price sets an enticing violet perfume over restrained black cherry, plum skin and pepper notes. At a cool 13.5%, it's refreshingly medium-bodied, charged with energetic acidity and finely ground, gravelly tannins. Screwcap. 13.5% alc. **Rating** 94 **To** 2021 $19 TS

Trinders Margaret River Cabernet Merlot 2011 Rating 94 To 2026 $32
Margaret River Cabernet Sauvignon 2011 Rating 94 To 2031 $90
Wilyabrup 2011 Rating 94 To 2031 $49
Wilyabrup 2010 Rating 94 To 2030 $49
Margaret River Zinfandel 2011 Rating 94 To 2018 $55

ŶŶŶŶŶ **Georgiana Margaret River Sauvignon Blanc 2012** Sourced predominantly
✪ from the cooler southern half of Margaret River, '12 is one of her most graceful
expressions yet. Fragrant elegance of Granny Smith apple, grapefruit and lemon
blossom glides through an airy bouquet and a honed palate of zesty poise and
refreshing restraint. Screwcap. 12.5% alc. **Rating** 93 **To** 2013 $19 TS

Cape Naturaliste Vineyard ★★★★★

1 Coley Road (off Caves Road), Yallingup, WA 6282 **Region** Margaret River
T (08) 9755 2538 **www**.capenaturalistevineyard.com.au **Open** 7 days 10.30–5
Winemaker Ian Bell, Bruce Dukes, Craig Bent-White **Est.** 1997 **Dozens** 4200
Vyds 9.7ha
Cape Naturaliste Vineyard has a long and varied history going back 150 years, when it was
a coach inn for travellers journeying between Perth and Margaret River. Later it became a
dairy farm, and in 1970 a mining company purchased it, intending to extract nearby mineral
sands. The government stepped in and declared the area a national park, whereafter (in 1980)
Craig Brent-White purchased the property. The vineyard is planted to cabernet sauvignon,
shiraz, merlot, semillon and sauvignon blanc, and is run on an organic/biodynamic basis. The
quality of the wines would suggest that the effort is well worthwhile, especially with Bruce
Dukes' skills recognised when he was named Winemaker of the Year at the WA Wine Industry
Awards '11. Exports to Singapore and Indonesia.

ŶŶŶŶŶ **Torpedo Rocks Single Vineyard Margaret River Shiraz 2010** Medium to
full red-purple; hand-picked and matured for 2 years in French barriques. It fully
reflects this pedigree, with an intense, but no more than medium- to full-bodied,
palate; red and black cherry fruit has a dusting of spice, fine-grained tannins and
perfectly judged oak. Screwcap. 14.5% alc. **Rating** 95 **To** 2025 $35
Torpedo Rocks Single Vineyard Margaret River Cabernet Merlot 2010
The colour is still full crimson-purple; low-yielding vines, hand-picking and skilled
winemaking (including 24 months in French oak) have resulted in a high-quality
wine; it is endowed with rich cassis and redcurrant fruit, and an authentic varietal
touch of black olive. Screwcap. 14.5% alc. **Rating** 95 **To** 2025 $35
**Torpedo Rocks Single Vineyard Margaret River Cabernet Sauvignon
2010** Counterintuitively, while deep and healthy, the colour is not quite as bright
as that of its sibling; both spent 24 months in French oak. The difference between
the two wines is revealed most tellingly in the authoritative tannins of this wine –
authoritative, but not dry or tough; just what the wine needs. Screwcap. 14% alc.
Rating 94 To 2030 $35

ŶŶŶŶŶ **Single Vineyard Margaret River Sauvignon Blanc 2012** Estate-produced;
✪ aromas of cut grass, snow pea, thyme and capsicum lead into a palate where gentle
tropical fruits emerge to add overall flavour balance courtesy of passionfruit and
guava. Bargain. Screwcap. 12.7% alc. **Rating** 93 **To** 2014 $18
✪ **Single Vineyard Margaret River Shiraz 2010** Full purple-crimson; a rich
and succulent Shiraz that spent 24 months (a little too long?) in French barriques;
it has particularly good mouthfeel to the medium-bodied palate, and some will
enjoy the fruit/oak combination, which is in no way threatened by tannins. Good
wine, excellent value. Screwcap. 14.5% alc. **Rating** 91 **To** 2020 $20

Capel Vale ★★★★★

118 Mallokup Road, Capel, WA 6271 **Region** Geographe
T (08) 9727 1986 www.capelvale.com **Open** 7 days 10–4
Winemaker Justin Hearn **Est.** 1974 **Dozens** 50 000 **Vyds** 90ha
Established by Perth-based medical practitioner Dr Peter Pratten and wife Elizabeth in 1974. The first vineyard adjacent to the winery was planted on the banks of the quiet waters of Capel River. The very fertile soil gave rise to extravagant vine growth, providing 95% of the winery's intake until the mid 1980s. The viticultural empire has since been expanded, spreading across Geographe (15ha), Mount Barker (15ha), Pemberton (32ha) and Margaret River (28ha); the most recent arrivals are petit verdot, sangiovese, tempranillo and nebbiolo. Unfavourable weather conditions in 2010 meant that Capel Vale did not make all its icon single vineyard wines in that year. Exports to all major markets.

♟♟♟♟♟ **Single Vineyard Series The Scholar Margaret River Cabernet Sauvignon 2010** Full crimson-purple; a high-quality cabernet, flooded with cassis, redcurrant and briar on the full-bodied palate; good tannins and oak management have put the final touches on a stylish wine. Screwcap. 14.5% alc. **Rating** 95 **To** 2035 $75
Single Vineyard Series Whispering Hill Mount Barker Riesling 2012 Pale straw-green; an elegant wine, with a fragrant bouquet and a lissom palate of lime and lemon fruit that uncoils itself on the finish and lingering aftertaste. Its future lies before it, and is assured. Screwcap. 11% alc. **Rating** 94 **To** 2020 $33
Cellar Exclusive Mount Barker Riesling 2011 A serious challenger for the most words on a long, two-paragraph back label that say precisely nothing. However, the wine does speak for itself having built flavour already, with succulent, sweet lime juice flavours that continue to expand through the finish and aftertaste. Screwcap. 11.5% alc. **Rating** 94 **To** 2018 $27
Regional Series Pemberton Semillon Sauvignon Blanc 2012 Light straw-green; a finely balanced and structured wine, seamlessly joining lemon citrus, cut grass and gently tropical aromas and flavours, a touch of passionfruit on the farewell. Screwcap. 13% alc. **Rating** 94 **To** 2014 $25
Single Vineyard Series Whispering Hill Mount Barker Shiraz 2011 Medium crimson-purple; this is a precise portrayal of Mount Barker shiraz: no more than medium-bodied; supple cherry and berry fruit; spices and pepper; and fine-grained tannins, here complemented by cedary oak. Screwcap. 14.5% alc. **Rating** 94 **To** 2026 $55
Single Vineyard Series The Scholar Margaret River Cabernet Sauvignon 2011 Bright crimson-purple; it opens with cassis and plum, then adds an atypical touch of chocolate, before a flood of French oak comes through to coat the back-palate and finish, with finally some bramble/capsicum notes from the cabernet fruit. Screwcap. 14.5% alc. **Rating** 94 **To** 2036 $75

♟♟♟♟♀ **Regional Series Mount Barker Shiraz 2011** **Rating** 93 **To** 2021 $27
Cellar Exclusive Margaret River Semillon Sauvignon Blanc 2012 **Rating** 92 **To** 2015 $27
Regional Series Margaret River Chardonnay 2011 **Rating** 92 **To** 2014 $25
Cellar Exclusive Pemberton Chardonnay 2011 **Rating** 92 **To** 2015 $27
✪ **Debut Merlot 2011** Clear red-purple; while only light- to medium-bodied, the wine speaks clearly of its variety and the cool regions in which the grapes were grown; there is enticing tension between the red berry/plum fruits on the one side and the savoury/black olive/earth notes on the other. Screwcap. 14% alc. **Rating** 92 **To** 2014 $18
Regional Series Margaret River Cabernet Merlot 2010 **Rating** 92 **To** 2023 $25
Regional Series Margaret River Cabernet Sauvignon 2011 **Rating** 92 **To** 2031 $27
Regional Series Margaret River Cabernet Merlot 2011 **Rating** 90 **To** 2020 $27

Capital Wines ★★★★★

Grazing Restaurant, Royal Hotel, Cork Street, Gundaroo, NSW 2620
Region Canberra District
T (02) 6236 8555 **www**.capitalwines.com.au **Open** Mon–Fri 10–5, w'ends 9–5
Winemaker Andrew McEwin **Est.** 1986 **Dozens** 5000 **Vyds** 5ha

This is the venture of Mark and Jennie Mooney (of the Royal Hotel at Gundaroo) and Andrew and Marion McEwin (of Kyeema Wines). They joined forces to found Capital Wines, which purchased Kyeema Wines and related contract winemaking in 2008. The venture has seen the creation of The Ministry Series wines, with clever graphic design and generally invigorated marketing efforts. The estate vineyard is still an important source, supplemented by grape purchases. Whether by coincidence or not, consecutive releases of the wines are of impressive quality, and have led to a substantial increase in production and sales. The cellar door operates in conjunction with the Grazing Restaurant in Gundaroo, in the 1830s stone stables.

ＹＹＹＹＹ **The Whip Canberra District Riesling 2012** Bright, light straw-green; fresh, ✪ crisp and lively, with intense lime and lemon sherbet fruit coursing along the palate, thence to the finish and aftertaste; its foundation is its crystalline acidity. Screwcap. 11.1% alc. **Rating** 94 **To** 2024 $19
The Ambassador Canberra District Tempranillo 2011 Deep purple; it's not often a back label talks about the beauty of another producer's wine; the explanation turned on this Tempranillo winning top gold at the Canberra Regional Wine Show (no year specified), but being beaten by a Mount Majura blend for the relevant trophy. This is indeed a very good Tempranillo, supple, rich and smooth, with layers of red and black fruit. Screwcap. 13.2% alc. **Rating** 94 **To** 2016 $27
The Black Rod 2009 Principally shiraz, with a small amount of cabernet sauvignon and merlot, given 3 years' lees contact. Full garnet-red, it is a very complex wine, with spice and licorice overtones to the black cherry and plum fruit; the overall balance is excellent, as is the mouthfeel. One from left field. Crown seal. 14.4% alc. **Rating** 94 **To** 2017 $36

ＹＹＹＹ   **The Swinger Sauvignon Blanc 2012 Rating** 89 **To** 2014 $19
The Treasury Late Picked Riesling 2011 Rating 89 **To** 2014 $25

Capogreco Winery Estate ★★★

3078 Riverside Avenue, South Mildura, Vic 3500 **Region** Murray Darling
T (03) 5022 1431 **Open** Mon–Sat 10–5
Winemaker Bruno and Domenico Capogreco **Est.** 1976 **Dozens** NA **Vyds** 33ha
Italian-owned and run, the wines are a blend of Italian and Australian Riverland influences. The estate has 13ha of chardonnay, 14ha of shiraz and 6ha of cabernet sauvignon, and also produces other varieties. All of the wines are entirely made at Capogreco, using traditional, well-established winemaking practices. Exports to the UK and Canada.

ＹＹＹＹ   **Museum Release Nuovo Millennio Cabernet Sauvignon 2000** Developed colour; the wine spent 9 years in 2500-l American oak vats, and was bottled in Aug '10 without fining or acid adjustment. A curio, but has stood the test of its long sojourn in vat well. Cork. 14% alc. **Rating** 89 **To** 2015 $50

Carlei Estate & Carlei Green Vineyards ★★★★★

1 Alber Road, Upper Beaconsfield, Vic 3808 **Region** Yarra Valley
T (03) 5944 4599 **www**.carlei.com.au **Open** W'ends 11–6, or by appt
Winemaker Sergio Carlei **Est.** 1994 **Dozens** 10 000 **Vyds** 2.25ha
Sergio Carlei has come a long way in a short time, graduating from home winemaking in a suburban garage to his own (commercial) winery in Upper Beaconsfield. Carlei Estate falls just within the boundaries of the Yarra Valley. Along the way Carlei acquired a Bachelor of Wine Science from CSU, and established a vineyard with organic and biodynamic accreditation adjacent to the Upper Beaconsfield winery. His contract winemaking services are now a major part of the business, and showcase his extremely impressive winemaking talents. Exports to the US, Singapore and China.

ŶŶŶŶŶ Estate Directors' Cut Central Victoria Shiraz 2010 Deep crimson-purple; redolent of spice, licorice and dark fruits on the bouquet and full-bodied palate; while the tannins are obvious, the fruit and oak provide balance. A cellaring special. Diam. 14.7% alc. Rating 95 To 2035 $95

ŶŶŶŶŶ Estate Tasmania Riesling 2012 Rating 93 To 2020 $25
Green Vineyards Heathcote Shiraz 2009 Rating 92 To 2020 $27
Estate Nebbiolo 2010 Rating 92 To 2017 $59
Estate Nord Heathcote Shiraz 2009 Rating 91 To 2019 $59
Green Vineyards Sauvignon Blanc 2012 Rating 90 To 2014 $25
Green Vineyards Heathcote Shiraz 2010 Rating 90 To 2017 $27
Estate Sud Heathcote Shiraz 2009 Rating 90 To 2018 $59

Carpe Diem Vineyards   ★★★★

213 Johnson Road, Wilyabrup, WA 6280 **Region** Margaret River
T (08) 9755 6118 **www**.carpediemvineyards.com.au **Open** By appt
Winemaker Gianfranco Anderle **Est.** 2003 **Dozens** 2500 **Vyds** 12.2ha
When Gianfranco and Francesca Anderle first visited WA in 2000, they immediately fell in love with the Margaret River region. They promptly returned to Italy, sold up, and returned to purchase their 30ha Wilyabrup property in 2001. Vineyard plantings began in '03 and continued until '05, with a mix of Margaret River staples (5.5ha of sauvignon blanc and semillon, and 3.3ha of cabernet sauvignon and merlot), the Italian connection cemented with further plantings of sangiovese, nebbiolo, malbec, vermentino and pinot grigio. Gianfranco is a qualified oenologist from Conegliano (northern Italy), the oldest wine school in Europe, and already had 22 years of winemaking experience when he arrived in Australia.

ŶŶŶŶŶ Schiaffo Margaret River Sauvignon Blanc 2012 Bright, light green-straw; an interesting combination of above-average texture and structure with tropical, rather than grassy/citrus/green pea, fruit flavours. Works well; some element of oak? Screwcap. 12.8% alc. Rating 91 To 2015 $26
Platinum Selection Margaret River Cabernet Sauvignon 2010 The wine has a different flavour register from many Margaret River cabernets, with a cedar/mocha overtone to the bouquet; this changes to crushed tobacco leaf and ground coffee on the palate, reminiscent of aged Chateau Haut Brion. Difficult to point. Screwcap. 13.8% alc. Rating 91 To 2020 $38
Platinum Selection Margaret River Malbec 2011 Less than 100 dozen made; the colour is good, as is the rich varietal fruit with a mix of confit and glossy dark cherry and plum fruit; the oak is within bounds, and the wine has the structure often missing from Malbec. Screwcap. 14.2% alc. Rating 91 To 2021 $45
Decantato Margaret River Sangiovese Merlot Cabernet Sauvignon 2012 The surreal label stands out like no other, no matter what colour scheme is adopted. The colour of the wine itself is not inspiring, but it turns out to have a lot of everything else: cassis, spice, olive, oak and tannins, each sparking off the other. Screwcap. 13.5% alc. Rating 90 To 2020 $26
Margaret River Sangiovese 2011 A very respectable Sangiovese, with its array of cherry (red, sour, glacé and spiced) aromas and flavours framed by the usual sangio tannins on the medium-bodied palate. Screwcap. 13.5% alc. Rating 90 To 2016 $26

ŶŶŶŶ L'Attimo Riserva Speciale Margaret River Sangiovese 2009 Rating 89 To 2016 $75

Carriages   ★★★

Halls Road, Pokolbin, NSW 2320 **Region** Hunter Valley
T (02) 4998 7591 **www**.thecarriages.com.au **Open** 7 days 10–dark
Winemaker Andrew Thomas (Contract) **Est.** 1999 **Dozens** 600 **Vyds** 2ha
Set on 16ha of picturesque grounds and she-oak forest, the vineyard produces small parcels of chardonnay and shiraz. Much of the vineyard work is undertaken by hand by a small team;

the wines are contract-made by Andrew Thomas. Carriages Shiraz and Chardonnay are typical of the modern Hunter Valley style, the Chardonnay elegant and crisp without heavy oak overload. A 10-room boutique hotel is set in a garden of its own within the vineyard. Not to be confused with The Carriages in the Goulburn Valley (see separate entry).

ŸŸŸŸ **Scarlett's Promise Single Vineyard Hunter Valley Chardonnay 2011** Picked after 7 days in excess of 40°C, and there are signs of adjusted acidity on the finish and aftertaste, resulting in a broken line. Gleaming green-yellow; one-third of the wine was fermented and matured in new French oak for 12 months. 80 dozen made. Screwcap. 13% alc. **Rating** 88 **To** 2014 $30

Hunter Valley Shiraz 2009 Medium red-purple; matured in American barriques, introducing vanilla notes on the bouquet and palate alike; made by Andrew Thomas, which is a surprise, for the wine does not convince. Screwcap. 13% alc. **Rating** 87 **To** 2016 $30

Casa Freschi

PO Box 45, Summertown, SA 5141 **Region** Langhorne Creek
T 0409 364 569 **www.**casafreschi.com.au **Open** Not
Winemaker David Freschi **Est.** 1998 **Dozens** 2000 **Vyds** 7.55ha
David Freschi graduated with a degree in oenology from Roseworthy College in 1991 and spent most of the decade working in California, Italy and NZ. In '98 he and his wife decided to trade in the corporate world for a small family-owned winemaking business, with a core of 2.4ha of vines established by his parents in '72; an additional 1.85ha of nebbiolo has now been planted adjacent to the original vineyard. Says David, 'The names of the wines were chosen to best express the personality of the wines grown in our vineyard, as well as to express our heritage.' A second 3.2ha vineyard has subsequently been established in the Adelaide Hills, planted to chardonnay, pinot gris, riesling and gewurztraminer. Exports to Canada and Singapore.

ŸŸŸŸŸ **Ragazzi Adelaide Hills Pinot Grigio 2012** Barrel-fermented and briefly matured in used French oak, the wine has greater impact and texture than many. Why Casa Freschi has chosen to label this pinot grigio is beyond my comprehension. Yes it is crisp and bright, but it's much more than that. Screwcap. 12.5% alc. Rating 94 To 2014 $25

ŸŸŸŸŸ **La Signorina 2012 Rating** 92 **To** 2017 $30 BE
La Signora 2010 Rating 92 **To** 2018 $45

Cascabel

Rogers Road, Willunga, SA 5172 (postal) **Region** McLaren Vale
T (08) 8557 4434 **www.**cascabelwinery.com.au **Open** Not
Winemaker Susana Fernandez, Duncan Ferguson **Est.** 1997 **Dozens** 2500 **Vyds** 4.9ha
Cascabel's proprietors, Duncan Ferguson and Susana Fernandez, have planted a mosaic of southern Rhône and Spanish varieties. The choice of grapes reflects the winemaking experience of the proprietors in Australia, the Rhône Valley, Bordeaux, Italy, Germany and NZ – and also Susana's birthplace, Spain. Production has moved steadily towards the style of the Rhône Valley, Rioja and other parts of Spain. Exports to the UK, the US, Hong Kong, Japan and China.

ŸŸŸŸŸ **Couloir 2012** A wolf (roussanne) in sheep's clothing (colour); it spent 10 months in used French oak, giving texture to its honeysuckle/quince flavours. Will repay cellaring. Screwcap. 12.5% alc. **Rating** 91 **To** 2017 $25

Eden Valley Riesling 2012 Bright straw-green; a crisp, dry minerally style, the citrus/lemon fruit still lurking in the shadows – the wine will transform itself over the next 3–5 years. Screwcap. 11.5% alc. **Rating** 90 **To** 2020 $20

✪ **Joven 2012** From Cascabel's younger (Joven) tempranillo vines, matured in used French oak for only 3 months to retain as much fruit freshness as possible. The aromas and flavours are an amalgam of cherry/sour cherry, with tamarillo on the finish. Great tapas wine. Screwcap. 13.5% alc. **Rating** 90 **To** 2015 $20

Casella Wines ★★★★

Wakely Road, Yenda, NSW 2681 **Region** Riverina
T (02) 6961 3000 **www**.casellawines.com.au **Open** Not
Winemaker Alan Kennett, Frank Mallamace, Randy Herron **Est.** 1969
Dozens 12 million **Vyds** 1397ha
A modern-day fairytale success story, transformed overnight from a substantial, successful but non-charismatic business making 650000 dozen in 2000. Its opportunity came when leading US distributor WJ Deutsch & Sons formed a partnership with Casella and, for the first time, imported wines as well as distributing them. The partners built their US presence at a faster rate than any other brand in history. It has been aided in all markets by making small batches (500 dozen or so) of gold medal-standard Reserve and Limited Release wines. It is not generally realised just how large its estate vineyards are, with pinot noir (53.76ha), merlot (59.87ha), semillon (62.92ha), sauvignon blanc (83.96ha), riesling (114.77ha), pinot gris (192.67ha), cabernet sauvignon (218.44ha) and shiraz (380.78ha). Exports to all major markets.

ΨΨΨΨΨ **yellow tail Reserve Special Selection Shiraz 2010** Good depth and clarity
✪ to the colour; with plum, cherry and chocolate all making their presence felt on the bouquet and medium-bodied palate; the tannin management is particularly good, sustaining the finish and aftertaste. Impressive at this price, and there is no sweetness evident. Diam. 14% alc. **Rating** 91 **To** 2017 $15

ΨΨΨΨ **yellow tail Reserve Special Selection Merlot 2010 Rating** 89 **To** 2014 $15
✪ **yellow tail Pinot Grigio 2011** Bright, fresh and crisp, in correct grigio style, and whatever residual sugar there may be, it is not obvious in a wine with plenty of citrus, pear and apple fruit. Exceptionally good value. Screwcap. 11.5% alc. **Rating** 87 **To** 2013 $10

Cassegrain ★★★★

764 Fernbank Creek Road, Port Macquarie, NSW 2444 **Region** Hastings River
T (02) 6582 8377 **www**.cassegrainwines.com.au **Open** 7 days 9–5
Winemaker John Cassegrain (Chief), Michelle Heagney (Senior) **Est.** 1980
Dozens 60000 **Vyds** 34.9ha
Cassegrain has continued to evolve and develop. It still draws on the original Hastings River vineyard of 4.9ha, the most important varieties being semillon, verdelho and chambourcin, with pinot noir and cabernet sauvignon making up the numbers. However, Cassegrain now part-owns and manages Richfield Vineyard (see separate entry) in the New England region, with 30ha of chardonnay, verdelho, semillon, shiraz, merlot, cabernet sauvignon and ruby cabernet. These estate vineyards are supplemented by grapes purchased from Tumbarumba, Orange and the Hunter Valley. Exports to the UK, the US, and other major markets.

ΨΨΨΨΨ **Fromenteau Reserve Chardonnay 2011** A blend of Orange and New
England fruit, early-picked to preserve acidity. White peach, honeydew melon and citrus are the major flavour contributors, the oak influence subtle. An easy-access, but elegant, wine. Screwcap. 12% alc. **Rating** 91 **To** 2017 $35

✪ **Merlot Cabernet Sauvignon 2011** Light red-purple; the bouquet is fragrant, driven by red berry fruits; how the wine could be described as 'luscious and full-bodied' (on the back label) is beyond my comprehension; it is medium-bodied, with a silky texture and attractive red fruit flavours, the finish well balanced. Screwcap. 14% alc. **Rating** 91 **To** 2016 $20

✪ **Stone Circle Chardonnay 2010** Bright straw-green; a surprise until you find the Tumbarumba and New England source of the grapes; while unwooded, time in bottle has added a dimension to the very good and intense varietal expression coming from the Tumbarumba component. Screwcap. 12.5% alc. **Rating** 90 **To** 2017 $15

Reserve Shiraz 2009 All up, a well-made medium-bodied wine that clearly expresses its cool-climate origins, with red and black cherry fruit, spices and fine-boned tannins; the light twist of mint/eucalypt does not disfigure the wine, and the oak is subtle. Screwcap. 13.5% alc. **Rating** 90 **To** 2018 $35

Edition Noir Shiraz Sangiovese 2009 Light to medium red-purple; a blend of New England and Central Ranges grapes; an uncommon blend that works very well; the light- to medium-bodied palate has red and black cherry to the fore, the tannins fine and soft. Drinking at its best now. Screwcap. 13.5% alc. **Rating** 90 To 2014 $25

ŶŶŶŶ　Semillon 2007 Rating 89 To 2014 $20
Edition Noir Pinot Noir 2010 Rating 89 To 2013 $25
Shiraz 2010 Rating 89 To 2015 $20
Stone Circle Semillon Sauvignon Blanc 2012 Rating 88 To 2014 $15
Edition Noir Three Tiers 2012 Rating 88 To 2015 $25
Edition Noir Merlot 2011 Rating 88 To 2015 $25
Noble Cuvee NV Rating 88 To 2013 $15
Edition Noir Sauvignon Blanc 2011 Rating 87 To 2013 $25
Chardonnay 2012 Rating 87 To 2014 $20
Edition Noir Pinot Gris 2012 Rating 87 To 2014 $25
Shiraz 2011 Rating 87 To 2014 $20
✪　Q Cabernet Merlot 2011 Medium red-purple; a surprise packet at its price, with plenty of blackcurrant and plum cake flavour, and no green characters. Ready now, and good value. Screwcap. 13.5% alc. **Rating** 87 To 2014 $10

Castelli Estate ★★★★★

380 Mount Shadforth Road, Denmark, WA 6333 **Region** Great Southern
T (08) 9364 0400 **www.**castelliestate.com.au **Open** By appt
Winemaker Mike Garland, Andrew Hoadley **Est.** 2007 **Dozens** 5000
Castelli Estate will cause many small winery owners to go green with envy. When Sam Castelli purchased the property in late 2004, he was intending simply to use it as a family holiday destination. But because there was a partly constructed winery he decided to complete the building work and lock the doors. However, wine was in his blood courtesy of his father, who owned a small vineyard in Italy's south. The temptation was too much, and in '07 the winery was commissioned, with 20 tonnes of Great Southern fruit crushed under the Castelli label, and annual increases thereafter. There is room for expansion because the winery actually has a capacity of 500 tonnes, and the underground cellar is fully climate controlled. Fruit is sourced from some of the best vineyards in WA, including the Hadley Hall, Kalgan River, Whispering Hill and Omodei vineyards. These are geographically distributed across WA's southern regions, including Frankland River, Mount Barker, Pemberton and Porongurup.

ŶŶŶŶŶ　Pemberton Chardonnay 2012 Vibrant green hue; this wine embodies the very essence of modern Australian chardonnay, poised, precise, complex, layered and refreshing; grapefruit, cashew, fine oak spices and a little charry complexity; the palate is scintillating, with laser-like acidity providing an extremely long and harmonious ride from start to finish. Screwcap. 13.4% alc. **Rating** 96 To 2022 $32 BE
Frankland River Cabernet Sauvignon 2011 Deep crimson, purple hue; the bouquet is incredibly pure and precise, offering cassis, cedar and violets at this early stage; the palate is seamless, effortlessly flowing from start to the extraordinarily long and fine-grained tannin finish; worth watching evolve over time. Screwcap. 14.8% alc. **Rating** 96 To 2030 $32 BE
Porongurup Riesling 2012 There is generosity and purity in this wine, which shows fresh lime, citrus blossom and touch of ginger; the palate shows wonderful line and grace, with enough flesh and concentration to persist evenly for a staggeringly long finish. Screwcap. 11.7% alc. **Rating** 95 To 2025 $24 BE
Great Southern Shiraz 2011 Bright purple hue; the bouquet offers an expressive blend of mulberry, clove and mocha; the medium-bodied palate is fresh and lively with tightly wound fruits sitting neatly alongside firm tannins and fresh acidity; worth cellaring to let all components fully integrate. Screwcap. 14.4% alc. **Rating** 94 To 2025 $32 BE

Il Cavaliere 2010 This is a muscular 56/37/7% blend of cabernet sauvignon, shiraz and malbec with blue and black fruits, florals and spice all playing a role; the full tale is revealed on the palate, as the chewy tannins and masses of fruit play against each other, both trying to gain dominance, but neither accomplishing the feat. Screwcap. 14.7% alc. **Rating** 94 **To** 2025 $70 BE

ŢŢŢŢŸ **Pemberton Merlot 2011 Rating** 92 **To** 2020 $24 BE
Checkmate Sauvignon Blanc Semillon 2012 Rating 91 **To** 2015 $18 BE
Checkmate Cabernet Merlot 2011 Rating 91 **To** 2018 $18 BE
Geographe Tempranillo 2011 Rating 90 **To** 2017 $24 BE

Castle Rock Estate   ★★★★★

2660 Porongurup Road, Porongurup, WA 6324 **Region** Porongurup
T (08) 9853 1035 **www**.castlerockestate.com.au **Open** 7 days 10–5
Winemaker Robert Diletti **Est.** 1983 **Dozens** 4500 **Vyds** 11.2ha
An exceptionally beautifully sited vineyard (riesling, pinot noir, chardonnay, sauvignon blanc, cabernet sauvignon and merlot), winery and cellar door on a 55ha property with sweeping vistas from the Porongurups, operated by the Diletti family. The standard of viticulture is very high, and the vineyard itself ideally situated (quite apart from its beauty). The two-level winery, set on a natural slope, maximises gravity flow, in particular for crushed must feeding into the press. The Rieslings have always been elegant and have handsomely repaid time in bottle; the Pinot Noir is the most consistent performer in the region; the Shiraz is a great cool-climate example; and Chardonnay has joined a thoroughly impressive quartet, elegance the common link. Rob Diletti's excellent palate and sensitive winemaking mark Castle Rock as one of the superstars of WA. Exports to China.

ŢŢŢŢŢ **A&W Reserve Great Southern Riesling 2011** Bright quartz-green; a wine of the highest quality, its extreme length and seamless union of citrus, apple and minerally acidity sheer perfection. Screwcap. 12% alc. **Rating** 97 **To** 2026 $28
Great Southern Riesling 2012 Light, bright straw-green; the scented bouquet has nuances of wild flowers and herbs, together with the more usual lime blossom; the pristine palate has the hallmark intensity and magical acidity that will see the wine unfold its full glory over the next decade and long thereafter. From the Porongurup subregion. Screwcap. 12% alc. **Rating** 96 **To** 2025 $25
Diletti Chardonnay 2010 Bright straw-green; a vividly flavoured wine with grapefruit, apple and white peach, then a vibrantly crisp finish, the 10 months in French oak not daring to interrupt the flow of the incisive, elegant palate. Screwcap. 12.5% alc. **Rating** 96 **To** 2020 $30
Great Southern Pinot Noir 2011 Clear, bright crimson; immediately proclaims its variety from the first whiff; elegant, intense red berry fruits are backed by silky, fine tannins, oak seen but not heard. Should give eastern states pinots from '11 a hard time in the show ring. Screwcap. 13.5% alc. **Rating** 96 **To** 2019 $35
Great Southern Riesling OD 2012 Pale quartz-green; the highly perfumed/blossom-filled bouquet leads into a delicious palate with lime juice flavours enhanced by 10g/l of residual sugar; the finish is long and lingering. Screwcap. 12.5% alc. **Rating** 94 **To** 2025 $20

ŢŢŢŢŸ **Great Southern Chardonnay 2012** Fermentation in 2–3-year-old barrels has
✪   introduced texture and structure, but left the fruit to express itself clearly, with mouthfilling nectarine and white peach fruit to the fore; the acidity sits where it should. Screwcap. 13% alc. **Rating** 93 **To** 2014 $19
✪   **Great Southern Sauvignon Blanc 2012** From low-yielding 16-year-old estate vines, cold-fermented with some cloudy juice; mainly in the snow pea and grass end of the flavour spectrum, its strength is in the texture and structure running through the length of the palate and into the aftertaste. Screwcap. 13% alc. **Rating** 92 **To** 2014 $20

Catherine Vale Vineyard ★★★★☆

656 Milbrodale Road, Fordwich, NSW 2330 **Region** Hunter Valley
T (02) 6579 1334 **www.**catherinevale.com.au **Open** W'ends & public hols 10–5, or by appt
Winemaker Hunter Wine Services (John Hordern) **Est.** 1994 **Dozens** 1500 **Vyds** 4.45ha
Former schoolteachers Bill and Wendy Lawson have established Catherine Vale as a not-so-idle retirement venture. The lion's share of the vineyard planting is chardonnay and semillon, with smaller amounts of verdelho, arneis, dolcetto and barbera. The Lawsons chose to plant the latter three varieties after visiting the Piedmont region of Italy, pioneering the move to these varieties in the Hunter Valley. In 2012 Wendy received an OAM for her work in tourism, the environment and viticulture.

ΨΨΨΨΨ **Aged Release Semillon 1999** Glorious green colour; the caterpillar first tasted in '01 has now spread its shimmering butterfly wings, unusually delicate and as fresh as a spring day. On the face of it, an astounding bargain, but the cork gods will smite you down with an unknowable percentage of oxidised bottles. As long as you factor this in, go for it. 11% alc. **Rating** 94 **To** 2015 $18

ΨΨΨΨΨ ✪ **Semillon 2011** Bright, although pale, straw-green; has all the indicia of a young, high-quality Semillon emanating from mature vines, but which needs time to open up; good value, nonetheless, if you share my conviction about its future. Screwcap. 12.3% alc. **Rating** 90 **To** 2019 $15

🍇 Caudo Vineyard ★★★☆

River Boat Road, Cadell, SA 5321 **Region** Riverland
T 0427 351 911 **www.**caudovineyard.com.au **Open** 7 days 10–9
Winemaker Contract **Est.** 2011 **Dozens** NFP **Vyds** 120ha
Joe, Christine and Zac Caudo have been supplying grapes to wineries for 20 years. The first step towards vertical integration came with a partnership with Cellarmasters, who created their Caudo brand from grapes coming from their vineyard. The Caudos have now taken the next step of developing their own brands: Desert Edge, Mediterranean Fiesta, Murraylands, Hogwash Bench and Bubbly Summers. With well-made wines at $10, $12 and $15, those who don't wish to pay more than they have to for easy drinking wines should stop and take a look.

ΨΨΨΨΨ ✪ **Murraylands Shiraz 2012** Exceptional given its origin; the bouquet and palate are equally exceptional, bursting with cherry and plum fruit; the tannin and oak influences are slight, but so what. Great value for outdoor drinking with the likes of Paul Hogan. Screwcap. 13.5% alc. **Rating** 90 **To** 2014 $12

ΨΨΨΨ ✪ **Murraylands Rose 2012** A blend of cabernet, merlot and shiraz. Bright crimson, it is fragrant, fresh, crisp and dry – with distinct red berry fruit flavours from start to finish. Screwcap. 13% alc. **Rating** 89 **To** 2014 $15
Hogwash Blend The Sentinels Shiraz 2011 Rating 87 **To** 2013 $12
Murraylands Cabernet Sauvignon 2012 Rating 87 **To** 2015 $15
Mediterranean Fiesta Tempranillo Sangiovese Shiraz 2012 Rating 87 **To** 2014 $15

✪ **Bubbly Summers Sparkling Rose 2012** Even here, with this brilliantly coloured rose, Caudo holds the line. It's dry. Substitute it for prosecco and save half your money. Crown seal. 13.5% alc. **Rating** 87 **To** 2014 $12

Celestial Bay ★★★★★

33 Welwyn Avenue, Manning, WA 6152 (postal) **Region** Margaret River
T (08) 9450 4191 **www.**celestialbay.com.au **Open** Not
Winemaker Bernard Abbott **Est.** 1999 **Dozens** 8000 **Vyds** 60ha
Michael and Kim O'Brien had a background of farming in the Chittering Valley when they purchased their 104ha property. It is very much a family enterprise, with son Aaron studying viticulture and oenology at Curtin University, and daughter Daneka involved in marketing and sales. Under the direction of vineyard manager Sam Juniper, vines have been rapidly planted. The plantings are totally logical: semillon, sauvignon blanc, chardonnay, shiraz,

cabernet sauvignon, merlot, malbec and petit verdot. More than half of the grape production is sold at attractive (for Celestial Bay) prices. Winemaker Bernard Abbott celebrated his 27th Margaret River vintage in 2012. Exports to the UK, the US, Canada, Kenya, Singapore, Hong Kong and China.

🍷🍷🍷🍷🍷 **Margaret River Semillon Sauvignon Blanc 2012** Only Margaret River could
✪   produce a semillon-dominant blend with upfront tropical fruit, then a long and
          sustained finish with lemon/citrus brightening the whole palate. Outstanding
          value. Screwcap. 13% alc. **Rating** 94 **To** 2015 $20 BE
          White Zenith 2012 A blend of 55% semillon (25% barrel-fermented) and
          45% sauvignon blanc, with great focus and elegance, all the inputs symbiotic, and
          pointing to a long future; this is absolutely not simply a barrel selection of the
          standard SSB. Screwcap. 13.5% alc. **Rating** 94 **To** 2019 $35

🍷🍷🍷🍷   **Margaret River Chardonnay 2012 Rating** 89 **To** 2015 $20

Centennial Vineyards   ★★★★★

'Woodside', 252 Centennial Road, Bowral, NSW 2576 **Region** Southern Highlands
T (02) 4861 8722 **www**.centennial.net.au **Open** 7 days 10–5
Winemaker Tony Cosgriff **Est.** 2002 **Dozens** 10 000 **Vyds** 28.65ha
Centennial Vineyards, a substantial development jointly owned by wine professional John Large and investor Mark Dowling, covers 133ha of beautiful grazing land, with the vineyard planted to pinot noir (6.21ha), chardonnay (7.14ha), sauvignon blanc (4.05ha), tempranillo (3.38ha), pinot gris (2.61ha) and smaller plantings of savagnin, riesling, arneis, gewurztraminer and pinot meunier. Production from the estate vineyards is supplemented by purchases of grapes from other regions, including Orange. The consistency of the quality of the wines is wholly commendable, reflecting the skilled touch of Tony Cosgriff in a region that often throws up climatic challenges. Exports to the US, Denmark, Singapore, China and South Korea.

🍷🍷🍷🍷🍷 **Blanc de Blancs NV** From selected blocks in the estate vineyards in Bowral,
          aged for 42 months on lees prior to disgorgement. A vital and intense Blanc de
          Blancs, long and focused; grapefruit, stone fruit and some almond/creamy yeast
          nuances; a long and even finish. Diam. 12.5% alc. **Rating** 95 **To** 2015 $37
          Reserve Single Vineyard Riesling 924 2012 Pale straw-green; a pristine and
          pure green apple and citrus blossom bouquet; the palate is taut, linear, fresh and
          long, with laser-like acidity and an almost dry and chalky finish, simply thrilling in
          its intensity; should age beautifully. Screwcap. 9% alc. **Rating** 95 **To** 2022 $25 BE
          Reserve Single Vineyard Pinot Noir 2011 The colour is excellent, full and
          bright, and the wine has none of the woes of the '11; rather there is rich plum and
          cherry fruit on the bouquet and fleshy, supple palate alike; moreover, has time to
          go. Screwcap. 13.3% alc. **Rating** 94 **To** 2019 $30
          Reserve Single Vineyard Shiraz Viognier 2011 From the Crossing vineyard
          in Orange, the two varieties presumably co-fermented, because the colour is
          excellent; the bouquet and palate have distinct spice and licorice notes, the palate
          is generous and plush, with black cherry and plum to the fore; the oak is, as usual
          with Centennial, a bystander. Diam. 14.5% alc. **Rating** 94 **To** 2021 $30
          Pinot Noir Chardonnay Pinot Meunier NV A 68/28/4% blend sourced
          entirely from the estate vineyards at Bowral. The colour is very pale, despite the
          pinot noir dominance; the flavours are vibrant, more to do with citrus and stone
          fruit than with red fruits; despite the volume of fruit flavour, it retains elegance.
          Diam. 12.5% alc. **Rating** 94 **To** 2016 $28
✪   **Brut Rose NV** A 73/27% blend of estate-grown pinot noir and chardonnay, with
          a significant amount of reserve wine, allowing a complex blend of many parcels.
          Very pale salmon, excellent mousse; the strawberry notes of the fruit are attractive,
          highlighted rather than subdued by the slightly savoury notes of the finish and
          aftertaste. Surprise packet. Diam. 12.5% alc. **Rating** 94 **To** 2015 $28
✪   **Sparkling Shiraz NV** The shiraz for the base wine comes from Orange, made
          using the traditional method, and given lees contact. Tony Cosgriff has an
          unerring hand: here flavour intensity and complexity have been achieved with
          exceptional precision and balance. Diam. 14% alc. **Rating** 94 **To** 2018 $25

ⓉⓉⓉⓉⓉ **Woodside Single Vineyard Pinot Grigio 2012** Not for the first time,
✪ winemaker Tony Cosgriff has come up with something extra from this estate-grown wine. It has considerable focus, grip and length, with nashi pear/brown pear skin fruit and crunchy acidity. Near the top of the grigio pile. Screwcap. 11.8% alc. **Rating** 93 **To** 2014 $23

✪ **Woodside Single Vineyard Riesling 116 2012** Pale colour; the bouquet is restrained and savoury, with lemon rind, fennel and ginger; the palate delivers a little generosity from the 6g/l of residual sugar, finishing for the most part dry and chalky. Screwcap. 11% alc. **Rating** 92 **To** 2018 $20 BE

Reserve Wild Ferment Sauvignon Blanc 2011 Rating 92 **To** 2014 $25
Finale Late Autumn Chardonnay 2011 Rating 92 **To** 2016 $23
Reserve Single Vineyard Cabernet Sauvignon 2010 Rating 91 **To** 2020 $30 BE
Woodside Sauvignon Blanc 2012 Rating 90 **To** 2015 $22 BE
Reserve Single Vineyard Pinot Gris 2011 Rating 90 **To** 2015 $25 BE
Woodside Single Vineyard Pinot Noir 2011 Rating 90 **To** 2016 $25 BE

Ceravolo Estate ★★★☆

Suite 5, 143 Glynburn Road, Firle, SA 5070 (postal) **Region** Adelaide Plains
T (08) 8336 4522 **www**.ceravolo.com.au **Open** Not
Winemaker Joe Ceravolo, Michael Sykes, Ben Glaetzer (Contract) **Est.** 1985
Dozens 25 000 **Vyds** 23.5ha

Dentist turned vigneron and winemaker Joe Ceravolo, and wife Heather, have been producing single vineyard wines from their 16ha estate on the Adelaide Plains since 1999, enjoying wine show success, particularly with Shiraz, Petit Verdot, Merlot and Sangiovese. Their son Antony, with wife Fiona, is now working with them to take their family business into the next generation. The Ceravolos have also established vineyards (7.5ha) around their home in the Adelaide Hills, focusing on cooler-climate Italian varieties such as primitivo, piccolit, pinot grigio, dolcetto, barbera and cortese. Wines are released under Ceravolo, St Andrews Estate and export-only Red Earth labels. Exports to all major markets.

ⓉⓉⓉⓉ **Red Earth Adelaide Plains Shiraz 2011** More depth of colour than many
✪ '11s, likewise weight and flavour in the mouth; no one could accuse the wine of elegance or finesse, just very good value and abundant black fruits; great barbecue red. Cork. 14% alc. **Rating** 87 **To** 2015 $11

Ceres Bridge Estate ★★★

84 Merrawarp Road, Stonehaven, Vic 3221 **Region** Geelong
T (03) 5271 1212 **Open** By appt
Winemaker Challon Murdock, Nyal Condon **Est.** 1996 **Dozens** 500 **Vyds** 7.4ha

Challon and Patricia Murdock began the long, slow and at times very frustrating process of establishing their vineyard in 1996. They planted 1.8ha of chardonnay in that year, but 50% of the vines died over the next two years in the face of drought and inadequate water supply. Instead of deciding it was all too difficult, they persevered by planting 1.1ha of pinot noir in 2000, replanting in '01, and then in '05 signified the intention to become serious by planting between 0.5ha and 1ha each of shiraz, nebbiolo, sauvignon blanc, viognier, tempranillo and pinot grigio.

ⓉⓉⓉⓉ **Geelong Chardonnay 2011** Bright mid gold; ripe nectarine, fresh fig, hazelnut and spicy oak aromas are evident on the bouquet; medium-bodied, generous and sweet-fruited with a lingering tail of toasty oak on the finish. Screwcap. 12.5% alc. **Rating** 89 **To** 2016 $20 BE

Chaffey Bros Wine Co. ★★★★

26 Campbell Road, Parkside, SA 5063 (postal) **Region** Barossa Valley
T 0417 565 511 **www**.chaffeybros.com **Open** Not
Winemaker Daniel Chaffey Hartwig **Est.** 2008 **Dozens** 20 000

This is a negociant/virtual winery business, co-founded by Daniel Chaffey Hartwig, the fifth generation of the Chaffey family in the Australian wine business. Daniel's great-uncle Bill Chaffey founded Seaview Wines in McLaren Vale, and he in turn was a descendant of the Chaffey brothers who came to Australia to create the Sunraysia and Riverland regions as we know them today by designing and implementing the original irrigation schemes. Daniel, born and raised in the Barossa Valley, worked at Penfolds' cellar door. After eight years of selling and helping other people create wine labels, he became a bulk wine merchant dealing both in Australian and overseas wines. Chaffey Bros Wine Co. has developed a range of wines including Cornucopia's Finest, Hero Series, Rivers of Gold, The Killer and the Nosey Parker (the last two exclusive to Dan Murphy). Exports to the UK, Canada and China.

Synonymous The Barossa is Shiraz 2010 Deep purple-red; a rich, complex and powerful wine, bordering on too powerful; its black fruits, licorice and tar aromas are replayed on the palate, but with some chocolate borrowed from McLaren Vale. In the end, it all comes together, and is good value. Screwcap. 14.5% alc. **Rating** 93 **To** 2025 $24

Battle for Barrosa La Conquista! Tempranillo + Garnacha 2012 Vivid purple-crimson; we don't know the blend percentages, and hence the size of the forces of the combatants, but the outcome is a win-win; juicy red berry/cherry/ raspberry fruits are the order of the day, the tannins fine. Ready any time over the next 4 years. Screwcap. 13.9% alc. **Rating** 93 **To** 2017 $24

This Is Not Your Grandma's Eden Valley Riesling 2012 Bright, light straw-green; the floral bouquet offers lime and apple blossom aromas, the vibrant palate with chalky/minerally acidity providing the structure for the citrus fruit; will flourish with time in bottle. Screwcap. 12.3% alc. **Rating** 92 **To** 2022 $22

The Nosey Parker Barossa Shiraz 2010 Apart from the cheeky label, this is a good wine at its price; its colour is good; it has blackberry and mulberry fruit on a palate that is light- to medium-bodied, and not troubled by oak or, for that matter, tannins. Screwcap. 14.5% alc. **Rating** 88 **To** 2014 $14

Chain of Ponds ★★★★★

Adelaide Road, Gumeracha, SA 5233 **Region** Adelaide Hills
T (08) 8389 1415 **www.**chainofponds.com.au **Open** Fri–Sun 11–4
Winemaker Greg Clack **Est.** 1993 **Dozens** 30 000
The Chain of Ponds brand has been separated from the now-sold 200ha of vineyards, which were among the largest in the Adelaide Hills. It has contract growers throughout the Adelaide Hills for the label, two single vineyard reds from Kangaroo Island, and the Novello wines with a SA appellation. Exports to the UK, the US, Canada, Singapore, Hong Kong, the Philippines and China.

First Lady Barrel Fermented Adelaide Hills Sauvignon Blanc 2011 Light to medium straw-green; a particularly complex Sauvignon Blanc reflecting the cool, wet growing season and the use of oak; there is a stainless steel wire of acidity that runs through the centre of the wine, giving it grip and tenacity, and the ability to age for some years to come. Screwcap. 11% alc. **Rating** 94 **To** 2015 $30

Grave's Gate Adelaide Hills Shiraz 2010 Good crimson-purple hue and clarity; the black cherry fruit on the bouquet has a liberal dusting of spice and pepper, blackberry and bitter chocolate minor players chiming in on the palate; the sweet fruit on the finish is neatly balanced by firm tannins. Screwcap. 14.5% alc. **Rating** 92 **To** 2020 $19

The Ledge Adelaide Hills Shiraz 2010 Rating 92 **To** 2023 $38 BE

Black Thursday Adelaide Hills Sauvignon Blanc 2012 Light straw-green; a savoury and immediately satisfying wine, with flavours firmly in the asparagus/ capsicum/grass spectrum, not tropical; the one concession is the citrussy acidity on the finish. Screwcap. 12.5% alc. **Rating** 91 **To** 2014 $19

Corkscrew Rd Chardonnay 2011 Rating 91 **To** 2018 $35 BE

Corkscrew Rd Chardonnay 2005 Rating 90 **To** 2015 $38 BE

The Amadeus Cabernet Sauvignon 2010 Rating 90 **To** 2020 $38 BE

Chalice Bridge Estate ★★★★☆

796 Rosa Glen Road, Margaret River, WA 6285 **Region** Margaret River
T (08) 9319 8200 **www**.chalicebridge.com.au **Open** By appt
Winemaker Janice McDonald (Consultant) **Est.** 1998 **Dozens** 15 000 **Vyds** 122ha
Planting of the vineyard (now fully owned by the Edinger family) began in 1998; there are now 29ha of chardonnay, over 28ha each of cabernet sauvignon and shiraz, 12.5ha of semillon, 18ha of sauvignon blanc, 7.5ha of merlot and a small amount of savagnin; it is the second-largest single vineyard in Margaret River. Sensible pricing helps, cross-subsidised by the sale of the major part of the annual crop. Exports to the UK, Macau, Hong Kong and China.

⚗⚗⚗⚗⚗ **The Quest Margaret River Shiraz 2010** Mid garnet, purple; a fragrant bouquet of blue and black fruits, with sage, ironstone and violet highlights; medium-bodied and fresh, the tannins are fine-grained and ripe; long, expansive and harmonious on the finish. Screwcap. 14% alc. **Rating** 94 **To** 2020 $26 BE

⚗⚗⚗⚗⚗ **The Quest Margaret River Cabernet Sauvignon 2010 Rating** 92 **To** 2020 $26 BE
The Quest Margaret River Chardonnay 2011 Rating 91 **To** 2016 $26 BE

Chalk Hill ★★★★★

58 Field Street, McLaren Vale, SA 5171 **Region** McLaren Vale
T (08) 8323 6400 **www**.chalkhill.com.au **Open** Not
Winemaker Emmanuelle Bekkers **Est.** 1973 **Dozens** 25 000 **Vyds** 55ha
The growth of Chalk Hill has accelerated after passing from parents John and Diana Harvey to grapegrowing sons Jock and Tom. Both are heavily involved in wine industry affairs in varying capacities (Tom was a participant in the second intake of the Wine Industry Future Leaders Program). Further acquisitions mean the vineyards now span each subregion of McLaren Vale, and have been planted to both the exotic (savagnin, barbera and sangiovese) and the mainstream (shiraz, cabernet sauvignon, grenache, chardonnay and cabernet franc). Exports to most markets; exports to the US under the Alpha Crucis label, to Canada under the Wits End label.

⚗⚗⚗⚗⚗ **Alpha Crucis McLaren Vale Shiraz 2011** The vivid colour, flavour, texture, balance and length of this wine are still exceptional. So, too, is its sense of place, its typicity, for this is the essence of McLaren Vale shiraz, with black fruits, dark bitter chocolate and savoury tannins all present and correct. Screwcap. 14% alc. **Rating** 95 **To** 2031 $85
Alpha Crucis Titan McLaren Vale Shiraz 2010 Medium red-purple; an elegant, supple, medium-bodied Shiraz that speaks loudly of McLaren Vale in a good vintage. There is abundant fruit flavour, but no alcohol heat nor dead fruit anywhere on the radar screen; unsurprisingly, the tannin and alcohol balance is very good. Screwcap. 14% alc. **Rating** 94 **To** 2025 $28

⚗⚗⚗⚗⚗ **Luna McLaren Vale Shiraz 2012** Dense, deep purple-crimson; an extraordinary
✪ wine, with more blackberry fruit per dollar than any other shiraz I can recollect ever tasting; durif would be the only competitor. It is a velvety, luscious mouthful of fruit, dark chocolate and soft tannins, whatever oak used no longer visible – and not needed. Exceptional value. Screwcap. 15% alc. **Rating** 93 **To** 2025 $15
✪ **The Procrastinator 2011** An estate-grown blend of cabernet franc, cabernet sauvignon and shiraz. It has the classic cabernet franc characters of a perfumed bouquet and lively cedar/cigar box-like flavours, the other varieties in sympathetic support. Always the same, always a bargain. Screwcap. 14% alc. **Rating** 91 **To** 2017 $18

Chalkers Crossing ★★★★★

285 Grenfell Road, Young, NSW 2594 **Region** Hilltops
T (02) 6382 6900 **www**.chalkerscrossing.com.au **Open** Mon–Fri 9–5
Winemaker Celine Rousseau **Est.** 2000 **Dozens** 17 000 **Vyds** 27ha

Chalkers Crossing's Rockleigh Vineyard was planted in 1996–97, and is supplemented by purchased grapes from Tumbarumba. Winemaker Celine Rousseau was born in France's Loire Valley, trained in Bordeaux and has worked in Bordeaux, Champagne, Languedoc, Margaret River and the Perth Hills. This Flying Winemaker (now an Australian citizen) has exceptional skills and dedication. In 2012 a subsidiary of a substantial Hong Kong-based company (Nice Link Pty Ltd) acquired Chalkers Crossing, and has appointed Celine Rousseau as manager of the business in addition to her prior and continuing role as winemaker. Exports to the UK, Canada, Germany, Denmark, Sweden, Singapore, China and Hong Kong.

♛♛♛♛♛ **Hilltops Riesling 2012** Another in a long series of fine, pure and crystalline
✪   Rieslings from Chalkers Crossing, lime foremost, green apple in the background; the high natural acidity, and low pH, gives the wine its minerally character, and underwrites its future. Screwcap. 12.5% alc. **Rating** 94 **To** 2022 $18
✪   **Hilltops Semillon 2011** Pale straw-green; fermented in used French barriques, then kept in those barrels on lees for 12 months; it is a textured and vibrant wine, the oak simply adding to the texture of the lemon-acccented fruit, acidity a given, and providing excellent length. Screwcap. 11.5% alc. **Rating** 94 **To** 2021 $18

♛♛♛♛♛ **Tumbarumba Chardonnay 2011** **Rating** 92 **To** 2018 $25
✪   **Tumbarumba Sauvignon Blanc 2012** Light straw-green; partially barrel-fermented in French barriques and given lees contact; a finely structured wine in a cut grass, pea pod and citrus spectrum, with just a breath of passionfruit. Screwcap. 12% alc. **Rating** 91 **To** 2014 $18
        Hilltops Cabernet Sauvignon 2011 **Rating** 90 **To** 2020 $35

Chalmers   ★★★★☆

PO Box 2263, Mildura, Vic 3502 **Region** Murray Darling/Heathcote
T 0400 261 932 **www**.chalmerswine.com.au **Open** Not
Winemaker Sandro Mosele (Contract) **Est.** 1989 **Dozens** 8000 **Vyds** 26.5ha
Following the March 2008 sale of their very large vineyard and vine nursery propagation business, the Chalmers family has refocused its wine businesses. The main vineyard is an 80ha property on the Mt Camel Range in Heathcote, which provides the grapes for the individual variety, single vineyard Chalmers range (Vermentino, Fiano, Rosato, Nero d'Avola, Lagrein, Sangiovese, Sagrantino and Aglianico). The entry-level Montevecchio label is based around blends and more approachable styles. The second vineyard, at Mildura, is simply a contract grapegrower, other than a small nursery block housing the Chalmers' clonal selections. In '13 a program of micro-vinification of the rarer, and hitherto unutilised, varieties from the Nursery Block have begun.

♛♛♛♛♛ **Heathcote Fiano 2011** Bright straw-green; has that surge of intensity to its flavour than marks fiano; lees contact has added a creamy texture before a savoury finish. This is a variety with a future in Australia after the shouting dies down. Screwcap. 12.5% alc. **Rating** 94 **To** 2015 $35

♛♛♛♛♛ **Heathcote Vermentino 2012** **Rating** 90 **To** 2014 $25
        Montevecchio Bianco 2012 **Rating** 90 **To** 2014 $23
        Heathcote Rosato 2012 **Rating** 90 **To** 2013 $25
        Montevecchio Heathcote Rosato 2012 **Rating** 90 **To** 2013 $23
        Montevecchio Heathcote Moscato 2012 **Rating** 90 **To** 2013 $23 TS

Chambers Rosewood   ★★★★★

Barkly Street, Rutherglen, Vic 3685 **Region** Rutherglen
T (02) 6032 8641 **www**.chambersrosewood.com.au **Open** Mon–Sat 9–5, Sun 10–5
Winemaker Stephen Chambers **Est.** 1858 **Dozens** 10000 **Vyds** 50ha
Chambers' Rare Muscat and Rare Muscadelle (or Topaque or Tokay, what's in a name?) are the greatest of all in the Rutherglen firmament, the other wines in the hierarchy also magnificent. Stephen Chambers comes into the role as winemaker, the sixth generation of the Chambers family. Exports to the UK, the US, Belgium, Sweden and NZ.

TTTTT **Rare Rutherglen Muscat NV** Beautifully fragrant, with a sense of true age, depth and power; floral on entry, the acidity is extraordinary and gives the wine amazing life and nerve; the layers of flavour are almost countless, and this wine is truly something that every wine lover must experience at least once in their lives; one sip was taken for this entire note and the flavour is still building. 375ml. Cork. 18% alc. **Rating** 98 **To** 2014 $250

Rare Rutherglen Muscadelle NV Deep, dark burnt umber, with an olive rim; exceedingly complex, and contains some very old material contributing to the rancio characters; the wine adheres to the sides of the glass as you swirl it, but, notwithstanding its concentration, the innumerable flavours come together on an exceedingly long, yet effortless, finish. 375ml. Screwcap. 18% alc. **Rating** 98 **To** 2014 $250

Special Rutherglen Tokay NV Attractive olive-green hue; explosive toasted toffee, ground grilled nuts, a touch of cold tea and plenty of bitter chocolate; the palate is layered, long, luscious and completely delicious, and the dark chocolate character holds on for the longest time; staggering complexity. 375ml. Cork. 18% alc. **Rating** 96 **To** 2014 $100 BE

Grand Rutherglen Muscat NV Has moved well into the brown spectrum, with olive starting to appear on the rim; here the raisin fruit has concentrated and developed strong Christmas pudding, liqueured plum, and an array of Asian spices, wrapped up in a viscous drum roll of flavour. 375ml. Screwcap. 18% alc. **Rating** 96 **To** 2014 $55

Grand Rutherglen Special Muscadelle NV Mahogany, with olive rim; intense tea leaf, toffee, fish oil and coffee varietal character, the flavours blazing in the mouth. Chambers' Grand is almost anyone else's Rare. 375ml. Cork. 18% alc. **Rating** 96 **To** 2014 $100

Old Vine Rutherglen Muscadelle NV Chambers has chosen to use the grape varietal name, rather than Topaque (the approved substituted for the incorrect 'Tokay'). Bright golden-brown; the wine is, as expected, very complex, with a mix of vanilla, tea, spice, mocha and toffee characters; part of the secret of the wine is the perfectly balanced finish. 375ml. Screwcap. 18.5% alc. **Rating** 96 **To** 2014 $60

✪ **Old Vine Muscat NV** Is old enough to have lost any red hues, but is still fresh and youthful, with raisins and warm spices illuminating the bouquet and palate alike. It is one of those wines that is so well balanced and inviting, you might well regret the following morning how much you drank the night before. 375ml. Screwcap. 18% alc. **Rating** 94 **To** 2014 $20

Chanters Ridge ★★★★

440 Chanters Lane, Tylden, Vic 3444 **Region** Macedon Ranges
T 0427 511 341 **www.**chantersridge.com.au **Open** W'ends 10–4 by appt
Winemaker Hanging Rock Winery **Est.** 1995 **Dozens** 200 **Vyds** 2ha
Orthopaedic surgeon Barry Elliott, as well as running the surgery unit at Melbourne's Alfred Hospital, has became involved with the Kyneton Hospital. He and his wife acquired the 24ha property without any clear idea of what they might do with it; later his lifelong interest in wine steered him towards the idea of establishing a vineyard. He retained John Ellis as his consultant, and this led to the planting of pinot noir, and the first tiny make in 2000.

TTTTY **Macedon Ranges Pinot Noir 2009** Deeply coloured, and showing the muscular side of the region, with dark plum, ironstone and clove on the bouquet; warm on the palate, with plenty of liqueur-soaked dark fruits coming to the fore; the weight is commendable, the lack of finesse a slight concern. Screwcap. 12.5% alc. **Rating** 90 **To** 2016 $30 BE

TTTT **Clonal Selection Pinot Noir 2010 Rating** 88 **To** 2016 $35 BE

Chapel Hill ★★★★★

1 Chapel Hill Road, McLaren Vale, SA 5171 **Region** McLaren Vale
T (08) 8323 8429 **www**.chapelhillwine.com.au **Open** 7 days 11–5
Winemaker Michael Fragos, Bryn Richards **Est.** 1973 **Dozens** 40 000 **Vyds** 44ha
A leading medium-sized winery in the region. In 2000 Chapel Hill was sold to the Swiss
Thomas Schmidheiny group, which owns the respected Cuvaison winery in California as well
as vineyards in Switzerland and Argentina. Wine quality is as good as, if not better than, ever.
The production comes from the estate plantings of shiraz, cabernet sauvignon, chardonnay,
verdelho, savagnin, sangiovese and merlot, together with purchased grapes from McLaren Vale.
Exports to all other major markets.

ŸŸŸŸŸ The Vicar McLaren Vale Shiraz 2011 Dense, deep purple; from the best blocks
and vineyards of the vintage, the source two Inkwell Vineyard blocks, and one
Trembath Vineyard. This is the fullest bodied Chapel Hill '11 Shiraz, achieving its
power with less obvious effort, the black fruit, savoury chocolate, oak and tannin
contributions all in sync. Screwcap. 14.5% alc. **Rating** 94 **To** 2026 $75
Bush Vine McLaren Vale Grenache 2011 Light colour; from old vines,
with spiced red berry aromas and flavours that include raspberry and cherry, but
(happily) little confection characters, just those spices of the bouquet. Screwcap.
14.5% alc. **Rating** 94 **To** 2016 $35
McLaren Vale Mourvedre 2011 Yet another Chapel Hill wine from '11 with
amazing depth to its colour and hue, and even more to the plush, sweet, velvety
black fruits and ripe tannins. Saluté; Chapeaux. Screwcap. 14.5% alc. **Rating** 94
To 2026 $35

ŸŸŸŸŸ Road Block McLaren Vale Shiraz 2011 **Rating** 93 **To** 2021 $65
The Chosen Gorge Block McLaren Vale Cabernet Sauvignon 2011
Rating 93 **To** 2026 $65

✪ Parson's Nose McLaren Vale Shiraz 2011 Exceptional purple-crimson; it is
clear parts of McLaren Vale were able to harvest high-quality shiraz, here matured
in French oak (mainly used) that allows the plum-accented fruit free range; tannins
are soft and ripe. Excellent value. Screwcap. 14.5% alc. **Rating** 92 **To** 2015 $16
Il Vescovo McLaren Vale Sangiovese Rose 2012 **Rating** 90 **To** 2013 $22

✪ Abacus McLaren Vale Shiraz 2011 Deep purple-crimson; the startling colour
(for an '11 wine) is on a par with the curious back label description of the palate
as 'ethereal, opulent, chunky'. The wine is, in fact, a pleasing midpoint between
those descriptors, with black fruits, a thin coat of French oak, and no shortage of
tannins. Screwcap. 14.5% alc. **Rating** 90 **To** 2017 $20
McLaren Vale Cabernet Sauvignon 2011 **Rating** 90 **To** 2020 $35 BE
Il Vescovo McLaren Vale Sangiovese 2011 **Rating** 90 **To** 2020 $25

Chapman Grove Wines ★★★★★

PO Box 1460, Margaret River, WA 6285 **Region** Margaret River
T (08) 9364 3885 **www**.chapmangrove.com.au **Open** Not
Winemaker Bruce Dukes (Contract) **Est.** 2005 **Dozens** 10 000 **Vyds** 32ha
A very successful venture under the control of managing director Ron Fraser. The contract-
made wines come from the extensive estate vineyards planted to chardonnay, semillon,
sauvignon blanc, shiraz, cabernet sauvignon and merlot. The wines are released in three price
ranges: at the bottom end, the Dreaming Dog red varietals and blends; in the middle, the
standard Chapman Grove range; and, at the top, ultra-premium wines under the Atticus label.
Exports to Canada, Hong Kong, Singapore, the Philippines, Taiwan and China.

ŸŸŸŸŸ Atticus La Croyance Single Vineyard Barrel Aged Margaret River
Sauvignon Blanc Semillon 2011 The bouquet has barrel-fermented oak
aromas intermingling with hints of nettle and guava; the palate is lively and fresh,
with toasty oak notes a feature on the finish, but not obscuring the fruit. Screwcap.
12.6% alc. **Rating** 94 **To** 2016 $60

Atticus Single Vineyard Margaret River Chardonnay 2011 Mid green-gold; the complex bouquet displays grapefruit, nectarine and quality barrel-fermented oak; the fluid and very well-balanced, medium-bodied palate offers generous levels of fruit, good acidity and a long finish. Screwcap. 13.4% alc. **Rating** 94 **To** 2018 $60

Atticus Single Vineyard Margaret River Syrah 2011 Deep crimson, purple; highly expressive and perfumed, with dark cherry, plum, grilled cashew and violets on the bouquet; the palate is medium-bodied and focused, with fresh acidity and ample tannins sitting neatly with the fruit; there is a bitter amaro note on the finish, offering added complexity and length. Screwcap. 14.4% alc. **Rating** 94 **To** 2022 $60 BE

♟♟♟♟♟
✪ **Margaret River Semillon Sauvignon Blanc 2011** A highly expressive and pungent bouquet of green nettle, pea pod and tropical fruit; the palate is super zesty, with tangy acidity a feature, eventually softening on the fruitful finish. Screwcap. 12% alc. **Rating** 90 **To** 2014 $20 BE

Atticus Cabernet Sauvignon 2011 Rating 90 **To** 2018 $60 BE

Charles Cimicky ★★★★★

Hermann Thumm Drive, Lyndoch, SA 5351 **Region** Barossa Valley
T (08) 8524 4025 **www**.charlescimickywines.com.au **Open** Tues–Fri 10.30–3.30, or by appt
Winemaker Charles Cimicky **Est.** 1972 **Dozens** 20 000 **Vyds** 25ha
These wines are of very good quality, thanks to the sophisticated use of good oak in tandem with high-quality grapes. Historically, Cimicky was happy to keep an ultra-low profile, but he has relented sufficiently to send some (very impressive) wines. Exports to the US, Canada, Switzerland, Germany, Malaysia and Hong Kong.

♟♟♟♟♟ **Barossa Valley Shiraz Mataro 2010** Impenetrable colour; dark and brooding, with inky black fruits, mocha oak, saltbush and bramble complexity; the palate is full-blooded, extremely intense and loaded with black fruits, gravelly, chewy tannins and finishing with a harmonious mocha note from the judicious oak handling; will stand the test of time. Cork. 14% alc. **Rating** 94 **To** 2025 $35 BE

♟♟♟♟♟
✪ **Trumps Barossa Valley Shiraz 2010** As honest as they come for Barossa shiraz, and handsomely priced; plum and blackberry fruit, mocha oak and soft tannins result in a full-flavoured and very well-balanced palate with no hint of alcohol heat. Excellent value. Screwcap. 14% alc. **Rating** 92 **To** 2018 $20

Barossa Valley Durif 2010 Rating 92 **To** 2018 $40 BE
Invisible Man Barossa Valley Shiraz 2011 Rating 90 **To** 2018 $25 BE

Charles Melton ★★★★★

Krondorf Road, Tanunda, SA 5352 **Region** Barossa Valley
T (08) 8563 3606 **www**.charlesmeltonwines.com.au **Open** 7 days 11–5
Winemaker Charlie Melton **Est.** 1984 **Dozens** 15 000 **Vyds** 31ha
Charlie Melton, one of the Barossa Valley's great characters, with wife Virginia by his side, makes some of the most eagerly sought à la mode wines in Australia. Inevitably, the Melton empire has continued to grow in response to the insatiable demand. There are now 7ha at Lyndoch, 9ha at Krondorf and 1.6ha at Light Pass, the lion's share shiraz and grenache, and a small planting of cabernet sauvignon. An additional 30ha property was purchased in High Eden, with 10ha of shiraz planted in 2009, and a 5ha field planting of grenache, shiraz, mataro, carignan, cinsaut, picpoul and bourboulenc planted in '10. The expanded volume has had no adverse effect on the wonderfully rich, well-made wines. The original Krondorf village church (circa 1864) has been converted to guest accommodation. Exports to all major markets.

♟♟♟♟♟ **Grains of Paradise Shiraz 2010** An outstanding Shiraz from a great vintage, with layer upon layer of black fruits, spice and licorice framed by ripe tannins and oak, the latter perfectly balanced and integrated. Despite all of its complexity and power, it is elegant and little more than medium-bodied. Screwcap. 14.5% alc. **Rating** 97 **To** 2040 $60

The Kirche Barossa Valley Shiraz 2010 The church (kirche) at Krondorf is surrounded by the vines that produced the grapes for this supremely elegant, medium-bodied wine, most of which finished its primary fermentation in barriques (66% French, 34% American). It then spent 27 months on lees in those barrels; the result is a vibrant red and black-fruited palate, with perfect balance and mouthfeel. Screwcap. 14.5% alc. **Rating** 96 **To** 2035 $35

Sotto di Ferro NV Golden brown; an utterly seductive glass of caramelised cumquat and honey, viscous in the mouth, yet with freshness on the finish and aftertaste. Worth every cent. 375ml. Screwcap. 8% alc. **Rating** 96 **To** 2014 $55

Barossa Valley Rose of Virginia 2012 Brilliant puce; a vibrantly fresh and lively cascade of all the red fruits imaginable run through a long and perfectly balanced palate, the aftertaste demanding another mouthful. Screwcap. 13% alc. **Rating** 95 **To** 2014 $25

Barossa Valley Cabernet Sauvignon 2010 Medium red-purple; the mouthfeel is sensuously soft, and the flavours are right in the heartland of cabernet sauvignon, with a mix of redcurrant and blackcurrant fruit, the tannins ameliorated by the barrel-ferment influence, but still balanced (and needed). Screwcap. 14.5% alc. **Rating** 95 **To** 2030 $45

Richelieu 2010 **Rating** 94 **To** 2025 $60

Barossa Valley Cabernet Sauvignon 2009 **Rating** 94 **To** 2029 $60

ΨΨΨΨΨ The Father In Law Shiraz 2010 **Rating** 93 **To** 2025 $24
The Kirche Barossa Valley Shiraz 2009 **Rating** 93 **To** 2024 $34

Charles Sturt University Winery ★★★★☆

McKeown Drive (off Coolamon Road), Wagga Wagga, NSW 2650 **Region** Big Rivers Zone
T (02) 6933 2435 **www**.csu.edu.au/winery **Open** Mon–Fri 11–5, w'ends 11–4
Winemaker Andrew Drumm **Est.** 1977 **Dozens** 12 000 **Vyds** 25.1ha
The full-scale commercial winery (opened 2002), the $1 experimental winery (opened '01) and a new cellar door building have all been largely financed by the proceeds of the sales of the CSU wines, which always offer exceptional value. Following the university's acquisition of the former University of Sydney campus in Orange (Leeds Parade, open Fri-Sun 11–4), it now has 7.1ha of estate plantings at Wagga Wagga and 18ha of mature vineyards at Orange, the latter planted to chardonnay, sauvignon blanc, shiraz, cabernet sauvignon and merlot. Interestingly, this teaching facility is using screwcaps for all its wines, white and red, recalling its pioneering use in 1977. Since 2005 its sparkling wines have been released under crown seal.

ΨΨΨΨΨ R Riesling 2012 Bright straw-green; the citrus blossom bouquet leads into a
✪ delicious palate, full of lime and lemon juice fruit backed by crisp acidity; will live for a decade, but will it ever be better than now? Screwcap. 12.5% alc. **Rating** 94 **To** 2022 $20

ΨΨΨΨΨ Cellar Reserve Tumbarumba Chardonnay 2011 **Rating** 93 **To** 2018 $28

ΨΨΨΨ Sauvignon Blanc 2012 Part of the grapes come from Tumbarumba to
✪ supplement the estate-grown portion from Orange; an elegant and vibrant wine, citrus to the fore, hints of passionfruit in the background. Very good value. Screwcap. 12.5% alc. **Rating** 89 **To** 2014 $15

Charnwood Estate ★★★★

253 Burrundulla Road, Mudgee, NSW 2850 (postal) **Region** Mudgee
T (02) 6372 4577 **www**.charnwoodestate.com.au **Open** Not
Winemaker Jacob Stein **Est.** 2004 **Dozens** 1500 **Vyds** 2ha
In 2004 owner Greg Dowker planted the vineyard on a historic property just 5mins from the centre of Mudgee, nestled at the foot of the surrounding hills of the Cudgegong Valley. He has established shiraz (1.5ha) and merlot (0.5ha), the wines contract-made by former Flying Winemaker Jacob Stein.

ΨΨΨΨΨ **C&S Premium Shiraz 2011** Mid garnet, red; lifted and spicy with fresh herbs and black cherry the prominent features of the bouquet; the palate is angular, with firm tannins and raspy acidity, yet there is charm in its rustic appeal and lingering freshness on the finish. Screwcap. 13.5% alc. **Rating** 90 **To** 2018 $18 BE

ΨΨΨΨ **Charlie's Row Merlot 2011 Rating** 88 **To** 2018 $19 BE
Mudgee Rose 2012 Rating 87 **To** 2014 $17 BE

Charteris Wines ★★★★★

PO Box 800, Cessnock, NSW 2320 **Region** Central Otago, NZ
T (02) 4998 7701 **www.**charteriswines.com **Open** Not
Winemaker PJ Charteris **Est.** 2007 **Dozens** 170 **Vyds** 1.7ha
Owners Peter James (PJ) Charteris and partner Christina Pattison met at Brokenwood in the Hunter Valley in 1999. PJ was the chief executive winemaker at Brokenwood, and Christina was the marketing manager. Together they have over three decades of winemaking and wine marketing experience. For NZ-born PJ, finding a top pinot noir site in Central Otago (they claim to have searched both Australia and NZ for the right combination of site and variety) was a spiritual homecoming. They also have a vineyard with the gold-plated address of Felton Road, Bannockburn, planted to clones 115, 777 and Abel. In October 2011 PJ decided the time had come to focus on Charteris Wines, and not without considerable emotional regret on both sides, left Brokenwood. (Tasting notes available on www.winecompanion.com.au.)

Chateau Francois ★★★★★

Broke Road, Pokolbin, NSW 2321 **Region** Hunter Valley
T (02) 4998 7548 **Open** W'ends 9–5, or by appt
Winemaker Don Francois **Est.** 1969 **Dozens** 200
I have known former NSW Director of Fisheries Dr Don Francois for almost as long as I have been involved with wine, which is a very long time indeed. I remember his early fermentations of sundry substances other than grapes (none of which, I hasten to add, was the least bit illegal) in the copper bowl of an antiquated washing machine in his laundry. He established Chateau Francois one year before Brokenwood, and our winemaking and fishing paths have crossed many times since. Some years ago Don suffered a mild stroke, and no longer speaks or writes with any fluency, but this has not stopped him from producing a range of absolutely beautiful Semillons that flourish marvellously with age. I should add that he is even prouder of the distinguished career of his daughter, Rachel Francois, at the NSW bar. The semillon vines are now over 40 years old, producing exceptional wine that is sold for the proverbial song year after year. Five-star value.

ΨΨΨΨΨ **Pokolbin Semillon 2007** Gleaming green-yellow; it is remarkable how a wine with such finesse and delicacy can be so filled with every lemon flavour imaginable and add a few more notes (grapefruit and lime) for good measure. Screwcap. 12% alc. **Rating** 96 **To** 2020 $18
Pokolbin Semillon 2012 Bright quartz; has a proud track record of releases with around 5 years' bottle age, hence the '07 to accompany this '12 wine. Thus don't underestimate this wine, for there are all the markers for future development in the lemongrass and minerally acidity. Screwcap. 11% alc. **Rating** 94 **To** 2025 $18

ΨΨΨΨ **Pokolbin Shiraz 2010** Gentle sweet berry fruit, soft tannins and an airbrush of
✪ oak join forces to provide an easygoing wine that is ready now, although will hold. Screwcap. 12.5% alc. **Rating** 89 **To** 2015 $18
✪ **Pinot Noir Rougeur 2005** The palest of the three Rougeurs, but far deeper than rose; lively and fresh, with strawberry and spice; the wine has considerable length, and is well balanced. Cork. 13.3% alc. **Rating** 89 **To** 2014 $18
✪ **Pinot Noir Rougeur 2004** The brightest red-purple; the flavours move partly away from strawberry to cherry, but the freshness and balance remain intact, as does the length. Cork. 13.3% alc. **Rating** 89 **To** 2014 $18
Pinot Noir Rougeur 2003 Rating 88 **To** 2014 $18

Chateau Pâto

67 Thompsons Road, Pokolbin, NSW 2321 **Region** Hunter Valley
T (02) 4998 7634 **Open** By appt
Winemaker Nicholas Paterson **Est.** 1980 **Dozens** 500 **Vyds** 2.5ha

Nicholas Paterson took over responsibility for this tiny winery following the death of father David during the 1993 vintage. The lion's share of plantings is shiraz (the first plantings), with smaller blocks of chardonnay, marsanne, roussanne, viognier and mourvedre; most of the grapes are sold, with a tiny quantity of shiraz being made into a marvellous wine. David's legacy is being handsomely guarded. No wines received for the *2014 Wine Companion*, but a five-star rating has been maintained.

Chateau Tanunda

9 Basedow Road, Tanunda, SA 5352 **Region** Barossa Valley
T (08) 8563 3888 **www**.chateautanunda.com **Open** 7 days 10–5
Winemaker Stuart Bourne **Est.** 1890 **Dozens** 50 000 **Vyds** 95ha

This is one of the most historically significant winery buildings in the Barossa Valley, built from bluestone quarried at nearby Bethany in the late 1880s. It has been restored by the Geber family and a new basket-press winery has been installed. Chateau Tanunda owns almost 100ha of vineyards in Bethany, Eden Valley, Tanunda and Vine Vale, with additional fruit sourced from a group of 30 growers, including descendants of the Barossa's original settlers, covering the panoply of Barossan subregions. The wines are made from hand-picked grapes, basket-pressed, and are neither fined nor filtered. There is an emphasis on single vineyard and single subregion wines under the Terroirs of the Barossa label. The grand building houses the cellar door and Barossa Small Winemakers Centre, offering wines made by boutique winemakers. The acclaimed charity Masters Cricket match played biennially on the CCG (Chateau Cricket Ground) sees many of the world's greats grace its pitch. Exports to the UK, the US, Germany Switzerland, Sweden, Denmark, Belgium and China.

🍷🍷🍷🍷🍷 **The Chateau 100 Year Old Vines Shiraz 2010** The grapes come from four small plantings in different districts within the Barossa Valley; they are open-fermented, basket-pressed, and spend 2½ years in a mix of used and new American and French oak. The colour is deep and bright, and the bouquet, like the medium- to full-bodied palate, is full of blackberry, plum and licorice fruit; the tannins are plentiful and ripe, the oak balanced and integrated. Cork. 14.5% alc. **Rating** 95 To 2025 $99
The Whole Dam Family Shiraz Grenache Mourvedre Carignan Cinsault 2012 A 41/24/22/7/6% blend; the kalaedoscopic array of grapes were all separately fermented and matured in French oak for 10 months prior to blending. It is full of life, with both red and black fruits in joyful and juicy abandon, fine-grained tannins, and a splash of French oak. Cork. 14% alc. **Rating** 95 To 2022 $40

🍷🍷🍷🍷🍷 **The Chateau Old Bush Vine Grenache Rose 2012 Rating** 93 To 2015 $28
Old Vine Barossa Shiraz 2011 Rating 93 To 2026 $40
The Chateau Cabernet Sauvignon 2010 Rating 92 To 2025 $28
The Three Graces Barossa Cabernet Sauvignon Cabernet Franc Merlot 2010 Rating 92 To 2030 $28
The Three Graces Barossa Valley Marsanne Viognier Roussanne 2012 Rating 90 To 2016 $28
✪ **Medley Barossa Grenache Shiraz Mataro 2010** Good, although relatively light, colour; the three varieties are grown in different parts of the Barossa Valley, and this – coupled with the very good vintage – has produced a wine with abundant plum, blackberry and red cherry fruits. Punches well above its price weight. Screwcap. 14.5% alc. **Rating** 90 To 2015 $17

 Chatto

PO Box 54, Cessnock, NSW 2325 **Region** Southern Tasmania
T 0417 710 794 **www**.chattowines.com **Open** Not
Winemaker Jim Chatto **Est.** 2000 **Dozens** 200 **Vyds** 1.5ha
I have to disclose a personal interest here: in 1999 one of the associate judges put forward by
the organisers of the Tasmanian Wines Show (I was Chairman) was a youthful Jim Chatto, and
I had no idea of his wine career to that date. His judging was of the highest standard, and I
asked him where had he gained his judging experience. The answer was 'Nowhere, this is the
first time I have judged.' Thus it was no surprise that he quickly became recognised as having
one of the very best palates in Australia, and has proved to be an outstanding winemaker.
He and wife Daisy have long wanted to get a small Tasmanian pinot wine business up and
running, but having moved to the Hunter Valley in 2000, it took six years to find a site that
satisfied all of the criteria Jim considers ideal. It is a warm, well-drained site in one of the
coolest parts of Tasmania, looking out over Glaziers Bay. So far they have planted nine clones,
with a 5000 vines per hectare spacing. Exports to the UK.

ΨΨΨΨΨ   Pinot Noir 2012 Vivid, crystal clear, purple-crimson; open-fermented with 25%
whole bunches, and then matured in French puncheons (30% new). The bouquet
is highly perfumed, and the red and black fruit palate is as pure, refined and long
as everything suggests it should be. This is a pinot lovers' pinot par example.
Screwcap. 13% alc. **Rating** 96 **To** 2020 $45

Cherry Tree Hill

Hume Highway, Sutton Forest, NSW 2577 **Region** Southern Highlands
T (02) 8217 1409 **www**.cherrytreehill.com.au **Open** 7 days 9–5
Winemaker Anton Balog (Contract) **Est.** 2000 **Dozens** 4000 **Vyds** 13.5ha
The Lorentz family, then headed by Gabi Lorentz, began the establishment of the Cherry Tree
Hill vineyard in 2000 with the planting of 3ha each of cabernet sauvignon and riesling; 3ha
each of merlot and sauvignon blanc followed in '01, and, finally, 2ha of chardonnay in '02.
The inspiration was childhood trips on a horse and cart through his grandfather's vineyard in
Hungary. Gabi's son (and current owner) David completes the three-generation involvement
as manager of the business.

ΨΨΨΨΨ   Riesling 2010 Bright green-straw; later picking and 2 extra years in bottle invest
✪   the wine with a greater range of ripe citrus fruits than the '12; they manifest
themselves with the greatest impact on the aftertaste – not a common experience,
but a good one. Screwcap. 13.5% alc. **Rating** 94 **To** 2018 $20

ΨΨΨΨΨ   Riesling 2012 Pale straw-green; the fragrant lime and apple blossom bouquet
✪   and crisp palate are highly expressive of the variety; this will develop very well
given the way the '10 has moved, and may upstage it down the track. Screwcap.
12.1% alc. **Rating** 92 **To** 2020 $20
✪   Rose 2011 Salmon-pink; a rose with attitude, with a perfumed, spicy bouquet,
and a dry, but supple and long, palate, with red berry fruits hidden in the
background. Exceptional value. Screwcap. 13.5% alc. **Rating** 91 **To** 2014 $15

Chestnut Hill Vineyard

1280 Pakenham Road, Mount Burnett, Vic 3781 **Region** Gippsland
T (03) 5942 7314 **www**.chestnuthillvineyard.com.au **Open** W'ends & public hols
10.30–5.30, or by appt
Winemaker Charlie Javor **Est.** 1995 **Dozens** 1200 **Vyds** 3.5ha
Charlie and Ivka Javor started Chestnut Hill with small plantings of chardonnay, sauvignon
blanc and pinot noir in 1985 and have slowly increased the vineyards to 3.5ha. Less than
an hour's drive from Melbourne, the picturesque vineyard is situated among the rolling
hills in the Dandenongs near Mt Burnett. The label explains, 'Liberty is a gift we had never
experienced in our homeland' – this was Croatia, from which they emigrated in the late 1960s.

ŶŶŶŶŶ Mount Burnett Sauvignon Blanc 2012 Light straw-green; a Sauvignon Blanc with considerable attitude and intensity, tropical fruit running riot on the palate and aftertaste, guava and passionfruit to the fore on the long palate. Diam. 12.8% alc. **Rating** 94 **To** 2014 $27

ŶŶŶŶŶ **Mount Burnett Sauvignon Blanc 2011 Rating** 90 **To** 2014 $25

Chris Ringland ★★★★★

9 Stone Chimney Creek Vineyard, Flaxmans Valley, SA 5353 **Region** Eden Valley
T (08) 8564 3233 www.chrisringland.com **Open** By appt
Winemaker Chris Ringland **Est.** 1989 **Dozens** 500 **Vyds** 2.05ha
The wines made by Chris Ringland for his eponymous brand were at the very forefront of the surge of rich, old-vine Barossa shirazs discovered by Robert Parker. As a consequence of very limited production, and high-quality results, the wine assumed immediate icon status. The production of 100 dozen does not include a small number of magnums, double-magnums and imperials that are sold each year. The addition of 0.5ha planted in 1999, joining the 1.5ha planted in '10 has had little practical impact on availability. Exports (obviously in tiny quantities) to the US, Canada, Belgium, Spain, Singapore and NZ.

ŶŶŶŶŶ Reservation 2008 Open-fermented and taken to barrel to complete the last stages and to undergo mlf (both this and Barossa Ranges are normally wild yeast-fermented, but cultured yeast is added if necessary.) Deeply coloured, the bouquet and palate have immensely deep black fruits as the base, with spice, licorice and fruitcake the next layer, integrated oak and ripe tannins the framework. Screwcap. 16% alc. **Rating** 94 **To** 2028 $50
Barossa Ranges Shiraz 2005 I need to stress that the points for this wine could be much higher or much lower, for it defies conventional assessment. It tasted better 24 hours after it was first opened and tasted. Key descriptors are prune, licorice and dark chocolate; it is the quintessence of Ringland style, and the mouthfeel is unctuously rich and warm. Cork. 17.6% alc. **Rating** 94 **To** 2035 $500

ŶŶŶŶŶ CR Barossa Shiraz 2010 Deep red-purple; the rich bouquet of plum and
✪ blackberry leads into a supple and plush palate bringing a touch of dark chocolate into play. All the French oak inputs (2–3-year-old hogsheads, and/or planks in tanks) are deliberately kept low. The tannins on the finish are soft and ripe, and cellaring isn't needed. Screwcap. 15% alc. **Rating** 92 **To** 2015 $20

Chrismont ★★★★☆

251 Upper King River Road, Cheshunt, Vic 3678 **Region** King Valley
T (03) 5729 8220 www.chrismont.com.au **Open** 7 days 11–5
Winemaker Warren Proft **Est.** 1980 **Dozens** 23 000 **Vyds** 100ha
Arnold (Arnie) and Jo Pizzini's substantial vineyards in the Whitfield area of the upper King Valley have been planted with riesling, sauvignon blanc, chardonnay, pinot gris, cabernet sauvignon, merlot, shiraz, barbera, marzemino and arneis. The La Zona range ties in the Italian heritage of the Pizzinis and is part of the intense interest in all things Italian. It also produces a Prosecco, contract-grown in the King Valley. A second cellar door also operates 7 days 10–5 at Shop 1, 1605 Glenrowan-Myrtleford Road, Milawa. Exports to Singapore.

ŶŶŶŶŶ La Zona King Valley Arneis 2012 If you thought arneis was just another
✪ alternative white grape from Italy, its name more interesting than its taste, think again. This has an almost electric drive to its lemon/lemon zest/lime fruit, not sweet and sour, but with a skein of sweetness buried in a citrus conveyor belt. Screwcap. 12.5% alc. **Rating** 93 **To** 2014 $22
King Valley Pinot Gris 2012 Light straw-green; has delicious pear, apple and citrus fruit that flows seamlessly across the palate, the finish fresh and zesty. Top-drawer Pinot Gris. Screwcap. 13.5% alc. **Rating** 92 **To** 2014 $26
La Zona King Valley Pinot Grigio 2012 Light straw-green; this indeed is grigio, with a more grainy/minerally texture than the gris; however, it has plenty of drive to its varietal fruit, built around nashi pear and spiced apple. Screwcap. 12.5% alc. **Rating** 91 **To** 2014 $22

La Zona King Valley Sangiovese 2011 Light red-purple; has an exotic mix of red and black cherries, including morello and preserved cherries, plus spices and persistent savoury tannins. Cries out for Italian food. Very good outcome for the vintage. Screwcap. 13% alc. **Rating** 91 **To** 2014 $26

King Valley Chardonnay 2011 Light straw-green; the gentle stone fruit and honeydew melon have been given an airbrush of oak, exactly as much as was needed. Well made. Screwcap. 13.5% alc. **Rating** 90 **To** 2016 $24

La Zona King Valley Barbera 2011 Much deeper colour than the Sangiovese, bright and full. Here plum and blackberry have a crosscut of savoury/briary/earthy characters. Once again, demands something like bistecca fiorentina. Screwcap. 13.5% alc. **Rating** 90 **To** 2016 $26

✪ · **La Zona King Valley Marzemino Frizzante 2012** Deep colour; an upmarket variant of Lambrusco. Quite how and where I would wish to drink it is a difficult question; it is chock-full of fruits of the forest, chocolate and spice, and the overall balance is far better than I could have imagined. Strangely fascinating. Screwcap. 9.5% alc. **Rating** 90 **To** 2014 $20

✪ **La Zona King Valley Moscato 2011** Fragrant and fresh, showing grapey aromas with bath talc and a little floral lift and zesty acidity providing life and energy on the finish. Screwcap. 5.5% alc. **Rating** 90 **To** 2013 $16 BE

🍷🍷🍷🍷 **King Valley Riesling 2012** The floral bouquet signals a complex array of
✪ flavours to come, with lime, lemon and softer notes of honeysuckle and spice; close to its best now, but won't suffer from another year or two in bottle. Screwcap. 12% alc. **Rating** 89 **To** 2014 $16

La Zona King Valley Rosato 2012 Rating 89 To 2014 $18

La Zona King Valley Tempranillo 2011 Rating 88 To 2014 $26

Churchview Estate   ★★★★☆

8 Gale Road, Metricup, WA 6280 **Region** Margaret River
T (08) 9755 7200 **www**.churchview.com.au **Open** Mon–Sat 10–5
Winemaker Greg Garnish **Est.** 1998 **Dozens** 25 000 **Vyds** 65ha
The Fokkema family, headed by Spike Fokkema, immigrated from The Netherlands in the 1950s. Business success in the following decades led to the acquisition of the 100ha Churchview Estate property in '97, and to the progressive establishment of substantial vineyards (65ha planted to 15 varieties). Exports to all major markets.

🍷🍷🍷🍷🍷 **The Bartondale Margaret River Cabernet Sauvignon 2011** Good colour; has 5% malbec; this is an altogether seductive cabernet, with a supple but rich medium-bodied palate, cassis and redcurrant fruit flowing evenly throughout, oak totally integrated, the tannins ripe and velvety. 250 dozen made. WAK screwcap. 14.5% alc. **Rating** 95 **To** 2031 $55

🍷🍷🍷🍷🍷 **St Johns Limited Release Cabernet Sauvignon Malbec Merlot Petit Verdot 2011** Rating 93 To 2026 $35
The Bartondale Reserve Margaret River Shiraz 2011 Rating 92 To 2036 $55
St Johns Margaret River Zinfandel 2011 Rating 92 To 2016 $35
St Johns Margaret River Marsanne 2012 Rating 91 To 2019 $35
St Johns Margaret River Vintage Brut 2010 Rating 91 To 2014 $35
The Bartondale Cabernet Sauvignon 2010 Rating 90 To 2016 $55

Ciavarella Oxley Estate   ★★★★

Evans Lane, Oxley, Vic 3678 **Region** King Valley
T (03) 5727 3384 **www**.oxleyestate.com.au **Open** Mon–Sat 9–5, Sun 10–5
Winemaker Cyril and Tony Ciavarella **Est.** 1978 **Dozens** 2500 **Vyds** 1.6ha
Cyril and Jan Ciavarella's vineyard was begun in 1978, with plantings being extended over the years. One variety, aucerot, was first produced by Maurice O'Shea of McWilliam's Mount Pleasant 60 or so years ago; the Ciavarella vines have been grown from cuttings collected from an old Glenrowan vineyard before the parent plants were removed in the mid 1980s.

Tony Ciavarella left a career in agricultural research in mid 2003 to join his parents at Ciavarella. The family is justifiably proud of the breadth of the range of wines it offers.

ŢŢŢŢŢ **Noble Aucerot 2012** Deep gold colour, the high levels of botrytis provide orange marmalade and honey on the bouquet; the palate is very sweet, with high levels of acidity providing a clean and harmonious finish. 500ml. Screwcap. 9% alc. **Rating** 90 **To** 2016 $30 BE

ŢŢŢŢ **Shiraz Viognier 2011** **Rating** 89 **To** 2017 $22 BE
Chardonnay 2011 **Rating** 88 **To** 2015 $19 BE

Cirami Estate ★★★★

78 Nixon Road, Monash, SA 5342 **Region** Riverland
T (08) 8583 5366 **www.rvic.org.au** **Open** Not
Winemaker Alex Russell (Contract) **Est.** 2008 **Dozens** 1000 **Vyds** 46.4ha
Cirami Estate is owned by the Riverland Vine Improvement Committee Inc, a non-profit organisation, although it is a sizeable venture. It is named after Richard Cirami, who was a pioneer in clonal selection and variety assessment, and was on the RVIC committee for over 20 years, beginning in the early 1970s. Richard was made a Member of the Order of Australia in 2003 for his services to the wine industry. The vineyard includes 40 varieties at 0.3ha or greater, and another 2ha planted to over 60 varieties, the latter Cirami Estate's collection of nursery plantings.

ŢŢŢŢŢ **Riverland Lagrein 2012** Deep purple-crimson; theoretically, this cool climate Italian variety should be a square peg in a round hole in the hot Riverland climate, but it's not. Instead this is a wine with black and glace cherry fruit, spice and a splash of chocolate. Trophy Australian Alternative Wine Show '12. Screwcap. 14% alc. **Rating** 93 **To** 2017 $18
Riverland Montepulciano 2012 Good hue; an intriguing bouquet, with nuances of sage, cinnamon and cherry, the palate with a mix of savoury herb and spicy notes alongside the red cherry fruit and fine tannins; the modest alcohol assists the elegance of the wine. Screwcap. 13.5% alc. **Rating** 91 **To** 2015 $18

✪ **Riverland Savagnin 2012** Quartz-white; the bouquet has blossom spice and rose petal nuances, the palate has some of the green apple and citrus flavours, supported by acidity that the variety provides in cooler climates. An interesting, well-priced wine. Screwcap. 13% alc. **Rating** 90 **To** 2013 $15

✪ **Riverland Vermentino 2012** Some hints of spice and musk on the bouquet, then a lively, punchy palate with lime zest, and green apple; shows its suitability to warm regions. Screwcap. 13% alc. **Rating** 90 **To** 2015 $15
Riverland Graciano 2012 Full crimson-purple; a fragrant, warmly spiced bouquet leads into an attractive medium-bodied wine, with juicy mulberry and plum fruit; the lack of tannins does not strip the wine of character. Screwcap. 14.5% alc. **Rating** 90 **To** 2016 $18
Riverland Saperavi 2012 As befits the variety, the purple-crimson colour is so dense it is virtually impenetrable; licorice and boot leather on the bouquet are followed by a robust palate with brooding black fruits but, pleasingly, no surfeit of tannins. Screwcap. 15% alc. **Rating** 90 **To** 2017 $18

Clairault ★★★★☆

3277 Caves Road, Wilyabrup, WA 6280 **Region** Margaret River
T (08) 9755 6225 **www.clairaultwines.com.au** **Open** At Streicker
Winemaker Bruce Dukes **Est.** 1976 **Dozens** 12 000 **Vyds** 39.62ha
Bill and Ena Martin, with sons Conor, Brian and Shane, acquired Clairault several years ago and expanded the vineyards on the 120ha property, but in April 2012 sold the business to John Streicker, already a substantial vineyard owner, with his eponymous wines (see separate entry) made by Naturaliste Vintners. The 12ha of vines established by the former owners (most now over 35 years old) have been supplemented by another 27ha or so of vines, with a ratio of roughly 70% red varieties to 30% white. Deeply concerned about the environment and

consumer health, Clairault has joined with ERA (Environmentally Responsible Agriculture) to implement the elimination of chemical use and the introduction of biological farming. Exports to the UK, the US and other major markets.

ΥΥΥΥΥ Estate Margaret River Chardonnay 2011 Bright straw-green; hand-picked, whole bunch-pressed, wild yeast-fermented in French barriques, lees stirring and partial mlf have been precisely calibrated to produce a wine of remarkable complexity and intensity, intensity that increases further on the finish and aftertaste. WAK screwcap. 13% alc. Rating 95 To 2020 $38

ΥΥΥΥΥ Margaret River Chardonnay 2011 Rating 93 To 2018 $27
✪ Margaret River Cabernet Sauvignon Merlot 2010 Good retention of hue; a lively redcurrant and cassis fruit-driven wine, with a consistent message from both bouquet and medium-bodied palate; the tannins are fine, the oak subtle; good regional expression is another plus. WAK screwcap. 14% alc. Rating 92 To 2019 $22

ΥΥΥΥ Estate Margaret River Cabernet Sauvignon 2011 Rating 89 To 2020 $43

Clare Wine Co

PO Box 852, Nuriootpa, SA 5355 **Region** Clare Valley
T (08) 8562 4488 **www.**clarewineco.com.au **Open** Not
Winemaker Reid Bosward, Stephen Dew **Est.** 2008 **Dozens** 4000 **Vyds** 30.5ha
An affiliate of Kaesler Wines, its primary focus is on exports to China, Singapore and Hong Kong. Its vines are predominantly given over to shiraz (15ha) and cabernet sauvignon (9.5ha). It also has 3.8ha of riesling and 2.2ha of semillon, but no chardonnay, which is presumably purchased from other Clare Valley growers. The business is growing rapidly, production up from 2500 dozen.

ΥΥΥΥΥ Pyrite Shiraz 2010 Dense purple-red; the first release from the estate's Polish Hill vineyard, with its pyrite/slate soil; matured in French oak, 20% new. It is unequivocally full-bodied, with sombre black fruits, strong tannins and oak. How good might it have been with 14% alcohol we will never know. 555 dozen made Cork. 15% alc. Rating 91 To 2030 $40

Clarence House Wines

193 Pass Road, Cambridge, Tas 7170 (postal) **Region** Southern Tasmania
T (03) 6247 7345 **Open** Not
Winemaker Julian Alcorso, Alain Rousseau **Est.** 1998 **Dozens** 3000 **Vyds** 12ha
Clarence House was built in 1830 at Clarence Vale, Mt Rumney. The house has been kept in great condition, and in 1998 present owner, David Kilpatrick, began planting vines on a northeast-sloping block opposite the house. While pinot noir and chardonnay account for over 8ha of the total plantings, the remainder includes pinot blanc and tempranillo, rare in Tasmania. The wines are released under three labels: at the bottom Clarence Plains, made for early drinking; Clarence House Estate, complex wines reflecting the terroir of the region; and Clarence House Reserve, occasional releases from exceptional vintages.

ΥΥΥΥΥ Pinot Noir 2010 Very deep colour indeed; the bouquet and palate are as rich and concentrated as the colour suggests they should be; it is filled with satsuma plum and black cherry fruit, with plenty of spices to help build light and shade; tannins and oak are also present in the right amount. Should be very long lived. Screwcap. 13.7% alc. Rating 94 To 2025 $33
Vivace 2009 A blend of estate-grown pinot noir (two-thirds) and chardonnay (one-third) that spent 30 months on lees prior to disgorgement in Sept '12. A distinctly toasty style with spicy/savoury nuances and a pleasingly dry and very long finish. Cork. 12.3% alc. Rating 94 To 2016 $38

ΥΥΥΥ Pinot Blanc 2012 Rating 88 To 2014 $26
Pinot Blanc 2011 Rating 88 To 2014 $26
Sauvignon Blanc 2011 Rating 87 To 2013 $26

Clarendon Hills

Brookmans Road, Blewitt Springs, SA 5171 **Region** McLaren Vale
T (08) 8363 6111 **www.**clarendonhills.com.au **Open** By appt
Winemaker Roman Bratasiuk **Est.** 1990 **Dozens** 15 000 **Vyds** 63ha

Age and experience, it would seem, have mellowed Roman Bratasiuk – and the style of his wines. Once formidable and often rustic, they are now far more sculpted and smooth, at times bordering on downright elegance. Roman has taken another major step by purchasing a 160ha property high in the hill country of Clarendon at an altitude close to that of the Adelaide Hills. Here he has established a vineyard with single-stake trellising similar to that used on the steep slopes of Germany and Austria, which produces the Domaine Clarendon Syrah. He makes up to 20 different wines each year, all consistently very good, a tribute to the old vines. Knocking on the door of the Winery of the Year Award. Exports to the US and other major markets.

Astralis 2010 Sourced from a single vineyard in the cool Blewitt Springs area, the vines over 90 years old; whole bunches and whole berries are included, followed by 18 months in 100% new, high-quality, French oak; the extreme power of the palate is effortless, and the wine has a touch of elegance that will emerge in the decades to come. Cork. 14.5% alc. **Rating** 97 **To** 2045 $500

Brookman Clarendon Syrah 2010 Dense, inky purple-crimson, purple to the fore; hugely concentrated and complex with years, if not decades, to go before the bouquet fully opens up; the flavours of the full-bodied palate centre on blackberry, licorice, spice and a touch of tobacco; cedary new French oak and tannins are submerged in oceans of fruit. Cork. 14.5% alc. **Rating** 96 **To** 2040 $110

Onkaparinga Clarendon Syrah 2010 Deep crimson-purple; shares the extra dimension of texture and structure with the other '10 releases, but takes it into a palate of considerable vinosity, easily able to absorb the high level of new French oak; bitter chocolate runs through the fruit; fully reflects the excellent vintage. Cork. 14.5% alc. **Rating** 96 **To** 2040 $110

Brookman Clarendon Syrah 2009 Definitely in the new mode of Clarendon Hills. Deep, dark crimson-purple; an exceptionally complex bouquet with nuances of the roasted meats I normally find so elusive, together with tobacco and blackberry nuances; the impact of 18 months in 70% new French oak is obvious, as it is across all of the Clarendon Syrah and Cabernet range. The long and supple palate has lifted black fruit flavours supported by fine, ripe tannins. All in all, a lovely wine. Cork. 14.5% alc. **Rating** 96 **To** 2035 $125

Blewitt Springs Grenache 2010 The most elegant wine in the Grenache line-up, it is deep crimson and bright in colour; the bouquet is laden with vibrant red fruits, floral notes, thyme and sappy complexity; the definition of fruit is bell-clear, with succulent acidity and ample silky tannins prevailing on a long and expansive finish. Cork. 14.5% alc. **Rating** 96 **To** 2020 $75 BE

Piggott Range Clarendon Syrah 2010 Deep, dense purple-crimson; whole bunches (as well as the usual Clarendon Hills whole berry approach) are included in the fermentation, coupled with 100% new French oak; while full-bodied, this wine has more elegance and supple mouthfeel, the tannins slightly softer, though abundant. Cork. 14.5% alc. **Rating** 95 **To** 2040 $285

Moritz Clarendon Syrah 2010 Deep purple-crimson; aromas of dark chocolate and spice, then an impressive black-fruited palate with an element of austerity which makes a positive contribution to a very good wine. Cork. 14.5% alc. **Rating** 95 **To** 2035 $80

Onkaparinga Grenache 2010 Deeply coloured, combining red and black fruits with Asian spices and sappy elements; the palate is luscious and intense, densely packed with tannins, fruitcake spice, and while robust and chewy, maintains a certain level of freshness; this will keep the biggest of big red lovers happy indeed. Cork. 14.5% alc. **Rating** 95 **To** 2022 $90 BE

Romas Grenache 2009 Brighter purple-crimson than the other Clarendon Hills Grenaches from '09; the spicy fruit aromas cover both black and red fruits, and the palate is fuller bodied, with very good length and tannin balance; is wild yeast-fermented in new to 5-year-old French oak. An altogether impressive wine that has more structure and a longer future than Blewitt Springs. 650 dozen made. Cork. 14.5% alc. **Rating** 95 **To** 2030 $125

Sandown Cabernet Sauvignon 2010 Showing more red fruits than the other two cabernets, with a touch of violet and cigar box as well; the palate is lively and fresh and the acidity is a more prominent feature, providing a long, fragrant and even conclusion. Screwcap. 14.5% alc. **Rating** 95 **To** 2035 $70 BE

Liandra Clarendon Mourvedre 2010 Dense, deep, purple-crimson; has the weight, depth, textural complexity and flavour richness typical of Clarendon Hills, but no other maker. Fruit, oak and tannins are welded together in a seamless stream that will grace any red meat dish. The lack of coarse extraction is remarkable. Cork. 14.5% alc. **Rating** 95 **To** 2035 $65

Hickinbotham Clarendon Syrah 2010 **Rating** 94 **To** 2040 $110
Bakers Gully Clarendon Syrah 2010 **Rating** 94 **To** 2030 $70
Liandra Clarendon Syrah 2010 **Rating** 94 **To** 2030 $80
Clarendon Grenache 2010 **Rating** 94 **To** 2022 $65 BE
Romas Grenache 2010 **Rating** 94 **To** 2025 $110 BE
Kangarilla Grenache 2010 **Rating** 94 **To** 2025 $75 BE
Blewitt Springs Grenache 2009 **Rating** 94 **To** 2020 $85
Hickinbotham Cabernet Sauvignon 2010 **Rating** 94 **To** 2035 $110 BE

🍷🍷🍷🍷🍷 **Domaine Clarendon Syrah 2010** **Rating** 93 **To** 2025 $50
Hickinbotham Grenache 2010 **Rating** 93 **To** 2020 $65 BE
Brookman Cabernet Sauvignon 2010 **Rating** 92 **To** 2025 $70 BE
Brookman Merlot 2010 **Rating** 91 **To** 2022 $70 BE

Clarnette & Ludvigsen Wines ★★★★

Westgate Road, Armstrong, Vic 3377 **Region** Grampians
T 0427 971 835 **www**.ludvigsen.com.au **Open** By appt
Winemaker Leigh Clarnette **Est.** 2003 **Dozens** 1000 **Vyds** 14ha

This brings together two vastly experienced wine professionals, Leigh Clarnette as winemaker, and Kym Ludvigsen as viticulturist. Their career paths crossed in late 1993 when both were working for Seppelt. Kym has a 14ha vineyard in the heart of the Grampians, all but 1ha of chardonnay, 0.5ha of viognier and 0.25ha of riesling planted to rare clones of shiraz, sourced from old plantings in the Great Western area. Kym is presently the Chairman of the Australian Vine Improvement Association and a board member (and past Chairman) of the Victorian and Murray Vine Improvement Association. He operates a formal consultancy service (details on the website). In 2005 the wheel turned full circle when both were employed by Taltarni.

🍷🍷🍷🍷🍷 **Grampians Shiraz 2010** Medium red-purple; both the aromas and flavours of this medium-bodied wine reflect the cool Grampians climate, with spice and pepper seasoning the black cherry fruit and savoury tannins, French oak a subtle by-play. While already elegant, could surprise with more bottle age. Screwcap. 14% alc. **Rating** 92 **To** 2020 $25

✪ **Ampersand Grampians Chardonnay 2011** Produced from seven French clones imported by Seppelt in 1988, and salvaged from neglect by quarantine officials (these are not the Bernard Dijon clones). The flavour focus is on the citrus family – especially grapefruit – with a little green apple. A bright and zesty unoaked Chardonnay that drinks well now, but will grow in bottle over the next 5 years. Screwcap. 12.5% alc. **Rating** 90 **To** 2018 $17

🍷🍷🍷🍷 ✪ **Angry Rabbit Riesling 2012** Light straw-green; an unashamedly generous and full-flavoured Riesling, with toasty, minerally characters underlying its lime and bruised apple fruit. Priced to sell in a flash. Screwcap. 11.7% alc. **Rating** 89 **To** 2016 $15

Clayfield Wines

25 Wilde Lane, Moyston, Vic 3377 **Region** Grampians
T (03) 5354 2689 **www**.clayfieldwines.com **Open** Mon–Sat 10–5, Sun 11–4
Winemaker Simon Clayfield **Est.** 1997 **Dozens** 1000 **Vyds** 2.1ha
Former long-serving Best's winemaker Simon Clayfield and wife Kaye are now doing their
own thing. They planted 2ha of shiraz and merlot between 1997 and '99, later adding 0.1ha of
durif. Additional grapes are purchased from local growers and, when the quality is appropriate,
incorporated in the Grampians Shiraz. Production is modest, but the quality is high. No wines
received for the *2014 Wine Companion*, but a five-star rating has been maintained.

Claymore Wines

91 Main North Road, Leasingham, SA 5452 **Region** Clare Valley
T (08) 8843 0200 **www**.claymorewines.com.au **Open** 7 days 10–5
Winemaker Donna Stephens, Marnie Roberts **Est.** 1998 **Dozens** 12000 **Vyds** 27ha
Claymore Wines is the venture of a medical professional who imagined that it would lead
the way to early retirement (which, of course, it did not). The starting date depends on which
event you take: the first 4ha vineyard at Leasingham purchased in 1991 (with 70-year-old
grenache, riesling and shiraz); '96, when a 16ha block at Penwortham was purchased and
planted to shiraz, merlot and grenache; '97, when the first wines were made; or '98, when the
first releases came onto the market. The labels are inspired by U2, Pink Floyd and Lou Reed.
Exports to Canada, Denmark, Sweden, Malaysia, Taiwan, Hong Kong and China.

ΨΨΨΨΨ Joshua Tree Clare Valley Riesling 2012 Such is the high-tensile, pristine
lemon juice acidity that slices through its core that you'd be hard-pressed to find
a wine of such sheer longevity at this bargain price. Pristine lime blossom wafts
over a refined palate of classic, chalky Watervale minerality. Screwcap. 12.2% alc.
Rating 94 To 2027 $20 TS

ΨΨΨΨΨ You'll Never Walk Alone Clare Valley Grenache Mataro Shiraz 2010
Rating 90 To 2020 $20 BE

Cleggett Wines
★★★

Langhorne Creek Road, Langhorne Creek, SA 5255 **Region** Langhorne Creek
T (08) 8537 3133 **www**.cleggettwines.com.au **Open** 7 days 10–6
Winemaker Peter Leske (Consultant) **Est.** 2000 **Dozens** 1500 **Vyds** 74.86ha
The Cleggett family first planted grape vines at Langhorne Creek in 1911. In '77 a sport
(a natural mutation) of cabernet sauvignon produced bronze-coloured grapes; cuttings were
taken and increasing quantities of the vine were gradually established, and called malian. Ten
years later one of the malian vines itself mutated to yield golden-white bunches, and this in
turn was propagated with the name shalistin. There are now 4ha of shalistin and 2ha of malian
in bearing. Shalistin is made as a full-bodied but unoaked white wine; malian produces both
an early- and a late-harvest rose-style wine. Exports to Malaysia and China.

ΨΨΨΨ Langhorne Creek Shalistin White Cabernet Sauvignon 2012 Served blind
it would be nigh on impossible to guess the variety, for it doesn't have any of the
bite of cabernet sauvignon (nor sauvignon blanc). Screwcap. 13.5% alc. **Rating** 87
To 2014 $17
The Pearl Langhorne Creek Rose 2012 Made from Cleggett's bronze
cabernet sauvignon malian clone with a touch of cabernet sauvignon. It is delicate
and distinctly light-bodied, gently fruity but not sweet. Screwcap. 13.5% alc.
Rating 87 To 2014 $16
Langhorne Creek Pinot Noir 2011 A small amount made, hand-picked from
the best rows. A major surprise: this isn't a great Pinot Noir, nor even a very good
one, but it has some varietal character and texture, its shortcomings some green/
minty edges. Still … Screwcap. 12.5% alc. **Rating** 87 To 2015 $18

Clemens Hill

686 Richmond Road, Cambridge, Tas 7170 **Region** Southern Tasmania
T (03) 6248 5985 **www**.clemenshill.com.au **Open** By appt
Winemaker Winemaking Tasmania **Est.** 1994 **Dozens** 2000 **Vyds** 5.3ha
The Shepherd family acquired Clemens Hill in 2001 after selling their Rosabrook winery in the Margaret River. They also have a shareholding in Winemaking Tasmania, the contract winemaking facility run by Julian Alcorso, who makes the Clemens Hill wines. The estate vineyard includes pinot noir (3.3ha) and sauvignon blanc (2ha). Dr Rob Ware is becoming a partner with the Shepherds, the intention being that he will take over ownership and management when the Shepherds retire 'in the next year or two'. Rob has been in partnership with Fred Peacock at Bream Creek since 1989, and brings vast experience.

Sauvignon Blanc 2012 An 86/14% blend of sauvignon blanc and semillon, partly barrel-fermented. It is all about building texture and structure to the herb/grass/citrus fruit, tropical characters notable by their absence. Has undoubted cellaring capacity in the manner of white Bordeaux. Gold Tasmanian Wine Show '13. Screwcap. 11.9% alc. **Rating** 94 **To** 2016 $26
Reserve Pinot Noir 2010 Typical bold, generous style of Clemens Hill; a multilayered, supple palate with highly expressive varietal fruit in a black and red cherry spectrum. Screwcap. 14% alc. **Rating** 94 **To** 2019 $50

Pinot Noir 2011 Rating 89 **To** 2016 $34 BE

Clonakilla

Crisps Lane, Murrumbateman, NSW 2582 **Region** Canberra District
T (02) 6227 5877 **www**.clonakilla.com.au **Open** 7 days 10–5
Winemaker Tim Kirk, Bryan Martin **Est.** 1971 **Dozens** 10 000 **Vyds** 12ha
The indefatigable Tim Kirk, with an inexhaustible thirst for knowledge, is the winemaker and manager of this family winery founded by Tim's father, scientist Dr John Kirk. It is not at all surprising that the quality of the wines is excellent, especially the Shiraz Viognier, which has paved the way for numerous others to follow, but remains the best example in Australia. Exports to all major markets.

Shiraz Viognier 2012 Has the best colour of the '12 Clonakilla red wines, hardly a surprise; the bouquet is supremely fragrant, almost flowery/scented, the palate instantaneously imprinting its total harmony and balance; fruit, oak and tannins are all seamlessly interwoven, the length prodigious. Low yields were the secret. Screwcap. 13% alc. **Rating** 97 **To** 2032 $100
Canberra District Riesling 2012 The floral bouquet has hints of spice and white blossom, giving little warning of the intensity and purity of the lime juice palate that follows, drawn out to an exceptional length by the refreshing acidity. Screwcap. 12% alc. **Rating** 96 **To** 2025 $30
Canberra District Viognier 2012 Bright straw-green; a mouthfilling tapestry of flavours that are truly varietal: apricot, peach, ginger and spice, the last partly derived from barrel fermentation; the oak has been perfectly handled, and this is a lovely wine. Screwcap. 12% alc. **Rating** 96 **To** 2018 $50
Tumbarumba Chardonnay 2012 Whole bunch-pressed, (relatively) warm-fermented, and 11 months' maturation in French oak followed. Brightly coloured, it is a very complex Chardonnay in terms of flavour and texture, with cashew, fig, spice, white peach and grapefruit all engaged in an ever-changing courtly dance. Screwcap. 13% alc. **Rating** 95 **To** 2020 $40
Hilltops Shiraz 2012 The hue is good, although not particularly deep; an exercise in restraint and elegance, with finely detailed and strung beads of red and black berry fruit, silky tannins and a touch of French oak. Screwcap. 13% alc. **Rating** 95 **To** 2025 $32

O'Riada Canberra District Shiraz 2012 Strong purple-crimson; having survived the heavy rain at the end of Feb, the vines flourished in the fine, warm weather of Mar and Apr to produce shiraz of great depth and varietal character; black fruits, spice, pepper, licorice and sweet, fresh earth fill the senses. Screwcap. 13% alc. **Rating** 95 **To** 2030 $40

Shiraz Viognier 2011 Transparently clear purple-crimson; the perfumed bouquet of predominantly red fruits leads into a superfine palate with some darker fruit nuances; it is only on the finish and aftertaste that the quality of the wine fully expresses itself. Has gained a dimension of intensity/focus/length since first tasted. Screwcap. 13% alc. **Rating** 95 **To** 2025 $100

🍷🍷🍷🍷🍷 **Ceoltoiri 2011 Rating** 93 **To** 2016 $40
Hilltops Shiraz 2011 Rating 92 **To** 2019 $30 TS

Clos Clare ★★★★★

Old Road, Watervale, SA 5452 **Region** Clare Valley
T (08) 8843 0161 **www**.closclare.com.au **Open** W'ends & public hols 11–5
Winemaker Sam and Tom Barry **Est.** 1993 **Dozens** 1000 **Vyds** 2ha
Clos Clare was acquired by the Barry family in 2008. Riesling continues to be made from the 2ha unirrigated section of the original Florita Vineyard (the major part of that vineyard was already in Barry ownership) and newly introduced red wines are coming from a 49-year-old vineyard beside the Armagh site. Exports to the UK.

🍷🍷🍷🍷🍷 **Watervale Riesling 2012** Bright, light straw-green; from 42-year-old vines, the grapes whole bunch-pressed and cold-fermented; the bouquet is filled with blossom aromas, and the palate has remarkable depth to its layers of ripe citrus fruits, the length equally impressive. Drink now or later. Screwcap. 12.6% alc. **Rating** 95 **To** 2027 $25

Clovely Estate ★★★★

Steinhardts Road, Moffatdale via Murgon, Qld 4605 **Region** South Burnett
T (07) 3876 3100 **www**.clovely.com.au **Open** 7 days 10–4
Winemaker Luke Fitzpatrick, Kieran Carney **Est.** 1997 **Dozens** 25 000 **Vyds** 173.76ha
Clovely Estate has the largest vineyards in Qld, having established over 170ha of immaculately maintained vines at two locations just to the east of Murgon in the Burnett Valley (including 60ha of shiraz). The wines are sold in six tiers: Double Pruned at the top; followed by Estate Reserve; Left Field, featuring alternative varieties and styles; then the White Label and Shed ranges for everyday drinking; and at the bottom, First Picked, primarily designed for the export market at low price points. The estate also has a second cellar door and B&B at 210 Musgrave Road, Red Hill (open Tues–Sat 11–7). Exports to Denmark, Papua New Guinea, Taiwan and China.

🍷🍷🍷🍷🍷 **Estate Reserve South Burnett Shiraz 2010** Good hue and depth; the bouquet has aromas of spice, leather and chocolate running through its predominantly black fruits, the medium- to full-bodied palate picking up the theme, adding hints of licorice and oak; it has a juicy mouthfeel, finishing with appropriately fine tannins. Screwcap. 14% alc. **Rating** 92 **To** 2020 $28

🍷🍷🍷🍷 ✪ **Semillon Sauvignon Blanc 2012** South Burnett semillon and sauvignon blanc from two cool Vic vineyards. It has a handsome amount of citrus and gooseberry on a juicy, long and well-balanced palate. Great value. Screwcap. 12.3% alc. **Rating** 89 **To** 2014 $14

✪ **South Burnett Rose 2012** Light, bright pink; a fragrant red cherry, raspberry bouquet leads into a softly fruity palate, with a subliminal touch of residual sugar to boot. Cellar door killer. Screwcap. 13.5% alc. **Rating** 89 **To** 2014 $14
Left Field Grenache Shiraz Mourvedre 2012 Rating 88 **To** 2015 $20
Left Field Pinot Gris 2012 Rating 87 **To** 2013 $20

Clover Hill

60 Clover Hill Road, Lebrina, Tas 7254 **Region** Northern Tasmania
T (03) 6395 6114 **www**.cloverhillwines.com.au **Open** By appt
Winemaker Karina Dambergs **Est.** 1986 **Dozens** 8000 **Vyds** 23.9ha
Clover Hill was established by Taltarni in 1986 with the sole purpose of making a premium sparkling wine. It has 23.9ha of vineyards (chardonnay, pinot noir and pinot meunier) and its sparkling wine quality is excellent, combining finesse with power and length. In 2009 the American owner and founder of Clos du Val (Napa Valley), Taltarni and Clover Hill brought the management of these businesses and Domaine de Nizas (Languedoc) under the one management roof; the group is known as Goelet Wine Estates. Exports to the UK, the US and other major markets.

ŸŸŸŸŸ Cuvee Exceptionnelle Blanc de Blancs 2008 Bright straw-green. Has delicious white stone fruit, grapefruit, brioche and spice flavours, the length and the acid balance particularly good. Delicious now or later. Diam. 13% alc. Rating 95 To 2015 $55
Clover Hill 2008 An estate-grown blend of chardonnay, pinot noir and pinot meunier, whole bunch-pressed, then made using traditional method, with a minimum of 3 years on yeast lees. Pale, bright straw-green, it has a Tasmanian-given mix of delicacy and intensity, focus and complexity, riding high on a shaft of acidity, white flowers and citrus to the fore. Diam. 12.5% alc. Rating 94 To 2017 $47

ŸŸŸŸŸ Methode Traditionnelle Tasmanian Cuvee NV Rating 93 To 2016 $33

Clyde Park Vineyard ★★★★★

2490 Midland Highway, Bannockburn, Vic 3331 **Region** Geelong
T (03) 5281 7274 **www**.clydepark.com.au **Open** Mon–Fri 11–5, w'ends & public hols 12–4
Winemaker Terry Jongebloed, Scott Gerrard **Est.** 1979 **Dozens** 6500 **Vyds** 10.1ha
Clyde Park Vineyard, established by Gary Farr but sold by him many years ago, has passed through several changes of ownership. Now owned by Terry Jongebloed and Sue Jongebloed-Dixon, it has significant mature plantings of pinot noir (3.4ha), chardonnay (3.1ha), sauvignon blanc (1.5ha), shiraz (1.2ha) and pinot gris (0.9ha), and the quality of its wines is consistently exemplary. Exports to the UK and Hong Kong.

ŸŸŸŸŸ Block D Geelong Pinot Noir 2012 Vibrant, clear purple-crimson. Hand-picked, whole bunch, wild yeast, then maceration on skins; 11 months in French oak (35% new) on lees and wild mlf. A luxuriantly rich pinot, with layers of intense black cherry and plum fruit, and immaculate tannin structure. Great wine, will be very long-lived. Screwcap. 13.2% alc. Rating 97 To 2025 $55
Block G Geelong Shiraz 2012 Open-fermented, then matured in French oak (35% new) for 11 months with natural mlf. Dense purple-crimson, it is crammed with black cherry, blackberry, spice and licorice, the tannins ripe and the oak no more than background music. Very impressive full-bodied cool-climate Shiraz. Screwcap. 13.6% alc. Rating 96 To 2032 $55
Block B2 Geelong Pinot Noir 2012 Its colour is fractionally lighter than Block D; made almost identically, with a highly aromatic bouquet, and a more elegant palate; while fruit-driven, it is slightly more savoury/spicy, less intense. Bad luck to have to compete against Block D. Screwcap. 12.4% alc. Rating 95 To 2020 $55
Sauvignon Blanc 2012 A Sauvignon Blanc with well above-average complexity and richness, wild yeast and barrel fermentation for 30% of the juice having been used to full advantage, investing the wine with texture and structure; cashew notes sit alongside ripe citrus fruits. Screwcap. 12.5% alc. Rating 94 To 2014 $20
Block B3 Geelong Chardonnay 2012 All Penfolds P58 clone, hand-picked, whole bunch-pressed, then taken to French oak (35% new) with some lees returned; wild yeast-fermented and likewise mlf. It is a super-elegant style, and the 100% mlf was a brave, and ultimately correct, decision for the white peach fruit on the long, well-balanced palate. Screwcap. 12.3% alc. Rating 94 To 2019 $55

Geelong Pinot Noir 2012 Entirely estate-grown, with excellent deep, clear and bright colour; has very good varietal fruit in a blood plum and cherry spectrum; full and long in the mouth, with some foresty notes on the finish. A proud pinot. Screwcap. 13% alc. **Rating** 94 **To** 2019 $33

Geelong Pinot Noir 2010 Full, bright red-purple; there is remarkable consistency of style between this and its '09 sibling; both are 100% estate-grown and (presumably) made the same way, the two years had marked differences in weather during the growing season; the tasting note for the '09 applies to this wine as well. Screwcap. 13% alc. **Rating** 94 **To** 2017 $30

Geelong Pinot Noir 2009 The full colour shows no hint of age; in pinot terms, the wine borders on full-bodied due to the richness and intensity of the fruit rather than tannin extract; damson plum delivers the main flavour message, oak a delicate seasoning. Screwcap. 13% alc. **Rating** 94 **To** 2016 $30

Geelong Shiraz 2008 Good hue and depth; a complete contrast to the disappointing '09, with dark spice and berry aromas and flavours; the medium-bodied palate has good texture and structure thanks to ripe tannins that will sustain the wine for many years to come. Screwcap. 14% alc. **Rating** 94 **To** 2030 $30

ŶŶŶŶŶ **Reserve Geelong Chardonnay 2011** **Rating** 93 **To** 2017 $49
Geelong Chardonnay 2010 **Rating** 93 **To** 2017 $30
Geelong Pinot Gris 2012 **Rating** 93 **To** 2014 $30

✪ **Locale Geelong Shiraz 2010** The bright colour is a sign of things to come; there are notes of spice and pepper to the juicy and seductive well of black cherry, blood plum and licorice fruit. Exceptional value. Screwcap. 14% alc. **Rating** 93 **To** 2020 $20

Geelong Chardonnay 2012 **Rating** 90 **To** 2016 $30
Locale Geelong Pinot Noir 2011 **Rating** 90 **To** 2015 $20

ŶŶŶŶ
✪ **Geelong Rose 2011** Bright, light pink; a brisk, lively rose with obvious acidity running through the small red berry fruits of the palate. Good value for drinking in the coming spring. Screwcap. 12% alc. **Rating** 89 **To** 2013 $15

Coal Valley Vineyard   ★★★★★

257 Richmond Road, Cambridge, Tas 7170 **Region** Southern Tasmania
T (03) 6248 5367 **www.**coalvalley.com.au **Open** Wed–Sun 11–5
Winemaker Alain Rousseau, Todd Goebel **Est.** 1991 **Dozens** 1000 **Vyds** 4.5ha
Since acquiring Coal Valley Vineyard in 1999, Gill Christian and Todd Goebel have increased the original 1ha hobby vineyard to pinot noir (2.3ha), riesling, cabernet sauvignon, merlot, chardonnay and tempranillo. More remarkable were Gill and Todd's concurrent lives: one in India, the other in Tasmania (flying over six times a year), and digging 4000 holes for the new vine plantings. Todd makes the Cabernet Sauvignon onsite, and dreams of making all the wines. Exports to Canada.

ŶŶŶŶŶ **Pinot Noir 2011** Similar clear colour to Barilla Bay, slightly more purple in the mix; here the power and concentration are apparent from the word go, black cherry and plum at its core, surrounded by forest floor notes and firm, but balanced, tannins. Will repay cellaring. Screwcap. 13.5% alc. **Rating** 94 **To** 2021 $38

Barilla Bay Pinot Noir 2011 Clear crimson-purple; the bouquet is fresh and fragrant; the wine enters the mouth without any fanfare of trumpets, but uncoils its flavours as it accelerates through to the back-palate and finish, savoury, spicy tannins moving into forest floor notes. Screwcap. 13% alc. **Rating** 94 **To** 2021 $28

ŶŶŶŶŶ **Chardonnay 2011** **Rating** 90 **To** 2016 $32
✪ **Cabernet Merlot 2010** As Domaine A has shown, this region can, if tightly disciplined, produce distinguished Bordeaux blends. The colour is very good, and the cassis and black olive fruit is not caught in a barbed wire fence of tannins. One of the best such blends I have seen outside of Domaine A. Screwcap. 13.5% alc. **Rating** 90 **To** 2015 $25

Coastal Estate Vineyard   ★★★★

320 Grays Road, Paraparap, Vic 3240 **Region** Geelong
T 0437 180 664 **www.**coastalestate.com.au **Open** Not
Winemaker Suzanne Paton **Est.** 2007 **Dozens** 100 **Vyds** 2.3ha
Winter trips to Falls Creek have taken innumerable skiers into Brown Brothers' cellar door at Milawa. Suzanne and Colin's visits began in the early 1990s as 20-year-olds, and it changed their perspective on wine forever. Colin began studies in viticulture at Dookie, and then at CSU to complete his degree, coupled with working in the Yarra Valley for periods of time, and coming into the Sergio Carlei orbit. Counterintuitively, it is in fact Suzanne who has taken on the role of winemaker and sales. The vineyard is planted to 0.6ha each of sauvignon blanc and shiraz, and 1.1ha of pinot noir with MV6 and 115 clones. In 2010 they produced a Sauvignon Blanc, '11 was a disaster with the incessant rain, and in '12 the Sauvignon Blanc once again came to the fore, an amazing second vintage effort.

♀♀♀♀♀ **Surfcoast Hinterland Sauvignon Blanc 2012** Fermented in French oak to
✪   full advantage; the oak (25% new) imparts extra texture and structure, but does
   not impede the gooseberry and citrus flavours on the long palate. Excellent value.
   Screwcap. 12.5% alc. **Rating** 93 **To** 2014 $20

Coates Wines   ★★★★★

PO Box 859, McLaren Vale, SA 5171 **Region** McLaren Vale
T 0417 882 557 **www.**coates-wines.com **Open** Not
Winemaker Duane Coates **Est.** 2003 **Dozens** 1500
Duane Coates has a Bachelor of Science, a Master of Business Administration and a Master of Oenology from Adelaide University; for good measure he completed the theory component of the Masters of Wine degree in 2005. Having made wine in various parts of the world, and in SA for a number of important brands, he is more than qualified to make and market the Coates wines. Nonetheless, his original intention was to simply make a single barrel of wine employing various philosophies and practices outside the mainstream; there was no intention to move to commercial production. The key is organically grown grapes and the refusal to use additives and fining agents. A deliberately low level of new oak (20%) is part of the picture. Exports to the US, Canada, Germany and Sweden.

♀♀♀♀♀ **Langhorne Creek McLaren Vale The Syrah 2010** Certainly comes from
the big end of town, full-bodied and effusive, yet not clumsy; black fruits of every description, licorice, bitter chocolate and a nice dab of oak from 20 months in barrel all work very well, tannins providing the bow to tie the parcel. Screwcap. 14.5% alc. **Rating** 94 **To** 2030 $23
Organic McLaren Vale Syrah 2010 Wild yeast-fermented, then matured in French and Russian oak before being bottled without fining or filtration; the colour is good, the palate packed with power, the tannins flexing their muscles and needing time to soften. Screwcap. 14.5% alc. **Rating** 94 **To** 2025 $35
The Reserve McLaren Vale Langhorne Creek Syrah 2008 Only 120 dozen bottles released of a 53/47% blend that spent 28 months in new and one-year-old French and Russian oak before being bottled unfined and unfiltered; the effort has been worth it, producing a complex yet supple and smooth wine with lashings of dark fruits in a web of dark chocolate, the oak evident but integrated and balanced. Diam. 14% alc. **Rating** 94 **To** 2028 $73
Cabernet Sauvignon Merlot Malbec 2009 A 66/17/17% blend from Langhorne Creek, Adelaide Hills and Robe, which spent 28 months in oak 'with a natural approach to winemaking'. It is a generous wine with abundant black cherry and cassis fruit, the oak in balance, the tannins fine and soft. There are no 'natural wine' issues here. Screwcap. 13.5% alc. **Rating** 94 **To** 2029 $35
The VP Langhorne Creek Touriga Nacional 2008 Foot-trodden, then pressed and fortified by potent brandy spirit; spent 34 months in barrel before bottling, the colour sill a deep crimson. Duane Coates says cellaring for 25 years recommended, which is not surprising given the abundant black fruits, bitter chocolate and panforte flavours. Diam. 19.5% alc. **Rating** 94 **To** 2033 $33

ΨΨΨΨႵ The Consonance Red 2009 Rating 93 To 2020 $25
Langhorne Creek Touriga Nacional 2009 Rating 92 To 2024 $35
The Adelaide Hills Semillon Sauvignon Blanc 2012 Rating 91 To 2014 $25
Organic Adelaide Hills Pinot Noir 2010 Rating 91 To 2016 $28
Cuvee Consonance Shiraz 2011 Rating 90 To 2016 $30

Cobaw Ridge   ★★★★★

31 Perc Boyers Lane, Pastoria, Vic 3444 **Region** Macedon Ranges
T (03) 5423 5227 **www**.cobawridge.com.au **Open** Thurs–Mon 12–5
Winemaker Alan Cooper **Est.** 1985 **Dozens** 1200 **Vyds** 4.85ha
When the Coopers started planting in the early 1980s there was scant knowledge of the
best varieties for the region, let alone the Cobaw Ridge site. They have now settled on four
varieties, chardonnay and syrah always being part of the mix. Lagrein and pinot noir are more
recent arrivals to thrive; cabernet sauvignon (long ago) and vermentino (more recently) have
been removed. In their place a close-planted, multiclonal block of pinot noir, with a 1.25m ×
1.25m spacing, was established. Son Joshua has breezed through the wine science degree at
Adelaide University with multiple distinctions; in 2012 he crammed in vintages with Tyrrell's,
Heathcote Estate/Yabby Lake and Domaine de la Vougerai (Burgundy). Cobaw Ridge is
now fully certified biodynamic, and all winery operations are carried out according to the
biodynamic calendar. Exports to Canada and China.

ΨΨΨΨΨ Syrah 2010 Strong purple-red; co-fermented with a little viognier in a top
Macedon vintage; it has all the fragrance and elegance one would hope for, with
black cherry, plum, multi-spice and a sprinkle of cracked pepper, oak and tannins
in synergistic balance. Diam. 13.7% alc. Rating 94 To 2025 $50
Syrah Lagrein 2008 An 80/20% blend, the lagrein's contribution immediately
evident with the deep purple colour. Rising 4 years old, it still has youthful spicy
fruit on the concentrated mid-palate, the tannins demure, especially on the finish.
Diam. 13.9% alc. Rating 94 To 2023 $38

ΨΨΨΨႵ Lagrein 2010 Rating 93 To 2025 $60
L'altra Chardonnay 2010 Rating 90 To 2014 $43

Cofield Wines   ★★★★☆

Distillery Road, Wahgunyah, Vic 3687 **Region** Rutherglen
T (02) 6033 3798 **www**.cofieldwines.com.au **Open** Mon–Sat 9–5, Sun 10–5
Winemaker Damien Cofield **Est.** 1990 **Dozens** 13 000 **Vyds** 15.4ha
Sons Damien (winery) and Andrew (vineyard) have taken over responsibility for the business
from parents Max and Karen. Collectively, they have developed an impressively broad-based
product range with a strong cellar door sales base. The Pickled Sisters Café is open for lunch
Wed–Mon ((02) 6033 2377). A 20ha property at Rutherglen, purchased in 2007, is planted to
shiraz, durif and sangiovese. Exports to China.

ΨΨΨΨႵ Cabernet Sauvignon 2012 Clear red-purple; a lively, fresh, cassis-accented
cabernet, its medium body throwing all of the emphasis on that fruit, even
though there are tannins, and a dab of oak, to give structure. Screwcap. 13.6% alc.
Rating 93 To 2025 $24
✪ Viognier 2012 Has gone on the side of living with some phenolics in obtaining
the distinctive fruit flavours of apricot, peach and a touch of spice. Fortune favours
the bold. Screwcap. 12.8% alc. Rating 90 To 2014 $20
Minimal Footprint Quartz Vein Vineyard Organic Durif 2011 Good
purple-crimson hue, although not particularly deep (for a Durif); has an attractive
mix of red and black fruits, then reasonably firm tannins on the finish. Will
respond well to time in the cellar. Screwcap. 13.8% alc. Rating 90 To 2020 $35

ΨΨΨΨ Rutherglen Marsanne Viognier 2011 Rating 89 To 2015 $20
Alpine & King Valleys Sauvignon Blanc 2012 Rating 87 To 2013 $18

Coldstream Hills

31 Maddens Lane, Coldstream, Vic 3770 **Region** Yarra Valley
T (03) 5960 7000 **www**.coldstreamhills.com.au **Open** 7 days 10–5
Winemaker Andrew Fleming, Greg Jarratt, James Halliday (Consultant) **Est.** 1985
Dozens NA **Vyds** 100ha
Founded by the author, who continues to be involved as a consultant, but acquired by Southcorp in mid 1996, Coldstream Hills is now a small part of TWE, with 100ha of owned or managed estate vineyards as its base. Chardonnay and Pinot Noir continue to be the principal focus; Merlot came on-stream in 1997, Sauvignon Blanc around the same time, Reserve Shiraz later still. Vintage conditions permitting, Chardonnay, Pinot Noir and Cabernet Sauvignon are made in both varietal and Reserve form, the latter in restricted quantities. In 2010 a new, multimillion-dollar winery was erected around the original winery buildings. There is a plaque in the fermentation area commemorating the official opening on 12 October 2010 and naming the facility the 'James Halliday Cellar'. Exports to the UK, the US and Singapore.

🍷🍷🍷🍷🍷 **Deer Farm Vineyard Chardonnay 2011** A breathtaking single vineyard Upper Yarra Chardonnay of undeterred line and graceful persistence. Sensitively handled French oak provides a gentle overlay of nutmeg and vanilla to pristine aromas of lemon blossom, white peach, grapefruit and fig. The palate is a spectacular continuation of the same show, laced together by an intricate, silver thread of cool-season acidity and an undercurrent of fine minerality. 2 trophies, 4 gold medals. Cork. 12.5% alc. **Rating** 96 **To** 2019 $45 TS
Reserve Yarra Valley Chardonnay 2011 Brilliantly honed and desperately pristine, lifted by lemon blossoms on crisp dawn air, almost ripe white peaches and freshly picked grapefruit. The palate is an exactingly focused vector of white fruits, charged with impeccable poise and set to uncoil slowly over a decade and beyond. Struck flint and gunpowder complexity are understated, but acid drive and mineral texture are proclaimed for all to behold. 4 gold medals. Screwcap. 13% alc. **Rating** 96 **To** 2026 $60 TS
Limited Release Roslyn Vineyard Coal Valley Pinot Noir 2011 Coldstream Hills' foray into Tasmania's Coal Valley has yielded an impeccably assembled pinot with a promising future. The concentration and expression of southern Tasmanian pinot is exemplified in rose hip fragrance and deep-set blackberry and black cherry fruit, suspended eloquently by cool-climate acidity and finely structured fruit and oak tannins. 1 trophy, 3 gold medals. Screwcap. 13.5% alc. **Rating** 95 **To** 2019 $50 TS
Rising Vineyard Chardonnay 2011 The contrasting personalities of the Upper and Lower Yarra are exemplified in Deer Farm and Rising. Perhaps confusingly, Rising is the lower of the two, showcasing the more generous character of the Valley floor in yellow peach, golden delicious apple and orange flesh. It's held tightly in line by lively, cool-season acidity that leaves its grapefruit-accented finish crisp and fresh. Screwcap. 12.5% alc. **Rating** 94 **To** 2015 $45 TS

🍷🍷🍷🍷🍸 **Yarra Valley Sauvignon Blanc 2012 Rating** 92 **To** 2014 $33 TS
Yarra Valley Pinot Noir 2011 Rating 91 **To** 2017 $35 TS
Chardonnay Pinot Noir 2009 Rating 90 **To** 2014 $35 TS

Collector Wines

12 Bourke Street, Collector, NSW 2581 (postal) **Region** Canberra District
T (02) 6116 8722 **www**.collectorwines.com.au **Open** Not
Winemaker Alex McKay **Est.** 2007 **Dozens** 3000
Owner and winemaker Alex McKay makes two Canberra District Shirazs, the Marked Tree Red from parcels of shiraz from vineyards in and around Murrumbateman, and the Reserve from a single patch of mature shiraz grown on an elevated granite saddle near Murrumbateman. Exports to The Netherlands and Japan.

ΨΨΨΨΨ   **Reserve Shiraz 2011** Full crimson-purple; licorice, pepper and black fruits eloquently speak through the bouquet, the intense and long palate with blackberry fruit, powerful but balanced tannins and quality French oak all making the wine what it is. Screwcap. 12.8% alc. **Rating** 96 **To** 2031 $59

Marked Tree Red Shiraz 2011 Crimson-red; the fragrant bouquet has warm spices interwoven with red and black berry fruits, a theme that carries through on the supple, medium-bodied palate, tannins and oak in finely balanced support. Theoretically an impossible outcome for this and the Reserve Shiraz in '11. Screwcap. 13.1% alc. **Rating** 94 **To** 2021 $28

ΨΨΨΨ♀   **Lamp Lit Marsanne 2011** **Rating** 93 **To** 2025 $33

Colvin Wines   ★★★★

19 Boyle Street, Mosman, NSW 2088 (postal) **Region** Hunter Valley
T (02) 9908 7886 **www**.colvinwines.com.au **Open** Not
Winemaker Andrew Spinaze, Mark Richardson **Est.** 1999 **Dozens** 500 **Vyds** 5.2ha
In 1990 Sydney lawyer John Colvin and wife Robyn purchased the De Beyers Vineyard, which has a history going back to the second half of the 19th century. By '67, when a syndicate headed by Douglas McGregor bought 35ha of the original vineyard site, no vines remained. The syndicate planted semillon on the alluvial soil of the creek flats and shiraz on the red clay hillsides. When the Colvins acquired the property the vineyard was in need of attention. Up to '98 all the grapes were sold to Tyrrell's, but since '99 quantities have been made for the Colvin Wines label. These include Sangiovese, from a little over 1ha of vines planted by John in 1996 because of his love of the wines of Tuscany.

ΨΨΨΨ♀   **De Beyers Vineyard Shiraz 2011** Mid garnet, bright; fragrant cherry and plum aromas mingle with sage and leather on the bouquet; medium-bodied and softly textured, providing an early-drinking and accessible example of shiraz from the Hunter Valley. Screwcap. 13% alc. **Rating** 90 **To** 2018 $28 BE

ΨΨΨΨ   **De Beyers Vineyard Sangiovese 2011** **Rating** 87 **To** 2015 $25 BE
De Beyers Vineyard Sangiovese 2010 **Rating** 87 **To** 2015 $28 BE

Conte Estate Wines   ★★★★☆

270 Sand Road, McLaren Flat, SA 5171 **Region** McLaren Vale
T (08) 8383 0183 **www**.conteestatewines.com.au **Open** By appt
Winemaker Danial Conte **Est.** 2003 **Dozens** 5000 **Vyds** 77ha
The Conte family has a large vineyard, predominantly established since 1960 but with 2.5ha of shiraz planted 100 years earlier, in the 1860s. The vineyard includes shiraz, grenache, cabernet sauvignon, sauvignon blanc and chardonnay. While continuing to sell a large proportion of the production, winemaking has become a larger part of the business. Exports to the US, Canada and China.

ΨΨΨΨΨ   **Reserve Over the Hill McLaren Vale Shiraz 2009** Produced from vines planted in 1880, said to be the oldest in McLaren Vale, a claim others may challenge, but no matter – the vines are seriously old, and the wine is very good, awash with dark fruits, fine tannins and well-integrated French oak. May well outlive its cork. 14.5% alc. **Rating** 94 **To** 2029 $50

ΨΨΨΨ♀   **Rock Hill McLaren Vale Shiraz 2010** **Rating** 93 **To** 2020 $25
Reserve Hunt Road Cabernet Sauvignon 2009 **Rating** 93 **To** 2029 $40
The Numb Hand Pruner Grenache 2006 **Rating** 90 **To** 2015 $20
✪   **The Gondola McLaren Vale Grenache Shiraz 2006** There is a greater range to the flavours and texture of the wine, which is nonetheless close to its best right now. Very good at the price. Cork. 14.5% alc. **Rating** 90 **To** 2015 $20

ΨΨΨΨ   **Primrose Lane McLaren Vale Chardonnay 2011** **Rating** 89 **To** 2014 $15

Coobara Wines

473 Cromer Road, Birdwood, SA 5234 **Region** Adelaide Hills
T 0407 685 797 **www**.coobarawines.com.au **Open** By appt
Winemaker David Cook **Est.** 1992 **Dozens** 2500 **Vyds** 12ha
David Cook has worked in the wine industry for over 20 years, principally with Orlando but also with Jim Irvine, John Glaetzer and the late Neil Ashmead. As well as working full-time for Orlando, he undertook oenology and viticulture courses, and – with support from his parents – planted 4ha of cabernet sauvignon and merlot on the family property at Birdwood. In 1993 they purchased the adjoining property, planting 2ha each of riesling and pinot gris, and lifting the plantings of merlot and cabernet sauvignon to 4ha each. In 2003 David decided to commence wine production. Coobara is an Aboriginal word meaning 'place of birds'.

ΨΨΨΨ **Adelaide Hills Cabernet Merlot 2009** Developed tobacco and dried herb aromas are evident on the bouquet; the palate is forward and accessible, with tangy acid and fine drying tannins a feature on the finish. Screwcap. 14% alc. **Rating** 88 To 2015 $25 BE

Cooks Lot

Cassilis Road, Mudgee, NSW 2850 **Region** Mudgee
T (02) 9550 3228 **www**.cookslot.com.au **Open** Not
Winemaker Duncan Cook **Est.** 2002 **Dozens** 4000
Duncan Cook began making wines for his eponymous brand in 2002, while undertaking his oenology degree at CSU. He completed his degree in '10, and now works with a number of small growers from the Mudgee and Orange regions wishing to be part of the production of wines with characteristic/distinctive regional character. The modest prices of all wines is striking. Exports to China.

ΨΨΨΨΨ ✪ **Orange Sauvignon Blanc 2012** Pale straw-green; barrel fermentation in older oak and subsequent lees stirring have in no way diminished the striking passionfruit and green pea flavour profile; has very good length, and a lingering aftertaste. Drink in its exuberant youth. Screwcap. 12.9% alc. **Rating** 94 To 2013 $20

ΨΨΨΨΨ ✪ **Orange Shiraz 2011** Bright purple-red; attractive medium-bodied wine, with black cherry, satsuma plum, spice and pepper on the supple, smooth palate; has admirable length and balance, oak a bystander. Screwcap. 13% alc. **Rating** 93 To 2018 $20

✪ **Orange Semillon Sauvignon Blanc 2012** Quartz-white; a 60/40% blend, with lemon/lemongrass/citrus/mineral characters reflecting the dominant semillon component, passionfruit/tropical notes arriving on the finish and aftertaste. Quite possibly another year in bottle would improve what is already a very tidy wine. Screwcap. 12% alc. **Rating** 92 To 2014 $20

✪ **Orange Pinot Gris 2012** Light straw-green; partial barrel fermentation has, if anything, enhanced the pear and green apple varietal expression of a bracingly fresh Pinot Gris; sophisticated winemaking at work, with maximum rewards. Screwcap. 13.2% alc. **Rating** 91 To 2014 $20

Coolangatta Estate

1335 Bolong Road, Shoalhaven Heads, NSW 2535 **Region** Shoalhaven Coast
T (02) 4448 7131 **www**.coolangattaestate.com.au **Open** 7 days 10–5
Winemaker Tyrrell's **Est.** 1988 **Dozens** 5000 **Vyds** 10.5ha
Coolangatta Estate is part of a 150ha resort with accommodation, restaurants, golf course, etc; some of the oldest buildings were convict-built in 1822. It might be thought that the wines are tailored purely for the tourist market, but in fact the standard of viticulture is exceptionally high (immaculate Scott Henry trellising), and the contract winemaking is wholly professional. Coolangatta has a habit of bobbing up with gold medals at Sydney and Canberra wine shows, with gold medals for its mature Semillons.

🍷🍷🍷🍷🍷 **Aged Release Estate Grown Semillon 2007** Bright, light green-straw; a
✪   delicious Semillon, just entering the plateau of development, the citrus juice
with the sweetness of Bickfords lime juice, although the finish is dry; an absolute
bargain for drinking now or in 10 or so years' time. Screwcap. 11.3% alc.
Rating 95 To 2022 $28
Estate Grown Semillon 2012 Pale but bright straw-green; the unusually
perfumed/citrus blossom/spice bouquet leads into an intense, juicy palate, the
length drawn out by crisp, crunchy acidity; Tyrrell's hand at work as contract
winemaker. Screwcap. 10.5% alc. **Rating** 94 To 2022 $25

🍷🍷🍷🍷🍷 **Estate Grown Savagnin 2012 Rating** 93 To 2014 $25
Estate Grown Tempranillo 2011 Rating 92 To 2021 $30
Alexander Berry Chardonnay 2011 Rating 91 To 2016 $25
Estate Grown Tannat 2011 Rating 90 To 2021 $35

Coombe Farm Estate Wines   ★★★☆

11 St Huberts Road, Coldstream, Vic 3770 **Region** Yarra Valley
T (03) 9739 1131 **www**.coombefarm.com.au **Open** Thurs–Mon 10–5, Tues–Wed by appt
Winemaker Nicole Esdaile **Est.** 1999 **Dozens** 6000 **Vyds** 60ha
Coombe Farm Vineyard is owned by Pamela, Lady Vestey (Dame Nellie Melba's granddaughter),
Lord Samuel Vestey and The Right Honourable Mark Vestey. The vineyard is planted to pinot
noir (22ha), chardonnay (18ha), pinot gris (2.6ha), cabernet sauvignon (2ha), with smaller
amounts of merlot and arneis; the rest of the vineyard is currently under development. The
vast majority of the fruit is sold to eager winemakers in the region, with a small amount made
for Coombe Farm. Exports to the UK.

🍷🍷🍷🍷🍷 **Yarra Valley Chardonnay 2011** Delicate aromas of fresh pear and citrus
blossom are offset by caramel and grilled hazelnut; the palate is lively and fresh on
entry, with tangy acidity a feature, while the savoury finish reveals a long, grilled
nut conclusion. Screwcap. 12.5% alc. **Rating** 90 To 2017 $29 BE

🍷🍷🍷🍷 **Nellie Melba Yarra Valley Blanc de Blancs 2011** Rating 89 To 2016 $35
Yarra Valley Pinot Noir 2011 Rating 87 To 2016 $29 BE

🍇 Coonawarra Jack   ★★★☆

PO Box 322, Coonawarra, SA 5263 **Region** Coonawarra
T (08) 8736 3130 **www**.coonawarrajack.com **Open** Not
Winemaker Shannon Sutherland, Joe Cory **Est.** 2011 **Dozens** 5000 **Vyds** 221ha
The Lees family has been involved in agriculture for over a century, but it was left to Adrian
and Dennise Lees (and their son Matthew) to make the transition from general agriculture
into viticulture. Although the business was not formally established until 2011, the family
has built a very large winery and barrel storage area to accommodate the Limestone Coast-
sourced wines, and the far larger amount from the Murray Darling region, where the
family owns 220ha of vineyard. The Jack Estate label is used for wines from the Limestone
Coast, most of the grapes being purchased (the family owns 1ha of cabernet sauvignon in
Coonawarra). Rachel Lees is responsible for marketing, and Matthew (with a degree in civil
engineering) is the winery manager. Exports to the UK, the US and China.

🍷🍷🍷🍷🍷 **Jack Estate Cabernet Sauvignon 2010** Moderate colour, though the hue is
good; black fruits, earth, leather and overarching savoury notes show its 18 months
in a mix of used French and American oak barrels; some initial reduction
dissipated with aeration. Screwcap. 14.3% alc. **Rating** 90 To 2018 $20

🍷🍷🍷🍷 **Jack Estate Sauvignon Blanc 2012** Rating 89 To 2014 $18
Jack Estate Shiraz 2010 Rating 89 To 2018 $20
Jack Estate Chardonnay 2012 Rating 87 To 2014 $19

Cooper Burns

1 Golden Way, Nuriootpa, SA 5353 (postal) **Region** Barossa Valley
T (08) 8562 2865 **www**.cooperburns.com.au **Open** Not
Winemaker Mark Cooper, Russell Burns **Est.** 2004 **Dozens** 500
Cooper Burns is the winemaking partnership of Mark Cooper and Russell Burns. It is a
virtual winery focusing on small-batch, handmade wine from the Barossa Valley (grapes are
sourced from Kalimna, Koonunga Hill and Moppa at the northern end of the valley). In
2006 production was increased to add a Shiraz Viognier and Grenache to the existing single
vineyard Shiraz. Exports to the US and Hong Kong.

ΨΨΨΨΨ **Barossa Valley Grenache 2009** 150 dozen made from 90-year-old bush
✪ vines. This is an altogether superior Barossa Valley Grenache, with none of the
confectionery/Turkish Delight characters the region often imparts; instead there
are bright red berry/raspberry flavours on the supple, smooth, light- to medium-
bodied palate. Screwcap. 14.5% alc. **Rating** 94 **To** 2016 $22

ΨΨΨΨΨ **Barossa Valley Shiraz 2009 Rating** 93 **To** 2029 $35

Coral Sea Wines

PO Box 800, Orange, NSW 2800 **Region** South Australia
T 0417 010 066 **www**.coralseawines.com **Open** Not
Winemaker Contract **Est.** 1993 **Dozens** 8000
Coral Sea Wines is the virtual winery venture of John Cooley. The modestly priced range of
Sauvignon Blanc, Chardonnay, NV Cuvee, Merlot, Shiraz and Cabernet Merlot comes from
grapes 'grown in South Australia's premier regions'. The business is a passionate supporter of
the World Wildlife Fund's 'Save the Coral Sea Appeal'. Exports to Tonga, Fiji, Solomon Islands,
Vietnam and China.

ΨΨΨΨ **Merlot 2010** Has retained good hue, and likewise gentle plum and cassis varietal
✪ fruit; no attempt to add overt oak to the equation, either. Good value. Screwcap.
14% alc. **Rating** 87 **To** 2013 $13

Coriole

Chaffeys Road, McLaren Vale, SA 5171 **Region** McLaren Vale
T (08) 8323 8305 **www**.coriole.com **Open** Mon–Fri 10–5, w'ends & public hols 11–5
Winemaker Alex Sherrah **Est.** 1967 **Dozens** 35 000 **Vyds** 48.5ha
While Coriole was not established until 1967, the cellar door and gardens date back to 1860,
when the original farm houses that now constitute the cellar door were built. The oldest shiraz
forming part of the estate plantings dates back to 1917, and since '85, Coriole has been an
Australian pioneer of sangiovese and – more recently – the Italian white variety fiano, plus
barbera and nero d'Avola, have joined the fold. Shiraz has 65% of the plantings, and it is for
this variety that Coriole is best known, led by the super-premium Lloyd Reserve. Exports to
all major markets.

ΨΨΨΨΨ **Lloyd Reserve McLaren Vale Shiraz 2011** Full purple-crimson; absolutely
in the heartland of McLaren Vale, redolent of medium- to full-bodied blackberry,
licorice and plentiful dark chocolate; there is no issue whatsoever about the
tannins, which are perfectly pitched. Screwcap. 14% alc. **Rating** 95 **To** 2031 $85
Estate Grown McLaren Vale Shiraz 2010 Deep magenta; lifted black fruits,
mocha, licorice and a fragrant violet note are all evident on the bouquet; the
palate is full-bodied, with densely packed tannins and bright dark fruits wrestling
for ascendancy; the finish is long and full of mocha and fruitcake spice. Screwcap.
14% alc. **Rating** 94 **To** 2022 $30 BE
Scarce Earth Old Vine Willunga Shiraz 2011 Deep colour; strong dark
chocolate and rich black fruit aromas lead into a medium- to full-bodied palate
speaking loudly of its place and not at all of '11; its abundant fruit flavours are
supported by a mix of new (30%) and used French oak, the tannins perfectly
balanced. 93-year-old estate vines. District 3, the 100,000-year-old Christies Beach
Formation left by a major flood. Screwcap. 14% alc. **Rating** 94 **To** 2026 $50

ŸŸŸŸ♀ Scarce Earth Galaxidia Shiraz 2011 Rating 93 To 2022 $50 BE
Estate McLaren Vale Cabernet Sauvignon 2010 Rating 93 To 2030 $30
Estate Grown McLaren Vale Shiraz 2011 Rating 92 To 2020 $30 BE
Andy Kissane National Wine Poet McLaren Vale Cabernet Shiraz 2011
Rating 91 To 2018 $35 BE
McLaren Vale Fiano 2012 Rating 90 To 2015 $25
Redstone McLaren Vale Shiraz 2010 Rating 90 To 2030 $19
The Dancing Fig Shiraz Mourvedre 2011 Rating 90 To 2018 $25 BE
McLaren Vale Sangiovese 2011 Rating 90 To 2025 $25

✪ McLaren Vale Nero d'Avola 2012 Mocha oak notes sit atop savoury thyme
and bramble on the bouquet; light- to medium-bodied with freshness the pivotal
feature of the palate; fleshy, forward and best consumed sooner rather than later.
Screwcap. 13.5% alc. Rating 90 To 2015 $20 BE

ŸŸŸŸ McLaren Vale Chenin Blanc 2012 Light straw-green; comes into its own on
✪ the palate, with nashi pear and green apple flavours on the mid-palate morphing
into minerally acidity on the finish. Old vines contribute to the texture and
structure of a wine that will repay cellaring if (improbably) it is given the chance.
Screwcap. 12.5% alc. Rating 89 To 2020 $16

Cornwall Vineyard   ★★★★

368 Richmond Road, Cambridge, Tas 7170 **Region** Southern Tasmania
T (03) 6248 5757 **www**.cornwall.com.au **Open** By appt
Winemaker Frogmore Creek **Est.** 1998 **Dozens** 150 **Vyds** 0.5ha
Alec Harper and partner Peta Elliott purchased their 14ha property in 1997, and the following
year established a pinot noir vineyard. This may seem a small planting, but they obtained
cuttings from Alec's sister Brenda and brother-in-law Peter Bosworth at Morningside
Vineyard. Their garage was turned into a nursery, with lights on 24 hours a day, encouraging
the cuttings to strike and thus become rootlings ready to plant. Since then the duo has micro-
managed every task in the vineyard: when a caterpillar invasion occurred they spent every
evening with buckets in hand, picking off the caterpillars one at a time.

ŸŸŸŸ♀ Devil of a Red Pinot Noir 2011 Good hue and depth to the colour; packed
with the varietal fruit that Tasmania, the Coal River/Richmond area in particular,
seems able to produce year in, year out; plum and dark cherry fruit flavours
run through the length of the palate, joined by fine, powdery tannins on the
finish; these will sustain the wine for a decade. Screwcap. 13.3% alc. Rating 93
To 2020 $28

Cosmo Wines   ★★★

32 Warrs Avenue, Preston, Vic 3072 (postal) **Region** Yarra Valley
T 0408 519 461 **www**.cosmowines.com.au **Open** Not
Winemaker Lindsay Corby **Est.** 2008 **Dozens** 1500
Lindsay Corby started with fruit winemaking while still at high school, but it was not until
1985 that he began to study at CSU, gaining qualifications in viticulture and wine science.
Thereafter he gained practical experience in various roles, including cellar door sales,
laboratory work and vineyard management, leading in turn to teaching 'the art and science of
the vine and wine' at La Trobe University and managing the small campus vineyard. Just prior
to Christmas 2008 he found his first (and hopefully permanent) home at Bianchet Winery,
where he makes the Bianchet wines, and the Cosmo wines (all of which are made from
purchased grapes). Exports to China.

ŸŸŸŸ Corby Gippsland Lakes Pinot Noir 2010 Part of the wine spent 18 months
in 2-year-old French oak; the slightly hazy (turbid) colour has good hue and
depth; a thick texture and very ripe fruit on the palate don't gel. A creased cork.
13.7% alc. Rating 87 To 2014 $21

Costanzo & Sons

602 Tames Road, Strathbogie, Vic 3666 **Region** Strathbogie Ranges
T 0423 720 682 **www**.costanzo.com.au **Open** By appt
Winemaker Sergio Carlei (Contract) **Est.** 2011 **Dozens** NFP **Vyds** 6ha

This is the venture of Joe Costanzo and Cindy Heath, Joe having grapegrowing in his DNA. He was raised among his parents' 20ha vineyard in NSW on the Murray River, the family business selling grapes to Brown Brothers, Seppelt, Bullers and Miranda Wines. By the age of 17 he had decided to follow in their footsteps, working full-time in vineyards, and formally studied viticulture. For many years he and Cindy searched for the perfect vineyard, and in 2011 finally acquired one that had been planted between 1993 and '94 (to 1.5ha each of sauvignon blanc and chardonnay, and 3ha of pinot noir). In conjunction with contract winemaker Sergio Carlei, they decided to make Sauvignon Blanc in the mould of the late Didier Dagueneau's Loire Valley Silex and Domaine A's Lady A, both barrel-fermented Sauvignon Blancs. To say the 2012 realises that ambition is a masterly understatement.

PPPPP **Estate Grown Strathbogie Ranges Sauvignon Blanc 2012** The wine is 100% wild yeast barrel-fermented in what appears to be used oak. This approach needs grapes with above-average varietal flavour, and that is what went into this very well-made, complex wine; ripe citrus, gooseberry and kiwifruit are cradled in the textured palate. Screwcap. 13% alc. **Rating** 94 **To** 2015 $30

Courabyra Wines

805 Courabyra Road, Tumbarumba, NSW 2653 **Region** Tumbarumba
T (02) 6948 2462 **www**.courabyrawines.com **Open** W'ends 10–4, or by appt
Winemaker Alex McKay, Nick Spencer, Peta Baverstock **Est.** 2010 **Dozens** NFP
Vyds 36.3ha

This significant development in the Tumbarumba region brings together brother and sister Cathy Gairn and Stephen Morrison, although it has taken 25 years for the two families to form Courabyra Wines. Cathy and husband Brian purchased their land in 1985, and moved there permanently in '87. Cathy had a horticultural degree and experience in cut flower production, and this was their first business venture. After planting their 8.3ha vineyard to pinot noir, chardonnay and pinot meunier in '93, Cathy moved on to formal viticultural studies. Investment banker Stephen always came to help at harvest time. After looking for a cool-climate vineyard for many years, he found one under his nose, at 157 Courabyra Road, in '10. This is the oldest vineyard in Tumbarumba, established in 1981 by Ian Cowell, and thereafter for two decades owned by what is now TWE. Now known as Revee Estate, pinot noir (16ha) and chardonnay (8ha) take the lion's share of the plantings, with lesser amounts of sauvignon blanc, pinot gris and pinot meunier.

PPPPP **805 Tumbarumba Pinot Noir Chardonnay Pinot Meunier 2001** Amazingly, only slightly deeper colour than that of the '08 version of this wine; it is also fresh, although there are some nutty/creamy brioche characters to the finely structured palate; it has very good length and balance, the dosage relatively low. Trophy Best Sparkling Wine NSW Wine Awards '12. Cork. 13% alc. **Rating** 94 **To** 2015 $55

PPPPP **157 Tumbarumba Chardonnay 2011** **Rating** 92 **To** 2018 $26

✿ **1 of 11 Tumbarumba Sauvignon Blanc 2012** Has a very attractive blend of passionfruit and citrus on its fresh, delicate, yet long and well-balanced palate. Enjoy its freshness asap. Screwcap. 11.5% alc. **Rating** 91 **To** 2013 $18

805 Pinot Noir Chardonnay Pinot Meunier 2008 **Rating** 91 **To** 2015 $45

✿ **1 of 11 Tumbarumba Pinot Gris 2012** I'm not convinced there is any gris (as opposed to grigio) character to the wine; however, there are some citrus notes grafted onto the apple and pear fruit that add complexity. Screwcap. 11.5% alc. **Rating** 90 **To** 2014 $18

Cowaramup Wines

19 Tassel Road, Cowaramup, WA 6284 **Region** Margaret River
T (08) 9755 5195 **www**.cowaramupwines.com.au **Open** By appt
Winemaker Naturaliste Vintners (Bruce Dukes) **Est.** 1995 **Dozens** 5000 **Vyds** 17ha
Russell and Marilyn Reynolds run a biodynamic vineyard with the aid of sons Cameron (viticulturist) and Anthony (assistant winemaker). Plantings began in 1996 and have been expanded to include merlot, cabernet sauvignon, shiraz, semillon, chardonnay and sauvignon blanc. Notwithstanding low yields and the discipline that biodynamic grapegrowing entails, wine prices are modest. Wines are released under the Cowaramup Wines, Clown Fish and New School labels. No wines received for the *2014 Wine Companion*, but a five-star rating has been maintained.

Crabtree Watervale Wines

North Terrace, Watervale SA 5452 **Region** Clare Valley
T (08) 8843 0069 **www**.crabtreewines.com.au **Open** 7 days 10.30–4.30
Winemaker Kerri Thompson **Est.** 1979 **Dozens** 6000 **Vyds** 13.2ha
Wine industry executives Richard Woods and Rasa Fabian purchased Crabtree in 2007 and left Sydney corporate life for the ultimate seachange. Collectively, they had decades of sales and marketing experience, and remain adamant that Crabtree should be an estate brand, and therefore limited in volume. In 2013, Richard and Rasa decided to stand aside from management of the business, but remain shareholders. Kerri Thompson (see Wines by KT) continues as Crabtree's highly talented and very experienced winemaker, having a great record with Riesling.

ΨΨΨΨΨ **Riesling 2012** Bright straw-green; there is an extra dimension of fruit complexity to both the bouquet and palate compared to its Hilltop sibling, yet it retains its elegance and lightness of step, chalky acidity providing gentle restraint. Greatness waits around the corner. Screwcap. 12.5% alc. **Rating** 95 **To** 2027 $25

✪ **Shiraz 2010** Full crimson-purple; the bouquet throws the emphasis onto an array of black fruits, French oak also in the mix; the medium- to full-bodied palate continues the theme with exceptional balance and structure, the finish long and complete; has a long life ahead. Screwcap. 14% alc. **Rating** 95 **To** 2030 $25

✪ **Hilltop Vineyard Riesling 2012** Bright straw-green; the blossom-filled bouquet ranges through citrus, talc and spice, the palate following in lockstep behind, its flavours changing back and forth through to the long finish. Screwcap. 12.5% alc. **Rating** 94 **To** 2022 $22

✪ **Cabernet Sauvignon 2010** From the estate Windmill Block, open-fermented and matured in new, 1- and 2-year-old French barriques for 18 months; has a degree of savoury elegance to its medium-bodied palate not common in the Clare Valley, and in consequence has very good length. Screwcap. 14.5% alc. **Rating** 94 **To** 2030 $25

ΨΨΨΨΨ **Hilltop Vineyard Shiraz 2010 Rating** 91 **To** 2025 $22
Bay of Biscay Grenache Rose 2012 Rating 90 **To** 2014 $22 BE

🍇 Cradle of Hills

76 Rogers Road, Sellicks Hill, SA 5174 **Region** McLaren Vale
T (08) 8557 4023 **www**.cradle-of-hills.com.au **Open** By appt
Winemaker Paul Smith **Est.** 2009 **Dozens** 600 **Vyds** 6.88ha
Paul Smith's introduction to wine was an unlikely one: the Royal Australian Navy, and in particular the wardroom cellar, at the tender age of 19. A career change took Paul to the world of high-performance sports, and he met his horticulturist wife Trace, who originally studied botany in Melbourne before moving into horticulture. From 2005 they travelled the world with their two children, spending a couple of years in Europe, working in and learning about the great wine regions of Europe, and how fine wine is made. For his part, Paul secured a winemaking diploma, and they now have almost 7ha of cabernet sauvignon and shiraz (roughly 50% each). They supplement the shiraz with grenache and mourvedre to make their Route de Bonheur (Road to Happiness) grenache, mourvedre, shiraz blend.

ŸŸŸŸŸ McLaren Vale Shiraz Mourvedre 2010 A 68/25/7% blend of shiraz, mourvedre and grenache. Each parcel was separately picked, hand-sorted, crushed into small open fermenters, hand-plunged, basket-pressed and had 30 months' maturation in used French hogsheads, not fined or filtered. Good red-purple; the bouquet and medium-bodied palate focus on blackberry, plum and licorice, with a dash of dark chocolate; the tannins are fine-grained and very good, combining well with the oak. Screwcap. 14.5% alc. **Rating** 94 **To** 2020 $25

ŸŸŸŸŸ Coeur de L'Ete Cinsault Grenache 2012 **Rating** 93 **To** 2014 $19
Row 23 McLaren Vale Shiraz 2011 **Rating** 93 **To** 2025 $45
Route du Bonheur McLaren Vale GMS 2010 **Rating** 93 **To** 2020 $25
Row 23 McLaren Vale Shiraz 2010 **Rating** 92 **To** 2018 $55 TS
McLaren Vale Cabernet Shiraz 2010 **Rating** 92 **To** 2025 $25
✪ McLaren Vale Cabernet Shiraz 2009 Open-fermented and basket-pressed; spent 30 months in French and American oak, which has well and truly left its mark on the wine; however, there are also multiple layers of blackberry, blackcurrant and plum fruit to carry that oak. 111 dozen made. Screwcap. 14.5% alc. **Rating** 92 **To** 2024 $25

Craiglee ★★★★★

Sunbury Road, Sunbury, Vic 3429 **Region** Sunbury
T (03) 9744 4489 **www.**craiglee.com.au **Open** Sun, public hols 10–5, or by appt
Winemaker Patrick Carmody **Est.** 1976 **Dozens** 2500 **Vyds** 9.5ha
A winery with a proud 19th-century record, Craiglee recommenced winemaking in 1976 after a prolonged hiatus. Produces one of the finest cool-climate Shirazs in Australia, redolent of cherry, licorice and spice in the better (warmer) vintages, lighter bodied in the cooler ones. Mature vines and improved viticulture have made the wines more consistent (and even better) over the past 10 years or so. Exports to the UK, the US, Hong Kong and Italy.

ŸŸŸŸŸ Sunbury Chardonnay 2010 Pale, bright green-straw; a very well-made wine, with great intensity to its white stone fruit/grapefruit flavours, which are complexed by barrel ferment in quality oak; excellent length and balance. Screwcap. 13.5% alc. **Rating** 95 **To** 2017 $33
Sunbury Shiraz 2010 Clear red-purple; an archetypal fragrant Craiglee bouquet, with a panoply of spicy, peppery red and black cherry fruits precisely reflected in the light- to medium-bodied palate; it has perfect balance and length, and will surprise those who don't know the prior history of this proud label. Diam. 13.5% alc. **Rating** 95 **To** 2030 $52
Sunbury Viognier 2010 Glowing light green-straw; it's easy to like the wine even if you don't like viognier; peach and apricot flavours are not phenolic or heavy, and the acid balance is good; barrel fermentation in 3-year-old barriques has worked perfectly. Screwcap. 13.5% alc. **Rating** 94 **To** 2017 $33
Sunbury Shiraz 2009 A remarkably youthful purple-crimson hue; fragrant, clearly avoided any smoke issues, and the period of extreme heat preceded the final stages of ripening; has plum and black cherry fruit, with spice present but not obvious. Diam. 14% alc. **Rating** 94 **To** 2014 $52

ŸŸŸŸŸ Sunbury Shiraz Viognier 2010 **Rating** 92 **To** 2018 $45

Craigow ★★★★★

528 Richmond Road, Cambridge, Tas 7170 **Region** Southern Tasmania
T (03) 6248 5379 **www.**craigow.com.au **Open** 7 days Christmas to Easter (except public hols), or by appt
Winemaker Winemaking Tasmania (Julian Alcorso) **Est.** 1989 **Dozens** 800 **Vyds** 8.75ha
Hobart surgeon Barry Edwards and wife Cathy have moved from being grapegrowers with only one wine to a portfolio of several wines, while continuing to sell most of their grapes. Craigow has an impressive museum release program; the best are outstanding, while others show the impact of sporadic bottle oxidation (a diminishing problem with each vintage now under screwcap). In 2008 Craigow won the Tasmanian Vineyard of the Year Award. There is

a degree of poetic history: the first settler, who arrived in the 1820s, was a Scottish doctor (James Murdoch) who, among other things, grew opium poppies for medical use; by 1872 his descendants were making wine from grapes, gooseberries and cherries. There is some suggestion that the grapes, known then as black cluster, were in all probability pinot noir.

ΨΨΨΨΨ **Riesling 2012** Light straw-green; still tightly wound up, but well balanced; history shows how well the Craigow Rieslings develop over time. Gold medal Tasmanian Wine Show '13 Screwcap. 12.1% alc. **Rating** 94 **To** 2022 $28
Chardonnay 2012 Light straw-green; the fragrant flower-laden bouquet and elegant palate sing from the same page, the 10 months spent in French oak (not too much new) making less impact than the ruby grapefruit that provides the acidity for the finish. Screwcap. 13.8% alc. **Rating** 94 **To** 2018 $29
Botrytis Riesling 2011 Gleaming green-straw; extremely intense and luscious; all the rot is of the noble kind, giving the wine great length and complexity, acid (of course) critical. 375ml. Screwcap. 8% alc. **Rating** 94 **To** 2016 $26

ΨΨΨΨ **Sauvignon Blanc 2011** **Rating** 89 **To** 2014 $22

Craneford

Moorundie Street, Truro, SA 5356 **Region** Barossa Valley
T (08) 8564 0003 **www**.cranefordwines.com **Open** Mon–Fri 10–5, w'ends by appt
Winemaker Carol Riebke, John Glaetzer (Consultant) **Est.** 1978 **Dozens** 50000
Since Craneford was founded in 1978 it has undergone a number of changes of both location and ownership. The biggest change came in 2004 when the winery, by then housed in the old country fire station building in Truro, was expanded and upgraded. In '06 John Glaetzer joined the team as consultant winemaker, with Carol Riebke the day-to-day winemaker. Quality grapes are sourced from contract growers, and production has doubled – amazing in these tough times. Exports to all major markets.

ΨΨΨΨΨ **Basket Pressed Barossa Valley Shiraz 2010** Full purple-red; a rich, deeply layered, full-bodied Shiraz with blackberry, plum, licorice and dark chocolate on the bouquet and palate alike; its plush and velvety palate also shows the use of quality oak, and is supported by ripe tannins. Screwcap. 14.5% alc. **Rating** 94 **To** 2030 $28

ΨΨΨΨΨ **Barossa Valley GSM 2010** The standard grenache/shiraz/mourvedre blend. The
✪ colour is bright, although not deep; the aromas and flavours take in some black fruits alongside the dominant red berry nuances; it has a well above average texture and structure for this blend. Screwcap. 14.5% alc. **Rating** 93 **To** 2018 $24
Barossa Valley Cabernet Sauvignon 2010 **Rating** 93 **To** 2025 $28
Barossa Valley Merlot 2010 **Rating** 92 **To** 2020 $32
Quartet 2010 **Rating** 90 **To** 2025 $24

Crawford River Wines

741 Hotspur Upper Road, Condah, Vic 3303 **Region** Henty
T (03) 5578 2267 **www**.crawfordriverwines.com **Open** By appt
Winemaker John and Belinda Thomson **Est.** 1975 **Dozens** 4000 **Vyds** 11.5ha
Time flies, and it seems incredible that Crawford River celebrated its 35th birthday in 2010. Once a tiny outpost in a little-known wine region, Crawford River is now one of the foremost producers of Riesling (and other excellent wines) thanks to the unremitting attention to detail and skill of its founder and winemaker, John Thomson (and moral support from wife Catherine). His exceptionally talented elder daughter Belinda has returned part-time after completing her winemaking degree and working along the way in Marlborough (NZ), Bordeaux, Ribera del Duero (Spain), Bolgheri and Tuscany, and the Nahe (Germany), with Crawford River filling in the gaps. She continues working in Spain, effectively doing two vintages each year. Younger daughter Fiona is in charge of national sales and marketing. No wines received for the *2014 Wine Companion*, but a five-star rating has been maintained. Exports to the UK, Ireland, Canada, Japan and South-East Asia.

Credaro Family Estate

2175 Caves Road, Yallingup, WA 6282 **Region** Margaret River
T (08) 9755 1111 **www.credarowines.com.au Open** 7 days 10–5
Winemaker Dave Johnson **Est.** 1993 **Dozens** 10000 **Vyds** 93ha
The Credaro family first settled in Margaret River in 1922, migrating from Northern Italy. Initially a few small plots of vines were planted to provide the family with wine in the European tradition. However, things moved significantly in the '80s and '90s, and today the family has three separate vineyards, one previously known as Vasse River Wines. Roughly 25% of the grapes are vinified by the family, the remainder sold under contract to larger local producers. The estate produces two ranges: Beach Head and Credaro Family Estate. In recent years Credaro has had significant success in wine shows for both ranges; skilled winemaking and mature vines are the foundation. This in turn has led to the opening of a cellar door.

Margaret River Sauvignon Blanc Semillon 2012 A very complex, but wholly satisfying, blend that spent 8 months in new and used French barriques, a sojourn that in no way blurred the juicy fruits effortlessly cruising through tropical and citrus flavours, cleansed on the finish by crunchy acidity. Screwcap. 12.5% alc. Rating 94 **To** 2015 $24

Beach Head Margaret River Sauvignon Blanc Semillon 2012 As is so often the case, over-delivers on its price; tropical fruits are stirred into the citrus/grass components from the word go, but avoid any sweet and sour notes. Ready now, but has a year or two up its sleeve. Screwcap. 12.8% alc. **Rating** 90 **To** 2014 $18

Beach Head Margaret River Shiraz 2011 Full red-purple; a medium- to full-bodied palate delivers the blackberry and blood plum fruit promised by the bouquet, with an added splash of dark chocolate. No one could accuse the wine of elegance, but its good-humoured rustic generosity makes it good value. Screwcap. 14% alc. **Rating** 90 **To** 2021 $19

Margaret River Cane Cut Semillon 2012 Rating 90 **To** 2015 $25

Crittenden Estate

25 Harrisons Road, Dromana, Vic 3936 **Region** Mornington Peninsula
T (03) 5981 8322 **www.crittendenwines.com.au Open** 7 days 11–4
Winemaker Rollo Crittenden **Est.** 1984 **Dozens** 7000 **Vyds** 4.8ha
The wheel of fortune has turned full circle with son Rollo Crittenden returning to the (new) family wine business established by father Garry in 2003. In so doing, both father and son have severed ties with Dromana Estate, the old family business. For good measure, the Crittendens have taken a lease on a modern winery in Patterson Lakes, approximately 20mins north of their Dromana property. Capable of handling 200 tonnes of grapes, more than that required by Crittenden Estate, it has enabled Rollo to develop Latitude 38, a contract winemaking business. He was named Young Gun Australian Winemaker of the Year '10. Exports to the UK and the US.

The Zumma Chardonnay 2011 The bouquet offers savoury elements of smoky bacon, nectarine, solidsy complexity and spicy oak notes; the palate is electrifying with its intensity and linear acidity, providing a long, engaging, refreshing and expansive conclusion; simply a lovely wine in every respect. Screwcap. 12.7% alc. Rating 96 **To** 2022 $50 BE

Mornington Peninsula Chardonnay 2011 Pale gold, bright; an elegant and refined bouquet, revealing glimpses of pear, nectarine and cashew aromas; the palate is luscious on entry, focused and truly complex, as the fruit takes its time to unwind and, aided by linear acidity, finishes on a long and high note of compelling complexity. Screwcap. 13.2% alc. Rating 95 **To** 2018 $34 BE

Cri de Coeur Savagnin 2011 Rating 93 **To** 2016 $60 BE
The Zumma Pinot Noir 2011 Rating 93 **To** 2018 $50 BE
Fume Blanc Sauvignon 2011 Rating 92 **To** 2015 $27 BE

Cruickshank Callatoota Estate

5058 Golden Highway, Denman, NSW 2328 **Region** Hunter Valley
T (02) 6547 1088 **www**.cruickshank.com.au **Open** 7 days 9–5
Winemaker John Cruickshank, Atsuko Radcliffe **Est.** 1973 **Dozens** 6000 **Vyds** 26.63ha
The Cruickshank family moved its winery when the existing property was acquired by a
coal miner, and moved to Denman, where they were able to acquire a substantial existing
vineyard. The new vineyard is predominantly planted to cabernet sauvignon, verdelho, shiraz,
chardonnay and cabernet franc. Wine quality and style remain unchanged.

ŸŸŸŸ   **Cabernet Sauvignon Pressings 2009** The colour is no deeper than the
standard Cabernet, but there is more tannin, and in this instance, this makes it
the better wine, with more varietal expression. Screwcap. 13.1% alc. **Rating** 87
To 2015 $21
Hunter Valley Two Cabernets 2009 Light red-purple; a light- to medium-
bodied wine with regional earthy overtones to the red berry fruits of the cabernet
sauvignon and cabernet franc, the tannins and extract controlled. Screwcap.
13.1% alc. **Rating** 87 **To** 2015 $21
Hunter Valley Botrytis Verdelho 2010 Yellow-gold; there is no question about
the botrytis, but other moulds were also present; that said, it's a fair effort. Cork.
13.5% alc. **Rating** 87 **To** 2014 $25

Cullen Wines

4323 Caves Road, Wilyabrup, WA 6280 **Region** Margaret River
T (08) 9755 5277 **www**.cullenwines.com.au **Open** 7 days 10–4.30
Winemaker Vanya Cullen, Trevor Kent **Est.** 1971 **Dozens** 20 000 **Vyds** 49ha
One of the pioneers of Margaret River, which has always produced long-lived wines of highly
individual style from the mature estate vineyards. The vineyard has progressed beyond organic
to biodynamic certification and, subsequently, has become the first vineyard and winery in
Australia to be certified carbon neutral. This requires the calculation of all the carbon used and
carbon dioxide emitted in the winery; the carbon is then offset by the planting of new trees.
Winemaking is now in the hands of Vanya Cullen, daughter of the founders; she is possessed
of an extraordinarily good palate. It is impossible to single out any particular wine from the
top echelon; all are superb. Exports to all major markets.

ŸŸŸŸŸ   **Kevin John Margaret River Chardonnay 2010** Hand-picked, whole bunch-
pressed, and wild yeast-fermented in French barriques before spending a further
5 months in those barrels. The texture and mouthfeel are supple and round, the
white peach, cashew and fig flavours coursing in an unbroken stream through
to the prodigiously long finish and aftertaste. Screwcap. 13.7% alc. **Rating** 97
To 2020 $105
Diana Madeline 2010 A 77/10/6/4/3% blend of cabernet sauvignon, merlot,
petit verdot, malbec and cabernet franc. Medium-bodied and perfectly balanced, its
array of blackcurrant, redcurrant, earth and spice fruit flavours are clearly varietal.
Effortless grace, sure to develop beautifully over the next 20–30 years. Screwcap.
13% alc. **Rating** 96 **To** 2040 $115
Cullen Vineyard Margaret River Sauvignon Blanc Semillon 2010
A blend of 66% sauvignon blanc matured in new French oak for 5 months and
34% semillon with a wide range of picking dates. It shows no green/unripe fruit,
just aromatic citrus and herb notes on the long, intense palate that I can only
describe as slippery. Still dazzlingly precise, fresh and long, and has completely
absorbed the oak flavours. Screwcap. 11.5% alc. **Rating** 95 **To** 2016 $35

Cumulus Wines

PO Box 41, Cudal, NSW 2864 **Region** Orange
T (02) 6390 7900 **www**.cumuluswines.com.au **Open** During Orange Food Week (Apr)
and Wine Week (Oct)
Winemaker Debbie Lauritz, Matt Atallah **Est.** 2004 **Dozens** 200 000 **Vyds** 508ha

Cumulus Wines is now majority owned by the Berardo Group of Portugal (which has numerous wine investments in Portugal, Canada and Madeira). Over 500ha of mature vineyards focus on shiraz, cabernet sauvignon, chardonnay and merlot. The wines are released under three brands: Rolling, from the Central Ranges Zone; Climbing, solely from Orange fruit; and Cumulus, super-premium from the best of the estate vineyard blocks. One of an increasing number of wineries to use lightweight bottles. Patrick Auld repaid the Hunter Valley Vignerons who gave him a wine industry Living Legend award in 2012 by accepting the position of general manager at Cumulus in Jan '13. Exports to the UK, the US and other major markets.

ŸŸŸŸŸ **Climbing Orange Cabernet Sauvignon 2011** An attractive, juicy, light- to medium-bodied wine; the bouquet has fragrant red fruits allied with a touch of black olive, and the supple palate brings those red berry fruits to the fore, fine-grained tannins to the rear. Great achievement. Screwcap. 14% alc. Rating 94 To 2021 $24

ŸŸŸŸŸ **Cumulus Orange Chardonnay 2012** Rating 92 To 2017 $35
Rolling Sauvignon Blanc Semillon 2012 Rating 90 To 2014 $19

ŸŸŸŸ **Rolling Central Ranges Chardonnay 2012** Bright, light straw-green; all the
✪ focus is on varietal fruit expression; while light, it has good balance and mouthfeel to the mix of melon, white peach and grapefruit flavours. Ready now. Screwcap. 13% alc. **Rating** 89 To 2014 $19
✪ **Luna Rosa Rosado 2012** A 50/50% blend of grenache and mourvedre and of an Australian and Portuguese winemaking team that produced this brilliantly coloured, red berry-fruited wine; it has more texture to the finish than most but remains bone dry. Terrific for tapas. Screwcap. 11.5% alc. **Rating** 89 To 2014 $15

Cupitt's Winery ★★★★

58 Washburton Road, Ulladulla, NSW 2539 **Region** Shoalhaven Coast
T (02) 4455 7888 **www**.cupittwines.com.au **Open** Wed–Sun 10–5
Winemaker Rosie and Wally Cupitt **Est.** 2007 **Dozens** 2000 **Vyds** 4ha
Griff and Rosie Cupitt run a combined winery and restaurant complex, taking full advantage of the location on the south coast of NSW. Rosie studied oenology at CSU and has more than a decade of vintage experience, taking in France and Italy; she also happens to be the Shoalhaven representative for Slow Food International. The Cupitts have 4ha of vines centred on sauvignon blanc, cabernet franc and semillon, and also buy viognier and shiraz from Tumbarumba, shiraz, chardonnay and sauvignon blanc from the Southern Highlands, and verdelho from Canowindra (Cowra). Rosie has been joined in the winery by son Wally.

ŸŸŸŸŸ **Rosie's Pinot Noir Rose 2012** Pale salmon, bright; delicately perfumed, with wild strawberry and sage evident on the bouquet; the palate is taut and finely textured, finishing with a fresh fennel note that is refreshing and intriguing; the price may deter some rose fans. Screwcap. 12.5% alc. **Rating** 90 To 2014 $30 BE

ŸŸŸŸ **Mia Bella Arneis 2012** Rating 88 To 2015 $26 BE
Woodlands Sauvignon 2011 Rating 87 To 2014 $26 BE
Late Harvest Chardonnay Sauvignon Blanc 2011 Rating 87 To 2016 $28 BE

Curlewis Winery ★★★★☆

55 Navarre Road, Curlewis, Vic 3222 **Region** Geelong
T (03) 5250 4567 **www**.curlewiswinery.com.au **Open** By appt
Winemaker Rainer Breit **Est.** 1998 **Dozens** 2000 **Vyds** 2.8ha
Rainer Breit and partner Wendy Oliver purchased their property in 1996 with 1.6ha of what were then 11-year-old pinot noir vines. Rainer, a self-taught winemaker, uses the full bag of pinot noir winemaking tricks: cold-soaking, hot fermentation, post-ferment maceration, part inoculated and part wild yeast use, prolonged lees contact, and bottling the wine neither fined nor filtered. While self-confessed 'pinotphiles', they planted some chardonnay, supplemented by a little locally grown shiraz and chardonnay. Rainer and Wendy sold the business in

May 2011 to Leesa Freyer and Stefano Marasco, but Rainer will stay on as winemaker until '14, with a phased exit strategy. Leesa and Stefano are passionate Pinot Noir drinkers, and also own and operate the Yarra Lounge in Yarraville, Melbourne. Exports to Canada, Sweden, the Maldives, Malaysia, Singapore and Hong Kong.

ŸŸŸŸŸ **Geelong Pinot Noir 2011** Fractionally brighter, although no deeper colour than Bel Sel; less spicy, and with more red fruits; the tannins are of gossamer weight, and in each case care has been taken not to use too much oak. Screwcap. 12% alc. **Rating** 92 **To** 2016 $40
Geelong Syrah 2010 Bright crimson hue; a lively wine, with a fragrant bouquet reflecting red fruits and French oak; not bottled until Dec '12, and there is some sharpness to the palate that will in all probability soften in bottle, and given the benefit of the doubt. Screwcap. 13.5% alc. **Rating** 90 **To** 2020 $40

ŸŸŸŸ **Bel Sel Geelong Pinot Noir 2011 Rating** 89 **To** 2014 $25

Curly Flat   ★★★★★

263 Collivers Road, Lancefield, Vic 3435 **Region** Macedon Ranges
T (03) 5429 1956 **www**.curlyflat.com **Open** W'ends 12–5, or by appt
Winemaker Phillip Moraghan, Matt Regan **Est.** 1991 **Dozens** 6000 **Vyds** 13ha
Phillip Moraghan and Jenifer Kolkka began developing Curly Flat in 1992, drawing in part on Phillip's working experience in Switzerland in the late '80s, and with a passing nod to Michael Leunig. With ceaseless help and guidance from the late Laurie Williams (and others), they have painstakingly established 8.5ha of pinot noir, 3.5ha of chardonnay and 1ha of pinot gris, and a multi-level, gravity-flow winery. Exports to the UK, Japan and Hong Kong.

ŸŸŸŸŸ **The Curly Pinot Noir 2010** A 3-tonne vineyard selection producing 244 dozen that was matured in 100% new French oak for 22 months. It has another dimension of intensity and length, its aromas and flavours linked to black cherry and foresty notes from 100% whole-bunch fermentation. Great Pinot. WAK screwcap. 14.2% alc. **Rating** 97 **To** 2024 $60
Pinot Noir 2010 Healthy, clear red-purple; offers a mix of spicy/savoury and French oak nuances running through the plum and red cherry fruit of the bouquet; the palate is perfectly balanced, and the 22 months in 30% new French oak barrels were judged to perfection. WAK screwcap. 13.8% alc. **Rating** 95 **To** 2020 $48
Lacuna Chardonnay 2011 Unoaked but with lees contact for 9 months; part wild, part inoculated fermentation, mlf occurring naturally. Bright straw-green; throwing all the focus on the fruit has worked very well, for the palate is full of flavour spanning nectarine, white peach and grapefruit, with a slightly creamy note ex mlf and lees contact. Screwcap. 13% alc. **Rating** 94 **To** 2018 $36

Curtis Family Vineyards   ★★★☆

514 Victor Harbor Road, McLaren Vale, SA 5171 **Region** McLaren Vale
T 0439 800 484 **www**.curtisfamilyvineyards.com **Open** Not
Winemaker Mark and Claudio Curtis **Est.** 1973 **Dozens** 10 000
The Curtis family traces its history back to 1471, and, more importantly, 1499, when Paolo Curtis was appointed by Cardinal de Medici to administer Papal lands in the area around Cervaro. (The name Curtis is believed to derive from Curtius, a noble and wealthy Roman Empire family.) The family has been growing grapes and making wine in McLaren Vale since 1973, having come to Australia some years previously. Exports to the US, Canada, Thailand and China.

ŸŸŸŸ **McLaren Vale Shiraz 2009** Medium red-purple; the decidedly curious wording
✪ of the back label discloses (inter alia) that the wine was matured in new American and French 'hogsheads' (sic). It is indeed oaky, but there is also a clear affirmation of its region of origin, with good black fruits and ripe tannins, and is very well priced. Screwcap. 14% alc. **Rating** 90 **To** 2020 $20

ŸŸŸŸ **Fifth Realm McLaren Vale Shiraz 2010 Rating** 89 **To** 2016 $30

Cuttaway Hill Wines ★★★★

PO Box 881, Mittagong, NSW 2575 **Region** Southern Highlands
T (02) 4889 4790 **www.**cuttawayhillwines.com.au **Open** By appt
Winemaker Mark Bourne, Jeff Aston **Est.** 1998 **Dozens** 10000 **Vyds** 30ha
While the Bourne family did not acquire Cuttaway Hill from the founding O'Neil family until 2011, Mark Bourne produced the region's first sparkling wines in '04 under the Cuttaway Hill Laurence label. Until '11 Mark's principal focus was viticulture, and he was the founding president of the Southern Highlands Vignerons Association, and chief organiser of the Australian Highlands Wine Show. While he continues those involvements, he is now in charge of all aspects of the Cuttaway Hill business. Exports to the US, Canada and China.

♟♟♟♟♀ Pinot Gris 2012 While there have been no (disclosed) winemaking flourishes, this has unusual depth and complexity to its multiple layers of flavours, ranging from pear all the way through to pineapple, but not exaggerated nor phenolic. Screwcap. 13.5% alc. **Rating** 93 **To** 2014 $28
Sauvignon Blanc 2012 Light green-straw; the fragrant grassy bouquet leads into a palate with tropical nuances running alongside citrussy acidity; a good outcome for a challenging vintage. Screwcap. 12% alc. **Rating** 90 **To** 2014 $22

♟♟♟♟ Semillon Sauvignon Blanc 2012 Rating 89 **To** 2014 $22
Merlot 2010 Rating 88 **To** 2014 $22

Cypress Post ★★★

269 Jimmy Mann Road, Stanthorpe, Qld 4380 **Region** Granite Belt
T (07) 3375 4083 **www.**cypresspost.com.au **Open** Not
Winemaker Mark Ravenscroft (Contract) **Est.** 2000 **Dozens** 160 **Vyds** 3.2ha
The Olsen family – headed by doctors Michael (a consultant botanist) and Catherine – has a strong botanical and conservation background continuing over two generations. The property has been registered under the Land for Wildlife program and will continue to be run on these principles, blending science and caring for the future. Plantings include shiraz (2ha), viognier, marsanne (1ha each) and pinot gris (0.5ha). The 2009, '10 and '11 vintages all suffered various nature-inflicted vicissitudes, significantly reducing the amount of wine available for sale.

♟♟♟♟ 2000 Granite Belt Viognier Marsanne 2012 A 70/30% blend with a label that breaks every law of marketing, 'Cypress Post' in tiny typeface, and almost transparent against the pale glass bottle. There is a very large orange oval, with a large '2000' occupying most of the space, but without any explanation for it. Perhaps it's all a cunning way to distract attention from the wine in the glass. Screwcap. 12.5% alc. **Rating** 87 **To** 2014 $23

D'Angelo Estate ★★★☆

41 Bayview Road, Officer, Vic 3809 **Region** Yarra Valley
T 0417 055 651 **www.**dangelowines.com.au **Open** W'ends 12–5, or by appt
Winemaker Benny D'Angelo **Est.** 1994 **Dozens** 3000 **Vyds** 15ha
The business dates back to 1994, when Benny D'Angelo's father planted a small block of pinot noir for home winemaking. One thing led to another, with Benny taking over winemaking and doing well in amateur wine shows. This led to the planting of more pinot and some cabernet sauvignon. Expansion continued with the 2001 acquisition of a 4ha site at Officer, which has been planted to six clones of pinot noir, and small parcels of cabernet sauvignon and shiraz. Grapes are also purchased from a wide range of vineyards, stretching from Gippsland to Langhorne Creek.

♟♟♟♟♀ Officer Pinot Grigio 2011 Vibrant green hue; savoury aromas are offset by lemon zest, bath talc and pear; juicy, concentrated and revealing lively acidity and a dry chalky and distinctly savoury long and harmonious finish. Screwcap. 13.4% alc. **Rating** 90 **To** 2015 $20 BE

ŶŶŶŶ   Officer Sauvignon Blanc 2011 Rating 88 To 2015 $20 BE
Officer Lady Chardonnay 2011 Rating 88 To 2016 $25 BE
Officer Pinot Grigio 2012 Rating 88 To 2015 $20 BE
Officer Sauvignon Blanc 2012 Rating 87 To 2014 $20 BE

d'Arenberg   ★★★★★

Osborn Road, McLaren Vale, SA 5171 **Region** McLaren Vale
T (08) 8329 4888 **www.**darenberg.com.au **Open** 7 days 10–5
Winemaker Chester Osborn, Jack Walton **Est.** 1912 **Dozens** 270 000 **Vyds** 197.2ha
Nothing, they say, succeeds like success. Few operations in Australia fit this dictum better
than d'Arenberg, which has kept its almost 100-year-old heritage while moving into the 21st
century with flair and élan. At last count the d'Arenberg vineyards, at various locations, have
24 varieties planted, as well as 120 growers in McLaren Vale. There is no question that its past,
present and future revolve around its considerable portfolio of richly robed red wines, Shiraz,
Cabernet Sauvignon and Grenache being the cornerstones, but with over 20 varietal and/or
blend labels spanning the gulf between Roussanne and Mourvedre. The quality of the wines
is unimpeachable, the prices logical and fair. It has a profile in both the UK and the US that
far larger companies would love to have, underlined by the *Wine & Spirits Magazine* (US)
accolade of Winery of the Year '09. d'Arenberg celebrated 100 years of family grapegrowing
in '12 on the property that houses the winery, cellar door and restaurant (together with some
of the oldest estate vines). Exports to all major markets.

ŶŶŶŶŶ   The Piceous Lodestar Shiraz 2011 The vines were 42 years old when the
grapes for this wine were picked on Mar 19, the trellis an unromantic double
cordon sprawl; more to the point was the District 7 Blanch Point Formation
geology of 35 million-year-old fossil limestone. There was nothing remarkable
about the vinification nor the 20 months in used French and American oak
spanning '98 to '09, but the wine is exceptional, overflowing with black fruits and
a lick of dark chocolate in a richly textured palate ticking all the boxes for line,
length and balance. Screwcap. 14.5% alc. **Rating** 96 **To** 2036 $102

The Garden of Extraordinary Delights Single Vineyard McLaren Vale
Shiraz 2010 The wine shares the excellent colour of the group, with a fragrant
bouquet punctuated by soot/earth/olive nuances along with the black fruits. The
palate soars and dives like a kite, with juicy fruit and a tannin millefeuille, those
tannins perfectly pitched. Screwcap. 14% alc. **Rating** 96 **To** 2040 $99

The Bamboo Scrub Shiraz 2010 This is the coolest of the subregions,
endowing the wine with a fragrant bouquet of dark fruits merging with the red
on the palate that has a fine structure built on classy tannins, the end result a wine
with effortless power and drive. Screwcap. 13.9% alc. **Rating** 95 **To** 2035 $99

The Amaranthine Shiraz 2010 Once again, the colour is impeccable, the
bouquet a mix of dark and milder chocolate and cooking spices; licorice joins the
dark chocolate on the palate that has delicious mouthfeel thanks to the very fine
tannins. Screwcap. 13.8% alc. **Rating** 95 **To** 2045 $99

✪   The Footbolt McLaren Vale Shiraz 2010 Medium purple-crimson; a
mouthfilling, medium- to full-bodied shiraz, flooded with roughly equal amounts
of blackberry, licorice, dark chocolate oak and tannins; the balance is good, as is
the outlook for the wine. Screwcap. 14% alc. **Rating** 94 **To** 2020 $20

JRO Afflatus Shiraz 2010 The bouquet is distinctly savoury, with earth, spice
and dark olive nuances, the palate multi-dimensional thanks to 3D tannins, yet
finishing fresh and harmonious. Screwcap. 13.9% alc. **Rating** 94 **To** 2040 $99

The Fruit Bat Shiraz 2010 Bright crimson-purple, the fragrant bouquet leading
into a supple, medium-bodied palate with juicy, sweet red fruits, structure coming
from fine tannins and subtle oak. Screwcap. 14.1% alc. **Rating** 94 **To** 2030 $99

The Swinging Malaysian Shiraz 2010 Is built in an austere mode, with
more earth, tar and dark chocolate nuances; has impressive structure and more
texture than most of the wines in the line-up. Screwcap. 13.8% alc. **Rating** 94
To 2040 $99

The Vociferate Dipsomaniac Shiraz 2010 The colour is very bright, especially on the rim; a distinctly different bouquet with nuances of brush/silage, the palate with full-on black fruits and tannins to match; those tannins are not dry, the overall balance excellent. Screwcap. 14.3% alc. **Rating** 94 **To** 2040 $99

The Sticks & Stones McLaren Vale Tempranillo Grenache Tinta Cao Souzao 2009 The only thing missing from this is the Iberian Peninsula's bulls' (aka puppy dogs') tails. It has retained exceptional colour and no less exceptional power, yet the red cherry fruits, supported by forest berries, are still vibrant, the tannins good. Screwcap. 14.1% alc. **Rating** 94 **To** 2024 $32

✪ The Noble Botryotinia Fuckeliana 2011 Deep golden-yellow; if ever a very rich, fully botrytised Sauvignon Blanc were to come from the Adelaide Hills, it was '11; the wine has cumquat, peach and mandarin fruit alongside honeyed nuances, and the balancing acidity is spot on. Drink now. 375ml. Screwcap. 10.5% alc. **Rating** 94 **To** 2013 $20

The Noble Mud Pie McLaren Vale Viognier Marsanne Pinot Gris 2011 Yellow-gold; said to be vineyard botrytis, and the '11 vintage would have certainly helped; multiple layers of every glacé and dried fruit you can imagine. 375ml. Screwcap. 8.2% alc. **Rating** 94 **To** 2015 $22

🍷🍷🍷🍷︎ The Little Venice Shiraz 2010 **Rating** 93 **To** 2030 $99
The Blind Tiger Shiraz 2010 **Rating** 93 **To** 2040 $99

✪ The High Trellis McLaren Vale Cabernet Sauvignon 2010 Full purple-crimson; lush blackcurrant on the bouquet and palate is the mainstay of an attractive medium-bodied wine, integrated oak and ripe tannins partners in crime. A drink today or in 10 years style, a regional dark chocolate nuance on the farewell. WAK screwcap. 14.3% alc. **Rating** 93 **To** 2020 $20

Galvo Garage Cabernet Sauvignon Merlot Petit Verdot Cabernet Franc 2009 **Rating** 93 **To** 2024 $32

DADD Adelaide Hills Chardonnay Pinot Noir Pinot Meunier NV **Rating** 93 **To** 2014 $28

Shipsters' Rapture Shiraz 2010 **Rating** 92 **To** 2030 $99
The Other Side Shiraz 2010 **Rating** 92 **To** 2040 $99
The Twentyeight Road Mourvedre 2011 **Rating** 92 **To** 2020 $40

✪ The Broken Fishplate Adelaide Hills Sauvignon Blanc 2012 Pale quartz-green; has considerable generosity to its array of tropical fruits, spanning passionfruit, kiwifruit and crunchy pineapple. Ready right now. Screwcap. 13.1% alc. **Rating** 91 **To** 2013 $20

Tyche's Mustard Shiraz 2010 **Rating** 91 **To** 2045 $99
The Love Grass McLaren Vale Shiraz 2010 **Rating** 91 **To** 2020 $25 BE
The Vintage Fortified Shiraz 2008 **Rating** 91 **To** 2023 $40

🍷🍷🍷🍷 The Stump Jump McLaren Vale Riesling Marsanne Sauvignon Blanc
✪ Roussanne 2011 d'Arenberg over-delivers with this fresh, crisp wine, honeysuckle citrus and apple all at play. An extra year in bottle might help. Screwcap. 12.3% alc. **Rating** 88 **To** 2014 $13

✪ The Stump Jump McLaren Vale Grenache Shiraz Mourvedre 2011 Mid garnet; a bright and juicy medium-bodied wine, showing spicy red fruits and enough structure of tannin and acidity to provide a little bit of fun and short-term enjoyment. Screwcap. 14.3% alc. **Rating** 88 **To** 2016 $13 BE

Dal Zotto Wines   ★★★★

Main Road, Whitfield, Vic 3733 **Region** King Valley
T (03) 5729 8321 **www.**dalzotto.com.au **Open** 7 days 10–5
Winemaker Michael Dal Zotto **Est.** 1987 **Dozens** 15 000 **Vyds** 48ha
The Dal Zotto family is a King Valley institution; ex-tobacco growers, then contract grapegrowers, they are now primarily focused on their Dal Zotto range. Led by Otto and Elena, and with sons Michael and Christian handling winemaking and sales/marketing respectively, the family is producing increasing amounts of wine of exceptionally consistent quality from its

substantial estate vineyard. The cellar door is in the centre of Whitfield, and is also home to their Trattoria (open weekends). One of the first to produce Prosecco in Australia.

ŸŸŸŸŸ **King Valley Rosato 2012** Bright, light pink; 'made from Italian varieties' we
✪ are told; whatever they may be, this is a superior rose, with abundant red fruit and spice flavours, the finish long, and with excellent grip adding authority. Screwcap. 12.5% alc. **Rating** 93 **To** 2014 $18
King Valley Nebbiolo 2009 Given its age, this is pretty impressive; yes, it has those slightly bitter almond characters that are part of the scenery, but the tannins are not mouth-ripping – they are more savoury than anything else. Screwcap. 13.5% alc. **Rating** 92 **To** 2017 $45
King Valley Arneis 2011 While not particularly distinctive, is crisp and well made, doubtless part of the reason why it won a Blue-Gold medal at the Sydney International Wine Competition '13; there is some citrus pith/zest on the finish. Screwcap. 12.5% alc. **Rating** 91 **To** 2014 $27

ŸŸŸŸ **King Valley Riesling 2012 Rating** 89 **To** 2018 $18
King Valley Pinot Grigio 2012 Rating 89 **To** 2014 $22
King Valley Barbera 2011 Rating 87 **To** 2014 $25

Dalfarras
★★★☆

PO Box 123, Nagambie, Vic 3608 **Region** Nagambie Lakes
T (03) 5794 2637 **Open** At Tahbilk
Winemaker Alister Purbrick, Alan George **Est.** 1991 **Dozens** 5500 **Vyds** 20.97ha
The personal project of Alister Purbrick and artist wife Rosa (née Dalfarra), whose paintings adorn the labels of the wines. Alister, of course, is best known as winemaker at Tahbilk (see separate entry), the family winery and home, but this range of wines is intended to (in Alister's words) 'allow me to expand my winemaking horizons and mould wines in styles different from Tahbilk'. Exports to Sweden.

ŸŸŸŸ **Tempranillo 2011** Mid garnet; ripe cola and dark cherry aromas on the bouquet;
✪ the palate is juicy, forward and shows moderate length and plenty of interest. Screwcap. 13.5% alc. **Rating** 89 **To** 2016 $16 BE
Marsanne Roussanne Viognier 2010 Fully developed, with lemon curd, straw and biscuit dough on display; the palate is unctuous and rich, with depth winning out over freshness. Screwcap. 12.5% alc. **Rating** 87 **To** 2014 $15 BE

Dalrymple Vineyards
★★★★★

1337 Pipers Brook Road, Pipers Brook, Tas 7254 **Region** Northern Tasmania
T (03) 6382 7229 **www.**dalrymplevineyards.com.au **Open** Not
Winemaker Peter Caldwell **Est.** 1987 **Dozens** 4000 **Vyds** 17ha
Dalrymple was established many years ago by the Mitchell and Sundstrup families; the vineyard and brand were acquired by Hill-Smith Family Vineyards in late 2007. Plantings are split between pinot noir and sauvignon blanc, and the wines are made at Jansz Tasmania. In September 2010 Peter Caldwell was appointed as 'Vigneron', responsible for the vineyard, viticulture and winemaking. He brings with him 10 years' experience at Te Kairanga Wines (Martinborough, NZ), and most recently two years with Josef Chromy Wines. His knowledge of pinot noir and chardonnay is obviously comprehensive. In Dec 2012 Hill-Smith Family Vineyards acquired the 120ha property on which the original Frogmore Creek Vineyard was established; 10ha of that property will be pinot noir specifically for Dalrymple, and will be known as the Mount Lord Vineyard.

ŸŸŸŸŸ **Cottage Block Pinot Noir 2011** The colour is a clear, vivid crimson-purple; the ultra-fragrant red berry fruit/rose petal aromas of the bouquet lead into a supremely elegant, yet confident, palate; here silky tannins join a hint of briar on the finish to provide the necessary complexity. Screwcap. 13% alc. **Rating** 95 **To** 2020 $50

Single Site Block CV90 Pinot Noir 2011 While there is little or no difference in hue or clarity, and the alcohol is lower, this wine has the depth and restrained complexity the '11 standard pinot doesn't achieve to the same degree; there are still savoury elements, but the varietal fruit carries the day. Screwcap. 13% alc. Rating 94 To 2020 $55

ŢŢŢŢŢ Pinot Noir 2011 Rating 93 To 2017 $36

Dalwhinnie

448 Taltarni Road, Moonambel, Vic 3478 **Region** Pyrenees
T (03) 5467 2388 **www.**dalwhinnie.com.au **Open** 7 days 10–5
Winemaker David Jones, Gary Baldwin (Consultant) **Est.** 1976 **Dozens** 4500 **Vyds** 26ha
David and Jenny Jones are making wines with tremendous depth of fruit flavour, reflecting the relatively low-yielding but very well-maintained vineyards. A 50-tonne contemporary high-tech winery now allows the wines to be made onsite. In 2011 David and Jenny celebrated 30 years of winemaking at Dalwhinnie. Ironically, no red wines were made in that year due to rain. Exports to the UK and other major markets.

ŢŢŢŢŢ Moonambel Chardonnay 2011 David Jones has long been the leader of chardonnay in the Pyrenees, and this rendition is full of energy and life; the bouquet reveals lemon pith, smoky oak and struck quartz; the palate is racy and taut, with the acidity and mineral personality working seamlessly. Screwcap. 13% alc. Rating 95 To 2022 $42 BE
The Eagle Shiraz 2010 Deep crimson-purple hue; aromas of black and blue fruits, Asian spices and ironstone are evident on the bouquet; the palate is medium-bodied and restrained with fine-grained tannins a feature of the long graphite-laden finish; seems to be in a dip at this point in time, but given the benefit of the doubt Screwcap. 13.5% alc. Rating 94 To 2022 $150 BE

ŢŢŢŢ The Hut Chardonnay 2012 Rating 89 To 2016 $23 BE

 # Dan Hugoes Wines ★★★

15 Mary Street, Hawthorn, Vic 3111 (postal) **Region** South Eastern Australia
T (03) 9819 4890 **Open** Not
Winemaker Benjamin Edwards, Rob Dolan **Est.** 2012 **Dozens** 5000
This is the venture of Zhijun (George) Hu, who has started a virtual winery with the primary purpose of exporting to China and elsewhere in South-East Asia. Rob Dolan has been retained as winemaker for the wines made from Yarra Valley grapes.

ŢŢŢŢ Cellar 519 Barossa Valley Shiraz 2010 Relatively developed colour for the vintage; the fruit has been enveloped in American oak on both the bouquet and palate; strictly for those who enjoy vanillin oak. Cork. 14.5% alc. Rating 87 To 2015 $20

Dandelion Vineyards

PO Box 138, McLaren Vale, SA 5171 **Region** McLaren Vale
T (08) 8556 6099 **www.**dandelionvineyards.com.au **Open** Not
Winemaker Elena Brooks **Est.** 2007 **Dozens** NFP **Vyds** 124.2ha
This is a highly impressive partnership between Peggy and Carl Lindner (40%), Elena and Zar Brooks (40%) and Fiona and Brad Rey (20%). It brings together vineyards spread across the Adelaide Hills, Eden Valley, Langhorne Creek, McLaren Vale, Barossa Valley and the Fleurieu Peninsula. Elena is not only the beautiful wife of industry dilettante Zar, but also an exceptionally gifted winemaker. It may be a dauntingly competitive marketplace, but there can be few more promising ventures than this one. Eye-catching pricing of every wine bar the icon Red Queen Shiraz. Exports to all major markets.

ΨΨΨΨΨ Red Queen of the Eden Valley Shiraz 2010 Full crimson-purple; the grapes come from the 99-year-old Kroehn Vineyard; hand-picked, open-fermented and basket-pressed to French barriques, and matured for 2½ years. A seriously complex wine, awash with red berry and black fruits, the tannins fine but persistent, the overall balance impeccable; the French oak will disappear into the wine as it ages. 420 dozen made. Screwcap. 14% alc. **Rating** 96 To 2045 $85

✪ Lion's Tooth of McLaren Vale Shiraz Riesling 2009 Has 3% riesling; vivid crimson-purple, and the flavours are positively opulent, the tannins plump and ripe; there is a delicious savoury/spicy/cedary aspect to the palate, which revels in its moderate alcohol. Screwcap. 13.5% alc. **Rating** 95 To 2024 $28

Wonderland of the Eden Valley Riesling 2012 Medium to full yellow-green; the aromatics of the bouquet bring together every expression imaginable of lime and lemon, the palate following suit, minerally/chalky acidity providing both drive and structure. Screwcap. 12.5% alc. **Rating** 94 To 2022 $28

Fairytale of the Barossa Rose 2012 From 85-year-old estate-grown grenache, hand-picked, with free-run juice wild yeast-fermented in used French barriques with 12 weeks lees contact. Pale, bright puce, it has a vibrant bouquet and palate, with the full kit and caboodle of small red fruits, the finish long, crisp and dry. Worth the price. Screwcap. 13.5% alc. **Rating** 94 To 2014 $28

Lionheart of the Barossa Shiraz 2011 From vines around 100 years old, open-fermented with wild yeast, then spending 18 months in mainly used French oak barriques. Even more deeply coloured than Dandelion's Lioness, with a full array of black fruits on the medium-bodied palate. Some sophisticated handling in the winery has produced a remarkable result. Screwcap. 14% alc. **Rating** 94 To 2025 $28

Lion's Tooth of McLaren Vale Shiraz Riesling 2010 An avant-garde approach, with the crushed shiraz fermented on top of riesling skins, open-fermented and hand-plunged before finishing its fermentation in predominantly older French oak, then 18 months in that oak. Makes a clarion call of its region, black fruits and dark chocolate vying for supremacy, with really attractive texture and structure. Screwcap. 14.5% alc. **Rating** 94 To 2025 $28

ΨΨΨΨΨ Lioness of McLaren Vale Shiraz 2011 **Rating** 93 To 2021 $28
Lionheart of the Barossa Shiraz 2010 **Rating** 93 To 2020 $28
Pride of the Fleurieu Peninsula Cabernet Sauvignon 2010 **Rating** 93 To 2020 $28
Legacy of the Barossa 30 Year Old Pedro Ximenez NV **Rating** 93 To 2014 $28
Pride of the Fleurieu Peninsula Cabernet Sauvignon 2011 **Rating** 91 To 2018 $28
Wishing Clock of the Adelaide Hills Sauvignon Blanc 2012 **Rating** 90 To 2013 $28
Damsel of the Barossa Merlot 2011 **Rating** 90 To 2016 $28

Darling Park   ★★★★☆

232 Red Hill Road, Red Hill, Vic 3937 **Region** Mornington Peninsula
T (03) 5989 2324 **www**.darlingparkwinery.com **Open** 7 days 11–5
Winemaker Judy Gifford **Est.** 1989 **Dozens** 2000 **Vyds** 7ha
Josh and Karen Liberman have energetically expanded the range of Darling Park's wines while maintaining a high quality standard. The Art of Wine club offers back vintages, as well as previews of upcoming releases. Wine labels feature artworks from the owners' collections; artists include Sidney Nolan, Arthur Boyd, John Perceval and Charles Blackman. The most important source of grapes for the venture is Hugh Robinson, who produces some of the best grapes available for sale on the Mornington Peninsula. The arrangement with Darling Park is a permanent one, with purchase by area, rather than by tonnes of grapes produced.

🍷🍷🍷🍷🍷 Pinot Noir 2009 After the shrivelling heatwave of vintage '09, any Mornington pinot capable of holding its freshness 3 years later is deserving of legend status. A pretty, primary fruit brightness is layered with ripe, secondary red berry and red cherry fruit, exotic spice and notes of dried herbs. It upholds a silky structure and fine, drying tannins. Screwcap. 14.3% alc. **Rating** 93 **To** 2014 $36 TS

David Franz   ★★★★★

PO Box 677, Tanunda, SA 5352 **Region** Barossa Valley
T 0419 807 468 **www**.david-franz.com **Open** By appt
Winemaker David Franz Lehmann **Est.** 1998 **Dozens** 4700 **Vyds** 29.54ha
David Franz (Lehmann) is one of Margaret and Peter Lehmann's sons, and took a very circuitous path around the world before establishing his eponymous winery. Wife Nicki accompanied him on his odyssey and they, together with three children, two dogs, a mess of chickens and a surly shed cat, all happily live together (albeit privately) in their house and winery. The utterly unique bottles stem from (incomplete) university studies in graphic design (and subsequently interior design); his degree in hospitality business management is less relevant, for visits to the winery, aka the shed, are strictly by appointment only. An extended family of five share the work in the vineyard and the shed. Exports to the UK, the US, Canada, India, Singapore, Japan, Indonesia, Hong Kong and China.

🍷🍷🍷🍷🍷 225 Cabernet Sauvignon 2002 Still has both depth and bright crimson-purple colour; only a single barrique (260 bottles) made, bottled after 4 years in new American oak and still has abundant power and extract, impatient for the next 10 years to pass; has the savoury, slightly minty, character of the very cool '02 vintage. Cork. 15.2% alc. **Rating** 95 **To** 2032 $150
Long Gully Road Ancient Vine Semillon 2011 From 125-year-old vines, basked-pressed and barrel-fermented with partial mlf; the free-run juice was cold-fermented for 3 months in stainless steel; the barrel and tank components were then matured on stirred lees for another 9 months. It is every bit as powerful and complex as the protracted making would suggest, reaching a crescendo on the finish. Screwcap. 12.3% alc. **Rating** 94 **To** 2020 $26
Cellar Release Survivor Vine Red Rose 2008 Amazing retention of crimson hue, perhaps due to the field blend block of eight red and white varieties co-planted in 1923, and only 32 dozen made! It has been fermented to dryness, but has a cornucopia of red berry fruits on the bouquet and palate. Gets full rose points for uniqueness. Screwcap. 12.8% alc. **Rating** 94 **To** 2015 $29
Alternative View Shiraz 2008 David Franz says this 'is all about the biggest, baddest shiraz I could make', a two-barrel selection that spent 48 months in oak. Anyone who buys it sight unseen will not feel short-changed. The points in no way reflect my personal taste, but it does deliver on David's promise. Screwcap. 15.9% alc. **Rating** 94 **To** 2030 $85

🍷🍷🍷🍷🍷 Cellar Release Eden Valley Riesling 2009 **Rating** 93 **To** 2020 $39
Smoking Jim Chopping Block Merlot 2010 **Rating** 93 **To** 2025 $33
Alexander's Reward 2008 **Rating** 93 **To** 2020 $42
✪ Sticky Botrytis Semillon 2011 Picked at around 24 baume, with 80% botrytis, the highest level seen since '74. The wine has an exceptional honeyed viscosity with some cumquat/mandarin/peach as well as remnants of lime; a touch more acidity could have made a spectacular wine. Screwcap. 10.5% alc. **Rating** 92 **To** 2020 $16
Brother's Ilk Moskos' Birdwood Vineyard Adelaide Hills Chardonnay 2011 **Rating** 91 **To** 2017 $42
Red Rose 2010 **Rating** 91 **To** 2014 $23
Eden Valley Riesling 2012 **Rating** 90 **To** 2016 $28
Benjamin's Promise Shiraz 2008 **Rating** 90 **To** 2030 $42
Georgie's Walk Cellar Release Cabernet Sauvignon 2005 **Rating** 90 **To** 2018 $63 BE

David Hook Wines ★★★★★

Cnr Broke Road/Ekerts Road, Pokolbin, NSW 2320 **Region** Hunter Valley
T (02) 4998 7121 **www**.davidhookwines.com.au **Open** 7 days 10–5
Winemaker David Hook **Est.** 1984 **Dozens** 7000 **Vyds** 8ha
David Hook has over 25 years' experience as a winemaker for Tyrrell's and Lake's Folly, also doing the full Flying Winemaker bit with jobs in Bordeaux, the Rhône Valley, Spain, the US and Georgia. The estate-owned Pothana Vineyard has been in production for over 25 years, and the wines made from it are given the 'Old Vines' banner. This vineyard is planted on the Belford Dome, an ancient geological formation that provides red clay soils over limestone on the slopes, and sandy loams along the creek flats; the former are for red wines, the latter for white. Exports to the US and Japan.

🍷🍷🍷🍷🍷 Reserve Central Ranges Riesling 2012 Pale straw-green; this is a brilliantly made off-dry Riesling, more notable for its lime-juicy acidity than the gossamer web of sweetness behind that acidity. Drink all day, every day. Screwcap. 10.5% alc. Rating 95 To 2020 $25
Old Vines Pothana Vineyard Belford Semillon 2012 Pale quartz-green; a tight and bracing palate, with herb, lemon zest and minerally acidity driving the long, lingering finish, leaving the mouth fresh and asking for more. Will develop with sure-footedness. Screwcap. 10.5% alc. Rating 94 To 2025 $25
Old Vines Pothana Vineyard Belford Shiraz 2011 Bright, clear crimson-purple; the Hunter Valley, often tormented by vintage rain, had a very good vintage while much of the rest of eastern Australia swam in water. This medium-bodied wine has excellent texture and structure, red and black fruits folded in an embrace of quality oak and balanced, but persistent, tannins. Screwcap. 13.5% alc. Rating 94 To 2026 $40

🍷🍷🍷🍷🍷 Reserve Central Ranges Barbera 2011 Rating 90 To 2015 $30

🍷🍷🍷🍷 Reserve Central Ranges De Novo Bianco 2012 Rating 89 To 2014 $30
Reserve Hunter Valley De Novo Rosso 2011 Rating 89 To 2015 $30
Hunter Valley Mosto 2012 Rating 88 To 2013 $25

Dawson & James ★★★★★

1240B Brookman Road, Dingabledinga, SA 5172 **Region** Southern Tasmania
T (08) 8556 7326 **www**.dawsonjames.com.au **Open** Not
Winemaker Peter Dawson, Tim James **Est.** 2010 **Dozens** 900
Peter Dawson and Tim James had long and highly successful careers as senior winemakers for Hardys/Accolade wines. Tim jumped ship first, becoming managing director of Wirra Wirra for seven years until 2007, while Peter stayed longer with Constellation. Now both have consulting roles, and Peter is chairman of the Australian Wine Research Institute, Tim an active consultant. They have both long had a desire to grow and make wine in Tasmania, a desire which came to fruition in '10. Tragically, however, the vineyard on the Derwent River that was supplying them with grapes was hit by the Tasmanian bushfires at the end of February 2012, smoke taint preventing the use of the grapes. Exports to the UK and Singapore.

🍷🍷🍷🍷🍷 Chardonnay 2011 Bright straw-green; the immediate, laser-like precision of Tasmanian acidity (here 7.4g/l) is the core around which the other components of white peach, citrus and cashew/French oak are assembled. Gold medal Tas Wine Show '13. Screwcap. 12.7% alc. Rating 96 To 2021 $50
Chardonnay 2010 The wine is super-intense and very long in the mouth, with grapefruit to the fore, white peach following. There is a gentle touch of funk ex partial solids fermentation, the 11 months in 30% new Taransaud oak (what else?) not obvious, and 50% mlf leaving great natural acidity that accelerates the wine on the finish and aftertaste. Screwcap. 12% alc. Rating 96 To 2023 $42
Pinot Noir 2011 Bright, clear crimson-purple; the bouquet has abundant satsuma plum and black cherry fruit, the palate supple, smooth and mouthfilling while retaining elegance and freshness; the tannins are ultra-fine, but there is no shortage of structure, demure oak in the background. A beautifully made wine. Screwcap. 13.2% alc. Rating 96 To 2020 $54

Pinot Noir 2010 Excellent bright red-purple colour introduces a very fragrant, flowery, scented bouquet, then a supple, elegant and expressive palate with small berries and spices, silky tannins, and great drive; 10% whole bunches and 30% new Taransaud oak are the trimmings for a lovely Pinot in which the fruit does all the work. Screwcap. 13.5% alc. **Rating** 96 **To** 2017 $48

Dawson's Patch ★★★★

71 Kallista-Emerald Road, The Patch, Vic 3792 (postal) **Region** Yarra Valley
T 0419 521 080 **www.**dawsonspatch.com.au **Open** Not
Winemaker Jody Dawson, Martin Siebert **Est.** 1996 **Dozens** 350 **Vyds** 1.2ha
James and Jody Dawson own and manage this vineyard at the southern end of the Yarra Valley, planted to chardonnay and pinot noir. The climate here is particularly cool, and the grapes do not normally ripen until late April. Jody has completed a degree in viticulture through CSU. The tiny hand-crafted production (Chardonnay and Pinot Noir) is sold through local restaurants and cellars in the Olinda/Belgrave/Emerald area.

Yarra Valley Chardonnay 2011 Vivid green-gold hue; the bouquet packs plenty of punch, suggesting pear, grapefruit and charcuterie complexity; the palate reveals a laser-like backbone of acidity that drives the wine, and there is good concentration of flavour and depth. Screwcap. 13% alc. **Rating** 90 **To** 2017 $27 BE

De Beaurepaire Wines

182 Cudgegong Road, Rylstone, NSW 2849 **Region** Mudgee
T (02) 6379 1473 **www.**debeaurepairewines.com **Open** At Bridgeview Inn, Rylstone
Winemaker Jacob Stein (Contract) **Est.** 1998 **Dozens** NA **Vyds** 52.34ha
The large De Beaurepaire vineyard was planted by Janet and Richard de Beaurepaire in 1998, and is situated at an altitude of 570-600m. The altitude, coupled with limestone soils, and with frontage to the Cudgegong River, provides grapes (and hence wines) very different from the normal Mudgee wines. The vineyard is planted to shiraz, merlot, cabernet sauvignon, chardonnay, semillon, viognier, petit verdot, verdelho and pinot gris; most of the grapes are sold. Exports to Malaysia, Singapore and China.

Captain Starlight Series Semillon Sauvignon Blanc 2011 Pale straw-green; citrus and tropical fruit flavours are an unexpected outcome for such an early-picked wine; there is a touch of sweetness, but not enough to make it more than simply a fresh, well-balanced wine. Screwcap. 10.7% alc. **Rating** 88 **To** 2014 $19

De Bortoli

De Bortoli Road, Bilbul, NSW 2680 **Region** Riverina
T (02) 6966 0100 **www.**debortoli.com.au **Open** Mon–Sat 9–5, Sun 9–4
Winemaker Darren De Bortoli, Julie Mortlock, John Coughlan **Est.** 1928
Dozens 3 million **Vyds** 332ha
Famous among the cognoscenti for its superb Noble One, which in fact accounts for only a minute part of its total production, this winery turns out low-priced varietal and generic wines that are invariably competently made and equally invariably provide value for money. These come in part from estate vineyards, but also from contract-grown grapes. The rating is in part a reflection of the exceptional value for money offered across the range. In June 2012 De Bortoli received a $4.8 million grant from the federal government's Clean Technology Food and Foundries Investment Program. This grant supports an additional investment of $11 million by the De Bortoli family in their project 'Re-engineering Our Future for a Carbon Economy'. Exports to all major markets.

Noble One Botrytis Semillon 2009 Noble One has long established itself as the best Botrytis Semillon in Australia, and this vintage simply reinforces that reputation; luscious fruit, oak and acidity all play their part on the extremely long and complex palate. 500ml. Screwcap. 10.5% alc. **Rating** 96 **To** 2019 $64

Noble One Botrytis Semillon 2010 Mid orange, green hue; a hedonistic bouquet of apricot jam, biscuit dough, cinnamon and clove; the palate is extremely sweet, unctuous and long, with the caramel sugar lingering for a staggeringly long time. Screwcap. 10% alc. **Rating** 94 **To** 2017 $64 BE

✪ **Deen De Bortoli Vat 5 Botrytis Semillon 2008** Glowing gold-green; still extremely luscious and rich, with cascades of cumquat, honey and nougat flavours, balanced by good acidity. Gold medal International Wine & Spirits Competition, London '11 fully deserved. Great bargain. Best now, but should hold. 375ml. Screwcap. 10.5% alc. **Rating** 94 **To** 2015 $14

Old Boys Show Reserve Release 21 Years Old Barrel Aged Tawny NV Strong tawny colour; full of biscuity rancio attesting to the serious age of the wine; makes light of its alcohol, seeming much lower thanks to its fresh, well-balanced, finish. Screwcap. 19% alc. **Rating** 94 **To** 2014 $45

Black Noble NV Dark aged mahogany; an absolutely unique barrel-aged Botrytis Semillon (ex Noble One) with hyper-intense fruit cleansed by its volatile acidity — counterintuitive, of course. 500ml. Screwcap. 17.5% alc. **Rating** 94 **To** 2014 $38

🍷🍷🍷🍷🍷 **Deen De Bortoli Vat 8 Shiraz 2009** For those who read the tea leaves of
✪ wine shows, and their results, gold medals in Vienna and Berlin, plus a silver at Rutherglen make sense for a $13 wine that has kept remarkably fresh colour and red fruit flavours; as if this were not enough, it has very good tannin and oak inputs. Screwcap. 14.5% alc. **Rating** 91 **To** 2019 $13

✪ **Deen De Bortoli Vat 9 Cabernet Sauvignon 2010** Light to medium red-purple; the skill and attention to detail of the De Bortoli winemaking team has never been in question, but it has risen above itself with this wine; it has clear blackcurrant/cassis fruit on the bouquet and medium-bodied palate alike, with cedary/spicy oak (of whatever origin) also contributing to the package. Screwcap. 13.5% alc. **Rating** 90 **To** 2016 $13

✪ **Deen De Bortoli Vat 1 Durif 2010** Deep purple-crimson; it's hard to imagine how you would find greater depth in a table wine at this price, rippling with black fruits, licorice/anise and ripe tannins. Gold medal class 215(!) Rutherglen Wine Show '11. Screwcap. 13.5% alc. **Rating** 90 **To** 2015 $13

Show Liqueur Muscat NV Rating 90 **To** 2014 $25

🍷🍷🍷🍷 **Sacred Hill Semillon Sauvignon Blanc 2012** You simply don't expect this
✪ level of varietal expression and mouthfeel at this price; tropical fruits, lemon/citrus and echoes of grass and herb are framed in a perfectly balanced interplay between a touch of sweetness and acidity. Screwcap. 12.1% alc. **Rating** 89 **To** 2013 $8

✪ **DB Family Selection Shiraz 2012** Light red-purple; cleverly made by a skilled winemaking team which has added an extra dimension of texture to the light-bodied plum and cherry fruit; has a whisper of oak and a juicy finish. Screwcap. 13.5% alc. **Rating** 88 **To** 2014 $9

✪ **La Bossa Sauvignon Blanc 2012** An interesting move to include 5% NZ sauvignon blanc; the wine is not particularly expressive of its variety, but does have good structure and length. Screwcap. 11.4% alc. **Rating** 87 **To** 2013 $9

✪ **Sacred Hill Unwooded Colombard Chardonnay 2012** One of the early blends of colombard, used by Wolf Blass and others, using the acid retention ability of colombard to full advantage; a wine that does not rely on sugar to provide its flavour. Screwcap. 12.3% alc. **Rating** 87 **To** 2013 $8

✪ **DB Reserve Pinot Noir 2011** Fresh red-purple; the only regional specification is South Eastern Australia — as broad as they come. There is no doubt about the cherry/strawberry pinot noir character on the bouquet and mid-palate, but the wine falters on the finish. No complaints at this price. Screwcap. 12.5% alc. **Rating** 87 **To** 2014 $13

✪ **Sacred Hill Shiraz Cabernet 2011** Light, bright and clear crimson; a light-bodied wine with delicious red fruits doing all the talking. If you want a wine to drink tonight and don't have a fat wallet, go no further. Screwcap. 13.5% alc. **Rating** 87 **To** 2013 $13

✪ **La Bossa Merlot 2010** You don't expect any of the savoury/black olive varietal character of higher priced merlots to appear in a wine at this price level, but they are there; indeed, more sweet fruit is needed to balance them. Screwcap. 13% alc. Rating 87 To 2013 $9

✪ **Deen De Bortoli Vat 4 Petit Verdot 2010** Bright colour, with jubey blackberry fruit on the bouquet and palate; fleshy and fresh, and excellent value. Screwcap. 14% alc. **Rating** 87 **To** 2015 $13

✪ **Trevi Original NV** A very clever wine indeed, and amazing value; there is plenty of sweetness ex the residual sugar, but there is also fruit flavour. Screwcap. 10% alc. **Rating** 87 **To** 2013 $6

✪ **La Bossa Pink Moscato 2011** Back in the moscato zone: distinctly sweet and fruity, but with enough acidity to prevent it cloying. Screwcap. 8% alc. **Rating** 87 **To** 2013 $9

De Bortoli (Hunter Valley)   ★★★★☆

532 Wine Country Drive, Pokolbin, NSW 2325 **Region** Hunter Valley
T (02) 4993 8800 **www.**debortoli.com.au **Open** 7 days 10–5
Winemaker Steve Webber **Est.** 2002 **Dozens** 10 000 **Vyds** 36ha
De Bortoli extended its wine empire in 2002 with the purchase of the former Wilderness Estate, giving it an immediate and significant presence in the Hunter Valley courtesy of the 26ha of established vineyards, including semillon vines over 40 years old. The subsequent purchase of the adjoining 40ha property increased the size of the business. The intention is to convert the vineyards to biological farming practices, with composting and mulching already used to reduce the need for irrigation. Exports to all major markets.

♟♟♟♟♟ **Hunter Valley Semillon 2004** Brilliant green-gold; has developed superbly since
✪   receiving a gold medal at the Sydney Wine Show '06; a taint touch of CO_2 has no doubt helped, and the wine has the freshness of (and other similarities to) cool-climate riesling, with lime and honey the drivers. Sensational value through the cellar door. Screwcap. 11.5% alc. Rating 94 To 2020 $20

♟♟♟♟♟ **Hunter Valley Shiraz 2011** Rating 91 To 2031 $20

De Bortoli (Victoria)   ★★★★★

Pinnacle Lane, Dixons Creek, Vic 3775 **Region** Yarra Valley
T (03) 5965 2271 **www.**debortoliyarra.com.au **Open** 7 days 10–5
Winemaker Stephen Webber, Sarah Fagan, Andrew Bretherton **Est.** 1987 **Dozens** 350 000
Vyds 237ha
The quality arm of the bustling De Bortoli group, run by Leanne De Bortoli and husband Steve Webber, ex-Lindemans winemaker. The top label (De Bortoli), the second (Gulf Station) and the third (Windy Peak) offer wines of consistently good quality and excellent value – the complex Chardonnay and the Pinot Noirs are usually of outstanding quality. The volume of production, by many times the largest in the Yarra Valley, simply underlines the quality/value for money ratio of the wines. This arm of the business has vineyards in the Yarra and King valleys. Exports to all major markets.

♟♟♟♟♟ **Reserve Release Yarra Valley Chardonnay 2011** Reinforces the fact that this was an excellent vintage for Yarra Valley chardonnay; light straw-green, it has beautiful white peach, melon and nectarine fruit aromas and flavours; there is an element of citrus in the acidity, no more obvious than the almost transparent touch of oak. Screwcap. 12% alc. Rating 96 To 2021 $47

   Estate Grown Yarra Valley Sauvignon 2011 It takes a rare talent to capture sauvignon's most zesty lime character without a hint of green pea, asparagus or capsicum in a freak cold vintage like '11. De Bortoli has pulled it off with impressive precision, crisp purity and even longevity. A tense acid backbone supports a fine, mineral structure of grapefruit pith-like texture. Screwcap. 12.5% alc. Rating 94 To 2016 $22 TS

Reserve Release Yarra Valley Syrah 2011 Bright crimson-purple; has that little bit extra of everything: more aroma, more red and black fruits, possibly more French oak and definitely more tannins. It has the attention to detail that is Steve Webber's credo. Screwcap. 13% alc. **Rating** 94 **To** 2021 $45

ŸŸŸŸŸ   Gulf Station Yarra Valley Chardonnay 2010 A complex yet elegant wine, the
✪   elegance enhanced by the early picking and high natural acidity. The flavours are much more in the grapefruit citrus range than stone fruit, which may not please others as much as me. Screwcap. 12.5% alc. **Rating** 93 **To** 2014 $20
Riorret Emu Yarra Valley Pinot Noir 2011 **Rating** 93 **To** 2018 $42
✪   Windy Peak Heathcote Shiraz 2012 Vivid, deep purple-crimson; it's a sign of the times that a wine such as this should be part of the Windy Peak range, comprehensively over-delivering with its densely packed, succulent black fruits held in a web of soft tannins and soft acidity. Outstanding value. Screwcap. 14.5% alc. **Rating** 93 **To** 2025 $14
✪   Gulf Station Yarra Valley Shiraz Viognier 2010 Bright red-purple; a small amount of viognier is included. The complex yet eminently approachable wine has an aromatic bouquet of the red and black fruits that drive the fresh, medium-bodied palate, oak and tannins both making a positive contribution. Outstanding value. Screwcap. 13% alc. **Rating** 93 **To** 2025 $18
Vinoque Amphi Vineyard Chardonnay 2011 **Rating** 92 **To** 2020 $25
✪   Gulf Station Yarra Valley Chardonnay 2011 Barrel-fermented in used French oak and lees stirring have built the creamy texture of the palate to precisely the right level, leaving the mix of stone fruit and honeydew melon free to combine with the citrussy acidity on the finish. Screwcap. 12.5% alc. **Rating** 92 **To** 2016 $18
✪   Vinoque Roundstone Vineyard Yarra Valley Gamay Noir 2012 Medium to full red-purple; gamay noir is simply gamay, the grape that makes Beaujolais – in similar style to this. The rounded mouthful (and mouthfeel) of polished black cherries, with a passing hint of stem and a dry finish, is right on the money. Screwcap. 12.5% alc. **Rating** 92 **To** 2014 $24
Estate Grown Yarra Valley Syrah 2011 **Rating** 92 **To** 2019 $28
Reserve Release Yarra Valley Pinot Noir 2011 **Rating** 91 **To** 2017 $45
✪   Reserve Release Yarra Valley EZ 2012 Light straw-green; fine and fresh, with lime and apple fruit supported by a minimal level of residual sugar, acidity playing an equal role in shaping this off-dry blend of gewurztraminer, riesling and pinot gris. Screwcap. 12% alc. **Rating** 91 **To** 2018 $18
La Boheme Act Three Yarra Valley Pinot Gris and Friends 2012 **Rating** 90 **To** 2014 $20
✪   BellaRiva King Valley Pinot Grigio Vermentino 2012 A field blend (ie interplanted varieties) hand-picked and tank-fermented. The vermentino adds a dimension to the citrus-accented finish with perfectly balanced acidity and sweetness. Screwcap. 12.5% alc. **Rating** 90 **To** 2014 $18
La Boheme Act Three Dry Pinot Noir Rose 2012 **Rating** 90 **To** 2014 $20
✪   La Boheme Act Two Yarra Valley Dry Pinot Noir Rose 2012 Pale salmon-pink; the spicy bouquet is followed by a well-balanced palate with a reprise of the spice of the bouquet accompanied by small red fruits; scores for its delicacy rather than power, needing a touch more acidity on the finish. Screwcap. 13% alc. **Rating** 90 **To** 2013 $20
✪   BellaRiva King Valley Sangiovese Merlot 2011 Bright, light red; the blend works very well indeed, the symbiotic red fruit flavours showing no sign of green fruit; a delicious light-bodied palate ready and waiting for a dish of fresh pasta. Screwcap. 13.5% alc. **Rating** 90 **To** 2014 $18
Rococo Yarra Valley Blanc de Blancs NV **Rating** 90 **To** 2013 $22

ŸŸŸŸ   Windy Peak Sauvignon Blanc Semillon 2011 Light straw-green; you get
✪   a lot of flavour complexity for $14. Lemon juice, apple and gooseberry fruits are lengthened by juicy acidity. Great value. Screwcap. 11.5% alc. **Rating** 89 **To** 2013 $14

✪ **Windy Peak Yarra Valley Cabernet Merlot 2010** Light, bright crimson-purple; fresh red and blackcurrant fruit on the bouquet flow through onto the equally fresh palate, where fine tannins provide good texture and structure. Emphatic value. Screwcap. 13% alc. **Rating** 89 **To** 2015 $14

✪ **Windy Peak Yarra Valley Pinot Noir 2011** Similar colour to Gulf Station – clear red; the fresh red fruits have a spicy/savoury/foresty backdrop that is clearly varietal; a wine to be enjoyed over the next 12 months, no longer, but good Pinot value. Screwcap. 13% alc. **Rating** 88 **To** 2013 $14

De Iuliis ★★★★★

1616 Broke Road, Pokolbin, NSW 2320 **Region** Hunter Valley
T (02) 4993 8000 **www.dewine.com.au Open** 7 days 10–5
Winemaker Michael De Iuliis **Est.** 1990 **Dozens** 10 000
Three generations of the De Iuliis family have been involved in the establishment of their 45ha vineyard. The family acquired the property in 1986 and planted the first vines in 1990, selling the grapes from the first few vintages to Tyrrell's but retaining increasing amounts for release under the De Iuliis label. Winemaker Michael De Iuliis has completed postgraduate studies in oenology at the Roseworthy campus of Adelaide University and was a Len Evans Tutorial scholar. He has lifted the quality of the wines into the highest echelon.

♟♟♟♟♟ **Limited Release Hunter Valley Shiraz 2011** Full purple-crimson; combines power and seemingly effortless elegance; there is some oak alongside the black cherry and plum fruits on the bouquet and palate, and the fruit caresses the palate with the lightest footfall. These '11 De Iuliis Shirazs can be drunk now without any hesitation, but will have a very long future. Screwcap. 13.5% alc. **Rating** 96 **To** 2036 $60

Sunshine Vineyard Hunter Valley Semillon 2012 This vineyard, planted on the sandy soils of Black Creek, was responsible for the great Lindemans Semillons of the '50s and '60s, De Iuliis now buying some of the grapes to produce this classic Semillon; its lemon and lime fruit persist on the finish for an interminable time. Destined to be a classic. Screwcap. 11.5% alc. **Rating** 95 **To** 2032 $25

Steven Vineyard Hunter Valley Shiraz 2011 Deep purple-crimson, with the most purple of the De Iuliis '11 Shirazs. Juicy black cherry and blackberry show the first signs of the earthy, leathery, regional complexity that will take at least 10 years to fully manifest itself. Screwcap. 13% alc. **Rating** 95 **To** 2036 $40

LDR Vineyard Hunter Valley Shiraz 2011 The colour is excellent; this is a rich, succulent and supple wine awash with plum and blackberry fruit, hints of earth (with more to come) and ripe tannins. Screwcap. 13% alc. **Rating** 95 **To** 2031 $40

Limited Release Hunter Valley Chardonnay 2011 A strict barrel selection resulted in 250 dozen bottles. The colour is still very pale, but the wine has remarkable intensity and grip to its long palate. One of the peculiarities of the Hunter Valley climate is that 12.5% alcohol translates to 13% to 13.5% in many other regions when assessing the present and future of this very stylish wine. Screwcap. 12.5% alc. **Rating** 94 **To** 2020 $35

Hunter Valley Shiraz 2011 Bright purple-crimson; the bouquet and palate sing the same song, with plum the main theme, warm spices including cinnamon the obbligato; the medium-bodied palate is seductively smooth and supple, with a fresh finish and aftertaste. Screwcap. 13.7% alc. **Rating** 94 **To** 2021 $25

♟♟♟♟♙ **Aged Release Hunter Valley Semillon 2006 Rating** 93 **To** 2026 $30

✪ **Hunter Valley Semillon 2012** Pale straw-green; the bouquet is fresh and clean, but it is only on the palate that the wine bursts into exuberant life, with intense lemon sherbet flavours that course through the long palate. An interesting facet is Michael De Iuliis' practice of picking the grapes a little riper than most. Great value. Screwcap. 11.5% alc. **Rating** 92 **To** 2025 $18

Hunter Valley Verdelho 2012 Rating 90 **To** 2014 $18

De Salis Wines

Lofty Vineyard, 125 Mount Lofty Road, Orange, NSW 2800 **Region** Orange
T 0403 956 295 **www**.desaliswines.com.au **Open** 7 days 11–5
Winemaker Charles Svenson **Est.** 1999 **Dozens** 3500 **Vyds** 8.7ha
This is the venture of research scientist Charles (Charlie) Svenson and wife Loretta. Charlie became interested in winemaking when, aged 32, he returned to study microbiology and biochemistry at the University of NSW. His particular area of interest (for his PhD) was the yeast and bacterial fermentation of cellulosic waste to produce ethanol. In 2009, after a prolonged search, Charlie and Loretta purchased a vineyard first planted in 1993 and known as Wattleview (now renamed Lofty Vineyard). At an altitude of 1050m it is the highest vineyard in the Orange GI, and their winery was built and equipped in time for the '09 vintage. In '12, De Salis vinified shiraz, cabernet franc and cabernet sauvignon from vineyards in Boree Lane (near Canobolas-Smith).

ꙮꙮꙮꙮꙮ **Wild Fume Blanc 2011** Gleaming yellow-green; evidently barrel-fermented with wild yeast, the bouquet and palate certainly supporting the assumption; it is a complex, rich style, with some overtones of white Bordeaux, and may well have a few years of healthy life left. Screwcap. 12.5% alc. **Rating** 91 **To** 2014 $28
Chardonnay 2011 Gleaming green-straw; picked just as the fruit ripened, preserving the substantial natural acidity; the overall balance is good; the fruit firmly in the grapefruit/citrus end of the spectrum, but with enough stone fruit to satisfy. Screwcap. 12.5% alc. **Rating** 91 **To** 2018 $35

ꙮꙮꙮꙮ **Lofty Pinot Noir 2011** **Rating** 89 **To** 2015 $65
Pinot Noir 2011 **Rating** 89 **To** 2014 $45
St Em M 2010 **Rating** 88 **To** 2015 $38
Nina Semillon Sauvignon Blanc 2009 **Rating** 87 **To** 2015 $28

Deakin Estate

Kulkyne Way, via Red Cliffs, Vic 3496 **Region** Murray Darling
T (03) 5018 5555 **www**.deakinestate.com.au **Open** Not
Winemaker Dr Phil Spillman **Est.** 1980 **Dozens** 400 000 **Vyds** 373ha
Part of the Katnook Estate, Riddoch and Deakin Estate triumvirate, which constitutes the Wingara Wine Group, now fully owned by Freixenet of Spain. Deakin Estate draws from its own vineyards, making it largely self-sufficient, and produces wines of consistent quality and impressive value, thanks in no small part to the skills and expertise of winemaker Phil Spillman. Exports to all major markets.

ꙮꙮꙮꙮꙮ **Cabernet Sauvignon 2010** Light to medium red-purple; another Cabernet
✪ from the '10 vintage to make a mockery of its price; this is a strongly varietal wine, with red and blackcurrant fruit at its heart, the tannins fine and ripe, oak barely seen. Screwcap. 13.5% alc. **Rating** 90 **To** 2015 $10

ꙮꙮꙮꙮ **Artisans Blend Chardonnay Pinot Grigio 2012** The label design suggests a
✪ $30 bottle, not a $10 bottle. It may be autosuggestion, but the wine in the glass has a delicious combination of stone fruit, pear and apple with particularly good mouthfeel. Screwcap. 12% alc. **Rating** 89 **To** 2014 $10

✪ **Merlot 2010** Light to medium red-purple; a nicely composed and balanced medium-bodied wine that displays all of the positive varietal characters of merlot, astutely merging cassis/plum with savoury/spicy black olive notes against a fine web of tannins. Screwcap. 13.5% alc. **Rating** 89 **To** 2014 $10

✪ **Shiraz 2012** Very good hue; is flooded with all-up flavour and texture; plum and blackberry varietal fruit is supported by tannins and an infusion of oak ex chips of staves – it matters not. Screwcap. 13.5% alc. **Rating** 88 **To** 2015 $10

✪ **Chardonnay 2012** A prime example of Riverland chardonnay, with an attractive array of stone fruit, melon and fig flavours; a tribute to the vintage and discipline in the vineyard and winery. Screwcap. 13% alc. **Rating** 87 **To** 2014 $10

✪ **Pinot Noir 2011** Very respectable colour; how did Deakin pull this from the rainy sky of '11 (or any other vintage, for that matter)? It is definably pinot noir, its Achilles heel the savoury/stalky tannins. Demands food to capture those tannins, but that's a small price for a very small cost. Screwcap. 13% alc. **Rating** 87 **To** 2014 $10

✪ **Moscato 2012** Clean and fresh, with green apple and grape aromas and flavours; very sweet, but the tangy acidity provides contrast and energy. Screwcap. 6% alc. **Rating** 87 **To** 2014 $10 BE

Deep Woods Estate

889 Commonage Road, Yallingup, WA 6282 **Region** Margaret River
T (08) 9756 6066 **www**.deepwoods.com.au **Open** Wed–Sun 11–5, 7 days during hols
Winemaker Julian Langworthy, Ben Rector **Est.** 1987 **Dozens** 30000 **Vyds** 16ha
The Gould family acquired Deep Woods Estate in 1992, when the first plantings were four years old. In 2005 the business was purchased by Perth businessman Peter Fogarty and family, who also own Lake's Folly in the Hunter Valley, and Millbrook in the Perth Hills. The 32ha property has 16ha plantings of cabernet sauvignon, shiraz, merlot, cabernet franc, chardonnay, sauvignon blanc, semillon and verdelho. Vineyard and cellar door upgrades are underway. Julian Langworthy was appointed winemaker in the wake of Janice McDonald's move to Howard Park. Exports to Germany, Malaysia, Singapore, Japan and China.

ᵀᵀᵀᵀᵀ **Margaret River Cabernet Sauvignon Merlot 2010** Medium to full red-purple; from 25-year-old estate-grown vines; in the mainstream of Margaret River style, its mix of red and blackcurrant fruit with a web of pleasantly savoury tannins giving both texture and structure to the medium-bodied, but long, palate. Screwcap. 14% alc. **Rating** 94 **To** 2025 $32

Reserve Margaret River Cabernet Sauvignon 2010 Deep magenta; expressive aromas of cassis, crushed leaf and olive on the bouquet; the palate is medium- to full-bodied with taut acidity and ample tannins delivering a long and unevolved finish; allowing some time will see this soften and become complete. Screwcap. 14.5% alc. **Rating** 94 **To** 2025 $60 BE

ᵀᵀᵀᵀᵀ **Margaret River Sauvignon Blanc 2012** Pale quartz; a zesty, zingy offering
✪ of citrus, passionfruit and fresh snow pea fruit on the bouquet and palate alike; Margaret River at its best in terms of varietal fruit expression. Screwcap. 12.5% alc. **Rating** 93 **To** 2014 $22

Block 7 Margaret River Shiraz 2011 Rating 93 **To** 2022 $30 BE
Margaret River Shiraz et al 2010 Rating 92 **To** 2020 $28

✪ **Margaret River Chardonnay 2012** Vibrant green hue; the toasty oak bouquet also reveals nectarine and fennel aromas; the palate is vibrant and fresh, with a fine backbone of acidity providing length. Screwcap. 13% alc. **Rating** 90 **To** 2016 $20 BE

Margaret River Verdelho Verde 2012 Rating 90 **To** 2014 $20

Deetswood Wines

Washpool Creek Road, Tenterfield, NSW 2372 **Region** New England
T (02) 6736 1322 **www**.deetswoodwines.com.au **Open** Fri–Mon 10–5, or by appt
Winemaker Deanne Eaton **Est.** 1996 **Dozens** 1000 **Vyds** 2.4ha
Deanne Eaton and Tim Condrick established their micro-vineyard in 1996, planting semillon, chardonnay, pinot noir, shiraz, merlot, viognier and cabernet sauvignon. At the end of the 19th century, German immigrant Joe Nicoll planted vines here and made wines for family use, and there is still one vine surviving from those original plantings. The wines are consistent both in quality and style, offering further proof that this is a very interesting area.

ᵀᵀᵀᵀᵀ **Platypus Port 2007** A very presentable wine that could once be called Vintage Port. The baume is not too high, and the spirit clean, leaving the spicy black fruits in command. While I agree with Deetswood that it could drink well into 2020, the medicine-type plastic button and cork closure may upset the occasional apple cart. 18% alc. **Rating** 90 **To** 2020 $20

Deisen

PO Box 61, Tanunda, SA 5352 **Region** Barossa Valley
T 0413 362 963 **www**.deisen.com.au **Open** Not
Winemaker Sabine Deisen **Est.** 2001 **Dozens** 1200

Deisen once again proves the old adage that nothing succeeds like success. In the first year, 3.5 tonnes of grapes produced five barrels of Shiraz and two of Grenache. Since that time, production has grown slowly but steadily, along with bits and pieces of traditional winemaking equipment (small crushers, open tanks and hand-plunging, now housed in a slightly larger tin shed). The number of wines made and the tiny quantities of some (20 dozen is not uncommon) is staggering. The style of all the wines is remarkably similar: sweet and luscious fruit; soft, ripe tannins; and a warmth from the alcohol (toned down in recent releases). Limited numbers of magnums of back vintages are available. Most of the 2010 wines are due for release Sept–Nov '13. Exports to the US.

ΨΨΨΨΨ **Tim's Block Barossa Shiraz 2010** Deep crimson-purple; this is a full-bodied blockbuster, but the density of the black fruits and dark chocolate, the tannins and the alcohol absorb the generous helping of oak. The end result is a balanced wine in the Deisen idiom. 60 dozen made. Screwcap. 15.5% alc. **Rating** 94 To 2025 $39

Backblock Barossa Shiraz 2010 Deep red-purple; matured for 30 months in French oak (30% new). The alcohol was deliberate, occasioned by a desire to make a wine with great depth of flavour; its savoury bitter chocolate and black fruit flavours, coupled with the oak, make light work (in an overall full-bodied context) of the alcohol. Strangely compelling. 60 dozen made. Due for release Mar '14. Screwcap. 15.5% alc. **Rating** 94 To 2030 $65

ΨΨΨΨΩ **Meadows Barossa Shiraz 2010 Rating** 93 To 2025 $32
Barossa Shiraz Cabernet Sauvignon 2010 Rating 93 To 2030 $32
Winter Sun Shiraz Mataro 2010 Rating 92 To 2025 $36

del Rios of Mt Anakie

2320 Ballan Road, Anakie, Vic 3221 **Region** Geelong
T (03) 9497 4644 **www**.delrios.com.au **Open** W'ends 10–5
Winemaker Gus del Rio **Est.** 1996 **Dozens** 5000 **Vyds** 17ha

Gus del Rio, of Spanish heritage, established a vineyard in 1996 on the slopes of Mt Anakie, northwest of Geelong (chardonnay, pinot noir, cabernet sauvignon, sauvignon blanc, shiraz, merlot and marsanne). The vines are hand-pruned, the fruit is hand-picked and the wines are made onsite in the fully equipped winery, which includes a bottling and labelling line able to process over 150 tonnes. Exports to China.

ΨΨΨΨΩ **Reserve Geelong Chardonnay 2011** Light straw-green; has many similarities to the varietal, but there is more barrel-ferment oak, and a more complex white peach and grapefruit play; some grilled nut nuances are also evident. Screwcap. 13% alc. **Rating** 92 To 2020 $45

Geelong Cabernet Sauvignon 2009 Medium crimson-purple; still youthful, the flavours cover the full range of cassis, mint and leaf, but end up sweet, not sour; the tannin structure is fine, the oak subtle. Screwcap. 14% alc. **Rating** 92 To 2020 $30

Mayhem @ Anakie Three Feisty Femmes 2012 Full straw-green; as is the style of del Rios, a wine as much about texture and mouthfeel as varietal character; here ripe, fleshy stone fruit fills the palate in a somewhat retro Chardonnay style. Screwcap. 13.5% alc. **Rating** 90 To 2016 $30

Geelong Marsanne 2010 Light straw-green; showing the leisurely development of the variety, honeysuckle alongside the citrus; there is something going on with the finish, most probably phenolics. Screwcap. 13.6% alc. **Rating** 90 To 2015 $45

Geelong Pinot Noir 2011 Light to medium red-purple; a creditable outcome from the challenging vintage, with plummy fruit and fine, ripe tannins; no mint or green flavours anywhere. Screwcap. 13.5% alc. **Rating** 90 To 2016 $30

Geelong Botrytis Chardonnay 2011 Green-gold; obviously, a high level of botrytis, with the suspicion of some less noble rot, but redeemed by its very good balance and acidity. 375ml. Screwcap. 12.5% alc. **Rating** 90 **To** 2015 $30

🍷🍷🍷🍷 **Geelong Chardonnay 2011 Rating** 89 **To** 2017 $30
Geelong Sauvignon Blanc 2012 Rating 88 **To** 2014 $25
Geelong Chardonnay 2010 Rating 88 **To** 2015 $35

Delamere Vineyard   ★★★★☆

Bridport Road, Pipers Brook, Tas 7254 **Region** Northern Tasmania
T (03) 6382 7190 **www**.delamerevineyards.com.au **Open** 7 days 10–5
Winemaker Shane Holloway, Fran Austin **Est.** 1983 **Dozens** 3500 **Vyds** 6.5ha
Delamere was one of the first vineyards planted in the Pipers Brook area. It had previously been a diverse fruit orchard and market garden, attesting to the fertile soils. A new chapter has opened for Delamere, with Shane Holloway and wife Fran Austin (ex Bay of Fires) now in charge of viticulture and winemaking. The journey has begun (Delamere was purchased by Shane, Fran and their respective families in 2007), but there are challenges and equally great opportunities lying ahead. The old vines still need some TLC, but there was also 4ha of pinot noir and chardonnay planted at the end of '12.

🍷🍷🍷🍷🍷 **Chardonnay 2011** Wild yeast-fermented in Burgundy-coopered oak, with partial mlf. Bright straw-green, it has the hallmark Tasmanian minerally acidity that creates the framework for the white stone fruits and pink grapefruit flavours on the long palate and aftertaste. Screwcap. 13% alc. **Rating** 94 **To** 2021 $40

🍷🍷🍷🍷🍷 **Rose 2012** Tank-fermented pinot noir free-run juice has given a fragrant,
✪ blossomy bouquet and a fresh, strawberry-filled palate, crisp acidity lengthening the fresh, clean finish. Screwcap. 12.5% alc. **Rating** 93 **To** 2015 $20
Naissante Pinot Gris 2012 Rating 92 **To** 2014 $27
Pinot Noir 2011 Rating 92 **To** 2022 $42

Delatite   ★★★★★

26 High Street, Mansfield, Vic 3722 **Region** Upper Goulburn
T (03) 5775 2922 **www**.delatitewinery.com.au **Open** 7 days 11–5
Winemaker Andy Browning **Est.** 1982 **Dozens** 8500 **Vyds** 26ha
With its sweeping views across to the snow-clad Alps, this is uncompromising cool-climate viticulture, and the wines naturally reflect that. Increasing vine age (many of the plantings are well over 25 years old), and the adoption of organic (and partial biodynamic) viticulture, seems also to have played a role in providing the red wines with more depth and texture; the white wines are as good as ever. In 2011 Vestey Holdings Limited, the international pastoral giant, acquired a majority holding in Delatite, and has said it represents 'the first of what they hope will be a number of agricultural businesses here'. It coincides with a modest increase in estate plantings. Exports to Denmark, China, Japan and Malaysia.

🍷🍷🍷🍷🍷 **Dead Man's Hill Gewurztraminer 2012** Brilliant straw-green; for long
✪ regarded as one of the best Gewurztraminers in Australia, but this takes things a little further, with wild yeast fermentation and some oak maturation. Ginger, lychee, rose petal, spice and musk are all at home in the richly textured palate. Screwcap. 13.5% alc. **Rating** 96 **To** 2022 $25
Riesling 2012 Light straw-green; flooded with juicy lime and lemon fruit; far more showing at this stage than the normally ultra-reserved Delatite style. Wild yeast fermentation was used, vintage played a role, and also conferred the spine of acidity. Screwcap. 12.5% alc. **Rating** 94 **To** 2022 $25
RJ Limited Edition Shiraz 2010 The fragrant bouquet and light- to medium-bodied palate have a refrain of warm spice and pepper as a background to the main melody of red and black cherry fruit; the tannins and oak have been skilfully handled. Screwcap. 13% alc. **Rating** 94 **To** 2025 $50

Late Harvest Riesling 2012 Akin to a dry Mosel (drier even than Kabinett) to be enjoyed anytime, anywhere, with (almost) every food style, none better than Asian. Beautifully balanced, and very long in the mouth. Screwcap. 11% alc. Rating 94 To 2020 $25

ΨΨΨΨ Catherine Gewurztraminer 2012 Rating 92 To 2017 $25
Chardonnay 2012 Rating 90 To 2016 $25
Pinot Gris 2012 Rating 90 To 2014 $25

Della Fay Wines   ★★★★☆

3276 Caves Road, Yallingup, WA 6284 **Region** Margaret River
T (08) 9755 2747 **www**.kellysvineyard.com.au **Open** By appt
Winemaker Michael Kelly **Est.** 1999 **Dozens** 3000 **Vyds** 8ha
This is the venture of the Kelly family, headed by district veteran Michael Kelly, who gained his degree in wine science from CSU before working at Seville Estate and Mount Mary in the Yarra Valley, and Domaine Louis Chapuis in Burgundy, then coming back to WA and working for Leeuwin Estate and Sandalford. From there he became the long-term winemaker at Fermoy Estate, but he and his family laid the ground for their own brand, buying prime viticultural land in Caves Road, Yallingup, in 1999. They planted 1.2ha each of cabernet sauvignon, merlot, nebbiolo, vermentino and sauvignon blanc, 1.1ha of chardonnay, and 0.5ha each of malbec and petit verdot. It is an eclectic mix of French, Italian and Spanish varieties, and shiraz from the Geographe region will also be included. 'Della Fay' honours the eponymous Kelly family matriarch. Exports to China.

ΨΨΨΨΨ Margaret River Chardonnay 2011 The grapes come from the warmer Yallingup area, and that of much cooler Karriedale; 100% barrel-fermented, it has a glowing yellow-green colour, and a supple, fine palate with white flesh stone fruit cosseted by quality oak. Attractive to drink now, but will be around for some years yet. Screwcap. 13.5% alc. Rating 94 To 2016 $32

ΨΨΨΨ Margaret River Vermentino 2012 Rating 91 To 2014 $18 BE
Geographe Shiraz 2011 Rating 90 To 2018 $32 BE

 ## Denton Viewhill Vineyard   ★★★★★

160 Old Healesville Road, Yarra Glen, Vic 3775 **Region** Yarra Valley
T (03) 9012 3600 **Open** By appt
Winemaker Contract **Est.** 1996 **Dozens** 840 **Vyds** 32ha
This is the venture of leading Melbourne architect John, and son Simon, Denton. John and Simon began the establishment of the vineyard with a first stage planting in 1997, and two more thereafter, lifting the total plantings to their present level in 2004. The name Viewhill derives from the fact that a granite plug 'was created 370 million years ago, sitting above the surrounding softer sand stones and silt stones of the valley'. Significant numbers of granite floaters had to be removed when creating the vineyards, and on the higher parts, holes for the trellis end-posts had to be drilled. This granite base is most unusual in the Yarra Valley, and together with the natural amphitheatre that the plug created, has consistently produced exceptional grapes. The principal varieties planted are pinot noir, chardonnay and shiraz, with lesser quantities of nebbiolo, cabernet sauvignon, merlot, cabernet franc and petit verdot. Substantial quantities of the grape production are sold, Coldstream Hills being the major offtaker. William Downie makes the Pinot Noir, Mac Forbes the Chardonnay, Barney Flanders the Shiraz and Luke Lambert the Nebbiolo.

ΨΨΨΨΨ DM Chardonnay 2010 From close-planted Gin Gin clone, and these grapes hold the key along with the site; delicious stone fruit and melon, rather than grapefruit, and the oak is subtle. Screwcap. 12.5% alc. Rating 94 To 2017 $45
DM Pinot Noir 2010 Light crimson-purple, it has an interesting, contrasting, juicy/savoury palate with layers of red and black cherry/berry fruit, and a long, lingering finish. Screwcap. 13.5% alc. Rating 94 To 2017 $45

DM Shiraz 2010 Medium purple-crimson; has a complex, fragrant bouquet and medium-bodied palate, with fine spicy nuances and an open-weave texture to the mouthfeel; the flavours are in the red and black cherry range, the finish long and relaxed. 153 dozen made. Screwcap. 13.5% alc. **Rating** 94 **To** 2025 $45

🍷🍷🍷🍷🍷 **Dead Mouse Shed Pinot Noir 2010 Rating** 92 **To** 2017 $30

Derwent Estate   ★★★★☆

329 Lyell Highway, Granton, Tas 7070 **Region** Southern Tasmania
T (03) 6263 5802 **www**.derwentestate.com.au **Open** Mon–Fri 10–4 (Sun–Fri 10–4 Nov–Jan)
Winemaker Winemaking Tasmania (Julian Alcorso) **Est.** 1992 **Dozens** 2500 **Vyds** 10.08ha
Three generations of the Hanigan family are involved in the management of their historic Mt Nassau property, owned by the family since 1913. Given that over the last 100 years or so the property has at various times been involved with sheep, cattle, vegetable production, seed crops and the production of lime, the addition of viticulture in '92 was not surprising. The vineyard has grown in stages, the grapes bound for Bay of Fires wines and Penfolds Yattarna. The grapes retained by Derwent Estate have produced consistently good wines.

🍷🍷🍷🍷🍷 **Pinot Noir 2011** Bright, clear crimson-purple hue; glossy cherry fruit with some spice, and also very attractive savoury/spicy tannins. Gold and The Wine Society Trophy for People's Choice Tasmanian Wine Show '13. Screwcap. 13.9% alc. **Rating** 94 **To** 2019 $35

🍷🍷🍷🍷🍷 **Pinot Gris 2012 Rating** 90 **To** 2014 $25

Deviation Road   ★★★★☆

214 Scott Creek Road, Longwood, SA 5153 **Region** Adelaide Hills
T (08) 8339 2633 **www**.deviationroad.com **Open** 7 days 10–5
Winemaker Kate and Hamish Laurie **Est.** 1999 **Dozens** 6000 **Vyds** 11.05ha
Deviation Road was created in 1998 by Hamish Laurie, great-great-grandson of Mary Laurie, SA's first female winemaker. He initially joined with father Dr Chris Laurie in 1992 to help build the Hillstowe Wines business; the brand was sold to Banksia Wines in 2001, but the Laurie family retained the vineyard, which now supplies Deviation Road with its grapes. Wife Kate joined the business in '01, having studied winemaking and viticulture in Champagne, then spending four years at her family's Stone Bridge winery in Manjimup. All the wines come from the family vineyards, but they only account for a small portion of the annual grape production of those vineyards. It also has 3ha of pinot noir and shiraz at Longwood, where its new cellar door is situated. Exports to the UK, the US and Hong Kong.

🍷🍷🍷🍷🍷 **Adelaide Hills Pinot Gris 2011** It is clear that those who kept botrytis and the mildews at bay made some excellent Pinot Gris from Adelaide Hills in '11; this has a juicy, lemony accent to its apple fruit, complexity coming from partial barrel fermentation; great length and balance. Screwcap. 12% alc. **Rating** 94 **To** 2014 $23

🍷🍷🍷🍷🍷 **Adelaide Hills Pinot Noir 2010 Rating** 92 **To** 2015 $32
Ironbark Adelaide Hills Shiraz Cabernet 2010 Rating 91 **To** 2015 $18 TS
Loftia Adelaide Hills Vintage Brut 2010 Rating 91 **To** 2015 $34
Altair Adelaide Hills Brut Rose NV Rating 90 **To** 2015 $28

🌿 Devil's Corner   ★★★★☆

The Hazards Vineyard, Sherbourne Road, Apslawn, Tas 7190 **Region** East Coast Tasmania
T (03) 6257 8881 **www**.brownbrothers.com.au **Open** 7 days 9–5 (Nov–Apr)
Winemaker Tom Ravech **Est.** 1999 **Dozens** 50 000 **Vyds** 175ha
This is one of the separately managed operations of Brown Brothers' Tasmanian interests, taking in the relatively new The Hazards Vineyard as its chief source of supply. That vineyard is planted to pinot noir, chardonnay, sauvignon blanc, pinot gris, riesling, gewurztraminer and savagnin. The avant-garde, striking and (for me) attractive labels mark a decided change from

the past, and also distinguish Devil's Corner from the other Tasmanian activities of Brown Brothers. Exports to all major markets.

🍷🍷🍷🍷 **Riesling 2012** Tropical nuances to the core of citrus fruits are left field for
✪   Tasmania, but make for a very attractive early-drinking style. Screwcap. 12% alc.
           Rating 92 **To** 2016 $20

✪   **Pinot Grigio 2012** Has a distinct blush-pink colour from some skin contact, and
           a vibrant, juicy palate that caused the judges to give it a gold medal at the Adelaide
           Wine Show '12. There are haunting echoes of strawberry and citrus. Screwcap.
           13% alc. **Rating** 92 **To** 2014 $20

✪   **Pinot Grigio 2011** Pinot Grigio's varietal integrity bursts through the
           understated restraint of the '11 season in bolts of lemon blossom, crunchy pear and
           lemon zest. This is fantastic value in Tassie Grigio, impressively balanced, persistent
           and textural. Screwcap. 13.5% alc. **Rating** 92 **To** 2014 $20 TS

           Pinot Noir 2011 Bright, clear crimson-purple; the perfumed bouquet of rose
           petals and red fruits leads into a red fruit palate that is supple, yet not too supple,
           because there is a fine web of gossamer tannins. Welcomes you into its bosom
           right now. Screwcap. 13.5% alc. **Rating** 91 **To** 2016 $22

✪   **Sauvignon Blanc 2012** Pale quartz-green; passionfruit and sweet citrus fruits
           drive the bouquet, a touch of grass joining those fruits on the palate. Screwcap.
           13% alc. **Rating** 90 **To** 2014 $20

✪   **Chardonnay 2012** Unoaked, but has good varietal expression courtesy of a
           seamless, almost creamy, mix of stone fruit, citrus and melon fruit flavours, the
           acidity well balanced. Screwcap. 12.5% alc. **Rating** 90 **To** 2015 $20

✪   **Chardonnay 2011** Unashamedly Tasmanian, unashamedly '11 and unashamedly
           bargain-priced, this is an eminently refreshing aperitif Chardonnay. It carries the
           high-tensile acidity of the vintage with delicate poise, presenting white peach
           and lemon blossom in a particularly taut and honed guise. Screwcap. 12.5% alc.
           Rating 90 **To** 2014 $20 TS

✪   **Chardonnay Pinot Noir NV** A blend of chardonnay, pinot noir and pinot
           meunier from the estate vineyards in the Tamar Valley. Made using the Charmat
           method. Faint pink blush; has good mousse, and is particularly vibrant and fresh;
           a fruit-driven aperitif style, with crunchy Tasmanian acidity. Cork. 12% alc.
           Rating 90 **To** 2014 $22

Devil's Lair   ★★★★★

Rocky Road, Forest Grove via Margaret River, WA 6285 **Region** Margaret River
T 1300 651 650 **www**.devils-lair.com **Open** Not
Winemaker Oliver Crawford **Est.** 1981 **Dozens** NFP **Vyds** 130ha
Having rapidly carved out a high reputation for itself through a combination of clever packaging and impressive wine quality, Devil's Lair was acquired by Southcorp in 1996. The estate vineyards have been substantially increased since, now with sauvignon blanc, semillon, chardonnay, cabernet sauvignon, merlot, shiraz, cabernet franc and petit verdot, supplemented by grapes purchased from contract growers. An exceptionally successful business; production has increased from 40 000 dozen to many times greater, in no small measure due to its Fifth Leg and Dance With the Devil wines. Exports to the UK, the US and other major markets.

🍷🍷🍷🍷🍷 **9th Chamber Margaret River Chardonnay 2009** The inaugural release of
           this estate-grown wine, only produced in the best vintages; fermented and matured
           in second-use French oak, the lees stirred for 10 months. The bouquet brings
           grapefruit, nectarine and white peach fruit into play, the oak imparting spicy/nutty
           characters; the palate is incredibly rich and unctuous, yet retains elegance thanks
           to its multilayered texture and tight focus. Elegant and intense. Screwcap. 13% alc.
           Rating 97 **To** 2025 $100

           Margaret River Chardonnay 2011 Bright straw-green; a seamless union of
           perfectly ripened chardonnay and subtle French oak; the flavours are in the white
           flesh stone fruit spectrum, citrussy acidity providing length and balance. Screwcap.
           13% alc. **Rating** 95 **To** 2019 $50

✪ **Fifth Leg Shiraz 2011** Deep purple-crimson; blackberry, black cherry, licorice and fruitcake chase each other around the bouquet and medium- to full-bodied palate, and the chase has no end. The theory of Fifth Leg is that it should provide an easy-drinking fruit-driven style, and on that premise it fails. On any other, it is awesomely good, and a great candidate for a minimum 5-year stay in the cellar. Screwcap. 14.5% alc. **Rating** 94 **To** 2026 $18

Margaret River Cabernet Sauvignon 2011 Bright crimson-purple; a perfectly ripened cabernet, full of blackcurrant fruit, the tannins ripe, the palate long; the one question is the amount of French oak showing at this stage, but the overall balance will ensure its future harmonious development. Screwcap. 14.5% alc. **Rating** 94 **To** 2031 $50

🍷🍷🍷🍷🍷 **The Hidden Cave Margaret River Cabernet Shiraz 2011** Medium
✪ crimson-purple; this wine must make cabernet shiraz blends more common in Margaret River, for the union is boldly synergistic, producing a gamut of red and black fruit flavours that are naturally complementary. Screwcap. 14.5% alc. **Rating** 93 **To** 2030 $23

Fifth Leg Cabernet Sauvignon Shiraz Merlot 2011 Rating 92 **To** 2017 $18
The Hidden Cave Sauvignon Blanc Semillon 2012 Rating 91 **To** 2014 $23
The Hidden Cave Chardonnay 2012 Rating 91 **To** 2015 $23
✪ **Fifth Leg Rose 2011** Vivid magenta-pink, it is all about red fruits, from strawberries to cherries to wild strawberries with their faintly savoury edge. There is the barest hint of sweetness on the finish, making it a top aperitif style. Screwcap. 13% alc. **Rating** 91 **To** 2012 $18

Dance with the Devil Shiraz Tempranillo 2011 Rating 91 **To** 2021 $25

🍷🍷🍷🍷 **Fifth Leg Crisp Chardonnay 2012** Pale straw-green; crisp in name, and crisp
✪ in nature, with tangy citrus/lime/grapefruit flavours, and a lively, minerally finish; not even a whisper of oak. Screwcap. 12.5% alc. **Rating** 89 **To** 2014 $18

Dexter Wines ★★★★★

210 Foxeys Road, Merricks North, Vic 3926 (postal) **Region** Mornington Peninsula
T (03) 5989 7007 **www.**dexterwines.com.au **Open** Not
Winemaker Tod Dexter **Est.** 2006 **Dozens** 1300 **Vyds** 7.1ha
Through a series of seemingly unrelated events, Tod Dexter arrived in the US with the intention of enjoying some skiing; having done that, he became an apprentice winemaker at Cakebread Cellars, a well-known Napa Valley winery. After seven years he returned to Australia and the Mornington Peninsula, and began the establishment of the vineyard, planted to pinot noir (4ha) and chardonnay (3.1ha). To keep the wolves from the door he became winemaker at Stonier, and leased his vineyard to Stonier, the grapes always used in the Stonier Reserve range. Having left Stonier to become Yabby Lake winemaker, and spurred on by turning 50 in 2006 (and at the urging of friends), he and wife Debbie decided to establish the Dexter label. Exports to the UK and the US.

🍷🍷🍷🍷🍷 **Mornington Peninsula Chardonnay 2011** Bright, light straw-green; a very distinguished wine, with great precision, length and drive to its pristine varietal fruit, hovering between stone fruit and citrus; the oak has been skilfully handled, supporting but never intruding, the long finish perfectly balanced. 700 dozen made. Screwcap. 12.5% alc. **Rating** 96 **To** 2020 $38

🍷🍷🍷🍷🍷 **Mornington Peninsula Pinot Noir 2011 Rating** 90 **To** 2016 $49

Di Fabio Estate ★★★★★

5 Valleyview Drive, McLaren Vale, SA 5171 (postal) **Region** McLaren Vale
T (08) 8383 0188 **www.**difabioestatewines.com.au **Open** Not
Winemaker Goe Di Fabio **Est.** 1994 **Dozens** 6000 **Vyds** 38.91ha
Di Fabio Estate is the venture of brothers Goe and Tony Di Fabio. Their parents Giovanni and Maria Di Fabio purchased their first vineyard in McLaren Vale in 1966 (with a tradition stretching back further to Italy) and became long-term contract grapegrowers for other

winemakers. The business carried on by their sons has a 56ha property at McLaren Vale, and 8.5ha at Waikerie. The plantings are dominated by 12.5ha of grenache, 10.5ha of shiraz, and 3.6ha of mourvedre; petit verdot, merlot, chardonnay, cabernet franc, sauvignon blanc and semillon are also grown. Exports to Macau, Singapore and China.

🍷🍷🍷🍷🍷 **Bush Vine McLaren Vale Shiraz 2010** Excellent colour; very well made, with an aromatic dark-fruited bouquet, then a medium- to full-bodied palate showcasing McLaren Vale shiraz with its wanton display of succulent plum, dark chocolate and blackberry. It has the balance and length to navigate the years ahead without a tremor. Screwcap. 14.5% alc. **Rating** 95 **To** 2035 $35

Marietta GSM McLaren Vale Grenache Shiraz Mataro 2010 Medium red-purple; has the complexity and abundance of rich red and black fruits that McLaren Vale achieves regularly and eludes the Barossa Valley; the structure of the wine is truly excellent, with succulent fruit framed by savoury tannins, oak a bystander. Screwcap. 14.5% alc. **Rating** 94 **To** 2020 $41

 # Di Sciascio Family Wines

2 Pincott Street, Newtown, Vic 3220 **Region** Various
T 0417 384 272 **www.**disciasciofamilywines.com.au **Open** Not
Winemaker Matthew Di Sciascio **Est.** 2012 **Dozens** 1500

Matthew Di Sciascio's journey through wine has been an odyssey of Homeric proportions, with wife Susan and seven-year-old daughter Lulu joining along the way. His working life began as an apprentice boilermaker in his father's family business. In 1991 he accompanied his father on a trip to Italy, where a shared bottle of wine in the kitchen of his uncle sowed a seed that first flowered back in Australia, helping with garage winemaking by his father and friends, and hobby winemaking courses at Cellar Plus. When the family business was sold in '97, the vinous pace increased, with vineyard work in the Yarra Valley and enrolment in Dookie Agricultural College's viticultural course. It accelerated further with the establishment of Bellbrae Estate (with wife Susan at his side) in Geelong with Matthew heading the partnership, and enrolling (in 2002) in the new Deakin University Wine and Science degree, graduating in '05 as co-dux, with a vintage at the celebrated Masciarelli Winery in Abruzzo as the price. In '08 and '09 he was winemaker at both Otway Estate and Bellbrae Estate, but in Dec '10 the responsibility for seriously ill parents and a young daughter led to the decision to sell his share of Bellbrae to his financial partners, and (in '12) to start this venture, while continuing to gain experience by working the '13 vintage at Galli Estate in Sunbury.

🍷🍷🍷🍷🍷 **D'Sas Drumborg Riesling 2012** Pale straw-green; a flavoursome Riesling, with ripe apple and citrus fruit; there may be a low level of residual sugar to balance the often penetrating acidity; whether this is a good thing or not is open to debate. Screwcap. 11.8% alc. **Rating** 90 **To** 2017 $24

D'Sas Heathcote Sangiovese 2012 Light, but bright, crimson-purple; attractive spicy, red cherry fruit on the bouquet and mid-palate is trimmed to a degree by sangiovese tannins on the finish; the problem was recognised and the wine fined with egg whites; the potential is there for limited (2–3 years) cellaring. Screwcap. 13% alc. **Rating** 90 **To** 2017 $27

🍷🍷🍷🍷 **D'Sas King Valley Pinot Gris 2012** **Rating** 89 **To** 2013 $22

Diamond Creek Estate

18 Merrigang Street, Bowral, NSW 2576 **Region** Southern Highlands
T (02) 4872 3311 **www.**diamondcreekestate.com.au **Open** Thurs–Sun 11–4
Winemaker Eddy Rossi **Est.** 1997 **Dozens** 2500 **Vyds** 6ha

Helen Hale purchased Diamond Creek Estate in late 2002, by which time the chardonnay, sauvignon blanc, riesling, pinot noir and cabernet sauvignon planted in 1997 by the prior owner had come into bearing. The vineyard is established at 680m on rich basalt soil, the north-facing slope being relatively frost-free. Since Helen acquired the property, some of the grapes have been sold to Southern Highlands Winery, but most have been retained for release under the Diamond Creek Estate label: the wines include Riesling, Sauvignon Blanc, Pinot Noir, Cabernet Sauvignon and the highly successful Noble Diamond. Exports to Asia.

¶¶¶¶ **Pinot Noir 2010** Mid garnet; the bouquet displays spiced plum and savoury aromas; the palate is firm and dry, yet maintains varietal integrity. Screwcap. 12.7% alc. **Rating** 87 **To** 2015 $22 BE

Diamond Valley Vineyards ★★★★★

PO Box 5155, Wonga Park, Vic 3115 **Region** Yarra Valley
T (03) 9722 0840 **www**.diamondvalley.com.au **Open** Not
Winemaker James Lance **Est.** 1976 **Dozens** 4000 **Vyds** 12ha
One of the Yarra Valley's finest producers of Pinot Noir and an early pacesetter for the variety, making wines of tremendous style and crystal-clear varietal character. They are not Cabernet Sauvignon lookalikes but true pinot noir, fragrant and intense. The Chardonnays show the same marriage of finesse and intensity, and the Cabernet family wines shine in the warmer vintages. In early 2005 the brand and wine stocks were acquired by Graeme Rathbone, the Lances continuing to own the vineyard and winery, and make the wine. The vineyards and winery were burnt in the Black Saturday bushfires of February '09; re-establishment is well underway. Exports to the UK.

¶¶¶¶¶ **Reserve Yarra Valley Pinot Noir 2007** Has exceptional colour for a 6-year-old Pinot; has built impressively on its start, the very complex palate with a Catherine Wheel of red and dark fruits, spices and all-important fine tannins on the long, lingering finish. Screwcap. 13% alc. **Rating** 96 **To** 2016 $60
Reserve Yarra Valley Chardonnay 2007 Glorious quartz-green, deeper than '10, but without any yellow; a very complex and very distinguished Chardonnay, with strong similarities to White Burgundy, especially with its talcy tannins; will be full of interest for years to come. Screwcap. 13.5% alc. **Rating** 95 **To** 2020 $36
Yarra Valley Chardonnay 2010 Bright quartz-green; wild yeast-fermented, and immaculately balanced throughout, with a posy of nectarine, white peach and French oak aromas that flow through seamlessly to the palate, with some creamy/ nutty notes on the finish. Screwcap. 13% alc. **Rating** 94 **To** 2017 $24
Yarra Valley Pinot Noir 2010 The colour is still youthful; the bouquet has dark fruit and multi-spice aromas, the palate taking these to another level, with a savoury bent giving the texture, complexity and drive only the best Pinots have. Screwcap. 13.5% alc. **Rating** 94 **To** 2018 $28

Diggers Bluff ★★★★

PO Box 34, Tanunda, SA 5352 **Region** Barossa Valley
T 0417 087 566 **www**.diggersbluff.com **Open** By appt
Winemaker Timothy O'Callaghan **Est.** 1998 **Dozens** 1000 **Vyds** 1.9ha
Timothy O'Callaghan explains that his family crest is an Irish hound standing under an oak tree; the Diggers Bluff label features his faithful hound Digger under a mallee tree. He is a third-generation O'Callaghan winemaker, and – reading his newsletter – it's not too hard to guess who the second generation is represented by. Diggers Bluff has cabernet sauvignon, shiraz, grenache, alicante and mataro, all old vines. Exports to Canada, Singapore and Hong Kong.

¶¶¶¶¶ **Watch Dog 2010** A cabernet shiraz blend sealed with a high-quality cork, its deep crimson-purple colour also reassuring. It is crammed full to bursting with blackcurrant and blackberry fruit, licorice and supple tannins; the vanilla oak also contributes. 14.5% alc. **Rating** 93 **To** 2030 $32
✪ **Stray Dog 2010** A blend of grenache, shiraz and mourvedre, the colour good; it is as full-bodied as the high alcohol would suggest, but the finish isn't unduly warm, and the array of red and black fruits, mocha, vanilla and leather all come together well. Well priced. Screwcap. 15.5% alc. **Rating** 90 **To** 2018 $18

DiGiorgio Family Wines   ★★★★☆

Riddoch Highway, Coonawarra, SA 5263 **Region** Coonawarra
T (08) 8736 3222 **www**.digiorgio.com.au **Open** 7 days 10–5
Winemaker Peter Douglas **Est.** 1998 **Dozens** 25 000 **Vyds** 353.53ha
Stefano DiGiorgio emigrated from Abruzzi, Italy, in 1952. Over the years, he and his family
gradually expanded their holdings at Lucindale. In '89 he began planting cabernet sauvignon
(99ha), chardonnay (10ha), merlot (9ha), shiraz (6ha) and pinot noir (2ha). In 2002 the
family purchased the historic Rouge Homme winery, capable of crushing 10 000 tonnes of
grapes, and its surrounding 13.5ha of vines, from Southcorp. Since that time the Coonawarra
plantings have been increased to almost 230ha, the lion's share to cabernet sauvignon. The
enterprise is offering full winemaking services to vignerons in the Limestone Coast Zone.
Exports to all major markets.

🍷🍷🍷🍷🍷 **Francesco Reserve Limestone Coast Cabernet Sauvignon 2008** Medium
to full red-purple; has retained good colour and flavour; it spent 2 years in French
barriques, the oak now absorbed by the cassis, blackberry and mulberry fruit;
earthy tannins are still largely untamed, but fit within the overall context of the
wine. ProCork. 14% alc. **Rating** 93 **To** 2025 $80

✪ **Lucindale Limestone Coast Botrytis Semillon 2011** Undoubted, although
relatively light, botrytis influence, and 6 months in new French hogsheads, has
produced a very appealing dessert style, with peach, apricot, musk and citrus all
contributing to the balanced palate and lingering finish. Fresh fruit or fruit pastries
would be an ideal match. 500ml. Screwcap. 12% alc. **Rating** 92 **To** 2017 $20

Francesco Reserve Limestone Coast Cabernet Sauvignon 2006 A
thoroughly stained ProCork is not a happy sight, and it is difficult to ignore it; the
wine is very savoury and lean, rather than the plum satin texture suggested on the
back label. On the other hand, it is true to type with its mint and licorice nuances.
14% alc. **Rating** 91 **To** 2016 $80

Coonawarra Tempranillo 2010 Medium purple-red; has a precise, clear-cut
expression of tempranillo through its red and black cherry fruit, fine-grained
tannins adding to the palate, oak incidental. Screwcap. 13.5% alc. **Rating** 91
To 2017 $23

Lucindale Limestone Coast Chardonnay 2012 Quartz-white; seemingly
unoaked, but has plenty of verve to its grapefruit and white peach fruit, resulting
in a long, fresh palate. Screwcap. 13.5% alc. **Rating** 90 **To** 2014 $18

Emporio Coonawarra Merlot Cabernet Sauvignon Cabernet Franc 2009
A 47/41/12% blend; while the colour is not deep, the hue is good; there is also
more flavour courtesy of cassis fruit and new French oak, and the finish has good,
albeit positive, tannins. Screwcap. 14% alc. **Rating** 90 **To** 2019 $23

🍷🍷🍷🍷 **Kongorong Riesling 2012** Rating 89 To 2016 $19
Coonawarra Fortified Shiraz 2008 Rating 89 To 2014 $33
Sterita Limestone Coast Shiraz 2010 Rating 88 To 2016 $15
Lucindale Limestone Coast Sauvignon Blanc 2012 Rating 87 To 2013 $18
Coonawarra Cabernet Sauvignon 2009 Rating 87 To 2015 $23
Lucindale Cabernet Sauvignon 2009 Rating 87 To 2016 $20

Dinny Goonan   ★★★★

880 Winchelsea-Deans Marsh Road, Bambra, Vic 3241 **Region** Geelong
T 0438 408 420 **www**.dinnygoonan.com.au **Open** 7 days Jan, w'ends & public hols
Nov–Jun, or by appt
Winemaker Dinny and Angus Goonan **Est.** 1990 **Dozens** 1200 **Vyds** 5.5ha
The establishment of Dinny Goonan dates back to 1988 when Dinny bought a 20ha
property near Bambra, in the hinterland of the Otway Coast. Dinny had recently completed
a viticulture diploma at CSU, and initially a wide range of varieties was planted in what is
now known as the Nursery Block, to establish those best suited to the area. As these came
into production Dinny headed back to CSU, where he completed a wine science degree.

Ultimately, it was decided to focus production on shiraz and riesling, with more extensive planting of these varieties. In '07 a 'sticky' block was added (semillon, sauvignon blanc), with the first harvest in '11.

ꝐꝐꝐꝐꝐ Early Harvest Riesling 2012 Pale straw-green; I'm not sure whether early or late harvest is the most helpful; both are essentially meaningless; it is only just into off-dry, but is finely structured and balanced; its lime and apple juice, coupled with very good natural acidity, will see it develop well over time. Screwcap. 11% alc. **Rating** 93 **To** 2027 $27

✪ **Single Vineyard Riesling 2012** Pale straw-green; an attractive, full-flavoured Riesling that retains elegance; there are lime juice and passionfruit flavours, and the acidity is balanced. Screwcap. 13% alc. **Rating** 92 **To** 2016 $20

ꝐꝐꝐꝐ **Viognier 2011** Pale straw-green; so early picked it is very difficult to discern any
✪ varietal character; it is possible this may develop with age, and the wine has the necessary balance. Screwcap. 11% alc. **Rating** 87 **To** 2015 $25

Dionysus Winery

1 Patemans Lane, Murrumbateman, NSW 2582 **Region** Canberra District
T (02) 6227 0208 **www.**dionysus-winery.com.au **Open** W'ends & public hols 10–5, or by appt
Winemaker Michael O'Dea **Est.** 1998 **Dozens** 1000 **Vyds** 4ha
Michael and Wendy O'Dea founded the winery while they had parallel lives as public servants in Canberra, but they have now retired, and devote themselves full-time to the winery. They purchased their property at Murrumbateman in 1996, and planted chardonnay, sauvignon blanc, riesling, viognier, merlot, pinot noir, cabernet sauvignon and shiraz between '98 and 2001. Michael has completed an associate degree in winemaking at CSU, and is responsible for viticulture and winemaking; Wendy has completed various courses at the Canberra TAFE and is responsible for wine marketing and (in their words) 'nagging Michael and being a general slushie'.

ꝐꝐꝐꝐꝐ Canberra District May Riesling 2012 May Riesling can mean many things: I have encountered dry or near-dry examples, but this is well into Spatlese territory, with pulsating sweetness to its lime juice flavours, brought back into balance by its acidity. 375ml. Screwcap. 10% alc. **Rating** 92 **To** 2020 $24

✪ **Canberra District Sauvignon Blanc 2012** Light straw-green; the perfumed bouquet has passionfruit at its core, but white flowers also make their mark; the palate is delicate, but has excellent balance and length to the mix of citrus, grass and tropical fruit flavours. Screwcap. 12.1% alc. **Rating** 91 **To** 2014 $20

🍂 Dirty Three

150 Holgates Road, Leongatha South, Vic 3953 **Region** Gippsland
T 0413 547 932 **www.**dirtythreewines.com.au **Open** By appt
Winemaker Marcus Satchell **Est.** 2012 **Dozens** 500 **Vyds** 4ha
The three people in question are winemaker Marcus Satchell, sales and marketer Cameron Mackenzie, and PR livewire Stuart Gregor. Each has a real-life job, this simply representing a bit of (serious) fun. They have acquired a 4ha vineyard planted in 1998 to 3.1ha of pinot noir, and a total of 0.9ha of riesling and chardonnay.

ꝐꝐꝐꝐꝐ South Gippsland Pinot Noir 2012 From the estate block; small batches were destemmed, then whole berries were wild-fermented and matured on lees in French oak (35% new) for 11 months. The colour is crimson-purple, the bouquet charged with satsuma plum and black cherry fruit, the structure round and supple, the finish long and fresh. Screwcap. 12.7% alc. **Rating** 94 **To** 2020 $40

Riesling 2012 Nigh on water-white; one-third wild yeast-fermented in used oak, the remainder in stainless steel, and with dirty (cloudy) solids juice. In the manner of some cool-region Rieslings, the acidity is more obvious than the residual sugar, and the wine has formidable length. Screwcap. 9.7% alc. **Rating** 94 **To** 2018 $27

Disaster Bay Wines

133 Oaklands Road, Pambula, NSW 2549 **Region** South Coast Zone
T (02) 6495 6869 **www**.disasterbay.com.au **Open** Not
Winemaker Dean O'Reilly, Nick O'Leary **Est.** 2000 **Dozens** 200 **Vyds** 1.2ha
Dean O'Reilly has a 15-year background in the distribution of fine table wines, culminating
in employment by Möet Hennessy Australia. In 2009 he was one of 12 wine professionals
selected to participate in the week-long Len Evans Tutorial. The wines are made with Nick
O'Leary; the grapes come from the block owned by Dean adjacent to the Pambula River.

Sauvignon Blanc Semillon 2012 The two varieties were picked and fermented
together in barrel or stainless steel tank, all the wine then matured for a period in
oak. That oak is very obvious, the sweetness less overt but nonetheless there. Good
cellar-door style. Screwcap. 13% alc. **Rating** 87 **To** 2015 $20

Dixons Creek Estate

1620 Melba Highway, Dixons Creek, Vic 3775 **Region** Yarra Valley
T (03) 5965 2553 **www**.graememillerwines.com.au **Open** 7 days 10–5
Winemaker Graeme Miller, Shaun Crinion **Est.** 2004 **Dozens** 5000 **Vyds** 30.4ha
Graeme Miller is a Yarra Valley legend in his own lifetime, having established Chateau Yarrinya
(now De Bortoli) in 1971, and as a virtual unknown winning the Jimmy Watson Trophy in
'78 with the '77 Chateau Yarrinya Cabernet Sauvignon. He sold Chateau Yarrinya in 1986
and established a vineyard that has steadily grown to over 30ha, with chardonnay, pinot gris,
cabernet sauvignon, cabernet franc, carmenere, shiraz, pinot noir, sauvignon blanc, petit verdot
and merlot. An onsite winery was built in 2004. Graeme's son Daniel has been working in
the business since '11; while the business was on the market in March '13, Daniel will work
to refocus operations if it is not sold. Exports to China.

Quatrain 2007 Has retained excellent hue; a 78/10/9/3% blend of cabernet
sauvignon, petit verdot and cabernet franc that must have had formidable tannins
when young, but is now well balanced; black and redcurrant fruit is bolstered by
those tannins on the long palate. Cork. 13.4% alc. **Rating** 92 **To** 2020 $35

Yarra Valley Pinot Noir 2010 **Rating** 89 **To** 2015 $28
Yarra Valley Chardonnay 2012 **Rating** 88 **To** 2015 $22

Doc Adams

2/41 High Street, Willunga, SA 5172 **Region** McLaren Vale
T (08) 8556 2111 **www**.docadamswines.com.au **Open** By appt
Winemaker Michael Brown **Est.** 2005 **Dozens** 5000 **Vyds** 27ha
Doc Adams is a partnership between viticulturist Adam Jacobs and orthopaedic surgeon
Dr Darren Waters (and their respective wives). Adam graduated from CSU with a degree
in viticulture and has had over 20 years' experience as a consultant viticulturist, first in the
Mornington Peninsula and then McLaren Vale, Coonawarra, Adelaide Hills and Langhorne
Creek. Darren has grown low-yielding shiraz vines in McLaren Vale since 1998, using all of his
time off from his surgical practice. The estate-grown Shiraz is open-fermented, and is matured
in 80% new French and 20% new American oak for 18 months. The Pinot Gris comes from
a single low-yielding Adelaide Hills vineyard; the wine is given 24 hours' skin contact, which
leads to the light-golden colour and palate richness. Exports to China.

McLaren Vale Shiraz 2010 Good depth and hue; a medium- to full-bodied,
supple and harmonious Shiraz which won the trophy for Best McLaren Vale Shiraz
at the McLaren Vale Wine Show '12. Its regional expression of shiraz is effortless,
with the full range of black fruits, fine tannins and a breath of dark chocolate.
Screwcap. 14.5% alc. **Rating** 94 **To** 2020 $25
McLaren Vale GSM 2010 The Hogarth painting of binge drinking revelry by
men old enough to know better is a bold label ploy in these nanny state days.
The wine fully deserved its gold medal at the McLaren Vale Wine Show '12,
rippling with red fruits, dark chocolate and supple tannins, its balance and structure
excellent. Screwcap. 14.5% alc. **Rating** 94 **To** 2025 $25

Dog Trap Vineyard

262 Dog Trap Road, Yass, NSW 2582 **Region** Canberra District
T (02) 6226 5898 **www**.dogtrapvineyard.com.au **Open** By appt
Winemaker Dr Dennis Hart, Dr Roger Harris, Brian Sinclair **Est.** 1996 **Dozens** 1000
Vyds 6.1ha

The somewhat ghoulish name and label illustration is a reminder of bygone days when wild dogs were caught in traps in much the same way as rabbits. It certainly means the name of the venture will be remembered. Planting of the vineyard began in 1996, with a smaller addition in '98. The property was purchased by Dr Dennis Hart and Ms Julian White in December 2003, and until '06 the grapes were sold to Constellation's Kamberra winery. In '07 the crop was completely destroyed by a violent but localised hailstorm, so the first wines were not made until '08. Shiraz and cabernet sauvignon were the initial plantings, and more recently riesling and pinot gris were added.

Canberra District Shiraz 2010 Very light colour; a light-bodied wine that does, however, have varietal fruit in a red berry spectrum, and a gentle wash of French and American oak. Cheap at twice the price, and ready now. Screwcap. 13% alc. **Rating** 87 **To** 2014 $12

DogRidge Wine Company

129 Bagshaws Road, McLaren Flat, SA 5171 **Region** McLaren Vale
T (08) 8383 0140 **www**.dogridge.com.au **Open** 7 days 11–5
Winemaker Fred Howard **Est.** 1991 **Dozens** 10000 **Vyds** 56ha

Dave and Jen Wright had a combined background of dentistry, art and a CSU viticultural degree when they moved from Adelaide to McLaren Flat to become vignerons. They inherited vines planted in the early 1940s as a source for Chateau Reynella fortified wines, and their viticultural empire now ranges from 2001 plantings to some of the oldest vines remaining in the immediate region today. At the McLaren Flat vineyards, DogRidge has 60+-year-old shiraz and grenache. Part of the grape production is retained, but most is sold to other leading wineries. Exports to the UK, the US and other major markets.

Shirtfront McLaren Vale Shiraz 2010 A generous and sweet black-fruited wine, showing mocha, mulberry, licorice and cinnamon on the bouquet; fleshy, forward and soft-centred for early consumption, the generosity of fruit is the key. Ready to go now and for the medium term. Screwcap. 14.5% alc. **Rating** 90 **To** 2020 $25 BE

DogRock Winery

114 De Graves Road, Crowlands, Vic 3377 **Region** Pyrenees
T (03) 5354 9201 **www**.dogrock.com.au **Open** By appt
Winemaker Allen Hart **Est.** 1999 **Dozens** 1000 **Vyds** 6.2ha

This is the micro-venture (but with inbuilt future growth to something slightly larger) of Allen (now full-time winemaker) and Andrea (viticulturist) Hart. Having purchased the property in 1998, the planting of shiraz, riesling, tempranillo, grenache, chardonnay and marsanne began in 2000. Given Allen's former post as research scientist/winemaker with Foster's, the attitude taken to winemaking is unexpected. The estate-grown wines are made in a low-tech fashion, without gas cover or filtration, the Harts saying 'all wine will be sealed with a screwcap and no DogRock wine will ever be released under natural cork bark'. DogRock installed the first solar-powered irrigation system in Australia, capable of supplying water 365 days a year, including at night or in cloudy conditions; irrigation can be continued by water taken from a header dam, automatically refilled when sunlight returns.

Pyrenees Riesling 2012 Fascinating wine; fermented using wild yeasts and kept on lees for 6 months, with no fining agents used nor any acid added (and not needed with a pH of 3.1 and t/a of 6.75g/l) It has great structure from its minerally backbone, and citrus expands dramatically on the finish and aftertaste. Top stuff. Screwcap. 12% alc. **Rating** 94 **To** 2022 $22

ŸŸŸŸŸ   Single Vineyard Pyrenees Shiraz 2011 Rating 91 To 2021 $25
Single Vineyard Pyrenees Grenache 2011 Rating 90 To 2016 $28

Dolan Family Wines   ★★★★

PO Box 500, Angaston, SA 5353 **Region** Barossa Valley
T 0438 816 034 **Open** Not
Winemaker Nigel and Timothy Dolan **Est.** 2007 **Dozens** 1000
Nigel is a fifth-generation member of the Dolan family, son Tim the sixth: truly, wine is in their blood. Nigel's father Bryan enrolled in the first oenology course offered by Roseworthy, graduating in 1949. His 30-year career at Saltram included the capture of the inaugural Jimmy Watson Trophy in '62. There was no nepotism involved when Nigel was appointed chief winemaker of Saltram in 1992, winning major accolades during his 15 years in that role before moving to Wyndham Estate as chief winemaker. Currently he is a consulting winemaker as well as having principal responsibility for Dolan Family Wines. Nigel's son Tim is a graduate of the Adelaide University oenology course, and has worked internationally for a number of Flying Winemaker vintages as well as working in Australia for Kangarilla Road, and most recently for Peter Lehmann Wines, close to home in the Barossa Valley. This is a virtual winery business for both, with neither vineyards nor winery – just lots of experience. Exports to Hong Kong.

ŸŸŸŸŸ   **Rifleman's Clare Valley Riesling 2012** Pale quartz; reflects in full measure the
✪   very good vintage for Clare Valley riesling; smooth but intense lime/lemon citrus flavours on the palate mirror the bouquet; it has line, balance and length, and will develop with extreme grace. Screwcap. 12% alc. **Rating** 93 To 2022 $20
Barossa Shiraz Tempranillo 2010 Still bright crimson-purple; this medium-bodied wine has ample, soft black and red fruits, and positive oak; the percentage of tempranillo would appear to be relatively small, but that's as may be. Screwcap. 14.5% alc. **Rating** 90 To 2020 $24

Domain Day   ★★★★☆

24 Queen Street, Williamstown, SA 5351 **Region** Barossa Valley
T (08) 8524 6224 **www**.domainday.com.au **Open** 7 days 12–5
Winemaker Robin Day **Est.** 2000 **Dozens** 8000 **Vyds** 15.5ha
This is a classic case of an old dog learning new tricks, and doing so with panache. Robin Day had a long and distinguished career as winemaker, chief winemaker, then technical director of Orlando; he participated in the management buy-out, and profited substantially from the on-sale to Pernod Ricard. He hastened slowly with the establishment of Domain Day, but there is nothing conservative about his approach in his vineyard at Mt Crawford, high in the hills (at 450m) of the southeastern extremity of the Barossa Valley, two sides of the vineyard bordering the Eden Valley. While the mainstream varieties are merlot, pinot noir and riesling, he has trawled Italy, France and Georgia for the other varieties: viognier, sangiovese, saperavi, lagrein, garganega, sagrantino and nebbiolo. Robin says, 'Years of writing descriptions for back labels have left me convinced that this energy is more gainfully employed in growing grapes and making wine.' Robin provides tutored tastings in the vineyard, showcasing alternative varieties (by appointment). Exports to Canada and China.

ŸŸŸŸŸ   **One Serious Mt Crawford Riesling 2011** Light, bright straw-green; an
     intense, tightly wound riesling with a backbone of slatey minerality, then a long, finely focused and balanced palate attesting to the very cool vintage. A seriously long life ahead. Screwcap. 12% alc. **Rating** 94 To 2026 $22

ŸŸŸŸŸ   **One Serious Mt Crawford Sangiovese 2009** Rating 92 To 2017 $30
One Serious Mt Crawford Sangiovese 2007 Rating 91 To 2017 $30
Mt Crawford Garganega 2011 Rating 90 To 2013 $22
One Serious Mt Crawford Pinot Noir 2009 Rating 90 To 2016 $35
Dolcezza Late Harvest Garganega 2008 Rating 90 To 2015 $20

Domaine A

Tea Tree Road, Campania, Tas 7026 **Region** Southern Tasmania
T (03) 6260 4174 **www**.domaine-a.com.au **Open** Mon–Fri 10–4
Winemaker Peter Althaus **Est.** 1973 **Dozens** 5000 **Vyds** 11ha
The striking black label of the premium Domaine A wine, dominated by the single, multicoloured 'A', signified the change of ownership from George Park to Peter Althaus many years ago. The wines are made without compromise, and reflect the low yields from the immaculately tended vineyards. They represent aspects of both Old World and New World philosophies, techniques and styles. Exports to the UK, Canada, Denmark, Switzerland, Taiwan, Hong Kong, Singapore, Japan and China.

♡♡♡♡♡ **Lady A Sauvignon Blanc 2010** Picked in small batches, fermented in new
French oak, matured on lees for 12 months before being bottled, then given
a further 2 years on cork. Green-straw, this is a unique Sauvignon Blanc with
unparalleled intensity and complexity, its array of grass, capsicum and citrus
flavours, the oak at once obvious yet seamless. Cork. 14% alc. **Rating** 96
To 2020 $60
Cabernet Sauvignon 2006 A 90/4/4/2% blend of cabernet sauvignon,
cabernet franc, merlot and petit verdot matured in new French barriques for
3 years, than matured in bottle in the cellar for a further 2 years. Full, deep colour;
an uncompromisingly full-bodied Bordeaux-style blend, the red and black fruits
not challenged – rather, heavily supported – by the oak and tannins. Cork. 14%
alc. **Rating** 95 **To** 2026 $120
Cabernet Sauvignon 2007 A 90/4/4/2% blend of cabernet sauvignon,
cabernet franc, merlot and petit verdot matured in new French barriques for
3 years. Medium red-purple; spicy blackcurrant aromas flow into the palate where
the black fruits stand toe to toe with the tannins, and ultimately prevail, laying the
base for a very long life. Diam. 13.5% alc. **Rating** 94 **To** 2037 $120

♡♡♡♡♡ **Pinot Noir 2009** **Rating** 93 **To** 2024 $90

Domaine Asmara

Gibb Road, Toolleen, Vic 3551 **Region** Heathcote
T (03) 5433 6133 **www**.domaineasmara.com **Open** 7 days 9–6.30
Winemaker Sanguine Estate **Est.** 2008 **Dozens** 2500 **Vyds** 12ha
Chemical engineer Andreas Greiving had a lifelong dream to own and operate a vineyard, and the opportunity came along with the global financial crisis. He was able to purchase a vineyard planted to shiraz (7ha), cabernet sauvignon (2ha), cabernet franc, durif and viognier (1ha each), and have the wines contract-made. The venture is co-managed by dentist wife Hennijati. Exports to the UK and China.

♡♡♡♡♡ **Reserve Heathcote Shiraz 2010** Deep crimson-purple; the fragrant and
expressive bouquet with spicy black fruits introduces a high-quality Shiraz, with
supple black fruits, spices and licorice, supported by integrated oak and fine,
ripe tannins. The balance ensures its long life. Screwcap. 14.5% alc. **Rating** 95
To 2030 $45

♡♡♡♡♡ **Heathcote Viognier 2012** **Rating** 90 **To** 2014 $25

Domaine Chandon

727 Maroondah Highway, Coldstream, Vic 3770 **Region** Yarra Valley
T (03) 9738 9200 **www**.chandon.com.au **Open** 7 days 10.30–4.30
Winemaker Dan Buckle, Glenn Thompson, Adam Keath **Est.** 1986 **Dozens** 120 000
Vyds 106.9ha
Established by Möet & Chandon, this is one of the two most important wine facilities in the Yarra Valley; the tasting room has a national and international reputation, having won a number of major tourism awards in recent years. The sparkling wine product range has evolved, and there has been increasing emphasis placed on the table wines, now released under

the Domaine Chandon label. An energetic winemaking team under the leadership of Dan Buckle has maintained the high quality standards. Exports to all major markets.

🍷🍷🍷🍷🍷 **Barrel Selection Chardonnay 2012** Pale quartz; in the heart of contemporary practices of chardonnay sculpting in the Yarra Valley, all designed to throw the emphasis onto fruit purity and length of flavour; the intensity and persistence of the grapefruit/white peach flavours have completely absorbed the oak, leaving only the imprint on texture. Screwcap. 13% alc. **Rating** 96 **To** 2020 **$46**

Barrel Selection Pinot Noir 2012 Full, clear purple-crimson, outstanding for pinot noir; has exceptional length and depth to its palate, with the red and black cherry flavours signalled by the bouquet; a feature is the quality of the tannins, which are fine-grained and persistent; high-quality oak also contributes. Screwcap. 12.5% alc. **Rating** 96 **To** 2022 **$50**

Vintage Collection Cuvee 500 2008 The King Valley provides the pinot noir, the chardonnay coming from Macedon and Strathbogie Ranges. Exceptionally pale colour for its age, but has good mousse; the bouquet and palate are complex, with the suggestion of some controlled aldehyde adding to the impact and length. Food style. Diam. 12.5% alc. **Rating** 95 **To** 2016 **$45**

Vintage Yarra Valley Cuvee 2008 This blend of 60/40% pinot noir and chardonnay was made with a final blend of 18 individual base wines. Excellent mousse to the pale colour, which has a faint touch of pink from the dominant pinot noir component; has exceptionally good mouthfeel and balance, all adding up to elegance on a major scale. Diam. 12.5% alc. **Rating** 95 **To** 2016 **$40**

Prestige Cuvee 2004 Follows the Domaine Chandon path of multi-region, multi-varietal blend, the same approach adopted in Champagne. Bright straw-green; extended lees contact has built texture and depth; toasty/brioche on the bouquet, the palate adding length; very good acid balance. Diam. 12.5% alc. **Rating** 95 **To** 2016 **$89**

Yarra Valley Chardonnay 2011 **Rating** 94 **To** 2017 **$28**
Yarra Valley Pinot Noir 2012 **Rating** 94 **To** 2019 **$34**
Heathcote Shiraz 2010 **Rating** 94 **To** 2025 **$34**
Vintage Brut 2009 **Rating** 94 **To** 2014 **$40**
Blanc de Blancs 2009 **Rating** 94 **To** 2014 **$40**
Tasmanian Cuvee 2009 **Rating** 94 **To** 2017 **$40**

🍷🍷🍷🍷 **Yarra Valley Chardonnay 2012** **Rating** 93 **To** 2019 **$28**
Sauvignon Blanc 2012 **Rating** 92 **To** 2014 **$25**
Pinot Gris 2012 **Rating** 92 **To** 2013 **$28**
Z*D Blanc de Blancs 2009 **Rating** 92 **To** 2014 **$40**
Pinot Noir Rose 2012 **Rating** 91 **To** 2013 **$25**
Brut NV **Rating** 91 **To** 2015 **$29**
Brut Rose NV **Rating** 91 **To** 2015 **$29**
Chandon Sparkling Pinot Noir Shiraz NV **Rating** 91 **To** 2014 **$29**
Yarra Valley Pinot Noir 2011 **Rating** 90 **To** 2014 **$34**

Domaine Rogha Crois Wines ★★★☆

PO Box 436, Bungendore, NSW 2621 **Region** Canberra District
T (02) 6238 0500 **www.**drcwine.com.au **Open** Not
Winemaker Malcolm Burdett, Andrew McEwin, Greg Gallagher **Est.** 1998 **Dozens** 400
Vyds 2ha

David and Lyn Crossley purchased their property on the Lake George escarpment in 1998, planting clonally selected pinot noir, pinot gris, cabernet franc and merlot over the following two years. Their inspiration was the pioneering work done by Dr Edgar Riek. The vineyard is on a steep hillside at 800–840m, often snow-covered in winter, but is protected from frosts by its slope. The small size of the vineyard facilitates micro-management of the vines throughout the year. The name is Gaelic for 'quality cross'.

ŶŶŶŶŶ **Cuvee 2010** A blend of pinot noir and chardonnay made in the traditional method and spending 2 years on lees; clean, fresh and well balanced, it has good length. Complexity will come with a few more years on cork (or on lees if progressively disgorged). Zork SPK. 12.8% alc. **Rating** 90 **To** 2015 $37

Domaines Tatiarra ★★★★☆

2 Corrong Court, Eltham, Vic 3095 (postal) **Region** Heathcote
T 0428 628 420 **www**.tatiarra.com **Open** Not
Winemaker Ben Riggs **Est.** 1991 **Dozens** 4500 **Vyds** 13.4ha
Domaines Tatiarra Ltd. is an unlisted public company, its core asset being a 60ha property of Cambrian earth identified and developed by Bill Hepburn, who sold it to the company in 1991. It produces only one varietal wine: Shiraz. The majority of the wine comes from the Tatiarra (an Aboriginal word meaning 'beautiful country') property, but the Trademark Shiraz is an equal blend of McLaren Vale and Heathcote wine. The wines are made at the Scotchmans Hill winery in Geelong, with Ben Riggs commuting between there and McLaren Vale as required. Exports to the UK, the US, Canada, Denmark, Switzerland, Singapore and China.

ŶŶŶŶŶ **Culled Barrel Heathcote Shiraz 2010** Uninspiring colour turns out to be
✪ irrelevant, for the wine has plenty of blackberry, licorice and spice fruit supported by ripe tannins and good oak. Ben Riggs' skills to the fore. Screwcap. 14.5% alc. **Rating** 92 **To** 2025 $23
Cambrian Heathcote Shiraz 2009 Full crimson-purple; a full-bodied, rich and unctuous wine, the crosscut of spicy/savoury notes partially obscuring the alcohol level. I simply don't understand why it was necessary to delay picking for so long. Screwcap. 15.5% alc. **Rating** 91 **To** 2029 $43

Dominique Portet ★★★★★

870–872 Maroondah Highway, Coldstream, Vic 3770 **Region** Yarra Valley
T (03) 5962 5760 **www**.dominiqueportet.com **Open** 7 days 10–5
Winemaker Ben Portet **Est.** 2000 **Dozens** 12 000 **Vyds** 4.3ha
Dominique Portet was bred in the purple. He spent his early years at Chateau Lafite (where his father was régisseur) and was one of the very first Flying Winemakers, commuting to Clos du Val in the Napa Valley, where his brother was winemaker. He then spent over 20 years as managing director of Taltarni and Clover Hill in Tasmania. After retiring from Taltarni, he moved to the Yarra Valley, a region he had been closely observing since the mid 1980s. In 2001 he found the site he had long looked for and in the twinkling of an eye built his winery and cellar door, planting a quixotic mix of viognier, sauvignon blanc and merlot next to the winery. Son Ben is now executive winemaker, leaving Dominique with a roving role as de facto consultant and brand marketer. Ben (32) has a winemaking CV of awesome scope, covering all parts of France, South Africa, California and four vintages at Petaluma. Exports to Canada, Denmark, India, Dubai, Hong Kong, Singapore, Malaysia, China and Japan.

ŶŶŶŶŶ **Yarra Valley Chardonnay 2011** Pale straw-green; immediately commands attention with texture and structure that effortlessly carry the elegant white peach and rockmelon fruit; citrus-tinged acidity draws out the finish and aftertaste. Overall, has uncommon elegance and length. Screwcap. 13% alc. **Rating** 96 **To** 2020 $36
Andre Pierre Yarra Valley Heathcote Shiraz Cabernet 2008 Medium purple-crimson; a wine built for the ages; a complex web of blackberry, blackcurrant and spices; high-quality oak and tannins threaded through the entire palate are all in imperious balance. Cork. 14.5% alc. **Rating** 94 **To** 2038 $150
Yarra Valley Brut Rose LD NV Full salmon-pink; a traditional method pinot noir and chardonnay blend sourced entirely from the Yarra Valley, 'LD' standing for light dosage, not late disgorged. That dosage is in fact precisely balanced; more would have obscured the spicy red berry and white peach fruit. An elegant wine. Diam. 13% alc. **Rating** 94 **To** 2015 $28

ŶŶŶŶŶ **Heathcote Shiraz 2011 Rating** 93 **To** 2026 $48
Yarra Valley Sauvignon Blanc 2012 Rating 92 **To** 2014 $28

✪ **Fontaine Yarra Valley Pyrenees Rose 2012** Very pale, but bright, pink; a blend of cabernet sauvignon, merlot and shiraz with a fragrant, flowery bouquet, and perfectly weighted palate, its delicate red fruits given structure by admirable acidity (and no sweetness). Screwcap. 13% alc. **Rating** 92 **To** 2014 $22

Donny Goodmac ★★★★

PO Box 467, Healesville, Vic 3777 **Region** Yarra Valley
T (03) 5962 3779 **www**.donnygoodmac.com.au **Open** Not
Winemaker Kate Goodman **Est.** 2002 **Dozens** 500

The improbable name is a typically whimsical invention of the three proprietors: Donny is contributed by Stuart Gregor, whose marketing and PR prowess has hitherto prevented an entry for the venture in the *Wine Companion*. Kate Goodman is the (genuinely) good part of the team, while Cameron MacKenzie is the 'mac'. Kate and Cameron both work full-time at Punt Road, where Kate is chief winemaker. What started as a little bit of fun in 2002 (less than 50 dozen made) has grown to the dizzy heights of 600 dozen, utilising old-vine shiraz from the Pyrenees, and chardonnay and cabernet sauvignon from a couple of old vineyards in the Coldstream area of the Yarra Valley.

🍷🍷🍷🍷 **Individual Vineyard Pyrenees Shiraz 2010** The three partners should know how to spell 'its' in possessive usage (not it's) on the back label, which is about the only negative I can find to write about this elegant, spicy/juicy/black cherry medium-bodied wine. Matured in French oak (33% new) following a gentle, non-interventionist fermentation of grapes relishing the end of a long, hot drought, it is very well balanced. Screwcap. 13.2% alc. **Rating** 93 **To** 2025 $35

Dorrien Estate ★★★★★

Cnr Barossa Valley Way/Siegersdorf Road, Tanunda, SA 5352 **Region** Barossa Valley
T (08) 8561 2200 **www**.cellarmasters.com.au **Open** Not
Winemaker Corey Ryan (Chief) **Est.** 1982 **Dozens** 1 million

Dorrien Estate is the physical base of the vast Cellarmasters network that, wearing its retailer's hat, is by far the largest direct-sale outlet in Australia. It also makes wine for many producers across Australia at its modern winery, which has a capacity of 14.5 million litres of wine in tank and barrel; however, a typical make of each wine will be little more than 1000 dozen. Most of the wines made for others are exclusively distributed by Cellarmasters. (Chateau Dorrien is an entirely unrelated business.) Acquired by Woolworths in May 2011. Exports to the UK and NZ.

🍷🍷🍷🍷🍷 **Dorrien Estate Bin 1A Chardonnay 2011** An innovative blend of Margaret River, Coal River (Tasmania) and Mount Benson grapes has worked brilliantly. Barrel fermentation in French oak has brought out the abundant white peach, nectarine and grapefruit flavours of the long palate; Bin 1A is the pinnacle of the vintage for Dorrien Estate. Screwcap. 13.5% alc. **Rating** 95 **To** 2018 $36

✪ **Mockingbird Hill Clare Valley Riesling 2012** Made from a single vineyard in the Watervale area. Pale quartz-green, it has an impressive mix of lime, lemon and crisp, minerally, acidity; the length, finish and aftertaste cannot be faulted. No need to comment on the great value. Screwcap. 12% alc. **Rating** 94 **To** 2022 $21

Redemption Landmark Release Tumbarumba Chardonnay 2011 Has marked intensity thanks in part to its high natural acidity, and has an extremely long, citrus/grapefruit palate that has soaked up the oak in which it was fermented. Will flourish. Screwcap. 12% alc. **Rating** 94 **To** 2020 $47

Dorrien Estate Bin 1 Barossa Valley Shiraz 2010 Bright crimson-purple; reflects the very good vintage, with an array of black fruits, dark chocolate, spice, and cedary oak that is balanced and integrated, as are the tannins. Screwcap. 14.5% alc. **Rating** 94 **To** 2030 $44

Shark's Block McLaren Vale Shiraz 2010 Deep purple-crimson; has a clear-cut sense of place, with black fruits, dark chocolate and cedar aromas and flavours; the medium-bodied structure is supported by fluffy tannins on the long, almost juicy, finish. Screwcap. 14% alc. **Rating** 94 **To** 2025 $39

Krondorf Symmetry Barossa Valley Shiraz 2010 Good hue; a very well made medium- to full-bodied wine, with black fruits (cherry and berry) shot through with ripe tannins and integrated oak; excellent balance. Screwcap. 14.5% alc. **Rating** 94 **To** 2030 $45

Black Wattle Vineyards Icon Mount Benson Cabernet Sauvignon 2010 Deep crimson-purple; a prolific gold medal wine show winner over the years, and this full-bodied Cabernet has the complexity and depth to its blackcurrant and cedar flavours, plus ripe tannins, to continue that success. Will be very long-lived. Screwcap. 14.5% alc. **Rating** 94 **To** 2040 $46

Dorrien Estate Bin 1 Barossa Valley Cabernet Sauvignon 2010 Moderately deep red-purple, bright and clear; has an abundance of juicy cassis and redcurrant fruit with spicy/cedary oak; the Barossa Valley only gives cabernet sauvignon a chance to express itself as clearly as this in occasional vintages, and the oak has also been well chosen and handled. Screwcap. 14.5% alc. **Rating** 94 **To** 2030 $43

Dorrien Estate Bin 1A Cabernet Sauvignon 2010 Bin 1A is said to be the pinnacle of wine made at the estate, yet this is significantly less expensive than either the Icon Black Wattle or Bin 1 Cabernet Sauvignons. Moreover, it comes from the Margaret River in a Burgundy-shaped bottle, and the colour is light albeit with good hue; it is an elegant, medium-bodied wine with cassis to the fore, spice and cedary oak and fine tannins framing the fruit. Screwcap. 13% alc. **Rating** 94 **To** 2025 $37

Black Wattle Vineyards Icon Cabernet Sauvignon 2009 Cabernet fruit is in a redcurrant rather than blackcurrant/cassis spectrum, although both fruits contribute; it is a wine that leaves it until its finish and juicy aftertaste to really shine, and as such is slightly lateral – the cabernet tannins are so fine they can be missed. Screwcap. 14% alc. **Rating** 94 **To** 2029 $46

♀♀♀♀♀ **Black Wattle Icon Chardonnay 2011 Rating** 93 **To** 2016 $42
Tolley Elite Shiraz 2010 Rating 93 **To** 2025 $38
Black Wattle Sauvignon Blanc 2012 Rating 92 **To** 2014 $25
Krondorf Symmetry Chardonnay 2011 Rating 92 **To** 2019 $31
Black Wattle Chardonnay 2011 Rating 91 **To** 2017 $27
Dorrien Estate The Growers Shiraz 2011 Rating 91 **To** 2021 $26
Mockingbird Hill Reserve Shiraz 2010 Rating 90 **To** 2025 $28
The Ridge Cabernet Sauvignon 2011 Rating 90 **To** 2015 $23

Dowie Doole   ★★★★☆

276 California Road, McLaren Vale, SA 5171 **Region** McLaren Vale
T (08) 8323 8875 **www**.dowiedoole.com **Open** By appt
Winemaker Chris Thomas **Est.** 1996 **Dozens** 25 000 **Vyds** 44.35ha
Dowie Doole was born of the frustration following the 1995 vintage, which led friends Norm Doole and Drew Dowie to form a partnership to take control of the destiny of their grapes. In '98, Leigh Gilligan, a McLaren Vale veteran, was appointed to take overall control of the business, and joined the partnership. Founding winemaker Brian Light has stepped back to a consultancy role following the appointment of Chris Thomas as winemaker in 2011. Sami Gilligan, Lulu Lunn and Dave Gartelmann share responsibility for the five vineyards in which Dowie Doole has an interest, all managed using sustainable viticulture practices. Exports to the UK, the US, Canada, Denmark, Germany, Hong Kong, Thailand and China.

♀♀♀♀♀ **Scarce Earth California Road 74 Block McLaren Vale Shiraz 2010** Full red-purple; certainly has a strong sense of place, with its generous display of blackberry, plum and dark chocolate; the medium- to full-bodied palate has excellent texture, structure and balance. Diam. 14.5% alc. **Rating** 94 **To** 2025 $45

♀♀♀♀♀ **Second Nature Adelaide Hills Sauvignon Blanc 2012** Pale straw-green; the
✪ wine takes a millisecond before its impact hits the palate, with green apple, citrus zest and minerally acidity driving through the length of the palate, lingering long on the aftertaste. Screwcap. 13% alc. **Rating** 93 **To** 2014 $18

McLaren Vale Shiraz 2010 Rating 93 To 2030 $25
McLaren Vale Cabernet Sauvignon 2010 Rating 93 To 2030 $25

✪ McLaren Vale Chenin Blanc 2012 Mainly sourced from the 80-year-old vines, believed to be the oldest in Australia of this variety, on Drew Dowie's vineyard in the cool Blewitt Springs area. The wine has excellent intensity and length, with a mix of citrus, melon and lychee flavours, and a crisp, clean finish. Screwcap. 13% alc. Rating 91 To 2016 $16

Downing Estate Vineyard ★★★★★

19 Drummonds Lane, Heathcote, Vic 3523 **Region** Heathcote
T (03) 5433 3387 **www**.downingestate.com.au **Open** Long w'ends & public hols 11–5, or by appt
Winemaker John Ellis **Est.** 1994 **Dozens** 1000 **Vyds** 10ha
Bob Downing purchased 24ha of undulating land in 1994, and has established a dry-grown vineyard planted to shiraz (7.2ha), cabernet sauvignon (2.4ha) and merlot (0.4ha). At any one time, a number of vintages of each wine are available for sale. Exports to Canada, Singapore and China.

🍷🍷🍷🍷🍷 Reserve Heathcote Shiraz 2010 Full, deep purple-crimson; spent 22 months in French oak barriques, and only the best four barriques were selected for this wine, with a total make of 90 dozen. The depth of the plum and blackberry fruit, and the soft tannins, easily carry the oak. Screwcap. 14% alc. Rating 95 To 2030 $85
Heathcote Shiraz Cabernet Sauvignon 2010 A 60/40% blend, with good depth to the still youthful crimson-purple hue; a complex medium- to full-bodied wine, it fuses blackberry, blackcurrant, spice and cedary French oak into a coherent whole, ripe tannins lined up in support. Will outlive some who taste it. Screwcap. 14% alc. Rating 94 To 2035 $34

🍷🍷🍷🍷🍷 Heathcote Merlot 2010 Rating 90 To 2018 $25

Drakesbrook Wines ★★★★

PO Box 284, Waroona, WA 6215 **Region** Peel
T 0427 944 503 **www**.drakesbrook.com.au **Open** Not
Winemaker Bernard Worthington **Est.** 1998 **Dozens** NA **Vyds** 10.46ha
Bernard (Bernie) Worthington, a Perth-based property specialist, developed a serious interest in wine and spent four years looking for a site which met all his criteria: ample water, easy access to a major city and supporting tourist attractions. During that time he also completed a wine-growing course at CSU. His interests coalesced when he found Drakesbrook, a 216ha property taking its name from the Drakesbrook River which flows through it. An hour's drive from Perth, it has views out to the ocean and is adjacent to the Lake Navarino tourist resort. He has subdivided the property, retaining 121ha. The vineyard is planted to semillon, chardonnay, shiraz, merlot, petit verdot, cabernet franc and cabernet sauvignon.

🍷🍷🍷🍷🍷 Wild Bird Savagnin 2012 Drakesbrook believes it is the only winery in WA to grow and make Savagnin, but if it continues to make wines such as this, others will soon follow. It has intense citrus pith/zest and mineral flavours on the long palate and fresh finish. Screwcap. 12% alc. Rating 91 To 2014 $25
Peel Cabernet Franc 2010 All in all a surprise packet, with good colour, texture and structure to the red fruits and contrasting olive notes of the palate; well made in every respect. Screwcap. 14.5% alc. Rating 90 To 2015 $25

🍷🍷🍷🍷 Wild Bird Chardonnay 2011 Rating 89 To 2013 $17
White Tail 2011 Rating 88 To 2014 $16
Wild Bird Grenache Shiraz Merlot 2011 Rating 88 To 2017 $17
Wild Bird Rose 2011 Rating 87 To 2013 $17
Peel Shiraz 2010 Rating 87 To 2014 $19
Wild Bird Malbec 2011 Rating 87 To 2016 $30
Wild Bird Mourvedre 2011 Rating 87 To 2015 $19

Drayton's Family Wines ★★★★

555 Oakey Creek Road, Cessnock, NSW 2321 **Region** Hunter Valley
T (02) 4998 7513 **www**.draytonswines.com.au **Open** Mon–Fri 8–5, w'ends &
public hols 10–5
Winemaker Andrew Leembruggen, Max and John Drayton **Est.** 1853 **Dozens** 60 000
Vyds 72ha
This substantial Hunter Valley producer has suffered more than its share of misfortune over
the years, but has risen to the challenges. Winemaker William (Will) Rikard-Bell, badly
injured in the winery explosion of 2007, retired prior to the '11 vintage to pursue separate
business interests in Orange with wife Kimmy. They parted on good terms, and Drayton's
was able to secure the services of Andrew Leembruggen as chief winemaker after 13 years
with McWilliam's Mount Pleasant. Exports to Ireland, Vietnam, Singapore, Taiwan and China.

ΨΨΨΨΨ **Heritage Vines Cabernet 2011** The youthful crimson colour introduces a
wine with unexpected varietal character in a strong blackcurrant mode backed by
good tannins and quality oak. Screwcap. 13.5% alc. **Rating** 93 **To** 2025 $60
Heritage Vines Liqueur Verdelho NV Golden brown; by far the richest and
most complex of the three Heritage Vines wines, viscous and rich, with abundant
rancio; nuts, Christmas cake, burnt toffee and honey are all present. Added an
additional trophy to its haul at the Hunter Valley Wine Show '12. 500ml. Diam.
17.5% alc. **Rating** 93 **To** 2013 $60
Heritage Vines Tawny 1978 Golden brown; the barrels must have been kept
in a warm part of the shed for the nutty viscosity the wine has to develop; there is
some rancio (although not as much as needed for higher points) and the wine is
a surprise packet and sure-fire cellar-door material. 500ml. Screwcap. 17.5% alc.
Rating 91 **To** 2013 $60
Heritage Vines Chardonnay 2011 Bright straw-green; a well-made wine with
good mouthfeel and balance to its nectarine and rockmelon fruit, the finish with
crisp acidity, any oak incidental to the main game. The price may cause some
raised eyebrows. Screwcap. 12.5% alc. **Rating** 90 **To** 2015 $60
Bin 5555 Hunter Valley Shiraz 2011 Mid crimson, bright; a fragrant and
bright red-fruited bouquet, also showing a splash of spicy oak; the palate is light-
to medium-bodied, fresh and polished on the finish. Screwcap. 14% alc. **Rating** 90
To 2018 $20 BE

ΨΨΨΨ **Vineyard Reserve Pokolbin Chardonnay 2011** Rating 88 **To** 2016 $30 BE
Heritage Vines Muscat NV Rating 88 **To** 2013 $60
William Shiraz 2007 Rating 87 **To** 2018 $45 BE

Dromana Estate ★★★★☆

555 Old Moorooduc Road, Tuerong, Vic 3933 **Region** Mornington Peninsula
T (03) 5974 4400 **www**.dromanaestate.com.au **Open** Wed–Sun 11–5
Winemaker Duncan Buchanan **Est.** 1982 **Dozens** 30 000 **Vyds** 53.9ha
Since it was established 30 years ago, Dromana Estate has always been near or at the cutting
edge, both in marketing terms and in terms of development of new varietals, most obviously
the Italian range under the 'i' label. Dromana Estate is owned by the investors of a publicly
listed company, operating under the name of Mornington Winery Group Limited. It includes
the Dromana Estate, Mornington Estate and David Traeger (see separate entry) labels.
Expanded production has seen export markets increase. Exports to the US, Canada and China.

ΨΨΨΨΨ **Mornington Estate Sauvignon Blanc 2012** Green-quartz; a combination of
tank and barrel fermentation has worked very well indeed, adding texture without
trimming the length or tropical-accented varietal expression, finishing with citrussy
acidity. Screwcap. 13% alc. **Rating** 94 **To** 2014 $25

ΨΨΨΨΨ **Mornington Estate Chardonnay 2011** Rating 93 **To** 2018 $25
Chardonnay 2011 Rating 92 **To** 2017 $35
i Mornington Peninsula Arneis 2010 Rating 90 **To** 2015 $22 BE
Mornington Peninsula Pinot Noir 2011 Rating 90 **To** 2016 $35 BE

Dryridge Estate

The Six Foot Track, Megalong Valley, NSW 2785 **Region** Central Ranges Zone
T (02) 4787 5625 **www**.dryridge.com.au **Open** W'ends from 11 am, or by appt
Winemaker Madrez Wine Services (Chris Derrez, Lucy Maddox) **Est.** 2000
Dozens 1000 **Vyds** 3.8ha

Bob and Barbara Tyrrell (no relation to Tyrrell's of the Hunter Valley) have pioneered commercial viticulture in the Megalong Valley, adjacent to the Blue Mountains National Park. They have 1.8ha of riesling, 1.1ha of shiraz and 0.9ha of cabernet sauvignon, and a further 0.9ha to be planted (possibly fiano) in due course. The vines are set on typically east-facing rolling hillsides, with granitic-derived light, sandy clay loam soils of moderately low fertility. Sunrise Lodge provides 4.5-star accommodation overlooking the vineyard.

ŸŸŸŸŸ **Blue Mountains Riesling 2012** Pale quartz-white; an attractive Riesling in every respect, with good varietal expression achieved at a modest alcohol level, the flavours right in the heartland of lime/lemon citrus fruit, and balanced by crisp acidity. Screwcap. 11.5% alc. **Rating** 91 **To** 2018 $25

✪ **Nellie's Cabernet Rose 2011** Pale crimson-purple; the fragrant bouquet has a mix of redcurrant and herb reflecting its variety, the palate well balanced and long, the finish supple and fruity, but not sugar-sweet. Screwcap. 12.5% alc. **Rating** 90 **To** 2014 $20

Ducketts Mill

1678, Scotsdale Road, Denmark, WA 6333 **Region** Denmark
T (08) 9840 9844 **www**.duckettsmillwines.com.au **Open** 7 days 10–4
Winemaker Harewood Estate (James Kellie) **Est.** 1997 **Dozens** 800 **Vyds** 8ha

Ducketts Mill is a twin operation with Denmark Farmhouse Cheese, both owned and operated by Ross and Dallas Lewis. They have the only cheese factory in the Great Southern region, and rely on James Kellie to make the wines from the extensive estate plantings (riesling, chardonnay, semillon, sauvignon blanc, merlot, cabernet franc, ruby cabernet and cabernet sauvignon). Some of the grapes are sold, some made into Riesling, Semillon Sauvignon Blanc, Late Harvest Riesling, Rose, Merlot and Three Cabernets and sold at low prices.

ŸŸŸŸŸ **Denmark Shiraz 2009** Good hue; a light- to medium-bodied Shiraz that has a
✪ complex range of flavours encompassing blackberry, red cherry, spice, licorice and cedary oak, in turn supported by persistent, feathery tannins. Screwcap. 14.5% alc. **Rating** 90 **To** 2017 $18

ŸŸŸŸ **Denmark Merlot 2009** Rating 87 **To** 2014 $16
Denmark Three Cabernets 2010 Rating 87 **To** 2014 $16
Denmark Late Harvest Riesling 2011 Rating 87 **To** 2015 $14

Ducks in a Row Winemakers

11 Stonehouse Lane, Aldinga, SA 5173 **Region** McLaren Vale
T 0413 445 534 **www**.ducksinarow.com.au **Open** By appt
Winemaker Glenn James-Pritchard **Est.** 2009 **Dozens** 1200

This is a life and winemaking partnership that (in their words) 'draws on the experience and knowledge of two people who fell for each other over their shared love of wine'. The two are former Foster's/Treasury Wine Estates senior winemaker Glenn James-Pritchard and wine marketer wife Amanda. I suspect she was responsible for the following words, 'Glenn is the brains behind the entire operation. Amanda is an avid product sampler and sometimes nails a press release. Other times she offends journalists with her use of the term "balls".' As well as giving up secure employment with guaranteed income, they have decided to forsake the security of mainstream varieties such as shiraz and chardonnay, instead focusing on aglianico, fiano and vermentino for white wines, mataro for the first red.

ΨΨΨΨΨ **Tempranillo Graciano Mataro 2011** All McLaren Vale-grown grapes, a 45/45/10% blend. It spent 1 week on skins with vigorous hand-plunging, then basket-pressed to old hogsheads. The colour is deep, the bouquet with strong black fruit aromas, and the seemingly inevitable touch of dark chocolate; a strong spice character runs through the palate, originally with red pepper, ageing into green pepper; outstanding tannin management is the key to an exceptionally good wine. Screwcap. 13.5% alc. **Rating** 96 **To** 2025 $25

Fiano 2011 100% from the Chalmers vineyard in Heathcote. Fermented with wild yeast, with no acid added at any stage, nor SO_2 until shortly prior to bottling after 12 months on lees. Winemaker Glenn James-Pritchard says, 'I was scared of its flavour' early in the maturation phase. It has an entirely unexpected streak of minerality underpinning the texture and structure, and contributing to the salivating effect of the wine in the mouth; it is multidimensional, yet precise, and has exceptional length. Screwcap. 12.8% alc. **Rating** 95 **To** 2016 $25

Pandora's Amphora 2011 A 45/45/10% blend of vermentino, fiano and muscat giallo, all from Chalmers vineyard in Heathcote. Picked on the same day; after destemming, the must was taken straight to an amphora where it remained for 7 months, during which time it went through a natural mlf, then basket-pressed and matured for 7 months in a used puncheon. It was bottled without any form of filtration or stabilisation, and is faintly hazy, albeit with a bright yellow colour (no orange wine here). In terms of its weight and mouthfeel, it is a red wine masquerading as a white, but the mouth-coating flavours, with nuances of cinnamon, honeycomb and dried fruits, are emphatically white. 567 bottles made, sold in three-packs. Cork. 14% alc. **Rating** 95 **To** 2018 $80

Vermentino 2012 60% of the grapes come from Heathcote, 40% from the Barossa Valley, the two components made separately. The wine has exceptional texture, richness and depth, a by-product of wild yeast ferment on juice with full solids, and no SO_2 added until shortly prior to bottling. Matured in old oak. Screwcap. 12.8% alc. **Rating** 94 **To** 2016 $25

Mataro 2010 Made from a single planting of 63-year-old vines in McLaren Vale. It is medium- to full-bodied, with masses of dark/black fruits, with a density to the flavour and mouthfeel greater than the other reds, although not Pandora's Amphora. There are also licorice and dark chocolate flavours with inbuilt tannins. Screwcap. 14.5% alc. **Rating** 94 **To** 2040 $25

Nero d'Avola 2011 Sourced from Chalmers vineyard in Heathcote, and picked in two lots, 1 week apart. It has a brilliant crimson colour, and literally explodes in the mouth, intensely spicy yet savoury, red cherry and sour cherry each competing for space. This is a red wine masquerading as a white, with its post mlf analysis of 3.2pH and 7.2g/L acidity. Hard to imagine a better lunch wine. Screwcap. 12.5% alc. **Rating** 94 **To** 2020 $25

Dudley Wines   ★★★☆

1153 Willoughby Road, Penneshaw, Kangaroo Island, SA 5222 **Region** Kangaroo Island
T (08) 8553 1333 **www**.dudleywines.com.au **Open** 7 days 10–5
Winemaker Brodie Howard **Est.** 1994 **Dozens** 3500 **Vyds** 14ha

Jeff and Val Howard own Dudley Wines and its three vineyards on Kangaroo Island's Dudley Peninsula: the Porky Flat Vineyard, Hog Bay River and Sawyers. It is the quirky vineyard names that give the wines their distinctive identities. The Howards not only look after viticulture, but also join in the winemaking process. Most of the wines are sold through licensed outlets on Kangaroo Island.

ΨΨΨΨΨ **Grassy Flat Kangaroo Island Sauvignon Blanc 2012** Light straw-green;
✪   there is an unusually intense and focused stream of ripe citrus and tropical fruits
running down the centre of the palate, and lingering well into the aftertaste.
Screwcap. 12% alc. **Rating** 93 **To** 2014 $20

ΨΨΨΨ **MacDonnell Kangaroo Island Merlot 2009** **Rating** 87 **To** 2014 $20

Duke's Vineyard ★★★★★

Porongurup Road, Porongurup, WA 6324 **Region** Porongurup
T (08) 9853 1107 **www**.dukesvineyard.com **Open** 7 days 10–4.30
Winemaker Robert Diletti **Est.** 1998 **Dozens** 3500 **Vyds** 10ha
When Hilde and Ian (Duke) Ranson sold their clothing manufacturing business in 1998, they were able to fulfil a long-held dream of establishing a vineyard in the Porongurup subregion of Great Southern with the acquisition of a 65ha farm at the foot of the Porongurup Range. They planted shiraz and cabernet sauvignon (3ha each) and riesling (4ha). Hilde, a successful artist, designed the beautiful, scalloped, glass-walled cellar door sales area, with its mountain blue cladding. The appointment of Rob Diletti as winemaker has underwritten the quality of the wines.

🍷🍷🍷🍷🍷 Magpie Hill Reserve Riesling 2012 Light straw-green; the bouquet has nuances of citrus, herb and spice; the palate is a different matter, with a vibrant shaft of lime and lemon buttressed by flinty acidity on the lingering finish and aftertaste. Screwcap. 12.3% alc. **Rating** 96 **To** 2027 $27

✪ Single Vineyard Porongurup Riesling 2012 Pale quartz-green; its clarity and finesse are accentuated by its bone-dry, lingering finish. Perfectly balanced lime, apple and mineral aromas and flavours guarantee this wine will develop superbly over 10–20+ years. Screwcap. 11.9% alc. **Rating** 96 **To** 2032 $20

Invitation Winemaker James Kellie Riesling 2012 A scented, blossom-filled bouquet leads into a palate that is delicate, yet offers a bewitching array of flavours spanning apple, lime and passionfruit; however delicious it is today, its best years are in front of it. Screwcap. 11.5% alc. **Rating** 94 **To** 2022 $27

🍷🍷🍷🍷 Magpie Hill Reserve Cabernet Sauvignon 2010 **Rating** 93 **To** 2030 $30
Magpie Hill Reserve Sparkling Shiraz 2010 **Rating** 92 **To** 2017 $30

✪ Porongurup Cabernet Sauvignon 2010 Medium red-purple; less new French oak allows the fruit, even though less rich that of Magpie Hill Reserve, to express itself better. Drink this while its big brother settles down. WAK screwcap. 13.2% alc. **Rating** 91 **To** 2020 $20

Magpie Hill Reserve Sparkling Riesling 2010 **Rating** 90 **To** 2014 $27

✪ Single Vineyard Autumn Riesling 2012 Barely off-dry, its acidity partially masking the residual sugar; apple, pear and citrus fruits drive the crisp and lively palate. Will improve and expand with age. Screwcap. 11.5% alc. **Rating** 90 **To** 2018 $19

Dutschke Wines ★★★★★

Lot 1 Gods Hill Road, Lyndoch, SA 5351 **Region** Barossa Valley
T (08) 8524 5485 **www**.dutschkewines.com **Open** By appt
Winemaker Wayne Dutschke **Est.** 1998 **Dozens** 6000 **Vyds** 67ha
Wayne Dutschke spent over 20 years working in Australia and overseas for companies large and small before joining his uncle (and grapegrower) Ken Semmler to form Dutschke Wines. In addition to outstanding table wines, he has a yearly release of fortified wines (doubtless drawing on his time at Baileys of Glenrowan); these sell out overnight, and have received the usual stratospheric points from Robert Parker Jr. The quality of the wines is in fact exemplary. Exports to the US, Canada, Denmark, Germany and The Netherlands.

🍷🍷🍷🍷🍷 Oscar Semmler Lyndoch Barossa Valley Shiraz 2010 Full crimson-purple; the quality of the vintage shines through in this distinguished wine, with its array of juicy dark fruits and spice framed by quality oak and fine, persistent tannins. At the start of a long, multifaceted life. Screwcap. 14.8% alc. **Rating** 96 **To** 2040 $60

Single Barrel St Jakobi Vineyard 78 & 95 Blocks Lyndoch Barossa Valley Cabernet Shiraz 2010 Deep purple-crimson; moves across into the bigger is better, biggest is most, camp, but you have to admire the wine, with more layers of black fruits than might seem possible, high-quality oak and tannins to sustain it for upwards of 50 years. Screwcap. 15% alc. **Rating** 96 **To** 2060 $125

St Jakobi Single Vineyard Lyndoch Barossa Valley Shiraz 2010 Impressive purple-crimson colour; more open and accessible than the Oscar Semmler at this early stage, with ripe plum and black fruit aromas and flavours; the palate supple and round, tannins and oak in a harmonious support role. Screwcap. 14.8% alc. Rating 95 To 2030 $38

80 Block St Jakobi Merlot 2011 Rating 92 To 2016 $25
GHR Neighbours Barossa Valley Shiraz 2011 Rating 91 To 2015 $25
Willow Bend Shiraz Cabernet Merlot 2011 Rating 91 To 2021 $22

Eagle Vale Estate ★★★★☆

7087 Caves Road, Margaret River, WA 6285 **Region** Margaret River
T (08) 9757 6477 **www**.eaglevalewine.com **Open** Mon–Fri 10–4.30, w'ends by appt
Winemaker Guy Gallienne **Est.** 1997 **Dozens** 15000 **Vyds** 11.5ha
Eagle Vale is the venture of Colorado businessman Steve Jacobs and the management/ winemaking team of Chantal and Guy Gallienne. The Galliennes come from the Loire Valley, although Guy secured his winemaking degree at Roseworthy College/Adelaide University. The vineyard is managed on a low-impact basis, without pesticides (guinea fowls do the work) and with minimal irrigation. All the wines are made from estate-grown grapes. Exports to the UK, the US, the Seychelles, China and Hong Kong.

Whispering Lake Single Vineyard Margaret River Chardonnay 2008 Glowing yellow-green; has developed very well indeed; while the white peach core of the varietal fruit has taken on some attractive buttery notes, the citrussy acidity provides a perfect frame to hold the overall flavours together. Screwcap. 14% alc. Rating 94 To 2016 $38

Whispering Lake Cabernet Sauvignon 2005 Rating 93 To 2020 $35

Earthworks Wines ★★★☆

PO Box 551, Tanunda, SA 5352 **Region** Barossa Valley
T (08) 8561 3200 **www**.earthworkswines.com **Open** Not
Winemaker Tyson Bitter, Andrew La Nauze **Est.** 2003 **Dozens** 10000 **Vyds** 15ha
Earthworks was founded by the Lindner and Bitter families in 2003. Both have been centrally involved in the Barossa wine industry for many years, and were able to persuade the marketing arm of the Hill-Smith Family/Yalumba, Negociants Australia, to handle the domestic distribution of the wine. When the arrangement was extended internationally via Negociants International, part of the business was purchased by the Hill-Smith Family, reinforcing their sales, winemaking and marketing efforts with an equity position in Earthworks.

The Gypsy Barossa Valley Shiraz 2009 Hand-picked grapes from old vines are wild yeast-fermented in old oak vats. The colour is bright, and the medium-bodied palate is perfectly balanced, showing red and black fruits at the core of the wine, soft tannins and subtle oak completing the picture. Screwcap. 13.5% alc. Rating 90 To 2020 $26

Eastern Peake ★★★★★

67 Pickfords Road, Coghills Creek, Vic 3364 **Region** Ballarat
T (03) 5343 4245 **www**.easternpeake.com.au **Open** 7 days 11–5
Winemaker Owen Latta **Est.** 1983 **Dozens** 1500 **Vyds** 5.5ha
Norm Latta and Di Pym established Eastern Peake, 25km northeast of Ballarat on a high plateau overlooking the Creswick Valley, over 20 years ago. In the early years the grapes were sold to the late Trevor Mast of Mount Chalambar and Mount Langi Ghiran, but the 5ha of vines are now dedicated to the production of Eastern Peake wines. Son Owen Latta has been responsible for the seismic increase in the quality of the wines.

ΨΨΨΨΨ **OB Terroir Pinot Noir 2010** Good hue, although slightly turbid; the bouquet has red fruits, spices and herbs all in play, the long palate with urgency and drive, taking and building on the characters of the bouquet. Impressive Pinot. Screwcap. 13% alc. **Rating** 94 **To** 2018 $60

Wash Block Syrah 2009 Strong purple-red hue; a very attractive wine, the use of syrah appropriate given its very cool climate origins and the perfumed bouquet of spicy red fruits; the palate surprises by bringing some black cherry into play, and there is not even a hint of unripe fruit. Grapes grown by the Wash family. Screwcap. 13% alc. **Rating** 94 **To** 2029 $35

ΨΨΨΨΨ **Pinot Tache Blanc du Noir 2012 Rating** 91 **To** 2014 $25
Intrinsic Pinot Noir 2011 Rating 91 **To** 2017 $35

Echelon   ★★★★★
68 Anzac Street, Chullora, NSW 2190 **Region** Various
T (02) 9790 8567 **www**.echelonwine.com.au **Open** Not
Winemaker Various **Est.** 2009 **Dozens** NFP
Echelon is the brainchild of Nicholas Crampton, a wine marketer who understands wine (by no means a usual occurrence). He persuaded McWilliam's (Echelon's owner) to give free rein to his insights, and enlisted the aid of McWilliam's chief winemaker Corey Ryan. Ryan relinquished that role on 30 June 2012, but continues to have a consultancy role. Brands under the Echelon umbrella are Last Horizon (single vineyard wines from Tasmania, made by Adrian Sparks), Partisan (from McLaren Vale), Armchair Critic and Under & Over (from established vineyards in the best regions) and Zeppelin (made by Corey Ryan and Kym Teusner, sourced from Barossa vineyards either owned by Teusner or Sons of Eden, and often up to 80 years old). Few wineries in Australia so over-deliver on quality at their price point.

ΨΨΨΨΨ **Partisan Communication Road McLaren Vale Shiraz 2010** Deep purple-crimson; a very distinguished Shiraz, its black fruits laced with bitter chocolate and cedary oak, tannins in perfect balance. Won the prestigious Stodart Trophy at the Queensland Wine Show '11. Screwcap. 14.5% alc. **Rating** 96 **To** 2050 $40

Armchair Critic Reserve Heathcote Shiraz 2010 Considerable concentration of satsuma plum and blackberry fruit is intricately interwoven with classically Heathcote, tightly defined, iron-like tannins and impressively lively acidity. A newcomer worth discovering, but do leave it in its armchair to mellow for at least a decade first. Screwcap. 14% alc. **Rating** 95 **To** 2030 $40 TS

✪ **Zeppelin Eden Valley Riesling 2012** Terroir and the hand of man working in perfect unison; the fragrant, flowery citrus blossom bouquet sets the scene for the flavours of the fore- and mid-palate, before crisp, cleansing acidity extends the length and finish, the balance impeccable. Screwcap. 12% alc. **Rating** 94 **To** 2022 $21

✪ **The Armchair Critic Tumbarumba Chardonnay 2011** Pale straw-green; the intensity and impact of this wine is of another order compared to most others in its price range; grapefruit just shades the white flesh stone fruit and Jonathan apple that define the bouquet and palate; the finish is long and seamless, and any oak used has been totally absorbed. Screwcap. 13% alc. **Rating** 94 **To** 2018 $19

Last Horizon Tamar Valley Chardonnay 2011 Bright green-straw; whole bunch-pressed; wild yeast-fermented with solids; 35% new French barriques; minimal mlf. All the right moves have been made with this wine, which has exceptional finesse and elegance, and that life-sustaining Tasmanian acidity. Screwcap. 12% alc. **Rating** 94 **To** 2018 $35

Last Horizon Huon Valley Pinot Noir 2010 A five-clone blend (D512, MV6, 113, 114 and 115) co-fermented with 20% whole bunches, then 9 months in French oak (30% new); it has very good colour, and is as rich and complex as its elevage would suggest; supple, fresh plum fruit is neatly balanced by fine tannins and palpable French oak. Screwcap. 13.9% alc. **Rating** 94 **To** 2018 $40

✪ **Zeppelin Single Vineyard Barossa Valley Shiraz 2010** Red-purple; hand-picked and fermented in open vats with daily hand plunging, then 18 months in older oak; a really enjoyable mouthfeel, and mouthful, of juicy wine that soars on the finish. One of those wines that combines finesse, elegance and intensity. Screwcap. 14.5% alc. **Rating** 94 **To** 2020 $19

✪ **Zeppelin Northern Barossa Valley Grenache 2010** Made by Kym Teusner from 80-year-old vineyards, open-fermented and basket-pressed; the colour is truly exceptional for Barossa Valley grenache, a sure indicator of the rich and powerful wine to follow, with red and black cherry fruit supported by firm tannins. Screwcap. 15% alc. **Rating** 94 **To** 2018 $19

ΤΤΤΤΤ **Last Horizon Tamar Valley Pinot Noir 2011** Bright purple-crimson, very
✪ good; destemmed and cold-soaked for 6 days, then fermented and aged for 8 months in 30% new French oak; an attractive bouquet, then a full, supple mouthfeel to the layers of red cherry and plum fruit balanced and lengthened by fine tannins. Screwcap. 14% alc. **Rating** 93 **To** 2017 $24
Zeppelin Amelie Shiraz 2010 Rating 93 **To** 2025 $27
Zeppelin Ferdinand Shiraz 2010 Rating 92 **To** 2020 $38 BE

✪ **Partisan McLaren Vale Shiraz 2011** Very good purple-red; intense care in the vineyard during the growing season must have been used, mirrored in the winery; it is fragrant, well balanced, medium-bodied, and shows no hint of bodybuilding of its palate; the flavours of plum and blackberry have a wisp of dark chocolate, but little oak (and no more needed). Screwcap. 14% alc. **Rating** 91 **To** 2016 $18

✪ **Under & Over Tumbarumba Chardonnay 2011** I'm not quite sure what to attach to the statement that the wine 'was vinified with minimal oak influence'; what is certain is the volume of nectarine, peach and grapefruit flavours to be found in the wine, together with some textural notes that could equally easily have come from lees contact. Whatever, exceptional value. Screwcap. 12.5% alc. **Rating** 90 **To** 2013 $13
Last Horizon East Coast Pinot Gris 2012 Rating 90 **To** 2014 $24

ΤΤΤΤ **Under & Over Tumbarumba Chardonnay 2012** 'Vinified with minimal oak
✪ influence' we are told; hardly surprising given the price of the wine. It is very typical Tumbarumba, especially at this alcohol level, with a strong citrus/grapefruit accent, making it an upmarket (in quality) Sauvignon Blanc substitute. Screwcap. 12% alc. **Rating** 89 **To** 2014 $14

✪ **Under & Over King Valley Pinot Gris 2012** Pale quartz; looks as if sauvignon blanc yeast was used, for there are striking tropical/grapefruit flavours, nothing to do with pinot gris, but quite pleasant – and good value. Screwcap. 12.5% alc. **Rating** 88 **To** 2014 $14

✪ **Under & Over Heathcote Shiraz 2011** Bright crimson-purple; some very adroit winemaking has been used here; the colour and bouquet are excellent, but there is some lack of line on the palate, with dusty tannins entering the fray. That said, it offers great value. Screwcap. 14% alc. **Rating** 88 **To** 2015 $14

Echo Hill Wines ★★★☆

120 Adams Peak Road, Broke, NSW 2330 (postal) **Region** Hunter Valley
T 0439 462 651 **Open** Not
Winemaker Nick Paterson (Contract) **Est.** 1998 **Dozens** 1000 **Vyds** 4ha
The Day, Epper and Butler families respectively bring Australian, French and NZ background and heritage to Echo Hill. They retained local vigneron Andrew Margan, with 40 years' hands-on experience in growing and making wine, as a consultant in the early stages of the venture, including the selection of varieties and design of the vineyard blocks. They have also very sensibly started small, with only 2ha each of chardonnay and shiraz planted on the property, and virtually unlimited room for expansion. Next, they retained one of the best contract winemakers in the region, Nick Paterson, who guides the making of the wine from the grapes on the vine to wine in the bottle. Particularly for the Chinese market, the screwcaps provide far better protection during transport, warehousing, retail sale, and maturation in bottle. Exports to China.

ŶŶŶŶŶ **Hunter 808 Shiraz 2011** One of the most hyperbolic back labels I have read for a long time, the one useful fact being the role of Nick Paterson (who doesn't know how to make a disappointing wine) as winemaker. The medium-bodied palate has excellent texture and structure, blackberry fruits with a sixth sense of Hunter Valley soil, allied with subtle French oak. Screwcap. 12.9% alc. **Rating** 92 To 2026 $25

ŶŶŶŶ **Hunter Valley Chardonnay 2012 Rating** 88 To 2014 $25

Eclectic Wines   ★★★★☆

687 Hermitage Road, Pokolbin, NSW 2320 (postal) **Region** Hunter Valley
T 0410 587 207 www.eclecticwines.com.au **Open** At Hunter Valley Gardens Cellars
Winemaker First Creek Wines **Est.** 2001 **Dozens** 2500
This is the venture of Paul and Kate Stuart, nominally based in the Hunter Valley, where they live and have a vineyard planted to shiraz and mourvedre; 'nominally', because Paul's 30 years in the wine industry have given him the marketing knowledge to sustain the purchase of grapes from various regions, including the Hunter Valley, Canberra and interstate. He balances the production and sale of his own wines under the Eclectic label with acting as an independent marketing and sales consultant to other producers, avoiding a conflict of interest by selling his clients' wine in different markets from those in which he sells his own. Exports to Denmark, The Netherlands, Germany and China.

ŶŶŶŶŶ **Pewter Label Hunter Valley Shiraz 2011** Bright crimson-purple; abundant satsuma plum and cherry fruit on the bouquet and a palate that is supported by well-judged oak and ripe tannins. So well balanced, it is as good now as it will be in 20 years' time (and vice versa). Screwcap. 13.8% alc. **Rating** 94 To 2030 $28

ŶŶŶŶ **Pewter Label Hunter Valley Verdelho 2012 Rating** 88 To 2014 $25
Pewter Label Hunter Valley Semillon 2012 Rating 87 To 2014 $25

Eden Hall   ★★★★★

6 Washington Street, Angaston, SA 5353 **Region** Eden Valley
T (08) 8562 4590 www.edenhall.com.au **Open** 7 days 11–5
Winemaker Kym Teusner, Christa Deans, Phil Lehmann (Contract) **Est.** 2002
Dozens 2000 **Vyds** 32.6ha
David and Mardi Hall purchased the historic Avon Brae estate in 1996. The 120ha property has been planted to cabernet sauvignon (the lion's share, with 13ha), riesling (9.25ha), shiraz (6ha) and smaller plantings of merlot, cabernet franc and viognier. The majority of the production is contracted to Yalumba, St Hallett and McGuigan Simeon, with 10% of the best grapes held back for the Eden Hall label. The Riesling, Shiraz Viognier and Cabernet Sauvignon are all excellent, the red wines outstanding. Exports to the US, Malaysia and China.

ŶŶŶŶŶ **Riesling 2012** A single vineyard wine which faithfully reflects the terroir of
✪ the Eden Valley, already full of lemon and lime fruit; most will be consumed well before its likely maturity date 7–10 years out, for it is perfectly balanced right now. Screwcap. 12.2% alc. **Rating** 94 To 2022 $20
Block 4 Shiraz 2010 Not only a single vineyard, not even a single block, but comes from selected rows of Block 4, and not bottled until Jan '13. The strong crimson-purple colour introduces a wine full of fleshy red and black fruits, a sprinkle of spice, fully resolved tannins and quality oak. The balance is such that it can be enjoyed at any time over the next 20+ years. Screwcap. 14% alc. **Rating** 94 To 2035 $40
Block 3 Cabernet Sauvignon 2010 Made from selected rows of grapes on Block 3. The lengthy sojourn in oak (bottled Jan '13) has in no way harmed this rich Cabernet, the colour deep purple–crimson, the varietal fruit bell-clear, the tannins rounded, and the oak integrated. Screwcap. 14% alc. **Rating** 94 To 2030 $40

Eden Road Wines

3182 Barton Highway, Murrumbateman, NSW 2582 **Region** Canberra District
T (02) 6226 8800 **www.**edenroadwines.com.au **Open** Wed–Sun 11–4
Winemaker Nick Spencer, Hamish Young **Est.** 2006 **Dozens** 9500 **Vyds** 3ha
The name of this business, now entirely based in the Canberra District, reflects an earlier stage of its development, when it also had a property in the Eden Valley. That has now been separated, and Eden Road's operations since 2008 centre on Hilltops, Canberra District and Tumbarumba. Eden Road has relocated to Murrumbateman, where it purchased the former Doonkuna winery and mature vineyard, marketing greatly assisted by winning the Jimmy Watson Trophy '09. Exports to the UK, the US, the Maldives and Hong Kong.

🍷🍷🍷🍷🍷 Maragle Chardonnay 2011 A restrained and pure expression of the variety, showing pear, citrus blossom and wet slate on the bouquet; the palate is taut and tightly wound, slowly revealing layers of citrus fruit and green apple; while at the high end of acidity, the freshness this delivers is engaging, linear and harmonious. Screwcap. 12.5% alc. **Rating** 95 **To** 2025 $45 BE
Tumbarumba Chardonnay 2012 Bright pale gold; a fragrant and complex array of aromas, with citrus blossom, nectarine and grilled hazelnut on the bouquet; the palate is taut and linear, with an underlying wet slate minerality, but enough flesh to provide a long, layered and complex conclusion. Screwcap. 12.5% alc. **Rating** 94 **To** 2018 $36 BE
Courabyra Tumbarumba Chardonnay 2011 The array of aromas is savoury and refined, showing wet chalk, citrus blossom, fresh-cut green apple and fennel; the palate is incredibly high in acid, a function of the vintage, but the subtlety of this high-altitude vineyard has been maintained and expressed in this wine, which could possibly live for two decades; will be intriguing to watch. Screwcap. 12% alc. **Rating** 94 **To** 2031 $45 BE
Tumbarumba Pinot Noir 2012 Light garnet colour, and with an obvious presence of spicy whole-bunch aromas, combining in harmony with ripe red cherry and Asian spices on the bouquet; the palate reveals silky tannins, vibrant, pure and concentrated red fruits, with a long, supple and elegant conclusion; Screwcap. 13% alc. **Rating** 94 **To** 2020 $36 BE
Courabyra Pinot Noir 2011 The high level of spicy whole-bunch (40%) and cold tea aromas is set to challenge, with black cherry and fine oak spices also on display; the tannins are prominent at this early stage, tightly wound and fine-grained, and the lively acidity drives the palate to an expansive conclusion; more time will be rewarded. Screwcap. 12.5% alc. **Rating** 94 **To** 2018 $45 BE
Canberra Shiraz 2011 Light but bright hue; a very elegant wine with a core of red cherry and plum fruit, supported rather than challenged by superfine tannins and oak (10% new French puncheons). Making a better Shiraz given the vintage would have been nigh on impossible, but it is probable this wine will principally appeal to lovers of Pinot Noir. Screwcap. 12.9% alc. **Rating** 94 **To** 2018 $50

🍷🍷🍷🍷🍷 Gundagai Shiraz 2011 **Rating** 93 **To** 2020 $45 BE
✪ The Long Road Shiraz 2010 Light to medium crimson-purple; all about elegance, from its spicy, perfumed red berry bouquet to its vibrantly fresh light- to medium-bodied palate, reflecting maturation in 3-4-year-old French puncheons plus a small component kept in stainless steel until bottling. The grapes were grown in Gundagai, not normally noted for elegance on any scale, let alone this. Screwcap. 13.4% alc. **Rating** 93 **To** 2020 $22
Museum Release Canberra Riesling 2009 **Rating** 92 **To** 2018 $30 BE
The Long Road Pinot Noir 2012 **Rating** 92 **To** 2018 $26 BE
The Long Road Chardonnay 2011 **Rating** 90 **To** 2018 $22 BE
The Long Road Shiraz 2011 **Rating** 90 **To** 2018 $24 BE
Off-Dry Canberra Riesling 2012 **Rating** 90 **To** 2018 $30 BE

Edenmae Estate Wines ★★★★

7 Miller Street, Springton, SA 5235 **Region** Eden Valley
T (08) 8568 2685 **www**.edenmae.com.au **Open** Fri–Sun 10–5
Winemaker David Redhead **Est.** 2007 **Dozens** 1000 **Vyds** 12ha
In 2006 David and Michelle Redhead moved from Melbourne to the Barossa, thence moving to work in various parts of the world but always returning to the Barossa. They purchased a 36ha property on the southernmost crest of the Eden Valley, for long known as Holmes Estate Wines. It had fallen on hard times, and been abandoned for three years. Hard work has restored it to its former glory, with tree lots, dams and open areas for grazing alpaca, lambs, ponies, geese and hens, and is managed on organic principles, certification some way around the corner. The varied nature of the property lends itself to farm stay, which is one of its attractions. There are 4ha each of riesling and shiraz, and 2ha each of pinot noir and cabernet sauvignon, most 38 years old, with some 10-year-old shiraz and 30-year-old pinot.

🍷🍷🍷🍷🍷 **Single Vineyard Jess Shiraz 2010** The grapes come from the three estate shiraz blocks planted in '74, '94 and '95, and the wine spent 2 years in 100% new French and American oak. Deep purple-crimson, it certainly shows the impact of the oak, but also aniseed, licorice, bitter chocolate and blackberry fruits. There is a huge amount of flavour demanding time to calm down. Screwcap. 14% alc. **Rating** 92 **To** 2030 $22

Single Vineyard Eden Valley Riesling 2012 Pale quartz-green; hand-picked and whole bunch-pressed, it is a fragrant and delicate wine, with apple and lime blossom aromas that directly translate to the flavours of the palate; it is pure free-run, and (counterintuitively) a little too fine. Screwcap. 11.5% alc. **Rating** 90 **To** 2016 $17

🍷🍷🍷🍷 **Cooper Shiraz 2008 Rating** 89 **To** 2023 $28

Edwards Wines ★★★★

687 Ellensbrook Road, Cowaramup, WA 6284 **Region** Margaret River
T (08) 9755 5999 **www**.edwardswines.com.au **Open** 7 days 10.30–5
Winemaker Michael Edwards **Est.** 1993 **Dozens** 12 000 **Vyds** 24.8ha
Edwards Wines is a family-owned and operated winery. Brothers Michael (formerly a winemaker at Voyager Estate) and Christo are the winemaker and viticulturist, respectively. The vineyard includes cabernet sauvignon (7.8ha), shiraz (5.2ha), sauvignon blanc (4.6ha), chardonnay (3.5ha), semillon (2.7ha) and merlot (1ha). The consistency in the quality of the wines is admirable. Exports to all major markets.

🍷🍷🍷🍷🍷 **Tiger's Tale Margaret River Cabernet Merlot 2011** A 70/16/14% blend
✪ of cabernet sauvignon, merlot and shiraz; the bouquet and palate send the same message of perfectly ripe fruit that has been appropriately treated in the winery; redcurrant, blackcurrant and blackberry all contribute, and the medium-bodied palate is well balanced. Great value. Screwcap. 14% alc. **Rating** 93 **To** 2021 $18

1847 ★★★

PO Box 919 Rowland Flat, SA 5352 **Region** Barossa Valley
T (08) 8524 5328 **www**.eighteenfortyseven.com **Open** Not
Winemaker Derek Fitzgerald **Est.** 1996 **Dozens** 20 000 **Vyds** 35.86ha
1847 is wholly owned by Treasure Valley Wines Pty Ltd, which is in turn Chinese-owned. Derek Fitzgerald became winemaker in 2012, after eight vintages at Thorn-Clarke Wines and one at Robert Oatley Vineyards in Mudgee. He is understandably excited about the plans for the business, which crushed over 600 tonnes of Barossa grapes in '13, sourced partly from estate vineyards and partly from a group of growers. A 1000-tonne winery will be built for the '14 vintage, to handle the core production destined to sell at $35 a bottle or more, together with new varieties and blends to be released over the coming years. Needless to say, China and Vietnam will be the major market destinations. Exports to Vietnam and China.

♥♥♥♥ Home Block Barossa Valley Petit Verdot 2010 Deep garnet, purple hue; lifted on the bouquet, showing pure red fruits, violets and sage; the palate is taut with tannins and racy acidity on the medium-bodied finish. Cork. 12.4% alc. **Rating** 88 **To** 2017 $35 BE

Lily's Late Harvest 2011 Deep gold; showing a little botrytis with straw and apricot notes on the bouquet; the palate is luscious and has good texture, finishing with a little grip and bitterness that simply adds freshness as a foil to the sugar on offer. 375ml. Screwcap. 11.8% alc. **Rating** 88 **To** 2016 $23 BE

Ekhidna

Cnr Kangarilla Road/Foggo Road, McLaren Vale, SA 5171 **Region** McLaren Vale
T (08) 8323 8496 **www.ekhidnawines.com.au Open** 7 days 11–5
Winemaker Matthew Rechner **Est.** 2001 **Dozens** 3500
Matt Rechner entered the wine industry in 1988, and spent most of the intervening years at Tatachilla in McLaren Vale, starting as laboratory technician and finishing as operations manager. Frustrated by the constraints of large winery practice, he decided to strike out on his own in 2001 via the virtual winery option. His long experience has meant he is able to buy grapes from high-quality producers. A restructuring has seen the arrival of Ekhidna (the old spelling of echidna) and the disappearance of Paper Eagle brands. Exports to the US, Canada, NZ, India and China.

♥♥♥♥♀ Rarefied McLaren Vale Shiraz 2010 A sealed tank, whole-bunch carbonic maceration for 7 days preceded destemming the grapes, which were then returned to the tank for a 7-day cold soak at 6°–8°C, whereafter the normal fermentation took place over 10–14 days, maturation in 100% new French oak, the result being a massively complex, although not hot, palate. It won't appeal to all, but others with a decade or more in mind will cellar it. Screwcap. 14.5% alc. **Rating** 93 **To** 2040 $90

Linchpin McLaren Vale Shiraz 2010 Good purple-crimson; the wine spent 27 months in predominantly French oak, some of which seems to have been new, for it plays a major role in shaping the medium- to full-bodied palate; black fruits, licorice and dark chocolate are accompanied by ample tannins. Demands time and understanding. Screwcap. 14.5% alc. **Rating** 92 **To** 2035 $40

Sparkling Shiraz NV Full red-purple, showing some development. This is an amazing wine: how can you achieve flavour ripeness (assuming this had zero dosage) at 11%? It ought not to be possible, but you can see the slight gap at the end of the palate – infinitely preferable to sweetening ex dosage. Cork. 11% alc. **Rating** 91 **To** 2015 $25

✪ **McLaren Vale Shiraz 2010** Medium red-purple; this wine allows the region and variety to speak in a quiet voice, not with a megaphone; plum and blackberry fruit, dark chocolate and a coat of oak drive the flavours of the palate. Screwcap. 14.5% alc. **Rating** 90 **To** 2020 $20

Elan Vineyard

17 Turners Road, Bittern, Vic 3918 **Region** Mornington Peninsula
T (03) 5989 7209 **www.elanvineyard.com.au Open** First w'end of month, public hols 11–5, or by appt
Winemaker Selma Lowther **Est.** 1980 **Dozens** 400 **Vyds** 2.5ha
Selma Lowther, then fresh from CSU (as a mature-age student) made an impressive debut with her spicy, fresh, crisp Chardonnay, and has continued to make tiny quantities of appealing and sensibly priced wines. Most of the grapes from the estate vineyards are sold; production remains minuscule. There is a rotunda and children's playground overlooking the vineyard.

♥♥♥♥♀ Blanc de Blanc 2009 Estate-grown and bottle-fermented, with no indication of time on lees. It is fresh and tight, with just a hint of vanilla under its citrus and stone fruit flavours; good length and balance. Diam. 12% alc. **Rating** 90 **To** 2016 $25

Elderton

★★★★★

3–5 Tanunda Road, Nuriootpa, SA 5355 **Region** Barossa Valley
T (08) 8568 7878 **www**.eldertonwines.com.au **Open** Mon–Fri 9–5, w'ends, hols 11–4
Winemaker Richard Langford **Est.** 1982 **Dozens** 45 000 **Vyds** 75ha
The founding Ashmead family, with mother Lorraine supported by sons Allister and Cameron, continues to impress with its wines. The original source was 30ha of fully mature shiraz, cabernet sauvignon and merlot on the Barossa floor; subsequently 16ha of Eden Valley vineyards (shiraz, cabernet sauvignon, chardonnay, zinfandel, merlot and roussanne) were incorporated into the business. The Rohrlach Vineyard, with 75-year-old shiraz, is under long-term lease and managed by the Ashmead family. The Command Shiraz is justifiably regarded as its icon wine; energetic promotion and marketing both in Australia and overseas are paying dividends. Elderton has followed in the footsteps of Cullen by becoming carbon neutral. Exports to all major markets.

🍷🍷🍷🍷🍷 **Command Single Vineyard Barossa Shiraz 2010** A very elegant and refined Shiraz that fully lives up to its reputation; fragrant red and black fruits have a garland of spicy oak on the bouquet, a message that is faithfully reproduced on the long, medium-bodied palate. Screwcap. 14.8% alc. **Rating** 95 **To** 2030 $110
Greenock Two Grenache Shiraz Mourvedre 2012 Deep, but vivid, crimson-purple, exceptional for a blend such as this, but then so is the palate (and bouquet). It has all the black fruit flavours of shiraz, but the mouthfeel and weight of grenache. There are tannins, but they are very soft, and it is left to quality oak to provide the finish. Screwcap. 14.5% alc. **Rating** 94 **To** 2022 $30
✪ **Eden Valley Cabernet Sauvignon 2012** Bright crimson-purple; a totally delicious Cabernet, putting a great vintage, a very good region, and skilled winemaking into a synergistic union; it is full of cassis, redcurrant and a touch of black olive, these fruit flavours precisely matched with French oak. The price is barely believable. Screwcap. 14% alc. **Rating** 94 **To** 2027 $20
Barossa Cabernet Sauvignon 2010 Excellent colour; fragrant cassis and redcurrant aromas lead into a juicy palate with pristine varietal flavours framed by quality oak and ripe, soft but persistent, tannins; the balance shouldn't deceive you – it will happily see out 20 years. Screwcap. 14.5% alc. **Rating** 94 **To** 2030 $30

🍷🍷🍷🍷🍷 **Eden Valley Shiraz 2012** Bright purple-crimson, full and deep; the bouquet and
✪ medium-bodied palate are flooded with red and black cherry, poached plum and a farewell touch of licorice on the finish; there is ample structure to carry the high-quality fruit. Great value. Screwcap. 14% alc. **Rating** 93 **To** 2020 $20
Greenock One Shiraz 2012 Rating 92 **To** 2025 $30
Western Ridge Grenache Carignan 2012 Rating 92 **To** 2018 $50
✪ **Eden Valley Riesling 2012** Light to medium yellow-green; has considerable drive and persistence to its mix of lime, lemon and citrus zest; bone dry, with good acidity on the finish. Screwcap. 10.5% alc. **Rating** 91 **To** 2018 $20

 # Eldorado Road

1317 Eldorado Road, Eldorado, Vic 3678 (postal) **Region** North East Victoria Zone
T (03) 5725 1698 **www**.eldoradoroad.com.au **Open** Not
Winemaker Paul Dahlenburg, Loretta Schulz **Est.** 2010 **Dozens** 215
Paul Dahlenburg (nicknamed Bear), Loretta Schulz (Laurie) and their children have leased a 2ha block of shiraz planted in the 1890s with rootlings supplied from France (doubtless grafted) in the wake of phylloxera's devastation of the Glenrowan and Rutherglen plantings. Francois de Castella (head of the Department of Agriculture) was foremost in the importation, but Lindemans (and one other) were also involved. Bear and Laurie knew about the origins of the vineyard, which was in a state of serious decline after years of neglect. The owners of the vineyard were aware of its historic importance, and, while unwilling or unable to look after the vineyard themselves, were more than happy to lease it. Four years of tireless work in the vineyard, reconstructing the old vines, has finally resulted in tiny amounts of exceptionally good Shiraz. They have also planted a small area of nero d'Avola and durif. In the meantime

they are purchasing small amounts of nero d'Avola from Glenrowan and durif from Rutherglen, allowing the release of tiny quantities of three wines.

♥♥♥♥♥ **Persévérance Old Vine Shiraz 2010** One of the inspired decisions was the picking date, investing the wine with effortless balance in the wake of open fermentation and basket-pressing, the mix of one new French oak barrel, one used, more of the same. Don't be fooled into drinking it today or tomorrow just because it is so delicious now. Screwcap. 13% alc. **Rating** 96 **To** 2030 $60

Onyx Durif 2010 Deep, dense purple-crimson; from a single mature vineyard in Rutherglen, it is a wine in heroic style, built for heroic customers. It has all but dismissed the new and used French oak in which it was matured, and simply needs time for the tumult to die down, and for its black fruits to relax — as they will. Screwcap. 14.5% alc. **Rating** 94 **To** 2025 $35

♥♥♥♥♀ **Quasimodo Shiraz Durif Nero d'Avola 2010** **Rating** 93 **To** 2023 $28

Eldredge ★★★★★

Spring Gully Road, Clare, SA 5453 **Region** Clare Valley
T (08) 8842 3086 **www.**eldredge.com.au **Open** 7 days 11–5
Winemaker Leigh Eldredge **Est.** 1993 **Dozens** 5000 **Vyds** 20.96ha
Leigh and Karen Eldredge have established their winery and cellar door in the Sevenhill Ranges at an altitude of 500m above Watervale. Their mature estate vineyard is planted to shiraz, cabernet sauvignon, merlot, riesling, sangiovese and malbec. Both the Rieslings and red wines have had considerable wine show success in recent years. Exports to the UK, the US, Canada, Singapore and China.

♥♥♥♥♥ **Clare Valley Riesling 2012** Bright straw-green; the fragrant blossom-filled
✪   bouquet leads into a seriously engaging palate that has already built intense fruit, with some overtones of Mosel Valley, although the wine is dry. Lovely today, in 5 years or 10. Screwcap. 12% alc. **Rating** 95 **To** 2022 $17

✪   **Blue Chip Clare Valley Shiraz 2010** A classic example of Blue Chip Shiraz; the colour is excellent, and the depth of the black fruits (principally blackberry) has prevented the oak from riding roughshod over it; licorice and tar add further complexity. WAK screwcap. 14.5% alc. **Rating** 94 **To** 2030 $25

✪   **RL Clare Valley Cabernet Sauvignon 2010** A blend of cabernet sauvignon, malbec and shiraz matured in American and French oak. It is wholeheartedly full-bodied, with a flood of juicy black fruits set on a bed of ripe tannins, oak a minor partner. Screwcap. 14.8% alc. **Rating** 94 **To** 2030 $25

♥♥♥♥♀ **Clare Valley Sangiovese Rose 2012** Bright pink; the fragrant bouquet of rose
✪   petal and spiced plums is replicated on the attractive palate, which is to all intents and purposes dry, yet softly fruity. Screwcap. 14% alc. **Rating** 92 **To** 2014 $17

✪   **Clare Valley Semillon Sauvignon Blanc 2012** A 60/40% blend fermented in stainless steel, and early bottled to (successfully) retain maximum fruit expression and freshness. Whether the Clare Valley is a hospitable environment for the blend is an open question, but the wine has done well in this instance; it is bright, with vibrant, citrussy fruit. Screwcap. 12.4% alc. **Rating** 90 **To** 2014 $17

Eldridge Estate of Red Hill ★★★★★

120 Arthurs Seat Road, Red Hill, Vic 3937 **Region** Mornington Peninsula
T (03) 5989 2644 **www.**eldridge-estate.com.au **Open** Mon–Fri 12–4, w'ends & hols 11–5
Winemaker David Lloyd **Est.** 1985 **Dozens** 800 **Vyds** 2.8ha
The Eldridge Estate vineyard was purchased by Wendy and David Lloyd in 1995. Major retrellising work has been undertaken, changing to Scott Henry, and all the wines are estate-grown and made. David has also planted several Dijon-selected pinot noir clones (114, 115 and 777), which have been contributing since 2004, likewise the Dijon chardonnay clone 96. An interesting move has been the development of the Euroa Creeks range (Early Harvest Shiraz, Shiraz and Reserve Shiraz), made from contract-grown grapes (a long-term contract)

from the northern end of Heathcote: an interesting grafting of the skills of a cool-climate pinot noir grower and maker onto the far bigger wine base of Heathcote shiraz. Exports to the UK, Canada and Singapore.

🍷🍷🍷🍷🍷 **Chardonnay 2011** Bright, light straw-green; a tangy, fragrant, fruit-driven style, the nectarine and white peach fruit underpinned by a crisp finish; oak is the sky over the landscape of the painting. Screwcap. 13% alc. **Rating** 93 **To** 2018 $40

Gamay 2011 Excellent colour for the vintage; one of a handful of Gamays made in Australia, and often the best; it has developed attractive spicy/savoury nuances underlying the summer berries that David Lloyd seeks, and which prolong and give texture to the finish. Screwcap. 13% alc. **Rating** 93 **To** 2015 $35

✪ **PTG12 2012** PTG is a take on Passetoutgrains, the now rare Burgundian blend of pinot noir and gamay; here the blend is 51% gamay/49% pinot; the vibrant purple-crimson colour blazes in the glass. It has low SO_2, and David Lloyd would like to see it consumed prior to the end of '13. It is loaded with plum and cherry fruit, and the acidity on the dry finish is admirable. Screwcap. 13% alc. **Rating** 93 **To** 2013 $25

Pinot Noir 2011 A mix of MV6, G5V15, Pommard, 114, 115 and 777 clones that were matured in 30% new French oak. Has good colour and more juicy plummy/black cherry fruit than many from the vintage. The texture is a highlight of a good Pinot. Screwcap. 13.5% alc. **Rating** 93 **To** 2016 $50

Single Clone Pinot Noir 2011 Clone MV6. Very good colour with slightly more purple than that of its sibling. Here the flavours stay in the satsuma/yellow plum spectrum, with an attractive twist and citrussy acidity on the finish. Screwcap. 13.5% alc. **Rating** 92 **To** 2015 $50

Elgee Park ★★★★★

24 Junction Road, Merricks North, Vic 3926 **Region** Mornington Peninsula
T (03) 5989 7338 **www**.elgeeparkwines.com.au **Open** At Merricks General Wine Store
Winemaker Geraldine McFaul (Contract) **Est.** 1972 **Dozens** 1600 **Vyds** 4.4ha
The pioneer of the Mornington Peninsula in its 20th-century rebirth, owned by Baillieu Myer and family. The vineyard is planted to riesling, chardonnay, viognier (some of the oldest vines in Australia), pinot gris, pinot noir, merlot and cabernet sauvignon. The vineyard is set in a picturesque natural amphitheatre with a northerly aspect looking out across Port Phillip Bay towards the Melbourne skyline.

🍷🍷🍷🍷🍷 **Family Reserve Mornington Peninsula Chardonnay 2011** Gleaming green-yellow; the cool vintage shows to maximum effect in this very good wine, barrel-fermented in French oak and matured in oak for 11 months; it has extremely attractive white peach and cashew flavours on the mid-palate, grapefruit acidity on the finish. Screwcap. 13.5% alc. **Rating** 95 **To** 2017 $40

Mornington Peninsula Cuvee Brut 2009 An estate-grown 60/40% blend of chardonnay and pinot noir, it was bottled Jul '09, and disgorged Oct '12. Quartz-green; while elegant and youthful, the balance and mouthfeel are very good, as is the slight savoury twist on the dry finish. Diam. 13% alc. **Rating** 94 **To** 2015 $45

🍷🍷🍷🍷🍷 **Family Reserve Riesling 2012 Rating** 92 **To** 2022 $25

Elgo Estate ★★★☆

2020 Upton Road, Upton Hill, via Longwood, Vic 3664 **Region** Strathbogie Ranges
T (03) 9328 3766 **www**.elgoestate.com.au **Open** Not
Winemaker Sam Plunkett **Est.** 1999 **Dozens** 5000 **Vyds** 100ha
Elgo Estate, owned by the Taresch family, is located high in the hills of the Strathbogie Ranges, 125km northeast of Melbourne, a stone's throw from the southern end of the Heathcote region. Elgo Estate is committed to sustainable viticulture reflecting and expressing the characteristics of this cool-climate region. All of the wines are 100% estate-grown from their three vineyards in the region, with plantings dating back to the early 1970s. Elgo Estate was the first winery in Australia to be fully powered by self-generated renewable wind energy.

The installation of a 30m tall 150 kW wind turbine in 2007 enables Elgo to save around 400 tonnes of greenhouse gas emissions per year, while generating enough electricity to power the winery twice over, the excess green electricity being fed back into the main power grid. In '12 Elgo purchased the Mount Helen Vineyard from Robert Kirby (previously used for the Cooralook wines). Exports to China.

ŸŸŸŸ♀ **Strathbogie Ranges Cabernet Sauvignon 2006** As expected, the colour is developed, but healthy. Quite why it has been held back for so long prior to release, I don't know, but it's ready now or soonish; the tannins and oak are spicy, and mesh well with the blackcurrant fruit of the medium-bodied palate. Screwcap. 13.5% alc. **Rating** 90 **To** 2016 $26

ŸŸŸŸ ✪ **Allira Strathbogie Ranges Cabernet Merlot 2010** Light red-purple; while only light- to medium-bodied, the aromas and flavours are fresh and lively, traversing cassis, redcurrant and plum, with silky tannins. If there is a touch of citrussy acidity, it adds, rather than detracts. Excellent value. Screwcap. 14% alc. **Rating** 89 **To** 2014 $14
Strathbogie Ranges Chardonnay 2008 **Rating** 88 **To** 2014 $22

Eling Forest Winery

Hume Highway, Sutton Forest, NSW 2577 **Region** Southern Highlands
T (02) 4878 9155 www.elingforest.com.au **Open** 7 days 8–5
Winemaker Jeff Aston **Est.** 1987 **Dozens** 4100 **Vyds** 5.95ha
Eling Forest's mentally agile and innovative founder (the late) Leslie Fritz celebrated his 80th birthday not long after he planted the first vines here in 1987. He celebrated his 88th birthday by expanding the vineyards from 3ha to 4ha, primarily with additional plantings of Hungarian varieties. He also developed a Cherry Port and is also using spinning cone technology to produce various peach-based liqueurs, utilising second-class peach waste. In a major change of direction, winemaker Jeff Aston leased the winery and vineyard in 2012, and produces wines under the Eling Forest label, and for other local producers.

ŸŸŸŸ♀ **Southern Highlands Riesling 2012** Pale, bright straw-green; the alcohol tells you there will be some residual sugar, and doesn't lie; this is a delicate wine that will flourish in bottle as the sweetness makes room for the citrus flavours to develop. Screwcap. 10% alc. **Rating** 91 **To** 2019 $35

Ellender Estate ★★★

Leura Glen, 260 Green Gully Road, Glenlyon, Vic 3461 **Region** Macedon Ranges
T (03) 5348 7785 www.ellenderwines.com.au **Open** W'ends & public hols 11–5, or by appt
Winemaker Graham Ellender **Est.** 1996 **Dozens** 900 **Vyds** 4.1ha
Graham and Jenny Ellender have established pinot noir (2.7ha), chardonnay (1ha), sauvignon blanc (0.2ha) and pinot gris (0.1ha). Wine style is restricted to those varieties true to the ultra-cool climate of the Macedon Ranges: Pinot Noir, Pinot Rose, Chardonnay and sparkling. Exports to the United Arab Emirates.

ŸŸŸŸ **Rosetta Macedon Ranges Pinot Rose 2011** Pale bronze-pink; from very early-picked estate-grown pinot noir, whole bunch-pressed, with brief skin contact along the way; it is strictly savoury, with lemony acidity. Screwcap. 11.8% alc. **Rating** 87 **To** 2014 $24
Reserve Macedon Ranges Pinot Noir 2009 Strong colour; made from three (unspecified) clones, separately fermented and matured before blending; it is generously flavoured, but the varietal expression is problematic. Screwcap. 13.9% alc. **Rating** 87 **To** 2015 $42

 Elliot Rocke Estate

Craigmoor Road, Mudgee, NSW 2850 **Region** Mudgee
T (02) 6372 7722 www.elliotrockeestate.com **Open** 7 days 10–4
Winemaker Contract **Est.** 1999 **Dozens** NA

Elliot Rocke Estate has vineyards dating back to 1987, when the property was known as Seldom Seen. Plantings are made up of 9ha of semillon, 4.3ha of shiraz and chardonnay, 2.2ha of merlot and 2ha each of cabernet sauvignon and traminer, with 0.5ha of doradillo. A change of ownership and the appointment of a new viticulturist has seen lower-yielding vines, a pesticide-free approach, retrellising and the pulling out of some of the poorer performing vineyard blocks. The aim is to significantly lift the quality of the wine. Exports to Switzerland, Indonesia, Thailand, Singapore, China and Japan.

ⲦⲦⲦⲦⲴ **Mudgee Shiraz 2010** Light crimson-purple; vibrant and fresh red cherry fruit
✪ on both the bouquet and palate has made light of the 50% new oak in which the wine was matured; it has good balance, line and length, and is already drinking well. Good value. Screwcap. 12.8% alc. **Rating** 92 **To** 2020 $23

✪ **Mudgee Semillon Sauvignon Blanc 2011** Pale straw-green; a well-made wine; the bouquet is fragrant, heralding the juicy palate, which gains intensity on the back-palate and finish with a surge of citrus, passionfruit and kiwifruit. Good value. Screwcap. 11.5% alc. **Rating** 90 **To** 2014 $19

✪ **Mudgee Chardonnay 2010** A well-made wine typical of the discipline and skill of the winemaking across the Elliot Rocke range. A delicate touch of French oak lifts the nectarine and grapefruit flavours, also adding to their length. Good value for short- to medium-term drinking. Screwcap. 12.5% alc. **Rating** 90 **To** 2015 $19

ⲦⲦⲦⲦ **Mudgee Traminer Riesling 2012** **Rating** 89 **To** 2013 $19
Mudgee Merlot 2011 **Rating** 88 **To** 2015 $23

Ellis Wines ★★★★

3025 Heathcote-Rochester Road, Colbinabbin, Vic 3559 (postal) **Region** Heathcote
T 0413 293 796 **www**.elliswines.com.au **Open** Not
Winemaker Guy Rathjen **Est.** 1998 **Dozens** 700 **Vyds** 54.6ha
Bryan and Joy Ellis own this family business, with sales manager Paul Flanagan, Bryan's son-in-law; seven of the vineyard blocks are named after family members. For 10 years the Ellises were content to sell the grapes to a range of producers including Taltarni, Domaine Chandon, Mount Langi Ghiran and Heathcote Winery. However, since 2009 a portion of the crop has been vinified.

ⲦⲦⲦⲦⲴ **Signature Label Viognier 2012** The bright, full green-gold colour is a tell-tale sign that 40% of the wine was partially barrel-fermented and matured in French oak for 5 months; it doesn't heighten the varietal expression, but it certainly makes for a much more interesting wine. Screwcap. 13.9% alc. **Rating** 92 **To** 2015 $24
Premium Shiraz 2011 The colour is good, reflecting the selection of only two barrels to make this supple medium- to full-bodied wine; while American oak has been used, it works well, enhancing rather than diminishing the black cherry and blackberry fruit, which has those touches of eucalypt mint so common in Central Victoria. Screwcap. 14.5% alc. **Rating** 92 **To** 2021 $33

ⲦⲦⲦⲦ **Signature Label Cabernet Sauvignon 2011** **Rating** 89 **To** 2015 $25
Signature Label Cabernet Merlot 2011 **Rating** 87 **To** 2014 $26

Elmswood Estate ★★★★★

75 Monbulk-Seville Road, Seville, Vic 3139 **Region** Yarra Valley
T (03) 5964 3015 **www**.elmswoodestate.com.au **Open** W'ends 12–5, or by appt
Winemaker Mal Stewart (Sparkling), Dylan McMahon **Est.** 1981 **Dozens** 3000 **Vyds** 8ha
Elmswood Estate has planted cabernet sauvignon, chardonnay, merlot, sauvignon blanc, pinot noir, shiraz and riesling on the red volcanic soils of the far southern side of the Yarra Valley. The cellar door operates from 'The Pavilion', a fully enclosed glass room situated on a ridge above the vineyard, with 180° views of the Upper Yarra Valley. It seats up to 110 guests, and is a popular wedding venue. Music events are held on the third Sunday of each month. Exports to China.

Reserve Yarra Valley Chardonnay 2011 Bright, light straw-green; a selection of the best barrels, and a light year removed from its sibling in both style and quality; there is vibrant white peach, grapefruit and nectarine on the fragrant bouquet and a long, intense palate. Screwcap. 12% alc. **Rating** 95 **To** 2018 $50
Yarra Valley Cabernet Merlot 2008 Has retained good hue and depth; the red earth, southern side of the Yarra Valley enjoyed the warmth of the '08 vintage; this medium- to full-bodied wine has the full hand of blackcurrant/cassis/plum fruit, with ripe tannins and quality oak lending the right amount of support. Diam. 14.2% alc. **Rating** 94 **To** 2023 $35

Yarra Valley Chardonnay 2008 **Rating** 91 **To** 2016 $33

Eloquesta ★★★☆

10 Stroud Avenue, Dubbo, NSW 2830 (postal) **Region** Mudgee
T 0458 525 899 **www**.eloquesta.com.au **Open** Not
Winemaker Stuart Olsen **Est.** 2008 **Dozens** 800 **Vyds** 6ha
The full name of the business is Eloquesta by Stuart Olsen, Stuart being the sole owner and winemaker. He is a trained scientist and teacher, gaining winemaking experience since 2000, variously working at Cirillo Estate, Lowe Family Wines and Torbreck, as well as a German winery in the Rheinhessen. His aim in Mudgee is to make the two varieties that he believes grow consistently well year after year in the cooler foothills of Mudgee and Rylstone: Shiraz and Petit Verdot, with an occasional bucket of Viognier.

Mudgee Shiraz Petit Verdot 2010 A 55/42/3% blend of shiraz, petit verdot and viognier; an artisanal approach with whole-berry/whole-bunch ferments, foot-stamped, then hand-plunged daily for 2 more weeks, aged in French, Hungarian and Russian oak. Given the problems of the vintage with persistent rain, a considerable achievement, with rich red and black fruits and no shortage of oak. Good hue, and has settled down well over the past 12 months. Screwcap. 14.5% alc. **Rating** 90 **To** 2017 $28

Emersleigh Estate NR

71 Stewart Road, Emerald, Vic 3782 **Region** Yarra Valley
T (03) 5968 4613 **Open** Sun 11–5, some pub hols 11–5
Winemaker Jeff Wright, Kilchurn Wines **Est.** 2001 **Dozens** 500 **Vyds** 2ha
Emersleigh Estate fulfils a dream of more than 30 years for John Wall and wife Michelle. In 1996 they began the planting of their vineyard, with 1.3ha of pinot noir, 0.5ha chardonnay, and a few rows each of sauvignon blanc and shiraz. They have two brands: Off the Wall for table wine, and Emersleigh for sparkling. It is the latter that John finds most fascinating: in its concept and culture, but, most of all, in the drinking of it. They plan to eventually process all sparkling wine onsite.

Eperosa ★★★★★

24 Maria Street, Tanunda, SA 5352 **Region** Barossa Valley
T 0428 111 121 **www**.eperosa.com.au **Open** By appt
Winemaker Brett Grocke **Est.** 2005 **Dozens** 400
Eperosa owner Brett Grocke qualified as a viticulturist in 2001, and, through Grocke Viticulture, consults and provides technical services to over 200ha of vineyards spread across the Barossa Valley, Eden Valley, Adelaide Hills, Riverland, Langhorne Creek and Hindmarsh Valley. He is ideally placed to secure small parcels of grapes of the highest quality, and treats these with traditional, no-frills winemaking methods: destemmed, macerated prior to fermentation, open-fermented, hand-plunged, basket-pressed, then 18 months in used French oak barrels. The wines are of impeccable quality.

Elevation Eden Valley Shiraz 2011 Deep colour; the bouquet reveals liqueur-soaked plums with a slight vegetal, herbal underlay; the palate is medium-bodied and fleshy, with fine tannins and fresh acidity a feature; a lively, fresh and accessible example. Cork. 14.2% alc. **Rating** 92 **To** 2018 $40 BE

Elevation Moppa Springs Shiraz 2011 Mid garnet, bright; the bouquet reveals a confected red fruit character, offset by spicy oak notes; the palate is fleshy, forward and fresh, and while lacking complexity, vibrancy and purity are the bedrock of the wine. Cork. 13.1% alc. **Rating** 90 **To** 2018 $40 BE

ԶԶԶԶ **L.R.C. Greenock Barossa Valley Shiraz 2011 Rating** 89 **To** 2018 $40 BE
Totality Barossa Valley Mataro 2011 Rating 88 **To** 2016 $30 BE

Eppalock Ridge   ★★★★
6 Niemann Street, Bendigo, Vic 3550 (postal) **Region** Heathcote
T 0409 957 086 **www.**eppalockridge.com **Open** Not
Winemaker Don Lewis, Narelle King, Rod Hourigan **Est.** 1979 **Dozens** 3000
Sue and Rod Hourigan gave up their careers in fabric design and television production at the ABC in 1976 to chase their passion for fine wine. This took them first to McLaren Vale, with Sue working in the celebrated Barn Restaurant, and Rod starting at d'Arenberg; over the next three hectic years both worked vintages at Pirramimma and Coriole while undertaking the first short course for winemakers at what is now CSU. They then moved to Redesdale in 1979 and established Eppalock Ridge on a basalt hilltop overlooking Lake Eppalock. The 10ha of shiraz, cabernet sauvignon, cabernet franc and merlot are capable of producing wines of high quality. Exports to China.

ԶԶԶԶԶ **Susan's Selection Heathcote Shiraz Cabernet Merlot 2010** Very bright,
✪   clear, crimson-purple; a sophisticated and complex 60/25/15% blend; it is
       medium-bodied, with an array of spicy/savoury red and black fruits, and fine,
       persistent tannins. Classy packaging is another plus for a wine of exceptional value.
       Screwcap. 14% alc. **Rating** 93 **To** 2020 $20
       Heathcote Shiraz 2010 Everything from picking to bottling is done by hand;
       this medium-bodied wine spent 14 months in French and American oak (mainly
       used) and has a seductive mix of dark berry and spice/pepper flavours. The tannins
       have been particularly well judged, lifting the finish and aftertaste. Screwcap.
       14% alc. **Rating** 92 **To** 2020 $28

Ernest Hill Wines   ★★★★
307 Wine Country Drive, Nulkaba, NSW 2325 **Region** Hunter Valley
T (02) 4991 4418 **www.**ernesthillwines.com.au **Open** 7 days 10–5
Winemaker Mark Woods **Est.** 1999 **Dozens** 6000 **Vyds** 12ha
This is part of a vineyard originally planted in the early 1970s by Harry Tulloch for Seppelt Wines; it was later renamed the Pokolbin Creek Vineyard, and later still (in '99) the Wilson family purchased the upper (hill) part of the vineyard, and renamed it the Ernest Hill vineyard. It is now planted to semillon, shiraz, chardonnay, verdelho, traminer, merlot, tempranillo and chambourcin. Exports to the US and China.

ԶԶԶԶԶ **William Henry Shiraz 2011** Deeper colour than the '11 Shareholders, with
       more purple evident; the palate, and especially the fruit profile, has another level of
       flavour and texture, plum and blackberry in the lead, leather and earth in the rear,
       coupled with ripe tannins. Diam. 13.7% alc. **Rating** 92 **To** 2026 $40
       The Dam Merlot 2011 Light to medium red-purple; matured in used French
       oak for 12 months; merlot does its best in cooler climates than that of Mudgee,
       which makes this red berry and plum Merlot especially meritorious, tannins and
       oak spot on. Screwcap. 13% alc. **Rating** 92 **To** 2018 $25
       Andrew Watson Tempranillo 2011 Tempranillo seems to give a smile wherever
       it is grown, in this case in the Hunter Valley. The colour is good, the black cherry
       fruit and ripe tannins in a supple duet. Screwcap. 12.9% alc. **Rating** 91 **To** 2018 $25
       Alexander Chardonnay 2011 Light straw-green; partial barrel fermentation
       and maturation for 10 months in new French oak have imparted a generous kiss
       of cashew and vanilla to the fruit; while that fruit has good varietal character, it
       has struggled to carry the oak, but may build somewhat over the next few years.
       Screwcap. 13% alc. **Rating** 90 **To** 2016 $35

ŶŶŶŶ   Shareholders Shiraz 2011 Rating 89 To 2019 $30
Alexander Chardonnay 2010 Rating 87 To 2013 $35

Ernest Schuetz Estate Wines

Edgel Lane, Mudgee, NSW 2850 **Region** Mudgee
T 0402 326 612 **www.ernestschuetzestate.com.au Open** Fri & Mon 11–3, w'ends 10–4
Winemaker Jacob Stein **Est.** 2003 **Dozens** 4300 **Vyds** 4.1ha
Ernest Schuetz's involvement in the wine industry started in 1988 at the age of 21. Working in various liquor outlets and as a sales representative for Miranda Wines, McGuigan Simeon and, later, Watershed Wines, gave him an in-depth understanding of all aspects of the wine market. In 2003 he and wife Joanna purchased the Arronvale Vineyard (first planted in '91) in the micro-valley of Menah, at an altitude of 530m. When the Schuetzs acquired the vineyard it was planted to merlot, shiraz and cabernet sauvignon, and they have since grafted 1ha to riesling, pinot blanc, pinot gris, zinfandel and nebbiolo. The estate plantings have been complemented by other varieties purchased from other growers. A new cellar door was opened in March '12 at the old Frog Rock site. Ernest Shuetz has had outstanding success at the Mudgee Wine Show.

ŶŶŶŶŶ   Epica Amarone Method Mudgee Cabernet Shiraz 2010 Dedicated to
Ernest Shuetz's father (died '12). It is a 55/40/5% blend of cabernet sauvignon, shiraz and merlot, the hand-picked bunches dried on racks for an average of 14 days, and after fermentation, aged in new French oak for 30 months. The colour is bright red-purple; full-bodied, but in no way extractive; it is only on the very complex, spicy, lifted finish that you catch sight of the Amarone method. A major success; 900 numbered bottles made. Cork. 14.9% alc. **Rating** 94 **To** 2030 $60

ŶŶŶŶŶ   Terra X Mudgee Shiraz 2010 Good colour; has abundant black fruits –
✪   blackberry, blackcurrant, cherry and plum – supported by ripe, soft tannins; oak is
a passenger, not a driver. Good value. Screwcap. 14.5% alc. **Rating** 90 **To** 2025 $18
Family Reserve Black Springs Vineyard Cabernet Sauvignon 2010
Rating 90 **To** 2018 $28

 Espier Estate   ★★★

Room 1208, 401 Docklands Drive, Docklands, Vic 3008 **Region** South Eastern Australia
T (03) 9078 7034 **www.jnrwine.com Open** Mon–Fri 9–5
Winemaker Sam Brewer **Est.** 2007 **Dozens** 20 000
This is the venture of Robert Luo and Jacky Lin, owners of JNR Wine Group, which in turns own Espier. Winemaker Sam Brewer has made wine for Southcorp and De Bortoli in Australia, and overseas in the US and China, and has been closely linked with the business since its establishment. The principal focus of the business is export to Asian countries, with China and Hong Kong the main areas of interest. Much of the volume is linked to contract-made wines for the Chinese market under the Espier Estate label, priced from entry level to premium. Heathcote is the focus for the latter, the entry- to mid-level sourced from supplies across Southeastern Australia, with Sam Brewer providing the relevant style and price specifications. Exports to Asia.

ŶŶŶŶ   Feel Reserve Heathcote Shiraz 2010 Good full purple-red colour; a solidly
constructed wine built around a choc-mint core and firm tannins; more power and extract than finesse. Cork. 14% alc. **Rating** 88 **To** 2019 $25

Evans & Tate   ★★★★★

Cnr Metricup Road/Caves Road, Wilyabrup, WA 6280 **Region** Margaret River
T (08) 9755 6244 **www.mcwilliamswinesgroup.com Open** 7 days 10.30–5
Winemaker Matthew Byrne, Lachlan McDonald **Est.** 1970 **Dozens** 450 000
Vyds 53.33ha
The 40-year history of Evans & Tate has been one of constant change and, for decades, expansion, moving to acquire large wineries in SA and NSW. For a series of reasons, nothing

to do with the excellent quality of its Margaret River wines, the empire fell apart in 2005; it took an interminable time before McWilliam's finalised its acquisition of the Evans & Tate brand, cellar door and vineyards (although not the winery) in December '07. Remarkably, wine quality was maintained through the turmoil, and shows no sign whatsoever of faltering. Exports to all major markets.

Metricup Road Margaret River Cabernet Merlot 2011 Deep magenta; the highly expressive bouquet offers cassis, redcurrant, cedar, violet and a little leafy complexity; the medium- to full-bodied palate is very fresh, taut and focused, with layers of fine tannins melting away before pristine fruit; beautifully constructed and incredible value. Screwcap. 14.5% alc. **Rating** 96 **To** 2025 $24 BE

Redbrook Margaret River Cabernet Sauvignon 2010 Deep, vibrant garnet; the bouquet offers a complex array of red and black fruits, crushed leaf, cigar box and violets; medium- to full-bodied with a gorgeous silky texture; fine-grained tannins coat the mouth as the fruit slowly reveals, with the zesty acidity providing cut and thrust; long, layered and supremely age-worthy. Screwcap. 14.2% alc. **Rating** 96 **To** 2030 $38 BE

Metricup Road Margaret River Chardonnay 2011 Pale gold, green hue; pure grapefruit aromas sit neatly alongside complex grilled cashew complexity; the palate is tightly wound and powerful, with zesty acidity providing a foil for the intense fruit on offer; long and precise, with latent power aplenty. Screwcap. 13.5% alc. **Rating** 95 **To** 2018 $24 BE

Pemberton Chardonnay 2011 Bright, pale straw-green; the fragrant bouquet is fruit- rather than barrel ferment-driven, and there is an immediate replay on the juicy palate, the flavours ranging through white peach, grapefruit and nectarine; very good balance and length. Screwcap. 13.9% alc. **Rating** 95 **To** 2020 $30

Redbrook Margaret River Chardonnay 2010 Light straw-green; the bouquet is full of struck match funky complexity, but the opulence of the layered stone fruit and rockmelon fruit on the palate dismisses the challenge of the bouquet; barrel-ferment oak is, of course, an important part of the message. Screwcap. 13.5% alc. **Rating** 95 **To** 2020 $30

Porongurup Pinot Noir 2011 Good depth to its crimson-purple colour; one of the richest Pinot Noirs yet to come from Porongurup, but not sacrificing its clear-cut varietal character; cherry and plum are woven together in a silk and velvet brocade. Major surprise; a benchmark for the future? Screwcap. 13.5% alc. **Rating** 95 **To** 2020 $36

Metricup Road Margaret River Shiraz 2010 Rating 94 To 2020 $24
Frankland River Shiraz 2010 Rating 94 To 2025 $38
Redbrook Shiraz 2009 Rating 94 To 2024 $38
Redbrook Cabernet Sauvignon 2009 Rating 94 To 2024 $38

Redbrook Margaret River Shiraz 2010 Rating 93 To 2030 $38
Redbrook Margaret River Chardonnay 2011 Rating 92 To 2016 $30
Classic Margaret River Shiraz 2011 Bright medium red-purple; has everything that could be expected at this price point from Margaret River: crystal clear varietal character to its blackberry and black cherry fruit, offset by nuances of spice and an infusion of oak; the soft tannins mean it is ready right now. Screwcap. 14.5% alc. **Rating** 91 **To** 2016 $20

Frankland River Riesling 2012 Rating 90 To 2020 $25 BE
Classic Margaret River Sauvignon Blanc 2012 Pale colour, bright; a pungent bouquet of nettle and citrus blossom; the palate is dry, lively and fresh, with gooseberry notes lingering on the finish. Screwcap. 12.5% alc. **Rating** 90 **To** 2014 $20 BE

Gnangara Cabernet Merlot 2011 Mid garnet; bright and fresh on the bouquet with red fruits, leafy complexity and a little floral lift; the palate is medium-bodied, focused and fresh, with fine tannins aplenty supported by lively acidity; excellent value. Screwcap. 14.5% alc. **Rating** 90 **To** 2018 $16 BE

Margaret River Malbec 2011 Rating 90 To 2020 $38 BE

Evans Wines

Barossa Valley Way, Nuriootpa, SA 5355 **Region** Barossa Valley
T 0417 442 768 **www**.evanswine.com **Open** Not
Winemaker Emma Norbiato **Est.** 1973 **Dozens** 15 000 **Vyds** 24.28ha
Evans Wines traces its history back to the 1970s when the late, revered, Len Evans formed a small, separate (from Rothbury Estate) business with then general manager of Rothbury Estate, Denis Power. Then, and now, its principal focus was on exports, the wines coming from various parts of Southeastern Australia. It is now fully owned by a group of wine industry professionals, headed by the Calabria family (of Westend Estate), which has a majority shareholding. The wines come in two ranges: Nine Stones and Bulletin Place. Nine Stones is varietal (Shiraz) and region (Barossa Valley, McLaren Vale and Hilltops) specific. Bulletin Place is a lower-priced range of varietal wines without regional ascription. Winemaker Emma Norbiato has had over a decade of experience, previously working at Casella Wines, Lindemans and Penfolds. Exports to the UK, the US and NZ.

Nine Stones Barossa Shiraz 2010 Medium purple-crimson; this medium- to full-bodied shiraz has good varietal black fruit flavours, speaking of its regional origin, and also of the very good vintage; it all hangs together convincingly. Good value. Screwcap. 14% alc. **Rating** 89 **To** 2016 $15

Nine Stones Hilltops Shiraz 2010 Medium crimson-purple; has a more fragrant bouquet and slightly brighter fruit, both reflecting the cooler region whence this wine comes; oak is very much part of the wine, as it is with the Nine Stones Barossa. Good value. Screwcap. 14% alc. **Rating** 89 **To** 2016 $15

Nine Stones Barossa Shiraz 2011 Medium red-purple; the wine has some shiraz fruit at its heart, and is well balanced; there is more vinosity here than expected, and the balance to the black fruits is good. Screwcap. 14% alc. **Rating** 87 **To** 2015 $15

Nine Stones Hilltops Shiraz 2011 Light to medium red-purple; there are more red fruits and spices here than in the Nine Stones Barossa, but not as much mid-palate presence. That said, the balance is fairly good. Screwcap. 13.5% alc. **Rating** 87 **To** 2014 $15

Nine Stones McLaren Vale Shiraz 2010 Medium crimson-purple; is a little lighter-bodied than its Nine Stones siblings, not expectedly, but there is a regional marker in the touch of chocolate. Needs more conviction. Screwcap. 14% alc. **Rating** 87 **To** 2015 $15

Evoi Wines ★★★★★

92 Dunsborough Lakes Drive, Dunsborough, WA 6281 **Region** Margaret River
T 0407 131 080 **www**.evoiwines.com **Open** By appt
Winemaker Nigel Ludlow **Est.** 2006 **Dozens** 600
NZ-born Flying Winemaker Nigel Ludlow has roosted in Margaret River for the past nine years, and has no intention of leaving, the beaches, scenery, lifestyle and wine quality all reasons to stay. Evoi's tiny production is dovetailed into Nigel's other winemaking responsibilities in the region. Exports to the UK and Hong Kong.

The Satyr Reserve 2011 A blend of cabernet sauvignon, petit verdot, merlot and malbec that has a gold medal sticker from the Blackwood Valley and a WA Boutique Wine Show, an apparent show hybrid that meant this Margaret River wine was able to enter; only 200 dozen made. It has an excellent, deep purple-crimson hue, its expansive and lush display of cassis fruits framed by quality French oak and ripe tannins. Screwcap. 14.5% alc. **Rating** 95 **To** 2031 $42

Reserve Margaret River Chardonnay 2011 Hand-picked, basket-pressed, barrel-fermented in new and 1-year-old French barriques. Bright quartz-green, it is as much about texture and structure as it is about the honeydew melon, fig and stone fruit flavours. Blue-Gold Sydney International Wine Competition '13. Screwcap. 14% alc. **Rating** 94 **To** 2016 $42

Eyre Creek

Main North Road, Auburn, SA 5451 **Region** Clare Valley
T 0418 818 400 **www**.eyrecreekwines.com.au **Open** W'ends & public hols 10–5,
Mon–Fri as per sign
Winemaker Stone Bridge Wines (Angela Meaney) **Est.** 1998 **Dozens** 2500 **Vyds** 2.9ha
John and Glenise Osborne, well-known Auburn hoteliers, established Eyre Creek in 1998. In
2008 they opened their cellar door, a renovated 100-year-old dairy, just north of Auburn. They
grow dryland shiraz and grenache; the production is sold at the cellar door, by mail order and
at selected bottle shops and restaurants in Adelaide and Sydney.

Clare Valley Grenache Rose 2010 Mid pink; a savoury bouquet of bramble
and red fruits; the palate is fresh for its age, with a taut acid line holding the fragile
fruit together. Screwcap. 12% alc. **Rating** 87 **To** 2013 $18 BE

Faber Vineyard

233 Haddrill Road, Baskerville, WA 6056 **Region** Swan Valley
T (08) 9296 0209 **www**.fabervineyard.com.au **Open** W'ends 11–4
Winemaker John Griffiths **Est.** 1997 **Dozens** 2000 **Vyds** 4.5ha
Former Houghton winemaker, now university lecturer and consultant John Griffiths teamed
with wife, Jane Micallef, to found Faber Vineyard. They have established shiraz, verdelho
(1.5ha each), brown muscat, chardonnay and petit verdot (0.5ha each). Says John, 'It may be
somewhat quixotic, but I'm a great fan of traditional warm-area Australian wine styles – those
found in areas such as Rutherglen and the Barossa, wines made in a relatively simple manner
that reflect the concentrated ripe flavours one expects in these regions. And when one
searches, some of these gems can be found from the Swan Valley.' Possessed of an excellent
palate, and with an impeccable winemaking background, the quality of John's wines is
guaranteed, although the rating is also quixotic. Exports to Hong Kong and China.

Reserve Swan Valley Shiraz 2010 Deep colour; comes in a massive, heavy
bottle that is a true portent of the full-bodied wine within; everything is in
abundance – black fruits, licorice, dark chocolate and tar – but in balance with
the tannins and oak. Shows what the Swan Valley can do if given the chance. The
wine-stained cork is a worry. 14.5% alc. **Rating** 94 **To** 2025 $58

Frankland River Cabernet 2010 Rating 93 To 2025 $48
Petit Verdot 2011 Rating 92 To 2021 $28
Riche Shiraz 2011 Rating 91 To 2019 $26

Far Ago Hill Wines

1371 Tugalong Road, Canyonleigh, NSW 2577 **Region** Southern Highlands
T (02) 9557 0089 **www**.faragohill.com **Open** Not
Winemaker Lark Hill (Sue Carpenter) **Est.** 2003 **Dozens** 600 **Vyds** 2.5ha
Katrina Hill lays it on the line when she describes herself as a mad, crazy, female vigneron,
and continues, 'What on earth possessed us (my ex husband and I) to plant a vineyard – I
will never know! "Grape change" seemed like a great idea at the time, and totally different
from interior design (me) and psychiatry (him). I don't think you understand how much
hard work a vineyard is, despite warnings, until you actually do it. Wombats, birds, the worst
sunburn I have ever had, and pruning for 14 weekends through the freezingness of winter!
Not exactly romantic.'

Reserve Canyonleigh Pinot Gris 2012 Full-on pink, almost into rose; the
maceration pre-pressing has led to this colour, and also to a slightly phenolic finish,
but there's no shortage of flavour. Screwcap. 12.8% alc. **Rating** 89 **To** 2014 $29

Feet First Wines

32 Parkinson Lane, Kardinya, WA 6163 (postal) **Region** Western Australia
T (08) 9314 7133 **www.feetfirstwines.com.au Open** Not
Winemaker Contract **Est.** 2004 **Dozens** 5000
This is the business of Ross and Ronnie (Veronica) Lawrence, who have been fine wine wholesalers in Perth since 1987, handling top-shelf Australian and imported wines. It is a virtual winery, with both grapegrowing and winemaking provided by contract. The wines are released in two ranges, the Feet First wines at around $17 a bottle, then three Limited Release wines (Shiraz, Grenache Barbera and Chardonnay) at around $30 a bottle.

Shiraz 2010 Bright, clear crimson-purple; red and black fruits course through the bouquet and elegant, fresh, medium-bodied palate, the alcohol seeming lower than it is; blackberry and plum are interwoven with spice, pepper and fine, gently savoury tannins. Has impeccable balance and length. Screwcap. 14.5% alc. **Rating** 95 **To** 2030 $30

Semillon Sauvignon Blanc 2012 Both varieties come from Margaret River, the grassy/lemony semillon matched by the gentle tropical aromas and flavours of the sauvignon blanc. A delicate style that won't frighten the horses, and offers obvious value. Screwcap. 12.8% alc. **Rating** 89 **To** 2014 $17
Chenin Blanc 2012 Rating 87 **To** 2014 $17

Fermoy Estate

838 Metricup Road, Wilyabrup, WA 6280 **Region** Margaret River
T (08) 9755 6285 **www.fermoy.com.au Open** 7 days 10–5
Winemaker Liz Dawson, Coralie Lewis-Garnier **Est.** 1985 **Dozens** 20 000 **Vyds** 17ha
A long-established estate-based winery with 17ha of semillon, sauvignon blanc, chardonnay, cabernet sauvignon and merlot. The Young family acquired Fermoy Estate in 2010, and built a new, larger cellar door, which opened in '13, signalling the drive to increase domestic sales. Notwithstanding its significant production, it is happy to keep a relatively low profile, however difficult that may be given the quality of the wines Liz Dawson is making. Exports to the US, Europe and Asia.

Margaret River Cabernet Sauvignon 2011 Strong red-purple; estate-grown from 25-year-old vines; has exemplary varietal expression, cassis foremost, black olive/earth as a counterpoint; the tannins are firm but balanced. Screwcap. 14.5% alc. **Rating** 94 **To** 2026 $30

Reserve Margaret River Semillon 2011 Rating 91 **To** 2016 $40 BE
Margaret River Cabernet Sauvignon 2010 Rating 91 **To** 2025 $30
Margaret River Chardonnay 2012 Rating 90 **To** 2016 $30 BE
Margaret River Merlot 2011 Rating 90 **To** 2018 $30 BE

Fernfield Wines

112 Rushlea Road, Eden Valley, SA 5235 **Region** Eden Valley
T (08) 8564 1041 **www.fernfieldwines.com.au Open** Fri–Mon 11–4
Winemaker Bronwyn Lillecrapp, Shannon Plummer **Est.** 2002 **Dozens** 1500
The establishment date of 2002 might, with a little poetic licence, be shown as 1864. Bryce Lillecrapp is the fifth generation of the Lillecrapp family; his great-great-great-grandfather bought land in the Eden Valley in 1864, subdividing it in 1866, establishing the township of Eden Valley and building the first house, Rushlea Homestead. Bryce restored this building as a bicentennial project; it now serves as Fernfield Wines' cellar door. He heads up Fernfield as grapegrower, with his wife Bronwyn chief winemaker, son Shannon cellar hand and assistant winemaker, and daughter Rebecca the wine marketer.

Eden Valley Merlot 2010 Deep crimson; a vibrant bouquet of spiced plum, mocha and tar; the palate is surprisingly fresh, although it does show some heat from the 15.4% alc/vol, yet manages to sustain life and varietal integrity. Screwcap. **Rating** 88 **To** 2016 $20 BE

Wayward Blend Eden Valley Cabernet Sauvignon Merlot Cabernet Franc 2010 Deep crimson; a very ripe and blackberry pastille-like bouquet, with mocha and fruitcake; richly textured, and deeply fruited, with a long sweet and charry finish. Screwcap. 15.2% alc. **Rating** 88 **To** 2018 $20 BE

Ferngrove ★★★★★

276 Ferngrove Road, Frankland River, WA 6396 **Region** Frankland River
T (08) 9855 2378 **www.**ferngrove.com.au **Open** Mon–Sat 10–4
Winemaker Kim Horton **Est.** 1997 **Dozens** NFP **Vyds** 210.4ha
After 90 years of beef and dairy farming heritage, Murray Burton ventured into premium grapegrowing and winemaking in 1997. Today the venture he founded has two large vineyards in Frankland River planted to the leading varieties, including shiraz, cabernet sauvignon, chardonnay, sauvignon blanc, merlot and semillon, with a small but important planting of malbec. The operation centres around the Ferngrove Vineyard, with its large rammed-earth winery and tourist complex. Part of the vineyard production is sold as grapes, part as juice or must, part as finished wine, and the pick of the crop is made for the Ferngrove label. The consistency of its wines across a wide range of price points is wholly admirable. Acquired Killerby (Margaret River) in 2008. Exports to the UK, the US and other major markets.

🍷🍷🍷🍷🍷 **The Stirlings Shiraz Cabernet Sauvignon 2009** Brilliant purple-crimson; spent 20 months in French oak, and its quality is immediately obvious, fruit and oak seamlessly joined, the blackcurrant, blackberry and licorice fruit woven through with fine tannins and quality oak; medium-bodied, the tannins fine and ripe, the balance impeccable. Screwcap. 13.5% alc. **Rating** 96 **To** 2034 $70

✪ **Cossack Frankland River Riesling 2012** Bright straw-green; another lovely wine under the Cossack label; the fruit aromas and flavours almost shimmer in their complexity, with lime, lemon and a whisper of mandarin; great value. Screwcap. 13% alc. **Rating** 95 **To** 2022 $23

Majestic Frankland River Cabernet Sauvignon 2010 Bright hue; an ultra-powerful, intense and long palate; despite the power, the tannins are supple, and the oak balance and integration good. An extremely impressive wine. Screwcap. 13.5% alc. **Rating** 95 **To** 2030 $32

Frankland River Sauvignon Blanc 2012 The aromatic bouquet has tropical fruits in abundance, as does the palate, with passionfruit to the fore, backed by citrus; the intensity, texture and length of the wine lift it well clear of the ruck, aided by crisp acidity on the finish. Screwcap. 14% alc. **Rating** 94 **To** 2014 $20

✪ **Leaping Lizard Shiraz 2011** Clear, full purple-crimson; has a fragrant, spicy/peppery cool-climate bouquet leading into a very lively and juicy medium-bodied palate with a display of black cherry/blackberry/satsuma plum flavours, oak and tannins playing a secondary role. Screwcap. 13.5% alc. **Rating** 94 **To** 2020 $18

Dragon Frankland River Shiraz 2011 Good hue and depth; a supple and smooth medium-bodied palate, the mix of gently savoury/spicy black fruits picking up precisely the message of the fragrant bouquet; the palate is long and very well balanced, the tannins ripe. Shows flavour achieved at a modest alcohol level. Screwcap. 13% alc. **Rating** 94 **To** 2026 $32

Dragon Frankland River Shiraz 2010 Mid crimson, purple hue; restrained and complex on the bouquet with black cherry, blackberry, sage and ironstone minerality on display; the palate is taut and full of gravelly tannins; fresh acidity and a long, spicy finish. Screwcap. 13.5% alc. **Rating** 94 **To** 2022 $32 BE

King Frankland River Malbec 2011 Bright purple-crimson; has the texture and structure so often missing from varietal Malbecs, but without distracting from the plush plum/plum jam fruit of the variety. Will be as good to drink in 10 years as it is today. Screwcap. 13% alc. **Rating** 94 **To** 2020 $32

King Frankland River Malbec 2010 A pre-fermentation cold soak, and further maturation post an 8-day fermentation preceded 20 months' maturation in predominantly new French and American oak; medium crimson-purple, the juicy red and black berry fruits and silky tannins signalling the unqualified success of the winemaking. Screwcap. 13.5% alc. **Rating** 94 **To** 2025 $30

🍷🍷🍷🍷🍷 Majestic Frankland River Cabernet Sauvignon 2011 Rating 93 To 2030 $32
✪ Leaping Lizard Semillon Sauvignon Blanc 2012 Pale straw-green; a bright
and breezy blend of tropical fruits, tinned passionfruit and a little pineapple
introduce the wine before lemon citrus flavours take hold, aided by crisp, crunchy
acidity on the finish. Screwcap. 13.5% alc. Rating 92 To 2014 $18
✪ Leaping Lizard Cabernet Sauvignon Merlot 2010 Strong crimson;
perfectly ripened cassis/blackcurrant fruit with undertones of spice leads into a
well-balanced, medium-bodied palate, both tannin and controlled French oak
contributing to a complete wine. Screwcap. 13.5% alc. Rating 92 To 2020 $18
✪ Frankland River Off Dry Riesling 2012 Lightly frizzante and showing lime,
wet slate and bath talc on the bouquet; the palate is lively and fresh, fun-filled and
a simple pleasure to consume, finishing dry and chalky; pass the spicy Asian food
please. Screwcap. 11% alc. Rating 92 To 2018 $20 BE
Leaping Lizard Sauvignon Blanc 2012 Rating 90 To 2013 $18
Diamond Frankland River Chardonnay 2011 Rating 90 To 2017 $25 BE
✪ Frankland River Shiraz 2010 Deep garnet; showing some developed leather
and earth notes, with red and black fruits providing lift on the bouquet; the palate
is medium-bodied and soft on entry, with jubey red fruits giving way to firm
tannins on the savoury finish. Screwcap. 14% alc. Rating 90 To 2018 $20 BE

Fighting Gully Road

319 Whorouly South Road, Whorouly South, Vic 3735 **Region** Beechworth
T (03) 5727 1434 **www**.fightinggully.com **Open** By appt
Winemaker Mark Walpole, Adrian Rodda **Est.** 1997 **Dozens** 1000 **Vyds** 8.3ha
Mark Walpole and partner Carolyn De Poi began the development of their Aquila Audax
Vineyard in 1997, planting the first vines. It is situated between 530m and 580m above sea
level: the upper-eastern slopes are planted to pinot noir and the warmer western slopes to
cabernet sauvignon; there are also small quantities of shiraz, tempranillo, sangiovese and merlot.

🍷🍷🍷🍷🍷 Beechworth Shiraz 2010 Deep garnet; the dynamic duo of Mark Walpole and
Adrian Rodda have captured a fine combination of vibrant red and dark fruits,
and savoury wet slate, roasted meat and thyme on the bouquet; the palate offers
a refreshing mix of tannins and ample medium-grained tannins; the finish is
harmonious and surprisingly long. Screwcap. 13.5% alc. Rating 94 To 2022 $32 BE

🍷🍷🍷🍷🍷 Beechworth Pinot Noir 2011 Rating 90 To 2016 $24
Beechworth Sangiovese 2011 Rating 90 To 2017 $28 BE
Tempranillo 2009 Rating 90 To 2015 $28 BE

Fire Gully

Metricup Road, Wilyabrup, WA 6280 **Region** Margaret River
T (08) 9755 6220 **www**.firegully.com.au **Open** By appt
Winemaker Dr Michael Peterkin **Est.** 1988 **Dozens** 5000 **Vyds** 13.4ha
The Fire Gully vineyard has been established on what was first a dairy and then a beef farm.
A 6ha lake created in a gully ravaged by bushfires gave the property its name. In 1998 Mike
Peterkin of Pierro purchased the property; he manages the vineyard in conjunction with
former owners Ellis and Margaret Butcher. He regards the Fire Gully wines as entirely separate
from those of Pierro, being estate-grown: the vineyards are planted to cabernet sauvignon,
merlot, shiraz, semillon, sauvignon blanc, chardonnay, viognier and chenin blanc, and have
been increased by over 4ha in recent years. Exports to all major markets.

🍷🍷🍷🍷🍷 Margaret River Sauvignon Blanc Semillon 2012 Light straw-green; the
✪ bouquet is powerful and complex, accurately pointing to a rich and complex
palate that belies its low alcohol, and succeeds admirably with its array of ripe
lemon and gooseberry fruit. Screwcap. 12.5% alc. Rating 94 To 2015 $20

🍷🍷🍷🍷🍷 Margaret River Chardonnay 2011 Rating 93 To 2016 $26
Margaret River Shiraz Viognier 2010 Rating 92 To 2029 $26

ŶŶŶŶ   **Cabernet Sauvignon Merlot 2010** Good hue, but light; seemingly (from
✪   the back label) co-fermented; has supremely honest red and blackcurrant aromas
and flavours, and good mouthfeel, thanks to silky tannins. Screwcap. 13.5% alc.
Rating 89 **To** 2016 $19

Fireblock   ★★★★☆

28 Kiewa Place, Coomba Park, NSW 2428 (postal) **Region** Clare Valley
T (02) 6554 2193 **Open** Not
Winemaker O'Leary Walker **Est.** 1926 **Dozens** 3000 **Vyds** 6ha
Fireblock (formerly Old Station Vineyard) is owned by Bill and Noel Ireland, who purchased
the almost-70-year-old Watervale vineyard in 1995. The vines planted in 1926 (3ha of shiraz
and 2ha of grenache) are dry-grown, and the riesling (1ha) was replanted to the Geisenheim
clone in 2008 when town water became available. Watervale Riesling, Old Vine Shiraz and
Old Vine Grenache are skilfully contract-made, winning trophies and gold medals at capital
city wine shows. Exports to the US, Sweden and Malaysia.

ŶŶŶŶŶ   **Watervale Riesling 2012** Bright green-straw; the floral, blossom-filled bouquet
✪   is a promising opening stanza, and the palate picks up the story without losing a
beat; long, fine and intense, with lime and minerally acidity given an added twist
by a faint touch of passionfruit. Screwcap. 12% alc. **Rating** 94 **To** 2020 $17

ŶŶŶŶŶ   **Old Vine Clare Valley Shiraz 2010 Rating** 91 **To** 2020 $20
✪   **Old Vine Clare Valley Grenache 2008** Light but bright hue; the vines were
planted in 1926, and the wine has more structure and texture than most Clare
Valley Grenache; while the flavours are in the raspberry/red cherry spectrum, they
show no confection characters, and the soft tannins are neatly woven through the
palate. Screwcap. 14.5% alc. **Rating** 91 **To** 2015 $17

Firetail   ★★★★

21 Bessell Road, Rosa Glen, WA 6285 **Region** Margaret River
T (08) 9757 5156 **www**.firetail.com.au **Open** 7 days 11–5
Winemaker Contract **Est.** 2002 **Dozens** 1600 **Vyds** 5.3ha
Electrical engineer Jessica Worrall and chemical engineer Rob Glass worked in the oil and
gas industry in Australia and The Netherlands for 20 years before making a staged move into
grapegrowing and the establishment of Firetail. Their first move was the planting of a small
vineyard of merlot in Geographe, which produced its first wine in 2003; a more important
move was the acquisition of a somewhat neglected vineyard (and rammed-earth house) in
Margaret River. Here the Geographe merlot is supplemented by semillon, sauvignon blanc
and cabernet sauvignon, the Margaret River plantings dating back to 2004. Jessica is in the
final stages of completing her Masters of Viticulture at Wine Technology at the University of
Melbourne while managing the vineyard and the wine production, and Rob balances the
demands of the wine sales and marketing with consulting for the liquid natural gas business.
It comes as no surprise that the wines are contract-made. Exports to Hong Kong, Japan
and China.

ŶŶŶŶŶ   **Margaret River Cabernet Sauvignon 2011** Medium red-purple; the fragrant,
cassis-accented bouquet is mirrored on the medium-bodied palate; here the cassis
is framed by ripe tannins and cedary oak; an elegant wine that won a gold medal
at the Qantas Wine Show of WA '12. Diam. 13.2% alc. **Rating** 94 **To** 2021 $28

ŶŶŶŶ   **Margaret River Semillon Sauvignon Blanc 2011 Rating** 89 **To** 2014 $19

First Creek Wines   ★★★★★

600 McDonalds Road, Pokolbin, NSW 2320 **Region** Hunter Valley
T (02) 4998 7293 **www**.firstcreekwines.com.au **Open** 7 days 10–5
Winemaker Liz Jackson, Damien Stevens, Greg Silkman **Est.** 1984 **Dozens** 25 000
First Creek Wines is the brand of First Creek Winemaking Services, a company contract-
making wine for over 25 clients. Winemaker Liz Jackson had an exceptional year in 2011: she

was a finalist in the Gourmet Traveller Winemaker of the Year awards, winner of the Hunter Valley Winemaker of the Year, and won Best Red Wine of Show at the NSW Wine Awards for the Winemakers Reserve Shiraz 2010. At the James Halliday Chardonnay Challenge '12, the First Creek Winemakers Reserve Chardonnay 2011 was named top Hunter Valley Chardonnay, adding to its prior triple-trophy record. Exports to the UK, Sweden and China.

ΨΨΨΨΨ **Winemaker's Reserve Hunter Valley Chardonnay 2012** Bright straw-green; the complex bouquet has had plenty of winemaker attention, slightly funky and with solids fermentation aromas, but rapidly throws those characters off with its exceptionally intense and long grapefruit and white peach palate; oak has, of course, played an important role. Screwcap. 12.5% alc. **Rating** 95 **To** 2020 $60
Winemaker's Reserve Hunter Valley Semillon 2009 Bright, gleaming straw-green; reflects the 94 points (Jan '10), but also the first important stages of development, with lemon, lemongrass and minerally acidity developing in lockstep. Another 5 years should see the wine at the zenith of its powers, but even then with another decade of vibrant health. Screwcap. 11% alc. **Rating** 94 **To** 2024 $40
Winemaker's Reserve Hunter Valley Shiraz 2011 Deep crimson-purple; a very good full-bodied Hunter Valley Shiraz from a very good vintage, stacked with earthy blackberry fruit, tannins and oak to match. The back label writer's recommendation of (only) 'several years of careful cellaring' must have been a misprint for 'several decades'. Screwcap. 13% alc. **Rating** 94 **To** 2031 $50

ΨΨΨΨΨ **Winemaker's Reserve Semillon 2012 Rating** 93 **To** 2025 $40
Hunter Valley Chardonnay 2010 Rating 92 **To** 2015 $25

First Drop Wines ★★★★★

Beckwith Park, Tanunda Road, Nuriootpa, SA 5335 **Region** Barossa Valley
T (08) 8562 3324 **www**.firstdropwines.com **Open** Not
Winemaker Matt Gant **Est.** 2005 **Dozens** 10 000
The First Drop Wines of today has been transformed since its establishment in 2005. It now has a real winery, part of the old Penfolds winery at Nuriootpa, shared with Tim Smith Wines. The group of buildings is now called Beckwith Park, in honour of the man who did so much groundbreaking work for Penfolds (Ray Beckwith OAM, who died in 2012, but not before his 100th birthday; his other recognition came in the form of the Maurice O'Shea Award, rightly recognising that while Penfolds was his employer, the work he did on wine chemistry and wine bacterial disease was of huge importance). Various of the wines have had wine show success. Exports to the UK, the US, Canada, Denmark, Japan, Hong Kong, Singapore and NZ.

ΨΨΨΨΨ **Fat of the Land Seppeltsfield Single Vineyard Barossa Valley Shiraz 2010** Not surprisingly, the colour is impenetrable and the lashings of black fruits also display an alluring scent of vine sap complexity; the palate is full-blooded, yet shows refinement and integration of tannins, fruit and oak, with a staggeringly long, bright, acid finish. Cork. 14.5% alc. **Rating** 95 **To** 2030 $75 BE
The Cream Barossa Valley Shiraz 2010 Vivid purple hue; the bouquet offers an intriguing blend of red and black fruits, hints of licorice and bitter chocolate, and a seasoning of charry oak; the palate is evenly balanced, fresh and vacillates between medium- and full-bodied in a most pleasant manner; long, complex, juicy, focused and harmonious. Cork. 14.5% alc. **Rating** 95 **To** 2035 $100 BE
Fat of the Land Single Vineyard Greenock Barossa Valley Shiraz 2010 The very essence of blackberry pastille mixed with spicy vanillin oak; roasted meat and black olive are on the bouquet; the palate is unctuous and warm, yet is still looking for some time for all parts to come together. There is a depth of fruit and complexity that will satisfy lovers of the style, and see it evolve with grace over the coming years. Cork. 14.5% alc. **Rating** 94 **To** 2030 $75 BE

ΨΨΨΨΨ **Fat of the Land Ebenezer Shiraz 2010 Rating** 93 **To** 2025 $75 BE
Two Percent Barossa Shiraz 2010 Rating 93 **To** 2022 $35 BE
Mother's Milk Barossa Shiraz 2011 Rating 90 **To** 2017 $25 BE
Half & Half Barossa Shiraz Monastrell 2010 Rating 90 **To** 2017 $25 BE

5 Blind Mice

PO Box 243, Basket Range, SA 5138 **Region** Adelaide Hills
T (08) 8390 0206 **www.5blindmice.com.au Open** Not
Winemaker Jodie and Hugh Armstrong **Est.** 2004 **Dozens** 300
Owners Jodie and Hugh Armstrong say, 'What started out as an idea between friends and family to make something for ourselves to drink at home during the week has blossomed into a quest for something to stand proudly on its own.' The grapes are chosen from small sections of three of the vineyards that Jodie manages, and she and Hugh make the wines in garagiste facilities in the Adelaide Hills and McLaren Vale with the support of local oenological talent. Exports to Singapore.

PPPP **La Debutante McLaren Vale Shiraz 2011** Dense purple-crimson; the promise of the colour is fulfilled on the medium- to full-bodied palate, with spice and dark chocolate threaded through the black fruits; its Achilles heel is a lack of true fruit vinosity on the mid-palate. Screwcap. 13.5% alc. **Rating** 89 **To** 2015 $19
Adelaide Hills Pinot Noir 2010 Has retained the depth and crimson-purple hue of a young pinot, although 3 years old; ripe poached plum flavours dominate the fruit, forceful tannins the palate. The thumbprint of the winemaker is too strong, leading to an extractive palate. Cork. 13% alc. **Rating** 87 **To** 2016 $35

Five Geese

389 Chapel Hill Road, Blewitt Springs, SA 5171 (postal) **Region** McLaren Vale
T (08) 8383 0576 **www.fivegeese.com.au Open** Not
Winemaker Contract **Est.** 1999 **Dozens** 3000 **Vyds** 26ha
Sue Trott is passionate about her Five Geese wine, which is produced by Hillgrove Wines. The wines come from vines planted in 1927 and '65. The grapes were sold for many years, but in '99 Sue decided to create her own label and make a strictly limited amount of wine from the pick of the vineyards, which are run on organic principles. Exports to the UK, the US, Hong Kong, South Korea and Singapore.

PPPPP **Reserve McLaren Vale Shiraz 2010** The grapes come from the 50-year-old vines surrounding Sue Trott's house in Blewitt Springs. It has wonderful crimson-purple colour, a great dark berry bouquet, and a glorious palate, with layer upon layer of plum and dark chocolate fruit accompanied by velvety tannins, oak somewhere in the background. Screwcap. 14.5% alc. **Rating** 96 **To** 2040 $35

PPPPP **McLaren Vale Shiraz 2011** From Sue Trott's estate vineyard in the Blewitt Springs area; despite meticulous vineyard work, 50% of the grapes were discarded, and no Reserve wine was made in '11. It has excellent colour and bouquet, but its most attractive feature is the fluid line in the mouth, and the overall spicy/juicy balance between fruit, oak and tannins. Screwcap. 14.5% alc. **Rating** 93 **To** 2021 $22
The Gander's Blend Grenache Shiraz 2010 Rating 92 **To** 2017 $22
The Gander's Blend Grenache Shiraz 2011 Rating 90 **To** 2014 $22

PPPP **Flocking Ducks McLaren Vale Grenache Shiraz 2011** A 75/25% blend, a seriously humorous back label, and bright colour; due to detailed care, this is a pretty smart wine for casual drinking, its colour attesting to the sprightly red berry flavours to follow. Don't drink too much before talking about the wine by name. Screwcap. 13.5% alc. **Rating** 89 **To** 2014 $15

Flametree

Cnr Caves Road/Chain Avenue, Dunsborough, WA 6281 **Region** Margaret River
T (08) 9756 8577 **www.flametreewines.com Open** 7 days 10–5
Winemaker Cliff Royle, Julian Scott **Est.** 2007 **Dozens** 15 000
Flametree, owned by the Towner family (John, Liz and Rob), has had extraordinary success since its first vintage in 2007. The usual practice of planting a vineyard and then finding

someone to make the wine was turned on its head: a state-of-the-art winery was built, and grape purchase agreements entered into with various growers in the region. Gold medal after gold medal, and trophy after trophy followed, topped by the winning of the Jimmy Watson Trophy with its first red wine, the 2007 Cabernet Merlot. If all this were not enough, Flametree has secured the services of former long-serving winemaker at Voyager Estate, Cliff Royle. Exports to the UK, Sweden, Fiji, Singapore, the Maldives, Indonesia, Hong Kong and China.

ΨΨΨΨΨ **S.R.S. Margaret River Cabernet Sauvignon 2011** This is a Cabernet of the highest quality, its colour excellent, its blackcurrant fruit framed by ripe, persistent tannins and quality French oak, its long-term future assured. Screwcap. 14% alc. **Rating** 96 **To** 2041 $50

S.R.S. Wallcliffe Margaret River Chardonnay 2012 Bright green-straw; the intensity of the wine comes from grapes from the southern, coolest part of Margaret River; here length is more important than the depth of Margaret River Chardonnay as a whole; the flavour spectrum and mouthfeel are also distinctly different, firmly tied to grapefruit/citrus. Screwcap. 13% alc. **Rating** 95 **To** 2022 $50

S.R.S. Wallcliffe Margaret River Chardonnay 2011 S.R.S. is Flametree's subregional series, this wine coming from the Wallcliffe area, which (many years ago) I dubbed the Golden Triangle; this is an effortlessly generous, fruit-driven style, with the depth of flavour that is the mark of Margaret River, ripe stone fruit the core. Screwcap. 13.5% alc. **Rating** 95 **To** 2021 $50

S.R.S. Karridale Margaret River Sauvignon Blanc 2012 Part fermented in stainless steel, part in French oak, the wine has well above average intensity and length; guava, lychee and nectarine fruit is balanced by the citrus component that manifests itself with the acidity running through the length of the palate. Screwcap. 13% alc. **Rating** 94 **To** 2015 $33

Margaret River Chardonnay 2011 Bright straw-green; in best Margaret River style, brings together elegance and depth of flavour; it really shines with the creamy/nutty texture and lifted white peach characters that swell on the finish and aftertaste. Screwcap. 13.5% alc. **Rating** 94 **To** 2018 $30

Margaret River Cabernet Merlot 2011 Bright, full red-purple; a full-bodied blend, rich and textured after 14 months' maturation in French oak; fruit, oak and tannins all make their mark in a wine with the requisite balance for a long life. Screwcap. 14% alc. **Rating** 94 **To** 2031 $30

ΨΨΨΨΨ **Frankland River Shiraz 2011** **Rating** 93 **To** 2030 $30

Margaret River Sauvignon Blanc Semillon 2012 **Rating** 92 **To** 2014 $24

Margaret River Chardonnay 2012 **Rating** 92 **To** 2018 $25

✪ **Embers Margaret River Cabernet Sauvignon 2011** Deep crimson-purple; said to be made as an early-drinking style, with redcurrant fruit to the fore; it's a very good wine, but the amount of tannins and oak makes it a cellaring proposition, needing time to calm down. Screwcap. 14% alc. **Rating** 92 **To** 2026 $20

Margaret River Shiraz 2011 **Rating** 91 **To** 2019 $24

Embers Margaret River Semillon Sauvignon Blanc 2012 **Rating** 90 **To** 2013 $20

Flaxman Wines   ★★★★★

Lot 535 Flaxmans Valley Road, Angaston, SA 5353 **Region** Eden Valley
T 0411 668 949 **www.**flaxmanwines.com.au **Open** By appt
Winemaker Colin Sheppard **Est.** 2005 **Dozens** 1500 **Vyds** 2ha
After visiting the Barossa Valley for over a decade, and working during vintage with Andrew Seppelt at Murray Street Vineyards, Melbourne residents Colin and Fiona Sheppard decided on a seachange and found a small, old vineyard overlooking Flaxmans Valley. It consists of 1ha of 40+-year-old riesling, 1ha of 50+-year-old shiraz and a small planting of 40+-year-old semillon. The vines are dry-grown, hand-pruned and hand-picked, and treated – say the

Sheppards — as their garden. Yields are restricted to under 4 tonnes per hectare, and small amounts of locally grown grapes are also purchased.

ŶŶŶŶŶ **Shhh Eden Valley Cabernet 2010** Full crimson-purple; a luscious, cassis-filled wine; open-fermented and matured in French oak for 24 months; the texture is essentially soft and welcoming, the palate medium- rather than full-bodied. A lovely Cabernet. Screwcap. 14.5% alc. **Rating** 96 **To** 2040 $37
Eden Valley Shiraz 2010 Medium purple-crimson; from dry-grown vines up to 83 years old, matured in 25% new French oak for 24 months, and neither fined nor filtered. It is joyously full-bodied, with a tsunami of black fruits and ripe tannins. 120 dozen made. Screwcap. 14% alc. **Rating** 95 **To** 2035 $48
Eden Valley Riesling 2012 Pale quartz; a strikingly, almost painfully, intense Riesling, with teeth-chattering acidity, but enough fruit to make it worthwhile as a long-term cellaring proposition. Screwcap. 11% alc. **Rating** 94 **To** 2025 $27
Barossa Valley Mataro 2010 Light to medium purple-crimson; open-fermented, matured in used French oak for 24 months. Colin Sheppard pulls another rabbit from the hat with the delicious red fruits and superfine tannins of the palate. He seems to have the same intuitive touch as Boireann's Peter Stark in making small volumes of flawless wines. Screwcap. 14.5% alc. **Rating** 94 **To** 2025 $37

ŶŶŶŶŶ **The Stranger Barossa Shiraz Cabernet 2011** **Rating** 91 **To** 2018 $37
Eden Valley Dessert Semillon 2012 **Rating** 91 **To** 2015 $22

Fletcher Wines   ★★★☆

90 Gold Street, Collingwood, Vic 3066 **Region** Various
T 0403 302 729 **www.**fletcherwines.com **Open** By appt
Winemaker David Fletcher **Est.** 2009 **Dozens** 200
David Fletcher has a background that would make any Florentine Renaissance man proud. While completing his oenology course at Adelaide University, he worked filling flagons and tending vines at Tinlins in McLaren Vale. On graduation in 2003, he worked for O'Leary Walker in the Clare Valley for two years; for reasons not entirely self-evident, this inspired him to work in Burgundy, and in '04 he worked harvest at Domaine Chevrot. In love with Pinot, he moved to the Yarra Valley at the start of '06, where he stayed for three years as assistant winemaker at Sticks, while fitting in a northern hemisphere vintage each year, once in Kazakhstan, and twice in Italy for Ceretto. In '09, he became a grape liaison officer with Foster's, with responsibilities extending across Vic and parts of NSW. This job then offered him the opportunity to fill the same role in the Napa Valley and Santa Barbara County for Beringer, part of Foster's. Agatha Christie would quickly find the link that led David and wife Eleanor to establish Fletcher Wines, dedicated solely to making Nebbiolo from vines at least 10 years old.

ŶŶŶŶŶ **Malakoff Estate Vineyard Pyrenees Nebbiolo 2011** Fair colour given the variety and vintage, and indeed the savoury cherry flavour and mouthfeel are an attractive stage for the variety, the tannins fine and balanced. Diam. 14% alc. **Rating** 90 **To** 2018 $50

ŶŶŶŶ **The Minion Nebbiolo 2011** **Rating** 87 **To** 2015 $35

Flint's of Coonawarra   ★★★★

Flint Road, Coonawarra, SA 5263 **Region** Coonawarra
T (08) 8736 5046 **www.**flintsofcoonawarra.com.au **Open** By appt
Winemaker Contract **Est.** 2001 **Dozens** 2000 **Vyds** 84ha
Six generations of the Flint family have lived and worked in Coonawarra since 1840. Damian Flint and his family began the development of 84ha of cabernet sauvignon, shiraz and merlot in 1989, but it was not until 2000 that they decided to have a small portion of cabernet sauvignon contract-made. Damian and Sue oversee the day-to-day running of both the vineyard and the farm, with Matthew, who studied viticulture in the Barossa, managing the vineyard.

ΨΨΨΨΥ **Rostrevor Shiraz 2010** Good retention of crimson-purple hue; it's no surprise
⊘   prior vintages of this wine should have twice won the trophy for Best Shiraz
           at the Limestone Coast Wine Show; it has abundant and generous plum and
           blackberry fruit, and oak and tannins to match. Screwcap. 14.5% alc. **Rating** 92
           To 2025 $20

⊘   **Gammon's Crossing Cabernet Sauvignon 2010** Medium red-purple; has
           abundant varietal expression to its medium- to full-bodied palate, and the tannins
           to sustain it for many years to come. French oak, too, has made its contribution.
           Screwcap. 14.5% alc. **Rating** 92 **To** 2030 $20

Flying Fish Cove

Caves Road, Wilyabrup, WA 6284 **Region** Margaret River
T (08) 9755 6600 **www.**flyingfishcove.com **Open** 7 days 11–5
Winemaker Simon Ding, Damon Eastaugh **Est.** 2000 **Dozens** 19 000 **Vyds** 25ha
Flying Fish Cove has two strings to its bow: contract winemaking for others, and the
development of its own brand, partly based on 25ha of estate plantings. The long-serving
winemakers both had a circuitous journey before falling prey to the lure of wine. Simon Ding
finished an apprenticeship in metalwork in 1993, and took off to see the world; some of his
employment was in restaurants and bars, which sparked his interest in wine. On returning to
Australia in '96 he became a cellar hand at Fermoy Estate, which led him to the Bachelor of
Science Degree, graduating in four years (and a vintage in Italy), and joining the Flying Fish
Cove team in '98. Damon Easthaugh has always lived in WA, spending seven years studying
law, among other things, at the University of WA. Practising law did not have the same appeal
as winemaking, and Damon became a founding member of the winery. Exports to the US
and Singapore.

ΨΨΨΨΨ **The Wildberry Reserve Margaret River Cabernet Sauvignon 2011**
           Estate-grown, open-fermented and hand-plunged, then matured in French oak.
           This is a stylish, albeit luscious, medium-bodied wine awash with cassis, mulberry
           and redcurrant fruit, cedary oak and plush tannins. Screwcap. 14.5% alc. **Rating** 94
           To 2026 $35

ΨΨΨΨΥ **Margaret River Shiraz 2011** Full crimson-purple; an unashamedly full-bodied
⊘   Shiraz, with multiple layers of black fruits, licorice, spice, French oak and – in
           spades – tannins. While those tannins need time to resolve, I think the wine has
           the balance needed to prosper with age, and a gamble at this price is reasonable.
           Screwcap. 14.5% alc. **Rating** 93 **To** 2031 $22

⊘   **Margaret River Sauvignon Blanc Semillon 2012** Light straw-green; the
           wanton display of tropical fruits from the sauvignon blanc – including pineapple
           and banana – on the bouquet and palate keep the semillon at bay until the
           finish, lengthened and streamlined by the citrus acidity of the semillon. Screwcap.
           12.5% alc. **Rating** 92 **To** 2014 $22
           Margaret River Chardonnay 2011 **Rating** 91 **To** 2016 $22

Flynns Wines

Lot 5 Lewis Road, Heathcote, Vic 3523 **Region** Heathcote
T (03) 5433 6297 **www.**flynnswines.com **Open** Mon–Fri 11–2.30, w'ends 11.30–5
Winemaker Greg and Natala Flynn **Est.** 1999 **Dozens** 2000 **Vyds** 4.12ha
The Flynn name has a long association with Heathcote. In the 1970s John Flynn and Laurie
Williams established a 2ha vineyard next door to Mount Ida Vineyard, on the rich, red
Cambrian soil. It produced some spectacular wines before being sold in 1983. Greg and
Natala Flynn (no relation to John Flynn) spent 18 months searching for their property, 13km
north of Heathcote on the same red Cambrian soil. They have established shiraz, sangiovese,
verdelho, cabernet sauvignon and merlot. Greg is a Roseworthy marketing graduate, and has
had 23 years working at the coalface of retail and wholesale businesses, interweaving nine
years of vineyard and winemaking experience, supplemented by the two-year Bendigo TAFE
winemaking course. Just for good measure, wife Natala joined Greg for the last eight years of
vineyard and winemaking, and likewise completed the TAFE course.

ŶŶŶŶŶ **Heathcote Vermentino 2012** Light straw-green; this has great drive and complexity, amplified by 20% fermentation in new French oak; the intensity of citrus peel and apple fruit is compelling, as are the length of the finish and aftertaste. Screwcap. 13.5% alc. **Rating** 94 **To** 2016 $29

MC Heathcote Shiraz 2010 MC stands for multiple clones; black cherry, plum and blackberry fruit drive the bouquet and the medium- to full-bodied palate until the mix of oak and ripe tannins add another dimension to what will be a long-lived wine. Screwcap. 14.5% alc. **Rating** 94 **To** 2035 $35

James Flynn Heathcote Shiraz 2010 Good colour; a lavishly textured and structured Shiraz which spent 1 year in new oak, at which point the best barrels were chosen to spend another year in new French and American oak. That oak is obvious, but it is very well integrated and there is a considerable volume of black fruits and velvety tannins to balance the oak. Screwcap. 14.8% alc. **Rating** 94 **To** 2030 $70

ŶŶŶŶŶ **MC Heathcote Shiraz 2009** **Rating** 92 **To** 2029 $35
Heathcote Viognier 2012 **Rating** 90 **To** 2014 $28

Forbes & Forbes ★★★★☆

Mengler Hill Road, Angaston, Tanunda, SA 5352 **Region** Eden Valley
T (08) 8568 2709 **Open** Sat 11–5
Winemaker Colin Forbes **Est.** 2008 **Dozens** 600 **Vyds** 5ha
This venture is owned by Colin and Robert Forbes, and their respective partners. Colin says, 'I have been in the industry for a "frightening" length of time', beginning with Thomas Hardy & Sons in 1974.' Currently he is contract winemaking for McLean's Farm, Smallfry, John Dawkins and Partalunga Vineyard, as well as making the wines for Forbes & Forbes. The winemaking is carried out in the shed owned by McLean's Farm. While Colin is particularly attached to riesling, the property owned by the partners in Eden Valley has 2ha each of riesling and merlot, and 1ha of cabernet sauvignon.

ŶŶŶŶŶ **Eden Valley Riesling 2012** The little known Forbes & Forbes is a secret worth
✪ discovering for its approachable, value-for-money riesling. A wine of considerable persistence and exacting purity, with an enticing hint of white pepper to its pretty lime blossom and lemon zest perfume. Fine, softly textured minerality glides through a gentle, clean finish. Screwcap. 11.3% alc. **Rating** 93 **To** 2017 $22 TS

Forest Hill Vineyard ★★★★★

Cnr South Coast Highway/Myers Road, Denmark, WA 6333 **Region** Great Southern
T (08) 9848 0000 **www**.foresthillwines.com.au **Open** 7 days 10–4
Winemaker Clémence Haselgrove **Est.** 1965 **Dozens** 23 000 **Vyds** 65ha
This family-owned business is one of the oldest 'new' winemaking operations in WA, and was the site for the first grape plantings in Great Southern in 1965. The Forest Hill brand became well known, aided by the fact that a '75 Riesling made by Sandalford from Forest Hill grapes won nine trophies. The quality of the wines made from the oldest vines on the property is awesome (released under the numbered vineyard block labels). Betty Quick, co-founder of Forest Hill (and of cool-climate wine production in WA) received the Jack Mann Award for lifetime support of the WA wine industry in 2011. Exports to Taiwan, Hong Kong, Singapore and China.

ŶŶŶŶŶ **Block 1 Mount Barker Riesling 2012** The fragrant and flowery, talc and blossom-filled bouquet leads into a leisurely uncoiling palate of lime and lemon, with quite beautiful flavour, mouthfeel and balance. From the oldest riesling vines in WA. Screwcap. 11.7% alc. **Rating** 96 **To** 2027 $40

Estate Great Southern Shiraz 2011 Deep garnet, purple hue; pristine red and black fruits are evident on the bouquet, offset by violets, ironstone, a suggestion of pepper and spicy oak; the palate is lively, tightly wound and showing a wonderful tension between the fruit, acid and fine-grained tannins. Screwcap. 13.5% alc. **Rating** 95 **To** 2025 $32 BE

Block 9 Mount Barker Shiraz 2009 Deep garnet, red hue; charry oak dominates the red-fruited bouquet, with a suggestion of juniper, thyme and pepper; the palate is medium-bodied, with plenty of muscle and power in the firm tannins that support the tightly wound fruit; this needs time to relent and relax, so patience is advised. Screwcap. 13.5% alc. **Rating** 94 **To** 2025 $55 BE

Estate Great Southern Cabernet Sauvignon 2011 Deep crimson; a fragrant and poised bouquet offering redcurrant, blackcurrant, fine oak aromas and cedar; the palate is medium- to full-bodied and lively, with compact tannins, taut acidity and a sinewy structure that will need time to flesh out, but flesh out it will. Screwcap. 14% alc. **Rating** 94 **To** 2025 $32 BE

ₜₜₜₜₜ **Estate Great Southern Riesling 2012 Rating** 92 **To** 2022 $26 BE
Block 5 Cabernet Sauvignon 2009 Rating 92 **To** 2025 $65 BE
Highbury Fields Sauvignon Blanc 2012 Rating 91 **To** 2016 $22 BE
Highbury Fields Chardonnay 2012 Rating 91 **To** 2018 $22 BE
Highbury Fields Shiraz 2011 Rating 91 **To** 2020 $22 BE
Highbury Fields Sauvignon Blanc Semillon 2012 Rating 90 **To** 2015 $22 BE

Forester Estate ★★★★★

1064 Wildwood Road, Yallingup, WA 6282 **Region** Margaret River
T (08) 9755 2788 **www**.foresterestate.com.au **Open** By appt
Winemaker Kevin McKay, Todd Payne **Est.** 2001 **Dozens** 25 000 **Vyds** 33.5ha
Forester Estate is owned by Kevin and Jenny McKay. Kevin has built a 500-tonne winery, half devoted to contract winemaking, the other half for the Forester label. Winemaker Todd Payne has had a distinguished career, starting in the Great Southern, thereafter the Napa Valley, back to Plantagenet, then on to Esk Valley in Hawke's Bay, plus two vintages in the Northern Rhône Valley, one with the esteemed producer Yves Cuilleron in 2008. His move back to WA completes the circle. The estate vineyards are planted to sauvignon blanc, semillon, chardonnay, cabernet sauvignon, shiraz, merlot, petit verdot, malbec and alicante bouschet. Exports to Japan.

ₜₜₜₜₜ **Margaret River Cabernet Merlot 2010** A more complex blend than the front
✪ label would suggest: a 48/41/6/5% blend of cabernet sauvignon, merlot, malbec and petit verdot, matured for 18 months in French barriques (15% new). Has retained good colour, and has exemplary balance to its redcurrant and blackcurrant fruit, tannins and oak; the length and mouthfeel are also very good. Great value. Screwcap. 13.5% alc. **Rating** 95 **To** 2030 $22

Margaret River Sauvignon Blanc 2012 Partial barrel fermentation has left an indelible mark on the wine, a specialty of Margaret River; that mark is mainly textural, and does not impinge on the mix of snow pea, passionfruit and citrus fruit on the long palate. Screwcap. 13.5% alc. **Rating** 94 **To** 2015 $25

Margaret River Cabernet Sauvignon 2010 Bright and fragrant red fruit bouquet offering a suggestion of lavender and fine cedary oak notes; the palate is medium-bodied, fresh and focused and is ready to go now, although will age with grace over the medium term thanks to the fine tannins on the finish. Screwcap. 13.5% alc. **Rating** 94 **To** 2018 $38

ₜₜₜₜₜ **Margaret River Semillon Sauvignon Blanc 2012** A 50/48/2% blend of
✪ semillon, sauvignon blanc and chardonnay, with 5% fermented in used French oak barriques with the aid of selected yeasts. Deliberately made in a ripe style, but without losing its freshness and zest; tropical, stone fruit and citrus nuances all coalesce. Screwcap. 13% alc. **Rating** 93 **To** 2014 $22

Home Block Margaret River Shiraz 2010 Rating 92 **To** 2022 $40 BE
Margaret River Chardonnay 2011 Rating 90 **To** 2016 $38 BE

Foster e Rocco ★★★★★

PO Box 438, Heathcote, Vic 3523 **Region** Heathcote
T 0407 057 471 **Open** Not
Winemaker Adam Foster, Lincoln Riley **Est.** 2008 **Dozens** 750

Long-term sommeliers and friends Adam Foster and Lincoln Riley have established a business that has a very clear vision: food-friendly wine based on the versatility of sangiovese. They make their wine at Syrahmi, building it from the ground up, with fermentation in both stainless steel and used French oak barrels.

🍷🍷🍷🍷🍷 **Riserva Heathcote Sangiovese 2009** Excellent hue and depth; a thoroughly distinguished Sangiovese, with an autocratic Italian stamp to its character; there is a cherry kernel nuance to the bouquet along with the dark cherry/red cherry, and the admirably constructed and textured palate is all one could wish for. Screwcap. 13.5% alc. **Rating** 94 **To** 2020 $55

🍷🍷🍷🍷♀ **Nuovo Heathcote Sangiovese 2012 Rating** 93 **To** 2014 $25
Heathcote Sangiovese 2011 Rating 92 **To** 2015 $28
Heathcote Fiano 2011 Rating 90 **To** 2015 $28

Four Winds Vineyard   ★★★★★

9 Patemans Lane, Murrumbateman, NSW 2582 **Region** Canberra District
T 0432 060 903 **www.fourwindsvineyard.com.au Open** W'ends 10–5
Winemaker Jaime and Bill Crowe **Est.** 1998 **Dozens** 1500 **Vyds** 11.9ha
Graeme and Suzanne Lunney conceived the idea for Four Winds in 1997, planting the first vines in '98, moving to the property full-time in '99, and making the first vintage in 2000. Daughter Sarah looks after events and promotions, and youngest daughter Jaime, complete with a degree in Forensic Biology, has joined Bill in the winery. She brings with her several years' experience with the former Kamberra winery, and three vintages in the Napa Valley. Suzanne tends the gardens and the 100 rose bushes planted at the end of the vine rows.

🍷🍷🍷🍷🍷 **Canberra District Riesling 2012** Pale straw, bright; while quite a departure
✪ from many Australian Rieslings in terms of style, the bouquet offers savoury bath talc, green apple and struck flint aromas; the palate is intensely concentrated, with laser-like acidity providing purity and line; will challenge in the short term, but provide great joy with a little time. Screwcap. 10% alc. **Rating** 94 **To** 2022 $20 BE

Fowles Wine   ★★★★☆

Cnr Hume Freeway/Lambing Gully Road, Avenel, Vic 3664 **Region** Strathbogie Ranges
T (03) 5796 2150 **www.fowleswine.com.au Open** 7 days 9–5
Winemaker Victor Nash, Lindsay Brown **Est.** 1968 **Dozens** 50 000 **Vyds** 145ha
Formerly known as Plunkett Fowles, the Fowles family acquiring the remaining Plunkett family shareholding in the company in April 2012 (Sam Plunkett is taking the opportunity to pursue his Master of Wine degree). The large vineyard is primarily focused on riesling, chardonnay, shiraz and cabernet sauvignon, but also includes chardonnay, shiraz, cabernet sauvignon, sauvignon blanc, pinot noir, merlot, riesling, semillon, viognier, gewurztraminer, savagnin, tempranillo, lagrein, arneis, vermentino, pinot gris and sangiovese. Marketing is energetic, with the well-known Ladies Who Shoot Their Lunch label available as large posters. Exports to the UK, the US, Canada and China.

🍷🍷🍷🍷🍷 **The Rule Strathbogie Ranges Shiraz 2010** Attractive purple-crimson; a rich, medium- to full-bodied wine flooded with blackberry, plum, spice and dark chocolate flavours that persist right through to the finish; exemplary oak and tannin management. Screwcap. 14.2% alc. **Rating** 94 **To** 2030 $50

🍷🍷🍷🍷♀ **Stone Dwellers Riesling 2012 Rating** 93 **To** 2020 $22
✪ **Are you Game? Sauvignon Blanc 2011** Fermented with QA23, the renowned sauvignon blanc yeast strain; this has great drive and length to its mix of ripe citrus and tropical flavours, the acidity (8.4g/l) underpinning its freshness. Screwcap. 12% alc. **Rating** 92 **To** 2013 $17
Stone Dwellers Strathbogie Ranges Shiraz 2009 Rating 92 **To** 2024 $25
Ladies Who Shoot Their Lunch Strathbogie Ranges Shiraz 2010 Rating 91 **To** 2025 $35

Ladies Who Shoot Their Lunch Strathbogie Ranges Merlot Lagrein Tempranillo 2010 Rating 91 To 2018 $35 BE
Stone Dwellers Chardonnay 2011 Rating 90 To 2015 $25

✪ **Are you Game? Pinot Noir 2010** Medium red-purple, with good retention of hue; travels the fine line between dry red and true pinot flavours, coming down (just) on the right side on the finish and aftertaste, with spiced plum fruit spreading its wings and taking flight. Screwcap. 14% alc. **Rating** 90 To 2015 $17

Fox Creek Wines ★★★★★

Malpas Road, McLaren Vale, SA 5171 **Region** McLaren Vale
T (08) 8557 0000 www.foxcreekwines.com **Open** 7 days 10–5
Winemaker Scott Zrna **Est.** 1995 **Dozens** 40000 **Vyds** 21ha
Fox Creek has made a major impact since coming on-stream late in 1995. It is the venture of the Watts family: Jim (a retired surgeon), wife Helen and son Paul (a viticulturist); and Lyn Roberts. Kristin McLarty (née Watts) is marketing manager and Georgy Rogers (née Watts) is cellar door supervisor. Moves are afoot to introduce organic practices in the vineyards, with trials of an organically registered herbicide derived from pine oil for weed control. Although Fox Creek is not organic, they use sustainable vineyard practices, avoiding all systemic chemicals. The wines have enjoyed considerable show success. Exports to all major markets.

🍷🍷🍷🍷🍷 **Reserve McLaren Vale Shiraz 2010** Dense, opaque purple-crimson; this is, quite simply, the essence of McLaren Vale, its bouquet and full-bodied palate with multiple layers of blackberry and dark chocolate. This is the result of a barrel selection, and fully deserved its gold medal at the Melbourne Wine Show '12. Screwcap. 14.5% alc. **Rating** 96 To 2035 $70
Reserve McLaren Vale Cabernet Sauvignon 2010 Has won a miscellany of gold awards from Asia, London, NZ, Japan and – wait for it – Adelaide. Deep purple-crimson; it has abundant blackcurrant/cassis fruit, typical cabernet tannins and quality oak. Not made every year, but '10 was almost inevitable. Screwcap. 14.5% alc. **Rating** 94 To 2030 $41

🍷🍷🍷🍷🍷 **JSM McLaren Vale Shiraz Cabernet Sauvignon Cabernet Franc 2010** Rating 92 To 2025 $23
✪ **Shadow's Run McLaren Vale Shiraz Cabernet Sauvignon 2010** A gold medal sticker on the bottle at the '2012 National Canberra Wine Show' (there is no such thing – presumably it's the Royal Show) without the dates being specified doesn't comply with the regulations. But it's an exceptional achievement for a wine of this price; it has very good colour, and has layers of blackberry, blackcurrant and chocolate fruit, ripe tannins and imperceptible oak. At face value, a great bargain. Screwcap. 14.5% alc. **Rating** 92 To 2020 $13
Short Row McLaren Vale Shiraz 2011 Rating 90 To 2019 $29

🍷🍷🍷🍷 **Red Baron McLaren Vale Shiraz 2011** The colour is quite deep and dark;
✪ a briary and wiry black-fruited wine, very different from many '11s; has dark chocolate in generous proportions, semaphoring its sense of place. Gold medal NZ International Wine Show (no year specified). Screwcap. 14.5% alc. **Rating** 89 To 2016 $18

Fox Gordon ★★★★★

65 Beaulah Road, Norwood, SA 5067 **Region** Barossa Valley/Adelaide Hills
T (08) 8362 4442 www.foxgordon.com.au **Open** Not
Winemaker Natasha Mooney **Est.** 2000 **Dozens** 10000
This is the venture of Sam and Rachel Atkins (née Fox) and winemaker Natasha (Tash) Mooney. Tash has had first-class experience in the Barossa Valley, particularly during her time as chief winemaker at Barossa Valley Estate. The partners wanted to produce high-quality wine, but only small quantities, which would allow them time to look after their children; the venture was planned in the shade of the wisteria tree in Tash's back garden. The grapes come from dry-grown vineyards farmed under biodiversity principles, which, says Tash, makes the

winemaker's job easy. Classy packaging adds the final touch, and bargains abound. Exports to the UK, Canada, Germany, India, Singapore, Hong Kong and China.

ŢŢŢŢŢ **Hannah's Swing Barossa Valley Shiraz 2010** Full purple-crimson; one of those Shirazs that combine generosity of pure varietal expression with elegance and length; spicy plum and black cherry fruit is gently laced with strands of spice and licorice, oak and tannins precisely pitched on the long finish. Screwcap. 13.9% alc. **Rating** 96 **To** 2030 $45

King Louis Barossa Valley Cabernet Sauvignon 2010 Deep, full crimson-purple; a rich, full-bodied Cabernet with layer upon layer of blackcurrant, black olive, briar, earth and tar fruit flavours, the tannins not about to take a backward step, the oak likewise. Screwcap. 14.5% alc. **Rating** 95 **To** 2030 $45

✪ **Sassy Adelaide Hills Sauvignon Blanc 2012** Light straw-green; a delicious Sauvignon Blanc with fragrant passionfruit at the heart of its bouquet and palate, and also guava and citrus; despite its intense flavour, has a light-footed delicacy. Terrific value. Screwcap. 13.5% alc. **Rating** 94 **To** 2014 $15

ŢŢŢŢŢ
✪ **Eight Uncles Barossa Valley Shiraz 2011** Full purple-crimson; yet another rabbit pulled from the '11 hat. Not bottled until Dec '12, it has considerable depth to its display of red and black fruits, spice and earth flavours; the tannins are savoury, but neither green or dry, and the French oak in which the wine was matured is totally integrated. Top value. Screwcap. 13.8% alc. **Rating** 92 **To** 2020 $20

Charlotte's Web Adelaide Hills Pinot Grigio 2012 **Rating** 90 **To** 2014 $20

Foxeys Hangout   ★★★★★

795 White Hill Road, Red Hill, Vic 3937 **Region** Mornington Peninsula
T (03) 5989 2022 **www.**foxeys-hangout.com.au **Open** W'ends & public hols 11–5
Winemaker Tony and Michael Lee **Est.** 1998 **Dozens** 5000 **Vyds** 3.4ha
This is the venture of Tony Lee and journalist wife Cathy Gowdie. Cathy explains where it all began in 1998: 'We were not obvious candidates for a seachange. When we talked of moving to the country, friends pointed out that Tony and I were hardly back-to-nature types. "Do you own a single pair of shoes without heels?" asked a friend. But at the end of a bleak winter, we bought an old farmhouse on 10 daffodil-dotted acres at Red Hill and planted a vineyard.' They planted pinot noir, chardonnay, pinot gris and shiraz on the north-facing slopes of the old farm. The name (and the catchy label) stems from the tale of two fox-hunters who began a competition with each other in 1936, hanging their kills on the branches of an ancient eucalypt tree to keep count. The corpses have gone, but not the nickname for the area.

ŢŢŢŢŢ **Shiraz 2011** Has 3% co-fermented viognier, and was matured in French oak (25% new); the vibrant colour and fragrant bouquet do not deceive, for the palate has deliciously pitched black cherry, spice and licorice fruit. The laconic comment from the Lee brothers is 100% correct: 'Shiraz seemed to work better than pinot noir in '11. Don't know why.' Screwcap. 13.5% alc. **Rating** 94 **To** 2026 $45

ŢŢŢŢŢ **Scotsworth Farm Pinot Noir 2011** **Rating** 92 **To** 2016 $60
Late Harvest Pinot Gris 2011 **Rating** 92 **To** 2014 $28
Chardonnay 2011 **Rating** 91 **To** 2017 $30

✪ **The Red Fox Pinot Noir 2012** Bright, clear crimson-purple; hand-picked and wild-fermented, the whole approach to making the wine has been to focus attention on the very attractive red cherry fruit, and not on the minimal oak inputs. It works very well with a wine designed to be enjoyed while young. Screwcap. 13% alc. **Rating** 91 **To** 2015 $22

Pinot Gris 2011 **Rating** 90 **To** 2013 $28
Pinot Noir 2011 **Rating** 90 **To** 2016 $30

Frankland Estate ★★★★★

Frankland Road, Frankland, WA 6396 **Region** Frankland River
T (08) 9855 1544 **www**.franklandestate.com.au **Open** Mon–Fri 10–4, public hols &
w'ends by appt
Winemaker Hunter Smith, Brian Kent **Est.** 1988 **Dozens** 15 000 **Vyds** 34.5ha
A significant Frankland River operation, situated on a large sheep property owned by Barrie
Smith and Judi Cullam. The vineyard has been established progressively since 1988; the recent
introduction of an array of single vineyard Rieslings has been a highlight. The venture into the
single vineyard wines is driven by Judi's conviction that terroir is of utmost importance, and
the soils are indeed different. The climate is not, and the difference between the wines is not
as clear-cut as theory might suggest. The Isolation Ridge Vineyard is now organically grown.
Frankland Estate has held several important International Riesling tastings and seminars over
recent years. Exports to all major markets.

ΨΨΨΨΨ **Isolation Ridge Vineyard Riesling 2012** Bright straw-green; as ever, a
distinguished Riesling with its interwoven display of lime, apple and mineral that
opens on the bouquet and expands along the length of the palate and its long,
lazily uncoiling aftertaste. Screwcap. 11.5% alc. **Rating** 96 **To** 2027 $32
Smith Cullam Riesling 2012 Only 9g/l of residual sugar, yet the wine has
remarkable length and balance, acidity more obvious than that touch of sweetness.
The result is a wine unique to Frankland Estate, which has adopted European
philosophy but used its (Frankland Estate's) own model. Screwcap. 10.5% alc.
Rating 96 **To** 2022 $45
Netley Road Vineyard Riesling 2012 Pale, bright straw-green; the fragrant
flowery bouquet leads into delicious palate, with sweet lime juice flavours tingling
the front of the tongue, thereafter joined by minerally acidity on the vibrant finish.
Screwcap. 11% alc. **Rating** 95 **To** 2022 $27
Isolation Ridge Vineyard Shiraz 2010 Strong purple-crimson; a complex,
medium- to full-bodied wine, with a symbiotic and synergistic union between its
abundant black fruits and plentiful ripe, velvety tannins. Absolutely guaranteed to
thrive over decades to come. Screwcap. 14% alc. **Rating** 95 **To** 2030 $32
Smith Cullam Shiraz Cabernet 2010 Full, bright crimson-purple; if attention
to detail is one of the indicia of high-quality wine, this has it in spades; the
bouquet is at once spicy and savoury, a lattice work for the intense yet fine black
fruits of the long, perfectly balanced, medium-bodied palate. Screwcap. 14.3% alc.
Rating 95 **To** 2030 $55
Olmo's Reward 2010 A crimson-purple, estate-grown blend of cabernet franc,
merlot, cabernet sauvignon and malbec, with cabernet franc and merlot the major
components, making it a rare assemblage. It pays (inadvertent?) homage to the
right bank of Bordeaux with its small black and red berry fruits, fine-grained
savoury tannins and integrated oak. Screwcap. 14% alc. **Rating** 95 **To** 2025 $40

ΨΨΨΨΨ **Rocky Gully Riesling 2012** Pale quartz; this may be the entry point riesling
✪ for Frankland Estate, but it is totally delicious; the low alcohol is an unqualified
success, highlighting the display of citrus fruit and possibly a subliminal touch of
sweetness; grainy acidity provides an emphatic finish. Screwcap. 11% alc. **Rating** 93
To 2022 $18
Poison Hill Vineyard Riesling 2012 **Rating** 93 **To** 2022 $27
✪ **Rocky Gully Shiraz 2011** Light to medium crimson-purple; there is a lift to
the fragrance of the bouquet and the juicy flavours of the palate from the small
but significant contribution of viognier; its light- to medium-bodied palate has
excellent balance, and the wine will be at its best over the next 3 or so years.
Screwcap. 14.5% alc. **Rating** 93 **To** 2015 $18
Isolation Ridge Vineyard Cabernet Sauvignon 2010 **Rating** 93
To 2025 $27
Isolation Ridge Vineyard Chardonnay 2011 **Rating** 90 **To** 2017 $27

○   **Rocky Gully Cabernets 2011** Bright colour; while only light- to medium-
bodied, and with no pretensions to glory, this comprehensively over-delivers, with
its bright, flavoursome cascade of red fruits effortlessly captured in the bottle, then
the glass. I wouldn't quarrel with anyone who polished off their bottles quickly,
but it will probably be equally good in another 5 years. Screwcap. 13.5% alc.
Rating 90 **To** 2017 $17

Franklin Tate Estates   ★★★★☆

Gale Road, Kaloorup, WA 6280 **Region** Margaret River
T (08) 9267 8555 **www**.franklintateestates.com.au **Open** Not
Winemaker Rory Clifton-Parks **Est.** 2010 **Dozens** 21000 **Vyds** 101.11ha
This is the second business established by Franklin and Heather Tate since the demise of
Evans & Tate. In 2007 they came up with Miles From Nowhere (see separate entry), but this
is a quite separate business, with 101ha of vines (Miles From Nowhere has 47ha). The lion's
share of the plantings go to sauvignon blanc and semillon (24ha each), chardonnay (22ha),
shiraz (17ha) and cabernet sauvignon (8ha), with minor plantings of verdelho, petit verdot and
viognier. Rory Clifton-Parks has been the winemaker for both incarnations. The Tate range is
price-pointed at $15, and the Tate Alexanders Vineyard at $25; they all represent good value for
estate-produced Margaret River wines, and it's not surprising to see the export focus. Exports
to Canada, Malaysia, Singapore, Thailand, Hong Kong and China.

♟♟♟♟♟ **Tate Alexanders Vineyard Margaret River Shiraz 2011** Excellent purple-
crimson; a complex medium- to full-bodied Shiraz stacked with blackberry, black
cherry and licorice aromas and flavours; the tannins are savoury but balanced, oak
likewise. Slick packaging, and over-delivers at its price, but a few years in the cellar
would reward. Screwcap. 14% alc. **Rating** 93 **To** 2026 $25
Tate Alexanders Vineyard Margaret River Chardonnay 2011 Straw-green;
there are some buttery/toasty oak notes on the bouquet, but the focus changes to
the white peach/nectarine fruit on the fresh palate, which is distinctly light on its
feet. Screwcap. 13% alc. **Rating** 92 **To** 2017 $25
Tate Alexanders Vineyard Margaret River Cabernet Sauvignon 2011
Has good colour and depth; the bouquet and medium-bodied palate present a mix
of cassis, black olive, and hints of leaf and mint; fine tannins and oak add to the
texture and structure. Screwcap. 14% alc. **Rating** 91 **To** 2021 $25

♟♟♟♟   **Tate Margaret River Sauvignon Blanc Semillon 2012** A light-bodied,
○   pleasant blend, its mid-palate flavours in a gentle tropical/stone fruit spectrum
before moving to citrus on the finish. Refreshing style, and well priced. Screwcap.
12.5% alc. **Rating** 88 **To** 2014 $15
Tate Margaret River Chardonnay 2012 Rating 88 **To** 2014 $15
Tate Margaret River Shiraz 2011 Rating 87 **To** 2014 $15

Fraser Gallop Estate   ★★★★★

547 Metricup Road, Wilyabrup, WA 6280 **Region** Margaret River
T (08) 9755 7553 **www**.frasergallopestate.com.au **Open** By appt
Winemaker Clive Otto, Kate Morgan **Est.** 1999 **Dozens** 14000 **Vyds** 20ha
Nigel Gallop began the development of the vineyard in 1999, planting cabernet sauvignon,
semillon, petit verdot, cabernet franc, malbec, merlot and multi-clone chardonnay. The vines
are dry-grown with modest yields, followed by kid-glove treatment in the winery. The first
vintage was 2002, the wine being contract-made offsite, but with Clive Otto (formerly of
Vasse Felix) on board, a 300-tonne winery was built onsite in '08, with highly qualified
assistant Kate Morgan joining the team for that vintage. Right from the word go, the wines
have had richly deserved success in wine shows and journalist reviews. Exports to the UK,
Canada, Switzerand and Hong Kong.

ŸŸŸŸŸ **Parterre Margaret River Semillon Sauvignon Blanc 2012** A 64/36% blend,
wild-fermented, then matured for 9 months in a mix of new French and stainless
steel barriques. It has a remarkable texture and intensity to its mouthfeel, the
herb and citrus flavours allied with nutty oak, and destined to last for many years.
Screwcap. 13% alc. **Rating** 96 **To** 2020 $36
Parterre Wilyabrup Margaret River Chardonnay 2012 Mid gold, vibrant
hue; the extremely youthful and unevolved the bouquet offers spicy oak, nectarine,
grapefruit and struck flint aromas; the palate is tightly wound, with racy, laser-like
acidity, charry oak and fine fruit slowly expanding across the finish. Screwcap.
12.5% alc. **Rating** 96 **To** 2022 $33 BE
Parterre Wilyabrup Margaret River Cabernet Sauvignon 2011 Bright
mid crimson; a highly polished and perfumed bouquet of red fruits, violets, cedar
and fine pencil lead oak aromas; full-bodied, yet elegantly proportioned, the palate
is long and layered, unevolved, and with all of the ingredients for a long and
interesting future. Screwcap. 14.5% alc. **Rating** 94 **To** 2025 $40 BE

ŸŸŸŸŸ **Margaret River Semillon Sauvignon Blanc 2012** **Rating** 90 **To** 2015 $23 BE
Margaret River Chardonnay 2012 **Rating** 90 **To** 2020 $23 BE

Fratelli ★★★★

18 High Street, Yea, Vic 3717 (postal) **Region** Victoria
T 0419 117 858 **www.**fratelliwines.com.au **Open** Not
Winemaker Andrew Santarossa **Est.** 2007 **Dozens** 3000
This is the virtual winery operation of three brothers of Italian heritage with a love of wine:
Andrew, Michael and Anthony Santarossa. Andrew, the eldest, is a winemaker with over
10 years' experience making wines in Oregon, the Margaret River and the Yarra Valley. The
handsomely packaged wines are sourced from various regions across Victoria; it has enjoyed
significant growth over the past few years.

ŸŸŸŸŸ **Yarra Valley Chardonnay 2011** A vibrantly zesty chardonnay sourced from
the Upper Yarra Valley, with grapefruit and white peach aromas and flavours
soaring across the palate, oak irrelevant to the expression of the fruit. Terrific value
from this vintage, which produced such good Chardonnays. Screwcap. 13% alc.
Rating 93 **To** 2019 $24
RedCote Heathcote Shiraz 2010 Bright purple-red hue; has energetic red
and black fruits on the bouquet and medium-bodied palate; this energy sits hand
in glove with elegance, oak and tannins well balanced and integrated. Screwcap.
14% alc. **Rating** 93 **To** 2025 $45
Upper Goulburn Riesling 2012 Pale colour, green hue; the fragrant bouquet
offers lime juice, green apple and flint; the tangy palate is lively and fresh, finishing
bone dry and with a distinctive and attractive mineral-laden conclusion. Screwcap.
12% alc. **Rating** 91 **To** 2018 $22 BE

Freeman Vineyards ★★★★★

101 Prunevale Road, Prunevale, NSW 2587 **Region** Hilltops
T (02) 6384 4299 **www.**freemanvineyards.com.au **Open** By appt
Winemaker Dr Brian Freeman, Xanthe Freeman **Est.** 2000 **Dozens** 5000 **Vyds** 45ha
Dr Brian Freeman has spent much of his long life in research and education, in the latter role
as head of CSU's viticulture and oenology campus. In 2004 he purchased the 30-year-old
vineyard previously known as Demondrille. He has also established a vineyard next door, and
in all has 14 varieties that range from staples such as shiraz, cabernet sauvignon, semillon and
riesling through to more exotic, trendy varieties such as tempranillo, and on to corvina and
rondinella. He has had a long academic interest in the effect of partial drying of grapes on
the tannins and, living at Prunevale, was easily able to obtain a prune dehydrator to partially
raisin the two varieties.

ŢŢŢŢŢ **Altura Vineyard Shiraz 2010** This is the first Altura release from Freeman, and the result is impressive, as the bouquet displays an elegant personality of red fruit, bramble, spice and a touch of pepper; the palate is medium-bodied and fine-boned with ample fine-grained tannins a harmonious feature of the long, slightly charry finish. Screwcap. 13.5% alc. **Rating** 94 **To** 2020 $25 BE

Rondinella Corvina Secco 2009 Light, clear red; follows the tried and true path of partial grape drying in a prune dehydrator, and is a blend unique to Brian Freeman. It takes understanding, but is much easier than nebbiolo, with its mix of spice, nutmeg, raisins and plum all balanced by life-giving acidity. Screwcap. 14.5% alc. **Rating** 94 **To** 2024 $35

ŢŢŢŢŢ **Altura Vineyard Tempranillo 2012 Rating** 93 **To** 2017 $25 BE

Fortuna Pinot Gris Plus 2011 Rating 90 **To** 2016 $25 BE

✪ **Rondo Rondinella Rose 2012** The pale burnt orange blush suggests a dry savoury rose, and this follows on the bouquet and palate; anise, wild strawberry and bramble aromas are followed by a dry and grippy palate that is refreshing and moreish; perfect with charcuterie. Screwcap. 13.5% alc. **Rating** 90 **To** 2015 $20 BE

Freycinet   ★★★★★

15919 Tasman Highway via Bicheno, Tas 7215 **Region** East Coast Tasmania
T (03) 6257 8574 **www.**freycinetvineyard.com.au **Open** 7 days 10–5 (Nov–Apr), 10–4 (May–Oct)
Winemaker Claudio Radenti, Lindy Bull **Est.** 1980 **Dozens** 6000 **Vyds** 14.83ha

The Freycinet vineyards are beautifully situated on the sloping hillsides of a small valley. The soils are brown dermosol on top of Jurassic dolerite, and the combination of aspect, slope, soil and heat summation produces red grapes with unusual depth of colour and ripe flavours. One of Australia's foremost producers of pinot noir, with an enviable track record of consistency – rare in such a temperamental variety. The Radenti (sparkling), Riesling and Chardonnay are also wines of the highest quality. In 2012 Freycinet acquired a portion of the neighbouring Coombend property from Brown Brothers. The 42ha property extends to the Tasman Highway, and also includes a 5.75ha mature vineyard and a 4.2ha olive grove. Exports to the UK and Singpapore.

ŢŢŢŢŢ **Pinot Noir 2010** Purple-crimson; a perfect demonstration of the value of fully mature 31-year-old vines; the fragrance of the bouquet has intensified since Dec '11; it has multiple layers of fruit with a silky sweetness to the flavours, tannins there, as is the oak, but it is the integrity of the fruit that makes all the difference to a superb Tasmanian Pinot. Screwcap. 14.5% alc. **Rating** 96 **To** 2015 $65

Radenti Chardonnay Pinot Noir 2001 A 60/40% estate-grown blend fermented in this bottle, and given more than 8 years on yeast lees, resulting in a blend of richness and texture, with spicy and creamy fruit on the mid-palate before a finely balanced, almost juicy, finish. A perennial favourite of mine, for which I make no apology. Cork. 12.5% alc. **Rating** 96 **To** 2015 $50

Pinot Noir 2011 Deeper colour than that of the Louis '11, with more purple in the hue; this is an imposing Pinot, with layers of dark berry fruits and persistent though balanced and integrated tannins, coupled with some new oak. Its power and length make this the ultimate Pinot cellaring special, and not yet ready. Screwcap. 14% alc. **Rating** 95 **To** 2025 $70

Chardonnay 2011 Bright green-straw; barrel-fermented in French oak and lees stirring have tamed the often fierce Tasmanian acidity, with a nectarine, white peach and melon trifecta the winning formula, the oak influence subtle, the finish long. Screwcap. 13.5% alc. **Rating** 94 **To** 2020 $38

Louis Pinot Noir 2011 Good depth to the colour, the bouquet and palate proclaiming their Tasmanian origin, with dark plum and black cherry fruit; has considerable depth to the structure and texture, yet is far more accessible than its sibling. Screwcap. 13.5% alc. **Rating** 94 **To** 2020 $34

Botrytis 2011 Made from heavily botrytised sauvignon blanc and riesling, an unusual double if ever there was one. It is very complex, very luscious and well balanced by its spear of Tasmanian acidity. 500ml. Screwcap. 9% alc. **Rating** 94 To 2016 $25

ΨΨΨΨΥ **Riesling 2012 Rating** 93 To 2022 $26
Cabernet Sauvignon Merlot 2008 Rating 90 To 2023 $34

Frogmore Creek ★★★★★

699 Richmond Road, Cambridge, Tas 7170 **Region** Southern Tasmania
T (03) 6248 4484 **www**.frogmorecreek.com.au **Open** 7 days 10–5
Winemaker Alain Rousseau, John Bown **Est.** 1997 **Dozens** 18 000
Frogmore Creek is a Pacific Rim joint venture, the owners being Tony Scherer of Tasmania and Jack Kidwiler of California. The business has grown very substantially, first establishing its own organically managed vineyard, and thereafter by a series of acquisitions. First was the purchase of the Hood/Wellington Wines business previously owned by Andrew Hood; next was the purchase of the large Roslyn Vineyard near Campania; and finally (in Oct 2010) the acquisition of Meadowbank Estate, where the cellar door is now located. In Dec '12 the original Frogmore Creek vineyard was sold to Hill-Smith Family Vineyards. Exports to the US, Japan, Indonesia and South Korea.

ΨΨΨΨΨ **Chardonnay 2011** Bright straw-green; a seductive and delicious wine that fills and caresses the mouth in a way that is not in the Tasmanian mainstream, thanks to the absence of strident acidity. There is a creamy/nutty aspect to the white peach fruit from the barrel fermentation that adds to the expression of that fruit on the long, fine palate. Screwcap. 13.1% alc. **Rating** 96 To 2021 $30
Chardonnay 2010 Bright green-straw; a seriously good wine, its climate/terroir speaking as clearly as its varietal character. While the barrel-ferment oak characters are quite obvious, it is the intensity of the luscious stone fruit flavours backed by lingering minerally acidity that drive the palate. Chassagne or Puligny-Montrachet is the question. Screwcap. 13.5% alc. **Rating** 96 To 2020 $30
Botrytis Riesling 2011 The sheer, pristine purity of the wine is astonishing. A brilliantly pale, green-tinted hue announces pure kaffir lime, pepper and gorgeous lemon freshness. It's very sweet, but tastes nothing like it, tightly hugging rails of cool vintage acidity. Screwcap. 8% alc. **Rating** 95 To 2031 $65 TS
Iced Riesling 2011 Gleaming green-gold; an outstanding example of the style, with an awesome 153g/l residual sugar balanced by 11.8g/l of total acidity; the intensity of flavour, and its extreme length, have more in common with the sweetest (trockenbeerenauslese style) wines of Austria and Germany than with any other Australian wine. Screwcap. 8% alc. **Rating** 95 To 2031 $26
Riesling 2011 Bright, light green-gold; the aromatic bouquet has a sunburst of lime, lemon and grapefruit, the palate treading in its steps, but with some acid restraint that will serve it well over the decade. Screwcap. 12.5% alc. **Rating** 94 To 2021 $24
Evermore Gewurztraminer 2011 Like the '10 Evermore Riesling, fermented on skins, but without any oak ageing. Has distinct overtones of Alsace gewurztraminer, with layers of varietal flavour ranging through musk, spice and cumquat, the finish emphatic. You can't sit on the fence with this wine. Screwcap. 13.1% alc. **Rating** 94 To 2016 $38

ΨΨΨΨΥ **Evermore Riesling 2010 Rating** 92 To 2017 $38
42°S Chardonnay 2010 Rating 91 To 2016 $22

 # Fullarton Estate Wines ★★★☆

Level 1/133 Archer Street, North Adelaide, SA 5006 (postal) **Region** Barossa
T (08) 7324 2942 **www**.fullartonestatewines.com.au **Open** At Gomersal Wines
Winemaker Peter Pollard **Est.** 2012 **Dozens** 10 000

This is the venture of Hongwei Hao, who has built up a broad-based wine business in a relatively short period of time, its principal focus on China, but also including the Australian and other international markets. As well as producing its own eponymously labelled wines, it has shares in Project Wine and Gomersal Wines (see separate entry). Project Wine is a major, state-of-the-art grape processing, winemaking and storage facility under the control of senior winemaker Peter Pollard. The product range has been intelligently structured, with support brands under the Stella Creek, Gomersal, Parson's Paddock, Bird's Eye View and Tail Spin labels. Fullarton Estate labels range from simple SA GI through to Langhorne Creek, Barossa Valley and Barossa Valley Reserve, all either Shiraz or Cabernet Sauvignon. Exports to China.

ŢŢŢŢŢ **Reserve Barossa Valley Shiraz 2009** Good colour; the 2 years the wine spent in French and American oak is certainly very evident, and also though less would have been better, there are attractive plum, blackberry and mocha flavours on the medium-bodied palate. Cork. 14.8% alc. **Rating** 90 **To** 2017 $40

ŢŢŢŢ **Langhorne Creek Shiraz 2011 Rating** 88 **To** 2016 $17
Langhorne Creek Cabernet Sauvignon 2011 Rating 87 **To** 2014 $17

Gaelic Cemetery Wines   ★★★★☆

PO Box 54, Sevenhill, SA 5453 **Region** Clare Valley
T (08) 8843 4370 **www**.gaelic-cemeterywines.com **Open** Not
Winemaker Neil Pike, John Trotter, Steve Baraglia **Est.** 2005 **Dozens** 250 **Vyds** 6.5ha
This is a joint venture of winemaker Neil Pike, viticulturist Andrew Pike and Adelaide retailers Mario and Ben Barletta. It hinges on a single vineyard owned by Grant Arnold, planted in 1996, adjacent to the historic cemetery of the region's Scottish pioneers. Situated in a secluded valley of the Clare hills, the low-cropping vineyard, say the partners, 'is always one of the earliest ripening shiraz vineyards in the region and mystifyingly produces fruit with both natural pH and acid analyses that can only be described as beautiful numbers'. The result is hands-off winemaking and maturation for 24 months in new and used Burgundian barriques. Exports to the UK, the US, Canada, Germany, Singapore, Taiwan and China.

ŢŢŢŢŢ **Clare Valley Riesling 2012** A tightly wound and restrained bouquet revealing lime juice, violets and wet slate aromas; the palate is taut, fresh and linear with chalky acidity playing a prominent role on the long finish; designed for extended cellaring. Screwcap. 12% alc. **Rating** 94 **To** 2025 $35 BE

ŢŢŢŢŢ **Celtic Farm Clare Valley Riesling 2012 Rating** 92 **To** 2020 $20 BE

Galafrey   ★★★★☆

Quangellup Road, Mount Barker, WA 6324 **Region** Mount Barker
T (08) 9851 2022 **www**.galafreywines.com.au **Open** 7 days 10–5
Winemaker Kim Tyrer **Est.** 1977 **Dozens** 4000 **Vyds** 13.1ha
Relocated to a purpose-built but utilitarian winery after previously inhabiting the exotic surrounds of the old Albany wool store, Galafrey makes wines with plenty of robust, if not rustic, character, drawing grapes in the main from estate plantings. Following the death of husband/father/founder Ian Tyrer, Kim and Linda Tyrer have taken up the reins, announcing, 'There is girl power happening at Galafrey Wines!' There is a cornucopia of back vintages available, some superb and underpriced, at the cellar door. Exports to China and Japan.

ŢŢŢŢŢ **Reserve Dry Land Mount Barker Riesling 2012** Light straw-green; this fully deserves its Reserve tag, with the intensity, drive and length the standard wine lacks; here lime, lime zest and lemon are built around a vibrant core of minerally acidity, the finish and aftertaste as fresh as a spring day. Screwcap. 12% alc. **Rating** 94 **To** 2025 $29

ŢŢŢŢŢ **Dry Grown Mount Barker Shiraz 2009 Rating** 93 **To** 2029 $28
Dry Grown Mount Barker Merlot 2011 Rating 91 **To** 2021 $28
Dry Grown Mount Barker Merlot 2009 Rating 91 **To** 2024 $28
Dry Land Mount Barker Riesling 2012 Rating 90 **To** 2017 $20

Gallagher Wines ★★★★

2770 Dog Trap Road, Murrumbateman, NSW 2582 **Region** Canberra District
T (02) 6227 0555 **www**.gallagherwines.com.au **Open** W'ends & public hols 10–5
Winemaker Greg Gallagher **Est.** 1995 **Dozens** 2000 **Vyds** 2ha

Greg Gallagher was senior winemaker at Taltarni for 20 years, working with Dominique Portet. He began planning a change at much the same time as did Portet, and, together with wife Libby, started establishing a small vineyard at Murrumbateman in 1995, now planted to 1ha each of chardonnay and shiraz. Between 1999 and 2004 Greg was winemaker at CSU, and now acts as both winemaker and consultant for a dozen or so wineries in or near the Canberra District.

♀♀♀♀♀ **Canberra District Shiraz 2009** Has retained good depth and hue; the bouquet and medium-bodied palate offer cherry, plum and chocolate aromas and flavours, supported on the palate by silky tannins and subtle oak. Screwcap. 13.7% alc. **Rating** 91 **To** 2020 $25

♀♀♀♀ **Canberra District Sauvignon Blanc 2012** Despite its low alcohol, this is
✪ fairly and squarely in the middle of the tropical fruit rainbow, with the two p's: passionfruit and (green) pineapple. Well made and priced. Screwcap. 11.5% alc. **Rating** 89 **To** 2014 $20

✪ **Canberra District Chardonnay 2012** A pleasant light- to medium-bodied unwooded – or should I say fruit-driven – style with just enough fruit brightness to catch attention. The flavours are not clichés, with apple and pear contributing as much as citrus and stone fruit, and some will enjoy it for its point of difference and/or price. Screwcap. 12.7% alc. **Rating** 89 **To** 2015 $20
Canberra District Merlot 2010 Rating 89 **To** 2014 $25

Galli Estate ★★★★★

1507 Melton Highway, Plumpton, Vic 3335 **Region** Sunbury
T (03) 9747 1444 **www**.galliestate.com.au **Open** 7 days 11–5
Winemaker Ben Ranken **Est.** 1997 **Dozens** 10000 **Vyds** 160ha

Galli Estate has two distinct vineyards: Heathcote, which produces the red wines (Shiraz, Sangiovese, Nebbiolo, Tempranillo, Grenache and Montepulciano), and the cooler climate vineyard at Plumpton in the Sunbury region, producing the whites (Chardonnay, Pinot Grigio, Sauvignon Blanc and Fiano). All wines are estate-grown and made. Since the death of Lorenzo Galli in 2004, his wife Pamela has continued his dream, and has developed export markets in Canada, Singapore, China and Hong Kong.

♀♀♀♀♀ **Artigiano Block Two Heathcote Shiraz 2009** Bright purple-crimson; takes what Camelback has, but builds on it impressively, with a mix of red and black fruits, quality oak and fine-grained tannins on the long, medium-bodied palate. Screwcap. 14% alc. **Rating** 94 **To** 2021 $30
Lorenzo 2009 Light to medium red-purple; a spicy, savoury Shiraz from a fiery, smoky vintage, but shows no sign of the issues faced in the Yarra Valley and elsewhere; this has tenacity and length on the palate to its spicy black cherry fruit and fine-grained tannins. Screwcap. 14% alc. **Rating** 94 **To** 2024 $42
Artigiano Heathcote Sangiovese 2010 Very light colour, but the hue is good, as is the purity of the varietal expression, its bright red cherry flavours nipped by a nice touch of spicy/savoury tannins; good balance of fruit, oak and tannins. Screwcap. 13.5% alc. **Rating** 94 **To** 2017 $30

♀♀♀♀♀ **Artigiano Sunbury Chardonnay 2011 Rating** 93 **To** 2016 $30
✪ **Artigiano Sunbury Pinot Grigio 2012** Pale quartz; the normal pattern is for what should be called grigios to be named gris, because the latter commands a higher price. Here the roles are (happily) reversed; it has delicious nashi pear and crunchy green apple flavours on a long, balanced palate. Screwcap. 13.5% alc. **Rating** 93 **To** 2014 $20

✪   **Heathcote Tempranillo Grenache Mourvedre 2011** Bright crimson-purple;
the unconventional blend works well, with fragrant red fruits and red flowers
on the bouquet, followed by juicy red cherry, raspberry and spice on the palate.
Screwcap. 13.5% alc. **Rating** 93 **To** 2018 .$20

Adele Tempranillo 2011 Rating 92 **To** 2016 $35

✪   **Camelback Heathcote Shiraz 2011** Purple-red; an attractive bouquet and ripe
fruit palate, with its juicy plum and black cherry fruit, tannins and oak very well
balanced and integrated. Screwcap. 14.5% alc. **Rating** 91 **To** 2017 $20

Camelback Heathcote Nebbiolo Rose 2012 Rating 90 **To** 2014 $20

✪   **Camelback Heathcote Shiraz 2010** Light, clear purple-crimson; the fresh, red-
fruited bouquet and palate, with an airbrush of oak and superfine tannins, make a
wine ready for immediate enjoyment. Screwcap. 14% alc. **Rating** 90 **To** 2015 $18

Adele Shiraz 2009 Rating 90 **To** 2019 $35

Gallows Wine Co

Lennox Road, Carbunup River, WA 6280 **Region** Margaret River
T (08) 9755 1060 **www**.gallows.com.au **Open** 7 days 10–5
Winemaker Charlie Maiolo, Neil Doddridge **Est.** 2008 **Dozens** 10 000 **Vyds** 27ha
This is the venture of the Maiolo family, headed by winemaker Charlie. The macabre name
is that of one of the most famous surf breaks on the Margaret River coast. The vineyard is
planted to semillon, sauvignon blanc, chardonnay, pinot noir, shiraz, merlot and cabernet
sauvignon. The site climate is strongly influenced by Geographe Bay, 5km to the north, and
facilitates the production of wines with a large spectrum of flavours and characteristics.

🍷🍷🍷🍷🍷   **The Bommy Margaret River Semillon Sauvignon Blanc 2012** Pale quartz;
the semillon component is the senior partner, contributing a lemon zest character
to the bouquet and palate, but the sauvignon blanc also makes its presence felt,
with tropical/gooseberry flavours coming through on the mid to back-palate.
A most enjoyable wine. Screwcap. 13% alc. **Rating** 93 **To** 2015 $26

The Gallows Margaret River Merlot 2011 Good hue and depth; there is an
undoubted synergy between Margaret River and merlot, allowing the varietal fruit
expression free rein, with redcurrant, black olive and cedar aromas and flavours on
the medium-bodied palate, tannins and oak well controlled. Screwcap. 14.5% alc.
Rating 92 **To** 2016 $24

The Bommy Margaret River Chardonnay 2011 Pale straw-green; the
hallmark depth of Margaret River Chardonnay, and its display of peach, fig and
melon fruit, come through strongly. At its best now. Screwcap. 14% alc. **Rating** 90
To 2014 $30

The Bommy Margaret River Cabernet Sauvignon 2010 Light colour; the
level of extract, and the quality of the oak, is less refined than that of Bin 1A, but
it's still a handy cabernet. Screwcap. 13% alc. **Rating** 90 **To** 2020 $31

🍷🍷🍷🍷   **The Bommy Margaret River Shiraz 2010 Rating** 88 **To** 2018 $31
The Gallows Margaret River Shiraz 2011 Rating 87 **To** 2016 $24

Gapsted

3897 Great Alpine Road, Gapsted, Vic 3737 **Region** Alpine Valleys
T (03) 5751 1383 **www**.gapstedwines.com.au **Open** 7 days 10–5
Winemaker Shayne Cunningham, Michael Cope-Williams, Tony Pla Bou **Est.** 1997
Dozens 95 000 **Vyds** 256.1ha
Gapsted is the major brand of the Victorian Alps Winery, which started life (and continues) as
a large-scale contract winemaking facility. However, the quality of the wines made for its own
brand (Gapsted) has led to the expansion of production not only under that label, but under
a raft of cheaper, subsidiary labels including Tobacco Road, Coldstone, Buckland Gap, Snowy
Creek, Waterstone Bridge, and doubtless others in the pipeline. Its vineyards extend across the
Alpine Valleys and (mostly) the King Valley. Its vineyard holdings have increased from 166ha to
the present level, the winemaking team expanded with the arrival of Tony Pla Bou. Exports
to the UK, Germany, Denmark, Singapore, China and Japan.

ΨΨΨΨΨ **Ballerina Canopy Durif 2009** Has retained its deep purple colour, and its rich, full-bodied palate; it spent 26 months in barrel, seamlessly integrating that oak with the cornucopia of predominantly black fruits, spice and licorice on the sideline. The tannins, often a problem with this variety, are in perfect balance. Cork. 14% alc. **Rating** 94 **To** 2024 $31

ΨΨΨΨΨ **Limited Release Petit Manseng 2011 Rating** 92 **To** 2015 $23
Limited Release Saperavi 2008 Rating 92 **To** 2020 $27

Garagiste ★★★★★

4 Lawrey Street, Frankston, Vic 3199 (postal) **Region** Mornington Peninsula
T 0439 370 530 **www**.garagiste.com.au **Open** Not
Winemaker Barnaby Flanders **Est.** 2006 **Dozens** 1500 **Vyds** 3ha
Barnaby Flanders was a co-founder of Allies Wines (see separate entry) in 2003, with some of the wines made under the Garagiste label. Allies has now gone its own way, and Barnaby has a controlling interest in the Garagiste brand. The future will focus on the Mornington Peninsula, and in particular grapes from Tuerong and Moorooduc in the north, with sand-based soils, the brown loam/red volcanic soils of Merricks and Merricks North in the middle, and the red volcanic soils of Red Hill and Main Ridge in the most elevated southern sector. Pinot noir and chardonnay will be the varieties used, and the wines will be made with wild yeasts, minimally handled and bottled without fining or filtration.

ΨΨΨΨΨ **Merricks Mornington Peninsula Chardonnay 2011** A singularly good Chardonnay, with greater intensity and drive than many of its Mornington Peninsula compatriots; the fruit is on the cusp between citrus/grapefruit and white peach/nectarine, oak a subtle by-play. Screwcap. 13% alc. **Rating** 94 **To** 2020 $45
Le Stagiaire Mornington Peninsula Pinot Gris 2012 Let no man put asunder the matrimonial bonds between the Mornington Peninsula and pinot gris – there is almost always an undefinable something extra in these wines, even without the sophisticated winemaking involved here. There are layers to the fruit flavour and structure, the fruit almost luscious, headed well into stone fruit. Screwcap. 13.5% alc. **Rating** 94 **To** 2016 $29

ΨΨΨΨΨ **Le Stagiaire Mornington Peninsula Rose 2012 Rating** 93 **To** 2014 $28
Red Hill Mornington Peninsula Pinot Noir 2011 Rating 92 **To** 2015 $45
Merricks Mornington Peninsula Pinot Noir 2011 Rating 90 **To** 2014 $45

Gartelmann Hunter Estate ★★★★★

701 Lovedale Road, Lovedale, NSW 2321 **Region** Hunter Valley
T (02) 4930 7113 **www**.gartelmann.com.au **Open** Mon–Sat 10–5, Sun 10–4
Winemaker Jorg Gartelmann, Liz Jackson **Est.** 1970 **Dozens** 6600
In 1996 Jan and Jorg Gartelmann purchased what was previously the George Hunter Estate – 16ha of mature vineyards, most established by Oliver Shaul in '70. In a change of emphasis, the vineyard was sold, and Gartelmann now sources its grapes from the Hunter Valley and other NSW regions, including the cool Rylstone area in Mudgee. Exports to the US, Germany, Singapore and China.

ΨΨΨΨΨ **Old Vines Mudgee Shiraz 2011** Has deeper colour than Wilhelm, and substantially more fruit; the palate is no more than medium-bodied, but the black cherry and spice-laden palate has arresting intensity; the tannins are superfine, the oak evident but integrated. Screwcap. 13.5% alc. **Rating** 94 **To** 2025 $30
Diedrich Shiraz 2011 Deep crimson, purple hue; the bouquet reveals lifted toasty oak with dark plum, sage and licorice; the palate is medium-bodied, fleshy and generous, with a taut backbone of acidity and ample fine-grained tannins; long and linear to conclude. Screwcap. 14.5% alc. **Rating** 94 **To** 2022 $45 BE
Rylstone Petit Verdot 2011 Good purple hue; the stars were in alignment over this wine, which spent 16 months in new and used French and American oak, enough to polish the sometimes rough-edged tannins of the variety, yet not obscure that fresh cassis fruit on the long finish. Screwcap. 14.5% alc. **Rating** 94 **To** 2020 $35

ŶŶŶŶŶ Sarah Elizabeth Chardonnay 2012 Rating 93 To 2017 $30
Benjamin Semillon 2009 Rating 91 To 2020 $45 BE
Mudgee Merlot 2011 Rating 90 To 2018 $25

Gatt Wines ★★★★☆

PO Box 295, Tanunda, SA 5352 **Region** Eden Valley
T (08) 8564 1166 **www**.gattwines.com **Open** At Taste Eden Valley, Angaston
Winemaker Jo Irvine, David Norman (Contract) **Est.** 1972 **Dozens** 8000 **Vyds** 50.65ha
When you read the hyperbole that sometimes accompanies the acquisition of an existing
wine business, about transforming it into a world-class operation, it is easy to sigh and move
on. When Ray Gatt acquired Eden Springs, he proceeded to translate words into deeds. As
well as the 19.82ha Eden Springs Vineyard, he also acquired the historic Siegersdorf Vineyard
(19.43ha) on the Barossa floor, and the neighbouring Graue Vineyard (11.4ha). He then put
contract winemakers Joanne Irvine and David Norman in charge, tapping into their long-
established credentials. It was hardly surprising that a string of wine show medals should
be bestowed on the wines, my personal appreciation of the wines also no surprise. Perhaps
the most obvious feature is the exceptional value for money they represent. The change of
name from Eden Springs to Gatt Wines in 2011 was sensible; Eden Springs was no longer
appropriate given the vineyard holdings in the Barossa Valley. Exports to Denmark, South
Korea, Hong Kong, China and Japan.

ŶŶŶŶŶ Eden Springs High Eden Riesling 2009 Pale colour, and still showing a
vivid green hue, the bouquet is slowly and gracefully evolving with lemon zest,
struck flint and fresh brioche all on display; the palate is lively, fresh and still with
plenty of energy and nerve; tangy and bone dry to conclude. Screwcap. 11.5% alc.
Rating 94 To 2020 $25 BE

ŶŶŶŶŶ High Eden Single Vineyard Cabernet Sauvignon 2010 Rating 92 To 2022
$55 BE

Gembrook Hill ★★★★★

Launching Place Road, Gembrook, Vic 3783 **Region** Yarra Valley
T (03) 5968 1622 **www**.gembrookhill.com.au **Open** By appt
Winemaker Timo Mayer, Andrew Marks **Est.** 1983 **Dozens** 2500 **Vyds** 6ha
Ian and June Marks established Gembrook Hill, one of the oldest vineyards in the coolest
part of the upper Yarra Valley, usually harvested some four weeks later than the lower parts of
the region. Son Andrew assists Timo Mayer on the winemaking front, each also having his
own respective labels (see separate entries for The Wanderer and Mayer). The northeast-facing
vineyard is in a natural amphitheatre and most vines are almost 30 years old; the low-yielding
vines are not irrigated, are hand-pruned and harvested (plantings consist of sauvignon blanc,
chardonnay and pinot noir). The minimal approach to winemaking produces wines of a
consistent style with finesse and elegance. Exports to the UK, Denmark, Japan and Malaysia.

ŶŶŶŶŶ Yarra Valley Sauvignon Blanc 2011 Pale colour, and showing lemon blossom,
nettle, wet slate and fennel on the bouquet; the palate is fine-boned and vibrant,
with lacy acidity providing a long and harmonious finish. Screwcap. 13% alc.
Rating 94 To 2015 $33 BE

ŶŶŶŶŶ Village Yarra Valley Pinot Noir 2010 Rating 91 To 2017 $30

Gemelli Estate ★★★

163 Palmers Lane, Pokolbin, NSW 2320 **Region** Hunter Valley
T (02) 4998 7910 **www**.gemelliestate.com.au **Open** Fri–Mon 10–4
Winemaker Peter Went, Daniel Binet **Est.** 2011 **Dozens** 350 **Vyds** 2.8ha
Rebecca and Michael Boyd purchased what is now called Gemelli Estate in 2011, inheriting
a 20-year-old vineyard and a cellar door that has been on the site since the mid 1990s. The
10ha property has 1.6ha of chardonnay, and 0.6ha each of merlot and muscat, the latter
used to produce moscato. The Cabernet Merlot obviously utilises purchased grapes for the
cabernet component.

ŦŦŦŦ **Warrens last Drop! Merlot 2011** Light colour, although the hue is good; a soft, plush, light- to medium-bodied palate stays strictly between the rails of the red fruits, with oak and tannins spectators on either side. Drink now while the fruit is in full flower. Screwcap. 13% alc. **Rating** 89 **To** 2014 $20

Methode Traditionelle 2011 The package (bottle, etc) and process of traditional method are capital intensive, and it is these that explain the price more than the wine in the bottle. That said, it is crisp and fresh, and (unexpectedly) not sweet. Crown seal. 12% alc. **Rating** 87 **To** 2013 $30

Gemtree Vineyards   ★★★★★

Elliot Road, McLaren Flat, SA 5171 **Region** McLaren Vale
T (08) 8323 8199 **www**.gemtreevineyards.com.au **Open** Mon–Fri 10–5, w'ends 11–5
Winemaker Mike Brown **Est.** 1998 **Dozens** 30000 **Vyds** 133.16ha
The Buttery family, headed by Paul and Jill, and with the active involvement of Melissa as viticulturist, have been grapegrowers in McLaren Vale since 1980, when they purchased their first vineyard. The vineyards are managed biodynamically and recently achieved organic certification. The wine portfolio is of high quality, and is also full of interest. In 2012 Chinese interests acquired a major shareholding in the business, and this led to Gemtree's acquisition of the Kangarilla winery and its surrounding vineyard in '13 from the O'Brien family. It's a friendly deal, as the Kangarilla brand stays with the O'Briens, and they will continue to make their wines there in conjunction with those of Gemtree. Exports to the UK, the US, Canada, South Korea, Vietnam, China and NZ.

ŦŦŦŦŦ **White Lees Shiraz 2009** The use of the 'white lees' is to preserve freshness and the result would support the theory; fresh, ripe red and black fruits, with fruitcake spice, mocha oak notes and light floral hints; the palate is juicy, unctuous and warm, with a long, fine-grained tannin finish that is plush and more than a little hedonistic. Cork. 14.5% alc. **Rating** 95 **To** 2022 $70 BE

ŦŦŦŦŶ **Moonstone McLaren Vale Savagnin 2012** Quartz-white; a zesty, spicy
✪ wine in a predominantly citrus zest/pith/juice spectrum attesting to the variety's relationship with gewurztraminer; good length and balance, the finish bright. Screwcap. 13.5% alc. **Rating** 90 **To** 2014 $16

✪ **Tatty Rd Shiraz 2012** Vivid purple hue; an unadulterated bouquet of blackberry and bitter chocolate; the palate is young, fresh and vital, constructed for maximum early-drinking enjoyment; a perfect little barbecue or pizza wine. Great value. Screwcap. 13.5% alc. **Rating** 90 **To** 2016 $12 BE

Uncut McLaren Vale Shiraz 2011 Rating 90 **To** 2018 $25 BE

ŦŦŦŦ **Tigers Eye McLaren Vale Shiraz 2010** Impenetrable colour; the bouquet is
✪ full of black fruits and charry mocha oak aromas; the palate is dense, with charry oak the dominant theme; big-boned and chewy to conclude. Screwcap. 14.5% alc. **Rating** 89 **To** 2018 $18 BE

Geoff Merrill Wines   ★★★★★

291 Pimpala Road, Woodcroft, SA 5162 **Region** McLaren Vale
T (08) 8381 6877 **www**.geoffmerrillwines.com.au **Open** Mon–Fri 10–5, w'ends 12–5
Winemaker Geoff Merrill, Scott Heidrich **Est.** 1980 **Dozens** 65000 **Vyds** 45ha
If Geoff Merrill ever loses his impish sense of humour or his zest for life, high and not-so-high, we shall all be the poorer. The product range consists of three tiers: premium (varietal); Reserve, being the older (and best) wines, reflecting the desire for elegance and subtlety of this otherwise exuberant winemaker; and, at the top, Henley Shiraz. His Mount Hurtle wines are sold exclusively through Vintage Cellars/Liquorland. Exports to all major markets.

ŦŦŦŦŦ **Reserve McLaren Vale Shiraz 2010** This succulent and sumptuous offering sings with perfumed violets, black plums and juicy blackberries that linger long and supple through an impressively fruit-focused palate, propelled by soft, fine-grained tannins. Screwcap. 14.6% alc. **Rating** 95 **To** 2020 $75 TS

Reserve Cabernet Sauvignon 2006 A 70/30% blend of McLaren Vale and Coonawarra grapes; it has retained very good hue, and is still at the start of what will be a long journey; it is flush with blackcurrant fruit supported by ripe tannins and oak from 21 months in barrel; positively juicy, and has great length. Cork. 14.5% alc. **Rating** 95 **To** 2031 $40

Pimpala Vineyard McLaren Vale Cabernet Merlot 2006 Light to medium red-purple; a testament to the quality and staying power of the '06 vintage; the bouquet is fragrant, with some spice and truffle notes, red berry and cassis on the finely structured, medium-bodied palate, oak and tannins well balanced and totally integrated. Approaching its best-by date. Cork. 14.5% alc. **Rating** 94 **To** 2016 $36

🍷🍷🍷🍷🍷 Bush Vine McLaren Vale Grenache Rose 2012 The grapes come from
✪ 80-year-old bush vines in the cool Blewitt Springs area. Pale but vivid puce, it has a fragrant and flowery bouquet, and a palate that is bone dry yet filled with spicy red fruit flavours. Screwcap. 14.5% alc. **Rating** 92 **To** 2013 $21

Reserve Chardonnay 2009 **Rating** 90 **To** 2014 $27
Wickham Park McLaren Vale Merlot 2008 **Rating** 90 **To** 2016 $27

Geoff Weaver ★★★★★

2 Gilpin Lane, Mitcham, SA 5062 (postal) **Region** Adelaide Hills
T (08) 8272 2105 **www.**geoffweaver.com.au **Open** Not
Winemaker Geoff Weaver **Est.** 1982 **Dozens** 3200 **Vyds** 12.3ha
This is the full-time business of former Hardys chief winemaker Geoff Weaver. He draws upon a little over 12ha of vineyard established between 1982 and '88, and invariably produces immaculate Riesling and Sauvignon Blanc, and one of the longest-lived Chardonnays to be found in Australia, with intense grapefruit and melon flavour. The beauty of the labels ranks supreme with Pipers Brook. Exports to Hong Kong and Singapore.

🍷🍷🍷🍷🍷 Lenswood Chardonnay 2010 Bright green-straw; wild yeast-fermented in French oak, plus mlf and lees contact, have given the extra complexity and texture sought by Geoff Weaver, but have also left the fragrant bouquet and the juicy, vibrant fruit and natural acidity in charge of the palate; the finish is very long and beautifully balanced. Screwcap. 13.5% alc. **Rating** 96 **To** 2018 $40

Lenswood Cabernet Merlot 2000 The decision to keep a part of the make for extended bottle age, and thus a museum release, has been fully justified. This is a rare opportunity to buy a fully mature wine direct from the cellar of the maker. All the components of dark berry fruits, oak and tannins have joined seamlessly and harmoniously. There will, I suppose, be some bottle variation, but it's hard to imagine a more perfect bottle than this one. Cork. 13.5% alc. **Rating** 96 **To** 2020 $40

Lenswood Sauvignon Blanc 2012 Pale straw-green; year in, year out, one of the most elegant (and most reliable) Sauvignon Blancs on the market; kiwifruit, citrus and a dab of white peach drive the fragrant bouquet and fresh palate, the finish dry and almost savoury. Prior history shows the wine does not have to be consumed immediately. Screwcap. 12.5% alc. **Rating** 95 **To** 2014 $26

Lenswood Riesling 2012 Surprisingly developed colour; a wine full of aromas and flavours, its richness and generosity already inviting drinking. However, the finish and aftertaste will sustain the wine over years, during which time the opulence of the lime and lemon fruit will grow further. Screwcap. 12.5% alc. **Rating** 94 **To** 2020 $26

Ghost Rock Vineyard ★★★★☆

1055 Port Sorrell Road, Northdown, Tas 7307 **Region** Northern Tasmania
T (03) 6428 4005 **www.**ghostrock.com.au **Open** Wed–Sun & public hols 11–5 (7 days Dec–Feb)
Winemaker Jeremy Dineen (Contract) **Est.** 2001 **Dozens** 3100 **Vyds** 16ha
Cate and Colin Arnold purchased the former Patrick Creek Vineyard (planted in 1989) in 2001. They run a printing and design business in Devonport and were looking for a suitable

site to establish a vineyard. The vineyard (pinot gris, pinot noir, sauvignon blanc, chardonnay and riesling) is planted on a sheltered slope with a northeasterly aspect. The increase in plantings (and consequent production) has allowed the Arnolds to supply markets throughout the mainland.

ΨΨΨΨΨ **Catherine Sparkling 2007** Excellent mousse; time on lees and on cork (this is the second disgorgement, Dec '11) has significantly improved the wine since first tasted Jan '11; long, intense and with some pleasing tannin grip on the finish. Diam. 12.5% alc. **Rating** 94 **To** 2016 $45

ΨΨΨΨΨ **Oulton Estate Chardonnay 2012 Rating** 92 **To** 2017 $25
Casper's Block Pinot Noir 2010 Rating 92 **To** 2017 $36
Sauvignon Blanc 2012 Rating 90 **To** 2014 $25
Ol' Man's Ghost Pinot Gris 2012 Rating 90 **To** 2014 $26

Giaconda ★★★★★

30 McClay Road, Beechworth, Vic 3747 **Region** Beechworth
T (03) 5727 0246 **www**.giaconda.com.au **Open** By appt
Winemaker Rick Kinzbrunner **Est.** 1985 **Dozens** 3000
These wines have a super-cult status and, given the tiny production, are extremely difficult to find; they are sold chiefly through restaurants and by mail order (via their website). All have a cosmopolitan edge befitting Rick Kinzbrunner's international winemaking experience. The Chardonnay is one of Australia's greatest in normal vintage conditions, and is now made and matured in the underground wine cellar hewn out of granite. This permits gravity flow, and a year-round temperature range of 14–15°C, promising even more for the future. Exports to the UK and the US.

ΨΨΨΨΨ **Chardonnay 2011** Vibrant green; the power and extreme complexity of the bouquet literally leap out of the glass, yet the palate lifts the bar further, eerily like a Grand Cru White Burgundy – Chevalier Montrachet comes to mind. The mouthfeel is staggeringly deep, yet full of energy, driving the wine through to an exceptionally long finish. This will surely rival the '96 Giaconda Chardonnay, its drink-to date ultra-conservative. Screwcap. 13% alc. **Rating** 98 **To** 2026 $150

Gibson Barossavale ★★★★★

190 Willows Road, Light Pass, SA 5355 **Region** Barossa Valley
T (08) 8562 3193 **www**.gibsonwines.com.au **Open** 7 days 11–5
Winemaker Rob Gibson **Est.** 1996 **Dozens** 10 000 **Vyds** 14.2ha
Rob Gibson spent much of his working life as a senior viticulturist for Penfolds. While at Penfolds he was involved in research tracing the characters that particular parcels of grapes give to a wine, which left him with a passion for identifying and protecting what is left of the original vineyard plantings in wine regions around Australia. He has two vineyards in the Barossa Valley, at Stockwell (shiraz, mataro and grenache) and Light Pass (merlot), and one in the Eden Valley (shiraz and riesling), and also purchases grapes from McLaren Vale and the Adelaide Hills. The 7000-dozen Loose End brand (launched in 2007) has been sold. Exports to the US, Denmark, Hong Kong, Japan, China and Singapore.

ΨΨΨΨΨ **Australian Old Vine Collection Barossa Shiraz 2009** The vines that produced the grapes for this wine were planted between the mid 1850s and early 1900s, the vines now spanning three centuries. It has spicy/cedary/savoury aspects, and while the black fruit core has great intensity, the wine is light on its feet, with an open weave to its texture, and great line, balance and length. Cork. 14.5% alc. Rating 96 To 2030 $110
Gibson Reserve Shiraz 2010 Deep purple-crimson. There are mountains of mouth-coating black fruits plus the contribution of 2½ years in mainly French oak, which has helped soften the still-sufficient tannins. There are no signs of dead fruit, nor heat from the alcohol. Will improve further with decades in bottle. Screwcap. 14.5% alc. **Rating** 95 **To** 2040 $44

✪ **Gibson Eden Valley Riesling 2012** I have always felt Eden Valley Riesling should be less minerally/talcy than Clare, with slightly more lime juice (and similar acidity). This is a prime example, ready to enjoy here and now or in 5 years. Screwcap. 12% alc. **Rating** 94 **To** 2018 $20

Gibson Reserve Merlot 2010 A 42/9/45/4% blend of Barossa merlot and Barossa cabernet, Adelaide Hills merlot and Fleurieu merlot, matured in French oak. The colour is excellent, as are the complexity, the mouthfeel, the varietal expression and the fine-grained but balanced tannins. A convincing mouthful of harmonious flavours. Screwcap. 14% alc. **Rating** 94 **To** 2025 $44

♟♟♟♟♟ **The Dirtman Barossa Shiraz 2010** Rating 91 To 2020 $27
Gibson Adelaide Hills Pinot Gris 2012 Rating 90 To 2014 $20

♟♟♟♟ **Gibson Isabelle Cabernet Merlot 2009** Rating 88 To 2016 $27
Wilfreda Blend 2009 Rating 87 To 2015 $27
Botrytis Semillon 2010 Rating 87 To 2014 $20

gilbert by Simon Gilbert ★★★★☆

PO Box 773, Mudgee, NSW 2850 **Region** Various
T (02) 6373 1371 **www**.thegilbertsarecoming.com.au **Open** Not
Winemaker Simon Gilbert **Est.** 2010 **Dozens** 2050
For some time now Simon Gilbert has devoted himself to his consultancy and wine brokering business Wineworks of Australia. As that business has grown, and with the sale of the Prince Hill winery to the Watson Wine Group, Simon has returned to the winery wearing his Wineworks of Australia hat, overseeing the winemaking of the estate-grown grapes, all of which will be exported. Separate from his consultancy business, he has established gilbert by Simon Gilbert, and also makes the wines for this label at the same winery. Grapes are sourced from premium locations across Australia, and not restricted to the same localities each year. Distribution is limited to specialist wine retailers and restaurants.

♟♟♟♟♟ **Mudgee Orange Saignee Sangiovese Shiraz Barbera 2012** Bright pale
✪ pink; this is one of the most highly perfumed bouquets I can recollect ever encountering, a vivid combination of strawberry and nettle leaf, followed by an incisive and mouth-watering palate with no concession whatsoever to sweetness. Truly exceptional. Screwcap. 12% alc. **Rating** 96 **To** 2015 $24

♟♟♟♟♟ **Orange Pinot Grigio 2012** Rating 92 To 2014 $26
✪ **g & Co Mudgee Shiraz Sangiovese Barbera 2011** Medium purple-crimson; an unusual blend, and while shiraz and oak lead the aromas and flavours, the contribution of the sangiovese (in particular) and barbera can be seen, introducing sidelights of red fruits to the chorus of blackberry flavour. Excellent value. Screwcap. 14% alc. **Rating** 90 **To** 2018 $18

Gilberts ★★★★☆

30138 Albany Highway, Kendenup via Mount Barker, WA 6323 **Region** Mount Barker
T (08) 9851 4028 **www**.gilbertwines.com.au **Open** Wed–Mon 10–5
Winemaker Plantagenet (Cath Oates) **Est.** 1980 **Dozens** 4000 **Vyds** 13.5ha
Once a part-time occupation for sheep and beef farmers Jim and Beverly Gilbert, but now a full-time and very successful one. The mature vineyard (shiraz, chardonnay, riesling and cabernet sauvignon), coupled with contract winemaking at Plantagenet, has long produced very high-class Riesling, and now also makes excellent Shiraz. The Three Devils Shiraz is named in honour of their sons. Exports to Singapore.

♟♟♟♟♟ **Cellar Reserve Cane Cut Riesling 2012** A delightful and varietal bouquet of meyer lemon, candied orange, ginger and anise; the luscious palate is focused and sweet, with the acid in complete balance to the sugar; excellent purity of expression and seriously long. 375ml. Screwcap. 11% alc. **Rating** 94 **To** 2020 $25 BE

♟♟♟♟ **Mount Barker Riesling 2012** Rating 92 To 2022 $22 BE

Gilligan ★★★★

PO Box 235, Willunga, SA 5172 **Region** McLaren Vale
T 0412 423 131 **www.**gilligan.com.au **Open** Not
Winemaker Mark Day, Leigh Gilligan **Est.** 2001 **Dozens** 1200 **Vyds** 5.74ha
Leigh Gilligan is a 20-year marketing veteran, mostly with McLaren Vale wineries (including Wirra Wirra). The Gilligan family has just over 4ha of shiraz and 0.4ha each of grenache, mourvedre, marsanne and roussanne, selling part of the production. In 2001 they persuaded next-door neighbour Drew Noon to make a barrel of Shiraz, which they drank and gave away. Realising they needed more than one barrel, they moved to Maxwell Wines, with help from (former) Maxwell winemaker Mark Day, and have now migrated to Mark's Koltz Winery at Blewitt Springs Exports to the UK, the US, Canada, Germany, Denmark, Thailand and Hong Kong.

♥♥♥♥   **McLaren Vale Roussanne Marsanne 2012** Deep glowing green-gold; looks as if it has had extended skin contact, and its fruit has dried out/been hidden by phenolics. Screwcap. 13.5% alc. **Rating** 87 **To** 2013 $25
McLaren Vale Shiraz Mourvedre Grenache 2011 Good colour for the vintage; there has been a concerted effort to build and extract structure; it has succeeded, but the fruit has been overwhelmed. Screwcap. 15% alc. **Rating** 87 **To** 2015 $25

Gioiello Estate ★★★★

PO Box 250, Tullamarine, Vic 3043 **Region** Upper Goulburn
T 0437 240 502 **www.**gioiello.com.au **Open** Not
Winemaker Scott McCarthy (Contract) **Est.** 1987 **Dozens** 4000 **Vyds** 8.97ha
The Gioiello Estate vineyard was established by a Japanese company and originally known as Daiwa Nar Darak. Planted between 1987 and '96, it accounts for just under 9ha on a 400ha property of rolling hills, pastures, bushland, river flats, natural water springs and billabongs. The early wines produced were sold only in Japan, but their quality was demonstrated by the 1994 Daiwa Nar Darak Chardonnay, which won the George Mackey Award for Best Wine Exported from Australia in '95. It is now owned by the Schiavello family, which is contemplating increasing the plantings with Italian varieties such as nebbiolo and arneis. The gold medal won by the 2007 Reserve Chardonnay at the 18th Annual Concours des Vins du Victoria in November '08 proved the Mackey Award was no fluke.

♥♥♥♥♀   **Upper Goulburn Chardonnay 2012** Full yellow-green; considerable colour
✪   development given that it was 'matured with minimal oak'. Altogether interesting, for the fruit flavours are of peach and melon rather than the grapefruit/citrus expected at this alcohol level. All of which says little about the overall quality of the wine, which is good. Screwcap. 12.6% alc. **Rating** 90 **To** 2015 $20
Mt Concord Upper Goulburn Syrah 2011 Hand-picked, crushed into open fermenters, then matured in French oak for 18 months. It has bright red fruits on the bouquet and medium-bodied palate alike, and despite the cool region and '11 vintage, the flavours are (just) ripe, and are certainly fresh. Screwcap. 13.2% alc. **Rating** 90 **To** 2018 $25

Gipsie Jack Wine Co ★★★★

Wellington Road, Langhorne Creek, SA 5255 **Region** Langhorne Creek
T (08) 8537 3029 **www.**gipsiejack.com.au **Open** 7 days 10–5
Winemaker John Glaetzer, Ben Potts **Est.** 2004 **Dozens** 12 000
One might have thought the partners of Gipsie Jack have enough wine on their plate already, but some just can't resist the temptation, it seems. The two in question are John Glaetzer and Ben Potts, who made a little over 500 dozen from two growers in their inaugural vintage in 2004 (that quantity has increased substantially since). Glaetzer and Potts say, 'We want to make this label fun, like in the "old days". No pretentiousness, no arrogance, not even a back label. A great wine at a great price, with no discounting.' Exports to Switzerland, Hong Kong, Singapore and China.

ŸŸŸŸŸ John Glaetzer & Ben Potts Langhorne Creek Blanc de Blancs 2008 A
100% chardonnay base, made in the traditional method, the fine mousse attesting
to the time it has spent on lees; there is plenty of citrus-accented fruit, plus
bready/yeasty complexity ex those lees. Cork. 11.5% alc. **Rating** 90 **To** 2014 $32

Girraween Estate ★★★

41 Hickling Lane, Wyberba, Qld 4383 **Region** Granite Belt
T (07) 4684 3186 **www**.girraweenestate.com.au **Open** W'ends & public hols 10–5,
or by appt
Winemaker Mike Hayes **Est.** 1985 **Dozens** 1000 **Vyds** 3.5ha
In 2009 Steve Messiter and wife and Lisa purchased Bald Mountain from its founders, Denis
and Jackie Parsons. Steve is a chemical engineer with a Masters degree, has studied winemaking,
and has overseen the complete rejuvenation of the vineyard, including the removal of the lyre
trellis and 40% of the vines. Mike Hayes (Symphony Hill) advises on vineyard management
and makes the wine. Underwent a name change to Girraween Estate in 2011.

ŸŸŸŸ Granite Belt Unwooded Chardonnay 2012 Pale quartz-green; has more
citrus to the bouquet and palate than its alcohol would suggest, but does have
length and good mouthfeel. Better than many such wines, and has been well made.
Screwcap. 13% alc. **Rating** 89 **To** 2014 $24
Sauvignon Blanc 2012 Quartz-white; fairly and squarely in the grassy/herbal/
green pea spectrum, but does have vibrancy and freshness. Screwcap. 11% alc.
Rating 87 **To** 2014 $20

GISA ★★★★

578 The Parade, Auldama, SA 5072 **Region** South Australia
T (08) 8338 2123 **www**.gisa.com.au **Open** Not
Winemaker Mat Henbest **Est.** 2006 **Dozens** 10000
Mat and Lisa Henbest have chosen a clever name for their virtual winery – GISA stands for
Geographic Indication South Australia – neatly covering the fact that the grapes for their
wines come variously from the Adelaide Hills (Sauvignon Blanc), McLaren Vale (Shiraz
Viognier) and Barossa Valley (Reserve Shiraz). It in turn reflects Mat's long apprenticeship in
the wine industry, as a child living on his parents' vineyard, then working in retail trade while
he pursued tertiary qualifications, and thereafter wholesaling wine to the retail and restaurant
trade. He then moved to Haselgrove, where he spent five years working closely with the small
winemaking team, refining his concept of style, and gaining experience on the other side of
the fence of the marketing equation. Exports to China.

ŸŸŸŸŸ Round Barossa Valley Shiraz 2010 Retains its youthful purple-crimson hue;
✪ the bouquet and palate are perfectly ripe, consistent with alcohol between 13%
and 14%, but where on earth did the 12% come from? Matured in 2–3-year-old
American oak, the supple plum, black cherry and blackberry fruits are sustained by
ripe tannins. Screwcap. 12% alc. **Rating** 92 **To** 2025 $18
Piccadilly Chardonnay 2012 The utterly bizarre back label says the grapes were
hand-picked, cold-soaked for 3 days and whole bunch-pressed. You can't 'cold
soak' whole bunches. One hundred per cent barrel-fermented in 50% new French
oak. An elegant wine is the outcome, with good varietal character that has soaked
up the oak. Screwcap. 13% alc. **Rating** 91 **To** 2016 $30
✪ Round Adelaide Hills Sauvignon Blanc 2012 Pale quartz; I had trouble
understanding the strange (but not unpleasant) note to the bouquet until I learned
that some semillon from the Kuitpo Forest area had been blended in, giving a
bath powder nuance to the tropical lychee of the bouquet and palate. It all comes
together well. Screwcap. 12.5% alc. **Rating** 90 **To** 2014 $18

ŸŸŸŸ Arc Adelaide Hills Semillon Sauvignon Blanc 2012 **Rating** 88 **To** 2014 $12

Gisborne Peak

69 Short Road, Gisborne South, Vic 3437 **Region** Macedon Ranges
T (03) 5428 2228 **www.**gisbornepeakwines.com.au **Open** 7 days 11–5
Winemaker John Ellis **Est.** 1978 **Dozens** 1800 **Vyds** 5.5ha
Bob Nixon began the development of Gisborne Peak way back in 1978, planting his dream vineyard row by row. (Bob is married to Barbara Nixon, founder of Victoria Winery Tours.) The tasting room has wide shaded verandahs, plenty of windows and sweeping views. The vineyard is planted to pinot noir, chardonnay, semillon, riesling and lagrein.

ŦŦŦŦŦ **Top Block Macedon Ranges Pinot Noir 2010** Slightly better hue than Foundation Block, deeper and with some purple; cherry, spice and plum elbow any savoury notes out of the way, giving a consistent message on both bouquet and palate. A very appealing wine. Screwcap. 12.9% alc. **Rating** 93 **To** 2017 $28
Macedon Ranges Riesling 2012 Pale straw-green; has more lime and lemon fruit on the bouquet and palate than is usual for young Macedon Rieslings, but has not sacrificed acidity to achieve its fruit profile. Delicious now, but will develop with poise. Screwcap. 12.1% alc. **Rating** 92 **To** 2025 $24
Macedon Ranges Chardonnay 2010 Light straw-green; has cruised through the first 3 years of its life, still fresh and elegant, its delicately tangy fruit the driver, sensibly leaving oak in the back seat. Will please Chablis lovers in particular. Screwcap. 12.5% alc. **Rating** 91 **To** 2016 $27

ŦŦŦŦ **Foundation Block Pinot Noir 2010 Rating** 89 **To** 2016 $28

Glaetzer Wines

PO Box 824 Tanunda, SA 5352 **Region** Barossa Valley
T (08) 8563 0947 **www.**glaetzer.com **Open** Not
Winemaker Ben Glaetzer **Est.** 1996 **Dozens** 15 000 **Vyds** 20ha
Colin Glaetzer and son Ben are almost as well known in SA wine circles as Wolf Blass winemaker John Glaetzer, Colin's twin brother. Glaetzer Wines purchases all its grapes from the Ebenezer subregion of the Barossa Valley, principally from fifth-generation growers. Its wines (Amon-Ra Shiraz, Anaperenna (Shiraz Cabernet Sauvignon), Bishop Shiraz and Wallace Shiraz Grenache) are all made under contract at Barossa Vintners. Exports to all major markets.

ŦŦŦŦŦ **Amon-Ra Unfiltered Barossa Valley Shiraz 2011** Deep crimson-purple, exceptional for the vintage; a courageous decision to leave the grapes on the vine and profit from the much-improved weather in April has resulted in a voluptuously plush wine; the only chink in its armour is the finish, which does point to the alcohol. Cork. 15.5% alc. **Rating** 94 **To** 2021 $100
Bishop Barossa Valley Shiraz 2010 Deep purple-crimson; sourced from the dry-grown Ebenezer Vineyard; the complex bouquet of black fruits, licorice and mocha flows seamlessly into the medium- to full-bodied palate, its savoury, spicy nature showing no hint of overripe fruit nor alcohol heat, just structured tannins. Screwcap. 15.1% alc. **Rating** 94 **To** 2030 $33

Glaetzer-Dixon Family Winemakers ★★★★★

197 Goulburn Street, West Hobart, Tas 7000 (postal) **Region** Southern Tasmania
T (03) 6248 5844 **www.**gdfwinemakers.com **Open** Not
Winemaker Nick Glaetzer **Est.** 2008 **Dozens** 900
History does not relate what Nick Glaetzer's high-profile Barossa Valley winemaker relatives thought of his decision to move to Tasmania in 2005, commencing a search for cool-grown, super-premium vineyards to make cutting edge cool-climate styles. Obviously wife Sally approves, and Nick has a full-time job as one of the winemakers at Frogmore Creek. While his winemaking career began in the Barossa Valley, he then reached into scattered parts of the New World and Old World alike, working successively in Languedoc, the Pfalz, Margaret

River, Riverland, Sunraysia, the Hunter Valley and Burgundy. It is a virtual winery operation, an eminently sensible first step. Exports to Hong Kong.

ŦŦŦŦŦ Reveur Pinot Noir 2010 Bright, clear purple-crimson; the highly fragrant bouquet has scents of rose petals, wild strawberries and truffle that keep drawing you back before you taste it; the palate is every bit as entrancing, long and complete, its supple red and black fruits with highlights of spice and forest floor to add flavour and texture contrast. This will be exceptionally long-lived, and really needs a minimum of 5 years to relax. Screwcap. 13.4% alc. **Rating** 96 To 2030 $56

Reveur Pinot Noir 2009 Deep crimson-purple; cherry, plum and a touch of exotic spices fill the bouquet; a very complex and long palate opens with plush, rich plum fruit, but as the wine travels across the mouth towards the finish, it changes pace, with a juicy elegance offset by touches of savoury tannins. Screwcap. 13.4% alc. **Rating** 96 To 2025 $56

Uberblanc Goldpunkt Riesling 2012 A blend of 60% from the Coal Valley (Southern Tasmania) and 40% from the Tamar Valley (Northern Tasmania), with each small batch of exceptional quality. Cold-fermented until virtually dry (2g/l residual sugar), with a low pH (3.03) investing the wine with a pronounced mineral structure. It is absolutely certain to develop in bottle for many years to come. Screwcap. 11.3% alc. **Rating** 95 To 2032 $36

Uberblanc Riesling 2012 60% Tamar Valley, 40% Coal Valley. In a very distinctive style, fermented to near dryness (3% residual sugar), offset by high acidity (8.5g/l) accentuating the impression of dryness; also kept on lees for 5 months. The wine has abundant lime zest characters, its minerality stemming from the very low pH (2.9), its juicy lime-infused finish a lovely contrast. Screwcap. 11.4% alc. **Rating** 94 To 2032 $24

Avance Pinot Noir 2012 Full, healthy purple-crimson; always on the market first, and made in a light-bodied, minimalist style, says Nick Glaetzer, but sneaking in some co-fermented pinot gris. All things are relative, and by mainland standards, this is definitely not light-bodied; it is simply full of luscious cherry and plum fruit, plus a savoury tannin twist on the finish. Screwcap. 13.8% alc. **Rating** 94 To 2020 $30

ŦŦŦŦ♀ Avance Pinot Noir 2011 Rating 91 To 2014 $30 TS

Glen Eldon Wines   ★★★★☆

143 Nitschke Road, Krondorf, SA 5352 **Region** Barossa Valley
T (08) 8568 2644 **www**.gleneldonwines.com.au **Open** By appt
Winemaker Richard Sheedy **Est.** 1997 **Dozens** 6000 **Vyds** 50ha
Owners Richard and Mary Sheedy (and their four children) have established the Glen Eldon property in the Eden Valley. The shiraz and cabernet sauvignon come from their vineyards in the Barossa Valley; riesling, viognier and merlot from contract-grown fruit; the riesling from the Eden Valley. Exports to the US, Canada and China.

ŦŦŦŦ♀ Barossa Grenache 2010 Deep garnet; ripe red fruits, mocha and cinnamon are evident on the bouquet; the palate is unctuous and thickly textured, with a backbone of chewy tannins and saltbush a feature on the finish. Screwcap. 14.5% alc. **Rating** 90 To 2017 $30 BE

ŦŦŦŦ Eden Valley Riesling 2012 Rating 87 To 2015 $20 BE

Glenfell   ★★★★☆

410/2 Queen Street, Melbourne, Vic 3000 (postal) **Region** Barossa Valley
T (03) 9629 8850 **www**.glenfell.com.au **Open** Not
Winemaker Natasha Mooney **Est.** 2008 **Dozens** 500 **Vyds** 3ha
In 2008 Peter Katsoulotos acquired 1.6ha of 20-year-old cabernet sauvignon planted on the sandy, deep, well-drained soils of the Greenock area. Although not declared on the label

of the Cabernet Sauvignon, it does in fact contain 3% tempranillo. Exports to Hong Kong and China.

ℙℙℙℙℙ **Barossa Valley Shiraz 2010** Deep crimson-purple; has a rich, full-bodied and voluptuous (perhaps a little too much so) swathe of plum, blackberry and licorice fruit; it has absorbed the 18 months it spent in new French oak, and needs to lose some of its puppy fat. Cork. 15% alc. **Rating** 92 **To** 2020 $45

Glenguin Estate ★★★★★

Milbrodale Road, Broke, NSW 2330 **Region** Hunter Valley
T (02) 6579 1009 **www**.glenguinestate.com.au **Open** 7 days 10–5
Winemaker Robin Tedder MW, Rhys Eather **Est.** 1993 **Dozens** 2000 **Vyds** 8ha
Glenguin Estate was established by the Tedder family, headed by Robin Tedder MW, close to Broke and adjacent to Wollombi Brook. The backbone of the production comes from 20-year-old plantings of semillon and shiraz. Tannat (1ha) and a new planting of grafted semillon, with cuttings from Braemore/HVD, complete the picture. Vineyard manager Andrew Tedder, who has considerable experience with organics and biodynamics, is overseeing the ongoing development of Glenguin's organic program. Exports to the UK, Hong Kong and NZ.

ℙℙℙℙℙ **Aged Release Aristea Hunter Valley Shiraz 2007** Very healthy colour; 100 dozen made from grapes from 60-year-old estate vines in an excellent vintage, skilled winemaking doing the rest. Black cherry, plum, cedar and a hint of spicy/earthy nuances are held within a web of fine tannins and quality oak. Screwcap. 14% alc. **Rating** 95 **To** 2037 $60

Aged Release The Old Broke Block Semillon 2007 Glowing yellow-gold; has developed that magic amalgam of citrus, honey and lightly browned toast with an electric tang of acidity, the finish long and balanced. 100 dozen made. Screwcap. 11.5% alc. **Rating** 94 **To** 2022 $25

Glenwillow Wines ★★★★☆

Bendigo Pottery Tourist Complex, 146 Midland Highway, Epsom, Vic 3551
Region Bendigo
T 0428 461 076 **www**.glenwillow.com.au **Open** Fri–Mon 11–5
Winemaker Greg Dedman **Est.** 1999 **Dozens** 750 **Vyds** 2.8ha
Peter and Cherryl Fyffe began their vineyard at Yandoit Creek, 10km south of Newstead, in 1999, planting 1.8ha of shiraz and 0.3ha of cabernet sauvignon, later branching out with 0.6ha of nebbiolo and 0.1ha of barbera. The vineyard, planted on a mixture of rich volcanic and clay loam interspersed with quartz and buckshot gravel, has an elevated, north-facing aspect, which minimises the risk of frost. Wines are released under the elegantly designed Glenwillow label.

Goaty Hill Wines ★★★★☆

530 Auburn Road, Kayena, Tas 7270 **Region** Northern Tasmania
T 1300 819 997 **www**.goatyhill.com **Open** 7 days 10–5
Winemaker Jeremy Dineen (Contract) **Est.** 1998 **Dozens** 5000 **Vyds** 19.5ha
The partners in Goaty Hill Wines are close friends from two families who moved from Victoria to make wine in the pristine climate of the Tamar Valley. Partners include Kristine Grant, Markus Maislinger, and Natasha and Tony Nieuwhof. Most of the estate-grown grapes are now made into the Goaty Hill brand, although they still sell some of their premium sparkling fruit to Jansz Tasmania. There aren't any goats on the property, but there is, according to the owners, a friendly collection of children and dogs.

ℙℙℙℙℙ **Riesling 2012** Bright, light green-straw; the floral lime and apple blossom bouquet leads into a palate stacked with intense lime juice flavour built around the core of firm acidity; has admirable length and persistence. Screwcap. 12.4% alc. **Rating** 94 **To** 2022 $25

ℙℙℙℙℙ **Maia 2010** **Rating** 92 **To** 2015 $38

 PPPP   Pinot Noir 2011 Rating 89 To 2016 $34
Gewurztraminer 2012 Rating 88 To 2015 $28

Golden Ball   ★★★★★

1175 Beechworth-Wangaratta Road, Beechworth, Vic 3747 **Region** Beechworth
T (03) 5727 0284 www.goldenball.com.au **Open** By appt
Winemaker James McLaurin **Est.** 1996 **Dozens** 800 **Vyds** 4ha
The Golden Ball vineyard is on one of the original land grants in the Beechworth region.
The vineyard was planted by James and Janine McLaurin in 1996, mainly to shiraz, cabernet
sauvignon, merlot and malbec, with lesser plantings of petit verdot, sagrantino and savagnin.
The wines are vinified separately and aged in one-third new French oak, the remainder 2–3
years old. The low yields result in intensely flavoured wines, which are to be found in a Who's
Who of Melbourne's best restaurants and a handful of local and Melbourne retailers, including
Randall's at Albert Park. Exports to Singapore.

PPPPP   là-bas Beechworth Chardonnay 2010 Gleaming green-straw; from Smith's
Vineyard, planted in 1978, the oldest in Beechworth. A top-class Chardonnay by
any standard, with wonderful varietal expression of white stone fruits and a hint
of melon, the balance of fruit and oak impeccable. Screwcap. 13% alc. **Rating** 96
To 2018 $45
Cherish a la provencale 2012 Pale salmon-pink; 100% shiraz, specifically
picked for this rose; the bouquet has an unusual cinnamon/spice fragrance, then a
different, but equally appealing, palate with strawberry and lemon flavours, and a
supple, but dry, finish. Screwcap. 12.8% alc. **Rating** 95 To 2014 $26
Beechworth Shiraz 2009 Full red-purple; the complex black fruits and roast
meat aromas of the bouquet herald an impressively structured medium- to full-
bodied palate, where fine-grained tannins and juicy fruits allow each other to state
their case. Diam. 14% alc. **Rating** 94 To 2029 $55
Beechworth Shiraz 2006 Outstanding retention of purple-crimson hue; an
altogether elegant and vibrant wine, the medium-bodied palate bursting with red
cherry and red berry fruits, spice and a touch of Central Victorian mint in the
background. Diam. 13.8% alc. **Rating** 94 To 2018 $60
egalitaire Rouge 2010 A 60/30/10% blend of merlot, shiraz and cabernet
sauvignon, matured in French oak, 25% new. Has retained a bright purple-red
hue, the fragrant bouquet introducing a silky, red berry, light- to medium-bodied
palate that flows evenly, with picture-perfect line and length. Screwcap. 13.5% alc.
Rating 94 To 2025 $30
Gallice Beechworth Cabernet Merlot Malbec 2006 Medium red-purple,
less vibrant than the Shiraz, but good for its age; fruit, oak and tannins have been
seamlessly fused together pre- and post-bottling; the cassis/redcurrant fruit at the
core of the wine is quite delicious. Diam. 13.8% alc. **Rating** 94 To 2018 $70

PPPPP   Beechworth Shiraz 2005 Rating 93 To 2017 $80
Beechworth Shiraz 2004 Rating 92 To 2016 $80
Gallice Beechworth Cabernet Merlot Malbec 2004 Rating 92 To 2016 $80
Gallice Beechworth Cabernet Merlot Malbec 2005 Rating 90 To 2014 $80

Golden Grove Estate   ★★★★★

Sundown Road, Ballandean, Qld 4382 **Region** Granite Belt
T (07) 4684 1291 www.goldengroveestate.com.au **Open** 7 days 9–4
Winemaker Raymond Costanzo **Est.** 1993 **Dozens** 4000 **Vyds** 12.4ha
Golden Grove Estate was established by Mario and Sebastian Costanzo in 1946, producing
stone fruits and table grapes for the fresh fruit market. The first wine grapes (shiraz) were
planted in 1972, but it was not until '85, when ownership passed to son Sam and his wife
Grace, that the use of the property began to change. In 1993 chardonnay and merlot joined
the shiraz, followed by cabernet sauvignon, sauvignon blanc and semillon. The baton has been
passed down another generation to Ray Costanzo, who has lifted the quality of the wines
remarkably, and has also planted tempranillo, durif, barbera, malbec, mourvedre, vermentino

and nero d'Avola. Its consistent wine show success over recent years with alternative varieties is impressive.

🍷🍷🍷🍷🍷 **Granite Belt Durif 2011** Inky purple-crimson; has typically dense and largely impenetrable fruit, but even at this stage the balance of the wine is evident; blackberry, licorice and some Asian spices fill the palate, tannins and oak bystanders now, but will be involved down the track. Top gold Australian Small Winemakers Show '11. Screwcap. 14.1% alc. **Rating** 95 **To** 2030 $30

Granite Belt Mourvedre 2011 Full purple-crimson; has a more open weave to its texture and structure, with spicy/earthy nuances to its core of red fruits; as in all these wines, balance is the key. Top gold Australian Small Winemakers Show '11. Screwcap. 14.4% alc. **Rating** 95 **To** 2021 $28

✪ **Granite Belt Sauvignon Blanc 2012** Pale straw-green; partial wild yeast barrel fermentation in new French oak has added texture, but not diminished the fresh flavours, which sit in the middle of the tropical spectrum, with kiwifruit, guava and lychee; citrussy acidity provides a balanced and long finish. Screwcap. 12.5% alc. **Rating** 94 **To** 2014 $18

Granite Belt Vermentino 2012 Partial wild yeast barrel fermentation in new French and American oak won it the trophy for Best Old Wine at the Queensland Wine Show '12, and the trophy for Best Other Variety or Blend at the Cowra Wine Show '12. You see why on the lingering aftertaste, which is truly remarkable. Screwcap. 13.5% alc. **Rating** 94 **To** 2014 $22

Granite Belt Tempranillo 2011 Full crimson-purple; full-bodied and firmly structured, the palate has more than sufficient depth to its black cherry fruit to carry the tannins and oak that are seamlessly woven through the palate. Gold medal Australian Small Winemakers Show '11. Screwcap. 14.5% alc. **Rating** 94 **To** 2026 $28

Granite Belt Malbec 2011 Deep purple-crimson; the plush weight of the wine immediately manifests itself in the mouth with the typical jam/confit flavours of malbec; the finish is fresh, and this is the most approachable of the Golden Grove red wines at the moment. Screwcap. 14% alc. **Rating** 94 **To** 2021 $28

🍷🍷🍷🍷 **Mediterranean Red NV Rating** 89 **To** 2018 $18

Golding Wines   ★★★☆

52 Western Branch Road, Lobethal, SA 5241 **Region** Adelaide Hills
T (08) 8389 5120 **www.**goldingwines.com.au **Open** 7 days 11–4
Winemaker Michael Sykes, Darren Golding **Est.** 2002 **Dozens** 5000 **Vyds** 18.53ha
The Golding family has lived in the Lobethal area of the Adelaide Hills for several generations, and has trimmed its once larger viticultural holdings to concentrate on their Western Branch Road vineyard, planted to sauvignon blanc, savagnin, chardonnay, pinot gris and pinot noir. The brand was created in 2002, the owners being Darren and Lucy Golding. Exports to Hong Kong, the Philippines, Malaysia, Singapore and China.

🍷🍷🍷🍷 **Block 2 Adelaide Hills Chardonnay 2010** Pale straw-green; a very complex wine, with intense fruit and oak doing battle at dawn; the unusual peppery finish is somewhat unsettling. Screwcap. 13.5% alc. **Rating** 89 **To** 2015 $30

Gomersal Wines   ★★★★

Lyndoch Road, Gomersal, SA 5352 **Region** Barossa Valley
T (08) 8563 3611 **www.**gomersalwines.com.au **Open** 7 days 10–5
Winemaker Barry White **Est.** 1887 **Dozens** 5000 **Vyds** 20ha
The 1887 establishment date has a degree of poetic licence. In 1887 Friedrich W Fromm planted the Wonganella Vineyards, following that with a winery on the edge of the Gomersal Creek in 1891 that remained in operation for 90 years, finally closing in 1983. In 2000 a group of friends 'with strong credentials in both the making and consumption end of the wine industry' bought the winery and re-established the vineyard, planting 17ha of shiraz, 2ha of mourvedre and 1ha of grenache via terraced bush vines. The Riesling comes from purchased

grapes, the Grenache Rose, Grenache Shiraz Mataro and Shiraz from the replanted vineyard. Exports to the US, Ireland, China and NZ.

ΨΨΨΨΩ **Barossa Valley Shiraz 2009** Has retained healthy red-purple colour; the wine is crammed to the rafters with confit black fruits, licorice and dark chocolate, all reflecting the very low yield of 1 tonne per acre; oak also makes its contribution. A cellaring special. Screwcap. 14.9% alc. **Rating** 93 **To** 2034 $25
Barossa Valley Mataro 2008 From estate-grown bush vines yielding 0.5 tonne per acre. Its alcohol takes it way out of left field; given the microscopic yield, I don't understand why flavour/phenological ripeness should not have been achieved at much lower baume levels. That said, the heat from the alcohol wasn't as great as expected, and the ripe, confit red flavours are attractive. Screwcap. 16.2% alc. **Rating** 92 **To** 2023 $100
Barossa Valley Grenache Shiraz Mataro 2008 A 35/33/32% blend that spent 2½ years in oak; this, and the alcohol, have given rise to a wine more like a liqueur chocolate and cherry drink. It will have its fanatical supporters, but is way off in left field. Screwcap. 16.2% alc. **Rating** 90 **To** 2030 $50

ΨΨΨΨ **Shiraz Rose 2012 Rating** 87 **To** 2014 $15

Good Catholic Girl Wines ★★★☆

Box 526, Clare, SA 5453 **Region** Clare Valley
T 0419 822 909 www.goodcatholicgirl.com.au **Open** Not
Winemaker Julie Ann Barry **Est.** 2005 **Dozens** 460 **Vyds** 1ha
Good Catholic Girl is the venture of Julie Ann Barry, one of the many children of the late Jim Barry. She says, 'Having been born into a Catholic wine family, in vintage, my fate was sealed. My Limerick Vineyard was planted in the Armagh area of the Clare Valley in 1997, with cuttings taken from my father's famed Armagh shiraz vines planted across the paddock.' The Shiraz is named The James Brazill, Jim Barry's Christian names. She takes up the story thus: 'In 2008 I made my first Clare Valley Riesling, "Teresa", named after my mother, who is the true GCG (good Catholic girl), and loves Clare Riesling, and who may in time consume my entire production of 108 dozen!' 2011 dealt Julie a double blow with the loss of the fruit for the James Brazill Shiraz and the contract-grown Teresa Riesling. Exports to the US.

ΨΨΨΨΩ **The James Brazill Clare Valley Shiraz 2009** Dense purple-crimson; a massively dense wine, the crop decimated by drought; 3 years in French oak have passed in a blink of the eye. If the alcohol doesn't bother you, the wine might live well into the hereafter, and that should by rights bother you if you can't take it with you. WAK screwcap. 16.5% alc. **Rating** 91 **To** 2049 $30

ΨΨΨΨ **Teresa Clare Valley Riesling 2012 Rating** 89 **To** 2016 $25
Hail Mary full of grace Clare Valley Cabernet Sauvignon 2010 Rating 89 **To** 2016 $25
The James Brazill Clare Valley Shiraz 2010 Rating 88 **To** 2020 $32

Goona Warra Vineyard ★★★☆

790 Sunbury Road, Sunbury, Vic 3429 **Region** Sunbury
T (03) 9740 7766 www.goonawarra.com.au **Open** 7 days 10–5
Winemaker John Barnier, Christopher Collier **Est.** 1863 **Dozens** 3000 **Vyds** 6.92ha
A historic stone winery, originally established under this name by a 19th-century Victorian premier. A brief interlude as part of The Wine Investment Fund in 2001 is over, the Barniers having bought back the farm. Excellent tasting facilities, an outstanding venue for weddings and receptions, and lunch on Sunday. Exports to Canada, China, Taiwan and South Korea.

ΨΨΨΨΩ **Sunbury Chardonnay 2010** Bright green-straw; whole bunch-pressed; wild yeast-fermented, then 12 months' maturation on lees, zero mlf. The result is a very likeable peachy/buttery style, saved from looking retro by its fresh acidity. Diam. 13% alc. **Rating** 91 **To** 2016 $27

♥♥♥♥ Sunbury Baldini Rose 2012 Pale crimson; the bouquet and palate are led by
✪ cherry, cherry pip and spice aromas and flavours, with good length and balance.
Gold medal Concours des Vins du Victoria '12. Screwcap. 13.5% alc. **Rating** 89
To 2014 $15
Sunbury Semillon Sauvignon Blanc 2012 **Rating** 88 To 2014 $22
Sunbury Pinot Noir 2010 **Rating** 88 To 2014 $33

Gooree Park Wines

Gulgong Road, Mudgee, NSW 2850 **Region** Mudgee
T (02) 6378 1800 **www**.gooreepark.com.au **Open** Mon–Fri 10–5, w'ends 11–4
Winemaker Andrew Ewart **Est.** 2008 **Dozens** 1800 **Vyds** 546ha
Gooree Park Wines is part of a group of companies owned by Eduardo Cojunagco, other
companies including a thoroughbred horse stud and a pastoral enterprise (cattle, sheep and
farming) and vineyards based in Mudgee and Canowindra. Eduardo's interest in all forms of
agriculture has resulted in the planting of over 500ha of vines, starting with the Tullamour
Vineyard in Mudgee in 1996, the Fords Creek in Mudgee in '97, and Mt Lewis Estate at
Canowindra in '98. A cellar door was opened at the horse stud in 2008, and a number of
events are staged covering Eduardo's various interests. The wines are made in three ranges:
Gooree Park at the entry level, Crowned Glory semi-premium, and Don Eduardo premium.

♥♥♥♥♡ Don Eduardo Mudgee Shiraz 2006 A wine named after a horse named after a
person. The hue is very good given the wine is 7 years old, and still has some fresh
red berry fruits woven through the American oak, the tannins fine, the balance
good. Cork. 13.9% alc. **Rating** 91 To 2016 $35
Desert War Mudgee Shiraz 2007 Desert War was the 2007 Horse of the
Year, which tells me that while I might know a thing or two about wine, I know
next to nothing about horses other than Black Caviar and Makybe Diva. This is a
fleshy and rich medium- to full-bodied palate, with layers of red and black fruits
complexed by vanillin American oak and ripe tannins. Cork. 13.5% alc. **Rating** 90
To 2030 $25

♥♥♥♥ Sauvignon Blanc 2012 **Rating** 87 To 2013 $16
Merlot 2012 **Rating** 87 To 2014 $16
Cabernet Sauvignon 2012 **Rating** 87 To 2015 $16
Chardonnay Pinot Noir 2010 **Rating** 87 To 2014 $24

Gotham

PO Box 343, Mona Vale, NSW 1660 **Region** South Australia
T 0412 124 811 **www**.gothamwines.com.au **Open** Not
Winemaker Bruce Clugston **Est.** 2004 **Dozens** 150 000
Bruce Clugston, with a long involvement in the wine industry, purchases grapes from various
vineyards in Langhorne Creek, McLaren Vale, Barossa Valley and Clare Valley. This is one of the
larger virtual wineries in SA, and its production underlines its commercial success. Extensive
sales through Get Wines Direct, and also exports, have led to rising production. Exports to the
US, Canada, Denmark, Germany, Malaysia, Thailand, Indonesia, Japan and NZ.

♥♥♥♥♡ Stalking Horse McLaren Vale Shiraz 2010 Full red-purple; the primary and
✪ mlf were completed and the wine matured for 20 months in 1-year-old American
oak. The result is an even stronger expression of McLaren Vale terroir, with layers
of black fruits, bitter chocolate and exemplary tannins. This is all about the quality
of the grapes. Screwcap. 14.2% alc. **Rating** 93 To 2025 $21
✪ Regional Vineyard Series Barossa Valley Shiraz 2010 Light to medium
red-purple; open-fermented in tank completing that fermentation in 20% new
and 80% 1-year-old French oak, and matured for 18 months in those barrels; the
black fruits show the impact of oak, but within bounds. The tannins are fine but
give texture and support to the black fruits of the palate. Seriously good value.
Screwcap. 14.5% alc. **Rating** 91 To 2017 $17

✪ **Regional Vineyard Series McLaren Vale Shiraz 2010** Good colour; the primary and mlf were completed in new American oak, the wine then racked to a mix of new and 1-year-old American oak, where it spent the next 20 months; medium-bodied and well-balanced; has some residual sugar that merges into the overall palate mouthfeel and adds to, rather than detracts from, the wine. Screwcap. 14.9% alc. **Rating** 90 **To** 2016 $17

🍷🍷🍷🍷 ✪ **Clare Valley Riesling 2012** May not be the best Clare Valley riesling from this great riesling vintage, but it's a pretty handy wine, with good balance to its generous citrus fruit and acidity. Great value for present drinking. Screwcap. 12% alc. **Rating** 89 **To** 2015 $15

Regional Vineyard Series Langhorne Creek Shiraz 2010 Rating 89 **To** 2015 $17

✪ **Wine Men of Gotham Pinot Grigio 2011** Clearly the best of the wines in the Wine Men of Gotham Range, which is ironic; zesty and crisp, it is in truth a halfway house between gris and grigio; obviously, outstanding value. Screwcap. 11.5% alc. **Rating** 88 **To** 2014 $9

✪ **Wine Men of Gotham Shiraz Grenache 2012** Light red-purple; the wine is light-bodied, but has respectable red berry fruits and fine tannins; best of all, it's not sweet. I'll never get used to the comic strip label, but the value offered by the wine is obvious. Screwcap. 13% alc. **Rating** 87 **To** 2014 $10

Goundrey ★★★☆

Location 10460, Vasse Highway, Nannup, WA 6275 **Region** Western Australia Zone
T 1800 088 711 **www**.goundreywines.com.au **Open** Not
Winemaker Garth Cliff **Est.** 1976 **Dozens** NFP

Goundrey is part of the Accolade Wines group empire. In 2008 it was put on the market by CWA, together with its 237ha of estate vineyards. In 2009 it was purchased by comparative minnow West Cape Howe. The Goundrey brand has been retained by CWA, and significant quantities of wine will continue to be made from its WA base, with 100% of the Goundrey-grown grapes sold back to CWA pursuant to an ongoing contract with West Cape Howe. Exports to Hong Kong and Pacific Islands.

🍷🍷🍷🍷🍷 ✪ **Homestead Cabernet Merlot 2011** A fine, fragrant and polished bouquet of red fruits, jasmine and cedar; the medium-bodied palate follows suit, with an alluring level of plush red fruits in complete harmony with the tannin and fresh acidity on offer; long and expansive and batting well above its weight in terms of price. Screwcap. 13.5% alc. **Rating** 92 **To** 2020 $17 BE

Grace Farm ★★★

45 Keane Street, Peppermint Grove, WA 6011 **Region** Margaret River
T (08) 9384 4995 **www**.gracefarm.com.au **Open** By appt
Winemaker Jonathan Mettam **Est.** 2006 **Dozens** 3500 **Vyds** 7.86ha

Grace Farm is a 47ha property purchased in 2003 by Perth businessman John Mair and wife Elizabeth. It had remained natural forest until 1952, when it was partially cleared to graze cattle; today the remnant forest adjoins a national park. Vineyard planting commenced in '06, the first stage completed in '11.

Graillot ★★★★★

19–21 Russell Street, Abbotsford, Vic 3067 (postal) **Region** Heathcote
T 1300 610 919 **www**.graillotaustralia.com.au **Open** Not
Winemaker Alain Graillot, Sandro Mosele **Est.** 2010 **Dozens** 900

Graillot is owned by Robert Walters, well known for his role with Bibendum Wine Co., which (inter alia) imports fine wines from various parts of Europe, with France to the fore. He has imported the wines of Alain Graillot, one of the superstars of the northern Rhône Valley (in Crozes-Hermitage) for many years. The two have become good friends during that time, but in 2010 that friendship took a new turn. For a number of years prior, Robert had been making small quantities of Heathcote Shiraz with guidance from Sandro Mosele from the Colbinabbin area, but was not satisfied with the results. Having visited the vineyard from which the grapes had been supplied, Alain was sufficiently convinced of the potential to become winemaker/consultant for the business, which is owned and financed by Robert.

� **Heathcote Shiraz 2011** No problems whatsoever with the colour, full purple-red, and even less with the bouquet and palate. There was no disease in the vineyard, and the ripening conditions were considered ideal by the Graillot team. The luscious, mouthfilling black fruits are absolutely remarkable outside WA and Tasmania; this is the richest and most distinguished '11 vintage red from Eastern Australia I have tasted in the more than 6000 wines to pass across my palate this year. Screwcap. 13% alc. **Rating** 97 **To** 2041 $52

Project Syrah No. 2 2011 This also has excellent hue. In theory, this is a bolder, more obviously Australian wine; in this vintage it isn't, but it needs no apology. It doesn't have the fleshy opulence of the Heathcote Shiraz, instead with an elegance to its medium-bodied fruits of red and black cherry, oak evident, but not obtrusive. Another success? Absolutely. Screwcap. 13% alc. **Rating** 94 **To** 2026 $35

Gralyn Estate ★★★★☆

4145 Caves Road, Wilyabrup, WA 6280 **Region** Margaret River
T (08) 9755 6245 **www**.gralyn.com.au **Open** 7 days 10.30–4.30
Winemaker Dr Bradley Hutton **Est.** 1975 **Dozens** 3000 **Vyds** 4.5ha
Under the eagle eye of Merilyn Hutton, Gralyn Estate has established a high reputation for its wines. The primary focus is on the full-bodied red wines, which are made in a distinctively different style from most from Margaret River, with an opulence reminiscent of some of the bigger wines from McLaren Vale. The age of the vines (35+ years) and the site are significant factors. Lesser amounts of chardonnay and fortified wines are also made.

♥♥♥♥♥ **Reserve Margaret River Cabernet Sauvignon 2009** Deep crimson; a polished blend of red and black fruits, with cedar, black olive and a generous seasoning of fine French oak; the full-bodied palate is tightly wound and densely packed with fine-grained tannins, concluding a long and sophisticated finish. Screwcap. 13.9% alc. **Rating** 94 **To** 2025 $110 BE

♥♥♥♥♀ **Reserve Margaret River Chardonnay 2011 Rating** 93 **To** 2018 $55 BE
Reserve Margaret River Shiraz 2009 Rating 92 **To** 2022 $110 BE

Grampians Estate ★★★★★

1477 Western Highway, Great Western, Vic 3377 **Region** Grampians
T (03) 5354 6245 **www**.grampiansestate.com.au **Open** 7 days 10–5
Winemaker Hamish Seabrook, Don Rowe, Tom Guthrie **Est.** 1989 **Dozens** 1200
Vyds 8ha
Graziers Sarah and Tom Guthrie began their diversification into wine in 1989, but their core business continues to be fat lamb and wool production. Both activities were ravaged by the 2006 bushfires, but each has recovered, that of their grapegrowing and winemaking rising like a phoenix from the ashes. They have acquired the Garden Gully winery at Great Western, giving them a cellar door and a vineyard of 2.4ha of 130-year-old shiraz, and 3ha of 80-year-old riesling vines. The cellar door features wine tutorials.

♥♥♥♥♥ **Streeton Reserve Shiraz 2009** Bright purple-crimson; an intensely flavoured and very long palate, with berry fruits, mainly black, spice and pepper, has been achieved with effortless ease; 18 months' maturation in French and American oak has simply provided the means to achieve this. Will be very long-lived. Screwcap. 13.8% alc. **Rating** 96 **To** 2035 $65

Mafeking Shiraz 2010 Bright crimson-purple; sourced from several Grampians vineyards in addition to the estate Mafeking Vineyard, which is still recovering from the '06 bushfire; the medium-bodied palate offers a beguiling mix of red and black cherry, spice and mocha/cedar flavours, the tannins fine and balanced. Screwcap. 13.5% alc. **Rating** 94 **To** 2025 $25

Rutherford Sparkling Shiraz 2009 The colour still retains some purple hue; good mousse; the red fruits have distinct spicy notes, and the flavours are very attractive. However, there is some sweetness from the high baume to the fruit and obvious dosage. It is going to have sufficient support to sell out very quickly, but could have been even better. Despite all this, I can't deny it gold medal points. Crown seal. 14.7% alc. **Rating** 94 To 2016 $35

Granite Hills   ★★★★★

1481 Burke and Wills Track, Baynton, Vic 3444 **Region** Macedon Ranges
T (03) 5423 7273 www.granitehills.com.au **Open** 7 days 11–6
Winemaker Llew Knight, Ian Gunter **Est.** 1970 **Dozens** 6000 **Vyds** 10.8ha
Granite Hills is one of the enduring classics, pioneering the successful growing of riesling and shiraz in an uncompromisingly cool climate. It is based on riesling, chardonnay, shiraz, cabernet sauvignon, cabernet franc, merlot and pinot noir (the last also used in its sparkling wine). The Rieslings age superbly, and the Shiraz is at the forefront of the cool-climate school in Australia. Exports to Canada, Germany, Mauritius, Hong Kong, Singapore and China.

ΨΨΨΨΨ **Knight Macedon Ranges Riesling 2012** Pale quartz-green; the vines are now 40 years old, the wine in typical Granite Hills style, ultra-pure, refined and with strong minerality, its long-term future absolutely guaranteed. Screwcap. 12.5% alc. **Rating** 94 To 2025 $25
TOR Macedon Ranges Chardonnay 2009 Bright, youthful colour; a touch of Burgundian funk on the bouquet carries over to the complex, and still very lively, palate; here stone fruit and grapefruit flavours are both spun around a framework of minerally acidity. Screwcap. 13.5% alc. **Rating** 94 To 2019 $45
TOR Macedon Ranges Pinot Noir 2009 Deeper colour than its vintage sibling, with more purple in the hue; a strict fruit selection takes this wine into another class, with its rich and supple array of damson plum and black cherry fruit supported by quality French oak and ripe, but refined, tannins. Screwcap. 13.5% alc. **Rating** 94 To 2019 $45
Knight Macedon Ranges Shiraz 2006 The colour is bright, as is the flavour of spicy red fruits; this is a Peter Pan, like others from Granite Hills that have gone before it. If you like light- to medium-bodied red wines, there can be few better than this. Screwcap. 14.5% alc. **Rating** 94 To 2021 $35
TOR Macedon Ranges Syrah 2006 Provides another dimension to its sibling, with more tannin structure, more oak, from a selection of the best grapes. I'm not convinced it's a quality difference, but it is certainly a different style. Screwcap. 14.5% alc. **Rating** 94 To 2026 $45
✪ **Knight The Gordon 2007** A 51/29/20% blend of cabernet sauvignon, cabernet franc and merlot matured in French and American barrels for 3 years. While this period of barrel maturation often proves too much for the fruit, it works well here – plus further time in bottle. The colour is still vibrant, the typical spice of Granite Hills adding to the finely structured cassis fruit. Why only $30? Screwcap. 14.5% alc. **Rating** 94 To 2017 $30

ΨΨΨΨΨ **Knight Macedon Ranges Chardonnay 2012 Rating** 93 To 2019 $30
Knight Macedon Ranges Pinot Noir 2009 Rating 91 To 2016 $30

Grant Burge   ★★★★★

279 Krondorf Road, Barossa Valley, SA 5352 **Region** Barossa Valley
T (08) 8563 3700 www.grantburgewines.com.au **Open** 7 days 10–5
Winemaker Grant Burge, Craig Stansborough, Matt Pellew **Est.** 1988 **Dozens** 400 000
Vyds 356ha
As one might expect, this very experienced industry veteran makes consistently good, full-flavoured and smooth wines based on the pick of the crop of his extensive vineyard holdings; the immaculately restored/rebuilt stone cellar door sales buildings are another attraction. Abednego joins Shadrach and Meshach at the top of the range. In 1999 Grant Burge repurchased the farm from Mildara Blass by acquiring the Krondorf winery in Tanunda

(not the brand) in which he made his first fortune, in 1986. He renamed it Barossa Vines and opened a cellar door offering casual food. A second cellar door (Illaparra) is open at Murray Street, Tanunda. Exports to all major markets.

🍷🍷🍷🍷🍷 **The Vigneron 1887 Barossa Shiraz 2010** Full crimson-purple; only 230 dozen made from a single block planted in 1887; it is more elegant and lighter in the mouth than the alcohol would suggest; maturation in mainly new French oak for 30 months has aided its cause, as do the fine tannins supporting the black fruits. Screwcap. 15% alc. **Rating** 95 **To** 2035 $75

Meshach 2008 Full crimson-purple; from the 85-year-old Filsell Vineyard, the wine matured for 2 years in new American and French oak hogsheads, and a further 2 years in the cellar. It is an incredibly rich and plush Shiraz, with black fruits, oak and dark chocolate all competing for attention. Will surely outlive its cork. 14.5% alc. **Rating** 95 **To** 2023 $180

Abednego Barossa Shiraz Grenache Mourvedre 2009 A 44/31/25% blend, each component fermented separately and given prolonged skin contact after fermentation, then matured in 2500-litre vats for 16 months. The colour is bright and clear, the palate an exercise in the synergy that these three varieties can provide, the core of red fruit flavours surrounded by savoury black olive notes; excellent tannin and oak handling. Diam. 13% alc. **Rating** 95 **To** 2030 $70

Shadrach 2009 Barrel and bottle ageing has led to the first stages of colour change; overall this Cabernet has remarkable synergy to its flavour, structure and texture inputs, resulting in a supple, ultra-smooth and beautifully balanced exercise in blackcurrant/cassis fruit. Cork. 14.5% alc. **Rating** 95 **To** 2034 $90

Shadrach 2008 Good colour for its age, showing no loss of the crimson edge; has very good varietal fruit thanks in part to the Corryton Park estate vineyards in the coolest part of the Barossa Valley that provided 80% of the wine before it spent 21 months in 75% new French oak; blackcurrant fruit is married with typical cabernet tannins, adding length to a high-quality wine. Cork. 14.5% alc. **Rating** 95 **To** 2033 $90

Filsell Old Vine Barossa Shiraz 2010 **Rating** 94 **To** 2030 $40

The Holy Trinity Barossa Grenache Shiraz Mourvedre 2010 **Rating** 94 **To** 2020 $45

🍷🍷🍷🍷♀ **The Vigneron The Natural Shiraz 2010** **Rating** 93 **To** 2030 $50

Corryton Park Barossa Cabernet Sauvignon 2010 **Rating** 93 **To** 2030 $45

The Vigneron Barossa Nebbiolo 2010 **Rating** 92 **To** 2018 $30

The Vigneron Wild Ferment Pinot Gris 2011 **Rating** 91 **To** 2013 $30

✪ **5th Generation Barossa Sauvignon Blanc Semillon 2012** An altogether surprising wine given its varietal composition, even if the sauvignon blanc comes from the Eden Valley; there is passionfruit, citrus and crisp acidity to burn; drink now or a little later. Screwcap. 13.5% alc. **Rating** 90 **To** 2014 $19

✪ **Moscato Frizzante 2012** There is no question Australian makers are trying hard with moscato, realising the market. Here part of the wine is the striking custom-made bottle, but the contents are also commendable, the grapey flavours enhanced by lemony acidity that balances the sweetness. Screwcap. 8% alc. **Rating** 90 **To** 2013 $17

10 Year Old Tawny NV **Rating** 90 **To** 2014 $30

Greedy Sheep

PO Box 530, Cowaramup, WA 6284 **Region** Margaret River
T (08) 9755 7428 **www.**greedysheep.com.au **Open** Not
Winemaker Dave Johnson **Est.** 2005 **Dozens** 4000 **Vyds** 6ha

Mining engineer Darren Guiney and electrical engineer wife Bridget lived and worked all around Australia in remote locations, but in 2004 decided to find a place to settle permanently. Margaret River was an obvious choice, for it was there they were married in 1999. They purchased the property in '04; it had been planted to cabernet sauvignon, merlot, cabernet franc and malbec in '99. It pays to have a sense of humour, for in January '05 1000 sheep found their way into the vineyard, eating everything green within their reach, including unripe grapes, which must have challenged their digestion.

🍷🍷🍷🍷🍷 **Margaret River Sauvignon Blanc Semillon 2012** Bright straw-green; the
✪ blossom-filled bouquet leads into a palate that opens with citrus and herbs, then swells on the finish as tropical fruits fill the mouth and the aftertaste. Screwcap. 12.5% alc. **Rating** 92 **To** 2014 $19

✪ **Margaret River Rose 2012** Vivid crimson-puce; fragrant red berry fruits drive the bouquet and palate; the vibrant flavours also take in a mix of red and morello cherry, the finish crisp and clean. Screwcap. 13.6% alc. **Rating** 91 **To** 2013 $19

Greenstone Vineyard ★★★★★

319 Whorouly South Road, Whorouly South, Vic 3735 **Region** Heathcote
T (03) 5727 1434 **www**.greenstoneofheathcote.com **Open** By appt
Winemaker Sandro Mosele (Contract), Alberto Antonini, Mark Walpole **Est.** 2002
Dozens 2500 **Vyds** 20ha
This is one of the most interesting ventures to emerge over the past few years, bringing together David Gleave MW, born and educated in Canada, now a long-term UK resident, who manages an imported wine business and writes widely about the wines of Italy; Alberto Antonini, a graduate of the University of Florence, with postgraduate degrees from Bordeaux and University of California (Davis), and Italian Flying Winemaker; and Mark Walpole, for 20 years manager of Brown Brothers' 700ha of vineyards before retiring in 2010. The partners have chosen what they consider an outstanding vineyard on the red soil of the Heathcote region, planted to 17ha of shiraz, 2ha of sangiovese and 1ha of monastrell (mourvedre). Exports to the UK, the US and other major markets.

🍷🍷🍷🍷🍷 **Heathcote Shiraz 2011** Deep crimson; fragrant and compelling on the bouquet with red and black fruits, sage and ironstone minerality aromas on display; the palate is muscular and tannic, though ripe and generous, and the fresh acidity so commonly found on the greenstone soils of Heathcote provides a linear framework for the ample fruit to adorn; long and savoury to conclude. Screwcap. 13% alc. **Rating** 94 **To** 2022 $35 BE

Heathcote Shiraz 2010 Medium purple-crimson; the very fragrant bouquet of spicy red berry fruits leads into a tightly focused and very elegant palate with a mix of savoury/earthy red and black fruits, the tannins fine and long, oak playing a pure support role. Screwcap. 13.5% alc. **Rating** 94 **To** 2035 $35

Heathcote Sangiovese 2010 Light, clear red colour; in the manner of the variety, has more intensity and drive than the colour might suggest; there is a delicious sour cherry edge to the main game of darker cherry and tannin flavours. Screwcap. 13.5% alc. **Rating** 94 **To** 2020 $65

🍷🍷🍷🍷🍷 **Rosso di Colbo Heathcote Sangiovese 2011 Rating** 93 **To** 2021 $28

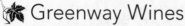 # Greenway Wines ★★★

PO Box 1290, North Sydney, NSW 2060 **Region** Hunter Valley
T (02) 9401 2080 **Open** Not
Winemaker Michael McManus **Est.** 2009 **Dozens** 290 **Vyds** 2.5ha
This is the venture of John Marinovich and Anne Greenway, who purchased the vineyard in 2009 after many years of dreaming of becoming vignerons. They acquired a vineyard that had been first planted in 1999, with 2ha of merlot, the remainder shiraz and a little gewurztraminer. They say, 'We were not prepared for how beautiful our little vineyard would be. It's located just south of the township of Broke, bordered by the foothills of the Brokenback mountains on one side, and skirted by Wollombi Brook on the other.'

🍷🍷🍷🍷 **Momento Hunter Valley Rose 2011** The back label is festooned with microscopic print (in grey) that might be informative if it were readable. Light crimson-purple; the bouquet is fresh, the palate tight and firm, happily allowed to speak for itself without any sugar coating. Good food style. Screwcap. 11.5% alc. **Rating** 88 **To** 2013 $20

Momento Hunter Valley Merlot 2010 Very savoury/earthy regional characters are uppermost, but the light- to medium-bodied palate, balance and mouthfeel are in tune with the essential character of the variety. Screwcap. 12.5% alc. **Rating** 88 **To** 2016 $24

Greg Cooley Wines ★★★★

Lot 1 Main North Road, Clare, SA 5453 **Region** Clare Valley
T (08) 8843 4284 **www.**gregcooleywines.com.au **Open** 7 days 10.30–5
Winemaker Greg Cooley **Est.** 2002 **Dozens** 3000
Greg Cooley says, 'I followed the traditional path to winemaking via accountancy, fraud squad, corporate investigations, running a Wendy's Supa Sundaes franchise and then selling residential property. I left the property market in Brisbane just as the boom started in 2001 and moved to the beautiful Clare just about when the wine glut started.' He explains, 'All my wines are named after people who have been of influence to me in my 45 years and their influence is as varied as the wine styles – from pizza shop owners to my greyhound's vet and South Australian author Monica McInerney.' I have to confess that I am taken by Greg's path to glory because my move through law to wine was punctuated by the part-ownership of two greyhounds that always wanted to run in the opposite direction from the rest of the field. After years of selling direct through wine lunches and internet sales, in April '11 Greg Cooley and partner Kelli Shanahan took the plunge, establishing a new cellar door on Main North Road, Clare.

🍷🍷🍷🍷🍷 **Valerie Beh Watervale Riesling 2012** Mid straw, green hue; the bouquet reveals fresh lime juice, straw and lemon zest; the palate is bone dry, angular and zesty, finishing with a struck quartz mineral note. Screwcap. 11.8% alc. **Rating** 90 **To** 2017 $22 BE
Five Year Olds and Dogs Clare Valley Rose 2012 Pale pink, bright; a vibrant and fresh, red-fruited bouquet with a little exotic Turkish Delight note; the palate is fresh and fragrant on entry, dry and chalky to conclude. Screwcap. 13.5% alc. **Rating** 90 **To** 2015 $22 BE
Dopity Brownhill Sparkling Shiraz NV Bottle-fermented; relatively light, but bright, red; has abundant red berry fruits, and needed the relatively high dosage to seek to cover its phenolics. Blue-gold Sydney International Wine Competition '13. Cork. 14.5% alc. **Rating** 90 **To** 2016 $29

🍷🍷🍷🍷 **Glynn and Pini Clare Valley Merlot Cabernet Franc 2010** Rating 88 **To** 2016 $25 BE
Bennett and Byrne Reserve Shiraz 2010 Rating 87 To 2018 $38 BE

Grey Sands ★★★★☆

Cnr Kerrisons Road/Frankford Highway, Glengarry, Tas 7275 **Region** Northern Tasmania
T (03) 6396 1167 **www.**greysands.com.au **Open** By appt
Winemaker Peter Dredge, Bob Richter **Est.** 1989 **Dozens** 800 **Vyds** 3.5ha
Bob and Rita Richter began the establishment of Grey Sands in 1989, slowly increasing the plantings to the present total. The ultra-high density of 8900 vines per hectare reflects the experience gained by the Richters during a three-year stay in England, when they visited many vineyards across Europe, as well as Bob's graduate diploma from Roseworthy College. Plantings include pinot noir, merlot, pinot gris and malbec.

🍷🍷🍷🍷🍷 Pinot Noir 2009 Full red-purple; a complex, mouth-filling Pinot Noir just short of being luscious (a good thing); it has multiple layers of spiced plum fruits, damson and blood plum, but finishes with life, freshness and length. Diam. 13% alc. Rating 94 To 2020 $40
🍷🍷🍷🍷🍷 **Romanesque 2010** Rating 91 To 2025 $35

Griffin Wines ★★★★☆

Tynan Road, Kuitpo, SA 5172 **Region** Adelaide Hills
T (08) 8388 3279 **www.**griffinwines.com **Open** By appt
Winemaker Phil Christiansen, Simon Parker **Est.** 1997 **Dozens** 1500 **Vyds** 26.12ha

The Griffins (Trevor, Tim, Mark and Val) planted pinot noir, merlot, chardonnay, sauvignon blanc and shiraz in 1997, having owned the property for over 30 years; the vines are cane-pruned and the grapes hand-picked. Situated 3km from Kuitpo Hall, its 350m elevation gives sweeping views over the valley below.

No. 1 Adelaide Hills Shiraz 2010 Bright, clear purple-crimson; the bouquet is fragrant, with the bright black cherry and blackberry fruits that drive the medium-bodied, but intense, palate; both oak and tannins are evident, but do not challenge the fruit, simply support it. Screwcap. 14.5% alc. **Rating** 94 To 2025 $21

No. 2 Adelaide Hills Sauvignon Blanc 2012 Rating 92 To 2014 $18
No. 5 Adelaide Hills Unwooded Chardonnay 2012 Light, bright green-straw; the fragrant bouquet of white peach, white flowers and grapefruit is faithfully replicated on the fresh and lively palate; unoaked Chardonnay of impressive style and quality. It can be done. Screwcap. 13.2% alc. **Rating** 92 To 2015 $12
No. 4 Adelaide Hills Merlot 2010 Rating 90 To 2018 $18

Groom ★★★★★

28 Langmeil Road, Tanunda, SA 5352 (postal) **Region** Barossa Valley
T (08) 8563 1101 **www.**groomwines.com **Open** Not
Winemaker Daryl Groom **Est.** 1997 **Dozens** 4000 **Vyds** 27.8ha
The full name of the business is Marschall Groom Cellars, a venture owned by David and Jeanette Marschall and their six children, and Daryl and Lisa Groom and their four children. Daryl was a highly regarded winemaker at Penfolds before he moved to Geyser Peak in California. Years of discussion between the families resulted in the purchase of a 35ha block of bare land adjacent to Penfolds' 130-year-old Kalimna Vineyard. Shiraz was planted in 1997, giving its first vintage in '99, the wine blended with the output from two vineyards, one 100 years old, the other 50 years old. The next acquisition was an 8ha vineyard at Lenswood in the Adelaide Hills, planted to sauvignon blanc. In 2000, 3.2ha of zinfandel was planted on the Kalimna Bush Block. Not surprisingly, a substantial part of the production is exported to the US (and also to Canada, Hong Kong and Taiwan).

Barossa Valley Shiraz 2010 Deeply coloured, the bouquet is full of red and black fruits coupled with licorice, the medium- to full-bodied palate intense and long; has immensely appealing fruit, with a supple, silky mouthfeel. A fitting reflection of an outstanding vintage. Cork. 14.2% alc. **Rating** 96 To 2030 $49

Adelaide Hills Sauvignon Blanc 2012 Pale straw-green; centrefold Adelaide Hills sauvignon blanc, with a full display of just about every fruit aroma and flavour imaginable, ranging from citrus through apple, stone fruit and ultimately fresh tropical fruits; the acidity frames this wanton display, and prevents going over the top. Screwcap. 13.5% alc. **Rating** 94 To 2014 $24

Bush Block Barossa Valley Zinfandel 2011 Rating 93 To 2016 $30

Grosset

King Street, Auburn, SA 5451 **Region** Clare Valley
T (08) 8849 2175 **www.**grosset.com.au **Open** Wed–Sun 10–5 from Sept for approx 6 weeks
Winemaker Jeffrey Grosset, Brent Treloar **Est.** 1981 **Dozens** 11 000 **Vyds** 22.2ha
Jeffrey Grosset has assumed the unchallenged mantle of Australia's foremost Riesling maker in the wake of John Vickery stepping back to a consultancy role for Richmond Grove. Grosset's pre-eminence in Riesling making is recognised both domestically and internationally; however, he merits equal recognition for the other wines in his portfolio: Semillon Sauvignon Blanc from Clare Valley/Adelaide Hills, Chardonnay and Pinot Noir from the Adelaide Hills; and Gaia, a Bordeaux blend from the Clare Valley. These are all benchmarks. His quietly spoken manner conceals a steely will, exemplified by his long and ultimately successful battle to prevent the use of 'riesling' on flagons and bottles as a generic description, rather than

varietal, and his subsequent success in having the Clare Valley Riesling makers migrate en masse to screwcaps, unleashing a torrent of change across Australia. Trial plantings (2ha) of fiano, aglianico, nero d'Avola and petit verdot suggest some new wines may be gestating. Exports to all major markets.

ΨΨΨΨΨ **Polish Hill Riesling 2012** Light straw-green; there is a purity to the bouquet that sets it apart from almost all other '12 Rieslings, a purity echoed in the faultless balance of the palate, taut lime and mineral driving through on the finish and lingering aftertaste. Great now, greater still in another decade; attention to detail is in Jeffrey Grosset's DNA. Screwcap. 12.5% alc. **Rating** 97 **To** 2032 $50
Clare Valley Adelaide Hills Semillon Sauvignon Blanc 2012 Bright straw-green; as ever, a tour de force of winemaking, with a seamless union between the lemon juice of the Clare semillon and the kiwifruit and lychee of the Adelaide Hills sauvignon blanc; oak has been used as a vehicle, and comprehensively absorbed by the wine. Screwcap. 12.5% alc. **Rating** 96 **To** 2018 $33
Piccadilly Adelaide Hills Chardonnay 2010 Has exceptional fruit intensity and focus, the flavours ricocheting around the mouth, and covering all the bases from grapefruit through to white peach and nectarine. Barrel-fermented in French oak, but this, at best, provides one part of the structural framework, more coming from the fruit and acidity. Screwcap. 13.5% alc. **Rating** 96 **To** 2019 $53
Alea Off-dry Clare Valley Riesling 2012 Bright straw-green; perfect balance allows the sweetness and acidity to engage in foreplay before the real business of the palate gets underway; once again, Jeffrey Grosset proves his mastery of all aspects of Riesling. Screwcap. 11.8% alc. **Rating** 96 **To** 2020 $33
Springvale Watervale Riesling 2012 Light straw-green; while finely strung and articulated, is more generous – particularly on the palate – than the Polish Hill River, making it a candidate for earlier consumption, its layers of lime, lemon and apple irresistible. Screwcap. 12.5% alc. **Rating** 95 **To** 2022 $37
Piccadilly Adelaide Hills Chardonnay 2011 Vibrant green hue; the pristine bouquet reveals nectarine, hazelnut, charry oak and citrus blossom; the palate is poised and precise, with taut lemony acidity in harmony with the fruit and the toasty oak; long and linear. Screwcap. 13.5% alc. **Rating** 95 **To** 2018 $56 BE
Gaia 2010 Rating 94 **To** 2025 $68 BE

ΨΨΨΨΩ **Adelaide Hills Pinot Noir 2011 Rating** 93 **To** 2018 $66 BE

Gundog Estate   ★★★★★

101 McDonalds Road, Pokolbin, NSW 2320 **Region** Hunter Valley
T (02) 4998 6873 **www**.gundogestate.com.au **Open** 7 days 10–5
Winemaker Matthew Burton **Est.** 2006 **Dozens** 500 **Vyds** 5ha
After five years as chief winemaker for Wandin Hunter Valley, Matthew Burton moved on in 2010 in the wake of the exit of Wandin founders James and Philippa Davern. He is now making four different Hunter Semillons and Shiraz from the Hunter Valley and Murrumbateman. He and wife Renee run the cellar door from the historic Pokolbin school house, next to the old Rosemount/Hungerford Hill building on McDonalds Road. They are also constructing a cellar door at the Gundaroo family property in the Canberra District owned by parents Sharon and Geoff, which has 2.5ha each of chardonnay and cabernet sauvignon.

ΨΨΨΨΨ **Hunter's Semillon 2012** Right in the heart of classic Hunter Valley Semillon style, leaving not a scintilla of doubt about its future, when it will burst forth with mouth-filling fruit around its fifth birthday; in the meantime, the lemongrass, herb and citrus undertones combine with the minerally acidity to make a great foil for fresh seafood on a summer day. Screwcap. 10.5% alc. **Rating** 94 **To** 2025 $25
Burton McMahon Yarra Valley Chardonnay 2012 From two Upper Yarra vineyards; whole bunch-pressed and wild-fermented, matured in a mix of French barriques and hogsheads. Has all the intensity that the Upper Yarra Valley confers on the grapefruit and white peach fruit, and which has soaked up the oak; the length of the palate is very good. Screwcap. 13% alc. **Rating** 94 **To** 2020 $40

Canberra District Shiraz 2012 The last release of this wine was in '09; this reflects unrelenting work in the vineyard throughout the troubled growing season, and ruthless fruit selection at harvest, resulting in a yield of just over 1 tonne per acre. Strong purple-red, the bouquet and palate tightly focused on spicy black and red cherry fruit, the oak well judged, tannin management likewise giving an attractive flourish on the finish. Screwcap. 13% alc. **Rating** 94 **To** 2025 $35

Hunter's Shiraz 2011 Very good colour; sourced from two vineyards in the Lovedale and Pokolbin areas; open-fermented, and matured in French oak puncheons for 10 months. This is a delicious wine showing the modern face of Hunter Valley shiraz to full advantage, its black fruits supported by notes of spice and cedar, the tannins round and soft. Screwcap. 14% alc. **Rating** 94 **To** 2035 $30

ΨΨΨΨΨ **Squire's Gundagai Canberra District Shiraz 2012** Rating 93 To 2022 $30
Wild Hunter Valley Semillon 2012 Rating 92 To 2016 $30
Poacher's Hunter Valley Semillon 2012 Rating 92 To 2022 $30
Burton McMahon Gippsland Pinot Noir 2012 Rating 92 To 2017 $40
Canberra District Rose 2012 Rating 90 To 2014 $25
Off-Dry Hunter Valley Semillon 2012 Rating 90 To 2018 $25

Haan Wines
★★★★☆

148 Siegersdorf Road, Tanunda, SA 5352 **Region** Barossa Valley
T (08) 8562 4590 **www**.haanwines.com.au **Open** Not
Winemaker Liz Heidenreich (Contract) **Est.** 1993 **Dozens** 4500 **Vyds** 16.3ha
Hans and Fransien Haan established their business in 1993 when they acquired a vineyard near Tanunda. The plantings are shiraz (5.3ha), merlot (3.4ha), cabernet sauvignon (3ha), viognier (2.4ha), cabernet franc (1ha) and malbec, petit verdot and semillon (0.4ha each). Oak undoubtedly plays a role in the shaping of the style of the Haan wines, but it is perfectly integrated, and the wines have the fruit weight to carry the oak. Exports to the UK, China and other major markets.

ΨΨΨΨΨ **Barossa Valley Shiraz Cabernet Sauvignon 2010** The shiraz was matured in American oak barriques, the cabernet sauvignon in French oak barriques; in each instance I suspect the fermentation was finished in those barriques. Happily, there is ample blackberry, cherry and minty blackcurrant fruit to carry the oak; the tannins are fine and ripe. Screwcap. 14.5% alc. **Rating** 94 **To** 2020 $25

ΨΨΨΨΨ **Barossa Valley Merlot Cabernet Franc 2010** Rating 93 To 2025 $25

Hackersley
★★★★

1133 Ferguson Road, Dardanup, WA 6236 **Region** Geographe
T (08) 9381 6247 **www**.hackersley.com.au **Open** Thurs–Sun 10–4
Winemaker Jeff Ovens **Est.** 1997 **Dozens** 1500 **Vyds** 12ha
Hackersley is a partnership between the Ovens, Stacey and Hewitt families, friends since their university days, and with (so they say) the misguided belief that growing and making their own wine would be cheaper than buying it. They found a 'little piece of paradise in the Ferguson Valley just south of Dardanup', and in 1998 they planted just under 8ha, extended since then to 11.5ha, of the mainstream varieties; interestingly, they turned their back on chardonnay. Most of the crop is sold to Houghton, but a small quantity is made for the Hackersley label.

ΨΨΨΨΨ **Ferguson Valley Shiraz 2010** Medium crimson-purple; the wine spent
✪ 18 months in French and American oak; the bouquet has a fragrant and vibrant display of red and black fruits, that vibrancy also foremost on the medium-bodied palate, with its juicy black fruit flavours; the tannins are fine, and the oak integrated. Exceptional value. Screwcap. 13.5% alc. **Rating** 93 **To** 2025 $20

Hahndorf Hill Winery ★★★★★

38 Pain Road, Hahndorf, SA 5245 **Region** Adelaide Hills
T (08) 8388 7512 **www**.hahndorfhillwinery.com.au **Open** 7 days 10–5
Winemaker Larry Jacobs **Est.** 2002 **Dozens** 4000 **Vyds** 6.5ha

Larry Jacobs and Marc Dobson, both originally from South Africa, purchased Hahndorf Hill Winery in 2002. Larry gave up a career in intensive-care medicine in 1988 when he bought an abandoned property in Stellenbosch and established the near-iconic Mulderbosch Wines. When Mulderbosch was purchased at the end of '96, the pair migrated to Australia and eventually found their way to Hahndorf Hill. In 2006, their investment in the winery and cellar door was rewarded by induction into the South Australian Great Tourism Hall of Fame. In '07 they began converting the vineyard to biodynamic status, and they were one of the first movers in implementing a carbon offset program. Having successfully grown and made multi medal-winning blaufrankish wines, they have successfully imported three clones of gruner veltliner from Austria, and their first vintage was made in '10. In '12 their Gruner Veltliner, Blaufrankisch and Sauvignon Blanc all received gold medals in Australian or international wine shows. Exports to the UK, Singapore and China.

♥♥♥♥♥ **Adelaide Hills Sauvignon Blanc 2012** Pale quartz, flecked with green; stands out from the ruck thanks to its excellent texture and structure, which highlight its citrus and passionfruit aromas and flavours, and its long, cleansing finish. Screwcap. 13% alc. **Rating** 94 **To** 2014 $23
Adelaide Hills Pinot Grigio 2012 Quartz-white; has an uncommon degree of intensity and length to the palate with mandarin, fresh ginger and pear all contributing; finishes with a zesty burst of citrussy acidity. Grigio doesn't come much better. Screwcap. 13% alc. **Rating** 94 **To** 2014 $25
GRU Adelaide Hills Gruner Veltliner 2012 Bright, light straw-green; a wine brimming with character and attitude, with its aromas of citrus, pepper and rocket through to the end of an exceptionally long and persistent palate; the balance is very good. Screwcap. 12.5% alc. **Rating** 94 **To** 2019 $28

♥♥♥♥♡ **Zsa Zsa Zweigelt Adelaide Hills Rose 2012** **Rating** 93 **To** 2014 $25
Blueblood Adelaide Hills Blaufrankisch 2011 **Rating** 93 **To** 2018 $35
Adelaide Hills Rose 2012 **Rating** 91 **To** 2014 $22
Single Vineyard Adelaide Hills Shiraz 2010 **Rating** 90 **To** 2025 $30

Hainault ★★★☆

255 Walnut Road, Bickley, WA 6076 **Region** Perth Hills
T (08) 9293 8339 **www**.hainault.com.au **Open** W'ends & public hols 11–5, or by appt
Winemaker Damian Hutton (Contract) **Est.** 1980 **Dozens** 1500 **Vyds** 5.5ha

Lyn and Michael Sykes became the owners of Hainault in 2002. The Hainault vineyard is nestled in jarrah forest high in the Perth Hills; at 400m it is the highest vineyard in WA, and one of the coldest. It was originally selected as Gungin orchard early last century and was replanted as a vineyard in 1978 by Peter Fimmel, one of the pioneers of the Perth Hills wine region. The close-planted vines are hand-pruned and hand-picked, and the pinot noir is very sensibly used to make a sparkling wine, rather than a table wine. Exports to China.

♥♥♥♥♡ **Bickley Valley Cabernet Sauvignon 2010** Good hue and depth; estate-grown
✪ hand-picked grapes, the wine spending 12 months in French and American oak; a surprise packet, with layers of blackcurrant, earth and black olive varietal cabernet supported by firm tannins and oak. Screwcap. 13.5% alc. **Rating** 92 **To** 2025 $20
✪ **Bickley Valley Semillon 2012** Stainless steel-fermented, and taken to new French oak for 3 months' maturation; the base wine is sufficiently intense and powerful to absorb the oak, and the lemony/minerally palate has good grip and length. Could well be interesting down the track. Screwcap. 12.5% alc. **Rating** 90 **To** 2020 $20

♥♥♥♥ **Bickley Valley Chardonnay 2010** **Rating** 89 **To** 2016 $20
Bickley Valley Classic White 2011 **Rating** 89 **To** 2014 $20
Bickley Valley Rose 2011 **Rating** 87 **To** 2014 $20

Halifax Wines

190 Binney Road, McLaren Vale, Willunga, SA 5172 **Region** McLaren Vale
T 0412 257 149 **www.**halifaxwines.com.au **Open** By appt
Winemaker Peter Butcher **Est.** 2000 **Dozens** 1000 **Vyds** 4ha
Owner/operators Peter Butcher and Lizzie Tasker produce small quantities of hand-made, vineyard-specific wines from their estate vineyard (4ha of shiraz) and from other growers who share their views on quality and sustainability. A minimalist approach is taken in the winery with small open fermenters, gentle handling and maturation in older French oak barrels. Says Peter, 'We seek to make wines which reflect their sense of place and the seasons in which they are grown.' Exports to the US, Sweden, Hong Kong, Singapore and China.

Per Se Block Shiraz 2010 A Shiraz of genuine restraint, with tightly coiled black plum, blackberry and black cherry fruit and a slowly emerging fragrance of pretty violets. Old French oak is invisible in the flavour spectrum, lending gentle support to finely poised tannins. Screwcap. 14% alc. **Rating** 94 To 2020 $60 TS

Hamelin Bay

McDonald Road, Karridale, WA 6288 **Region** Margaret River
T (08) 9758 6779 **www.**hbwines.com.au **Open** 7 days 10–5
Winemaker Julian Scott **Est.** 1992 **Dozens** 12000 **Vyds** 23.5ha
The Hamelin Bay vineyard was established by the Drake-Brockman family, pioneers of the region. Richard Drake-Brockman's great-grandmother, Grace Bussell, is famous for her courage when, in 1876 aged 16, she rescued survivors of a shipwreck not far from the mouth of the Margaret River. Richard's great-grandfather Frederick, known for his exploration of the Kimberley, read about the feat in Perth's press and rode 300km on horseback to meet her, and they married in 1882. Hamelin Bay's vineyard and winery are located within a few kilometres of Karridale, at the intersection of the Brockman and Bussell Highways, which were named in honour of both these pioneering families. Exports to the UK, Canada, Malaysia, Singapore and China.

Five Ashes Vineyard Margaret River Cabernet Sauvignon 2009 Has retained its crimson-purple hue; shows its cool Karridale origin in its austere, but correct, varietal character; blackcurrant fruit has a framework of powerful, but not dry, tannins. Will repay patience. Screwcap. 14% alc. **Rating** 94 To 2024 $32

Five Ashes Vineyard Margaret River Shiraz 2009 **Rating** 93 To 2024 $32
Five Ashes Vineyard Margaret River Semillon Sauvignon Blanc 2012 **Rating** 92 To 2014 $24
Five Ashes Vineyard Margaret River Merlot 2011 **Rating** 91 To 2020 $24
Rampant Red Margaret River Shiraz Cabernet Merlot 2010 Medium red-purple; a somewhat rustic, ballsy blend, with a highly spiced Christmas cake bouquet, and more of the same on the palate, with a few spoonfuls of tannins added for good measure. Screwcap. 14.5% alc. **Rating** 90 To 2015 $19

Hand Crafted by Geoff Hardy

PO Box 2370, McLaren Vale SA 5171 **Region** South Australia
T (08) 8383 2700 **www.**handcraftedbygeoffhardy.com.au **Open** Not
Winemaker Geoff Hardy **Est.** 2005 **Dozens** 6000 **Vyds** 3.4ha
Hand Crafted is a collection of wines made from Geoff Hardy's vineyards around SA, including the Angus Vineyard (200ha) at Langhorne Creek, Wirrega Vineyard (160ha) on the Limestone Coast and the Adelaide Hills (45ha); distinctly separate from K1 (Adelaide Hills) and Pertaringa (McLaren Vale).

McLaren Vale Shiraz 2010 Dense purple-crimson; an impressive estate-grown wine, speaking as eloquently of its place as its variety; black cherry, plum, spice, licorice and dark chocolate all contribute in varying ways to its bouquet and medium- to full-bodied palate, with balanced oak and tannins. Screwcap. 14.5% alc. **Rating** 95 To 2025 $30

McLaren Vale Shiraz 2009 Bright, clear crimson-purple; an elegant, fragrant wine that carries the same regional expression as the '10, but a very different vintage message, here on the light side of medium-bodied, red fruits dominant, the tannins fine. Screwcap. 14.5% alc. **Rating** 94 **To** 2019 $30

Adelaide Hills Shiraz Viognier Mourvedre 2010 Bright, clear red-purple; the shiraz and viognier were co-fermented, and subsequently blended with the mourvedre; the result is a medium-bodied but multifaceted wine, with spicy/savoury characters on the way through before red cherry, raspberry and black cherry emerge on the finish and aftertaste. Screwcap. 14.5% alc. **Rating** 94 **To** 2020 $30

ŢŢŢŢŢ McLaren Vale Aglianico 2011 **Rating** 93 **To** 2015 $30 BE
Limestone Coast Lagrein 2010 **Rating** 93 **To** 2025 $30
Adelaide Tempranillo 2011 **Rating** 91 **To** 2015 $30
Langhorne Creek Viognier 2012 **Rating** 90 **To** 2015 $25 BE
Langhorne Creek Savagnin 2012 **Rating** 90 **To** 2014 $25 BE
Langhorne Creek Graciano 2010 **Rating** 90 **To** 2016 $30
McLaren Vale Tannat 2010 **Rating** 90 **To** 2018 $30 BE

Hanging Rock Winery ★★★★★

88 Jim Road, Newham, Vic 3442 **Region** Macedon Ranges
T (03) 5427 0542 **www.**hangingrock.com.au **Open** 7 days 10–5
Winemaker John Ellis **Est.** 1983 **Dozens** 40 000 **Vyds** 14.5ha
The Macedon area has proved very marginal in spots, and the Hanging Rock vineyards, with their lovely vista towards the Rock, are no exception. John Ellis has thus elected to source additional grapes from various parts of Victoria to produce an interesting and diverse range of varietals at different price points. In 2011 John and Anne's children Ruth and Robert returned to the fold: Robert obtained his oenology degree at Adelaide University in '06, since working as a Flying Winemaker in Champagne, Burgundy, Oregon and Stellenbosch. Most recently he worked as winemaker at Hewitson. Ruth has a degree in wine marketing from Adelaide University, and began work at the winery before leaving to work with Hanging Rock's Victorian distributors for 18 months. Exports to the UK, the US and other major markets.

ŢŢŢŢŢ Jim Jim Macedon Ranges Pinot Noir 2011 John Ellis, take a bow. Bright, clear crimson-purple; this is an extremely attractive Pinot Noir, with pure varietal fruit driving both bouquet and palate; the supple, silky palate has an array of red fruits and good oak. There is the faintest touch of green, perhaps ex stalks (I'm not sure), which I have deliberately overlooked in giving the wine 94 points, not 93. Screwcap. 12.5% alc. **Rating** 94 **To** 2016 $40

Heathcote Shiraz 2010 Strong, deep purple-crimson; a voluptuously rich wine with plush blackberry fruit, American steam-bent oak (18 months, 100% new) and dusty tannins; the three components need to knit and will take some years to do so, but have the requisite balance. Diam. 14.3% alc. **Rating** 94 **To** 2025 $70

Reserve Heathcote Shiraz 2005 The wine-stained Diam strongly suggests heat storage issues somewhere along the way; the stains are old and the ripe fruit of the wine doesn't show any adverse impact. It's certainly in the mainstream of Heathcote Shiraz style, with a strong injection of vanilla, the tannins still there, but round and soft. 15% alc. **Rating** 94 **To** 2018 $105

ŢŢŢŢŢ The Jim Jim Macedon Ranges Sauvignon Blanc 2012 Quartz-white;
✪ from vines below the winery planted in 1984, and typically low yielding. The grapes were picked in three stages of ripeness, and 10% were fermented in new French barriques; the result is a complex wine, every bit as much from fruit as oak, and with excellent balance and mouthfeel. Screwcap. 13.2% alc. **Rating** 93 **To** 2014 $27

Macedon Cuvee NV **Rating** 93 **To** 2017 $50
Macedon Brut Rose NV **Rating** 91 **To** 2015 $30

Happs ★★★★★

575 Commonage Road, Dunsborough, WA 6281 **Region** Margaret River
T (08) 9755 3300 **www**.happs.com.au **Open** 7 days 10–5
Winemaker Erl Happ, Mark Warren **Est.** 1978 **Dozens** 16000 **Vyds** 35.2ha
One-time schoolteacher, potter and winemaker Erl Happ is the patriarch of a three-generation family. More than anything, Erl has been a creator and experimenter, building the self-designed winery from mudbrick, concrete form and timber, and designing and making the first crusher. In 1994 he began an entirely new vineyard at Karridale, planted to no less than 28 different varieties, including some of the earliest plantings in Australia of tempranillo. The Three Hills label is made from varieties grown at the 30ha Karridale vineyard. Erl passed on to son Myles a love of pottery, and Happs Pottery now has four potters, including Myles. Exports to Denmark, The Netherlands, Malaysia, Hong Kong, China and Japan.

🍷🍷🍷🍷🍷 **Three Hills Shiraz 2011** Deep crimson; fragrant choc-mint aromas complement the dark berry fruit of the bouquet; the palate is medium-bodied and fleshy, with silky tannins and fruit in complete harmony; the finish is even, warmly textured and long. Screwcap. 14.5% alc. **Rating** 94 **To** 2020 $55 BE

🍷🍷🍷🍷🍷 **Three Hills Charles Andreas 2011 Rating** 90 **To** 2018 $36 BE

Harbord Wines ★★★★

PO Box 41, Stockwell, SA 5355 **Region** Barossa Valley
T (08) 8562 2598 **www**.harbordwines.com.au **Open** Not
Winemaker Roger Harbord **Est.** 2003 **Dozens** 3000
Roger Harbord is a well-known and respected Barossa winemaker, with over 20 years' experience, the last 10 as chief winemaker for Cellarmasters Wines, Normans and Ewinexchange. He has set up his own virtual winery as a complementary activity; the grapes are contract-grown (sources include Vine Vale, Moppa, Greenrock and Marananga), and he leases winery space and equipment to make and mature the wines. Exports to the UK, the US, France, Singapore and China.

🍷🍷🍷🍷🍷 **The Tendril Barossa Shiraz 2010** Full purple-crimson; a Barossa wine looking back to McLaren Vale thanks to its infusion of bitter chocolate into the rich blackberry and dark plum fruit; the tannin and oak management has been perfectly managed; while medium- to full-bodied, has delicious, juicy mouthfeel. Screwcap. 14% alc. **Rating** 93 **To** 2025 $25

Harcourt Valley Vineyards ★★★★☆

3339 Calder Highway, Harcourt, Vic 3453 **Region** Bendigo
T (03) 5474 2223 **www**.harcourtvalley.com.au **Open** 7 days 11–5 (11–6 during daylight saving)
Winemaker Quinn Livingstone **Est.** 1976 **Dozens** 2000 **Vyds** 4ha
Harcourt Valley Vineyards (planted 1975) has the oldest planting of vines in the Harcourt Valley. Using 100% estate-grown fruit Quinn Livingstone (second-generation winemaker) is making a number of small-batch wines. The vines are hand-tended and minimal fruit handling is used in the winemaking process. A new tasting area overlooks the vines; it has a large window that allows visitors to see the activity in the winery. In both 2011 and '12 Harcourt Valley won seven trophies at regional wine shows. Founder Barbara Broughton died in '12, aged 91, and Quinn's mother, Barbara Livingstone, has now retired. Exports to China.

🍷🍷🍷🍷🍷 **Barbara's Bendigo Shiraz 2011** Gold medals at the Melbourne Wine Show
✪ '12 and Daylesford Wine Show (plus a trophy) were richly deserved. This is a lovely, supple, deeply fruited wine, with plum, black cherry and mocha flowing through to the finish and aftertaste of the medium- to full-bodied palate. A triumph for the vintage. Screwcap. 13.6% alc. **Rating** 95 **To** 2031 $25

ŶŶŶŶŶ **Bendigo Riesling 2011** The cooler vintage gives this wine an advantage over
✪ '12 Harcourt Valley Riesling; while still full-flavoured, it is in a tighter lime juice
spectrum, and the palate has good length, as does the aftertaste. Screwcap. 11% alc.
Rating 92 **To** 2017 $20
Old Vine Bendigo Cabernet Sauvignon 2010 Rating 92 **To** 2020 $60
Sightings Shiraz 2011 Rating 90 **To** 2015 $20
Bendigo Cabernet Sauvignon 2011 Rating 90 **To** 2018 $25

Hardys   ★★★★★

202 Main Road, McLaren Vale, SA 5171 **Region** McLaren Vale
T (08) 8329 4124 **www.**hardys.com.au **Open** Mon–Fri 10–4.30, Sat 10–5, Sun 11–5
Winemaker Paul Lapsley (Chief) **Est.** 1853 **Dozens** NFP
The 1992 merger of Thomas Hardy and the Berri Renmano group may well have had some
elements of a forced marriage when it took place, but the merged group prospered mightily
over the next 10 years. So successful was it that a further marriage followed in early 2003,
with Constellation Wines of the US the groom, BRL Hardy the bride, creating the largest
wine group in the world (the Australian arm of the business is known as Constellation Wines
Australia, or CWA); but it is all now part of the Accolade Wines group. The Hardys wine
brands are headed by Eileen Hardy Chardonnay and Shiraz and Thomas Hardy Cabernet
Sauvignon; then the Sir James range of sparkling wines; next the HRB Riesling, Chardonnay,
Shiraz and Cabernet; then the expanded Oomoo range; and, at the bottom of the price
pyramid, the Nottage Hills wines. Exports to all major markets.

ŶŶŶŶŶ **HRB Shiraz 2009** D649. Vivid crimson-purple, exceptional for its age; the
✪ bouquet is fragrant and opulent, with the minority McLaren Vale component
more expressive than that of the Clare Valley; the full-bodied palate restores the
balance in more ways than one, with a complex yet fresh array of black fruits,
licorice and dark chocolate, the oak integrated, the tannins ripe. Great value.
Screwcap. 14% alc. **Rating** 96 **To** 2034 $29
HRB Riesling 2011 D650. A synergistic blend of Clare Valley and Tasmanian
riesling, lifting the citrus fruit profile of the Clare component and balancing that
with the acidity and texture of the Tasmanian component; the flavour coats the
mouth, and won't let go. A cellaring special, although there is a case to be made
for opening a bottle tonight. Screwcap. 12.5% alc. **Rating** 95 **To** 2031 $26
Thomas Hardy Cabernet Sauvignon 2010 Deep, bright garnet; an elegant
and highly perfumed rendition of this Australian classic, showing pure red fruits,
cassis, violets and bath talc; the medium-bodied palate is beautifully detailed, fine-
boned and full of silky tannins and seductive fruit; long, expansive, subtle and
ageworthy. Screwcap. 13.5% alc. **Rating** 95 **To** 2025 $105 BE
HRB Chardonnay 2011 D652. This cool-region blend (52% Pemberton, 48%
Yarra Valley) shows barrel fermentation inputs, with a hint of toasty oak on the
bouquet, but does not obscure the floral fruit alongside it; on the palate nectarine,
white peach and some grapefruit gain ascendancy, the oak simply providing the
framework. Screwcap. 13.2% alc. **Rating** 94 **To** 2019 $29
HRB Chardonnay 2010 D651. Sourced from Pemberton and the large Upper
Yarra Valley vineyard of Hardys. Unexpectedly rich and generous, although not the
least flabby, the richness is balanced by lingering citrussy/lemony acidity on the
long and persuasive palate. Screwcap. 13.5% alc. **Rating** 94 **To** 2018 $26
Sir James Vintage Pinot Noir Chardonnay 2007 Bottle-fermented, with
several years on yeast lees, and made under the direction of sparkling wine maestro
Ed Carr. It is sourced from the Upper Yarra Valley and Tumbarumba regions.
Bright green-gold, and, while obviously has bottle-developed complexity, there is a
really attractive juicy wellspring of white stone fruit on the palate and a little yeast-
derived brioche to add a final touch. Cork. 12.5% alc. **Rating** 94 **To** 2015 $27

♥♥♥♥♀ Sir James Vintage Pinot Noir Chardonnay 2008 Rating 93 To 2014 $27

✪ Nottage Hill Cabernet Sauvignon 2010 Crunchy black and redcurrants, capsicum and cassis are supported by a well-defined tannin structure which will sustain it for a few years. An impressively balanced and drinkable quaffer, the highlight of Nottage Hill '10. Screwcap. 13.5% alc. Rating 90 To 2015 $10 TS

♥♥♥♥
✪ Nottage Hill Pinot Grigio 2012 A pale straw-green hue and zesty, taut palate very much confirm a Grigio style rather than gris. It's refreshingly varietal at this bargain price point, defined by crisp, clean lemon juice and crunchy pear flavours, edging into lime zest. Screwcap. 12.5% alc. Rating 88 To 2013 $10 TS

✪ Nottage Hill Merlot 2011 A surprise package for '11 merlot at such a low price. With a bouquet of violet perfume and a palate of blackcurrants and blackberries, there's no mistaking its varietal credentials. Soft, supple tannins support a fruit-focused finish. Screwcap. 13.5% alc. Rating 88 To 2013 $10 TS

✪ Nottage Hill Shiraz 2012 Deep magenta, vivid hue; bright blackberry fruit aromas are offset by a strong charry mocha oak note; medium-bodied, with tangy acidity and gravelly tannins a notable feature on the finish. Screwcap. 13.5% alc. Rating 87 To 2016 $11 BE

✪ Nottage Hill Shiraz 2011 Some adroit work in the winery has invested the wine with well above average colour for the vintage (its South Eastern Australian GI precludes help from WA); the medium- to full-bodied palate, too, has unexpected weight given the combination of price and vintage. Its limitation is the slightly heavy/claustrophobic impact of the palate. Screwcap. 13.5% alc. Rating 87 To 2014 $10

✪ Nottage Hill Cabernet Shiraz 2011 Light, bright red; another example of the skills of the major wine producers to deal with extremely adverse vintage conditions; juicily fresh, it is ready to go right now. Screwcap. 13.5% alc. Rating 87 To 2013 $10

Hare's Chase   ★★★★★

PO Box 46, Melrose Park, SA 5039 **Region** Barossa Valley
T (08) 8277 3506 **www**.hareschase.com **Open** Not
Winemaker Peter Taylor **Est.** 1998 **Dozens** 5000 **Vyds** 16.8ha
Hare's Chase is the creation of two families who own a 100-year-old vineyard in the Marananga Valley area of the Barossa Valley. The simple, functional winery sits at the top of a rocky hill in the centre of the vineyard, which has some of the best red soil available for dry-grown viticulture. The winemaking arm of the partnership is provided by Peter Taylor, former Southcorp group red winemaker, with over 30 vintages' experience. No wines received for the *2014 Wine Companion*, but a five-star rating has been maintained. Exports to the US, Canada, Switzerland, Singapore, Hong Kong, Malaysia and China.

Harewood Estate   ★★★★★

Scotsdale Road, Denmark, WA 6333 **Region** Denmark
T (08) 9840 9078 **www**.harewood.com.au **Open** Fri–Mon 10–4, 7 days during school hols
Winemaker James Kellie, Paul Nelson **Est.** 1988 **Dozens** 15 000 **Vyds** 10ha
In 2003 James Kellie, for many years a winemaker with Howard Park, and responsible for the contract making of Harewood's wines since 1998, purchased the estate with his father and sister as partners. Events moved quickly thereafter: a 300-tonne winery was constructed, offering both contract winemaking services for the Great Southern region and the ability to expand the Harewood range to include subregional wines that demonstrate the differences in style across the region. In January '10 James, with wife Careena, purchased his father's and sister's shares in the business, and are now 100% owners. Exports to the UK, the US, Denmark, Hong Kong, Malaysia, Macau, Singapore, China and Japan.

♥♥♥♥♥ Reserve Great Southern Riesling 2012 Pale quartz; the grapes come from Porongurup, its reputation as a riesling region growing day by day. This has all the fragrance, elegance and purity of the region, with beautifully balanced citrus fruit and minerally acidity. Is delicious now, but in 5 years will be a world beater. Screwcap. 12% alc. Rating 96 To 2027 $34

Mount Barker Riesling 2012 Bright straw-green; the bouquet is instantly expressive and appealing, with lime and green apple fruit to the fore, picked up seamlessly by the palate; has clever retention of just enough residual sugar to flesh out the finish, yet balanced by acidity. Screwcap. 11% alc. **Rating** 94 **To** 2022 $22

Porongurup Riesling 2012 Bright, light straw-green; has the hallmark effortless balance of Porongurup riesling, so at ease with itself you can underestimate its capacity to unfurl its intense, complex, lime and mineral aromas and flavours over many years. Screwcap. 12% alc. **Rating** 94 **To** 2025 $22

Reserve Great Southern Semillon Sauvignon Blanc 2012 Separate parcels of semillon and sauvignon blanc were barrel-fermented in French oak, leading to an expressive bouquet, and an even more striking mouthfeel, with a seamless array of citrus, green pea, white peach and gooseberry fruit running through to the long finish. Screwcap. 13.5% alc. **Rating** 94 **To** 2016 $25

Reserve Great Southern Shiraz 2010 A blend of shiraz from Frankland River and Mount Barker, matured for 20 months in new and 1-year-old French barriques. Strong crimson-purple; black cherry dominates, coupled with blackberry, the tannins ripe; the oak contribution is obvious, but well balanced and integrated. Screwcap. 14.5% alc. **Rating** 94 **To** 2030 $34

Reserve Great Southern Cabernet Sauvignon 2010 The grapes were grown in Denmark and Frankland River; matured for 24 months in new and used French barriques. Has energy and drive, with blackcurrant fruit and cedary oak playing major roles; the somewhat challenging tannins are the only issue, and given the benefit of the doubt. Screwcap. 14% alc. **Rating** 94 **To** 2025 $34

ŸŸŸŸŸ
✪ **Frankland River Riesling 2012** The same bright, light straw-green of the trio; this is the fullest of the three regional rieslings, with ripe citrus fruit amplified by sweetness that doesn't seek to hide its light under a bushel; the wine may surprise in 5 years' time. Screwcap. 12% alc. **Rating** 93 **To** 2022 $22

✪ **Great Southern Shiraz 2011** From Frankland River and Mount Barker, and spent 12 months in barriques (of unspecified oak type and age). Strong purple-crimson; emphatic black fruits are fortified further with a generous helping of oak, and good tannins. Great value. Screwcap. 14.5% alc. **Rating** 93 **To** 2020 $21

Great Southern Sauvignon Blanc Semillon 2012 **Rating** 92 **To** 2014 $22

✪ **Great Southern Shiraz Cabernet 2011** Small batch-selected from vineyards across Great Southern, matured for 18 months in French and American oak. The bouquet and medium- to full-bodied palate have blackberry, blackcurrant, plum and a twist of dark chocolate; tannins and oak both contribute to a generous wine. Screwcap. 14.5% alc. **Rating** 92 **To** 2021 $21

✪ **Great Southern Cabernet Merlot 2011** Uses the usual Harewood Estate small-batch winemaking processes. This is a well-made Merlot with clear-cut varietal character; no more than medium-bodied, its plum/cassis fruit has a nice touch of black olive and earth on the spicy finish, the oak positive, but not over the top. Screwcap. 14% alc. **Rating** 92 **To** 2018 $21

Great Southern Chardonnay 2012 **Rating** 91 **To** 2017 $25
Great Southern Chardonnay 2011 **Rating** 91 **To** 2018 $34

Harrington Glen Estate

88 Townsend Road, Glen Aplin, Qld 4381 **Region** Granite Belt
T (07) 4683 4388 **www**.harringtonglenwines.com.au **Open** 7 days 10–4, Sat & public hols 10–5
Winemaker Stephen Oliver **Est.** 2003 **Dozens** 700 **Vyds** 3.44ha
The Ireland family planted cabernet sauvignon, shiraz, merlot and verdelho vines in 1997, with follow-on plantings of muscat, viognier and pinot gris. Red grapes not required for cellar door production are sold to local producers, and some white grapes are purchased from other Granite Belt producers. It is somehow appropriate that the accommodation offered by Harrington Glen is in fact a former Victorian Railways train carriage now embedded within the accommodation building.

ΥΥΥΥΩ **Granite Belt Cabernet 2008** Has a string of medals from Qld and Aus small maker wine shows; the colour is excellent for its age, with crimson-purple through to the rim; has abundant cassis and black fruits on the full-bodied palate, just enough to carry the powdery tannins on the finish. Screwcap. 13.5% alc. **Rating** 93 **To** 2020 $40

✪ **Granite Belt Petit Verdot 2011** Striking, deep purple-crimson; a totally fruit-driven and intense wine showing how petit verdot responds to a climate theoretically too warm; cassis and choc-mint flavours flow from the glass into the mouth without any warning (other than the colour) of their approach. Will win a bevy of admirers for its instant gratification. Screwcap. 15.2% alc. **Rating** 90 **To** 2016 $20

ΥΥΥΥ **Vineyard 88 Granite Belt Verdelho 2012** **Rating** 89 **To** 2014 $20

Hart & Hunter

PO Box 120, Cessnock, NSW 2320 **Region** Hunter Valley
T 0401 605 219 **www**.hartandhunter.com.au **Open** At Small Winemakers Centre, Pokolbin
Winemaker Damien Stevens, Jodie Belleville **Est.** 2009 **Dozens** 1500
This is the venture of winemaking couple Damien Stevens and Jodie Belleville, together with Daniel and Elle Hart. It is a virtual winery, the grapes being purchased from single vineyards, and made at First Creek Wines, where Damien and Jodie are full-time winemakers. In 2010, and again in '11, the venture had significant wine show success, and production has leapt from 350 dozen to its present level. Exports to the UK.

ΥΥΥΥΥ **Single Vineyard Series The Hill Shiraz 2011** There is a unique chalky mineral texture to Hart & Hunter's The Hill Vineyard, which blesses this wine with grace and a silky persona. Great concentration of beautifully primary black plum and black cherry fruit is nuanced with violets and licorice, lingering long and seamlessly. A standout of a great vintage. Screwcap. 13.5% alc. **Rating** 95 **To** 2026 $40 TS

Hart of the Barossa

Cnr Vine Vale Road/Light Pass Road, Tanunda, SA 5352 **Region** Barossa Valley
T 0412 586 006 **www**.hartofthebarossa.com.au **Open** By appt
Winemaker Michael and Alisa Hart, Troy Kalleske (Consultant) **Est.** 2007 **Dozens** 2000
Vyds 6.5ha
The ancestors of Michael and Alisa Hart arrived in SA in 1845; their first address (with seven children) was a hollow tree on the banks of the North Para River. Michael and Alisa personally tend the vineyard, which is the oldest certified organic vineyard in the Barossa Valley, and includes a patch of 110-year-old shiraz. The quality of the wines coming from these vines is exceptional; unfortunately there is only enough to fill two hogsheads a year (66 dozen bottles). The other wines made are also impressive, particularly given their prices.

ΥΥΥΥΥ **The Faithful Limited Release Old Vine Shiraz 2010** Medium crimson-
✪ purple. Only two new French hogsheads can be made from the four half-rows of vines planted over 110 years ago; spent 30 months in that oak, but the rich, voluptuous black fruits and dark chocolate balance that oak with ease. Comes in a massive bottle, and glory be, a screwcap. The half-century cellaring potential is conservative. 14.3% alc. **Rating** 96 **To** 2060 $79

The Brave Limited Release Shiraz 2010 Impenetrable purple; an incredibly rich and unctuous wine, flooded with blackberry and dark chocolate fruit, the American and French oak in which it was matured long since swallowed by the fruit, although the oak does help build the mocha and fruitcake characters. Screwcap. 14.5% alc. **Rating** 94 **To** 2035 $28

ΥΥΥΥΩ **The Blesing Cabernet Sauvignon 2010** **Rating** 93 **To** 2030 $32
The Blesing Cabernet Sauvignon 2011 **Rating** 90 **To** 2020 $32

Hartz Barn Wines

1 Truro Road, Moculta, SA 5353 **Region** Eden Valley
T 0408 857 347 **www.**hartzbarnwines.com.au **Open** By appt
Winemaker David Barnett **Est.** 1997 **Dozens** 1600 **Vyds** 11ha
Formed in 1997 by Penny Hart (operations director), David Barnett (winemaker/director), Katrina Barnett (marketing director) and Matthew Barnett (viticulture/cellar director), which may suggest that the operation is rather larger than it in fact is. The business name and label have an unexpectedly complex background too, involving elements from all the partners. The grapes come from the 11ha Dennistone Vineyard, which is planted to merlot, shiraz, riesling, cabernet sauvignon, chardonnay and lagrein. Exports to Japan and NZ.

ΤΤΤΤΩ **General Store Reserve Barossa Shiraz 2010** Good colour; a very convincing wine, at peace with itself notwithstanding the depth of the medium- to full-bodied palate. Here, blackberry, plum and dark chocolate are given additional complexity by positive oak and ripe tannins. Will have a long life. Screwcap. 14% alc. **Rating** 93 **To** 2030 $30

ΤΤΤΤ **General Store Reserve Eden Valley Riesling 2012 Rating** 88 **To** 2015 $25

Harvey River Bridge Estate

Third Street, Harvey, WA 6220 **Region** Geographe
T (08) 9729 2085 **www.**harveyriverbridgeestate.com.au **Open** 7 days 10–4
Winemaker Stuart Pierce, Jurie du Plessis **Est.** 1999 **Dozens** 40 000
This highly focused business is owned by the Sorgiovanni and Scolaro families, who also own the successful fruit juice and dairy product company Harvey Fresh. It has contract growers with 50ha of vines spread throughout the Geographe region, with the wines being made in the company-owned winery and juice factory. Exports to the UK, the US, Canada, Singapore and China.

ΤΤΤΤΤ **Joseph River Estate Reserve Margaret River Cabernet Sauvignon 2011**
✪ A successor to the '09 vintage Jimmy Watson Trophy winner; the colour is deep but bright, the bouquet and palate flush with blackcurrant/cassis fruit, the tannins ripe and perfectly balanced; together with the oak they have a slightly savoury cast that adds to the appeal of a very good wine. Screwcap. 14.5% alc. **Rating** 96 **To** 2041 $38

ΤΤΤΤΩ **Joseph River Estate Reserve Margaret River Cabernet Sauvignon 2010** **Rating** 93 **To** 2020 $38

Haselgrove Wines

187 Sand Road, McLaren Vale, SA 5171 **Region** McLaren Vale
T (08) 8323 8706 **www.**haselgrove.com.au **Open** By appointment Mon–Fri 10–4
Winemaker Greg Clack, Matthew Copping **Est.** 1981 **Dozens** 40 000 **Vyds** 9.7ha
In 2008 the business was acquired by four Italian-Australian wine stalwarts: Don Totino, Don Luca, Tony Carrocci and Steve Maglieri. The wines are released in four ranges: at the top, the Il Padrone (The Boss); next the Bella Vigna (Beautiful Vineyard) Series; then the First Cut Series; and at the entry level, the 'H' by Haselgrove Series. Exports to the UK, Denmark, Hong Kong, China and NZ.

ΤΤΤΤ **First Cut Adelaide Hills Pinot Grigio 2012** A pleasant wine with gentle
✪ peach, pear and apple fruit, and an attractive subtext of sweetness that is not residual sugar. Screwcap. 12.5% alc. **Rating** 88 **To** 2014 $16

Hastwell & Lightfoot

204 Foggos Road, McLaren Vale, SA 5171 **Region** McLaren Vale
T (08) 8323 8692 **www.**hastwellandlightfoot.com.au **Open** By appt
Winemaker James Hastwell **Est.** 1988 **Dozens** 5000 **Vyds** 16ha

Established in 1988 by Mark and Wendy Hastwell and Martin and Jill Lightfoot with a focus on growing quality grapes for McLaren Vale wineries. Having initially sold much of the production, they have made a significant commitment to the Hastwell & Lightfoot brand, producing wines from estate-grown varieties. The vines are grafted onto devigorating American rootstocks that restrain the development of dead fruit characters in warmer seasons. James Hastwell, son of Mark and Wendy, has his winery just 2km from the vineyard, which means that fruit is moved quickly into the winery. Ferments are conducted in 2- and 3-tonne temperature-controlled open fermenters. Exports to the UK, Canada, Denmark, Norway, Germany, Malaysia, Taiwan, Singapore and China.

♀♀♀♀♀ **Single Block Scarce Earth McLaren Vale Shiraz 2010** Medium red-purple; dark chocolate, mocha and fruit oak aromas and flavours are regional enough, a twist of black fruits and licorice on the finish lifting the wine; however, the vanilla oak is very obvious at this stage. Screwcap. 14.5% alc. **Rating** 90 **To** 2018 $28
McLaren Vale Cabernet Sauvignon 2009 Has retained good hue and depth; the wine in fact contains 12% cabernet franc, and deserves the self-bestowed epithet 'A wine made for eating'. Black fruits, dark chocolate and mocha, and robust tannins, fill the full-bodied palate, leaving just enough daylight for the cabernet franc to wave its hand. Screwcap. 14.5% alc. **Rating** 90 **To** 2029 $23

♀♀♀♀ **McLaren Vale Cabernet Franc 2010 Rating** 87 **To** 2016 $23

Hat Rock Vineyard   ★★★

2330 Portarlington Road, Bellarine, Vic 3221 (postal) **Region** Geelong
T (03) 5259 1386 **www**.hatrockvineyard.com.au **Open** By appt
Winemaker Ray Nadeson (Contract) **Est.** 2000 **Dozens** 300 **Vyds** 2ha
Steven and Vici Funnell began the development of Hat Rock in 2000, planting pinot noir. The vineyard derives its name from a hat-shaped rocky outcrop on the Corio Bay shore, not far from the vineyard, a landmark named by Matthew Flinders when he mapped the southern part of Australia.

♀♀♀♀ **Bellarine Peninsula Pinot Noir 2011** Clear, light red-purple; the bouquet is fragrant and enticing, a siren allure that so often in '11 leads into a palate that has pretty fruits, but lacks fruit flesh; no issue with the winemaking. Screwcap. 13.5% alc. **Rating** 89 **To** 2015 $30

Hay Shed Hill Wines   ★★★★★

511 Harmans Mill Road, Wilyabrup, WA 6280 **Region** Margaret River
T (08) 9755 6046 **www**.hayshedhill.com.au **Open** 7 days 9–5
Winemaker Michael Kerrigan **Est.** 1987 **Dozens** 24 000 **Vyds** 18.55ha
Mike Kerrigan, highly regarded former winemaker at Howard Park, acquired the business in late 2006 (with co-ownership by the West Cape Howe syndicate) and is now the full-time winemaker. He had every confidence he could dramatically lift the quality of the wines, which is precisely what he has done. Exports to the UK, the US, Singapore, China and Hong Kong.

♀♀♀♀♀ **Block 1 Margaret River Semillon Sauvignon Blanc 2012** Made from some of the oldest vines (dry grown) of semillon and sauvignon blanc in Margaret River with some barrel ferment. It is a wine of startling intensity and length, the oak swept away by the tsunami of citrus, grass and snow pea flavours; a long, bone-dry finish. Screwcap. 12.8% alc. **Rating** 96 **To** 2022 $28
Block 2 Margaret River Cabernet Sauvignon 2010 Bright crimson-purple; made from the oldest cabernet planted on the estate, and brings together elegant cassis and red berry fruit with quality French oak, the tannins persistent yet particularly fine. Screwcap. 14% alc. **Rating** 96 **To** 2030 $48
Margaret River Chardonnay 2012 Pale, bright green-straw; a precisely made Chardonnay, with attention to detail from the decision to pick through to the aftertaste of the wine in the glass. It has great purity, the fruit sucking saliva from the mouth on the long finish. Screwcap. 13% alc. **Rating** 94 **To** 2019 $25

Pitchfork Margaret River Cabernet Merlot 2010 Excellent retention of colour, even brighter than when first tasted 12 months ago. This has all the character one expects from higher priced Margaret River Cabernet Merlots; there is abundant cassis fruit framed by quality French oak and persistent, ripe tannins. Has undoubted development potential. Screwcap. 14% alc. Rating 94 To 2025 $17

Margaret River Cabernet Sauvignon 2011 The strong purple-crimson colour and rich, cassis-laden bouquet are followed by a deeply flavoured, medium-to full-bodied palate, fruit dominant, but with noticeable tannins and good-quality oak. Screwcap. 14% alc. Rating 94 To 2031 $28

ΨΨΨΨΩ ✪ Margaret River Sauvignon Blanc Semillon 2012 Estate-grown, the vines fully mature. An elegant wine, the aromas and flavours largely in the snow pea, grass and citrus spectrum, the semillon an important partner (though its percentage is not specified). Screwcap. 12.5% alc. Rating 93 To 2015 $22

✪ Margaret River Shiraz Tempranillo 2011 Deep purple-crimson; the percentage contribution of the two varieties is not specified, but shiraz is the flavour and structure leader of the band; that said, the array of red and black cherry fruit has been given complexity by the tempranillo. A wholly successful blend at an enticing price. Screwcap. 14% alc. Rating 93 To 2018 $20

✪ Margaret River Cabernet Merlot 2011 Deep crimson-purple hue; the bouquet is enticing, and the palate continues the theme with juicy cassis and redcurrant fruit, 12 months in French oak judged to perfection, contributing to both texture and flavour. Great value. Screwcap. 14% alc. Rating 93 To 2024 $22

Margaret River Malbec 2010 Rating 93 To 2030 $30

✪ Pitchfork Riesling 2012 A crisp, bracing style, with inflections of slate and herb to its citrus zest and pith fruit; the energy and tightness of the package make this a cellar special at a great price. Screwcap. 12.5% alc. Rating 92 To 2025 $17

✪ Pitchfork Pink 2012 Pale, vivid pink; the flowery bouquet leads into a fresh, dry palate that has a delicious line of red berry fruit running through the length of the palate; if there is residual sugar, it's not obvious. 'Made from Margaret River grapes.' Do tell. Screwcap. 13% alc. Rating 92 To 2014 $17

✪ Pitchfork Margaret River Semillon Sauvignon Blanc 2012 Uses contract-grown grapes; some tropical notes come into play alongside citrus and grassy nuances; good acidity freshens and lengthens the finish of a very attractive wine for immediate consumption. Screwcap. 12.5% alc. Rating 90 To 2014 $17

Hazyblur Wines ★★★★

Lot 5 Angle Vale Road, Virginia, SA 5120 Region Kangaroo Island
T (08) 8380 9307 www.hazyblur.com Open By appt
Winemaker Ross Trimboli Est. 1998 Dozens 3500 Vyds 5ha

Robyne and Ross Trimboli hit the jackpot with their 2000 vintage red wines, sourced from various regions in SA, including one described by Robert Parker Jr as 'Barotta, the most northerly region in SA' (it is in fact Baroota, and is not the most northerly), with Parker points ranging between 91 and 95. One of the wines was a Late Harvest Shiraz, tipping the scales at 17% alcohol, and contract-grown at Kangaroo Island. It is here that the Trimbolis have established their own vineyard, planted to cabernet sauvignon, shiraz, pinot noir and pinot gris. Exports to the UK, the US, Canada, Denmark, Taiwan, Malaysia, Singapore, Hong Kong, China and Japan.

ΨΨΨΨΩ Kangaroo Island Pinot Gris 2012 Distinct pink; a fragrant bouquet speaks clearly of the variety, as does the palate; pear, peach and a touch of citrus provide the aromas and flavours on the gentle palate. Screwcap. 13.5% alc. Rating 90 To 2014 $28

Kangaroo Island Cabernet Sauvignon 2010 Medium to full red-purple; a reduced yield has produced a concentrated wine, with blackcurrant fruit and an edge of bitter chocolate; the structure is firm, with ample tannins for the long term. Screwcap. 15% alc. Rating 90 To 2030 $28

Head in the Clouds

36 Neate Avenue, Belair, SA 5052 **Region** Adelaide Hills
T 0404 440 298 **www.**headintheclouds.com **Open** Not
Winemaker Tom Robinson **Est.** 2008 **Dozens** 250

This is very much the part-time business of winemaker Tom Robinson and sales manager Ashley Coats. In a potential demarcation dispute, Tom Robinson won the Gourmet Traveller Wine Magazine/Wine Communicators Australia New Wine Writer Award '12, and holds a Masters degree in French literature. Each of them has a part-time teaching job at Mercedes College, Tom lecturing in French, Ashley head of the Arts Faculty. Tom's journey through wine is a prodigious one, covering the US for many years, and more recently Australia. With a production of 250 dozen, they have travelled below the Halliday radar up to this point, but have been making wines under the Head in the Clouds banner since 2008.

♟♟♟♟♟ **Wild Ferment Chardonnay 2012** Bright quartz-green; a more than useful Chardonnay at this price, with greater texture and flavour than all but a handful of its price peers; it has white and yellow stone fruit flavours picked up and accelerated by the benison of wild ferment on the finish and aftertaste, where the flavour moves more to citrus. Screwcap. 13% alc. **Rating** 92 **To** 2015 $15

Sellicks Hill The Waves Vineyard McLaren Vale Grenache 2010 Light red-purple; fresh spicy red fruits in a light- to medium-bodied framework; has no Turkish Delight/confection, a thoroughly good thing, but as expected for McLaren Vale; restrained oak a plus. Screwcap. 15.3% alc. **Rating** 90 **To** 2016 $25

The Tempest McLaren Vale Gnarly Zin Mo 2009 Light colour showing expected development; an eclectic blend of grenache, zinfandel and mourvedre, it has greater presence and more vibrant juicy red fruits than expected, the tannins neatly weighted. Screwcap. 14.5% alc. **Rating** 90 **To** 2015 $18

Sellicks Hill The Waves Vineyard McLaren Vale Mourvedre 2010 Good colour; the wine is varietal and also regional, but cannot help but display its alcohol; food might well prove the perfect antidote, for there is a lot to like about the texture and flavour of this wine. Screwcap. 15.5% alc. **Rating** 90 **To** 2016 $25

♟♟♟♟ **The Aurora McLaren Vale Grenache Rose 2011** Pale pink; a neatly constructed and structured rose, with wild strawberry, raspberry and spice on a palate that is neither dry nor sweet – but is good value. Screwcap. 13% alc. **Rating** 89 **To** 2014 $15

Head Wines ★★★★★

Lot 1 Stonewell Road, Stonewell, SA 5352 **Region** Barossa Valley
T 0413 114 233 **www.**headwines.com.au **Open** Not
Winemaker Alex Head **Est.** 2006 **Dozens** 2500 **Vyds** 7.5ha

Head Wines is the intriguing, and highly focused, venture of Alex Head, who came into the wine industry in 1997 with a degree in biochemistry from Sydney University. Experience in fine wine retail stores, wholesale importers and an auction house was followed by vintage work at wineries he particularly admired: Tyrrell's, Torbreck, Laughing Jack and Cirillo Estate. The labelling and naming of the wines reflects his fascination with the Northern Rhône Valley, and, in particular, Côte-Rôtie. The two facing slopes in Côte-Rôtie are known as Côte Blonde and Côte Brune. Head's Blonde comes from an east-facing slope in the Stonewell area of the Barossa Valley, while The Brunette comes from a very low-yielding vineyard in the Moppa area. In each case, open fermentation (with whole bunches included) and basket-pressing precedes 15 months in seasoned French hogsheads.

♟♟♟♟♟ **The Brunette Single Vineyard Syrah 2011** Alex Head has pulled a rabbit from the hat with the depth of colour to this wine, and a second rabbit with the fully ripe and generous fruit, bordering on sweet, with layers of satsuma plum and blackberry; judicious use of oak has added the final dimension. One of the best Barossa Valley Shirazs from '11. Screwcap. 13.4% alc. **Rating** 95 **To** 2025 $50

The Blonde Single Vineyard Stonewell Shiraz Viognier 2011 Excellent crimson-purple hue of medium depth; the perfumed red berry bouquet is followed by a juicy red fruit palate with no hint of under-ripe fruit; the tannin and oak management is exemplary. Screwcap. 13.5% alc. Rating 94 To 2018 $40

ŸŸŸŸŸ Barossa Valley Grenache Rose 2012 Rating 93 To 2014 $25
Head Red Barossa Valley GSM 2012 Rating 92 To 2015 $25
The Contrarian Single Vineyard Marananga Barossa Valley Syrah 2011 Rating 91 To 2017 $30

✪ Head Red Barossa Valley Shiraz 2011 Exceptional purple-crimson for the vintage, magic needed in the vineyard and winery alike to achieve this outcome; it isn't particularly fleshy, but does have balance, and hasn't been over-oaked. Screwcap. 13% alc. Rating 90 To 2015 $20
Old Vine Barossa Valley Grenache 2011 Rating 90 To 2015 $30

Heafod Glen Winery ★★★★☆

8691 West Swan Road, Henley Brook, WA 6055 **Region** Swan Valley
T (08) 9296 3444 **www**.heafodglenwine.com.au **Open** Wed–Sun 10–5
Winemaker Liam Clarke **Est.** 1999 **Dozens** 2500 **Vyds** 3ha
A combined vineyard and restaurant business, each set on outdoing the other, each with major accolades. Founder Neil Head taught himself winemaking, but in 2007 employed Liam Clarke (with a degree in viticulture and oenology), and a string of significant show successes for Verdelho, Viognier and Reserve Chardonnay has followed. Chesters Restaurant was awarded Best Tourism Restaurant in '08 and Best Restaurant at a Winery – Perth and Surrounds '09. Exports to Japan.

ŸŸŸŸŸ Family Reserve Methode Champenoise Pinot Noir 2008 The base wine is a 91/9% blend of pinot noir and chardonnay; this wine (traditional method) is a late release that spent 55 months on lees prior to disgorgement. It has aged very impressively indeed, and the dosage has been exactly pitched to the delicate red fruits of the palate. Zork SPK. 12.5% alc. Rating 94 To 2015 $80

ŸŸŸŸŸ HB2 Vineyard Swan Valley Semillon 2012 Rating 93 To 2016 $27
Family Reserve Chandala Creek Vineyard Perth Hills Chardonnay 2011 Rating 90 To 2016 $50

Heartland Wines ★★★★

The Winehouse, Wellington Road, Langhorne Creek, SA 5255 **Region** Langhorne Creek
T (08) 8333 1363 **www**.heartlandwines.com.au **Open** 7 days 10–5
Winemaker Ben Glaetzer **Est.** 2001 **Dozens** 50 000
A joint venture of industry veterans: winemakers Ben Glaetzer and Scott Collett, and wine industry management specialist Grant Tilbrook. It uses grapes grown in the Limestone Coast and Langhorne Creek, predominantly from vineyards owned by the partners. It currently exports 60% of its make to 36 international markets. The wines are principally contract-made at Barossa Vintners and are excellent value for money. Exports to all major markets.

ŸŸŸŸŸ Langhorne Creek Pinot Gris 2012 Light straw-green; fresh and fruity, but its aroma and flavour spectrum is very different from the normal pear and apple, here headed more to citrus and stone fruit. Any less enjoyable? No. Screwcap. 13.5% alc. Rating 90 To 2014 $22

✪ Langhorne Creek Shiraz 2010 Purple-crimson; the inherent softness of Langhorne Creek shiraz and a copious infusion of vanillin oak seem appropriate given the wine was made by Ben Glaetzer, John Glaetzer's brother (of Wolf Blass fame). Screwcap. 14.8% alc. Rating 90 To 2016 $20

✪ Langhorne Creek Cabernet Sauvignon 2010 Medium red-purple; manages to combine the soft mid-palate of Langhorne Creek with cabernet tannins on the finish, but do so in a way that doesn't break the line of the wine; likewise, maturation in French hogsheads hasn't threatened the fruit. Screwcap. 14.5% alc. Rating 90 To 2016 $20

Heaslip Wines ★★★★

PO Box 878, Clare, SA 5453 **Region** Clare Valley
T (08) 8842 3242 **www**.heaslipwines.com.au **Open** Not
Winemaker Paulett Wines (Neil Paulett), Cardinham Estate (Scott Smith) **Est.** 2005
Dozens 600 **Vyds** 5ha
The Heaslip family, headed by Marie Heaslip, son Anthony and wife Philippa Stansell, pooled their resources to buy the vineyard (planted to cabernet sauvignon, shiraz and riesling) in 2004, after it had been on the market for some time. It is dry-grown, fertilised with organic fertilisers, all fungicides are organic, and no insecticides are used. The tough '07 vintage produced no grapes, but the organic approach, coupled with minimal use of tractors in the vineyard, is paying dividends. Anthony and Philippa live and work in the Northern Territory for most of the year, leaving management of the property to Marie. Exports to the US, Europe and NZ.

🍷🍷🍷🍷🍷 **Dry Grown Handpicked Clare Valley Riesling 2012** Pale quartz-green; an elegant and fragrant wine, the bouquet flowery, the palate crisp and fresh; here lime, apple and slate intermingle, promising a long life. Screwcap. 12% alc. **Rating** 93 **To** 2022 $18

✪ **Dayspring Dry Grown Clare Valley Shiraz 2010** Exceptionally deep purple-crimson; the vineyard is dry grown and organic which explains the concentration and focus of the fruit. The palate is medium- to full-bodied, and is inhabited by savoury black fruits and fine tannins, the lowish alcohol giving the wine freshness. Top value. Screwcap. 13.8% alc. **Rating** 93 **To** 2025 $18

🍷🍷🍷🍷 **Philly's Block Cabernet Sauvignon 2010 Rating** 89 **To** 2017 $18

Heathcote Estate

98 High Street, Heathcote, Vic 3523 **Region** Heathcote
T (03) 5433 2488 **www**.yabbylake.com **Open** 7 days 10–5
Winemaker Tom Carson, Chris Forge **Est.** 1988 **Dozens** 5000 **Vyds** 34ha
Heathcote Estate is a thoroughly professional venture, a partnership between Louis Bialkower, founder of Yarra Ridge, and Robert G. Kirby, owner of Yabby Lake Vineyards, director of Escarpment Vineyards (NZ) and chairman of Village Roadshow Ltd. They purchased a prime piece of Heathcote red Cambrian soil in 1999, planting shiraz (30ha) and grenache (4ha). The wines are matured exclusively in French oak (50% new). The arrival of the hugely talented Tom Carson as Group Winemaker has added lustre to the winery and its wines, notwithstanding a number of challenging vintages for the Heathcote region as a whole. The cellar door, situated in an old bakery in the Heathcote township, provides a relaxed dining area. Exports to the US, the UK, Canada, Sweden, Singapore, Hong Kong and China.

🍷🍷🍷🍷🍷 **Single Block Release Block F Shiraz 2010** Even better colour than that of Block A; while the similarities are more obvious than the differences, the texture of this medium- to full-bodied palate is more open, with a more spicy spectrum, the tannins (while fully ripe) finer, the French oak fractionally more evident. Chacun à son gout. Screwcap. 14.5% alc. **Rating** 96 **To** 2045 $80
Single Block Release Block A Shiraz 2010 Deep purple-crimson; a densely packed, full-bodied wine with layer upon layer of black fruits, licorice, dark chocolate, high-quality French oak and ripe, velvety tannins. Because the balance is so outstanding, this Shiraz has a 50-year future, the screwcap guaranteeing its development. 14.5% alc. **Rating** 96 **To** 2060 $80
Single Block Release Block F Shiraz 2009 Bright crimson; spicy red berry aromas leap out of the glass and cascade across the medium-bodied palate; depth and complexity are achieved by stealth, the ripeness strictly fruit (not alcohol) expressed, oak and tannins precisely lined up in support. All about the terroir, not so much the winemaking. Screwcap. 14.5% alc. **Rating** 96 **To** 2034 $80
Single Vineyard Shiraz 2011 Good depth and hue to the colour; a rabbit pulled out of the '11 vintage hat, with more than average conviction; the perfumed bouquet leads into a palate driven by dark berry fruits with obvious spice and quality French oak supports. Screwcap. 14% alc. **Rating** 94 **To** 2026 $45

Grenade Noir 2012 In Australia, grenache noir is simply a fancy name for grenache, but then this is a fancy Grenache. The result from a top vintage such as '12 is vibrant raspberry and rich cherry fruit, fine tannins and very good length. Most importantly, it doesn't have confection/Turkish Delight characters on its lingering back-palate and aftertaste. Screwcap. 14% alc. **Rating** 94 **To** 2020 $30

Heathcote Winery ★★★★☆

183–185 High Street, Heathcote, Vic 3523 **Region** Heathcote
T (03) 5433 2595 **www**.heathcotewinery.com.au **Open** 7 days 10–5
Winemaker Rachel Brooker **Est.** 1978 **Dozens** 8000 **Vyds** 15.25ha
The cellar door of Heathcote Winery is situated in the main street of Heathcote, housed in a restored miner's cottage built by Thomas Craven in 1854 to cater for the huge influx of gold miners. The winery is immediately behind the cellar door, and processed the first vintage in 1983, following the planting of the vineyards in '78. In '97 the winery was purchased by an independent group of wine enthusiasts, led by Stephen Wilkins. When first established, the emphasis was on white wines, but it has since moved decisively in the direction of Shiraz and Shiraz Viognier, with 60% of the total plantings devoted to shiraz. Part of this move came with the establishment of the Slaughterhouse Paddock Vineyard, 3km north of Heathcote, with 4ha of shiraz. Exports to China.

♆♆♆♆♆ **The Wilkins Shiraz 2008** Strong red-purple; grapes from three different blocks were open-fermented and basket-pressed, then spent 15 months in barriques from Burgundian coopers. It was bottle-matured for another 2 years prior to release. And yes, the wine repaid all this attention, with resplendent plum and black cherry fruit, supple tannins and balanced French oak. Just under 80 dozen made. Screwcap. 14.5% alc. **Rating** 95 **To** 2030 $95

♆♆♆♆♀ **Curagee Shiraz 2010 Rating** 93 **To** 2025 $60
Mail Coach Shiraz 2010 Rating 91 **To** 2020 $33

Hedberg Hill ★★★★

701 The Escort Way, Orange, NSW 2800 **Region** Orange
T (02) 6365 3428 **www**.hedberghill.com.au **Open** W'ends 10–5
Winemaker Wallace Lane Wine Company (Philip Kerney) **Est.** 1998 **Dozens** 1000 **Vyds** 5.6ha
Peter and Lee Hedberg have established their hilltop vineyard 4km west of Orange, with 0.8ha each of cabernet sauvignon, merlot, tempranillo, chardonnay, viognier, sauvignon blanc and riesling. The cellar door, opened in June 2010, has great views of Mt Canobolas and the surrounding valleys. The appointment of Wallace Lane/Phil Kerney as winemaker has seen a significant increase in quality, however difficult the '11 vintage proved to be.

♆♆♆♆♀ **Peter's Orange Riesling 2012** Light straw-green; the floral bouquet has lime
✪ and apple blossom aromas that swell on the delicious lime juice palate; while generous, it has the acidity to age with grace. Screwcap. 12.8% alc. **Rating** 93 **To** 2020 $18
Orange Late Harvest Riesling 2011 Orange-bronze; botrytis and barrel ageing have resulted in a wine with abundant flavour and sweet fruit, yet also the all-important acidity to give it length and life. 375ml. Screwcap. 14% alc. **Rating** 92 **To** 2016 $25
Lara's Orange Chardonnay 2011 Pale quartz; an elegant, light-bodied Chardonnay barrel-fermented in used French barriques and aged on lees; white peach and melon fruit flavours have good balance, and just a touch of creamy/nutty notes. Screwcap. 13% alc. **Rating** 90 **To** 2016 $22

♆♆♆♆ **Oscar's Orange Cabernet Sauvignon 2010 Rating** 88 **To** 2015 $22
Claudia's Orange Viognier 2011 Rating 87 **To** 2014 $22

Heemskerk ★★★★★

131 Cascade Road, South Hobart, Tas 7004 (postal) **Region** Southern Tasmania
T 1300 651 650 **www**.heemskerk.com.au **Open** Not
Winemaker Anna Pooley (former) **Est.** 1975 **Dozens** NFP **Vyds** 5.2ha
The Heemskerk brand established by Graham Wiltshire when he planted the first vines in 1965 (in the Pipers River region) is a very different business these days. It is part of TWE, and sources its grapes from three vineyards: the Riversdale Vineyard in the Coal River Valley for riesling; the Lowestoft Vineyard in the Derwent Valley for pinot noir; and the Tolpuddle Vineyard in the Coal River Valley for chardonnay.

ŶŶŶŶŶ **Derwent Valley Pinot Noir 2010** Positive crimson-purple; the fragrant red berry and spice bouquet leads into a palate with cherry and plum fruit balanced to perfection by savoury/foresty characters; it has great line, length and balance, the French oak inputs totally integrated. Screwcap. 14% alc. **Rating** 96 **To** 2020 $60
Abel's Tempest Chardonnay 2011 Bright straw-green; has utterly harmonious mouthfeel and equally well-balanced flavours, first the fruit in a white stone fruit citadel, and second in the fruit-oak-acidity triangle. Will drink at any time over the next 5–7+ years. Screwcap. 13% alc. **Rating** 95 **To** 2018 $25
Coal River Valley Chardonnay Pinot Noir 2008 Very pale straw-green. Has abundant mousse, and a vibrant mix of white peach and citrus fruit, with minimum yeast influence, the palate long and fine. Diam. 12% alc. **Rating** 95 **To** 2014 $60
Abel's Tempest Pinot Noir 2011 Bright crimson; has a very attractive and expressive bouquet full of red berry fruits and spice, the palate bringing those characters onto the palate, there supported by fine tannins with some savoury characters. Screwcap. 13.5% alc. **Rating** 94 **To** 2018 $32

ŶŶŶŶŶ **Abel's Tempest Sauvignon Blanc 2012 Rating** 93 **To** 2014 $25
Coal River Valley Chardonnay 2011 Rating 93 **To** 2017 $50
Abel's Tempest Chardonnay Pinot Noir 2010 Rating 93 **To** 2016 $32

Heggies Vineyard ★★★★★

Heggies Range Road, Eden Valley, SA 5235 **Region** Eden Valley
T (08) 8561 3200 **www**.heggiesvineyard.com **Open** By appt
Winemaker Peter Gambetta **Est.** 1971 **Dozens** 15 000 **Vyds** 62ha
Heggies was the second of the high-altitude (570m) vineyards established by the Hill-Smith family. Plantings on the 120ha former grazing property began in 1973; the principal varieties are riesling, chardonnay, viognier and merlot. There are then two special plantings: a 1.1ha reserve chardonnay block, and 27ha of various clonal trials. Exports to all major markets.

ŶŶŶŶŶ **Eden Valley Botrytis Riesling 2012** The perfectly poised acidity and fine, chalk mineral texture of Heggies Vineyard define one of SA's most impeccably crafted and enticingly drinkable Botrytis Rieslings. Glorious white peach, lemon, apricot and honey flavours maintain succulent generosity and pristine balance. Screwcap. 11% alc. **Rating** 95 **To** 2022 $29 TS
Eden Valley Riesling 2012 Light straw-green; ripe lime and Granny Smith apple aromas burst into rollicking song on the palate as they meet grainy acidity. There is so much on offer now, there is no reason to wait. Screwcap. 12.5% alc. **Rating** 94 **To** 2020 $24

ŶŶŶŶŶ **Eden Valley Chardonnay 2011 Rating** 92 **To** 2015 $30

Heidenreich Estate ★★★☆

PO Box 99, Tanunda, SA 5352 **Region** Barossa Valley
T (08) 8563 2644 **www**.heidenreichvineyards.com.au **Open** By appt
Winemaker Noel Heidenreich, Mark Jamieson **Est.** 1998 **Dozens** 2000 **Vyds** 47.3ha

The Heidenreich family arrived in the Barossa in 1857, with successive generations growing grapes ever since. It is now owned and run by Noel and Cheryl Heidenreich who, having changed the vineyard plantings and done much work on the soil, were content to sell the grapes from their 45ha (at three different sites) of shiraz, cabernet sauvignon, cabernet franc, viognier and chardonnay until 1998, when they and friends crushed a tonne of shiraz, cabernet sauvignon and cabernet franc. Production has increased to around 2000 dozen, much exported to San Diego (US), and a little sold locally, the remainder exported to Hong Kong and China.

ŸŸŸŸŸ **The Old School Principals Barossa Valley Shiraz 2010** Bright crimson-purple; the bouquet has an attractive display of black fruits neatly framed by touches of oak, the medium-bodied palate with lithe and lively black cherry and plum fruit, the tannins soft and round. Screwcap. 14.5% alc. **Rating** 93 **To** 2025 $30

ŸŸŸŸ **The Old School Masters Barossa Valley Cabernet Merlot 2010 Rating** 88 **To** 2016 $20

Heirloom Vineyards   ★★★★★

PO Box 39, McLaren Vale, SA 5171 **Region** Adelaide Zone
T (08) 8556 6099 **www**.heirloomvineyards.com.au **Open** Not
Winemaker Elena Brooks **Est.** 2006 **Dozens** NFP
This is (yet another) venture for Zar Brooks and his wife Elena. They met during the 2000 vintage, and one thing led to another, as they say. Dandelion Vineyards and Zonte's Footstep came along first, and continue, but other partners are involved in those ventures. The lofty aims here are to preserve the best of tradition, the old world of wine, the unique old vineyards of SA, and to champion the best clones of each variety, embracing the principles of organic and biodynamic farming. I don't doubt for one moment the sincerity of the underlying sentiments, but there's a fair degree of Brooksian marketing spin involved. Having said that, the quality of their first wines was outstanding, easily putting Heirloom Vineyards into the Best New Wineries list. Exports to all major markets.

ŸŸŸŸŸ **Eden Valley Shiraz 2010** Medium crimson-purple; there are spicy aromas to the black fruits of the bouquet, and the structure and texture of the medium-bodied palate is outstanding, the blackberry and licorice flavours supported by perfect tannins, oak seamlessly joined to the whole parade; has wonderful length. Screwcap. 14% alc. **Rating** 96 **To** 2035 $35
Barossa Valley Shiraz 2010 Medium crimson-purple; balance and harmony are the keywords, an expressive red and black fruit bouquet leading into a gently juicy palate framed by fine, soft tannins and quality oak; this medium-bodied Shiraz easily carries its alcohol Screwcap. 14.5% alc. **Rating** 94 **To** 2025 $40

Helen's Hill Estate   ★★★★★

16 Ingram Road, Lilydale, Vic 3140 **Region** Yarra Valley
T (03) 9739 1573 **www**.helenshill.com.au **Open** 7 days 10–5
Winemaker Scott McCarthy **Est.** 1984 **Dozens** 12000 **Vyds** 53ha
Helen's Hill Estate is named after the previous owner of the property, Helen Fraser. Venture partners Andrew and Robyn McIntosh and Roma, Allan and Christine Nalder combined childhood farming experience with more recent careers in medicine and finance to establish and manage the day-to-day operations of the estate. The estate produces two labels: Helen's Hill Estate and Ingram Rd, both labels made onsite by Scott McCarthy. Scott started his career early by working vintages during school holidays before gaining diverse and extensive experience in the Barossa and Yarra valleys, Napa Valley, Languedoc, the Loire Valley and Marlborough. The winery, cellar door complex and elegant 140-seat restaurant command some of the best views in the valley. Exports to Hong Kong, the Maldives and China.

ŸŸŸŸŸ Breachley Block Single Vineyard Yarra Valley Chardonnay 2012 Mid
gold, bright hue; ripe aromas of white peach, spicy oak and some oak-derived
complexity; the palate is generously textured, with ample levels of fruit and fresh
acidity, and a lingering tail of toasty oak that is in harmony with the wine; enjoy
in the short to medium term. Screwcap. 12.2% alc. **Rating** 93 **To** 2016 $30 BE
The Nemesis Single Vineyard Yarra Valley Arneis 2011 Fresh pear,
straw and spice are evident on the bouquet, with the palate providing a twist of
bitterness on the finish, in keeping with a European-styled white; will be fun to
pair with food. Screwcap. 12.8% alc. **Rating** 90 **To** 2014 $30 BE

ŸŸŸŸ Ingram Rd Yarra Valley Sauvignon Blanc 2012 **Rating** 87 **To** 2015 $19 BE
The Nemesis Yarra Valley Arneis 2012 **Rating** 87 **To** 2015 $30 BE

Helm   ★★★★★

19 Butt's Road, Murrumbateman, NSW 2582 **Region** Canberra District
T (02) 6227 5953 **www**.helmwines.com.au **Open** Thurs–Mon 10–5
Winemaker Ken and Stephanie Helm **Est.** 1973 **Dozens** 4000 **Vyds** 17ha
Ken Helm is an energetic promoter of his wines and of the Canberra District generally.
For some years now his wines have been of the highest standard, the Rieslings receiving
conspicuous show success and critical acclaim. Plantings have steadily increased, with riesling
(8ha), cabernet sauvignon (6ha), shiraz, gewurztraminer and chardonnay (1ha each), plus
smaller plantings of other varieties. Exports to Macau and Hong Kong.

ŸŸŸŸŸ Premium Canberra District Riesling 2012 Pale quartz; has far better balance
than its sibling, Classic Dry, at this stage, and it's not hard to see why Ken Helm
describes it as 'the vintage of my lifetime'; its ultra-cool conditions (including frost
in Jan '11) have produced a lean and racy wine; pure lime juice fruit on the ultra-
long palate and lingering aftertaste; will be exceptionally long-lived thanks to its
low pH (and arresting acidity). Screwcap. 10.3% alc. **Rating** 96 **To** 2032 $48
Classic Dry Canberra District Riesling 2012 Pale quartz; an almost painfully
intense palate, with unsweetened lime and lemon juice flavours resting on
a bedrock of minerally acidity reflecting the low pH. Must be cellared for a
minimum of 5 years. Screwcap. 10.5% alc. **Rating** 94 **To** 2032 $30

ŸŸŸŸŸ Half Dry Canberra District Riesling 2012 **Rating** 92 **To** 2015 $25
Canberra District Botrytis Riesling 2012 **Rating** 92 **To** 2017 $30

Hemera Estate   ★★★★★

1516 Barossa Valley Way, Lyndoch, SA 5351 **Region** Barossa Valley
T (08) 8524 4033 **www**.rosswines.com **Open** 7 days 10–5
Winemaker Alex Peel **Est.** 1999 **Dozens** 15 000 **Vyds** 44ha
Darius and Pauline Ross laid the foundation for Ross Estate Wines when they purchased
a vineyard that included two blocks of 75- and 90-year-old grenache. Also included were
blocks of 30-year-old riesling and semillon, and 14-year-old merlot; plantings of chardonnay
sauvignon blanc, cabernet sauvignon, cabernet franc, shiraz and tempranillo have followed.
Ross Estate was sold in 2012, and the business was in the process of changing its name to
Hemera Estate as the *2014 Wine Companion* was going to print. Exports to the US, Canada,
Denmark, Germany, Hong Kong and China.

ŸŸŸŸŸ Hemera Estate JDR Barossa Shiraz 2010 Full crimson-purple; a striking
full-bodied Shiraz, with layers of blackberry, plum, licorice and spice, French and
American oak testifying to a lengthy sojourn in bottle. The tannin structure is
exceptional, both adding to the flavours, but also introducing savoury, dry notes to
the finish. Screwcap. 14.5% alc. **Rating** 96 **To** 2035 $75
Hemera Estate Tier 1 2008 Utterly exceptional colour for an '08 wine, still
vivid purple-crimson; it is full-bodied, with black fruits to the fore, and fine,
ripe tannins. Quality oak also makes a balanced but positive contribution to a
remarkable wine. Screwcap. 14.5% alc. **Rating** 96 **To** 2035 $125

ROSS Limited Release Barossa GSM 2010 Very good hue; a most impressive example of what the Barossa Valley can achieve at its best with this blend; the medium-bodied palate has a totally satisfying array of red and black fruits, licorice and spice; the gently savoury tannins are a symbiotic backdrop. Screwcap. 14.5% alc. **Rating** 95 **To** 2020 $45

Ross Estate Single Vineyard Barossa Merlot 2010 From a vintage that gave Barossa every chance to impress; as well as the plum and mulberry fruit, there is a fine crosshatch of dark, savoury, black olive and forest in the background. Don't expect this every year. Screwcap. 14.5% alc. **Rating** 94 **To** 2025 $30

Hemera Estate Limited Release Cabernet Sauvignon 2010 Excellent full purple-crimson; a full-bodied Cabernet with luscious cassis, ripe fruit, and a framework of French oak; it has a long finish, and relaxes its grip slightly on the finish, which adds to its appeal. Screwcap. 14.5% alc. **Rating** 94 **To** 2030 $75

Ross Estate Single Vineyard Barossa Cabernet Sauvignon 2010 Good colour; an immediately attractive medium-bodied Cabernet with a juicy character to the blackcurrant and redcurrant varietal fruit, neatly offset by fine savoury tannins on a particularly long and well-balanced finish. Screwcap. 14.5% alc. **Rating** 94 **To** 2025 $35

ROSS Limited Release Barossa Lyndoch 2010 A blend of estate-grown cabernet sauvignon, cabernet franc and merlot, with a rich and succulent array of blackcurrant, redcurrant and spicy Christmas cake memories, oak and tannins moulded into the fruit. Vale 2010. Screwcap. 14.5% alc. **Rating** 94 **To** 2025 $45

♥♥♥♥♡ **Ross Estate Single Vineyard Barossa Shiraz 2010** Rating 92 To 2020 $35

Henley Hill Wines   ★★★☆

1 Mount Morton Road, Belgrave South, Vic 3160 (postal) **Region** Yarra Valley
T 0414 563 439 **www.**henleyhillwines.com.au **Open** Not
Winemaker Travis Bush (Contract) **Est.** 2003 **Dozens** 3350 **Vyds** 12.28ha
The history of Henley Hill dates back to 1849, when Rowland Hill began growing crops in the Yarra Valley; the home was built in the 1860s by David Mitchell, Dame Nellie Melba's father. The property adjoined Gulf Station, but when that property was sold in the 1930s the home was moved to Henley and re-erected by Clive and Hilda Hill. Clive then purchased an 80ha property adjoining Gulf Station, completing a full circle for the origins of the Henley name. In 2003 Debbie Hill (Clive's granddaughter), Errol Campbell (Debbie's father-in-law) and Nick and Andrew Peterson planted chardonnay, sauvignon blanc, pinot gris and shiraz. Errol, Nick and Andrew are long-time partners in various business ventures in the hospitality industry and property development. Exports to Sweden.

♥♥♥♥ **Yarra Valley Shiraz 2011** Bright, clear crimson-purple; the wine may only be light- to medium-bodied, and is not complex, but does have attractive plum and blackberry fruit, and a slippery/silky mouthfeel. Vineyard discipline and winery skills have resulted in a very creditable wine. Screwcap. 12.5% alc. **Rating** 89 **To** 2017 $22

Henry's Drive Vignerons   ★★★★

41 Hodgson Road, Padthaway, SA 5271 **Region** Padthaway
T (08) 8765 5251 **www.**henrysdrive.com **Open** 7 days 10–4
Winemaker Renae Hirsch **Est.** 1998 **Dozens** 150 000 **Vyds** 94.9ha
Named after the proprietor of the 19th-century mail coach service that once ran through their property, Henry's Drive Vignerons is the wine operation established by Kim Longbottom and her late husband Mark. Kim is continuing to build the family tradition of winemaking with brands such as Henry's Drive, Parson's Flat, The Trial of John Montford, Dead Letter Office, Pillar Box, Morse Code and The Postmistress. Exports to the UK, the US, Canada, Denmark, Singapore, China and NZ.

♍♍♍♍♍ Dead Letter Office Shiraz 2010 Deep, dense purple-crimson; as powerful and ✪ concentrated as the colour suggests, with black fruits, loads of bitter chocolate, spice and licorice on the full-bodied palate; happily, the tannins are controlled. Very well priced for a cellaring special. Screwcap. 14.5% alc. **Rating** 93 **To** 2030 $23

Reserve Padthaway Shiraz 2010 Deep, dark purple-red; a full-bodied Shiraz from the word go, charged with black fruits, dark chocolate, earth, licorice and oak; legs on the side of the glass are unusually obvious too. Screwcap. 15% alc. **Rating** 93 **To** 2030 $55

Reserve Padthaway Shiraz 2009 Full, dense purple-red; a very rich and exotic wine that largely manages to carry its alcohol, even on the aftertaste; blackberry, prune, plum and a dash of licorice are all in play. It's always a question how wines with high alcohol like this will develop, but I'll give it the benefit of the doubt. Screwcap. 15.5% alc. **Rating** 93 **To** 2029 $55

Parson's Flat Padthaway Shiraz Cabernet 2010 Full red-purple; I'm not enthralled by the oak, but there is a considerable volume of blackberry, blackcurrant, redcurrant and plum fruit on the bouquet and medium- to full-bodied palate alike; the tannins, too, are on the money. Screwcap. 14.5% alc. **Rating** 91 **To** 2030 $30

✪ **Morse Code Padthaway Shiraz 2010** Medium red-purple; a full-flavoured wine punching way above its price weight; the supple Padthaway profile to the black fruits is not quite sufficient to carry the oak, but that's hardly a capital crime. Screwcap. 14.5% alc. **Rating** 90 **To** 2016 $12

♍♍♍♍ Pillar Box Sangiovese Cabernet Franc Rose 2012 Rating 89 **To** 2013 $18

Padthaway Shiraz 2010 Rating 89 **To** 2020 $30

✪ **Pillar Box Red Padthaway Shiraz Cabernet Sauvignon Merlot 2010** Solid purple-red colour; reflects the good vintage with its array of red and black fruits, oak and tannins merely the postmen. Compelling value for now or later casual drinking. Screwcap. 14.5% alc. **Rating** 89 **To** 2016 $14

The Trial of John Montford Cabernet Sauvignon 2010 Rating 89 **To** 2025 $30

Pillar Box Reserve Cabernet Sauvignon 2010 Rating 88 **To** 2016 $18

Henschke   ★★★★★

1428 Keyneton Road, Keyneton, SA 5353 **Region** Eden Valley
T (08) 8564 8223 **www.**henschke.com.au **Open** Mon–Fri 9–4.30, Sat 9–12, public hols 10–3
Winemaker Stephen Henschke **Est.** 1868 **Dozens** 30 000 **Vyds** 121.72ha
Regarded as the best medium-sized red wine producer in Australia, Henschke has gone from strength to strength over the past three decades under the guidance of winemaker Stephen and viticulturist Prue Henschke. The red wines fully capitalise on the very old, low-yielding, high-quality vines and are superbly made with sensitive but positive use of new small oak: Hill of Grace is second only to Penfolds Grange as Australia's red wine icon (since 2005 sold with a screwcap). Exports to all major markets.

♍♍♍♍♍ Hill of Grace 2008 Deep purple-crimson, even after 5 years. It is explosively rich and decadent, with oceans of sumptuous black fruits which have soaked up the new and used French oak, and carry the alcohol with contemptuous ease. The grapes were picked early each morning between 9 and 13 March. Each block was separately made and matured, and the final blend is not made until shortly before bottling. Vino-Lok. 14.5% alc. **Rating** 98 **To** 2038 $600

Mount Edelstone 2010 So perfectly balanced and composed, its latent power may not be realised; black and red cherry fruits at its heart are complexed by lesser notes of plum and blackberry; the tannins are superb, the oak of high quality, and totally integrated on the very long, silky finish of this outstanding medium-bodied Shiraz. Vino-Lok. 14.5% alc. **Rating** 97 **To** 2035 $118

Tappa Pass Vineyard Selection Eden Valley Shiraz 2010 Bright colour; the bouquet is firmly in a black fruit spectrum, with blackberry and a touch of smoked meat/charcuterie; the medium- to full-bodied palate follows on with a complex array of flavours, each demanding to be heard, as do the savoury tannins and oak. Will be very, very, long-lived. Vino-Lok. 14.5% alc. **Rating** 96 **To** 2040 $84

Cyril Henschke 2009 An 81/13/6% blend of cabernet sauvignon, cabernet franc and merlot; French oak (40% new). Dark, dense red-purple; classic density and power, blackcurrant, superb cedary tannins, harmonious flavour/texture; just enough savoury/earthy notes. Screwcap. 14%alc. **Rating** 96 **To** 2039 $135

Julius Eden Valley Riesling 2012 Straw-green; lemon competes on equal ground with lime on the blossom-filled bouquet and brightly framed palate, slatey/minerally acidity balancing all that has gone before. A long future in store. Screwcap. 11.5% alc. **Rating** 95 **To** 2027 $33

Johann's Garden 2012 A 66/29/5% blend of grenache, viognier and shiraz (for structure); 3-4-year-old oak 12 months then blended for bottling. Good colour; considerable texture, almost viscous; liqueur cherry/raspberry; spicy, wonderful grenache; very good mouthfeel; black fruits, licorice, glossy finish. Screwcap. 14.5% alc. **Rating** 95 **To** 2019 $45

Lenswood Blanc de Noir NV 100% estate-grown pinot noir; there is a beguiling fruity sweetness to the finish, although the dosage is low. Bottle fermented and left on lees in bottle to age; multiple vintages from '97 to '09 were combined in an assemblage-style blend in March '11. Crown seal. 12% alc. **Rating** 95 **To** 2014 $50

Green's Hill Lenswood Riesling 2012 Rating 94 **To** 2022 $25

✪ **Peggy's Hill Eden Valley Riesling 2012** Light straw-green; the alcohol reflects early picking to retain maximum acidity, not the retention of residual sugar; lime, apple and scented bath talc are seamlessly joined on the fragrant bouquet and long palate alike; a great vintage also played its part in demonstrating the sort of value Riesling can provide. Screwcap. 11.5% alc. **Rating** 94 **To** 2022 $20

Joseph Hill Gewurztraminer 2012 Rating 94 **To** 2020 $30

Louis 2010 Rating 94 **To** 2025 $23

Coralinga Adelaide Hills Sauvignon Blanc 2012 Rating 94 **To** 2014 $27

Eleanor's Cottage Eden Valley Adelaide Hills Sauvignon Blanc Semillon 2012 Rating 94 **To** 2015 $24

Littlehampton Innes Vineyard Adelaide Hills Pinot Gris 2012 Rating 94 **To** 2015 $28

Keyneton Euphonium 2010 Rating 94 **To** 2035 $49

Stone Jar Tempranillo Graciano 2010 Rating 94 **To** 2018 $45

🍷🍷🍷🍷🍷 **Louis 2012 Rating** 93 **To** 2017 $25

Cranes Eden Valley Chardonnay 2012 Rating 93 **To** 2018 $28

Henry's Seven 2012 Rating 93 **To** 2017 $32

The Rose Grower Nebbiolo 2010 Rating 93 **To** 2020 $55

Hentley Farm Wines ★★★★★

Cnr Jenke Road/Gerald Roberts Road, Seppeltsfield, SA 5355 **Region** Barossa Valley
T (08) 8562 8427 **www**.hentleyfarm.com.au **Open** 7 days 10–5
Winemaker Andrew Quin **Est.** 1999 **Dozens** 10 000 **Vyds** 38.21ha
Keith and Alison Hentschke purchased Hentley Farm in 1997, as an old vineyard and mixed farming property. Keith has thoroughly impressive credentials, having studied agricultural science at Roseworthy, and then wine marketing, obtaining an MBA. During the 1990s he had a senior production role with Orlando, before moving on to manage one of Australia's largest vineyard management companies, and from 2002 to '06 he worked with Nepenthe. Shiraz (26.83ha), grenache (6.46ha), cabernet sauvignon (4ha), zinfandel (0.78ha) and viognier (0.14ha) are now in production. The vineyard, situated among rolling hills on the banks of Greenock Creek, has red clay loam soils overlaying shattered limestone, lightly rocked slopes and little topsoil. Exports to the US and other major markets.

🍷🍷🍷🍷🍷 **The Creation Barossa Valley Shiraz 2011** Each year winemaker Andrew Quin selects a single block which he feels has something unique to offer; this vintage led to the decision to rack-dry the grapes for 2 weeks prior to crushing and fermentation. The colour is a deep, dense purple-crimson; the palate is concentrated, luscious and velvety. One has the image of a giant umbrella opened above Block G (keeping the rain at bay), the end result this remarkable full-bodied wine, the alcohol lost in the folds of the fruit. Cork. 15% alc. **Rating** 96 **To** 2026 $115

Barossa Valley Shiraz 2010 Deep crimson-purple; a wine built for the ages, overflowing with black fruits and quality oak on the bouquet that feed through to the full-bodied palate, joined there by ripe, savoury tannins. Yes, this is a big wine, but everything is in great balance. Top-quality grapes, top-quality wine. Screwcap. 14.7% alc. **Rating** 96 **To** 2040 $32

Museum Release The Beast Barossa Valley Shiraz 2008 This is full-bodied, yet not without elegance, and while blackberry, plum and dark chocolate are emerging, it is a little strange that the museum release for a wine with a drink-to date of 2033 should come only 3 years after the initial release. Cork. 15% alc. **Rating** 96 $105

Museum Release The Beauty Barossa Valley Shiraz 2008 Deep purple-crimson; this is less imposingly monumental than the Museum Release Clos Otto, although this is a relative assessment; it is full of black fruits, licorice, dark chocolate and ripe, but balanced, tannins; these have sufficient power to carry the alcohol. Cork. 15% alc. **Rating** 95 **To** 2030 $70

The Beast Barossa Valley Shiraz 2011 A very complex bouquet and palate bring blackberry, plum, licorice, spice and dark chocolate, the tannins full and ripe, oak well handled. This is another example of the remarkable terroir of Hentley Farm. Cork. 14.6% alc. **Rating** 94 **To** 2026 $80

Clos Otto Barossa Valley Shiraz 2011 Full purple-crimson, excellent for the vintage. It must have taken courage (and constant vineyard work) to achieve this alcohol, needed for the development of the plush, spiced plums and blackberry fruit, with a farewell savoury twist. Cork. 15% alc. **Rating** 94 **To** 2026 $150

Museum Release Clos Otto Barossa Valley Shiraz 2008 Dark, deep colour; a huge wine in a huge bottle and velvet back label. I am an unabashed admirer of Hentley Farm's red wines, but this operates firmly on the principle of bigger is better, and biggest is best. Cork. 15% alc. **Rating** 94 **To** 2038 $200

Museum Release The Beauty Barossa Valley Shiraz 2007 A sister to the more highly rated and priced Hentley Farm The Beast, and I prefer this wine; here distinct dark chocolate nuances join forces with the blackberry fruit and quality oak to provide a more rich, supple and round palate, the length and finish without any break in line. Cork. 15% alc. **Rating** 94 **To** 2027 $70

ŢŢŢŢŢ **Eden Valley Riesling 2012** **Rating** 93 **To** 2022 $23 BE
Museum Release The Beast Shiraz 2007 **Rating** 93 **To** 2022 $103
✪ **Barossa Valley Cabernet Sauvignon 2012** Medium crimson-purple; three east-facing blocks with minimal topsoil produced high-quality cabernet grapes, and were picked early enough to preserve authentic black olive/forest notes to the central pillar of cassis fruit; the tannins are fine-grained, the oak well integrated and balanced. Screwcap. 14% alc. **Rating** 93 **To** 2027 $25
von Kasper Cabernet Sauvignon 2011 **Rating** 93 **To** 2026 $80
Barossa Valley Rose 2011 **Rating** 92 **To** 2013 $23
The Noble Exception 2011 **Rating** 92 **To** 2014 $26
Barossa Valley Viognier 2012 **Rating** 91 **To** 2014 $43 BE
The Stray Mongrel 2012 **Rating** 91 **To** 2019 $25
✪ **Barossa Valley Rose 2012** Vivid fuchsia; the red cherry/raspberry aroma of the estate-grown grenache is a direct line to the pure fruit flavours of the palate, fruity yet bone dry. Won't fall over, but best young. Screwcap. 12.8% alc. **Rating** 90 **To** 2014 $19
The Beauty Barossa Valley Shiraz 2011 **Rating** 90 **To** 2017 $23 BE
Barossa Valley Shiraz 2011 **Rating** 90 **To** 2020 $25

Henty Estate   ★★★★★

657 Hensley Park Road, Hamilton, Vic 3300 (postal) **Region** Henty
T (03) 5572 4446 **www.henty-estate.com.au** **Open** Not
Winemaker Peter Dixon **Est.** 1991 **Dozens** 1400 **Vyds** 7ha
Peter and Glenys Dixon have hastened slowly with Henty Estate. In 1991 they began the planting of 4.5ha of shiraz, 1ha each of cabernet sauvignon and chardonnay, and 0.5ha of

riesling. In their words, 'we avoided the temptation to make wine until the vineyard was mature', establishing the winery in 2003. Encouraged by neighbour John Thomson, they have limited the yield to 3–4 tonnes per hectare on the VSP-trained, dry-grown vineyard.

ΤΤΤΤΤ **Riesling 2012** Light, bright straw-green; underlines what a great region (however
✪ forgotten in general riesling dissertations) Henty is; superfine, elegant and intense, with lime, apple and minerally acidity wound together in a seamless stream. Great bargain. Screwcap. 11.5% alc. **Rating** 95 **To** 2027 $20
Edward Shiraz 2010 Very good purple-crimson hue and depth; the fruit achieved full physiological ripeness allowing maturation in 100% new oak, half French, half Hungarian; intense, but supple, spicy black fruits run side by side with the oak. Screwcap. 13.7% alc. **Rating** 95 **To** 2030 $40

ΤΤΤΤΥ **Chardonnay 2011** Hand-picked and basket-pressed, with a portion matured in
✪ new French oak for 9 months. A classic cool-climate style with grapefruit to the fore on the long, juicy palate that has absorbed the oak. Great value. Screwcap. 12.8% alc. **Rating** 93 **To** 2020 $20
Shiraz 2010 Rating 93 **To** 2025 $24
✪ **Wannon Run Shiraz 2010** The colour is slightly less bright than that of its siblings, the black fruits and licorice supported by oak from shaved French barrels and staves in tank; the fruit is definitely the driver, with a juicy finish, the tannins superfine. Screwcap. 13.7% alc. **Rating** 90 **To** 2020 $16

Herbert Vineyard ★★★★

Bishop Road, Mount Gambier, SA 5290 **Region** Mount Gambier
T 0408 849 080 **www.**herbertvineyard.com.au **Open** By appt
Winemaker David Herbert **Est.** 1996 **Dozens** 550 **Vyds** 2.4ha
David and Trudy Herbert have planted 1.9ha of pinot noir, and a total of 0.5ha of cabernet sauvignon, merlot and pinot gris (the majority of the pinot noir is sold for sparkling wine). They have built a two-level (mini) winery overlooking a 1300-sq metre maze planted in 2000, which is reflected in the label logo.

ΤΤΤΤΥ **Barrel Number 1 Mount Gambier Pinot Noir 2010** One must assume that a single barrel was used to create this wine, and while there is a prominent seasoning of charry oak, there are red cherry and cold tea also on display; the palate is light-to medium-bodied, persistent and finely tannic. Screwcap. 13% alc. **Rating** 90 **To** 2017 $37 BE

ΤΤΤΤ **Mount Gambier Pinot Noir + 2011 Rating** 87 **To** 2015 $24 BE

Hesketh Wine Company ★★★★

76 Halifax Street, Adelaide, SA 5000 **Region** Various
T (08) 8232 8622 **www.**heskethwinecompany.com.au **Open** Not
Winemaker Various **Est.** 2006 **Dozens** 20 000
The Hesketh Wine Company is a New World version of the French négociant éleveur, commonly known in Australia as a virtual winery, and is owned by Jonathon Hesketh, wife Trish and children. Jonathon spent seven years as the Global Sales & Marketing Manager of Wirra Wirra, two and a half years as General Manager of Distinguished Vineyards in NZ working with the Möet Hennessy wine and champagne portfolio, plus the Petaluma group. He also happens to be the son of Robert Hesketh, one of the key players in the development of many facets of the SA wine industry. The model for Hesketh Wine Company is to find wines that best express the regions they come from. Exports to the US, Canada, Thailand, Singapore and NZ.

ΤΤΤΤΥ **Thirsty Dog Coonawarra Cabernet Sauvignon 2010** Good hue; flooded
✪ with cassis fruit on the bouquet and palate alike, although oak also makes a contribution; the tannins are soft, adding to the overall fleshy and welcoming appeal of the wine. Screwcap. 14% alc. **Rating** 92 **To** 2018 $20

The Protagonist Barossa Shiraz 2010 An elegant expression of the region with red fruits a feature on the bouquet, also showing licorice and a splash of briary complexity; the palate is juicy, fun-packed and uncomplicated, with a long and even finish. Screwcap. 14.5% alc. **Rating** 91 **To** 2016 $23 BE

Scissor Hands Clare Valley Riesling 2012 Bright colour, and restrained on the bouquet, offering glimpses of lemon pith and lime juice; the palate is dry, taut and showing plenty of grip on the finish; a little time will be rewarded. Screwcap. 12.5% alc. **Rating** 90 **To** 2018 $23 BE

Bright Young Things Adelaide Hills Sauvignon Blanc 2012 A vibrant combination of crushed nettle, cut grass and tropical fruit is evident on the bouquet; the palate shows good concentration and a fleshy finish that is long and harmonious; balance is the key. Screwcap. 13.5% alc. **Rating** 90 **To** 2015 $23 BE

Usual Suspects McLaren Vale Shiraz 2010 Good colour; a tribute to the '10 vintage, with barrel fermentation and maturation in older oak leaving clear air for the black fruits supported by fine and savoury tannins. Uncomplicated, and all the better for that. Screwcap. 14.5% alc. **Rating** 89 **To** 2018 $20

The Protagonist Barossa Shiraz 2009 While the colour isn't entirely convincing, once the wine enters the mouth it's a different story, with very attractive plum and blackberry fruit, soft but positive tannins, and oak a bystander. Good value. Screwcap. 14% alc. **Rating** 89 **To** 2017 $20

Wild at Heart Rose 2012 Rating 88 **To** 2014 $15 BE

Rules of Engagement Pinot Gris 2012 Rating 87 **To** 2014 $15 BE

Hewitson   ★★★★★

1 Seppeltsfield Road, Dorrien, SA 5355 **Region** Adelaide Zone
T (08) 8212 6233 **www.**hewitson.com.au **Open** 7 days 9–5
Winemaker Dean Hewitson **Est.** 1996 **Dozens** 35 000 **Vyds** 4.5ha

Dean Hewitson was a winemaker at Petaluma for 10 years, during which time he managed to do three vintages in France and one in Oregon as well as undertaking his Masters at the University of California (Davis). It is hardly surprising that the wines are immaculately made from a technical viewpoint. Dean has managed to source 30-year-old riesling from the Eden Valley and 70-year-old shiraz from McLaren Vale; he also makes a Barossa Valley Mourvedre from vines planted in 1853 at Rowland Flat and Barossa Valley Shiraz and Grenache from 60-year-old vines at Tanunda. Between 2008 and '10 Dean progressively established his own winery at Dorrien, completing it in time to process the '10 vintage. A new cellar door opened mid 2012. Exports to the UK, the US and other major markets.

Old Garden Barossa Valley Mourvedre 2010 Clear crimson; a wine that is complete and confident in itself, effortlessly filling the bouquet and palate with its small red and black fruits, a shimmer of tannins throughout, and a lingering finish. Vines planted 1853. Screwcap. 14.5% alc. **Rating** 97 **To** 2030 $120

Private Cellar Barossa Valley Shiraz Mourvedre 2010 Purple-crimson; it's not hard to understand why Dean Hewitson boldly puts 'cellaring potential 20 years' on the front label; this is a complex and intense wine, from exceedingly old vines; satsuma plum, liqueur cherries, spice and fruitcake fill the palate from start to finish, the tannins fine and ripe, oak merely a vehicle. Screwcap. 14% alc. **Rating** 96 **To** 2040 $120

The Dorrien Bank Barossa Valley Shiraz 2010 Bright purple-crimson; the bouquet has red and black fruits in a fine web of French oak, the medium-bodied palate providing endless amounts of the same, the tannins at once savoury and silky. Screwcap. 14% alc. **Rating** 95 **To** 2035 $50

Gun Metal Eden Valley Riesling 2012 Pale straw-green; a classically restrained and precise Riesling, the lime, lemon and apple flavours built around a framework of crisp, steely acidity. Screwcap. 12% alc. **Rating** 94 **To** 2027 $26

The Mad Hatter McLaren Vale Shiraz 2010 From a single Blewitt Springs vineyard. Strong crimson-purple, it immediately shows the impact of over 20 months' maturation in new French oak; the fruit is there, and the mouthfeel is silky and supple, so there is no doubt the oak influence will become progressively less obvious than it is now. Screwcap. 14.5% alc. **Rating** 94 **To** 2030 $70

Miss Harry 2010 Predominantly grenache and shiraz, with small amounts of mourvedre, carignan and cinsaut, sourced from 25 separate vineyard plots, five over 100 years old. Full, clear crimson-purple; medium-bodied, there is wonderful tension between the array of predominantly black fruits and the savoury tannins on the finish, with added complexity from quality oak. The only question is why it is so underpriced. Screwcap. 14% alc. **Rating** 94 **To** 2030 $23

ŶŶŶŶŶ **LuLu Adelaide Hills Sauvignon Blanc 2012 Rating** 92 **To** 2013 $23
Truffle Row Shiraz Marsanne Roussanne 2011 Rating 92 **To** 2019 $35
Ned & Henry's Shiraz Mourvedre 2011 Rating 90 **To** 2014 $25

Heydon Estate ★★★★★

325 Tom Cullity Drive, Wilyabrup, WA 6280 **Region** Margaret River
T (08) 9755 6995 **www.**heydonestate.com.au **Open** Thurs–Mon 10–5
Winemaker Mark Messenger **Est.** 1988 **Vyds** 10ha
Margaret River dentist George Heydon (and wife Mary) have been involved in the region's wine industry since 1995. They became 50% partners in Arlewood, and when that partnership was dissolved in 2004 the Heydons relinquished their interest in the Arlewood brand but retained the property and the precious 2ha of cabernet sauvignon and 2.5ha of Gingin clone chardonnay planted in '88. Additional plantings from '95 include Dijon chardonnay clones, sauvignon blanc, semillon, shiraz and petit verdot. The first Cabernet made under the Heydon ownership, the '04 W.G. Grace Cabernet Sauvignon, won the trophy for Best Cabernet Sauvignon at the Margaret River Wine Show '06. The estate is now biodynamic, near-neighbour Vanya Cullen having no doubt inspired the decision. And if it wasn't already very obvious, George is a cricket tragic. Exports to the UK, Singapore and Hong Kong.

ŶŶŶŶŶ **W.G. Grace Single Vineyard Margaret River Cabernet Sauvignon 2008**
Deep crimson, purple hue; the essency bouquet delivers a fragrant and alluring array of cassis, violets, cedar and well-handled high-quality oak; the palate is focused and fleshy on entry, with fine-grained tannins aplenty, providing drive to the luscious fruits of offer. Screwcap. 14% alc. **Rating** 96 **To** 2030 $60 BE
The Willow Single Vineyard Margaret River Chardonnay 2008 Pale gold, green; ripe grapefruit, fresh fig, straw and charry oak are all evident on the bouquet; the palate is lean, with the fruit slow to reveal itself as the strong charry oak dominates on the mid-palate; quite extraordinary given the age of the wine. Screwcap. 13% alc. **Rating** 94 **To** 2020 $50 BE

Higher Plane ★★★★★

165 Warner Glen Road, Forest Grove, WA 6286 **Region** Margaret River
T (08) 9755 9000 **www.**higherplanewines.com.au **Open** At Juniper Estate
Winemaker Mark Messenger **Est.** 1996 **Dozens** 2500 **Vyds** 14.55ha
In late 2006 Higher Plane was purchased by Roger Hill and Gillian Anderson (of Juniper Estate), but kept as a stand-alone brand, with different distributors, etc. The Higher Plane vineyards are planted to all of the key varieties, chardonnay and sauvignon blanc foremost, with cabernet sauvignon, merlot, tempranillo, fiano, semillon, cabernet franc, malbec and petit verdot making up the rest of the plantings. Exports to Canada, Denmark and Hong Kong.

ŶŶŶŶŶ **Margaret River Chardonnay 2011** Whole bunch-pressed direct to French oak barrels for fermentation and 10 months' lees contact, the wine a best barrels selection. In the modern Australian style, tightly focused on the fruit rather than the oak, white peach/grapefruit with natural acidity all coalescing on the long palate. Screwcap. 12.5% alc. **Rating** 95 **To** 2021 $35

Margaret River Sauvignon Blanc 2011 Hand-picked and whole bunch-pressed direct to barrel for fermentation and 10 months' lees contact. A final barrel selection was made of a notably fresh, crisp and lively wine, with bell-clear varietal fruit expression and well-integrated oak. Astute winemaking. Screwcap. 12.5% alc. Rating 94 To 2014 $27

 South by Southwest Margaret River Chardonnay 2011 Some straw colour development along with the green; an extremely elegant Chardonnay, with all the Margaret River qualities on show, and in perfect balance, white stone fruit to the fore along with some melon; the French oak influence is fully integrated and balanced on the long palate. Screwcap. 13.5% alc. **Rating** 93 To 2016 $20
Margaret River Merlot 2011 Rating 91 To 2021 $35

Hill-Smith Estate   ★★★☆

Flaxmans Valley Road, Eden Valley, SA 5235 **Region** Eden Valley
T (08) 8561 3200 **www**.hillsmithestate.com **Open** By appt
Winemaker Kevin Glastonbury **Est.** 1979 **Dozens** 5000 **Vyds** 12ha
The vineyard sits at an altitude of 510m, providing a cool climate that extends the growing season; rocky, acidic soil, coupled with winter rainfall and dry summers, results in modest crops of sauvignon blanc. As an added bonus, the vineyard is surrounded by conservation park.

Eden Valley Sauvignon Blanc 2012 The 33-year-old sauvignon blanc vines are some of the oldest in Australia. Wild yeast-fermented, the wine has good tactile character, but expression of varietal character is modest. Screwcap. 13% alc. Rating 89 To 2014 $24

Hillbillé   ★★★★☆

Blackwood Valley Estate, Balingup Road, Nannup, WA 6275 **Region** Blackwood Valley
T (08) 9481 0888 **www**.hillbille.com **Open** By appt
Winemaker Woodlands Wines (Stuart Watson), Naturaliste Vintners (Bruce Dukes)
Est. 1998 **Dozens** 5000 **Vyds** 18ha
Gary and Rai Bettridge have planted chardonnay, shiraz, cabernet sauvignon, merlot, semillon, sauvignon blanc and viognier on their 75ha family property. The vineyard is situated in the Blackwood Valley between Balingup and Nannup, which the RAC describes as 'the most scenic drive in the southwest of WA'. Part of the grape production is sold to other makers, the remainder vinified for the Hillbillé label. Exports to Japan, Singapore, Hong Kong and China.

 Estate Cabernet Merlot 2010 Good purple-crimson; a most attractive blend, awash with juicy cassis, redcurrant and plum fruit; the French oak is positive, the tannins fine and ripe; the overall balance of the medium-bodied palate cannot be faulted. Screwcap. 13.8% alc. **Rating** 94 To 2020 $18

 Estate Semillon Sauvignon Blanc 2012 Pale straw-green; considered unnecessary to give the percentage contribution of the varieties on the back label, but it does have its share of tropical fruits to accompany the citrus/lemongrass flavours of the semillon. Screwcap. 13% alc. **Rating** 90 To 2014 $18

Hillcrest Vineyard   ★★★★★

31 Phillip Road, Woori Yallock, Vic 3139 **Region** Yarra Valley
T (03) 5964 6689 **www**.hillcrestvineyard.com.au **Open** By appt
Winemaker David and Tanya Bryant **Est.** 1970 **Dozens** 1000 **Vyds** 8.1ha
The small, effectively dry-grown vineyard was established by Graeme and Joy Sweet, who ultimately sold it to David and Tanya Bryant. The pinot noir, chardonnay, merlot and cabernet sauvignon grown on the property have always been of the highest quality and, when Coldstream Hills was in its infancy, were particularly important resources for it. For some years the wines were made by Phillip Jones (Bass Phillip), but the winemaking is now carried out onsite by David and Tanya Bryant.

🍷🍷🍷🍷🍷 **Premium Yarra Valley Pinot Noir 2010** Not only are the colours of the three Hillcrest Pinots from 2010 identical, but so is the stated alcohol on the label, a statistic that has a degree of elasticity at the best of times. This is far superior to the other two wines, however good they may be, with plum and black cherry aromas introducing gorgeous supple, round and mouth-filling palate with its layers of richly robed fruit and spice flavours. Diam. 13.1% alc. **Rating** 97 **To** 2020 $60
Premium Yarra Valley Cabernet Sauvignon 2010 Strong colour; has the depth (and, to a degree, width) that is the hallmark of Hillcrest cabernet. Intense blackcurrant fruit, and a suggestion of black olive, are just the starting point, the ultimate strength – and future – of the wine lying with its outstanding fine tannin structure. Cork. 13.1% alc. **Rating** 96 **To** 2030 $60
Premium Yarra Valley Chardonnay 2011 Gleaming green-yellow; a wine that manages to combine complexity with finesse, its barrel-ferment characters submerged in the interplay of white peach, grapefruit and nectarine flavours, plus balanced acidity. Cork. 12.6% alc. **Rating** 95 **To** 2020 $60
Reserve Chardonnay 2010 Full green-yellow; a complex, rich and layered wine, with white peach, nectarine, fig and cashew all contributing to the bouquet and palate; a prior sample was the result of random oxidation, and bore no resemblance to this wine. Cork. 12.9% alc. **Rating** 94 **To** 2015 $100

🍷🍷🍷🍷🍷 **Village Yarra Valley Chardonnay 2011** **Rating** 92 **To** 2018 $25
Premium Yarra Valley Pinot Noir 2011 **Rating** 92 **To** 2018 $60
Village Yarra Valley Pinot Noir 2011 **Rating** 90 **To** 2016 $25

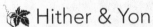 Hither & Yon ★★★★

17 High Street, Willunga, SA 5172 **Region** McLaren Vale
T (08) 8556 2082 **www.**hitherandyon.com.au **Open** Fri–Mon 9–3
Winemaker Richard Leask **Est.** 2012 **Dozens** 1000 **Vyds** 82ha
At first blush it might seem strange that Richard and Malcolm Leask have taken so long to take the plunge and establish their own grapegrowing and winemaking business, having arrived in McLaren Vale with their parents in the 1970s to begin grapegrowing. Admittedly, they were young at the time, but have since clocked up tens of thousands of hours prowling every corner of the region they love so much. The key change came in Dec 2011 when they sold their 50% interest in the Pertaringa brand to co-owners Geoff Hardy and family. Part of the change was the acquisition by Richard and Malcolm of 100% of the Pertaringa vineyard, and they now have over 80ha of vines spread across the region. The first releases are from '11, a tough act, but with much more to come. For the foreseeable future, they will be grapegrowers more than winemakers. Richard makes the wines at Kangarilla Road, and Malcolm is in charge of production, marketing and sales. While shiraz dominates the Old Jarvie (formerly Pertaringa) and Breakneck Vineyards, the smaller Sand Road and Hunt Road plantings have emerging varieties aglianico, nero d'Avola, red frontignac, tannat and white frontignac.

🍷🍷🍷🍷🍷 **McLaren Vale Shiraz 2011** Deep purple-red; a big, bold, muscular Shiraz from 'that vintage', with black fruits, dark chocolate and layers of tannins; a single vineyard, single block wine snatched from the jaws of defeat. ProCork. 14.5% alc. **Rating** 93 **To** 2026 $44
McLaren Vale Cabernet Sauvignon 2011 Very good hue and depth for the vintage; the bouquet promises, and the palate delivers, ripe cassis fruit, dark chocolate and spice; there is no shortage of tannins, maybe even a surfeit. ProCork. 14.5% alc. **Rating** 93 **To** 2026 $44

Hobbs of Barossa Ranges ★★★★★

Cnr Flaxman's Valley Road/Randalls Road, Angaston, SA 5353 **Region** Barossa Valley
T 0427 177 740 **www.**hobbsvintners.com.au **Open** At Artisans of Barossa
Winemaker Pete Schell, Chris Ringland (Consultant) **Est.** 1998 **Dozens** 1100 **Vyds** 6.22ha
Hobbs of Barossa Ranges is the high-profile, if somewhat challenging, venture of Greg and Allison Hobbs. The estate vineyards revolve around 1ha of shiraz planted in 1908, another hectare planted in '88, a further planted in '97, and 1.82ha planted in 2004. In '09 0.4ha

of old white frontignac was removed, giving space for another small planting of shiraz. The viticultural portfolio is completed with 0.6ha of semillon planted in the 1960s, and an inspired 0.6ha of viognier ('88). All of the wines made by Peter Schell (at Spinifex) push the envelope. The only conventionally made wine is the Shiraz Viognier, with a production of 130 dozen. Gregor is an Amarone-style Shiraz in full-blooded table wine mode, and a quartet of dessert wines are produced by cane cutting followed by further desiccation on racks. Exports to the US, France, The Netherlands, Russia, Taiwan, Hong Kong and China.

ŢŢŢŢŢ **Gregor Shiraz 2010** As ever, a challenging wine, best understood in the context of Italian Amarone. The estate-grown, hand-picked grapes are placed on trays and partially dried; after fermentation the wine spent 24 months in new French oak. It has, of course, a large volume of rich flavour, yet is graceful, not extractive. Cork. 15.7% alc. **Rating** 95 **To** 2030 $130

Shiraz 2010 Deeply coloured, the wine has even higher alcohol than Gregor. This spent 24 months in new French oak, and is trenchantly full-bodied, with black fruits, bitter chocolate and persistent tannins. 130 dozen made. Cork. 15.8% alc. **Rating** 94 **To** 2025 $130

Viognier 2006 The colour is a glorious gold tinged with green; this wine was better when first tasted 3 years ago than the '06 White Fronti, and still is, the acidity fresher, the wine with more texture to its luscious tangerine, cumquat and honey flavours. 375ml. Screwcap. 9.4% alc. **Rating** 94 **To** 2015 $39

ŢŢŢŢŢ ✪ **Semillon 2007** Deep, but bright gold; hand-picked then rack-dried before fermentation; intensely sweet, and without the complexity of botrytis; it doesn't really improve with age, just slowly loses its sweetness. 375ml. Screwcap. 10.1% alc. **Rating** 92 **To** 2014 $39

White Frontignac 2006 **Rating** 92 **To** 2015 $39
Shiraz Viognier 2010 **Rating** 91 **To** 2018 $110

Hochkirch Wines   ★★★☆

Hamilton Highway, Tarrington, Vic 3301 **Region** Henty
T (03) 5573 5200 **Open** 11–5 by appt
Winemaker John Nagorcka **Est.** 1997 **Dozens** 4000 **Vyds** 8ha
Jennifer and John Nagorcka have developed Hochkirch in response to the very cool climate: growing season temperatures are similar to those in Burgundy. A high-density planting pattern was implemented, with a low fruiting wire taking advantage of soil warmth in the growing season, and the focus was placed on pinot noir (5ha), with lesser quantities of riesling, chardonnay, semillon and shiraz. The Nagorckas have moved to certified biodynamic viticulture: vines are not irrigated, and no synthetic fungicides, pesticides or fertilisers are used. Jennifer and John, together with Jennifer's sister Dianne, are also owners of the Tarrington Vineyards label. Exports to Japan.

ŢŢŢŢŢ **Riesling 2011** Pale straw-green; has lovely tingling fruit sherbet flavours on the tip of the tongue, but the decision to use cork is bizarre – as the '10 Tarrington Vineyards Chardonnay shows. 12.1% alc. **Rating** 90 **To** 2013 $35

ŢŢŢŢ **Tarrington Vineyards Chardonnay 2010** **Rating** 89 **To** 2016 $33
Tarrington Vineyards Pinot Noir 2010 **Rating** 88 **To** 2014 $45
Syrah 2009 **Rating** 88 **To** 2015 $45

Hoddles Creek Estate   ★★★★★

505 Gembrook Road, Hoddles Creek, Vic 3139 **Region** Yarra Valley
T (03) 5967 4692 **www.**hoddlescreekestate.com.au **Open** By appt
Winemaker Franco D'Anna, Lucas Hoorn, Chris Beadle **Est.** 1997 **Dozens** 20 000
Vyds 33.3ha
In 1997, the D'Anna family decided to establish a vineyard on the property that had been in the family since 1960. The vineyards (chardonnay, pinot noir, sauvignon blanc, cabernet sauvignon, pinot gris, merlot and pinot blanc) are hand-pruned and hand-harvested. A 300-tonne, split-level winery was completed in 2003. Son Franco is the viticulturist and

winemaker; he started to work in the family liquor store at 13, graduating to chief wine buyer by the time he was 21, then completed a Bachelor of Commerce degree at Melbourne University before studying viticulture at CSU. A vintage at Coldstream Hills, then consulting help from Peter Dredge of Red Edge and Mario Marson (ex Mount Mary), has put an old head on young shoulders. Exports to South Africa, Singapore and Japan.

ŸŸŸŸŸ **1er Yarra Valley Chardonnay 2011** Bright straw-green; has the finesse and intensity typical of Hoddles Creek Estate Chardonnays, with white flesh stone fruit built on a platform of minerally acidity. The wine has almost entirely absorbed the new and used French oak in which it was fermented. Screwcap. 13.2% alc. Rating 95 To 2018 $40

✪ **Wickhams Road Yarra Valley Chardonnay 2012** Light straw-green; the Yarra Valley gives this barrel-fermented wine the edge over its Geelong counterpart; it achieves all the elegance and varietal expression, but with an extra dimension to its white peach and citrus fruit flavours; the French oak has simply been a vehicle; filtered, but not fined. Screwcap. 13% alc. Rating 94 To 2017 $17

Yarra Valley Chardonnay 2011 Light straw-green; Franco d'Anna has long proved his mastery of chardonnay; it is beautifully balanced, its fruit aromas and flavours at the very heart of white stone fruit, albeit supported by citrussy acidity and barrel fermentation in used French oak barriques. Screwcap. 13.2% alc. Rating 94 To 2017 $20

ŸŸŸŸŸ **Wickhams Road Gippsland Chardonnay 2012** Light straw-green; an
✪ ultimate exercise in elegance, achieving intense varietal flavour in a light-bodied frame, the oak (15% new French) perfectly integrated. Screwcap. 13% alc. Rating 93 To 2017 $17

✪ **Wickhams Road Gippsland Pinot Noir 2012** Bright, clear crimson; a perfectly made Pinot Noir from an outstanding vintage at a bargain price; red and black cherry fruit is the foundation of the bouquet and palate alike, oak a vehicle, not an end in itself. Great now for its purity, and in 3-4 years time for its added complexity. Screwcap. 13.2% alc. Rating 93 To 2019 $17

✪ **Wickhams Road Mornington Peninsula Pinot Noir 2012** Bright, clear crimson with a touch of purple; counterintuitively, is slightly more fleshy in the mouth than the Wickhams Road Gippsland Pinot, with some plum joining the cherry; the bouquet, too, is a little more complex. So the style is different, but the quality and development outlook are the same. Screwcap. 13.5% alc. Rating 93 To 2019 $17

1er Yarra Valley Pinot Blanc 2012 Rating 90 To 2016 $40

Hoeyfield ★★★

17 Jetty Road, Birchs Bay, Tas 7162 **Region** Southern Tasmania
T (03) 6267 4149 **Open** By appt
Winemaker Contract **Est.** 1995 **Dozens** 150 **Vyds** 0.5ha
Richard and Jill Pringle-Jones run a postage stamp-sized vineyard of 0.25ha each of pinot noir and chardonnay, planted on a vine-by-vine basis. When they purchased Hoeyfield in 2004, plantings of chardonnay and pinot noir had spread over 1998, '00, and '02; Richard and Jill added more pinot noir (the new Dijon clone 777) in '04 and '05. Following Richard's retirement from sharebroking, Hoeyfield takes up much of his retirement time.

ŸŸŸŸ **D'Entrecasteaux Channel Pinot Noir 2011** Light red; from one of the coolest parts of Tasmania, it has a haunting, perfumed bouquet, the light-bodied palate translating that perfume into strawberry compote, herbs and spices. Does need a little more conviction. Screwcap. 13.5% alc. Rating 89 To 2015 $25

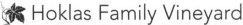

Hoklas Family Vineyard NR

PO Box 521, Tanunda, SA 5352 **Region** Barossa Valley
T (08) 8524 9006 **www.hoklaswines.com.au** **Open** Not
Winemaker Dean Hoklas **Est.** 2004 **Dozens** 120 **Vyds** 1ha

The property on which the micro vineyard is established has been in the Hoklas family since 1860, and it is known that a vineyard was planted on the property in the 1890s (a time of boom) and removed in the 1900s, possibly due to World War I. In 2001 fifth-generation Dean and wife Julie, together with sons Caleb and Isaac, planted 0.7ha of shiraz and 0.3ha of cabernet sauvignon, and the vineyard has since been trained, pruned and hand-picked by the family and friends. Dean, with 15 years of winery experience, manages the winemaking, making the wines in a restored stone barn built in the late 1800s.

Hollick ★★★★☆

Riddoch Highway, Coonawarra, SA 5263 **Region** Coonawarra
T (08) 8737 2318 **www**.hollick.com **Open** Mon–Fri 9–5, w'ends & public hols 10–5
Winemaker Ian Hollick, Matthew Caldersmith **Est.** 1983 **Dozens** 30000 **Vyds** 87ha
Owned by Ian and Wendy Hollick, and winner of many trophies (including the most famous of all, the Jimmy Watson), its wines are well crafted. The lavish cellar door and restaurant complex is one of the focal points for tourism in Coonawarra. The Hollicks have progressively expanded their vineyard holdings: the first is the Neilson's Block, one of the original John Riddoch selections, but used as a dairy farm from 1910 to '75, when the Hollicks planted cabernet sauvignon and merlot. The second is the Wilgha Vineyard, with mature dry-grown cabernet sauvignon and shiraz. The last is the Red Ridge Vineyard in Wrattonbully, which includes trial plantings of tempranillo and sangiovese. Exports to most major markets.

ᵠᵠᵠᵠᵠ Bond Road Chardonnay 2011 Mid gold, bright; the bouquet offers fragrant nectarine, lemon curd and anise; the palate is racy and fine, with fresh acidity highlighting the grapefruit notes; lively and focused on the finish. Screwcap. 13% alc. **Rating** 91 **To** 2017 $32 BE
Tannery Block Coonawarra Cabernet Sauvignon Merlot 2011 Mid garnet; the bouquet offers red and black fruit, black olive and bay leaf aromas; the medium-bodied palate is supple and fleshy, with fine tannins a feature of the harmonious finish; even and poised. Screwcap. 13.5% alc. **Rating** 91 **To** 2018 $30 BE
Down the Lane Cabernet Sauvignon Shiraz Merlot 2010 A savoury bouquet of red and blackcurrant, fresh earth, green olive and touch of eucalypt; the medium-bodied palate is bright, fragrant and fresh, with fine tannins lingering evenly on the finish. Screwcap. 14.5% alc. **Rating** 90 **To** 2020 $25 BE
The Nectar 2012 Bright colour, showing lifted fresh apricot, lavender and a little brulée complexity; luscious on the palate, but light on its feet; consuming in the full flush of youth and purity is certainly encouraged. 375ml. Screwcap. 11.5% alc. **Rating** 90 **To** 2016 $30 BE

ᵠᵠᵠᵠ Savagnin 2012 Rating 88 **To** 2014 $25
Sauvignon Blanc Savagnin Semillon 2012 Rating 88 **To** 2015 $25 BE

Holm Oak ★★★★★

11 West Bay Road, Rowella, Tas 7270 **Region** Northern Tasmania
T (03) 6394 7577 **www**.holmoakvineyards.com.au **Open** 7 days 11–5 Sept–June, 11–4 Jun–Aug
Winemaker Rebecca Duffy **Est.** 1983 **Dozens** 6000 **Vyds** 11.62ha
Holm Oak takes its name from its grove of oak trees, planted around the beginning of the 20th century and originally intended for the making of tennis racquets. In 2004 Ian and Robyn Wilson purchased the property. The vineyard is planted (in descending order) to pinot noir, cabernet sauvignon, chardonnay, riesling, sauvignon blanc and pinot gris, with small amounts of merlot, cabernet franc and arneis. In '06 the Wilsons' daughter Rebecca (with extensive winemaking experience in Australia and California) became winemaker at the onsite winery, and husband Tim Duffy (a viticultural agronomist) took over management of the vineyard. Exports to Japan.

ᵠᵠᵠᵠᵠ Chardonnay 2011 Still pale straw-green, the wine has exceptional drive and energy to its very long palate, white peach and nectarine to the fore, but with some creamy, almost spicy, notes adding complexity. Brilliant winemaking. Screwcap. 12.7% alc. **Rating** 95 **To** 2020 $30

Riesling 2012 A restrained and pure expression, with lemon blossom, green apple, lime and coriander on display; the palate continues the purity theme, with taut acidity and an extremely long mineral-laden finish; will age with grace. Screwcap. 12.3% alc. **Rating** 94 **To** 2030 $25 BE

Sauvignon Blanc 2012 Pale straw-green; delivers far, far more than many Tasmanian Sauvignon Blancs; it is the vibrant kiwifruit and passionfruit aromas and flavours that make the wine so enjoyable, the finish and aftertaste especially commendable. Screwcap. 12.7% alc. **Rating** 94 **To** 2013 $25

Pinot Gris 2012 Stands out like a beacon when tasted amid Australian mainland Pinot Gris with its ultra-fresh, bracing and penetrating pear, apple and citrus flavours which spear through to the long, lingering finish. This is absolutely not boring. Screwcap. 13% alc. **Rating** 94 **To** 2014 $25

The Wizard Pinot Noir 2010 Created from just six rows of vines, with whole bunches in the fermentation, as well as plenty of new oak; red cherry, spiced plum, a touch of mint and sappy notes are on the bouquet; the palate is finely detailed, with fresh acidity and elegant fine-grained tannins a refreshing feature on the long finish. Screwcap. 14% alc. **Rating** 94 **To** 2022 $60 BE

ՔՔՔՔ **Arneis 2011 Rating** 92 **To** 2014 $25
Pinot Noir 2011 Rating 92 **To** 2017 $32 BE
TBR Duffy Moscato 2012 Rating 90 **To** 2013 $22 BE

Home Hill ★★★★★

38 Nairn Street, Ranelagh, Tas 7109 **Region** Southern Tasmania
T (03) 6264 1200 **www**.homehillwines.com.au **Open** 7 days 10–5
Winemaker Gilli and Paul Lipcombe **Est.** 1994 **Dozens** 2000 **Vyds** 6ha
Terry and Rosemary Bennett planted their first 0.5ha of vines in 1994 on gentle slopes in the beautiful Huon Valley. Between '94 and '99 the plantings were increased to 3ha of pinot noir, 1.5ha of chardonnay and 0.5ha of sylvaner. Home Hill has had great success with its exemplary Pinot Noir, a consistent wine show major award winner. At the '13 Tasmanian Wine Show, the '10 Kelly's Reserve Pinot Noir won three trophies, including Best Wine of Show; in a show notable for the small number of medal awards, its other entries accumulated a further gold and three silver medals for Pinot Noirs.

ՔՔՔՔՔ **Kelly's Reserve Pinot Noir 2010** Has positively flowered over the past year, and has more yet to give. It has excellent colour, and that assured richness of the best Tasmanian Pinots; the palate has great complexity to its berry fruits, yet retains focus, high-quality tannins providing the final element. Seven trophies Tas Wine Show '13. Screwcap. 13.8% alc. **Rating** 96 **To** 2020 $50

Kelly's Reserve Pinot Noir 2011 The relatively light colour is no guide to the extravagant display of red berry fruits, sustained and complexed by quality tannins. Gold Tas Wine Show '13. Screwcap. 13.5% alc. **Rating** 95 **To** 2019 $50

Honey Moon Vineyard ★★★★★

PO Box 544, Echunga SA 5153 **Region** Adelaide Hills
T 0419 862 103 **www**.honeymoonvineyard.com.au **Open** Not
Winemaker Jane Bromley, Hylton McLean **Est.** 2005 **Dozens** 500 **Vyds** 0.8ha
Jane Bromley and Hylton McLean planted 0.4ha each of pinot noir (clones 777, 114 and 115) and shiraz (selected from two old vineyards known for their spicy fruit flavours) in 2003. The moon is a striking feature in the landscape, particularly at harvest time when, as a full moon, it appears as a dollop of rich honey in the sky – hence the name. The first vintage was '05, but Jane has been making wine since '01, with a particular interest in Champagne; Hylton is a winemaker, wine science researcher and wine educator with over 20 years' experience.

ՔՔՔՔՔ **Adelaide Hills Shiraz 2010** Medium crimson-purple. A very elegant and harmonious wine, its dark berry fruits nestled in a gentle basket of oak and superfine tannins. Totally delicious. Screwcap. 14% alc. **Rating** 95 **To** 2025 $48

✪ **Adelaide Hills Fancy Rose 2012** Bright, light salmon-pink; a blend of pinot noir, shiraz and a touch of chardonnay fermented and aged in used French barriques; predictably, there is more texture and mouthfeel than normal, but there are also juicy fruit flavours. Screwcap. 12.5% alc. **Rating** 94 **To** 2014 $20

Honeytree Estate ★★★★☆

130 Gillards Road, Pokolbin, NSW 2321 **Region** Hunter Valley
T (02) 4998 7693 **www**.honeytreewines.com **Open** Wed–Fri 11–4, w'ends 10–5
Winemaker Monarch Winemaking Services (Liz Jackson) **Est.** 1970 **Dozens** 1200
Vyds 9.8ha
The Honeytree Estate vineyard was first planted in 1970 and for a period of time wines were produced. It then disappeared, but the vineyard has since been revived by Dutch-born Henk Strengers and family. The vineyard includes semillon, cabernet sauvignon, shiraz and a little clairette. Jancis Robinson comments that the wine 'tends to be very high in alcohol, a little low in acid and to oxidise dangerously fast', but in a sign of the times, the first Honeytree Clairette sold out so quickly (in four weeks) that 2.3ha of vineyard has been grafted over to clairette. Exports to The Netherlands.

🍷🍷🍷🍷🍷 **Veronica Hunter Valley Semillon 2011** Quartz-white; a classy Semillon from
✪ 40-year-old vines with a fragrant bouquet and lively, lemony/grassy flavours on the crisp palate; chalky/minerally acidity will give the wine a long life. Screwcap. 10.8% alc. **Rating** 93 **To** 2026 $20
Paul Alexander Old Vines Hunter Valley Shiraz 2011 Produced from 40-year-old estate shiraz, matured for 19 months in 30% new French and American oak; good hue and depth; reflects the good Hunter Valley vintage with most attractive plum and black cherry fruit, fine, ripe tannins and a positive contribution by the oak. Screwcap. 13% alc. **Rating** 93 **To** 2026 $30
Hunter Valley Clairette 2012 Honeytree Estate has for long been the last champion of the variety in the Hunter Valley. It is quite floral, with elements of citrus and musk on the palate. Screwcap. 12.1% alc. **Rating** 90 **To** 2015 $25

Houghton ★★★★★

Dale Road, Middle Swan, WA 6065 **Region** Swan Valley
T (08) 9274 9540 **www**.houghton-wines.com.au **Open** 7 days 10–5
Winemaker Ross Pamment **Est.** 1836 **Dozens** NFP
Houghton's reputation was once largely dependent on its (then) White Burgundy, equally good when young or 10 years old. In the last 20 years its portfolio has changed out of all recognition, with a kaleidoscopic range of high-quality wines from the Margaret River, Frankland River, Great Southern and Pemberton regions to the fore. The Jack Mann and Gladstones red wines stand at the forefront, the Wisdom range covering all varietal bases in great style. Nor should the value-for-money brands (Stripe, The Bandit and others) be ignored. To borrow a saying of the late Jack Mann, 'There are no bad wines here.' With a history of more than 175 years, its future now lies in the hands of Accolade Wines. Exports to Asia.

🍷🍷🍷🍷🍷 **Gladstones Margaret River Cabernet Sauvignon 2010** Bright, clear crimson; as befits its name, a very distinguished and expressive wine from the first whiff of its bouquet through to the finish; the grapes are grown in the Wilyabrup area, with ultra-classic cassis and redcurrant fruit that easily carries the fine-grained tannins and high-quality oak. Screwcap. 14% alc. **Rating** 97 **To** 2040 $73
Wisdom Pemberton Sauvignon Blanc 2012 Pale colour, bright; elegantly constructed, with aromas of citrus blossom, nettle, bath talc and tropical fruits; the palate is taut and energetic, finely detailed and showing a struck flint complexity and dry chalky finish that are alluring and compelling. Screwcap. 13% alc. **Rating** 95 **To** 2016 $28 BE
CW Ferguson Great Southern Cabernet Malbec 2008 Deep magenta; an elegantly perfumed bouquet of cassis, cigar box, clove and violets from the malbec; the palate is fresh and focused, belying its age, with fine-grained tannins and elegant, yet powerful, fruit. Screwcap. 14% alc. **Rating** 95 **To** 2025 $57 BE

✪ **Margaret River Cabernet Sauvignon 2011** Deep crimson-purple; an expressive cassis-laden bouquet leads into a complex medium- to full-bodied palate where the cassis is joined by French oak, a suggestion of dark chocolate and persistent ripe tannins to carry the wine on for a decade or 2. Screwcap. 13.5% alc. Rating 94 To 2026 $19

Wisdom Margaret River Cabernet Sauvignon 2011 Revealing the crushed leaf and red fruit character that is often a hallmark of the region on the bouquet; the palate is medium to full-bodied with seductive charry oak notes; will drink well from the moment it is released and well in to the future. Screwcap. 13.5% alc. Rating 94 To 2022 $32 BE

🍷🍷🍷🍷🍷 **Gladstones Margaret River Cabernet Sauvignon 2011** Rating 92 To 2022 $73 BE

✪ **Shiraz 2011** Bright crimson-purple; it is only with the global shiraz resources of WA and its ever-reliable climate that a wine of this quality could be available at this price; there are spicy cool-climate notes with a contrast of soft, almost silky cherry and plum fruit, and the tannins are similarly fine. To be enjoyed now, while its freshness is at its maximum. Screwcap. 13.5% alc. Rating 91 To 2014 $14

✪ **Cabernet Sauvignon 2011** Great value, on a par with that of Houghton Margaret River Cabernet of the same vintage, the latter a better wine, but (naturally) more expensive; here fragrant and breezy cassis is woven through with fine tannins on the light- to medium-bodied palate, and a touch of oak also appears. Screwcap. 13.5% alc. Rating 91 To 2016 $14

✪ **Cabernet Sauvignon 2012** Good colour; packs a lot of varietal character on both bouquet and palate into a budget-priced package; there is blackcurrant fruit, good savoury tannins and cigar box oak, whether or not from barrels beside the point. Amazing value. Screwcap. 13.5% alc. Rating 90 To 2016 $14

🍷🍷🍷🍷 ✪ **Red Classic Cabernet Shiraz Merlot 2011** Good colour; the bouquet is fragrant, the medium-bodied palate with the full range of red and black berries, gentle tannins and an infusion of oak. Like the Cabernet, ridiculously good value. Screwcap. 13.5% alc. Rating 89 To 2016 $14

Houlaghans Valley Wines ★★★

242 Summer Hill Road, Temora, NSW 2666 **Region** Gundagai
T (02) 6924 7265 **www.**houlaghansvalleywines.com.au **Open** Fri–Mon 10–8 (1st Sun each month 1.30–8)
Winemaker Kosciusko Wines (Chris Thomas), Lankeys Creek (Steve Thompson)
Est. 1997 **Dozens** 1000 **Vyds** 2.6ha
The estate-owned vineyard is planted on the Summer Hill sheep grazing and cropping property owned by the Hughes family, headed by third-generation Ken and Toddy, fourth-generation Barney and Angela, and their children, fifth-generation Georgia and Brandon all resident. In 1997 Ken followed in the footsteps of his grandfather, who began contract grapegrowing in 1869, those vines lost in the mists of time. Estate vines are led by 1.6ha of shiraz, with smaller amounts of tempranillo, viognier and chardonnay.

Hugh Hamilton Wines ★★★★☆

94 McMurtrie Road, McLaren Vale, SA 5171 **Region** McLaren Vale
T (08) 8323 8689 **www.**hughhamiltonwines.com.au **Open** 7 days 11–5
Winemaker Peter Leske **Est.** 1991 **Dozens** 30 000 **Vyds** 29.03ha
Hugh Hamilton is the fifth generation of the famous Hamilton family, who first planted vineyards at Glenelg in 1837. A self-confessed black sheep of the family, Hugh embraces non-mainstream varieties such as sangiovese, tempranillo and viognier, and is one of only a few growing saperavi. Production comes from estate plantings and a vineyard in Blewitt Springs of 85-year-old shiraz and 65-year-old cabernet sauvignon. The irreverent black sheep packaging was the inspiration of daughter Mary (CEO). The cellar door is lined with the original jarrah from Vat 15 of the historic Hamilton's Ewell winery, the largest wooden vat ever built in the southern hemisphere. Exports to the UK, the US, Canada, Sweden, Finland, Malaysia and China.

♥♥♥♥♡ **Blackblood I Cellar Vineyard McLaren Vale Shiraz 2011** Black fruits, saltbush, fruitcake spice, licorice and a little briary complexity; the palate is dense and chewy, with some red fruit highlights to the mid-palate, and then the prodigious tannins take control on the long finish. Screwcap. 15% alc. **Rating** 93 To 2022 $70 BE

Black Ops McLaren Vale Shiraz Saperavi 2010 Bright crimson; the 7% saperavi made a savoury contribution to the blend, and maybe to the spicy tannins; notes of black chocolate join the blackberry fruits of the palate; good length. Screwcap. 14.5% alc. **Rating** 93 To 2020 $30

The Rascal McLaren Vale Shiraz 2011 Mocha oak and licorice complexity are offset by dark black fruits on the bouquet; the palate is full of compact tannins, fresh acidity and lingering mocha oak notes on the moderately long finish. Screwcap. 15% alc. **Rating** 90 To 2018 $30 BE

Jekyll & Hyde McLaren Vale Shiraz Viognier 2011 Deep colour and lifted in perfume, with confiture black fruits and licorice in spades; the palate is unctuous and showing a little alcoholic warmth, no surprise at 15.2% alc/vol; a style for the hedonistic lover of big, fragrant reds. Screwcap. **Rating** 90 To 2018 $50 BE

The Oddball McLaren Vale Saperavi 2011 Impenetrable colour; the dark fruited and essency bouquet offers cola, sage and roasted meat complexity; incredibly dense on the palate, the chewy tannins are a massive mouthful, but the volume of fruit is up to the task; big-boned and high in impact; for lovers of massive red wines. Cork. 15% alc. **Rating** 90 To 2018 $50 BE

♥♥♥♥ **Members Only Shearer's Cut Black Sheep Block Shiraz 2011** Rating 89 To 2017 $25 BE

The Mongrel McLaren Vale Sangiovese 2012 Rating 89 To 2016 $25 BE
The Scallywag McLaren Vale Chardonnay 2012 Rating 88 To 2014 $20
The Loose Cannon Viognier 2012 Rating 88 To 2014 $23 BE
The Ratbag McLaren Vale Merlot 2011 Rating 88 To 2016 $25 BE
The Villain Cabernet Sauvignon 2011 Rating 88 To 2017 $30 BE

Hugo ★★★

246 Elliott Road, McLaren Flat, SA 5171 **Region** McLaren Vale
T (08) 8383 0098 **www.**hugowines.com.au **Open** Mon–Fri 9.30–5, Sat 12–5, Sun 10.30–5
Winemaker John Hugo **Est.** 1982 **Dozens** 7000 **Vyds** 25ha
Came from relative obscurity to prominence in the late 1980s with some lovely ripe, sweet reds, which, while strongly American oak-influenced, were quite outstanding. It picked up the pace again after a dull period in the mid '90s, but seems to have drifted back again. The estate plantings include shiraz, cabernet sauvignon, chardonnay, grenache and sauvignon blanc, with part of the grape production sold to others. Exports to the UK, the US and Canada.

♥♥♥♥ **McLaren Vale Cabernet Sauvignon 2010** Medium red-purple; picked at the right time, then spent 15 months in French and American oak; there are some pleasant cassis and chocolate fruit flavours, but the wine needs more depth and structure, and less American oak. Screwcap. 14.5% alc. **Rating** 88 To 2015 $25

Humbug Reach Vineyard ★★★★

72 Nobelius Drive, Legana, Tas 7277 **Region** Northern Tasmania
T (03) 6330 2875 **www.**humbugreach.com.au **Open** Not
Winemaker Paul McShane, Bass Fine Wines (Guy Wagner) **Est.** 1988 **Dozens** 200
Vyds 1ha
The Humbug Reach Vineyard was established in the late 1980s on the banks of the Tamar River with plantings of pinot noir; riesling and chardonnay followed. Since '99 it has been owned by Paul and Sally McShane, who proudly tend the 6000 vines on the property. After frost decimated the 2007 vintage, Sally and Paul, wanting to become involved in winemaking, brought the process closer to home, with Guy Wagner making the Riesling and Chardonnay, Paul making the Pinot Noir (commuting from the Sustainability Institute at Monash University in Melbourne to do so).

ᵀᵀᵀᵀᵀ **Pinot Noir 2011** Good colour; has immaculate varietal expression with its plum and black cherry aromas and flavours; northern Tasmania had its share of challenges in '11, but not as severe as those of Vic, and this wine has been very well made. Screwcap. 13% alc. **Rating** 93 **To** 2019 $28
Riesling 2012 Pale quartz; the low pH and natural acidity intensify the minerality in the wine, the fruit in a green apple/citrus spectrum, unsweetened lemon on the finish. Needs a 3-year probation, but should graduate with honours. Screwcap. 12% alc. **Rating** 92 **To** 2025 $25

ᵀᵀᵀᵀ **Chardonnay 2011 Rating** 89 **To** 2017 $32

Hungerford Hill ★★★★★

1 Broke Road, Pokolbin, NSW 2320 **Region** Hunter Valley
T (02) 4998 7666 www.hungerfordhill.com.au **Open** Sun–Thurs 10–5, Fri–Sat 10–6
Winemaker Adrian Lockhart **Est.** 1967 **Dozens** 50 000 **Vyds** 5ha
Since acquiring Hungerford Hill a decade ago, the Kirby family has sought to build on the Hungerford Hill story that began over 40 years ago. James Kirby was involved in his family's engineering business during its growth to become one of Australia's leading automotive refrigeration and air-conditioning manufacturers. The winemaking team, now guided by Adrian Lockhart, continues to make wines from the Hunter Valley and from the cool-climate regions of Hilltops and Tumbarumba. The cellar door complex sits at the gateway to the Hunter Valley at One Broke Road and has been the recipient of significant awards. Exports to all major markets.

ᵀᵀᵀᵀᵀ **Collection Majors Lane Vineyard Hunter Valley Semillon 2008** Youthful and fresh, showing just a little lemon curd, with struck flint an interesting addition; the palate is taut and racy, with chalky acidity and grip a feature on the focused, and ever so slightly toasty, finish. Screwcap. 9.5% alc. **Rating** 95 **To** 2022 $35 BE
Collection Majors Lane Vineyard Hunter Valley Semillon 2011 Bright green with some straw; has already developed delicious varietal fruit, with some of the riesling crossover citrus along with lemon zest lemon curd flavours. Can be drunk with pleasure, but will give even more in 5 years. Screwcap. 10.5% alc. **Rating** 94 **To** 2020 $35
Collection Hesperia Vineyard Tumbarumba Chardonnay 2010 Glowing yellow-green; has the fruit freshness that is the mark of top-quality Tumbarumba Chardonnays, and also their ability to soak up oak, here new French; the finish is long and incisive. Screwcap. 13% alc. **Rating** 94 **To** 2016 $40
Dalliance Methode Traditional 2008 A bottle-fermented blend of chardonnay and pinot noir with a light pink-bronze colour; it is a very delicate and fresh wine, particularly given its age; the balance and mouthfeel are particularly impressive for an aperitif style, freshness the key word. Diam. 13% alc. **Rating** 94 **To** 2016 $30

ᵀᵀᵀᵀᵀ **Heavy Metal Shiraz 2010 Rating** 92 **To** 2025 $45 BE
Epic Hunter Valley Shiraz 2007 Rating 92 **To** 2035 $55 BE
Collection Hillside Vineyard Shiraz 2009 Rating 90 **To** 2019 $55

Huntington Estate ★★★★★

Cassilis Road, Mudgee, NSW 2850 **Region** Mudgee
T 1800 995 931 www.huntingtonestate.com.au **Open** Mon–Sat 10–5, Sun & public hols 10–4
Winemaker Tim Stevens **Est.** 1969 **Dozens** 15 000 **Vyds** 43.8ha
Since taking ownership of Huntington Estate from the founding Roberts family, Tim Stevens has sensibly refrained from making major changes. On the wine side, the policy of having older vintage wines available is continuing, making the cellar door a first port of call for visitors to Mudgee. On the other side, the Music Festival suffers only one problem: there are simply not enough tickets to satisfy the demand. It really has a well-deserved life of its own, and I can see no reason why it should not do so for years to come. Most Successful Exhibitor Mudgee Wine Show '12.

♥♥♥♥♥ Mudgee Shiraz 2009 Bin 14. Deep purple-crimson colour still in evidence; the
✪   most powerful and full-bodied of the '13 releases by Huntington Estate, with black
      fruits, chocolate, vanilla oak and ripe tannins all jostling for primacy, and none
      succeeding. From Block 14; vies every year for inclusion with Special Reserve.
      Screwcap. 14% alc. **Rating** 94 **To** 2025 $22
      Block 3 Mudgee Cabernet Sauvignon 2009 Full red-purple; the three '09
      Cabernets from Huntington Estate all demonstrate the ability of parts of Mudgee
      to produce wines with cool-climate varietal expression. As the flagship wine, and
      the most expensive of the three, it duly delivers as a powerful, savoury, black-
      fruited wine, with the type of tannin profile that is seldom found outside cabernet
      (nebbiolo etc exceptions). Screwcap. 13.2% alc. **Rating** 94 **To** 2030 $70

♥♥♥♥♀ Barrel Fermented Mudgee Chardonnay 2012 **Rating** 91 **To** 2016 $22
✪   **Mudgee Merlot 2011** Bright crimson-purple hue; full of juicy red berry fruits
      on the bouquet and a fresh, light- to medium-bodied palate which finishes with a
      faint twitch of black olive. Screwcap. 13.2% alc. **Rating** 90 **To** 2017 $20
      Special Reserve Mudgee Cabernet Sauvignon 2009 Rating 90
      To 2019 $33

Hurley Vineyard   ★★★★★

101 Balnarring Road, Balnarring, Vic 3926 **Region** Mornington Peninsula
T (03) 5931 3000 **www.**hurleyvineyard.com.au **Open** 1st w'end each month 11–5,
or by appt
Winemaker Kevin Bell **Est.** 1998 **Dozens** 1000 **Vyds** 3.5ha
It's never as easy as it seems. Despite leading busy city lives, Kevin Bell and wife Tricia Byrnes
have done most of the hard work in establishing Hurley Vineyard themselves, with family and
friends. Most conspicuously, Kevin has completed the Applied Science (Wine Science) degree
at CSU, drawing on Nat White for consultancy advice, and occasionally from Phillip Jones of
Bass Phillip and Domaine Fourrier in Gevrey Chambertin. He has not allowed a significant
heart issue to prevent him continuing with his first love.

♥♥♥♥♥ Estate Mornington Peninsula Pinot Noir 2011 The only wine made by
      this estate in '11, it is light garnet colour, set with spicy dark cherry fruit, charry
      oak and a little brambly complexity on the bouquet; the light- to medium-
      bodied palate is lively, revealing plump fruits, silky tannins and a long, even and
      distinguished conclusion. Excellent execution in a challenging vintage and will
      stand the test of time. Diam. 13.7% alc. **Rating** 94 **To** 2020 $50 BE

Hutton Vale Vineyard   ★★★★

Stone Jar Road, Angaston, SA 5353 **Region** Eden Valley
T (08) 8564 8270 **www.**huttonvale.com **Open** By appt
Winemaker Torbreck Vintners, Murray Street Vineyard (Andrew Seppelt) **Est.** 1960
Dozens 600 **Vyds** 27ha
John Howard Angas (who arrived in SA in 1843, aged 19, charged with the responsibility
of looking after the affairs of his father, George Fife Angas) named part of the family estate
Hutton Vale. It is here that John Angas, John's great-great-grandson, and wife Jan tend 27ha
of vines. Almost all the grapes are sold, but a tiny quantity has been made by the who's who
of the Barossa Valley, notably David Powell of Torbreck. Jan is also chair of Regional Food SA.

♥♥♥♥♀ Eden Valley Riesling 2012 Hutton Vale presents a generous and enticing appeal
      in '12, without ever deviating from the focused definition and taut structure that
      defines this site. An electric green hue anticipates kaffir lime and white pepper
      purity, but there's more to this vintage, finishing with layers of Pink Lady apples,
      even almost ripe fig. Screwcap. 12% alc. **Rating** 93 **To** 2022 $28 TS

Hutton Wines

PO Box 1214, Dunsborough, WA 6281 **Region** Margaret River
T 0417 923 126 **www.**huttonwines.com **Open** Not
Winemaker Michael Hutton **Est.** 2006 **Dozens** 300
This is another venture of the Hutton family of Gralyn fame, with Michael Hutton, who returned to the Margaret River region in 2005, establishing this micro-business the following year, while continuing his architectural practice. Tiny quantities of Semillon Sauvignon, Chardonnay and Cabernet Sauvignon are produced, hardly enough to threaten Gralyn.

ΨΨΨΨΨ **Triptych Margaret River Chardonnay 2011** Vibrant green hue; the bouquet
offers nectarine, hazelnuts and well-handled spicy oak; the palate is taut, racy
and mouth-watering, with a long, expansive and complex grilled cashew finish.
Screwcap. 12.8% alc. **Rating** 94 **To** 2018 $40 BE

ΨΨΨΨΨ **Triptych Margaret River Semillon 2012 Rating** 92 **To** 2016 $25 BE

Idavue Estate

470 Northern Highway, Heathcote, Vic 3523 **Region** Heathcote
T (03) 5433 3464 **www.**idavueestate.com **Open** W'ends & public hols 10.30–5
Winemaker Andrew and Sandra Whytcross **Est.** 2000 **Dozens** 600 **Vyds** 5.7ha
Owners and winemakers Andrew and Sandra Whytcross both undertook a two-year winemaking course through the Bendigo TAFE; with assistance from son Marty, they also look after the vineyard, which is planted to shiraz (3ha), cabernet sauvignon (1.9ha), and semillon and chardonnay (0.4ha each). The red wines are made in typical small-batch fashion with hand-picked fruit, hand-plunged fermenters and a basket press.

ΨΨΨΨΨ **Heathcote Shiraz 2010** Hand-picked estate-grown fruit open-fermented and
basket-pressed; has obviously spent time in new oak, with plush blackberry fruit,
plum cake and vanillin flavours supported by soft, ripe tannins. Diam. 14% alc.
Rating 93 **To** 2022 $28
Blue Note Heathcote Shiraz 2009 Good colour depth and hue; a medium- to
full-bodied Shiraz with considerable depth to its fruit, texture and structure; there
are savoury overtones to its blackberry and plum fruit, part tannin-derived, part
oak. Diam. 14% alc. **Rating** 93 **To** 2029 $35
The Barrelhouse Heathcote Shiraz 2010 Shares many of the characters of its
sibling, but is slightly more savoury and less oaky, the tannins a little more obvious.
While the fermentation regime is the same, it seems oak is the major difference.
In the end result, it is as much a question of style as of quality. Screwcap. 14% alc.
Rating 92 **To** 2020 $25
Heathcote Shiraz 2009 The hue is not as good as that of the '09 Blue Note, but
is nonetheless deep. Spice, licorice and leather overtones to the black fruits fit well
with the savoury back-palate and finish. Diam. 14% alc. **Rating** 91 **To** 2027 $25
Heathcote Cabernet Sauvignon 2009 Still retains a purple/crimson edge
to its colour; it has good varietal definition, the cassis and mulberry fruit with
a hint of chocolate, and fine tannins courtesy of basket-pressing. Diam. 14% alc.
Rating 91 **To** 2019 $25

Idle Hands Wines

18 The Avenue, Lorn, NSW 2320 **Region** Hunter Valley
T 0439 544 446 **Open** Not
Winemaker Contract **Est.** 2005 **Dozens** NFP
Brothers Michael and Peter Tonkin bought the Kurrajong Vineyard in 2004; 2.15ha of verdelho had been planted in 1991, the shiraz 1.5ha and semillon 1.2ha followed in '94. Idle Hands wines are all estate-grown.

ŶŶŶŶŶ **Hunter Reserve Semillon 2008** Pale, light straw-green; all the Idle Hands
✪ Semillons come from the same vineyard, and this surely demonstrates that 10.5%
alcohol is far better than 12.5%. It is flinty, crisp and fresh, still on the upwards
track, an ideal match for tapas. Screwcap. **Rating** 91 **To** 2018 $16

ŶŶŶŶ **Hunter Reserve Semillon 2010 Rating** 88 **To** 2014 $16

Indigo Wine Company ★★★★★

1221 Beechworth-Wangaratta Road, Everton Upper, Vic 3678 **Region** Beechworth
T (03) 5727 0233 **www**.indigovineyard.com.au **Open** Wed–Sun 11–4
Winemaker Brokenwood (Simon Steele) **Est.** 1999 **Dozens** 1950 **Vyds** 46.15ha
Indigo Wine Company has a little over 46ha of vineyards planted to 11 varieties, including the
top French and Italian grapes. The business was and is primarily directed to growing grapes
for sale to Brokenwood, but since 2004 increasing amounts have been vinified for the Indigo
label. The somewhat incestuous nature of the whole business sees the Indigo wines being
made at Brokenwood.

ŶŶŶŶŶ **Secret Village Beechworth Chardonnay Roussanne 2010** I absolutely
did not expect this blend to be more interesting, and to have more flavour, than
the Chardonnay, but it is and it does. The length, in particular, is a feature, with
citrus rind and Granny Smith apple flavours around a minerally core. Screwcap.
13.5% alc. **Rating** 94 **To** 2017 $32
Beechworth Pinot Grigio 2012 Pale straw colour; this is Pinot Gris with
attitude; its flavours of pear, pear skin and apple are conventional, but its texture,
structure and intensity are all as uncommon as they are welcome. If you like
grigio, go for it. Screwcap. 13.5% alc. **Rating** 94 **To** 2014 $20
Secret Village Beechworth Shiraz 2010 Bright, clear crimson-purple;
the fragrant, almost flowery, bouquet is filled with bright red fruits, the palate
underwriting and highlighting the red cherry, strawberry and gently spicy flavours.
While only light- to medium-bodied, the purity and precision of this wine are
outstanding. Screwcap. 14% alc. **Rating** 94 **To** 2020 $45

ŶŶŶŶŶ **Chardonnay 2012 Rating** 93 **To** 2017 $27
Chardonnay 2010 Rating 93 **To** 2017 $27
Cabernet Sauvignon Sangiovese 2012 Rating 90 **To** 2016 $25

Ingoldby ★★★★☆

GPO Box 753, Melbourne, Vic 3001 **Region** McLaren Vale
T 1300 651 650 **www**.ingoldby.com.au **Open** Not
Winemaker Kelly Healy **Est.** 1983 **Dozens** NFP
Part of TWE, with the wines now having a sole McLaren Vale source. Over the years,
Ingoldby has produced some excellent wines, which can provide great value for money.

ŶŶŶŶŶ **McLaren Vale Cabernet Sauvignon 2010** Deep, bright crimson-purple; a
small portion of sangiovese has been added to significantly enhance the savoury
nature of the medium- to full-bodied palate, yet without obscuring the touch of
regional bitter chocolate or the blackcurrant at the heart of a potentially long-lived
wine. Screwcap. 14.5% alc. **Rating** 94 **To** 2030 $20

ŶŶŶŶŶ **McLaren Vale Grenache Shiraz 2011** A light but vivid hue heralds a wine that
✪ was not blindsided by the vintage; it has an array of predominantly red fruits, but
licorice and dark chocolate, and some spiced plum, also make their appearance;
well-handled oak and tannins complete the picture. Screwcap. 14% alc. **Rating** 93
To 2021 $20

Inkwell ★★★☆

PO Box 33, Sellicks Beach, SA 5174 **Region** McLaren Vale
T 0430 050 115 **www**.inkwellwines.com **Open** By appt
Winemaker Dudley Brown **Est.** 2003 **Dozens** 800 **Vyds** 12ha

Inkwell was born in 2003 when Dudley Brown returned to Australia from California and bought a somewhat rundown vineyard on the serendipitously named California Road. He inherited 5ha of neglected shiraz, and planted an additional 7ha to viognier (2.5ha), zinfandel (2.5ha) and heritage shiraz clones (2.5ha). The five-year restoration of the old vines and establishment of the new reads like the ultimate handbook for aspiring vignerons, particularly those who are prepared to work non-stop. The reward has been rich – almost all the grapes are sold, and the grapes go from a mid range commercial rating to near the top of the tree. The first toe in the water of commercial winemaking came in '06 with 140 dozen produced. Dudley is adamant the production will be capped at 2000 dozen. Exports to the US and Canada.

ΨΨΨΨႵ **McLaren Vale Shiraz 2010** Full crimson-purple; a powerful, full-bodied estate-grown wine with a panoply of rich black fruits, bitter chocolate and well-integrated and balanced French oak, finishing with firm but ripe tannins. It's hard to criticise the alcohol, but one cannot help but wonder how great the wine would have been at 14%. Screwcap. 14.9% alc. **Rating** 93 **To** 2030 $35

ΨΨΨΨ **The Inkling McLaren Vale Shiraz Primitivo 2010** Rating 89 To 2016 $25
The Infidel McLaren Vale Primitivo 2010 Rating 89 To 2018 $30

Innocent Bystander ★★★★★

336 Maroondah Highway, Healesville, Vic 3777 **Region** Yarra Valley
T (03) 5962 6111 **www.**innocentbystander.com.au **Open** Mon–Fri 10–10, w'ends 8–10
Winemaker Phil Sexton, Steve Flamsteed, Tim Shand **Est.** 1997 **Dozens** 70000 **Vyds** 32ha
Innocent Bystander is owned by accomplished brewer and winemaker Phil Sexton. A pioneer in both industries, Phil co-founded Matilda Bay and Little Creatures breweries and Devils Lair winery in Margaret River. Innocent Bystander produces distinctive wines from its Yarra Valley vineyards, each a symbiotic expression of variety and region. Giant Steps focuses on single vineyard wines, showcasing some of the Yarra Valley's finest sites. Wines under the Innocent Bystander, Giant Steps and Mea Culpa labels are fastidiously produced onsite in the heart of Healesville, providing a busy backdrop behind the soaring glass walls for visitors to its award-winning restaurant and cellar door. Exports to the UK, the US and other major markets.

ΨΨΨΨΨ Giant Steps Sexton Vineyard Yarra Valley Chardonnay 2011 Bright yellow-green; has an extra degree of elegant and intensity, with some grapefruit and citrus acidity joining creamy cashew notes that build through the length of the palate; has a high quality, lingering finish. Screwcap. 12.6% alc. **Rating** 94 To 2018 $40
Giant Steps Tarraford Vineyard Yarra Valley Chardonnay 2011 Bright yellow-green; distinguished by its finely detailed structure and length, the fruit expression restrained but unequivocally varietal. Oak has its place in all three '11 Giant Steps Chardonnays, contributing more to texture than to structure. Screwcap. 12.8% alc. **Rating** 94 To 2018 $40
Giant Steps Arthurs Creek Vineyard Yarra Valley Chardonnay 2011 Gleaming yellow-green; a generous mouth-filling wine, with white peach and melon fruit on the fore-palate, then moving into a more elegant mode on the finish and aftertaste. Screwcap. 13% alc. **Rating** 94 To 2018 $40
Giant Steps Arthurs Creek Vineyard Yarra Valley Chardonnay 2008 Glowing yellow-green; an extremely complex funky Burgundian bouquet, but the palate is decidedly elegant and delicate, nectarine and citrus fruit to the fore. Screwcap. 12.7% alc. **Rating** 94 To 2016 $40
Mea Culpa Yarra Valley Shiraz 2011 Light to medium red-purple; the grapes come from the low-yielding 30-year-old Tarraford Vineyard; whole bunches in open fermenters have produced a spicy edge to the flavours, the medium-bodied palate has a more complex flavour profile than usual in '11, the finish long and satisfying. Screwcap. 13.5% alc. **Rating** 94 To 2021 $60

ΨΨΨΨႵ Innocent Bystander Yarra Valley Pinot Noir 2012 Rating 93 To 2019 $30
Giant Steps Sexton Vineyard Pinot Noir 2011 Rating 92 To 2017 $50
Innocent Bystander Yarra Valley Pinot Gris 2012 Rating 90 To 2014 $25

✪ Innocent Bystander Yarra Valley Shiraz 2011 Rating 90 To 2016 $30
Moscato 2012 Pale pink in a hot pink can, following in the footsteps of Barokes; made from Muscat of Hamburg/Black Muscat using pressure fermentation and 'bottled' (there are in fact also 750ml bottles of the wine); it is intensely grapey/juicy, its residual sugar balanced by lemony acidity. Can. 5.5% alc. Rating 90 To 2013 $5

Ironbark Hill Vineyard ★★★★☆

694 Hermitage Road, Pokolbin, NSW 2321 Region Hunter Valley
T (02) 6574 7085 www.ironbarkhill.com.au Open 7 days 10–5
Winemaker Damian Stevens, Keith Tulloch Est. 1990 Dozens 12000 Vyds 16.5ha
Ironbark Hill Estate is owned by Peter and Leesa Drayton and Michael and Julie Dillon. Peter's father, Max Drayton, and brothers John and Greg, run Drayton's Family Wines. The estate plantings include shiraz, chardonnay, semillon, cabernet sauvignon, tempranillo, merlot, verdelho and tyrian. Peter is a commercial/industrial builder, so constructing the cellar door was a busman's holiday. Ironbark Hill features an atmospheric function venue and wedding chapel set among the vines, with events organised and catered for by the award-winning Pokolbin restaurant, Café Enzo. Exports to Vietnam, Hong Kong and China.

ŶŶŶŶŶ Peter Drayton Premium Release Shiraz 2011 Quite how they achieved such layers of deep blackberry and dark plum fruit depth, at just 12.5% alcohol, is quite a profound mystery. Finely poised tannins carry the long and seamless finish. It's harmonious, graceful, concentrated, silky and downright delicious. Screwcap. Rating 95 To 2021 $38 TS

ŶŶŶŶŶ Semillon 2012 Rating 91 To 2018 $22
✪ Merlot Rose 2012 Estate-grown; light magenta; the bouquet and palate are driven by strawberry and raspberry fruit, brightened by citrussy acidity on the finish. Screwcap. 12.5% alc. Rating 90 To 2014 $20

Ironwood Estate ★★★★

2191 Porongurup Road, Porongurup, WA 6234 Region Porongurup
T (08) 9853 1126 www.ironwoodestatewines.com.au Open Wed–Mon 11–5
Winemaker Wignalls Wines (Michael Perkins) Est. 1996 Dozens 2500 Vyds 5ha
Ironwood Estate was established in 1996 under the ownership of Mary and Eugene Harma. An estate vineyard planted to riesling, sauvignon blanc, chardonnay, shiraz, merlot and cabernet sauvignon (in more or less equal amounts) has been established on a northern slope of the Porongurup Range. Exports to Japan and Singapore.

ŶŶŶŶŶ Porongurup Merlot 2011 Light, bright, clear crimson; the perfumed bouquet leads into a light- to medium-bodied palate with excellent varietal definition, red fruits to the fore, trimmed by just a touch of black olive, and suitably fine-grained tannins. Screwcap. 13.5% alc. Rating 93 To 2016 $25
Reserve Porongurup Chardonnay 2012 Hand-picked, and barrel-fermented in French oak. Right from the slightly funky bouquet, this is a Chardonnay with attitude, balancing ripe stone fruit with pronounced acidity and, to a lesser degree, oak. Its one issue is that the reflection of that attitude equals a lack of finesse. Screwcap. 14.5% alc. Rating 91 To 2017 $25

ŶŶŶŶ Porongurup Cabernet Merlot 2011 Good depth and hue; at the top end
✪ of Porongurup weight and flavour, but doesn't go over the top; blackcurrant and plum fruit flavours are enriched by ripe tannins and a generous infusion of cedary oak. Good value. Screwcap. 14.5% alc. Rating 89 To 2016 $20

Irvine

PO Box 308, Angaston, SA 5353 **Region** Eden Valley
T (08) 8564 1046 **www**.irvinewines.com.au **Open** At Taste of Eden Valley, Angaston
Winemaker Joanne Irvine **Est.** 1980 **Dozens** 8000 **Vyds** 9.5ha
Industry veteran Jim Irvine, who has successfully guided the destiny of so many SA wineries, quietly introduced his own label in 1991. The vineyard from which the wines are sourced was planted in '83 to an eclectic mix of merlot (4.2ha), chardonnay (3.1ha), pinot gris (1ha), petit meslier, zinfandel (0.5ha each) and tannat (0.2ha). The flagship is the rich Grand Merlot. Jim has stepped back to allow daughter Joanne to receive the recognition and praise for the wines she makes for the brand (and, for that matter, others). Exports to the UK, Germany, Taiwan, Malaysia, Singapore, Hong Kong and China.

ΨΨΨΨΨ **James Irvine Eden Valley Grand Merlot 2008** Colour development consistent with its age and vintage; remarkably, has largely absorbed 36 months in Allier oak; its texture is supple and silky, and while this is a thoroughly unique approach to the variety, it works. Cork. 15% alc. **Rating** 94 **To** 2023 $130

ΨΨΨΨΨ **Estate Barossa Merlot 2010 Rating** 90 **To** 2020 $28

Jack Rabbit Vineyard

85 McAdams Lane, Bellarine, Vic 3223 **Region** Geelong
T (03) 5251 2223 **www**.jackrabbitvineyard.com.au **Open** 7 days 10.30–5
Winemaker Nyall Condon **Est.** 1989 **Dozens** 6000 **Vyds** 2ha
Jack Rabbit Vineyard is the reincarnation of Kilgour Estate following its acquisition by David and Lyndsay Sharp of Leura Park Estate. Its 2ha of vineyards (planted equally to pinot noir and cabernet sauvignon), take second place to its restaurant and function facilities, with the opening of the House of Jack Rabbit tasting room, cellar door and café (open 7 days for lunch, Fri–Sat for dinner). The estate vineyards are supplemented by contract-grown fruit, and production has increased sharply with wine show success.

ΨΨΨΨΨ **Bellarine Peninsula Riesling 2012** Light straw-green; a crisp and pure Riesling, with considerable drive and intensity to the lemon and lime citrus fruits, punchy acidity drawing out the long finish. Given its maritime climate, is most impressive – as is the price. Screwcap. 11.6% alc. **Rating** 93 **To** 2020 $30
Bellarine Peninsula Pinot Noir 2011 Clear and vivid purple-crimson; fresh, clear and engaging cherry fruit on the bouquet and palate sets the scene; notwithstanding the low alcohol, there are no green characters, rather nuances of game and forest. Screwcap. 12% alc. **Rating** 90 **To** 2017 $30

ΨΨΨΨ **Bellarine Peninsula Sauvignon Blanc 2012 Rating** 89 **To** 2013 $30
Bellarine Peninsula Chardonnay 2011 Rating 89 **To** 2015 $30
Bellarine Peninsula Pinot Grigio 2012 Rating 89 **To** 2013 $30
Bellarine Peninsula Rose 2012 Rating 89 **To** 2013 $30
Bellarine Peninsula Blanc de Blanc 2011 Rating 88 **To** 2013 $30

Jacob's Creek

Barossa Valley Way, Rowland Flat, SA 5352 **Region** Barossa Valley
T (08) 8521 3000 **www**.jacobscreek.com **Open** 7 days 10–5
Winemaker Bernard Hickin **Est.** 1973 **Dozens** NFP
Jacob's Creek is one of the largest-selling brands in the world, and the global success of the basic Jacob's Creek range has had the perverse effect of prejudicing many critics and wine writers who fail (so it seems) to objectively look behind the label and taste what is in fact in the glass. Jacob's Creek has four ranges, and all the wines have a connection, direct or indirect, with Johann Gramp, who built his tiny stone winery on the banks of the creek in 1847. The four-tier range consists of Icon (Johann Shiraz Cabernet); then Heritage (Steingarten Riesling, Reeves Point Chardonnay, Centenary Hill Barossa Shiraz and St Hugo Coonawarra Cabernet); then Regional Reserve (all of the major varietals); and finally Classic (ditto). Exports to the UK, the US, China and other major markets.

ŸŸŸŸŸ **St Hugo Barossa Grenache Shiraz Mataro 2010** Bright crimson-purple; a 45/32/23% blend, the grenache from two 40-year-old and one 83-year-old blocks, the mataro from bush-pruned vines at Greenock. Lifted aromatics, layers of red and black fruits, and supple, fine tannins and a balanced touch of oak on the very long finish. Gold medals Melbourne, Adelaide, Hobart and National Wine Shows, all in '11. Screwcap. 14.1% alc. **Rating** 96 **To** 2018 $50

Steingarten Barossa Riesling 2012 Pale straw-green; it has a scented array of lime blossom, pith and rind, with a haunting nuance of jasmine. The palate has great tension built around its mineral backbone, giving it wonderful line, length and balance. The '12 vintage is an outstanding one for Eden and Clare Valley Riesling, and this wine does the vintage proud. Screwcap. 12.1% alc. **Rating** 95 **To** 2032 $35

Steingarten Barossa Riesling 2011 Bottle no. 17903. Early picking and fermentation until dry has made for a delicate style with a crisp, lingering finish; apple, lime and lemon are all present. Screwcap. 10.8% alc. **Rating** 95 **To** 2031 $32

St Hugo Shiraz Cabernet 2009 A Barossa shiraz (61%) and Coonawarra cabernet (39%) blend made famous by Max Schubert, but the first for St Hugo. The rich and juicy plum fruit of the shiraz is given structure and complexity by the blackcurrant, black olive and ripe tannins of the cabernet. A stone-cold certainty to age very well. Screwcap. 14% alc. **Rating** 94 **To** 2030 $50

St Hugo Coonawarra Cabernet Sauvignon 2008 Bright crimson-purple; this is the 27th release of St Hugo, and fittingly has won a trophy and five gold medals, with more likely; it has an abundance of blackcurrant fruit plus nuances of regional earth and mint, then the tannins, providing structure for long and distinguished ageing. Screwcap. 14.5% alc. **Rating** 94 **To** 2030 $50

ŸŸŸŸŸ
✪ **Reserve Adelaide Hills Chardonnay 2011** Continues the move to regional wines in the middle/upper echelons of Jacob's Creek, and does so to great effect in this cool vintage that needed vigilance in the vineyard. Here zesty white peach and nectarine fruit lead the bouquet and palate, oak in a support role allied with toasty cashew characters. Screwcap. 12.5% alc. **Rating** 93 **To** 2017 $18

✪ **Reserve Coonawarra Cabernet Sauvignon 2010** Good crimson-purple; an attractive, sweet-fruited, medium-bodied wine, its Coonawarra parentage not in doubt; mint, mulberry, blackcurrant and black olive are all contributors to the central story, finely judged tannins bringing it to a close. Screwcap. 14% alc. **Rating** 91 **To** 2018 $18

✪ **Reserve Barossa Riesling 2012** Though its name and front label unfortunately don't proclaim it, this is resolutely Eden Valley in sourcing and expression. Its pretty, fresh fragrance is characterised by lemon blossom, lime zest and riper notes of mandarin and red apple. The palate balances lively citrus freshness with ripe stone fruit character, rounded out by a touch more fruit sweetness than it really needs on the finish. Screwcap. 12.5% alc. **Rating** 90 **To** 2015 $18 TS

✪ **Sparkling Rose NV** Jacob's Creek has yet again nailed the most drinkable of the bottom-shelf sparkling roses this year. Refreshingly clean and fruit-focused, it's laced with pretty rose petal fragrance and flavours of red cherries and strawberries. Subtle tannin texture brings impressive balance to an off-dry finish. Cork. 11.5% alc. **Rating** 90 **To** 2013 $14 TS

JaJa   ★★★★

PO Box 3015, Strathmore, Vic 3041 **Region** Barossa Valley
T 0411 106 652 **www**.jaja.com.au **Open** Not
Winemaker Troy Kalleske (Contract) **Est.** 2003 **Dozens** 600
Brothers Bert and Pierre Werden are the faces behind www.winestar.com.au, which they describe as Australia's leading online fine wine retailer. While it seemed a natural progression for them to develop JaJa as a family label, they say, 'Being in retail was a huge advantage in learning what not to do.' On the positive side was the decision to concentrate on Barossa shiraz, the Stonewell subdistrict, 50-year-old vines, and the services of Troy Kalleske as winemaker. The Starlite wines are region-specific, small-batch wines that are sold to on-premise and fine

wine off-premise businesses. Bert and Pierre say, 'The further we delved into the resources of our partner wineries, the more it became abundantly clear that the recent economic hardship had slowed the ability of even the biggest names to find a home either domestically or internationally for their premium fruit. The result was a vintage Mornington Peninsula bubbly, a single vineyard, high altitude Adelaide Hills chardonnay, and a Barossa shiraz, with more than a smidgeon of old vine material.' Exports to Singapore and Hong Kong.

♀♀♀♀♀ **JaJa Barossa Shiraz 2008** Dense, inky colour; the full-bodied palate is crammed to the gills with blackberry, prune, licorice and dark chocolate flavours which obscure both the tannins and the oak, both of which are there. If you are looking for a high-class barbecue wine, this will do the trick. Screwcap. 14.9% alc. **Rating** 93 **To** 2028 $30

James Estate

951 Bylong Valley Way, Baerami, NSW 2333 **Region** Hunter Valley
T (02) 6547 5168 **www.**jamesestatewines.com.au **Open** 7 days 10–4.30
Winemaker Graeme Scott **Est.** 1997 **Dozens** 15 000 **Vyds** 86ha
James Estate has had an unsettled corporate existence at various times since 1997, but has recently straightened the ship. Graeme Scott has been installed as senior winemaker, having previously worked with Jim Chatto and Ross Pearson at First Creek, and The Rothbury Estate before that. The newly appointed winemaking team has appreciably lifted the quality of the wines, with (I guess) more to come. Exports to China.

♀♀♀♀♀
⚙ **Reserve Hunter Valley Semillon 2012** Pale green-quartz; the typical intensity, the spread of aromas and flavours in the 'new' style, with specific cultured yeast(s) helping build the citrus and pear fruits, but without detracting from the sharply focused, laser-like line of the palate. Screwcap. 10% alc. **Rating** 94 **To** 2025 $23

♀♀♀♀♀
⚙ **Reserve Hunter Valley Fume 2012** A semillon/sauvignon blanc blend barrel-fermented in used French oak, the sauvignon blanc playing a nominal role; this is all about lemony/grassy fruit and the textural contribution of the barrel ferment. Works very well, with some years to go if you wish to see how it builds with age – as it will. Screwcap. 11% alc. **Rating** 93 **To** 2016 $23

⚙ **The Estate Hunter Valley Shiraz 2011** Deep crimson, bright; a fragrant bouquet of red and blue fruits are offset by a fine seasoning of spicy oak; mid weight on the palate with taut acidity and fine tannins remaining on the fresh finish. Great value. Screwcap. 13% alc. **Rating** 90 **To** 2020 $16 BE

♀♀♀♀
⚙ **The Estate Hunter Valley Rose 2012** Light, bright magenta; made from cabernet franc, and has a very unusual palate, gyrating from red berry to pepper and spice and then back again, the mid-palate with fruit (and sugar?) sweetness followed by a dry finish. Screwcap. 13% alc. **Rating** 89 **To** 2014 $16

Jamiesons Run

Coonawarra Wine Gallery, Riddoch Highway, Coonawarra, SA 5263 **Region** Coonawarra
T (08) 8737 1300 **www.**jamiesonsrun.com.au **Open** 7 days 10–5
Winemaker Andrew Hales **Est.** 1987 **Dozens** NFP
The wheel has turned full circle for Jamiesons Run. It started out as a single-label, mid market, high-volume brand developed by Ray King during his time as CEO of Mildara. It grew and grew until Mildara, having many years since been merged with Wolf Blass, decided to rename the Mildara Coonawarra winery Jamiesons Run, with the Mildara label just one of a number falling under the Jamiesons Run umbrella. Now the Jamiesons Run winery is no more – Foster's sold it, but retained the brand; the cellar door has moved to shared accommodation at the Coonawarra Wine Gallery. Exports to Asia.

♀♀♀♀♀
⚙ **Chardonnay 2012** Clever winemaking provides a meaty complexity to the nectarine and melon fruit on the bouquet; the palate is fresh and lively, with concentration and complexity to command respect. Top gold Sydney Wine Show '13. Outstanding value. Screwcap. 13.5% alc. **Rating** 94 **To** 2016 $16 BE

ŢŢŢŢ Sauvignon Blanc Semillon 2012 Rating 88 To 2013 $16
Merlot 2011 Rating 87 To 2014 $16
Cabernet Sauvignon 2011 Rating 87 To 2016 $16
Cabernet Shiraz Merlot 2011 Rating 87 To 2016 $16

Jamsheed   ★★★★★

157 Faraday Street, Carlton, Vic 3053 (postal) **Region** Yarra Valley
T 0409 540 414 **www**.jamsheed.com.au **Open** Not
Winemaker Gary Mills **Est.** 2003 **Dozens** 1000
Jamsheed is the venture of Gary Mills, proprietor of Simpatico Wine Services, a boutique
contract winemaking company established at the Hill Paddock Winery in Healesville. The
wines are sourced from a 30-year-old, low-yielding vineyard, and are made using indigenous/
wild yeasts and minimal handling techniques. For the short-term future the business will focus
on old vine sites in the Yarra Valley, but will also include Grampians and Heathcote Shiraz. The
name, incidentally, is that of a Persian king recorded in the Annals of Gilgamesh. No wines
received for the *2014 Wine Companion*, but a five-star rating has been maintained.

Jane Brook Estate Wines   ★★★★

229 Toodyay Road, Middle Swan, WA 6056 **Region** Swan Valley
T (08) 9274 1432 **www**.janebrook.com.au **Open** 7 days 10–5
Winemaker Mark Baird **Est.** 1972 **Dozens** 15 000 **Vyds** 18.2ha
Beverley and David Atkinson have worked tirelessly to build up the Jane Brook Estate wine
business over the past 40 years. All wines are produced from the estate vineyards in Swan Valley
(6.5ha) and Margaret River (11.7ha). Exports to Singapore and China.

ŢŢŢŢŢ Atkinson Family Reserve Cabernet Sauvignon 2010 'Atkinson Family' is
selected as the best wine of the vintage, but with no indication of its vineyard
origin. The crimson–purple hue is excellent, although not especially deep; the
medium-bodied palate is elegant, with vibrant cassis fruit to the fore, the tannins
fine, the finish long, French oak totally integrated. Screwcap. 14.3% alc. **Rating** 94
To 2025 $50

ŢŢŢŢ? Back Block Shiraz 2011 Rating 90 To 2020 $25

Jansz Tasmania   ★★★★★

1216b Pipers Brook Road, Pipers Brook, Tas 7254 **Region** Northern Tasmania
T (03) 6382 7066 **www**.jansztas.com **Open** 7 days 10–4.30
Winemaker Natalie Fryar **Est.** 1985 **Dozens** 38 000 **Vyds** 30ha
Jansz is part of Hill-Smith Family Vineyards, and was one of the early sparkling wine labels in
Tasmania, stemming from a short-lived relationship between Heemskerk and Louis Roederer.
Its 15ha of chardonnay, 12ha of pinot noir and 3ha of pinot meunier correspond almost
exactly to the blend composition of the Jansz wines. It is the only Tasmanian winery entirely
devoted to the production of sparkling wine (although the small amount of Dalrymple Estate
wines are also made here), and is of high quality. Part of the former Frogmore Creek Vineyard
purchased by Hill-Smith Family Vineyards in Dec 2012 will be dedicated to the needs of Jansz
Tasmania. Exports to all major markets.

ŢŢŢŢŢ Premium Vintage Rose 2008 The whole bunch-pressed pinot noir base wine
was barrel-fermented and spent 9 months in aged French oak before secondary
fermentation in this bottle, followed by 36 months on lees prior to disgorgement.
Fraises du bois (forest strawberries) provide much of the aroma and flavour for
a seriously attractive rose, which has excellent length and a lingering, mouth-
watering finish. Cork. 12.5% alc. **Rating** 96 To 2017 $48

Premium Vintage Cuvee 2007 Whole bunch-pressed, bottle-fermented chardonnay and pinot noir taken through 100% mlf, then kept on yeast lees for 48 months prior to being disgorged. The wine combines complexity and full flavour with delicacy, the dosage precisely calibrated. Lovely now or later. Cork. 12% alc. Rating 95 To 2016 $45

🍷🍷🍷🍷🍷 **Premium Non Vintage Cuvee** Rating 92 To 2014 $30

Jasper Hill ★★★★★

Drummonds Lane, Heathcote, Vic 3523 **Region** Heathcote
T (03) 5433 2528 **www**.jasperhill.com **Open** By appt
Winemaker Ron Laughton, Emily McNally **Est.** 1979 **Dozens** 2500 **Vyds** 26.5ha
The red wines of Jasper Hill are highly regarded and much sought after. Over the past decade drought has caused some variation in style and weight, but as long as vintage conditions allow, these are wonderfully rich and full-flavoured wines, albeit with high levels of alcohol. The vineyards are dry-grown (hence drought problems) and are managed organically. Exports to the UK, the US, Canada, France, Denmark, Hong Kong and Singapore.

🍷🍷🍷🍷🍷 **Georgia's Paddock Heathcote Riesling 2012** It cannot be compared to a Clare or Eden Valley Riesling of the same age: that of Jasper Hill is much bolder and richer, finesse inevitably a trade-off. But in the top vintages – and this was one – is succulently juicy, its lime juice flavours flowing evenly across the tongue, with a long, balanced finish. Cork. 13% alc. Rating 94 To 2022 $40
The Sisters Heathcote Shiraz 2011 The decision was taken to blend Emily's and Georgia's Paddocks on the basis that the sum was greater than the parts. The colour is good, the bouquet fragrant and perfumed, the medium-bodied palate with juicy red black fruits, distinct cracked pepper and spice fruit. Has improved out of all recognition over the past 9 months. Cork. 13.5% alc. Rating 94 To 2021 $73

jb Wines

PO Box 530, Tanunda, SA 5352 **Region** Barossa Valley
T 0408 794 389 **www**.jbwines.com **Open** By appt
Winemaker Joe Barritt **Est.** 2005 **Dozens** 1000 **Vyds** 18ha
The Barritt family has been growing grapes in the Barossa since the 1850s, but this particular venture was established in 2005 by Lenore, Joe and Greg Barritt. It is based on shiraz, cabernet sauvignon and chardonnay (with tiny amounts of zinfandel, pinot blanc and clairette) planted between 1972 and '03. Greg runs the vineyard operations; Joe, with a Bachelor of Agricultural Science degree from Adelaide University, followed by 10 years of winemaking in Australia, France and the US, is now the winemaker. Exports to Hong Kong.

🍷🍷🍷🍷 **Barossa Valley Shiraz 2009** Medium red-purple, showing early stages of development; a pleasant Shiraz with notably sweet fruit/mocha/fruitcake flavours, the tannins soft. Screwcap. 14% alc. Rating 89 To 2019 $30
Lola Barossa Valley Zinfandel 2009 Given its age, has good colour, although not deep; the bouquet is aromatic, with a mix of spicy fruits and fresh baked cake, the medium-bodied palate with spiced fruits and a hint of preserved lemon. Screwcap. 13.5% alc. Rating 89 To 2016 $25
Barossa Valley Cabernet Sauvignon 2009 Good colour for the vintage; has plenty of generous black fruits along with mocha oak and soft tannins. Ready now, but will hold. Screwcap. 14% alc. Rating 88 To 2016 $25
Joseph's Barossa Valley Clairette 2012 Clairette was grown in the Hunter Valley until the 1970s. Has a distinct chalky/grippy palate, and a dry finish. Screwcap. 12.8% alc. Rating 87 To 2014 $25

Jeir Creek

122 Bluebell Lane, Murrumbateman, NSW 2582 **Region** Canberra District
T (02) 6227 5999 **www**.jeircreekwines.com.au **Open** Thurs–Mon & hols 10–5
(w'ends only during Aug)
Winemaker Rob Howell **Est.** 1984 **Dozens** 3000 **Vyds** 8ha
Rob and Kay Howell, owner–founders of Jeir Creek, celebrated 25 years of involvement
in 2009. Rob runs the technically advanced winery, while Kay looks after the cellar door.
Predominantly an estate-based business, the plantings comprise chardonnay, cabernet
sauvignon (2ha each), riesling, sauvignon blanc, shiraz (1ha each) and smaller plantings of pinot
noir, viognier and muscat.

Canberra District Riesling 2012 Bright straw-green; the floral, faintly spicy
bouquet introduces a palate with some Germanic overtones to its delicate blend of
lime, apple/apple blossom and acidity; scores well thanks to its finish and lingering
aftertaste. Screwcap. 12.2% alc. **Rating** 93 **To** 2018 $20
Reserve Canberra District Cabernet Merlot 2010 The colour is not entirely
convincing; a lateral approach saw the first year spent in 3-year-old French oak
barriques, the second in new French oak puncheons; a conventional approach
is new oak first up, older thereafter. But it does basically work, the fruit flavour
spectrum of black fruits encircled by cedary oak. In a perfect world, slightly less
oak would have been even better. Screwcap. 13.8% alc. **Rating** 92 **To** 2025 $40
Les Trois Filles Canberra District Chardonnay Pinot Noir 2008 Traditional
method used with now prolonged time on lees, the release timed for the 25th
anniversary of Jeir Creek and to recognise the contribution of Rob and Kay
Howell's three daughters (Kate, Anna and Jess). Still pale green-straw, it has
added complexity to the long palate of apple and citrus fruit, the dosage perfect.
Disgorged Nov '12. Crown seal. 12.2% alc. **Rating** 92 **To** 2017 $30

Canberra District Sparkling Shiraz 2009 **Rating** 89 **To** 2017 $30

Jenner & You

Cnr Catholic Church Road/Burra Road, Mintaro, SA 5415 **Region** Clare Valley
T 0429 697 323 **www**.ajwines.com.au **Open** By appt
Winemaker Contract **Est.** 2009 **Dozens** 1000 **Vyds** 5ha
Andrew Jenner and his father Vincent have 2ha each of shiraz and riesling and 0.8ha of cabernet
sauvignon at their family-operated Larkey's Corner Vineyard at Mintaro in the Clare Valley. The
wines are made by respected local winemakers Neil Pike and Steve Baraglia at Pikes.

Mintaro Creek Clare Valley Riesling 2012 Pale quartz; the fragrant and floral
bouquet leads into a delicious palate, filled with lime fruit, then tightened nicely
on the long finish by bright acidity. Top value. Screwcap. 12.3% alc. **Rating** 94
To 2020 $20

Larkey's Corner Clare Valley Shiraz 2011 **Rating** 88 **To** 2016 $25

Jim Barry Wines

Craig's Hill Road, Clare, SA 5453 **Region** Clare Valley
T (08) 8842 2261 **www**.jimbarry.com **Open** Mon–Fri 9–5, w'ends, hols 9–4
Winemaker Peter Barry **Est.** 1959 **Dozens** 80 000 **Vyds** 249ha
The patriarch of this highly successful wine business, Jim Barry, died in 2004, but the business
continues under the active management of several of his many children. There is a full range
of wine styles across most varietals, but with special emphasis on Riesling, Shiraz and Cabernet
Sauvignon. The ultra-premium release is The Armagh Shiraz, with the McCrae Wood red
wines not far behind. Jim Barry Wines is able to draw upon mature Clare Valley vineyards,
plus a small holding in Coonawarra. Exports to all major markets.

ŶŶŶŶŶ **The Armagh Shiraz 2010** Deep but bright purple-crimson; a deeply woven bouquet of blackberry, blackcurrant and plum flows through into the rich, multilayered palate; oak and ripe tannins are also plentiful. A 30-year life is conservative. Screwcap. 14.5% alc. **Rating** 97 **To** 2040 $215

PB Shiraz Cabernet Sauvignon 2010 Bright, full crimson-purple colour is a good start to a full-bodied and rich wine; a junior brother to The Armagh, with similar densely woven black fruits, dark chocolate, ripe tannins and positive but balanced oak. Screwcap. 14.5% alc. **Rating** 95 **To** 2035 $60

The Benbournie Cabernet Sauvignon 2010 Strong, deep, purple-crimson; while the varietal character is not in doubt, the cassis/blackberry and plum fruit is richer than the First Eleven, although not riper in terms of alcohol – admirably controlled with each wine. Screwcap. 13.5% alc. **Rating** 95 **To** 2035 $90

Watervale Riesling 2012 Pale green-quartz; a classically structured and balanced Riesling, already with plenty of zesty lime flavours underpinned by good acidity; will develop very well over many years. Its structure is particularly impressive. Screwcap. 12.4% alc. **Rating** 94 **To** 2025 $18

The Lodge Hill Dry Riesling 2012 Bright straw-green; there is more on show here than with The Florita; ripe citrus blossom on the bouquet dictates the path the palate takes, again with lashings of citrus fruit needing the acidity it duly finds on the finish. Screwcap. 12.5% alc. **Rating** 94 **To** 2022 $23

The Florita Clare Valley Riesling 2012 From one of the most distinguished vineyards in the Clare Valley, appropriate given the classic restraint of the wine, more hidden than heralded at this stage; the bouquet has notes of citrus and bath powder, the elegant, finely boned palate built around its talcy acidity. Have no fears for its future. Screwcap. 12.3% alc. **Rating** 94 **To** 2027 $50

The McRae Wood Clare Valley Shiraz 2010 No shrinking violet, this rendition captures the brightness of the vintage with fragrant red and black fruits, mocha, licorice and sage on the bouquet; the palate offers a succulent core of vibrant red fruits, fresh acidity and a long, pure and evenly balanced conclusion. Screwcap. 14% alc. **Rating** 94 **To** 2022 $50 BE

First Eleven Coonawarra Cabernet Sauvignon 2010 Medium red-purple, fresh, although not deep; the bouquet announces the clear-cut varietal character of cassis, black olive and a touch of herb, the oak well balanced and integrated, the tannins likewise. Screwcap. 13.5% alc. **Rating** 94 **To** 2030 $55

The Benbournie Cabernet Sauvignon 2009 The last Benbournie under cork. The colour is bright crimson-purple, the flavours more luscious and ripe than the '10, although here, too, the alcohol has been carefully controlled. Not quite as precise as the '10. 13.5% alc. **Rating** 94 **To** 2029 $90

ŶŶŶŶŷ **Three Little Pigs 2010** **Rating** 90 **To** 2015 $21

Jim Brand Wines

PO Box 18, Coonawarra, SA 5263 **Region** Coonawarra
T (08) 8736 3252 www.jimbrandwines.com.au **Open** Not
Winemaker Brand family, Bruce Gregory (consultant) **Est.** 2000 **Dozens** 2000 **Vyds** 9.5ha
The Brand family story starts with the arrival of Eric Brand in Coonawarra in 1950, when he married Nancy Redman and purchased a 24ha block from the Redman family, relinquishing his job as a baker and becoming a grapegrower. It was not until '66 that the first Brand's Laira wine was made. The Brand family sold the Brand's Laira winery in '94 to McWilliam's, Jim Brand staying on as chief winemaker right up until he died in 2005, after a long battle with cancer, unable to fulfil his ambition to make quality wine under his name. His son Sam, with help from locals, including Bruce Gregory at Majella, has now realised his father's dream, with the release of the '08 and '09 wines, made from the family's holding of 8ha of cabernet sauvignon and 1.5ha of shiraz.

ŢŢŢŢŢ Silent Partner Coonawarra Cabernet Sauvignon 2010 Deeply coloured
and deeply fruited, with blackcurrant pastille, smoky oak and a touch of geranium;
the palate is full-bodied and full-blooded, with ample chewy tannins dominating
the fruit at this early stage; a little time will see the big parts all come together.
Screwcap. 14% alc. **Rating** 90 **To** 2020 $33 BE

Jinglers Creek Vineyard   ★★★☆

288 Relbia Road, Relbia, Tas 7258 (postal) **Region** Northern Tasmania
T (03) 6344 5121 **www**.jinglerscreekvineyard.com.au **Open** Thurs–Sun 11–5
Winemaker Bass Fine Wines (Guy Wagner) **Est.** 1998 **Dozens** 250 **Vyds** 2ha
Irving Fong came to grapegrowing later in life, undertaking the viticulture course at
Launceston TAFE when he was 67 years old (he also met his second wife there). They have
1.8ha of pinot noir, and small plantings of pinot gris, sauvignon blanc and chardonnay.

ŢŢŢŢŢ Riesling 2011 Bright green-straw; a rich wine, lime marmalade on toast already
on show. Ready now. Screwcap. 12.7% alc. **Rating** 90 **To** 2016 $24

 # Jirra Wines at Jeir Station   ★★★★

Jeir Station, 2443 Barton Highway, Yass, NSW 2582 **Region** Canberra District
T (02) 6227 5671 **www**.jirrawines.com.au **Open** Not
Winemaker Canberra Winemakers **Est.** 2007 **Dozens** 2000 **Vyds** 4ha
The present day Jeir Station, while a substantial 120ha, was once part of a 6500ha grazing
property owned by the Johnston family between 1825 and 1918. The old homestead was
built around 1835 by convict labour, and still stands today. In 2000 present owners Colin and
Kay Andrews planted shiraz, cabernet sauvignon, chardonnay, viognier and sangiovese; they
have the wines contract-made by Rob Howell and Greg Gallagher of Canberra Winemakers.

ŢŢŢŢŢ Canberra District Shiraz 2006 Developed, but healthy, colour sets the scene for
✪ a very attractive Shiraz reflecting Canberra's coolness; obvious (but not excessive)
French oak maturation; the tannins are still present, but in no way impede the
juicy fresh fruit of the finish. Great opportunity for a mature wine of significant
quality. Screwcap. 14.5% alc. **Rating** 92 **To** 2016 $16
✪ Canberra District Cabernet Merlot 2006 Very good retention of hue and
depth; a wine of considerable flesh and depth, albeit passing into secondary/savoury
flavours (as one would expect at this age); the balance of fruit, oak and tannins is
very good, the wine a bargain. Screwcap. 14.8% alc. **Rating** 91 **To** 2016 $16

John Duval Wines   ★★★★★

PO Box 622, Tanunda, SA 5352 **Region** Barossa Valley
T (08) 8562 2266 **www**.johnduvalwines.com **Open** At Artisans of Barossa
Winemaker John Duval **Est.** 2003 **Dozens** 8000
John Duval is an internationally recognised winemaker, having been the custodian of Penfolds
Grange for almost 30 years as part of his role as chief red winemaker at Penfolds. In 2003
he established his eponymous brand, and begun providing consultancy services to clients
in various parts of the world. On the principle 'if not broken, don't fix', he is basing his
business on shiraz and shiraz blends from old-vine vineyards in the Barossa Valley. The brand
name Plexus denotes combining the different elements of shiraz/grenache/mourvedre into a
coherent structure. Exports to the UK, the US, Canada, Switzerland, Hong Kong and China.

ŢŢŢŢŢ Eligo Barossa Valley Shiraz 2010 Essency black fruits, savoury roasted meat
aromas and fragrant wood spices are all evident on the bouquet; the palate is full-
bodied and muscular with prodigious tannins lying in wait beneath the succulent
black fruits on offer. Cork. 14.5% alc. **Rating** 95 **To** 2030 $105 BE

ŢŢŢŢŢ Plexus Barossa Valley Marsanne Roussanne Viognier 2012 Rating 90
To 2017 $30 BE

John Gehrig Wines

Oxley-Milawa Road, Oxley, Vic 3678 **Region** King Valley
T (03) 5727 3395 **www**.johngehrigwines.com.au **Open** 7 days 10–5
Winemaker Ross Gehrig **Est.** 1976 **Dozens** 5600 **Vyds** 6ha
This family-founded and owned winery has passed on to the second generation, headed by
Ross Gehrig. The estate vineyard is a patchwork quilt of riesling, chenin blanc, chardonnay,
pinot meunier, pinot noir, muscat, lagrein, cabernet sauvignon, merlot, malbec, cabernet franc,
petit verdot, durif and gamay, allowing – indeed demanding – Ross to make wines in a wide
variety of styles. He continues to enjoy particular success with Riesling and Chenin Blanc.

ፕፕፕፕፕ King Valley Riesling 2012 An exceptional wine given that Oxley is in the low-
altitude section of the King Valley. It has a flowery bouquet of citrus and apple
blossom, the palate infused with lime juice, the long finish marked by crisp acidity,
yet leaving the lime flavours on the aftertaste. Screwcap. 11.5% alc. Rating 94
To 2020 $22

ፕፕፕፕፕ RG King Valley Riesling 2009 Rating 93 To 2019 $32
King Valley Durif Vintage Port 2006 Rating 91 To 2020 $25

John Kosovich Wines

Cnr Memorial Avenue/Great Northern Highway, Baskerville, WA 6056 **Region** Swan Valley
T (08) 9296 4356 **www**.johnkosovichwines.com.au **Open** 7 days 10–5.30
Winemaker Anthony Kosovich **Est.** 1922 **Dozens** 4000 **Vyds** 12.5ha
John Kosovich Wines operated as Westfield Wines until 2003, when it changed its name to
honour John's 50th vintage. The name change did not signify any change in either philosophy
or direction for this much-admired producer of a surprisingly elegant and complex
Chardonnay. The other wines are more variable, but from time to time there have been
attractive Verdelho and excellent Cabernet Sauvignon. Since 1998, wines partly or wholly
from the family's planting at Pemberton have been made, the Swan Valley/Pemberton blends
released under the Bronze Wing label.

ፕፕፕፕፕ Liqueur Verdelho NV Deeply flavoured, with burnt toffee, smoky oak, roasted
nut brittle and rancio complexity; the palate is luscious and complex, with taut
acidity and well-handled freshening of spirit duly noted and applauded. 375ml.
Diam. 19% alc. Rating 94 To 2014 $65 BE

ፕፕፕፕፕ Pemberton Chardonnay 2012 Rating 90 To 2016 $28 BE
Swan Valley Petit Verdot 2011 Rating 90 To 2016 $28 BE

John's Blend

18 Neil Avenue, Nuriootpa, SA 5355 (postal) **Region** Langhorne Creek
T (08) 8562 1820 **www**.johnsblend.com.au **Open** At The Winehouse, Langhorne Creek
Winemaker John Glaetzer **Est.** 1974 **Dozens** 2000 **Vyds** 23ha
John Glaetzer was Wolf Blass' right-hand man almost from the word go, the power behind the
throne of the three Jimmy Watson trophies awarded to Wolf Blass Wines – in 1974, '75 and
'76 – and a small matter of 11 Montgomery trophies for the Best Red Wine at the Adelaide
Wine Show. This has always been a personal venture on the side, as it were, by John and wife
Margarete, officially sanctioned of course, but really needing little marketing effort. Exports to
Canada, Switzerland, Indonesia, Singapore and Hong Kong.

ፕፕፕፕፕ Margarete's Langhorne Creek Shiraz 2010 The colour is good, and the
standard completion of the primary fermentation in 100% new oak, followed
by mlf in that oak, and a further 25 months' maturation in barrels has taken full
advantage of the vintage. Well priced, and in pure Glaetzer 'no wood, no good'
style. Cork. 14.5% alc. Rating 95 To 2025 $35

Individual Selection Langhorne Creek Cabernet Sauvignon 2009
Full red-purple; a Guigal-like 38 months' maturation in new French oak
hogsheads of two distinct parcels blended shortly prior to bottling. It cannot really
be compared to other Australian Cabernet Sauvignons; if accepted on its own
terms, is very good. Cork. 14.5% alc. **Rating** 94 **To** 2029 $35

Johnston Oakbank

18 Oakwood Road, Oakbank, SA 5243 **Region** Adelaide Hills
T (08) 8388 4263 **www**.johnston-oakbank.com.au **Open** Mon–Fri 10.30–4.30, w'ends 11–5
Winemaker David O'Leary (Contract), Geoff Johnston **Est.** 2002 **Dozens** 5000 **Vyds** 49ha
Johnston's has two distinct vineyards: the Galbraith Vineyard (22ha), adjacent to the Oakbank
racecourse, was planted in 1993 to chardonnay (12ha) and pinot noir (5ha) for sparkling
wine, and cabernet sauvignon (5ha). In '98 40ha was purchased in Balhannah, where 27ha of
sauvignon blanc, merlot, pinot noir and shiraz had been planted by the Wenzel family (part of
this production is sold to other makers). Exports to the US and Hong Kong.

ΨΨΨΨΨ **Adelaide Hills Sauvignon Blanc 2012** Bright straw-green; has tension rarely
✪ encountered in Sauvignon Blanc as grass, citrus and passionfruit – with a strong
undertow of crisp acidity – engage in a tug-of-war for flavour dominance, none
winning. Top-class value and quality. Screwcap. 12% alc. **Rating** 94 **To** 2014 $18

ΨΨΨΨΨ **Adelaide Hills Pinot Noir 2010** Rating 90 To 2018 $20

Jones Road

2 Godings Road, Moorooduc, Vic 3933 **Region** Mornington Peninsula
T (03) 5978 8080 **www**.jonesroad.com.au **Open** W'ends 11–5
Winemaker Sticks (Travis Bush) **Est.** 1998 **Dozens** 7500 **Vyds** 26.5ha
It's a long story, but after establishing a very large and very successful herb-producing business
in the UK, Rob Frewer and family migrated to Australia in 1997. By a circuitous route they
ended up with a property on the Mornington Peninsula, promptly planting pinot noir and
chardonnay, then pinot gris, sauvignon blanc and merlot; they have since leased another
vineyard at Mt Eliza, and purchased Ermes Estate in 2007.

ΨΨΨΨΨ **Nepean Mornington Peninsula Chardonnay 2012** Pale, bright quartz-green;
immediately seizes attention with its fragrant bouquet and an intense grapefruit
and white peach palate, the fruit having entirely absorbed the oak. Will be long-
lived. 130 dozen made. Screwcap. 13% alc. **Rating** 94 **To** 2020 $50
Mornington Peninsula Chardonnay 2011 Hand-picked, whole bunch-
pressed, wild yeast-fermented in a range of oak barrels. It is very lively and
refreshing; if any mlf has been used, it is not obvious; the palate is long and precise,
the balance excellent. Screwcap. 12.5% alc. **Rating** 94 **To** 2018 $30
Nepean Mornington Peninsula Pinot Noir 2012 The best estate-grown
pinot noir; matured for 9 months in a mix of new and used barriques from
Burgundian coopers. Light, bright crimson; both the fragrant bouquet and palate
are complex, albeit with only light-bodied red cherry/strawberry spice fruits; has
very good line and length. Screwcap. 13.5% alc. **Rating** 94 **To** 2019 $50

ΨΨΨΨΨ **Mornington Peninsula Pinot Gris 2011** Rating 92 To 2014 $25

Jones Winery & Vineyard

Jones Road, Rutherglen, Vic 3685 **Region** Rutherglen
T (02) 6032 8496 **www**.joneswinery.com **Open** Mon, Thurs, Fri 10–4, w'ends 10–5
Winemaker Mandy Jones **Est.** 1860 **Dozens** 1000 **Vyds** 9.22ha
Jones Winery & Vineyard was established in 1860 and stands testament to a rich winemaking
tradition. Since 1927, the winery has been owned and operated by the Jones family. Two
blocks of old vines have been preserved (including 1.69ha of shiraz), supported by further
blocks progressively planted between '75 and 2008. Today, Jones Winery & Vineyard is jointly
operated by winemaker Mandy Jones, who brings 14 years of experience working at Chateau

Carsin in Bordeaux, France, and her brother Arthur Jones. Together they produce a small range of boutique wines. Exports to Finland.

♀♀♀♀♀ **Rutherglen Old Tawny NV** A deeply coloured tawny and very rich, with raisins, toasted nuts, florals and licorice all evident; the rancio pulls through on the finish, providing freshness and a long nutty finish. 500ml. Vino-Lok. 19% alc. **Rating** 93 To 2014 $42 BE

Rutherglen Shiraz 2010 Deep garnet; a restrained bouquet of red and black fruits, with a little wood spice on display; the palate reveals plush tannins and a medium-bodied aspect that lingers harmoniously on the finish. ProCork. 12.5% alc. **Rating** 92 To 2018 $30 BE

Rutherglen Malbec 2011 Mid magenta; vibrant and perfumed on the bouquet with blue fruits, vine sap, spice and thyme on display; the palate is lively and fresh, juicy and direct, with fine tannins and a freshness that belies the warm origins; an excellent example of the variety. Screwcap. 13.5% alc. **Rating** 92 To 2018 $35 BE

LJ 2008 Deep garnet; the bouquet reveals dark fruits, mocha and prune aromas; ample levels of sweet fruit coat the palate, with a savoury backbone of tannin, leather and licorice; a Shiraz at the warm end of the spectrum, and executed with aplomb. ProCork. 14.8% alc. **Rating** 91 To 2018 $65 BE

JW Dry Red Shiraz 2010 Mid garnet, bright; a savoury bouquet of red fruits, licorice, sage and toast; the palate is medium-bodied and fragrant, accessible and fully ripe, despite the modest 12% alc. on the label; a luncheon wine in every respect. Screwcap. **Rating** 90 To 2016 $22 BE

Josef Chromy Wines   ★★★★★

370 Relbia Road, Relbia, Tas 7258 **Region** Northern Tasmania
T (03) 6335 8700 **www**.josefchromy.com.au **Open** 7 days 10–5
Winemaker Jeremy Dineen **Est.** 2004 **Dozens** 28 000 **Vyds** 60ha

Joe Chromy just refuses to lie down and admit that the wine industry in Tasmania is akin to a financial black hole. After escaping from Czechoslovakia in 1950, establishing Blue Ribbon Meats, using the proceeds of that sale to buy Rochecombe and Heemskerk vineyards, then selling those and establishing Tamar Ridge before it, too, was sold, Joe is at it again; this time he's invested $40 million in a wine-based but multifaceted business, including a major building development in Launceston. If this were not remarkable enough, Joe is in his eighties, and has recovered from a major stroke. The foundation of the new wine business was the purchase of the large Old Stornoway Vineyard at a receivership sale in 2003; in all, there are 60ha of 10-year-old vines, the lion's share to pinot noir and chardonnay. He retained Jeremy Dineen as winemaker, and the winery was completed prior to the '07 vintage. Chromy's grandson, Dean Cocker, is business manager of the restaurant, function and wine centre, which has spectacular views over White Hills to Ben Lomond, the vineyard and the lakes. The homestead is now a dedicated wine centre and cellar door, offering WSET (Wine & Spirit Education Trust) courses. Exports to the UK, the US and other major markets.

♀♀♀♀♀ **Vintage 2005** Full straw, faintest bronze overlay; a bottle-fermented blend of pinot noir and chardonnay that clearly spent many years on lees prior to disgorgement, needing relatively little dosage; a gentle wine with very good mouthfeel. Diam. 12.1% alc. **Rating** 95 To 2014 $45

DELIKAT SGR Riesling 2012 A pristine and apple-laden bouquet, with wet slate also playing a role; the palate offers laser-like acidity and extraordinary purity and length; a refreshing wine for either end of a meal. Screwcap. 7.5% alc. **Rating** 95 To 2020 $26 BE

Riesling 2011 Light straw-green; intense lime and spice aromas lead into an equally intense palate, complete with the grippy Tasmanian (in the best sense) acidity, lengthening the palate and finish. Screwcap. 12% alc. **Rating** 94 To 2026 $26

Sauvignon Blanc 2011 Light straw-green; replete with expressive fruit on the bouquet and palate, the flavours positively luscious, with lychee, passionfruit and guava all in play, balanced by Tasmanian acidity on the finish. Screwcap. 12% alc. **Rating** 94 To 2013 $26

Chardonnay 2011 This is sure to challenge most, as the bouquet offers an intense introduction into struck match and charry complexity (sulphide), with ripe lemon and hazelnut also on display; the palate is full-bodied, and while the acidity is fine and linear, the overall impression is of a full-flavoured wine with lots of grip. Screwcap. 13.5% alc. **Rating** 94 **To** 2022 $34 BE

Pinot Noir 2011 The features of this wine are an insight into its creator, with savoury 'European' notes a dominant feature; dark plums, cold tea, Asian spices and a damp forest floor on the bouquet lead to a silky and alluring palate, where the quite substantial tannins lurk in waiting, to reveal an extremely long and expansive conclusion. Screwcap. 13.5% alc. **Rating** 94 **To** 2020 $34 BE

Vintage 2008 A bottle-fermented blend of pinot noir and chardonnay with extended time on lees, but low dosage leaves the intense fruit flavours and underlying acidity in high relief; the finish is long and bracing. Diam. 12.1% alc. **Rating** 94 **To** 2015 $40

Botrytis Riesling 2011 Bright golden-green; unashamedly sweet and no less complex, with lime, marmalade and butterscotch flavours; likely near the peak of its development. 375ml. Screwcap. 9.5% alc. **Rating** 94 **To** 2016 $26

ΥΥΥΥΥ **PEPIK Sparkling Rose NV Rating** 93 **To** 2015 $30
ZDAR Chardonnay 2009 Rating 92 **To** 2016 $50 BE
Pinot Noir 2010 Rating 92 **To** 2017 $34
Non Vintage Rating 92 **To** 2015 $30
PEPIK Sparkling Sekt NV Rating 92 **To** 2015 $30
Delikat SGR Riesling 2011 Rating 92 **To** 2021 $26

✪ **PEPIK Pinot Noir 2012** Brightly coloured, offering red and spiced black cherries on the bouquet, and following with a plump and juicy palate; a joyful wine to put a smile on your face, especially at this price. Screwcap. 13.5% alc. **Rating** 91 **To** 2016 $22 BE
Riesling 2012 Rating 90 **To** 2020 $26 BE

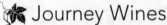 Journey Wines ★★★★

1a/29 Hunter Road, Healesville, Vic 3777 (postal) **Region** Yarra Valley
T 0427 298 098 **www**.jackrussellwines.com.au **Open** Not
Winemaker Damian North **Est.** 2011 **Dozens** 730
The name chosen by Damian North for his virtual winery is particularly appropriate given the winding path he has taken before starting (with his wife and three youngish children) his virtual winery. Originally a sommelier at Tetsuya's when it was still at Rozelle (and at Pier) he was inspired to enrol in the oenology course at CSU, gaining his first practical winemaking experience as assistant winemaker at Tarrawarra Estate for a number of years. Then, with family in tow, he moved to Oregon's Benton-Lane Winery to make Pinot Noir for several years, before returning to become assistant winemaker at Leeuwin Estate for five years, indulging in his other vinous passion, Chardonnay. The wheel has turned full circle as the family has returned to the Yarra Valley, securing 1.2ha of chardonnay and 0.8ha of pinot noir under contract arrangements with three distinguished vineyards, and making the wines at Medhurst.

ΥΥΥΥΥ **Yarra Valley Chardonnay 2011** Striking straw-green; the cool vintage produced many top-quality Chardonnays from the Yarra Valley; this is no exception, with its purity of varietal flavour, and hallmark regional line and length. Will develop with extreme grace. Screwcap. 12.5% alc. **Rating** 93 **To** 2020 $30
Yarra Valley Pinot Noir 2011 Pale colour; it is a very pretty wine, with a perfumed cherry/strawberry bouquet, then strawberry and cream flavours running through to the finish. Likely to give the most pleasure over the next few years, but could surprise with its tenacity. Screwcap. 12.5% alc. **Rating** 90 **To** 2014 $32

Juniper Estate ★★★★★

98 Tom Cullity Drive, Cowaramup, WA 6284 **Region** Margaret River
T (08) 9755 9000 **www**.juniperestate.com.au **Open** 7 days 10–5
Winemaker Mark Messenger **Est.** 1973 **Dozens** 12000 **Vyds** 19.5ha

When Roger Hill and Gillian Anderson purchased the Wrights' vineyard in 1998, the 10ha vineyard was already 25 years old, but in need of retrellising and a certain amount of nursing to bring it back to health. All of that has happened, along with the planting of additional shiraz and cabernet sauvignon. The Juniper Crossing wines use a mix of estate-grown grapes and grapes from other Margaret River vineyards, while the Juniper Estate releases are made only from the estate plantings. Exports to the UK, Ireland, Canada, Denmark, Hong Kong, the Philippines and Singapore.

ŸŸŸŸŸ **Margaret River Chardonnay 2011** Produced from Mendoza and 95 clone grapes; whole bunch-pressed direct to barrel (40% new) for 10 months. Has that depth and generosity typical of Margaret River, with ripe, white flesh fruit and creamy/cashew oak on the well-balanced palate. Screwcap. 13% alc. **Rating** 95 To 2031 $34

Margaret River Cabernet Sauvignon 2010 Bright crimson-purple; has brushed away the impact of 15 months of maturation in French oak, still fresh and vibrant with an abundance of cassis fruit and a strong substrate of tannins. A long life ahead. Screwcap. 14.5% alc. **Rating** 94 To 2035 $50

ŸŸŸŸŸ **Margaret River Semillon 2011 Rating** 93 To 2017 $27

✪ **Juniper Crossing Margaret River Shiraz 2010** Vivid crimson-purple, bright and clear; the wine finished its fermentation in the French and American oak barrels in which it was thereafter matured; potent red and black fruits and licorice and spice on the bouquet and medium- to full-bodied palate are, joined and complexed by oak and substantial tannins. Screwcap. 14.5% alc. **Rating** 93 To 2030 $20

Margaret River Shiraz 2010 Rating 93 To 2030 $35

✪ **Juniper Crossing Margaret River Cabernet Sauvignon Merlot 2009** Bright and clear colour; a very elegant, medium-bodied wine with a fragrant red fruit bouquet, and sufficient tannins and French oak to provide complexity. Typical high-quality Margaret River style. Screwcap. 14.5% alc. **Rating** 93 To 2019 $20

✪ **Juniper Crossing Margaret River Cabernet Sauvignon Merlot 2010** A 75/21% primary blend, the remainder cabernet franc, malbec and shiraz. An extended fermentation was followed by 4 months in French oak (15% new); the bright crimson-purple colour announces a fresh, medium-bodied palate with a bright mix of red and black fruits supported by dusty tannins. Screwcap. 14% alc. **Rating** 91 To 2017 $20

Aquitaine 2011 Rating 90 To 2014 $34

Juniper Crossing Tempranillo 2011 Rating 90 To 2016 $22

K1 by Geoff Hardy   ★★★★☆

Tynan Road, Kuitpo, SA 5172 **Region** Adelaide Hills
T (08) 8388 3700 **www**.k1.com.au **Open** Fri–Sun & public hols 11–5
Winemaker Geoff Hardy, Shane Harris **Est.** 1980 **Dozens** 7000 **Vyds** 36.5ha
The ultra-cool Kuitpo vineyard in the Adelaide Hills was planted by Geoff Hardy in 1987 after searching the hills for an ideal location for premium wine production. As this was the first significant vineyard planted in the region it became known as the K1 Vineyard. All fruit for Geoff Hardy's K1 brand is sourced from this vineyard, perched on the southwestern ridge of the Adelaide Hills above McLaren Vale Exports to the US, Canada, The Netherlands, Switzerland, Malaysia, Hong Kong and Singapore.

ŸŸŸŸŸ **Tzimmukin 2009** Deep colour; a blend of shiraz and cabernet sauvignon, revealing dark fruits of cassis, prune, black olive and cedar; the palate is fleshy and still fresh, mid weight and light on its feet, slowly revealing abundant fine-grained tannins and a savoury conclusion. ProCork. 15% alc. **Rating** 94 To 2022 $95 BE

ŸŸŸŸŸ **Gold Label Cabernet Sauvignon 2010 Rating** 93 To 2018 $35 BE
Gold Label Gruner Veltliner 2012 Rating 90 To 2015 $28

Kabminye Wines

Krondorf Road, Tanunda, SA 5352 **Region** Barossa Valley
T (08) 8563 0889 **www.**kabminye.com **Open** 7 days 11–5
Winemaker Rick Glastonbury **Est.** 2001 **Dozens** 1500 **Vyds** 1.5ha
Richard and Ingrid Glastonbury's cellar door is on land settled in the 1880s by Ingrid's ancestor, Johann Christian Henschke. Kabminye is an Aboriginal word meaning 'morning star', and was given to the hamlet of Krondorf as a result of the anti-German sentiment during World War II (since changed back to the original Krondorf). The cellar door and café opened in 2003; SA Tourism has since used the building as a sustainable tourism case study. The vineyard is planted to durif, shiraz, mourvedre, carignan, cinsaut, princess black muscat and black frontignac. Exports to the UK, Malaysia, Hong Kong and China.

ΨΨΨΨΨ **Ken & Neville 2010** A blend of mataro, cinsaut and 'with a good dash of
✪ grenache' dedicated to two veteran Barossa Valley grapegrowers. The light red-purple colour is good for this blend, and the flavours are terrific, red and black fruits contesting primacy, neither winning; the tannin structure is equally good. Great value. Screwcap. 14.5% alc. **Rating** 94 **To** 2020 $24

ΨΨΨΨΨ **Barossa Valley Durif 2011 Rating** 92 **To** 2021 $28

Kaesler Wines

Barossa Valley Way, Nuriootpa, SA 5355 **Region** Barossa Valley
T (08) 8562 4488 **www.**kaesler.com.au **Open** 7 days 10–5
Winemaker Reid Boshard, Stephen Dew **Est.** 1990 **Dozens** 22 000 **Vyds** 50ha
The first members of the Kaesler family settled in the Barossa Valley in 1845. The vineyards date back to '93, but the Kaesler family ownership ended in 1968. After several changes, the present (much-expanded) Kaesler Wines was acquired by a small group of investment bankers (who have since acquired Yarra Yering), in conjunction with former Flying Winemaker Reid Boshard and wife Bindy. Reid's experience shows through in the wines, which now come from estate vineyards, 40ha adjacent to the winery, and 10ha in the Marananga area. The latter includes shiraz planted in 1899, with both blocks seeing plantings in the 1930s, '60s, then each decade through to the present. Exports to all major markets.

ΨΨΨΨΨ **Alte Reben Barossa Valley Shiraz 2010** The shiraz is grown on the 113-year-old estate vineyard. The colour is spectacular, as is the profound depths of the blackberry, liqueur-soaked plum, licorice, bitter chocolate and spice fruit, oak a further adornment. Cork. 14.5% alc. **Rating** 97 **To** 2040 $120
Old Vine Barossa Valley Shiraz 2010 Dense purple-crimson; the grapes come from three estate vineyards, 40, 60 and 112 years old; it spent 18 months in French oak, and was neither fined nor filtered; it is a massive wine, with luscious black fruits, its tannins and oak relatively unobtrusive, something that cannot be said of the alcohol. Nonetheless, a great example of its genre. Cork. 15.5% alc. **Rating** 95 **To** 2030 $70
The Bogan 2009 Sourced from two estate vineyards, one planted 1899, the other in 1965, matured in American and French oak for 15 months, neither fined nor filtered. This Shiraz has a luxuriant display of sweet fruit wrapped in Swiss chocolate; carries its alcohol well thanks to spicy/savoury tannins on the finish. Cork. 15% alc. **Rating** 95 **To** 2029 $50
✪ **Old Vine Barossa Valley Semillon 2012** Quartz-white; made from estate vines over 50 years old; winemaker Reid Boshard has grasped the nettle, picked early at Hunter Valley baume levels, and not fiddled around with oak. This will develop superbly, already having an attention-getting display of lemon, apple and lime, buttressed by crystalline acidity. Screwcap. 10.5% alc. **Rating** 94 **To** 2027 $17
Old Bastard Barossa Valley Shiraz 2010 Deep red-purple; definitely and definitively in the biggest is best school of thought and practice; from the single vineyard planted in 1893, and crammed with ripe black fruits, ripe tannins and oak, almost suffocating in its density. Cork. 15.5% alc. **Rating** 94 **To** 2030 $200

Alte Reben Barossa Valley Mataro 2010 Matured in used French for
20 months; has retained good hue, and has a deliciously glossy array of plums of
various kinds on the palate and an ever so slightly spicy/savoury/juicy finish. Cork.
15% alc. **Rating** 94 **To** 2025 $80

ⓉⓉⓉⓉⓎ **Avignon 2009 Rating** 93 **To** 2024 $30
Barossa Valley Viognier 2011 Rating 90 **To** 2015 $25
Stonehorse Shiraz 2011 Rating 90 **To** 2017 $25
Stonehorse Shiraz Grenache Mourvedre 2010 Rating 90 **To** 2020 $20

Kalleske   ★★★★★

6 Murray Road, Greenock, SA 5360 **Region** Barossa Valley
T (08) 8563 4000 **www**.kalleske.com **Open** Mon–Fri by appt
Winemaker Troy Kalleske **Est.** 1999 **Dozens** 8000 **Vyds** 42ha
The Kalleske family has been growing and selling grapes on a mixed farming property at
Greenock for over 100 years. Sixth-generation Troy Kalleske, with brother Tony, established
the winery and created the Kalleske label in 1999. The vineyard is planted to shiraz (27ha),
grenache (6ha), mataro (2ha), chenin blanc, durif, viognier, zinfandel, petit verdot, semillon
and tempranillo (1ha each). The vines vary in age, with the oldest dating back to 1875, and
the overall average age is about 50 years; all grown organically. Exports to all major markets.

ⓉⓉⓉⓉⓉ **Johann Georg Old Vine Single Vineyard Barossa Valley Shiraz 2010**
Dense purple-red; the grapes were hand-picked from the vineyard planted in
1875. The yield of 1 tonne/hectare is obvious in this densely black-fruited wine,
with its undercurrent of spicy, savoury, ripe tannins, the French and American
oak integrated courtesy of the last phase of primary ferment carried out in barrel.
Barossa Valley Shiraz at its best. Screwcap. 14.5% alc. **Rating** 96 **To** 2050 $120
Eduard Old Vine Barossa Valley Shiraz 2010 Certified biodynamic; deep
crimson-purple, from vines planted between 1905 and '71. It is a prime example
of high-quality full-bodied Barossa Valley Shiraz; the question is whether it would
have been even better with 14% alc/vol. Unfined and unfiltered. Screwcap.
15% alc. **Rating** 94 **To** 2040 $85
Old Vine Single Vineyard Barossa Valley Grenache 2010 It is richer and
with greater depth and structure than many Barossa Valley Grenaches, and its
varietal expression has been retained through maturation in older hogsheads for
2 years. A red wine equivalent of cherries and ice cream. Screwcap. 15.5% alc.
Rating 94 **To** 2025 $45
✪   **Clarry's Barossa Valley GSM 2012** Deep purple-crimson; biodynamically
grown estate blocks have produced a delicious medium-bodied wine, aged in used
oak hogsheads for 6 months to focus all the attention on the opulent array of red
and black cherry, raspberry and blackberry fruit. This vintage was as great as '11
was not. Screwcap. 14.5% alc. **Rating** 94 **To** 2017 $19

ⓉⓉⓉⓉⓎ **Moppa Barossa Valley Shiraz 2011 Rating** 92 **To** 2021 $28
Greenock Barossa Valley Shiraz 2011 Rating 92 **To** 2026 $38
✪   **Clarry's Barossa Valley GSM 2011** Fourth-generation Clarry Kalleske spent
70 years tending the vines on this Greenock vineyard until his retirement in the
1990s; the wine is made by the sixth and seventh generations. It is a real surprise
packet, its energy and fresh red fruit drive coming from the low alcohol; if ever
there was proof that biodynamics can help vines weather the storm of incessant
rain, this is it. Screwcap. 14% alc. **Rating** 92 **To** 2018 $18
Merchant Single Vineyard Barossa Valley Cabernet Sauvignon 2010
Rating 92 **To** 2020 $28
Old Vine Barossa Valley Grenache 2011 Rating 91 **To** 2020 $45
Merchant Cabernet Sauvignon 2011 Rating 91 **To** 2020 $28
JMK Barossa Valley Shiraz VP 2010 Rating 91 **To** 2014 $23
JMK Barossa Valley Shiraz VP 2009 Rating 91 **To** 2029 $23

✪ **Florentine Single Vineyard Barossa Valley Chenin Blanc 2012** From estate vines planted in 1985; apparently hand-picked at night, and whole bunch-pressed, then wild-fermented in hogsheads (50%) and tank (50%), with some lees stirring until bottled after 5 months. The hard work has helped invest the wine with structure and texture it would otherwise have lacked. Screwcap. 13.5% alc. **Rating** 90 **To** 2015 $18
Buckboard Single Vineyard Barossa Valley Durif 2011 Rating 90 **To** 2020 $23

Kangarilla Road Vineyard ★★★★★

Kangarilla Road, McLaren Vale, SA 5171 **Region** McLaren Vale
T (08) 8383 0533 www.kangarillaroad.com.au **Open** Mon–Fri 9–5, w'ends 11–5
Winemaker Kevin O'Brien **Est.** 1997 **Dozens** 65 000 **Vyds** 14ha
In Jan 2013 Kangarilla Road founders Kevin O'Brien and wife Helen succeeded in breaking the mould for winery sales, and crafted a remarkable win-win outcome. They sold their winery and surrounding vineyard to Gemtree Vineyards, which has had its wine made at Kangarilla Road since '01 under the watchful eye of Kevin. The O'Briens have retained their adjacent JOBS Vineyard and the brand name. The Kangarilla Road wines will continue to be made by Kevin at the winery. Luck of the Irish, perhaps. Exports to the UK, the US and other major markets.

🍷🍷🍷🍷🍷 **Scarce Earth Project McLaren Vale Shiraz 2011** There is simply more of everything in this wine; strong aromas of mocha, fruitcake spice, prunes and black fruits are all on display; the palate is tannic, unyielding at this early stage, with black fruits in abundance and a lingering mocha note on the long unevolved finish. Screwcap. 14.5% alc. **Rating** 94 **To** 2022 $60 BE

🍷🍷🍷🍷🍷 **Q McLaren Vale Shiraz 2010 Rating** 93 **To** 2020 $70 BE
The Devil's Whiskers McLaren Vale Shiraz 2011 Rating 90 **To** 2018 $32 BE
McLaren Vale Cabernet Sauvignon 2011 Rating 90 **To** 2018 $20 BE
Terzetto 2010 Rating 90 **To** 2016 $22

KarriBindi ★★★☆

RMB 111, Scott Road, Karridale, WA 6288 (postal) **Region** Margaret River
T (08) 9758 5570 www.karribindi.com.au **Open** Not
Winemaker Naturaliste Vintners (Bruce Dukes) **Est.** 1997 **Dozens** 2000 **Vyds** 32.05ha
KarriBindi is owned by Kevin and Yvonne Wealand. The name is partly derived from Karridale and the surrounding karri forests, and from Bindi, the home town of one of the members of the Wealand family. In Nyoongar, 'karri' means strong, special, spiritual, tall tree and 'bindi' means butterfly, hence the label's picture of a butterfly soaring through karri trees. The Wealands have established sauvignon blanc (15ha), chardonnay (6.25ha), cabernet sauvignon (4ha), plus smaller plantings of semillon, shiraz and merlot. The major part of the grape production is sold under contract to Vasse Felix and Leeuwin Estate, with limited amounts released under the KarriBindi label. The core range includes Sauvignon Blanc, Semillon Sauvignon Blanc, Shiraz and Chardonnay Pinot. Exports to Singapore and China.

🍷🍷🍷🍷 **Margaret River Chardonnay Pinot 2010** Light straw-green, good mousse; pleasantly fruity, with a dry finish; not complex, and will be at its best over the next year or so. Cork. 12.5% alc. **Rating** 89 **To** 2014 $28
Margaret River Cabernet Merlot 2011 Mid garnet; simple red fruits with some cedary complexity; medium-bodied, simple and fragrant on the palate, and best consumed as a young wine. Screwcap. 13.5% alc. **Rating** 87 **To** 2016 $20 BE

Kate Hill Wines ★★★★☆

101 Glen Road, Huonville, Tas 7109 (postal) **Region** Southern Tasmania
T (03) 6223 5641 www.katehillwines.com.au **Open** Not
Winemaker Kate Hill **Est.** 2008 **Dozens** 1000

When Kate Hill (and husband Charles) came to Tasmania in 2006, Kate had worked as a winemaker in Australia and overseas for 10 years. Kate's wines are made from grapes from a number of vineyards across southern Tasmania, the aim being to produce approachable, delicate wines. Exports to the UK and Singapore.

PPPPP **Pinot Noir 2011** Full red-purple; fragrant plum and black cherry aromas translate directly onto the fore-palate, and are joined along the way by some savoury/foresty/stemmy notes to add complexity and texture. A little lean? Screwcap. 13% alc. **Rating** 93 **To** 2018 $35

Riesling 2012 Bright quartz-green; a potent and rich Riesling, crammed with sweet lemon and lime fruit, the shattering acidity of some Tasmanian Rieslings nowhere to be seen; indeed, could have done with more. Screwcap. 11.8% alc. **Rating** 92 **To** 2018 $27

PPPP **Cabernet Merlot 2010 Rating** 89 **To** 2016 $24

Katnook Estate ★★★★★

Riddoch Highway, Coonawarra, SA 5263 **Region** Coonawarra
T (08) 8737 0300 **www.katnookestate.com.au Open** Mon–Sat 10–5, Sun 11–5
Winemaker Wayne Stehbens **Est.** 1979 **Dozens** 90000 **Vyds** 198ha
Second in size only to Wynns Coonawarra Estate in the region, Katnook has made significant strides since its acquisition by Freixinet, the Spanish Cava producer; at one time selling most of its grapes, it now sells a maximum of 10%. The historic stone woolshed in which the second vintage in Coonawarra (1896) was made, and which has served Katnook since 1980, has been restored. Likewise, the former office of John Riddoch has been fully restored and is now the cellar door, and the former stables now serve as a function area. Well over half the total estate plantings are cabernet sauvignon and shiraz, other varieties of importance being chardonnay, merlot, sauvignon blanc and pinot noir. The Odyssey Cabernet Sauvignon and Prodigy Shiraz are the icon duo at the top of a multi-tiered production. Exports to all major markets.

PPPPP **The Caledonian Coonawarra Cabernet Shiraz 2010** The bright purple-crimson colour leads into a fresh and vibrant bouquet and palate, with a cascade of juicy red and black fruits supported by fine tannins and integrated oak. An impressive reprise of the '87 Jimmy Watson winner (a rather lesser wine). Cork. 14.5% alc. **Rating** 96 **To** 2025 $50

Coonawarra Cabernet Sauvignon 2010 The freshness of the vintage is easy to see within this wine, with fresh blackcurrant and red fruit aromas, black olive and finely tuned oak handling; the palate is full-bodied and impressive in concentration, revealing plenty of oak and tannin. Screwcap. 13.5% alc. **Rating** 95 To 2022 $40 BE

Coonawarra Shiraz 2010 Deep, bright crimson; restrained and savoury aromas of black fruits, sage and spicy mocha oak; the palate is medium- to full-bodied, with tightly packed tannins and fresh black fruits, offset by a lingering mocha and floral violet note to conclude. Screwcap. 13.5% alc. **Rating** 94 **To** 2022 $40 BE

PPPPP **Coonawarra Merlot 2010 Rating** 93 **To** 2020 $40 BE
Coonawarra Riesling 2012 Rating 92 **To** 2018 $22 BE
Coonawarra Sauvignon Blanc 2012 Rating 91 **To** 2015 $25 BE
Odyssey Cabernet Sauvignon 2009 Rating 90 **To** 2018 $100 BE

Katoa Wines ★★★★

PO Box 10, Heathcote, Vic 3523 **Region** Heathcote
T 0401 088 214 **Open** Not
Winemaker Michael Katoa **Est.** 2005 **Dozens** 200
Michael Katoa was introduced to wine at a young age at the behest of his mother, with tastings of up and coming producers in NZ's rapidly developing wine industry. A move to Australia led to work in bars and restaurants, then as a wine retailer. Next came experience working in vineyards and wineries around the Mornington Peninsula, and thereafter Heathcote, with

overlapping studies in wine science and viticulture at CSU. He and wife Natasha intend to make Heathcote their permanent home, and ultimately establish a vineyard and winemaking facility of their own. In the meantime, they are purchasing small amounts of shiraz and viognier from local growers, with sangiovese (Natasha has Italian heritage) also in the mix.

♟♟♟♟♟ **Heathcote Shiraz 2010** Full red-purple; a powerful Shiraz, with sombre black fruits and anise/licorice to the fore; there are also tar and bitter chocolate nuances that add to the character and quality of the wine. Very clever label with a cut-out glass. Screwcap. 14.5% alc. **Rating** 93 **To** 2030 $32

Kay Brothers Amery Vineyards ★★★★★

57 Kays Road, McLaren Vale, SA 5171 **Region** McLaren Vale
T (08) 8323 8211 www.kaybrothersamerywines.com **Open** Mon–Fri 9–5, w'ends & public hols 11–5
Winemaker Colin Kay, Andy Coppard **Est.** 1890 **Dozens** 12 000 **Vyds** 22ha
A traditional winery with a rich history and just over 20ha of priceless old vines; while the white wines have been variable, the red wines and fortified wines can be very good. Of particular interest is Block 6 Shiraz, made from 100-year-old vines; both vines and wines are going from strength to strength. Exports to the UK, the US, Canada, Switzerland, France, Germany, Malaysia, Indonesia, Hong Kong, Singapore, Japan and NZ.

♟♟♟♟♟ **Block 6 McLaren Vale Shiraz 2010** The estate-grown grapes from 118-year-old vines were open-fermented, basket-pressed, and the wine then spent 20 months in new American and Baltic oak. The colour is deep and the palate full-bodied, with multiple layers of blackberry fruit that have largely absorbed the oak. Screwcap. 14.5% alc. **Rating** 95 **To** 2050 $75
Hillside McLaren Vale Shiraz 2010 Strong colour; a generous, full-bodied Shiraz, replete with black fruits, savoury notes and ample tannins, all presented with a backdrop of mocha/vanillin oak. Very good wine with a long future. Screwcap. 14.5% alc. **Rating** 94 **To** 2035 $40
Basket Pressed McLaren Vale Shiraz 2010 Deep crimson; a perfumed bouquet in keeping with regional mulberry, fruitcake and bitter chocolate expectation; the palate is lively and reveals the freshness of the vintage; medium-bodied, with ample levels of juicy fruit, gravelly tannins and mocha oak on the finish. Screwcap. 14.5% alc. **Rating** 94 **To** 2025 $25 BE

♟♟♟♟♟ **Cuthbert McLaren Vale Cabernet Sauvignon 2010** **Rating** 93 **To** 2025 $40
McLaren Vale Shiraz 2011 **Rating** 92 **To** 2022 $25 BE
McLaren Vale Mataro 2011 **Rating** 90 **To** 2018 $25 BE

Keith Tulloch Wine ★★★★★

Hermitage Road, Pokolbin, NSW 2320 **Region** Hunter Valley
T (02) 4998 7500 www.keithtullochwine.com.au **Open** 7 days 10–5
Winemaker Keith Tulloch **Est.** 1997 **Dozens** 9000 **Vyds** 7.4ha
Keith Tulloch is, of course, a member of the Tulloch family, which has played such a leading role in the Hunter Valley for over a century. Formerly a winemaker at Lindemans and then Rothbury Estate, he has developed his own label since 1997. There is the same almost obsessive attention to detail, the same almost ascetic intellectual approach, the same refusal to accept anything but the best as that of Jeffrey Grosset. Exports to the UK, the US, Canada, Sweden and Hong Kong.

♟♟♟♟♟ **The Doctor Hunter Valley Shiraz 2011** A barrel selection of 140 dozen bottles made by Dr Harry Tulloch, Keith Tulloch's father, and named in his honour. The purple colour is very deep, the wine particularly intense and long, and (in Harry's words) more 'lean and refined' than many of the best wines from this outstanding Hunter Valley Shiraz vintage. Screwcap. 14.5% alc. **Rating** 96 **To** 2036 $70

Field of Mars Block 2A Hunter Valley Semillon 2012 Bright green-quartz; the wine is almost painfully intense, with its piercing acidity knifing through the lemon juice/mineral/lemongrass flavours. 100 dozen made from estate 4-year-old dry-grown vines. Screams out for patience; think of a 2-year-old First Growth Bordeaux. Screwcap. 10.5% alc. **Rating** 95 **To** 2027 $40

Museum Release Hunter Valley Semillon 2006 Brilliant straw-green; a very good example of the magical transformation of Hunter Valley semillon with 5–7 years' bottle age; the wine retains its purity and line of 5 years ago, yet has built sweet lemon and honeycomb flavours, with further time to develop even richer characters. Screwcap. 10.5% alc. **Rating** 95 **To** 2021 $45

The Kester Hunter Valley Shiraz 2011 Strong colour; a potent, full-bodied Shiraz reflecting extended maceration after the conclusion of the primary fermentation, plus generous use of new French oak. It has multiple layers of dark berry and polished leather fruit; given the screwcap, its life is almost unlimited. 14.5% alc. **Rating** 95 **To** 2041 $65

Museum Release Kester Hunter Valley Shiraz 2005 All of the components have now welded themselves seamlessly together on the bouquet and medium-bodied palate; it has reached the first stage of maturity, with a delicious combination of red and black berry fruits, superfine tannins and subtle French oak. Screwcap. 14.5% alc. **Rating** 95 **To** 2030 $70

Hunter Valley Semillon 2012 Rating 94 To 2022 $28
Field of Mars Hunter Valley Chardonnay 2012 Rating 94 To 2020 $45
Hunter Valley Shiraz Viognier 2011 Rating 94 To 2026 $32
Forres Blend 2010 Rating 94 To 2025 $38
Hunter Valley Botrytis Semillon 2011 Rating 94 To 2016 $35

ŶŶŶŶŶ **Tumbarumba Chardonnay 2012** Rating 93 To 2017 $30
Field of Mars Block 1 Hunter Valley Shiraz 2010 Rating 93 To 2025 $70
Tumbarumba Chardonnay 2011 Rating 92 To 2016 $30

Kellermeister ★★★★★

Barossa Valley Highway, Lyndoch, SA 5351 **Region** Barossa Valley
T (08) 8524 4303 **www.kellermeister.com.au Open** 7 days 9.30–5.30
Winemaker Matthew Reynolds, Andrew Cockram **Est.** 1976 **Dozens** 35 000 **Vyds** 2ha
Kellermeister is owned by Ralph Wesley Jones and is now the exclusive brand for all wines made by it, including the flagship Wild Witch Shiraz. For a variety of reasons, one being the financial failure of Dan Philips' The Grateful Palate, there have been structural changes to the business, including the appointment of Mark Pearce (most recently ex Wirra Wirra) as CEO, Matt Reynolds as chief winemaker, and assistant winemaker Andrew Cockram. Matt began his career with Kay Brothers Amery Vineyards in McLaren Vale, thereafter working with Jeffrey Grosset making Riesling, joining Kellermeister in 2005. Kellermeister was awarded Best Shiraz in the World, Best Australian Shiraz and Best Barossa Shiraz at the International Wine Challenge (London) '12, the largest wine competition in the world. Exports to the US, Canada, Switzerland, Denmark, Israel, Taiwan, China and Japan.

ŶŶŶŶŶ **Wild Witch Barossa Shiraz 2009** The hue is good, although of moderate (ie normal) depth; the wine has an utterly unexpected elegant and gentle footfall, the fruits as much red as they are black; the tannins are fine, and the oak balanced and integrated. A delicious wine in every respect, radically different from the '10 Shirazs. Screwcap. 14.5% alc. **Rating** 95 **To** 2030 $85

Black Sash Barossa Valley Shiraz 2010 Deep red-purple; made from old vines, and laden with more or less equal portions of black fruits, dark chocolate, mocha and oak, licorice also in play. Obviously full-bodied, but the fruit isn't dead, and the tannins are balanced. Screwcap. 14.5% alc. **Rating** 94 **To** 2030 $55

Dry Grown Barossa Valley Shiraz 2010 Full red-purple; has a very different texture and structure from that of Black Sash, with more light and shade, more freshness and clearer blackberry, black cherry and plum fruits. Oak and tannins play precisely determined roles. Screwcap. 14.5% alc. **Rating** 94 **To** 2030 $32

ŶŶŶŶŶ   **The Wombat General Hand Picked Eden Valley Riesling 2012** Quartz-
✪   white; the delicate, flowery/blossom aromas of the bouquet lead into a fresh, lively
         and precise palate with lime and green apple to the fore, the finish lengthened by
         citrussy acidity. Screwcap. 12% alc. **Rating** 93 **To** 2020 $22
         Individual Selection Reserve Riesling 2011 Rating 93 To 2026 $28
         The Pious Pioneer Barossa Shiraz 2010 Rating 90 To 2020 $25
         The Runaway Ring Late Harvest Riesling 2012 Rating 90 To 2018 $22

Kelvedon

PO Box 126, Swansea, Tas 7190 **Region** East Coast Tasmania
T (03) 6257 8283 **www**.kelvedonestate.com.au **Open** Not
Winemaker Winemaking Tasmania (Julian Alcorso) **Est.** 1998 **Dozens** 2000 **Vyds** 9ha
Jack and Gill Cotton began planting the Kelvedon Vineyard with 1ha of pinot noir in 1998.
The Cotton family has owned and managed the historic East Coast property since 1829,
grapegrowing coming very late in the piece. The plantings were extended in 2000–01 by
an additional 5ha, half to pinot noir and half to chardonnay, followed by a further 2ha of
chardonnay in '10. The chardonnay and 1ha of pinot noir plantings are under contract to
Accolade Wines. One hectare of sauvignon blanc has also been established to provide a second
wine under the Kelvedon label; the Pinot Noir can be of excellent quality.

ŶŶŶŶŶ   **Pinot Noir 2011** Bright, clear purple-crimson; has an abundance of rich, ripe
         (but not overripe) plum fruit on the bouquet and palate; the mouthfeel is round
         and supple, the balance exemplary, the oak restrained. Screwcap. 13.9% alc.
         Rating 94 To 2020 $37

ŶŶŶŶŶ   **Chardonnay 2011** Rating 92 To 2021 $37
         Sauvignon Blanc 2012 Rating 91 To 2014 $27

Kennedy   ★★★

Maple Park, 224 Wallenjoe Road, Corop, Vic 3559 (postal) **Region** Heathcote
T (03) 5484 8293 **www**.kennedyvintners.com.au **Open** Not
Winemaker Sandro Mosele (Contract) **Est.** 2002 **Dozens** 1000 **Vyds** 29.2ha
Having been farmers in the Colbinabbin area of Heathcote for 27 years, John and Patricia
Kennedy were on the spot when a prime piece of red Cambrian soil on the east-facing slope
of Mt Camel Range became available for purchase. They planted 20ha of shiraz in 2002. As
they gained knowledge of the intricate differences within the site, and worked with contract
winemaker Sandro Mosele, further plantings of shiraz, tempranillo and mourvedre followed in
'07. The Shiraz is made in small open fermenters, using indigenous yeasts and gentle pigeage
before being taken to French oak (20% new) for 12 months' maturation prior to bottling.

ŶŶŶŶ   **Cambria Heathcote Shiraz 2009** Mid garnet, showing a little development;
        there is a strong vegetal presence, with prune, plum and mocha also on show;
        medium-bodied, with fragrant acidity and a moderately long finish. Diam.
        13.5% alc. **Rating** 87 **To** 2017 $32 BE

Kennedy & Wilson

203 Maroondah Highway, Healesville, Vic 3777 (postal) **Region** Port Phillip Zone
T (03) 9017 4746 **www**.kennedyandwilson.com.au **Open** Not
Winemaker Peter and James Wilson **Est.** 2005 **Dozens** 700
Kennedy & Wilson is a partnership between brothers James and Peter Wilson, and Juliana
Kennedy. James, previously a chemical engineer, completed his Master of Oenology degree at
Adelaide University in 2006, and is currently completing a PhD. Peter worked under Bailey
Carrodus at Yarra Yering from 1986–96, and established Kennedy & Wilson chocolates in '96
before joining Stuart Wines as chief winemaker in 2003. Juliana, ex-CEO of a smartcard/sim
card company and the business mind behind the chocolate venture, now describes herself
as 'manager of the worldwide Kennedy & Wilson conglomerate'. A sense of humour is an
essential ingredient in this business. The grapes come from the Quarry Ridge Vineyard in

Kilmore, at an elevation of 400m, on the southern side of the Great Dividing Range. The chardonnay and one of the pinot noir blocks are over 20 years old; the balance of the vineyard was planted in 1998. The climate is very cool indeed, the hand-picked fruit ripening between April and May.

🍷🍷🍷🍷🍷 **Quarry Ridge Vineyard Semillon 2012** If the Hunter Valley can pick semillon with a potential 10.5% alcohol (or lower) why shouldn't the Yarra Valley follow the same path, although sensibly stopping at 11.5%? It is bright, with lemon zest and pith, and a complex texture. Screwcap. **Rating** 91 **To** 2018 $20

Kenred Shiraz   ★★★★

1819 Sunraysia Highway, Redbank, Vic 3477 **Region** Pyrenees
T (03) 5467 7192 **www**.kenred.com.au **Open** W'ends & public hols 10.30–4.30, or by appt
Winemaker Michael Unwin **Est.** 2002 **Dozens** 400 **Vyds** 3ha
Kenred is the venture of Fay and Ken Keech. The vineyard is planted solely to shiraz, with the single clone, SA 1654. The northwest boundary features a pine plantation, and a short walk through that plantation brings you to an ornamental lake; alternatively, barbecue and picnic facilities are available adjacent to the winery. The grapes are hand-picked, basket-pressed and made with minimum intervention.

🍷🍷🍷🍷🍷 **Single Vineyard Pyrenees Shiraz 2010** Medium to full crimson-purple; a generously flavoured wine, although only medium-bodied thanks to fine tannins; juicy black cherry, blackberry and spice fruits are the fulcrum around which the tannins and oak move. Screwcap. 13.5% alc. **Rating** 92 **To** 2025 $30

Kerrigan + Berry   ★★★★★

PO Box 221, Cowaramup, WA 6284 **Region** South West Australia Zone
T (08) 9755 6046 **www**.kerriganandberry.com.au **Open** At Hay Shed Hill
Winemaker Michael Kerrigan, Gavin Berry **Est.** 2007 **Dozens** 1200
Owners Michael Kerrigan and Gavin Berry have been making wine in WA for a combined period of over 40 years, and say they have been most closely associated with the two varieties that in their opinion define WA: riesling and cabernet sauvignon. This is strictly a weekend and after-hours venture, separate from their respective roles as chief winemakers at Hay Shed Hill and West Cape Howe. They have focused on what is important, and explain, 'We have spent a total of zero hours on marketing research, and no consultants have been injured in the making of these wines.' The Riesling is made from the Langton Vineyard in Mount Barker, with some of the oldest riesling vines in WA (planted in the 1970s). The Cabernet Sauvignon is a blend of grapes from Mount Barker (the Landsdale Vineyard) and Margaret River (the Hay Shed Hill vineyard). Exports to the UK and Singapore.

🍷🍷🍷🍷🍷 **Mt Barker Great Southern Riesling 2012** The purity of varietal expression on the bouquet is paralleled by the tightly carved green apple, citrus and mineral of the palate. This is a classic Riesling simply needing time to burst into a shimmering display of flavours that will seek every corner of the mouth, and linger long after it is swallowed. Screwcap. 12% alc. **Rating** 96 **To** 2032 $28

Kersbrook Hill   ★★★★☆

1498 South Para Road, Kersbrook, SA 5231 **Region** Adelaide Hills
T (08) 8389 3301 **www**.kersbrookhill.com.au **Open** 7 days 10–5.30
Winemaker Simon Greenleaf, Peter Schell, Ryan Haynes **Est.** 1998 **Dozens** 8000
Vyds 11ha
Paul and Mary Clark purchased what is now the Kersbrook Hill property, then grazing land, in 1997, planting 0.4ha of shiraz on a reality-check basis. Encouraged by the results, they increased the plantings to 3ha of shiraz and 1ha of riesling two years later. Yet further expansion of the vineyards has seen the area under vine increased to 11ha, cabernet sauvignon (with 6ha) the somewhat unusual frontrunner. Mark Whisson is consultant viticulturist (Mark has been growing grapes in the Adelaide Hills for over 20 years). Exports to the US, Singapore, Hong Kong and China.

ŸŸŸŸŸ **Grace Louise Adelaide Hills Cabernet Sauvignon 2010** A single French barrique chosen from the entire production; spent 18 months in that barrique; medium red-purple, it has very clear varietal expression, a certain black olive severity adding to, rather than detracting from, the appeal of the wine. Screwcap. 14% alc. **Rating** 94 **To** 2025 $50

ŸŸŸŸŸ **Adelaide Hills Riesling 2011 Rating** 93 **To** 2020 $25
Adelaide Hills Chardonnay 2011 Rating 92 **To** 2016 $25
Adelaide Hills Riesling 2012 Rating 91 **To** 2016 $25
Don's Acre Adelaide Hills Shiraz 2008 Rating 90 **To** 2014 $120

Kidman Wines   ★★★★

13713 Riddoch Highway, Coonawarra, SA 5263 **Region** Coonawarra
T (08) 8736 5071 **www**.kidmanwines.com.au **Open** 7 days 10–5
Winemaker Sid Kidman **Est.** 1984 **Dozens** 6000 **Vyds** 17.2ha
Sid Kidman planted the first vines on the property in 1971, and has been managing the vineyard ever since. Over the years it has grown to its present size, with cabernet sauvignon, shiraz, riesling and sauvignon blanc. The cellar door is housed in the old stables on the Kidman property; they were built in 1859 and are a great link with the district's history. Susie and Sid have recently been joined by their son George, who becomes the fourth generation of the Kidman family to be involved with the property. Exports to Malaysia and China.

ŸŸŸŸŸ ✪ **Coonawarra Cabernet Sauvignon 2010** Estate-grown and matured for 18 months in French oak. The colour is very good, and varietal cabernet is clear-cut on both the bouquet and palate; the blackcurrant fruit has notes of tar and earth, the tannins firm but not dry, the oak disciplined. Well worth cellaring, and well priced. Screwcap. 14% alc. **Rating** 91 **To** 2030 $21

✪ **Coonawarra Shiraz 2010** Medium purple-red, good retention; the wine spent 18 months in American oak, seemingly mostly old, for it is the red and black fruits of the medium-bodied palate that come through most clearly, and expand on the juicy finish. Screwcap. 13.5% alc. **Rating** 90 **To** 2020 $19

ŸŸŸŸ **Coonawarra Sauvignon Blanc 2012 Rating** 87 **To** 2014 $16

Kies Family Wines   ★★★

Barossa Valley Way, Lyndoch, SA 5381 **Region** Barossa Valley
T (08) 8524 4110 **www**.kieswines.com.au **Open** 7 days 9.30–4
Winemaker Wine Wise Consultancy **Est.** 1969 **Dozens** 5000 **Vyds** 33ha
The Kies family has been resident in the Barossa Valley since 1857; the present generation of winemakers is the fifth. Until 1969 the family sold almost all their grapes, but in that year they launched their own brand, Karrawirra. The coexistence of Killawarra forced a name change in 1983 to Redgum Vineyard; this business was subsequently sold. Later still, Kies Family Wines opened for business, drawing upon vineyards (up to 100 years old) that had remained in the family throughout the changes, offering a wide range of wines through the 1880 cellar door. Exports to the UK, Singapore, Hong Kong, China and Japan.

ŸŸŸŸ **Klauber Block Barossa Valley Shiraz 2009** Very good colour retention; the old vine material seems to have been matured in oak of lesser quality than it deserved, sending discordant messages on the bouquet and palate. Screwcap. 14.5% alc. **Rating** 87 **To** 2016 $27

Kilikanoon   ★★★★★

Penna Lane, Penwortham, SA 5453 **Region** Clare Valley
T (08) 8843 4206 **www**.kilikanoon.com.au **Open** Thurs–Mon 11–5
Winemaker Kevin Mitchell **Est.** 1997 **Dozens** 40 000 **Vyds** 330ha
Kilikanoon has travelled in the fast lane since winemaker Kevin Mitchell established it in 1997 on the foundation of 6ha of vines owned by him and father Mort. With the aid of investors its 40 000-dozen production comes from over 300ha of estate-owned vineyards, and access to the

best grapes from a total of 2266ha across SA. In Feb '13 Warren Randall (ex Seppelt sparkling winemaker in the 1980s) increased his already very substantial shareholding in Seppeltsfield to over 90%, and divested Seppeltsfield of its former ownership of Kilikanoon. At the time of going to print it is unclear how the separation of Kilikanoon from Seppeltsfield will impact on Kilikanoon's future operations. Exports to most major markets.

ΨΨΨΨΨ **Attunga 1865 Clare Valley Shiraz 2010** The venerable old vines dating back to the 1860s have produced a stunning wine that is a multilayered, complex and compelling for its elegance, restraint and latent power; the bouquet is pure fruited, with blackberry, red fruits, violets and a fine seasoning of spicy oak; the silky texture of the palate is enthralling, and the acidity provides lift and length. Screwcap. 14.5% alc. **Rating** 97 **To** 2035 $250 BE
Reserve Clare Valley Cabernet Sauvignon 2010 Impenetrable colour, purple hue; epic in its concentration and purity, the fruit is pure cassis seasoned with fine oak and a touch of sage; the palate is juicy on entry, with the densely packed tannins barely having a voice with the succulent fruit on offer; will age with grace. Screwcap. 14% alc. **Rating** 96 **To** 2030 $49 BE
Mort's Reserve Watervale Riesling 2012 Pale colour; the bouquet is reserved and almost in hiding, offering glimpses of lime zest, green apple and lanolin; the palate follows suit, with restraint the central theme, yet the fine, dry and tightly wound acidity provides a very long finish; will certainly reward patient cellaring. Screwcap. 12.5% alc. **Rating** 95 **To** 2025 $35 BE
Green's Vineyard Barossa Valley Shiraz 2010 Deeply coloured, and showing vibrant aromas of black fruits, red licorice, sage, wet slate minerality and spicy oak; the palate remains light on its feet, and while some warmth from high alcohol is noticeable, it merely complements the hedonistic fruit on offer. Screwcap. 14.5% alc. **Rating** 95 **To** 2025 $80 BE
Oracle Clare Valley Shiraz 2010 Once again, impenetrable colour, yet there is a lift to the perfume redolent of fresh crushed blackberry, vine sap, mocha and spicy oak that is alluring; the palate is thickly textured on entry, with juicy acidity providing lift and lightness on the long and fine-grained tannin finish. Screwcap. 14.5% alc. **Rating** 95 **To** 2025 $80 BE
Mort's Block Watervale Riesling 2012 **Rating** 94 **To** 2025 $22 BE
✪ **Killerman's Run Shiraz 2010** Deep crimson, purple hue; when first tasted in January the wine had a highly expressive and fragrant bouquet, the sweet-fruited medium-bodied palate warm, generous and fresh, finding a balance between ripeness and savoury complexity. It has flourished since then, the underlying freshness now even more evident. Screwcap. 14.5% alc. **Rating** 94 **To** 2025 $20
Crowhurst Reserve Barossa Valley Shiraz 2010 **Rating** 94 **To** 2025 $120 BE
Blocks Road Clare Valley Cabernet Sauvignon 2010 **Rating** 94 **To** 2025 $33 BE

ΨΨΨΨΨ **Miracle Hill McLaren Vale Shiraz 2010** **Rating** 93 **To** 2022 $80 BE
Exodus Barossa Valley Shiraz 2010 **Rating** 93 **To** 2022 $40 BE
Killerman's Run Shiraz Grenache 2011 **Rating** 93 **To** 2018 $20 BE
Killerman's Run Shiraz 2011 **Rating** 90 **To** 2016 $20 BE
Covenant Clare Valley Shiraz 2010 **Rating** 90 **To** 2018 $40 BE

Killara Estate   ★★★☆

773 Warburton Highway, Seville East, Vic 3139 **Region** Yarra Valley
T (03) 5961 5877 **www.**killaraestate.com.au **Open** Wed–Sun 11–5
Winemaker Travis Bush, Mac Forbes **Est.** 1997 **Dozens** 8000 **Vyds** 29.5ha
The Palazzo family, headed by Leo, sold its Killara vineyard in November 2010 to Yarragum Agrifoods, which is now well known as the viticultural home of Thousand Candles. The family continues to own and run the 36ha Sunnyside Vineyard on the corner of Warburton Highway and Sunnyside Road. Wines produced include Pinot Grigio, Sauvignon (Blanc), Dolcino (late-harvest viognier) and Sangiovese (the latter made by Mac Forbes).

The cellar door and Racers and Rascals Café (open Wed-Sun 10-4) enjoy sweeping views of the valley and mountain ranges. Exports to the UK and China.

ᵀᵀᵀᵀᵀ **Yarra Valley Chardonnay 2011** Pale colour, bright hue; restrained and focused on the bouquet, showing zesty lemon juice, pear and a delicate seasoning of spicy oak; the acidity is like a laser beam and cuts across the palate, and while a little challenging, is also a lively ride; a long and fine finish. Screwcap. 12.5% alc. **Rating** 92 **To** 2018 $25 BE

ᵀᵀᵀᵀ **Racers & Rascals Yarra Valley Shiraz 2012 Rating** 89 **To** 2017 $20 **Sparkling Shiraz 2008 Rating** 88 **To** 2014 $25

Killerby ★★★★

4259 Caves Road, Wilyabrup, WA 6280 **Region** Margaret River
T (08) 9755 5983 **www.**killerby.com.au **Open** 7 days 10–5
Winemaker Marco Pinares **Est.** 1973 **Dozens** NFP
In June 2008, the winery established by the late Dr Barry Killerby in 1973 was purchased by the Ferngrove wine group, and the estate vineyard was acquired by Sandalford. In 2012 a 13ha vineyard on Caves Road was leased, planted to chardonnay, semillon, sauvignon, blanc, cabernet sauvignon and shiraz, supplementing the 3ha of estate cabernet sauvignon. While the wines are made at Ferngrove, a substantial cellar door was opened in Jul '12, offering a broad range of products from across the southwest of the state.

ᵀᵀᵀᵀᵀ **Margaret River Sauvignon Blanc 2012** Pale straw-green; barrel-fermented in mainly used French oak, some new, and spent 2 months in that oak; has a mix of tropical, herbal and minerally notes, the oak also making its presence felt. Screwcap. 13.8% alc. **Rating** 90 **To** 2014 $26

ᵀᵀᵀᵀ **Margaret River Chardonnay 2011 Rating** 89 **To** 2015 $30 **Merchant Trader Margaret River Semillon Sauvignon Blanc 2012 Rating** 88 **To** 2015 $20

Killibinbin ★★★★

PO Box 10, Langhorne Creek, SA 5255 **Region** Langhorne Creek
T (08) 8537 3382 **www.**killibinbin.com.au **Open** Not
Winemaker Jim Urlwin **Est.** 1997 **Dozens** 3000 **Vyds** 10ha
In late 2010 Guy and Liz Adams (of Metala Vineyards fame) acquired the Killibinbin brand. The wines will continue to be sourced solely from the Metala Vineyards (10ha are dedicated to Killibinbin), and the primary market will be the US, currency exchange hurdles permitting. Exports to the UK, Canada, Sweden, Denmark and Taiwan.

ᵀᵀᵀᵀᵀ **Scream Shiraz 2009** Dense purple-crimson; the colour is a cue for the luscious black fruits of the bouquet and palate, crammed with licorice, spice and dark chocolate on top of the blackberry; the tannins, too, are built to size, the oak likewise. Screwcap. 14.8% alc. **Rating** 93 **To** 2034 $30
The Shadow 2009 Developed colour; a blend of shiraz and cabernet sauvignon grown on the Metala Vineyards, with a savoury array of black fruits, dark chocolate, ripe tannins and vanilla oak; in Killibinbin style, focusing on flavour not elegance, notwithstanding the modest alcohol. Screwcap. 13.8% alc. **Rating** 91 **To** 2024 $27
Scaredy Cat 2009 I really can't hack the label design; ok for a $10 bottle, but not at this level. The colour is good, the medium- to full-bodied flavours rich and dark (there is no information on the variety/ies) with a dark chocolate overlay, the tannins ripe. Screwcap. 14% alc. **Rating** 91 **To** 2024 $24
The Shadow 2008 Good retention of colour; a 900-dozen blend of shiraz and cabernet from the Metala Vineyard; it is so lavishly coated with dark chocolate you wonder whether you will uncover the black fruits; they briefly appear on the mid-palate before dark chocolate comes again on the finish. Strangely, it all works. Screwcap. 15% alc. **Rating** 90 **To** 2023 $27

ᵀᵀᵀᵀ **Cabernet Sauvignon 2010 Rating** 89 **To** 2018 $30

Killiecrankie Wines

PO Box 6125, Lansell Plaza, Vic 3555 **Region** Bendigo
T (03) 5435 3155 **Open** Not
Winemaker John Monteath **Est.** 2000 **Dozens** 120 **Vyds** 1ha
This is the venture of John Monteath and Claire Wills; John moved to the Bendigo region in
1999 to pursue his interest in viticulture and winemaking, and while helping to establish the
vineyard from which the grapes are sourced, gained experience at Water Wheel, Heathcote
Estate, Balgownie Estate and Blackjack wineries. The original vineyard was planted in 2000 to
four shiraz clones, and is the backbone of the Bendigo wine. The small crop is hand-picked,
with the resultant wines made in true garagiste style. Small parcels of premium fruit are
also sourced from a limited number of meticulously tended vineyards in the Bendigo and
Heathcote regions. No wines received for the *2014 Wine Companion*, but a five-star rating
has been maintained.

Kimbarra Wines

422 Barkly Street, Ararat, Vic 3377 **Region** Grampians
T (03) 5352 2238 www.kimbarrawines.com.au **Open** Mon–Fri 9–4.30, or by appt
Winemaker Peter Leeke, Ian MacKenzie, Adam Wadewitz **Est.** 1990 **Dozens** 1000
Vyds 12ha
Peter Leeke has established 9ha of shiraz, 2ha of riesling and 1ha of cabernet sauvignon,
varieties that have proved best suited to the Grampians region. The particularly well-made,
estate-grown wines deserve a wider audience.

Great Western Riesling 2012 Bright green-straw; the bouquet and palate tell
the same story: sweet lime/lemon juice in contrast with grated skin and pith in a
quasi-savoury mould. A high-quality, complex wine, full of interest and pleasure.
Screwcap. 13.3% alc. **Rating** 94 **To** 2020 $25
Aged Release Great Western Riesling 2003 The light green-quartz colour
is exceptional, and the bouquet and palate are no less youthful; gentle lime and
lemon fruit runs through its length, and it will continue to give pleasure for some
years yet. Screwcap. 13.3% alc. **Rating** 94 **To** 2018 $35

Great Western Cabernet Sauvignon 2009 Rating 93 **To** 2029 $29

Kimbolton Wines

The Winehouse Cellar Door, Lot 93 Wellington Road, Langhorne Creek, SA 5255
Region Langhorne Creek
T (08) 8537 3359 www.kimboltonwines.com.au **Open** 7 days 10–5
Winemaker Greg Follett (Contract) **Est.** 1998 **Dozens** 1000 **Vyds** 56.2ha
The Kimbolton property originally formed part of the Potts Bleasdale estate; in 1946 it was
acquired by Henry and Thelma Case, parents of the current owners, Len and wife Judy Case.
Since that time the grapes from vineyard plantings of cabernet sauvignon, shiraz, chardonnay,
sauvignon blanc, zinfandel and montepulciano have been sold to leading wineries. However,
in '98 the decision was taken to retain a small amount of cabernet sauvignon and shiraz to
supply the Kimbolton Wines label established in that year (the name comes from a medieval
town in Bedfordshire, UK, from which some of Judy's ancestors emigrated).

The Rifleman Langhorne Creek Shiraz 2010 Inky purple hue; the bouquet
offers a blackberry pastille-laden expression, with spicy oak notes a prominent
feature; the palate is thickly textured and rich, and while at the warm and
chocolatey end of the flavour spectrum, remains light on its feet on the finish.
Screwcap. 14.9% alc. **Rating** 92 **To** 2022 $50 BE

House Block Shiraz 2010 Rating 87 **To** 2017 $20 BE
The Rifleman Cabernet Sauvignon 2010 Rating 87 **To** 2018 $50 BE

King River Estate

3556 Wangaratta-Whitfield Road, Wangaratta, Vic 3678 **Region** King Valley
T (03) 5729 3689 www.kingriverestate.com.au **Open** 7 days 11–5
Winemaker Trevor Knaggs **Est.** 1996 **Dozens** 3000 **Vyds** 16ha
Trevor Knaggs, with the assistance of his father Collin, began the establishment of King River Estate in 1990, making the first wines in '96. The initial plantings were 3.3ha each of chardonnay and cabernet sauvignon, followed by 8ha of merlot and 3ha of shiraz. More recent plantings have extended the varietal range to include verdelho, viognier, barbera and sangiovese. Biodynamic practices have been used in the vineyard since 2008. Exports to China and Singapore.

King Valley Saperavi 2011 Saperavi stood its (colour) ground in '11; boot leather, licorice, earth and plum aromas and flavours are supported on the medium- to full-bodied palate by good tannins and controlled oak. Diam. 14.4% alc. **Rating** 91 **To** 2021 $35

Kingsdale Wines

745 Crookwell Road, Goulburn, NSW 2580 **Region** Southern New South Wales Zone
T (02) 4822 4880 www.kingsdale.com.au **Open** W'ends & public hols 10–5, or by appt
Winemaker Howard Spark **Est.** 2001 **Dozens** 1200 **Vyds** 2.8ha
Howard and Elly Spark established their vineyard (shiraz, sauvignon blanc, chardonnay, merlot and semillon) south of the burgeoning Southern Highlands region, falling into the Southern NSW Zone. It sits 700m above sea level on deep red soils with iron-rich sediments (doubtless causing the colour) and limestone. The limestone-clad cellar door overlooks Lake Sooley, 7mins' drive from Goulburn.

Goulburn Semillon Sauvignon Blanc 2012 Pale colour; a highly expressive and pungent bouquet of nettle and fresh lemon; the palate is bone dry, taut and minerally, finishing with lingering tail of guava and gun flint. Screwcap. 10% alc. **Rating** 89 **To** 2014 $20 BE

Kingsley Grove

49 Stuart Valley Drive, Kingaroy, Qld 4610 **Region** South Burnett
T (07) 4162 2229 www.kingsleygrove.com **Open** 7 days 10–5
Winemaker Michael, Patricia and Simon Berry **Est.** 1998 **Dozens** 3000 **Vyds** 8.8ha
Michael and Patricia Berry, and Edward Devereux, have a substantial vineyard of 8.8ha near Kingaroy. It is planted to verdelho, chardonnay, semillon, shiraz, merlot, sangiovese, chambourcin and cabernet sauvignon, and the wines are made in a winery built in 2001 and extended in '03, Michael Berry having undertaken viticulture studies at Melbourne University. Exports to Southeast Asia.

Verdelho 2009 Yellow-green; the best of the Kingsley Grove white wines, a touch of residual sugar adding to the honeyed buttery characters that are starting to build with bottle age; has a year or two yet to run. Screwcap. 13.5% alc. **Rating** 87 **To** 2014 $18
Merlot 2005 Has retained remarkable colour, tannins and alcohol; must have been a monster in its youth. It has a few technical issues, but gets points for its sheer resilience. Screwcap. 14.8% alc. **Rating** 87 **To** 2015 $18

Kingston Estate Wines

Sturt Highway, Kingston-on-Murray, SA 5331 **Region** South Australia
T (08) 8243 3700 www.kingstonestatewines.com **Open** By appt
Winemaker Bill Moularadellis, Brett Duffin, Helen Foggo, Donna Hartwig **Est.** 1979
Dozens 70 000 **Vyds** 500ha
Kingston Estate, under the direction of Bill Moularadellis, has its production roots in the Riverland region, but has long-term purchase contracts with growers in the Clare Valley, Adelaide Hills, Coonawarra, Langhorne Creek and Mount Benson. It has also spread its net

to take in a wide range of varietals, mainstream and exotic, under a number of different brands at various price points. Exports to all major markets.

Pinot Gris 2012 A fresh, crisp, no-frills Pinot Gris that derives classic brown pear and green apple fruit from its regional origins; happily, it shows no sweetness on the finish. Well priced. Screwcap. 12.5% alc. **Rating** 88 **To** 2014 $15

Cabernet Sauvignon 2011 Light to medium red-purple; has attractive varietal fruit on the bouquet and entry to the mouth, but the slightly sweet finish jars however much it will be appreciated by the punters. From the Mount Lofty Ranges and Mount Benson. Screwcap. 14% alc. **Rating** 87 **To** 2014 $15

Kirrihill Wines

Wendouree Road, Clare, SA 5453 **Region** Clare Valley
T (08) 8842 4087 **www.**kirrihillwines.com.au **Open** 7 days 10–4
Winemaker Hamish Seabrook, Marnie Roberts **Est.** 1998 **Dozens** 35 000
A large development, with an 8000-tonne, $12 million winery making and marketing its own range of wines, also acting as a contract maker for several producers. Focused on the Clare Valley and Adelaide Hills, grapes are sourced from specially selected parcels of Kirribilly's 1300ha of managed vineyards, as well as the Edwards and Stanway families' properties in these regions. The quality of the wines is thus no surprise. The Companions range comprises blends of both regions, while the Single Vineyard Series aims to elicit a sense of place from the chosen vineyards. Exports to all major markets.

Single Vineyard Series Slate Creek Clare Valley Riesling 2012 Light straw-green; a very fine, fresh and tightly sculpted Riesling coming from Kirrihill's Slate Creek Vineyard; has exceptional length, and balanced lime-accented fruit with slatey (what else?) minerality. Screwcap. 12% alc. **Rating** 94 **To** 2027 $18

Single Vineyard Series Tullymore Vineyard Clare Valley Shiraz 2010 Deep crimson-purple; a mouth-filling, rich, full-bodied Shiraz, with dense blackberry and dark chocolate fruit framed by cedar and vanilla oak and soft, ripe tannins. A very good drink now or much later style; equally good value. Screwcap. 14.5% alc. **Rating** 93 **To** 2030 $22

Single Vineyard Series Barton Springs Adelaide Hills Sauvignon Blanc 2012 Light straw-green; an attractive, well-balanced Sauvignon Blanc with its bouquet and palate encompassing the full range of aromas and flavours from herb and snow pea through to passionfruit. Screwcap. 13% alc. **Rating** 91 **To** 2013 $18

KJB Wine Group

82 Ridge Street, Northgate, Qld 4013 (postal) **Region** McLaren Vale
T 0409 570 694 **Open** Not
Winemaker Adam Hooper, Kurt Brill **Est.** 2008 **Dozens** 500
KJB Wine Group (formerly Oenotria Vintners) is the venture of Kurt Brill, who began his involvement in the wine industry in 2003, largely through the encouragement of his wife Gillian. He commenced the wine marketing course at the University of Adelaide, but ultimately switched from that to the winemaking degree at CSU. His main business is the distribution company Grace James Fine Wines, but he also runs a virtual winery operation, purchasing cabernet sauvignon and shiraz from vineyards in McLaren Vale. Needless to say, he participates as far as possible in the winemaking process. Exports to the UK.

Land of the Vines McLaren Vale Shiraz 2011 Good colour; spent 18 months in American and French oak hogsheads, which helped shape the blackberry, dark chocolate and plum cake flavours; the tannins are soft but accumulate on the finish. Screwcap. 14.5% alc. **Rating** 88 **To** 2016 $23

Land of the Vines McLaren Vale Cabernet Sauvignon 2011 The slightly dull colour is no doubt due to the vintage, as is the lack of drive on the back-palate and finish; however, 16 months in French and American oak has partially compensated. Screwcap. 14.5% alc. **Rating** 87 **To** 2014 $23

Knappstein   ★★★★★

2 Pioneer Avenue, Clare, SA 5453 **Region** Clare Valley
T (08) 8841 2100 **www**.knappstein.com.au **Open** Mon–Fri 9–5, Sat 11–5, Sun &
public hols 11–4
Winemaker Glenn Barry **Est.** 1969 **Dozens** 40 000 **Vyds** 114ha
Knappstein's full name is Knappstein Enterprise Winery & Brewery, reflecting its history
before being acquired by Petaluma, and since then part of Lion Nathan's stable. The substantial
mature estate vineyards in prime locations supply grapes both for the Knappstein brand and
for wider Petaluma use. Exports to all major markets.

♦♦♦♦♦ **Hand Picked Clare Valley Riesling 2012** Pale straw-green; a very good
✪ example of a great vintage for Clare Valley Riesling, winning the title of Wine of
the Year at the SA Wine Awards; has multiple layers of lime/citrus fruit without
any phenolic static. Delicious now or in 10 or 20 years. Screwcap. 13% alc.
Rating 96 To 2027 $20

✪ **The Insider Limited Release Clare Valley Shiraz Malbec 2012** Whole
bunch fermentation is more common in cooler and/or maritime climates, but has
worked very well here; both it and the malbec have heightened the red fruits of
the palate, these in turn given texture and structure by the whole-bunch tannins;
oak has barely raised its head. WAK screwcap. 13% alc. **Rating** 94 **To** 2025 $22
Enterprise Vineyard Clare Valley Cabernet Sauvignon 2010 Good colour;
the wine is uncompromisingly full-bodied, blackcurrant the major fruit driver,
but with enthusiastic support from persistent tannins and a lot of French oak. I
don't normally give points for where the wine will be in 5 years, but do so in this
instance. Screwcap. 14% alc. **Rating** 94 **To** 2035 $40

♦♦♦♦♀ **Ackland Vineyard Watervale Riesling 2012** Rating 92 To 2018 $30

Knee Deep Wines   ★★★★★

160 Johnson Road, Wilyabrup, WA 6280 **Region** Margaret River
T (08) 9755 6776 **www**.kneedeepwines.com.au **Open** 7 days 10–5
Winemaker Bruce Dukes, Bob Cartwright **Est.** 2000 **Dozens** 8800 **Vyds** 20ha
Perth surgeon and veteran yachtsman Phil Childs and wife Sue acquired a 34ha property in
Wilyabrup in 2000. This was planted to chardonnay (3.2ha), sauvignon blanc (4ha), semillon
(1.48ha), chenin blanc (4ha), cabernet sauvignon (6.34ha) and shiraz (1.24ha). The name, Knee
Deep, was inspired by the passion and commitment needed to produce premium wine and as
a tongue-in-cheek acknowledgement of jumping in 'boots and all' during a testing time in the
wine industry, the grape glut building more or less in tune with the venture.

♦♦♦♦♦ **Kim's Limited Release Margaret River Chardonnay 2010** Bright straw-
green; as complex and intense as the standard '11 is straightforward; barrel-ferment
inputs are evident, but it's the grapefruit and white peach flavours that drive the
wine through to its finish. Screwcap. 13.5% alc. **Rating** 95 **To** 2018 $45
Hayley's Limited Release Margaret River Shiraz 2010 Bottle 2643 of 3150,
and the heaviest (bottle) in Christendom. Deeper colour than the standard release,
but similar hue; a substantial, but integrated and balanced oak contribution takes
the perfectly ripened fruit flavours (saturated plum to the fore) and gives them
shape, texture and structure. Screwcap. 14% alc. **Rating** 95 **To** 2030 $45

♦♦♦♦♀ **Margaret River Sauvignon Blanc 2012** Light straw-green; an attractive wine
✪ with a suite of aromas and flavours, some of which can crop up in Semillon and/
or Riesling; citrus is dominant, passionfruit and stone fruit also evident; good
length and overall balance. Screwcap. 12% alc. **Rating** 93 **To** 2014 $22
Kelsea's Limited Release Margaret River Cabernet Sauvignon 2010
Rating 93 To 2030 $45
Margaret River Shiraz 2010 Rating 92 To 2020 $28

Knots Wines

A8 Shurans Lane, Heathcote, Vic 3552 **Region** Heathcote
T (03) 5441 5429 **www**.thebridgevineyard.com.au **Open** Select w'ends, or by appt
Winemaker Lindsay Ross **Est.** 1997 **Dozens** 1000 **Vyds** 4.75ha
This venture of former Balgownie winemaker Lindsay Ross and wife Noeline is part of a broader business known as Winedrops, which acts as a wine production and distribution network for the Bendigo wine industry. The Knots wines are sourced from long-established vineyards, providing shiraz (4ha), malbec (0.5ha) and viognier (0.25ha). The viticultural accent is on low-cropping, with concentrated flavours, the winemaking emphasis on flavour, finesse and varietal expression.

ŸŸŸŸŸ **The Bridge Shurans Lane Heathcote Shiraz 2009** The distorted Diam hasn't enjoyed the diameter of the long neck of the expensive bottle; this to one side, this is an opulent, fleshy, black-fruited wine with good tannins and oak support on the palate. 14% alc. **Rating** 93 **To** 2020 $55
The Bridge Shurans Lane Heathcote Shiraz Viognier 2010 Bright, medium red-purple; there is an aromatic lift from the juicy viognier, controlled alcohol assisting the expression of the fragrant red and black fruits on the bouquet and supple, medium-bodied palate; good oak. Diam. 13% alc. **Rating** 93 **To** 2028 $45
The Bridge Shurans Lane Heathcote Shiraz Sangiovese 2010 Slightly more purple hue than its siblings; there are more spicy nuances here, but in all three wines the bouquet is impressive; black and red cherry fruit is the driver, the tannins fine and integrated, as is the oak. Diam. 13.5% alc. **Rating** 93 **To** 2028 $45
The Bridge Shurans Lane Heathcote Shiraz Malbec 2010 Darker colour than the Shiraz Viognier; here the emphasis shifts firmly to black fruits, licorice and some bitter chocolate, the medium- to full-bodied palate with a greater use of ripe tannins. Diam. 14% alc. **Rating** 91 **To** 2030 $45
The Bridge Shurans Lane Heathcote Shiraz Viognier 2009 Medium red-purple; has a generosity of flavour, albeit without the usual amount of lifted red fruits co-fermented viognier usually imparts, but there is more life and focus on the finish than the Shiraz Malbec. Diam. 14% alc. **Rating** 90 **To** 2017 $45

ŸŸŸŸ **The Bridge Shurans Lane Shiraz Malbec 2009 Rating** 89 **To** 2017 $45

Knotting Hill Estate Vineyard

247 Carter Road, Wilyabrup WA 6280 **Region** Margaret River
T (08) 9755 7733 **www**.knottinghill.com.au **Open** 7 days 11–5
Winemaker Flying Fish Cove (Simon Ding) **Est.** 1997 **Dozens** 4000 **Vyds** 37.5ha
The Gould family has been farming in WA since 1907, and still owns the land grant taken up on their arrival from Scotland. In 1997 the family decided to diversify, and acquired Knotting Hill, their Wilyabrup property in the Margaret River. In '98 they propagated 56 000 cuttings by hand in an onsite nursery, supervised plantings, created a 5.5ha dam, and built the 45m bridge entry to the local limestone cellar door. In 2002 they leased the wheat farm, and have since devoted all their time to Knotting Hill. The spectacular vineyard is established on a natural amphitheatre, with the lake at the bottom.

ŸŸŸŸŸ **Margaret River Sauvignon Blanc 2012** Light straw-green; a lively and fragrant
✪ bouquet introduces a similarly lively and fresh palate, with citrus providing a contrast to its passionfruit and white peach fruit; the finish is juicy and appealing. Top value. Screwcap. 12.5% alc. **Rating** 92 **To** 2014 $20
Margaret River Cabernet Sauvignon 2011 Medium to full red-purple; a rich and fleshy Cabernet with none of the dry tannins of the '11 Cabernet Merlot; here blackcurrant/cassis fruit is enveloped in cedary French oak adding to the weight and texture of the wine. Screwcap. 13.5% alc. **Rating** 92 **To** 2026 $35
✪ **Margaret River Semillon Sauvignon Blanc 2012** A 60/40% blend, still pale quartz-green; fresh grassy aromas change tack on the juicy palate, where sweet citrus and tropical fruits are seamlessly interwoven through to the long finish. Well priced. Screwcap. 12.5% alc. **Rating** 91 **To** 2015 $20

✪ **Margaret River Verdelho 2012** Light straw-green; an unexpected burst of flavour, juicy and with a distinct undertone of citrus, the finish bright and zesty. May even benefit from a few years in bottle. Screwcap. 12.5% alc. **Rating** 90 **To** 2015 $20

🍷🍷🍷🍷 **Margaret River Shiraz 2011** **Rating** 89 **To** 2021 $28

Koonara ★★★★★

44 Main Street, Penola, SA 5277 **Region** Coonawarra
T (08) 8737 3222 **www**.koonara.com **Open** 7 days 10–6
Winemaker Peter Douglas **Est.** 1988 **Dozens** 10 000 **Vyds** 9ha
Koonara is a sister, or, more appropriately, a brother company to Reschke Wines. The latter is run by Burke Reschke, Koonara by his brother Dru. Both are sons of Trevor Reschke, who planted the first vines on the Koonara property in 1988. The initial planting was of cabernet sauvignon, followed by shiraz in '93 and additional cabernet sauvignon in '98. Peter Douglas, Wynns' chief winemaker before moving overseas for some years, has returned to the district and is consultant winemaker. The Bay of Apostles range was released in 2008, with four of the five wines under the label sourced from Vic. A Bay of Apostles cellar door has been opened in the main street of Apollo Bay on the Great Ocean Road. In '10–11 organic management of the vineyard was initiated. Exports to Canada, Singapore and China.

🍷🍷🍷🍷🍷 **Ezra's Gift Family Reserve Coonawarra Shiraz 2010** Dense purple-crimson; the exceptional colour does not deceive; despite its very low yield, 1 tonne per acre, it is no more than medium-bodied, but the clarity of the black cherry and blackberry fruit, its fine-grained tannins, and integrated French oak are all seamlessly joined. Screwcap. 14.2% alc. **Rating** 96 **To** 2025 $30

The Marquise Mt Gambier Chardonnay 2012 Some pretty nifty winemaking decisions have been taken, including the time to pick, a wild ferment, half in new French oak (other half in tank), both components undergoing mlf; this is an elegant wine with grapefruit to the fore, but leaving space for a white peach contribution. Screwcap. 12.8% alc. **Rating** 94 **To** 2019 $25

✪ **Angel's Peak Coonawarra Shiraz 2008** Excellent crimson-purple hue; fully deserves its 2 gold (1 at Limestone Coast Wine Show '11) medals. The oak contribution is obvious, but by no means excessive, adding to the mouthfeel and without impinging on the blackberry and plum fruit; finishes with soft tannins. Sensational value. Screwcap. 13.5% alc. **Rating** 94 **To** 2023 $18

🍷🍷🍷🍷 **Ambriel's Gift Family Reserve Coonawarra Cabernet Sauvignon 2010** **Rating** 93 **To** 2025 $35

The Seductress Shiraz 2010 **Rating** 92 **To** 2025 $25

Bay of Apostles Pinot Noir 2010 **Rating** 91 **To** 2016 $25

Koonowla Wines ★★★★★

PO Box 45, Auburn, SA 5451 **Region** Clare Valley
T (08) 8849 2270 **www**.koonowla.com **Open** Not
Winemaker O'Leary Walker Wines **Est.** 1997 **Dozens** 5000 **Vyds** 100ha
It's not often that a light as large as this can be hidden under a bushel. Koonowla is a historic Clare Valley property; situated just east of Auburn, it was first planted with vines in the 1890s, and by the early 1900s was producing 60 000 litres of wine annually. A disastrous fire in '26 destroyed the winery and wine stocks, and the property was converted to grain and wool production. Replanting of vines began in '85, and accelerated after Andrew and Booie Michael purchased the property in '91; there are now 40ha of cabernet sauvignon, 36ha of riesling, 20ha of shiraz, and 2ha each of merlot and semillon. In an all-too-familiar story, the grapes were sold until falling prices forced a change in strategy; now a major part of the grapes is vinified by the infinitely experienced David O'Leary and Nick Walker, with the remainder sold. Exports to the UK, the US, Scandinavia, Malaysia, NZ and China.

🍷🍷🍷🍷🍷 **The AJM Reserve Clare Valley Shiraz 2010** Has the deepest colour of the Koonowla '10 Shirazs, and is a selection of the best French and American oak barriques of the vintage; it throbs with black fruits, licorice and cedar/vanilla oak, the tannins warm and ripe. Yes, it's high in alcohol, but the flavours carry the burden with aplomb. Screwcap. 15% alc. **Rating** 95 **To** 2035 $35

🍷🍷🍷🍷🍷 **Clare Valley Riesling 2012 Rating** 93 **To** 2020 $20

✪ **Clare Valley Shiraz 2010** Full red-purple; both the bouquet and medium- to full-bodied palate have an intriguing edge of spice, and oak also plays a positive role in framing the black fruits and ripe tannins of the long, balanced palate. Screwcap. 14.5% alc. **Rating** 93 **To** 2020 $22

✪ **The Ringmaster Clare Valley Riesling 2012** Bright, full straw-green; has abundant fruit: lime, lemon and (unusually) grapefruit all sweep past in a three-way dance with each other. No need for patience, nor a stuffed wallet. Screwcap. 12.5% alc. **Rating** 90 **To** 2016 $16

✪ **The Ringmaster Clare Valley Shiraz 2010** Relatively light colour; 18 months in used French and American oak has been a positive, not overwhelming the fruit and freshness of this light- to medium-bodied wine; the blackberry fruit has a spicy edge and good acidity. Terrific value as an early-drinking style. Screwcap. 14.5% alc. **Rating** 90 **To** 2015 $16

✪ **The Ringmaster Clare Valley Cabernet Sauvignon 2010** Good colour; matured in 2- and 3-year-old French oak hogsheads, there is an unexpected but enjoyable juicy aspect to the black fruits, and also some spicy/cedary nuances. Good balance makes the wine enjoyable now, or into the future. Screwcap. 14.5% alc. **Rating** 90 **To** 2017 $16

Kooyong   ★★★★★

PO Box 153, Red Hill South, Vic 3937 **Region** Mornington Peninsula
T (03) 5989 4444 **www.**kooyongwines.com.au **Open** At Port Phillip Estate
Winemaker Sandro Mosele **Est.** 1996 **Dozens** 10 000 **Vyds** 33.4ha
Kooyong, owned by Giorgio and Dianne Gjergja, released its first wines in 2001. The vineyard is planted to pinot noir (20ha), chardonnay (10.4ha) and, more recently, pinot gris (3ha). Winemaker Sandro Mosele is a graduate of CSU, and has a deservedly high reputation. He also provides contract winemaking services for others. The Kooyong wines are made at the spectacular new winery of Port Phillip Estate, also owned by the Gjergjas. Exports to the UK, the US, Canada, Sweden, Singapore, Hong Kong, Japan and China.

🍷🍷🍷🍷🍷 **Estate Mornington Peninsula Chardonnay 2011** Pale gold, green; restrained and pure on the bouquet with nectarine, pear and citrus blossom on display; the tightly wound palate is nothing short of electrifying, with superb concentration and a fine balance of fruit and acidity drawing the wine to an extraordinarily long finish. Screwcap. 13% alc. **Rating** 96 **To** 2022 $43 BE

Single Vineyard Selection Haven Pinot Noir 2010 Deep crimson; pure dark fruits are abundant on the bouquet, with Asian spices and well-handled oak; the palate starts with a refreshing blend of red and dark fruits and tangy acidity, and then makes way for a rush of firm but fine tannins, common in top-quality Burgundies, but not in Australia. A Pinot built for cellaring: 15 years should not tire it. Screwcap. 13% alc. **Rating** 96 **To** 2025 $75

Clonale Mornington Peninsula Chardonnay 2012 Mid gold, vivid green hue; the highly expressive and savoury bouquet offers fresh grapefruit, nectarine, charcuterie and struck match in equal measure; the palate is racy and fresh, with the concentration of fruit offering generosity and providing the framework for the diligent winemaking on display; long and harmonious, and good value. Screwcap. 13% alc. **Rating** 95 **To** 2018 $33 BE

Single Vineyard Selection Faultline Chardonnay 2011 While in many ways the most restrained of the three Chardonnays, there is a latent complexity and power waiting to be released; the bouquet offers cashew, grapefruit and clove; the palate offers richness and depth, with an extraordinarily long cashew-laden conclusion. Screwcap. 13% alc. **Rating** 95 **To** 2022 $60 BE

Single Vineyard Selection Ferrous Pinot Noir 2011 Mid garnet, bright; the Ferrous vineyard always exhibits brightness on the bouquet, with alluring red fruits, ironstone, generous new oak and some sappy complexity; the palate is juicy and fresh, with typically racy acidity and fine-grained tannins. Screwcap. 13.5% alc. Rating 95 To 2022 $75 BE
Single Vineyard Selection Farrago Chardonnay 2011 Rating 94 To 2020 $60 BE
Single Vineyard Selection Meres Pinot Noir 2011 Rating 94 To 2016 $75 BE

ĭĭĭĭĭ Estate Mornington Peninsula Pinot Noir 2011 Rating 92 To 2018 $53 BE
Single Vineyard Selection Haven Pinot Noir 2011 Rating 92 To 2020 $75 BE
Beurrot Mornington Peninsula Pinot Gris 2012 Rating 90 To 2016 $31 BE
Massale Mornington Peninsula Pinot Noir 2011 Rating 90 To 2014 $33 TS

Krinklewood Biodynamic Vineyard ★★★★

712 Wollombi Road, Broke, NSW 2330 **Region** Hunter Valley
T (02) 6579 1322 www.krinklewood.com **Open** W'ends 10–5
Winemaker Damien Stevens, Rod Windrim **Est.** 1981 **Dozens** 5000 **Vyds** 19.9ha
A boutique, family-owned biodynamic vineyard, Krinklewood produces 100% estate-grown wines reflecting the terroir of the Broke Fordwich subregion of the Hunter Valley. The cellar door is set among Provençal-style gardens that overlook the vineyard, with the Wollombi Brook and Brokenback range providing a spectacular backdrop. In 2010 the winery was extended and upgraded, including the installation of a Vaslin Bucher basket press.

ĭĭĭĭĭ Semillon 2012 Pale quartz; classic Hunter Semillon, with a gently flowery/fragrant bouquet hinting at the mix of grass, citrus and sweet pea flavours on the long, clean palate; the balance is exemplary. Screwcap. 10.8% alc. **Rating** 93 To 2020 $22
Chardonnay 2012 Light straw-green; a very well composed and balanced Chardonnay with clear white peach and nectarine fruit, subtle oak playing a minor chord for the wine. Screwcap. 12.8% alc. **Rating** 91 To 2017 $28
Basket Press Chardonnay 2011 Developed straw-yellow; basket pressed and wild yeast-fermented in French puncheons with no additives of any kind; natural winemaking at its best, will be snapped up without tasting; is in fact a very nice, rich chardonnay. Screwcap. 12.5% alc. **Rating** 90 To 2014 $38

ĭĭĭĭ Wild White 2012 Very early picked verdelho (and 2% gewurztraminer) produces
✪ a wine with utterly unexpected length and aftertaste, even if unsweetened lemon juice is a descriptor that may frighten the timid. Take a ride, and find out. Screwcap. 11% alc. **Rating** 89 To 2015 $16
Spider Run White 2010 **Rating** 89 To 2015 $35
Francesca Rose 2012 **Rating** 87 To 2013 $24
Basket Press Shiraz 2010 **Rating** 87 To 2017 $35 BE

Kurrajong Downs ★★★

Casino Road, Tenterfield, NSW 2372 **Region** New England
T (02) 6736 4590 www.kurrajongdownswines.com **Open** Thurs–Mon 9–4
Winemaker Symphony Hill (Mike Hayes) **Est.** 2000 **Dozens** 1500 **Vyds** 4.4ha
Jonus Rhodes arrived at Tenterfield in 1858, lured by the gold he mined for the next 40 years, until his death in 1898. He was evidently successful, for the family now runs a 2800ha cattle-grazing property on which Lynton and Sue Rhodes began the development of their vineyard, at an altitude of 850m, in 1996. Plantings include pinot noir, shiraz, cabernet sauvignon, chardonnay, semillon, gewurztraminer and tempranillo.

ĭĭĭĭ Tenterfield Shiraz 2011 Mid garnet; a fragrant bouquet of red fruits, sage and fresh earth; the palate is light-bodied and juicy, with fresh acidity and fine tannins providing energy on the finish; uncomplicated and best consumed sooner rather than later. Screwcap. 13.2% alc. **Rating** 87 To 2016 $21 BE

Kurrajong Vineyard/KV Wines   ★★★

614 Hermitage Road, Pokolbin, NSW 2320 **Region** Hunter Valley
T (02) 6574 7117 www.kv.com.au **Open** By appt
Winemaker Cameron Webster, Gary Maclean, Desmond Young **Est.** 1990 **Dozens** 400
Vyds 6.5ha

Owners Desmond and Susan Young began making fruit wines when they moved to the UK in 1980. Elderberry, and rosehip and fig, gave way to wine grape juice obtained from France. When they returned to Australia 24 years later, they decided they wanted to make red wine, and Susan wanted a place with enough rain to have a good garden. They chose the Hunter Valley, but without realising how often the rain fell at the wrong time for the vineyard. This hasn't deterred them, and, moreover, Hunter Semillon has entrenched itself.

🍷🍷🍷🍷 **KV Hunter Valley Merlot Rose 2012** Pale salmon-pink; rose petal/spice/ strawberry aromas on the bouquet, the palate delicate, but well balanced, and with a pleasantly dry finish. Screwcap. 11% alc. **Rating** 89 **To** 2014 $18

Kurtz Family Vineyards   ★★★★

731 Light Pass Road, Angaston, SA, 5353 **Region** Barossa Valley
T 0418 810 982 www.kurtzfamilyvineyards.com.au **Open** By appt
Winemaker Steve Kurtz **Est.** 1996 **Dozens** 3000 **Vyds** 15.04ha

The Kurtz family vineyard is at Light Pass, with 9ha of shiraz, the remainder planted to chardonnay, cabernet sauvignon, semillon, sauvignon blanc, petit verdot, grenache, mataro and malbec. Steve Kurtz has followed in the footsteps of his great-grandfather Ben Kurtz, who first grew grapes at Light Pass in the 1930s. During a career working first at Saltram, and then Foster's until 2006, Steve gained invaluable experience from Nigel Dolan, Caroline Dunn and John Glaetzer, among others. Exports to the US, Canada, Macau, Hong Kong and China.

🍷🍷🍷🍷🍷 **Boundary Row Barossa Valley Grenache Shiraz Mataro 2009** A
✪ 52/30/18% blend that has retained very good colour, and goes a long way to carrying its alcohol courtesy of the layers of black and red fruits that, while complex, are not jammy. Screwcap. 15.5% alc. **Rating** 92 **To** 2024 $20
Boundary Row Barossa Valley Cabernet Sauvignon 2010 Full, deep purple-crimson; a very handy Barossa Valley cabernet, flooded with cassis and mint on the bouquet and palate; mint (as in eucalypt) is frowned on by some (especially Kiwis), and may well be foreign, but it makes for a pretty delicious wine. Screwcap. 14% alc. **Rating** 92 **To** 2025 $25

🍷🍷🍷🍷 **Seven Sleepers Barossa Valley Shiraz 2010** Medium to full purple-red; has a
✪ core of blood plum fruit to its bouquet and palate, allied with a generous helping of oak. Excellent value. Screwcap. 14% alc. **Rating** 89 **To** 2015 $15

Kyneton Ridge Estate   ★★★★★

90 Blackhill School Road, Kyneton, Vic 3444 **Region** Macedon Ranges
T (03) 5422 7377 www.kynetonridge.com.au **Open** W'ends & public hols 10–5, or by appt
Winemaker John and Luke Boucher **Est.** 1997 **Dozens** 1000 **Vyds** 4ha

Established by John Boucher and partner Pauline Russell in the shadow of Black Mountain, an ideal environment for pinot noir and chardonnay vines. With five generations of winemaking behind them, John and Luke Boucher continue the quest for quality and refinement. Being boutique winemakers, they maintain the traditional hand-making processes that complement the character of the wines. New facilities have recently been introduced to enhance the production process for all the sparkling wines. The additional production capacity gives the opportunity to source additional suitable quality parcels of shiraz and cabernet sauvignon from the Macedon and Heathcote regions.

🍷🍷🍷🍷🍷 **Premium Macedon Ranges Pinot Noir 2009** Has retained excellent hue and depth to the colour; made in the same manner as the '07, but is very different, with a more open texture and greater finesse to its spicy red fruits. Its multiple gold medals are well deserved. Screwcap. 13.5% alc. **Rating** 94 **To** 2018 $45

Premium Macedon Ranges Pinot Noir 2007 Aged release. Very good colour for its age; estate-grown, hand-plunged in open fermenters, then pressed and taken to French oak for 12 months; it has an almost velvety texture to its panoply of dark small berry/cherry fruit. Screwcap. 13.5% alc. **Rating** 94 **To** 2018 $52

 Fortunate Land Chardonnay 2006 Rating 90 **To** 2016 $35

La Curio

Cnr Fogg Road/Kangarilla Road, McLaren Vale, SA 5171 **Region** McLaren Vale
T (08) 8323 7999 **www**.lacuriowines.com **Open** By appt
Winemaker Adam Hooper **Est.** 2003 **Dozens** 1400
La Curio has been established by Adam Hooper, who purchases small parcels of grapes from vineyards in McLaren Vale with an average age of 40 years, the oldest 80 years. The wines are made at Redheads Studio, a boutique winery in McLaren Vale that caters for a number of small producers. The manacles depicted on the striking label are those of Harry Houdini, and the brand proposition is very cleverly worked through. Winemaking techniques, too, are avant-garde, and highly successful. Exports to the UK, Canada and Sweden.

 The Nubile McLaren Vale Grenache Shiraz 2011 Deep garnet; essency pastille red fruits are evident on the bouquet; the palate is firm and textured, forward and lively, showing a fragrant savoury finish that is evenly balanced. Screwcap. 14.5% alc. **Rating** 88 **To** 2017 $21 BE
The Original Zin McLaren Vale Primitivo 2011 Sweet and simple fruitcake and red berry fruit aromas are evident on the bouquet; the palate is juicy, forward and while slightly short, will accommodate those who appreciate the user-friendly nature of the variety. Screwcap. 14.5% alc. **Rating** 87 **To** 2015 $21 BE

La Linea ★★★★☆

36 Shipsters Road, Kensington Park, SA 5068 (postal) **Region** Adelaide Hills
T (08) 8431 3556 **www**.lalinea.com.au **Open** Not
Winemaker Peter Leske **Est.** 2007 **Dozens** 2500 **Vyds** 9ha
La Linea is a partnership of experienced wine industry professionals, including Peter Leske and David LeMire MW. Peter was among the first to recognise the potential of tempranillo in Australia, and his knowledge of it is reflected in the three wine styles made from the variety: Tempranillo Rose, the Tempranillo blended from several Adelaide Hills vineyards, and Norteno, from a single vineyard at the northern end of the Hills. Two Rieslings are produced under the Vertigo label: TRKN (short for trocken), and the off-dry 25GR (25g/l residual sugar).

Adelaide Hills Tempranillo Rose 2012 An idyllic season has captured the alluring character of tempranillo within a rose of impressive balance and stylistic restraint. It achieves both refreshing delicacy and characterful, flavoursome presence of savoury tomato, rose water and fresh wild strawberries. It concludes impeccably bone dry, nuanced with finely integrated texture and taut acidity. Screwcap. 12.5% alc. **Rating** 92 **To** 2013 $21 TS

La Pleiade ★★★★☆

c/- Jasper Hill, Drummonds Lane, Heathcote, Vic 3523 **Region** Heathcote
T (03) 5433 2528 **Open** By appt
Winemaker Ron Laughton, Michel Chapoutier **Est.** 1998 **Dozens** 500 **Vyds** 9ha
This is the joint venture of Michel and Corinne Chapoutier and Ron and Elva Laughton. In spring 1998 a vineyard using Australian and imported French shiraz clones was planted. The vineyard is run biodynamically, and the winemaking is deliberately designed to place maximum emphasis on the fruit quality. Exports to the UK, the US and other major markets.

ŶŶŶŶŶ Heathcote Shiraz 2010 Medium red-purple; while I remain to be convinced
the baume (and hence alcohol) level was necessary, it is fair to say that the wine
carries it without undue protest; there is a complex array of spicy red and black
fruits in a web of fine but persistent tannins, plus French oak on a palate notable
more for its length than its weight. Cork. 15% alc. **Rating** 95 **To** 2030 $68

ŶŶŶŶŶ Heathcote Shiraz 2009 **Rating** 93 **To** 2029 $68

Laanecoorie

4834 Bendigo-Maryborough Road, Betley,Vic 3472 **Region** Bendigo
T (03) 5468 7260 **www**.laanecoorievineyard.com **Open** W'ends & public hols 11–5,
Mon–Fri by appt
Winemaker Graeme Jukes, John Ellis (Contract) **Est.** 1982 **Dozens** 1000
John and Rosa McQuilten's vineyard (shiraz, cabernet franc, merlot and cabernet sauvignon)
produces grapes of high quality, and competent contract winemaking does the rest, the
vicissitudes of vintages in recent years permitting. Exports to China.

Lake Breeze Wines

Step Road, Langhorne Creek, SA 5255 **Region** Langhorne Creek
T (08) 8537 3017 **www**.lakebreeze.com.au **Open** 7 days 10–5
Winemaker Greg Follett **Est.** 1987 **Dozens** 18000 **Vyds** 90ha
The Folletts have been farmers at Langhorne Creek since 1880, and grapegrowers since the
1930s. Most of the grape production is sold, but the quality of the Lake Breeze wines has been
exemplary, with the red wines particularly appealing. Lake Breeze also owns and makes the
False Cape wines from Kangaroo Island. Exports to the UK, the US and other major markets.

ŶŶŶŶŶ Winemaker's Selection Langhorne Creek Shiraz 2010 Vivid purple-
crimson; a barrel selection, with only 290 dozen made. The bouquet and palate are
flooded with luscious choc-mint fruit, the texture velvety, yet not the least heavy,
the palate with great length. Screwcap. 14.8% alc. **Rating** 95 **To** 2030 $38
Arthur's Reserve Cabernet Sauvignon Petit Verdot Malbec 2009 An
85/9/6% blend. The deep, bright purple-crimson colour is outstanding, and the
bouquet and medium- to full-bodied palate live up to the promise of the colour,
with lush blackcurrant/cassis and mulberry fruit; the tannins are ripe and balanced,
the oak integrated. Screwcap. 14% alc. **Rating** 95 **To** 2039 $35
Section 54 Langhorne Creek Shiraz 2010 Vivid purple hue; the bouquet
offers a vibrant melange of blue and black fruits, violets and wood spice; the
medium-bodied palate is zesty, fresh and focused, with a fine balance of tannin and
acid for the fruit on offer. Screwcap. 14.5% alc. **Rating** 94 **To** 2020 $24 BE
False Cape The Captain Kangaroo Island Cabernet Sauvignon 2010
Deep crimson-purple; a lusciously rich Cabernet, its bouquet and palate in
complete harmony with layers of cassis/blackcurrant fruit framed by ripe tannins
and quality French oak. Screwcap. 14% alc. **Rating** 94 **To** 2030 $28
The Drake Cabernet Shiraz 2010 The colour is not as vibrant as the Arthur's
Reserve, although good by normal standards; here the stage is occupied by
blackcurrant, blackberry, earth and tar, the tannins ripe, the oak balanced. Screwcap.
14.5% alc. **Rating** 94 **To** 2025 $70

ŶŶŶŶŶ Bernoota Langhorne Creek Shiraz Cabernet 2010 **Rating** 91 **To** 2018 $22
Reserve Langhorne Creek Chardonnay 2012 **Rating** 90 **To** 2016 $24 BE
Langhorne Creek Cabernet Sauvignon 2010 **Rating** 90 **To** 2018 $24

ŶŶŶŶ False Cape Unknown Sailor Cabernet Merlot 2010 Deep magenta; essency
✪ blackcurrant pastille aromas mingle with olive and wood spice; the palate is fleshy,
juicy and reveals more essency fruit on the finish. Screwcap. 14% alc. **Rating** 89
To 2018 $18 BE

Lake George Winery ★★★★

Old Federal Highway, Lake George, NSW 2581 **Region** Canberra District
T (02) 9948 4676· **www**.lakegeorgewinery.com.au **Open** 7 days 10–5
Winemaker Nick Spencer, Hamish Young **Est.** 1971 **Dozens** 4000 **Vyds** 20ha
Lake George Winery was established by legend-in-his-own-lifetime Dr Edgar Riek, who has contributed so much to the Canberra District and the Australian wine industry. It has now passed into good hands, and the plantings of 40-year-old chardonnay, pinot noir, cabernet sauvignon, semillon and merlot have been joined by shiraz and tempranillo, pinot gris, viognier, pinot noir and malbec. In March 2008 Lake George acquired the Madew vineyard, providing yet more grape resources. The winemaking techniques include basket-pressing and small-batch barrel maturation under the expert eyes of consultant winemaker Alex McKay, now retired, and replaced by the equally expert Nick Spencer. Exports to China.

🍷🍷🍷🍷🍷 **Riesling 2012** Light straw-green; a crisp and fresh Riesling, with a mix of
lime and mineral aromas and flavours. Made in the teeth of a rainy vintage,
which seems to have slightly diluted the impact of the fruit. Screwcap. 11.5% alc.
Rating 91 **To** 2018 $25
Chardonnay 2012 Early picking led to the decision to take the wine through
mlf, which was 100% correct, for even with this effected, the acidity is still very
much part of the citrus/grapefruit palate, the nutty/creamy nuance ex mlf not
prominent. Screwcap. 12.5% alc. **Rating** 91 **To** 2020 $24

Lake's Folly ★★★★★

2416 Broke Road, Pokolbin, NSW 2320 **Region** Hunter Valley
T (02) 4998 7507 **www**.lakesfolly.com.au **Open** 7 days 10–4 while wine available
Winemaker Rodney Kempe **Est.** 1963 **Dozens** 5000 **Vyds** 12.2ha
The first of the weekend wineries to produce wines for commercial sale, long revered for its Cabernet Sauvignon and nowadays its Chardonnay. Very properly, terroir and climate produce a distinct regional influence and thereby a distinctive wine style. The winery continues to enjoy an incredibly loyal clientele, with much of each year's wine selling out quickly Lake's Folly no longer has any connection with the Lake family, having been acquired some years ago by Perth businessman Peter Fogarty. Peter's family company previously established the Millbrook Winery in the Perth Hills, so is no stranger to the joys and agonies of running a small winery. Curiously, it is the Chardonnay that justifies the rating.

🍷🍷🍷🍷🍷 **Hill Block Chardonnay 2012** The Folly Chardonnays are never fined or
stabilised, and less than a gram of malic acid is added; this wine is fully barrel-
fermented, with quite cloudy juice, and spends 8 months on lees. Vibrant green-
gold hue; it has a complex bouquet, and a layered palate of white peach around a
talc and mineral core; its drive is exceptional, offering power with grace. Screwcap.
13.5% alc. **Rating** 96 **To** 2022 $80
Hunter Valley Cabernets 2011 An estate-grown 61/18/13/8% blend of
cabernet sauvignon, shiraz, petit verdot and merlot. Great terra rossa soil, 50-year-
old vines, and a top vintage have been putty in the hands of Rodney Kempe.
Bright, clear crimson hue; there is a profusion of blackcurrant/cassis, black olive,
spice and red cherry fruit. Cork. 13% alc. **Rating** 96 **To** 2036 $65
Hill Block Chardonnay 2011 Only 250 dozen bottles produced from the vines
on top of the hill behind the winery. While the same alcohol as the traditional
wine, this has a mouth-coating richness to its fruit that sets it apart, but doesn't
cloy. Screwcap. 14% alc. **Rating** 95 **To** 2019 $70
Hunter Valley Chardonnay 2012 The fermentation is started in tank, and the
wine is transferred to barrel (French oak, around 30% new) when halfway through
fermentation. Pale green-gold hue; it is finer, and more grainy than Hill Block,
its nectarine-accented fruit with a distinct minerally thread, the oak imparting a
garnish of subtle grilled nuts. An altogether elegant wine from 38-year-old vines.
Screwcap. 13% alc. **Rating** 95 **To** 2020 $65

Hunter Valley Chardonnay 2011 Bright straw-green; it is a question of style, not quality, which differentiates this wine from Hill Block. Here the accent is on fruit purity and linearity, with more citrus and less richness. This is Corton compared to the Montrachet of Hill Block, and it is (in this instance) my preferred wine. Screwcap. 14% alc. **Rating** 95 **To** 2020 $65

Hunter Valley Chardonnay 2008 Very light straw-green; highly fragrant, with elements of citrus and peach blossom; a fine, intense palate reflecting the modest alcohol, verging on cool-climate grapefruit, and best of all, not swamped by oak. Screwcap. 12.7% alc. **Rating** 95 **To** 2018 $60

Hunter Valley Cabernets 2010 Rating 94 **To** 2020 $65

Lambert Estate

Barossa Valley Way, Tanunda, SA 5352 **Region** Barossa Valley
T (08) 8563 3375 **www**.lambertestate.com.au **Open** 7 days 11–5
Winemaker Kirk Lambert, Vanessa Herrera **Est.** 1986 **Dozens** 15 000 **Vyds** 40ha
James (Jim) and Pamela Lambert are the owners of the renamed Lambert Estate Wines (previously Stanley Lambert Wines), with son Kirk now winemaker. Like his parents, Kirk was born in Wisconsin, and followed his parents' footsteps to the University of Wisconsin. Graduating as a mechanical engineer, he worked for several years for General Electric, but decided to move to Australia, and after working in the vineyard and winery for some years, obtained his Masters degree in oenology from the University of Adelaide. In 2003 Jim and Pamela purchased a 24ha vineyard planted in 1986; they subsequently expanded this to 40ha, with shiraz, riesling, chardonnay, cabernet sauvignon, zinfandel, tempranillo, grenache, mourvedre, merlot and viognier. Exports to the US, Canada, Germany, China and other major markets.

ΨΨΨΨ **Thoroughbred Barossa Valley Cabernet 2009** Mid garnet, bricking; showing development through leather notes with mere suggestions of red fruits and olive; medium-bodied with a little freshness on the finish, but should be consumed in the short term. Diam. 14.5% alc. **Rating** 87 **To** 2016 $30 BE

Lambloch Estate

2342 Broke Road, Pokolbin, NSW 2320 **Region** Hunter Valley
T (02) 4998 6722 **www**.lambloch.com **Open** 7 days 10–5
Winemaker Scott Stephens **Est.** 2008 **Dozens** 2000 **Vyds** 8ha
Whether it be upmarket housing or mining tenements, the address is all important. When Jas Khara acquired the 8ha vineyard now known as Lambloch Estate, it adjoined Lake's Folly and was directly opposite McWilliam's Rosehill Vineyard. All three share the red volcanic soils not often found in the Hunter Valley. With a strong marketing background in brand creation, he has invested in a new cellar door on Broke Road (itself an all-important artery) with large open areas overlooking the vines and a backdrop of the Brokenback Range in the middle distance. Currently almost all of the production is sold in Belgium, Hong Kong, Macau, Singapore, Thailand, Malaysia and China.

ΨΨΨΨΨ **The Loch 2011** Awesomely deep vivid purple-crimson; Lambloch's 50-year-old vines have now produced three outstanding Shirazs in a row. This is absolutely flooded with blackberry fruit, so much so that the oak you know must be there is hidden; the tannins are also there, but ripe and totally integrated (and balanced). Screwcap. 13.5% alc. **Rating** 96 **To** 2021 $75

ΨΨΨΨΨ **Hunter Valley Shiraz 2011 Rating** 93 **To** 2020 $30

Lambrook Wines

6 Coorara Avenue, Payneham South, SA 5070 **Region** Adelaide Hills
T 0437 672 651 **www**.lambrook.com.au **Open** By appt
Winemaker Adam Lampit, Michael Sykes **Est.** 2008 **Dozens** 3000

This is a virtual winery created by the husband and wife team of Adam and Brooke Lampit. With almost two decades of industry experience between them, they began purchasing sauvignon blanc, shiraz and pinot noir (for sparkling) in 2008, having the wine made by Sam Scott. Adam's experience came through working with Stonehaven, Norfolk Rise and Bird in Hand, while Brooke also worked at Norfolk Rise before moving to work for Wine Australia.

♀♀♀♀♀ **Adelaide Hills Shiraz 2010** Good crimson-purple; the fragrant red and black
✪ cherry bouquet leads into a complex medium-bodied palate, with cherry and
plum fruit backed by fine, but persistent, tannins, the oak incidental. Trophy
Adelaide Hills Wine Show Best $20 & Under Red Wine. 750 dozen made.
Excellent value. Screwcap. 14.5% alc. **Rating** 94 **To** 2020 $20

♀♀♀♀ **Adelaide Hills Sauvignon Blanc 2012** Pale quartz; should have considerable
✪ appeal to lovers of Marlborough Sauvignon Blanc; the bouquet and palate run
almost entirely in a tropical spectrum, with guava, passionfruit and lychee to the
fore. 750 dozen made. Screwcap. 12.5% alc. **Rating** 89 **To** 2014 $16

Lamont's Winery   ★★★★★

85 Bisdee Road, Millendon, WA 6056 **Region** Swan Valley
T (08) 9296 4485 **www**.lamonts.com.au **Open** Thurs–Sun 10–5
Winemaker Digby Leddin **Est.** 1978 **Dozens** 7000 **Vyds** 2ha
Corin Lamont is the daughter of the late Jack Mann, and oversees the making of wines in a style that would have pleased her father. Lamont's also boasts a superb restaurant run by granddaughter Kate Lamont. The wines are going from strength to strength, utilising both estate-grown and contract-grown (from southern regions) grapes. Lamont's restaurant in Perth, open for lunch and dinner Mon–Fri, offers food of the highest quality, and is superbly situated. The Margaret River cellar door is open 7 days 11–5 for wine tasting, sales and lunch. Full details of Lamont's venues are available on their website.

♀♀♀♀♀ **Hand Picked Frankland Riesling 2012** Pale quartz, almost white; a very well
made, exceptionally focused wine, with intense lime fruit wrapped in a steely
embrace of acidity, and a long, lingering finish. Will be magnificent once it passes
its fifth birthday. Screwcap. 12.5% alc. **Rating** 96 **To** 2027 $30
Mount Barker Riesling 2012 Similar colour to its Frankland sibling; another
high-quality wine, but of radically different style; here it is led by a sunburst of
juicy lime fruit (and a ghost of passionfruit), the acidity definitely adequate, but
not as prominent. Screwcap. 12.7% alc. **Rating** 94 **To** 2020 $25
Margaret River Semillon Sauvignon Blanc 2012 Light straw-green; an
impressive wine; while the aromas and flavours of grass, snap pea and kiwifruit are
in line with regional expectations, it's the authority of the texture and structure
that stand out, immeasurably extending the finish and aftertaste. Screwcap.
12.5% alc. **Rating** 94 **To** 2015 $20

♀♀♀♀♀ **Chardonnay 2012 Rating** 93 **To** 2020 $30
Chittering Verdelho 2012 Rating 90 **To** 2016 $25
The Bunyip 2012 Rating 90 **To** 2013 $20

 ## Lana   ★★★☆

2 King Valley Road, Whitfield, Vic 3678 **Region** King Valley
T (03) 5729 9278 **www**.lanawines.com.au **Open** 7 days 11–5
Winemaker Joel Pizzini **Est.** 2011 **Dozens** 2000
This is a new venture of siblings Carlo, Joel and Natalie Pizzini, whose grandparents migrated to Australia from Lana, a town in Italy's Trentino-Alto Adige region at the foot of the Italian Alps. The strikingly labelled wines are made by Joel from grapes purchased from King Valley producers, and are a promising start.

♀♀♀♀♀ **King Valley Prosecco 2012** Pale quartz; is in no-holds-barred Prosecco style,
akin to plunging into an ice bath; in the right context, perfect, in the wrong,
painful. Crown seal. 11% alc. **Rating** 90 **To** 2014 $25

ȲȲȲȲ   Il Nostro Gallo 2010 Rating 89 To 2015 $30
King Valley Pinot Grigio 2011 Rating 88 To 2014 $25

Landhaus Estate   ★★★★★

PO Box 2135, Bethany SA 5352 **Region** Barossa Valley
T (08) 8353 8442 **www**.landhauswines.com.au **Open** Not
Winemaker Kane Jaunutis **Est.** 2002 **Dozens** 5000
The Jaunutis family (John, Barbara and son Kane) purchased Landhaus Estate in 2002, followed by 'The Landhaus' cottage and 1ha vineyard at Bethany. Bethany is the oldest German-established town in the Barossa (1842) and the cottage was one of the first to be built. Kane has worked vintages for Mitolo and Kellermeister, as well as managing East End Cellars, one of Australia's leading fine wine retailers, while John brings decades of owner/management experience and Barbara 20 years in sales and marketing. Rehabilitation of the estate plantings and establishing a grower network has paid handsome dividends. A commendable decision not to make any wine in 2011 means no new wines could be submitted for the *2014 Wine Companion*; the rating has been retained. Exports to Canada, Singapore and China.

ȲȲȲȲȲ   Barossa Valley Cabernet Sauvignon 2010 Bright crimson; abounds with juicy red and black small berry fruits on the bouquet and supple palate; as yet it still has to build texture, but the wellspring of fruit will provide that in the future. Screwcap. 14% alc. **Rating** 94 To 2025 $50

Langmeil Winery   ★★★★★

Cnr Para Road/Langmeil Road, Tanunda, SA 5352 **Region** Barossa Valley
T (08) 8563 2595 **www**.langmeilwinery.com.au **Open** 7 days 10.30–4.30
Winemaker Paul Lindner, Tyson Bitter **Est.** 1996 **Dozens** 35000 **Vyds** 25.3ha
Vines were first planted at Langmeil (which possesses the oldest block in Australia) in the 1840s, and the first winery on the site, known as Paradale Wines, opened in 1932. In '96, cousins Carl and Richard Lindner with brother-in-law Chris Bitter formed a partnership to acquire and refurbish the winery and its 5ha vineyard (planted to shiraz, and including 2ha planted in 1843). Another vineyard was acquired in '98, which included cabernet sauvignon and grenache. In late 2012 the Lindner family put a succession plan into action: Richard and Shirley Lindner, and their sons Paul and James, have acquired 100% ownership of the business. In terms of management, little changes, Paul has been chief winemaker and James the sales and marketing manager since the winery began in '96. Exports to all major markets.

ȲȲȲȲȲ   Valley Floor Barossa Shiraz 2010 Bright crimson-purple; a beautiful wine from this wondrous vintage; a selection from 19 vineyard sites, open-fermented, basket-pressed and matured in quality American oak; its juicy flavours caress the mouth, the oak balance is spot on, and not imparting overt vanilla, the tannins equally good. Screwcap. 14.5% alc. **Rating** 96 To 2025 $30
The Freedom 1843 Barossa Shiraz 2010 Created from the world's oldest existing shiraz vines; there is profound restraint and depth of character on the bouquet, with dark fruits, fresh pitch and charry oak on display; the palate is lively and fresh, with vibrant acidity and silky fine-grained tannins providing an even and fine conclusion. Screwcap. 15% alc. **Rating** 96 To 2035 $100 BE
Orphan Bank Barossa Shiraz 2010 The bouquet shows fragrant red fruits, licorice and sappy complexity; the palate is medium-bodied, revealing toasted oak nuances; slippery fine-grained tannins and fresh acidity on the long and harmonious finish. Screwcap. 15% alc. **Rating** 94 To 2025 $50 BE

ȲȲȲȲȲ   Eden Valley Dry Riesling 2012 Rating 92 To 2019 $25 BE
Jackaman's Barossa Valley Cabernet 2010 Rating 92 To 2025 $50 BE

Lanz Vineyards

220 Scenic Road, Lyndoch, SA 5351 **Region** Barossa Valley
T 0417 858 967 **www**.lanzvineyards.com **Open** By appt
Winemaker Michael Paxton **Est.** 1998 **Dozens** 1750 **Vyds** 15ha

The major part of the grape production from the vineyards is sold to premium producers in the Barossa Valley. However, Marianne and Thomas Lanz take enough of the grapes to make their Shiraz and Grenache Shiraz Mourvedre. Their choice of Michael Paxton as winemaker is no accident; he is a committed biodynamic grower (together with father David) and the Lanzs are aiming at the 'three L' wine style: Lower alcohol, Lower intervention, and Lower carbon footprint. Exports to Switzerland, Germany and Singapore.

🍷🍷🍷🍷 **Limited Edition The Grand Reserve Barossa Valley Shiraz 2010** Positive crimson-purple colour; an elegant and persuasive wine, with excellent life and energy underwriting its mix of red and black fruits, spice and mocha and driving through to the finish. The Barossa Valley does not need to hit the consumer with an alcohol hammer. Screwcap. 13.5% alc. **Rating** 94 **To** 2020 $39

🍷🍷🍷 **Scenic Road Barossa Valley Shiraz 2011** **Rating** 88 **To** 2015 $25

Lark Hill

521 Bungendore Road, Bungendore, NSW 2621 **Region** Canberra District
T (02) 6238 1393 **www**.larkhillwine.com.au **Open** Wed–Mon 10–5
Winemaker Dr David, Sue and Chris Carpenter **Est.** 1978 **Dozens** 4000 **Vyds** 10.5ha

The Lark Hill vineyard is situated at an altitude of 860m, offering splendid views of the Lake George escarpment. The Carpenters have made wines of real quality, style and elegance from the start, but have defied all the odds (and conventional thinking) with the quality of their Pinot Noirs in favourable vintages. Significant changes have come in the wake of son Christopher gaining three degrees, including a double in wine science and viticulture through CSU, the progression towards biodynamic certification of the vineyard and the opening of a restaurant in 2007. They have also planted 1ha of gruner veltliner; it is hard to understand why there have been so few plantings of this high-quality Austrian variety. In '11 Lark Hill purchased one of the two Ravensworth vineyards from Brian Martin, with plantings of sangiovese, shiraz, viognier, roussanne and marsanne; they will also be converting it (renamed Dark Horse) to biodynamic farming. Exports to the UK.

🍷🍷🍷🍷🍷 **Canberra District Auslese Riesling 2012** Bright green-gold; a small section of the vineyard was deliberately exposed to botrytis and the '12 vintage obliged. This is crammed with orange and cumquat conserve balanced by brilliant and persistent acidity. Top-quality wine. Screwcap. 9.5% alc. **Rating** 95 **To** 2018 $25

Canberra District Gruner Veltliner 2012 Bright green-yellow; opens with the white pepper and spice nuances for which the variety is known, but changes gear on the energetic palate with a rainbow of flavours from citrus through to stone fruit, finishing with good acidity. Screwcap. 12.5% alc. **Rating** 94 **To** 2020 $40

✪ **Canberra District Pinot Noir 2012** Light, but bright red-purple; a cherry/ cherry blossom/spice bouquet leads into a juicy, lively palate with flavours precisely tracking the bouquet, and excellent mouthfeel and balance. The vintage wasn't an easy one, and this biodynamic wine comes through with flying colours (this from a biodynamic sceptic). Screwcap. 12.5% alc. **Rating** 94 **To** 2018 $30

🍷🍷🍷🍷 **Canberra District Chardonnay 2012** **Rating** 93 **To** 2017 $35

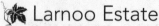

Larnoo Estate   NR

'Larnoo', Larnoo Road, Yea, Vic 3717 **Region** Upper Goulburn
T (03) 5797 2748 **Open** Not
Winemaker Bill Gurry **Est.** 1997 **Dozens** NA

This is likely to be a once-only entry in the *Wine Companion*, for it makes its appearance after well-known investment banker Bill Gurry decided to rip out the 120ha of vines he had planted in 1996-97. In the early years, all went well, but then the combination of drought, bushfires and frost suggested grazing cattle might have a positive, rather than negative, cash flow. There are still substantial quantities of wines from 2005 and (mainly) '06, with a price tag between $115 and $119 per dozen. Bill adds 'the wines are still drinking well, and we are running out of stock'.

Larry Cherubino Wines   ★★★★★

15 York Street, Subiaco, WA 6008 **Region** Western Australia
T (08) 9382 2379 **www.**larrycherubino.com **Open** Not
Winemaker Larry Cherubino, Peter Dillon **Est.** 2005 **Dozens** 6000 **Vyds** 70ha
Larry Cherubino has had a particularly distinguished winemaking career, first at Hardys Tintara, then Houghton, and thereafter as consultant/Flying Winemaker in Australia, NZ, South Africa, the US and Italy. In 2005 he started Larry Cherubino Wines and has developed three ranges: at the top is Cherubino (Riesling, Sauvignon Blanc, Shiraz and Cabernet Sauvignon); next The Yard, five single vineyard wines from WA; and at the bottom the Ad Hoc label, all single-region wines. The range and quality of his wines is extraordinary, the prices irresistible. The runaway success of the business (owned by Larry and wife Edwina) has seen the accumulation of 70ha of vineyards, the appointment of two additional winemakers, and Larry's own appointment as Director of Winemaking at Robert Oatley Vineyards. Exports to the UK, the US, Canada, Ireland, Switzerland, Hong Kong, South Korea, Singapore, China and NZ.

🍷🍷🍷🍷🍷 **Cherubino Porongurup Riesling 2012** Pale quartz-green; if ever a Riesling was built for a very long future, this is it; ultra-careful selection of high-quality grapes means that Cherubino's role as a winemaker has been limited to ensuring the fermentation has left the wine bone dry, the magic coming from the fruit expression on the finish and the quite beautiful mouthfeel. Screwcap. 11.5% alc. **Rating** 97 **To** 2032 $35

Cherubino Laissez Faire Syrah 2011 Bright purple-crimson; startlingly powerful and concentrated syrah, with savoury/spicy black fruits occupying all but a small part of the space given to the firm tannins and oak. It is not the least extractive, its power coming naturally from the fruit. Screwcap. 13.5% alc. **Rating** 97 **To** 2041 $49

Cherubino Laissez Faire Riesling 2012 Hand-harvested and sorted grapes were wild yeast-fermented, and little was added during fermentation, some SO_2 at bottling – an almost natural wine. There is an array of lime and apple blossom aromas, lime persisting on the long palate, given extra balance by a subliminal touch of residual sugar. Screwcap. 11% alc. **Rating** 96 **To** 2027 $29

Cherubino Frankland River Shiraz 2011 Deep purple-crimson; has all the gravitas and depth expected of Frankland River, its sombre black fruits with splashes of spice and licorice on the bouquet and palate alike; tannins and oak provide the textural framework for the fruit; a long and distinguished full-bodied Shiraz. Screwcap. 14.5% alc. **Rating** 96 **To** 2036 $65

The Yard Riversdale Vineyard Frankland River Cabernet Sauvignon 2011 Medium to full red-purple; the blackcurrant fruit of Frankland River leaps out of the glass, vibrant and pure, intense and penetrating. There is also a symbiotic union between the tannins, fruit and oak. Screwcap. 14.2% alc. **Rating** 96 **To** 2036 $35

Cherubino Pemberton Sauvignon Blanc 2012 Light straw-green; there is an uncommon depth to the wine, with a display of tropical fruit on the bouquet and the mid-palate, before tightening up with a lingering minerally/savoury finish and aftertaste. Works very well. Screwcap. 13.2% alc. **Rating** 95 **To** 2014 $35

The Yard Riversdale Vineyard Frankland River Shiraz 2011 A distinctly savoury and complex bouquet has notes of licorice, polished leather and a hint of smoked meat, followed by a fresh, medium-bodied palate with a strong contribution from foresty/savoury tones to its blackberry fruit; the tannins are ripe, and prolong the finish. Screwcap. 13.9% alc. **Rating** 95 **To** 2031 $35

The Yard Acacia Vineyard Frankland River Shiraz 2011 Deep purple-crimson; the expressive bouquet has spice and pepper overtones of black fruits, the palate with fresh fruit flavours (black cherry/plum) and fine-grained tannins of the highest quality, oak playing a pure support role on the long finish. Sensibly priced. Screwcap. 13.6% alc. **Rating** 95 **To** 2026 $35

Cherubino Margaret River Cabernet Sauvignon 2011 Medium red-purple; while the flavours are complex, they are essentially soft; oak and tannins join seamlessly with the fruit, and you ultimately realise this is all about texture and length. Screwcap. 14% alc. **Rating** 95 **To** 2031 $75

Cherubino Frankland River Cabernet Sauvignon 2011 This is a deadly serious Cabernet, with multiple layers of black fruits on a foundation of no less serious tannins, oak in a pure support role. Destined for a very long life. 95 dozen made. Screwcap. 14.5% alc. **Rating** 95 **To** 2040 $109

The Yard Riversdale Vineyard Frankland River Riesling 2012 **Rating** 94 **To** 2022 $25

Ad Hoc Wallflower Great Southern Riesling 2012 **Rating** 94 **To** 2025 $21

The Yard Channybearup Vineyard Pemberton Sauvignon Blanc 2012 **Rating** 94 **To** 2014 $25

Pedestal Sauvignon Blanc Semillon 2012 **Rating** 94 **To** 2014 $25

Cherubino Margaret River Chardonnay 2012 **Rating** 94 **To** 2020 $49

✪ Ad Hoc Middle of Everywhere Frankland River Shiraz 2011 Full crimson-purple; the bouquet is full of spice, licorice, pepper and black fruits, the palate with blackberry to the fore before a savoury touch of tobacco comes into play; the tannins are ripe but persistent, the oak subtle. Screwcap. 14% alc. **Rating** 94 **To** 2021 $21

Pedestal Margaret River Cabernet Merlot 2011 **Rating** 94 **To** 2025 $25

♟♟♟♟♟ Ad Hoc Straw Man Margaret River Sauvignon Blanc Semillon 2012 **Rating** 93 **To** 2015 $21

✪ Ad Hoc Cruel Mistress Great Southern Pinot Noir 2012 Healthy bright crimson-purple colour; has clear varietal character, with a mix of red and black cherry, plum and a touch of forest floor to add complexity and typicity. Will gain further complexity. Screwcap. 13.5% alc. **Rating** 93 **To** 2018 $25

The Yard Pusey Road Vineyard Margaret River Cabernet Sauvignon 2011 **Rating** 93 **To** 2026 $35

Ad Hoc Cruel Mistress Pinot Noir 2011 **Rating** 90 **To** 2015 $25

Laughing Jack ★★★★★

Cnr Seppeltsfield Road/Stonewell Road, Marananga, SA 5355 **Region** Barossa Valley
T (08) 8562 3878 www.laughingjackwines.com.au **Open** By appt
Winemaker Shawn Kalleske **Est.** 1999 **Dozens** 3000 **Vyds** 38.88ha
The Kalleske family has many branches in the Barossa Valley. Laughing Jack is owned by Shawn, Nathan, Ian and Carol Kalleske, and Linda Schroeter. The lion's share of the vineyard is planted to shiraz, with lesser amounts of semillon, chardonnay, riesling and grenache. Vine age varies considerably, with old dry-grown shiraz the jewel in the crown. A small part of the production is taken for the Laughing Jack Shiraz. As any Australian knows, the kookaburra is also called the laughing jackass, and there is a resident flock of kookaburras in the stands of blue and red gums surrounding the vineyards. Exports to Hong Kong and China.

♟♟♟♟♟ Greenock Barossa Valley Shiraz 2010 Deep purple-crimson; aromas of black fruits, licorice, tobacco leaf and spice spiral out of the glass, dark chocolate adding its weight on the majestic palate, where savoury tannins provide flavour balance and the structure to last for many decades to come. Screwcap. 14.5% alc. **Rating** 96 **To** 2045 $40

Moppa Block Barossa Valley Shiraz 2009 The colour is still crimson-purple, the bouquet catching attention, the full-bodied palate sweeping all before it; here abundant black fruits, quality oak and ample ripe tannins are still nowhere near maturity, but have a gold-plated future. 60 dozen made. Cork. 14.5% alc. **Rating** 95 **To** 2039 $55

Old Vine Moppa Barossa Valley Grenache 2009 Has retained excellent colour, and has more structure than many other Barossa Valley Grenaches; the firm red berry flavours have enough savoury nuances to lift this wine into the top echelon. Cork. 14.5% alc. **Rating** 94 **To** 2020 $45

ᵽᵽᵽᵽᵽ **Jack's Barossa Valley Shiraz 2011 Rating** 90 **To** 2016 $20

Laurance of Margaret River ★★★★★

3518 Caves Road, Wilyabrup, WA 6280 **Region** Margaret River
T (08) 9755 6199 **www**.laurancewines.com **Open** 7 days 10–5
Winemaker Naturaliste Vintners (Bruce Dukes) **Est.** 2001 **Dozens** 8000 **Vyds** 23ha
Founder and chairwoman Dianne Laurance is the driving force behind this family-owned and run business, with sons Brendon (Executive Director) and Danny (Special Events Manager) representing the next generation. The 100ha property has vines (planted in 1996 to three clones of chardonnay, plus sauvignon blanc, shiraz, cabernet sauvignon, semillon and merlot), beautiful gardens, artwork and sculptures. The quality of the wines can be lost behind the oddly shaped bottles, reminiscent of Perrier-Jouët's Belle Epoque deluxe Champagne. Exports to Singapore, Hong Kong, Malaysia, Thailand and China.

ᵽᵽᵽᵽᵽ **Icon Cabernet 2010** Full crimson-purple; this is a superior wine from an estate that regularly produces very good wine; the fruit ripeness is suspended on a high wire between cassis fruit and fine, savoury tannins, the mid-palate partly oak-filled, partly fruit-filled. Screwcap. 14% alc. **Rating** 96 **To** 2025 $42
Chardonnay 2011 Gleaming, bright straw-green; high-quality estate-grown fruit shines through the barrel-ferment French oak background, the flavours giving equal space to white peach, honeydew melon and grapefruit flavours; oak is a positive, yet subtle, contributor. Screwcap. 13.5% alc. **Rating** 94 **To** 2022 $38
Shiraz 2010 Medium crimson-purple; fragrant cherry, plum and spice aromas on the bouquet are joined by quality oak on the juicy, well-balanced medium-bodied palate. Seductive style. Screwcap. 13.8% alc. **Rating** 94 **To** 2020 $30
Red 2010 Strong purple-crimson; Laurance is consistently producing wines with impressive regional and varietal expression across the board, and does so here; cassis and redcurrant fruit is given length, texture and structure by ripe tannins and balanced French oak. Screwcap. 14% alc. **Rating** 94 **To** 2025 $29

ᵽᵽᵽᵽᵽ **Semillon Sauvignon Blanc 2011 Rating** 93 **To** 2015 $26
Chardonnay 2010 Rating 93 **To** 2019 $38
✪ **Rose 2011** Pale magenta; a well-made wine with real presence; bright red berry/cherry fruits fill the palate without diminishing its vibrancy; its acidity will sustain it over the next 12–18 months. Screwcap. 13% alc. **Rating** 93 **To** 2014 $15
Merlot 2010 Rating 93 **To** 2018 $26
White 2010 Rating 90 **To** 2017 $29

Laurel Bank ★★★★

130 Black Snake Lane, Granton, Tas 7030 **Region** Southern Tasmania
T (03) 6263 5977 **www**.laurelbankwines.com.au **Open** By appt
Winemaker Winemaking Tasmania (Julian Alcorso) **Est.** 1987 **Dozens** 1100 **Vyds** 3.5ha
Laurel (hence Laurel Bank) and Kerry Carland began planting their vineyard in 1986 to sauvignon blanc, riesling, pinot noir, cabernet sauvignon and merlot. They delayed the first release of their wines for some years and (by virtue of the number of entries they were able to make) won the trophy for Most Successful Exhibitor at the Hobart Wine Show '95. Things have settled down since; wine quality is very reliable.

ᵽᵽᵽᵽᵽ **Riesling 2012** An exotic style of Riesling, revealing nectarine, pepper and fresh celery notes on the bouquet; the palate is chalky in texture, but has a long, lively and generous conclusion. Screwcap. 11.9% alc. **Rating** 91 **To** 2018 $22 BE

Cabernet Merlot 2009 Deeply coloured, with concentrated and essency blackcurrant pastille, dried herbs and cedar on the bouquet; medium- to full-bodied with ample fine-grained tannins playing a prominent role on the palate; surprisingly fleshy and generous for a Tasmanian cabernet blend. Screwcap. 13.9% alc. **Rating** 91 **To** 2018 $28 BE

ＹＹＹＹ **Sauvignon Blanc 2012 Rating** 88 **To** 2014 $22 BE

Lavina Wines

12 Beltunga Close, Blewitt Springs, SA 5171 **Region** McLaren Vale
T (08) 8383 0928 **www**.lavinawines.com.au **Open** Mon–Fri 9–5,
Winemaker Tim Whitrow **Est.** 2004 **Dozens** 50 000 **Vyds** 1.5ha
Lavina Wines is owned by Sam and Victoria Daw, who continue to rapidly build and expand the Lavina brand along with its sub-brands and private label to both domestic and overseas markets. The estate vineyards surrounding the winery are strictly showpiece, with an odd combination of 1ha of cabernet franc and 0.5ha of shiraz. The vast amount of the intake comes from over 40 contract growers and wineries with 8000ha of vineyards, the degree of difficulty being increased by the preference for biodynamically grown fruit. The winery itself is state-of-the-art, with a new-generation mechanised sorting table, and equipped with every other bit of whizz-bang equipment needed. Exports to most major markets.

ＹＹＹＹＹ **Elicere McLaren Vale Cabernet Franc 2012** Bright colour, with a floral and blue-fruited bouquet, offset by cassis and marzipan; the palate is lively, fresh, focused and surprisingly long for cabernet franc as a mono-varietal; user friendly, but with serious intent. Cork. 13.5% alc. **Rating** 91 **To** 2018 $35 BE
Elicere McLaren Vale Shiraz 2010 Deep colour, bright hue; the lifted bouquet offers dark fruits, mocha, a generous seasoning of toasty new oak and fruitcake spice; the palate is densely structured, with freshness of fruit offsetting the concentration. Cork. 14.5% alc. **Rating** 90 **To** 2022 $35 BE
The Aurum Release McLaren Vale Shiraz 2010 Deep colour, and showing black fruits, pitch, fruitcake and leather on the bouquet; the palate reveals some freshness of fruit and acidity to offset the concentration; the finish is harmonious and even. Enjoying the wine will be one thing, forgiving the olive oil bottle is another, but perhaps beauty is in the eye of the beholder. Cork. 14.5% alc. **Rating** 90 **To** 2022 $50 BE

ＹＹＹＹ **Grand Royale McLaren Vale Shiraz 2010 Rating** 89 **To** 2020 $120 BE
Elicere McLaren Vale Grenache Shiraz 2010 Rating 89 **To** 2017 $35 BE
Grand Royale McLaren Vale Cabernet Sauvignon 2010 Rating 89 **To** 2018 $95 BE
Elicere McLaren Vale Cabernet Sauvignon 2010 Rating 88 **To** 2017 $35 BE

Leaning Church Vineyard

76 Brooks Road, Lalla, Tas 7267 **Region** Northern Tasmania
T (03) 6395 4447 **www**.leaningchurch.com.au **Open** 7 days 10–5
Winemaker Jeremy Dineen **Est.** 1988 **Dozens** 1500 **Vyds** 6.3ha
In 2011 Mark and Sarah Hirst purchased the then 20-year-old Lalla Gully Vineyard from long-term owner Taltarni. Sarah has a background in journalism, media, event management and wine marketing; Mark has years of experience in agriculture, accounting and business management. It's difficult not to describe that as a match made in heaven.

ＹＹＹＹＹ **Chardonnay 2011** Light straw-green; delicate but positive fruit, and grainy, minerally acidity. They typically take a few years to open up, but as long as the balance is there – as it is here – will do so. Screwcap. 12.5% alc. **Rating** 93 **To** 2020 $38
Riesling 2012 Very pale colour; made in the style of a Mosel kabinett, the fermentation stopped with substantial residual sugar remaining; the flavours are of lime, sweet apple and (even) pineapple. A touch more acidity might have been useful. Screwcap. 8% alc. **Rating** 90 **To** 2017 $25

Sauvignon Blanc 2012 Pale straw-green; has tropical fruits on the fore-palate, then moves swiftly to pronounced lemon citrus acidity on the back-palate and finish. Why Tasmania should struggle with this variety remains a mystery. Screwcap. 11.7% alc. **Rating** 90 **To** 2013 $28

Pinot Noir 2010 Light, bright and clear colour that shows no sign of ageing; the bouquet is fragrant and fresh, and the once prominent tannins have softened considerably. The wine is still on the savoury edge of the spectrum, but that makes it complex. Screwcap. 13.2% alc. **Rating** 90 **To** 2016 $30

YYYY   **Merlot 2011 Rating** 87 **To** 2015 $32

Leasingham   ★★★★★

PO Box 57, Clare, SA 5453 **Region** Clare Valley
T 1800 088 711 **www.**leasingham-wines.com.au **Open** Not
Winemaker Charlie Seppelt (former) **Est.** 1893 **Dozens** NFP
Leasingham has experienced death by a thousand cuts. First, its then owner CWA sold its Rogers Vineyard to Tim Adams in 2009, and unsuccessfully endeavoured to separately sell the winemaking equipment and cellar door, while retaining the winery. In January '11 Tim Adams was able to buy the winery, cellar door and winemaking equipment, making the once-proud Leasingham a virtual winery. Exports to all major markets.

YYYYY   **Classic Clare Riesling 2008** Gleaming straw-green; in the year of its birth the wine received 94 points (Sept), and, as anticipated, has developed superbly. Even now, its laser-like citrus fruit and echoes of honey have years to go, building yet greater complexity along the way. Screwcap. 11% alc. **Rating** 96 **To** 2023 $43

Classic Clare Sparkling Shiraz 2005 This release was disgorged in May '11. A rich and complex wine, it is a perennial gold medal and trophy winner in the absence of Seppelt vintage sparkling Shirazs; it is (seductively) slightly sweet, and slightly oaky, both qualities at the heart of the style. Cork. 14% alc. **Rating** 95 **To** 2018 $49

YYYY   **Bin 61 Clare Valley Shiraz 2010 Rating** 93 **To** 2025 $22 BE
Bin 7 Clare Valley Riesling 2012 Rating 91 **To** 2020 $22 BE
Bin 56 Clare Valley Cabernet Malbec 2010 Rating 90 **To** 2018 $22 BE

Leayton Estate   ★★★

PO Box 325, Healesville, Vic 3777 **Region** Yarra Valley
T (03) 5962 3042 **www.**leaytonestate.com.au **Open** Not
Winemaker Graham Stephens **Est.** 1997 **Dozens** 300 **Vyds** 1.6ha
Yet another partnership between medicine and winemaking: Dr Graham Stephens is a GP in Healesville, and together with wife Lynda has established a vineyard (split evenly between chardonnay and pinot noir) and a supplementary olive plantation on a 12ha property west of Healesville. One-third of the grapes are sold to Sergio Carlei, the remainder retained for the Leayton Estate label. Graham is still working full-time as a doctor, but intends to gradually wind back his medical hours and spend more time in the vineyard and winemaking.

YYYY   **Yarra Valley Chardonnay 2010** Bright straw-green; an interesting wine with plenty of varietal flavour, but suggests there may have been some fermentation issues. ProCork. 12.3% alc. **Rating** 88 **To** 2013 $20

Leconfield   ★★★★★

Riddoch Highway, Coonawarra, SA 5263 **Region** Coonawarra
T (08) 8737 2326 **www.**leconfieldwines.com **Open** Mon–Fri 11–4.30, w'ends & public hols 11–4
Winemaker Paul Gordon, Tim Bailey **Est.** 1974 **Dozens** 25 000 **Vyds** 43.7ha
Sydney Hamilton purchased the unplanted property that was to become Leconfield in 1974, having worked in the family wine business for over 30 years until his retirement in the mid '50s. When he acquired the property and set about planting it, he was 76, and

reluctantly bowed to family pressure to sell Leconfield to nephew Richard in '81. Richard has progressively increased the vineyards to their present level, over 75% to cabernet sauvignon, for long the winery's specialty. Exports to the UK, Canada, Denmark, Switzerland, Belgium, Japan, Malaysia, Hong Kong, Singapore, the Philippines, Vietnam, China and NZ.

ΥΥΥΥΥ **Coonawarra Cabernet Sauvignon 2011** Deep crimson; pure cassis, red fruits and cigar box aromas all combine on the alluring bouquet; the full-bodied palate is lusciously fruited, with fresh acidity and even-handed oak that merely seasons the refined fruit. Screwcap. 13.5% alc. **Rating** 94 **To** 2025 $34 BE
Coonawarra Cabernet Sauvignon 2010 Includes 7% McLaren Vale fruit, and has 3% cabernet franc and 1% petit verdot. Crimson-purple; the bouquet and palate are flooded with cassis, blackberry and cedary oak, the soft tannins make the wine fleshy and approachable now, notwithstanding its long future. Screwcap. 14.5% alc. **Rating** 94 **To** 2030 $34

ΥΥΥΥΥ **Old Vines Coonawarra Riesling 2012** **Rating** 92 **To** 2022 $25
Coonawarra Merlot 2011 **Rating** 91 **To** 2017 $25 BE

Leeuwin Estate   ★★★★★

Stevens Road, Margaret River, WA 6285 **Region** Margaret River
T (08) 9759 0000 **www**.leeuwinestate.com.au **Open** 7 days 10–5
Winemaker Paul Atwood, Tim Lovett, Phil Hutchinson **Est.** 1974 **Dozens** 60 000
Vyds 121ha
This outstanding winery and vineyard is owned by the Horgan family, founded by Denis and Tricia, who continue their involvement, with son Justin Horgan as general manager. The Art Series Chardonnay is, in my opinion, Australia's finest example, based on the wines of the last 30 vintages. The move to screwcap brought a large smile to the faces of those who understand just how superbly the wine ages. The large estate plantings, coupled with strategic purchases of grapes from other growers, provide the base for high-quality Art Series Cabernet Sauvignon and Shiraz; a hugely successful, quick-selling Art Series Riesling and Sauvignon Blanc; and lesser-priced wines such as Prelude Chardonnay and Siblings Sauvignon Blanc Semillon. Exports to all major markets.

ΥΥΥΥΥ **Art Series Margaret River Chardonnay 2009** Craftmanship of the highest order in the vineyard and winery have combined to create a perfect example with this wine. The intensity and power unwind effortlessly, but with multiple aroma and flavour messages from the barrel fermentation and subsequent maturation of the fully ripe, pink grapefruit and peach at its core. Screwcap. 14.5% alc. **Rating** 97 **To** 2024 $96
Art Series Margaret River Chardonnay 2010 Pale green-gold; a restrained bouquet offering pure grapefruit and cashew aromas; the palate reveals a swathe of pure fruit, showing a vintage of purity rather than complexity, the latent power is held in check by linear acidity and well-handled French oak; long, expansive and absolutely in keeping with its lineage. Screwcap. 14% alc. **Rating** 95 **To** 2025 $89 BE
Art Series Margaret River Shiraz 2010 Bright, clear crimson-purple; a vibrantly fresh wine; red berry and cherry fruit is at the core of the bouquet and medium-bodied palate of an elegant and delicious wine. Screwcap. 14% alc. **Rating** 94 **To** 2030 $37

ΥΥΥΥΥ **Prelude Vineyards Margaret River Chardonnay 2011** **Rating** 92 **To** 2014 $32 TS
Art Series Margaret River Riesling 2012 **Rating** 90 **To** 2015 $22 BE

Lenton Brae Wines   ★★★★★

3887 Caves Road, Margaret River, WA 6285 **Region** Margaret River
T (08) 9755 6255 **www**.lentonbrae.com **Open** 7 days 10–6
Winemaker Edward Tomlinson **Est.** 1983 **Dozens** NFP **Vyds** 9ha

Former architect and town planner Bruce Tomlinson built a strikingly beautiful winery (now heritage listed by the Shire of Busselton), which is now in the hands of winemaker son Edward, who consistently makes elegant wines in classic Margaret River style. Exports to Indonesia, Singapore and China.

ŶŶŶŶŶ **Margaret River Semillon Sauvignon Blanc 2012** Light straw-green; this wine
✪   is often more reserved in its youth, but here is full to the brim with citrus from
           the semillon and a cascade of tropical fruits from the sauvignon blanc, passionfruit,
           lychee and guava to the fore. Great now, but will age well. Screwcap. 12% alc.
           Rating 95 **To** 2017 $25

✪   **Southside Margaret River Chardonnay 2011** Barrel-fermented and matured
           in French oak, the palate is exceptionally intense and incisive, the fruit having
           easily absorbed the oak and showing its potent grapefruit base, nectarine and
           white peach each playing second fiddle; the high natural acidity will see this wine
           through to the next decade without batting an eyelid. Exceptional value. Screwcap.
           13.5% alc. **Rating** 95 **To** 2025 $25
           Wilyabrup Chardonnay 2011 Estate-grown, with four clones fermented and
           matured in new and used French oak. Provides a total contrast to Lenton Brae's
           '12 Southside, with vivid fruit spanning white peach and citrus/grapefruit, oak a
           vehicle, the finish long and cleansing. Screwcap. 13% alc. **Rating** 95 **To** 2020 $50
           Wilyabrup Cabernet Sauvignon 2011 The hue is good, though the colour
           is slightly light, almost certainly a consequence of the correct decision to pick
           earlier rather than later; the result is a fresh, crunchy cassis-driven suite of flavours
           couched in a fine tannin web and quality oak; the bouquet, too, is fragrant.
           Screwcap. 13.5% alc. **Rating** 94 **To** 2026 $60

ŶŶŶŶŶ **Margaret River Cabernet Merlot 2011** Rating 93 **To** 2031 $25
           Southside Margaret River Chardonnay 2012 Rating 91 **To** 2018 $25

Leo Buring   ★★★★★

Sturt Highway, Nuriootpa, SA 5355 **Region** Eden Valley/Clare Valley
T 1300 651 650 **www**.leoburing.com.au **Open** Not
Winemaker Peter Munro **Est.** 1934 **Dozens** NFP
Between 1965 and 2000, Leo Buring was Australia's foremost producer of Rieslings, with a rich legacy left by former winemaker John Vickery. After veering away from its core business with other varietal wines, it has now been refocused as a specialist Riesling producer. The top of the range are the Leopold Derwent Valley Riesling and the Leonay Eden Valley Riesling, under a changing DW bin no. (DWO for 2011, DWP for '12 etc), supported by Clare Valley Riesling and Eden Valley Riesling at significantly lower prices, and expanding its wings to Tasmania and WA.

ŶŶŶŶŶ **Leonay Riesling 2012** DWP 18. Pale straw-green; the floral bouquet gives the
           wine a flying start, and the juicy, lissom palate does not disappoint, filled with
           lime and lemon fruit before finishing with minerally acidity. Watervale. Screwcap.
           12% alc. **Rating** 95 **To** 2025 $40

ŶŶŶŶŶ **Dry Clare Valley Riesling 2012** Pale straw-green; in classic Clare style, with
✪   purity of varietal fruit in a citrus and ripe apple spectrum, balanced acidity
           giving the wine length and an appealing finish. Screwcap. 12% alc. **Rating** 93
           To 2020 $20
           Medium Sweet Eden Valley Riesling 2012 Rating 92 **To** 2017 $20 TS

Leogate Estate Wines   ★★★★★

1693 Broke Road, Pokolbin, NSW 2320 **Region** Hunter Valley
T (02) 4998 7499 **www**.leogate.com.au **Open** 7 days 10–5
Winemaker Mark Woods **Est.** 2009 **Dozens** 10 000 **Vyds** 60ha
Since purchasing the substantial Brokenback Vineyard in 2009 (a key part of the original Rothbury Estate, with vines over 40 years old), Bill and Vicki Widin have wasted no time.

Initially the Widins leased the Tempus Two winery, but prior to the '13 vintage they completed the construction of their own winery and cellar door. They have also expanded the range of varieties to supplement the long-established 28ha of shiraz, 18ha of chardonnay and 4ha of semillon, with between 1 and 2.5ha of each of verdelho, viognier, gewurztraminer, pinot gris, tempranillo and merlot. In '12 the Leogate Reserve Semillon won a trophy, two gold and three silver medals, while the three Shirazs accumulated five trophies, six gold and numerous silver medals. Small wonder that Mark Woods continues to make the wines.

ΨΨΨΨΨ **Western Slopes Reserve Hunter Valley Shiraz 2011** Has even deeper and slightly more purple colour than that of The Basin, and throughout its bouquet and palate the same comparison applies; this magnificently rich and complex wine will live for at least 50 years if given half-decent cellaring conditions. Three trophies, five gold medals (including the National Wine Show) and six silver medals. Screwcap. 14% alc. **Rating** 97 **To** 2060 $55

The Basin Reserve Hunter Valley Shiraz 2011 Extraordinarily deep purple-crimson, shades of the fabled 1965 Lindemans Bins 3100 and 3110; the bouquet has great balance between intense, ripe fruit and oak, the medium- to full-bodied palate building on this foundation with waves of blackberry, plum and black cherry fruit, the tannins ripe and supple. The surprise is that it only won two gold medals (and two silver) in '12. Screwcap. 14% alc. **Rating** 96 **To** 2050 $55

Reserve Hunter Valley Semillon 2010 Pale straw-green; an aromatic bouquet offering a mix of grassy/herbal and lemon citrus characters, the palate nigh-on explosive in its intensity and length. From the Brokenback Vineyard. Trophy Boutique Wine Awards '12. Screwcap. 11.4% alc. **Rating** 95 **To** 2025 $25

H10 Block Reserve Hunter Valley Chardonnay 2011 Part wild yeast-fermented in new French hogsheads, part stainless steel-fermented with cultured yeast. The slightly riper fruit has responded well to the more adventurous winemaking; while the citrussy acidity is good, there are also some creamy, nutty characters. Screwcap. 13.5% alc. **Rating** 94 **To** 2017 $33

ΨΨΨΨΥ **Creek Bed Reserve Chardonnay 2011 Rating** 91 **To** 2016 $33

Lerida Estate   ★★★★★

The Vineyards, Old Federal Highway, Lake George, NSW 2581 **Region** Canberra District
T (02) 6295 6640 **www.**leridaestate.com.au **Open** 7 days 10–5
Winemaker Malcolm Burdett **Est.** 1999 **Dozens** 5000 **Vyds** 7.93ha

Lerida Estate, owned by Jim Lumbers and Anne Caine, owes a great deal to the inspiration of Dr Edgar Riek, planted as it is immediately to the south of his former Lake George vineyard, and also planted mainly to pinot noir (there are also smaller plantings of pinot gris, chardonnay, shiraz, merlot, cabernet franc and viognier). The Glenn Murcutt–designed winery, barrel room, cellar door and café complex has spectacular views over Lake George. The Shiraz Viognier and Pinot Noir enjoy continuing wine show success. Exports to China.

ΨΨΨΨΨ **Lake George Canberra District Botrytis Pinot Gris 2012** There is no doubt about the botrytis, nor the purity of the infection; a luscious array of pear, peach and citrus flavours put it well and truly onto the dessert wine list. 375ml. Screwcap. 11.2% alc. **Rating** 94 **To** 2015 $35

ΨΨΨΨΥ **Lake George Chardonnay 2011 Rating** 90 **To** 2015 $25
Pinot Grigio 2012 Rating 90 **To** 2014 $25
Lake George Pinot Noir 2011 Rating 90 **To** 2015 $27
Lake George Shiraz Viognier 2010 Rating 90 **To** 2018 $50

Lethbridge Wines   ★★★★★

74 Burrows Road, Lethbridge, Vic 3222 **Region** Geelong
T (03) 5281 7279 **www.**lethbridgewines.com **Open** Thurs–Sun & public hols 10.30–5, or by appt
Winemaker Ray Nadeson, Maree Collis, Alexander Byrne **Est.** 1996 **Dozens** 3000 **Vyds** 7ha

Lethbridge was founded by scientists Ray Nadeson, Maree Collis and Adrian Thomas. In Ray's words, 'Our belief is that the best wines express the unique character of special places.' As well as understanding the importance of terroir, the partners have built a unique straw-bale winery, designed for its ability to recreate the controlled environment of cellars and caves in Europe. Winemaking is no less ecological: hand-picking, indigenous yeast fermentation, small open fermenters, pigeage and minimal handling of the wines throughout the maturation process are all part and parcel of the highly successful Lethbridge approach. Ray also has a special touch with chardonnay, and has a successful contract winemaking limb to the business. Exports to the UK.

Geelong Pinot Gris 2011 Part of the crop was frozen as whole bunches, then pressed while frozen, increasing the base flavour; fermented in new 2500-litre oval casks and given extended lees contact, the outcome is a Pinot Gris that still has varietal expression of nashi pear and a dressing of citrus juice; no heaviness on the mid-palate or long, lingering finish. Screwcap. 12.5% alc. **Rating** 95 **To** 2014 $30

Leura Park Estate ★★★★★

1400 Portarlington Road, Curlewis, Vic 3222 **Region** Geelong
T (03) 5253 3180 **www.**leuraparkestate.com.au **Open** W'ends & public hols 10.30–5, 7 days Jan, or by appt
Winemaker Darren Burke **Est.** 1995 **Dozens** 8000 **Vyds** 15.94ha
Leura Park Estate's vineyard is planted to chardonnay (50%), pinot noir, pinot gris, sauvignon blanc and shiraz. Owners David and Lyndsay Sharp are committed to maintaining minimal interference in the vineyard, and have expanded the estate-grown wine range (Sauvignon Blanc, Pinot Gris, Chardonnay, Pinot Noir and Shiraz) to include Vintage Grande Cuvee (Pinot Noir Chardonnay). The next step was the erection of an onsite winery prior to the 2010 vintage, leading to increased production and ongoing wine show success. Exports to South Korea and Singapore.

Limited Release Block 1 Reserve Chardonnay 2011 Hand-picked, whole bunch-pressed, wild yeast-fermented, and matured in French oak for 12 months. A very elegant and vibrantly fresh wine with white peach, nectarine and grapefruit in a near-invisible web of oak; perfectly balanced acidity. Starred in the James Halliday Chardonnay Challenge '12 (it bears my name, but I did not judge). Screwcap. 13.7% alc. **Rating** 96 **To** 2019 $45
Voix de la Terre Hand-Picked Reserve Sauvignon Blanc 2011 The otherwise gushing back label does contain some useful information, including whole bunch-pressing and some French oak barrel ferment, and these steps do indeed show through in what is a very good Sauvignon Blanc, with nicely balanced pea pod and tropical fruit flavours, the finish crisp, dry and long. Screwcap. 13.3% alc. **Rating** 94 **To** 2014 $30

25 d'Gris Bellarine Peninsula Pinot Gris 2012 **Rating** 93 **To** 2014 $30
Bellarine Peninsula Pinot Noir 2011 **Rating** 93 **To** 2019 $40
Nine Yards and Counting Chardonnay 2009 **Rating** 92 **To** 2019 $25
Bellarine Peninsula Sauvignon Blanc 2012 **Rating** 90 **To** 2013 $30
Bellarine Peninsula Shiraz 2011 **Rating** 90 **To** 2019 $40

 # Levantine Hill Estate ★★★★☆

Level 1, 461 Bourke Street, Melbourne, Vic 3000 **Region** Yarra Valley
T (03) 8602 0831 **www.**levantinehill.com.au **Open** Not
Winemaker Rob Dolan **Est.** 2009 **Dozens** 1560 **Vyds** 23.6ha
All things considered, this is the most ambitious project in the Yarra Valley since the establishment of Domaine Chandon a quarter of a century ago. It is the venture of Lebanese-born Elias Jreissati and wife Colleen, Elias already having two rags to riches stories under his belt. Their vast house in Hill Road has a helipad, cutting the trip to Ely's Melbourne CBD office to 17 minutes, and the sight of the house at night lit up with hundreds of lights is not easily missed. Nor is the towering frame of Rob (Sticks) Dolan, whose long legs attest to his

early years as an AFL footballer. Rob has over 20 years' experience winemaking in the Yarra Valley, and has been buying grapes from the older of the two vineyards owned by Levantine Hill (purchased three years ago) for over eight years. That vineyard is 17 years old, and after its acquisition by Levantine Hill, has had over half the vines removed, leaving 18ha of the best blocks of pinot noir, shiraz, cabernet sauvignon, merlot, sauvignon blanc and semillon. The new plantings in Hill Road are a little over 5ha of chardonnay, pinot noir and a single site blend of cabernet sauvignon, merlot, malbec and petit verdot. The entire focus of the business is on quality, completely regardless of cost, with low yields and small lot fermentation. Leading Melbourne architect Fender Katsalidis has been retained to design a world-class cellar door, restaurant, fresh food outlet and high-end accommodation for a building on the Maroondah Highway vineyard; the cellar door is planned to open in '14, and will be the first stage of a five-year building program.

ΨΨΨΨΨ Sauvignon Blanc Semillon 2012 The first wine of this new development, crafted by Rob Dolan from barrel-fermented sauvignon blanc and tank-fermented semillon. A prominent new oak presence is surprisingly well integrated, energising enticing purity of lemon blossom aromas and flavours of preserved lemon, nettles and roast nuts. Screwcap. 13% alc. **Rating** 94 **To** 2017 $35 TS

Light's View/Pure Vision Organic Wines ★★★☆

PO Box 258, Virginia, SA 5120 **Region** Adelaide Plains
T 0412 800 875 **www.**lightsviewwines.com.au **Open** Not
Winemaker David Norman, Jim Irvine, Ken Carypidis **Est.** 2001 **Dozens** 10 000
Vyds 55ha
The Carypidis family runs two brands: Pure Vision (15ha of certified organically grown grapes), and Light's View (with a much larger planting of conventionally grown grapes). Growing grapes under a certified organic regime is much easier if the region is warm to hot and dry, conditions unsuitable for botrytis and downy mildew. You are still left with weed growth (no herbicides are allowed) and powdery mildew (sulphur sprays are permitted) but the overall task is much simpler. The Adelaide Plains, where Pure Vision's vineyard is situated, is such a region, and owner Ken Carypidis has been clever enough to secure the services of Jim Irvine as co-winemaker. Exports to the US, Canada, Taiwan and China.

ΨΨΨΨΨ ✪ Nature's Step Wild Ferment Organic Chardonnay 2012 The wine has utterly unexpected vibrancy and grip, with its mix of ripe stone fruit and tangy citrus aromas and flavours on a long and fresh palate. A convincing advertisement for organic wines. Screwcap. 13.5% alc. **Rating** 90 **To** 2015 $10

ΨΨΨΨ ✪ Nature's Step Organic Wild Ferment Pinot Grigio 2012 Wild yeast-fermented, with the faintest bronze hint on the colour; a remarkably good outcome, fresh acidity underpinning the spice, nashi pear and apple flavours. Great value. Screwcap. 12.6% alc. **Rating** 89 **To** 2013 $10

✪ Light's View Shiraz 2010 Blackberry, black cherry, plum and dark chocolate (plus a dab of French and American oak) coalesce on the medium-bodied palate, the tannins soft and unobtrusive. Great bargain for immediate casual drinking, from a very good vintage. Cork. 14.3% alc. **Rating** 89 **To** 2014 $14

✪ Pure Vision Organic Cabernet Sauvignon 2011 Has the colour lacking in the '11 Light's View Cabernet, and is a powerful testament to the merits of organic grapegrowing and skilled winemaking. Blackcurrant fruit is in abundance; maturation in used French and American oak for the better part of a year has been equally successful. Screwcap. 13.5% alc. **Rating** 89 **To** 2014 $17

✪ Nature's Step Organic Wild Ferment Sauvignon Blanc 2012 Pale quartz; the Adelaide Plains' hot climate is a hostile environment for downy mildew, but poses problems for Sauvignon Blanc, here met with wild yeast fermentation building structure; the tropical flavours are enhanced by cleverly managed residual sugar and acidity. Screwcap. 12.6% alc. **Rating** 88 **To** 2013 $10

Pure Vision Organic Shiraz 2011 **Rating** 88 **To** 2015 $17
Pure Vision Organic Merlot 2011 **Rating** 88 **To** 2014 $17
Light's View The Virginian Merlot 2010 **Rating** 87 **To** 2013 $14

Lightfoot & Sons ★★★★☆

Myrtle Point Vineyard, 717 Calulu Road, Bairnsdale, Vic 3875 (postal) **Region** Gippsland
T (03) 5156 9205 **www**.lightfootwines.com **Open** Not
Winemaker Alastair Butt, Tom Lightfoot **Est.** 1995 **Dozens** 4000 **Vyds** 29.3ha

Brian and Helen Lightfoot have established pinot noir, shiraz, chardonnay, cabernet sauvignon and merlot, the lion's share to pinot noir and shiraz. The soil bears a striking resemblance to that of Coonawarra, with terra rossa over limestone. The vines are irrigated courtesy of a licence allowing the Lightfoots to pump water from the Mitchell River, and most of the grapes are sold (as originally planned) to other Vic winemakers. With the arrival of Alastair Butt (formerly of Brokenwood and Seville Estate), supported by son Tom, production has increased, and may well rise further. Second son Rob has also come on board, bringing 10 years' experience in sales and marketing.

🍷🍷🍷🍷🍷 Myrtle Point Single Vineyard Pinot Noir 2011 Light red-purple; while the '11 vintage has reduced the volume of red fruits that would otherwise be present, there are fragrant cherry notes to the bouquet and palate; the spicy, savoury nuances are part of the DNA of the wine, and are in balance. Screwcap. 12.8% alc. **Rating** 94 **To** 2018 $26

🍷🍷🍷🍷 Myrtle Point Single Vineyard Chardonnay 2011 Pale quartz; a classy chardonnay that has capitalised on the cool vintage by retaining natural acidity, and restraining the new oak influence; barrel fermentation and lees contact have given texture to the elegant stone fruit, melon and citrus fruit. Screwcap. 13% alc. **Rating** 93 **To** 2019 $24

Limited Release Myrtle Point Single Vineyard Shiraz 2010 **Rating** 93 **To** 2020 $50

✪ Myrtle Point Single Vineyard Rose 2012 Light, bright pale pink; made from estate-grown pinot noir; the fragrant bouquet has cherry blossom and cinnamon spice aromas that flow onto the palate, there lifted by a track of lemony acidity. Screwcap. 12.7% alc. **Rating** 90 **To** 2014 $20

Myrtle Point Single Vineyard Shiraz 2011 **Rating** 90 **To** 2017 $24

Lillian ★★★★☆

PO Box 174, Pemberton, WA 6260 **Region** Pemberton
T (08) 9776 0193 **Open** Not
Winemaker John Brocksopp **Est.** 1993 **Dozens** 300 **Vyds** 3.2ha

Long-serving (and continuing consultant) viticulturist to Leeuwin Estate, John Brocksopp established 2.8ha of the Rhône trio of marsanne, roussanne and viognier, and 0.4ha of shiraz. The varietal mix may seem à la mode, but it in fact comes from John's early experience working for Seppelt at Barooga in NSW, and his years in the Barossa Valley. Exports to the UK.

🍷🍷🍷🍷🍷 Lefroy Brook Pemberton Pinot Noir 2011 Good purple-red; the fragrant bouquet offers spiced dark cherry aromas picked up seamlessly by the beautifully proportioned palate; a resounding testament to Pemberton's ability to produce high-quality pinot in the right spot, and with the right calls in the winery. Compelling wine. Screwcap. 14% alc. **Rating** 94 **To** 2018 $26

🍷🍷🍷🍷 Pemberton Viognier 2010 **Rating** 91 **To** 2015 $21

Lillypilly Estate ★★★★☆

47 Lillypilly Road, Leeton, NSW 2705 **Region** Riverina
T (02) 6953 4069 **www**.lillypilly.com **Open** Mon–Sat 10–5.30, Sun by appt
Winemaker Robert Fiumara **Est.** 1982 **Dozens** 15 000 **Vyds** 27.9ha

Botrytised white wines are by far the best offering from Lillypilly, with the Noble Muscat of Alexandria unique to the winery; these wines have both style and intensity of flavour and can age well. However, table wine quality is always steady. Exports to the UK, the US, Canada and China.

⟡⟡⟡⟡⟡ **Museum Release Noble Harvest 2006** Full gold, tinged with green; immensely luscious and richly complex, with multiple layers of botrytised cumquat, orange and peach, luscious citrus acidity providing balance. 375ml. Screwcap. 11% alc. **Rating** 94 **To** 2015 $39

⟡⟡⟡⟡⟡ **Noble Harvest 2011 Rating** 93 **To** 2016 $25
✪ **Shiraz 2010** Good colour; this was a vintage to remember in the Riverina, and in particular its reds, led by shiraz. This is medium-bodied, with black and red fruits lingering long on the palate, tannins and oak bit players in the background. Screwcap. 13.5% alc. **Rating** 90 **To** 2018 $18

⟡⟡⟡⟡ **Moscato 2011** Not entirely moscato (minimal bubbles), but does have muscat
✪ fruit, and balanced sweetness. Gold medal Vienna International Wine Challenge '12. Screwcap. 10% alc. **Rating** 89 **To** 2013 $15

Lindemans (Coonawarra)   ★★★★★

Coonawarra Wine Gallery, Riddoch Highway, Coonawarra, SA 5263 **Region** Coonawarra
T (08) 8737 1300 **www**.lindemans.com **Open** 7 days 10–5
Winemaker Brett Sharpe **Est.** 1908 **Dozens** NFP
Lindemans' Coonawarra vineyards have assumed a greater importance than ever thanks to the move towards single region wines. Moreover, the three key labels of Limestone Ridge Vineyard Shiraz Cabernet, St George Vineyard Cabernet Sauvignon and Pyrus Cabernet Sauvignon Merlot Cabernet Franc are all of high quality. Exports to the UK, the US, Canada and NZ.

⟡⟡⟡⟡⟡ **Pyrus Cabernet Sauvignon Merlot Cabernet Franc 2010** Deep crimson-purple; has more depth and complexity than recent vintages, and has relished its 18-month sojourn in new and used French oak; the flavours are a classic mix of blackcurrant and a twist of black olive, the tannins fine and polished. A long life ahead. Screwcap. 14% alc. **Rating** 96 **To** 2035 $65
Limestone Ridge Vineyard Shiraz Cabernet 2010 Excellent crimson-purple; the wine has that special quality of merging power with elegance, intensity with finesse; the quality of the blackberry and mulberry fruit has been neatly framed by 18 months' maturation in a mix of new and used French and American oak; the tannins are fine and supple and the wine has the balance for long-term ageing. Screwcap. 14% alc. **Rating** 95 **To** 2035 $65
St George Vineyard Cabernet Sauvignon 2010 Bright crimson-purple; the wine spent 18 months in a mix of new and used French oak barriques; it has excellent structure to the medium-bodied palate, and the balance between redcurrant and more savoury/olive fruit is strengthened by the oak. Screwcap. 14% alc. **Rating** 95 **To** 2035 $65

Lindemans (Hunter Valley)

McDonalds Road, Pokolbin, NSW 2320 **Region** Hunter Valley
T (02) 4998 7684 **www**.lindemans.com.au **Open** 7 days 10–5
Winemaker Wayne Falkenberg, Brett Sharpe **Est.** 1843 **Dozens** NFP
Just when I expected it least, Lindemans has produced some seriously good wines from the Hunter Valley, and one half of the Lindeman winemaking or marketing side (without talking to the other half) has exhumed some of the Bin number systems that were used in the glory days of the 1960s, admittedly without total consistency. Thus for white wines, 50 or 55 were the last two digits used for what was named Riesling, 70 for what was named White Burgundy, and 75 for what was called Chablis; with the shiraz-based wines, the last two digits were either 00, 03 or 10. The most famous were the 1965 Claret and Burgundy releases Bin 3100 and Bin 3110, and Chablis 1967 Bin 3475. Enquiries about the present system were, it seems, not understood. Exports to the UK, the US and other major markets.

ΨΨΨΨΨ Limited Release Reserve Hunter Valley Shiraz 2011 Bin 1100. Historically the bin number finishing with 00 was the best of the vintage; this wine came from Block 5 on the old Ben Ean Vineyard, and spent 12 months in used French oak. Deep crimson, this is a throwback to Lindemans' glory days: not to the freakish '65 Bins 3100 and 3110 that stand unchallenged, but I wish I could live long enough to see this full-bodied, black-fruited wine peak 30 or so years hence. Screwcap. 13.5% alc. **Rating** 96 **To** 2045 $50

ΨΨΨΨΨ Limited Release Hunter Valley Shiraz 2011 **Rating** 93 **To** 2026 $50

Lindemans (Karadoc)   ★★★

44 Johns Way, Karadoc, Vic 3496 **Region** Murray Darling
T (03) 5051 3285 **www.**lindemans.com.au **Open** 7 days 10–4.30
Winemaker Wayne Falkenberg **Est.** 1974 **Dozens** NFP
Now the production centre for all the Lindemans and Leo Buring wines, with the exception of special lines made in Coonawarra. The very large winery allows all-important economies of scale, and is the major processing centre for TWE's beverage wine sector (casks, flagons and low-priced bottles). Exports to all major markets.

ΨΨΨΨ Early Harvest Semillon Sauvignon Blanc 2012 Light straw-green; some
✪ very sophisticated winemaking has gone on with this vibrant lime/lemon-infused wine that is indeed crisp and refreshing – the only question is it too much of a good thing for buyers with lower expectations? Screwcap. 8.5% alc. **Rating** 89 **To** 2014 $15

✪ Bin 65 Chardonnay 2012 More depth to the straw-green colour than many prior to their first birthday; it also has distinctly greater structure and varietal flavour than most sub-$10 Chardonnays. If all the blend batches are as good as this one, show success may follow. Screwcap. 13% alc. **Rating** 89 **To** 2014 $10

✪ Bin 50 Shiraz 2012 Excellent crimson-purple; there is an abundance of plum and blackberry fruit on the medium-bodied palate; of course it doesn't
- have complexity, but it's terrific value for casual drinking, and while few will even dream of cellaring it, a year or two in bottle could bring a surprise result. Screwcap. 13.5% alc. **Rating** 88 **To** 2014 $10

✪ Bin 95 Sauvignon Blanc 2012 Pale quartz; you would not expect a fanfare of trumpets from a wine of this price point (or be gravely disappointed if you did) but it has been cleverly made to preserve its juicy citrus fruit background, the hint of sweetness perfectly balanced. Screwcap. 11.5% alc. **Rating** 87 **To** 2014 $10

✪ Bin 50 Shiraz 2011 Light, bright red; a totally remarkable achievement, with a burst of fresh red fruits, and only a touch of green/mint on the finish. Screwcap. 12.5% alc. **Rating** 87 **To** 2013 $10

Lindenderry at Red Hill   ★★★★★

142 Arthurs Seat Road, Red Hill, Vic 3937 **Region** Mornington Peninsula
T (03) 5989 2933 **www.**lindenderry.com.au **Open** W'ends 11–5
Winemaker Lindsay McCall, Sandro Mosele, Barnaby Flanders **Est.** 1999 **Dozens** 2000
Vyds 3.35ha
Lindenderry at Red Hill is a sister operation to Lancemore Hill in the Macedon Ranges and Lindenwarrah at Milawa. It has a five-star country house hotel, conference facilities, a function area, day spa and restaurant on 16ha of gardens, but also has a little over 3ha of immaculately maintained vineyards, planted equally to pinot noir and chardonnay more than 15 years ago.

ΨΨΨΨΨ Mornington Peninsula Chardonnay 2011 Interesting wine. The nuggets of nutty/complexity suggest mlf (as well as barrel fermentation), but the shaft of citrussy acidity points in another direction, with terrific energy and drive. Screwcap. 13% alc. **Rating** 95 **To** 2019 $40

Macedon Ranges Pinot Noir 2008 Still retains bright, clear crimson, amazing; so is the vibrant red cherry fruit, clear and precise, long and well balanced. It should be enjoyed now, but having mooched along for 5 years to this point, another 5 won't hurt it. Screwcap. 14% alc. **Rating** 94 **To** 2018 $40

Reserve Macedon Ranges Pinot Noir 2008 Deeper colour than the varietal with more purple; two very different wines from the same vineyard and the same winemaker; obviously, more work was done with this wine during fermentation, and seemingly more new oak was used. Each has its merits – great merits. This too will repay further cellaring. Screwcap. 14% alc. **Rating** 94 **To** 2023 $60

Linfield Road Wines

65 Victoria Terrace, Williamstown, SA 5351 **Region** Barossa Valley
T (08) 8524 7355 **www.**linfieldroadwines.com **Open** 7 days 10–5
Winemaker Daniel Wilson, Natasha Mooney **Est.** 2002 **Dozens** 2500 **Vyds** 19ha
Linfield Road produces small batches of single vineyard wines from the Wilson family vineyard at Williamstown. The story began in 1860 when Edmund Major Wilson planted the first vines on the outskirts of Williamstown. Since Edmund's first plantings, the Wilson family has fostered a viticulture tradition that now spans five generations; three generations of the family currently live and work on the property. The vineyard is located at the very southern edge of the Barossa. It is situated high above the valley floor, leading to cooler nights and longer ripening periods. This results in elegant red and white wines with good structure. Exports to the US, Canada, Hong Kong, South Korea, Singapore, Japan and China.

ŸŸŸŸŸ The Stubborn Patriarch Single Vineyard Barossa Shiraz 2011 Deep crimson-purple; exceptional for the vintage, a quality that carries forward through the bouquet and palate; has amazing velvety depth to the polished black cherry, licorice and spice fruit, tannins and oak perfectly pitched. Not as good as the exceptional '10, but so outperforms the '11 vintage that it gets the same points. Screwcap. 14.4% alc. **Rating** 94 **To** 2021 $28

ŸŸŸŸŸ The Pruner Grenache 2011 Rating 92 **To** 2018 $30

 ## Lion Mill **NR**

700 Lion Street, Mount Helena, WA 6082 **Region** Perth Hills
T (08) 9295 6537 **www.**lionmillvineyards.com **Open** W'ends & public hols 11–5, or by appt
Winemaker MyattsField Vineyards (Josh and Rachael Davenport) **Est.** 1999 **Dozens** 500 **Vyds** 1.25ha
Patrick and Ann Bertola purchased the property on which the Lion Mill Vineyard now stands in 1996, and began planting the first vines in '99. The Lilliputian plantings are split fairly equally among shiraz, tempranillo, zinfandel, semillon and cabernet sauvignon, with minor plantings of merlot, petit verdot, durif and graciano. The wines made to date have had significant success in the Perth Hills Wine Show, showing that small can indeed be beautiful.

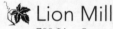 ## Lisa McGuigan Wines

18 College St, Sydney, NSW 2000 (postal) **Region** Various
T 0418 424 382 **www.**lisamcguiganwines.com **Open** Not
Winemaker Liz Jackson **Est.** 2010 **Dozens** 6000
Lisa McGuigan is a fourth-generation member of a famous Hunter Valley winemaking dynasty, started many decades ago by Perc McGuigan, and more recently (and perhaps more famously) led by Brian McGuigan. In 1999 Lisa started Tempus Two from her garage, and under the McGuigan-Simeon (now Australian Vintage) umbrella, the volume rose to 250 000 dozen before she left in 2007 to start a retail wine business. Now she has turned full circle, starting her own business in the Hunter Valley (taking grapes from various regions), and using the winemaking skills of Liz Jackson, whom she had headhunted for Tempus Two, and who is now chief winemaker at First Creek Wines.

ŸŸŸŸŸ Hunter Valley Shiraz 2011 Hand-picked shiraz was given a brief cold soak before fermentation was initiated in small, hand-plunged, open fermenters, the wine then matured in French oak for 12 months. It has excellent colour, the medium-bodied palate alive with plush blackberry and plum fruit, sustained by velvety tannins. Modern Hunter Valley shiraz at its best. Screwcap. 13.5% alc. **Rating** 94 **To** 2026 $30

🍷🍷🍷🍷🍷 Adelaide Hills Pinot Noir 2011 Rating 93 To 2018 $30
Wild Thing Hunter Valley Semillon 2012 Rating 91 To 2016 $25
Hunter Valley Chardonnay 2011 Rating 91 To 2016 $30
Pinot Grigio 2012 Rating 90 To 2013 $25

Little Brampton Wines   ★★★

PO Box 61, Clare, SA 5453 **Region** Clare Valley
T (08) 8843 4201 **www**.littlebramptonwines.com.au **Open** At The Little Red Grape,
Sevenhill
Winemaker Contract **Est.** 2001 **Dozens** 500 **Vyds** 10ha
Little Brampton Wines is a boutique, family-owned business operated by Alan and Pamela
Schwarz. They purchased their 24ha property in the heart of the Clare Valley in the early
1990s (Alan had graduated from Roseworthy in '81). The property had produced grapes since
the 1860s, but the vineyard had been removed during the Vine Pull Scheme of the 1980s. The
Schwarzs have replanted riesling (2ha), shiraz and cabernet sauvignon (4ha each) on northwest
slopes at 520m; a small proportion of the production is vinified for the Little Brampton label.
Exports to the UK and Singapore.

🍷🍷🍷🍷 Flagpole Clare Valley Riesling 2012 From the Flagpole Block in front of the
Schwarz family home; has plenty of ripe citrus flavour, but not the bright acidity
of the best of this vintage. Screwcap. 12.5% alc. **Rating** 88 **To** 2016 $22

Little Bridge   ★★★

106 Brooks Road, Bywong, NSW 2621 **Region** Canberra District
T (02) 6236 9620 **www**.littlebridgewines.com.au **Open** W'ends & public hols 11–4
Winemaker Canberra Winemakers, Lark Hill, Mallaluka Winemakers **Est.** 1996
Dozens 1000 **Vyds** 5.5ha
Little Bridge is a partnership between long-term friends John Leyshon, Rowland Clark,
John Jefferey and Steve Dowton. There are 2ha of chardonnay, pinot noir, riesling and merlot
planted at Folly Run; 2ha of shiraz, cabernet sauvignon, sangiovese, cabernet franc and malbec
at Mallaluka; and 1.5ha of riesling, chardonnay and mourvedre at Brooks Creek. Canberra
Winemakers makes the white wines, Lark Hill the Pinot Noir, and Mallaluka the other reds.
Steve purchased Brooks Creek Vineyard in 2009 (largely derelict, and being rehabilitated), and
it is here that the Little Bridge cellar door is situated. Exports to Singapore and China.

🍷🍷🍷🍷 Canberra District Cabernet Sauvignon 2010 Medium red-purple; the wine
✪ spent 24 months in French oak, and has plenty of robust flavour and structure;
it does not aspire to elegance, but will provide good drinking over the next
3–5 years; neatly priced. Screwcap. 13.2% alc. **Rating** 89 **To** 2017 $20

Littles   ★★★★☆

Cnr Palmers Lane/McDonalds Road, Pokolbin, NSW 2321 **Region** Hunter Valley
T (02) 4998 7626 **www**.littleswines.com.au **Open** Fri–Sun 10–4.30
Winemaker Rhys Eather (Contract) **Est.** 1984 **Dozens** 2000 **Vyds** 21.6ha
Littles is managed by the Kindred family, the ownership involving a number of investors. The
winery has mature vineyards planted to shiraz (7.3ha), cabernet sauvignon (4.5ha), semillon
(4.3ha), pinot noir (3.4ha), chardonnay (1.3ha) and marsanne (0.8ha). Littles' Daisy Hill
vineyard is a replanting of vineyards from the old Daisy Hill winery, which was one of the
most substantial wineries in the Hunter Valley. The Daisy Hill winery won many awards, the
most notable being a trophy from the 1855 Paris International Exhibition in the late 19th
century. In the mid 1950s a fierce bushfire swept through Pokolbin and destroyed the winery
and vineyards. Exports to Germany, Taiwan and Japan.

🍷🍷🍷🍷🍷 Hunter Valley Marsanne 2011 From 30-year-old estate vines, 25% matured
in 1-year-old French oak for 3 months; has honeysuckle and pear aromas and
flavours, and both the balance and structure promise rewards for those with
patience. Screwcap. 12.5% alc. **Rating** 91 **To** 2021 $22

🍷🍷🍷🍷 Reserve Hunter Valley Chardonnay 2011 Rating 87 To 2014 $25

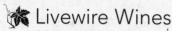 Livewire Wines

PO Box 369, Portarlington, Vic 3223 **Region** Geelong
T 0439 024 007 **www.livewirewines.com.au Open** Not
Winemaker Anthony Brain **Est.** 2011 **Dozens** 600

Anthony Brain started working life as a chef, but in the late 1990s 'took a slight bend into the wine industry'. He started gathering experience in the Yarra Valley, and simultaneously started oenology studies at CSU. Margaret River followed, as did time in SA before returning to the Yarra, working at De Bortoli from 2003 to '07 (undertaking vintages in the Hunter, King and Yarra Valleys). Five vintages as winemaker at Bellarine Estate followed, giving him 'a platform and understanding of the Geelong region and the opportunity to learn more about sites, viticulture and winemaking decisions'. In '13 he resigned from Bellarine Estate, having made some of his own Livewire wines on the way through, albeit coming up against the '11 vintage challenges.

ΨΨΨΨΨ **Geelong Shiraz 2010** Medium red-purple; 100% whole bunch-fermented, foot-stamped, basket-pressed, 12 months' barrel maturation and not filtered. A potent wine with strong savoury/meaty flavours directly flowing from the whole-bunch fermentation, the tannins lean but somehow entirely suited to the wine. Screwcap. 13.8% alc. **Rating** 92 **To** 2030 $36

ΨΨΨΨ **Geelong Pinot Noir 2011 Rating** 89 **To** 2014 $36
Jolt Geelong Heathcote Shiraz 2011 Rating 88 **To** 2017 $22

Lloyd Brothers ★★★★★

34 Warners Road, McLaren Vale, SA 5171 **Region** McLaren Vale
T (08) 8323 8792 **www.lloydbrothers.com.au Open** 7 days 11–5
Winemaker Ross Durbidge **Est.** 2002 **Dozens** 3000 **Vyds** 13.21ha

Lloyd Brothers Wine and Olive Company is owned and operated by David and Matthew Lloyd, third-generation McLaren Vale vignerons. Their 25ha estate overlooks the township, and is planted to 12ha shiraz, 0.81ha bush vine grenache and 0.4ha bush vine mataro. The shiraz planting allows the creation of a full range of styles, including Rose, Sparkling Shiraz, Fortified Shiraz and Estate Shiraz, along with the White Chalk Shiraz, so named because of the white chalk used to mark each barrel during the classification process.

ΨΨΨΨΨ **Hand Picked McLaren Vale Shiraz 2008** Deep colour; open-fermented and
✪ matured for 20 months in new and used French and American oak; utterly classic full-bodied McLaren Vale style, black fruits, dark chocolate and savoury tannins seamlessly wound together. Screwcap. 14.5% alc. **Rating** 95 **To** 2033 $25
White Chalk McLaren Vale Shiraz 2008 Spent 21 months in new and used French and American oak, and was a selection of the 10 best barrels. It is massively powerful and concentrated, showing resplendent flavours, but the high alcohol will always show through. Screwcap. 15% alc. **Rating** 94 **To** 2028 $45

ΨΨΨΨΨ **Caesar Adelaide Hills Sauvignon Blanc 2012** This is one of the largest
✪ alpaca studs in the world and Caesar is the name of one of the top stud males. The bouquet has some flowery aromas, and the palate an array of fruits from citrus to tropical. Not a heavyweight, but finishes with cleansing acidity. Screwcap. 13.5% alc. **Rating** 90 **To** 2014 $13
Spartacus McLaren Vale Shiraz 2011 Rating 90 **To** 2016 $13

ΨΨΨΨ **Daredevil McLaren Vale Rose 2012** Bright puce; spice and red berries drive
✪ the bouquet and mid-palate, followed by dusty acidity on the finish; unusual, but gives texture. Excellent value. Screwcap. 13.6% alc. **Rating** 88 **To** 2014 $13

Lobethal Road Wines ★★★★★

2254 Onkaparinga Valley Road, Mount Torrens, SA 5244 **Region** Adelaide Hills
T (08) 8389 4595 **www.lobethalroad.com Open** W'ends & public hols 11–5
Winemaker Michael Sykes (Contract) **Est.** 1998 **Dozens** 1500 **Vyds** 5.1ha

Dave Neyle and Inga Lidums bring diverse but very relevant experience to the Lobethal Road vineyard, the lion's share planted to shiraz (3.1ha), with smaller amounts of chardonnay, tempranillo, sauvignon blanc and graciano. Dave has been in vineyard development and management in SA and Tasmania since 1990. Inga brings 25 years' experience in marketing and graphic design in Australia and overseas, with a focus on the wine and food industries. The property is managed with minimal chemical input, and uses solar power in the pursuit of an environmentally sustainable product and lifestyle.

Adelaide Hills Sauvignon Blanc 2012 Light straw–green; a cut well above the average, with considerable intensity and drive to its omnibus collection of herb, freshly mown grass, guava, pineapple and gooseberry fruits, the finish zesty and crisp. Screwcap. 12.4% alc. **Rating** 94 **To** 2014 $20

Bacchant Adelaide Hills Shiraz 2010 Light, but relatively bright, hue; the fragrant bouquet leads into a bright and lively light- to medium-bodied palate, with spicy red fruits and well-integrated French oak, the tannins appropriately fine. Scores for its elegance, not its power. Screwcap. 14% alc. **Rating** 94 **To** 2020 $42

Adelaide Hills Pinot Gris 2012 Rating 92 **To** 2014 $22

Lofty Valley Wines

100 Collins Road, Summertown, SA 5141 **Region** Adelaide Hills
T 0400 930 818 www.loftyvalleywines.com.au **Open** By appt
Winemaker Brendon Keys **Est.** 2004 **Dozens** 1000 **Vyds** 3ha
Medical practitioner Brian Gilbert began collecting wine when he was 19, flirting with the idea of becoming a winemaker before being headed firmly in the direction of medicine by his parents. Thirty or so years later he purchased a blackberry- and gorse-infested 12ha property in the Adelaide Hills, eventually obtaining permission to establish a vineyard. Chardonnay (2ha) was planted in 2004, and 1ha of pinot noir in '07, both on steep slopes. Exports to Singapore.

Single Vineyard Adelaide Hills Shiraz 2011 Medium purple-crimson; the fragrant spiced red cherry bouquet leads into a silky and supple light- to medium-bodied palate with a graceful display of fresh black and red cherry fruit, the tannins fine. Outstanding success. Screwcap. 13% alc. **Rating** 94 **To** 2017 $32

Single Vineyard Chardonnay 2011 Rating 93 **To** 2018 $27
Single Vineyard Pinot Noir 2011 Rating 91 **To** 2015 $32
Running Deer Shiraz 2009 Rating 91 **To** 2029 $25

Logan Wines

Castlereagh Highway, Apple Tree Flat, Mudgee, NSW 2850 **Region** Mudgee
T (02) 6373 1333 www.loganwines.com.au **Open** 7 days 10–5
Winemaker Peter Logan **Est.** 1997 **Dozens** 40 000
Logan is a family-owned and operated business with emphasis on cool-climate wines from Orange and Mudgee. The business is run by husband and wife team Peter (winemaker) and Hannah (sales and marketing). Wines are released from three ranges: Logan (from Orange), Weemala and Apple Tree Flat. Exports to the UK, the US, Japan and other major markets.

Weemala Orange Riesling 2012 Light straw-green; offers an ever-changing display of tropical fruits combined with lime and grapefruit; then counterpoised acidity and an airbrush of residual sweetness. It all comes together well. Screwcap. 11.5% alc. **Rating** 93 **To** 2020 $18

Hannah Orange Rose 2012 Pale pink; there are elements of spice on both the perfumed bouquet and palate; a twist of lemony acidity on the finish gives the wine energy and life. Screwcap. 12.5% alc. **Rating** 91 **To** 2013 $22

Orange Cabernet Merlot 2010 A fresh, light- to medium-bodied wine with pleasing redcurrant, blackcurrant and plum fruit, with just enough tannin and oak support to provide some texture and complexity. Screwcap. 13.5% alc. **Rating** 91 **To** 2017 $28

✪ **Weemala Orange Pinot Gris 2012** There is no question: pinot gris does best in cool climates. While the flavours are somewhat amorphous, pear, apple, melon and even ginger all melding into each other, the outcome is pleasant enough, and this will suit casual lunches devoted to conversation. Screwcap. 13% alc. **Rating** 90 To 2013 $18

Orange Shiraz 2010 Light to medium crimson-purple; a medium-bodied wine with cherry, plum, spice and oak all contributing to the bouquet and palate, the tannins fine and ripe. Drink while it retains its freshness. Screwcap. 13.5% alc. **Rating** 90 To 2018 $28

ϼϼϼϼ **Weemala Orange Gewurztraminer 2012** Rating 89 To 2014 $18
Orange Sauvignon Blanc 2012 Rating 89 To 2013 $22
Ridge of Tears Orange Shiraz 2010 Rating 89 To 2017 $45
Weemala Central Ranges Shiraz Viognier 2010 Rating 89 To 2015 $18
Weemala Orange Pinot Noir 2011 Rating 88 To 2015 $18
Ridge of Tears Mudgee Shiraz 2010 Rating 88 To 2015 $45
Orange Chardonnay 2011 Rating 87 To 2013 $25

Lonely Vineyard

61 Emmett Road, Crafers West, SA 5152 (postal) **Region** Eden Valley
T 0413 481 163 www.lonelyvineyard.com.au **Open** Not
Winemaker Michael Schreurs **Est.** 2008 **Dozens** 400 **Vyds** 1.5ha
This is the venture of winemaker Michael Schreurs and Karina Ouwens, a commercial lawyer from Adelaide. Daughter Amalia Schreurs can 'hoover a box of sultanas in record time' while Meesh, the family cat, 'treats Karina and Amalia well, and Michael with the contempt he deserves. As cats do.' One or other of the partners (perhaps both) has a great sense of humour. Michael's winemaking career in Australia began with Seppelt Great Western winery for three years, followed by six years at Henschke, and, more recently, The Lane Vineyard in the Adelaide Hills, backed up by stints in Burgundy, the Rhône Valley, the US and Spain. No red wines were made in 2011.

ϼϼϼϼϼ **Eden Valley Riesling 2012** The quality of the label design sets you off on the right foot; the quality of the bouquet with its spice and curry powder nuances, and the length of the citrus and apple-flavoured palate simply add to the appeal; its acidity will underwrite a long life. Screwcap. 12.5% alc. **Rating** 93 To 2025 $28

Longleat Wines

105 Old Weir Road, Murchison, Vic 3610 **Region** Goulburn Valley
T (03) 5826 2294 www.murchisonwines.com.au **Open** W'ends & most public hols 10–5, or by appt
Winemaker Guido Vazzoler **Est.** 1975 **Dozens** 4000 **Vyds** 8.1ha
Sandra (ex-kindergarten teacher turned cheesemaker) and Guido Vazzoler (ex-Brown Brothers) acquired the long-established Longleat Estate vineyard in 2003 (renaming it Murchison Wines), after living on the property (as tenants) for some years. The mature vineyard comprises 3.2ha of shiraz, 2.3ha of cabernet sauvignon, 0.8ha each of semillon, sauvignon blanc and chardonnay, and 0.2ha of petit verdot. Exports to Hong Kong and China.

ϼϼϼϼϼ **Murchison Cabernet Sauvignon 2010** Estate-grown and matured in French oak for 12 months; the colour is good, as befits the vintage, the bouquet with slightly smoky/tarry/spicy aromas, almost into star anise; the juicy nature of the medium-bodied palate comes as a pleasing surprise, giving an even flow through to the harmonious finish. Screwcap. 14% alc. **Rating** 91 To 2020 $22

✪ **Murchison Semillon 2012** Has clear-cut varietal character; it has depth and texture to its grass, lemon curd and lanolin flavours, held in check with good acidity and length; only medium-term cellaring needed to build its body and flesh. Screwcap. 13% alc. **Rating** 90 To 2015 $15

ŸŸŸŸ
✪
Murchison Rose 2011 Salmon-pink; the spicy bouquet leads into a positively juicy palate, with both red berry and citrus fruit intended to partly mimic a white wine, and succeeding; the finish is dry. Screwcap. 12% alc. **Rating** 89 **To** 2014 $15
Murchison Shiraz 2010 Rating 87 **To** 2016 $22

Longview Creek Vineyard

150 Palmer Road, Sunbury, Vic 3429 **Region** Sunbury
T (03) 9740 2448 **www.**longviewcreek.com.au **Open** Sun 12–5, Sat by appt
Winemaker Bill Ashby **Est.** 1988 **Dozens** 400 **Vyds** 2.2ha
Bill and Karen Ashby purchased the Longview Creek Vineyard from founders Dr Ron and Joan Parker in 2003. It is situated on the brink of the spectacular Longview Gorge. The bulk of the chardonnay (0.9ha), pinot noir (0.7ha) and chenin blanc (0.2ha) was planted between 1988 and '90. Thereafter a little cabernet franc and riesling were planted.

ŸŸŸŸ
Riesling 2012 Pale green-quartz; has good varietal expression, and freshness from crisp acidity; the flavours span apple and citrus, though not particularly long or intense. Screwcap. 11.5% alc. **Rating** 89 **To** 2015 $18
Sparkling Chenin Blanc 2011 Made using the traditional method, and is a crisp, refreshing wine, with relatively low dosage a major plus. Diam. 13% alc. **Rating** 88 **To** 2014 $25

Longview Vineyard

Pound Road, Macclesfield, SA 5153 **Region** Adelaide Hills
T (08) 8388 9694 **www.**longviewvineyard.com.au **Open** 7 days 11–5
Winemaker Ben Glaetzer (Contract) **Est.** 1995 **Dozens** 20 000 **Vyds** 63.74ha
The Saturno family purchased Longview from founder Duncan MacGilvray in 2007, with members of the extended family now also involved in many aspects of the business. Shiraz and cabernet sauvignon are the major varieties, followed by chardonnay, and smaller plantings of alternative varieties of gruner veltliner (as part of the Adelaide Hills Vine Improvement Society). A significant investment has been made in upgrading the function facilities, and in rejuvenating the vineyard. Exports to the UK, the US, Ireland, Denmark, The Netherlands, Malaysia, Taiwan, Hong Kong, China and NZ.

ŸŸŸŸŸ
✪
Epitome Late Harvest Riesling 2012 Deeply coloured, and showing plenty of rich botrytis character in the form of apricot conserve and a touch of peanut brittle; the palate is very sweet, unctuous and hedonistic, and will satisfy the sweetest of tooth. 375ml. Screwcap. 11.5% alc. **Rating** 92 **To** 2016 $20 BE
Whippet Adelaide Hills Sauvignon Blanc 2012 Bright colour, and offering a pungent blend of fresh-cut grass, passionfruit and straw on the bouquet; the lemony acidity is linear and fine, providing thrust and cut to the juicy fruit on offer. Screwcap. 12.5% alc. **Rating** 90 **To** 2014 $20 BE

ŸŸŸŸ
Boat Shed Adelaide Hills Nebbiolo Rose 2012 **Rating** 89 **To** 2013 $20
Yakka Adelaide Hills Shiraz 2010 **Rating** 88 **To** 2017 $27 BE
Queenie Adelaide Hills Pinot Grigio 2012 **Rating** 87 **To** 2013 $20

Lost Lake

14591 Vasse Highway, Pemberton, WA 6260 **Region** Pemberton
T (08) 9776 1251 **www.**lostlake.com.au **Open** 7 days 10–4
Winemaker Katie Masters **Est.** 1990 **Dozens** 4500 **Vyds** 7.82ha
Previously known as Eastbrook Estate, Lost Lake's origins go back to 1990, to the acquisition of an 80ha farming property which was subdivided into three portions: 16ha, now known as Picardy, were acquired by Dr Bill Pannell, 18ha became the base for Lost Lake, and the remainder was sold. The initial plantings in 1990 were of pinot noir and chardonnay, followed by shiraz, sauvignon blanc, merlot and cabernet sauvignon. Steve and Karen Masters acquired the property in 2006 and moved from Perth to live there full-time.

♟♟♟♟♟ Barrel Selection Pemberton Pinot Noir 2011 Light, clear red-purple; the spicy, savoury bouquet and fore-palate do not hint at the way the red fruits swell on the back-palate, finish and aftertaste; French oak has been adroitly handled. Screwcap. 14.5% alc. **Rating** 94 To 2017 $35

♟♟♟♟♟ Barrel Select Pemberton Cabernet Sauvignon 2010 **Rating** 93
To 2025 $35
Single Vineyard Pemberton Pinot Noir 2011 **Rating** 90 To 2016 $25

Lou Miranda Estate   ★★★★★

Barossa Valley Way, Rowland Flat, SA 5352 **Region** Barossa Valley
T (08) 8524 4537 **www**.loumirandaestate.com.au **Open** Mon–Fri 10–4, w'ends 11–4
Winemaker Lou Miranda **Est.** 2005 **Dozens** 20000 **Vyds** 23.29ha
Lou Miranda's daughters Lisa and Victoria are the driving force behind the estate, albeit with continuing hands-on involvement from Lou. The jewels in the crown of the estate plantings are 0.5ha of mourvedre planted in 1897 and 1.5ha of shiraz planted in 1907. The remaining vines have been planted gradually since '95, the varietal choice widened by cabernet sauvignon, merlot, chardonnay and pinot grigio. The cellar door works on the principle that there should be a wine for every conceivable taste. Exports to the UK and other major markets.

♟♟♟♟♟ Angel's Vineyard Old Vine Barossa Valley Shiraz Mourvedre 2010 Spent 20 months in barrel but is deliciously fresh and elegant, with as much red fruit as black fruit flavour, its juicy mouthfeel set within a garland of fine tannins. Cork. 14.5% alc. **Rating** 96 To 2025 $38
Rare Rutherglen Aged 30 Years Muscat NV Extreme age is very obvious; very complex, but expert Rutherglen winemakers might well be tempted to add some younger, fresher material to add verve; as it is, very good with raisined muscat grapes. Screwcap. 17% alc. **Rating** 94 To 2014 $70

♟♟♟♟♟ Cordon Cut Barossa Valley Shiraz 2010 **Rating** 93 To 2025 $37
Leone Barossa Valley Sparkling Shiraz NV **Rating** 90 To 2016 $27

Lowe Wines   ★★★★☆

Tinja Lane, Mudgee, NSW 2850 **Region** Mudgee
T (02) 6372 0800 **www**.lowewine.com.au **Open** 7 days 10–5
Winemaker David Lowe, Liam Heslop **Est.** 1987 **Dozens** 15000 **Vyds** 21.8ha
Lowe Wines has undergone a number of changes in recent years, the most recent the acquisition of Louee and its two vineyards. The first is at Rylstone with 10ha, led by shiraz, cabernet sauvignon, petit verdot and merlot, with chardonnay, cabernet franc, verdelho and viognier making up the balance. The second is on Nullo Mountain, bordered by the Wollemi National Park, at an altitude of 1100m, high by any standards, and often the coolest location in Australia. Here 4.45ha of cool-climate varieties (riesling, sauvignon blanc, chardonnay, pinot noir, pinot gris and nebbiolo) have been planted. Lowe Wines continues with its organic profile, with just over 20ha of its own. Exports to the UK and Japan.

♟♟♟♟♟ Mudgee Blue Shiraz Cabernet 2011 Crimson-purple; a traditional Mudgee blend, perhaps, but a very good one, with plum, blackberry and blackcurrant all on display on the generous medium- to full-bodied palate; the handling of oak and tannins is impressive. Screwcap. 14% alc. **Rating** 94 To 2030 $30

♟♟♟♟♟ Nullo Mountain Riesling 2012 **Rating** 93 To 2020 $60
Nullo Mountain Sauvignon Blanc 2012 **Rating** 93 To 2014 $30
Louee Nullo Mountain Rylstone Pinot Grigio 2012 **Rating** 92 To 2014 $30
Block 5 Reserve Mudgee Shiraz 2011 **Rating** 92 To 2031 $75
Gentleman's Daughter Orange Pinot Noir Chardonnay 2010 **Rating** 92
To 2017 $45
Headstone Organic Mudgee Primitivo Rose 2012 **Rating** 90 To 2014 $25
Organic Zinfandel 2010 **Rating** 90 To 2018 $45

Lucas Estate

329 Donges Road, Severnlea, Qld 4352 **Region** Granite Belt
T (07) 4683 6365 **www**.lucasestate.com.au **Open** Tues–Sat 10.30–4.30, 1st Sun each month
Winemaker Louise Samuel **Est.** 1999 **Dozens** 1000 **Vyds** 2.7ha

Louise Samuel and her late husband Colin Sellers purchased Lucas Estate in 2003. The wines
are made from the estate vineyard (at an altitude of 825m), which is planted to chardonnay,
cabernet sauvignon, muscat hamburg, merlot, verdelho and shiraz, and also from purchased
grapes. A new winery was completed in time for the '08 vintage, with a pneumatic press for
the white wines, leaving the basket press for reds. Later that year Colin succumbed to cancer;
after it had been diagnosed 18 months earlier, he and Louise agreed that Lucas Estate should
continue, and that is what she is doing.

Estate Granite Belt Chardonnay 2009 Has had show success in three
local derbies, its raw power doubtless the reason it attracted the judges. Yes, it's
a bit rough around the edges, but there is a lot of flavour in the glass. Screwcap.
13.5% alc. **Rating** 89 **To** 2014 $35

Granite Belt Petit Verdot 2008 Still has remarkable colour, as is the wont of
petit verdot, and enough depth of fruit to carry the tannins. Screwcap. 15% alc.
Rating 89 **To** 2018 $40

Granite Belt Unwooded Tempranillo 2010 Bright red-purple; given its
unwooded elevage, and its screwcap closure, reduction might have been seen
as inevitable. Well, it isn't reduced, and it does have attractive red cherry fruits.
Screwcap. 12% alc. **Rating** 89 **To** 2015 $22

**The Surveyor Granite Belt Cabernet Sauvignon Merlot Cabernet Franc
Petit Verdot 2008** Very extractive, which will prolong its life in bottle, but not
ameliorate the rugged tannins. Screwcap. 14% alc. **Rating** 87 **To** 2018 $28

Lucinda Estate Vineyard

108 Parr Street, Leongatha, Vic 3953 **Region** Gippsland
T 0417 337 270 **www**.lucindaestate.com.au **Open** Thurs–Mon 11–4
Winemaker Andrew Gromotka **Est.** 1990 **Dozens** 700 **Vyds** 3.64ha

Owners Lucinda and Andrew Gromotka planted their vineyard in 1990, the lion's share to
pinot noir, with 0.4ha each of shiraz and chardonnay. It is an east-facing block, the soil ancient
volcanic deep red clay loam, with buckshot giving a high ironstone content. Andrew is both
winemaker and viticulturist. He also purchases shiraz from Heathcote.

Reserve South Gippsland Pinot Noir 2010 A complex and potent wine,
with hints of bramble and forest floor to the palate in particular; despite the sample
being a half-bottle (750ml bottles are available), has obvious development potential.
Screwcap. 13.5% alc. **Rating** 93 **To** 2019 $35

South Gippsland Syrah 2009 Good retention of colour; has an abundantly
juicy/spicy array of red and black fruits on the bouquet and palate alike, the length
and intensity of the fruit very good. Screwcap. 13.5% alc. **Rating** 93 **To** 2024 $28

Estate Gippsland Pinot Noir 2010 Strong, clear and deep red-purple; spicy
plum and black cherry fruit aromas on the bouquet are replicated on the full-
flavoured palate, with slightly more emphasis on the glossy black cherry fruit.
Needs, and will repay, cellaring. Screwcap. 14% alc. **Rating** 91 **To** 2017 $28

Heathcote Shiraz 2011 Very good colour; needs no apologies for the vintage,
with its lush red and black fruit aromas and flavours, with an offset touch of spice,
controlled oak and ripe tannins. Screwcap. 13.5% alc. **Rating** 91 **To** 2021 $35

South Gippsland Syrah 2010 Light to medium red-purple; has a fragrant, very
spicy, red berry bouquet and light- to medium-bodied palate; the tannins are fine,
and the oak is well integrated. Screwcap. 12.8% alc. **Rating** 91 **To** 2020 $28

Gippsland Chardonnay 2011 Rating 89 **To** 2015 $24
Lucinda Gippsland Pinot Noir 2011 Rating 89 **To** 2016 $22
Lucinda Two Vineyards Shiraz 2011 Rating 89 **To** 2016 $26

Sparkling Red 2007 Rating 89 To 2015 $26
Reserve South Gippsland Chardonnay 2010 Rating 88 To 2015 $35
Estate Gippsland Pinot Noir 2011 Rating 88 To 2014 $28

Luke Lambert Wines   ★★★★☆

PO Box 1297, Healesville, Vic 3777 **Region** Yarra Valley
T 0448 349 323 **www**.lukelambertwines.com.au **Open** By appt
Winemaker Luke Lambert **Est.** 2003 **Dozens** 1500 **Vyds** 4.5ha
Luke Lambert graduated from CSU's wine science course in 2002, aged 23, cramming in
winemaking experience at Mount Pleasant, Coldstream Hills, Mount Prior, Poet's Corner,
Palliser Estate in Martinborough, and Badia di Morrona in Chianti. With this background he
has established a virtual winery, purchasing grapes from quality-conscious growers in the Yarra
Valley and Heathcote. He has now settled in the Yarra Valley, leasing slightly less than 1ha of
Heathcote nebbiolo, and similar amounts of Yarra Valley shiraz and nebbiolo (newly grafted).
The wines are wild yeast-fermented and bottled without fining or filtration. Exports to the
UK and the US.

♀♀♀♀♀ Yarra Valley Syrah 2011 Deep, bright crimson; the fresh blackberry bouquet,
and a suggestion of black pepper are evenly proportioned; the medium-
bodied palate reveals rapier-like acidity, superfine tannins and an almost plush
conclusion; in the style of modern cool-climate Australian Shiraz that shares
many characteristics with the Rhône Valley. Diam. 13.5% alc. Rating 94 To 2025
$40 BE

♀♀♀♀♀ Yarra Valley Chardonnay 2011 Rating 90 To 2017 $30 BE

M. Chapoutier Australia   ★★★★★

141–143 High Street, Heathcote, Vic 3523 **Region** Pyrenees
T (03) 5433 2411 **www**.mchapoutieraustralia.com **Open** Mon–Sat 9–5, Sun 10–5
Winemaker Michel Chapoutier, Eduard Guerin **Est.** 1998 **Dozens** 20000 **Vyds** 51.9ha
M. Chapoutier Australia is the eponymous offshoot of the famous Rhône Valley producer.
Having disposed of its plantings in Mount Benson, the business now focuses on vineyards in
the Pyrenees, Heathcote and Beechworth, with collaboration from Ron Laughton of Jasper
Hill and Rick Kinzbrunner of Giaconda. After first establishing a vineyard in Heathcote
adjacent to Jasper Hill (see La Pleiade), Chapoutier purchased the Malakoff Vineyard in the
Pyrenees to create Domaine Terlato & Chapoutier (the Terlato & Chapoutier joint venture
was established in 2000 with its first vintage in '04; Terlato still owns 50% of the Malakoff
Vineyard). In '09 Michel Chapoutier purchased two neighbouring vineyards, Landsborough
Valley and Shays Flat, all three sites within 5km of each other; all these are now fully owned
by Domaine Tournon. (Domaine Tournon consists of Landsborough and Shays Flat Estates in
the Pyrenees and Lady's Lane estate in Heathcote.) Exports to all major markets.

♀♀♀♀♀ Domaine Terlato & Chapoutier L-Block Pyrenees Shiraz 2009 A powerful
shiraz, with clearly articulated black fruits basted with a sprinkle of spice and
pepper; the oak has been well handled, but the best feature is the outstanding
texture and weight of the tannins. Cork. 13.5% alc. Rating 95 To 2034 $60
Tournon Shays Flat Vineyard Pyrenees Shiraz 2010 Deep purple-crimson;
the complex bouquet has black fruits, polished shoe leather and a dusting of spice;
the palate brings juicy red and black fruit flavours onto centre stage, finishing with
a savoury/spicy flourish. Screwcap. 14% alc. Rating 94 To 2025 $35
Domaine Terlato & Chapoutier lieu dit Malakoff Pyrenees Shiraz 2009
Blackberry, black cherry and licorice aromas on the bouquet flow through to the
medium-bodied palate, where spice comes more into play, along with persistent,
powdery tannins running through from start to finish. Cork. 14% alc. Rating 94
To 2029 $40

ᵀᵀᵀᵀᵀ Lady's Lane Vineyard Heathcote Shiraz 2009 Rating 93 To 2029 $60
✪   Domaine Terlato & Chapoutier Shiraz Viognier 2010 Like all the Terlato
       shirazs, has braille imprinted on the label, a nice touch. Delivers plenty of flavour
       and structure on the medium-bodied palate, with plum, black cherry and spice to
       the fore, savoury tannins on the finish. Screwcap. 14% alc. Rating 92 To 2020 $18
       Tournon Shays Flat Vineyard Pyrenees Shiraz 2011 Rating 90
       To 2018 $30

ᵀᵀᵀᵀ   Tournon Mathilda Shiraz 2010 Medium red-purple; made for reasonably early,
✪   relaxed consumption, and succeeds admirably; it's driven by its fresh red berry
       fruits, but does have some fine tannin support, and the overall mouthfeel and
       balance are good. Screwcap. 13.5% alc. Rating 89 To 2015 $15

Macedon Ridge Wines   ★★★★★
PO Box 35, Mount Macedon, Vic 3441 **Region** Macedon Ranges
T (03) 5427 0047 **www**.macedonridge.com.au **Open** Not
Winemaker Scott Ireland, Andrew Koerner **Est.** 1985 **Dozens** 1500 **Vyds** 3ha
The Macedon Ridge vineyard was established in 1984 on the northern slopes of
Mt Macedon. Right from the outset the aim was to produce sparkling wines, and, with this
in mind, 1.5ha each of chardonnay and 1ha of pinot noir were established. Owners Geoff and
Leesa Mackay are responsible for the meticulous management of the vines.

ᵀᵀᵀᵀᵀ Blanc de Blanc 2008 Bright straw-green; 100% chardonnay made using
       the traditional method, and spends a minimum of 42 months on lees prior to
       disgorgement. Despite this long time, it is fresh and fruit-foremost, thanks in part
       to keeping the dosage to a minimum. Cork. 12.6% alc. Rating 94 To 2015 $40
       Sparkling Rose 2005 Pale salmon-pink; while made using the traditional
       method, and (like the '08 Blanc de Blanc) spending at least 42 months on lees;
       it has more spicy, biscuity flavours to accompany the strawberry fruits, and the
       balance is very good. Cork. 12% alc. Rating 94 To 2015 $40

ᵀᵀᵀᵀᵀ Brut NV Rating 90 To 2013 $28

McGlashan's Wallington Estate   ★★★★☆
225 Swan Bay Road, Wallington, Vic 3221 **Region** Geelong
T (03) 5250 5760 **www**.mcglashans.com.au **Open** W'ends & public hols 11–5, 7 days in
Jan, or by appt
Winemaker Robin Brockett (Contract) **Est.** 1996 **Dozens** 1500 **Vyds** 10ha
Russell and Jan McGlashan began the establishment of their vineyard in 1996. Chardonnay
(6ha) and pinot noir (4ha) make up the bulk of the plantings, the remainder shiraz and pinot
gris (1ha each); the wines are made by Robin Brockett, with his usual skill and attention to
detail. Local restaurants around Geelong and the Bellarine Peninsula take much of the wine,
although a newly opened cellar door offering food and music will see an increase in direct
sales. No Shiraz was made in 2011 due to the wet vintage.

ᵀᵀᵀᵀᵀ Bellarine Peninsula Shiraz 2010 Deep, dense purple-crimson; a luscious,
       velvety wine with great depth to the confit plum, black cherry and licorice
       flavours, tannins and French oak lazing somewhere in the background. A cellaring
       special. Screwcap. 14.5% alc. Rating 94 To 2030 $34

ᵀᵀᵀᵀᵀ Bellarine Peninsula Chardonnay 2011 Rating 90 To 2016 $28

McGuigan Wines   ★★★★☆
Cnr Broke Road/McDonalds Road, Pokolbin, NSW 2321 **Region** Hunter Valley
T (02) 4998 7400 **www**.mcguiganwines.com.au **Open** 7 days 9.30–5
Winemaker Peter Hall **Est.** 1992 **Dozens** 1.5 million
A publicly listed company – the ultimate logical expression of Brian McGuigan's marketing
drive and vision, which is on a par with that of Wolf Blass in his heyday. The overall size of the

company has been increased by the acquisition of Simeon Wines; Yaldara and Miranda, now also part of the business. In '07 McGuigan Simeon acquired Nepenthe, a move that surprised many, and in '08 the group was renamed Australian Vintage Limited, a slightly curious moniker. CEO Neil McGuigan has been a serial winner of International Winemaker of the Year awards in the UK. Exports to all major markets.

🍷🍷🍷🍷🍷 **Personal Reserve Shiraz 2011** Deep crimson-purple, striking for the Hunter Valley; a full-bodied Shiraz (again rare) with multiple layers of blackberry, leather and licorice fruit superimposed on a latticework of ripe tannins and good oak. Needs extended cellaring. Diam. 14.5% alc. **Rating** 94 **To** 2036 $50

🍷🍷🍷🍷🍷 **Bin Series No. 9000 Hunter Valley Semillon 2012** Quartz-white; attractive
✪ young semillon with an abundance of juicy lemon and gooseberry fruit flavours more commonly found in Sauvignon Blanc, making it a drink now or later proposition. Screwcap. 11% alc. **Rating** 93 **To** 2020 $13
The Shortlist Hunter Valley Semillon 2007 Rating 92 **To** 2017 $35
✪ **Expressions Adelaide Hills Sauvignon Blanc 2012** The Adelaide Hills grapes provide a mix of tropical fruits, kiwifruit and a citrussy/grassy finish, tropical notes coming back on the aftertaste. Screwcap. 12.5% alc. **Rating** 90 **To** 2013 $16

McGuigan Wines (Barossa Valley)   ★★★★★

Chateau Yaldara, Hermann Thumm Drive, Lyndoch, SA 5351 **Region** Barossa Valley
T (08) 8524 0225 **www.**mcguiganwines.com.au **Open** 7 days 10–5
Winemaker James Evers **Est.** 1947 **Dozens** 5000
At the end of 1999, Yaldara became part of the publicly listed Simeon Wines, the intention being that it (Yaldara) should become the quality flagship of the group. Despite much expenditure and the short-lived stay of at least one well-known winemaker, the plan failed to deliver the expected benefits. In 2002 McGuigan Wines made a reverse takeover for Simeon, and the various McGuigan brands now fill the role intended for Yaldara. Exports to all major markets.

🍷🍷🍷🍷🍷 **The Shortlist Adelaide Hills Chardonnay 2011** Light straw-green; there is a
✪ delightful tension between white peach and citrus/grapefruit acidity, 8 months in French oak a distant memory. Screwcap. 13% alc. **Rating** 95 **To** 2021 $29
The Shortlist Barossa Valley Shiraz 2010 Medium red-purple; an expressive and fragrant bouquet leads into a harmonious palate; the wine spent 16 months in new French and American oak, but the red and black fruits are not obscured by that oak, and the tannins are finely balanced. It all works very well. Screwcap. 14% alc. **Rating** 94 **To** 2025 $29
The Shortlist Coonawarra Cabernet Sauvignon 2010 Matured for 16 months in new French and American oak, but the fruit has by and large managed to deal with the oak, its freshness (not its weight) aiding its cause; some lateral decision making on display here. Screwcap. 13% alc. **Rating** 94 **To** 2025 $29

🍷🍷🍷🍷🍷 **Farms Barossa Valley Shiraz 2010 Rating** 93 **To** 2025 $70 BE
Hand Made Langhorne Creek Shiraz 2010 Rating 90 **To** 2022 $45 BE
The Shortlist Barossa Valley GSM 2010 Rating 90 **To** 2018 $29

McHenry Hohnen Vintners   ★★★★★

5962 Caves Road, Margaret River, WA 6285 **Region** Margaret River
T (08) 9757 7600 **www.**mchv.com.au **Open** 7 days 10.30–4.30
Winemaker Trent Carroll **Est.** 2004 **Dozens** 10000 **Vyds** 56ha
McHenry Hohnen is owned by the McHenry and Hohnen families, sourcing grapes from four vineyards owned by various members of the families. Vines have been established on the McHenry, Calgardup Brook, Rocky Road and McLeod Creek properties. A significant part of the grape production is sold to others (including Cape Mentelle). The family members with direct executive responsibilities are leading Perth retailer Murray McHenry and Cape Mentelle founder and former long-term winemaker David Hohnen. In 2007 David received

the inaugural Len Evans Award for Leadership. Exports to the UK, Ireland, Sweden, Indonesia, Japan, Singapore, Hong Kong and NZ.

ΨΨΨΨΨ **Calgardup Brook Vineyard Margaret River Chardonnay 2012** This has the lightest colour of the three; the soils here, just inland from the coast, are sandy and schisty, and well weathered; it is intense and elegant, with white stone fruit and grapefruit at its core. Screwcap. 13% alc. **Rating** 94 **To** 2020 $37
Burnside Vineyard Margaret River Chardonnay 2012 Has the brightest straw-green colour of the three individual vineyard '12 Chardonnays; all three were wild-fermented in old (inert) oak and concrete vessels; the black micaceous soil is unique, and the wine has the greatest generosity and longest finish and aftertaste. Screwcap. 13% alc. **Rating** 94 **To** 2019 $37
Rocky Road Vineyard Margaret River Cabernet Sauvignon 2011 Wild-fermented, then matured in old (inert) oak or concrete vessels, with the aim (successful) of focusing on the fruit, which is fully flavour-ripe (even a touch of dark chocolate). Screwcap. 14.5% alc. **Rating** 94 **To** 2031 $37
Tiger Country 2009 A cosmopolitan, medium-bodied blend of tempranillo, graciano and petit verdot. There is a range of red and black fruit flavours, with spicy cherry on the mid-palate, and firm, balanced tannins on the finish, contributed by the petit verdot. Screwcap. 14.5% alc. **Rating** 94 **To** 2024 $32

ΨΨΨΨΨ
✪ **Margaret River Semillon Sauvignon Blanc 2012** Has all the usual Margaret River attributes, but with more generosity; the many herbal and tropical components are so fused it is pointless to pick any out for special comment. Just enjoy this hedonistic wine. Screwcap. 12.5% alc. **Rating** 93 **To** 2014 $22
✪ **Margaret River Sauvignon Blanc 2012** Straw-green; both the colour and texture suggest some oak contact, but there is no mention of this on the label; regardless, it is generously endowed with a complex web of flavours in a tropical spectrum before finishing with citrussy acidity. Screwcap. 12.5% alc. **Rating** 92 **To** 2014 $22
Rocky Road Vineyard Chardonnay 2012 Rating 91 **To** 2016 $37
Margaret River Shiraz 2011 Rating 91 **To** 2017 $22
Rocky Road Vineyard Zinfandel 2011 Rating 90 **To** 2021 $37

McIvor Estate ★★★★

80 Tooborac-Baynton Road, Tooborac, Vic 3522 **Region** Heathcote
T (03) 5433 5266 **www**.mcivorestate.com.au **Open** W'ends & public hols 10–5, or by appt
Winemaker Various (contract) **Est.** 1997 **Dozens** 2000
McIvor Estate is situated at the base of the Tooborac Hills, at the southern end of the Heathcote wine region, 5km southwest of Tooborac. Gary and Cynthia Harbour have planted 5.3ha of marsanne, roussanne, shiraz, cabernet sauvignon, merlot, nebbiolo and sangiovese.

ΨΨΨΨΨ **Marsanne Roussanne 2012** Light straw-green; a tangy and very lively wine, the aromas yet to strike a consistent chord, but the palate is very clearly defined, with precise citrus/apple flavours folded in crunchy acidity. Should improve markedly if given the chance. Screwcap. 12.8% alc. **Rating** 90 **To** 2018 $30

McKellar Ridge Wines ★★★★☆

Point of View Vineyard, 2 Euroka Avenue, Murrumbateman, NSW 2582
Region Canberra District
T (02) 6258 1556 **www**.mckellarridgewines.com.au **Open** Sun 12–5, or by appt Sept–Jun
Winemaker Dr Brian Johnston **Est.** 2000 **Dozens** 600 **Vyds** 5.5ha
Dr Brian Johnston and his wife Janet are the partners in McKellar Ridge Wines. Brian has completed a postgraduate diploma in science at CSU, focusing on wine science and wine production techniques. The wines come from low-yielding mature vines (shiraz, cabernet sauvignon, chardonnay, merlot and viognier) and have had significant show success. They are made using a combination of traditional and new winemaking techniques, the emphasis being on fruit-driven styles.

🍷🍷🍷🍷︎ Trio Canberra District Cabernet Sauvignon Merlot Cabernet Franc
2011 Bright but light hue; the bouquet is fragrant, and the juicy redcurrant and
blackcurrant fruits on the light- to medium-bodied palate are supported by fine-
grained tannins and attractive French oak; a top-flight return from the vintage.
Screwcap. 13.5% alc. **Rating** 93 **To** 2020 $28
Canberra District Shiraz Viognier 2011 Very good purple-crimson; the
fragrant bouquet (and the colour) point to the viognier inclusion, as does the fruit
profile; the finish is lifted, with contrasting tannins, the latter slightly dry. Screwcap.
13% alc. **Rating** 90 **To** 2021 $28

🍷🍷🍷🍷 Canberra District Sauvignon Blanc 2012 Rating 88 To 2014 $18

McLaren Ridge Estate

Whitings Road, McLaren Vale, SA 5171 **Region** McLaren Vale
T (08) 8383 0504 **www**.mclarenridge.com **Open** 7 days 11–5
Winemaker Brian Light **Est.** 1997 **Dozens** 5000 **Vyds** 6ha
Peter and Heather Oliver have 4ha of shiraz and 2ha of grenache, planted over 50 years ago
on the ridge that now gives their estate its name. The cellar door opened in 2007, and luxury
vineyard accommodation is available. Exports to the UK and Canada.

🍷🍷🍷🍷🍷 Fork in the Road Old Oval Estate Shiraz 2010 One of the Scarce Earth
✪ series; bright, full purple-crimson; fills the senses with its opulent black fruits and
dark chocolate aromas and flavours; the medium- to full-bodied palate has ripe
tannin and positive oak contributions, and the finish is balanced. A long life ahead.
Screwcap. 14.7% alc. **Rating** 94 **To** 2030 $15

McLaren Vale III Associates ★★★★☆

130 Main Road, McLaren Vale, SA 5171 **Region** McLaren Vale
T 1800 501 513 **www**.associates.com.au **Open** Mon–Fri 9–5, w'ends 11–4
Winemaker Brian Light **Est.** 1999 **Dozens** 20000 **Vyds** 34ha
McLaren Vale III Associates is a very successful boutique winery. Its signature wine is Squid Ink
Shiraz. Mary Greer, Managing Director, Reg Wymond, Director and Brian Light, Winemaker
have over 80 years' combined experience in the wine industry. An impressive portfolio of
estate-grown wines allows them control over quality and consistency, thus enjoying success
in Australian and International wine shows (in 2011 they won 10 gold medals and a trophy).
Exports to the US, Canada, Indonesia, Hong Kong, Singapore and China.

🍷🍷🍷🍷︎ Four Score Grenache 2010 Light to medium red-purple; produced from
80-year-old estate vines, matured in used French and American oak for 2 years.
Its display of juicy red raspberry and cherry fruits has a touch of Barossa Valley
Turkish Delight, which some will welcome, others raise an eyebrow. Screwcap.
14.5% alc. **Rating** 92 **To** 2020 $30

🍷🍷🍷🍷 Backbone GSM 2010 Rating 89 To 2017 $35

McLean's Farmgate

barr-Eden Vineyard, Menglers Hill Road, Tanunda, SA 5352 **Region** Eden Valley
T (08) 8564 3340 **www**.mcleansfarm.com **Open** W'ends 10–5, or by appt
Winemaker Bob and Wilma McLean **Est.** 2001 **Dozens** 6000 **Vyds** 5.3ha
The ever-convivial, bigger-than-life, Bob McLean has covered a lot of wine turf over the
past 40 years. The farm shed on the home property produces 1000 dozen of red wine; the
remainder of the production is contract-made by some very savvy winemakers. There are now
three brands: barr-Eden, from the dry-grown estate vineyard and sold only ex cellar for private
buyers and some trade; McLean's Farmgate, made in lots of 250–300 dozen each when special
parcels of grapes become available from 'a few old chums'; and McLean's Farm, 100% Barossa
fruit and made through the Dorrien Estate facility. These wines are sold through Cellarmasters,
but with some restaurant listings. The barr-Eden Vineyard, at an altitude of around 500m, is
one of the highest in the Eden Valley, and the annual blend of some or all of its grenache,

shiraz and mataro is strictly dependent on the quality and character of the components from year to year. Exports to the UK.

🍷🍷🍷🍷🍷 **barr-Eden Riesling 2012** Quartz-white; the floral bouquet has hints of talc and apple blossom, the palate adds the expected citrus that joins the apple in a seamless stream. Whether the wine is left field, or my palate has wandered there, I don't know; either way, I like the wine. Screwcap. 12% alc. **Rating** 93 **To** 2022 $30
Barossa Master Shiraz 2010 The grapes come from a single 50-year-old block high in the Eden Valley; the red and black fruits are framed by supple tannins and positive vanillin oak. Screwcap. 14.5% alc. **Rating** 93 **To** 2035 $52
barr-Eden Shiraz Mataro Grenache 2010 Relatively light, but bright, colour; has the elegance that the Eden Valley can impart on this blend (from 2513 shiraz, 1946 mataro, and 603 grenache vines); those numbers help explain that finesse, and the attractive red fruits. Screwcap. 14.5% alc. **Rating** 93 **To** 2020 $35
Greenock Grown Barossa Shiraz 2009 Medium to full purple-red; an unashamedly full-bodied wine, redolent of plum, blackberry, licorice and dark chocolate; tannins and oak line up in support of a wine created in the image of its larger-than-life creator, Bob McLean. Screwcap. 14.5% alc. **Rating** 90 **To** 2029 $25

🍷🍷🍷🍷 **Eden Valley Riesling 2012** **Rating** 89 **To** 2015 $21
Reserve Barossa Valley Grenache Shiraz Mataro 2010 **Rating** 89 **To** 2017 $27

McLeish Estate ★★★★★

462 De Beyers Road, Pokolbin, NSW 2320 **Region** Hunter Valley
T (02) 4998 7754 **www**.mcleishhunterwines.com.au **Open** 7 days 10–5, or by appt
Winemaker Andrew Thomas (Contract) **Est.** 1985 **Dozens** 8000 **Vyds** 17.3ha
Bob and Maryanne McLeish have established a particularly successful business, based on estate plantings of semillon, chardonnay, verdelho, shiraz, merlot and cabernet sauvignon. The wines are of consistently high quality, and more than a few have accumulated show records leading to gold medal-encrusted labels. The quality of the grapes is part of the equation, the other the skills of contact winemaker Andrew Thomas. Exports to the UK, the US and Asia.

🍷🍷🍷🍷🍷 ✪ **Hunter Valley Semillon 2009** Pale straw-green; a very intense and expressive bouquet of citrus, lemon to the fore, then an equally intense and pervasive palate, with almost freakish intensity of citrus fruit; the finish lingers long. Still available, and travelling without a tremor. Screwcap. 11% alc. **Rating** 96 **To** 2020 $23
✪ **Reserve Hunter Valley Chardonnay 2009** Light green-straw; intense white peach and grapefruit flavours run through the long palate, oak at once present yet largely irrelevant. Has continued to develop well over the past 3 years. Screwcap. 12.8% alc. **Rating** 94 **To** 2015 $25

🍷🍷🍷🍷🍷 ✪ **Dwyer Hunter Valley Rose 2012** Bright, light pink; made from merlot, and arguably the best use of this variety in the Hunter Valley; certainly this is a delicious and pure rose with sweet red fruits dancing across the delicate, finely balanced palate. Screwcap. 12% alc. **Rating** 93 **To** 2014 $18
Reserve Hunter Valley Shiraz 2011 **Rating** 93 **To** 2021 $35
Hunter Valley Cabernet Sauvignon 2008 **Rating** 93 **To** 2023 $35
Jessica's Hunter Valley Botrytis Semillon 2009 **Rating** 92 **To** 2015 $25
✪ **Hunter Valley Semillon Chardonnay 2011** A 60/40% blend, the chardonnay barrel-fermented in 1-year-old French barriques; a wine that is altogether superior to the usual anodyne blend; citrus, honey and lemon flavours are seamlessly welded, the finish well balanced. Screwcap. 12% alc. **Rating** 91 **To** 2016 $18

🍷🍷🍷🍷 **Hunter Valley Verdelho 2011** **Rating** 89 **To** 2014 $18

McPherson Wines ★★★★

6 Expo Court, Mount Waverley, Vic 3149 **Region** Nagambie Lakes
T (03) 9263 0200 **www**.mcphersonwines.com.au **Open** Not
Winemaker Jo Nash **Est.** 1993 **Dozens** 400 000 **Vyds** 262ha

McPherson Wines is not well known in Australia but is, by any standards, a substantial business. Its wines are largely produced for the export market, with some sales in Australia. Made at various locations from the estate vineyards and supplemented with contract-grown grapes, they represent very good value. For the record, McPherson Wines is a joint venture between Andrew McPherson and Alister Purbrick (Tahbilk), both of whom have had a lifetime of experience in the industry. Exports to all major markets.

♀♀♀♀♀ **Chapter Three Chardonnay 2011** The flagship of McPherson's wines; barrel-fermentation in French oak provides a medium-bodied Chardonnay with gently ripe peachy fruit that marries well with the nutty/creamy notes; enhanced by its citrus acidity on the finish. Screwcap. 13% alc. **Rating** 93 **To** 2015 $30

Basilisk Riesling 2012 Bright straw-green; has that particular generosity of Central Victoria/Goulburn Valley riesling, its perfumed bouquet leading into a supple, smooth, citrus-accented palate. Drink now or later. Screwcap. 12% alc. **Rating** 92 **To** 2022 $19

❂ **Basilisk Shiraz Mourvedre 2011** Good colour; a medium-bodied wine with good depth and a complex array of red and black fruits framed by French oak and ripe tannins. Not many in South Eastern Australia did as well at this price level in '11. Screwcap. 14% alc. **Rating** 91 **To** 2016 $18

♀♀♀♀ **Basilisk Sauvignon Blanc 2012 Rating** 89 **To** 2015 $20 BE

❂ **Verdelho 2012** Light straw-green; hits right in the heart of verdelho varietal character, with fruit salad to the fore; nor would I argue with the suggestion by Angus McPherson that there are some traces of Turkish delight; the texture of the palate is a strong point. Screwcap. 14% alc. **Rating** 89 **To** 2015 $11

❂ **Shiraz 2011** The back label reads, 'concentrated, robust and full bodied', but don't believe a word of it. This restrained, pepper-laden and spice-accented shiraz encapsulates the cool '11 season remarkably well. Finely textured and softly structured tannins support bright rhubarb and mixed berry compote flavours. Screwcap. 14% alc. **Rating** 89 **To** 2013 $11 TS

Pickle's McPherson Sauvignon Blanc 2012 Rating 87 **To** 2013 $13
Andrew McPherson Shiraz 2012 Rating 87 **To** 2016 $13 BE
Curious Shiraz 2012 Rating 87 **To** 2016 $13 BE
Curious Shiraz 2011 Rating 87 **To** 2014 $12

McWilliam's   ★★★★★

Jack McWilliam Road, Hanwood, NSW 2680 **Region** Riverina
T (02) 6963 3400 **www**.mcwilliamswinesgroup.com **Open** Mon–Fri 10–4, Sat 10–5
Winemaker Jim Chatto **Est.** 1916 **Dozens** NFP **Vyds** 445ha
The best wines to emanate from the Hanwood winery are from other regions, notably the Barwang Vineyard at Hilltops (see separate entry), Coonawarra (Brand's Laira), Yarra Valley, Tumbarumba and Eden Valley. As McWilliam's viticultural resources have expanded, it has been able to produce regional blends from across Australia of startlingly good value. The 2006 sale of McWilliam's Yenda winery to Casella has led to a major upgrade in both the size and equipment at the Hanwood winery, now the nerve centre of the business. The winery rating is strongly reliant on the exceptional value for money of the Hanwood Estate and Inheritance brands. Exports to all major markets via a major distribution joint venture with Gallo and PLB Group.

♀♀♀♀♀ **Morning Light Riverina Botrytis Semillon 2010** Deep golden-yellow; incredibly rich and luscious, but not heavy; botrytis provides the necessary cut and complexity, acidity the balance. 375ml. Screwcap. 10.5% alc. **Rating** 95 **To** 2019 $25

♀♀♀♀♀ **Catching Thieves Margaret River Chardonnay 2011** The flavours
❂ encompass stone fruits, melon and citrus, sustained by good acidity. Any-time Chardonnay. Screwcap. 13.5% alc. **Rating** 91 **To** 2015 $19

✪ **Catching Thieves Margaret River Cabernet Merlot 2011** A complex, savoury/earthy medium-bodied blend, with notes of black olive running alongside dusty cassis nuances; the tannins are typical of the region. Screwcap. 14% alc. **Rating** 91 **To** 2021 $17

✪ **Catching Thieves Margaret River Semillon Sauvignon Blanc 2012** Pale quartz; the blend components are joined at the hip, neither seeking to dominate the other, gentle tropical notes woven through the grassy citrus of the semillon. Another year won't hurt. Screwcap. 12% alc. **Rating** 90 **To** 2014 $19

✪ **Hanwood Estate Chardonnay 2009** Bright straw-green; as is so often the case, is ridiculously good value; the varietal character is crystal clear, yet the wine has considerable complexity and texture, reflecting its multi-region (some first class) origins. Screwcap. 13.5% alc. **Rating** 90 **To** 2014 $12

✪ **Hanwood Estate Cabernet Sauvignon 2009** Light to medium red-purple; light-bodied, perhaps, but has an evenly balanced and long palate with gentle cassis fruit and fine tannins in support, oak likewise. First tasted a year ago, and has lost none of its freshness or elegance. Screwcap. 13.5% alc. **Rating** 90 **To** 2016 $12

🍷🍷🍷🍷
✪ **Inheritance Semillon Sauvignon Blanc 2012** It's hard to imagine that it could not have some WA contribution even if the sauvignon blanc specific yeast has been used. This has a delicious array of tropical/passionfruit flavours cleansed by citrussy acidity on the finish. Ludicrously good value. Screwcap. 12% alc. **Rating** 89 **To** 2014 $7

✪ **Inheritance Semillon Sauvignon Blanc 2011** Straw-green; the ripe, tropical fruit nuances are clearly those of the sauvignon blanc, semillon providing the lemon-accented citrus. Still remarkably fresh and crisp when retasted Sept '12, with good length and balance, the tropical notes having slightly receded. Exceptional value. Screwcap. 11.5% alc. **Rating** 89 **To** 2013 $7

✪ **Hanwood Estate Chardonnay 2010** Full straw-green; impeccable quality at the price, the cooler-grown components having more to say than those from the Riverland (and elsewhere); oak has been deliberately kept to a minimum. Screwcap. 13.5% alc. **Rating** 89 **To** 2013 $12

✪ **Inheritance Riesling 2012** Its citrus/grapefruit varietal expression is utterly correct, and the wine does not rely on residual sugar for its flavour; moreover, it will repay mid term cellaring. Screwcap. 13% alc. **Rating** 88 **To** 2015 $7

✪ **Hanwood Estate Cabernet Sauvignon 2011** Bright colour; fragrant and varietal with cassis and a touch of cedar on the bouquet; the palate is lively and fresh, with the tannins a little unresolved and assertive for complete harmony; still, excellent value. Screwcap. 13% alc. **Rating** 88 **To** 2018 $14 BE

✪ **Inheritance Shiraz Cabernet 2012** Bright in colour and in character, with juicy red and black fruits on the bouquet and palate; a juicy and fresh early-drinking style. Screwcap. 13.5% alc. **Rating** 87 **To** 2016 $7 BE

McWilliam's Mount Pleasant ★★★★★
Marrowbone Road, Pokolbin, NSW 2320 **Region** Hunter Valley
T (02) 4998 7505 **www**.mcwilliamswinegroup.com **Open** 7 days 10–5
Winemaker Jim Chatto **Est.** 1921 **Dozens** NFP **Vyds** 119ha
McWilliam's Elizabeth and the glorious Lovedale Semillon are generally commercially available with four to five years of bottle age; they are undervalued treasures with a consistently superb show record. The individual vineyard wines, together with the Maurice O'Shea memorial wines, add to the lustre of this proud name. Exports to all major markets.

🍷🍷🍷🍷🍷 **Original Vineyard OP&OH Hunter Valley Shiraz 2010** The Old Paddock was planted by Maurice O'Shea in 1921, the Old Hill was first planted in 1880. The wine has silky elegance and ultimate poise, its red fruits are cradled by fine tannins and just a hint of new oak. I feel sad that I will be long dead before the wine reveals all it has to show. Screwcap. 14.9% alc. **Rating** 97 **To** 2050 $50

Lovedale Single Vineyard Hunter Valley Semillon 2007 Festooned with gold medals, the wine is undoubtedly superb, coming as it does from a good vintage and a very great vineyard. The interesting part is the CO_2 prickle that underwrites the longer term future of an already beautiful lemon and mineral-accented wine. Screwcap. 11.5% alc. **Rating** 96 **To** 2022 $60

ΨΨΨΨΨ **High Paddock Hunter Valley Shiraz 2010** **Rating** 92 **To** 2022 $27 BE
✪ **Florence Adelaide Hills Sauvignon Blanc 2012** The Adelaide Hills origin does appear on the front label, but I continue to be troubled by the Mount Pleasant brand; it is packed with gooseberry, paw paw and tropical fruits, with a low-level touch of sweetness. Screwcap. 13.5% alc. **Rating** 91 **To** 2013 $18

✪ **Jack Coonawarra Cabernet Sauvignon 2011** Deep crimson; highly polished red and black fruits, lanolin and a hint of eucalypt; medium-bodied fine-grained tannins are in harmony with the gentle fruit; long and expansive to conclude. Good value. Screwcap. 13% alc. **Rating** 91 **To** 2020 $19 BE
Elizabeth Semillon 2007 **Rating** 90 **To** 2017 $24

Maglieri of McLaren Vale ★★★★

GPO Box 753, Melbourne, Vic 3001 **Region** McLaren Vale
T 1300 651 650 **Open** Not
Winemaker Kate Hongell **Est.** 1972 **Dozens** 10 000
One of the better-kept secrets among the wine cognoscenti, but not among the many customers who drink thousands of cases of white and red Lambrusco every year; an example of niche marketing at its profitable best. It was a formula that proved irresistible to Beringer Blass, which acquired Maglieri in 1999. The Lambrusco is no more, but attractive Shiraz and Cabernet Sauvignon have more than filled the void.

ΨΨΨΨΨ **Shiraz 2010** Medium crimson-purple; blackberry, plum and black cherry aromas flow through to the medium-bodied palate, there joined by a touch of dark chocolate and controlled oak. Good wine at the price. Screwcap. 14% alc. **Rating** 91 **To** 2020 $23
✪ **Cabernet Sauvignon 2010** Medium red-purple; the bouquet and palate walk the same line, with blackcurrant, blackberry and earthy/bitter chocolate aromas and flavours, then tannins and oak completing the course. Good value. Screwcap. 14% alc. **Rating** 90 **To** 2025 $20

Magpie Estate ★★★★★

PO Box 126, Tanunda, SA 5352 **Region** Barossa Valley
T (08) 8562 3300 **Open** Not
Winemaker Rolf Binder, Noel Young **Est.** 1993 **Dozens** 5000
This is a partnership between Rolf Binder and Cambridge (UK) wine merchant Noel Young. It came about in 1993, when there was limited demand for – or understanding of – Southern Rhône-style blends based on shiraz, grenache and mourvedre. Initially a small, export-only brand, the quality of the wines was such that it has grown over the years, although the intention is to limit production. The majority of the wines are reasonably priced, the super-premiums more expensive. Exports to the UK, the US, Canada, Austria, Finland, Belgium and the Bahamas.

ΨΨΨΨΨ **The Election Barossa Valley Shiraz 2010** Deep, bright purple-crimson; spent 22 months in French and American oak; a rich and opulent wine, flooded with blackberry, plum, licorice and dark chocolate. It has very good balance, and will still be developing a decade hence. Screwcap. 14% alc. **Rating** 94 **To** 2035 $60
The Sack Barossa Valley Shiraz 2010 Good colour; has an abundance of complex black fruits, with licorice, spice and charcuterie add-ons flowing through the bouquet and medium-bodied palate; the tannins and oak also play their part in shaping a high-quality wine. Screwcap. 14% alc. **Rating** 94 **To** 2030 $32

ΨΨΨΨΨ **The Call Bag Barossa Valley Mourvedre Grenache 2010** **Rating** 93 **To** 2020 $25

The Black Sock Barossa Valley Mourvedre 2010 Rating 92 To 2020 $28

 The Schnell Barossa Valley Grenache Shiraz 2010 Solid crimson-purple; there is an abundance of blackberry, cherry and plum fruit, with a swathe of French and American oak around that fruit, the tannins ripe. Screwcap. 14% alc. Rating 90 To 2016 $18

Main Ridge Estate ★★★★★

80 William Road, Red Hill, Vic 3937 **Region** Mornington Peninsula
T (03) 5989 2686 **www**.mre.com.au **Open** Mon–Fri 12–4, w'ends 12–5
Winemaker Nat White **Est.** 1975 **Dozens** 1200 **Vyds** 2.8ha
Quietly spoken and charming founder/owners Nat and Rosalie White preside over their immaculately maintained vineyard and equally meticulously run winery. Their site is a particularly cool one, and if global warming proves to be a permanent part of the landscape, they say they will not be complaining.

ΨΨΨΨΨ Mornington Peninsula Chardonnay 2011 Made with infinite attention to detail from some of the oldest chardonnay vines on the Mornington Peninsula; all the fruit and oak components are fused so seamlessly together that it is hard, if not impossible, to unpick the many strands. Screwcap. 12.5% alc. Rating 96 To 2020 $55

Mainbreak Wines ★★★★

199 McDonald Road, Karridale, WA 6288 (postal) **Region** Margaret River
T (08) 9758 6779 **www**.mainbreak.net.au **Open** Not
Winemaker Contract **Est.** 2009 **Dozens** 3000
This is a small side venture to Hamelin Bay, also owned by Mainbreak Wines proprietors Richard and Roslyn Drake-Brockman. The grapes are sourced from the southern end of Margaret River and the business has grown under the direction of winemaker and keen surfer Julian Scott. The label underlines the association between the region and its outstanding surf beaches.

ΨΨΨΨΨ Surfers Point Margaret River Shiraz 2011 Deep crimson-purple; flooded
 with black fruits plus touches of bitter chocolate and licorice; the controlled tannins keep the focus on the fruit of the medium- to full-bodied palate. Ten years will not begin to tire it. Screwcap. 14% alc. Rating 93 To 2026 $19

Surfers Point Margaret River Sauvignon Blanc Semillon 2012 Gentle tropical characters of kiwifruit, passionfruit and guava manifest themselves on the bouquet and well-balanced palate alike. Has achieved these flavours without any heaviness. Good value. Screwcap. 12.5% alc. Rating 90 To 2014 $19

Maipenrai Vineyard & Winery ★★★★

1516 Sutton Road, Sutton, NSW 2620 (postal) **Region** Canberra District
T (02) 8588 1217 **www**.maipenrai.com.au **Open** Not
Winemaker Brian Schmidt **Est.** 2000 **Dozens** 250 **Vyds** 1.1ha
What a story this is, far too rich for just a few lines. It begins at Harvard, in 1992–93, where American-born Brian Schmidt and (now) wife (Australian) Jennifer Gordon were both working on their PhDs. Brian is presently a Laureate Fellow at the Australian National University's Mount Stromlo Observatory and in 2011 shared the Nobel Prize for Physics. Prior to emigrating to Canberra in 1995, he had formed a research team of 20 astronomers on five continents who used distant exploding stars to trace the expansion of the universe back in time; between then and now he has been awarded a constellation of awards and fellowships. In '99 he and Jennifer purchased a property with a beautiful sloped hillside, and planted six clones of pinot noir; he was 33 at the time, and figured that by the time he was ready to retire, the vineyard would be well and truly into the prime of its life. An astronomer's view indeed. A 0.1ha trial of ultra-close spaced shiraz and viognier is underway.

▼▼▼▼⚲ **Canberra District Pinot Noir 2010** There is some good pinot fruit here, but it is a great pity the wine was not fined, for the tannins are dry and not balanced – time is unlikely to cure this imbalance. Vino-Lok. 13.6% alc. **Rating** 90 To 2016 $33

Majella   ★★★★★

Lynn Road, Coonawarra, SA 5263 **Region** Coonawarra
T (08) 8736 3055 **www**.majellawines.com.au **Open** 7 days 10–4.30
Winemaker Bruce Gregory **Est.** 1969 **Dozens** 25 000 **Vyds** 55ha
Majella is one of the foremost grapegrowers in Coonawarra, with important vineyards, principally shiraz and cabernet sauvignon, plus a little riesling and merlot. The Malleea is one of Coonawarra's greatest wines, The Musician one of Australia's most outstanding red wines selling for less than $20. Exports to the UK, the US and other major markets.

▼▼▼▼▼ **Coonawarra Cabernet Sauvignon 2010** Deep purple-crimson; a profound, full-bodied Cabernet awash with cassis/blackcurrant, mulberry and Coonawarra earth, the tannins ripe and the oak in a support role. From a top-quality vineyard that has revelled in the vintage to produce a very long-lived Cabernet. Screwcap. 14.5% alc. **Rating** 96 To 2040 $33
The Malleea 2010 Vivid purple; this long-established iconic cabernet shiraz blend has hit the jackpot this vintage, with lush juicy blackcurrant, mulberry and blackberry fruit set in a wreath of ripe tannins and quality oak. Diam. 14.5% alc. **Rating** 96 To 2035 $75
Coonawarra Shiraz 2010 Bright purple-crimson; the fragrant bouquet exudes red cherry, damson plum and a dash of spice, the supple and harmonious medium-bodied palate bringing with it soft tannins and appreciable oak. A harmonious wine. Screwcap. 14.5% alc. **Rating** 94 To 2025 $30

▼▼▼▼⚲ **Coonawarra Riesling 2012 Rating** 90 To 2016 $17

▼▼▼▼ **Melody Coonawarra Rose 2012** Full, bright, clear red; red fruits surge from
✪ the bouquet, and on entry to the palate; thereafter it tones its message down, no bad thing, and ends pleasantly dry. Screwcap. 12.5% alc. **Rating** 89 To 2014 $15

Majors Lane Wines   ★★★★

64 Majors Lane, Lovedale, NSW 2320 **Region** Hunter Valley
T (02) 4930 7328 **www**.majorslane.com **Open** 7 days 10–5
Winemaker Daniel Binet, Andrew Thomas, David Hook **Est.** 1987 **Dozens** 800
Vyds 9.4ha
Elizabeth and Elvis Metelovski acquired Majors Lane Wines in 2010, inheriting a fully mature vineyard planted to shiraz, chardonnay, semillon, chambourcin and pinot gris. They say they are seeking to differentiate the wines by having each variety made by a winemaker with a track record for the variety in question. Thus Andrew Thomas is making the Semillon, David Hook the Pinot Grigio and Daniel Binet the Shiraz.

▼▼▼▼⚲ **Peppercorn Block Hunter Valley Shiraz 2011** Light, clear crimson-purple; already showing some of the regional markers of polished leather and fresh earth to accompany the fragrant bouquet and elegant, medium-bodied, palate; the tannin structure is a feature. Screwcap. 13.8% alc. **Rating** 93 To 2026 $25
Top Block Hunter Valley Chardonnay 2011 Light straw-green; a full-flavoured (but not broad) and juicy mouthfeel is quite striking, its flavours poised between citrus and quasi tropical, oak present but incidental. Unusual, but quite seductive. Screwcap. 13% alc. **Rating** 91 To 2016 $25

 Mak Vineyards   ★★★★

PO Box 119, Mooroolbark, Vic 3138 **Region** Various
T 0405 631 557 **www**.shooflywines.com **Open** Not
Winemaker Ben Riggs, Behn Payton, Garry Wall **Est.** 2003 **Dozens** 50 000

This is a far flung, export-oriented, business. It purchases a little over 620 tonnes of grapes each vintage, the lion's share (surprisingly) riesling (250 tonnes), followed by shiraz (200 tonnes) and chardonnay (50 tonnes); the remainder is made up of pinot noir, gewurztraminer, merlot, dolcetto and muscat gordo blanco. Ben Riggs makes Shoo Fly Shiraz and Chardonnay at Vintners McLaren Vale; Shoo Fly Pinot Noir is made by Behn Payton at Punt Road in the Yarra Valley; Frisk Riesling is made by Garry Wall at King Valley Wines. The bulk of exports go the the US, Canada and Ireland.

♛♛♛♛♀ **Shoo Fly Yarra Valley Pinot Noir 2012** Excellent, deep and clear, red-purple;
✪ the cherry/spice aromas of the bouquet are followed by a strongly structured palate, its black cherry and plum fruit supported by savoury/foresty tannin-derived nuances. Screwcap. 13.5% alc. **Rating** 93 **To** 2020 $14

✪ **Shoo Fly Adelaide Hills Chardonnay 2011** Bright, pale straw-green; the role of the oak has been reduced to a minimum, but the wine has considerable texture and structure, lees contact a likely contributor; the fresh grapefruit and mineral-accented palate has well above-average length. A grand bazaar bargain. Screwcap. 13.5% alc. **Rating** 92 **To** 2018 $14

✪ **Shoo Fly Shiraz 2012** Full purple-crimson; the complex black fruits and spice bouquet leads into a richly robed, medium- to full-bodied palate where fruit, tannins and an infusion of smoky oak all coalesce. Exceptionally well priced. Screwcap. 14.5% alc. **Rating** 92 **To** 2020 $14

♛♛♛♛ **Shoo Fly Buzz Cut 2009 Rating** 87 **To** 2014 $14

Malcolm Creek Vineyard   ★★★★

33 Bonython Road, Kersbrook, SA 5231 **Region** Adelaide Hills
T (08) 8389 3619 **www**.malcolmcreekwines.com.au **Open** By appt
Winemaker Peter Leske **Est.** 1982 **Dozens** 900 **Vyds** 2ha
Malcolm Creek was set up as the retirement venture of Reg Tolley, who decided to upgrade his retirement by selling the venture to Bitten and Karsten Pedersen in 2007. The wines are invariably well made and develop gracefully; they are worth seeking out, and are usually available with some extra bottle age at a very modest price. Exports to the UK, the US, Denmark and Malaysia.

♛♛♛♛♀ **Adelaide Hills Sauvignon Blanc 2012** Pale colour, bright; an attractively
✪ adorned bouquet of tropical fruit, fresh-cut grass and a cool nettle note for effect; the palate is juicy and generous, focused and lively. Screwcap. 13% alc. **Rating** 90 **To** 2014 $17 BE

Ashwood Estate Adelaide Hills Cabernet Sauvignon 2009 Estate-grown, hand-picked, and spent 20 months in French oak; the medium- to full-bodied palate has gently spicy blackcurrant fruit framed by cedary oak and gentle tannins. Cork. 13.5% alc. **Rating** 90 **To** 2020 $25

Malone Wines   ★★★★

PMB 47, Naracoorte, SA 5271 **Region** Wrattonbully
T 0408 854 706 **www**.malonewines.com.au **Open** Not
Winemaker Paulett **Est.** 2005 **Dozens** 700 **Vyds** 23ha
The third and fourth generations of the Malone family continue to farm the Talinga property, owned by the family since 1930. The planting of vines in '98 was a minor diversification from the core businesses of producing prime lamb, hay and pasture seed. The decision was taken to focus on shiraz and cabernet sauvignon, with most of the grapes being sold, and limited amounts made under the Malone label.

♛♛♛♛♀ **Wrattonbully Cabernet Sauvignon 2010** It has generous blackcurrant and
✪ mulberry fruit on its medium- to full-bodied palate, the oak integrated and balanced, the tannins ripe. Screwcap. 13.5% alc. **Rating** 93 **To** 2025 $25

Wrattonbully Shiraz 2010 Deep crimson-purple; a full-bodied, rich and plush wine, with black fruits, mocha, vanilla and chocolate on the bouquet and palate alike; the tannins are ripe and generous. A Shiraz for a cold night. Screwcap. 14.5% alc. **Rating** 92 **To** 2025 $28

Mandala ★★★★★

1568 Melba Highway, Dixons Creek, Vic 3775 **Region** Yarra Valley
T (03) 5965 2016 **www**.mandalawines.com.au **Open** 7 days 10–5
Winemaker Scott McCarthy (Contract) **Est.** 2007 **Dozens** 9000 **Vyds** 29ha

Mandala was officially opened in July 2008 by owner Charles Smedley. The estate vineyard has vines up to 20 years old, but the spectacular restaurant and cellar door complex is a more recent addition. The vineyards are primarily at the home base, Dixons Creek, with chardonnay (8ha), cabernet sauvignon (6ha), sauvignon blanc and pinot noir (4ha each), shiraz (2ha) and merlot (1ha), and a separate 4ha vineyard planted entirely to pinot noir at Yarra Junction with an impressive clonal mix. The restaurant has deservedly achieved considerable praise.

🍷🍷🍷🍷🍷 **Matriarch Yarra Valley Pinot Noir 2010** Amazingly deeply coloured, the same opaque purple SA Shiraz achieved in '10. If this sets the standard for Matriarch, it may be another 10 years before we see another pinot noir Matriarch. There are black cherry and black plum fruits in the pinot range. Nearly impossible to rationally point. Screwcap. 13% alc. **Rating** 94 **To** 2030 $50

Rock Yarra Valley Shiraz 2010 A rich, plush shiraz with black fruits dominant, and given complexity by spicy/peppery/savoury notes; exceptional flavour from perfectly ripened grapes. Screwcap. 14% alc. **Rating** 94 **To** 2030 $50

Butterfly Yarra Valley Cabernet Sauvignon 2010 Full purple-red; an altogether serious Cabernet Sauvignon filled to the brim with blackcurrant fruit, bound into a long palate by persistent tannins, which, while imposing, are not dry. This is bound to repay cellaring. Screwcap. 14% alc. **Rating** 94 **To** 2030 $50

🍷🍷🍷🍷 **Yarra Valley Chardonnay 2011** **Rating** 93 **To** 2020 $28

Yarra Valley Merlot 2010 **Rating** 93 **To** 2025 $39

✪ **Yarra Valley Sauvignon Blanc 2012** Light, clear straw-green; it overflows with a full range of tropical fruits, from lychee to pineapple to passionfruit. All this needs food for the second glass. Screwcap. 12.5% alc. **Rating** 92 **To** 2013 $20

Mandalay Estate ★★★★

Mandalay Road, Glen Mervyn via Donnybrook, WA 6239 **Region** Geographe
T (08) 9732 2006 **www**.mandalayroad.com.au **Open** 7 days 11–5
Winemaker Fermoy Estate (Liz Dawson), Faber Vineyard (John Griffiths) **Est.** 1997 **Dozens** 300 **Vyds** 4.2ha

Tony and Bernice O'Connell left careers in science and education to establish plantings of shiraz, chardonnay, zinfandel and cabernet sauvignon on their property in 1997. What started off as a fun venture has quickly turned into serious grapegrowing and winemaking. A hands-on approach with low yields has brought out the best characteristics of the grape varieties and the region. Most of the grapes are sold to Fermoy Estate.

🍷🍷🍷🍷 ✪ **Mandalay Road Sauvignon Blanc Semillon 2012** A 55/45% blend from the Margaret River. Both varieties contribute to the complex structure and flavour set; the characters range from passionfruit to herb and then to lemon sherbet. Impressive wine; terrific value. Screwcap. 13.1% alc. **Rating** 93 **To** 2014 $18

✪ **Mandalay Road Geographe Shiraz 2008** Good retention of hue; a fragrant and elegant wine that has showed no hint of tiring since first tasted 3 years ago (89 points). Indeed, its perfectly balanced, juicy red fruits and spices call for that important extra point. Screwcap. 14.1% alc. **Rating** 90 **To** 2018 $18

Mandurang Valley Wines ★★★★

77 Fadersons Lane, Mandurang, Vic 3551 **Region** Bendigo
T (03) 5439 5367 **www**.mandurangvalleywines.com.au **Open** W'ends & public hols 11–5, or by appt
Winemaker Wes Vine, Steve Vine **Est.** 1994 **Dozens** 4000 **Vyds** 2.5ha

Wes and Pamela Vine planted their first vineyard at Mandurang in 1976 and started making wine as a hobby. An additional vineyard was established in '97. Wes (a former school principal) became full-time winemaker in '99. Son Steve has progressively taken greater responsibility for the winemaking, while Wes is spending more time developing export markets. Pamela manages the cellar door cafe. Expansive lawns and gardens provide the opportunity for visitors to enjoy wine and food outdoors. Exports to China.

🍷🍷🍷🍷🍷 **Bendigo Merlot 2012** Bright crimson-purple; an attractive Merlot, the
✪ bouquet with ripe cassis and plum fruit that also drives the palate, joined there by gentle tannins and perceptible oak; good overall balance and length. Good value. Screwcap. 13.5% alc. **Rating** 92 **To** 2020 $22

🍷🍷🍷🍷 **Bendigo Shiraz 2010 Rating** 89 **To** 2016 $28
Bendigo Riesling 2012 Rating 88 **To** 2015 $22
Sauvignon Blanc 2012 Rating 87 **To** 2014 $22

Manorbier Vineyard ★★★☆

Barana Road, Cootamundra, NSW 2590 **Region** Gundagai
T (02) 6942 3835 **www**.manorbiervineyard.com **Open** Not
Winemaker Capital Wines (Andrew McEwin) **Est.** 2004 **Dozens** 300 **Vyds** 4.40ha
Richard and Suzie Wood purchased the 46ha Manorbier property near Cootamundra in 1988, breeding Angus cattle until 2004, when they decided to diversify with the planting of 4ha of shiraz on a north-facing hill. Yield is kept low, and the grapes are hand-picked.

🍷🍷🍷🍷 **Shiraz 2007** Has held its hue well, and is unexpectedly the best of the Manorbier Shirazs so far produced, however young the vines may have been. No longer commercially available. Screwcap. 13% alc. **Rating** 89 **To** 2017
Cootamunda Gundagai District Shiraz 2009 Hazy red-purple; the bouquet has plummy fruit backed by vanillin oak, the medium-bodied palate following suit, the tannins soft. Has the ripeness missing from the '10 wines. Screwcap. 13.1% alc. **Rating** 88 **To** 2014 $22
Shiraz Rose 2012 Bright, light crimson-purple; I'm not sure why this wine is self-styled 'unique', as it is a typical example of early-picked shiraz, with slightly green nuances neatly balanced by a subliminal touch of sugar sweetness. Screwcap. 11.5% alc. **Rating** 87 **To** 2013 $18
Allan Hope Cootamunda Gundagai District Shiraz 2008 Diffuse colour; ripe plum fruit and oak make for a pleasant, although unremarkable, wine. Includes 10% tempranillo. Screwcap. 13.7% alc. **Rating** 87 **To** 2015 $29

Mansfield Wines ★★★★

201 Eurunderee Lane, Mudgee, NSW 2850 **Region** Mudgee
T (02) 6373 3871 **www**.mansfieldwines.com.au **Open** Thurs–Tues & public hols 10–5, or by appt
Winemaker Bob Heslop **Est.** 1975 **Dozens** 1000 **Vyds** 5.5ha
Ian McLellan and family purchased Mansfield Wines from his cousin Peter Mansfield in late 1997. Before and after that time, the original plantings, which included chardonnay, frontignac, sauvignon blanc, cabernet sauvignon, merlot and shiraz, were removed, to be replaced by a Joseph's coat patchwork of savagnin, vermentino, petit manseng, parellada, tempranillo, touriga, zinfandel and tinta cao, supported by grenache, mourvedre and pedro ximinez. Souzao and carignan are more recent arrivals.

🍷🍷🍷🍷🍷 **Dos Cabras 2010** A 50/25/25% blend of tempranillo, monastrell and garnacha
✪ (grenache); the colour is light and shows some development; the flavours of spiced plum and cherry fruit are soft and welcoming, with a fruitcake finish that is appealing. Diam. 14% alc. **Rating** 90 **To** 2015 $19
Touriga Nacional 2011 Strong, deep red-purple; another distinctly different wine, going beyond the crude measure of alcohol; here black fruits, licorice, leather and dark chocolate clamour for attention in the crucible of the alcohol. Diam. 15.5% alc. **Rating** 90 **To** 2020 $23

🍷🍷🍷🍷 **Monastrell Garnacha 2011 Rating** 89 **To** 2016 $19

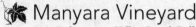 Manyara Vineyard ★★★★☆

380 Onkaparinga Valley Road, Balhannah, SA 5242 **Region** Adelaide Hills
T 0458 495 225 **www**.manyaravineyard.com.au **Open** By appt
Winemaker Simon Greenleaf, Michael Hall (Contract) **Est.** 1995 **Dozens** 300 **Vyds** 7.5ha
Manyara Vineyard was established by the extended Lipman family, including the Munros, Herzbergs and Forwoods, on Eve and Rex Lipman's Manyara property, then acknowledged as one of Australia's finest rearing and pre-training establishments for thoroughbreds. They planted chardonnay, sauvignon blanc, pinot noir, cabernet sauvignon, merlot, malbec and petit verdot, the last four to make a Bordeaux blend.

🍷🍷🍷🍷🍷 **Lipman Adelaide Hills Pinot Noir 2011** Bright, clear red–purple; the
✪   perfumed bouquet leads into a beautifully weighted and proportioned palate; the flavours are spun around a core of cherry fruit, but with flourishes of spice, herb and sour cherry. Screwcap. 13% alc. **Rating** 94 **To** 2018 $25

🍷🍷🍷🍷🍷 **Adelaide Hills Chardonnay 2010 Rating** 91 **To** 2016 $25

Marchand & Burch ★★★★★

241 Scotsdale Road, Denmark, WA 6333 **Region** Great Southern
T (08) 9848 2345 **www**.burchfamilywines.com.au **Open** 7 days 10–4
Winemaker Pascal Marchand, Jeff Burch **Est.** 2006 **Dozens** 1100 **Vyds** 8.46ha
A joint venture between Canadian-born and Burgundian-trained Pascal Marchand and Burch Family Wines, which owns Howard Park. Grapes are sourced from single vineyards, and in most cases, from single blocks within those vineyards (4.51ha of chardonnay and 4ha of pinot noir, in each case variously situated in Mount Barker and Porongurup). Biodynamic practices underpin the viticulture in the selected Australian and French vineyards, and Burgundian viticultural techniques have been adopted in the Australian vineyards (eg narrow rows and high-density plantings, Guyot pruning, vertical shoot positioning, and leaf and lateral shoot removal). Several blocks are planted with multiple, rather than single, clones. Exports to the UK, the US and other major markets.

🍷🍷🍷🍷🍷 **Porongurup Chardonnay 2011** Bright straw-green; it has exceptional drive and intensity to the long, lingering palate, fruit flavours in the nectarine, white peach and grapefruit spectrum; oak has played its part in creating a wine with great texture and structural complexity, its destiny far in the future. The aftertaste lingers for minutes. Screwcap. 13% alc. **Rating** 96 **To** 2021 $70

Marcus Hill Vineyard ★★★★☆

560 Banks Road, Marcus Hill, Vic 3222 (postal) **Region** Geelong
T (03) 5251 3797 **www**.marcushillvineyard.com.au **Open** Not
Winemaker Darren Burke (Contract), Richard Harrison **Est.** 2000 **Dozens** 1000 **Vyds** 3ha
In 2000, Richard and Margot Harrison, together with 'gang pressed friends', planted 2ha of pinot noir overlooking Port Lonsdale, Queenscliff and Ocean Grove, a few kilometres from Bass Strait and Port Phillip Bay. Since then chardonnay, shiraz, more pinot noir, and three rows of pinot meunier have been added. The vineyard is run with minimal sprays, and the aim is to produce elegant wines that truly express the maritime site.

🍷🍷🍷🍷🍷 **Bellarine Peninsula Chardonnay 2011** Light straw-green; fermented and matured for 12 months in a mix of new and used French oak, and taken partway through mlf; this approach has worked well, taming the acidity, introducing some creamy/nutty nuances, but not compromising the white peach varietal fruit. Screwcap. 13% alc. **Rating** 94 **To** 2020 $27

🍷🍷🍷🍷🍷 **Bellarine Peninsula Pinot Gris 2012** Barrel-fermented and matured for
✪   6 months on lees; minimal colour pickup, but has certainly gained the texture needed for gris; nashi pear flavours are ripe, particularly on the mid-palate, and there is a tangy cut to the finish. Screwcap. 13.5% alc. **Rating** 91 **To** 2014 $20

✪ **Bellarine Peninsula Rose 2012** Bright colour; a blend of 90% pinot noir and shiraz, cabernet franc and chardonnay fermented and aged in used French barriques; the emphasis is on the fruit profile, which is fresh and slightly citrussy. Screwcap. 12% alc. **Rating** 91 **To** 2014 $18

✪ **People Madly Stomping Bellarine Peninsula Pinot Noir 2011** Full red-purple; a very complex bouquet with dark fruits, bramble and spice; the palate follows suit, but has some of the green edge of the '11 standard version; this is a much better wine, but could have been better still. Screwcap. 13% alc. **Rating** 91 **To** 2017 $19

Margan Family   ★★★★★

1238 Milbrodale Road, Broke, NSW 2330 **Region** Hunter Valley
T (02) 6579 1317 **www**.margan.com.au **Open** 7 days 10–5
Winemaker Andrew Margan **Est.** 1997 **Dozens** 25 000 **Vyds** 98ha
Andrew Margan, following in his father's footsteps, entered the wine industry over 20 years ago, and has covered a great deal of territory since, working as a Flying Winemaker in Europe, then for Tyrrell's. Andrew and wife Lisa now have almost 100ha of fully mature vines at their Ceres Hill property at Broke, and lease the nearby Vere Vineyard. Wine quality is consistently good. The rammed-earth cellar door and restaurant are highly recommended. Exports to the UK, the US and other major markets.

♟♟♟♟♟ **Hunter Valley Semillon 2012** Bright straw-green; the ripe – almost sweet –
✪ citrus and lemongrass flavours flood the mouth, yet are balanced by the good acidity. Screwcap. 12% alc. **Rating** 94 **To** 2020 $18
Limited Release Semillon 2011 While Andrew Margan prefers to pick the semillon at a higher baume than many of his peers, the pH is only 3.03; thus while there is a seductive array of ripe lemon/citrus fruit, with honey just around the corner, there is a bedrock of minerally acidity for the long-term future. Screwcap. 11.5% alc. **Rating** 94 **To** 2026 $35
Aged Release Semillon 2008 Bright, glowing straw-green; an elegant Semillon now on the journey to its ultimate destination, the first signs of honey and beeswax appearing, toast around the corner, lemony acidity a constant. Screwcap. 10.5% alc. **Rating** 94 **To** 2020 $40
Limited Release Shiraz 2011 Excellent crimson-purple; an impressive medium- to full-bodied wine that has taken full advantage of the good vintage; it verges on succulent, with layers of blackberry and plum fruit, Hunter leather and earth still locked up. Screwcap. 13.5% alc. **Rating** 94 **To** 2031 $60
Limited Release Shiraz Mourvedre 2011 Good crimson-purple colour; the bouquet offers black cherry, plum and a hint of spice, the medium-bodied palate taking those flavours, adding positive tannins to build the very good structure, but not diminishing its freshness. Screwcap. 13.5% alc. **Rating** 94 **To** 2026 $45

♟♟♟♟♟ **Limited Release Barbera 2011 Rating** 93 **To** 2020 $49
✪ **Hunter Valley Chardonnay 2012** Full straw-green; from 40-year-old vines, and partially matured in new French oak barriques for 6 months; picked at the right time to protect acidity and enliven the white peach and melon varietal fruit. Great value. Screwcap. 13% alc. **Rating** 92 **To** 2016 $18
Limited Release Chardonnay 2012 Rating 92 **To** 2016 $35
✪ **Hunter Valley Shiraz 2011** The hue of the wine is bright, although not deep; the supple, medium-bodied palate shows the maturation in new and used French oak, but not to distraction, and the tannins are fine and soft. Bargain price. Screwcap. 13.5% alc. **Rating** 92 **To** 2021 $20

Margaret Hill Vineyard   ★★★★★

Level 12, North Tower, 454 Collins Street, Melbourne, Vic 3000 (postal) **Region** Heathcote
T (03) 9836 2168 **www**.guangtiangroup.com.au **Open** Not
Winemaker Ben Portet **Est.** 1996 **Dozens** 970 **Vyds** 12.5ha

Formerly known as Toolleen Vineyard, the new name was chosen by owner Linchun Bao (and wife Chunye Qiu) when they acquired the business from the Huang family in 2010. They began upgrading the vineyard equipment and irrigation system, and restoring full health and vigour to the vineyard, which is equally split between cabernet sauvignon and shiraz. Wines are released under the Margaret Hill and Kudo labels. Exports to China.

ŶŶŶŶŶ **Kudo Heathcote Shiraz 2011** Dense purple-crimson; a remarkable wine from this difficult vintage; it has the dark plum and black cherry aromas and flavours typical of Heathcote, allied with spice and licorice, and excellent texture and harmony in the mouth. Cork. 14.6% alc. **Rating** 95 **To** 2030 $80
Kudo Heathcote Cabernet Sauvignon 2011 Another distinguished wine in any context, especially that of '11. Blackcurrant, a touch of earth, quality oak and ripe tannins are seamlessly united on the medium- to full-bodied, well-balanced, palate. Cork. 13.8% alc. **Rating** 94 **To** 2026 $80

Marienberg/Fern Hill Estate   ★★★☆

PO Box 120, Denman, NSW 2328 **Region** McLaren Vale
T (02) 6547 5168 **www.**marienberg.com.au **Open** Not
Winemaker Graeme Scott **Est.** 1966 **Dozens** 4000
Marienberg (founded by Australia's first female owner/vigneron, Ursula Pridham), along with Fern Hill Estate and Basedow (see separate entry), became part of the James Estate empire in 2003. A revamping of the packaging and labelling, plus acquisition of grapes from the Adelaide Hills to supplement those from McLaren Vale, has been accompanied by a move away from retail to restaurant/on-premise sales. Exports to Canada.

ŶŶŶŶŶ **Marienberg Reserve Cabernet Sauvignon 2010** An attractive McLaren Vale Cabernet, with lively cassis/blackcurrant on the medium-bodied palate, the region supplying the dark chocolate; good oak handling also a plus. Does not need patience. Screwcap. 13.5% alc. **Rating** 90 **To** 2018 $25

ŶŶŶŶ **Marienberg Limeburners Cottage Shiraz 2009** Rating 88 **To** 2014 $16

Maritime Estate   ★★★★

65 Tucks Road, Red Hill, Vic 3937 **Region** Mornington Peninsula
T 0432 931 890 **www.**maritime-estate.com.au **Open** Not
Winemaker Sandro Mosele **Est.** 1988 **Dozens** 800 **Vyds** 4.55ha
Maritime Estate is the venture of the Ruljancich family since brothers John and Kevin purchased the property in 1993. Plantings were expanded in '95 to their present level of 2.7ha of MV6, 114, 115 and 777 clones of pinot noir, 1ha of chardonnay and 0.8ha of pinot gris. The family's involvement with wine dates back to the early 1800s, with vines on the tiny Dalmatian island of Vis, Croatia. The Ruljancichs migrated to Australia in 1946, but the vineyard on Vis was still being attended until the '80s by John and Kevin's uncle. John died in 2007, but the business continues on under the care of Kevin and John's children, Jane, Paul and Sally.

ŶŶŶŶŶ **Mornington Peninsula Chardonnay 2011** Pale, bright quartz; an elegant and delicate wine, the accent on stone fruit and pear; looks very much as if taken through mlf, and given little contact with new oak. Screwcap. 12.5% alc. **Rating** 91 **To** 2016 $34

ŶŶŶŶ **Mornington Peninsula Pinot Noir 2011** Rating 88 **To** 2014 $36
Mornington Peninsula Pinot Gris 2011 Rating 87 **To** 2014 $24

Marius Wines   ★★★★★

PO Box 545, Willunga, SA 5172 **Region** McLaren Vale
T 0402 344 340 **www.**mariuswines.com.au **Open** By appt
Winemaker Roger Pike, James Hastwell **Est.** 1994 **Dozens** 1000 **Vyds** 1.8ha

Roger Pike says he has loved wine for over 30 years and that over a decade ago he decided to do something about it, ripping up the front paddock and planting shiraz in 1994. He sold the grapes from the '97–99 vintages, but when the '98 vintage became a single vineyard wine (made by the purchaser of the grapes), selling in the US at $40, the temptation to make his own wine became irresistible. No wines were made in 2009 due to the impact of the short heatwave at a critical point in the middle of veraison. Rather than compromise with a second label, he decided to skip the vintage altogether, and was richly rewarded with an array of high-quality wines from '10. No wines were received in time for the *2014 Wine Companion*, but the five-star rating is maintained.

Marq Wines ★★★★★

2 Gibson Drive, Dunsborough, WA 6281 (postal) **Region** Margaret River
T 0411 122 662 **www**.marqwines.com.au **Open** Not
Winemaker Mark Warren **Est.** 2011 **Dozens** 1500
Mark Warren has a degree in wine science from CSU and a science degree from the University of WA; to complete the circle, he is currently lecturing in wine science and wine sensory processes at Curtin University, Margaret River. He also has 22 years' experience in both the Swan Valley and Margaret River, and his current major commercial role is producing the extensive Happs range as well as wines under contract for several other Margaret River wine brands. When all of this is added up, he is responsible for 60 to 70 individual wines each year, now including six wines under his own Marq Wines label. A quick look at the list of Vermentino, Fiano, Wild Ferment Chardonnay, Gamay, Tempranillo and Malbec, and Cut & Dry Shiraz (Amarone style) points to the underlying philosophy: an exploration of the potential of alternative varieties and unusual winemaking methods by someone with an undoubted technical understanding of the processes involved. The wines are produced in very small amounts.

ΨΨΨΨΨ **Wild Ferment Margaret River Chardonnay 2011** Bright straw-green; the fragrant bouquet announces a very smart wine; wild yeast-fermented, it has outstanding mouthfeel, line and length; white peach and some creamy/nutty notes add interest to the palate. Screwcap. 12.5% alc. **Rating** 95 **To** 2020 $28
Wild and Worked Margaret River Sauvignon Blanc Semillon 2012 I really get the gun smoke component of this wild yeast-fermented wine; the flavours build progressively each time it is tasted. The best feature is the focused, tight and long back-palate and finish. Screwcap. 12.5% alc. **Rating** 94 **To** 2016 $25
Margaret River Vermentino 2012 Positively exuberant and mouth-watering, it has a network of fibres of acidity punctuating the grapefruit and pear flavours, the finish long, crisp and dry. Screwcap. 10.6% alc. **Rating** 94 **To** 2016 $25
Margaret River Tempranillo 2011 Bright crimson-purple; a notably complex Tempranillo, with more texture and structure than many; the medium- to full-bodied palate has both black fruit notes and the typical red cherry on the finish; distinctly varietal. Screwcap. 14% alc. **Rating** 94 **To** 2020 $28
Margaret River Malbec 2011 Deeply coloured purple-crimson; this has a kaleidoscope of black and red fruits, quality tannins providing all the texture and structure one could wish for. Screwcap. 14.9% alc. **Rating** 94 **To** 2021 $28

ΨΨΨΨΨ **Margaret River Fiano 2012 Rating** 92 **To** 2015 $25
Cut and Dry Margaret River Shiraz 2011 Rating 92 **To** 2021 $35
Margaret River Gamay 2011 Rating 91 **To** 2014 $25

Marri Wood Park

Caves Road, Yallingup, WA 6282 **Region** Margaret River
T 0438 525 580 **www**.marriwoodpark.com.au **Open** 7 days 12–5
Winemaker Ian Bell, Bob Cartwright, John Frazer **Est.** 1993 **Dozens** 1500 **Vyds** 7ha
Marri Wood Park has 2.2ha of chenin blanc, 1.6ha of sauvignon blanc, 1.5ha of cabernet sauvignon, with semillon, malbec and merlot making up the total; part of the grape production is sold to other makers. The budget-priced Guinea Run range takes its name from the guinea fowl which are permanent vineyard residents, busily eating the grasshoppers, weevils and bugs

that cluster around the base of the vines. The vineyard is certified 'In Conversion Biodynamic' and since 2009, the wines have been biodynamic.

🍷🍷🍷🍷🍷 **Reserve Margaret River Chenin Blanc 2006** First tasted Mar '08. Chenin Blanc from the Loire Valley can be cellared for many decades; this is behaving in the same way. It is incredibly fresh, and with the protection of its screwcap, will hold for many years to come. For the young (or young at heart), worthy of two or three bottles to find out. 12.2% alc. **Rating** 94 **To** 2036 $50
Reserve Margaret River Cabernet Sauvignon 2009 Hand-picked and matured in oak for 20 months. Savoury/briary/spices are fused with blackcurrant fruit and firm, but ripe, tannins – fused so tightly they cannot be unpicked for further analysis or description. Screwcap. 14.2% alc. **Rating** 94 **To** 2025 $40

🍷🍷🍷🍷 **Dessert Chenin Blanc 2012 Rating** 89 **To** 2014 $20
Grandis Brut Reserve 2009 Rating 88 **To** 2013 $30

Marsh Estate   ★★★★

Deasy's Road, Pokolbin, NSW 2321 **Region** Hunter Valley
T (02) 4998 7587 **www**.marshestate.com.au **Open** Mon–Fri 10–4.30, w'ends 10–5
Winemaker Andrew Marsh **Est.** 1971 **Dozens** 4000 **Vyds** 32ha
Through sheer consistency, value for money and unrelenting hard work, the Marsh family has built up a sufficiently loyal cellar door and mailing list clientele to allow all the production to be sold direct. Wine style is straightforward, with oak playing a minimal role, and prolonged cellaring paying handsome dividends.

🍷🍷🍷🍷🍷 **Vat S Hunter Valley Shiraz 2011** Aged in American oak; bright colour, with a savoury bacon, oak and dark berry fruit bouquet; the palate is juicy, fresh and lively, with the charry oak a fitting counterpoint to the jubey fruit on offer. Screwcap. 13% alc. **Rating** 90 **To** 2022 $30 BE
Sinclair Hunter Valley Shiraz 2011 Deeply coloured and showing ripe and essency red fruit aromas, with generous vanillin French oak; the palate follows suit, with red and black fruits coming to the fore, and the toasty oak a lingering footnote; some time in bottle is needed. Screwcap. 13.5% alc. **Rating** 90 **To** 2020 $55

🍷🍷🍷🍷 **Vat R Hunter Valley Shiraz 2011 Rating** 88 **To** 2020 $40 BE

Mason Wines   ★★★☆

27850 New England Highway, Glen Aplin, Qld 4381 **Region** Granite Belt
T (07) 4684 1341 **www**.masonwines.com.au **Open** Wed–Sun 10–4
Winemaker Anthony Rametta **Est.** 1998 **Dozens** 2000 **Vyds** 30.5ha
Robert and Kim Mason set strict criteria when searching for land suited to viticulture: a long history of commercial stone fruit production with well-drained, deep soil. The first property was purchased in 1997, the vines planted thereafter. A second property was purchased in 2000, and a cellar door was constructed. They have planted cabernet sauvignon, chardonnay, shiraz, merlot, viognier, semillon, verdelho, sauvignon blanc and petit verdot. Exports to Japan.

🍷🍷🍷🍷 **Cellar Collection Granite Belt Chardonnay 2011** A well-made wine, with some French oak barrel ferment evident, as well as peachy fruit and a twist of lemon juice/lemon zest. Screwcap. 13.5% alc. **Rating** 89 **To** 2016 $25
Granite Belt Verdelho 2012 Pale straw-green; largely follows in the footsteps of the fruit salad pattern, but has more zesty/lemony acidity than many. Screwcap. 13% alc. **Rating** 88 **To** 2014 $18
Granite Belt Rose 2012 Clear purple-crimson; while the colour may suggest a rich/sweet rose style, the alcohol is a far better guide to an early-picked, fresh, bone-dry palate; paradoxically, a tiny tweak of a few grains of residual sugar might have made a very good rose. Screwcap. 11.5% alc. **Rating** 88 **To** 2013 $15

Cellar Collection Granite Belt Shiraz Viognier 2011 The contribution of the French and American oak in which the wine was matured is more evident than that of the viognier; there is some good shiraz here, too, but it is smothered by the oak – a frustrating near miss. Screwcap. 13.5% alc. **Rating** 87 **To** 2016 $28
Cellar Collection Granite Belt Cabernet Sauvignon 2010 Good colour; there is plenty of ripe cassis fruit; the tannins needed to be fined or polished, and further time in bottle should help, for there is balance between the parts. Screwcap. 14% alc. **Rating** 87 **To** 2015 $30

Massena Vineyards
★★★★★

PO Box 54, Tanunda, SA 5352 **Region** Barossa Valley
T (08) 8564 3037 **www**.massena.com.au **Open** At Artisans of Barossa
Winemaker Dan Standish, Jaysen Collins **Est.** 2000 **Dozens** 5000 **Vyds** 4ha
Massena Vineyards draws upon 1ha each of mataro (mourvedre), saperavi, petite syrah and tannat at Nuriootpa, also purchasing grapes from other growers. It is an export-oriented business, although the wines can be purchased by mail order, which, given both the quality and innovative nature of the wines, seems more than ordinarily worthwhile. Exports to the UK, the US and other major markets.

♥♥♥♥♥ **Barossa Valley Barbera 2012** Deep, vivid purple-crimson; absolutely loaded with satsuma plum and red and black cherry on the juicy palate, tannins and oak entirely subsumed by the waves of fruit. Screwcap. 13.5% alc. **Rating** 94 **To** 2020 $25
Barossa Valley Primitivo 2012 The bright, full colour is a sure sign of success, and the pleasing, light- to medium-bodied, display of cherry, raspberry and mulberry fruit flavours confirms the colour. Top class Primitivo. Screwcap. 14.5% alc. **Rating** 94 **To** 2018 $25

♥♥♥♥♡ **The Eleventh Hour 2010 Rating** 93 **To** 2025 $35
The Surly Muse 2012 Rating 92 **To** 2015 $22

Massey Wines/two rooms Wines
★★★★☆

53A Stoneyfell Road, Stonyfell, SA 5066 **Region** McLaren Vale/Adelaide Hills
T 0408 077 769 **www**.masseywines.com.au **Open** Not
Winemaker Bevan and Harry Ferguson **Est.** 2004 **Dozens** 1000
This is the venture of Bevan and Catherine Ferguson, representing a fork in the road for Bevan. His winemaking career commenced at Rockford in 1995, then Larkhill, Evans & Tate, Petaluma and, finally, Coriole in 2002. Having secured grape purchase agreements with loyal growers in McLaren Vale and Adelaide Hills, and also sharefarming a small parcel of eight-year-old vines at Blewitt Springs, Massey Wines began production in '04. The wines are made in shared accommodation at the historic Stonyfell winery.

♥♥♥♥♥ **Massey McLaren Vale Grenache Shiraz Mourvedre Rose 2012** Pale salmon-pink; wild-fermented in used French oak; the finely structured and balanced palate has rose petal, rose hip and strawberry fruit with attractive spicy hints throughout. Screwcap. 13% alc. **Rating** 94 **To** 2014 $22

♥♥♥♥♡ **Massey Huey's Patch McLaren Vale Shiraz 2007 Rating** 93 **To** 2022 $38
Massey Reserve Pinot Noir 2010 Rating 90 **To** 2015 $35

Massoni
★★★★☆

30 Brasser Avenue, Dromana, Vic 3936 **Region** Pyrenees/Mornington Peninsula
T (03) 5981 0711 **www**.massoniwines.com **Open** Not
Winemaker Fred Ursini, Robert Paul, Nic Baxter **Est.** 1984 **Dozens** 25000 **Vyds** 269ha
Massoni is a substantial business owned by the Pellegrino and Ursini families, and is a venture with two completely distinct arms. In terms of vineyard and land size, by far the largest is the GlenKara vineyard in the Pyrenees (269ha). It endured years of drought, which finally broke in 2010, with production increasing from 9600 dozen to its present level. It also has 8.5ha on

the Mornington Peninsula where Massoni started, and where it gained its reputation. In Feb '12 Massoni purchased the former Tucks Ridge/Red Hill winemaking facility at Dromana.

🍷🍷🍷🍷 **Mornington Peninsula Chardonnay 2011** Barrel-fermented in French oak; has retained light, bright colour and a crisp, vibrant palate with very good acidity; citrus melon and stone fruit are the major players, and the overall balance and length are strong points. Screwcap. 13.5% alc. **Rating** 93 **To** 2019 $25
Pyrenees Ranges Sangiovese 2011 Clear, bright red; the highly fragrant bouquet proclaims sangiovese with its spiced morello cherry aromas; inevitably, and properly, there are savoury, sour cherry notes on the palate that make this such a good (Italian) food wine. Screwcap. 13.6% alc. **Rating** 91 **To** 2018 $30

 # Matchbox Wine Co.

GPO Box 181, Sydney, NSW 2001 **Region** Clare Valley
T 0403 773 871 **www**.matchboxwine.com **Open** Not
Winemaker Nav Singh **Est.** 2012 **Dozens** 1500
Matchbox Wine Co. brings together the winemaking skills of Nav Singh and the public relations skills and experience of Louise Radman. Together they have over 30 years of street cred, underlined by the fact that this is a virtual winery, with neither vineyards nor winery to finance. Nav was born in India, but came to Australia to study winemaking, since gaining experience in the Clare, Eden and Yarra Valleys, plus numerous vintages in Burgundy and Bordeaux. Louise has been one of the lucky few to be selected for the Len Evans Tutorial, and is now employed by Domain A as Head of Marketing and Public Relations. Exports to the US, Hong Kong and Singapore.

🍷🍷🍷🍷 **Clare Valley Syrah 2012** The fragrant red berry bouquet is followed by a medium- to full-bodied palate, the mouthfeel slightly thick, reflecting the interaction of fruit, licorice, ripe tannins and oak. Should slim down nicely with a few years in bottle. Screwcap. 14% alc. **Rating** 92 **To** 2027 $30
Clare Valley Malbec 2012 The highly fragrant bouquet and spicy, juicy palate reflect the excellent vintage, and the decision to limit the time in barrel was the correct decision. The notorious lack of structure of malbec has been cleverly turned to an advantage. Screwcap. 14% alc. **Rating** 92 **To** 2015 $30
Clare Valley Riesling 2012 Wild-fermented and given time on lees; the flavours are complex, the singularity of the lemon/lime varietal fruit yet to build and define itself – this will happen with time. Screwcap. 12% alc. **Rating** 90 **To** 2020 $30

Maverick Wines

Lot 141 Light Pass Road, Vine Vale, Moorooroo, SA 5352 **Region** Barossa Valley
T (08) 8563 3551 **www**.maverickwines.com.au **Open** By appt
Winemaker Ronald Brown **Est.** 2004 **Dozens** 10000 **Vyds** 35.82ha
This is the very successful venture of Ronald Brown, Jeremy Vogler and Adrian Bell. Taking advantage of excess grape production in Australia, the partners have acquired four vineyards in key areas of the Eden Valley and Barossa Valley, with vines ranging in age from 40 to over 140 years. The wines are made in small batches in tanks of 0.5–3-tonne capacity, and are then matured in French oak. Maverick has achieved listings in top restaurants and fine wine retailers in Australia and internationally. Exports to the UK, the US, Canada, France, Scandinavia, Russia, Cambodia, Malaysia, Thailand, Singapore, Hong Kong, Japan and China.

🍷🍷🍷🍷🍷 **Trial Hill Eden Valley Shiraz 2009** The bouquet of plush dark fruits offers a flinty minerality and floral lift that speaks of elegance alongside power; on the palate fine-grained tannins and fresh acidity sit alongside dense dark fruit of almost epic proportions. Cork. 14.5% alc. **Rating** 95 **To** 2025 $70 BE
The Maverick Barossa Shiraz 2009 Impenetrable colour; the bouquet is dominated by the lavish use of new oak, yet seductive and super-ripe dark fruits, spice and bitter chocolate are also on display; the palate is big-boned, and oaky, with time needed to settle down all aspects. Cork. 14.7% alc. **Rating** 94 **To** 2025 $100 BE

Paraview Barossa Valley Shiraz 2009 Laden with black fruits, cold tea, prunes and licorice on the bouquet; the palate is lively and fresh, with fine tannins and a lingering mocha note in keeping with the style. Cork. 13.5% alc. **Rating** 94 To 2025 $40 BE

♀♀♀♀♀ **Old Ben Barossa Shiraz 2010 Rating** 93 To 2020 $50 BE
Trial Hill Eden Valley Riesling 2012 Rating 92 To 2019 $25
Greenock Rise Barossa Valley Shiraz 2010 Rating 92 To 2020 $60 BE

Maximus Wines

Cnr Foggo Road/Penny's Road, McLaren Vale, SA 5171 **Region** McLaren Vale
T (08) 8323 8777 **www**.maximuswinesaustralia.com.au **Open** Fri–Mon & public hols 11–4
Winemaker Scott Rawlinson **Est.** 2007 **Dozens** NA **Vyds** 1.82ha
Sailing master Rowland Short, having run one of Australia's most successful sailing schools, decided (in his words) 'to brave the choppy waters of the Australian wine industry' by establishing Maximus Wines in partnership with wife Shelley. They purchased a shiraz vineyard, and built a cellar door into the side of a hill, with a barrel store underneath for maturing cask and bottled wine. Grapes are purchased from other vineyards in McLaren Vale, and the wines are contract-made by local winemaker Scott Rawlinson.

♀♀♀♀♀ **Adelaide Hills Pinot Gris 2012** Vibrant hue; the bouquet is pure fresh-cut pear with lemon and bath talc; the palate is lively, fresh and fragrant, offering good concentration and a taut dry finish. Screwcap. 13.4% alc. **Rating** 93 To 2014 $25 BE
Premium McLaren Vale GSM 2011 Brightly coloured and showing distinctly savoury aromas of tar, licorice, thyme and mocha; the palate is somewhat tannic, but has good fruit weight and a juicy, fresh and accessible finish. Screwcap. 14.6% alc. **Rating** 92 To 2018 $25 BE

♀♀♀♀ **Adelaide Hills Sauvignon Blanc 2012 Rating** 88 To 2014 $20 BE
Emperor Series Cabernet Sauvignon 2011 Rating 88 To 2020 $50 BE

Maxwell Wines

Olivers Road, McLaren Vale, SA 5171 **Region** McLaren Vale
T (08) 8323 8200 **www**.maxwellwines.com.au **Open** 7 days 10–5
Winemaker Alexia Roberts **Est.** 1979 **Dozens** 24000 **Vyds** 37.5ha
Over the past 30 years Maxwell Wines has carved out a reputation as a premium producer in McLaren Vale. The brand has produced some excellent red wines in recent years, making the most of the solid limestone hill in the Seaview area on which the winery and vineyards are situated. The majority of the vines on the estate were planted in 1972, and include 19 rows of the highly regarded Reynella Selection cabernet sauvignon. The Ellen Street shiraz block in front of the winery was planted in '53. During vintage, visitors to the elevated cellar door can watch the gravity-flow operations in the winery as the winemaking team plunge and pump-over the red ferments. Owned and operated by Mark Maxwell. Exports to all major markets.

♀♀♀♀♀ **Minotaur Reserve McLaren Vale Shiraz 2010** Delivers a fine impression of freshness and concentration; luscious on entry, the fruit is lifted by fine acidity and ample, fine-grained tannins; the long mocha oak finish complements the fruit with aplomb. Cork. 15% alc. **Rating** 94 To 2022 $75 BE

♀♀♀♀♀ **Four Roads McLaren Vale Grenache 2011 Rating** 91 To 2015 $22
Adelaide Hills Chardonnay 2011 Rating 90 To 2017 $22 BE
✪ **Silver Hammer McLaren Vale Shiraz 2011** Deep, bright garnet; a dark and brooding bouquet of black fruits, mocha, licorice and sea salt; the palate is medium-bodied and muscular, with gravelly tannins and fresh acidity in balance. Screwcap. 14% alc. **Rating** 90 To 2018 $18 BE
Ellen Street McLaren Vale Shiraz 2010 Rating 90 To 2020 $40 BE

Mayer   ★★★★★

66 Miller Road, Healesville, Vic 3777 **Region** Yarra Valley
T (03) 5967 3779 **www**.timomayer.com.au **Open** By appt
Winemaker Timo Mayer **Est.** 1999 **Dozens** 1000 **Vyds** 2.4ha
Timo Mayer, also winemaker at Gembrook Hill Vineyard, teamed with partner Rhonda
Ferguson to establish Mayer Vineyard on the slopes of Mt Toolebewoong, 8km south of
Healesville. The steepness of those slopes is presumably 'celebrated' in the name given to the
wines (Bloody Hill). There is just under 2.5ha of vineyard, the lion's share to pinot noir and
smaller amounts of shiraz and chardonnay – all high-density plantings. Mayer's winemaking
credo is minimal interference and handling, and no filtration. Exports to the UK, Germany,
Denmark, Singapore and Japan.

ŸŸŸŸŶ **Bloody Hill Yarra Valley Chardonnay 2011** Pale straw-green; the extremely
funky and somewhat reduced bouquet cannot be blamed on the screwcap; this
is in the far left field, with the funky notes continuing on the palate. One man's
meat … Diam. 12.5% alc. **Rating** 91 **To** 2017 $38

Mayfield Vineyard   ★★★★☆

954 Icely Road, Orange, NSW 2800 **Region** Orange
T (02) 6365 9292 **www**.mayfieldvineyard.com **Open** W'ends 10–4
Winemaker Antonio D'Onise, Simon Gilbert **Est.** 1998 **Dozens** 12 000 **Vyds** 20.1ha
The property – including the house in which owners Richard and Kathy Thomas now live,
and its surrounding arboretum – has a rich history as a leading Suffolk sheep stud, founded
upon the vast fortune accumulated by the Crawford family via its biscuit business in the UK.
The estate vineyard has 8.4ha of sauvignon blanc, 3.4ha each of cabernet sauvignon and
merlot, 3.2ha of pinot noir, and slightly less than 1ha each of sangiovese and chardonnay.
Exports to the UK and Asia.

ŸŸŸŸŶ **Icely Road Orange Sangiovese 2009** Bright red–purple; a very interesting
 Sangiovese, its fruit spectrum extending from cherry to raspberry to plum, yet not
losing focus or becoming too heavy; instead, there is a juicy, supple mouthfeel. Has
developed exceptionally well. Screwcap. 13.3% alc. **Rating** 93 **To** 2016 $20

✪ **Icely Rd Orange Sauvignon Blanc 2012** Another demonstration of the bond
between variety and place; while the tropical/passionfruit varietal expression is
very obvious, the wine has a combination of delicacy and vibrancy. Great value.
Screwcap. 12.7% alc. **Rating** 92 **To** 2014 $20

Single Vineyard Orange Pinot Noir 2007 Has held on tenaciously, indeed
improved, since first tasted 3 years ago. Fragrant and elegant, its cherry-accented
fruit is held in a near invisible net of tannins and equally integrated oak.
A rare opportunity to buy fully mature Pinot. Screwcap. 13.5% alc. **Rating** 90
To 2015 $35

Single Vineyard Orange Cabernet Sauvignon 2010 Bright, light purple-
red; the fragrant, cassis-accented bouquet leads into a light- to medium-bodied
palate with the same fruit message as the bouquet, but complexed by some slightly
minty/dried herb notes, and fine tannins. Diam. 14% alc. **Rating** 90 **To** 2020 $45

ŸŸŸŸ **Reserve Chardonnay 2011 Rating** 87 **To** 2016 $35 BE

Maygars Hill Winery   ★★★★☆

53 Longwood-Mansfield Road, Longwood, Vic 3665 **Region** Strathbogie Ranges
T 0402 136 448 **www**.maygarshill.com.au **Open** By appt
Winemaker Contract **Est.** 1997 **Dozens** 900 **Vyds** 3.2ha
Jenny Houghton purchased this 8ha property in 1994, planting shiraz (1.9ha) and cabernet
sauvignon (1.3ha), and establishing a stylish B&B cottage. The name comes from Lieutenant
Colonel Maygar, who fought with outstanding bravery in the Boer War in South Africa in
1901, and was awarded the Victoria Cross. In World War I he rose to command the 8th Light

Horse Regiment, winning yet further medals for bravery. He died on 1 November 1917. No wines were made in 2011 due to poor vintage conditions. Exports to Fiji.

ŢŢŢŢŢ Reserve Shiraz 2008 Is a totally logical step onwards since last tasted 3 years ago, all of its components very much alive, and all in harmony. The tasting note then read '... the wine relies on the complex interaction of savoury/spicy notes with red and black cherry fruit; has good length and balance'. So, the same points, and the same drink-to date. Screwcap. 14.5% alc. **Rating** 94 **To** 2018 $34

ŢŢŢŢŢ Reserve Cabernet Sauvignon 2008 Rating 93 **To** 2020 $34

Mayhem & Co.   ★★★★★
49 Collingrove Avenue, Broadview, SA 5083 **Region** Adelaide Hills
T 0468 384 817 **www.**mayhemandcowine.com.au **Open** Not
Winemaker Brendon Keys **Est.** 2009 **Dozens** 1000
A venture between Andrew Hill and winemaker Brendon Keys. Andrew and Brendon worked together many years ago at Wirra Wirra, and they have combined their skills in order to create the Mayhem & Co. brand. Brendon has made wine in Australia, NZ, the US and Argentina, and Andrew has worked vintages at Wirra Wirra and Chapel Hill, before taking on senior sales and marketing roles with Koonara, Tomich Hill and Reschke Wines. The wines are made from grapes purchased from various local growers in the Adelaide Hills, Eden Valley and McLaren Vale. Exports to Hong Kong and China.

ŢŢŢŢŢ Hipster Eden Valley Riesling 2012 Bright straw-green; has excellent structure and minerally texture, lemon, lime and apple providing the fruit for the long finish. 260 dozen made. Screwcap. 12.4% alc. **Rating** 94 **To** 2022 $26
Newcomer Adelaide Hills Pinot Noir 2012 Deep (for pinot noir) crimson-purple; a complex Pinot with attitude, it offers a three-way split between cherry/strawberry primary fruit, a crosscut of herbs, and excellent tannins; the overall texture and length are compelling. Screwcap. 13.5% alc. **Rating** 94 **To** 2018 $36

Mazza Wines   ★★★★
PO Box 480, Donnybrook, WA 6239 **Region** Geographe
T (08) 9201 1114 **www.**mazza.com.au **Open** Not
Winemaker Contract **Est.** 2002 **Dozens** 450 **Vyds** 4ha
The inspiration for this venture of David and Anne Mazza was the great wines of Rioja and the Douro Valley, as well as the opportunity to continue a long-standing family tradition of making wine. So they planted the key varieties of those two regions: tempranillo, graciano, bastardo, sousao, tinta cao and touriga nacional. They believe they are the only Australian vineyard to present this collection of varieties on a single site, and I am reasonably certain they are correct in this belief.

ŢŢŢŢŢ Bastardo Rose 2012 The colour may be pale, but the flavours and mouthfeel are not, with red berry and orange peel flavours, and an urgent drive on the palate sustained by punchy acidity. Screwcap. 13.5% alc. **Rating** 92 **To** 2014 $18

Meadow Croft Wines   ★★★
221 Woodlands Road, Mittagong, NSW 2575 **Region** Southern Highlands
T (02) 4878 5344 **Open** By appt
Winemaker Jonathan Holgate **Est.** 1998 **Dozens** 300 **Vyds** 1.2ha
Carl and Linda Bahls have 20ha of prime grazing country, but decided on a minor diversification by planting 0.6ha each of chardonnay and cabernet sauvignon. 'While chardonnay was a natural choice of fruit for a cool climate, cabernet sauvignon was a gamble, albeit a calculated one.' The cabernet sauvignon gamble has had varying degrees of success, much influenced by the vintage conditions of each year. This variable to one side, it has received meticulous care in the vineyard, and from the winemaking team of Jonathan Holgate at High Range Vintners (overseen by Nick Bulleid MW).

Medhurst ★★★★★

24–26 Medhurst Road, Gruyere, Vic 3770 **Region** Yarra Valley
T (03) 5964 9022 **www.**medhurstwines.com.au **Open** Thurs–Mon & public hols 11–5, or by appt
Winemaker Matt Steel **Est.** 2000 **Dozens** 5000 **Vyds** 15.2ha
The wheel has come full circle for Ross and Robyn Wilson. In the course of a very distinguished corporate career, Ross was CEO of Southcorp when it brought the Penfolds, Lindemans and Wynns businesses under the Southcorp banner. Robyn spent her childhood in the Yarra Valley, her parents living less than a kilometre away as the crow flies from Medhurst. Immaculately sited and tended vineyard blocks, most on steep, north-facing slopes, promise much for the future. A large winery was built in 2011; despite its size, it focuses on small-batch production, and also provides contract winemaking services to other wine producers. The winery was recognised for its architectural excellence at the Victorian Architecture Awards '12. Medhurst has redesigned the cellar door to include 'Medhurst and More' which offers high-quality food to match their wines. Exports to Hong Kong and China.

ŶŶŶŶŶ **Reserve Yarra Valley Chardonnay 2011** The first Reserve release from Medhurst; only one puncheon (616 bottles) was made. It is a wine all about texture and structure, with citrus zest, apple and mineral flavours, and will be long-lived. Screwcap. 12.5% alc. **Rating** 95 **To** 2021 $50
Yarra Valley Sauvignon Blanc 2012 The bouquet is decidedly complex, both it and the palate showing the oak influence, but not over the top; the flavours range from sweet pea to passionfruit, and the finish is fresh and bright. Screwcap. 12.2% alc. **Rating** 94 **To** 2014 $24
Yarra Valley Chardonnay 2012 Very elegant, the mouthfeel and the flavours each sending precisely the same message of elegance and harmony, white peach at the heart of that message. Screwcap. 13.2% alc. **Rating** 94 **To** 2020 $30
Yarra Valley Chardonnay 2011 Pale, bright green-straw; a particularly lively and intense wine, fruit-driven notwithstanding barrel fermentation; grapefruit is followed by white peach and brisk acidity on the finish. Screwcap. 12.7% alc. **Rating** 94 **To** 2016 $30
Yarra Valley Cabernet 2010 Medium to full red-purple; restrained oak and relatively early picking have given the wine the character of classic cabernet from the 1970s or '80s, a return of considerable merit; it has all the necessary length and very good balance. Screwcap. 12.8% alc. **Rating** 94 **To** 2022 $32

ŶŶŶŶŶ **Yarra Valley Pinot Noir 2011** **Rating** 93 **To** 2015 $42
Yarra Valley Rose 2012 **Rating** 90 **To** 2013 $24
Yarra Valley Shiraz 2010 **Rating** 90 **To** 2020 $32

Meehan Vineyard ★★★★

4536 McIvor Highway, Heathcote, Vic 3523 **Region** Heathcote
T 0407 058 432 **www.**meehanvineyard.com **Open** W'ends & public hols 10–5
Winemaker Phil Meehan **Est.** 2003 **Dozens** 750 **Vyds** 2ha
In 1999, after their children had left the nest, Phil and Judy Meehan decided to return to the country and grow grapes for sale to wineries. In that year they took the first step, planting a small pinot noir vineyard at Bannockburn. It then took until April 2003 to find a near-perfect site, just within the Heathcote town boundary, its northeast-facing gentle slope on the famous Cambrian soil. Phil graduated with a Diploma of Winemaking and a Diploma of Viticulture in '05, saying, 'After a mere six years of study I only learned, after all that time, just how much more to winemaking there was to learn.' Exports to the UK.

ŶŶŶŶŶ **Heathcote Shiraz 2010** Light to medium red-purple; despite its alcohol, the wine is fresh and only medium-bodied, with oriental spices, a dusting of pepper, and attractive small-berry fruit flavours. Screwcap. 15% alc. **Rating** 92 **To** 2020 $28

Meerea Park ★★★★★

2198 Broke Road, Pokolbin, NSW 2320 **Region** Hunter Valley
T (02) 4998 7474 **www.meereapark.com.au Open** 7 days 10–5
Winemaker Rhys Eather **Est.** 1991 **Dozens** 12000

All the wines are produced from grapes purchased from growers primarily in the Pokolbin area, but also from the Upper Hunter, and as far afield as Young. It is the brainchild of Rhys Eather, a great-grandson of Alexander Munro, a leading vigneron in the mid 19th century; he makes the wine at the former Little's Winery at Palmers Lane in Pokolbin, purchased in 2007. Exports to the US, Germany, The Netherlands, Hong Kong, Singapore and China.

ŸŸŸŸŸ **Alexander Munro Individual Vineyard Hunter Valley Semillon 2007** The colour has vivid green tinges; the bouquet foreshadows a totally delicious palate with ripe citrus reaching into passionfruit flavours, and a long finish tied together with gentle acidity. Screwcap. 11.5% alc. **Rating** 96 **To** 2020 $35

Terracotta Individual Vineyard Hunter Valley Shiraz 2010 Purple-crimson; blackberry and plum fruit has a juicy drive and energy that courses through the palate to the finish and aftertaste; the tannins are balanced, and contribute more than the oak. Screwcap. 14% alc. **Rating** 95 **To** 2035 $65

Alexander Munro Individual Vineyard Hunter Valley Shiraz 2010 An air of violets and white pepper hovers over focused, ripe black plum and blackberry fruits, on a supportive bed of finely textured, soft tannins. There are nuances of exotics, thanks to a healthy inclusion of stalks in the ferment. Screwcap. 14% alc. **Rating** 95 **To** 2020 $75 TS

Hell Hole Individual Vineyard Hunter Valley Semillon 2011 It is as distinguished as it is fine and delicate; its balance and length are exemplary. Lemongrass and herb are threaded through the acidity which guarantees a long life ahead. Screwcap. 11% alc. **Rating** 94 **To** 2031 $25

Alexander Munro Individual Vineyard Hunter Valley Semillon 2008 Bright, light straw-green; well on the way to developing the full majesty of mature Semillon; lemon, lime and lemongrass intermingle with hints of lanolin which add flesh to the texture. Screwcap. 10.5% alc. **Rating** 94 **To** 2023 $40

Hell Hole Individual Vineyard Hunter Valley Shiraz 2010 Crimson-purple; luscious black fruits, with a hint of licorice, are swathed in a silky web of oak and tannins; has great mouthfeel to a long, medium-bodied palate. Screwcap. 13.5% alc. **Rating** 94 **To** 2030 $60

ŸŸŸŸŸ **The Aunts Individual Vineyard Shiraz 2010 Rating** 93 **To** 2025 $30
XYZ Hunter Valley Shiraz 2010 Rating 93 **To** 2015 $25
Indie Hunter Valley Shiraz Pinot 2010 Rating 92 **To** 2030 $40

Merilba Estate ★★★★

3611 Kingstown Road, Uralla, NSW 2358 **Region** New England
T (02) 6778 9145 **www.merilbaestatewines.com.au Open** W'ends 11–4
Winemaker Shaun Cassidy **Est.** 1998 **Dozens** 3000 **Vyds** 11ha

This impressive venture is owned and run by Shaun and Kassy Cassidy and John and Annette Cassidy. With the exception of Tempranillo and Gewurztraminer, all of the wines are estate-grown and made, all coming from the New England region. Sean also makes the wines for Thunder Ridge (see separate entry). The converted Cobb & Co. stables on the property provide the cellar door and a function and wedding venue.

ŸŸŸŸŸ **New England Semillon Sauvignon Blanc 2012** Pale, but bright, straw-green; a 57/43% blend that has ample depth to its mix of ripe lime citrus and tropical passionfruit flavours. Screwcap. 12.8% alc. **Rating** 91 **To** 2014 $25

New England Shiraz 2011 Medium red-purple; the bouquet and palate have an unexpected hint of chocolate, which adds flavour and texture to this well-constructed, medium-bodied Shiraz; red and black cherry are the dominant fruit flavours, the tannins ripe and soft. Screwcap. 14.5% alc. **Rating** 91 **To** 2021 $25

Mermerus Vineyard

60 Soho Road, Drysdale, Vic 3222 **Region** Geelong
T (03) 5253 2718 **www.**mermerus.com.au **Open** Sun 11–4
Winemaker Paul Champion **Est.** 2000 **Dozens** 500 **Vyds** 2.5ha

Paul Champion has established pinot noir, chardonnay and riesling at Mermerus since 1996. The wines are made from the small but very neat winery on the property, with small-batch handling and wild yeast fermentation playing a major part in the winemaking, oak taking a back seat. Paul also acts as contract winemaker for small growers in the region.

ŶŶŶŶŶ **Bellarine Peninsula Pinot Noir 2011** Crystal-clear red-purple; shows the Janus faces of the '11 vintage: the wine is very light in colour and body, yet perfumed with red cherry and strawberry fruit, unimpeded by tannins and/or oak. The one imperative is to drink it now. Screwcap. 13% alc. **Rating** 90 To 2013 $28

ŶŶŶŶ **Bellarine Peninsula Riesling 2012** **Rating** 88 To 2014 $20

Merricks Creek Wines

44 Merricks Road, Merricks, Vic 3916 **Region** Mornington Peninsula
T (03) 5989 8868 **www.**pinot.com.au **Open** Not
Winemaker William Downie **Est.** 1998 **Dozens** 650 **Vyds** 2ha

The pinot noir vineyard established by Peter and Georgina Parker has consistently produced grapes of exceptional quality. It is planted to a sophisticated collection of pinot noir clones, and includes a small planting at an ultra-high density of 0.5m spacing, which produces the Close Planted Pinot Noir. Retaining William Downie as (part-time) winemaker will be seen by many as a coup, as his dedication to pinot noir is well known. No wines received for the *2014 Wine Companion*, but a five-star rating has been maintained.

Merricks Estate

Thompsons Lane, Merricks, Vic 3916 **Region** Mornington Peninsula
T (03) 5989 8416 **www.**merricksestate.com.au **Open** 1st w'end of month, daily 26–31 Dec, each w'end in Jan & public hol w'ends 12–5
Winemaker Paul Evans, Alex White **Est.** 1977 **Dozens** 2500 **Vyds** 4ha

Melbourne solicitor George Kefford, with wife Jacky, runs Merricks Estate as a weekend and holiday enterprise. Right from the outset it has produced distinctive, spicy, cool-climate Shiraz, which has accumulated an impressive array of show trophies and gold medals. As the current tasting notes comprehensively demonstrate, the fully mature vineyard and skilled contract winemaking are producing top-class wines across the full varietal spectrum.

ŶŶŶŶŶ **Mornington Peninsula Shiraz 2008** A deliciously vibrant medium-bodied Shiraz, with spice, pepper and a flood of juicy cherry fruit; the tannins and oak are present, but are of secondary importance. Drink it while it retains this vibrancy. Screwcap. 13% alc. **Rating** 95 To 2018 $34
Mornington Peninsula Chardonnay 2012 Light straw-green; it is very lively, with a strong chord of citrussy acidity running the length of its white peach and grapefruit palate. Screwcap. 12.5% alc. **Rating** 94 To 2019 $32
Mornington Peninsula Chardonnay 2011 Light straw-green; a very fresh and fragrant bouquet reflects the very cool vintage that was a boon for chardonnay, grapefruit and white peach providing the fruit flavours and the marked acidity that will give the wine a long life. Screwcap. 13% alc. **Rating** 94 To 2023 $27
Mornington Peninsula Pinot Noir 2008 Light, bright red-purple, excellent given its age; has the distinctive stamp of '08, its rich, ripe fruit flavours filling the mouth; released after the '09. A great opportunity to buy a mature Pinot of high quality. Screwcap. 13.5% alc. **Rating** 94 To 2016 $38

ŶŶŶŶŶ
✪ **Thompson's Lane Pinot Noir 2012** Offers a fragrant red cherry character, offset by a little dried herb complexity; light-bodied and full of juicy red fruits on the palate, the zesty acidity provides life and energy in this drink-early style of Pinot Noir. Screwcap. 12.5% alc. **Rating** 90 To 2016 $20 BE

Merum Estate

PO Box 840, Denmark, WA 6333 **Region** Pemberton
T (08) 9848 3443 **www**.merumestate.com.au **Open** Not
Winemaker Harewood Estate (James Kellie) **Est.** 1996 **Dozens** 3700 **Vyds** 10ha
Merum Estate stirred from slumber after morphing from grower and winemaker to pure grapegrowing after the 2006 vintage. Mike Melsom is the link with the past, for it was he and partner Julie Roberts who were responsible for the extremely good wines made in '05 and '06. The wines are released at three levels: the entry point Curious Nature, then the Signature range, and finally the Estate Premium Reserve range.

ŸŸŸŸŸ Premium Reserve Pemberton Shiraz 2010 Strong purple-crimson; an unusual but seductive wine, with a wonderful array of aromas and flavours; spice, licorice, black pepper, black cherry, plum and blackberry all flow backwards and forwards across the ever-enticing palate, the finish impeccable thanks to high-quality tannins. Screwcap. 14.5% alc. **Rating** 95 **To** 2030 $30
Premium Reserve Pemberton Semillon 2012 Light straw-green; a complex barrel-fermented wine with layers of flavour in a lemongrass and lychee range, oak adding a dimension to both the flavour and texture. Screwcap. 12.5% alc. **Rating** 94 **To** 2019 $30
Premium Reserve Pemberton Semillon 2011 It does not – and cannot – meet Hunter Valley Semillon on the same platform. Here French oak has been used to subtly add another dimension to the bouquet and palate, which already has a hint of honey and a whiff of passionfruit to embroider the core of citrus fruit. Screwcap. 13% alc. **Rating** 94 **To** 2021 $30
✪ Pemberton Semillon Sauvignon Blanc 2011 Light straw-green; a notably fresh, crisp and vibrant wine with a fragrant bouquet, then a lively, light-bodied but intense, palate where cut grass and snow pea flavours intermingle with citrus and apple, slatey/minerally acidity a constant refrain on the long, clean finish. Screwcap. 13.5% alc. **Rating** 94 **To** 2014 $20
Premium Reserve Pemberton Chardonnay 2011 Pale straw-green; a complex, but well-balanced and lively wine; white peach, nectarine and grapefruit are the flavour drivers on the long, focused palate. Screwcap. 14% alc. **Rating** 94 **To** 2020 $35

ŸŸŸŸŸ Curious Nature Semillon Sauvignon Blanc 2011 Pale quartz-green; lifted
✪ aromas of grass at one extreme, passionfruit at the other lead into a particularly interesting palate that, while anchored on citrus/mineral notes, has a rich and complex finish. Screwcap. 14% alc. **Rating** 93 **To** 2014 $15
✪ Curious Nature Remarkable Red Shiraz Cabernet 2010 Full crimson; a 71/29% blend of Pemberton and Great Southern fruit, with a highly spiced bouquet of black fruits, black cherry and blackcurrant riding high on the palate, licorice, cedary oak and tannins the stirrups. Screwcap. 14.5% alc. **Rating** 92 **To** 2020 $15
✪ Pemberton Semillon Sauvignon Blanc 2012 Juicy/fleshy citrus and gooseberry fruit to accompany the grassy fruit; good acidity also comes to the party. Well priced. Screwcap. 13% alc. **Rating** 90 **To** 2015 $20
✪ Curious Nature Wondrous Premium White 2010 A blend of semillon, chardonnay, sauvignon blanc and viognier, a modern interpretation of classic dry white; I haven't the faintest idea how this blend could be as synergistic as it is. All in all, has far more personality than the vast majority of these shotgun blends. Still very crisp and fresh. Screwcap. 13.5% alc. **Rating** 90 **To** 2013 $15

Miceli

60 Main Creek Road, Arthurs Seat, Vic 3936 **Region** Mornington Peninsula
T (03) 5989 2755 **www**.miceli.com.au **Open** W'ends 12–5, public hols by appt
Winemaker Anthony Miceli **Est.** 1991 **Dozens** 4000 **Vyds** 5.5ha
This may be a part-time labour of love for general practitioner Dr Anthony Miceli, but that hasn't prevented him taking the whole venture very seriously. He acquired the property in 1989

specifically to establish a vineyard, planting 1.8ha in '91. Subsequent plantings have brought it to its present size, with pinot gris, chardonnay and pinot noir the varieties grown. Between '91 and '97 Dr Miceli completed the wine science course at CSU and he now manages both vineyard and winery. One of the top producers of sparkling wine on the Peninsula.

♟♟♟♟♟ **Lucy's Choice Mornington Peninsula Pinot Noir 2009** Medium red-purple; the bouquet and palate are full of plum, cherry, spice and oak aromas and flavours; the power and length of the palate are particularly impressive. Screwcap. 13.5% alc. Rating 94 To 2018 $35

♟♟♟♟♟ **Olivia's Mornington Peninsula Chardonnay 2009** Rating 91 To 2017 $28

Michael Hall Wines ★★★★★

10 George Street, Tanunda, SA 5352 (postal) **Region** Mount Lofty Ranges Zone
T 0419 126 290 **www**.michaelhallwines.com **Open** Not
Winemaker Michael Hall **Est.** 2008 **Dozens** 1200
For reasons no longer relevant (however interesting), Michael Hall was once a jewellery valuer for Sotheby's in Switzerland. He came to Australia in 2001 to pursue winemaking, a lifelong interest, and undertook the wine science degree at CSU, graduating as dux in '05. His vintage work in Australia and France is a veritable who's who: in Australia with Cullen, Giaconda, Henschke, Shaw + Smith, Coldstream Hills and Veritas; in France with Domaine Leflaive, Meo-Camuzet, Vieux Telegraphe and Trevallon. He is now involved full-time with his eponymous brand, along with some teaching at the Nuriootpa TAFE; the Adelaide Hills Sang de Pigeon Pinot Noir was made in '11, together with a Stonewell Valley Roussanne. The wines are as impressive as his CV suggests they should be. Exports to the UK.

♟♟♟♟♟ **Stonewell Valley Barossa Valley Shiraz 2010** Full purple-crimson; hand-picked, wild yeast-fermented, pressed direct to French oak (30% new Francois Freres) with 18 months on lees, bottle 2106 of 3700. A gloriously luscious array of black fruits, licorice and quality oak, the tannins supple, the balance excellent. Diam. 14.4% alc. Rating 95 To 2035 $40
Flaxman's Valley Eden Valley Syrah 2010 Purple-crimson; this has irresistible texture to its panoply of black fruits, chocolate and cedary/spicy oak flavours; the tannins are ripe and complete. Diam. 14.4% alc. Rating 95 To 2030 $40
Piccadilly Adelaide Hills Chardonnay 2011 Bright green-quartz; a fragrant bouquet with some grilled nut aromas, then a tangy, juicy palate of grapefruit, apple and white peach. Screwcap. 12.8% alc. Rating 94 To 2019 $40
Sang de Pigeon Barossa Shiraz Saignee 2012 Light, bright crimson; a totally delicious rose, with intense spiced red berry fruits on the bouquet and palate; a long, even and balanced palate. Roses don't come much better than this. Screwcap. 13.5% alc. Rating 94 To 2014 $22

♟♟♟♟♟ **Piccadilly Adelaide Hills Sauvignon Blanc 2012** Rating 92 To 2014 $31
Stonewell Valley Barossa Valley Roussanne 2011 Rating 92 To 2016 $34

Michael Unwin Wines

2 Racecourse Road, Beaufort, Vic 3373 **Region** Western Victoria Zone
T (03) 5349 2021 **www**.michaelunwinwines.com.au **Open** Mon–Fri 8.30–5, Sat 11–4.30, Sun 12–4.30
Winemaker Michael Unwin **Est.** 2000 **Dozens** 2500 **Vyds** 8ha
Michael Unwin, a veteran of over 30 vintages, learned the art of winemaking around the world with some of the most influential and forward-thinking winemakers of the time. The winery location was chosen because it is the geographical centre of the best viticultural areas in Western Victoria. The grapes come from three vineyards in the Pyrenees, two in the Grampians and one in the Henty region. In all, approximately 2ha of shiraz and 1ha each of cabernet sauvignon, sangiovese, barbera, durif, riesling and chardonnay are grown or contracted.

ＹＹＹＹ **Umbrella Man Sangiovese 2011** Mid garnet colour; the savoury bouquet offers turned earth, dark cherry and prune aromas; the palate follows suit, with a tobacco leaf note on the medium-bodied and drying finish. Screwcap. 13.5% alc. **Rating** 88 **To** 2016 $28 BE

Umbrella Man Single Vineyard Petit Verdot 2011 Deeply coloured, with essency blackberry pastille and lifted floral notes, typical of the variety; also typical is the slightly hollow palate, yet there is energy and direction enough to be more than a mere curio. Screwcap. 13.5% alc. **Rating** 88 **To** 2016 $28 BE

Michelini Wines

Great Alpine Road, Myrtleford, Vic 3737 **Region** Alpine Valleys
T (03) 5751 1990 **www.**micheliniwines.com.au **Open** 7 days 10–5
Winemaker Greg O'Keefe **Est.** 1982 **Dozens** 10 000 **Vyds** 34.5ha

The Michelini family are among the best-known grapegrowers in the Buckland Valley of North East Victoria. Having migrated from Italy in 1949, they originally grew tobacco, diversifying into vineyards in '82. The main vineyard (16.74ha), on terra rossa soil, is at an altitude of 300m, mostly with frontage to the Buckland River. The Devils Creek Vineyard (17.69ha) was planted in '91 on grafted rootstocks, merlot and chardonnay taking the lion's share. The winery can handle 1000 tonnes of fruit, which eliminates the problem of moving grapes out of a declared phylloxera area. Exports to China.

ＹＹＹＹＹ **Alpine Valleys Pinot Grigio 2011** Pinot grigio enjoys the Alpine and King
✪ Valleys in much the same way as it does the Mornington Peninsula; here pear, apple and citrus come together in a single stream, the finish long and minerally. Screwcap. 13.5% alc. **Rating** 90 **To** 2015 $18

Mike Press Wines

PO Box 224, Lobethal, SA 5241 **Region** Adelaide Hills
T (08) 8389 5546 **www.**mikepresswines.com.au **Open** Not
Winemaker Mike Press **Est.** 1998 **Dozens** 12 000 **Vyds** 22.7ha

Mike and Judy Press established their Kenton Valley Vineyards in 1998, when they purchased 34ha of land in the Adelaide Hills. Over the next two years they planted mainstream cool-climate varieties (merlot, shiraz, cabernet sauvignon, sauvignon blanc, chardonnay and pinot noir), intending to sell the grapes to other wine producers. Even an illustrious 42-year career in the wine industry did not prepare Mike for the downturn in grape prices that followed, and that led to the development of the Mike Press wine label. They produce high-quality Sauvignon Blanc, Chardonnay, Pinot Noir, Merlot, Shiraz, Cabernet Merlot and Cabernet Sauvignon, which are sold at mouth-wateringly low prices. Exports to Denmark.

ＹＹＹＹＹ **MP One Single Vineyard Adelaide Hills Shiraz Cabernet 2009** This is the flagship wine for the Mike Press stable; it is medium- to full-bodied, with blackberry, blackcurrant and plum fruit, vanillin oak and plentiful fine tannins all contributing. Screwcap. 14.8% alc. **Rating** 94 **To** 2029 $25

ＹＹＹＹＹ **Adelaide Hills Sauvignon Blanc 2012** As ever, the estate-grown Mike Press
✪ wines punch way above their price weight; citrus, grass and tropical aromas and flavours are intertwined, providing a palate with good structure and length. Screwcap. 13.5% alc. **Rating** 93 **To** 2013 $13

✪ **Single Vineyard Adelaide Hills Merlot 2010** Good colour; as usual with Mike Press, punches way above its fruit weight, with lush redcurrant and blackcurrant fruit framed by positive oak (French and American) and gentle, fully ripened tannins. Ludicrous value. Screwcap. 14.8% alc. **Rating** 93 **To** 2020 $14

✪ **Single Vineyard Adelaide Hills Chardonnay 2012** Pale straw-green; a fresh and lively unwooded Chardonnay with an edge of all-important grapefruit to the stone fruit at the heart of the wine; no frills, simply honest value. Screwcap. 13.5% alc. **Rating** 90 **To** 2015 $12

Miles from Nowhere ★★★★

PO Box 197, Belmont, WA 6984 **Region** Margaret River
T (08) 9267 8555 **www.**milesfromnowhere.com.au **Open** Not
Winemaker Rory Clifton-Parks **Est.** 2007 **Dozens** 15 000 **Vyds** 46.9ha

Miles from Nowhere is the born-again business of Franklin (Frank) and Heather Tate; Frank was CEO of Evans & Tate for many years. The demise of Evans & Tate has been well chronicled, but has not prevented the Tates from doing what they know best. The plantings of petit verdot, chardonnay, shiraz, sauvignon blanc, semillon, viognier, cabernet sauvignon and merlot are scattered across the Margaret River region, miles from nowhere. Production has risen from 6000 dozen to its current level; the vineyards have also increased significantly (from 36ha), with excess grapes being sold. Exports to the UK, Canada, Sweden and Thailand.

♇♇♇♇♀ **Limited Lot Margaret River Semillon 2012** A portion of this wine has seen barrel fermentation and adds a layer to the fresh-cut grass, crushed nettle and straw notes on the bouquet; the palate is generous and fleshy, finishing bone dry and chalky. Screwcap. 11.5% alc. **Rating** 90 **To** 2015 $23 BE

Best Blocks Margaret River Semillon Sauvignon Blanc 2012 Light straw-green; early picking has heightened the lemon/citrus aspects of the wine, and partial barrel fermentation has added texture; the length and balance are good. Screwcap. 11.7% alc. **Rating** 90 **To** 2014 $27

Best Blocks Margaret River Shiraz 2011 Lavish use of new oak is evident in this wine, with blackberry, pepper and clove a feature; the palate is extremely dry at this early stage, needing time for the tightly wound fruit to make its way past the toasty oak. Screwcap. 14% alc. **Rating** 90 **To** 2020 $27 BE

♇♇♇♇ **Margaret River Shiraz 2011 Rating** 89 **To** 2018 $21 BE

Milhinch Wines ★★★★

27 Gerald Roberts Road Seppeltsfield, SA 5355 **Region** Barossa Valley
T 0412 455 553 **www.**seizetheday.net.au **Open** By appt
Winemaker Contract **Est.** 2003 **Dozens** 1200 **Vyds** 4ha

In 1999 Peter Milhinch and Sharyn Rogers established 2ha each of shiraz and cabernet sauvignon near Greenock Creek, which flows through their property. At the foot of their vineyard is award-winning Seppeltsfield Vineyard Cottage, a restored 1860s German settlers' cottage offering luxury accommodation for one couple. The cottage restoration and Peter and Sharyn's wine production began in 2003, when Peter was recovering from a serious illness. The Seize the Day phrase on their wine labels acknowledges their journey through adversity, as Peter notes 'Carpe Diem – we never know what tomorrow may bring!'

♇♇♇♇♀ **Seize the Day Barossa Valley Shiraz 2010** From the small estate vineyard near Greenock Creek. Deep crimson-purple, it is filled to the brim with blackberry, licorice and tar, the full-bodied palate well balanced despite the onslaught of this fruit and accompanying tannins. Screwcap. 14.5% alc. **Rating** 93 **To** 2030 $30

♇♇♇♇ **Seize the Day Rose 2012 Rating** 89 **To** 2013 $20
Seize the Day Shiraz Cabernet 2010 Rating 89 **To** 2020 $30
Seize the Day Cabernet Sauvignon 2010 Rating 89 **To** 2024 $50

Millbrook Winery ★★★★☆

Old Chestnut Lane, Jarrahdale, WA 6124 **Region** Perth Hills
T (08) 9525 5796 **www.**millbrookwinery.com.au **Open** 7 days 10–5
Winemaker Damian Hutton **Est.** 1996 **Dozens** 20 000 **Vyds** 7.8ha

The strikingly situated Millbrook Winery is owned by highly successful Perth-based entrepreneur Peter Fogarty and wife Lee. They also own Lake's Folly in the Hunter Valley and Deep Woods Estate in Margaret River, and have made a major commitment to the quality end of Australian wine. Millbrook draws on vineyards in the Perth Hills planted to sauvignon blanc, semillon, chardonnay, viognier, cabernet sauvignon, merlot, shiraz and petit verdot. The wines (Millbrook and Barking Owl) are of consistently high quality. Exports to Germany, Malaysia, Hong Kong, Singapore, China and Japan.

�♥ LR Shiraz 2011 Deep crimson, purple hue; the bouquet exhibits layers of black fruits, fresh leather, mocha and ironstone; the palate is fleshy, bordering on unctuous, with generosity of fruit sitting neatly alongside fresh acidity and refreshing tannins. Screwcap. 14% alc. **Rating** 94 **To** 2022 $45 BE

♥♥♥♥♀ Viognier 2011 Clear-cut varietal expression on the bouquet and palate alike, ranging through apricot, peach and ginger, the last coming through on the finish and aftertaste. Screwcap. 14% alc. **Rating** 93 **To** 2014 $22

Barking Owl Shiraz 2010 Positive purple-crimson; most likely a regional blend (unspecified), with 5% viognier co-fermented; it certainly has a very fragrant and flowery red berry bouquet; the medium-bodied palate has spicy red and black cherry fruit and fine tannins. Screwcap. 14% alc. **Rating** 92 **To** 2016 $18

Great Southern Riesling 2012 Rating 91 **To** 2017 $22

Margaret River Sauvignon Blanc 2012 Rating 91 **To** 2013 $22

Barking Owl Sauvignon Blanc Semillon 2012 Light straw-green; a crisp and fresh blend, the two components fused into a passionfruit and gooseberry medley dressed with lemony acidity. Screwcap. 12.5% alc. **Rating** 90 **To** 2014 $18

Cabernet Sauvignon Malbec 2011 Rating 90 **To** 2020 $28 BE

Geographe Tempranillo 2012 Rating 90 **To** 2016 $28 BE

LR Liqueur Muscat NV Rating 90 **To** 2014 $60 BE

Milton Vineyard ★★★★★

14635 Tasman Highway, Cranbrook, Tas 7190 **Region** East Coast Tasmania
T (03) 6257 8298 www.miltonvineyard.com.au **Open** 7 days 10–5
Winemaker Winemaking Tasmania (Julian Alcorso) **Est.** 1992 **Dozens** 6500 **Vyds** 9.5ha
Michael and Kerry Dunbabin have one of the most historic properties in Tasmania, dating back to 1826. The property is 1800ha, meaning the vineyard (2.7ha of pinot noir, 1.4ha of riesling, 1.2ha of pinot gris and 1ha of gewurztraminer) has plenty of room for expansion. Michael says, 'I planted some of the newer pinot clones in 2001, but have yet to plant what I reckon will prove to be some of the best vineyard sites on the property.' Exports to Japan.

♥♥♥♥♥ Pinot Noir 2011 Bright, clear red-purple; the fragrant dark cherry bouquet leads directly into the palate, with more dark cherry joined by plum and a touch of spice; fine, persistent tannins on the back-palate provide texture and length. Gold medal Hobart Wine Show '12. Screwcap. 13.9% alc. **Rating** 94 **To** 2018 $30

Chardonnay Pinot Noir 2009 Estate-grown; the fruit flavours are very intense and long, with grapefruit/citrus to the fore, backed by just a touch of stone fruit. Not to be denied. Diam. 12.1% alc. **Rating** 94 **To** 2017 $35

♥♥♥♥♀ Iced Riesling 2012 Rating 90 **To** 2020 $30

Minko Wines ★★★★

13 High Street, Willunga, SA 5172 **Region** Southern Fleurieu
T (08) 8556 4987 www.minkowines.com **Open** Wed–Sun 11–5, Sat 9.30–5
Winemaker James Hastwell, Linda Domas **Est.** 1997 **Dozens** 1600 **Vyds** 10.4ha
Mike Boerema (veterinarian) and Margo Kellet (ceramic artist) established the Minko Vineyard on their cattle property at Mt Compass. The vineyard, which uses biodynamic methods, is planted to pinot noir, merlot, cabernet sauvignon, chardonnay, pinot gris and savagnin; 60ha of the 160ha property is heritage listed. Exports to the UK.

♥♥♥♥♀ Methode Traditionelle Blanc de Blancs 2010 Virtually colourless; chardonnay from Minko's Mt Compass Vineyard on the Fleurieu Peninsula spent over 2 years on yeast lees; grapefruit flavours come through loud and clear on the bright, tightly focused palate. Crown seal. 11.5% alc. **Rating** 92 **To** 2016 $35

✪   **Fleurieu Peninsula Chardonnay 2012** Bright quartz; barrel-fermented and then matured in French oak for 3 months; it has zesty grapefruit pitch, apple and melon fruit; and good acidity is a given. Good value. Screwcap. 12.5% alc. Rating **90** To 2016 $20

♈♈♈♈   **Fleurieu Peninsula Pinot Grigio 2012** Rating **89** To 2014 $19
Mount Compass Reserve Cabernet Sauvignon 2010 Rating **89** To 2018 $35

Minnow Creek

5 Hillside Road, Blackwood, SA 5051 (postal) **Region** McLaren Vale
T 0404 288 108 **www**.minnowcreekwines.com.au **Open** Not
Winemaker Tony Walker **Est.** 2005 **Dozens** 1800
Former Fox Creek winemaker Tony Walker has set up Minnow Creek in partnership with William Neubauer; the grapes are grown by Don Lopresti at vineyards just west of Willunga. The name of the venture reflects the intention of the partners to keep the business focused on quality rather than quantity, and to self-distribute much of the wine through the large number of highly regarded Adelaide restaurants. Exports to the US, Canada and Germany.

♈♈♈♈♈   **The Black Minnow Adelaide Sangiovese Cabernet Sauvignon Malbec**
✪   **2010** A 76/19/5% blend with a bright, although relatively light, colour reflecting the sangiovese component that also drives the very attractive, juicy red fruit flavours of the wine; the mouthfeel and balance are also good. Great value. Screwcap. 13.5% alc. **Rating** 92 To 2016 $20

✪   **The Silver Minnow Adelaide Hills Sauvignon Blanc 2012** Bright straw-quartz; part of the wine was wild-fermented in French oak, and adds texture to the base of tropical and ripe stone fruits. Screwcap. 13% alc. **Rating** 91 To 2014 $20

Mintaro Wines

Leasingham Road, Mintaro, SA 5415 **Region** Clare Valley
T (08) 8843 9150 **www**.mintarowines.com.au **Open** 7 days 10–4.30
Winemaker Peter Houldsworth **Est.** 1984 **Dozens** 4000 **Vyds** 10ha
Mintaro Wines' vineyards were planted in 1962, and were incorporated into a functioning winery complex in '85 by the present owner and winemaker, Peter Houldsworth. There are five vineyards in the Mintaro and Polish Hill districts of the Clare Valley, one-third planted to riesling, the remainder divided equally between cabernet sauvignon and shiraz. Exports to Singapore.

♈♈♈♈♈   **Clare Valley Riesling 2012** Pale straw-green; one of the best Mintaro Rieslings for a number of years, taking full advantage of the exceptional vintage, with juicy lime fruit running through a long, well-balanced palate. Screwcap. 11% alc. **Rating** 92 To 2020 $22
Clare Valley Cabernet Sauvignon Shiraz 2010 Strong red-purple; a neatly balanced mix of blackcurrant and blackberry bridged by red berry notes and some vanillin oak drive the medium- to full-bodied palate, tannins also playing a role. Screwcap. 15% alc. **Rating** 90 To 2020 $22

♈♈♈♈   **Belles Femmes 2010** Rating **87** To 2018 $28

Mr Mick

7 Dominic Street, Clare, SA 5453 **Region** Clare Valley
T (08) 8842 2555 **www**.mrmick.com.au **Open** 7 days 10–5
Winemaker Tim Adams, Brett Schutz **Est.** 2011 **Dozens** 10 000
This is the venture of Tim Adams and wife Pam Goldsack, the name chosen to honour KH (Mick) Knappstein, a legend in both the Clare Valley and the broader Australian wine community. Tim worked at Leasingham Wines with Mick between 1975 and '86, and knew him very well. When Tim and Pam acquired the Leasingham winery in January 2011, together

with its historic buildings, it brought the wheel full circle. Various commentators (including myself) have used Mick's great one-liner 'There are only two types of people in the world: those who were born in Clare, and those who wished they had been.' This is a separate business from the eponymous Tim Adams Wines. Exports to China.

PPPP **Shiraz 2010** Good colour; an honest, generously flavoured and structured Shiraz,
✪ with plum and black cherry/blackberry fruit, tannins and oak sufficient for the
task. Screwcap. 14% alc. **Rating** 89 **To** 2018 $15

✪ **Tempranillo 2009** The colour is not deep, but the hue is remarkably fresh, perhaps due to spending over 2 years in French oak and tank. It is light-bodied, with typical cherry flavours, plus a twist of lemon on the finish. Good value. Screwcap. 13.5% alc. **Rating** 89 **To** 2016 $15

Rose 2012 An unusual rose, described (accurately) on the back label as having raspberry, strawberry, lychee and white peach characters, which suggests it may be a blend of white and red wines with a little residual sweetness. Equally, it may simply be grenache. Screwcap. 13% alc. **Rating** 87 **To** 2013 $15

Mr Riggs Wine Company ★★★★★

281 Main Road, McLaren Vale, SA 5171 **Region** McLaren Vale
T (08) 8557 0808 **www**.mrriggs.com.au **Open** At Penny's Hill 7 days 10–5
Winemaker Ben Riggs **Est.** 2001 **Dozens** 20 000 **Vyds** 7.5ha
After a quarter of a century of winemaking experience, Ben Riggs is well established under his own banner. Ben sources the best fruit from individual vineyards in McLaren Vale, Clare Valley, Adelaide Hills, Langhorne Creek, Coonawarra, and from his own Piebald Gully Vineyard (shiraz and viognier). Each wine is intended to express the essence of not only the vineyard, but also the region's terroir. The vision of the Mr Riggs brand is unpretentious and personal, 'to make the wines I love to drink'. Exports to the US, Canada, Denmark, Sweden, Germany, The Netherlands, Switzerland, China, Hong Kong, Singapore, Japan and NZ.

PPPPP **d'Adelaide Hills Montepulciano 2011** From Caj Amadio's Kersbrook Vineyard in the warmest part of the Adelaide Hills; has exceptional colour for the vintage, and a generous amount of sour cherry and other savoury flavours. Impressive wine. Screwcap. 14% alc. **Rating** 91 **To** 2017 $27

PPPP **The Gaffer McLaren Vale Shiraz 2011** **Rating** 89 **To** 2018 $22
Ein Riese Adelaide Hills Riesling 2012 **Rating** 88 **To** 2016 $22 BE

Mistletoe Wines ★★★★★

771 Hermitage Road, Pokolbin, NSW 2320 **Region** Hunter Valley
T (02) 4998 7770 **www**.mistletoewines.com.au **Open** 7 days 10–6
Winemaker Nick Paterson **Est.** 1989 **Dozens** 5000 **Vyds** 5.5ha
Mistletoe Wines, owned by Ken and Gwen Sloan, can trace its history back to 1909, when a vineyard was planted on what was then called Mistletoe Farm. The Mistletoe Farm brand made a brief appearance in the late '70s. The wines are made onsite by Nick Paterson, who has had significant experience in the Hunter Valley. The quality and consistency of these wines is irreproachable, as is their price. Mistletoe has also been steadily building museum stock for sale, with several years' bottle age.

PPPPP **Noble Viognier 2012** Full yellow-gold; this has been seriously botrytised, with gloriously sweet, luscious fruit absolutely true to the variety, yet with a vibrant and long finish. A freakish wine. 375ml. Screwcap. 10% alc. **Rating** 96 **To** 2017 $20

Reserve Hunter Valley Shiraz 2011 The best parcel of estate, dry-grown shiraz was matured in new French puncheons; the depth of flavour is far greater than that of the Home Vineyard, part due to the integrated French oak, part to the intense red and black fruits. Screwcap. 13.8% alc. **Rating** 95 **To** 2030 $50

Reserve Hunter Valley Semillon 2012 Quartz-white; at the very dawn of its life, with lemon zest, lemongrass and prominent acidity all making their mark; the old vines and skilled winemaking provide any assurance you need to cellar the wine for over 10 years. Screwcap. 9.1% alc. **Rating** 94 **To** 2025 $24

Barrel Fermented Hunter Valley Rose 2011 Crushed and chilled shiraz was given 24 hours skin contact, then pressed and barrel-fermented in used French oak. This is a rose with considerable attitude, tangy and savoury, with a very long palate and aftertaste. Screwcap. 12.5% alc. **Rating** 94 **To** 2014 $20

ŸŸŸŸŸ Hunter Valley Chardonnay 2011 Pale, bright straw-green; an elegant wine,
✪ the grapes – as usual – picked at optimum ripeness to give a delicious mix of stone fruit, melon and citrus. Very good value. Screwcap. 13% alc. **Rating** 93 **To** 2018 $22
Reserve Hunter Valley Chardonnay 2011 **Rating** 93 **To** 2020 $40
✪ Hunter Valley Chardonnay 2012 An elegant and fresh chardonnay picked at precisely the right time, and given exactly the right oak treatment, its mix of citrus and stone fruit given free varietal expression. Screwcap. 13% alc. **Rating** 92 **To** 2015 $22
Home Vineyard Hunter Valley Shiraz 2011 **Rating** 92 **To** 2024 $30
Hilltops Cabernet 2011 **Rating** 92 **To** 2026 $25
✪ Silvereye Hunter Valley Semillon 2012 Here the level of sweetness is apparent, but still less than (say) most off-dry Rieslings; the lemon juice is palpable, and I think it is marginally better balanced than the Home Vineyard, and better enjoyed while relatively young. Screwcap. 8.1% alc. **Rating** 92 **To** 2017 $20
Home Vineyard Hunter Valley Semillon 2012 **Rating** 90 **To** 2025 $22

Misty Glen Wines   ★★★★

293 Deasys Road, Pokolbin, NSW 2320 **Region** Hunter Valley
T (02) 4998 7781 www.mistyglen.com.au **Open** Fri, Sun, Mon 10–4, Sat 10–5, or by appt
Winemaker Contract **Est.** 1985 **Dozens** 2000 **Vyds** 6.85ha
Vicci Lashmore-Smith and Eric Smith purchased the Wright Family Wines business in December 2009. Part of the vineyard dates back to 1985, supplemented by an additional 3ha planted between '00 and '02; the varieties planted are chardonnay, cabernet sauvignon, semillon, chambourcin, shiraz and sauvignon blanc.

ŸŸŸŸŸ Hunter Valley Semillon 2011 Pale, but bright, colour; has begun to develop some secondary flavours (in semillon terms) with the emergence of lemon zest/pith over the bed of grainy acidity; has the requisite balance for the future. Screwcap. 10.5% alc. **Rating** 90 **To** 2017 $20
Hunter Valley Semillon 2010 Straw-green; already shows positive development, supporting the idea (from the '11) that prolonged cellaring will not be necessary; the lemon flavours are evident, but I think the wine is in transition, with better things to come. Screwcap. 10.4% alc. **Rating** 90 **To** 2016 $20

ŸŸŸŸ Hunter Valley Chardonnay 2010 **Rating** 89 **To** 2015 $25
Hunter Valley Shiraz 2009 **Rating** 89 **To** 2019 $25

Mitchell

Hughes Park Road, Sevenhill via Clare, SA 5453 **Region** Clare Valley
T (08) 8843 4258 www.mitchellwines.com **Open** 7 days 10–4
Winemaker Andrew Mitchell **Est.** 1975 **Dozens** 30 000 **Vyds** 75ha
One of the stalwarts of the Clare Valley, established by Jane and Andrew Mitchell, producing long-lived Rieslings and Cabernet Sauvignons in classic regional style. The range now includes very creditable Semillon, Grenache and Shiraz. A lovely old stone apple shed provides the cellar door and upper section of the upgraded winery. Children Angus and Edwina are now working in the business, heralding generational changes. Over the years the Mitchells have established or acquired 75ha of vineyards on four excellent sites, some vines over 50 years old; all are managed organically, with the use of biodynamic composts for the past decade. Exports to the UK, the US, Canada, Singapore, Hong Kong, China and NZ.

🍷🍷🍷🍷🍷 **McNicol Clare Valley Shiraz 2005** Healthy red-purple; has developed slowly but surely over the past 8 years, and is approaching the point where it will enter a long plateau of maximum expression. The bouquet is complex, but still with a fresh display of plum fruit; the palate adds nuances of spice and oak, but plum is the key to the wine, supported as it is by fine tannins. Lovely wine in every respect. Screwcap. 14.5% alc. **Rating** 96 **To** 2025 $40

Watervale Riesling 2012 Light straw-green; the fragrant bouquet tells of the citrus and green apple flavours to come on the long, focused palate, lengthened and balanced by very good minerally acidity. Screwcap. 13% alc. **Rating** 94 **To** 2022 $22

McNicol Clare Valley Riesling 2009 Glowing quartz-green; a complex bouquet of citrus and wild flowers leads into an equally complex palate, with ripe citrus and a hint of tropical fruit; there is balancing acidity, and no need for patience. Screwcap. 13.5% alc. **Rating** 94 **To** 2016 $35

🍷🍷🍷🍷🍷 **Peppertree Vineyard Clare Valley Shiraz 2010 Rating** 93 **To** 2030 $27
✪ **Clare Valley Semillon 2012** Barrel-fermented in used oak; the power of the fruit from the 37-year-old estate vines is more than sufficient to justify the approach, the citrus/lemongrass flavours of the semillon running through to the very finish of the palate. Screwcap. 12% alc. **Rating** 92 **To** 2020 $22

Sevenhill Vineyard Cabernet Sauvignon 2009 Rating 91 **To** 2024 $27

Mitchell Harris Wines ★★★★★

38 Doveton Street North, Ballarat, Vic 3350 **Region** Pyrenees
T 0417 566 025 **www**.mitchellharris.com.au **Open** Sun–Tues 11–6, Wed 11–9, Thurs–Sat 11–11
Winemaker John Harris **Est.** 2008 **Dozens** 800
Mitchell Harris Wines is a partnership between Alicia and Craig Mitchell and Shannyn and John Harris, the latter winemaker for this eponymous producer. John began his career at Mount Avoca, then spent eight years as winemaker at Domaine Chandon in the Yarra Valley, cramming in northern hemisphere vintages in California and Oregon. While the total make is not large, a lot of thought has gone into the creation of each of the wines. In 2012 a multipurpose space was created in an 1880s brick workshop and warehouse, the renovation providing a cellar door and education facility. They intend to install some winemaking equipment to allow visitors the opportunity to participate in small-scale winemaking.

🍷🍷🍷🍷🍷 **Pyrenees Sauvignon Blanc Fume 2012** Partial wild fermentation and subsequent oak maturation have been wholly responsible for the left-field style, although this approach is being used by an increasing number of Australian winemakers to combat the Marlborough tsunami. Here it works well, giving an almost creamy texture to the wine without obscuring the predominantly citrus fruit, which provides all-important freshness and zest to the finish. Screwcap. 13% alc. **Rating** 94 **To** 2015 $23

🍷🍷🍷🍷🍷 **Pyrenees Shiraz 2011 Rating** 93 **To** 2021 $30
Pyrenees Mataro Grenache Shiraz 2011 Rating 92 **To** 2018 $27

Mitchelton ★★★★★

Mitchellstown via Nagambie, Vic 3608 **Region** Nagambie Lakes
T (03) 5736 2222 **www**.mitchelton.com.au **Open** 7 days 10–5
Winemaker Travis Clydesdale **Est.** 1969 **Dozens** 12000 **Vyds** 148ha
Mitchelton was founded by Ross Shelmerdine, who had a vision splendid for the very expensive and very striking winery, restaurant, observation tower and surrounding vineyards. Suffice it to say that the expected volume of tourism did not eventuate, and that the business became embroiled in a long-running dispute. Phylloxera, too, struck the vineyard. In 1994 it was acquired by Petaluma, but once again, did not deliver the expected financial return, notwithstanding the long and faithful service of chief winemaker Don Lewis, and notwithstanding the quality of its best wines. In Aug 2012 a new chapter opened for

Mitchelton, with the completion of an acquisition agreement by Gerry Ryan OAM, and son Andrew. Gerry founded caravan company Jayco in 1975, and as a consequence of the success of that company, has a virtually unlimited budget to take Mitchelton to the next level. Winemaker Travis Clydesdale has had a long association with Mitchelton, dating back 30 years when, as a small boy, his father was cellar manager. Exports to all major markets.

ŦŦŦŦŦ **Marsanne 2011** Pale gold, green hue; a highly expressive bouquet of nectarine, straw and honeysuckle; a lively palate, with a long, expansive and intriguingly complex finish. Screwcap. 13% alc. **Rating** 94 **To** 2017 $23 BE
Heathcote Shiraz 2010 A fragrant and perfumed bouquet of red and blue fruits, lavender and sage; the palate is medium-bodied, precise and focused, with fine red fruits lingering harmoniously with fine-grained tannins on the evenly balanced, supple and elegant finish. Screwcap. 14.5% alc. **Rating** 94 **To** 2022 $40 BE

ŦŦŦŦŦ **Blackwood Park Riesling 2012** An exotic bouquet of lime juice, orange zest,
✪ coriander and a touch of musk; the palate is lively, with taut acidity prominent, making way for a complex bitter amaro conclusion that is full of blanched almonds. Screwcap. 12.5% alc. **Rating** 90 **To** 2018 $19 BE
Chardonnay 2011 Rating 90 **To** 2016 $22 BE
Shiraz 2011 Rating 90 **To** 2018 $22 BE
Blackwood Park Botrytis Riesling 2012 Rating 90 **To** 2016 $22 BE

Mitolo Wines   ★★★★★
PO Box 520, Virginia, SA 5120 **Region** McLaren Vale
T (08) 8282 9012 **www**.mitolowines.com.au **Open** Not
Winemaker Ben Glaetzer **Est.** 1999 **Dozens** 20 000
Mitolo has had a meteoric rise since Frank Mitolo decided to turn a winemaking hobby into a business. In 2000 he took the plunge into the commercial end of the business, inviting Ben Glaetzer to make the wines. Split between the Jester range and single vineyard wines, Mitolo began life as a red wine-dominant brand, but now also produces Rose and Vermentino. Exports to all major markets.

ŦŦŦŦŦ **Jester McLaren Vale Sangiovese Rose 2012** Pale pink; a classic Sangiovese
✪ Rose, more spicy and savoury than sweet and fruity, though there are ample cherry nuances to fill out the palate. Has very good balance and length; a cut above most. Screwcap. 12.5% alc. **Rating** 93 **To** 2014 $22
Savitar McLaren Vale Shiraz 2010 Deep crimson-purple; the wine does express its regional origin courtesy of the earthy dark chocolate subtext, but the question is why was it necessary to end up with such high alcohol? Savoury bitter chocolate, prune, blackberry and licorice are the drivers of the palate. Screwcap. 15.2% alc. **Rating** 93 **To** 2020 $80
Reiver Barossa Valley Shiraz 2010 Deep crimson-purple; the hand of the winemaker is more obvious in these wines than that of the terroir, alcohol being only one part of the story; this has slightly more fruit and less dark chocolate, but the overall extract is similar. Screwcap. 15% alc. **Rating** 92 **To** 2030 $58
Jester McLaren Vale Vermentino 2012 It is obvious that vermentino can and does deliver considerable concentration of ripe flavours at low alcohol levels, thus retaining natural acidity; lime, honeysuckle and a dusting of white pepper are all present. Screwcap. 11% alc. **Rating** 91 **To** 2014 $22
G.A.M. McLaren Vale Shiraz 2010 Deep purple-crimson; the wine is so potent and concentrated on the spice, licorice, dark chocolate and black-fruited bouquet and palate that you don't initially think about the alcohol, but it progressively becomes more obvious. Screwcap. 15.4% alc. **Rating** 91 **To** 2030 $58
Serpico McLaren Vale Cabernet Sauvignon 2010 Dense crimson-purple; a predictably huge wine; we absolutely know McLaren Vale does not need to ripen cabernet to such extreme levels; it is a double pity, because there is some attractive fruit under the canopy of alcohol. Screwcap. 15.5% alc. **Rating** 90 **To** 2020 $80

Molly's Cradle

356 Tuckers Lane, North Rothbury, NSW 2335 **Region** Hunter Valley
T (02) 9979 1471 **www**.mollyscradle.com.au **Open** By appt
Winemaker Gary Reed **Est.** 2002 **Dozens** 10 000 **Vyds** 9ha
Steve Skidmore and Deidre Broad created the Molly's Cradle brand concept in 1997, moving
to reality with the first planting of estate vines in 2000, the first vintage following in '02.
They have 2ha each of verdelho, chardonnay, merlot and shiraz, plus 1ha of petit verdot, but
also look to other regions to supplement the estate-grown grapes. Thus, for the time being,
shiraz comes from Wrattonbully, merlot from Mudgee and sauvignon blanc (for blending with
Hunter semillon) from Orange. A significant part of the business is the luxury Cradle Lodge,
built as a '5-star adult retreat comfortably accommodating up to three couples'. Exports to
Indonesia and Malaysia.

ꭩꭩꭩꭩ   **Single Vineyard Range Hunter Valley Petit Verdot 2009** Strong colour, as
ever with this variety; likewise it has good blackcurrant/berry fruit on the mid-
palate, finishing with strong tannins on the finish – as yet, a little tough. Screwcap.
12.7% alc. **Rating** 89 **To** 2016 $25
Hunter Valley Sauvignon Blanc Semillon 2011 A 57/43% blend from the
Upper and Lower Hunter Valley; here the flavours of the two varieties are so
seamlessly joined that they cancel each other out, which is no bad thing. Screwcap.
12% alc. **Rating** 88 **To** 2014 $20
Mudgee Shiraz 2009 Light red-purple; what is there is well balanced, with ripe
plum and cherry fruit; however, needs more conviction and fruit weight for higher
points. Screwcap. 13.8% alc. **Rating** 87 **To** 2015 $20
Vignerons Selection Cradle Shiraz 2006 If you like lots and lots of oak in
your wine, this is your answer; if you don't, limit yourself to a glass with food at
hand. Screwcap. 15% alc. **Rating** 87 **To** 2013 $38
Mudgee Merlot 2009 The colour is developed, and the wine is light-bodied,
but the pomegranate noted on the bouquet and palate by winemaker Gary Reed
is not a figment of his imagination; the wine has retained a fresh finish. Screwcap.
14.7% alc. **Rating** 87 **To** 2013 $20

Mongrel Vineyard

571 Spring Flat Road, Mudgee, NSW 2850 **Region** Mudgee
T (02) 6372 2681 **www**.mongrelwine.com.au **Open** W'ends & public hols 10–5, or by appt
Winemaker Michael Slater, Jacob Stein, David Lowe **Est.** 1998 **Dozens** 700 **Vyds** 1ha
In 1986 Sue and David Fairlie-Cuninghame purchased a 50ha property on Spring Flat, 6km
east of the Mudgee township. It was a weekend retreat, and the main occupation was (and
remains) fattening steers. But wine was in their blood: both were founding members of The
Rothbury Estate, and Sue was Executive Editor Food & Wine at *Vogue Entertaining* for over
10 years, adding, 'I was influenced by many leading winemakers from all over the world, but
not one of them ever told me what bloody back-breaking work it is, the discipline required
and how dodgy the returns.' So it was that in 1998 they planted a shiraz vineyard on their
property, using six of the principal clones. The name was chosen because of the uncontrollable
vigour of the vines, itself a legacy of the time when a sheepyard had existed where the vines
were planted, providing the soil with an inexhaustible supply of nitrogen.

ꭩꭩꭩꭩ   **Rose 2012** Very pale pink; it is juicily fruity, with some citrus elements, but not
grassy/green. A very interesting wine, having no similarity to the roses of Bandol
in the South of France, the back label notwithstanding. Screwcap. 11.3% alc.
Rating 89 **To** 2014 $23
Barbera 2011 Medium red-purple; has a mix of blueberry, mulberry and cherry
fruits, with low structure and texture despite its alcohol; is not going to offend
anyone. Screwcap. 14% alc. **Rating** 87 **To** 2015 $23

Montalto   ★★★★★

33 Shoreham Road, Red Hill South, Vic 3937 **Region** Mornington Peninsula
T (03) 5989 8412 **www**.montalto.com.au **Open** 7 days 11–5
Winemaker Simon Black **Est.** 1998 **Dozens** 7000 **Vyds** 18.7ha

John Mitchell and family established Montalto in 1998, but the core of the vineyard goes
back to '86. There are 6ha of pinot noir, 3ha of chardonnay, 1ha of pinot gris, and 0.5ha
each of semillon and riesling. Intensive vineyard work opens up the canopy, with yields
ranging between 1.5 and 2.5 tonnes per acre. Wines are released under two labels, the flagship
Montalto and Pennon, the latter a lower-priced second label. A significant change has been
the decision to lease five vineyards that deliberately span the extremes of the Peninsula, giving
vastly greater diversity of pinot noir sources, and greater insurance against weather extremes.
There is also a broad range of clones adding to that diversity. The leased vineyards are known
within Montalton as the Tuerong Block, the Merricks Block, Hawkins Hill and Black Rabbit.
Watch this space. Exports to China.

ŸŸŸŸŸ **Single Vineyard Hawkins Hill Mornington Peninsula Chardonnay 2011**
Bright green-straw; a perfectly balanced mix of melon, stone fruit and grapefruit
on the bouquet and distinctly juicy palate; the oak is subtle, the acidity particularly
good. Trophy Concours des Vins '12. Screwcap. 13.5% alc. **Rating** 95 **To** 2018 $55
Estate Mornington Peninsula Chardonnay 2011 Pale bright gold;
a beguiling combination of freshness and complexity with nectarine, pear,
charcuterie and cashew on the bouquet; the palate appears soft on entry, but the
spine of acidity punches through and delivers the luscious stone fruits to the long,
linear and refreshing finish. Screwcap. 13% alc. **Rating** 94 **To** 2017 $39 BE
Estate Mornington Peninsula Pinot Noir 2011 Mid, bright garnet; smoky
bacon bone aromas derived from oak sit comfortably alongside fragrant red cherry
and Asian spices; the palate is linear and pure-fruited, silky in texture, and shows
good concentration and persistence, especially considering the challenges of the
vintage. Screwcap. 13.5% alc. **Rating** 94 **To** 2018 $48 BE

ŸŸŸŸŸ **Single Vineyard The Eleven Mornington Peninsula Chardonnay 2011**
Rating 93 **To** 2017 $55
Pennon Hill Shiraz 2011 Rating 91 **To** 2018 $30 BE
Estate Mornington Peninsula Riesling 2012 Rating 90 **To** 2018 $25 BE
Pennon Hill Sauvignon Blanc 2012 Rating 90 **To** 2014 $23
Pennon Hill Pinot Grigio 2012 Rating 90 **To** 2014 $23

Montara   ★★★★

76 Chalambar Road, Ararat, Vic 3377 **Region** Grampians
T (03) 5352 3868 **www**.montaragrampianswines.com **Open** Fri–Sun 11–4
Winemaker Leigh Clarnette **Est.** 1970 **Dozens** 2500 **Vyds** 19.2ha

Gained considerable attention for its Pinot Noirs during the 1980s, and continues to
produce wines of distinctive style under the near seven-year ownership of no less than the
six siblings of the Stapleton family. As I can attest from several visits over the years, the view
from the cellar door is one of the best in the Grampians region. Exports to the US, Ireland
and China.

ŸŸŸŸŸ **Chalambar Road Grampians Shiraz 2009** The bouquet is in intriguing blend
of charry oak, graphite, red fruits and fresh leather; medium-bodied and with
plenty of fresh acidity and ample chewy tannins; more time is needed, but the
ingredients for enjoyment are in place. Cork. 14% alc. **Rating** 92 **To** 2022 $70 BE

ŸŸŸŸ **Grampians Riesling 2012 Rating** 89 **To** 2016 $17 BE
Grampians Sauvignon Blanc 2012 Rating 87 **To** 2014 $17 BE

Montgomery's Hill

South Coast Highway, Upper Kalgan, Albany, WA 6330 **Region** Albany
T (08) 9844 3715 **www**.montgomeryshill.com.au **Open** 7 days 11–5
Winemaker The Vintage Wineworx, Bill Crappsley (Consultant) **Est.** 1996 **Dozens** 6000
Montgomery's Hill is 16km northeast of Albany on a north-facing slope on the banks of the
Kalgan River. Previously used as an apple orchard, it is a diversification for the third generation
of the Montgomery family. Chardonnay, cabernet sauvignon, cabernet franc, sauvignon blanc,
shiraz and merlot were planted in 1996–97. The wines are made with a gentle touch.

Albany Sauvignon Blanc 2012 The vines are grown on a steep, rocky gravelly
patch on the bank of a small river. Distinct herb and snow pea influences on the
bouquet come through strongly on the palate; as distinctive as it is generous, crisp
acidity driving the long finish. Screwcap. 13% alc. **Rating** 94 **To** 2014 $18

Albany Shiraz 2011 Good colour; an elegant, cool-grown style, picked at the
optimum moment, giving dark cherry fruit and spicy/peppery fruit flavours equal
play, the palate supported by fine tannins and positive oak; exceptional value once
again. Screwcap. 13.5% alc. **Rating** 94 **To** 2021 $20

Albany Chardonnay 2010 While sharing some of the '11 characters, this wine
has more intensity, drive and persistence to its grapefruit and white peach flavours,
with cashew oak and figgy nuances incidental to the main game. Screwcap.
12% alc. **Rating** 93 **To** 2016 $22

Albany Unwooded Chardonnay 2010 Light straw-green; a vibrant example of
the unwooded style, with more than sufficient juicy white peach and nectarine to
fill the palate with flavour through to the long finish and aftertaste. Excellent value.
Screwcap. 12% alc. **Rating** 92 **To** 2016 $18

Albany Sauvignon Blanc 2011 Pale straw-green; as you swirl the glass, the
overwhelming aromas are of snow peas, the palate with continuing notes of herbs
and grainy minerally acidity. Screwcap. 14% alc. **Rating** 90 **To** 2016 $18

Albany Chardonnay 2011 Rating 90 **To** 2016 $22

Monument Vineyard

Cnr Escort Way/Manildra Road, Cudal, NSW 2864 **Region** Central Ranges Zone
T (02) 9679 2922 **www**.monumentvineyard.com.au **Open** At Borenore Store (02) 6365 2261
Winemaker Chris Derrez **Est.** 1998 **Dozens** 5000 **Vyds** 97ha
In the early 1990s five mature-age students at CSU, successful in their own professions,
decided to form a partnership to develop a substantial vineyard and winery. After a lengthy
search, a large property at Cudal was identified, with ideal terra rossa basalt-derived soil over
a limestone base. The property has just under 100ha under vine, planted in 1998 and '99. Ten
years later in 2009, brothers Andrew, Phillip and Stephen Jones acquired the business, which
also includes a state-of-the-art cage-free poultry farm, and over 100 head of cattle.

Verdelho 2011 Pale straw-green; no problems with a well-made Verdelho
offering typical tropical fruit salad flavours. Screwcap. 14% alc. **Rating** 87
To 2013 $16

Moody's Wines

'Fontenay', Stagecoach Road, Orange, NSW 2800 **Region** Orange
T (02) 6365 9117 **www**.moodyswines.com **Open** W'ends 10–5, or by appt
Winemaker Madrez Wine Services (Chris Derrez) **Est.** 2000 **Dozens** 200 **Vyds** 2ha
Tony Moody's great-grandfather started a retail chain of shops in Merseyside, England, under
the banner Moody's Wines; the business was sold in 1965 to a brewery seeking to minimise
competition. Tony planted 1ha of shiraz 'in a promising sheep paddock' in 2000, and has
subsequently added 1ha of sauvignon blanc. Moody's is in the east of the Orange region, with
lighter rainfall than the west, the soils clay rather than red earth.

ŸŸŸŸŸ Orange Sauvignon Blanc 2012 Navigated a path through rain, mildew and a last-minute hailstorm, to a trophy for Best Sauvignon Blanc at the Orange Wine Show '12; the bouquet is fresh and clean, leaving it to the intense palate to display a seductive mix of gooseberry, tropical and citrus flavours. The trophy and gold medal sticker on the bottle should be in the Guinness Book of Records for its size. Screwcap. 12.5% alc. **Rating** 94 **To** 2014 $25

ŸŸŸŸŸ Rose de Fontenay 2011 Rating 90 **To** 2014 $18

Moombaki Wines ★★★★★

341 Parker Road, Kentdale via Denmark, WA 6333 **Region** Denmark
T (08) 9840 8006 **www**.moombaki.com **Open** 7 days 11–5
Winemaker Harewood Estate (James Kellie) **Est.** 1997 **Dozens** 800 **Vyds** 2.4ha
David Britten and Melissa Boughey (with three young sons in tow) established vines on a north-facing gravel hillside, with picturesque Kent River frontage. Not content with establishing the vineyard (cabernet sauvignon, shiraz, cabernet franc, malbec and chardonnay), they put in significant mixed tree plantings to increase wildlife habitats. It is against this background that they chose Moombaki as their vineyard name: it is a local Aboriginal word meaning 'where the river meets the sky'. Exports to Malaysia and Singapore.

ŸŸŸŸŸ Shiraz 2010 Equal amounts of Frankland River and estate Denmark grapes were combined to make this wine, which spent 22 months in French oak. The hue is good, although not particularly deep, and the intensity and power of the dark, spicy/savoury fruits come as a surprise; add the impact of high-grade tannins, and the result is a top-quality wine. Screwcap. 14.5% alc. **Rating** 95 **To** 2040 $35
Chardonnay 2010 Bright straw-green; all or some of the extra month in oak, the extra year in bottle, and the vintage have invested this wine with greater presence and complexity than the '11, without taking away its elegance; here white peach and melon are co-drivers with grapefruit, and the oak imparts some creamy/nutty nuances. Screwcap. 13.5% alc. **Rating** 94 **To** 2015 $33
Shiraz 2009 Is the same 50/50% blend of Frankland River and Denmark as the '10; a very good wine, with potent black fruits, licorice and spice; has great energy and length. Screwcap. 14% alc. **Rating** 94 **To** 2034 $40
Cabernet Sauvignon Cabernet Franc Malbec 2009 A 66/18/16% blend, and like the '10, matured for 24 months in French oak; the depth of the colour is similar, but here the fruit has greater depth, and accommodates the oak; it shows its cool-grown origins in the flavour of its cassis/blackcurrant fruit, nicely weighted by tannins to close. Screwcap. 14.5% alc. **Rating** 94 **To** 2024 $40

ŸŸŸŸŸ Cabernet Sauvignon Cabernet Franc Malbec 2010 Rating 93 **To** 2020 $35
Chardonnay 2011 Rating 90 **To** 2015 $29

Moonbark Estate Vineyard ★★★★

Lot 11 Moonambel-Natte Yallock Road, Moonambel, Vic 3478 (postal) **Region** Pyrenees
T 0439 952 263 **www**.moonbark.com.au **Open** Not
Winemaker Contract **Est.** 1998 **Dozens** 500 **Vyds** 1.75ha
This small family-owned and operated vineyard is located on a 17.1ha property in the Pyrenees region. Rod Chivers and his family have slowly established their vineyard with 1ha of shiraz, 0.5ha of merlot and 0.25ha of cabernet sauvignon planted on the red clay intermingled with quartz soils typical of the region.

ŸŸŸŸŸ Shiraz 2009 Good hue; curiously, this wine has significantly more to offer than the '10; plum, licorice and blackberry coalesce with the French and American oak and ripe tannins. Will drink well over the short to medium term. Screwcap. 14% alc. **Rating** 90 **To** 2020 $20

✪   **Merlot 2009** The colour isn't deep, but the retention of a youthful hue is good, and the palate is as powerful as you could possibly expect; here plum is the cornerstone, but has sufficient black olive/savoury notes to give it varietal integrity. Screwcap. 13.6% alc. **Rating** 90 **To** 2016 $20

🍷🍷🍷🍷   **Shiraz 2010 Rating** 87 **To** 2016 $20

Moondah Brook   ★★★★

Dale Road, Middle Swan, WA 6056 **Region** Swan Valley
T (08) 9274 9540 **www.**moondahbrook.com.au **Open** Not
Winemaker Courtney Treacher (former) **Est.** 1968 **Dozens** NFP
Part of Accolade Wines, Moondah Brook has its own special character, as it draws part of its fruit from the large Gingin vineyard, 70km north of the Swan Valley, and part from the Margaret River and Great Southern. From time to time it has exceeded even its own reputation for reliability with some quite lovely wines, in particular honeyed, aged Chenin Blanc, generous Shiraz and finely structured Cabernet Sauvignon. Exports to Canada, Pacific Islands and China.

🍷🍷🍷🍷   **Cabernet Sauvignon 2012** Good colour; blackcurrant is front and centre with
✪   this medium-bodied wine, oak on either side of the stage, giving some mocha/ fruitcake notes along with the soft tannins. Well priced. Screwcap. 13.5% alc. **Rating** 89 **To** 2016 $16
       Verdelho 2012 Has blendamix fruit salad flavours that serve the purpose well. Screwcap. 13.5% alc. **Rating** 87 **To** 2014 $16

Moores Hill Estate   ★★★★

3343 West Tamar Highway, Sidmouth, Tas 7270 **Region** Northern Tasmania
T (03) 6394 7649 **www.**mooreshill.com.au **Open** 7 days 10–5
Winemaker Julian Allport **Est.** 1997 **Dozens** 3000 **Vyds** 4.5ha
Planting of the Moores Hill Estate vineyard (jointly owned by winemaker Julian Allport with Fiona and Lance Weller) began in 1997 and progressively expanded, and now consists of pinot noir, chardonnay and riesling, with very small amounts of cabernet sauvignon and merlot. The vines are located on a northeast-facing hillside, 5km from the Tamar River and 30km from the Bass Strait. The cellar door is built from timber found on the property.

🍷🍷🍷🍷⸮   **Chardonnay 2011** An exactingly pure and honed Chardonnay, crafted with the deft touch of Julian Allport at Winemaking Tasmania. An immaculate bouquet of almond blossom and lemon fruit opens into a palate of delicate grapefruit and taut, persistent, cool '11 acidity. Cork. 12.6% alc. **Rating** 92 **To** 2018 $31 TS

🍷🍷🍷🍷   **Pinot Gris 2012 Rating** 87 **To** 2013 $27

Moorilla Estate   ★★★★★

655 Main Road, Berriedale, Tas 7011 **Region** Southern Tasmania
T (03) 6277 9900 **www.**moorilla.com.au **Open** Wed–Mon 9.30–5
Winemaker Conor van der Reest **Est.** 1958 **Dozens** 9400 **Vyds** 14.5ha
Moorilla Estate was the second winery to be established in Tasmania in the 20th century, Jean Miguet's La Provence beating it to the punch by two years. However, through much of the history of Moorilla Estate, it was the most important winery in the state, if not in size but as the icon. Magnificently situated on a mini-isthmus reaching into the Derwent River, and a lazy 20-min drive from the Hobart CBD, it has always been a must-visit for wine lovers and tourists. A new winery in 2010 saw a decrease of 80% from peak production to around 90 tonnes per year sourced entirely from the vineyards around Moorilla, and its St Matthias Vineyard (Tamar Valley). It's almost incidental that the new winery is part of an overall development said by observers (not Moorilla) to cost upwards of $150 million. It also houses the boutique brewery Moo Brew, but its raison d'être is the establishment of an art gallery (MONA) that has the highest atmospheric environment accreditation of any gallery in the Southern Hemisphere, housing both the extraordinary ancient and contemporary art

collection assembled by Moorilla's owner, David Walsh, and visiting exhibitions from major art museums around the world. The official opening of the Museum in Jan '11 was attended by 2000 guests from all corners of the globe.

🍷🍷🍷🍷🍷 **Muse Pinot Noir 2010** Bright, clear red-purple; a beautifully articulated and detailed Pinot; both bouquet and palate are alive with juicy red and black cherry fruit, the mouthfeel outstanding. Still in its primary phase, even more complexity will come with years in bottle. Screwcap. 13.8% alc. **Rating** 96 **To** 2023 $48

Muse St Matthias Vineyard Syrah 2010 Light to medium purple-crimson; a vibrantly juicy wine; spice and pepper stand alongside the bevy of red fruits and fine tannins; the most notable feature of a seriously good Shiraz is its extreme length and gossamer tannins. Screwcap. 13.7% alc. **Rating** 95 **To** 2025 $67

Muse Riesling 2010 Pale green; very well made, with a hint of sweetness within the lime juice flavour spectrum to provide balance with the high-toned Tasmanian acidity and notes of mineral. Screwcap. 12.8% alc. **Rating** 94 **To** 2025 $30

Muse St Matthias Vineyard Sauvignon 2011 Pale straw-green; this wine is complex, with some barrel-ferment characters and ripe fruit; the result is a palate that has more drive and length than Praxis. Screwcap. 13% alc. **Rating** 94 **To** 2014 $30

Muse Chardonnay 2010 A highly sophisticated winemaking approach has resulted in an equally sophisticated wine, the fruit moulded like putty in the winemakers' hands. There is enough tenacity in that fruit to keep its shape and varietal expression. Screwcap. 13.5% alc. **Rating** 94 **To** 2020 $45

🍷🍷🍷🍷🍷 **Praxis St Matthias Vineyard Sauvignon Blanc 2012** **Rating** 93 **To** 2014 $25
Muse Pinot Gris 2011 **Rating** 90 **To** 2014 $35
Praxis Pinot Noir 2011 **Rating** 90 **To** 2015 $30

Moorooduc Estate   ★★★★★

501 Derril Road, Moorooduc, Vic 3936 **Region** Mornington Peninsula
T (03) 5971 8506 **www**.moorooducestate.com.au **Open** Thurs–Mon 11–5
Winemaker Dr Richard McIntyre **Est.** 1983 **Dozens** 5000 **Vyds** 6.5ha
Richard McIntyre has taken Moorooduc Estate to new heights, having completely mastered the difficult art of gaining maximum results from wild yeast fermentations. Starting with the 2010 vintage, there has been a complete revamp of grape sources, and hence changes to the tiered structure of the releases. These changes were driven by the simple fact of life that the estate vineyards had no possibility of providing the 5000–6000 dozen bottles of wine sold each year. The entry point wines under the Devil Bend Creek label remain, as before, principally sourced from the Osborn Vineyard. The mid priced Chardonnay and Pinot Noir are no longer single estate vineyard wines. At the top come the Robson Vineyard Pinot Noir and Chardonnay, priced a little below the ultimate 'Ducs' (Moorooduc Vineyard). These have always been individual vineyards, and will remain so, but now clearly declared as such on the front labels. Exports to the UK, the US, Hong Kong and Singapore.

🍷🍷🍷🍷🍷 **The Moorooduc McIntyre Pinot Noir 2010** Bright, clear colour; the fragrant mix of red fruits, spice and forest on the bouquet leads into a silky, mouth-watering palate, with red fruits, fine tannins and precisely calibrated French oak all contributing to its balance and length. Screwcap. 14% alc. **Rating** 96 **To** 2018 $65

Chardonnay 2011 Light yellow-green; an elegant wine with a savoury embellishment from its wild yeast barrel fermentation of cloudy juice; the complexity of the fore- and mid-palate smoothes out on the long, fine finish. Screwcap. 12.5% alc. **Rating** 94 **To** 2018 $35

Moppity Vineyards   ★★★★★

Moppity Road, Young, NSW 2594 (postal) **Region** Hilltops
T (02) 6382 6222 **www**.moppity.com.au **Open** Not
Winemaker Jason Brown **Est.** 1973 **Dozens** 30 000 **Vyds** 73ha

Jason Brown and wife Alecia, with backgrounds in fine wine retail and accounting, purchased Moppity Vineyards in 2004; it was then already 31 years old. Initially they were content to sell the grapes to other makers, but that changed with the release of the '06 Shiraz, which won top gold in its class at the London International Wine & Spirit Competition. In Nov '09 the '08 Eden Road Long Road Hilltops Shiraz, made from Moppity Vineyards grapes, won the Jimmy Watson Trophy. These awards are among a cascade of golds for its Shirazs, Riesling, Tumbarumba Chardonnay and Cabernet Sauvignon. The consequence has been that production (and sales) have soared, and all of the grapes from the estate are now used for the Moppity Vineyards brand. The Lock & Key range provides exceptional value for money. Exports to the UK and China.

Reserve Hilltops Shiraz 2010 The whole kit and caboodle of nouveau cool-climate Shiraz making; good hue; the texture first and foremost and structure are outstanding, the length remarkable, and there is a dazzling array of black cherry, spice and pepper fruit on the palate and finish. Screwcap. 13.5% alc. **Rating** 97 To 2030 $60

Single Vineyard Hilltops Riesling 2012 Pale, gleaming straw-green; a perfectly modulated and structured riesling, with exemplary purity of varietal expression, the dry finish refusing to make any compromise. Moppity's suggestion, that the wine style has similarity to that of Burklin-Wolf in Germany's Pfalz region, is totally justified. Screwcap. 12.5% alc. **Rating** 95 To 2030 $25

Museum Release Reserve Hilltops Shiraz 2006 The colour is still deep, likely helped by the 5% viognier, and the bouquet has developed some savoury/secondary aromas of spice, licorice and forest to accompany the black fruits. Five gold medals, including top gold at the International Wine & Spirit Competition (London). Screwcap. 15% alc. **Rating** 94 To 2026 $75

Hilltops Cabernet Sauvignon 2010 A last-minute decision was made to declassify this from the Reserve label, albeit for no particular reason that I can see. It has juicy cassis and redcurrant fruit, the oak and tannins with precise support, the finish long and balanced. Screwcap. 13.5% alc. **Rating** 94 To 2025 $25

Hilltops Merlot 2010 Rating 93 To 2025 $25

Lock & Key Single Vineyard Hilltops Riesling 2012 Bright green-quartz; this is a serious riesling, with spice, green apple, citrus and slatey acidity running the length of the structured, dry palate. Screwcap. 11% alc. **Rating** 91 To 2020 $15

Botrytis Semillon 2009 Rating 90 To 2014 $25

Morambro Creek Wines   ★★★☆

PMB 98, Naracoorte, SA 5271 (postal) **Region** Padthaway
T (08) 8765 6043 **www**.morambrocreek.com.au **Open** Not
Winemaker Ben Riggs **Est.** 1994 **Dozens** 30 000 **Vyds** 178.5ha

The Bryson family has been involved in agriculture for more than a century, moving to Padthaway in 1955 as farmers and graziers. Since the '90s, they have progressively established large plantings of shiraz (88.5ha), cabernet sauvignon (47.5ha), chardonnay (34.5ha) and sauvignon blanc (8ha). The Morambro Creek and Mt. Monster wines have been consistent winners of wine show medals. Exports to the UK, the US and other major markets.

Jip Jip Rocks Padthaway Sauvignon Blanc 2012 Light straw-green; slightly unexpectedly, a Sauvignon Blanc with strong and consistent varietal expression on the bouquet and a palate neatly positioned in the centre of the palette of aromas and flavours that the variety offers, with guava, stone fruit, citrus and a touch of ginger. Screwcap. 13.5% alc. **Rating** 93 To 2014 $20

Jip Jip Rocks Padthaway Shiraz Cabernet 2011 Rating 89 To 2019 $20

Jip Jip Rocks Padthaway Unoaked Chardonnay 2012 There are three regions that can produce interesting unwooded chardonnay: Tumbarumba, Tasmania and Padthaway. The splash of grapefruit in the melon base makes this wine as enjoyable as it is. Screwcap. 13.5% alc. **Rating** 88 To 2013 $10

Jip Jip Rocks Padthaway Shiraz 2011 Rating 88 To 2015 $20

Mt. Monster Shiraz 2011 Rating 88 To 2014 $16
Mt. Monster Cabernet 2011 Rating 88 To 2015 $16
Jip Jip Rocks Sparkling Shiraz NV Rating 88 To 2014 $20
Mt. Monster Sauvignon Blanc 2012 Rating 87 To 2014 $16

Morgan Simpson   ★★★★

PO Box 39, Kensington Park, SA 5068 **Region** McLaren Vale
T 0417 843 118 **www**.morgansimpson.com.au **Open** Not
Winemaker Richard Simpson **Est.** 1998 **Dozens** 1500 **Vyds** 22.7ha
Morgan Simpson was founded by SA businessman George Morgan (since retired) and
winemaker Richard Simpson, who is a graduate of CSU. The grapes are sourced from the
Clos Robert Vineyard (where the wine is made), planted to shiraz (10.8ha), cabernet sauvignon
(3.8ha), mourvedre (3.5ha), semillon and chardonnay (1.8ha each), and were established by
Robert Allen Simpson in 1972. Most of the grapes are sold, the remainder used to provide
the reasonably priced, drinkable wines for which Morgan Simpson has become well known.

ΨΨΨΨΨ **Two Clowns McLaren Vale Chardonnay 2011** In one sense follows the
✪   Morgan Simpson philosophy of 'not broke, don't fix' via the laid-back back labels
       and modest prices, but in another is far more up with the times than the two
       clowns might admit. Early picking and sensitive oak handling have produced
       a thoroughly modern style of bright, fresh Chardonnay. Screwcap. 12.9% alc.
       Rating 92 To 2015 $18

✪   **Plan B McLaren Vale Mataro 2010** The colour has developed a little more
       quickly than expected, but on the other hand, it has also developed considerable
       complexity, reflecting the variety (red fruits), the region (chocolate) and oak
       (which is not a correct read, for Morgan Simpson eschew more than a light
       touch). Screwcap. 15.7% alc. **Rating** 92 To 2018 $18

✪   **Row 42 McLaren Vale Cabernet Sauvignon 2011** Good colour for the
       vintage; there is abundantly ripe, small-berry fruit flavours, again meritorious in
       the context of the vintage. Drink over the next few years for maximum pleasure.
       Screwcap. 14.5% alc. **Rating** 90 To 2016 $18

ΨΨΨΨ Basket Press McLaren Vale Shiraz 2009 Rating 89 To 2017 $22

Morningside Vineyard   ★★★★

711 Middle Tea Tree Road, Tea Tree, Tas 7017 **Region** Southern Tasmania
T (03) 6268 1748 **www**.morningsidevineyard.com.au **Open** By appt
Winemaker Peter Bosworth **Est.** 1980 **Dozens** 700 **Vyds** 2.8ha
The name Morningside was given to the old property on which the vineyard stands because
it gets the morning sun first; the property on the other side of the valley was known as
Eveningside. Consistent with the observation of the early settlers, the Morningside grapes
achieve full maturity with good colour and varietal flavour. Production will increase as the
vineyard matures, and as recent additions of clonally selected pinot noir (including 8104, 115
and 777) come into bearing. The Bosworth family, headed by Peter and wife Brenda, do all
the vineyard and winery work, with conspicuous attention to detail.

ΨΨΨΨΨ **Riesling 2012** Pale quartz; the bouquet and palate are still tightly bound up
       (especially the bouquet); the intense minerally/rocky palate does have unsweetened
       lemon, lime and green apple flavours, and I'm not worried about its future.
       Screwcap. 11.5% alc. **Rating** 93 To 2025 $24

       Pinot Noir 2011 Full red-purple; a potent, dark-fruited, full-bodied (for pinot
       noir) wine with layers of plum and black cherry fruit and substantial tannins.
       Needs several years yet. Diam. 13.5% alc. **Rating** 92 To 2020 $35

       Cabernets 2010 The Coal River/Richmond area (which also houses Domaine A)
       is one of the most likely parts of Tasmania to successfully ripen the cabernet family,
       and this a prime example. While blackcurrant is the dominant contributor, the
       tannins are soft and ripe, the fruit likewise. Diam. 14% alc. **Rating** 91 To 2020 $28

ΨΨΨΨ Chardonnay 2011 Rating 88 To 2014 $25

Morris

Mia Mia Road, Rutherglen, Vic 3685 **Region** Rutherglen
T (02) 6026 7303 **www**.morriswines.com.au **Open** Mon–Sat 9–5, Sun 10–5
Winemaker David Morris **Est.** 1859 **Dozens** 100 000 **Vyds** 96ha
One of the greatest of the fortified winemakers, ranking with Chambers Rosewood. Morris has changed its labelling system for its sublime fortified wines, with a higher-than-average entry point with the (Classic) Liqueur Muscat; Tokay, and the ultra-premium wines are being released under the Old Premium Liqueur (Rare) label. The oldest components of the Old Premium are entered in a handful of shows, but the trophies and stratospheric gold medal points they receive are not claimed for the Old Premium wines. The art of these wines lies in the blending of very old and much younger material. They have no equivalent in any other part of the world.

 Old Premium Rare Liqueur Muscat NV Deep olive-brown; exceptionally rich and luscious, but – even more – complex, with a dense array of oriental sweet spices, dried raisins, and (for me) childhood memories of mother's Christmas pudding laced with brandy. And, yes, this really does go with dark, bitter chocolate in any form. 500ml. Cork. 17.5% alc. **Rating** 98 **To** 2013 $75
Old Premium Grand Rutherglen Muscat NV Deep olive brown; dense spice, plum pudding and raisin aromas; utterly exceptional intensity and length; altogether in another dimension; while based upon some very old wine, is as fresh as a daisy. Cork. 17.5% alc. **Rating** 97 **To** 2014 $150
Old Premium Liqueur Tokay NV Mahogany, with an olive rim; aromas of Christmas cake and tea; incredibly viscous and rich, with layer upon layer of flavours ranging through ginger snap, burnt butterscotch, and every imaginable spice, the length and depth of the palate is as extraordinary, as is that of the aftertaste. 500ml. Screwcap. 18% alc. **Rating** 96 **To** 2014 $75

Morrisons Riverview Winery ★★★☆

Lot 2 Meerol Lane, Moama, NSW 2731 **Region** Perricoota
T (03) 5480 0126 **www**.morrisons.net.au **Open** 7 days 10–5
Winemaker John Ellis, Jen Pfeiffer **Est.** 1996 **Dozens** 1500 **Vyds** 10ha
Alistair and Leslie Morrison purchased this historic piece of land in 1995. Plantings began in 1996 with shiraz and cabernet sauvignon, followed in '97 by sauvignon blanc, and frontignac in '98. The award-winning restaurant has views of the vineyard, billabong and river, and caters for weddings with guests often arriving by paddle steamer.

 Reserve Shiraz 2009 Medium red-purple; Morrisons believes this to be the best shiraz it had produced up to '09, and I think that is correct. I'm less sure about its cellaring capacity, for while the earthy/cedary/savoury characters are presently in balance with the red and black fruits, those fruit characters will diminish as the others grow. Screwcap. 14.5% alc. **Rating** 89 **To** 2016 $35
Pink Fronti 2012 Pale bright pink; barely spritzy, but is fresh and lively, with attractive grape and strawberry fruit, finishing with crisp acidity. Screwcap. 10% alc. **Rating** 88 **To** 2013 $21
Muscat NV Very luscious and good varietal character – inevitably still simple and grapey, but is well priced as an entry point wine with multiple uses. Cork. 18% alc. **Rating** 87 **To** 2014 $17

Mosquito Hill Wines ★★★★☆

18 Trinity Street, College Park, SA 5069 (postal) **Region** Southern Fleurieu
T 0448 802 950 **www**.mosquitohillwines.com.au **Open** Not
Winemaker Glyn Jamieson, Peter Leske **Est.** 2004 **Dozens** 1200 **Vyds** 4.2ha
This is the venture of Glyn Jamieson, who happens to be the prestigious Dorothy Mortlock Professor and Chairman of the Department of Surgery of the University of Adelaide. His interest in wine dates back for decades, and in 1994 he commenced the part-time (distance) degree at CSU and says that while he never failed an exam, it did take him 11 years to

complete the course. His year in France directed him to Burgundy, rather than Bordeaux, hence the planting of chardonnay, pinot blanc and savagnin on the slopes of Mt Jagged on the Magpies Song Vineyard and pinot noir (clones 114 and MV6) on the Hawthorns Vineyard. The last few years have been very difficult indeed for Glyn and his family as Elizabeth battled cancer. However, he has emerged from this, building a small onsite winery for the first vintage in 2011, assisted by Mike Waller from the highly rated Calera Vineyard in California. Glyn went to Calera for the '11 vintage, with a further exchange planned for '12, which the early vintage nipped in the bud. Exports to the US, China and Hong Kong.

Reserve Single Vineyard Chardonnay 2012 Barrel-fermented and matured in French barriques, 30% new. It combines full flavour and elegance, the fruit with nectarine, white peach and melon, the oak in a creamy/nutty spectrum. Screwcap. 13.3% alc. Rating 94 To 2018 $50

Single Vineyard Chardonnay 2011 Rating 91 To 2016 $25
Single Vineyard Pinot Noir 2009 Clear red, some development (as expected); this is the best balanced of the three vintages of Mosquito Hill Pinots tasted together; the tannins, while present, are fine and silky; there are no green characters; indeed, if anything, the reverse, with poached red cherry fruit. Screwcap. 12.5% alc. Rating 91 To 2015 $20
Single Vineyard Pinot Noir 2010 Rating 90 To 2016 $22

Moss Brothers   ★★★★★

3857 Caves Road, Wilyabrup, WA 6280 **Region** Margaret River
T (08) 9755 6270 **www.**mossbrothers.com.au **Open** 7 days 10–5
Winemaker Bernie Stanlake **Est.** 1984 **Dozens** 7000 **Vyds** 9.6ha
Patriarch Jeff Moss began his wine career in 1947, first with Mildara, then the Victorian Government, while simultaneously developing a 20ha vineyard, followed by a five-year stint with Seppelt. In 1978 he and his family moved to WA, where he became vineyard manager for Houghton, part of his job entailing the identification of worthwhile vineyards in the cooler south of the state. The family took its first step in 1984 when it purchased the Caves Road property, commencing planting the following year. With various children involved in differing roles over the years, Moss Brothers has grown, most significantly with the construction of a 400-tonne winery in '92, which processes both estate-grown and purchased grapes for the Moss Brothers label, and provides contract winemaking services. Exports to Germany and Singapore.

Moses Rock Estate 3857 Caves Road The Wilyabrup 2011 Bright, full crimson-purple; an estate-grown blend of cabernet sauvignon, cabernet franc and petit verdot, with only 146 dozen made. The blend is both synergistic and symbiotic, the marriage of red and blackcurrant fruit, cedary oak and fine tannins utterly seamless. Screwcap. 14.5% alc. Rating 96 To 2030 $70
Black Label Single Vineyard Margaret River Chardonnay 2011 A very elegant, very intense and focused Chardonnay, with grapefruit and white peach fruit supported by subtle French oak; the finish and lingering aftertaste are also particularly impressive. Screwcap. 13.5% alc. Rating 95 To 2020 $35
Single Vineyard Margaret River Chardonnay 2010 Bright straw-green; estate-grown chardonnay, pressed direct to French oak barrels and matured for 9 months; has a seductive mouthfeel to its array of white peach, nectarine and melon fruit, oak in its due place. Screwcap. 14.5% alc. Rating 94 To 2018 $30

Moses Rock Estate 3857 Caves Road Margaret River Cabernet Sauvignon 2011 Rating 93 To 2031 $35
Moses Rock Estate 3857 Caves Road Margaret River Cabernet Franc & Merlot 2011 Rating 92 To 2026 $50
Moses Rock Estate Cabernet Shiraz 2011 Rating 90 To 2020 $22

Moss Wood

926 Metricup Road, Wilyabrup, WA 6284 **Region** Margaret River
T (08) 9755 6266 **www**.mosswood.com.au **Open** By appt
Winemaker Clare and Keith Mugford **Est.** 1969 **Dozens** 14 000 **Vyds** 18.14ha
Widely regarded as one of the best wineries in the region, capable of producing glorious Semillon in both oaked and unoaked forms, unctuous Chardonnay and elegant, gently herbaceous, superfine Cabernet Sauvignon which lives for many years. In 2000 Moss Wood acquired the Ribbon Vale Estate; the Ribbon Vale wines are treated as vineyard-designated within the Moss Wood umbrella. A bold new move for this conservative, long-established winery, has been the introduction of a Mornington Peninsula Pinot Noir to complement the estate-grown Margaret River Pinot Noir. Exports to all major markets.

ŸŸŸŸŸ Margaret River Cabernet Sauvignon 2009 Positive red-purple colour; in the mainstream of Moss Wood style: supple, round and impeccably balanced, yet with regal cabernet expression. Small wonder that Moss Wood has one of the most loyal mail/email lists in Australia. Screwcap. 14.5% alc. **Rating** 95 **To** 2029 $90
Margaret River Chardonnay 2011 Mid gold; grapefruit, cashew and struck flint are evident on the bouquet; the palate is restrained with a fleshy mid-palate and a lingering tail of mealy texture to finish; a fine and understated wine in keeping with the estate. Screwcap. 14% alc. **Rating** 94 **To** 2018 $65 BE
Mornington Peninsula Pinot Noir 2010 Bright, deep purple-crimson; a supple and rich Pinot, with an evocative bouquet of satsuma plum and red cherry, then the palate adding some sour cherry to the mix; oak and tannins are in precise support, the finish long and satisfying. Screwcap. 14% alc. **Rating** 94 **To** 2019 $45
Ribbon Vale Vineyard Margaret River Merlot 2010 Medium purple-red; there is no question this has totally authentic varietal character, with cassis tempered by black olive flavours, the result taking you to the Right Bank of Bordeaux; the tannins, too, are serious, and underwrite the future development. Screwcap. 13.5% alc. **Rating** 94 **To** 2025 $50
Ribbon Vale Vineyard Margaret River Cabernet Sauvignon Merlot 2010 Slightly less bright colour, with more red; is very much the half-brother of the Merlot, with darker fruit flavours, yet with every bit as much breed; fruit, oak and tannins are all in tune. Screwcap. 13.5% alc. **Rating** 94 **To** 2030 $50

ŸŸŸŸŸ Amy's 2011 **Rating** 93 **To** 2020 $38 BE
Ribbon Vale Vineyard Margaret River Semillon Sauvignon Blanc 2012 **Rating** 90 **To** 2015 $34 BE

Motton Terraces

119 Purtons Road, North Motton, Tas 7315 **Region** Northern Tasmania
T (03) 6425 2317 **Open** Tues–Sun 10–5
Winemaker Flemming Aaberg **Est.** 1990 **Dozens** 140 **Vyds** 1.5ha
Another of the micro-vineyards, which seem to be a Tasmanian specialty; Flemming and Jenny Aaberg planted slightly less than 0.5ha of chardonnay and riesling in 1990, and now have 0.5ha each of chardonnay, riesling and tempranillo. The exercise in miniature is emphasised by the permanent canopy netting to ward off possums and birds.

ŸŸŸŸŸ Riesling 2011 Gleaming straw-green; an incisive wine made in the off-dry style
✪ of Mosel Valley Kabinetts, with residual sweetness balanced by crunchy acidity; indeed, the wine approaches Spatlese level. Served icy cold, it will be ideal with fresh fruit. But why the diam? 9.1% alc. **Rating** 91 **To** 2016 $15

Mount Alexander Winery

410 Harcourt Road, Sutton Grange, Vic 3448 **Region** Bendigo
T (03) 5474 2567 **www**.mawine.com.au **Open** W'ends & public hols 10–5, or by appt
Winemaker Bill Blamires **Est.** 2001 **Dozens** 2000 **Vyds** 7.4ha

Bill and Sandra Blamires acquired their property after a two-year search of the southern Bendigo area for what they considered an ideal location. They have firmly planted their faith in shiraz (5.9ha), with merlot, cabernet sauvignon, chardonnay and viognier contributing 1.5ha. The winery was previously called Blamires Butterfly Crossing (because of the butterfly population on Axe Creek, which runs through the property), but was changed due to confusion with Angove's Butterfly Ridge.

ΨΨΨΨΨ **Cabernet Shiraz 2010** Medium red-purple; a 75/25% blend with attractive,
❂   juicy blackcurrant and plum fruit, touches of spice, fine tannins and subtle oak.
           Good value, ready now. Screwcap. 13.6% alc. **Rating** 90 **To** 2016 $19

Mount Avoca   ★★★★★

Moates Lane, Avoca, Vic 3467 **Region** Pyrenees
T (03) 5465 3282 **www**.mountavoca.com **Open** 7 days 10–5
Winemaker William Talbot **Est.** 1970 **Dozens** 10 000 **Vyds** 23.72ha
A winery that has long been one of the stalwarts of the Pyrenees region, owned by Matthew and Lisa Barry. The estate vineyards (shiraz, sauvignon blanc, cabernet sauvignon, chardonnay, merlot, cabernet franc and semillon) are organically managed, and provide the total intake of the winery. Owing to a series of unfortunate circumstances, Mount Avoca was unable to submit their full range of wines for the *2014 Wine Companion*. Exports to China.

ΨΨΨΨΨ **Pyrenees Shiraz 2010** Bright crimson-purple of medium depth;
           co-fermentation with a small percentage of viognier has produced an aromatic red
           berry and spice bouquet and an elegant, medium-bodied palate with good tannin
           and oak support. Screwcap. 13% alc. **Rating** 94 **To** 2025 $30

ΨΨΨΨ   **Pyrenees Sauvignon Blanc 2012 Rating** 89 **To** 2014 $21

Mount Beckworth   ★★★☆

46 Fraser Street, Clunes, Vic 3370 **Region** Ballarat
T (03) 5343 4207 **www**.mountbeckworthwines.com.au **Open** W'ends 11–5, or by appt
Winemaker Paul Lesock **Est.** 1984 **Dozens** 800 **Vyds** 4ha
The Mount Beckworth vineyard was planted between 1984 and '85, but it was not until '95 that the full range of wines under the Mount Beckworth label appeared. Until that time much of the production was sold to Seppelt (Great Western) for sparkling wine use. It is owned and managed by Paul Lesock, who studied viticulture at CSU, and wife Jane. The wines usually reflect the very cool climate.

ΨΨΨΨΨ **Pinot Noir 2010** Has retained very good hue; there is full physiological ripeness
❂   to the black cherry and dark plum fruit, but no loss of the touch of spice expected
           from such a cool climate. Shows how well the wine can develop in bottle.
           Screwcap. 12.5% alc. **Rating** 92 **To** 2016 $20

ΨΨΨΨ   **Cabernet Merlot 2010** Surely the most challenging blend (here 70/30%) for
❂   the region, but worked as well as it is every likely to in this vintage, with gently
           ripe red berry/cassis fruits, fine tannins and good oak. Screwcap. 13.5% alc.
           Rating 89 **To** 2016 $18
           Shiraz 2010 Rating 87 **To** 2014 $20

Mt Bera Vineyards   ★★★

PO Box 372, Gumeracha, SA 5233 **Region** Adelaide Hills
T (08) 8389 2433 **www**.mtberavineyards.com.au **Open** Not
Winemaker Kersbrook Hill **Est.** 1997 **Dozens** 600 **Vyds** 11.5ha
In 2008 Greg and Katrina Horner (plus four kids and a growing collection of animals) purchased Mt Bera from Louise Warner. Greg and Katrina grew up on farms, and the 75ha property, with its homestead built in the 1880s, was irresistible. The property overlook the Torrens Valley. For the time being, at least, most of the production is sold, but the intention is to increase the range and quantity of wines available. Exports to the UK.

♥♥♥♥ **3.13 Adelaide Hills Pinot Noir 2009** Slightly hazy colour suggests the wine was not filtered; there are distinct stewed fruit flavours that are not unpleasant, but do not serve pinot noir well. Given the modest alcohol, I have no idea how these characters developed. Screwcap. 13.2% alc. **Rating** 87 **To** 2014 $29

Mt Billy ★★★★★

58 Waterport Road, Port Elliott, SA 5212 **Region** Southern Fleurieu
T 0416 227 100 **www.**mtbillywines.com.au **Open** 7 days 10–5
Winemaker Dan Standish, Peter Schell, John Edwards **Est.** 2000 **Dozens** 2000 **Vyds** 2.4ha
Having been an avid wine collector and consumer since 1973, John Edwards (a dentist) and wife Pauline purchased a 3.75ha property on the hills behind Victor Harbor, planting chardonnay and pinot meunier. There have been various viticultural peregrinations since that time, involving the progressive grafting of all of the original plantings so that the vineyard (named 'No Secrets') now comprises 0.7ha each of shiraz and tempranillo, the balance to petite syrah, sangiovese and viognier, from which both varietal and blended wines are made, with the active involvement of John Edwards. Exports to Japan and China.

♥♥♥♥♥ **Soliloquy Southern Fleurieu Syrah 2009** Deep purple-crimson; an imperiously complex and sculpted wine, with a multitude of spice/pepper/anise/ French oak nuances around the heart of the palate, where five clones of shiraz have come together synergistically. Screwcap. 14.5% alc. **Rating** 96 **To** 2025 $30
Willie John Shiraz 2007 Bright crimson-purple; a very complex and stylish shiraz, its 100% new French oak woven through and around the quite spicy black fruits, fine tannins likewise seamlessly integrated. All in all, a singular achievement from the '07 vintage. Diam. 13.8% alc. **Rating** 96 **To** 2022 $100
Antiquity Shiraz 2007 Deep crimson-purple; an ultra-powerful mouth-filling display of black fruits – blackberry, prune, plum – and licorice; despite all this, is not brutish, as the tannins are soft and ripe, oak integration good. Diam. 14.5% alc. **Rating** 95 **To** 2030 $50
No Secrets Southern Fleurieu Chardonnay 2007 Vivid green-straw; an attractive cool-grown Chardonnay, the bouquet and palate with plenty of citrus and stone fruit characters, but it is the persistent aftertaste that is so striking – and so good. Screwcap. 13.3% alc. **Rating** 94 **To** 2017 $25

 # Mt Buff Wines ★★★☆

220 Mt Buffalo Road, Porepunkah, Vic 3740 **Region** Various
T 0417 346 948 **www.**mtbuffwines.com.au **Open** Not
Winemaker Bruce Holmes, Mario Marsen **Est.** 2007 **Dozens** NFP **Vyds** 10.9ha
Neil and Margaret Mulcahy have established their vineyard at the base of Mt Buffalo, and are rhapsodic about the beauty of the surrounding countryside and the view they enjoy from the house and vineyard. Their successful garden supply business was the initial trigger, in no small measure because it took them to the Mt Buffalo area. They have two highly experienced winemakers (not onsite), Bruce Holmes having started his career in the early 1970s, and Mario Marsen as winemaker at Mount Mary in the Yarra Valley before moving to Central Victoria.

♥♥♥♥♡ **Durif 2008** Still inky-purple, and still with untold layers of sombre black fruits, licorice, polished leather and dark chocolate. I'm not sure it will ever be better than it is now (the tannins are ripe and balanced), but neither am I sure how many decades it will live for. Screwcap. 15% alc. **Rating** 93 **To** 2040 $23

♥♥♥♥ **Prosecco 2012 Rating** 88 **To** 2014 $20

Mount Cathedral Vineyards ★★★★★

125 Knafl Road, Taggerty, Vic 3714 **Region** Upper Goulburn
T 0409 354 069 **www.**mtcathedralvineyards.com **Open** By appt
Winemaker Oscar Rosa, Nick Arena **Est.** 1995 **Dozens** 900 **Vyds** 5ha
The Rosa and Arena families established Mount Cathedral Vineyards at an elevation of 300m on the north face of Mt Cathedral. The first plantings were of 1.2ha of merlot and 0.8ha of

chardonnay, followed by 2.5ha of cabernet sauvignon and 0.5ha of cabernet franc in 1996. No pesticides or systemic chemicals are used in the vineyard. Oscar Rosa, chief winemaker, has a Bachelor of Wine Science degree from CSU, and gained practical experience working at Yering Station in the late '90s.

🍷🍷🍷🍷🍷 Reserve Cabernet Sauvignon 2010 This has the most exhilarating depth and hue to the colour of all the '10 Mount Cathedral reds, and moves from medium- to full-bodied territory, so the intensity is even greater, cassis still king, but tar, bitter chocolate, star anise and cigar leaf are all in the shadows behind; the tannins are formidable, yet not abrasive. Cork. 13.8% alc. **Rating** 95 **To** 2040 $40

✪ Merlot 2010 Amazing colour; the palate tracks the colour, with black fruits to the fore, and substantial tannins also present. As much like petit verdot as merlot, the points are for courage. Screwcap. 13.8% alc. **Rating** 94 **To** 2030 $24

✪ Cabernet Sauvignon 2010 Deep crimson-purple; despite the intensity of the cassis fruit, the wine has the elegance only achieved with a medium-bodied palate, the finish with admirable cabernet tannins and perfectly judged French oak. Screwcap. 13.8% alc. **Rating** 94 **To** 2025 $24

🍷🍷🍷🍷 Cabernet Merlot 2010 **Rating** 92 **To** 2030 $24

Mount Charlie Winery ★★★★☆

228 Mount Charlie Road, Riddells Creek, Vic 3431 **Region** Macedon Ranges
T (03) 5428 6946 **www**.mountcharlie.com.au **Open** Fri–Sun 10–4, or by appt
Winemaker Trefor Morgan **Est.** 1991 **Dozens** 600 **Vyds** 3ha

Mount Charlie's wines are sold principally by mail order and through selected restaurants. A futures program encourages mailing-list sales, with a substantial discount on the eventual release price. Owner/winemaker Trefor Morgan is perhaps better known as Professor of Physiology at Melbourne University. The vineyard is planted to 0.5ha each of chardonnay, sauvignon blanc, tempranillo, merlot, malbec and shiraz.

🍷🍷🍷🍷🍷 Beatrix Elsie 2008 A 50/50% blend of pinot noir and chardonnay, open-fermented, followed by 18 months in French and American barrels, mercifully all used. The wine has considerable mousse and freshness. A tribute to Macedon. Crown seal. 11.8% alc. **Rating** 94 **To** 2015 $32

🍷🍷🍷🍷 Chardonnay 2011 **Rating** 90 **To** 2016 $20

Mount Cole Wineworks ★★★☆

6669 Western Highway, Buangor, Vic 3375 **Region** Grampians
T (03) 5352 2311 **www**.mountcolewineworks.com.au **Open** 7 days 10–5
Winemaker Dr Graeme Bertuch **Est.** 1998 **Dozens** 1000 **Vyds** 6.5ha

Dr Graeme Bertuch's involvement in grapegrowing and winemaking goes back far further than the establishment of Mount Cole Wineworks. In 1977 he established Cathcart Ridge, but found the time demands on a rural doctor-cum-vigneron were too much. He sold Cathcart Ridge in '93, but did not sell the itch to grow grapes and make wine. He now has 3.5ha of shiraz and 1ha of viognier, and in 2007 purchased the somewhat neglected and rundown Mt Chalambar Vineyard previously owned by the late Trevor Mast. Since that time there has been a systematic, albeit gradual, resurrection of the vineyard. Exports to China.

🍷🍷🍷🍷 Fenix Rising Reserve Shiraz 2010 Spicy oak aromas of cinnamon and clove are evident on the bouquet, shading the red fruit beneath; medium-bodied with gravelly tannins and finishing with a strong mocha note. Screwcap. 13.5% alc. **Rating** 87 **To** 2018 $35 BE

Mount Eyre Vineyards ★★★★

173 Gillards Road, Pokolbin, NSW 2321 **Region** Hunter Valley
T 0438 683 973 **www**.mounteyre.com **Open** At Garden Cellars, Hunter Valley Gardens
Winemaker Rhys Eather **Est.** 1970 **Dozens** 4000 **Vyds** 45.5ha

This is the venture of two families whose involvement in wine extends in an unbroken line back several centuries: the Tsironis family in the Peleponnese, Greece, and the Iannuzzi family in Vallo della Lucania, Italy. Their vineyards are at Broke (the largest), with a smaller vineyard at Pokolbin. The three principal varieties planted are chardonnay, shiraz and semillon, with small amounts of merlot, viognier, chambourcin, verdelho, negro amaro, and nero d'Avola. Exports to the Maldives, the Malaysia, China and Hong Kong.

 Three Ponds Hunter Valley Verdelho 2012 Vibrant colour; lime juice, nectarine and straw are evident on the bouquet, with zesty acidity and good concentration a feature on the dry chalky finish. Screwcap. 12% alc. **Rating** 90 **To** 2015 $20 BE

Three Ponds Hunter Valley Shiraz 2010 **Rating** 88 **To** 2017 $25 BE

Mount Gisborne Wines ★★★★

83 Waterson Road, Gisborne, Vic 3437 **Region** Macedon Ranges
T (03) 5428 2834 **www.**mountgisbornewines.com.au **Open** Wed–Sun 10–6
Winemaker David Ell, Stuart Anderson (Consultant) **Est.** 1985 **Dozens** 1300 **Vyds** 3ha
David and Mary Ell began the development of their vineyard on fractured granitic and volcanic soils in 1986. Planting of the pinot noir and chardonnay was completed in '90, but a small plot of clone 115 pinot noir has recently been added. Balgownie Estate founder Stuart Anderson moved to Macedon many years ago, and has added his immense knowledge to the crucible of learning on the job. The wines are made in the small winery on the property. Exports to Canada, Singapore and Malaysia.

Macedon Ranges Pinot Noir 2011 Light but bright crimson-purple; its fragrant cherry and plum bouquet does not indicate the power of the dark cherry palate, nor its attendant tannins; these need to relax their grip, and should do so, but will the fruit have diminished? Screwcap. 14% alc. **Rating** 90 **To** 2017 $40

Mount Horrocks ★★★★★

The Old Railway Station, Curling Street, Auburn, SA 5451 **Region** Clare Valley
T (08) 8849 2243 **www.**mounthorrocks.com **Open** W'ends & public hols 10–5
Winemaker Stephanie Toole **Est.** 1982 **Dozens** 4500 **Vyds** 9.4ha
Owner/winemaker Stephanie Toole has never deviated from the pursuit of excellence in the vineyard and winery. She has three vineyard sites in the Clare Valley, each managed using natural farming and organic practices. Stephanie has continuously built on the business since becoming sole owner in 1993, with the cellar door in the old, renovated, Auburn railway station. The attention to detail and refusal to cut corners is obvious in all of her wines. Exports to the UK, the US and other major markets.

Watervale Shiraz 2010 Medium crimson-purple; the complex bouquet has multi-spice and oak aromas, plum and blackberry to the fore, licorice, dark chocolate and earth to the back; plump tannins join the fleshy fruit of the medium-bodied palate. Screwcap. 13.5% alc. **Rating** 95 **To** 2030 $37
Watervale Riesling 2012 Light straw-green; there is a volume of lime zest and slatey/minerally acidity that guarantee its long-term future; drink it now if you will, but a minimum of 5 years is needed to even begin to show its true nature. Screwcap. 12.5% alc. **Rating** 94 **To** 2027 $29
Clare Valley Semillon 2011 As always, 100% barrel-fermented, the percentage of new oak kept to a minimum to gain texture, but not diminish the varietal aromas and flavours that range from lemon to orange zest, with just a touch of spice on the finish. Screwcap. 13% alc. **Rating** 94 **To** 2026 $28
Clare Valley Cabernet Sauvignon 2010 Mid purple-crimson; has both texture and flavour complexity, cassis, spice and earthy fruit cradled by French oak; the tannins are ripe and round, the finish long and very well balanced. Screwcap. 14% alc. **Rating** 94 **To** 2025 $37

Cordon Cut Clare Valley Riesling 2012 Full, glowing green-gold; Stephanie Toole has this technique down pat; this is extravagantly luscious and fruity, with just enough acidity for balance and to draw out the finish. 375ml. Screwcap. 11.5% alc. **Rating** 94 **To** 2016 $35

Mount Langi Ghiran Vineyards   ★★★★★

Warrak Road, Buangor, Vic 3375 **Region** Grampians
T (03) 5354 3207 **www**.langi.com.au **Open** Mon–Fri 9–5, w'ends 10–5
Winemaker Kate Petering **Est.** 1969 **Dozens** 60 000
A maker of outstanding cool-climate peppery Shiraz, crammed with flavour and vinosity, and very good Cabernet Sauvignon. The Shiraz points the way for cool-climate examples of the variety. The business was acquired by the Rathbone family group in 2002, and the marketing integrated with the Yering Station and Xanadu Estate wines, a synergistic mix with no overlap. Exports to all major markets.

⚷⚷⚷⚷⚷ Billi Billi Shiraz 2009 The bright, clear red-purple colour has not changed since first tasted a year ago, nor has the fragrant bouquet; has a warm spice and pepper introduction to the red and black cherry fruit of the perfectly balanced medium-bodied palate; the quality of the wine comes through on the lingering finish and aftertaste. So well balanced it can be drunk now although it will repay 10 years' cellaring, and live for another 10 thereafter. Screwcap. 14% alc. **Rating** 95 **To** 2029 $18
Cliff Edge Grampians Riesling 2011 The highly scented bouquet of lime, apple blossom and talc leads into a deliciously fresh and intense palate following precisely in the footsteps of the bouquet, the finish as clear and fresh as a spring day. Screwcap. 12% alc. **Rating** 94 **To** 2021 $25
Cliff Edge Grampians Pinot Gris 2011 The estate vines were planted in '94, making them some of the oldest in Australia, and the extra levels of intensity and complexity show in the wine, with its pear, apple and ginger flavours, the palate of considerable length. Screwcap. 11% alc. **Rating** 94 **To** 2015 $25
Nowhere Creek Vineyard Shiraz 2010 Bright, full crimson-purple; the wine exhibits intense red and black fruits, spice, pepper and licorice on its bouquet, and its long, well-balanced palate. Screwcap. 13.5% alc. **Rating** 94 **To** 2025 $30
Trevor Mast Tribute Grampians Shiraz 2005 Has retained very good hue; it is filled with spicy black cherry and plum fruit, with touches of licorice and quality oak, the tannins supple. Screwcap. 15% alc. **Rating** 94 **To** 2025 $34

⚷⚷⚷⚷⚷ Langi Grampians Shiraz 2011 **Rating** 92 **To** 2020 $100
Cliff Edge Grampians Cabernet Sauvignon 2007 **Rating** 90 **To** 2016 $30

Mt Lofty Ranges Vineyard   ★★★★★

Harris Road, Lenswood, SA 5240 **Region** Adelaide Hills
T (08) 8389 8339 **www**.mtloftyrangesvineyard.com.au **Open** Fri–Sun & public hols 11–5, or by appt
Winemaker Peter Leske, Taras Ochota **Est.** 1992 **Dozens** 2000 **Vyds** 4.6ha
Mt Lofty Ranges is owned and operated by Sharon Pearson and Garry Sweeney. Nestled high in the Lenswood subregion of the Adelaide Hills at an altitude of 500m, the very steep north-facing vineyard (pinot noir, sauvignon blanc, chardonnay and riesling) is hand-pruned and hand-picked. The soil is sandy clay loam with a rock base of white quartz and ironstone, and irrigation is kept to a minimum to allow the wines to display vintage characteristics.

⚷⚷⚷⚷⚷ Hand Picked Lenswood Riesling 2012 An intense and perfumed lime and apple blossom bouquet, and a long, beautifully focused and lingering palate. This is a beautiful wine. Screwcap. 12.5% alc. **Rating** 96 **To** 2025 $22
Lenswood Sauvignon Blanc 2012 Quartz-green; a vibrantly fresh and lively Sauvignon Blanc that balances citrus and grassy notes with tropical passionfruit and guava; all of this is achieved with a light but sure touch. Drink asap while all of this zesty display survives. Screwcap. 13.5% alc. **Rating** 94 **To** 2013 $20

🍷🍷🍷🍷🍷 Lenswood Chardonnay 2011 Rating 90 To 2017 $25
Methode Traditionelle Pinot Noir Chardonnay 2011 Rating 90 To 2015 $35

Mount Majura Vineyard ★★★★★

RMB 314 Majura Road, Majura, ACT 2609 (postal) **Region** Canberra District
T (02) 6262 3070 **www**.mountmajura.com.au **Open** Thurs–Mon 10–5
Winemaker Dr Frank van de Loo **Est.** 1988 **Dozens** 4000 **Vyds** 9.31ha
The first vines were planted in 1988 by Dinny Killen on a site on her family property that had been especially recommended by Dr Edgar Riek; its attractions were red soil of volcanic origin over limestone, with reasonably steep east and northeast slopes providing an element of frost protection. The tiny vineyard established in '88 has been significantly expanded since it was purchased in '99. The pre-existing blocks of pinot noir and chardonnay have been joined by pinot gris, shiraz, tempranillo, riesling, graciano, mondeuse, cabernet franc and touriga. In addition, there has been an active planting program for the pinot noir, introducing Dijon clones 114, 155 and 777. All the grapes used to come from these estate plantings. Made light of the '11 vintage with its red wines.

🍷🍷🍷🍷🍷 Canberra District Riesling 2012 This is a cleverly made wine; the 7g/l of residual sugar (deliberately retained) has given some respite from the laser line of acidity strung through the lime and grapefruit flavours. Screwcap. 10% alc. **Rating** 94 To 2025 $25
Canberra District Shiraz 2011 Bright, clear crimson-purple; attention to detail in the winery has paid dividends, with a complex array of black cherry/blackberry fruit, spices to burn, ripe tannins and good oak integration; the overall mouthfeel of the medium-bodied palate is excellent. Screwcap. 13.5% alc. **Rating** 94 To 2026 $32
Dinny's Block 2009 A vineyard (or field) blend of cabernet franc, merlot and cabernet sauvignon. The colour is light, although the hue is good, and the bouquet and palate are full of delicious redcurrant and cassis fruit, with no problems whatsoever with the tannins. Screwcap. 14% alc. **Rating** 94 To 2020 $25
Canberra District Tempranillo 2011 Excellent, bright purple-crimson; matured in older oak, 11% new. An excellent outcome, with cherry/cherry stone fruit, and firm but fine tannins; has the structure and balance to age well. Screwcap. 13% alc. **Rating** 94 To 2021 $40

🍷🍷🍷🍷🍷 Canberra District Chardonnay 2011 Rating 92 To 2017 $30
TSG Tempranillo Shiraz Graciano 2011 Rating 90 To 2020 $30
Canberra District Graciano 2010 Rating 90 To 2018 $25

Mount Mary ★★★★★

Coldstream West Road, Lilydale, Vic 3140 **Region** Yarra Valley
T (03) 9739 1761 **www**.mountmary.com.au **Open** Not
Winemaker Sam Middleton **Est.** 1971 **Dozens** 4500 **Vyds** 12ha
Superbly refined, elegant and intense Cabernets and usually outstanding and long-lived Pinot Noirs fully justify Mount Mary's exalted reputation. The Triolet blend is very good; more recent vintages of Chardonnay are even better. Founder and long-term winemaker, the late Dr John Middleton, was one of the great, and truly original, figures in the Australian wine industry. He liked nothing more than to tilt at windmills, and would do so with passion. His annual newsletter grew longer as each year passed, although the paper size did not. The only change necessary was a reduction in font size, and ultimately very strong light or a magnifying glass (or both) was needed to fully appreciate the barbed wit and incisive mind of this great character. The determination of the family to continue the business is simply wonderful. Exports to the UK, the US, Denmark, Hong Kong, Singapore, South Korea and China.

🍷🍷🍷🍷🍷 Yarra Valley Pinot Noir 2010 Beautiful limpid crimson; a fragrant, perfumed bouquet of red fruits leads into a glorious palate that effortlessly caresses the mouth with its display of red fruits in a silken web in no way dependent on oak, just the finest tannins. Diam. 13.4% alc. **Rating** 97 To 2020 $130

Yarra Valley Chardonnay 2011 Gleaming yellow-green; white peach, melon and a touch of fig coalesce with subtle barrel ferment oak on the long and harmonious palate. Diam. 13.3% alc. **Rating** 96 **To** 2020 $86

Yarra Valley Chardonnay 2010 Bright green-quartz; there isn't a hair out of place, yet this is in some ways a challenging wine with its grapefruit zest/grapefruit juice/white peach flavours anchored on its minerally acidity, oak merely a vehicle. Diam. 13.4% alc. **Rating** 95 **To** 2017 $86

Triolet 2011 Pale straw-green; a wine built on structure and flavour, and with elegance, not power; there are dried grass, herb and talc flavours, the oak not contributing flavour, just texture. It has always been a wine that gets slammed in blind tastings when young, and sometimes when old, but when things go right, it's a great example of the genre. Diam. 12.7% alc. **Rating** 94 **To** 2020 $86

Quintet 2011 A scented, perfumed red berry bouquet leads into a juicy palate with no green notes, just a touch of mint; it is long and evenly balanced, and will provide much pleasure over the next 5 or so years; thereafter is in the lap of the gods. Diam. 12.5% alc. **Rating** 94 **To** 2018 $127

Quintet 2010 A 47/30/14/5/4% blend of cabernet sauvignon, cabernet franc, petit verdot and malbec, its colour bright crimson-purple; yet another wine to turn back the alcohol hands of time, albeit in the best possible way, for its vibrant black and redcurrant fruit rolls out for a seeming eternity on the palate and lingering aftertaste. Diam. 12.7% alc. **Rating** 94 **To** 2025 $130

ŢŢŢŢŢ Triolet 2010 **Rating** 93 **To** 2020 $86
Reflexion Cabernet Blend 2009 **Rating** 93 **To** 2017 $45 TS
Yarra Valley Pinot Noir 2011 **Rating** 92 **To** 2018 $127
Reflexion Pinot Noir 2009 **Rating** 92 **To** 2015 $45 TS

Mount Stapylton Wines   ★★★★

14 Cleeve Court, Toorak, Vic 3142 (postal) **Region** Grampians
T 0425 713 044 **www**.mtsv.com.au **Open** Not
Winemaker Don McRae, Caroline Mooney **Est.** 2002 **Dozens** 560 **Vyds** 2.2ha
Mount Stapylton Vineyard is planted on the historic Goonwinnow Homestead farming property at Laharum on the northwest side of the Grampians in front of Mt Stapylton. In 2010 founders Howard and Samantha Staehr sold the homestead property, but leased back the vineyard. The Little Yarra Station Vineyard (1.2ha planted in 2009) in the Yarra Valley provides the grapes for the Samantha Chardonnay and the Sophia Pinot Noir. The wines are listed with several iconic restaurants in Sydney and Melbourne.

ŢŢŢŢŢ Samantha Yarra Valley Chardonnay 2012 Pale straw-green; a very tightly constructed Chardonnay with a minerally framework to the fine grapefruit pith and apple fruit, the oak already receding back into the wine; needs time for the fruit to open for business. Screwcap. 13.1% alc. **Rating** 92 **To** 2020 $40

Sophia Yarra Valley Pinot Noir 2012 Bright, but distinctly light crimson; it has a perfumed bouquet and light-bodied palate, with fresh red fruits to the fore. For those who enjoy light-bodied pinots. Screwcap. 12.9% alc. **Rating** 91 **To** 2017 $40

Shirley Grampians Shiraz 2011 Good colour and clarity; a light- to medium-bodied wine matured in a mix of French and American oak; it has bright, fresh red berry fruits and fine-grained tannins, the oak subtle. Particularly good outcome for the vintage. Screwcap. 13% alc. **Rating** 91 **To** 2020 $40

Mt Terrible   ★★★★★

289 Licola Road, Jamieson, Vic 3723 **Region** Central Victoria Zone
T (03) 5777 0703 **www**.mtterrible-pinot.com **Open** By appt
Winemaker Andy Browning, John Eason **Est.** 2001 **Dozens** 400 **Vyds** 2ha
John Eason and wife Janene Ridley began the long, slow (and at times very painful) business of establishing their vineyard in 1992, just north of Mt Terrible — hence the choice of name. The original plantings were trials, DIY home winemaking likewise, aided by an extensive library of how-to books. In 2001 they found the courage to plant 2ha of pinot noir (MV6, 115, 114 and

777 clones) on a gently sloping, north-facing river terrace adjacent to the Jamieson River. The DIY trials persuaded John to have the first commercial vintage in 2006 contract-made by Jane Donat, then Delatite winemaker. Construction has begun on an underground fireproof wine cellar, with a cellar door to be built above. The Central Victoria Zone is shown as the region, as the vineyard is 5km outside the boundary of the Upper Goulburn region. Exports to the UK.

 Jamieson Pinot Noir 2010 From four estate-grown clones (114, 115, 777 and MV6), cold-soaked (with 20% whole bunches) for 5 days before open fermentation, then 18 months in French oak. This is a serious Pinot Noir, the whole bunches contributing to but not dominating the texture and structure of the wine; bright red fruits merge into a gently savoury/foresty backdrop, tannins perfectly pitched. Screwcap. 14% alc. **Rating** 94 **To** 2018 $42

Mt Toolleen ★★★★★

Level 12, North Tower, 459 Collins Street, Melbourne, Vic 3000 (postal)
Region Barossa Valley/Heathcote
T (03) 9885 1367 **www**.mttoolleen.com.au **Open** Not
Winemaker Mark Jamieson (Contract) **Est.** 2000 **Dozens** 1500 **Vyds** 17.5ha
Mt Toolleen is owned by a group of Melbourne investors in a somewhat complicated joint venture scheme that gives Mt Toolleen access to 100ha of shiraz grown in Barossa Valley, and ownership of a 17.5ha vineyard in Heathcote. Exports to Canada, China, Taiwan, United Arab Emirates and Hong Kong.

 Limited Release Adelaide Hills Chardonnay 2010 Bright, clear quartz-green; whole bunch-pressed, wild-fermented in French barriques (50% new), then matured for 20 months in those barrels. A fine, elegant, tautly structured wine, with exceptional line, length and balance; has devoured the new oak. 550 dozen made. Screwcap. 13.5% alc. **Rating** 95 **To** 2020 $23

Mount Torrens Vineyards ★★★★★

PO Box 1679, Mt Torrens, SA 5244 **Region** Adelaide Hills
T 0418 822 509 **www**.solstice.com.au **Open** Not
Winemaker Torbreck (David Powell, Craig Isbel) **Est.** 1996 **Dozens** 1000
Mount Torrens Vineyards has 2.5ha of shiraz and viognier, and the distinguished team of Mark Whisson as viticulturist and David Powell as contract winemaker. The excellent wines are available by mail order and through selected retailers, but are chiefly exported to the UK, the US and other major markets. No wines received for the *2014 Wine Companion*, but a five-star rating has been maintained.

Mount Trio Vineyard ★★★★★

2534 Porongurup Road, Mount Barker WA 6324 **Region** Porongurup
T (08) 9853 1136 **www**.mounttriowines.com.au **Open** When sign is out or by appt
Winemaker Gavin Berry, Andrew Siddell **Est.** 1989 **Dozens** 4000 **Vyds** 8.8ha
Mount Trio was established by Gavin Berry and wife Gill Graham (plus partners) shortly after they moved to the Mount Barker area in late 1988, Gavin to take up the position of chief winemaker at Plantagenet, which he held until 2004 when he and partners acquired the now very successful and much larger West Cape Howe. They have slowly built up the business, increasing estate plantings with riesling (2.7ha), shiraz (2.4ha), sauvignon blanc (2ha) and pinot noir (1.7ha). Exports to the UK, Denmark and China.

 Riesling 2012 Pale straw-green; the complex bouquet sets the scene for the palate, where citrus and apple flavours grapple with crunchy acidity. Just when you think the acidity wins the argument, the lingering aftertaste reveals the fruit once more. Screwcap. 12% alc. **Rating** 94 **To** 2025 $20

Shiraz 2011 An impressive wine; with a peacock's tail display of black cherry, spice and licorice embraced by fine tannins. Will cellar well, but there's no reason not to drink it today. Screwcap. 14.5% alc. **Rating** 94 **To** 2021 $20

ŦŦŦŦŶ **Great Southern Sauvignon Blanc 2012** Light straw-green; has crystal-clear
✪ varietal expression on the bouquet and palate alike, primarily in the snow pea/
herbal end, but with distinct flashes of tropical fruit along the way; the finish is
crisp and bright. Screwcap. 12.8% alc. **Rating** 92 **To** 2014 $16

✪ **Great Southern Chardonnay 2012** Bright straw-green; partly barrel-
fermented, the remainder stainless steel, and bottled before the end of the year to
preserve as much as possible of the fresh white-flesh stone fruit flavours. Excellent
value. Screwcap. 13% alc. **Rating** 90 **To** 2015 $16

Mount View Estate ★★★★★

Mount View Road, Mount View, NSW 2325 **Region** Hunter Valley
T (02) 4990 3307 **www**.mtviewestate.com.au **Open** Mon–Sat 10–5, Sun 10–4
Winemaker Scott Stephens **Est.** 1971 **Dozens** 3000 **Vyds** 16ha
Mount View Estate's vineyard was planted by the very knowledgeable Harry Tulloch over
40 years ago – he recognised the quality of the red basalt volcanic soils of the very attractive
hillside vineyard. John and Polly Burgess became the owners of Mount View Estate (8ha) in
2000, and in '04 purchased the adjoining Limestone Creek Vineyard (8ha); planted in 1982,
it fits seamlessly into the Mount View Estate production.

ŦŦŦŦŦ **Reserve Museum Release Hunter Valley Semillon 2006** While the vivid
green hue might suggest mere infancy, the bouquet reveals developed toast and
ripe lemon aromas; the palate is lively and linear, with a long and fresh toasty
finish. Screwcap. 10.3% alc. **Rating** 94 **To** 2020 $45 BE
Reserve Hunter Valley Shiraz 2011 Vibrant purple hue; the elegant and highly
perfumed bouquet offers blue fruits, Asian spices and the mandatory fresh leather
of the region; the palate is fleshy and generous, medium-bodied in aspect and
laden with fine-grained tannins and refreshing acidity; there is a strong note of
toasty oak on the finish. Screwcap. 13.5% alc. **Rating** 94 **To** 2022 $35 BE

ŦŦŦŦŶ **Reserve Limestone Creek Vineyard Hunter Valley Cabernet Franc 2011**
Rating 92 **To** 2022 $35 BE
Reserve Hunter Valley Semillon 2012 Rating 90 **To** 2025 $25 BE

Mount William Winery ★★★★★

890 Mount William Road, Tantaraboo, Vic 3764 **Region** Macedon Ranges
T (03) 5429 1595 **www**.mtwilliamwinery.com.au **Open** W'ends 11–5, or by appt
Winemaker David Cowburn (Contract), Murray Cousins **Est.** 1985 **Dozens** 1500
Vyds 7.5ha
Adrienne and Murray Cousins purchased a 220ha grazing property in 1985; the sheep and
Angus cattle remain the principal part of the general farming program, but between '87 and
'99 they established pinot noir, chardonnay, cabernet franc and merlot. The quality of the
wines has been consistently good, and they are sold through a stone cellar door, as well as at
a number of fine wine retailers around Melbourne.

ŦŦŦŦŦ **Pinot Noir Chardonnay 2004** A 50/50% blend, disgorged Jun '12. A touch of
pale pink/blush to the colour; an excellent wine; fine, elegant, yet intense and long;
a harmonious, balanced finish. Diam. 12% alc. **Rating** 96 **To** 2016 $40
Jorja-Alexis Pinot Rose 2003 Bright pink; the lively, spicy red fruits of the
palate are as attractive as they were when first tasted in Aug '10 (also receiving 95
points); a supple, delicious finish. Diam. 13% alc. **Rating** 95 **To** 2016 $45
Louise Clare NV VII. A blend of shiraz and pinot noir, with a little cabernet
family. The colour is clear red; the palate is very good, with a wholly attractive
savoury/spicy blend surrounding the red fruit core; the finish is long and well
balanced. Diam. 14% alc. **Rating** 95 **To** 2016 $50
**Special Late Disgorged 10 Years on Lees Macedon Blanc de Blancs
2000** Estate-grown, the follow-on to the excellent '99. Pale bright green-straw;
a crisp lemon/citrus-accented bouquet and palate; low dosage has left the wine
bright, fresh and crisp. Diam. 12.5% alc. **Rating** 94 **To** 2015 $100

Mountadam

High Eden Road, Eden Valley, SA 5235 **Region** Eden Valley
T (08) 8564 1900 **www**.mountadam.com.au **Open** By appt
Winemaker Con Moshos **Est.** 1972 **Dozens** 35 000 **Vyds** 80ha
Founded by the late David Wynn for the benefit of winemaker son Adam, Mountadam
was (somewhat surprisingly) purchased by Cape Mentelle (doubtless under the direction of
Möet Hennessy Wine Estates) in 2000. Rather less surprising was its sale in '05 to Adelaide
businessman David Brown, who has extensive interests in the Padthaway region. Con Moshos
(long-serving senior winemaker at Petaluma) has had a significant impact on lifting the
quality of the wines. One should hope so, because Con eats (well, almost), drinks and sleeps
Mountadam. Exports to the UK, France, Switzerland, Poland and Hong Kong.

𝟅 **High Eden Estate Chardonnay 2011** Barrel-fermented in French barriques
(70% new) with full mlf – absolutely the right call, for the fruit has soaked up the
oak, and minerally acidity provides a firm frame for that fruit. A distinguished wine
with a very long future. Screwcap. 13% alc. **Rating** 96 **To** 2021 $35

𝟅 **Barossa Chardonnay 2012** Very pale straw-green; deliberately made without
any oak contact to throw all the attention on the fine fruit, with flavours of white-
flesh stone fruit and grapefruit/lemon; it has excellent length, but needs to build
complexity with time in bottle. Screwcap. 14.1% alc. **Rating** 93 **To** 2020 $18
Eden Valley Riesling 2012 Rating 91 **To** 2018 $25 BE

𝟆 **High Eden Pinot Chardonnay NV Rating** 88 **To** 2013 $28

Mountford

Bamess Road, West Pemberton, WA 6260 **Region** Pemberton
T (08) 9776 1345 **www**.mountfordwines.com.au **Open** 7 days 10–4
Winemaker Andrew Mountford, Saxon Mountford **Est.** 1987 **Dozens** 3000 **Vyds** 6ha
English-born and trained Andrew Mountford and wife Sue were early movers when selecting
Pemberton for their vineyard. The cool climate and spectacular forested countryside were
important considerations in the move. Their strikingly packaged wines are produced from
permanently netted, dry-grown vineyards (pinot noir, chardonnay, merlot, cabernet franc,
cabernet sauvignon and sauvignon blanc). Exports to the UK.

𝟅 **Reserve Pemberton Pinot Noir 2010** The organically grown product of the
vintage, with pea-sized berries, and all the right responses in the winery (including
the picking decision). It is a very complex wine, with black cherry and plum fruit,
multi-spice and ripe, but balanced, tannins. Diam. 13% alc. **Rating** 93 **To** 2022 $45

𝟆 **Pemberton Sauvignon Blanc 2012 Rating** 89 **To** 2014 $21

Mudgee Wines

Henry Lawson Drive, Mudgee, NSW 2850 **Region** Mudgee
T (02) 6372 2244 **www**.mudgeewines.com.au **Open** 7 days 10–5
Winemaker Simon McMillan **Est.** 1963 **Dozens** 8000 **Vyds** 18ha
Things are very different at Mudgee Wines these days under the ownership of Bill Whalley
and Jane McLean. The focus of the vineyard (and hence the wines) is on cabernet sauvignon,
shiraz, durif, negro amaro and primitivo (including 1ha each of old bushvine shiraz and of
cabernet sauvignon), the two white wines Pinot Gris and Chardonnay. Exports to Sweden,
Finland, Hong Kong and China.

𝟅 **Reserve Shiraz 2011** Medium red-purple; confident winemaking has produced
an attractive, fleshy, medium- to full-bodied wine replete with blackberry, black
cherry, licorice and warm earth flavours, with tannins and oak management in
support. Diam. 13.4% alc. **Rating** 94 **To** 2026 $30

𝟅 **Reserve Cabernet Sauvignon 2011 Rating** 93 **To** 2026 $30
Reserve Verdelho 2012 Rating 90 **To** 2015 $25

Kama Sutra Wines The Union of the Butterfly Shiraz NV **Rating** 90
To 2020 $20
Reserve Durif 2011 Rating 90 To 2020 $30

Murdoch Hill   ★★★★★

260 Mappinga Road, Woodside, SA 5244 **Region** Adelaide Hills
T (08) 8389 7081 **www**.murdochhill.com.au **Open** By appt
Winemaker Michael Downer **Est.** 1998 **Dozens** 3000 **Vyds** 20.48ha
A little over 20ha of vines were established on the undulating, gum-studded countryside of
Charlie and Julie Downer's 60-year-old Erinka property, 4km east of Oakbank. In descending
order of importance, the varieties planted are sauvignon blanc, shiraz, cabernet sauvignon and
chardonnay. Son Michael, with a Bachelor of Oenology degree from Adelaide University, is
winemaker. Exports to the UK and China.

🍷🍷🍷🍷🍷 The Landau Single Vineyard Oakbank Adelaide Hills Syrah 2012
Deep but bright purple-crimson; juicy black cherry, black plum, licorice and spices
flood the bouquet and medium- to full-bodied palate; the finish is long, balanced
and harmonious. Diam. 13% alc. **Rating** 95 To 2032 $46
Single Vineyard Adelaide Hills Chardonnay 2012 The gleaming yellow-
green colour heralds an elegant but intense bouquet and palate; it has excellent
length to its citrus and stone fruit flavours, the oak virtually subliminal. Screwcap.
12.5% alc. **Rating** 94 To 2020 $25

🍷🍷🍷🍷🍷 Adelaide Hills Sauvignon Blanc 2012 An attractive, pure, hand-picked
✪   sauvignon blanc with its seamless blend of grass, citrus and stone fruit aromas and
flavours making a fresh and lively palate and finish. Very well priced. Screwcap.
12.5% alc. **Rating** 92 To 2014 $20
The Phaeton Single Vineyard Pinot Noir 2012 Rating 92 To 2020 $42

Murray Street Vineyard   ★★★★★

Murray Street, Greenock, SA 5360 **Region** Barossa Valley
T (08) 8562 8373 **www**.murraystreet.com.au **Open** 7 days 10–6
Winemaker Andrew Seppelt **Est.** 2001 **Dozens** NFP **Vyds** 46ha
Andrew Seppelt has moved with a degree of caution in setting up Murray Street Vineyard,
possibly because of inherited wisdom and the business acumen of partner Bill Jahnke, a
successful investment banker with Wells Fargo. Andrew is a direct descendant of Benno and
Sophia Seppelt, who built Seppeltsfield and set the family company on its path to fame. The
partnership has two vineyards, one block at Gomersal, the other at Greenock, with the lion's
share planted to shiraz, followed by grenache, mourvedre, viognier, marsanne, semillon and
zinfandel. Unusually good point of sale/propaganda material. Exports to the UK, the US,
Canada, Denmark, Laos, Macau, Malaysia, Singapore and Hong Kong.

🍷🍷🍷🍷🍷 Benno 2010 A classic Barossa Valley Shiraz from a great vintage that effortlessly
carries its alcohol; the bouquet and palate have plum and blackberry fruit on a
cushion of integrated oak and tannins; a slightly savoury twist adds to the interest
and complexity of the wine. Screwcap. 15% alc. **Rating** 96 To 2040 $75
Sophia 2010 Deep, intense crimson-purple; blackberry fruit, spice, dark
chocolate and licorice lead into a deeply flavoured and structured palate; tannins
run through its length, but yield on the finish to a surge of juicy fruit; the oak is
integrated and balanced. Screwcap. 15% alc. **Rating** 96 To 2040 $75
Greenock 2010 Full, deep crimson-purple; ripe blackberry fruit on the bouquet
leads through to a generous full-bodied palate, with blackberry and a touch of
licorice supported by ripe tannins and good oak; overall line, length and balance
are impeccable. Shiraz. Screwcap. 15% alc. **Rating** 95 To 2035 $55
✪   **Black Label Barossa Shiraz 2010** Good red-purple; a prime example of a
great Barossa Valley vintage, the bouquet fragrant, the palate elegant and medium-
bodied, supple and filled to the brim with perfectly ripened black fruits. Excellent
value. Screwcap. 14% alc. **Rating** 95 To 2025 $25

Red Label Shiraz 2010 Good colour; it's pretty useful, with an array of spice, dark chocolate and black fruits on the bouquet and medium-bodied palate. Over-delivers on its price. Screwcap. 14.5% alc. **Rating** 94 **To** 2030 $35
Gomersal 2010 The colour is good, although not as bright as Benno; the bouquet is subtly different, the palate markedly so, with a touch of confit fruit set against an edge of acidity; this actually injects life into the palate, and is not sweet and sour. Shiraz. Screwcap. 15% alc. **Rating** 94 **To** 2030 $55

ŸŸŸŸŸ **Black Label Barossa Semillon 2012 Rating** 92 **To** 2025 $20
Black Label Barossa Grenache 2010 Rating 91 **To** 2018 $25
✪ **Black Label Barossa Viognier 2011** Pale, bright colour; it may not be particularly varietal, but has shape and life to its palate, avoiding the blah finish of so many young vine viogniers looking for the home they will never find. Screwcap. 13% alc. **Rating** 90 **To** 2015 $20

Murrindindi Vineyards

30 Cummins Lane, Murrindindi, Vic 3717 **Region** Upper Goulburn
T 0438 305 314 **www**.murrindindivineyards.com **Open** Not
Winemaker Hugh Cuthbertson **Est.** 1979 **Dozens** 5000 **Vyds** 16ha
This small winery is owned and run by the Cuthbertson family, established by Alan and Jan as a minor diversification from their cattle property. Plantings began in 1978, increasing in '82 and '95 to their present level. Son Hugh, himself with a long and high-profile wine career, has overseen the marketing of the wines, including the Family Reserve and Don't Tell Dad brands. Exports to the UK, the US, Finland, Estonia and China.

ŸŸŸŸŸ **Don't Tell Dad Yea Valley Riesling 2012** Pale straw-green; the Upper
✪ Goulburn climate is cool and strongly continental, with cold nights and warm days, making ideal conditions for riesling; this is a very well made wine with varietal fruit, acidity and a barest hint of residual sugar on the mid-palate and finish. Screwcap. 12.5% alc. **Rating** 91 **To** 2022 $20

Murrumbateman Winery ★★★☆

Cnr Barton Highway/McIntosh Road, Murrumbateman, NSW 2582
Region Canberra District
T (02) 6227 5584 **www**.murrumbateman-winery.com.au **Open** Thurs–Mon & public hols 10–5
Winemaker Mark Farrell **Est.** 1972 **Dozens** NA
Murrumbateman Winery draws upon upon 4.5ha of estate-grown sauvignon blanc, shiraz and cabernet sauvignon. It also incorporates an à la carte restaurant and function room, together with picnic and barbecue areas.

ŸŸŸŸŸ **Shiraz Rose 2011** Pale magenta; has above-average flavour, with an almost citrussy zest to the strawberry/red cherry flavours of the palate. Screwcap. 11% alc. **Rating** 91 **To** 2014 $25

ŸŸŸŸ **Sauvignon Blanc 2011 Rating** 89 **To** 2014 $20
Riesling 2012 Rating 88 **To** 2017 $30
Sauvignon Blanc 2012 Rating 87 **To** 2013 $20

Mylkappa Wines ★★★

Mylkappa Road, Birdwood, SA 5234 **Region** Adelaide Hills
T (08) 8568 5489 **www**.mylkappawines.com.au **Open** Not
Winemaker Kirrihill Wines (Donna Stephens) **Est.** 1998 **Dozens** 2100 **Vyds** 36.3ha
Having left the Adelaide Hills in 1988 with their three children, Patricia and Geoff Porter returned 10 years later to purchase an old dairy farm at Birdwood. Since then the entire family has worked tirelessly to progressively establish a large vineyard planted to chardonnay (7.5ha), sauvignon blanc (15.7ha), two clones of pinot noir (5.8ha) and pinot gris (5.8ha). Much of the grape production is sold to other Adelaide Hills makers.

♟♟♟♟ **Adelaide Hills Chardonnay 2012** Crisp acidity, and grapefruit citrus (along
✪   with stone fruit) make this an enjoyable lunch time, beach or other casual occasion
       Chardonnay at unbeatable value. Screwcap. 13.5% alc. **Rating** 89 **To** 2014 $10

✪   **Adelaide Hills Pinot Grigio 2012** Quartz-pink; has clear-cut varietal character,
       with nashi pear, citrus and apple all contributing to the fresh palate. Obvious value.
       Screwcap. 13% alc. **Rating** 88 **To** 2013 $10

       Adelaide Hills Sauvignon Blanc 2012 Estate-grown, and has no shortage of
       flavours, primarily in the tropical spectrum; however, the texture, structure and
       focus are all somewhat blurred. It's hard to be too critical, given the price of the
       wine. Screwcap. 13.5% alc. **Rating** 87 **To** 2013 $10

Myrtaceae

53 Main Creek Road, Main Ridge, Vic 3928 **Region** Mornington Peninsula
T (03) 5989 2045 www.myrtaceae.com.au **Open** W'ends & public hols 12–5, 7 days
27 Dec to end Jan
Winemaker Julie Trueman **Est.** 1985 **Dozens** 300 **Vyds** 1ha
Owners John Trueman (viticulturist) and wife Julie (winemaker) began the planting of
Myrtaceae in 1985, intending to make a Bordeaux-style red blend. It became evident that
these late-ripening varieties were not well suited to the site, so the vineyard was converted to
chardonnay (0.6ha) and pinot noir (0.4ha) in '98. Part of the property is devoted to the Land
for Wildlife Scheme; the integrated Australian garden is a particular feature.

♟♟♟♟♀ **Mornington Peninsula Pinot Noir 2010** Light, clear crimson-red; while
       unashamedly light-bodied, the ripe strawberry/cherry fruit flavours are in sharp
       contrast to those of the '11; it also has deceptive length, but is best consumed soon.
       Screwcap. 13.5% alc. **Rating** 90 **To** 2015 $40

♟♟♟♟ **Mornington Peninsula Chardonnay 2010** **Rating** 89 **To** 2016 $40

Naked Run Wines

36 Parawae Road, Salisbury Plain, SA 5109 (postal) **Region** Clare Valley/Barossa Valley
T 0408 807 655 www.nakedrunwines.com.au **Open** Not
Winemaker Steven Baraglia **Est.** 2005 **Dozens** 1200
Naked Run Wines is the virtual winery of Jayme Wood, Bradley Currie and Steven Baraglia,
their skills ranging from viticulture through to production, and also all-important sales and
marketing. The riesling is sourced from Clare Valley, grenache from the Williamstown area of
the Barossa Valley, and shiraz from Greenock. The price/quality ratio is utterly exceptional.

♟♟♟♟♟ **The First Clare Valley Riesling 2012** Pale quartz; the bouquet has a pleasing
✪   floral lift, but the intensity of the lime/lemon sherbet flavour of the palate catches
       you by surprise; the aftertaste refuses to go away; its has enough Clare Valley
       minerality in its make-up to age well. Screwcap. 12% alc. **Rating** 94 **To** 2022 $20

✪   **The First Clare Valley Riesling 2011** Light straw-green; gentle lime/apple
       blossom aromas lead into a juicy palate, the flavours fairly and squarely in the
       lemon/lime spectrum; the long finish is very well balanced. Screwcap. 12.5% alc.
       Rating 94 **To** 2021 $20

♟♟♟♟♀ **Nikala Barossa Valley Grenache Rose 2011** Pale pink, still bright; made from
✪   70-year-old dry-grown vines, picked solely for this wine. It has excellent, fresh red
       fruits and confection/nougat notes that all hang together well. Screwcap. 12.5% alc.
       Rating 93 **To** 2014 $18

✪   **Sweet Kiss Clare Valley Riesling 2012** The sweetness is at Kabinett level,
       infusing the lime juice/fruit with life and zest, yet balanced by crisp acidity. Will
       develop well, but unlikely to ever be more enjoyable than now. Screwcap. 10% alc.
       Rating 92 **To** 2016 $15

       The First Clare Valley Riesling 2006 **Rating** 91 **To** 2016 $30

✪ **The Aldo Old Vine Grenache Shiraz 2011** From 70-year-old vines; open-fermented, basket-pressed and matured in used French barriques; it has good texture and weight to its raspberry and blackberry fruit flavours. Screwcap. 15% alc. **Rating** 91 **To** 2019 $20

✪ **The Aldo Old Vine Grenache Shiraz 2010** The hue is good; there is a freshness and elegance to the cherry and raspberry fruit expression, the tannins and French oak making a minimal impact. Screwcap. 15% alc. **Rating** 90 **To** 2015 $20

Nannup Ridge Estate
★★★★★

PO Box 2, Nannup, WA 6275 **Region** Blackwood Valley
T (08) 9756 2005 **www.**nannupridge.com.au **Open** Not
Winemaker Naturaliste Vintners (Bruce Dukes), Andries Mostert **Est.** 1998
Dozens 3500 **Vyds** 31ha
The business is owned by the Blizard and Fitzgerald families, who purchased the then unplanted property from the family that had farmed it since the early 1900s. Mark and Alison Blizard had in fact moved to the region in the early '90s and established a small vineyard on the banks of the beautiful Donnelly River. The partners established 31ha of mainstream varieties (and 1ha of tempranillo) backed by a (then) grape sale agreement with Constellation. They still regard themselves as grapegrowers, but have highly successful wines skilfully contract-made from the estate production. Terrific value is par for the course. Exports to China.

🍷🍷🍷🍷🍷 **Cabernet Sauvignon 2010** Very strong purple-red; blackcurrant/cassis/bramble fruit flavours are perfectly balanced with French oak and firm, but fine, tannins. The wine has a vibrancy and freshness to its fruit that has increased over the past year. Screwcap. 14.1% alc. **Rating** 95 **To** 2025 $25

✪ **Chardonnay 2012** From an estate block of the distinguished Dijon clone 95, and the wine shows it. It has a particular flavour of white peach and pear, oak in the background, but not competing with the fruit expression, which lingers long after the wine is swallowed. Screwcap. 13.5% alc. **Rating** 94 **To** 2016 $19

🍷🍷🍷🍷🍷 **Sauvignon Blanc 2012** Estate-grown, the vines are 5 years old. Pale quartz-
✪ green; the fragrant bouquet foretells a palate with an unusual but attractive array of citrus, gooseberry and white stone fruit flavours, cleansing acidity lengthening the finish and aftertaste. Screwcap. 12.4% alc. **Rating** 93 **To** 2014 $17

✪ **Chardonnay 2011** Bright, light green-straw; grapefruit and apple aromas find traction on the long, well-balanced palate. Since first tasted in Dec '11 has gained significantly in the bottle, in both the intensity of flavour and the length of the palate. Made by Bruce Dukes, the best contract winemaker in Western Australia. Two silver medals don't do it justice. Screwcap. 12.5% alc. **Rating** 92 **To** 2019 $18
Cabernet Sauvignon 2011 Rating 90 **To** 2018 $25

Nardone Baker Wines
★★★☆

PO Box 386, McLaren Vale, SA 5171 **Region** McLaren Vale
T (08) 8445 8100 **www.**nardonebaker.com **Open** Not
Winemaker Brian Light **Est.** 1999 **Dozens** 70 000
Italian-born Joe Nardone and English-born John Baker were brought together by the marriage of Joe's daughter and John's son. Son Franco Nardone runs what is a significant virtual winery, sourcing grapes from all over SA. There are five ranges, headed by The Wara Manta Reserve, followed by Nardone Baker, Blaxland's Legacy, Treeview Selection and then Wara Manta (non-reserve). Exports to the UK, the US, Italy, Singapore, China and Japan.

🍷🍷🍷🍷🍷 **The Wara Manta Reserve McLaren Vale Shiraz 2011** Deep red-purple; earthy, bitter chocolate, espresso bean aromas and flavours are regional, particularly within the confines of the challenging vintage. Interesting price. Cork. 14.5% alc. **Rating** 91 **To** 2020 $78

Narkoojee ★★★★★

170 Francis Road, Glengarry, Vic 3854 **Region** Gippsland
T (03) 5192 4257 **www.**narkoojee.com **Open** 7 days 10.30–4.30
Winemaker Harry and Axel Friend **Est.** 1981 **Dozens** 5000 **Vyds** 10.3ha
Narkoojee Vineyard (originally a dairy farm owned by the Friend family) is near the old goldmining town of Walhalla and looks out over the Strzelecki Ranges. The wines are produced from a little over 10ha of estate vineyards, with chardonnay accounting for half the total. Former lecturer in civil engineering and extremely successful amateur winemaker Harry Friend changed horses in 1994 to take joint control, with Axel Friend, of the family vineyard and winery, and hasn't missed a beat since; their skills show through with all the wines, none more so than the Chardonnay. Exports to Canada, Japan and China.

ᵶᵶᵶᵶᵶ Reserve Gippsland Pinot Noir 2011 Very good colour, no excuses needed for the vintage; full of red and black cherry, plum and raspberry fruit; the medium-bodied palate is remarkably smooth and supple. Screwcap. 13.5% alc. **Rating** 94 To 2020 $34

ᵶᵶᵶᵶᵵ Four Generations Gippsland Merlot 2009 Rating 93 To 2029 $45
Gippsland Pinot Noir 2011 Rating 91 To 2018 $25
Reserve Maxwell Gippsland Cabernet Sauvignon 2009 Rating 91 To 2024 $34
Reserve Isaac Gippsland Shiraz 2010 Rating 90 To 2020 $34

Nashwauk ★★★★★

PO Box 852, Nuriootpa, SA 5355 **Region** McLaren Vale
T (08) 8562 4488 **www.**nashwaukvineyards.com.au **Open** Not
Winemaker Reid Bosward, Stephen Dew **Est.** 2005 **Dozens** 5000 **Vyds** 20ha
This is an estate-based venture, with 17ha of shiraz, 2ha of cabernet sauvignon and 1ha of tempranillo, all except the tempranillo between 13 and 40+ years old. It is a stand-alone business of the Kaesler family, and the first time it has extended beyond the Barossa Valley. The striking label comes from satellite photos of the vineyard, showing the contour planting; the name Nashwauk comes from Canada's Algonquin language, meaning 'land between'. Exports to the US, Singapore, Malaysia and China.

ᵶᵶᵶᵶᵶ Beacon McLaren Vale Shiraz 2009 It is difficult to imagine how more of anything could be put into a red wine, notably more alcohol – which makes its presence felt. Not my style, but you have to admire its panache. Cork. 15.5% alc. **Rating** 95 To 2039 $120
Wrecked McLaren Vale Shiraz 2009 Deep purple-crimson, it is plush and velvety to the point of outright thickness, with unctuous black fruits, oak and dark chocolate bolstered by ripe tannins. We will never know what might have been achieved with 14% alc. Cork. 15.5% alc. **Rating** 94 To 2034 $70
McLaren Vale Cabernet Sauvignon 2010 Deep purple-crimson; the medium- to full-bodied wine spent 18 months in French oak barriques. Black and redcurrant fruit dominate proceedings, albeit with the expected contribution of oak tannins. Impressive wine. Screwcap. 14.5% alc. **Rating** 94 To 2030 $25

ᵶᵶᵶᵶᵵ McLaren Vale Shiraz 2010 Rating 93 To 2030 $25
McLaren Vale Tempranillo 2010 Rating 92 To 2017 $25

Native Point Wines ★★★★☆

718 Windermere Road, Windermere, Tas 7252 **Region** Northern Tasmania
T (03) 6328 1628 **www.**nativepoint.com **Open** 7 days 8–5, or by appt
Winemaker Winemaking Tasmania **Est.** 1999 **Dozens** 1500 **Vyds** 5ha
The story of Tim and Sheena High's adventure might well have been written by Hans Christian Andersen, complete with happy ending. In 1993 they decided to establish a vineyard and start producing wine in Tasmania. What made that decision out of the ordinary was that they were living in Denmark at that time. Born in the UK, they had relocated to Melbourne

in '87 for Tim's work in the dairy industry, but drank more wine than milk. Tim's career took them to Chicago, London, Minneapolis, Amsterdam and Auckland for extended periods. But the seed had been sown, and Sheena, with a degree in biology, began a four-year distance education applied science degree course in winemaking through CSU. It was a chance visit to Launceston for a dairy conference that led to their ultimate '94 purchase of a 40ha cattle grazing property that had previously been an apple orchard. Tim has now retired from the dairy business, and the pair devote themselves to Native Point Wines.

ŶŶŶŶŶ **Pinot Noir 2011** Crimson-purple; '11 Tasmanian pinot noir is in a very different category from that of the mainland; the bouquet and palate are complex and deep, even if fruit-dominated; black cherry, plum and sage flavours are supported by ripe tannins and good oak. Screwcap. 13.7% alc. **Rating** 94 **To** 2021 $38

ŶŶŶŶŶ **Sauvignon Blanc 2012 Rating** 90 **To** 2014 $25

Neagles Rock Wines

Lot 51 Main North Road, Clare, SA 5453 **Region** Clare Valley
T 0407 391 109 www.neaglesrock.com **Open** Not
Winemaker Jane Willson and various consultants **Est.** 1997 **Dozens** 3000 **Vyds** 17ha
The Neagles Rock story started back in 1997, with a blank sheet of paper and plenty of vision. The name comes from the eponymous Neagles Rock, perched above the home vineyard and overlooking southwest Clare, which was named after pastoralist George Neagle. Founder Jane Willson has recently relaunched the business under a new structure: the label and concept remain unchanged, but new products supporting the Neagles Rock story have been created, with Georges of Clare and Harvest Selection labels recently added. Born and raised in Clare, Jane only pursues varieties that are tried and tested from the region, namely Riesling, Shiraz and Cabernet Sauvignon. Exports to the UK, Canada, The Netherlands, Belgium, Denmark and China.

ŶŶŶŶŶ **Georges of Clare King George 2010** A blend of cabernet sauvignon and shiraz matured in new French and American oak; it has excellent balance and depth, but the cassis/blackberry fruit, ripe tannins and oak needs time to settle down. Cork. 14.5% alc. **Rating** 95 **To** 2035 $50
Clare Valley Riesling 2012 Bright straw-green; plays to the strengths of the great riesling vintage in the Clare Valley, awash with juicy lime and lemon fruit from the start to the minerally/slatey finish; very good length and balance. Screwcap. 12.5% alc. **Rating** 94 **To** 2022 $22

ŶŶŶŶŶ **Georges of Clare Shiraz 2010** Spent 22 months in French and American oak,
✪ but is all about its finely pitched, juicy, spicy black and red fruits; no more than medium-bodied, but has very good balance, drive and length, and is a standout bargain. Screwcap. 14.5% alc. **Rating** 93 **To** 2025 $22
✪ **Clare Valley Riesling 2011** Displays the tight focus and crunchy minerality of the vintage to full advantage; lime/lemon/apple fruit fill out the mid-palate, and the wine will age well. Screwcap. 12.5% alc. **Rating** 92 **To** 2020 $20
✪ **Mr Duncan Clare Valley Shiraz Cabernet 2010** Good crimson hue; a well-balanced, medium-bodied wine with blackberry, blackcurrant and spice aromas and flavours, the tannins ripe and refined, enhancing the supple mouthfeel. Screwcap. 14.5% alc. **Rating** 90 **To** 2020 $21

Nepenthe

Jones Road, Balhannah, SA 5242 **Region** Adelaide Hills
T (08) 8398 8888 www.nepenthe.com.au **Open** 7 days 10–4
Winemaker Alex Trescowthick **Est.** 1994 **Dozens** 40 000 **Vyds** 108.68ha
Nepenthe quickly established its reputation as a producer of high-quality wines, but when founder Ed Tweddell died unexpectedly in 2006, the business was purchased by McGuigan Simeon the following year. The winery was closed in '09, and winemaking operations transferred to Australian Vintage, McGuigan Simeon's principal SA winery. (The Nepenthe winery has since been purchased by Peter Leske and Mark Kozned, and provides contract

winemaking services via their Revenir venture.) Nepenthe has over 100ha of close-planted vineyards spread over four vineyards in the Adelaide Hills, with an exotic array of varieties. Exports to the UK, the US and other major markets.

ŦŦŦŦŦ **Gate Block Adelaide Hills Shiraz 2010** Medium crimson-purple; the latent energy of the wine starts to reveal itself on the spicy, red berry bouquet, coming into full focus on the light- to medium-bodied palate, with its length and finish seemingly preordained. Screwcap. 14% alc. **Rating** 94 **To** 2025 $32
Adelaide Hills Shiraz 2010 Clear crimson-purple; has bright red fruit and spice on the bouquet, with a truly medium-bodied spicy red fruit palate; there is a splash of toasty oak on the finish, along with silky tannins. A compelling example of cool-grown shiraz. Screwcap. 14.5% alc. **Rating** 94 **To** 2020 $20

ŦŦŦŦŦ **Gate Block Adelaide Hills Shiraz 2011 Rating** 93 **To** 2020 $36 BE
Winemaker's Selection Zinfandel Rose 2012 Rating 91 **To** 2014 $25
Ithaca Adelaide Hills Chardonnay 2011 Rating 90 **To** 2015 $32
✪ **Adelaide Hills Pinot Noir 2011** Good depth to the colour, with plenty of purple hue; a surprise packet, with more depth and ripe plum and cherry fruit flavours at this price; it shortens stride on the finish and aftertaste, but time may allow it to stretch out more. Screwcap. 14% alc. **Rating** 90 **To** 2016 $20

Newbridge Wines   ★★★

18 Chelsea Street, Brighton, Vic 3186 (postal) **Region** Bendigo
T (03) 9591 0330 **www**.newbridgewines.com.au **Open** At Newbridge Hotel, Newbridge
Winemaker Mark Matthews, Andrew Simpson **Est.** 1996 **Dozens** 300 **Vyds** 1ha
The Newbridge property was purchased by Ian Simpson in 1979 partly for sentimental family history reasons, and partly because of the beauty of the property, which is situated on the banks of the Loddon River. It was not until '96 that he decided to plant shiraz, and up to and including the 2002 vintage the grapes were sold to several local wineries. He retained the grapes and made wine in '03, and Ian saw that and the following two vintages take shape before his death. The property is now run by his son Andrew; the wines are contract-made by Mark Matthews, with enthusiastic support from Andrew.

ŦŦŦŦ **Bendigo Shiraz 2010** Medium red-purple; an attractive light- to medium-bodied Shiraz with a gentle mix of red and black fruits spice, gentle tannins and subtle oak. Ready now or at any time over the next few years. Screwcap. 13% alc. **Rating** 89 **To** 2016 $25

Newtons Ridge Estate   ★★★★

1170 Cooriemungle Road, Timboon, Vic 3268 **Region** Geelong
T (03) 5598 7394 **www**.newtonsridgeestate.com.au **Open** 7 days 11–5 Oct–Apr, or by appt
Winemaker David Falk **Est.** 1998 **Dozens** 1400 **Vyds** 4ha
Ownership of Newtons Ridge Estate passed to David and Carla Falk in 2012. They have operated a real estate and livestock agency in southwest Vic since 1989, with this property 'just a couple of ridges away'. When they heard that founder David Newton had become ill and was contemplating pulling out the vines, they were able to purchase the vineyard, completing a circle that began in the 1880s when Carla's family were among the first vignerons in Geelong; they produce wine in Switzerland to this day.

ŦŦŦŦŦ **Summer Wine Rose 2012** Pale pink; a fragrant bouquet and bright, juicy palate
✪ with strawberry fruit, distinctly citrussy acidity, and a long, dry finish. Very well made. Screwcap. 13.5% alc. **Rating** 91 **To** 2014 $20
Sauvignon Blanc 2012 Pale straw-green; a touch of smoke (or possibly reduction) on the bouquet and palate is not unpleasant, simply part of a sauvignon blanc with attitude, plus tropical, citrus and herb aromas and flavours. Screwcap. 13.2% alc. **Rating** 90 **To** 2014 $20

ŦŦŦŦ **Pinot Grigio 2012 Rating** 88 **To** 2014 $20

Ngeringa

119 Williams Road, Mount Barker, SA 5251 **Region** Adelaide Hills
T (08) 8398 2867 **www**.ngeringa.com **Open** Fri–Sun & public hols 11–5
Winemaker Erinn Klein **Est.** 2001 **Dozens** 2500 **Vyds** 5ha
Erinn and Janet Klein say, 'As fervent practitioners of biodynamic wine growing, we respect biodynamics as a sensitivity to the rhythms of nature, the health of the soil and the connection between plant, animal and cosmos. It is a pragmatic solution to farming without the use of chemicals.' It is not an easy solution, and the Kleins have increased the immensity of the challenge by using ultra-close vine spacing of 1.5m × 1m, necessitating a large amount of hand-training of the vines plus a tiny crawler tractor. They teamed up while studying at Adelaide University in 2000 (Erinn – oenology, Janet – viticulture/wine marketing), and then spent time looking at the great viticultural regions of the Old World, with a particular emphasis on biodynamics. Exports to the UK, the US, Canada, Austria, Sweden, Japan, Taiwan and China.

ΨΨΨΨΨ **Adelaide Hills Sangiovese 2010** Clear varietal expression of red cherries, warm spices and a hint of sour cherry, the tannins superfine but lengthening the finish. Delicious wine. Screwcap. 13.5% alc. **Rating** 94 **To** 2016 $35

ΨΨΨΨΨ **Adelaide Hills Tempranillo 2010** **Rating** 93 **To** 2016 $35
Adelaide Hills Pinot Noir 2010 **Rating** 91 **To** 2015 $35

Nicholson River

57 Liddells Road, Nicholson, Vic 3882 **Region** Gippsland
T (03) 5156 8241 **www**.nicholsonriverwinery.com.au **Open** 7 days 10–5 during hols, or by appt
Winemaker Ken Eckersley **Est.** 1978 **Dozens** 500 **Vyds** 8ha
Nicholson River's fierce commitment to quality in the face of the temperamental Gippsland climate and frustratingly small production has been handsomely repaid by some massive Chardonnays and impressive red wines (from estate plantings). Ken Eckersley refers to his Chardonnays not as white wines but as gold wines, and lists them accordingly in his newsletter.

ΨΨΨΨΨ **Chardonnay 2010** The first Nicholson River Chardonnays, made over 20 years ago, were spectacularly opulent; this is a more restrained wine, but the family resemblance is still there with complex mouth-filling peach, fig and cream flavours. Screwcap. 13.5% alc. **Rating** 92 **To** 2016 $45
Pinot Noir 2010 A potent, savoury style that retains a core of pinot varietal character via its cherry/sour cherry/plum fruit. Has commendable length and overall balance. Screwcap. 12.6% alc. **Rating** 90 **To** 2015 $32

Nick O'Leary Wines

129 Donnelly Lane, Bungendore, NSW 2621 **Region** Canberra District
T (02) 6161 8739 **www**.nickolearywines.com.au **Open** By appt
Winemaker Nick O'Leary **Est.** 2007 **Dozens** 3250
At the ripe old age of 28, Nick O'Leary had been involved in the wine industry for over a decade, working variously in retail, wholesale, viticulture and winemaking. Two years earlier he had laid the foundation for Nick O'Leary Wines, purchasing shiraz from local vignerons (commencing in 2006) and riesling (from '08). His wines have had extraordinarily consistent success in local wine shows and competitions since the first vintages.

ΨΨΨΨΨ **Riesling 2011** Pale, bright straw-green; the highly fragrant and floral bouquet leads into a pulsating, vibrant palate with lime, lemon and Granny Smith apple flavours; I enjoy the acidity that is part and parcel of many '11 Rieslings. Screwcap. 11.8% alc. **Rating** 95 **To** 2026 $25
Shiraz 2011 Positive crimson colour; there is no question this wine should be enjoyed before the Bolaro is approached; there are juicy plum and cherry flavours nestling comfortably on a bed of fine tannins. Screwcap. 13.5% alc. **Rating** 94 **To** 2021 $28

ŸŸŸŸ♀ Bolaro Shiraz 2011 Rating 93 To 2030 $58
         Shiraz 2010 Rating 93 To 2020 $28

Night Harvest   ★★★★★

PO Box 569, Dunsborough, WA 6280 **Region** Margaret River
T (08) 9756 7813 **www**.greenpiper.com.au **Open** Not
Winemaker Contract **Est.** 2005 **Dozens** 40 000 **Vyds** 300ha
This is the rags-to-riches story of Andy and Mandy Ferreira, who arrived in Margaret River in
1986 as newly married young migrants. They soon became involved in the construction and
establishment of the new vineyards of that time. Their vineyard-contracting business expanded
quickly when the region experienced rapid growth in the late '90s; they were involved in the
establishment of about 300ha of Margaret River vineyards, many of which they continue to
manage today. As their fortunes grew, they purchased their own property and produced their
first wines in 2005. Harvesting is a key part of their business, and currently they run seven
self-propelled harvesters and are responsible for harvesting the fruit from over 100 different
sites in the southwest. Hence the Night Harvest brand was born. Butler Crest was added as a
premium label. Exports to the UK, Thailand, Hong Kong and China.

ŸŸŸŸŸ **John George Reserve Margaret River Cabernet Sauvignon 2010**
         Estate-grown; a barrel selection made after 18 months in French oak; an intense,
         medium-bodied wine with exceptional length, the tannins and oak perfectly
         judged for the future of the wine. Needs time, but is certain to repay it. Cork.
         13.2% alc. **Rating** 96 **To** 2035 $35
         Butler Crest Margaret River Chardonnay 2011 Light straw-green; an
         elegant, fragrant chardonnay, picked at perfect ripeness to maximise its display of
         nectarine, white peach and grapefruit flavours unchallenged by oak. Screwcap.
         13.7% alc. **Rating** 94 **To** 2018 $30
         John George Reserve Margaret River Cabernet Sauvignon 2011
         Medium to full purple-red; here the medium-bodied array of cassis/blackcurrant
         and redcurrant is backed by fine tannins, and the cedary oak, while obvious, is well
         balanced and integrated. Screwcap. 14.3% alc. **Rating** 94 **To** 2026 $35

ŸŸŸŸ♀ **Butler Crest Margaret River Shiraz 2010** Rating 93 To 2025 $39
         Butler Crest Margaret River Shiraz 2011 Rating 91 To 2026 $37
         Reserve Margaret River Chardonnay 2011 Rating 90 To 2016 $21

ŸŸŸŸ   **Margaret River Semillon Sauvignon Blanc 2012** Light straw-green; a fresh,
✪   lively and crisp SSB that draws upon the grass/lemongrass of the semillon and
         the gently tropical notes of the sauvignon blanc. User-friendly over the next 18
         months. Screwcap. 12.7% alc. **Rating** 89 **To** 2014 $16

Nillahcootie Estate   ★★★

3630 Midland Highway, Lima South, Vic 3673 **Region** Upper Goulburn
T (03) 5768 2685 **www**.nillahcootieestate.com.au **Open** Mon–Thurs by appt, Fri 12–4,
Sat 11–11, Sun 12–5
Winemaker Kilchurn Wines (David Cowburn), Victor Nash **Est.** 1988 **Dozens** 1200
Karen Davy and Michael White decided to diversify their primary business of beef cattle
production on their 280ha property in 1988. Between then and 2001 they planted a little
over 8ha of grapes, initially content to sell the production to other local wineries; in '01 they
retained a small proportion of the grapes for winemaking, increasing it the following year to
its current level. In '01 they also purchased a 20ha property overlooking Lake Nillahcootie,
on which they have built a strikingly designed restaurant and cellar door.

ŸŸŸŸ   **Shiraz 2010** Everything about the wine points to its very cool region; the colour,
         the perfume, and the light to medium body. All this should have triggered the
         delicate use of oak, but more than necessary was employed. Whether this will
         disappoint those who taste it is an open question. Screwcap. 13.8% alc. **Rating** 89
         To 2020 $32

Merlot 2010 Light red-purple; the perfumed bouquet promises more than the light-bodied palate can deliver, the problem being the lack of texture/structure. Hard to know what more could be done, but the '05 puts the case that nothing more needs to be done. Screwcap. 13.4% alc. **Rating** 88 **To** 2016 $32

Merlot 2005 Good retention of hue; a fascinating riposte to the '10, and my commentary on it, for this '05 is also light-bodied, and is still very much present; a low pH may be a saving grace for a wine that has some of the character of Loire Valley cabernet franc. Screwcap. 13.5% alc. **Rating** 88 **To** 2014 $36

Nillumbik Estate

PO Box 24, Smiths Gully, Vic 3760 **Region** Yarra Valley
T (03) 9710 1773 **www**.nillumbikestate.com.au **Open** Not
Winemaker John Tregambe **Est.** 2001 **Dozens** 1250 **Vyds** 1.6ha
In establishing Nillumbik Estate, John and Chanmali Tregambe had the multi-generational winemaking experience of John's parents, Italian immigrants who arrived in Australia in the 1950s. The estate plantings of pinot noir are supplemented by cabernet sauvignon, chardonnay, shiraz and nebbiolo purchased variously from Sunbury, Heathcote and the King Valley.

Boomers Block Yarra Valley Shiraz 2009 Deep crimson colour, the bouquet showing almost syrup-like concentration of blackberry; the palate follows suit, and while pushing the boundaries of ripeness, the structure brings freshness to the finish. Screwcap. 14% alc. **Rating** 87 **To** 2016 $25 BE

Nine Fingers

PO Box 212, Lobethal, SA 5241 **Region** Adelaide Hills
T (08) 8389 6049 **Open** By appt
Winemaker Contract **Est.** 1999 **Dozens** 200 **Vyds** 1ha
Simon and Penny Cox established their sauvignon blanc vineyard after encouragement from local winemaker Robb Cootes of Leland Estate. They obviously have a sense of humour, which may not be shared by their youngest daughter Olivia. In 2002, 2-year-old Olivia's efforts to point out bunches that needed to be thinned resulted in Penny's secateurs cutting off the end of Olivia's finger. A race to hospital and successful microsurgery resulted in the full restoration of the finger; strangely, Olivia has shown little interest in viticulture since. Exports to Singapore.

Adelaide Hills Sauvignon Blanc 2012 Light straw-green; crisp, vibrant and juicy, with a delicious combination of citrus and passionfruit on a perfectly balanced palate. Great value. Screwcap. 12.4% alc. **Rating** 93 **To** 2014 $19

919 Wines

39 Hodges Road, Berri, SA 5343 **Region** Riverland
T (08) 8582 4436 **www**.919wines.com.au **Open** Wed–Sun & public hols 10–5
Winemaker Eric and Jenny Semmler **Est.** 2002 **Dozens** 3000 **Vyds** 17ha
Eric and Jenny Semmler have a special interest in fortified wines. Eric previously made fortified wines for Hardys at Berri Estates, and worked at Brown Brothers. Jenny has worked for Strathbogie Vineyards, Pennyweight Wines, St Huberts and Constellation. They have planted micro-quantities of varieties specifically for fortified wines. Notwithstanding their Riverland GI, they use minimal water application, deliberately reducing the crop levels, practising organic and biodynamic techniques. In 2011 they purchased the 12.3ha property at Loxton they now call 809 Vineyard. The 919 vineyard is certified biodynamic; the 809 vineyard is biodynamic (in conversion) with full certification anticipated in 2013.

Classic Topaque NV Relatively deep walnut-olive colour; a powerful and concentrated topaque with all the right ingredients; its viscosity suggests it is on the cusp of the grand classification, but also points to the potential of even more cask age. 500ml. Screwcap. 19% alc. **Rating** 91 **To** 2014 $39

Petit Manseng 2012 Has a distinct straw tinge, possibly from skin contact or oak (or both); the fore- and mid-palate also have some creamy notes before citrussy acidity comes through on the finish. Well worth seeking out. Screwcap. 13.5% alc. **Rating** 90 **To** 2014 $25

Vermentino 2012 One of the strengths of vermentino is its positive structure and texture, resting as it does on grainy acidity, the stone fruit, citrus pith and zest a counterpoint. Different from, but as interesting as, the Petit Manseng. Screwcap. 14% alc. **Rating** 90 **To** 2014 $25

🍷🍷🍷🍷 **Shiraz 2011 Rating** 89 **To** 2015 $40
Classic Tawny NV Rating 89 **To** 2014 $29

90 Mile Wines ★★★★

Main Goolwa Road, Middleton, SA 5213 **Region** Currency Creek
T 0430 313 548 **www**.90milewines.com **Open** Thurs–Sun 1–4
Winemaker Contract **Est.** 2009 **Dozens** 4500
This is the venture of corporate refugee Steve Ramsey, and Martin Kay, who has a long track record in marketing and sales roles in some of Australia's best-known wineries. In 2009 they opened their cellar door at the popular holiday destination of Middleton on the Fleurieu Peninsula. It is a virtual wine operation with neither winery nor vineyards of its own, simply wisdom. And, by the way, they happen to be stepfather and son respectively.

🍷🍷🍷🍷🍷 **Destination McLaren Vale Shiraz 2010** Deep purple-crimson; the bitter, dark chocolate bellwether of McLaren Vale leaps out of the glass on the bouquet and palate alike. The full-bodied palate adds black fruits and licorice in abundance, yet retains excellent balance and mouthfeel. A seriously good wine. Screwcap. 14.5% alc. **Rating** 94 **To** 2025 $40

🍷🍷🍷🍷 **Currency Creek Shiraz 2010 Rating** 89 **To** 2015 $20

Nintingbool ★★★★

56 Wongerer Lane, Smythes Creek, Vic 3351 (postal) **Region** Ballarat
T (03) 5342 4393 **www**.nintingbool.com **Open** Not
Winemaker Peter Bothe **Est.** 1998 **Dozens** 350 **Vyds** 2ha
Peter and Jill Bothe purchased the Nintingbool property in 1982 and built the home in which they now live in '84, using bluestone dating back to the goldrush period. They established an extensive Australian native garden and home orchard, but in '98 diversified with the planting of pinot noir, a further planting the following year lifting the total to 2ha. This is one of the coolest mainland regions, and demands absolute attention to detail (and a warm growing season) for success.

🍷🍷🍷🍷🍷 **Ballarat Pinot Noir 2010** Has embarked on a slow journey to maturity, having started to loosen its muscular palate; a remarkable wine in the context of Ballarat, with layers of dark fruits. Venison or wild boar will suit it admirably, as will further cellaring to continue its upward path since first tasted Dec '11. Screwcap. 13.7% alc. **Rating** 93 **To** 2020 $33

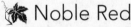 Noble Red ★★★★★

18 Brennan Avenue, Upper Beaconsfield, Vic 3808 (postal) **Region** Heathcote
T 0400 594 440 **www**.nobleredwines.com **Open** Not
Winemaker Adrian Munari **Est.** 2002 **Dozens** 300 **Vyds** 6ha
Noble Red is the venture of Roman and Margaret Sobiesiak, who acquired their property in 2002. There was 0.25ha of shiraz planted in the 1970s, and a progressive planting program has seen an increase to 6ha, shiraz (3.6ha) accounting for the lion's share, the remainder more or less equally split between tempranillo, mourvedre, merlot and cabernet sauvignon. Roman and Margaret deliberately adopted a dry-grown approach, which has meant slow

development during the prolonged drought, but their commitment remains undimmed. Visiting wine regions around the world and working within the industry locally has increased their determination, and they have been appropriately rewarded with the 2011 Shiraz.

🍷🍷🍷🍷🍷 Heathcote Shiraz 2011 Good colour for the vintage; an altogether impressive Shiraz from this unusually troubled vintage; it is medium-bodied, and full of energy and zest from the spice and licorice overtones to the black cherry and blackberry fruit; the fine but persistent tannins on the finish are particularly meritorious. Screwcap. 14% alc. **Rating** 94 **To** 2026 $28

Nocton Park

373 Colebrook Road, Richmond, Tas 7025 **Region** Southern Tasmania
T 0418 645 807 **www**.noctonpark.com.au **Open** By appt
Winemaker Winemaking Tasmania (Julian Alcorso) **Est.** 1998 **Dozens** 10000 **Vyds** 34ha
Prior to the 2010 vintage, Nocton Park emerged from two years' administration following the financial demise of its founders. Jerry Adler and viticulturist Richard Meyman now run the business, the 100ha property planted to pinot noir, chardonnay, merlot and sauvignon blanc. The site was originally earmarked by Peter Althaus of Domaine A (see separate entry), who, back in 1995, described it as the best vineyard land in the Coal River Valley. Exports to China.

🍷🍷🍷🍷🍷 Botrytis Semillon Chardonnay Sauvignon Blanc 2011 Massively sweet, but does have Tasmanian acidity to provide balance; the developed colour says this wine should be enjoyed asap. Screwcap. 8.6% alc. **Rating** 91 **To** 2013 $25

🍷🍷🍷🍷 Coal River Valley Merlot 2010 **Rating** 87 **To** 2014 $25

Noon Winery

Rifle Range Road, McLaren Vale, SA 5171 **Region** McLaren Vale
T (08) 8323 8290 **www**.noonwinery.com.au **Open** W'ends 10–5 in November (while stock is available)
Winemaker Drew Noon **Est.** 1976 **Dozens** 2200 **Vyds** 6ha
Drew and wife Raegan Noon returned to McLaren Vale and purchased Noon's from Drew's parents in 1996. Drew had previously spent many years as a consultant oenologist and viticulturist in Vic, and thereafter for a time as winemaker at Cassegrain. His rich red wines have a loyal following, and are eagerly snapped up by customers on the annual mailing list. Exports to the UK, the US, and other major markets.

🍷🍷🍷🍷🍷 Reserve Shiraz 2010 True to Noon, this is an unashamedly full-bodied Shiraz, putting forward impressive depth of glossy satsuma plums, blackberries, sarsaparilla, liquorice and mixed spice of considerable persistence. It finishes with fine, dusty tannins and warming alcohol. Cork. 14.7% alc. **Rating** 94 **To** 2017 $27 TS

🍷🍷🍷🍷 Eclipse 2010 **Rating** 93 **To** 2016 $27 TS

Norfolk Rise Vineyard

Limestone Coast Road, Mount Benson, SA 5265 **Region** Mount Benson
T (08) 8768 5080 **www**.norfolkrise.com.au **Open** Not
Winemaker Daniel Berrigan **Est.** 2000 **Dozens** 8000 **Vyds** 130.3ha
This is by far the largest and most important development in the Mount Benson region. It is ultimately owned by a privately held Belgian company, G & C Kreglinger, established in 1797. In early 2002 Kreglinger acquired Pipers Brook Vineyard; it will maintain the separate brands of the two ventures. The Mount Benson development commenced in '00, with a large vineyard and a 2000-tonne winery, primarily aimed at the export market. The business is moving away from the export of bulk wine to bottled wine, with significantly better returns to the winery. Exports to Europe and Asia.

🍷🍷🍷🍷🍷 **Sauvignon Blanc 2012** A mysterious label depicting a mountain range at home
✪　　　in NZ, not the basically flat Norfolk Rise vineyard and surrounds; however, the
wine is the glass is pleasing, vibrant and focused, with a mix of cut grass, snow pea
and passionfruit, the acidity bright and cleansing. Gold medal Melbourne Wine
Show '12. Screwcap. 12.5% alc. **Rating** 93 **To** 2014 $16

✪　　　**Merlot 2010** A fresh, bright and juicy Merlot, with redcurrant fruit to the fore
on a supple, medium-bodied palate, tannins appearing on the finish in convincing
manner. Bargain. Screwcap. 14% alc. **Rating** 93 **To** 2020 $16

🍷🍷🍷🍷 **Pinot Grigio 2012** Has the faintest touch of pink; it is crisp and lively, with
✪　　　ample depth to the pear and apple fruit. A sign of the times that it should be line-
priced with the red wines. Screwcap. 12.5% alc. **Rating** 89 **To** 2013 $16

✪　　　**Cabernet Sauvignon 2010** Estate-grown; given cold-soak maceration prior
to initiation of fermentation, thereafter spending 16 months in French oak; it has
attractive cassis fruit, but also the varietal tendency to back off on the mid-palate
before tannins return on the finish. Screwcap. 14% alc. **Rating** 89 **To** 2018 $16

Norton Estate

758 Plush Hannans Road, Lower Norton, Vic 3401 **Region** Western Victoria Zone
T (03) 5384 8235 **www**.nortonestate.com.au **Open** Fri–Sun 11–4, or by appt
Winemaker Best's Wines **Est.** 1997 **Dozens** 1300 **Vyds** 4.66ha
In 1996 the Spence family purchased a rundown farm at Lower Norton and, rather than farm
the traditional wool, meat and wheat, trusted their instincts and planted vines on the elevated,
frost-free, buckshot rises. The vineyard is halfway between the Grampians and Mt Arapiles,
6km northwest of the Grampians region, and will have to be content with the Western
Victoria Zone, but the wines show regional Grampians character and style. A traditional
Wimmera ripple-iron barn has been converted into a cellar door. Norton Estate decided to
sell all of its 2011 wine as cleanskins, and the '12 wines will not be bottled prior to publication.
However, the '10s are still available through the cellar door and wholesale.

🍷🍷🍷🍷🍷 **Wendy's Dedication Shiraz 2010** Dedicated to Wendy Spence, Norton's
founder, who picked the grapes, but died before the wine was bottled. It is full-
bodied, with great depth and will be a living reminder of her role for another two
decades. Screwcap. 14.5% alc. **Rating** 95 **To** 2030 $100

Arapiles Run Shiraz 2010 A complex, well-structured and -balanced wine, with
black fruits, spice and tannins running through the very long palate; seemingly
more oak than in the varietal. Screwcap. 14.2% alc. **Rating** 94 **To** 2025 $37

🍷🍷🍷🍷 **Shiraz 2010 Rating** 89 **To** 2020 $23
Sauvignon Blanc 2010 Rating 88 **To** 2011 $18

Nova Vita Wines

GPO Box 1352, Adelaide, SA 5001 **Region** Adelaide Hills
T (08) 8356 0454 **www**.novavitawines.com.au **Open** Not
Winemaker Peter Leske, Taras Ochota, Mark Kozned **Est.** 2005 **Dozens** 14000 **Vyds** 46ha
Mark and Jo Kozned did months of painstaking research before locating the property on which
they have now established their 30ha Woodlands Ridge Vineyard, planted to chardonnay,
sauvignon blanc, pinot gris and shiraz. They have subsequently established the Tunnel Hill
Vineyard near Forreston, with 16ha of pinot noir, shiraz, cabernet sauvignon, sauvignon blanc,
semillon, verdelho, merlot and sangiovese. The name Nova Vita reflects the beginning of the
Kozneds' new life, the firebird on the label coming from their Russian ancestry. It is a Russian
myth that only a happy or lucky person may see the bird or hear its song. The Kozneds have
joined forces with Peter Leske to form Revenir, a contract winemaking business that has
purchased the former Nepenthe winery, and is where the Nova Vita wines are made. Exports
to Malaysia, Singapore and China.

🍷🍷🍷🍷🍷 **Firebird Adelaide Hills Chardonnay 2011** Vibrant pale straw; a restrained and elegant bouquet of grapefruit, hazelnut, fennel and citrus blossom; the palate is linear and racy, with dry, chalky acidity providing a refreshing and textural conclusion. Screwcap. 12.5% alc. **Rating** 92 **To** 2018 $30 BE

Firebird Adelaide Hills Pinot Gris 2012 A fragrant bouquet of pear, anise and bath talc; the palate is lively, fresh, dry and chalky, finishing with a lingering fresh note in harmony with the fruit. Screwcap. 13% alc. **Rating** 90 **To** 2015 $20 BE

Nugan Estate ★★★★★

Kidman Way, Wilbriggie, NSW 2680 **Region** Riverina
T (02) 9362 9993 **www**.nuganestate.com.au **Open** Mon–Fri 9–5
Winemaker Daren Owers **Est.** 1999 **Dozens** 500 000 **Vyds** 491ha

Nugan Estate arrived on the scene like a whirlwind. It is an offshoot of the Nugan Group headed by Michelle Nugan (until her retirement in Feb '13), inter alia the recipient of an Export Hero Award in '00. In the mid 1990s the company began developing vineyards, and it is now a veritable giant, with five vineyards: Cookoothama (335ha), Manuka Grove (46ha) in the Riverina, Frasca's Lane (100ha) in the King Valley and McLaren Parish (10ha) in McLaren Vale. In addition, it has contracts in place to buy 1000 tonnes of grapes per year from Coonawarra. It sells part of the production as grapes, part as bulk wine and part under the Cookoothama and Nugan Estate labels. The wine business is now in the energetic hands of Matthew and Tiffany Nugan, Michelle's children. Exports to the UK, the US and other major markets.

🍷🍷🍷🍷🍷 **McLaren Parish Vineyard McLaren Vale Shiraz 2010** Strong purple-crimson; a medium- to full-bodied Shiraz in the mainstream of McLaren Vale style; 16 months in new and used French and American oak has given some mocha, and there is regional chocolate, these two inputs coming on top of fully ripe, plummy fruitcake flavours. Screwcap. 15% alc. **Rating** 93 **To** 2020 $23

✪ **Frasca's Lane King Valley Chardonnay 2010** Pale straw-green, exceptional given that the wine was fermented in and then spent 15 months in new and used French oak. No less surprising is the fresh display of nectarine, white peach and melon fruit. Screwcap. 13.5% alc. **Rating** 92 **To** 2017 $20

Alcira Vineyard Coonawarra Cabernet Sauvignon 2009 Cassis and mulberry fruit has a juicy mid-palate before fine tannins provide structure on the finish; the oak is surprisingly well balanced and integrated. Screwcap. 14% alc. **Rating** 92 **To** 2020 $23

✪ **Frasca's Lane King Valley Sauvignon Blanc 2012** Estate-grown, the bouquet offers predominantly tropical fruits that swell on the fruit-sweet palate, packed with pineapple, kiwifruit and ripe citrus flavours; has good length and aftertaste. Screwcap. 12.5% alc. **Rating** 91 **To** 2013 $20

✪ **Frasca's Lane King Valley Pinot Grigio 2011** While the wine is at the upper end of the price scale for Pinot Grigio, it has more complexity on the bouquet and palate than most, with a ripe display of honeysuckle, citrus and pear, the finish artfully balanced. Screwcap. 13% alc. **Rating** 90 **To** 2013 $20

🍷🍷🍷🍷 **Frasca's Lane Pinot Grigio 2012** **Rating** 89 **To** 2014 $20

River Road Vineyard Merlot 2007 **Rating** 89 **To** 2016 $23

✪ **Talinga Park Sauvignon Blanc 2012** This is a bargain, expressing clear varietal character throughout, in a thoroughly welcoming fashion; tropical fruits are followed by a deliberate touch of sweetness on the finish. Screwcap. 12% alc. **Rating** 88 **To** 2013 $10

Cookoothama Darlington Point Shiraz 2010 **Rating** 88 **To** 2015 $15

Cookoothama Darlington Point Chardonnay 2010 **Rating** 87 **To** 2012 $15

Nursery Ridge Estate

8514 Calder Highway, Red Cliffs, Vic 3496 **Region** Murray Darling
T (03) 5024 3311 **www**.nrewines.com.au **Open** Thurs–Sun, school & public hols 10–4.30
Winemaker Bob Shields **Est.** 1999 **Dozens** 3500 **Vyds** 60.8ha

The estate takes its name from the fact that the first vineyard was situated on the site of the original vine nursery at Red Cliffs. The holdings have since been expanded to plantings on three additional vineyards: Wilga Road, Cottrell's Hill Road and Calder. It is owned by four partners, the vineyards planted to shiraz, cabernet sauvignon, chardonnay, petit verdot, pinot noir, ruby cabernet and viognier. The well-priced wines are usually well made, with greater richness and depth of fruit flavour than most other wines from the region.

♀♀♀♀ **Cassia Shiraz 2012** Good colour; a well-made wine, picked while still retaining good acidity; the flavours of the medium-bodied palate straddle red and black berry fruits backed by good tannins and evident oak. Screwcap. 13% alc. **Rating** 89 **To** 2017 $18
Coorong Petit Verdot 2012 Medium to full red-purple; petit verdot, as ever, manages to produce wines with plenty of flavour even in high-yielding Riverland surroundings; here mocha/vanilla oak also adds to the flavour parcel. Screwcap. 15% alc. **Rating** 87 **To** 2015 $18

O'Leary Walker Wines   ★★★★★
Main Road, Leasingham, SA 5452 **Region** Clare Valley
T (08) 8843 0022 www.olearywalkerwines.com **Open** Mon–Sat 10–4, Sun 11–4
Winemaker David O'Leary, Nick Walker, Keeda Zilm **Est.** 2001 **Dozens** 19000 **Vyds** 35ha
David O'Leary and Nick Walker together had more than 30 years' experience as winemakers working for some of the biggest Australian wine groups when they backed themselves to establish their own brand. Initially the focus was on the Clare Valley, with 10ha of riesling, shiraz, cabernet sauvignon and semillon the main plantings; thereafter attention swung to the Adelaide Hills, where they now have 25ha of chardonnay, cabernet sauvignon, pinot noir, shiraz, sauvignon blanc and merlot. Exports to the UK, Ireland and Asia.

♀♀♀♀♀ **Polish Hill River Riesling 2012** Light straw-green; the wine has an extra
✪ degree of character courtesy of its lime juice and slate counterpoint, which comes through on the bouquet and palate alike; the length of flavour and lingering aftertaste are prodigious. Screwcap. 12.5% alc. **Rating** 95 **To** 2022 $22
Watervale Riesling 2012 Bright straw-green; the bouquet is classic Watervale, with lime and lemon blossom, the palate following on precisely, its length built on perfectly balanced fruit and acidity, the finish pure and bright. Died in the wool stayer. Screwcap. 12.5% alc. **Rating** 94 **To** 2022 $20

♀♀♀♀♀ **Adelaide Hills Sauvignon Blanc 2012** Bright straw-green; a stylish wine, with
✪ more structure and texture than the vast majority of Sauvignon Blancs at this price; the aromas and flavours encompass tropical fruits (passionfruit to the fore) ranging through to more grassy characters; crisp acidity on the finish ties it all in a neat parcel. Screwcap. 12% alc. **Rating** 93 **To** 2013 $18

Oak Valley Estate   ★★★
3055 Deakin Avenue, Sturt Highway, Mildura South, Vic 3502 **Region** Murray Darling
T (03) 5021 2379 www.oakvalleyestate.com.au **Open** 7 days 10–5
Winemaker Ferdinando DeBlasio **Est.** 2000 **Dozens** 1000 **Vyds** 10ha
Ferdinando DeBlasio left Italy bound for Australia when he was 13 years old, with both grandfather and father having made wine for home consumption every year. In 1963 he purchased a 20ha paddock on Oak Avenue (near Mildura airport) with 4ha of established vines. With the help of wife Joanne the plantings were slowly expanded, and completed by '72. Oak Valley Estate has 10ha of vineyards supplying the onsite winery.

♀♀♀♀ **Fiano 2011** A small omission of the vintage on the label, and inclusion of a
bronze medal at the Riverland Wine Show '12 may not do full justice to fiano in general, or to this wine in particular, with its attractive grainy pear and white peach fruit. Screwcap. 12.5% alc. **Rating** 88 **To** 2014 $16

Sweet Nellie Late Harvest Moscato 2010 A schizophrenic wine. On the one hand it is called Moscato, on the other it's a high-quality dessert wine that will develop beautifully with bottle age. So how do I assess it? I'll go with the dessert style. Screwcap. 11.5% alc. **Rating** 88 **To** 2014 $20

The Pink Contessa 2012 Pale pink; with its tinned strawberry taste and crisp finish, does the trick. Screwcap. 8% alc. **Rating** 87 **To** 2013 $15

Oakdene ★★★★★

255 Grubb Road, Wallington, Vic 3221 **Region** Geelong
T (03) 5256 3886 **www**.oakdene.com.au **Open** Sun–Tues 10–4
Winemaker Ray Nadeson, Robin Brockett **Est.** 2001 **Dozens** 5000 **Vyds** 11ha
Bernard and Elizabeth Hooley purchased Oakdene in 2001. Bernard focused on planting the vineyard (shiraz, pinot gris, sauvignon blanc, pinot noir, chardonnay, merlot, cabernet franc and cabernet sauvignon), while Elizabeth worked to restore the 1920s homestead. Ray Nadeson makes Chardonnay, Pinot Noir and Shiraz; Robin Brockett makes the Sauvignon Blanc. Much of the wine is sold through the award-winning Oakdene Restaurant and cellar door.

♟♟♟♟♟ **Jessica Single Vineyard Bellarine Peninsula Sauvignon 2012**
Barrel-fermented in French oak (20% new) and kept in that oak for 8 months' maturation. It works well, because the fruit was (and remains) intense, with grapefruit, passionfruit and citrus all in play on the very long and intense palate. Will develop well. Screwcap. 13% alc. **Rating** 95 **To** 2017 $28

♟♟♟♟♟ **Yvette Pinot Noir Chardonnay 2010 Rating** 93 **To** 2015 $35
Bellarine Peninsula Riesling 2012 Rating 92 **To** 2020 $23
✪ **Single Vineyard Sauvignon Blanc 2012** Bright, light straw-green; the passionfruit and lychee bouquet is followed by a fresh and juicy palate, bringing some additional stone fruit into play. A Sauvignon Blanc for all seasons. Screwcap. 13% alc. **Rating** 92 **To** 2014 $21
Single Vineyard Pinot Grigio 2012 Rating 91 **To** 2014 $23
Bellarine Peninsula Pinot Noir 2011 Rating 91 **To** 2016 $24

Oakridge Wines ★★★★★

864 Maroondah Highway, Coldstream, Vic 3770 **Region** Yarra Valley
T (03) 9738 9900 **www**.oakridgewines.com.au **Open** 7 days 10–5
Winemaker David Bicknell **Est.** 1978 **Dozens** 23000 **Vyds** 9.8ha
Winemaker and CEO David Bicknell has proved his worth time and again as an extremely talented winemaker. At the top of the brand tier is 864, all Yarra Valley vineyard selections, and only released in the best years (Chardonnay, Shiraz, Cabernet Sauvignon, Riesling); next is the Oakridge core label (the Chardonnay, Pinot Noir and Sauvignon Blanc come from the cooler Upper Yarra Valley, the Shiraz, Cabernet Sauvignon and Viognier from the Lower Yarra); and the Over the Shoulder range, drawn from all of the sources available to Oakridge (Sauvignon Blanc, Pinot Grigio, Pinot Noir, Shiraz Viognier, Cabernet Sauvignon). Exports to the UK, Canada, Papua New Guinea, Indonesia, Singapore, Hong Kong, Japan and China.

♟♟♟♟♟ **Local Vineyard Series Yarrawood Vineyard Yarra Valley Botrytis Riesling 2012** A pure and fragrant bouquet of nashi pear, lanolin, beeswax and coriander; the true excitement is revealed on the palate as purity of expression takes control, with fine acidity and a beautifully poised level of sweetness revealed languidly on the long and fine-boned finish. 375ml. Screwcap. 8.2% alc. **Rating** 96 **To** 2020 $40 BE
Local Vineyard Series Chardonnay Pinot Noir 2009 A 74/36% blend, using the traditional method, that spent 36 months on lees prior to disgorgement. A deliciously balanced wine, with creamy yeast notes spun through the vibrant white peach/citrus fruit, the dosage spot on. Diam. 11.8% alc. **Rating** 95 **To** 2014 $40

ŶŶŶŶŶ Local Vineyard Series Guerin, Oakridge & Syme Yarra Valley Fumare
2012 Rating 93 To 2015 $32
Local Vineyard Series Denton Vineyard Yarra Valley Pinot Noir 2011
Rating 93 To 2016 $38

✪ Over the Shoulder Yarra Valley Chardonnay 2012 Fresh pear, citrus blossom
and smoky oak aromas coexist on the restrained and elegant bouquet; the palate is
taut and energetic, with tangy acidity and a bone-dry, and enticingly long, chalky
finish. Screwcap. 12.4% alc. Rating 92 To 2018 $22 BE
Local Vineyard Series Syme Vineyard Yarra Valley Pinot Noir 2011
Rating 92 To 2015 $38
Over the Shoulder Pinot Noir 2012 Rating 90 To 2017 $22 BE
Local Vineyard Series Oakridge Vineyard Yarra Valley Pinot Noir 2011
Rating 90 To 2014 $38

Oakvale   ★★★★

1596 Broke Road, Pokolbin, NSW 2320 **Region** Hunter Valley
T (02) 4998 7088 **www**.oakvalewines.com.au **Open** 7 days 10–5
Winemaker Patrick Auld, James Becker **Est.** 1893 **Dozens** 3000 **Vyds** 29.4ha
For three-quarters of a century Oakvale was in the ownership of the founding Elliot family,
whose original slab hut homestead is now a museum. In 2010 it was purchased by the Becker
family, experienced grapegrowers and owners of the famed Steven's Vineyard. One of the
'must see' destinations in the Hunter, with vineyards now totalling almost 30ha.

ŶŶŶŶŶ Lemon Flower Semillon Sauvignon Blanc 2011 A blend of Hunter Valley
semillon and Southern Highlands sauvignon blanc that comes together well, with
a range of fresh-mown grass, herbs and ripe citrus notes; good overall balance and
length. Screwcap. 10.5% alc. Rating 90 To 2014 $18
Peppercorn Hunter Valley Shiraz 2011 Light crimson-purple; fresh, lively and
spicy aromas and flavours on the bouquet and medium-bodied palate, with black
cherry and blackberry fruits unhindered by oak. Will surprise with its longevity.
Screwcap. 13.5% alc. Rating 90 To 2020 $22

ŶŶŶŶ Hunter Valley Chardonnay 2012 Rating 89 To 2014 $22
Reserve Hunter Valley Chardonnay 2011 Rating 89 To 2014 $35
Hunter Valley Verdelho 2012 Rating 89 To 2014 $22
Hunter Valley Rose 2012 Rating 88 To 2013 $18

Observatory Hill Vineyard   ★★★★

107 Centauri Drive, Mt Rumney, Tas 7170 **Region** Southern Tasmania
T (03) 6248 5380 **www**.observatoryhill.com.au **Open** By appt
Winemaker Frogmore Creek (Alain Rousseau) **Est.** 1991 **Dozens** 1200 **Vyds** 3.1ha
Glenn and Chris Richardson's Observatory Hill Vineyard began in 1991, when Glenn and his
late father-in-law Jim Ramsey planted the first of the 8500 vines that now make up the estate.
Together with the adjoining property, owned by Chris' brother Wayne and his wife Stephanie,
the vineyard now covers just over 3ha. The name 'Observatory Hill' comes from the state's
oldest observatory, which is perched on the hill above the vineyard.

ŶŶŶŶŶ Vintner's Reserve Riesling 2009 A bronze medal at the Tasmanian Wine
Show '10 became a silver a the '12 show, neatly encapsulating the leisurely
development; even now it is still very elegant and fresh, with green apple and
citrus fruit not yet at full maturity. Screwcap. 12% alc. Rating 92 To 2020 $24
Chardonnay 2011 Tangy Tasmanian acidity places a ring around the peach,
melon and lychee fruit at the core of the wine; a twist of nutty French oak adds
complexity and length. Screwcap. 12.5% alc. Rating 90 To 2015 $26
Pinot Noir 2011 Light, clear red; the perfumed strawberry/wild strawberry
bouquet leads into an elegant, spicy, light- to medium-bodied palate, French oak
well handled. Screwcap. 13.1% alc. Rating 90 To 2015 $29

ŶŶŶŶ Blanc de Blanc 2009 Rating 89 To 2014 $38

Occam's Razor

c/- Jasper Hill, Drummonds Lane, Heathcote, Vic 3523 **Region** Heathcote
T (03) 5433 2528 **Open** By appt
Winemaker Emily McNally **Est.** 2001 **Dozens** 300 **Vyds** 2.5ha
Emily McNally (née Laughton) has decided to follow in her parents' footsteps after first seeing
the world and having a range of casual jobs. Having grown up at Jasper Hill, winemaking was
far from strange, but she decided to find her own way, buying the grapes from a small vineyard
owned by Jasper Hill employee Andrew Conforti and his wife Melissa. She then made the
wine 'with guidance and inspiration from my father'. The name comes from William of
Ockham (1285–1349), also spelt Occam, a theologian and philosopher responsible for many
sayings, including that appearing on the back label of the wine: 'what can be done with fewer
is done in vain with more'. The winery rating is based on the longer-term track record of
Occam's Razor. Cork. Exports to the UK, the US and Canada.

ᵽᵽᵽᵽ **Lo Stesso Heathcote Fiano 2011** Quite full straw-green for its age; has
mouth-filling fruit with a range of flavours from stone fruit to ripe citrus, and
good length. Cork. 13% alc. **Rating** 89 **To** 2015 $30
Heathcote Shiraz 2011 Light, clear red-purple; has ended up a millimetre short
of physiological ripeness; the savoury/minty flavours of the mid- to back-palate are
the problem, not the tannins. 14% alc. **Rating** 89 **To** 2016 $44

Oceans Estate

Courtney Road, Karridale, WA 6288 (postal) **Region** Margaret River
T (08) 9758 2240 **www.**oceansestate.com.au **Open** Not
Winemaker Frank Kittler **Est.** 1999 **Dozens** 6000 **Vyds** 21ha
Oceans Estate was purchased by the Tomasi family (headed by Frank and Attilia) in 1995, and,
between '99 and 2007, chardonnay, sauvignon blanc, semillon, pinot noir, merlot and cabernet
sauvignon were planted. Since '06 the wines have been made at the onsite winery, which is
big enough to handle the 180 to 220 tonnes of grapes that will come once the vineyards are
in full bearing. Exports to Hong Kong.

ᵽᵽᵽᵽᵽ **Margaret River Sauvignon Blanc 2011** Light, bright straw-green; the fragrant
✪ bouquet has a mix of tropical notes, fresh-mown grass and green bean; the palate is
well balanced, its energy and drive as impressive as they are unexpected. Screwcap.
12.8% alc. **Rating** 93 **To** 2014 $16
✪ **Margaret River Chardonnay 2010** Barrel fermentation in 100% new French
oak, and matured for 12 months in the same barrels; the fruit has emerged on
top of the oak, with a display in the white peach/grapefruit spectrum. Screwcap.
13.5% alc. **Rating** 92 **To** 2017 $18
Tomasi Vineyard Margaret River Cabernet Merlot 2009 A 75/25% blend
given precisely the same oak treatment as the Merlot; the cassis/blackcurrant fruit
is more powerful than that of the Merlot, and responds well to the cedary oak on
the medium- to full-bodied palate. Screwcap. 14% alc. **Rating** 91 **To** 2017 $15
✪ **Margaret River Semillon Sauvignon Blanc 2011** Pale straw-green; the
sauvignon blanc (40%) injects some tropical nuances into the lemon citrus of the
semillon; needs no cellaring, even though its semillon will provide the opportunity
for those wishing to experiment. Screwcap. 13% alc. **Rating** 90 **To** 2014 $16
✪ **Tomasi Vineyard Margaret River Merlot 2009** From a block of the oldest
vines on the property, 33% spending 2 years in new French oak, which imparts
pronounced cedar/cigar box flavours that mesh well with the savoury, black olive
notes on the palate. Screwcap. 13.5% alc. **Rating** 90 **To** 2016 $15

ᵽᵽᵽᵽ **Margaret River Semillon 2011** Light straw-green; in the typical Margaret
✪ River fashion, relatively rich and full-bodied (for an unwooded white) and will
stay the course, its ripe lemon flavours providing flesh for the future. Good food
wine. Screwcap. 13% alc. **Rating** 89 **To** 2016 $14

Ochota Barrels

Merchants Road, Basket Range, SA 5138 **Region** Adelaide Hills
T 0400 798 818 **www**.ochotabarrels.com **Open** Not
Winemaker Taras Ochota **Est.** 2008 **Dozens** 900 **Vyds** 0.5ha
Taras Ochota has had an incredibly varied career as a winemaker after completing his oenology degree at Adelaide University. He has made wine for top-end Australian producers, and has had a Flying Winemaker role in many parts of the world, most recently as consultant winemaker for one of Sweden's largest wine-importing companies, working on Italian wines from Puglia and Sicily. Wife Amber has accompanied him to many places, working in a multiplicity of technical and marketing roles. Taras' day job now is working for Peter Leske and Mark Kozned's new venture, Revenir, completing another circle, for part of his early career involved working with Peter at Nepenthe. Exports to the US and Canada.

The Shellac Vineyard Syrah 2012 Wonderful black fruits, licorice and quality oak on the palate, bolstered by perfect tannins on the very long and beautifully balanced finish. A truly exceptional wine, which will give pleasure whenever it is opened. Screwcap. 13.6% alc. **Rating** 97 **To** 2047 $50
Weird Berries in the Woods Gewurztraminer 2012 The colour points to some left-field winemaking of the Adelaide Hills-sourced grapes; it is richly textured, with a distinct nod to Alsace also evident in its phenolics. The polar opposite to Henschke's Joseph Hill. Screwcap. 12.3% alc. **Rating** 94 **To** 2018 $35
A Forest Pinot Noir 2012 A blend of two clones, 777 and MV6, its plush red and black cherry fruit set within a spicy, savoury gossamer web of fine tannins; despite the winery name, oak has been controlled. Cork. 13.3% alc. **Rating** 94 **To** 2019 $45

The Slint Vineyard Chardonnay 2012 Rating 93 **To** 2019 $45
The Green Room Grenache Noir Syrah 2012 Rating 93 **To** 2015 $30
The Fugazi Vineyard Grenache 2012 Rating 92 **To** 2018 $38

Oddfellows Wines

523 Chapel Road, Langhorne Creek, SA 5255 **Region** Langhorne Creek
T (08) 8537 3326 **www**.oddfellowswines.com.au **Open** Not
Winemaker David Knight **Est.** 1997 **Dozens** 5000 **Vyds** 46.1ha
Oddfellows is the name taken by a group of five individuals who decided to put their expertise, energy and investments into making premium wine. Langhorne Creek vignerons David and Cathy Knight were two of the original members, and in 2007 took over ownership and running of the venture. David worked with Greg Follett from Lake Breeze to produce the wines, gradually taking over more responsibility, and is now both winemaker and viticulturist. Exports to the UK, the US, Canada, Singapore, Indonesia, Hong Kong and China.

Langhorne Creek Cabernet Sauvignon 2008 The gold medal on the label is real, awarded at the Adelaide Wine Show '12. The colour is deep, the powerful palate with an amalgam of blackcurrant, tar, dark chocolate and earth, the tannins more vocal than is normal for Langhorne Creek, but in harmony with the strength and focus of the fruit. Screwcap. 14.6% alc. **Rating** 94 **To** 2028 $25

Langhorne Creek Shiraz 2008 Rating 89 **To** 2018 $25

Old Kent River

1114 Turpin Road, Rocky Gully, WA 6397 **Region** Frankland River
T (08) 9855 1589 **www**.oldkentriverwines.com.au **Open** At Kent River, Denmark
Winemaker Alkoomi (Andrew Cherry) **Est.** 1985 **Dozens** 1500 **Vyds** 17ha
Mark and Debbie Noack have earned much respect from their neighbours and from the other producers to whom they sell more than half the production from the vineyard on their sheep property. The quality of their wines has gone from strength to strength, Mark having worked particularly hard with his Pinot Noir. The Noacks have added a 2ha vineyard at Denmark to their much older 15ha vineyard at Rocky Gully.

ŶŶŶŶŶ **Frankland River Pinot Noir 2011** An early mover in pinot noir production in the Great Southern, and the first in Frankland River. The wine has generous, ripe plum-accented aromas and flavours; the colour is particularly auspicious, with depth and clarity. Screwcap. 13.5% alc. **Rating** 93 **To** 2018 $25

Old Plains   ★★★☆

71 High Street, Grange, SA 5023 (postal) **Region** Adelaide Plains
T 0407 605 601 **www.**oldplains.com **Open** Not
Winemaker Domenic Torzi, Tim Freeland **Est.** 2003 **Dozens** 3000 **Vyds** 14ha
Old Plains is a partnership between Tim Freeland and Domenic Torzi, who have acquired small parcels of old vine shiraz (3ha), grenache (1ha) and cabernet sauvignon (4ha) in the Adelaide Plains region. A portion of the wines, sold under the Old Plains, Longhop and Raw Power labels, is exported to the US, Denmark, Hong Kong, Singapore and China.

ŶŶŶŶŶ **Power of One Old Vine Shiraz 2010** Hand-picked, open-fermented and basket-pressed, the grapes from 50-year-old vines; matured in French oak for 24 months. Has a rich cocktail of blackberry, plum and prune fruits, trimmed by good acidity and ripe tannins. Screwcap. 14% alc. **Rating** 90 **To** 2018 $30

ŶŶŶŶ **Terreno Old Vine Grenache 2009 Rating** 89 **To** 2015 $30
Longhop Mount Lofty Ranges Shiraz 2011 Rating 87 **To** 2014 $16

Olivers Taranga Vineyards   ★★★★★

246 Seaview Road, McLaren Vale, SA 5171 **Region** McLaren Vale
T (08) 8323 8498 **www.**oliverstaranga.com **Open** 7 days 10–4
Winemaker Corrina Wright **Est.** 1841 **Dozens** 7000 **Vyds** 85.42ha
William and Elizabeth Oliver arrived from Scotland in 1839 to settle at McLaren Vale. Six generations later, members of the family are still living on the Whitehill and Taranga farms. The Taranga property has 15 grape varieties planted (the lion's share shiraz and cabernet sauvignon, with lesser quantities of chardonnay, chenin blanc, durif, fiano, grenache, mataro, merlot, petit verdot, sagrantino, semillon, tempranillo, viognier and white frontignac). Since 2000 the wine has been made by Corrina Wright (the Oliver family's first winemaker and a sixth-generation family member), and in '11 the family celebrated 170 years of grapegrowing. Exports to the US, Canada, Hong Kong and China.

ŶŶŶŶŶ **Small Batch Cadenzia McLaren Vale Grenache 2010** Light to medium purple-crimson; a very attractive Grenache that is relatively light-bodied, yet has remarkable intensity and length to its deliciously juicy array of red fruits; the key was the timing of the harvest. Screwcap. 14% alc. **Rating** 95 **To** 2017 $30
McLaren Vale Shiraz 2010 A first-class expression of regional shiraz character, with a skein of dark chocolate woven through blackberry, plum fruit and mocha; soft but persistent tannins. Screwcap. 14.5% alc. **Rating** 94 **To** 2025 $29
Corrina's McLaren Vale Shiraz Cabernet Sauvignon 2010 The two estate-grown components were co-fermented; layers of ultra-typical regional character are delivered via blackberry and blackcurrant flavours wrapped in a coating of dark chocolate and licorice. Yummy stuff indeed. Screwcap. 14.5% alc. **Rating** 94 **To** 2030 $30

ŶŶŶŶŶ **Small Batch McLaren Vale Fiano 2012** Fiano continues to impress when
✪ grown in temperate to warm regions, reflecting its birthplace in southern Italy. The lemon zest aromas gain intensity on the long, highly focused palate. Screwcap. 12.5% alc. **Rating** 93 **To** 2014 $24
McLaren Vale Shiraz 2011 Rating 92 **To** 2020 $29
Small Batch McLaren Vale Tempranillo 2011 Rating 90 **To** 2015 $32

Olsen

529 Osmington Road, Osmington, WA 6285 **Region** Margaret River
T (08) 9757 4536 **www**.olsen.com.au **Open** W'ends 11–5
Winemaker Jarrad Olsen **Est.** 1986 **Dozens** 825 **Vyds** 9.5ha
Steve and Ann Marie Olsen have planted cabernet sauvignon, chardonnay, semillon, verdelho and shiraz, which they tend with the help of their four children. It was the desire to raise their children in a healthy country environment that prompted the move to establish the vineyard, coupled with a long-standing dream to make their own wine. Not to be confused with Olsen Wines in Melbourne.

Margaret River Semillon Sauvignon Blanc 2012 Bright and fragrant aromas of nectarine and straw; fresh, lively and revealing a little smoky gun flint complexity on the finish. Screwcap. 12.8% alc. **Rating** 87 **To** 2014 $20 BE
Margaret River Cabernet Sauvignon 2010 Deep garnet; showing dried tobacco and confected red fruit notes on the bouquet; medium-bodied with orange zest, green olive and thyme; accessible for immediate consumption. Screwcap. 13.6% alc. **Rating** 87 **To** 2017 $20 BE

Olsen Wines Victoria

21 Carinish Road, Oakleigh South, Vic 3167 **Region** Port Phillip Zone
T (03) 9544 4033 **www**.vin888.com **Open** Mon–Fri 9.30–5
Winemaker Glenn Olsen **Est.** 1991 **Dozens** 50 000
Glenn Olsen, a science and engineering graduate of the University of Melbourne, has been involved in the wine industry since 1975, initially importing wines and spirits from Europe, then moving into retailing. In 1991, he and Angie Joson-Olsen started Olsen Wines, claiming to be Melbourne's first inner-suburban winery. Several others may dispute this claim, but that is perhaps neither here nor there. Most of the wines come from grapes grown on either the Murray River in Northeast Victoria (for the full-bodied Big Fella range), or in the Yarra Valley. Exports to the US and other major markets.

Yarra Valley Cabernet Sauvignon 2010 Good colour; the fractured, broken ProCork may not have helped this wine, which has a distinct late-picked character. 14.3% alc. **Rating** 87 **To** 2016 $25
Autumn Harvest Yarra Valley Riesling 2012 Light straw-green; a pleasant, well-balanced wine best suited to fresh fruit or cake desserts; is not particularly sweet. Screwcap. 11% alc. **Rating** 87 **To** 2014 $20

Onannon

PO Box 190, Flinders, Vic 3929 **Region** Port Phillip Zone
T 0448 900 229 **www**.onannon.com **Open** Not
Winemaker Sam Middleton, Kaspar Hermann, Will Byron **Est.** 2008 **Dozens** 700
Onannon is the venture of Sam Middleton, Kaspar Hermann and Will Byron, who donated the last two or three letters of their surnames to come up with Onannon. They have many things in common, not the least working vintages at Coldstream Hills, Will for six years, Sam for two (before ultimately returning to the family's winery, Mount Mary) and Kaspar for one. Since then they have bounced between vintages in Burgundy and Australia, Will accumulating the most frequent flyer points. Strictly speaking, I should disqualify myself from making any comment about them or their wine, but you would have to go a long way to find three more open-hearted and utterly committed winemakers; the world is their oyster, their ambitions unlimited.

Mornington Peninsula Pinot Noir 2012 Full, bright crimson-purple; here is an object lesson in the impact of terroir (in its full meaning), for the wine has a radically different expression of pinot noir, with plum firmly in the driver's seat, but don't think this has been overworked in the winery, because it hasn't. It combines its fluid line with texture, which – like the Gippsland Pinot – accelerates through to the finish. Diam. 13.7% alc. **Rating** 96 **To** 2022 $38

Gippsland Pinot Noir 2012 Light, bright red; sourced from a single vineyard, and a prime example of not judging Pinot Noir on its colour; the fragrant, perfumed bouquet of red berry fruits and spices are followed by a very long, silky palate that accelerates through to the finish and lingering aftertaste. 350 dozen made. Diam. 12.8% alc. **Rating** 94 **To** 2017 $38

Gippsland Pinot Noir 2011 Light, clear purple-red; the fragrant bouquet of black cherry and plum flows through to the attractive and particularly well-balanced palate; this is not a heavyweight Pinot, but nor is it weak, and in the context of '11, is an outstanding success. Diam. 13% alc. **Rating** 94 **To** 2017 $37

ᵀᵀᵀᵀᵀ Gippsland Chardonnay 2012 **Rating** 91 **To** 2018 $38
Mornington Peninsula Pinot Noir 2011 **Rating** 90 **To** 2014 $37

Optimiste   ★★★☆

Cnr Castlereagh Highway/Horseflat Lane, Mudgee, NSW 2850 **Region** Mudgee
T (02) 9967 3294 **www**.optimiste.com.au **Open** Fri–Sun 10–4
Winemaker Jacob Stein **Est.** 1998 **Dozens** 3000 **Vyds** 11ha
Steven and Sharlene Dadd had been growing grapes for over a decade before realising a long-held dream to launch their own wines under the Optimiste label. The name is inspired by their son's struggle with deafness and a quote by Helen Keller: 'Optimism is the faith that leads to achievement. Nothing can be done without hope and confidence.' The first vines planted were cabernet sauvignon, petit verdot and merlot, with more recent plantings of viognier, semillon, tempranillo and pinot gris (chardonnay is purchased). A 'Tasting House' opened in 2013. Exports to Singapore.

ᵀᵀᵀᵀ The Jewel Mudgee Botrytis Semillon Viognier 2012 High levels of botrytis and lifted acidity, with stewed apricot aromas, peanut brittle and straw on the bouquet; luscious and very sweet on the palate, with the finish even and poised, long and hedonistic. 375ml. Screwcap. 9.5% alc. **Rating** 88 **To** 2016 $25 BE

Paris in Spring Limited Release Mudgee Rose 2012 Pale salmon blush; the bouquet is all savoury in style, with fennel and earthy notes; the palate is bone dry, almost sitting within a white wine framework, finishing with a crisp and fragrant conclusion. Screwcap. 11.5% alc. **Rating** 87 **To** 2014 $20 BE

Orange Mountain Wines   ★★★★

10 Radnedge Lane, Orange, NSW 2800 **Region** Orange
T (02) 6365 2626 **www**.orangemountain.com.au **Open** Wed–Fri 9–3, w'ends 9–5
Winemaker Terry Dolle **Est.** 1997 **Dozens** 3500
Terry Dolle has a total of 5.5ha of vineyards, part at Manildra (established 1997) and the remainder at Orange (in 2001). The Manildra climate is distinctly warmer than that of Orange, and the plantings reflect the climatic difference, with pinot noir and sauvignon blanc at Orange, shiraz, cabernet sauvignon, merlot and viognier at Manildra. Exports to China.

ᵀᵀᵀᵀᵀ Limited Release Riesling 2012 Vibrant green hue; the bouquet has green apple, lemon rind, ginger and anise on display; the chalky, racy acidity is the prominent feature of the palate, with the moderately long finish bone dry and showing blanched almonds to conclude. Screwcap. 12% alc. **Rating** 90 **To** 2020 $25 BE

Limited Release Shiraz Viognier 2011 Deep garnet; a spicy and fragrant bouquet of red fruits and cinnamon; medium-bodied with ample medium-grained tannins, and taut acidity drawing out the slightly sinewy finish; time is needed for all parts to fully come together. Screwcap. 13.5% alc. **Rating** 90 **To** 2022 $38 BE

Limited Release Mountain Ice Viognier 2012 This is incredibly sweet and intense, taking the level of sweetness to its zenith, and offering candied orange, spice and a hint of musk for good measure; long and luscious. 375ml. Screwcap. 11% alc. **Rating** 90 **To** 2020 $25 BE

ᵀᵀᵀᵀ Limited Release Sauvignon Blanc 2012 **Rating** 88 **To** 2014 $22 BE

Oranje Tractor

198 Link Road, Albany, WA 6330 **Region** Albany
T (08) 9842 5175 **www**.oranjetractor.com **Open** Fri–Sun 11–5 (Tues–Sun during school hols)
Winemaker Rob Diletti **Est.** 1998 **Dozens** 1000 **Vyds** 2.9ha
The name celebrates the 1964 vintage, orange-coloured Fiat tractor acquired when Murray Gomm and Pamela Lincoln began the establishment of the vineyard. Murray was born next door, but moved to Perth to work in physical education and health promotion. Here he met nutritionist Pamela, who completed the wine science degree at CSU in 2000, before being awarded a Churchill Fellowship to study organic grape and wine production in the US and Europe. When the partners established their vineyard, they went down the organic path.

Fat Tyre Broke Spoke SB 2012 The connection between the name and the wine in the glass is decidedly tenuous, even with the back label explanation. All of which is completely irrelevant, for this is a top-class Sauvignon Blanc, full of multifaceted aromas and – in particular – flavours that hit the bull's eye at every point along the way. Screwcap. 12.5% alc. **Rating** 95 **To** 2013 $25
Top Paddock Shiraz 2011 Strong red-purple; a very seductive style, crammed full of stewed plum, black cherry, clove and licorice on the bouquet and palate; savoury tannins on the finish are an elixir giving the wine texture and balancing its sweet fruits. Screwcap. 14% alc. **Rating** 94 **To** 2024 $26

Sauvignon Blanc 2012 Rating 92 **To** 2014 $26
Reverse Riesling 2012 A Mosel Kabinett style, the gauge on the back label showing the wine to be well into the medium-sweet category. Its juicy, sweet fruit is very attractive, but the wine could have done better with greater acidity. Screwcap. 12% alc. **Rating** 91 **To** 2018 $20
Albany Rose 2012 Uses the sweetness scale on the back label normally restricted to riesling – showing the wine to be on the cusp between dry and sweet. And in the mouth it is precisely that, with red berry fruits running through to a long, well-balanced finish. Screwcap. 12.9% alc. **Rating** 90 **To** 2014 $19

Orlando

Barossa Valley Way, Rowland Flat, SA 5352 **Region** Barossa Valley
T (08) 8521 3111 **www**.orlandowines.com **Open** Not
Winemaker Bernard Hickin **Est.** 1847 **Dozens** NFP **Vyds** 1600ha
Orlando is the parent who has been divorced by its child, Jacob's Creek (see separate entry). While Orlando is 165 years old, Jacob's Creek is little more than 39 years old. For what are doubtless sound marketing reasons, Orlando aided and abetted the divorce, but the average consumer is unlikely to understand the logic, and – if truth be known – will care about it even less. The vineyard holding is for all brands (notably Jacob's Creek) and for all regions across SA, Vic and NSW; it will likely be less in coming years.

St Helga Eden Valley Riesling 2012 A note of mandarin provides a suggestion of generosity to St Helga's pristine lemon blossom and Granny Smith apple fruits. It's precise, crunchy, citrus-focused and accented with mouth-filling, slatey minerality and tense acidity. An impressive vintage for St Helga. Screwcap. 12.1% alc. **Rating** 94 **To** 2022 $20 TS

Ortus Wines

22 Nile Street, Port Adelaide, SA 5015 (postal) **Region** South Australia
T 0408 496 155 **www**.ortuswines.com.au **Open** Not
Winemaker Tim Geddes **Est.** 2011 **Dozens** 5500
While Ortus was not established until September 2011, its family history dates back to 1848 and the arrival of Johann Gottlieb Bittner from Prussia; the owner of Ortus, Julie Cooper, is a descendant of Johann. She has more than 15 years of experience in the winery industry working for small through to large multinational companies in sales and marketing.

Ortus purchases grapes from the Barossa Valley, Riverland, Coonawarra and McLaren Vale, producing three tiers of wines for both domestic and international markets. Exports to Canada, Sweden, South Korea and China.

ŶŶŶŶŶ **Coonawarra Cabernet Sauvignon 2011** Medium red-purple, bright and clear; the bouquet is fragrant, the light- to medium-bodied palate with cassis/blackcurrant, olive and earth flavours; the tannins are fine, the oak well balanced and integrated. Cork. 14% alc. **Rating** 91 **To** 2017 $30
Reserve Barossa Valley Shiraz 2011 The back label tells us of 'blackberry, blackcurrent (sic), cassis, dark chocolate, licorice, dark cherry, vanillin (sic) oak, ripe, dark-fruits (sic), jasmine blossom, five spice …', and it's true that some of those flavours are present. It's just a huge ask to get all this from '11; the '12 will surely be monumental. Cork. 14.5% alc. **Rating** 90 **To** 2020 $95

ŶŶŶŶ **Cabernet Shiraz 2012** Light, bright crimson-purple; it has totally surprising
✪   redcurrant, blackcurrant and blackberry fruit. Drink now, but the tannins will hold the wine for a few years yet. Screwcap. 14% alc. **Rating** 89 **To** 2016 $15

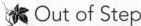 Out of Step   ★★★★★

6 McKenzie Avenue, Healesville, Vic 3777 (postal) **Region** Yarra Valley
T 0424 644 693 **www**.outofstepwineco.com **Open** Not
Winemaker David Chatfield, Nathan Reeves **Est.** 2012 **Dozens** 100
Out of Step is the micro virtual winery of David Chatfield and Nathan Reeves. David explains, 'I've worked in the music industry for a long time promoting tours for international acts, so I'm very familiar with financial risk, and am currently employed on a part-time basis as cellar hand at Oakridge (full-time during vintage).' Nathan works full-time as a cellar hand at Sticks, and both are getting close to finishing their winemaking degrees. Along the way they have variously chalked up experience at Stella Bella (Margaret River) and Vinify (California). Their initial foray with Sauvignon Blanc sourced from Lusatia Park was spectacular, and they have a Chardonnay from the vineyard that produces the Thousand Candles wines, and a Nebbiolo from Malakoff in the Pyrenees.

ŶŶŶŶŶ **Lusatia Park Vineyard Yarra Valley Sauvignon Blanc 2012** Bright, light
✪   straw-green; out of step because it thumbs its nose at Marlborough and nods to the Loire Valley. Has remarkable texture, imperatively gripping the mouth (in the best way) and leading into a long finish and aftertaste. Sauvignon Blanc with attitude is faint praise. Screwcap. 12.9% alc. **Rating** 95 **To** 2015 $23

Outlook Hill Vineyard   ★★★★

97 School Lane, Tarrawarra, Vic 3777 **Region** Yarra Valley
T (03) 5962 2890 **www**.outlookhill.com.au **Open** By appt
Winemaker Peter Snow, Al Fencaros **Est.** 2000 **Dozens** 1100 **Vyds** 5.4ha
After several years overseas, former Melbourne professionals Peter and Lydia Snow returned in 1997, planning to open a wine tourism business in the Hunter Valley. However, they had second thoughts, and in 2000 moved to the Yarra Valley, where they have now established five B&B cottages, a vineyard, and a cellar door outlet, backed by a constant temperature wine storage cool room. Exports to China.

ŶŶŶŶŶ **Gold Leaf Yarra Valley Pinot Noir 2011** Light red-purple; the Gold Leaf label is reserved for Outlook Hill's premium releases, and if you accept the vintage conditions, that is a fair call, for the wine has good varietal expression courtesy of its plum and dark cherry fruit, the mouthfeel supple, the finish long. Screwcap. 12.5% alc. **Rating** 92 **To** 2016 $28
Gold Leaf Reserve Yarra Valley Cabernet Merlot 2011 Good hue, although not deep; a fragrant red berry and spice bouquet, then a bright, juicy palate; notwithstanding the low alcohol, there are no green flavours, and the tannin/oak balance is good. Screwcap. 12.5% alc. **Rating** 90 **To** 2016 $25

Oxford Landing Estates

Pipeline Road, Nuriootpa, SA 5355 **Region** Riverland
T (08) 8561 3200 **www.oxfordlanding.com.au** **Open** By appt
Winemaker Andrew La Nauze **Est.** 1958 **Dozens** NFP **Vyds** 250ha
Oxford Landing Estate is, so the website tells us, 'A real place, a real vineyard. A place distinguished by clear blue skies, rich red soil and an abundance of golden sunshine.' In the 50+ years since the vineyard was planted, the brand has grown to reach all corners of the world. Success has been due to over-delivery against expectations at its price points, and it has largely escaped the scorn of the UK wine press. In 2008 a five-year experiment began to determine whether a block of vines could survive and produce an annual crop with only 10% of the normal irrigation. The result showed that the vines could survive, but with a crop production of between 40% and 65%. There is also 1ha of native vegetation for every hectare of vineyard. Outstanding packaging with custom-made, branded bottles. Exports to the UK, the US and NZ.

ŸŸŸŸ **Sauvignon Blanc 2012** Weaves the same magic as it has done for decades
✪ (since 1959!), bringing clear varietal character to the Riverland in a full-on tropical mode, pineapple and mango to the fore; the balance is very good, the palate long. Screwcap. 11% alc. **Rating** 89 **To** 2013 $9
✪ **Rose 2012** Bright, light crimson-purple; a fresh and fragrant red berry bouquet leads into a palate that, from the first moment, proclaims the absence of any residual sugar, yet is well balanced. A rose for all seasons, and truly excellent value. Screwcap. 12.5% alc. **Rating** 89 **To** 2014 $10
✪ **Chardonnay 2012** Bright green-straw; as always, Oxford Landing manages to conjure that little bit extra; the stone fruit is there, as is the citrus and acidity to cleanse the finish. Best right now. Screwcap. 13.5% alc. **Rating** 88 **To** 2013 $9
Pinot Grigio 2012 At this price point, and with its geographic origin, it is no surprise for the wine to be bland. Screwcap. 11.5% alc. **Rating** 87 **To** 2014 $10
✪ **Viognier 2012** Positive medium yellow-green; has considerable apricot and stone fruit aroma and palate, even if there is a hint of phenolics on the finish. None better at this price. Screwcap. 14.5% alc. **Rating** 87 **To** 2014 $10

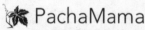 PachaMama ★★★☆

PO Box 2208, Sunbury, Vic 3429 **Region** Heathcote
T (03) 9500 0346 **www.pachamamawines.com.au** **Open** Not
Winemaker Don Lewis, Narelle King **Est.** 2010 **Dozens** 6630 **Vyds** 4.5ha
When David Jemmeson established PachaMama in 2010, he had already worked in the winery community for 30 years, his experience crossing the Tasman, and also into businesses such as Riedel. He also found time to travel to the Andean mountains, and says the liveliness, colour and vibrancy of South American culture was the inspiration for the brand (Pachamama is the Inca earth goddess). David also has a long history of interconnection with Don Lewis, dating back to their working together and developing the Mitchelton, Blackwood Park and Preece brands. David has 4.5ha of pinot gris, riesling and shiraz.

ŸŸŸŸŸ **Central Victoria Pinot Gris 2012** Very pale pink-bronze; as well as the
✪ expected pear, has some nougat nuances that add considerable interest to the palate and aftertaste. Screwcap. 13.8% alc. **Rating** 90 **To** 2014 $19

ŸŸŸŸ **Riesling 2012** **Rating** 89 **To** 2015 $20
Heathcote Shiraz 2010 **Rating** 88 **To** 2015 $25

Pages Creek

624 Middle Teatree Road, Teatree, Tas 7017 **Region** Southern Tasmania
T (03) 6260 2311 **www.pagescreekwine.com.au** **Open** By appt
Winemaker Winemaking Tasmania (Julian Alcorso) **Est.** 1999 **Dozens** 1600 **Vyds** 4.5ha
In 1999 Peter and Sue Lowrie planted a vineyard on their 20ha Pages Creek property, named after the creek that runs through it. They have cabernet sauvignon, pinot noir, chardonnay and merlot. The tiny first vintage (2002) was consumed at their wedding; the first full vintage was '03, and the Pages Creek label was launched in '04.

ΨΨΨΨΨ **Pinot Noir 2011** Deeply coloured, with the bouquet displaying dark cherry, spiced plum and a generous dollop of charry oak; the palate is fresh, full-blooded, with a certain charm. Screwcap. 13.9% alc. **Rating** 90 **To** 2017 $25 BE

ΨΨΨΨ **Sauvignon Blanc 2011 Rating** 88 **To** 2014 $25 BE
Merlot 2011 Rating 88 **To** 2017 $25 BE
Chardonnay 2010 Rating 87 **To** 2017 $25 BE

Palmarium   ★★★★★

395B Belmore Road, Balwyn, Vic 3103 (postal) **Region** Various
T 0422 546 825 **www.**palmarium.com.au **Open** Not
Winemaker John Ellis, Walter Clappis, Kym Teusner **Est.** 2010 **Dozens** 1300
Peter Mornement's philosophy is simple: to develop a portfolio of high-quality Shiraz from six premium regions. Each wine would be made by a winemaker in that region with an established reputation, and a simple instruction from Peter: buy the best fruit you can, and use the new oak of your choice. He has joined forces with John Ellis (of Hanging Rock) for Heathcote, and Walter Clappis and Kym Teusner (of their eponymous wineries) for McLaren Vale and Barossa Valley respectively. The wines are sold in six-bottle cases, the initial releases from Heathcote and McLaren Vale, only to subscribers.

ΨΨΨΨΨ Exemplar Heathcote Shiraz 2010 Combines power and intensity with elegance and balance; the fragrant bouquet is the opening chorus for the symphony of spice, licorice, black cherry and blackberry of the palate, where quality oak and ripe but firm tannins are the final act. Screwcap. 14% alc. Rating 96 To 2035 $65

Palmer Wines   ★★★★★

1271 Caves Road, Dunsborough, WA 6281 **Region** Margaret River
T (08) 9756 7024 **www.**palmerwines.com.au **Open** 7 days 10–5
Winemaker Mark Warren, Bruce Jukes **Est.** 1977 **Dozens** 6000 **Vyds** 51.39ha
Steve and Helen Palmer established their vineyard in 1977; the plantings have been increased over the years, and are now headed by cabernet sauvignon, sauvignon blanc, shiraz, merlot, chardonnay and semillon, with smaller amounts of malbec and cabernet franc. Recent vintages have had major success in WA and national wine shows, including Most Successful Exhibitor at the Australian Small Winemakers Show '11 and '12. Exports to Indonesia, Hong Kong and China.

ΨΨΨΨΨ Reserve Margaret River Shiraz 2010 Good colour; in the same mould as the '11 Reserve, with an extra degree of concentration to its bouquet and palate; predominantly black fruit-driven, with savoury tannins building an extra layer of complexity, oak making a positive but controlled contribution. Screwcap. 14.9% alc. Rating 95 To 2035 $45
Margaret River Chardonnay 2011 Light straw-yellow; a vibrant and stylish Chardonnay, picked relatively early to maximise the freshness of the citrus and stone fruit aromas and flavours, the oak deliberately restrained. Screwcap. 12.7% alc. Rating 94 To 2018 $28
Reserve Margaret River Shiraz 2011 Very good colour; this has more power and authority than the standard Shiraz, with savoury tannins providing grip, oak also obvious. It will prove to be the better wine in 10 years' time, but at the moment is on a par with its sibling. Screwcap. 14.9% alc. Rating 94 To 2036 $45
Margaret River Shiraz 2011 Deep purple-crimson; a rich, medium-bodied Shiraz, with fruit, oak and tannins all competing for primacy, and none succeeding, so good is the balance. Will always be enjoyable, now or much later, but a few more years in bottle will reward. Screwcap. 14.5% alc. Rating 94 To 2026 $28

ΨΨΨΨΨ Margaret River Cabernet Sauvignon 2011 Rating 93 To 2031 $28
Margaret River Cabernet Sauvignon 2010 Rating 93 To 2025 $28

✪   **Margaret River Semillon 2012** Light straw-green; a modern take on Margaret River semillon, picking relatively early, then letting the wine do the work. It is still at the dawn of its life, but the balance and length point to a prosperous future. Screwcap. 12.3% alc. **Rating** 92 **To** 2022 $23
Margaret River Shiraz 2010 Rating 92 **To** 2020 $28

✪   **Cabernets The Grandee 2011** Good red-purple; the only question is the amount of oak used with a medium-bodied Bordeaux blend; the cassis and redcurrant flavours are lively, well balanced and fresh; a near miss for a well-priced wine. Screwcap. 14.5% alc. **Rating** 92 **To** 2021 $23
Margaret River Sauvignon Blanc 2012 Rating 91 **To** 2014 $23
Margaret River Merlot 2010 Rating 91 **To** 2020 $23

✪   **Krackerjack Bin 112 2012** A good example of the ease with which Margaret River presents this style to suit wallets and palates alike; the soft citrus make the main running, but with some stone fruit/tropical nuances to add interest. Sauvignon Blanc/Semillon. Screwcap. 12.6% alc. **Rating** 90 **To** 2014 $20
Margaret River Semillon Sauvignon Blanc 2012 Rating 90 **To** 2014 $23

✪   **Krackerjack Bin 410 2010** Bright, light, green; packed with ripe fruit, it displays equal contributions of ripe stone fruit and citrus bolstered by a subtle touch of creamy cashew oak. Screwcap. 13.1% alc. **Rating** 90 **To** 2015 $20
Margaret River Malbec 2011 Rating 90 **To** 2018 $23

Paracombe Wines   ★★★★☆

294b Paracombe Road, Paracombe, SA 5132 **Region** Adelaide Hills
T (08) 8380 5058 **www**.paracombewines.com **Open** By appt
Winemaker Paul Drogemuller, James Barry **Est.** 1983 **Dozens** 15 000 **Vyds** 17.7ha
Paul and Kathy Drogemuller established Paracombe following the devastating Ash Wednesday bushfires in 1983. It has become a successful business, producing a range of wines that are never less than good, often very good. The wines are made onsite in the 250-tonne winery, with every part of the production process through to distribution handled from there. Exports to the UK and other major markets.

♛♛♛♛♛ **The Reuben 2009** A 56/19/11/10/4% blend of cabernet sauvignon, cabernet
✪   franc, merlot, malbec and shiraz showing a little development; the bouquet offers blackcurrant and choc-mint aromas; the full-bodied palate reveals a bright core of sweet fruit, and then tannins come through the finish. Screwcap. 14.5% alc.
Rating 91 **To** 2018 $21 BE

Holland Creek Adelaide Hills Riesling 2012 Pale colour, and delicate in character, with apple blossom and lemon rind on display; the palate is lean, fresh and focused, with a soft finish. Like all the Paracombe wines, well priced. Screwcap. 12.5% alc. **Rating** 90 **To** 2018 $20 BE

Adelaide Hills Chardonnay 2012 Pale colour, bright; restrained pear, citrus and anise aromas come together on the bouquet; the palate is taut and textured, with blanched almonds sitting alongside the fresh acidity with aplomb. Screwcap. 13.5% alc. **Rating** 90 **To** 2016 $21 BE

Adelaide Hills Red Ruby 2012 Vivid pink hue; bright, floral red-fruited bouquet, with a provençale garrigue note of complexity; the palate is dry, chalky and refreshing, offering a well-balanced and lively finish. Screwcap. 13.7% alc.
Rating 90 **To** 2014 $21 BE

Adelaide Hills Cabernet Sauvignon 2009 Mid crimson; vibrant cassis fruits are evident on the bouquet, offset by a touch of licorice; the palate is taut and savoury, with chewy tannins and lively acidity providing drive and energy on the finish. Screwcap. 14.5% alc. **Rating** 90 **To** 2018 $21 BE

Paradigm Hill

26 Merricks Road, Merricks, Vic 3916 **Region** Mornington Peninsula
T (03) 5989 9000 **www**.paradigmhill.com.au **Open** 1st w'end of month
Winemaker Dr George Mihaly **Est.** 1999 **Dozens** 1500 **Vyds** 4.2ha

Dr George Mihaly (with a background in medical research, biotechnology and pharmaceutical industries) and wife Ruth (a former chef and caterer) have realised a 30-year dream of establishing their own vineyard and winery, abandoning their previous careers to do so. George had all the necessary scientific qualifications, and built on those by making the 2001 Merricks Creek wines, moving to home base at Paradigm Hill in '02, all along receiving guidance and advice from Nat White of Main Ridge Estate. The vineyard, under Ruth's control with advice from Shane Strange, is planted to 2.1ha of pinot noir, 0.9ha of shiraz, 0.8ha of riesling and 0.4ha of pinot gris. Exports to China and Singapore.

🍷🍷🍷🍷🍷 **Les Cinq Mornington Peninsula Pinot Noir 2011** From the best five rows, made in very similar fashion to L'Ami Sage. While still having a savoury framework, there are more red berry fruits providing a supple mouthfeel; all up, a very elegant wine. Screwcap. 13.2% alc. **Rating** 95 **To** 2019 $80

Mornington Peninsula Pinot Gris 2012 One of two $50 Pinot Gris on the market: the only Pinot Gris to be barrel-fermented in 50% new and 50% second-use French oak, and the only Pinot Gris with a cellaring span (ex the back label) of 10–12+ years. As ever, this audacious approach works, making the wine complex, but not ponderous. Screwcap. 14% alc. **Rating** 94 **To** 2017 $50

L'Ami Sage Mornington Peninsula Pinot Noir 2011 Light, clear red-purple; wild yeast-fermented, and spent 18 months in French oak (30% new). It is a very savoury wine, with overt tannins needing to soften, which they will over time in bottle. 6200 made. Screwcap. 13.9% alc. **Rating** 94 **To** 2017 $60

🍷🍷🍷🍷🍷 **Mornington Peninsula Riesling 2012 Rating** 90 **To** 2015 $36

Paradise IV   ★★★★★

45 Dog Rocks Road, Batesford, Vic 3213 (postal) **Region** Geelong
T (03) 5276 1536 **www.paradiseivwines.com.au Open** Not
Winemaker Douglas Neal **Est.** 1988 **Dozens** 800 **Vyds** 3.1ha
The former Moorabool Estate has been renamed Paradise IV for the very good reason that it is the site of the original Paradise IV Vineyard, planted in 1848 by Swiss vigneron Jean-Henri Dardel. It is owned by Ruth and Graham Bonney. The vineyard is planted on decomposed granite over limestone, an ideal structure. The winery has an underground barrel room, and the winemaking turns around wild yeast fermentation, natural mlf, gravity movement of the wine and so forth. Exports to China.

🍷🍷🍷🍷🍷 **Geelong Chardonnay 2011** Pale straw-green; the wine is unexpectedly rich, indeed bordering on luscious, stone fruit interwoven with toasty/creamy/nutty nuances from oak and 80% mlf, then a balancing and cleansing line of acidity to the finish and aftertaste. Screwcap. 13.1% alc. **Rating** 94 **To** 2017 $49

The Bates' Ford Geelong Shiraz 2011 Good colour; has remarkable generosity and warmth (in the best sense) for the vintage; fragrant bouquet and medium-bodied palate with velvety plum and black cherry fruit. Screwcap. 13.5% alc. **Rating** 94 **To** 2021 $36

The Dardel 2011 Bright hue, with more purple than the Bates' Ford; has more structure and darker fruits, and may well have a longer life. Both these wines are exceptional for the vintage, for there have been no magic tricks in the winery, and neither needs any excuse. Screwcap. 13.5% alc. **Rating** 94 **To** 2031 $50

The Bates' Ford Geelong Shiraz 2010 Clear crimson-purple, it is light- to medium-bodied, with juicy red fruit flavours and a silky mouthfeel. It will probably surprise with its longevity, but will never be better than it is now. Screwcap. 12.8% alc. **Rating** 94 **To** 2018 $35

Paramoor Wines   ★★★★★

439 Three Chain Road, Carlsruhe via Woodend, Vic 3442 **Region** Macedon Ranges
T (03) 5427 1057 **www.paramoor.com.au Open** Fri–Mon 10–5
Winemaker William Fraser **Est.** 2003 **Dozens** 1500 **Vyds** 1.6ha

Paramoor Wines is the retirement venture of Will Fraser, formerly Managing Director of Kodak Australasia. To be strictly correct, he is Dr William Fraser, armed with a PhD in chemistry from Adelaide University. Much later he added a diploma of wine technology from the University of Melbourne to his qualifications. Paramoor is set on 17ha of beautiful country not far from Hanging Rock; it was originally a working Clydesdale horse farm, with a magnificent heritage-style barn now used for cellar door sales and functions. Will has planted 0.8ha each of pinot noir and pinot gris, and leases 2.6ha of vines in the lower Goulburn Valley (1.3ha shiraz, 0.9ha cabernet sauvignon, 0.4ha merlot). He also receives regular supplies of pinot noir and chardonnay grapes from another Macedon Ranges vineyard.

ŸŸŸŸŸ **Joan Picton Pinot Noir 2009** Deep colour, still holding crimson, no sign of colour change; a very classy Pinot, with satsuma plum, cherry and fruit spice driving the bouquet and palate alike; its balance is impeccable, as is the classic lift on the finish. Trophies Best Pinot Noir and Best Wine of Show Macedon Ranges Wine Exhibition '11. Diam. 13.3% alc. **Rating** 96 **To** 2021 $40
Joan Picton Pinot Noir 2010 Full crimson colour, although bright and clear; the rich bouquet of plum and black cherry leads into a powerful, layered palate with a reprise of the bouquet fruit before a spicy/foresty finish. A complex Pinot that manages to carry its alcohol without demur and will live for many years. Diam. 15% alc. **Rating** 94 **To** 2023 $35
The Fraser Shiraz Cabernet Sauvignon 2010 Excellent purple-crimson; very complex with blackberry and blackcurrant to the fore, and a powerful framework of tannins. Just when you think those tannins are over the top, a note of juicy fruit comes through on the finish. Diam. 14.9% alc. **Rating** 94 **To** 2025 $25
The Fraser Shiraz Cabernet Sauvignon 2009 Medium to full red-purple; skilled winemaking at work, the dark berry fruit flavours fresh, the oak balance good, the tannins likewise. Trophy Best Cabernet Blend Le Concours des Vins du Victoria '11. Diam. 14.5% alc. **Rating** 94 **To** 2029 $25
Uncle Fred Heathcote Cabernet Sauvignon 2011 Good hue, although lacks depth; there is much more varietal cabernet on the bouquet and juicy palate than expected, with cassis and cedar to the fore, tannins and oak in close support. Top class outcome for '11. Diam. 14.3% alc. **Rating** 94 **To** 2020 $25

ŸŸŸŸŸ **Sandhill Cabernet Sauvignon Merlot 2010 Rating** 93 **To** 2025 $25
✪ **Heathcote Rose 2012** The wine is composed of shiraz and small amounts (less than 10%) of pinot noir and pinot gris; the fruit-filled bouquet leads into an equally fruity palate with red and morello cherry leading the way, acidity balances a touch of sweetness. Screwcap. 13.9% alc. **Rating** 92 **To** 2014 $22
Kathleen Shiraz 2010 Rating 92 **To** 2030 $25
Master Angus Cabernet Sauvignon Merlot 2009 Rating 92 **To** 2020 $25

Paringa Estate   ★★★★★
44 Paringa Road, Red Hill South, Vic 3937 **Region** Mornington Peninsula
T (03) 5989 2669 **www**.paringaestate.com.au **Open** 7 days 11–5
Winemaker Lindsay McCall, Craig Thompson **Est.** 1985 **Dozens** 15 000 **Vyds** 24.7ha
Schoolteacher-turned-winemaker Lindsay McCall has shown an absolutely exceptional gift for winemaking across a range of styles, but with immensely complex Pinot Noir and Shiraz leading the way. The wines have an unmatched level of success in the wine shows and competitions Paringa Estate is able to enter, the limitation being the relatively small production of the top wines in the portfolio. His skills are no less evident in contract winemaking for others. Exports to the UK, Canada, Denmark, Ukraine, Singapore, Hong Kong, China and Japan.

ŸŸŸŸŸ **The Paringa Single Vineyard Pinot Noir 2009** A fraction of purple to the crimson colour; the super-fragrant bouquet leaps out of the glass, exuding black cherries and a dash of French oak; the palate has great elegance and length, oak and tannins an essential part of the future of a beautiful Pinot. Screwcap. 14% alc. **Rating** 97 **To** 2019 $90

Estate Pinot Noir 2010 Mid crimson, bright hue; a lifted bright and elegant perfume of red and black cherry, hoisin and Asian spices; the palate is racy and light on its feet, with lacy, fine tannins and a long and expansive, elegant structure. Screwcap. 14.5% alc. **Rating** 96 **To** 2020 $60 BE

The Paringa Single Vineyard Pinot Noir 2010 Mid garnet, vibrant hue; the bouquet offers a beguiling array of tea smoke, red cherry, Asian spices and a well-handled seasoning of toasty oak; the palate is lively, full of energy and fine-grained tannins, and is extremely long and expansive; the peacock's tail of flavour unwinds on the scintillating finish. Screwcap. 14.5% alc. **Rating** 96 **To** 2022 $90 BE

The Paringa Single Vineyard Shiraz 2009 Deep colour and brooding in character, with dark cherry, plum, black pepper and ironstone on the bouquet; the palate is densely packed with supple tannins and super-fresh acidity; the finish is extraordinarily long, pure and expansive; a little more of everything. Screwcap. 14.5% alc. **Rating** 96 **To** 2025 $80 BE

✪ Peninsula Shiraz 2012 Co-fermented with 5% viognier; the fragrant bouquet has the viognier lift to intense black cherry, blackberry and spice fruit aromas all reflected on the medium-bodied palate. Lyndsay McCall says shiraz was a standout in '12 and this wine, with its powerful texture and structure, shows he's right. Screwcap. 13.5% alc. **Rating** 95 **To** 2027 $25

Estate Shiraz 2010 Vibrant colour; a highly perfumed and spicy bouquet of red fruits, sage and Asian spices; the palate is fine-boned and linear, with latent power lingering beneath the fine-grained tannins; the conclusion is harmonious and expansive. Screwcap. 14% alc. **Rating** 95 **To** 2025 $50 BE

Peninsula Shiraz 2010 Lindsay McCall is a genius in the stratosphere of Australian shiraz. I cannot recall a Mornington Shiraz at this price of such exact black fruits and pepper, finely textured structure and outstanding persistence. Fruit concentration meets elegant, chalky structure. Screwcap. 14% alc. **Rating** 95 **To** 2018 $25 TS

Estate Chardonnay 2011 **Rating** 94 **To** 2018 $35 BE

♟♟♟♟♟ The Paringa Single Vineyard Chardonnay 2011 **Rating** 92 **To** 2016 $50 BE
Estate Riesling 2012 **Rating** 91 **To** 2020 $25 BE
Peninsula Chardonnay 2011 **Rating** 90 **To** 2016 $22 BE

🍇 Parish Lane Wines   ★★★☆

4 Moirs Road, Upper Kalgan, WA 6328 **Region** Great Southern
T (08) 9846 1220 **www**.parishlanewines.com.au **Open** By appt
Winemaker Mike Garland, Andrew Hoadley **Est.** 1997 **Dozens** 360
Richard and Julie Parish moved from Perth to Albany in 1995 seeking a lifestyle change, and planning to grow lavender. This they did for a couple of years until friends, who had a vineyard, suggested the small property would be ideal for growing grapes. They planted the first vines in '97, entering a steep learning curve. Both were teachers, Richard in primary school, Julie teaching cello in primary and high schools. The vineyard has 1ha of merlot, and 0.5ha each of chardonnay and pinot noir (the last as the result of a grafting program); cabernet sauvignon is purchased from a local grower. Quite apart from the problems of pests, birds and weather patterns, they own several dogs and an embodiment of Mr Ed the talking horse.

♟♟♟♟♟ Albany Merlot 2010 Presents a darker portrait of merlot than is usually the
✪ case, but much preferable to the plummy flavours of warm climates. Foresty/savoury/black olive nuances are slightly at odds with the dark chocolate, but it all works if you are searching for cool-climate merlot. Screwcap. 14% alc. **Rating** 90 **To** 2016 $20

♟♟♟♟ Albany Cabernet Merlot 2009 **Rating** 88 **To** 2016 $25
Methode Traditionale Albany Blanc de Blanc 2008 **Rating** 88 **To** 2015 $30

Parker Coonawarra Estate

Riddoch Highway, Coonawarra, SA 5263 **Region** Coonawarra
T (08) 8737 3525 **www.**parkercoonawarraestate.com.au **Open** 7 days 10–4
Winemaker Peter Bissell (Contract) **Est.** 1985 **Dozens** 7000
Parker Coonawarra Estate is at the southern end of Coonawarra, on rich terra rossa soil over limestone. Cabernet sauvignon is the predominant variety (17.45ha), with minor plantings of merlot and petit verdot. In 2012 the Rathbone Group wine interests were placed on the market for sale either as a group or individually. As the *2014 Wine Companion* was going to press, Parker Coonawarra was purchased by the Hesketh family. Exports to all major markets.

ŸŸŸŸŸ **First Growth 2010** Deep crimson-purple; as the often-pilloried name suggests, the best grapes from the estate vineyards are married with new French oak for an extended stay; luscious, perfectly ripened, cassis fruit blots out the competition (no mint here) and is harmoniously joined by supple tannins and quality French oak. Screwcap. 14% alc. **Rating** 96 **To** 2040 $110
Terra Rossa Cabernet Sauvignon 2010 The crimson-purple colour heralds a full-bodied Cabernet built for long-term cellaring. It is filled with blackcurrant, earth and mint fruit, flavours utterly true to the region, and the tannins need all that fruit (and vice versa). Screwcap. 14% alc. **Rating** 95 **To** 2035 $40
✪ **Favourite Son Shiraz 2010** Deep red-purple; a blend of Wrattonbully and Coonawarra shiraz, it has a striking bouquet with intense black and white pepper and licorice, moving to an unexpectedly supple, medium-bodied palate, with blackberry to the fore; the oak and tannins are a positive part of the very good texture and structure of the wine. Screwcap. 14.5% alc. **Rating** 94 **To** 2030 $25

ŸŸŸŸ   **Favourite Son Cabernet Merlot 2010 Rating** 88 **To** 2017 $25

Parri Estate

Sneyd Road, Mount Compass, SA 5210 **Region** Southern Fleurieu/McLaren Vale
T (08) 8554 9660 **www.**parriestate.com.au **Open** W'ends & public hols, and by appt
Winemaker Linda Domas **Est.** 1998 **Dozens** 15 000 **Vyds** 42ha
Alice, Peter and John Phillips have a business with a clear marketing plan and an obvious commitment to quality. The vineyard is planted to chardonnay, viognier, sauvignon blanc, semillon, savagnin, pinot noir, cabernet sauvignon and shiraz, using modern trellis and irrigation systems. In 2004 a second property, on Ingoldby Road, McLaren Vale, was acquired, with a second cellar door, with shiraz and cabernet sauvignon, and 70-year-old bush vine grenache. Exports to the UK and other major markets.

ŸŸŸŸŸ **Southern Fleurieu Estate Grown Savagnin 2012** Two batches picked at
✪ different baume levels, one clear juice, cool-fermented with cultured yeast, the other with cloudy juice, wild-fermented at warmer temperatures, up to 21°C; all this has resulted in good texture, with spice, ginger and pear flavours heightened by some sweetness on the finish. Screwcap. 12.5% alc. **Rating** 90 **To** 2015 $18
Shiraz Grenache 2010 Tasted shortly after bottling in Nov '12; the hue is very good, reflecting the shiraz component; a full-bodied wine that has benefited from its long oak maturation, the tannins ripe and integrated, shiraz black fruits more obvious than the red fruits ex grenache. Cork. 15% alc. **Rating** 90 **To** 2020 $22
Phillips Family Selection McLaren Vale Cabernet Shiraz 2008 This limited production blend (300 dozen) spent 16 months in French and American oak; it is medium-bodied, with fruit, oak and tannins neatly balanced, the black fruits with just a hint of regional dark chocolate. Cork. 14.5% alc. **Rating** 90 **To** 2016 $30

Passing Clouds ★★★★☆

30 Roddas Lane, Musk, Vic 3461 **Region** Macedon Ranges
T (03) 5348 5550 **www.**passingclouds.com.au **Open** 7 days 11–5
Winemaker Cameron and Graeme Leith **Est.** 1974 **Dozens** 3500 **Vyds** 10ha
Graeme and son Cameron Leith have undertaken a monumental vine change. They have moved the entire operation that started way back in 1974 in Bendigo to its new location

at Musk, near Daylesford. The vines at the original vineyard had been disabled by ongoing drought and all manner of pestilence, and it was no longer feasible to continue the business there. Sixteen semi-trailer loads later, all of their winemaking equipment and stock arrived at Musk, and the emphasis has moved to elegant Pinot Noir and Chardonnay, with a foot still in Bendigo courtesy of their friends, the Adams at Riola. Exports to the UK, the US and Europe.

ŸŸŸŸŸ **Daylesford Macedon Ranges Sparkling Chardonnay 2008** The grapes are estate-grown at an elevation of 771m, and the wine has been progressively disgorged, this wine the fourth disgorgement (in Nov '12). Good mousse; a super-elegant wine, with soft creamy nuances around its core of delicate stone fruit and red fruit flavours. Diam. 12.7% alc. **Rating** 94 **To** 2016 $41

ŸŸŸŸŸ **Graeme's Blend Shiraz Cabernet 2011** The purple-red colour makes light
✪ of the vintage, the red and black fruits of the palate likewise, with cherry, plum, blackberry and blackcurrant all in play; the tannins are soft, the oak integrated. Screwcap. 13.1% alc. **Rating** 93 **To** 2026 $30
Bendigo Shiraz 2011 **Rating** 92 **To** 2021 $30

Patina ★★★★

109 Summerhill Lane, Orange, NSW 2800 **Region** Orange
T (02) 6362 8336 **www**.patinawines.com.au **Open** W'ends 11–5, or by appt
Winemaker Gerald Naef **Est.** 1999 **Dozens** 3000 **Vyds** 3ha
Gerald Naef's home in Woodbridge in the Central Valley of California was surrounded by the vast vineyard and winery operations of Gallo and Robert Mondavi. It would be hard to imagine a more different environment than that provided by Orange. Gerald and wife Angie left California in 1981, initially establishing an irrigation farm in the northwest of NSW; 20 years later they moved to Orange, and by 2006 Gerald was a final-year student of wine science at CSU. He set up a micro-winery at the Orange Cool Stores, and his first wine was an '03 Chardonnay, made from vines planted in '99. At its first show it won the trophy for Best White Wine of Show – at the Orange Wine Show '06, of which I was Chairman. Dream starts seldom come better than this.

ŸŸŸŸŸ **Scandalous Orange Riesling 2012** Light straw-green; the higher residual sugar works well here, although not to the point of justifying the name; the play of residual sugar and acidity woven through the lime juice palate is evenly matched, so keeps attention on it. Screwcap. 11.9% alc. **Rating** 91 **To** 2016 $22

ŸŸŸŸ **Orange Riesling 2012** **Rating** 89 **To** 2017 $27

Patrick of Coonawarra ★★★★★

Cnr Ravenswood Lane/Riddoch Highway, Coonawarra, SA 5263 **Region** Coonawarra
T (08) 8737 3687 **www**.patrickofcoonawarra.com.au **Open** 7 days 10–4.30
Winemaker Luke Toccaciu **Est.** 2004 **Dozens** 7000 **Vyds** 79.5ha
Patrick Tocaciu (who died in 2013) was a district veteran, with prior careers at Heathfield Ridge Winery and Hollick Wines. He and his partners have over 41ha of vines at Wrattonbully, and another 38.5ha in Coonawarra. The Wrattonbully plantings cover all the major varieties, while the Coonawarra plantings give rise to the Home Block Cabernet Sauvignon. Patrick of Coonawarra also carries out contract winemaking for others. Son Luke, with a degree in oenology from Adelaide University and vintage experience in Australia and the US, has taken over in the winery. Exports to China and NZ.

ŸŸŸŸŸ **Estate Grown Riesling 2012** Pale straw-green; the wine is exuberantly fresh and tingling, with unsweetened lime juice and green apple to the fore, minerally acidity providing the framework for the development prior vintages of this wine have shown. Screwcap. 11% alc. **Rating** 94 **To** 2025 $29
Aged Riesling 2008 Glowing green-gold; despite, or perhaps due to, its low alcohol, the wine brings joyous ripe citrus fruit to fill the long palate from start to finish. It has the acidity to underwrite further development/ageing, when hints of toast will join the party. Screwcap. 11% alc. **Rating** 94 **To** 2018 $39

Limited Cellar Release Home Block Cabernet Sauvignon 2006
The grapes were grown at the Toccaciu Coonawarra estate, the wine matured for 26 months in French and American oak; this is a very attractive wine, which has cruised through 6, rising 7, years, the cassis and cedar flavours supported by very fine but persistent tannins. ProCork. 13.8% alc. **Rating** 94 **To** 2021 $49

�♀ **Mother of Pearl Sauvignon Blanc 2012** Well crafted, with the right calls on
✪ picking dates, then to simply cold-ferment clean juice with the correct sauvignon blanc-friendly yeast; flowery and fragrant, the palate balanced between citrus and passionfruit flavours. Screwcap. 11.5% alc. **Rating** 92 **To** 2014 $19
Estate Grown Wrattonbully Shiraz 2009 Rating 91 To 2019 $29

Patritti Wines   ★★★★★

13–23 Clacton Road, Dover Gardens, SA 5048 **Region** Adelaide Zone
T (08) 8296 8261 **www**.patritti.com.au **Open** Mon–Sat 9–5
Winemaker James Mungall, Ben Heide **Est.** 1926 **Dozens** 200 000
A traditional, family-owned business offering wines at modest prices, but with impressive vineyard holdings of 10ha of shiraz in Blewitt Springs and 6ha of grenache at Aldinga North. The surging production points to success in export markets, and also to the utilisation of contract-grown grapes as well as estate-grown. Quite how this has come about I don't know, but Patritti is currently releasing wines of very high quality at enticing prices, and a range of lesser quality wines at unfathomably low prices. The JPB Single Vineyard celebrates the arrival of Giovanni Patritti in Australia in 1925; he sold his wines under the 'John Patritti Brighton' label. Exports to the US and other major markets.

ppppp **Old Gate McLaren Vale Shire Shiraz 2010** Dense, inky purple-crimson; it has
✪ a highly expressive, but densely packed, full-bodied palate, black fruits at its heart, licorice, dark chocolate and oak providing a garland for the fruit. Ridiculously good value for a wine that demands 10 years, and will live for (at least) another 20 years thereafter. High-quality cork. 14.5% alc. **Rating** 94 **To** 2040 $18
✪ **Section 181 Single Vineyard McLaren Vale Grenache 2011** Only McLaren Vale's Blewitt Springs area can provide a wine with the density and structure of this wine, with its mix of raspberry and dark cherry in a thin coating of dark chocolate and ripe tannins, yet avoid heaviness. 15% alc. **Rating** 94 **To** 2020 $28

pppp♀ **Limited Release Barossa Valley Fortified Riesling 2004** Riesling was
✪ fortified and matured in oak for 8 years before release. Golden bronze, it is a vinous version of a toffee apple – and dangerously drinkable. The points are nominal. Cork. 17.5% alc. **Rating** 90 **To** 2014 $15

pppp **Barossa Valley Saperavi 2011** The inspiration for the wine came from a
✪ Georgian winemaker who worked at Patritti for a time; suitably impressed by a bottle of saperavi he provided, Patritti persuaded its oldest grower in the Barossa Valley to plant a small patch, and this is the first vintage. Here the variety easily accounted for the vintage with great colour, an array of berry fruits, and no excessive tannins. Cork. 14.5% alc. **Rating** 89 **To** 2016 $20

Paul Bettio Wines   ★★★

145 Upper King River Road, Cheshunt, Vic 3678 **Region** King Valley
T (03) 5729 8101 **www**.paulbettiowines.com.au **Open** Fri–Mon 10–5, or by appt
Winemaker Paul Bettio **Est.** 1995 **Dozens** 12 800 **Vyds** 21.8ha
The Bettio family settled in the King Valley during the 1950s. Paul and Helen Bettio have been growing cabernet sauvignon, merlot and sauvignon blanc beside the King River since '88. Paul's father Joe has the winery's second vineyard at Cheshunt, with chardonnay, merlot, barbera and pinot grigio.

pppp **King Valley Chardonnay 2010** Pale quartz; early picking has preserved natural
✪ acidity, and given a touch of tangy citrus to the gentle peach of the light-bodied palate. Obvious value. Screwcap. 12.1% alc. **Rating** 87 **To** 2014 $12

Paul Conti Wines ★★★★☆

529 Wanneroo Road, Woodvale, WA 6026 **Region** Greater Perth Zone
T (08) 9409 9160 **www**.paulcontiwines.com.au **Open** Mon–Sat 10–5, Sun by appt
Winemaker Paul and Jason Conti **Est.** 1948 **Dozens** 4000 **Vyds** 14ha

Third-generation winemaker Jason Conti has assumed control of winemaking, although father Paul (who succeeded his own father in 1968) remains involved in the business. Over the years Paul challenged and redefined industry perceptions and standards; the challenge for Jason is to achieve the same degree of success in a relentlessly and increasingly competitive market environment, and he is doing just that. Plantings at the Carabooda Vineyard have been expanded to include tempranillo, petit verdot and viognier, and pinot noir and chardonnay are purchased from Manjimup. In a further extension, a property has been acquired at Cowaramup in Margaret River, with sauvignon blanc, shiraz, cabernet sauvignon and semillon; muscat and malbec. Jason is a firm believer in organics, and the Swan Valley and Manjimup vineyards will soon join the family's Cowaramup organic vineyard. The original 2ha vineyard (shiraz) of the Mariginiup Vineyard remains the cornerstone. Exports to the UK, Malaysia, China and Japan.

ㅏㅏㅏㅏㅏ **Mariginiup Shiraz 2011** An enduring label – or wine – that has been consistently good over many vintages, but few better than this; it is medium-bodied, supple, and the red and black fruits are seamlessly cradled by ripe but soft tannins and subtle oak. Screwcap. 14.5% alc. **Rating** 95 **To** 2026 $28

ㅏㅏㅏㅏㅏ **Margaret River Chardonnay 2012** Stone fruit, melon and grapefruit are
❂ seamlessly integrated with a light touch of oak; the length is excellent, as is the value. Screwcap. 13.5% alc. **Rating** 92 **To** 2016 $20

❂ **Margaret River Cabernet Sauvignon 2011** Good colour; has a small proportion of merlo; it is medium- to full-bodied, with ripe blackcurrant fruit, a touch of cedar, and slightly dusty/furry tannins that need to soften and integrate, and should do so. Screwcap. 14.5% alc. **Rating** 90 **To** 2018 $20

❂ **Late Harvest Fronti 2012** Is utterly true to its label, with strong grapey flavours and considerable sweetness, balanced by acidity. I remember this style from 35 wines ago, when it was rarely encountered; this is better. Screwcap. 12% alc. **Rating** 90 **To** 2014 $18

Paul Nelson Wines ★★★★

11 Kemsley Place, Denmark, WA 6333 (postal) **Region** Great Southern
T 0406 495 066 **www**.paulnelsonwines.com.au **Open** Not
Winemaker Paul Nelson **Est.** 2009 **Dozens** 700

Paul Nelson started making wine with one foot in the Swan Valley, the other in the Great Southern, while completing a bachelor's degree in viticulture and oenology at Curtin University. He then worked successively at Houghton in the Swan Valley, Goundrey in Mount Barker, Santa Ynez in California, South Africa (for four vintages), hemisphere-hopping to the Rheinhessen, three vintages in Cyprus, then moving to a large Indian winemaker in Mumbai before returning to work for Houghton at Nannup. He has since moved on from Houghton to employment elsewhere, but (in partnership with wife Bianca Swart) makes small quantities of table wines.

ㅏㅏㅏㅏㅏ **Maison Madeleine 2012** Pale salmon-pink; a fragrant red berry bouquet takes on a fun third dimension on the palate; here strawberries and cream, and a touch of spice, are given unexpected tension and focus by citrussy acidity. Impressive rose. Screwcap. 14% alc. **Rating** 93 **To** 2014 $30

Grenache Mourvedre Tempranillo 2011 A searchlight, not candlelight, needed to read the label and see the grapes come from Geographe. The wine itself is a major surprise, with superb colour, and a lively and complex array of red berry fruits couched in a satin weave. Screwcap. 14.5% alc. **Rating** 93 **To** 2020 $45

Mount Barker Fume Blanc 2012 Light straw-green; this barrel-fermented sauvignon blanc is in Loire Valley style, with grainy acidity and grassy green pea components together with apple and kiwifruit; the oak does not contribute to the flavour, but to the texture. Screwcap. 13% alc. **Rating** 92 **To** 2014 $30

Paul Osicka ★★★★★

Majors Creek Vineyard at Graytown, Vic 3608 **Region** Heathcote
T (03) 5794 9235 **Open** By appt
Winemaker Paul and Simon Osicka **Est.** 1955 **Dozens** NFP **Vyds** 13ha

The Osicka family arrived in Australia from Czechoslovakia in the early 1950s. Vignerons in their own country, they settled at Graytown and commenced planting vines in '55. Their vineyard was the first new venture in Central and Southern Victoria for over half a century. With the return of Simon Osicka to the family business, there have been substantial changes. Prior to joining the family business full-time in 2010, Simon had senior winemaking positions at Houghton, Leasingham and as group red winemaker for CWA, interleaved with vintages in Italy, Canada, Germany and France, working at the prestigious Domaine J.L. Chave in Hermitage for the '10 vintage. The fermentation of the red wines has been changed from static to open fermenters, and French oak has replaced American oak. His handling of the '11 challenge was very impressive.

ŸŸŸŸŸ **Majors Creek Vineyard Heathcote Riesling 2012** Reconstruction of the
✪ vines over the '11 year paid dividends by protecting the grapes from sunburn; after fermentation the unsulphured wine was left on lees for 2 months to build weight and structure. It has citrus and herb nuances, and particularly attractive grainy acidity. Great Value. Screwcap. 12.9% alc. **Rating** 94 **To** 2022 $20
Majors Creek Vineyard Heathcote Shiraz 2011 The wine was open-fermented (14 days) and spent 16 months in French oak (30% new). The result is a most attractive medium-bodied Shiraz, with red and black cherry fruit and persistent spice, pepper and tannin nuances reflecting the cool season. Screwcap. 13.5% alc. **Rating** 94 **To** 2025 $35

ŸŸŸŸŸ **Majors Creek Vineyard Cabernet Sauvignon 2011 Rating** 92 **To** 2020 $35

Paulett ★★★★★

Polish Hill Road, Polish Hill River, SA 5453 **Region** Clare Valley
T (08) 8843 4328 **www.**paulettwines.com.au **Open** 7 days 10–5
Winemaker Neil Paulett, Kelvin Budarick **Est.** 1983 **Dozens** 14 000 **Vyds** 41.9ha

The Paulett story is a saga of Australian perseverance, commencing with the 1982 purchase of a property with 1ha of vines and a house, promptly destroyed by the terrible Ash Wednesday bushfires of the following year. Son Matthew has joined Neil and Alison Paulett as a partner in the business, responsible for viticulture on a much-expanded property holding, following the recent purchase of a large vineyard at Watervale. The winery and cellar door have wonderful views over the Polish Hill River region, the memories of the bushfires long gone. Exports to the UK, the US, Denmark, Singapore, Malaysia, China and NZ.

ŸŸŸŸŸ **Antonina Polish Hill River Riesling 2012** Painfully shy, yet its aristocratic breeding shines through its crunchy, minerally acidity; it is only on the aftertaste that the citrus and apple fruit breaks free. In 10 years anyone with this wine in their cellar will say it was well worth the wait. Screwcap. 11.5% alc. **Rating** 94 **To** 2032 $50
✪ **Polish Hill River Riesling 2012** Pale quartz-green; an elegant wine with a fragrant bouquet of lime and apple blossom which precisely translate to the flavours and structure of the palate. Classic Polish Hill River style; great value. Screwcap. 12% alc. **Rating** 94 **To** 2022 $24
Polish Hill River Aged Release Riesling 2008 Gleaming green-yellow; still young and vibrant, with lime and a touch of toast on the floral bouquet, then a supple, smooth and beautifully balanced palate. Drink today or in another 5 years; either way, you will be happy. Screwcap. 12.5% alc. **Rating** 94 **To** 2018 $50

ŸŸŸŸŸ **47/74 Malbec 2008 Rating** 92 **To** 2023 $80
Polish Hill River Shiraz 2009 Rating 91 **To** 2020 $24

ΥΥΥΥ **Cause & Effect Cabernet Merlot Shiraz Malbec 2009** The red wine
✪ brother to the '12 Riesling, both raising money for charity. This is the better wine
by some distance, with good colour and a robust personality, the multifaceted
red and black fruits with lots of flavour, and slightly coarse tannins. Screwcap.
13.5% alc. **Rating** 89 **To** 2018 $15

Paulmara Estates ★★★☆

47 Park Avenue, Rosslyn Park, SA 5072 (postal) **Region** Barossa Valley
T 0417 895 138 **www**.paulmara.com.au **Open** Not
Winemaker Paul Georgiadis, Neil Pike **Est.** 1999 **Dozens** 300 **Vyds** 11.8ha
Born to an immigrant Greek family, Paul Georgiadis grew up in Waikerie, where his family
had vineyards and orchards. His parents worked sufficiently hard to send him first to St Peters
College in Adelaide and then to do a marketing degree at Adelaide University. He became the
whirlwind grower-relations manager for Southcorp, and one of the best-known faces in the
Barossa Valley. Paul and wife Mara established a vineyard in 1995, planted to semillon, shiraz,
sangiovese, merlot and cabernet sauvignon. Part of the production is sold, and the best shiraz
makes the Syna Shiraz ('syna' being Greek for together).

ΥΥΥΥΥ **Limited Release Syna Barossa Valley Shiraz 2010** The colour is very good,
but – of course – the alcohol, and the attendant 'super-ripeness' (Georgiadis' own
words) are bound to create controversy even before the wine is tasted, coconut
oak another red rag for some. Nigh-on impossible to point, 92 a cowardly
compromise. Cork. 15.5% alc. **Rating** 92 **To** 2020 $50

ΥΥΥΥ **The Marriage Barossa Valley Coonawarra Shiraz Cabernet 2010**
Rating 88 **To** 2015 $25

Paxton ★★★★★

68 Wheaton Road, McLaren Vale, SA 5171 **Region** McLaren Vale
T (08) 8323 9131 **www**.paxtonvineyards.com **Open** 7 days 10–5
Winemaker Michael Paxton **Est.** 1979 **Dozens** 20 000 **Vyds** 74.5ha
David Paxton is one of Australia's best-known viticulturists and consultants. He founded
Paxton Vineyards in McLaren Vale with his family in 1979, and has since been involved in
various capacities in the establishment and management of vineyards in several leading regions
across the country. Son Michael, a former Flying Winemaker (with experience in Spain, South
America, France and Australia), is responsible for making the wines. There are five vineyards:
the Thomas Block (28ha), the Jones Block (22ha), Quandong Farm (19ha), Landcross Farm
(2ha) and Maslin Vineyard (3.5ha). All five are certified biodynamic, making Paxton one of
the largest biodynamic producers in Australia. A historic 1860s sheep farm, site of the original
village, houses Paxton's tasting rooms and cellar door. Exports to the UK, the US, Canada,
Denmark, Sweden, The Netherlands, Hong Kong, Taiwan and China.

ΥΥΥΥΥ **Elizabeth Jean 100 Year McLaren Vale Shiraz 2009** Deep garnet; there is
a sappy complexity to the bouquet that is beguiling, with ripe red fruits, well-
handled oak, and a hint of jasmine; the palate reveals more toasty oak notes, with
fine-grained tannins and velvety texture a feature of the long finish; an elegant
expression of the region. Screwcap. 14% alc. **Rating** 95 **To** 2025 $85 BE
Jones Block Single Vineyard McLaren Vale Shiraz 2010 A dark and layered
bouquet full of black fruits, red fruit highlight, hints of mocha and licorice; the
palate is full-blooded, ample and generous, with ripe chewy tannins and fresh
acidity lingering on the finish. Screwcap. 14.5% alc. **Rating** 94 **To** 2020 $37 BE

ΥΥΥΥΥ **Biodynamic Graciano Grenache 2011** **Rating** 93 **To** 2017 $30
✪ **The Guesser McLaren Vale Cabernet Shiraz 2010** A 52/58% blend; it has
abundant black fruits, licorice and bitter chocolate on the bouquet and medium-
to full-bodied palate, and a long life ahead for those who are patient. Screwcap.
14% alc. **Rating** 92 **To** 2025 $15
Quandong Farm Single Vineyard Shiraz 2011 **Rating** 91 **To** 2018 $30 BE

Cracker Barrels McLaren Vale Shiraz 2010 Rating 91 To 2017 $49 BE

✪ MV Biodynamic Vineyards McLaren Vale Shiraz 2011 Deep crimson; the bouquet reveals dark blackberry and thyme aromas, with a savoury edge; the palate is medium-bodied and lively, with chewy tannins and fresh acid offset by a little saltbush complexity. Screwcap. 14% alc. Rating 90 To 2018 $20 BE

✪ AAA McLaren Vale Shiraz Grenache 2011 Deep garnet; a decidedly savoury affair of bramble, Provençale garrigue and ripe red fruits; the palate is juicy on entry, tightening up with pronounced tannins and warmth on the finish. Screwcap. 14% alc. Rating 90 To 2016 $20 BE

Payne's Rise

10 Paynes Road, Seville, Vic 3139 **Region** Yarra Valley
T (03) 5964 2504 **www.**paynesrise.com.au **Open** Thurs–Sun 11–5, or by appt
Winemaker Franco D'Anna (Contract) **Est.** 1998 **Dozens** 800 **Vyds** 4ha
Tim and Narelle Cullen have progressively established 1ha each of cabernet sauvignon, shiraz, chardonnay and sauvignon blanc since 1998, supplemented by grapes purchased from local growers. They carry out all the vineyard work; Tim is also a viticulturist for a local agribusiness, and Narelle is responsible for sales and marketing. The contract-made wines have won several awards at the Victorian Wines Show.

🍷🍷🍷🍷🍷 Reserve Yarra Valley Chardonnay 2011 Pale, bright quartz-green; a super-intense, refined and tightly focused Chardonnay reflecting its Upper Yarra birthplace, with grapefruit to the fore, white peach to the rear, both built around crisp acidity. Screwcap. 13% alc. Rating 94 To 2018 $30

Peccavi Wines ★★★★☆

1121 Wildwood Road, Yallingup Siding, WA 6282 **Region** Margaret River
T 0409 544 630 **www.**peccavi-wines.com **Open** By appt
Winemaker Brian Fletcher **Est.** 1996 **Dozens** 5000 **Vyds** 16ha
Owner Jeremy Muller was introduced to the great wines of the world by his father when he was young, and says he spent many years searching New and Old World wine regions (even looking at the sites of ancient Roman vineyards in England), but did not find what he was looking for until one holiday in Margaret River. There he found a vineyard in Yallingup that was for sale, and he did not hesitate. He quickly put together a very impressive contract winemaking team, and appointed Colin Bell as chief viticulturist. The wines are released under two labels: Peccavi, for 100% estate-grown fruit (all hand-picked) and No Regrets, for wines that include contract-grown grapes and estate material. The quality of the wines is very good, reflecting the skills and experience of Brian Fletcher. Exports to the UK, Germany, Denmark, Malaysia, Singapore, Indonesia, Hong Kong and China.

🍷🍷🍷🍷🍷 Margaret River Cabernet Sauvignon 2010 Medium red-purple; the fragrant bouquet points to the medium-bodied palate that follows, with pure varietal expression (cassis and black olive), fine-grained tannins and good oak handling throughout. WAK screwcap. 14% alc. Rating 94 To 2025 $45

🍷🍷🍷🍷🍷 Margaret River Chardonnay 2011 Rating 92 To 2017 $45
Margaret River Shiraz 2010 Rating 92 To 2020 $40

Pedestal Vineyard Wines

PO Box 871, Canning Bridge, WA 6153 **Region** Margaret River
T (08) 6364 4862 **www.**pedestalwines.com.au **Open** Not
Winemaker Larry Cherubino **Est.** 2008 **Dozens** 1500 **Vyds** 14ha
This was a joint venture between land (and vineyard) owners Greg and Kerilee Brindle, and winemaker Larry Cherubino and wife Edwina, now fully owned by the latter. The vineyard (cabernet sauvignon, merlot, sauvignon blanc and semillon) was planted in 1998, the grapes being sold over the ensuing years to other winemakers in the region. Distribution by Bibendum on the eastern seaboard is testimony to the skills of Larry Cherubino, leading

to increased sales. This is a venture worth watching. No wines received for the *2014 Wine Companion*, but a five-star rating has been maintained.

Peel Estate   ★★★★☆

290 Fletcher Road, Karnup, WA 6176 **Region** Peel
T (08) 9524 1221 **www**.peelwine.com.au **Open** 7 days 10–5
Winemaker Will Nairn, Mark Morton **Est.** 1974 **Dozens** 4000 **Vyds** 16ha
Peel's icon wine is the Shiraz, a wine of considerable finesse and with a remarkably consistent track record. Every year Will Nairn holds a Great Shiraz Tasting for six-year-old Australian shirazs, and pits Peel Estate (in a blind tasting attended by 100 or so people) against Australia's best. It is never disgraced. The wood-matured Chenin Blanc is another winery specialty. Exports to the UK, Ireland, China and Japan.

ΨΨΨΨΨ **Old Vine Shiraz 2006** Bright and clear medium red-purple; the juicy red and black berry fruit has a faintly peppery, cranberry character in the background, and also shows the positive contribution of extended barrel maturation. Still remarkably fresh. Screwcap. 14.5% alc. **Rating** 94 **To** 2016 $35

ΨΨΨΨΨ **Wood Matured Chenin Blanc 2011** **Rating** 90 **To** 2017 $25

Penfolds

Tanunda Road, Nuriootpa, SA 5355 **Region** Barossa Valley
T (08) 8568 9408 **www**.penfolds.com **Open** 7 days 10–5
Winemaker Peter Gago **Est.** 1844 **Dozens** NFP
Penfolds is the star in the crown of Treasury Wine Estates (TWE), but its history predates the formation of TWE by close on 170 years. Over that period its shape has changed both in terms of its vineyards, its management, its passing parade of great winemakers, and its wines. There is no other single winery brand in the new, or the old, world with the depth and breadth of Penfolds. In 2013 the retail prices ranged from $18 to $785 for Grange, which is the cornerstone produced every year, albeit with the volume determined by the quality of the vintage, not by cash flow. There is now a range of regional wines with single varieties, and the so-called Bin Range of wines that include both regional blends and (in some instances) varietal blends. It may sound complicated, but given the size of the business, and the long-term history of the Bins (the oldest dating back to the early 1960s) it is not as difficult as one might imagine to understand the winemaking and commercial rationale. Despite the very successful Yattarna and Reserve Bin A Chardonnays, and some impressive Rieslings, this remains a red wine producer at heart. Exports to all major markets.

ΨΨΨΨΨ **Grange 2008** Contains 98/2% shiraz and cabernet sauvignon, and spent 19 months in new American oak hogsheads, in which it finished its fermentation. Densely coloured, it has an ultra-complex bouquet, with black fruits/anise/licorice, easily dealing with the oak; a remarkable wine in every way. The balance, texture and structure are faultless, so much so that the wine achieves elegance now, many years before you would expect that quality to be commented on. Cork. 14.3% alc. **Rating** 98 **To** 2060 $785
Bin 169 Coonawarra Cabernet Sauvignon 2010 A single vineyard wine, matured for 14 months in new, fine-grained French oak, in which it finished the final stages of its fermentation. The bouquet is laden with cassis of startling purity, and while cedary oak is a major player, it is so well integrated it doesn't overwhelm, let alone challenge, the fruit. The tannin support is as remarkable as any other aspect of this wine. Screwcap. 14.5% alc. **Rating** 98 **To** 2040 $350
Yattarna Chardonnay 2009 Pale straw-green; mineral/slate are decidedly uncommon characters to find on the bouquet, but they are certainly there once the wine is taken onto the palate, and thereafter back to the bouquet. While it is extremely tight and elegant, there is a delicious melodic trio of stone fruit, melon and citrus flavours. Screwcap. 12.5% alc. **Rating** 97 **To** 2022 $130

RWT Barossa Valley Shiraz 2009 Deep, dense purple-crimson; the bouquet sets the scene with interwoven black fruits and cedary French oak; the palate is exceedingly complex, intense and layered; the flavours are spicy, black-fruited, with licorice and bitter chocolate, fine, lingering tannins provide the framework. Screwcap. 14.5% alc. **Rating** 97 **To** 2040 $175

Grandfather Fine Old Liqueur Tawny NV Fully aged but bright tawny; the very complex Christmas cake bouquet has all manner of Asian spices asking to be heard; the palate is very luscious, yet is magically made elegant by its burnt sugar acidity. Cork. 20% alc. **Rating** 97 **To** 2014 $100

Great Grandfather Limited Release Rare Tawny NV Arguably the best of all Australian tawnies, with more luscious fruit than Seppelt DP90 (the other contender); luscious it may be, but it is also wonderfully elegant, with rancio and Christmas cake and toffee flavours on the mid-palate, moving to a spicy, dry and ultimately fresh finish. Cork. 19.5% alc. **Rating** 97 **To** 2014 $350

Reserve Bin A Chardonnay 2010 Bright straw-green; this is a supremely elegant wine, but in a different mode from the '09 and '08; the white stone fruit and grapefruit flavours are supple and have excellent balance with each other and with the subtle French oak; a little more cut and energy needed for that extra point. Screwcap. 13% alc. **Rating** 96 **To** 2018 $95

Yattarna Chardonnay 2010 There is an extremely charming blend of complexity and purity in this wine that offers ripe lemon, nectarine and fine oak spices on the bouquet; the palate is tightly wound, and while simply waiting for the appropriate amount of time to gain weight and fulfil its potential, will make it a real challenge to keep your hands off this now truly iconic Australian Chardonnay. Screwcap. 13% alc. **Rating** 96 **To** 2025 $130 BE

RWT Barossa Valley Shiraz 2010 Year in and year out there is an understated quietness to this wine that speaks volumes about the style, as everything is working together as one; the fruit, the oak, the tannins and the inherent complexity of some seriously old vine Barossa material shines through; freshness, vitality, harmony and ageworthiness are just a few words that do this excellent rendition of RWT justice. Screwcap. 14.5% alc. **Rating** 96 **To** 2050 $175 BE

Bin 707 Cabernet Sauvignon 2010 From the Barossa Valley, Padthaway, Wrattonbully and Adelaide Hills. Exceptional depth of crimson-purple colour sets the scene for a spectacular wine from this great vintage. The American oak is very obvious, but that's the style. Tastings over the years have shown that, when 10–20 years old, the components come together very well. Screwcap. 14.5% alc. **Rating** 96 **To** 2030 $350

Bin 707 Cabernet Sauvignon 2009 This deeply coloured, full-bodied Cabernet has an array of blackcurrant and redcurrant fruit drawn from the best cabernet vineyards of Penfolds (and from some growers). The oak and tannins add another dimension, and the wine will still be improving 20 years hence. Screwcap. 14.5% alc. **Rating** 96 **To** 2032 $250

Cellar Reserve Coonawarra Cabernet Sauvignon 2008 Superbly intense, focused and long; fruit, French oak and tannins all perfectly balanced, the palate spectacularly long. Screwcap. 14.5% alc. **Rating** 96 **To** 2033 $200

Bin 389 Cabernet Shiraz 2010 A 51/49% blend, matured for 14 months in American oak hogsheads (40% new). It is full-bodied, with layer upon layer of flavour, yet has a plush, welcoming character. The perfectly ripe blackcurrant and blackberry fruit has a coat of Belgian chocolate, the oak already submerged under the fruit. Screwcap. 14.5% alc. **Rating** 96 **To** 2045 $75

Cellar Reserve Barossa Valley Mataro 2010 A new age of Penfolds, one in which fruit leads over oak and structure, and expressive fruit is afforded magnificent space to be fresh, lively, poised, even elegant. All the while, it remains definitively Barossa and unmistakably Penfolds, with seamless persistence and concentrated blueberry and black plum fruit. Screwcap. 14.5% alc. **Rating** 96 **To** 2025 $50 TS

Bin 150 Marananga Barossa Valley Shiraz 2010 Impenetrable colour, purple hue; this subregional Barossa Shiraz exhibits a dark and brooding personality, complex and full of intrigue, with black fruits, ironstone, oak-derived spices and a floral lift; the palate is tightly wound, impressively proportioned and, while dark and dense, shows plenty of detail and excellent balance. Made for the long haul. Screwcap. 14.5% alc. **Rating** 95 **To** 2040 $75 BE

Bin 407 Cabernet Sauvignon 2010 As always, this is Australian cabernet with muscle, revealing flashes of both house style and purity of expression that can be achieved with multi-regional fruit; essency dark fruits and a hint of floral on the bouquet, with the muscular framework providing drive and energy on the palate; long and almost luscious, this is an excellent rendition of Bin 407. Screwcap. 14.5% alc. **Rating** 95 **To** 2030 $75 BE

Bin 51 Eden Valley Riesling 2012 **Rating** 94 **To** 2020 $33
Cellar Reserve Adelaide Hills Chardonnay 2012 **Rating** 94 **To** 2020 $34 BE
Bin 28 Kalimna Shiraz 2010 **Rating** 94 **To** 2025 $38 BE

ΨΨΨΨΨ St Henri 2009 **Rating** 93 **To** 2025 $95 BE
Bin 169 Coonawarra Cabernet Sauvignon 2009 **Rating** 93 **To** 2030 $350 BE
Cellar Reserve Barossa Valley Sangiovese 2010 **Rating** 93 **To** 2018 $50
Thomas Hyland Chardonnay 2012 **Rating** 92 **To** 2020 $25 BE
Bin 128 Coonawarra Shiraz 2011 **Rating** 92 **To** 2023 $38 BE
Bin 2 Shiraz Mourvedre 2011 **Rating** 92 **To** 2022 $38 BE
Koonunga Hill Shiraz Cabernet 2010 **Rating** 92 **To** 2025 $18
Cellar Reserve Barossa Valley Cabernet Sauvignon 2010 **Rating** 92 **To** 2025 $200 BE
Bin 138 Barossa Shiraz Grenache Mataro 2011 **Rating** 91 **To** 2025 $38 BE
Cellar Reserve Woodbury Vineyard Eden Valley Traminer 2012 **Rating** 90 **To** 2015 $34 BE
Cellar Reserve Adelaide Hills Semillon 2012 **Rating** 90 **To** 2016 $34 BE
Thomas Hyland Sauvignon Blanc 2012 **Rating** 90 **To** 2014 $25 BE

Penfolds Magill Estate   ★★★★★

78 Penfold Road, Magill, SA 5072 **Region** Adelaide Zone
T (08) 8301 5569 **www**.penfolds.com **Open** 7 days 10.30–5
Winemaker Peter Gago **Est.** 1844 **Dozens** NFP **Vyds** 5.2ha
This is the birthplace of Penfolds, established by Dr Christopher Rawson Penfold in 1844; his house is still part of the immaculately maintained property. It includes 5.2ha of precious shiraz used to make Magill Estate; the original and subsequent winery buildings, most still in operation or in museum condition; and the much-acclaimed Magill Restaurant, with panoramic views of the city, a great wine list and fine dining. All this 20 minutes' drive from Adelaide's CBD. Exports to the UK, the US and other major markets.

ΨΨΨΨΨ Shiraz 2010 Impenetrable colour; the bouquet of this flagship vineyard is dominated by sweet vanillin oak at this early stage, indicating that patience is a necessity to get the most out of this wine; beyond the lavish oak are layers of black fruits, licorice, spice and floral notes; there is a firmness to the tannins here that complements the depth of fruit on offer, the wine's parts in total harmony. Patience will be rewarded. Cork. 14.5% alc. **Rating** 95 **To** 2045 $130 BE

Penley Estate   ★★★★★

McLeans Road, Coonawarra, SA 5263 **Region** Coonawarra
T (08) 8736 3211 **www**.penley.com.au **Open** 7 days 10–4
Winemaker Kym Tolley, Greg Foster **Est.** 1988 **Dozens** 45 000 **Vyds** 111ha
Owner Kym Tolley describes himself as a fifth-generation winemaker, the family tree involving both the Penfolds and the Tolleys. He worked in the industry for 17 years before establishing Penley Estate and has made every post a winner since, producing a succession of

rich, complex, full-bodied red wines and stylish Chardonnays. These are made from precious estate plantings. Exports to all major markets.

ᵭᵭᵭᵭᵭ Special Select Coonawarra Shiraz 2010 Very good crimson-purple colour; a rich, multifaceted, medium- to full-bodied wine reflecting the excellent vintage, with plum, blackberry, spice and anise wrapped in quality oak. Trophy at Limestone Coast Wine Show '12. Cork. 14.5% alc. Rating 94 To 2035 $51

ᵭᵭᵭᵭᵭ
⬤ Phoenix Coonawarra Cabernet Sauvignon 2010 Vibrant deep crimson; a punchy and expressive cabernet bouquet with redcurrant, cassis, clove and olive on display; the palate is medium- to full-bodied, fleshy, and manages to create a long and even finish; designed for early consumption, but will stand the test of time in the medium term. Screwcap. 14.5% alc. **Rating** 93 To 2020 $20 BE

⬤ Condor Coonawarra Cabernet Shiraz 2010 Bright colour, with fresh red and black fruits, black olive and a gentle lift of thyme; the palate is medium-bodied, fleshy and succulent. Screwcap. 14.5% alc. **Rating** 90 To 2016 $20 BE

ᵭᵭᵭᵭ Aradia Coonawarra Chardonnay 2010 Rating 88 To 2014 $20
Hyland Coonawarra Shiraz 2010 Rating 88 To 2016 $20 BE
Gryphon Coonawarra Merlot 2010 Rating 88 To 2014 $20 BE

Penmara   ★★★★

Unit 8, 28 Barcoo St, Roseville, NSW 2069 (postal) **Region** Hunter Valley/Orange
T (02) 9417 7088 **www**.penmarawines.com.au **Open** Not
Winemaker Hunter Wine Services (John Hordern) **Est.** 2000 **Dozens** 25 000 **Vyds** 120ha
Penmara was formed with the banner 'Five Families: One Vision', pooling most of their grapes, with a central processing facility, and marketing focused exclusively on exports. The sites are Lilyvale Vineyards in New England; Tangaratta Vineyards at Tamworth; Birnam Wood and Martindale Vineyards in the Hunter Valley; and Highland Heritage at Orange. These vineyards give Penmara access to 120ha of shiraz, chardonnay, cabernet sauvignon, semillon, verdelho and merlot. Exports to South Korea, Malaysia, Singapore and China.

ᵭᵭᵭᵭᵭ
⬤ Family Select Orange Pinot Noir 2010 Medium red-purple; while the wine does not aspire to greatness, it is well within the comfort zone of pinot noir varietal character, with warm plum and dark cherry fruit to the fore, and an unexpectedly juicy finish. Screwcap. 14% alc. **Rating** 91 To 2015 $20

ᵭᵭᵭᵭ Family Select Orange Sauvignon Blanc 2012 Rating 88 To 2013 $20
Family Select Hunter Valley Chardonnay 2011 Rating 88 To 2014 $20
Family Select Hunter Valley Shiraz 2010 Rating 87 To 2016 $20

Penna Lane Wines   ★★★★

Lot 51 Penna Lane, Penwortham via Clare, SA 5453 **Region** Clare Valley
T (08) 8843 4033 **www**.pennalanewines.com.au **Open** Thurs–Sun 11–5, or by appt
Winemaker Peter Treloar, Chris Proud **Est.** 1998 **Dozens** 4500 **Vyds** 4.37ha
Penna Lane is located in the beautiful Skilly Valley, approximately 10km south of Clare. The estate vineyard (shiraz, cabernet sauvignon and semillon), is planted at an elevation of approximately 450m, which allows a long, slow ripening period, usually resulting in wines with intense varietal fruit flavours. The vines are virtually dry-grown, receiving only supplementary irrigation in the very dry years. Exports to Hong Kong, South Korea, Fiji, Vietnam, Thailand, China and Japan.

ᵭᵭᵭᵭᵭ Watervale Riesling 2011 One year after its birth, the colour is still very pale indeed; in this context the lime and passionfruit on the bouquet and palate come as a surprise. An attractive wine, but it's hard to guess how long it will live and flourish. Screwcap. 12.5% alc. **Rating** 91 To 2016 $18

Penny's Hill   ★★★★★

281 Main Road, McLaren Vale, SA 5171 **Region** McLaren Vale
T (08) 8557 0888 **www.**pennyshill.com.au **Open** 7 days 10–5
Winemaker Ben Riggs **Est.** 1988 **Dozens** 15000 **Vyds** 44ha
Founded in 1988 by Tony and Susie Parkinson, Penny's Hill produces high-quality Shiraz
(Footprint and The Skeleton Key) from its 18.4ha estate vineyard that, unusually for McLaren
Vale, is close-planted. Malpas Road Vineyard (15ha of shiraz, cabernet sauvignon and merlot)
and Goss Corner Vineyard (10.6ha of viognier, shiraz and merlot) complete the estate holdings,
and provide the fruit for the Cracking Black Shiraz. Penny's Hill also produces estate-grown
Grenache, Cabernet Sauvignon and Merlot (the Sauvignon Blanc and Chardonnay come
from 'estates of mates' vineyards in the Adelaide Hills), all wines with a distinctive 'red dot',
inspired by red dot 'sold' stickers on works of art in commercial galleries. Exports to the UK,
the US, Canada, Sweden, Denmark, Germany, Switzerland, Singapore, China and NZ.

♀♀♀♀♀ Footprint McLaren Vale Shiraz 2011 From a relatively young vineyard planted
in '91 to 5 clones; traditionally made with 7 days on skins, pressed at 2° baume and
matured for 18 months in used French and American oak. It has great balance and
mouthfeel, the flavours complex, yet supple and persistent. Screwcap. 14.5% alc.
Rating 95 To 2026 $65

♀♀♀♀♀ The Agreement Sauvignon Blanc 2012 A convincing example of the
❍   Adelaide Hills sauvignon blanc style, with texture and structure the foundation
stone; citrus/grapefruit, kiwi fruit and a hint of capsicum are all present, minerally
acidity lengthening the finish. Screwcap. 13% alc. **Rating** 92 **To** 2014 $19

❍   **Thomas Goss McLaren Vale Shiraz 2011** Deep crimson, red hue; the
bouquet offers a blend of red and black fruits, with an attractive floral lift of violets;
the uncomplicated palate is lively and fresh, juicy and fragrant, packing plenty of
punch into a compact finish; excellent value for the price. Screwcap. 14.5% alc.
Rating 92 **To** 2018 $15 BE

The Veteran Very Old Fortified NV Has an average age of over 20 years, and
is very complex – as well as very luscious. 500ml. Screwcap. 18.5% alc. **Rating** 92
To 2014 $30

❍   **The Black Chook Pinot Grigio 2012** Slight bronzing; the bouquet is the very
essence of fresh cut pear and bath talc; the palate is generous, fresh and delivers
the right amount of concentration to persist on the finish for a reasonable amount
of time; dry and chalky to conclude. Screwcap. 12.5% alc. **Rating** 90 **To** 2014
$17 BE

Edwards Road Cabernet Sauvignon 2011 Impenetrable colour, and dark
and brooding in character, with essency black fruits, salted caramel and licorice on
display; the full bodied palate is very tannic and gravelly in texture, with the ample
black fruits taking a back seat to the impressive muscle on display; a little time should
see this find better balance. Screwcap. 14.5% alc. **Rating** 90 **To** 2020 $24 BE

❍   **Thomas Goss Cabernet Sauvignon 2011** Bright and fragrant red fruits
are offset by pencilly oak and cedar; medium-bodied and fragrant on the palate,
showing fine varietal character and an evenly balanced finish. Screwcap. 14.5% alc.
Rating 90 **To** 2018 $15 BE

♀♀♀♀ The Black Chook Shiraz 2011 One of the most successful McLaren Vale
❍   Shirazs in this price range from '11; has regional dark chocolate, and no shortage
of black fruits; just a touch hollow. Screwcap. 14.5% alc. **Rating** 89 **To** 2015 $18

Cracking Black McLaren Vale Shiraz 2011 Rating 89 **To** 2016 $22

Malpas Road McLaren Vale Merlot 2011 Rating 89 **To** 2015 $19

❍   **Thomas Goss Clare Valley Riesling 2012** Generous aromas of ripe lemon,
flint and coriander all appear on the bouquet; the palate is juicy, accessible and
made for early consumption. Screwcap. 11.5% alc. **Rating** 88 **To** 2016 $15 BE

The Black Chook Langhorne Creek Rose 2012 Rating 88 **To** 2014 $17 BE

The Specialized Shiraz Cabernet Merlot 2011 Rating 88 **To** 2018 $35 BE

The Black Chook Sauvignon Blanc 2012 Rating 87 **To** 2013 $18

Pepper Tree Wines

Halls Road, Pokolbin, NSW 2321 **Region** Hunter Valley
T (02) 4909 7100 **www.**peppertreewines.com.au **Open** Mon–Fri 9–5, w'ends 9.30–5
Winemaker Scott Comyns **Est.** 1991 **Dozens** 50 000 **Vyds** 172.1ha
The Pepper Tree winery is part of a complex that also contains The Convent guest house
and Roberts Restaurant. In 2002 it was acquired by a company controlled by Dr John
Davis, who owns 50% of Briar Ridge. It sources the majority of its Hunter Valley fruit
from its Tallavera Grove vineyard at Mt View, but also has premium vineyards at Orange,
Coonawarra and Wrattonbully, which provide its Grand Reserve and Reserve (single region)
wines. Self-evidently, the wines are exceptional value for money. Following the departure of
winemaker Jim Chatto in 2013, his understudy Scott Comyns has slipped easily into the chair
of Chief Winemaker. Exports to the US, Canada, Denmark, Singapore and China.

ŸŸŸŸŸ **Single Vineyard Reserve Coquun Hunter Valley Shiraz 2011** Like all the
Pepper Tree Hunter Valley wines, is the epitome of elegance, yet has untold depths
of blackberry and plum fruit that have brushed aside the high-quality oak you
know is there, likewise the ripe, plum tannins. I will be long gone by the time this
wine reaches its peak. Screwcap. 14% alc. **Rating** 97 **To** 2051 $55
Single Vineyard Reserve Alluvius Hunter Valley Semillon 2009 Has
also left the station on the first stage of its train ride to maturity, the lime and
lemongrass flavours intensifying. Retains the 96 points given when first tasted in
Sept '09. Screwcap. 10.5% alc. **Rating** 96 **To** 2024 $45
Single Vineyard Limited Release Tallavera Hunter Valley Shiraz 2011
Full medium red-purple; a (tasting) buzz word these days is 'detailed', and it
certainly fits the precision of this medium-bodied wine; the red and black fruits
are effortlessly carried by ultra-fine tannins and subtle French oak. Screwcap.
13.5% alc. **Rating** 96 **To** 2041 $45
Single Vineyard Reserve Alluvius Hunter Valley Semillon 2012 The
bouquet and palate speak with the same voice of lemongrass, citrus and a touch
of talc, all classic denominators. But it is the texture of the minerally acidity on the
finish and aftertaste that tell you how great the wine will be when it reaches full
maturity in 10–20 years, and today's points will seem niggardly. Screwcap. 10.8%
alc. **Rating** 95 **To** 2027 $35
Single Vineyard Limited Release Hunter Valley Semillon 2009 There has
been barely any colour development over the 3½ years since the wine received
96 points out of the Hunter Valley Wine Show '09; tight lemon zest, lemon pith
and lemon juice, basically unsweetened, flavours still mark the wine. Screwcap.
11.2% alc. **Rating** 95 **To** 2020 $35
**Single Vineyard Limited Release Tallawanta Hunter Valley Semillon
2012** **Rating** 94 **To** 2027 $28
Single Vineyard Limited Release Hunter Valley Shiraz 2011 **Rating** 94
To 2031 $35

ŸŸŸŸŸ **Hunter Valley Marlborough Semillon Sauvignon Blanc 2012** When you
✪ can't beat them, join them, especially when you get a synergistic outcome such
as this, the grassy semillon bouncing off the full-on tropical passionfruit of the
Marlborough component. Screwcap. 11.5% alc. **Rating** 91 **To** 2014 $18

Pepperilly Estate Wines

Suite 16, 18 Stirling Highway, Nedlands, WA 6009 (postal) **Region** Geographe
T 0401 860 891 **www.**pepperilly.com **Open** Not
Winemaker Damian Hutton **Est.** 1999 **Dozens** 2500 **Vyds** 11ha
Partners Geoff and Karyn Cross, and Warwick Lavis, planted their vineyard in 1991 with 2ha
each of cabernet sauvignon, shiraz and sauvignon blanc, and 1ha each of semillon, viognier,
chardonnay, mourvedre and grenache. The vineyard has views across the Ferguson Valley to
the ocean, with sea breezes providing good ventilation.

Peregrine Ridge

19 Carlyle Street, Moonee Ponds, Vic 3039 (postal) **Region** Heathcote
T 0411 741 772 **www.peregrineridge.com.au Open** Not
Winemaker Graeme Quigley, Sue Kerrison **Est.** 2001 **Dozens** 1000 **Vyds** 5.5ha
Graeme Quigley and Sue Kerrison were wine lovers and consumers before they came to growing and making their own wine. Having purchased a property high on the Mt Camel Range (the name comes from the peregrine falcons that co-habit the vineyard and the ridgeline that forms the western boundary of the property), they progressively planted their vineyard solely to shiraz. Irrigation is used sparingly, with the yields restricted to 2.5 to 3.5 tonnes per hectare; the grapes are hand-picked into small baskets, transported direct to small open fermenters and made in small batches.

TTTT   American Oak Blend Heathcote Shiraz 2009 Deeply coloured, and densely concentrated, with lashings of mocha and sage sitting atop black fruits and prunes; the palate is big-boned and raw, with tangy acidity providing relief from the mocha flavours that dominate. Screwcap. 14.8% alc. **Rating** 88 **To** 2018 $45 BE

Pertaringa

Cnr Hunt Road/Rifle Range Road, McLaren Vale, SA 5171 **Region** McLaren Vale
T (08) 8323 8125 **www.pertaringa.com.au Open** Mon–Fri 10–5, w'ends & public hols 11–5
Winemaker Shane Harris, Geoff Hardy **Est.** 1980 **Dozens** 10 000 **Vyds** 64ha
The name 'Pertaringa' means 'belonging to the hills' and originates from the local Kaurna indigenous language. Tucked away in the cooler eastern foothills of McLaren Vale, Pertaringa was founded by highly respected viticulturists Geoff Hardy and Ian Leask. In December 2011, Geoff and his family acquired the Leask interest in Pertaringa to become the sole custodians of the brand. Geoff's commitment to industry innovation through clonal and varietal trials has seen, in recent times, the traditional range of Pertaringa wines complemented by the arrival of Tannat, Aglianico and the 'Tin Man' Spanish blend. Exports to the UK, the US and other major markets.

TTTTT   Undercover McLaren Vale Shiraz 2010 Deep purple-crimson; flooded with
✪   luscious and generous plum, dark chocolate and licorice fruit, the tannins ripe, the oak a bystander. One of those wines that drinks well today or in 20 years, and a great bargain by any standards. Screwcap. 14.5% alc. **Rating** 95 **To** 2030 $22

TTTTT   Scarecrow Sauvignon Blanc 2012 Very good texture and overall balance, the
✪   bouquet and palate with tropical fruit to start, then moving to a more citrussy/herbal finish, the acidity perfectly balanced. Screwcap. 13% alc. **Rating** 91 **To** 2014 $18
          Over The Top McLaren Vale Shiraz 2010 Rating 90 **To** 2018 $40 BE
          Rifle & Hunt Adelaide Cabernet Sauvignon 2010 Rating 90 **To** 2018 $40 BE

Petaluma

Spring Gully Road, Piccadilly, SA 5151 **Region** Adelaide Hills
T (08) 8339 9300 **www.petaluma.com.au Open** At Bridgewater Mill, 7 days 10–5
Winemaker Andrew Hardy, Mike Mudge, Penny Jones **Est.** 1976 **Dozens** 60 000
Vyds 240ha
The Petaluma range has been expanded beyond the core group of Croser Sparkling, Clare Valley Riesling, Piccadilly Chardonnay and Coonawarra (Cabernet Sauvignon/Merlot). Newer arrivals of note include Adelaide Hills Viognier and Adelaide Hills Shiraz. Bridgewater Mill is the second label, which consistently provides wines most makers would love to have as their top label. The SA plantings in the Clare Valley, Coonawarra and Adelaide Hills provide a more than sufficient source of estate-grown grapes for the wines. In Dec 2012 plans were announced for the building of a new winery at Woodside. It is a greenfield site, with views of Mt Lofty, and the multimillion-dollar investment has been enthusiastically welcomed by Andrew Hardy, and all at Petaluma. The first vintage at the new winery is expected in '15. Exports to all major markets.

ŦŦŦŦŦ **Hanlin Hill Clare Valley Riesling 2012** Bright straw-green; a distinguished Riesling with a long pedigree; the lemon blossom fragrance of the bouquet leads into a mouth-watering palate where the initial impact is of lime and lemon fruit before a burst of minerally acidity takes hold, then releases its grip on the aftertaste, allowing the fruit the last say. Screwcap. 13% alc. **Rating** 96 **To** 2030 $30

Piccadilly Valley Chardonnay 2010 Bright straw-green; time in bottle has served to increase the richness and generosity of the wine, with the layers of white peach and nectarine the product of a warmer than usual vintage, and a touch of Margaret River in its style make-up. Will be at its peak over the next few years. Screwcap. 13.5% alc. **Rating** 94 **To** 2015 $50

✪ **White Adelaide Hills Pinot Gris 2012** Decked out in the controversial fish and chips label of the new White series of red and white wines. A spectacularly intense wine with great line and length to its burst of nashi pear and apple fruit. This might well frighten the horses, and interrupt lunch conversation. Screwcap. 13% alc. **Rating** 94 **To** 2014 $23

White Coonawarra Cabernet Sauvignon 2010 Medium red-purple; after a 10-day fermentation, spent almost 2 years in French barriques; it has excellent blackcurrant/cassis fruit, typical cabernet tannins, and the oak has not been overplayed. Screwcap. 14.5% alc. **Rating** 94 **To** 2025 $27

ŦŦŦŦ♀ ✪ **White Adelaide Hills Coonawarra Sauvignon Blanc 2012** Follows an increasing trend to a small percentage of barrel fermentation in French oak, working perfectly here to provide an added touch of texture and structure to its mix of tropical fruits (guava and kiwifruit) plus a dab of grapefruit, the finish long and dry. Screwcap. 13.5% alc. **Rating** 93 **To** 2014 $23

Croser Pinot Noir Chardonnay NV Rating 92 **To** 2013 $25 TS

ŦŦŦŦ **White Adelaide Hills Chardonnay 2011 Rating** 88 **To** 2015 $23

Peter Lehmann   ★★★★★

Para Road, Tanunda, SA 5352 **Region** Barossa Valley
T (08) 8565 9555 **www**.peterlehmannwines.com **Open** Mon–Fri 9.30–5, w'ends & public hols 10.30–4.30
Winemaker Andrew Wigan, Ian Hongell, Peter Kelly **Est.** 1979 **Dozens** 750 000
Under the benevolent ownership of the Swiss/Californian Hess Group, Peter Lehmann has continued to flourish, making wines from all the major varieties at multiple price points. Its record with its Reserve Eden Valley Riesling (usually released when five years old) is second to none, and it has refined its Semillons to the point where it can take on the Hunter Valley at its own game with five-year-old releases, exemplified by the recent wines. At the base level, the Semillon is the largest seller in that category in the country (albeit significantly diminished by Marlborough Sauvignon Blanc sales). Yet it is as a red winemaker that Peter Lehmann is best known in both domestic and export markets, with some outstanding wines leading the charge. Grapes are purchased from 150 growers in the Barossa and Eden Valleys, and the quality of the wines has seen production soar. Chief winemaker Andrew Wigan notched up his 30th vintage in 2012. Exports to all major markets.

ŦŦŦŦŦ **Margaret Barossa Semillon 2008** Vivid green-straw; while the jury is out on the '08 Wigan Riesling, there are no qualms about this wine, with its fluid line of lemon, lemongrass and apple; its greatest strength is the structure derived from the perfect acidity. Screwcap. 11% alc. **Rating** 96 **To** 2028 $32

Margaret Barossa Semillon 2007 Gleaming green-yellow; a totally delicious wine, in a different world from the Hunter Valley, Clare Valley, WA or anywhere else great semillon is made. It has a stream of ripe citrus fruit that cascades along the tongue, continuing to the finish and aftertaste – yet it is fresh and vibrant. Screwcap. 11.5% alc. **Rating** 96 **To** 2027 $32

VSV 1885 Shiraz 2010 Strong, full red-purple; from vines owned by the Schrapel family, whose forebears planted them in 1885. The wine spent 12 months in French oak, which provides a perfect frame for the luscious berry and cherry fruit of the medium-bodied palate. Screwcap. 14.4% alc. **Rating** 96 **To** 2040 $60

VSV Orrock Shiraz 2009 From the southern Flinders Ranges; a very elegant wine, with exceptional mouthfeel to the array of juicy dark cherry and plum fruit, the tannins positively silky, the finish long, harmonious and utterly persuasive. Screwcap. 14.5% alc. **Rating** 96 **To** 2030 $60

Stonewell Barossa Shiraz 2009 Deep purple-crimson; the aromas and flavours are complex, yet seamlessly moulded in a supple display of black and red fruits, the tannins equally supple, the French oak totally integrated and balanced. Screwcap. 14.2% alc. **Rating** 96 **To** 2035 $100

✪ **Portrait Eden Valley Riesling Dry 2012** Bright, light straw-green; the wine provides a fascinating contrast to the Lehmann H&V Barossa Riesling, being firmer, more intense and filled with zesty lime juice flavours, bolstered and lengthened by good acidity; it carries its message through the length of the palate and aftertaste. Screwcap. 11% alc. **Rating** 94 **To** 2020 $18

Wigan Eden Valley Riesling 2007 Glowing yellow-green; a distinguished label, with a great history. This is a good wine, but doesn't have quite the same intensity and line of the best in its tasting line-up; that said, plenty of lime, honey and toast on display. Screwcap. 11.5% alc. **Rating** 94 **To** 2017 $32

✪ **H&V Shiraz 2010** The crimson-purple colour is an engaging start to a quality wine from a quality vintage; the medium-bodied palate ranges through spice, licorice, mocha, black cherry, plum and blackberry, the tannins fine but persistent, the balance underwriting a long future. Screwcap. 14.5% alc. **Rating** 94 **To** 2025 $20

Drawcard Barossa Shiraz 2010 Vivid and deep purple-crimson; it hits all the right buttons, with svelte black fruits ranging from black cherry to blackberry on the bouquet and medium- to full-bodied palate, where precisely weighted tannins and oak chime in. Screwcap. 14.5% alc. **Rating** 94 **To** 2025 $25

Eight Songs Barossa Shiraz 2009 Strong, healthy colour; both the bouquet and palate are complex, offering a range of dark/black berry fruits and integrated but noticeable French oak; the palate has excellent line and length, with the finish a high point of the wine. Screwcap. 14.5% alc. **Rating** 94 **To** 2030 $42

Drawcard Barossa Shiraz Mataro 2010 A full-bodied wine that does not go over the top, and reveals the complexity of its bouquet and palate as it is revisited time and again; black fruits, licorice, violets and eastern spices – plus a dash of dark Barossa soil. Screwcap. 14.5% alc. **Rating** 94 **To** 2025 $25

Mentor Barossa Cabernet Shiraz Malbec 2009 Very good colour, and has a generous palate of black and red fruits, earth, black olive and cedary oak. A medium- to full-bodied wine with a long future. Screwcap. 14% alc. **Rating** 94 **To** 2025 $42

Black Queen Sparkling Shiraz 2008 From two top-rated vineyards, spending 1 year in hogsheads before being bottled, then given 2 years on yeast lees; it is full of spicy black fruits and the dosage has been very well judged; the balance is excellent. Cork. 14% alc. **Rating** 94 **To** 2020 $42

🍷🍷🍷🍷🍷 **Wigan Eden Valley Riesling 2008** **Rating** 93 **To** 2018 $32
Futures Barossa Shiraz Cabernet 2010 **Rating** 93 **To** 2020 $26
Vine Vale Shiraz 2011 **Rating** 92 **To** 2025 $30

✪ **Portrait Barossa Shiraz 2010** Bright crimson-purple; the medium-bodied palate has excellent texture and structure, with fine spicy/savoury tannins running throughout underneath the black cherry, plum and dark chocolate flavours all signalled by the bouquet; oak, too, plays a positive role. Screwcap. 14.5% alc. **Rating** 92 **To** 2020 $18

✪ **H&V Eden Valley Riesling 2012** A floral bouquet and delicately lime-juicy palate are the by-product of the very low alcohol; citrus fruit, acidity and a hint of sweetness all chase each other across the palate. Adventurous winemaking. Screwcap. 10.5% alc. **Rating** 91 **To** 2016 $20

Lyndoch Shiraz 2011 **Rating** 91 **To** 2024 $30
Mentor Barossa Cabernet Shiraz Malbec 2010 **Rating** 91 **To** 2025 $42
H&V Barossa Valley Semillon 2012 **Rating** 90 **To** 2022 $20
H&V Eden Valley Chardonnay 2011 **Rating** 90 **To** 2015 $20
Lot #2 Stonewell Road Shiraz 2011 **Rating** 90 **To** 2023 $30
Futures Barossa Shiraz 2010 **Rating** 90 **To** 2018 $26

✪   **Portrait Barossa Cabernet Sauvignon 2010** Bright colour, with good depth; a more than useful commercial Cabernet Sauvignon (as per the back label), all the emphasis on the mix of juicy red and black fruits; ready right now, but will hold for a couple of years. Screwcap. 14.5% alc. **Rating** 90 **To** 2015 $18

♟♟♟♟   **Classic Range Shiraz Grenache 2011** Light, bright colour; some clever
✪   footwork in the vineyard and winery has been rewarded with this juicy, light-bodied wine. Screwcap. 14.5% alc. **Rating** 87 **To** 2013 $12

Pewsey Vale   ★★★★★

Eden Valley Road, Eden Valley, SA 5353 **Region** Eden Valley
T (08) 8561 3200 **www**.pewseyvale.com **Open** By appt
Winemaker Louisa Rose **Est.** 1847 **Dozens** 20 000 **Vyds** 50ha
Pewsey Vale was a famous vineyard established in 1847 by Joseph Gilbert, and it was appropriate that when the Hill-Smith family began the renaissance of the Adelaide Hills plantings in 1961, it should do so by purchasing Pewsey Vale and establishing 40ha of riesling and 4ha each of gewurztraminer and pinot gris. The Riesling has also finally benefited from being the first wine to be bottled with a Stelvin screwcap in 1977. While public reaction forced the abandonment of the initiative for almost 20 years, Pewsey Vale never lost faith in the technical advantages of the closure. A quick taste (or better, a share of a bottle) of five- to seven-year-old Contours Riesling will tell you why. Exports to all major markets.

♟♟♟♟♟   **Prima 24GR Eden Valley Riesling 2012** The lightness of touch of this wine is its special magic. The sweetness is as much of the fruit as its residual sugar, and the minerally acidity is a major part of the palate structure and flavour (lime and apple). One of the best yet. Screwcap. 10% alc. **Rating** 96 **To** 2027 $27
Prima 24GR Eden Valley Riesling 2011 Light straw-green; the 24g/l of residual sugar is perfectly balanced by acidity, and together they lift the flavour profile dramatically. There is no rule of any kind for when you should drink the wine between now and 2025, nor is there any rule about when not to drink it. Vino-Lok. 9.5% alc. **Rating** 96 **To** 2025 $27
The Contours Museum Reserve Eden Valley Riesling 2006 Sheer elegance and finesse, the floral bouquet and crisp acidity book-ending the wine, lime, lemon and apple on the way through. Still with decades to go. Screwcap. 12.5% alc. **Rating** 94 **To** 2036 $30

♟♟♟♟♀   **Eden Valley Riesling 2012 Rating** 93 **To** 2027 $23

Pfeiffer Wines   ★★★★★

167 Distillery Road, Wahgunyah, Vic 3687 **Region** Rutherglen
T (02) 6033 2805 **www**.pfeifferwines.com.au **Open** Mon–Sat 9–5, Sun 10–5
Winemaker Chris and Jen Pfeiffer **Est.** 1984 **Dozens** 20 000 **Vyds** 32ha
Family-owned and run, Pfeiffer Wines occupies one of the historic wineries (built in 1880) that abound in Northeast Victoria, and which is worth a visit on this score alone. In 2012 Chris Pfeiffer was awarded an Order of Australia Medal (OAM) for his services to the wine industry. Both hitherto and into the future, Pfeiffer's Muscats, Topaques and other fortified wines are a key part of the business. The arrival of winemaker daughter Jen, by a somewhat circuitous and initially unplanned route, has dramatically lifted the quality of the table wines, led by the reds. The results at the Victorian Wines Show '11 were unprecedented: trophies for the '10 Merlot and Shiraz, and top gold medals for the '10 Cabernet Sauvignon, NV Topaque and Classic Topaque. Watch this space. Exports to the UK, Canada, Belgium, Malaysia, Taiwan and China.

♟♟♟♟♟   **Rare Rutherglen Muscat NV** Significantly deeper and darker than the Grand, and voluptuously smooth and velvety, the first-up flavours a celestial smoothie of raisins, chocolate and coffee, thereafter opening up to allow the rancio to enter and freshen the mouth, and begin building the prodigiously long finish. A mere sip of a wine such as this will stay in your taste buds for literally minutes. 500ml. Screwcap. 17.5% alc. **Rating** 98 **To** 2014 $123

Rare Rutherglen Topaque NV Light, clear burnt amber, distinctly lighter than other Rutherglen Rare Topaques; consistently with the colour, it is very fine and detailed, yet displays the full array of toffee, cake, tea leaf and rich spices. Screwcap. 17.5% alc. **Rating** 97 **To** 2014 $123

Grand Rutherglen Muscat NV Deep brown grading to olive on the rim; exceptionally viscous for the Grand category, with layers of raisined fruit, dried fruits, Christmas cake and coffee; the rancio cuts in quite early, thus preventing any suggestion of cloying sweetness, the back-palate and finish drawing out so effortlessly that there is no alcohol hit or full-on sweetness. 500ml. Screwcap. 17.5% alc. **Rating** 97 **To** 2014 $84

✪ **Carlyle Cabernet Merlot 2010** Full crimson-purple; another tour de force of winemaking by Chris and daughter Jen Pfeiffer, with the balance and flavours one expects from much cooler regions than Rutherglen; cassis is the central flavour theme of the medium-bodied palate, texture and structure from ripe tannins and precisely judged oak. Screwcap. 14% alc. **Rating** 94 **To** 2020 $19

Seriously Fine Pale Dry Apera NV Bright light green-gold; a very good example of a flor fino style, fine, intense and bone dry, the finish and aftertaste lingering for a very long time. Screwcap. 17% alc. **Rating** 94 **To** 2014 $29

Seriously Nutty Medium Dry Apera NV Golden-orange; it has an average age of 25 years, with some of the components twice that age. It is no longer possible to use any of the classic Sherry names, but if it were permitted, this would be a dry Amontillado; it has wonderful nutty flavours on the mid-palate, with rancio evident but not overwhelming, and miraculously finishes dry. Screwcap. 21.5% alc. **Rating** 94 **To** 2014 $50

ⲨⲨⲨⲨⲨ **Shiraz 2011 Rating** 93 **To** 2018 $24

Classic Rutherglen Muscat NV Rating 93 **To** 2014 $29

✪ **Rutherglen Muscat NV** A rich and luscious style with abundant raisin, burnt toffee and Christmas pudding flavours, the finish lifted by a cut of rancio. 500ml. Screwcap. 17.5% alc. **Rating** 92 **To** 2014 $20

✪ **Riesling 2012** Straw-green; a neatly constructed wine, with plenty of varietal expression on both the floral bouquet and juicy palate; ripe lemon flavours are offset by balanced acidity. Will repay cellaring in the manner of all good rieslings. Screwcap. 12% alc. **Rating** 91 **To** 2020 $19

Classic Rutherglen Topaque NV Rating 91 **To** 2014 $29

✪ **Carlyle Shiraz 2011** Deep, bright garnet; a bright and effusive bouquet displaying red fruits, cracked pepper and fresh leather aromas; the palate is generous, soft and plushly textured, and there is plenty of pleasure to be had in the short term. Screwcap. 13.5% alc. **Rating** 90 **To** 2016 $19 BE

Merlot 2011 Rating 90 **To** 2016 $25

Cabernet Sauvignon 2011 Rating 90 **To** 2017 $24

Phaedrus Estate

220 Mornington-Tyabb Road, Moorooduc, Vic 3933 **Region** Mornington Peninsula **T** (03) 5978 8134 **www.**phaedrus.com.au **Open** W'ends & public hols 11–5 **Winemaker** Ewan Campbell, Maitena Zantvoort **Est.** 1997 **Dozens** 3500 **Vyds** 2.5ha Since Maitena Zantvoort and Ewan Campbell established Phaedrus Estate, they have gained a reputation for producing premium cool-climate wines. Their winemaking philosophy brings art and science together to produce wines showing regional and varietal character with minimal winemaking interference. The vineyard includes 1ha of pinot noir and 0.5ha each of pinot gris, chardonnay and shiraz. Exports to Hong Kong.

ⲨⲨⲨⲨⲨ **Reserve Mornington Peninsula Pinot Noir 2010** Far deeper colour than the standard '11 Pinot Noir of Phaedrus, with a purple hue. The best parcels of fruit were matured in two new and one second-use French oak puncheons for 20 months. 100 dozen bottles made of (in pinot terms) a full-bodied wine with dark cherry and plum fruit plus appreciable fruit and oak tannins. Screwcap. 13.9% alc. **Rating** 91 **To** 2016 $45

✪   **Mornington Peninsula Chardonnay 2011** All Bernard/Dijon clones, wild yeast barrel-fermented, and with 9 months' lees contact. A complex, generous wine, with plenty of stone fruit/fig/cashew flavours, but would it have been better if picked a week or so earlier? Screwcap. 13.4% alc. **Rating** 90 **To** 2016 $22
Mornington Peninsula Pinot Gris 2012 A 55-day slow ferment in tank ex low-yielding grapes; faint pink-bronze colour; it has strong varietal character on the bouquet and palate with spicy poached pear characters; needed a touch more acidity for even higher points. Screwcap. 13.9% alc. **Rating** 90 **To** 2014 $22
Mornington Peninsula Pinot Noir 2011 Light, bright red; a light mix of savoury and sweet red berry fruit makes for a fresh strawberry and forest floor wine, gentle handling and short maceration exactly the right response to the vintage. Screwcap. 13.4% alc. **Rating** 90 **To** 2015 $25

PHI   ★★★★★

Lusatia Park Vineyard, Owens Road, Woori Yallock, Vic 3139 **Region** Yarra Valley
T (03) 5964 6070 **www**.phiwines.com **Open** By appt
Winemaker Steve Webber **Est.** 2005 **Dozens** 1700 **Vyds** 7.5ha
This is a joint venture of two very influential wine families: De Bortoli and Shelmerdine. The key executives are Stephen Shelmerdine and Steve Webber (and their respective wives). It rests upon the selection and management of specific blocks of vines without regard to cost. Until 2010 the wines all came from the Lusatia Park Vineyard in the Yarra Valley, but in that year a Heathcote Syrah Grenache was made, and, if the opportunity arises, other wines will be added to the portfolio. The name, incidentally, is derived from the 21st letter of the ancient Greek alphabet, symbolising perfect balance and harmony. No wines received for the *2014 Wine Companion*, but a five-star rating has been maintained. Exports to the UK and China.

🍷🍷🍷🍷🍷   **Single Vineyard Yarra Valley Chardonnay 2011** Pale straw-green; a very refined style with primary emphasis on mouthfeel, texture and structure, paradoxically stemming from the fruit rather than the oak; it is creamy, yet fine, the stone fruit flavours subtle, the acidity gently drawing out the long finish. Screwcap. 12% alc. **Rating** 94 **To** 2020 $48

Philip Lobley Wines   ★★★★

1084 Eucalyptus Road, Glenburn, Vic 3717 (postal) **Region** Upper Goulburn
T (03) 5797 8433 **Open** Not
Winemaker Philip Lobley **Est.** 2008 **Dozens** 450 **Vyds** 2.82ha
The micro, patchwork-quilt vineyard was first planted by Philip Lobley in 1995 with pinot noir, merlot and cabernet sauvignon. In 2008 nebbiolo, semillon, sauvignon blanc and moscato giallo (or gold muskateller, thought to be a version of muscat a petits grains) were added. These are high-density plantings and yield is kept to 600–800g per vine. The red wines are wild yeast-fermented and neither filtered nor fined; the Yarra Valley Sauvignon Blanc (purchased) is whole bunch-pressed and wild yeast-fermented. The 2008 plantings were destroyed by the Black Saturday bushfires, and nebbiolo and moscato giallo have been replanted; 80% of the older wines recovered thanks to the good spring/summer rainfall of '10.

🍷🍷🍷🍷🍷   **Sauvignon Blanc 2011** A minor technicality is that while both the front and back labels show the region as Yea Valley, they also show that the grapes come from the Yarra Valley. Pressed directly to barrel, wild yeast-fermented and left on lees for 5 months. All about texture, with no colour, and just a flash of sour lemon fruit; only five barrels made. Diam. 11.8% alc. **Rating** 91 **To** 2014 $22

🍷🍷🍷🍷   **The Falcon 2010 Rating** 88 **To** 2015 $25

Philip Murphy Estate   ★★★★☆

484 Purves Road, Main Ridge, Vic 3928 (postal) **Region** Mornington Peninsula
T (03) 5989 6609 **www**.philipmurphyestate.com.au **Open** Not
Winemaker Philip Murphy **Est.** 2004 **Dozens** 200 **Vyds** 1ha

Few would know the challenges facing small, start-up wineries better than Philip Murphy. After the sale of his very substantial retail wine business to Coles, he and wife Jennifer decided to have a seachange and move down to the Mornington Peninsula. He then happened to meet Kevin Bell of Hurley Vineyard, who gave him the confidence to enrol in wine science at CSU in 2003. The Murphys built a new house, incorporating a winery and cellar door underneath. They planted chardonnay and pinot noir (the latter French clones and MV6), and the first experimental vintage followed in '07; the '08 was 'a big step forward', says Philip, and he's not wrong. And, of course, he has completely circumvented the sale challenges with the tiny make (although it may be expanded) by selling most of the wine through the mailing list and small amounts through the Pinot Shop in Launceston, and the Prince Wine Store and Como Wines & Spirits in Melbourne.

ΨΨΨΨΨ **Mornington Peninsula Chardonnay 2011** Bright green-straw; a prime example of the elegant and expressive Chardonnays that could be, and were, made in the cool '11 vintage. There is a full range of white peach, nectarine and melon fruit, grapefruit a minor component in the mix; the palate is very long and finely tuned, oak doing no more than providing the full stop at its conclusion. Diam. 13.5% alc. **Rating** 95 **To** 2020 $35

ΨΨΨΨΩ **Mornington Peninsula Pinot de la Maison 2011 Rating** 90 **To** 2016 $35

Philip Shaw Wines ★★★★★

Koomooloo Vineyard, Caldwell Lane, Orange, NSW 2800 **Region** Orange
T (02) 6365 2334 **www.**philipshaw.com.au **Open** 7 days 11–5
Winemaker Philip Shaw, Daniel Shaw **Est.** 1989 **Dozens** 25 000 **Vyds** 47ha
Philip Shaw, former chief winemaker of Rosemount Estate and then Southcorp, first became interested in the Orange region in 1985. In '88 he purchased the Koomooloo Vineyard and began extensive plantings, the varieties including shiraz, merlot, pinot noir, sauvignon blanc, cabernet franc, cabernet sauvignon and viognier. Son Daniel has joined Philip in the winery, at a time when the quality of the portfolio of wines goes from strength to strength. Exports to the UK, the US and other major markets.

ΨΨΨΨΨ **No. 11 Orange Chardonnay 2011** Bright straw-green; Philip Shaw's vast experience with chardonnay shines through in this perfectly structured and balanced wine; grapefruit, nectarine, white peach, cashew and oak form a seamless stream across the palate. Screwcap. 12.5% alc. **Rating** 95 **To** 2018 $35
No. 19 Orange Sauvignon Blanc 2012 Has considerable intensity and purity, with delicious fruit spanning grapefruit/citrus through to lychee/guava, all tightly spun together. Screwcap. 12.5% alc. **Rating** 94 **To** 2014 $25
No. 11 Orange Chardonnay 2012 Light to medium straw-green; has the textural and structural complexity that Philip Shaw has introduced in all of the Chardonnays he has made in his winemaking life, even if less baroque than his Roxburgh wines. Screwcap. 12% alc. **Rating** 94 **To** 2020 $35

ΨΨΨΨ **The Wire Walker Orange Pinot Noir 2012 Rating** 87 **To** 2015 $20
The Conductor Orange Merlot 2010 Rating 87 **To** 2014 $20

Piano Gully ★★★★

Piano Gully Road, Manjimup, WA 6258 **Region** Pemberton
T (08) 9316 0336 **www.**pianogully.com.au **Open** By appt
Winemaker Naturaliste Vintners **Est.** 1987 **Dozens** 3500 **Vyds** 6ha
The Piano Gully vineyard, established in 1987 on rich karri loam 10km south of Manjimup (but in the Pemberton region), includes chardonnay, sauvignon blanc, cabernet sauvignon, viognier, shiraz and merlot. The name of the road (and the winery) commemorates the shipping of a piano from England by one of the first settlers in the region. The horse and cart carrying the piano on the last leg of the long journey were within sight of their destination when the piano fell from the cart and was destroyed.

ŢŢŢŢ♀ **Chardonnay 2010** Light straw-green; notwithstanding the use of 100% new French oak, and at least 2 years in bottle, the wine is still tight and fresh with grapefruit, white peach and apple driving both the bouquet and palate; the finish is still bright. Screwcap. 13% alc. **Rating** 93 **To** 2016 $35
Shiraz 2009 Clear red; a light- to medium-bodied Shiraz that has cruised through the first 4 years of its life, with spice and cedar undertones to its red fruits; good short-term drinking. Screwcap. 13.5% alc. **Rating** 90 **To** 2015 $24

 # Piano Piano

852 Beechworth-Wangaratta Road, Everton Upper, Vic 3678 **Region** Beechworth
T (03) 5727 0382 **www**.pianopiano.com.au **Open** By appt
Winemaker Marc Scalzo **Est.** 2001 **Dozens** 1000 **Vyds** 5.1ha
'Piano piano' means 'slowly slowly' in Italian, and this is how Marc Scalzo and wife Lisa Hernan have approached the development of their business. Marc has a degree in oenology from CSU and many years' practical experience as a winemaker with Brown Brothers, and vintage experience with Giaconda and John Gehrig and Seresin Estate and Delegat's (NZ). In 1997 they planted 2.6ha of merlot, cabernet sauvignon, tempranillo and touriga nacional on their Brangie Vineyard in the King Valley; they followed up with 1.2ha of chardonnay ('06) and 0.8ha of shiraz ('08) on their Beechworth property.

ŢŢŢŢ♀ **Sophie's Block Chardonnay 2010** An impressively fine and youthful wine, with a touch of reduction, but has outstanding length and balance, the reduction will be long gone in a year or so. Screwcap. 13.4% alc. **Rating** 93 **To** 2018 $35
Sophie's Block Chardonnay 2011 Pale quartz-green; fresh and lively, but at the green apple and citrus, almost grassy, end point. Oak has not been used as a panacea, and it will appeal to those who have no truck with what they call 'oaky Chardonnays'. Screwcap. 13% alc. **Rating** 90 **To** 2016 $35

Pierrepoint Wines

271 Pierrepoint Road, Tarrington, Vic 3301 **Region** Henty
T (03) 5572 5553 **www**.pierrepointwines.com.au **Open** Mon–Fri 10–3, w'ends & public hols 11–5
Winemaker Scott Ireland (Contract) **Est.** 1998 **Dozens** 1200 **Vyds** 5ha
Mount Pierrepoint Estate was established by Andrew and Jennifer Lacey on the foothills of Mt Pierrepoint between Hamilton and Tarrington, at an altitude of 200m. The predominantly red buckshot soils of the vineyard are derived from ancient volcanic basalt, rich in minerals and free-draining. Two hectares each of pinot noir and pinot gris, and 1ha of chardonnay are planted on an ideal north-facing slope.

ŢŢŢŢŢ **Pinot Noir 2011** Bright, full crimson-purple, exceptional for the vintage; this colour does not deceive, for the wine has more plum and cherry fruit backed by firm, balanced tannins that are better than those of most '11 pinots. The yield of 1 tonne per acre also played its part. Screwcap. 13% alc. **Rating** 94 **To** 2017 $40

ŢŢŢŢ♀ **Pinot Gris 2011 Rating** 93 **To** 2014 $37
Alexandra Chardonnay 2011 Rating 91 **To** 2018 $25

Pierro

Caves Road, Wilyabrup via Cowaramup, WA 6284 **Region** Margaret River
T (08) 9755 6220 **www**.pierro.com.au **Open** 7 days 10–5
Winemaker Dr Michael Peterkin **Est.** 1979 **Dozens** 10 000 **Vyds** 7.85ha
Dr Michael Peterkin is another of the legion of Margaret River medical practitioners; for good measure, he married into the Cullen family. Pierro is renowned for its stylish white wines, which often exhibit tremendous complexity; the Chardonnay can be monumental in its weight and texture. That said, its red wines from good vintages can be every bit as good. Exports to the UK and other major markets.

ΨΨΨΨΨ Margaret River Chardonnay 2011 Pale, bright straw-green; a high-quality Chardonnay, showing the marriage of elegance and generosity that Margaret River can achieve like no other Australian region; white peach, nectarine and fig use sleight of hand to push whatever amount of new French oak was used into the background. Screwcap. 13.5% alc. **Rating** 96 **To** 2021 $78

L.T.C. 2012 Light straw-green; semillon and sauvignon have been relegated to the back label, the little touch of chardonnay promoted to the front label. The wine is filled with resounding luscious fruits oscillating between tropical and stone fruits. Screwcap. 13.5% alc. **Rating** 94 **To** 2016 $32

Reserve Margaret River Cabernet Sauvignon Merlot 2009 There are in fact cabernet franc, petit verdot and malbec also in the blend, matured in new French oak. It is part of a deliberate move to lower alcohol levels, elegance preferred over power, cerebral pleasure over hedonism. Screwcap. 13.5% alc. **Rating** 94 **To** 2024 $74

ΨΨΨΨΨ Cabernet Sauvignon Merlot L.T.C. 2010 **Rating** 92 **To** 2020 $38

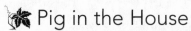 Pig in the House ★★★★

Balcombe Road, Billimari, NSW 2804 **Region** Cowra
T 0427 443 598 **www**.piginthehouse.com.au **Open** Fri–Sun 11–5
Winemaker Antonio D'Onise **Est.** 2002 **Dozens** 2000 **Vyds** 15ha
Jason and Rebecca O'Dea established their vineyard (5ha each of merlot, shiraz and cabernet sauvignon) on a block of land formerly used as home for 20 free-range pigs – making any explanation about the name of the business totally unnecessary. Given its prior use, one would imagine the vines would grow lustily, and it is no surprise that organic certification has been given by Biological Farmers of Australia. The O'Deas have in fact taken the process several steps further, using biodynamic preparations and significantly reducing all sprays. The wines made are good advertisements for organic/biodynamic farming.

ΨΨΨΨΨ Cabernet Sauvignon 2010 Light but bright purple-crimson; manages to get
✪   that bit extra from the region; perhaps its certified organic status helps. Whatever, the juicy cassis fruit is nicely tempered by gently savoury varietal tannins giving length and definition to the palate. Screwcap. 13.5% alc. **Rating** 91 **To** 2020 $22
✪   Shiraz 2011 Light purple-red; red and black cherry, plum and oak all compete for space in this medium-bodied wine; the back label food match suggestions of curry, roast vegetables or grilled fish are, if nothing else, novel. Screwcap. 14% alc. **Rating** 90 **To** 2016 $22

Pike & Joyce ★★★★★

PO Box 54, Sevenhill, SA 5453 **Region** Adelaide Hills
T (08) 8843 4370 **www**.pikeandjoyce.com.au **Open** Not
Winemaker Neil Pike, John Trotter, Steve Baraglia **Est.** 1998 **Dozens** 5000 **Vyds** 18.5ha
This is a partnership between the Pike family (of Clare Valley fame) and the Joyce family, related to Andrew Pike's wife, Cathy. The Joyce family have been orchardists at Lenswood for over 100 years, but also have extensive operations in the Riverland. Together they have established a vineyard planted to sauvignon blanc (5.9ha), pinot noir (5.73ha), pinot gris (3.22ha), chardonnay (3.18ha) and semillon (0.47ha). The wines are made at Pikes Clare Valley winery. Exports to the UK, Canada, The Netherlands, Taiwan, Singapore, Hong Kong, and Japan.

ΨΨΨΨΨ Adelaide Hills Sauvignon Blanc 2012 This quartz-green wine has a full
✪   display of multifaceted varietal aromas and flavours, catching snow pea/herbs at the one extreme, guava/passionfruit at the other. Adelaide Hills and sauvignon blanc have a symbiotic relationship. Screwcap. 13% alc. **Rating** 94 **To** 2014 $22
Adelaide Hills Chardonnay 2011 Light straw-green; a fresh, vibrant and elegant wine; barrel fermentation has not in any way interfered with the purity or line of the varietal expression of grapefruit and white peach; it has just added some delicate creamy/nutty notes. Screwcap. 13% alc. **Rating** 94 **To** 2017 $32

ΫΫΫΫΫ **Adelaide Hills Pinot Gris 2012** Pale straw-green; clearly in the Gris camp, with
✪   an attractive array of fruit flavours spanning spiced pear through to stone fruit;
           crisp, minerally finish. Screwcap. 13% alc. **Rating** 93 **To** 2014 $22

Pikes   ★★★★★

Polish Hill River Road, Sevenhill, SA 5453 **Region** Clare Valley
T (08) 8843 4370 **www**.pikeswines.com.au **Open** 7 days 10–4
Winemaker Neil Pike, Steve Baraglia **Est.** 1984 **Dozens** 35 000 **Vyds** 69.41ha
Owned by the Pike brothers: Andrew was for many years the senior viticulturist with
Southcorp, Neil was a winemaker at Mitchell. Pikes now has its own winery, with Neil
presiding. In most vintages its white wines, led by Riesling, are the most impressive. Planting
of the vineyards has been an ongoing affair, with a panoply of varietals, new and traditional,
reflected in the 2007 plantings of an additional 4.3ha of riesling (26ha in total), 3.5ha of
shiraz and a first-up planting of 1.24ha of savagnin. The Merle is Pikes' limited production,
flagship Riesling. Exports to the US, Canada, The Netherlands, Switzerland, Poland, Cyprus,
Singapore, Malaysia, Hong Kong, Taiwan, Japan and China.

ΫΫΫΫΫ **The Merle Clare Valley Riesling 2012** The J.T. came from the Hill Block
           planted in '84–85; this wine comes from The Thicket Block planted in '88; while
           only 500m apart, the wines are strikingly different, this one racier, longer and
           more slatey/minerally, yet also clothed with totally delicious lime juice flavours.
           Screwcap. 12% alc. **Rating** 96 **To** 2032 $45
✪   **Traditionale Clare Valley Riesling 2012** The '12 vintage had one overarching
           feature, high-quality Riesling, in its traditional strongholds of the Clare and Eden
           Valleys, yet its expression varied considerably from one maker to the next. Here
           lime juice flavours leap out of the glass, coating the mouth, yet supported by fine
           acidity. Screwcap. 12% alc. **Rating** 95 **To** 2027 $22
           The J.T. Clare Valley Riesling 2012 Honours John Trotter, who was a
           winemaker at Pikes for 12 years before dying of a heart attack mid vintage, all
           proceeds going to charity. It is a mouth-filling wine, with layers of juicy citrus fruit
           underpinned by lingering acidity. Screwcap. 12% alc. **Rating** 95 **To** 2027 $42
✪   **The Assemblage Clare Valley Shiraz Mourvedre Grenache 2010** Has a
           luscious array of blackberry, red and black cherry and plum fruits; the tannins are
           ripe and soft, the oak evident, but controlled; overall balance is a feature, as is the
           value. Screwcap. 14.5% alc. **Rating** 94 **To** 2020 $22
✪   **Luccio Sangiovese 2010** Has fresh, bright cherry fruit on the bouquet and
           palate, the tannins perfectly captured; Pikes' experience with the variety, and
           mature vines, shines through. Screwcap. 14.5% alc. **Rating** 94 **To** 2020 $18

ΫΫΫΫΫ **Luccio Clare Valley Sangiovese Carmenere Rose 2012** Italy meets France.
✪   We don't know the percentage of the carmenere, but it contributed to the bright
           colour and to the red cherry fruits ex the sangiovese. Grape rarity to one side, this
           is a very smart Rose. Screwcap. 13% alc. **Rating** 93 **To** 2014 $18
✪   **Olga Emmie Clare Valley Riesling 2012** Very pale quartz; off-dry, but not
           particularly sweet, which may be why there is no mention of its residual sweetness
           either front or back label; is nicely balanced, with crisp acidity cleansing the finish.
           Screwcap. 11.5% alc. **Rating** 92 **To** 2017 $20
           The Dogwalk Clare Valley Cabernet Merlot 2010 **Rating** 91 **To** 2025 $22
           Impostores Clare Valley Savignan 2012 **Rating** 90 **To** 2014 $20

Pimpernel Vineyards   ★★★★★

6 Hill Road, Coldstream, Vic 3770 **Region** Yarra Valley
T 0457 326 436 **www**.pimpernelvineyards.com.au **Open** W'ends & public hols 11–5,
or by appt
Winemaker Damien Archibald, Mark Horrigan **Est.** 2001 **Dozens** 2000 **Vyds** 6ha
Lilydale-based cardiologist Mark Horrigan's love affair with wine started long before he had
heard about either the Yarra Valley or his family's links, centuries ago, to Condrieu, France.

He is a direct descendant of the Chapuis family, his ultimate ancestors first buried in the Church of St Etienne in 1377. In a cosmopolitan twist, his father came from a Welsh mining village, but made his way to university and found many things to enjoy, not the least wine. When the family moved to Australia in 1959, wine remained part of everyday life and, as Mark grew up in the '70s, the obsession passed from father to son. In '97, while working at Prince Alfred Hospital (Sydney), Mark was offered a job in Melbourne, and within weeks of arriving had started looking for a likely spot in the Yarra Valley. In 2001 he and wife Fiona purchased the property on which they have built a (second) house, planted a vineyard, and erected a capacious winery designed by WA architect Peter Moran. In the course of doing so they became good friends of near-neighbour the late Bailey Carrodus.

ŸŸŸŸŸ **Chardonnay 2011** Pale quartz; wild yeast-fermented and 12 months' maturation in French barriques; has the finely tuned edge of most Yarra Valley Chardonnays in '11, although not as much thrust. Diam. 13% alc. **Rating** 93 **To** 2017 $38
Syrah 2011 Estate-grown, wild yeast-fermented shiraz with a tiny amount of viognier; the wine has a silky mouthfeel to its spicy red fruit flavours on the light-bodied, balanced palate. Diam. 13.4% alc. **Rating** 91 **To** 2017 $45
Viognier 2011 Achieves considerable varietal character, with peach, apricot and musk doing the talking, and has good acidity; the downside is the phenolic curtain between the fruit and the acidity. Diam. 13.8% alc. **Rating** 90 **To** 2016 $40

Pindarie   ★★★★☆

PO Box 341, Tanunda, SA 5352 **Region** Barossa Valley
T (08) 8524 9019 **www**.pindarie.com.au **Open** Mon–Fri 11–4, w'ends 11.5
Winemaker Peter Leske **Est.** 2005 **Dozens** 5000 **Vyds** 32.4ha
Owners Tony Brooks and Wendy Allan met at Roseworthy College in 1985. They came from very different family backgrounds: Tony was the sixth generation of farmers in SA and WA, and was studying agriculture; NZ-born Wendy was studying viticulture. On graduation Tony worked overseas managing sheep feedlots in Saudi Arabia, Turkey and Jordan, while Wendy worked for the next 12 years with Penfolds, commencing as a grower liaison officer and working her way up to become a senior viticulturist. She also found time to study viticulture in California, Israel, Italy, Germany, France, Portugal, Spain and Chile, working vintages and assessing vineyards for wine projects. In 2001 she completed a graduate diploma in wine business. In 2010 they opened a new cellar door and café (winning a major tourism award in '12), joining the original bluestone homestead and other buildings, taking in panoramic views of the locality. Exports to Malaysia, Hong Kong and China.

ŸŸŸŸŸ **Reserve Black Hinge Tempranillo 2010** The deluxe, super-tall bottle has been matched with a sophisticated cork; the fruit is as luscious and velvety as possible at this restrained alcohol level, with gently spiced plums running through its fine, silky tannins and quality oak. 13.5% alc. **Rating** 94 **To** 2023 $40

ŸŸŸŸŸ **Barossa Valley Shiraz 2010 Rating** 90 **To** 2025 $23
Barossa Valley Cabernet Sauvignon 2010 Rating 90 **To** 2018 $23
✪ **Bar Rossa Tempranillo Sangiovese Shiraz 2011** Light but bright hue; a fresh and lively red-fruited wine that has reached phenological ripeness in this adverse year, and has not been bulked up by added tannins. Ideal for early consumption. Screwcap. 13.5% alc. **Rating** 90 **To** 2015 $21

ŸŸŸŸ **La Femme Barossa Valley Savagnin 2012** Presumably planted in the belief
✪ that it was albarino; has a chalky freshness to its acidity that is part of its charm, as is its citrus zest/pith flavour, and floral bouquet. Well worth getting a few bottles and watching its progress. Screwcap. 13% alc. **Rating** 89 **To** 2015 $16

Pipers Brook Vineyard   ★★★★★

1216 Pipers Brook Road, Pipers Brook, Tas 7254 **Region** Northern Tasmania
T (03) 6382 7527 **www**.pipersbrook.com.au **Open** 7 days 10–5
Winemaker René Bezemer **Est.** 1974 **Dozens** 60 000 **Vyds** 185ha

The Pipers Brook Tasmanian empire has 185ha of vineyard supporting the Pipers Brook and Ninth Island labels, with the major focus, of course, being on Pipers Brook. Fastidious viticulture and winemaking, immaculate packaging and enterprising marketing create a potent and effective blend. Pipers Brook operates two cellar door outlets, one at headquarters, the other at Strathlyn. In 2001 it was acquired by Belgian-owned sheepskin business Kreglinger, which has also established the large Norfolk Island winery and vineyard at Mount Benson in SA (see separate entry). Exports to the UK, the US and other major markets.

▼▼▼▼▼ **Kreglinger Vintage Brut 2006** This blend of pinot noir and chardonnay was disgorged in late '10, and given additional cork age prior to release. Very pale, bright quartz-green; the palate is taut and precise, showing both its dominant pinot noir, and substantial freshness and crispness on the long, citrussy finish. Scores more for elegance than power. 12.5% alc. **Rating** 95 **To** 2019 $46

Estate Pinot Gris 2011 Pushes a radically different barrow from that of Moorilla Estate's Muse; while using some skin contact and some French oak handling, it does not lose its vibrant freshness nor the focus of its line and length; musk, pear and citrussy acidity leave the mouth looking for the next glass. Screwcap. 13.5% alc. **Rating** 94 **To** 2014 $34

Reserve Collection Pinot Noir 2006 Exceptional colour for a 6-year-old pinot; the key is a yield of less than 2 tonnes per hectare, which has provided not only this colour, but also a profoundly intense bouquet and palate with black cherry, forest, leather and game all clamouring to be heard. Screwcap. 13.5% alc. **Rating** 94 **To** 2020 $65

The Lyre Pinot Noir 2005 Deep garnet, bright; while oak is the prominent feature of the bouquet, the dark cherry fruit and Asian spices continue to provide an attractive perfume; the palate is dark and brooding, still fresh and full of fine-grained tannins and lively acidity; ageing with grace, and still plenty of gas in the tank. Cork. 13.5% alc. **Rating** 94 **To** 2018 $110 BE

Pipers 2008 A 50/50% blend of chardonnay and pinot noir disgorged June '12. Good mousse, light straw colour; shows the gentle complexing effect of over 4 years on yeast lees; still a fine-boned, elegant style, with very good balance and length. Diam. 12.5% alc. **Rating** 94 **To** 2015 $37

▼▼▼▼▽ **Ninth Island Pinot Noir 2011** Opportunity comes out of adversity, and one
✪ can only assume that some serious declassification from Pipers Brook has lifted its lowest tier wine in this challenging season. This is an incredible Pinot for the price. It's unashamedly light-bodied, yet more than compensates for weight in refinement and exactness of fragrant rose hip, pink pepper, red cherry and raspberry fruit. Screwcap. 13% alc. **Rating** 92 **To** 2014 $25 TS

Estate Pinot Noir 2010 Rating 92 **To** 2018 $42 BE
Estate Chardonnay 2009 Rating 91 **To** 2020 $34 BE
Ninth Island Sparkling NV Rating 90 **To** 2014 $27

Piromit Wines   ★★★★☆

113 Hanwood Avenue, Hanwood, NSW 2680 **Region** Riverina
T (02) 6963 0200 **www.**piromitwines.com.au **Open** Mon–Fri 10–4
Winemaker Belinda Morandin, Dom Piromalli **Est.** 1998 **Dozens** 100 000
I simply cannot resist quoting directly from the background information kindly supplied to me. 'Piromit Wines is a relatively new boutique winery situated in Hanwood, NSW. The 1000-tonne capacity winery was built for the 1999 vintage on a 14-acre site which was until recently used as a drive-in. Previous to this, wines were made on our 100-acre vineyard. The winery site is being developed into an innovative tourist attraction complete with an Italian restaurant and landscaped formal gardens.' It is safe to say this extends the concept of a boutique winery into new territory. Exports to Canada, Sweden and Italy.

▼▼▼▼▽ **The Sticky Italian Botrytis Semillon 2009** Deep gold, green; levels of botrytis
✪ with marmalade and ginger on the bouquet; the palate is sweet on entry, then dries out with burnt caramel and biscuit notes on the finish; long and luscious. 375ml. Screwcap. 11% alc. **Rating** 92 **To** 2018 $16 BE

Two Italian Boys Shiraz 2010 Deep garnet; ripe red fruits with a little clove spice are evident on the bouquet; the palate reveals some charry oak notes, fleshy fruit, and a little savoury roasted meat character on the finish; good value. Screwcap. 14% alc. **Rating** 89 **To** 2016 $13 BE

Two Italian Boys Vermentino 2012 Pale gold; fresh pear and straw are evident on the bouquet, with a lively citrus cut of acidity providing freshness and energy on the finish. Screwcap. 11.5% alc. **Rating** 88 **To** 2014 $13 BE

Two Italian Boys Pinot Grigio 2012 Rating 87 **To** 2014 $13 BE

Two Italian Boys Cabernet Sauvignon 2010 Rating 87 **To** 2015 $13 BE

Pirramimma

Johnston Road, McLaren Vale, SA 5171 **Region** McLaren Vale
T (08) 8323 8205 **www.**pirramimma.com.au **Open** Mon–Fri 10–4.30, w'ends & public hols 10.30–5
Winemaker Geoff Johnston **Est.** 1892 **Dozens** 30000 **Vyds** 82.7ha
A long-established family-owned company with outstanding vineyard resources. It is using those resources to full effect, with a series of intense old-vine varietals including Semillon, Sauvignon Blanc, Chardonnay, Shiraz, Grenache, Cabernet Sauvignon and Petit Verdot, all fashioned without over-embellishment. Wines are released under several ranges: Pirra, Stock's Hill, White Label, ACJ, Katunga, Eight Carat and Gilden Lilly. Exports to the UK, the US and other major markets.

War Horse Shiraz 2010 This, says Pirramimma, 'is our first definitive shiraz release in 120 years of winemaking', from 70-year-old contoured vines. It has received Rolls Royce treatment, including 100% new oak, and is akin to an essence of McLaren Vale shiraz, with sultry black fruits, dark chocolate, spices of all kinds, and ripe tannins. Cork. 14.8% alc. **Rating** 96 **To** 2040 $60

McLaren Vale Shiraz Viognier 2010 The bright purple-crimson colour is no surprise, nor is the top gold medal in its class at the Adelaide Wine Show '12; it has a bright display of spicy red and black fruits on its bouquet and medium-bodied palate, supported by silky tannins on the long finish. Screwcap. 15% alc. **Rating** 95 **To** 2025 $35

McLaren Vale Shiraz 2010 Medium purple-crimson; a very complex wine with ladles of spicy plum and blackberry fruit, a generous helping of new oak, some dark chocolate, and ripe tannins on the medium- to full-bodied palate. Screwcap. 15% alc. **Rating** 94 **To** 2025 $30

Old Bush Vine McLaren Vale Grenache 2010 From the War Horse Vineyard, the 45-year-old Katunga Block and from other old vineyards in the region. Brimming with red fruits of every description, it also has tannin structure to provide texture and length. Cork. 14.8% alc. **Rating** 94 **To** 2020 $25

McLaren Vale Grenache Shiraz 2010 The grenache comes from the 70-year-old vines on the War Horse Vineyard, the shiraz from the Johnson Prolific Block. The wine literally coats the tongue, but doesn't cloy, as the fruit coat disappears before the next sip is taken. Screwcap. 14.5% alc. **Rating** 94 **To** 2020 $30

McLaren Vale Petit Verdot 2010 The late-ripening petit verdot enjoys warm vintages, especially one such as '10 with its even accumulation of heat. It has superb colour, and while the tannins are firm, there is a mountain of black fruits and oak to carry those tannins. Screwcap. 14.5% alc. **Rating** 94 **To** 2030 $30

Katunga GTS 2009 A 52/26/22% blend of grenache, tannat and shiraz. This is a luscious wine, with a regional signal of dark chocolate fruit, and plum mixed in with the spicy parade of red fruits. Terrific value. Screwcap. 14.8% alc. **Rating** 93 **To** 2019 $20

McLaren Vale Cabernet Sauvignon 2010 Rating 93 **To** 2030 $30

303 Watervale Riesling 2012 Has already developed some straw-green colour, consistent with the attractive floral bouquet and attractive lime juice flavours of the palate; while accessible now, there is no hint that it will blow out or become tired any time soon. Screwcap. 12.5% alc. **Rating** 92 **To** 2020 $20

McLaren Vale Tannat 2010 Rating 92 To 2020 $30

✪ Eight Carat McLaren Vale Shiraz 2010 Bright red-purple; a richly flavoured wine with a mix of black cherry fruit and the regional dark chocolate signature; however, the vanillin oak has been a little too enthusiastically used. Screwcap. 14.5% alc. Rating 91 To 2018 $20

✪ Katunga McLaren Vale Shiraz 2010 The shiraz was co-fermented with a small percentage of viognier. The colour of this exultantly full-bodied wine is good, the palate overflowing with black fruits, licorice and dark chocolate, the tannins ripe and plentiful oak – a little too much so for some. Very good value. Screwcap. 15% alc. Rating 91 To 2020 $20

✪ Katunga GTS 2010 Grenache, tannat and shiraz, were separately fermented, and matured in different oaks, ranging from two-year-old French to much older American. The impact of the tannat and shiraz is very obvious, especially in the tannins; while some dark berry characters are in play, red fruits are dominant, keeping the wine lively and fresh. Cork. 14.5% alc. Rating 91 To 2018 $20

✪ Stock's Hill McLaren Vale Cabernet Sauvignon 2010 Medium red-purple; reflects the vintage (good) and the region (also good); it has unexpectedly juicy cassis fruit, fine-grained tannins and a dash of regional chocolate. The balance strongly suggests medium-term cellaring will be in order, although it can be enjoyed now. Excellent value. Screwcap. 14.5% alc. Rating 91 To 2018 $18

✪ French Oak McLaren Vale Chardonnay 2012 Different parcels from four vineyards were picked at different baume levels, and a portion of each, using eight different yeast strains, was barrel-fermented in new Quintessence French oak. The wine has length and balance, but not enough vinosity for higher points; that said, amazing value. Screwcap. 13.5% alc. Rating 90 To 2016 $20

🍷🍷🍷🍷
✪ Pirra McLaren Vale Grenache Shiraz 2011 50-year-old estate-grown grenache, plus shiraz from the Johnstone Road Vineyard, produces a supple, light-bodied blend of very sweet red berry fruit, fine tannins and mocha oak. Good value for immediate consumption. Screwcap. 14.5% alc. Rating 89 To 2015 $14

Pizzini   ★★★★★

175 King Valley Road, Whitfield, Vic 3768 **Region** King Valley
T (03) 5729 8278 **www.**pizzini.com.au **Open** 7 days 10–5
Winemaker Joel and Alfred Pizzini **Est.** 1980 **Dozens** 29 000 **Vyds** 48.7ha
Fred and Katrina Pizzini have been grapegrowers in the King Valley for over 30 years, with a substantial vineyard. Originally much of the grape production was sold, but today 80% is retained for the Pizzini brand, and the focus is on winemaking, which has been particularly successful. Their wines rank high among the many King Valley producers. It is not surprising that their wines should span both Italian and traditional varieties, and I can personally vouch for their Italian cooking skills. Katrina's A tavola! cooking school opened in 2010 with lessons in antipasti, gnocchi, ravioli, cakes and desserts, and of course, pasta. Exports to Japan.

🍷🍷🍷🍷🍷 Per gli Angeli 2006 Made from trebbiano grown in Northeast Victoria, matured in used oak until Jan '12, the name 'for the angels' referring to the evaporative loss over the 6 years' maturation. It has become immensely complex, gleaming gold in colour, and gloriously rich and vibrant, with toffee, cumquat, honey and citrus flavours. Screwcap. 14.1% alc. Rating 95 To 2020 $65

Il Barone 2009 A blend of cabernet sauvignon, shiraz, sangiovese and nebbiolo, separately fermented and matured for 18 months prior to blending, thereafter kept in bottle for 2 years. It has all been worth the effort; the complex dark fruits have spice and cedary nuances, and the tannins are fine and soft. Diam. 14.2% alc. Rating 94 To 2020 $45

King Valley Nebbiolo 2009 Leading out supple, finishing savoury and drawing out long and refined, it's ready to enjoy now, yet a very fine tannin profile will see it out for a decade. Layers of alluring violets, dried flowers, forest berries, mixed spice, anise and dried herbs characterise a complex, sophisticated style. Screwcap. 14.1% alc. Rating 94 To 2019 $48 TS

♥♥♥♥♡ **King Valley Riesling 2012** Pale quartz; the fragrant and flowery bouquet is
✪   followed by a burst of crisp, yet intensely fruity, flavour on the fore-palate, then
bright citrus and apple morph into lingering, cleansing acidity. Excellent value.
Screwcap. 11.5% alc. **Rating** 93 **To** 2020 $16

✪   **Whitefields King Valley Pinot Grigio 2011** How much is due to extra time
in bottle, the vintage or the site I don't know, but there are genuine layers of
flavour and aromas here, ranging through dried flowers, spice and – of course –
fresh and dried pear. Screwcap. 12.2% alc. **Rating** 93 **To** 2014 $27
King Valley Arneis 2012 Rating 91 **To** 2016 $22

✪   **Gundagai Shiraz 2006** Densely coloured; Pizzini finds blackberry, dark cherry,
black olives, dark chocolate, leather, earth, black pepper, plum and cherry in the
wine. So there you have it. My only additional comment is that it has aged very
well, and there is good texture, structure and balance to this bargain-priced wine.
Cork. 13.5% alc. **Rating** 91 **To** 2018 $20
King Valley Sangiovese 2011 Rating 91 **To** 2018 $25
King Valley Pinot Grigio 2012 Rating 90 **To** 2014 $19
King Valley Prosecco 2012 Rating 90 **To** 2012 $20 TS

Plan B   ★★★★

679 Calgardup Road, Forest Grove, WA 6286 **Region** Great Southern/Margaret River
T 0413 759 030 **www.**planbwines.com **Open** Not
Winemaker Bill Crappsley **Est.** 2005 **Dozens** 40 000 **Vyds** 20ha
This is a joint venture between Bill Crappsley, a 44-year veteran winemaker/consultant; Gary
Gosatti, of Arlewood Estate; and Terry Chellappah, wine consultant. The Shiraz is sourced
from Bill's Calgardup Vineyard, the remaining wines from Arlewood, and all are single vineyard
releases. It has been a notably successful Plan B under Terry's management, with significant
increases in production naturally following. Exports to the UK, Canada, Sweden, Norway,
Finland, Switzerland, Singapore, Hong Kong and China.

♥♥♥♥♡ **TV Margaret River Tempranillo 2007** TV stands for tempranillo viognier, the
✪   presence of a splash of the latter disclosed on the back label. Despite its age, the
hue is still light and the mouthfeel plush and soft, the flavours of red cherry true
to the variety. Excellent value. Screwcap. 14% alc. **Rating** 91 **To** 2015 $18

✪   **MB Frankland River Sauvignon Blanc 2012** An extremely clever back label:
'Made from free-range grapes; no mental blanc; won't strip the enamel from your
pearly whites you've spent a fortune on; succulent fruit'. All true, all tropical, all
hedonistic. Screwcap. 13.5% alc. **Rating** 90 **To** 2014 $18

✪   **ST Frankland River Shiraz 2010** Bright colour; while the front label only
shows shiraz, the back label says (an undefined percentage of) tempranillo is
included; an elegant, light- to medium-bodied wine with an array of plum and
cherry fruits, and fine tannins. Screwcap. 14% alc. **Rating** 90 **To** 2017 $18

Plantagenet   ★★★★★

Albany Highway, Mount Barker, WA 6324 **Region** Mount Barker
T (08) 9851 3111 **www.**plantagenetwines.com **Open** 7 days 10–4.30
Winemaker Cath Oates, Chris Murtha **Est.** 1974 **Dozens** 60 000 **Vyds** 130ha
Plantagenet was established by Tony Smith, who continues to be involved in its management
40 years later, notwithstanding that it has been owned by Lionel Samson & Son for many
years. He established five vineyards: Bouverie in 1968, Wyjup in '71, Rocky Horror 1 in
'88, Rocky Horror 2 in '97 and Rosetta in '99. These vineyards are the cornerstone of the
substantial production of consistently high quality wines: highly aromatic Riesling, tangy
citrus-tinged Chardonnay, glorious Rhône-style Shiraz and ultra-stylish Cabernet Sauvignon.
Exports to the UK, the US, Canada, China and Japan.

ŢŢŢŢŢ **Riesling 2012** Bright straw-green; one whiff and one sip will tell you why this
✪   wine has won trophies, including that for Best Wine of Show in the Qantas Wine
    Show of WA '12. The sheer quality of the lime-filled palate, with bursts of crunchy
    acidity and green apple, takes it out of the ordinary. The drink-to date will
    prove to be conservative, but reflects the pleasure the wine gives now. Screwcap.
    12.5% alc. **Rating** 96 **To** 2022 $25
    Shiraz 2011 Bright, medium deep red-purple; the bouquet is positively
    perfumed, with spice, pepper and licorice woven through the red fruits, fruits
    that drive the silky, medium-bodied palate through to its long finish; the oak
    and tannin management have been exemplary. Screwcap. 14.5% alc. **Rating** 95
    To 2026 $45
    Cabernet Sauvignon 2011 The healthy crimson-purple colour heralds an
    elegant, medium-bodied cabernet with a mix of cassis, mint, redcurrant and spice
    on its bouquet and medium-bodied palate; here the juicy fruit flavours are given
    complexity by quality French oak and fine-grained tannins. Screwcap. 14.6% alc.
    Rating 94 **To** 2026 $45

ŢŢŢŢŢ **Mount Barker Chardonnay 2012 Rating** 93 **To** 2019 $28
✪   **Omrah Great Southern Rose 2012** Made from tempranillo plus a
    small amount of shiraz. Pale pink, it has more attitude and length than many
    contemporary Roses; red cherry and strawberry flavours are lifted by the citrussy
    acidity on the dry, lingering finish. Screwcap. 13.8% alc. **Rating** 93 **To** 2014 $19
✪   **Omrah Great Southern Sauvignon Blanc Semillon 2012** Light straw-green;
    the relatively warm vintage has aided the near riotous expression of tropical fruits
    on the scented bouquet, joined by ripe citrus on the palate; the flavours linger on
    the aftertaste. Screwcap. 13% alc. **Rating** 92 **To** 2013 $18
✪   **Omrah Great Southern Cabernet Merlot 2010** Light crimson-purple; the
    fragrant cassis-accented bouquet leads into a very well balanced medium-bodied
    palate, the emphasis on the juicy redcurrant and blackcurrant fruit rather than oak
    or tannins; no need to delay. Screwcap. 13.5% alc. **Rating** 90 **To** 2014 $19

Poacher's Ridge Vineyard   ★★★★★

1630 Spencer Road, Narrikup, WA 6326 **Region** Mount Barker
T (08) 9857 6066 **www**.prv.com.au **Open** Fri–Sun 10–4, or by appt
Winemaker Robert Diletti (Contract) **Est.** 2000 **Dozens** 1000 **Vyds** 6.9ha
Alex and Janet Taylor purchased the Poacher's Ridge property in 1999; before then it had
been used for cattle grazing. The vineyard includes shiraz, cabernet sauvignon, merlot,
riesling, marsanne and viognier. Winning the Tri Nations '07 Merlot class against the might
of Australia, NZ and South Africa with its '05 Louis' Block Great Southern Merlot was a
dream come true.

ŢŢŢŢŢ **Louis' Block Great Southern Riesling 2012** The perfumed bouquet has lime
✪   blossom aromas to the fore, the fine, elegant and delicate palate with the inherent
    balance that guarantees its long-term future, although that balance also makes it
    accessible now. Screwcap. 12.5% alc. **Rating** 94 **To** 2027 $24
    Louis' Block Great Southern Cabernet Sauvignon 2011 Medium red-
    purple; this is an elegant, cool-grown Cabernet with equal measures of cassis and
    savoury black olive inputs; the fruit expression is bright, the tannins persistent, and
    the oak in measured support. Screwcap. 14% alc. **Rating** 94 **To** 2021 $28

ŢŢŢŢŢ **Louis' Block Great Southern Marsanne 2012** Fresh and crisp, with good
✪   varietal character already apparent courtesy of honeysuckle, peach and citrus fruit
    supported by bright acidity. Screwcap. 13.5% alc. **Rating** 91 **To** 2027 $20

Point Leo Road Vineyard   ★★★★☆

214 Point Leo Road, Red Hill South, Vic 3937 **Region** Mornington Peninsula
T 0406 610 815 **www**.pointleoroad.com.au **Open** By appt
Winemaker Simon Black, Andrew Thomson, David Cowburn **Est.** 1996 **Dozens** 1000
Vyds 3.6ha

John Law and family planted 1.9ha of pinot noir and 1.5ha of chardonnay in 1996 as contract growers for several leading Mornington Peninsula wineries. Plantings have been progressively expanded, now including small amounts of pinot gris, lagrein and gewurztraminer. Some of the grapes are now contract-made, and they have two labels: Point Leo Road for premium wines, and Point Break the second label.

ΨΨΨΨΨ Mornington Peninsula Chardonnay 2011 Bright straw-green; a vibrant and incisive wine, its stream of white peach and grapefruit flavours energetically coursing along the full length of the palate; oak is a bystander to a very attractive wine. Screwcap. 12.8% alc. **Rating** 94 **To** 2019 $26

ΨΨΨΨΨ Mornington Peninsula Pinot Grigio 2011 **Rating** 93 **To** 2014 $24
Point Break Pinot Gris 2011 **Rating** 91 **To** 2014 $22

Pokolbin Estate ★★★★★
McDonalds Road, Pokolbin, NSW 2321 **Region** Hunter Valley
T (02) 4998 7524 **www**.pokolbinestate.com.au **Open** 7 days 9–5
Winemaker Andrew Thomas (Contract) **Est.** 1980 **Dozens** 4000 **Vyds** 15.7ha
Pokolbin Estate has a very unusual, but very good, multi-varietal, multi-vintage array of wines available for sale at any one time. The Riesling is true Riesling, not misnamed Semillon, the latter being one of their best wines, and wines under screwcap going back six or seven vintages, and single vineyard offerings to boot, are available. No wines received for the *2014 Wine Companion*, but a five-star rating has been maintained.

Polperro/Even Keel ★★★★☆
76 Arthurs Seat Road, Red Hill, Vic 3937 **Region** Mornington Peninsula
T 0405 155 882 **www**.evenkeelwines.com **Open** By appt
Winemaker Samuel Coverdale **Est.** 2006 **Dozens** 3000 **Vyds** 10ha
Sam Coverdale lives on the Mornington Peninsula, makes wine there full-time and surfs part-time. Before taking up residence on the Peninsula, he obtained his degree in oenology from CSU, and accumulated 10 years of winemaking experience in Australia, France, Spain and Italy. Polperro is his single vineyard Mornington Peninsula range, and includes Pinot Noir, Chardonnay and Pinot Gris. Second label Even Keel uses grape varieties that best represent their region. Exports to Hong Kong.

ΨΨΨΨΨ Polperro Mill Hill Chardonnay 2011 While the vintage caused much heartache for pinot noir, it produced wonderfully fragrant and poised chardonnays. These have great length and precision in the fruit flavours of the palate, paying little heed to the French oak in which they were matured. This wine precisely demonstrates all those attributes. Diam. 12.9% alc. **Rating** 95 **To** 2021 $48

ΨΨΨΨΨ Even Keel Chardonnay 2011 **Rating** 93 **To** 2019 $29

ΨΨΨΨ Polperro Landividdy Lane Pinot Noir 2011 **Rating** 88 **To** 2015 $48
Polperro Mill Hill Pinot Noir 2011 **Rating** 87 **To** 2014 $48

Ponda Estate ★★★★☆
150 Rhinds Road, Wallington, Vic 3221 **Region** Geelong
T 0438 845 696 **www**.pondaestate.com.au **Open** Oct–Apr w'ends & public hols 10–5, or by appt
Winemaker Ray Nadeson, Darren Burke **Est.** 2000 **Dozens** 400
Ponda Estate's small vineyard is situated on the Bellarine Taste Trail, 15 minutes from Geelong and five minutes from Ocean Grove. The low-yielding vines are managed by owners Peter Congdon and Tracey Frigo, who are committed to using sustainable and organic viticultural practices. Babydoll sheep and chooks work the block to sort out weeds/bugs and provide fertiliser for the vines, and each year family and friends gather to help pick the grapes and celebrate harvest. Peter and Tracey also source a small amount of chardonnay from local growers.

♥♥♥♥♡ **Bellarine Peninsula Chardonnay 2011** Has a seamless stream of nectarine, white peach, melon and citrus, the oak well balanced and integrated. Screwcap. 13% alc. **Rating** 93 **To** 2018 $30

Bellarine Peninsula Pinot Noir 2011 Light, clear red; the bouquet is fragrant with cherry blossom aromas, and the palate, although light-bodied, has some really attractive red berry/cherry fruit flavours. Screwcap. 13% alc. **Rating** 93 **To** 2017 $30

Pondalowie Vineyards   ★★★★★

123 View Street, Bendigo, Vic 3550 **Region** Bendigo
T 0439 373 366 **www**.pondalowie.com.au **Open** W'ends 12–5, or by appt
Winemaker Dominic Morris, Krystina Morris **Est.** 1997 **Dozens** 2500 **Vyds** 10ha
Dominic and Krystina Morris both have strong winemaking backgrounds gained from working in Australia, Portugal and France. Dominic worked alternate vintages in Australia and Portugal from 1995 to 2012, and Krystina has also worked at St Hallett and Boar's Rock. They have established 5.5ha of shiraz, 2ha each of tempranillo and cabernet sauvignon, and a little malbec. Incidentally, the illustration on the Pondalowie label is not a piece of barbed wire, but a very abstract representation of the winery kelpie dog. Drought and flood successively devastated Pondalowie in '09 (only 3.3 tonnes harvested from 10ha of shiraz), '10 (no grapes harvested) and '11 (a total of 14 tonnes of mediocre fruit). However, Krystina says the '12 and '13 wines are fantastic. Exports to Hong Kong and Japan.

♥♥♥♥♥ **Vineyard Blend 2008** Dense, almost impenetrable colour; the bouquet has an exotic array of spice, cassis and black fruits. Licorice and dark chocolate join the band, along with ripe tannins and oak. Full of individuality, and great for lovers of big reds for long ageing, and all this for next to nothing. This is essentially the same tasting note I wrote a year ago, and I am astonished it is still available. Usually a blend of shiraz, cabernet sauvignon and tempranillo. Screwcap. 14% alc. **Rating** 94 **To** 2030 $19

Pooley Wines   ★★★★★

Belmont Vineyard, 1431 Richmond Road, Richmond, Tas 7025 **Region** Southern Tasmania
T (03) 6260 2895 **www**.pooleywines.com.au **Open** 7 days 10–5
Winemaker Matt Pooley **Est.** 1985 **Dozens** 4000 **Vyds** 14ha
Three generations of the Pooley family have been involved in the development of Pooley Wines, although the winery was previously known as Cooinda Vale. Plantings have now reached over 12ha in a region that is warmer and drier than most people realise. In 2003 the family planted pinot noir and pinot grigio (with more recent plantings of pinot noir and chardonnay) at Belmont Vineyard, a heritage property with an 1830s Georgian home and a second cellar door in the old sandstone barn and stables.

♥♥♥♥♥ **Coal River Riesling 2012** Vibrant green hue; a highly perfumed and lifted bouquet of apple blossom, nectarine, lemon zest and bath talc; the palate is long and extremely fine, and while absolutely delicious now, will continue to progress with grace. Screwcap. 11.5% alc. **Rating** 96 **To** 2025 $27 BE

Coal River Pinot Noir 2011 Light, bright crimson; a fragrant red cherry and damson plum aromas lead into a vibrant, fresh and well-balanced palate; here similar red fruit flavours are supported by fine, gently spicy, tannins; the oak has been well handled. Screwcap. 13.5% alc. **Rating** 95 **To** 2019 $35

Butchers Hill Pinot Noir 2011 Attractively spicy on the bouquet with black cherry, plum and a suggestion of jasmine all evident; the palate is fleshy, vibrant and lively, with fine-grained tannins providing thrust to the fine acid cut of the expansive and complex finish. Screwcap. 13.7% alc. **Rating** 95 **To** 2020 $45 BE

Late Harvest Riesling 2012 Pure green apple, bath talc, coriander and white nectarine aromas and flavours linger seamlessly; long and fine-boned, demure and delicious. Screwcap. 10.4% alc. **Rating** 95 **To** 2018 $35 BE

Butchers Hill Pinot Noir 2010 Bright, clear crimson, with good retention of hue; an expressive and fragrant bouquet leads into a well-constructed and textured palate, red cherry and spiced plum fruit supported by fine tannins. Screwcap. 13.4% alc. **Rating** 94 **To** 2020 $40

♀♀♀♀♀ **Margaret Pooley Tribute Riesling 2012 Rating** 93 **To** 2025 $40 BE

Poonawatta Estate   ★★★★★

Angaston Road, Eden Valley, SA 5235 **Region** Eden Valley
T (08) 8565 3248 **www**.poonawatta.com **Open** By appt
Winemaker Reid Bosward, Andrew Holt **Est.** 1880 **Dozens** 1500 **Vyds** 3.6ha
The Poonawatta Estate story is complex, stemming from 0.8a of shiraz planted in 1880. When Andrew Holt's parents purchased the Poonawatta property, the vineyard had suffered decades of neglect, and a slow process of restoration began. The strongest canes available from the winter pruning of the 1880s block were slowly and progressively dug into the stony soil of the site. It took seven years to establish the matching 0.8ha, and the yield is even lower than that of the 1880s block. The Riesling is produced from a single vineyard of 2ha hand-planted by the Holt family in the 1970s. Exports to France, Denmark and Hong Kong.

♀♀♀♀♀ **Sub-Regional Collection Single Vineyard Bob's Block Eden Valley Cabernet 2010** A very refined wine in terms of its texture and of its oak treatment; has an intense, juicy core of cassis running through its prodigiously long medium-bodied palate, the tannins perfectly tempered. A superb example of low alcohol Cabernet Sauvignon. Screwcap. 13.1% alc. **Rating** 97 **To** 2040 $60
Sub-Regional Collection Single Vineyard Bob's Block Eden Valley Shiraz 2010 Full purple-crimson; it's difficult to understand the back label: three wines in this series, Bob's Vineyards (plural) producing two of them. Only 400 bottles were produced of this lovely, supple and deeply flavoured wine from 60-year-old vines. Screwcap. 14.7% alc. **Rating** 96 **To** 2040 $60
The Centenarian Single Barrel Reserve Eden Valley Shiraz 2007 From the original Poonawatta vines planted 2 centuries ago. Exceptional colour for a 6-year-old wine from any vintage, let alone the problematic '07, noted for the toughness of its wines. This wine is the reverse, with softly luscious red and black fruits in a wreath of cedary oak. Cork. 14% alc. **Rating** 96 **To** 2037 $160
Sub-Regional Collection Single Vineyard Wayne's Block Eden Valley Cabernet 2010 Vivid purple-crimson; the medium- to full-bodied wine abounds with blackcurrant fruit and whispers of bitter chocolate and sweet earth, the tannins contributing to texture, structure and even flavour. Screwcap. 13.8% alc. **Rating** 96 **To** 2040 $60
Regional Series The Four Corners of Eden Valley Shiraz 2010 Full purple-crimson; a notably rich, concentrated and very complex full-bodied wine with an array of spice, pepper and licorice woven through its black fruits; the power comes from the integral flavours of the wine, not from its alcohol. Screwcap. 14.8% alc. **Rating** 95 **To** 2030 $30
Regional Series The Four Corners of Eden Valley Cabernet 2010 In most years the Eden Valley has a better climate for cabernet sauvignon than the Barossa Valley; '10 was so good that both regions prospered, and this is a special wine. It has juicy cassis fruit, and on the other, aristocratic tannins that are not abrasive or hard. Screwcap. 13.9% alc. **Rating** 95 **To** 2035 $30
The Eden Riesling 2012 Rating 94 **To** 2023 $26

Port Phillip Estate   ★★★★★

263 Red Hill Road, Red Hill, Vic 3937 **Region** Mornington Peninsula
T (03) 5989 4444 **www**.portphillipestate.com.au **Open** 7 days 11–5
Winemaker Sandro Mosele **Est.** 1987 **Dozens** 4000 **Vyds** 9.3ha
Port Phillip Estate has been owned by Giorgio and Dianne Gjergja since 2000. The ability of the site (enhanced, it is true, by the skills of Sandro Mosele) to produce outstanding Syrah,

Pinot Noir and Chardonnay, and very good Sauvignon Blanc, is something special. Whence climate change? Quite possibly the estate may have answers for decades to come. A futuristic, multimillion-dollar restaurant, cellar door and winery complex was opened prior to the '10 vintage. Exports to the UK, Canada and Singapore.

ŸŸŸŸŸ Mornington Peninsula Sauvignon 2012 Bright straw-green; it would be hard to imagine a greater contrast with the sauvignon blanc of Marlborough; here texture and structure take primacy, not fruit salad, with oak just the starting point. Screwcap. 13% alc. **Rating** 94 **To** 2016 $26
Mornington Peninsula Chardonnay 2011 The bouquet is fruit-driven, albeit with some oak, and the fore-palate opens quietly before it accelerates dramatically, its grapefruit and white peach spearing through to the finish and aftertaste, demanding the next glass. Screwcap. 13% alc. **Rating** 94 **To** 2018 $35
Salasso Mornington Peninsula Rose 2012 Pale salmon-pink; while the variety is not disclosed, it is a fair assumption to point to pinot noir; the strawberry bouquet and palate fruit is delicate, the palate has latent power, and bursts into song on the long finish. Lovely Rose. Screwcap. 13.5% alc. **Rating** 94 **To** 2015 $24

ŸŸŸŸŸ Quartier Pinot Gris 2012 Rating 93 **To** 2015 $30
Mornington Peninsula Shiraz 2011 Rating 93 **To** 2018 $38
Quartier Arneis 2012 Rating 92 **To** 2016 $30

Portsea Estate   ★★★★☆

PO Box 3148, Bellevue Hill, NSW 2023 **Region** Mornington Peninsula
T (02) 9328 6359 **www**.portseaestate.com **Open** By appt
Winemaker Tim Elphick, Chris Catlow **Est.** 2000 **Dozens** 1400 **Vyds** 3.14ha
Noted film maker Warwick Ross and sister (and silent partner) Caron Wilson-Hawley have moved fast and successfully since the first vintage in 2004. Having had the luxury of having their first seven vintages made at Paringa Estate by Lyndsay McCall and his team, they have built an onsite winery, and hired not one, but two, winemakers with impeccable pedigrees. By the time of publication, Warwick's film 'Red Obsession', with Andrew Caillard MW playing a leading role, will have been completed. It takes an inside look at Bordeaux, and will no doubt be devoured by audiences stretching from Shanghai to New York.

ŸŸŸŸŸ Stonecutters Block Mornington Peninsula Chardonnay 2011 Penfolds (P58) clone was the source, and just the first 33% of free-run juice was fermented and matured in French oak, 33% taken through mlf. The colour is a little deeper than the standard version, and the palate is much richer, and has absorbed the new oak. Screwcap. 13% alc. **Rating** 94 **To** 2019 $57

ŸŸŸŸŸ Mornington Peninsula Chardonnay 2011 Rating 90 **To** 2016 $29
Mornington Peninsula Pinot Noir 2011 Rating 90 **To** 2015 $40

Possums Vineyard   ★★★★

88 Adams Road, Blewitt Springs, SA 5171 **Region** McLaren Vale
T (08) 8272 3406 **www**.possumswines.com.au **Open** By appt
Winemaker Pieter Breugem **Est.** 2000 **Dozens** 3000 **Vyds** 53.4ha
Possums Vineyard is owned by Dr John Possingham and Carol Summers. They have two vineyards in McLaren Vale – one at Blewitt Springs, the other at Willunga – covering shiraz (23.6ha), cabernet sauvignon (16.9ha), chardonnay (7.7ha), with lesser plantings of viognier, malbec, pinot gris, sauvignon blanc and grenache. In 2007 they completed construction of a 500-tonne winery at Blewitt Springs and sell both bottled and bulk wine. Winemaker Pieter Breugem has come from South Africa via the US and Constellation Wines. Exports to the UK, Denmark, Germany, Singapore, Hong Kong and China.

ŸŸŸŸŸ Dr John's Willunga McLaren Vale Shiraz 2010 Vivid crimson-purple;
 proclaims its regional origin from the start through to the finish and aftertaste; dark berry fruit is wrapped in dark chocolate, fruit and oak tannins giving texture and balance. Great value. Screwcap. 14.5% alc. **Rating** 92 **To** 2019 $18

Poverty Hill Wines ★★★★

PO Box 76, Springton, SA 5235 **Region** Eden Valley
T (08) 8568 2220 **www.**povertyhillwines.com.au **Open** Fri–Mon 10–5
Winemaker John Eckert **Est.** 2002 **Dozens** 5000 **Vyds** 29ha

Poverty Hill Wines brings together men who have had a long connection with the Eden Valley. Robert Buck owns a small vineyard on the ancient volcanic soils east of Springton, producing both shiraz and cabernet sauvignon. Next is Stuart Woodman, who owns the vineyard with the riesling that produced glorious wines in the early 1990s; it also has high quality, mature-vine cabernet sauvignon. Finally, there is John Eckert, who once worked at Saltram. He not only works as winemaker at Poverty Hill, but manages Rob Buck's vineyard and his own small block of young riesling in the highlands of Springton. Prolonged drought to 2009, with extreme black frosts down to −14°C at night, gave way to incessant rain that devastated the '11 vintage. Poverty Hill indeed. Exports to the US, Hong Kong and NZ.

ⵠⵠⵠⵠⵠ **Eden Valley Riesling 2012** Light straw-green; another affirmation of the quality
✪ of the '12 vintage for Clare and Eden Valley riesling; a core of minerally, crunchy, acidity is surrounded by lime, lemon and green apple fruit; the overall mouthfeel and length all one can ask for. Screwcap. 12.5% alc. **Rating** 93 **To** 2027 $20

Prancing Horse Estate ★★★★★

39 Paringa Road, Red Hill South, Vic 3937 **Region** Mornington Peninsula
T (03) 5989 2602 **www.**prancinghorseestate.com **Open** First w'end each month, or by appt
Winemaker Sergio Carlei, Pascal Marchand, Patrick Piuze **Est.** 1990 **Dozens** 1500
Vyds 6ha

Anthony and Catherine Hancy acquired Lavender Bay Vineyard in early 2002, renaming it Prancing Horse Estate and embarking on increasing the estate vineyards, with 2ha each of chardonnay and pinot noir, and 0.5ha of pinot gris moving to organic farming in '03, progressing to biodynamic in '07. They appointed Sergio Carlei as winemaker, and the following year became joint owners, with Sergio, of Carlei Wines. An additional property 150m west of the existing vineyard has been purchased, and 2ha of vines was planted there in the spring of '10. Prancing Horse has become one of a small group of Australian wineries having wines specifically made for them in Burgundy. Pascal Marchand makes an annual release of Morey-St-Denis Clos des Ormes Premier Cru and Meursault Premier Cru Blagny, while Patrick Piuze makes four Chablis appellation wines. Exports to the UK, the US, France and Sweden.

ⵠⵠⵠⵠⵠ **Mornington Peninsula Chardonnay 2011** Light straw-green; fruit-driven, first and foremost; the barrel-ferment input ex French oak is subtle, and the early picking has highlighted the grapefruit/citrus components on the long palate and aftertaste. Screwcap. 11.5% alc. **Rating** 94 **To** 2020 $60
Mornington Peninsula Chardonnay 2010 Pale, bright straw-green; an elegant, perfectly balanced and articulated wine, so much so it might be possible to figuratively walk by it. On the elegant side of Mornington Peninsula Chardonnay, minerally/chalky acidity to the fore, white flesh stone fruit, apple and melon following. Screwcap. 13% alc. **Rating** 94 **To** 2017 $55

ⵠⵠⵠⵠⵠ **Mornington Peninsula Pinot Gris 2010 Rating** 92 **To** 2016 $40
The Pony Mornington Peninsula Chardonnay 2011 Rating 91 **To** 2016 $30

Pressing Matters ★★★★★

665 Middle Tea Tree Road, Tea Tree, Tas 7017 **Region** Southern Tasmania
T (03) 6268 1947 **www.**pressingmatters.com.au **Open** By appt 0408 126 668
Winemaker Winemaking Tasmania, Paul Smart **Est.** 2002 **Dozens** 1350 **Vyds** 7.1ha

Greg Melick simultaneously wears more hats than most people manage in a lifetime. He is a top-level barrister (Senior Counsel), a Major General (the highest rank in the Australian Army Reserve) and has presided over a number of headline special commissions and enquiries into subjects as diverse as cricket match-fixing allegations against Mark Waugh and others and the Beaconsfield mine collapse. Yet, if asked, he would probably nominate wine as his major focus in life. Having built up an exceptional cellar of the great wines of Europe, he has turned his attention to grapegrowing and winemaking, planting riesling (2.9ha) at his vineyard on Middle Tea Tree Road in the Coal River Valley. It is a perfect north-facing slope, the Mosel-style Rieslings sweeping all before them. It is moderately certain that Greg is waiting impatiently for his multi-clone pinot noir block to perform in a similar manner. Exports to Singapore.

ŸŸŸŸŸ **R139 Riesling 2010** Bright green-gold; since first tasted in January '11, when it won gold at the Tas Wine Show, it has developed another dimension of complexity to its pure, sweet lime juice aromas and flavours; the acidity is a perfect foil for its luscious sweetness. It will last for as long as you can keep your hands off it. 375ml. Screwcap. 9.2% alc. **Rating** 96 **To** 2020 $26
R9 Riesling 2012 Bright straw-green; shows the benefit of retention of a modest 9g/l of sugar, which is manifested not as sweetness per se (as it is masked by the high natural acidity and low pH of the wine), but as lime juice fruit; excellent length. Screwcap. 11% alc. **Rating** 95 **To** 2027 $29
R9 Riesling 2011 Showing a distinct wet slate and citrus blossom bouquet, with some exotic spices in tow; the touch of sugar gives the palate some weight and generosity, with chalky acidity providing grip and length on the finish. Screwcap. 10.4% alc. **Rating** 95 **To** 2025 $33 BE
R0 Riesling 2011 A tightly wound and restrained expression of lemon zest, nectarine and fennel; the palate is bone dry, challengingly so in fact, with generosity something that will come in the fullness of time; the acidity is bracing and refreshing, the finish long. Screwcap. 11% alc. **Rating** 94 **To** 2025 $33 BE

ŸŸŸŸŸ **R0 Riesling 2012 Rating** 93 **To** 2022 $29
Pinot Noir 2011 Rating 90 **To** 2015 $55 BE

Preveli Wines   ★★★★☆

Bessell Road, Rosa Brook, Margaret River, WA 6285 **Region** Margaret River
T (08) 9757 2374 **www.**preveliwines.com.au **Open** At Prevelly General Store, 7 days 10–8
Winemaker Fraser Gallop Estate (Clive Otto) **Est.** 1998 **Dozens** 4500 **Vyds** 7.5ha
While Preveli Wines is a relative newcomer, its owners, the Home family, have lived on the property for three generations. Vince and Greg Home also operate the Prevelly Park Beach Resort and Prevelly Liquor Store, where the wines are available for tasting. Fruit from the vineyard at Rosa Brook (3.5ha of semillon and 1ha each of pinot noir, merlot, cabernet sauvignon and sauvignon blanc) is supplemented by contracts with local growers. The wines are of impressive quality.

ŸŸŸŸŸ **Wild Thing Margaret River Sauvignon Blanc 2012** Hand-picked, whole bunch-pressed, wild yeast-fermented in either stainless steel or used French oak; the approach, coupled with early picking, has worked well. The wine has drive and precision, the flavours of citrus and passionfruit coupled with zesty acidity. May polarise opinions. Screwcap. 12.5% alc. **Rating** 94 **To** 2014 $23

ŸŸŸŸŸ **Margaret River Semillon Sauvignon Blanc 2012** Hand-picked and whole
✪ bunch-pressed, part of the semillon component fermented in used French oak; the result is a fragrant, high-toned bouquet and an intensely flavoured palate with passionfruit, gooseberry and citrus all showing their wares. Terrific value. Screwcap. 12% alc. **Rating** 93 **To** 2015 $19
Wild Thing Margaret River Pinot Rose 2012 Rating 90 **To** 2014 $23

Primo Estate   ★★★★★

McMurtrie Road, McLaren Vale, SA 5171 **Region** McLaren Vale
T (08) 8323 6800 **www.**primoestate.com.au **Open** 7 days 11–4
Winemaker Joseph Grilli, Daniel Zuzolo **Est.** 1979 **Dozens** 30000 **Vyds** 34ha
One-time Roseworthy dux Joe Grilli produces innovative and excellent wines. The biennial release of the Joseph Sparkling Red (in its tall Italian glass bottle) is eagerly awaited, the wine immediately selling out. Also unusual and highly regarded are the vintage-dated extra-virgin olive oils. However, the core lies with the La Biondina, Il Briccone Shiraz Sangiovese

and Joseph Cabernet Merlot. The business has expanded to take in both McLaren Vale and Clarendon, with plantings of colombard, shiraz, cabernet sauvignon, riesling, merlot, sauvignon blanc, chardonnay, pinot gris, sangiovese, nebbiolo and merlot. Exports to all major markets.

ƧƧƧƧƧ **Joseph Sparkling Red NV** Disgorged July '11; every year a hogshead of Joseph Moda Cabernet Sauvignon Merlot is added to the base wine, limiting the production to slightly less than 36 dozen bottles. It also means the style is very similar from one release to the next, the appeal of the red and black fruit flavours universal. Cork. 13.5% alc. **Rating** 96 **To** 2017 $70

Joseph Angel Gully Clarendon Shiraz 2010 Full red-purple; a distinguished wine from an excellent site and a top vintage; fine, ripe, savoury tannins, verging on minerally, are built into the medium-bodied palate, which is replete with an abundance of dark fruits leading through to the long, fresh finish. Screwcap. 14% alc. **Rating** 95 **To** 2030 $75

Shale Stone McLaren Vale Shiraz 2010 Good colour; seamlessly joins fruit from Primo's Clarendon and McMurtrie Road vineyards, the latter filling the mid-palate with notes of dark, bitter chocolate, book-ended by juicy, fresh black fruit, oak and tannins lined up in support. Screwcap. 14% alc. **Rating** 94 **To** 2020 $32

Joseph Moda McLaren Vale Cabernet Sauvignon Merlot 2010 A wine with a long and proud history, here with a profound depth to its blackcurrant fruit, supported by quality oak and positive tannins. The alcohol is achieved by partial drying of the grapes, and the wine is not porty. Screwcap. 15% alc. **Rating** 94 **To** 2030 $75

Zamberlan McLaren Vale Cabernet Sauvignon Sangiovese 2010 The skins of the just-fermented Joseph Moda Cabernet Sangiovese were added to the base cabernet sauvignon must, which was in turn fermented before going to barrel; you might think this would produce a tannic, heavy wine, but it doesn't. Rather, this is a medium-bodied wine with attractive berry fruit, finishing with dusty tannins. Screwcap. 14% alc. **Rating** 94 **To** 2025 $35

ƧƧƧƧƧ **Joseph d'Elena Adelaide Pinot Grigio 2012** **Rating** 92 **To** 2014 $28
✪ **La Biondina Colombard 2012** Pale straw-green; a wine that has always delivered more flavour and attitude than theoretically possible; intense grapefruit flavours spear through the length of the intensely focused palate. If you want an alternative to Chardonnay (or other mainstream varieties) try this, and leave pinot gris on the shelf. Screwcap. 12% alc. **Rating** 91 **To** 2024 $16

Il Briccone McLaren Vale Shiraz Sangiovese 2011 **Rating** 90 **To** 2018 $25

Principia ★★★★

139 Main Creek Road, Red Hill, Vic 3937 (postal) **Region** Mornington Peninsula
T (03) 5931 0010 **www.**principiawines.com.au **Open** By appt
Winemaker Darrin Gaffy **Est.** 1995 **Dozens** 500 **Vyds** 3.5ha

Darrin Gaffy's philosophy for Principia is minimal interference, thus the vines (pinot noir and chardonnay) are not irrigated, yields are restricted to 3.75 tonnes per hectare or less, and all wine movements are by gravity or by gas pressure, which in turn means there is no filtration, and both primary and secondary fermentation are by indigenous yeasts. 'Principia' comes from the word 'beginnings' in Latin: *The Principia* was Sir Isaac Newton's famous scientific work that incorporated his theory of gravitation and the laws of motion.

ƧƧƧƧ **Mornington Peninsula Chardonnay 2011** Gleaming green-straw; not bottled until Jan '13; wild yeast-fermented, French oak, no pumps and (hence) no filtration. The wine is certainly complex, but there is a cut of acidity (volatile?) on the finish and aftertaste. Screwcap. 13.5% alc. **Rating** 89 **To** 2015 $36

Printhie Wines ★★★★★

489 Yuranigh Road, Molong, NSW 2866 **Region** Orange
T (02) 6366 8422 **www.**printhiewines.com.au **Open** Mon–Sat 10–4, or by appt
Winemaker Drew Tuckwell **Est.** 1996 **Dozens** 20000 **Vyds** 33.1ha

Owned by the Swift family, Printhie has established itself at the forefront of quality viticulture and winemaking in Orange. The estate vineyards have matured and fruit intake is supplemented by contract growers. The new generation at Printhie continues to make its mark with Ed Swift, former President of the Orange Region Vignerons Association and a participant of the Future Leaders Program. Winemaker Drew Tuckwell is a Len Evans Tutorial scholar and participant in the Wine Communicators of Australia Young Guns and Gurus program (as a young gun). The wine portfolio has been consolidated: the entry-level Mountain Range now comprises just six wines (three white, three red), the Mount Canobolas Collection (MCC) range is a quasi-reserve range, and the Swift Family Heritage flagship range has been trimmed to just one red wine (a Cabernet Sauvignon/Shiraz blend). Exports to the US, Canada, Denmark, Ivory Coast and China.

MCC Riesling 2012 This wine strikes for the balance between sugar and acid with aplomb, and reveals candied orange, spices and ginger, with a generous texture; long and almost luscious, with a little grip to conclude. An excellent wine for spicy Asian foods. Screwcap. 12.5% alc. **Rating** 95 **To** 2025 $25 BE

MCC Sauvignon Blanc 2011 The full green-straw colour in part reflects full barrel fermentation in 2- and 6-year-old oak, with wild yeast and cloudy juice, battonage and possibly some mlf. This is certainly way out in left field, with a funky bouquet, but an unexpectedly juicy/fruity palate. Won't appeal to all, but it works for me. Screwcap. 13.5% alc. **Rating** 94 **To** 2015 $35

MCC Chardonnay 2011 A single vineyard wine, barrel-fermented with wild yeast, and taken through mlf to reduce acidity. Sophisticated winemaking has produced a very elegant and well-balanced wine, with all the length one could wish for. Screwcap. 12.5% alc. **Rating** 94 **To** 2017 $35

Mountain Range Orange Chardonnay 2012 Part barrel-, part tank-fermented; part wild yeast, part cultured yeast; partial mlf; fine lees and stirring. All this for $18! It's a very complex and attractive wine, its fruit running from grapefruit to stone fruit, the oak balanced, the length admirable. Screwcap. 13% alc. **Rating** 93 **To** 2014 $18

MCC Orange Shiraz 2011 Rating 92 **To** 2021 $35

Mountain Range Orange Sauvignon Blanc 2012 Light straw-green; a fragrant bouquet and juicy palate neatly straddle grass, citrus and tropical flavours. An Attractive wine. Screwcap. 12.5% alc. **Rating** 91 **To** 2014 $18

Swift Cuvee Brut NV Rating 91 **To** 2014 $40 TS

Mountain Range Orange Pinot Gris 2012 One hundred per cent estate-grown; some mlf, oak and lees are used to build texture and complexity, and duly succeed (helped by generous alcohol warmth). There is the full gamut of pear, peach and spice in the wine. Screwcap. 14% alc. **Rating** 90 **To** 2014 $18

Swift Family Heritage 2010 Rating 90 **To** 2018 $65 BE

Provenance Wines   ★★★★★

870 Steiglitz Road, Sutherlands Creek, Vic 3331 **Region** Geelong
T (03) 5281 2230 **www.provenancewines.com.au Open** By appt
Winemaker Scott Ireland, Sam Vogel **Est.** 1995 **Dozens** 1800 **Vyds** 5ha
Scott Ireland and partner Jen Lilburn established Provenance Wines in 1997 as a natural extension of Scott's years of winemaking experience, both here and abroad. Located in the Moorabool Valley, the winery team focuses on the classics in a cool–climate sense – Pinot Gris, Chardonnay and Pinot Noir in particular, as well as Shiraz. Fruit is sourced both within the Geelong region and further afield (when the fruit warrants selection). They are also major players in contract making in the Geelong region.

Tarrington Pinot Gris 2011 From the very cool Western Victorian town of Tarrington, but reached flavour ripeness in this challenging vintage; moreover, the almost fleshy pear and ginger fruit has very good line, length and balance. Screwcap. 13% alc. **Rating** 94 **To** 2014 $27

Golden Plains Pinot Noir 2011 Has more colour than many from the '11 vintage; a thoroughly attractive Pinot, with a fragrant bouquet then a juicy palate of red cherry, plum and spice, the finish with a slight twist of citrus. To be enjoyed now. Screwcap. 12.5% alc. **Rating** 94 **To** 2016 $32

🍷🍷🍷🍷🍷 **Geelong Shiraz 2011 Rating** 93 **To** 2021 $32
Geelong Nebbiolo 2010 Rating 93 **To** 2019 $32
Golden Plains Chardonnay 2011 Rating 92 **To** 2018 $29

Punch ★★★★★

2130 Kinglake Road, St Andrews, Vic 3761 (postal) **Region** Yarra Valley
T (03) 9710 1155 **www.**punched.com.au **Open** Not
Winemaker James Lance **Est.** 2004 **Dozens** 600 **Vyds** 3.45ha
In the wake of Graeme Rathbone taking over the brand (but not the real estate) of Diamond Valley, the Lances' son James and his wife Claire leased the vineyard and winery from David and Catherine Lance, including the 0.25ha block of close-planted pinot noir. In all, Punch has 2.25ha of pinot noir (including the close-planted), 0.8ha of chardonnay and 0.4ha of cabernet sauvignon. When the 2009 Black Saturday bushfires destroyed the crop, various grapegrowers wrote offering assistance, which led to the purchase of the grapes used for that dire year, and the beginning of the 'Friends of Punch' wines.

🍷🍷🍷🍷🍷 **Lance's Vineyard Chardonnay 2011** Light straw-green; a wine of exemplary poise and purity, wild-fermented and not filtered, the flavours moulded as much by stone fruit as citrus. Screwcap. 12.5% alc. **Rating** 94 **To** 2020 $45
Lance's Vineyard Close Planted Pinot Noir 2011 The hue is appreciably brighter, with more purple, than that of its sibling; the red cherry fruits are accompanied by violets on the bouquet, and a fine web of spicy, savoury nuances on the complex, albeit light, palate. A triumph of nature and nurture. Screwcap. 13% alc. **Rating** 94 **To** 2018 $90
Friends of Punch Berrys Creek Vineyard Noble Riesling 2011 A rarely encountered elegance and balance to a wine that technically must have been very difficult to make, but has emerged with the finest texture imaginable to its lime juice and apple fruit. 375ml. Screwcap. 8% alc. **Rating** 94 **To** 2020 $25

🍷🍷🍷🍷🍷 **Lance's Vineyard Yarra Valley Pinot Noir 2011 Rating** 92 **To** 2016 $55

Punt Road ★★★★★

10 St Huberts Road, Coldstream, Vic 3770 **Region** Yarra Valley
T (03) 9739 0666 **www.**puntroadwines.com.au **Open** 7 days 10–5
Winemaker Kate Goodman **Est.** 2000 **Dozens** 20 000 **Vyds** 63.5ha
Punt Road has been producing wine for over a decade, and is now under the sole ownership of the Napoleone family. The emphasis is firmly on wines produced from vineyards owned by the family; this has resulted in the introduction of the Airlie Bank range, a mostly sub-$20 Yarra Valley range made in a fruit-driven, lightly oaked style to complement the successful Punt Road range at the premium end of their offerings. There will also be more focus on small-production single vineyard wines in the coming vintages, especially under the Punt Road label. Exports to the UK, the US, Canada, Hong Kong, Japan, China and other major markets.

🍷🍷🍷🍷🍷 **Chemin Yarra Valley Chardonnay 2011** Avant-garde winemaking saw two-thirds whole bunch-pressed direct to barrel, the remainder destemmed and fermented on skins then pressed direct to barrel just prior to finishing that ferment. The approach has worked brilliantly, introducing a totally delicious creamy texture to the white peach fruit, the oak flavour minimal. Screwcap. 12% alc. **Rating** 96 **To** 2020 $40
Napoleone Vineyard Yarra Valley Chardonnay 2011 Whole bunch-pressed, a portion direct to barrel for wild yeast fermentation; 10 months in French oak (25% new), with lees stirring and partial mlf. Has the elegance, finesse and extreme length of high-quality Yarra Valley Chardonnay, the white peach fruit doing most of the talking. Screwcap. 12% alc. **Rating** 94 **To** 2019 $23

ŸŸŸŸ♀ Napoleone Vineyard Yarra Valley Pinot Noir 2012 Rating 93 To 2016 $29
Coldstream Vineyard Yarra Valley Cabernet Sauvignon 2011 Rating 92
To 2020 $29 BE
Napoleone Vineyard Yarra Valley Pinot Noir 2011 Rating 91 To 2017 $26
✪ Airlie Bank Yarra Valley Pinot Noir 2011 Bright mid crimson colour; the
bouquet offers a bright expression of the variety, with dark cherry plum and
a touch of spicy oak thrown in for good measure; the palate is driven by fresh
acidity and taut tannins; not overly long; the flavours are harmonious and the wine
generous. Screwcap. 12.5% alc. Rating 90 To 2017 $18 BE

Punters Corner ★★★★★

Cnr Riddoch Highway/Racecourse Road, Coonawarra, SA 5263 **Region** Coonawarra
T (08) 8737 2007 www.punterscorner.com.au **Open** Mon–Fri 10–4, w'ends 12–4,
public hols 10–2
Winemaker Balnaves (Peter Bissell) **Est.** 1988 **Dozens** 7000 **Vyds** 25.43ha
In 1988 David Muir and Robert Hance (and their wives) purchased a property on V&A
Lane and planted 16ha of vines. Since then the vineyard area has expanded considerably
with the development of a further three vineyards, including the cellar door block that is
situated on the Riddoch Highway. In 1996 a winery designed by Peter Bissell was built, and
in late '99 the Punters Corner Retreat accommodation centre was opened. While judging
the Limestone Coast Wine Show, I frequently had occasion to eat at the Retreat; it has won
various architectural and tourism awards. Punters Corner had a moment of glory when its '99
Spartacus Reserve Shiraz won the Jimmy Watson Trophy 2000. Exports to The Netherlands,
Malaysia, Singapore, Japan and China.

ŸŸŸŸŸ Sovereign Reserve Cabernet Sauvignon 2010 Double everything (including
the price) of the standard Punters Corner Cabernet, and you end up with this wine.
The colour is deep; add the oak (20 months in new French oak hogsheads), and the
layers of black fruits and tannins from the oldest (40-year-old) estate vines and you
have this lush, hedonistic wine. ProCork. 14.5% alc. Rating 96 To 2040 $60
✪ Single Vineyard Coonawarra Chardonnay 2011 Picking at the very low
baume of 11.4° might have made this wine look like a Sauvignon Blanc, but
that is not the case here, with white peach, melon and grapefruit all combining
synergistically. Great value. Screwcap. 12% alc. Rating 94 To 2016 $26
Spartacus Reserve Shiraz 2010 Spent 20 months in new French oak
barriques; this has obviously left its calling card, but there is also attractive
plummy/blackberry fruit; the tannins are fine and soft, sharing spice with the fruit
on the long finish. ProCork. 13.5% alc. Rating 94 To 2025 $60

ŸŸŸŸ♀ Coonawarra Cabernet Sauvignon 2010 Rating 93 To 2020 $30

Purple Hands Wines ★★★★★

PO Box 11, Williamstown, SA 5351 **Region** Barossa Valley
T 0401 988 185 www.purplehandswines.com.au **Open** Not
Winemaker Craig Stansborough **Est.** 2006 **Dozens** 2000 **Vyds** 8ha
This is a remarkable new (well, only six years old) venture, a partnership between Craig
Stansborough, who provides the winemaking know-how and an 8ha vineyard of shiraz,
northwest of Williamstown in a cooler corner of the southern Barossa, and Mark Slade,
who provides the passion. Don't ask me how this works – I don't know, but I do know they
are producing outstanding single vineyard wines (the grenache is contract-grown) of quite
remarkable elegance. The wines are made at Grant Burge, where Craig is chief winemaker.
Exports to China.

ŸŸŸŸŸ Old Vine Barossa Valley Grenache 2012 Has had the full works: hand-picked,
open-fermented in wax-lined concrete fermenters, wild yeast, hand-plunged, hot
ferment, basket-pressed, 11 months on lees in used puncheons. Best of all is the
brightness of the red fruits achieved on the bouquet and palate alike with only
13.5% alcohol. Bravo. Screwcap. Rating 96 To 2020 $30

Barossa Valley Mataro Shiraz Grenache 2012 Has very good colour, and greater depth than normal with this 48/32/20% blend; the bouquet and palate are also well in the leading group, with spicy red and black fruits neatly balanced in their range of flavours, tannins precisely judged. Has thrown down the gauntlet to McLaren Vale. Screwcap. 14% alc. **Rating** 95 **To** 2022 $30

ŶŶŶŶŶ **Adelaide Hills Pinot Gris 2012 Rating** 91 **To** 2014 $22
Barossa Valley Shiraz 2011 Rating 90 **To** 2020 $30

Pyren Vineyard ★★★★★

22 Errard Street North, Ballarat, Vic 3350 (postal) **Region** Pyrenees
T (03) 5467 2352 **www**.pyrenvineyard.com **Open** By appt
Winemaker Andrew Davey, Leighton Joy **Est.** 1999 **Dozens** 5000 **Vyds** 28ha
Brian and Kevyn Joy have planted 23ha of shiraz, 5ha of cabernet sauvignon and 1ha split between malbec, cabernet franc and petit verdot on the slopes of the Warrenmang Valley near Moonambel. Yield is restricted to between 1.5 and 2.5 tonnes per acre. Exports to the UK, the US, Vietnam and China.

ŶŶŶŶŶ **Yardbird Union 2011** A blend of cabernet sauvignon, cabernet franc, malbec and petit verdot that offers much to enjoy with its bright red fruits and fine tannins; has length and balance. Screwcap. 13.1% alc. **Rating** 94 **To** 2019 $30
Studio Ink 2010 Medium to full purple-red; a distinguished blend of cabernet sauvignon and shiraz; the black and red fruits of the medium-bodied palate are tied together by excellent tannins and well-controlled oak, all up providing very good mouthfeel, balance and length. Screwcap. 13.5% alc. **Rating** 94 **To** 2025 $30

ŶŶŶŶ **Broken Quartz Pyrenees Shiraz 2011 Rating** 88 **To** 2015 $20
Broken Quartz Pyrenees Cabernet Sauvignon 2011 Rating 88 **To** 2015 $20

Pyrenees Ridge Winery ★★★★★

532 Caralulup Road, Lamplough via Avoca, Vic 3467 **Region** Pyrenees
T (03) 5465 3320 **www**.pyreneesridge.com.au **Open** Thurs–Mon & public hols 11–5
Winemaker Graeme Jukes **Est.** 1998 **Dozens** 5000 **Vyds** 15.3ha
Notwithstanding the quite extensive winemaking experience (and formal training) of Graeme Jukes, this started life as small-scale winemaking in the raw version of the French garagiste approach. Graeme and his wife Sally-Ann now have 10ha of shiraz and 3ha cabernet sauvignon, with lesser amounts of chardonnay, merlot and a hatful of viognier. There are plans to plant a further 3–4ha of shiraz. After a fire in 2007 destroyed the winery and cellar door, the facility has been rebuilt, bigger and better than before. Exports to Canada, Germany, Denmark, South Korea, Hong Kong, Vietnam, China and Japan.

ŶŶŶŶŶ **Shiraz 2011** Deep colour; the bouquet is decidedly exotic, with essency red and black fruits, elements of geranium and candied orange on display; the fleshy medium-bodied palate reveals lashings of toasty oak, mocha and chewy tannins. Diam. 14.5% alc. **Rating** 91 **To** 2022 $28 BE
Rose 2012 Pale pink colour; the bouquet of this pinot noir rose shows fresh herbs, notably sage, and glimpses of citrus and wild strawberry; the palate is bone dry, linear and reveals struck quartz and finishes with a refreshing acid line. Screwcap. 12.5% alc. **Rating** 90 **To** 2015 $20 BE

Quarisa Wines ★★★★

743 Slopes Road, Tharbogang, NSW 2680 (postal) **Region** South Australia
T (02) 6963 6222 **www**.quarisa.com.au **Open** Not
Winemaker John Quarisa **Est.** 2005 **Dozens** 50 000
Quarisa Wines was established by John and Josephine Quarisa (and their three children). John has had a distinguished career as a winemaker spanning over 20 years, working for some of Australia's largest wineries, including McWilliam's, Casella and Nugan Estate. He was

also chiefly responsible in 2004 for winning the Jimmy Watson Trophy (Melbourne) and the Stodart Trophy (Adelaide). In a busman's holiday venture, the Quarisas set up a very successful family business using grapes from various parts of NSW and SA, made in leased space. Production has risen in a tough economic environment, value for money being part of the reason for success. Exports to the UK, Canada, Sweden, Switzerland, Israel, Indonesia, Malaysia, China, Hong Kong, South Korea, Thailand, Japan and NZ.

Treasures McLaren Vale Shiraz 2010 A bright and fragrant bouquet, showing blackberry, bitter chocolate, licorice and fruitcake spice; medium- to full-bodied, and certainly no shrinking violet; the freshness of fruit and acidity is commendable, as is the value. Screwcap. 14.5% alc. **Rating** 92 **To** 2018 $15 BE

Johnny Q Shiraz Viognier 2010 Vibrant purple hue; a perfumed and attractive bouquet of black fruits, violets, spice and leather; the palate is fleshy, medium-bodied and lively, with the viognier component barely discernible. Screwcap. 14.5% alc. **Rating** 92 **To** 2020 $12 BE

Johnny Q Shiraz 2010 Deeply coloured, and showing essency black fruits in abundance on the bouquet; the palate is fleshy, sweet-fruited and vibrant, with mocha and licorice a lingering note to the finish; well constructed and good value. Screwcap. 14.5% alc. **Rating** 90 **To** 2016 $12 BE

Treasures Adelaide Hills Chardonnay 2012 Rating 88 **To** 2016 $15 BE

Johnny Q Cabernet Sauvignon 2010 Deep magenta; essency and ripe blackberry pastille bouquet, with a touch of mocha; the palate is fleshy, generous and direct, with chewy tannins a lingering note on the finish. Screwcap. 14.5% alc. **Rating** 88 **To** 2018 $12 BE

Johnny Q Adelaide Hills Semillon Sauvignon Blanc 2012 Rating 87 **To** 2014 $12 BE

30 Mile Shiraz 2010 Deeply coloured, and deeply oaky, with pastille black fruits, mocha and fruitcake on display; the palate is very dry, with the tannins providing plenty of muscle for the fruit on offer; a big wine in every regard. Screwcap. 14.5% alc. **Rating** 87 **To** 2016 $10 BE

Quarry Hill Wines   ★★★☆

8 Maxwell Street, Yarralumla, ACT 2600 (postal) **Region** Canberra District
T 0414 574 460 **www**.quarryhill.com.au **Open** Not
Winemaker Collector Wines (Alex McKay) **Est.** 1999 **Dozens** 500 **Vyds** 4.5ha
Owner Dean Terrell is the ex-Vice Chancellor of the Australian National University and a Professor of Economics. The acquisition of the property, originally used as a quarry for the construction of the Barton Highway and thereafter as a grazing property, was the brainchild of his family, who wanted to keep him active in retirement. The vineyard was established in 1999, with further plantings in 2001 and '06; there are 2ha of shiraz, 1ha of sauvignon blanc, and 0.25ha each of savagnin, sangiovese, tempranillo, grenache, pinot noir and sagrantino. Only part of the production is released under the Quarry Hill label, as grapes are sold to other wineries, including Clonakilla and Collector Wines.

North Block Dry White 2012 Pale quartz; a 60/40% blend of savagnin and sauvignon blanc (just to keep everyone on their toes); there is a real cut and drive from the high acidity that demands food for safety, but is worth it. Screwcap. 11.5% alc. **Rating** 90 **To** 2014 $16

North Block Dry White 2011 Rating 89 **To** 2014 $16

Canberra District Shiraz 2010 Rating 87 **To** 2015 $18

Quartz Hill Vineyard   ★★★★☆

65 Lillicur West Road, Lamplough, Vic 3352 (postal) **Region** Pyrenees
T (03) 5465 3670 **www**.quartzhillwines.com.au **Open** Not
Winemaker Darrin Gaffy **Est.** 1995 **Dozens** 400 **Vyds** 3.6ha
Quartz Hill was established in 1995 with Shane and Michelle Mead relocating from Melbourne to run their vineyard in '99. After growing grapes for other wine labels for many

years, the First Quartz Hill wine came onto the market in '09. Winemaking is a family effort, with brother Darrin Gaffy from Principia on the Mornington Peninsula (see separate entry) as winemaker, all winemaking processes performed traditionally, by hand. Shane and Michelle grow their own shiraz and viognier, and, when available, purchase select parcels of fruit from other Pyrenees growers.

ΨΨΨΨΨ Pyrenees Viognier 2011 Straw-green; spent 18 months in French oak; it has good texture and balance, and has retained fruit freshness, plus a mix of apricot and citrus. A superior Viognier. Screwcap. 13.5% alc. **Rating** 91 **To** 2015 $32

ΨΨΨΨ Pyrenees Roussanne 2011 Rating 87 **To** 2014 $32

Quattro Mano ★★★★★

PO Box 189, Hahndorf, SA 5245 **Region** Barossa Valley
T 0430 647 470 **www.quattromano.com.au Open** By appt
Winemaker Anthony Carapetis, Christopher Taylor, Philippe Morin **Est.** 2006
Dozens 3500 **Vyds** 3.8ha
Anthony Carapetis, Philippe Morin and Chris Taylor have collective experience of over 50 years working in various facets of the wine industry, Philippe as a leading sommelier for over 25 years, and presently as Director of French Oak Cooperage, Anthony and Christopher as long-serving winemakers. The dream of Quattro Mano began in the mid 1990s, but only became a reality in 2006 (I'm still not sure how three equals four). They now have an eclectic range of wines, Tempranillo the cornerstone, extending at one extreme to the multi-Iberian Peninsula Duende, and to La Deft Pinot Noir and La Hada Barossa Valley Mourvedre at the other. It's an impressive, albeit small, business. Exports to the US and Japan.

ΨΨΨΨΨ La Gracia 2010 A 51/39/10% blend of tempranillo, touriga and tinta amarela, each variety fermented and matured separately in new and used French oak barriques, the best barrels blended after 20 months. A lovely wine, full of fragrance and perfume, spicy red and black fruits dancing on the light- to medium-bodied palate, and taking it through to a long, lingering finish; oak, tannins and alcohol are all simply vehicles for the fruit. Cork. 13% alc. **Rating** 96 **To** 2030 $50
La Reto Barossa Valley Tempranillo 2010 A 91/7/2% blend of tempranillo, tinta amarela and touriga. A complex fermentation regime, and 18 months in used French oak barriques, have resulted in a very, very good Tempranillo with great colour, and a more supple texture than most Australian Tempranillos. Screwcap. 13% alc. **Rating** 95 **To** 2025 $25

ΨΨΨΨΨ Duende Nina 2012 Rating 91 **To** 2013 $18

Quealy Balnarring Vineyard ★★★★☆

62 Bittern-Dromana Road, Balnarring, Vic 3926 **Region** Mornington Peninsula
T (03) 5983 2483 **www.quealy.com.au Open** 7 days 11–5
Winemaker Kathleen Quealy **Est.** 1982 **Dozens** 8000 **Vyds** 8ha
Kathleen Quealy and husband Kevin McCarthy lost no time after T'Gallant was purchased from them by Foster's in 2003. As they were fully entitled to do, they already had their ducks set up in a row, and in short order acquired Balnarring Estate winery (being significantly upgraded) and leased Earl's Ridge Vineyard near Flinders. In a move reminiscent of Janice McDonald at Stella Bella/Suckfizzle in Margaret River, they launched their business with Pobblebonk (a white blend) and Rageous (a red blend), plus a Pinot Noir and a Pinot Gris as a passing nod to convention. The estate plantings are 2ha each of pinot noir, tocai friulano and pinot gris, and 1ha each of chardonnay and muscat giallo. Kathleen (with five children) is a human dynamo. They also leased the Tussie Mussie Vineyard (planted to pinot gris) in Merricks in '13. Wines are also available at Merricks General Wine Store.

ΨΨΨΨΨ Balnarring Vineyard Chardonnay 2012 Light straw-green; a fragrant stone fruit, grapefruit and blossom bouquet leads into a fruit-driven palate, with the same flavours in play, the finish long and lingering. Screwcap. 12.5% alc. **Rating** 93 **To** 2018 $25

Pinot Grigio 2012 Pale quartz; has more texture and structure than most Pinot Gris, varietal nashi pear the dominant flavour, and sustaining the long finish. Reflects Kathleen Quealy's long love affair with the variety. Screwcap. 13% alc. **Rating** 93 **To** 2014 $28

Seventeen Rows Pinot Noir 2011 Light, clear purple-red; has greater intensity and focus than its varietal sibling, the fruit flavours headed to black cherry and a touch of plum, the tannins fine and savoury. Screwcap. 12.5% alc. **Rating** 93 **To** 2015 $50

Pyrenees Nebbiolo 2011 Light colour, but the hue is brighter than that of many Nebbiolos; there is attractive sour cherry fruit, then comes that lethal tannin structure nebbiolo almost always throws up as a roadblock – unless it is matched with Italian food, when all issues disappear. Screwcap. 14% alc. **Rating** 91 **To** 2020 $50

Balnarring Vineyard Pinot Noir 2011 Light, clear red; a smart wine given the vintage; its bright red colour introduces a light-bodied but fresh palate with red cherry and strawberry fruit; tailor made for drinking pleasure right now. Screwcap. 12.8% alc. **Rating** 90 **To** 2013 $28

Quilty Wines

16 Inglis Street, Mudgee, NSW 2850 (postal) **Region** Mudgee
T 0419 936 233 **www.**quiltywines.com.au **Open** Not
Winemaker Des Quilty, Jacob Stein **Est.** 2008 **Dozens** 700
Owner Des Quilty grew up in the Hunter Valley and studied agriculture at the University of New England. To support himself while at university, he drifted into viticulture, his first job after graduation at Tyrrell's as assistant vineyard manager. He was soon promoted and formed part of the Tyrrell's management team. Over the latter half of the '90s he worked for a rural outlet supplying products to Hunter Valley grape and wine producers, before moving to Mudgee as a viticulturist around 2000. While his focus remains on that region, he has also been involved in vineyards in Orange and Young. He ventured into small-scale winemaking in '08, relying on the depth of his experience to secure small parcels of top-quality grapes.

♈♈♈♈♈ **Black Thimble Single Vineyard Burrundulla Mudgee Shiraz 2011** The bouquet offers smoky oak as a dominant feature with blackberry, tea and bramble on display; the palate is medium-bodied and vibrant, with gravelly tannins in tune with the fruit, and while oak is dominant at this early stage, time should settle it down nicely. Screwcap. 13.5% alc. **Rating** 91 **To** 2018 $28 BE

Silken Thread Apple Tree Flat Mudgee Petit Verdot 2011 Bright colour, and an effusive personality, with dark cherry and floral violet notes coming to the fore; the palate is juicy, with a moderately long finish. Screwcap. 14% alc. **Rating** 90 **To** 2017 $22 BE

Racecourse Lane Wines

28 Racecourse Lane, Pokolbin, NSW 2320 **Region** Hunter Valley
T 0408 242 490 **www.**racecourselane.com.au **Open** By appt
Winemaker David Fatches (Contract) **Est.** 1998 **Dozens** 200 **Vyds** 5ha
Mike and Helen McGorman purchased their 15ha property in 1998. They have established shiraz, sangiovese, semillon, verdelho and viognier. Consultancy viticultural advice from Brian Hubbard, and winemaking by David Fatches (a long-term Hunter Valley winemaker, who also makes wine in France each year), has paid dividends. Exports to the UK.

♈♈♈♈♈ **Hunter Valley Verdelho 2004** Full golden-yellow; as much a testament to the
✪ screwcap as to the quality of verdelho; the wine is mature, yet fresh, with light honey and toast nuances, and a bargain for those looking for something different. 13.5% alc. **Rating** 90 **To** 2014 $19

♈♈♈♈ **Hunter Valley Semillon 2007 Rating** 89 **To** 2015 $19
Basket Press Hunter Valley Shiraz 2005 Rating 88 **To** 2014 $22

Radford Wines   ★★★★★

RSD 355, Eden Valley, SA 5235 (postal) **Region** Eden Valley
T (08) 8565 3256 **www**.radfordwines.com **Open** Not
Winemaker Gill and Ben Radford **Est.** 2003 **Dozens** 2000 **Vyds** 4.2ha
I first met Ben Radford when he was working as a head winemaker at the Longridge/
Winecorp group in Stellenbosch, South Africa. A bevy of international journalists grilled
Ben, a French winemaker and a South African about the wines they were producing for the
group. The others refused to admit there were any shortcomings in the wines they had made
(there were), while Ben took the opposite tack, criticising his own wines even though they
were clearly the best. He and wife Gill are now the proud owners of a vineyard in the Eden
Valley, with 1.2ha of riesling planted in 1930, another 1.1ha planted in '70, 1.7ha of shiraz
planted in 2000 and 0.2ha of mataro planted '10. Following Ben's appointment as winemaker
at Rockford in '07, executive winemaking responsibilities are now Gill's. Exports to the UK,
the US, Canada, Denmark and South Africa.

♥♥♥♥♥ Bio-Dynamically Grown Eden Valley Riesling 2012 The flowery and fragrant
bouquet has citrus, green apple and a tickle of spice; the palate is beautifully
detailed and refined, although with ample citrus/lemon/apple fruit running
through to its long finish. Vino-Lok. 12% alc. **Rating** 96 **To** 2030 $40
Quartz Garden Eden Valley Riesling 2012 The name reflects the belief of
the original vignerons who planted riesling in the Eden Valley two centuries ago
that quartz soils were the best for this variety. The wine has exemplary balance
and mouthfeel to its display of positive riesling aromas and flavours; full but not
phenolic or heavy. Screwcap. 12% alc. **Rating** 94 **To** 2020 $25

Raidis Estate   ★★★

147 Church Street, Penola, SA 5277 **Region** Coonawarra
T (08) 8737 2966 **www**.raidis.com.au **Open** Thurs–Sun 12–6, or by appt
Winemaker Amelia Anderson **Est.** 2006 **Dozens** 1600 **Vyds** 24.29ha
The Raidis family has lived and worked in Coonawarra for over 40 years. Chris Raidis was
only three years old when he arrived in Australia with his parents, who were market gardeners
in Greece before coming here. In 1994 he planted just under 5ha of cabernet sauvignon; son
Steven significantly expanded the vineyard in 2003 with sauvignon blanc, riesling, pinot gris,
merlot and shiraz. The cellar door was opened by then Deputy Prime Minister Julia Gillard
in Nov '09, an impressive example of pulling power.

 # Ramco Wine Group   ★★★

20 Payneham Road, Stepney, SA 5069 **Region** Adelaide
T (08) 8541 9013 **www**.ramcowinegroup.com **Open** Not
Winemaker Contract **Est.** 2004 **Dozens** 500 000 **Vyds** 180ha
Ramco is the venture of Scott Curtis who, in 2004, acquired the 180ha Murray Valley
vineyard originally planted by G Gramp & Sons in 1953. It is primarily aimed at the export
market, all of the wines (with five different labels, headed by Ramco Ridge, finishing with
Cock + Bull) priced between $7 and $10 on the Australian market. Exports to the UK, Hong
Kong and China.

♥♥♥♥ Ramco Ridge Shiraz 2006 A pleasant light-bodied wine from what was a very
✪   good vintage in almost all parts of South Eastern Australia. While the influence of
French and American oak is evident, it must have spent a lengthy sojourn in oak
to retain its freshness. Screwcap. 14.5% alc. **Rating** 87 **To** 2014 $10
Cock + Bull Limited Release Rubienne 2011 Amazing purple-crimson
colour from this CSIRO-bred variety. Despite the ferocious alcohol, the plum
and prune fruit flavours are the main play, tannins irrelevant. Screwcap. 16% alc.
Rating 87 **To** 2015 $7

Ravens Croft Wines   ★★★★

274 Spring Creek Road, Stanthorpe, Qld 4380 **Region** Granite Belt
T (07) 4683 3252 **www**.ravenscroftwines.com.au **Open** Fri–Sun 10.30–4.30
Winemaker Mark Ravenscroft **Est.** 2002 **Dozens** 800 **Vyds** 1.2ha

Mark Ravenscroft was born in South Africa, and studied oenology there. He moved to Australia in the early 1990s, and in '94 became an Australian citizen. His wines come from estate plantings of verdelho and pinotage, supplemented by contract-grown grapes from other vineyards in the region. A new winery has recently been completed. The rating has been retained, having regard to some very difficult vintages, especially 2011. Exports to Japan.

ΨΨΨΨΩ **The Waagee 2010** A bright crimson-purple hue announces a 60/30/10% blend of cabernet sauvignon, petit verdot and merlot that was matured for 20 months in a mix of new and 1-year-old oak; it has a mix of savoury/sultry/earthy nuances with splashes of red fruits, the tannins well weighted and integrated. Screwcap. 14% alc. **Rating** 93 **To** 2025 $40

Granite Belt Petit Verdot 2010 Strong crimson; the bouquet has a complex mix of predominantly black-fruits together with a smoky cigar box nuance; the medium-bodied palate is easier to access than most young petit verdots. Nice wine. Screwcap. 14.5% alc. **Rating** 90 **To** 2018 $30

ΨΨΨΨ **Granite Belt Verdelho 2012 Rating** 89 **To** 2014 $24

Ravensworth   ★★★★★

312 Patemans Lane, Murrumbateman, ACT 2582 **Region** Canberra District
T (02) 6226 8368 **www**.ravensworthwines.com.au **Open** Not
Winemaker Bryan Martin **Est.** 2000 **Dozens** 2000

Winemaker, vineyard manager and partner Bryan Martin (with dual wine science and wine growing degrees from CSU) has a background of wine retail, food and beverage in the hospitality industry, and teaches part-time in that field. He is also assistant winemaker to Tim Kirk at Clonakilla, after seven years at Jeir Creek. Judging at wine shows is another string to his bow. Ravensworth has two vineyards: Rosehill, planted in 1998 to cabernet sauvignon, merlot and sauvignon blanc; and Martin Block, planted in 2000–01 to shiraz, viognier, marsanne and sangiovese.

ΨΨΨΨΨ **Murrumbateman Riesling 2012** Bright quartz-green; an unambiguously
✪ delicious Riesling, its blossom-filled bouquet leading into a palate that delights in confusing you: one minute dry and slatey/minerally, the next with citrus and a sprinkling of sugar sweetness, but never lingering long on the tongue. Screwcap. 12% alc. **Rating** 95 **To** 2025 $20

Murrumbateman Shiraz Viognier 2012 First hail, then rain, endeavoured to destroy the crop, but only succeeded in sharply reducing the yield. It is strikingly fragrant, with spice, red fruits and the often talked about, but rarely seen (by me) violets. The polished, medium-bodied palate picks up the flavour cues of the bouquet, and tops and tails them with some very attractive savoury nuances. Screwcap. 13.5% alc. **Rating** 94 **To** 2025 $32

ΨΨΨΨΩ **The Grainery 2012 Rating** 92 **To** 2018 $30
✪ **Le Querce Canberra District Sangiovese 2012** Bright colour for the variety; a young Sangiovese that seeks to embrace you, not fend you off with a sharp pointed (tannin) stick; it will undoubtedly cellar well in the medium term, but the gain on the complexity roundabouts might see the loss of bright red fruits on the swings. Screwcap. 13% alc. **Rating** 91 **To** 2017 $22

✪ **Murrumbateman Marsanne 2011** Full straw colour; taking a cue from good marsanne (Tahbilk, Yeringberg, Yarra Yering), I would be confident that in 3+ years this already full-flavoured wine will be a show-stopper, capable of holding its own against red wines and red wine dishes (as well as more conventional matches). Screwcap. 12% alc. **Rating** 90 **To** 2017 $20

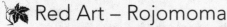 Red Art – Rojomoma

22 Julius Street, Tanunda, SA 5352 (postal) **Region** Barossa Valley
T 0421 272 336 **www**.rojomoma.com.au **Open** Not
Winemaker Bernadette Kaeding **Est.** 2004 **Dozens** 600 **Vyds** 5.4ha

Bernadette Kaeding purchased the vineyard site in 1996 when it had 1.49ha of 80-year-old dry-grown grenache; over the next few years she planted 3.95ha of shiraz, cabernet sauvignon, petit verdot and tempranillo. Until 2004 the grapes from the old and new plantings were sold to Rockford, Chateau Tanunda, Spinifex and David Franz. In that year she decided to make a small batch of wine and have it commercially bottled, and continued to accumulate wine until '11, when she began selling the wines under the Red Art label. All along she has sold part of the grape production, but has now reduced the buyers to two: Spinifex and David Franz. Bernadette has no plans to expand, 'My production and business continue to be small – and I like it that way.'

ŸŸŸŸŸ Raj's Pick Single Vineyard Barossa Valley Shiraz 2006 A very small amount of this wine from the best grapes from the vineyard is handmade, even to the handmade paper label wrapped (by hand) around the bottle. It has excellent balance and texture, the fruit in a plum and black cherry spectrum, the tannins fine and oak unobtrusive. Screwcap. 14.2% alc. **Rating** 95 **To** 2026 $57
Red Art Single Vineyard Barossa Valley Shiraz 2006 The colour is still vibrant; open-fermented, basket-pressed and matured in new and seasoned French and American oak; an elegant medium-bodied wine with spicy/savoury elements to its plum and black cherry fruit, the tannins exceptionally fine. A tribute to a great vintage. Screwcap. 14.2% alc. **Rating** 95 **To** 2021 $36
Red Art Single Vineyard Barossa Valley Shiraz 2010 Wild yeast-fermented, 5% whole bunch, macerated on skins for 2 weeks then basket-pressed, and matured in seasoned oak; a densely packed wine with a near-unlimited future. I might have preferred a gentler touch, but not the judges at the Barossa Wine Show '12, where it won two trophies. Screwcap. 14.4% alc. **Rating** 94 **To** 2035 $30

ŸŸŸŸŸ Red Art Single Vineyard Shiraz 2008 **Rating** 93 **To** 2028 $30
Red Art Single Vineyard Cabernet Sauvignon 2008 **Rating** 92 **To** 2023 $30
Red Art Single Vineyard Shiraz 2005 **Rating** 91 **To** 2025 $36
Red Art Single Vineyard Cabernet Sauvignon 2005 **Rating** 91 **To** 2020 $36
Red Art Single Vineyard Grenache Shiraz 2008 **Rating** 90 **To** 2016 $30
Red Art Single Vineyard Petit Verdot 2008 **Rating** 90 **To** 2020 $30
Red Art Single Vineyard Tempranillo 2008 **Rating** 90 **To** 2016 $30

Red Earth Estate

18L Camp Road, Dubbo, NSW 2830 **Region** Western Plains Zone
T (02) 6885 6676 **www**.redearthestate.com.au **Open** Thurs–Tues 10–5
Winemaker Ken Borchardt **Est.** 2000 **Dozens** 1500 **Vyds** 6.2ha

Red Earth Estate, owned by Ken and Christine Borchardt, is the focal point of grapegrowing and winemaking in the Western Plains Zone. They have planted riesling, verdelho, frontignac, grenache, shiraz, cabernet sauvignon and a small amount of torrentes (supplemented by purchased grapes). The winery has a capacity of 14000 dozen, and the Borchardts also offer contract winemaking facilities for others in the region. Exports to China.

ŸŸŸŸ Cabernet Sauvignon 2011 Lifted red fruit and spicy oak aromas are evident on the bouquet; medium-bodied with fresh acidity at the core, driving the red fruits home to an even conclusion. Screwcap. 13.2% alc. **Rating** 88 **To** 2018 $26 BE
Verdelho 2012 Fresh nectarine, lime and straw are evident on the bouquet; the palate is off-dry on entry, with fresh acidity and a chalky texture providing line to the blanched almond finish. Screwcap. 13.2% alc. **Rating** 87 **To** 2014 $22 BE

Red Edge

Golden Gully Road, Heathcote, Vic 3523 **Region** Heathcote
T 0407 422 067 **www.rededgewine.com.au Open** By appt
Winemaker Peter Dredge **Est.** 1971 **Dozens** 1500 **Vyds** 14ha

Red Edge's vineyard dates back to 1971 and the renaissance of the Victorian wine industry. In the early 1980s it produced the wonderful wines of Flynn & Williams, and was rehabilitated by Peter and Judy Dredge, producing two quite lovely wines in their inaugural vintage and continuing that form in succeeding years. Exports to the US, Canada and China.

🍷🍷🍷🍷🍷 Heathcote Shiraz 2010 While a step up in concentration from Degree, this wine exhibits a melange of red, blue and black fruits, with more slatey mineral character drawn from the earth; the palate is moving towards full-bodied, with fresh acidity and gravelly tannins a feature of the finish. A wine with presence and restraint. Screwcap. 14.2% alc. **Rating** 94 **To** 2022 $45 BE

🍷🍷🍷🍷🍷 Degree Heathcote Shiraz 2010 **Rating** 90 **To** 2018 $25 BE

Red Hill Estate ★★★★★

53 Shoreham Road, Red Hill South, Vic 3937 **Region** Mornington Peninsula
T (03) 5989 2838 **www.redhillestate.com.au Open** 7 days 11–5
Winemaker Barry Kooij **Est.** 1989 **Dozens** 25 000 **Vyds** 72.2ha

Red Hill Estate was established by Sir Peter Derham, and has three vineyard sites: Range Road, Red Hill Estate and The Briars. Taken together, the vineyards make Red Hill Estate one of the larger producers of Mornington Peninsula wines. The tasting room and restaurant have a superb view of Westernport Bay and Phillip Island. In 2007 it (surprisingly) merged with Arrowfield Estate in the Hunter Valley, both companies thereafter owned by the InWine Group until October '10, when InWine was acquired by Cheviot Bridge. Exports to the US, Canada, Ireland, Poland, Sweden, Singapore, Japan and Hong Kong.

🍷🍷🍷🍷🍷 P&Q Mornington Peninsula Chardonnay 2011 P&Q are the best two estate blocks, although this is the first time this wine has been kept separate; it coats the mouth with succulent stone fruit flavours, but the finish is cleansed and balanced by citrussy acidity. The substantial amount of new French oak used has been completely absorbed. Screwcap. 13.5% alc. **Rating** 95 **To** 2020 $65

Mossolini Mornington Peninsula Shiraz 2010 Good crimson-purple; a prime example of cool-grown but fully ripe fruit, with a delicious fusion of red and black cherry, licorice and spice, fine tannins spun around the fruit, oak positive but balanced. Screwcap. 14% alc. **Rating** 95 **To** 2025 $65

Merricks Grove Mornington Peninsula Chardonnay 2011 Brilliant green-straw; the complex bouquet of fruit and oak leads directly into a supple palate, with stone fruit, grapefruit and strong creamy cashew notes each contributing, yet not disrupting the line or focus. Screwcap. 13% alc. **Rating** 94 **To** 2019 $40

🍷🍷🍷🍷🍷 Blanc de Noirs Pinot Noir 2007 **Rating** 92 **To** 2015 $37

Merricks Grove Pinot Noir 2010 **Rating** 91 **To** 2014 $40

✪ Chardonnay 2011 It's a strange thing to find a Mornington Peninsula Chardonnay at this price, even if the oak contribution has been minimal. The decision to use mlf was correct, for the lemony/minerally acidity is on the high side. Summer shellfish style. Screwcap. 13% alc. **Rating** 90 **To** 2014 $19

Cellar Door Release Chardonnay 2009 **Rating** 90 **To** 2015 $25

M&N Mornington Peninsula Pinot Noir 2010 **Rating** 90 **To** 2014 $65

Blanc de Blanc Chardonnay 2007 **Rating** 90 **To** 2015 $37

Cordon Cut Pinot Gris 2011 **Rating** 90 **To** 2014 $25

Redbank Alpine Valleys Estates ★★★☆

Whitfield Road, King Valley, Vic 3678 **Region** King Valley
T 0411 404 296 **www.redbankwines.com Open** Not
Winemaker Nick Dry **Est.** 2005 **Dozens** 33 000 **Vyds** 15ha

The Redbank brand was for decades the umbrella for Neill and Sally Robb's Sally's Paddock. In 2005 Hill-Smith Family Vineyards acquired the Redbank brand from the Robbs, leaving them with the Redbank winery and Sally's Paddock label. Redbank Alpine Valley purchases grapes from the King Valley, Whitlands, Beechworth and the Ovens Valley (among other vineyards sources). Exports to all major markets.

The Long Paddock Shiraz 2010 Medium red-purple; a well-crafted medium-bodied wine, with far more texture and style to the plum and black cherry fruit than expected at this price. Will never be better than it is now, and that's pretty good. Screwcap. 13.5% alc. **Rating** 89 **To** 2015 $13

Sunday Morning King Valley Pinot Gris 2012 With some imagination, it is possible to see a little more fruit than Grigio would need, but not the rationale for the price. Screwcap. 13% alc. **Rating** 88 **To** 2014 $25

The Long Paddock Sauvignon Blanc 2012 No winemaking fault, but is almost devoid of varietal character. Screwcap. 12.5% alc. **Rating** 87 **To** 2014 $13

Redbox Vineyard & Winery ★★★

2 Ness Lane, Kangaroo Ground, Vic 3097 **Region** Yarra Valley
T (03) 9712 0440 **www**.redboxvineyard.com.au **Open** W'ends & public hols 11–6, or by appt
Winemaker Contract **Est.** 2004 **Dozens** 2000 **Vyds** 4ha
Colin and Clayton Spencer have moved quickly since establishing their business in 2004. Initially using grapes from several regions, they now only use Yarra Valley fruit, and likewise only use the Redbox label. The estate plantings are of 2ha of cabernet sauvignon, 0.8ha of chardonnay and 0.4ha of riesling, with an additional 0.8ha of cabernet sauvignon offsite.

Yarra Valley Cabernet Blanc 2012 Intriguing at best, with red fruits and a lot of fennel on the bouquet; the palate is soft and forward; should be consumed early and well chilled. Screwcap. 12% alc. **Rating** 87 **To** 2014 $18 BE

Redesdale Estate Wines ★★★★☆

46 Gibbards Lane, Redesdale, Vic 3444 **Region** Heathcote
T (03) 5425 3236 **www**.redesdale.com **Open** By appt
Winemaker Tobias Ansted (Contract) **Est.** 1982 **Dozens** 900 **Vyds** 4ha
Planting of the Redesdale Estate vines began in 1982 on the northeast slopes of a 25ha grazing property fronting the Campaspe River on one side. The rocky quartz and granite soil meant the vines had to struggle, and when Peter Williams and wife Suzanne Arnall-Williams purchased the property in '88 the vineyard was in a state of disrepair. They have rejuvenated the vineyard, planted an olive grove, and, more recently, erected a two-storey house surrounded by a garden, which is part of the Victorian Open Garden Scheme (and cross-linked to a villa in Tuscany).

Heathcote Shiraz 2005 Has developed serenely over the past 7+ years; the hue is a healthy red-purple, with no hint of brick, and plum, black cherry and spice still drive the medium-bodied palate; the oak and tannins are an integral part of the flavour and mouthfeel, but do not challenge the fruit. A lovely developed Australian red. Screwcap. 14% alc. **Rating** 94 **To** 2025 $50

Heathcote Shiraz 2009 Rating 88 **To** 2016 $40

Redgate ★★★★★

659 Boodjidup Road, Margaret River, WA 6285 **Region** Margaret River
T (08) 9757 6488 **www**.redgatewines.com.au **Open** 7 days 10–4.30
Winemaker Joel Page **Est.** 1977 **Dozens** 6500 **Vyds** 17.88ha
Founder and owner of Redgate, the late Bill Ullinger, chose the name not simply because of the nearby eponymous beach, but also because – so it is said – a local farmer (with a prominent red gate at his property) had run an illegal spirit-still 100 or so years ago, and its patrons would come to the property and ask whether there was any 'red gate' available.

True or not, Redgate was one of the early movers in Margaret River, now with close to 20ha of mature estate plantings (the majority to sauvignon blanc, semillon, cabernet sauvignon, cabernet franc, shiraz and chardonnay, with smaller plantings of chenin blanc and merlot). No wines received for the *2014 Wine Companion*, but a five-star rating has been maintained. Exports to Denmark, Switzerland, China and Japan.

Redman ★★★★

Main Road, Coonawarra, SA 5263 **Region** Coonawarra
T (08) 8736 3331 **www**.redman.com.au **Open** Mon–Fri 9–5, w'ends 10–4
Winemaker Bruce, Malcolm and Daniel Redman **Est.** 1966 **Dozens** 18 000 **Vyds** 34ha
In March 2008 the Redman family celebrated 100 years of winemaking in Coonawarra. The '08 vintage also marked the arrival of Daniel as the fourth-generation Redman winemaker. Daniel gained winemaking experience in Central Victoria, the Barossa Valley and the US before taking up his new position. It was felicitous timing, for the '04 Cabernet Sauvignon and '04 Cabernet Merlot were each awarded a gold medal from the national wine show circuit in '07, the first such accolades for a considerable time. The quality has stabilised at a level in keeping with the long-term history of the winery and its mature vines.

ȚȚȚȚȚ **The Redman 2004** Holding excellent colour; a 100th anniversary blend of cabernet sauvignon, merlot and shiraz that spent 2 years in French oak before being bottled. It has the regional mint and earth notes frequently encountered, and a medium- to full-bodied palate supported by firm tannins and the expected oak. Cork. 14% alc. **Rating** 92 **To** 2019 $74

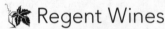 # Regent Wines ★★★★

762 Kenley Road, Kenley, Vic 3597 **Region** Swan Hill
T (03) 5038 8238 **www**.chislettnavel.com.au **Open** 7 days 10–5
Winemaker Alan Cooper, Brian Cooper (Contract) **Est.** 2007 **Dozens** 890
The main business activity of owners Greg and Susan Chislett is wholesale nursery and orchard production. They buy quality grapes and have the wines made by highly regarded boutique winemakers Alan Cooper and Brian Martin. Their wine business is named after the endangered parrot that frequents their property, and they use the proceeds from wine sales to plant habitat corridors on their property for the Regent Parrot.

ȚȚȚȚȚ **Tempranillo 2007** If anything, a touch deeper in colour than the '08, but also
✪   spent 15 months in used oak. The palate is richer and more concentrated, probably due to lower yields than normal in '07, and larger than normal in '08. A very delicious Tempranillo, with darker cherry flavours. Screwcap. 13.5% alc. **Rating** 92 **To** 2017 $16

✪   **Reserve Shiraz Viognier 2006** Has retained similar hue to that of the Shiraz; the two components were co-fermented, and the wine spent 30 months in barrel; the flavours of juicy red fruits are framed by gentle oak and fine tannins. Screwcap. 13.5% alc. **Rating** 91 **To** 2016 $16

✪   **Tempranillo 2008** Has retained a fresh red hue; the flavours, too, are fresh and bright, with vibrant red, black and sour cherries, acidity also playing a role. 15 months in used oak. Screwcap. 13.5% alc. **Rating** 90 **To** 2016 $16

ȚȚȚȚ **Vermentino 2012** Here grown in a cooler region than that of most Australian
✪   vermentinos, paradoxically with slightly sweeter fruit; holds to the core of honeysuckle, apple and white pepper of the variety. Profits go to provide habitat corridors for the Regent Parrot. Screwcap. 11% alc. **Rating** 89 **To** 2014 $15
Shiraz 2008 Rating 89 **To** 2015 $18
Lagrein 2011 Rating 87 **To** 2016 $18

Reillys Wines ★★★★

Cnr Leasingham Road/Hill Street, Mintaro, SA 5415 **Region** Clare Valley
T (08) 8843 9013 **www**.reillyswines.com.au **Open** 7 days 10–4
Winemaker Justin Ardill **Est.** 1994 **Dozens** 30 000 **Vyds** 85ha

This has been a very successful venture for Adelaide cardiologist Justin Ardill and wife Julie, beginning as a hobby in 1994, but growing significantly over the intervening years. They now have vineyards at Watervale, Leasingham and Mintaro, growing riesling, cabernet sauvignon, shiraz, grenache, tempranillo and merlot. Justin is also a partner in another Clare Valley venture (Rockridge, see separate entry). The cellar door and restaurant were built between 1856 and '66 by Irish immigrant Hugh Reilly; 140 years later they were restored by the Ardills, distant relatives of Reilly. Exports to the US, Canada, Ireland, Malaysia, China and Singapore.

ŸŸŸŸ♀ **Clare Valley Shiraz 2010** Strong colour; open-fermented and matured for
✪ 18 months in oak; a full-bodied, rich and opulent Shiraz, oozing black fruits, licorice and gently savoury tannins from every pore. Does not go over the top. Great value. Screwcap. 14.5% alc. **Rating** 92 **To** 2030 $18

✪ **Watervale Riesling 2012** A generously proportioned and fleshy Riesling, with lime and lemon fruit; the acidity is there, but is not obvious. Early-developing style, not typical of the vintage. Screwcap. 13% alc. **Rating** 90 **To** 2015 $18

Renards Folly

PO Box 499, McLaren Vale, SA 5171 **Region** McLaren Vale
T (08) 8556 2404 **www.**renardsfolly.com.au **Open** Not
Winemaker Tony Walker **Est.** 2005 **Dozens** 2000
The dancing foxes on the label, one with a red tail, give a subliminal hint that this is a virtual winery, owned by Linda Kemp (who looks after the marketing and sales) and Mark Dimberline. Aided by friend and winemaker Tony Walker, they source grapes from McLaren Vale, and allow the Vale to express itself without too much elaboration, the alcohol nicely controlled. Exports to the US, Canada, Germany and Singapore.

ŸŸŸŸ **McLaren Vale Shiraz 2011** Deep colour, and offering sumptuous blackberry, fruitcake and licorice on the bouquet; the palate is juicy and forward, accessible and fresh; lacking complexity, but pleasant and well constructed nonetheless. Screwcap. 14% alc. **Rating** 89 **To** 2017 $24 BE

Repertoire

PO Box 293, Cowaramup, WA 6284 **Region** Margaret River
T 0404 987 417 **www.**repertoirewines.com.au **Open** Not
Winemaker Richard Tattam, Mark Warren **Est.** 2008 **Dozens** 800
Repertoire is the virtual winery venture of Richard Tattam, who has turned his attention from sculpting bronze artworks to winemaking. He learnt to craft wines by working three vintages at Cullen Wines, two at Happs Three Hills winery, and two in France. The influence of Vanya Cullen has no doubt played a role in the decision of the business to be carbon neutral, while Richard's artistic credentials come through in the highly unusual labels and background stories of each of the wines to be found on the website.

ŸŸŸŸ♀ **Venturous Margaret River Grenache 2009** Bright, light red-purple; grown in the coolest, southern end of Margaret River, not in the theoretically better, northern, warmer part. The wine has attractive red fruits and a fine patina of tannins. Four barrels made. Screwcap. 14.3% alc. **Rating** 90 **To** 2015 $28

Reschke Wines

Level 1, 183 Melbourne Street, North Adelaide, SA 5006 (postal) **Region** Coonawarra
T (08) 8239 0500 **www.**reschke.com.au **Open** Not
Winemaker Peter Douglas (Contract) **Est.** 1998 **Dozens** 15 000 **Vyds** 155ha
It's not often that the first release from a new winery is priced at $100 per bottle, but that was precisely what Reschke Wines achieved with its 1998 Cabernet Sauvignon. The family has been a landholder in Coonawarra for 100 years, with a large holding that is part terra rossa, part woodland. Cabernet sauvignon (with 120ha) takes the lion's share of the plantings, with merlot, shiraz and petit verdot making up the balance. Exports to the UK, Canada, Germany, Hong Kong and Japan.

ŶŶŶŶŶ **Fume Sauvignon Blanc 2011** 'Fume' is explained on the back label as 'lightly touched by fine oak', and the wine lives up to that; despite its low alcohol, or perhaps thanks to it, the palate has an appealing mix of citrus, stone fruit and kiwifruit; good acidity on the finish. Vino-Lok. 11.5% alc. **Rating** 90 **To** 2014 $23
Pinot Noir 2010 Light red-purple; the claim on the back label that Mount Gambier is the coolest region on the Australian mainland is not correct: there are four cooler regions. Quite apart from climate quibbles and price grumbles, I would under no circumstances subject a Pinot Noir to the vagaries of cork. It has good varietal character, with some confit plum and cherry fruit, tannins and oak in balance. 13.4% alc. **Rating** 90 **To** 2015 $70
Vitulus Coonawarra Cabernet Sauvignon 2009 Developed red-purple hue; the very low yield (not much over 1 tonne per acre) and harvest in May might have been expected to produce a wine capable of handling a lot of oak. I don't know how long the wine spent in oak, or its composition, but less would have been better. A carping criticism of a wine that was nearly very good. Cork. 14.5% alc. **Rating** 90 **To** 2019 $28

ŶŶŶŶ **Pinot Gris 2011 Rating** 89 **To** 2013 $23
Aged Release Vitulus Cabernet Sauvignon 2005 Rating 87 **To** 2015 $40

Resolution Vineyard   ★★★★

4 Glen Street, South Hobart, Tas 7004 **Region** Southern Tasmania
T (03) 6224 9497 **www.**theresolutionvineyard.com **Open** By appt
Winemaker Frogmore Creek **Est.** 2003 **Dozens** 150 **Vyds** 0.8ha
Owners Charles and Alison Hewitt live in England and entrust the care of the property and vineyard to Alison's father Peter Brown, with support from former Parks & Wildlife ranger Val Dell. A love of red burgundy and fishing was sufficient for Charles to establish the vineyard, planted to three clones of pinot noir, in Tasmania, where Alison had spent most of her formative years. The vineyard is on a north-facing slope overlooking the D'Entrecasteaux Channel. Exports to the UK.

ŶŶŶŶŶ **Pinot Noir 2011** Good hue; has abundant spicy satsuma plum fruit aromas, the palate adding some savoury elements, and also tannins and acidity on the finish. Screwcap. 13.2% alc. **Rating** 90 **To** 2017 $25

Reynella   ★★★★★

Reynell Road, Reynella, SA 5161 **Region** McLaren Vale/Fleurieu Peninsula
T (08) 8392 2300 **Open** Mon–Fri 10–4
Winemaker Neville Rowe **Est.** 1838 **Dozens** NFP
John Reynell laid the foundations for Chateau Reynella in 1838; over the next 100 years the stone buildings and cellars, with patches of lawn and leafy gardens, were constructed. Thomas Hardy's first job in SA was with Reynella; he noted in his diary that he would be able to better himself soon. He did just that, becoming by far the largest producer in SA by the end of the 19th century; 150 or so years after Chateau Reynella's foundation CWA (now Accolade Wines) completed the circle by acquiring it and making it corporate headquarters, while preserving the integrity of the Reynella brand in no uncertain fashion. In a sign of the times, 'Chateau' has been dropped from its name. Exports to Canada, Europe and China.

ŶŶŶŶŶ **Cellar No. One Reserve McLaren Vale Shiraz 2005** Very good colour for a 7-year-old red; it comes from 80-year-old vines that, together with 20 months in French oak, invest the wine with exceptional intensity and length; spices of every description, black fruits, licorice, fruitcake and cedary oak are all part of the picture. Totally immaculate cork. 14% alc. **Rating** 96 **To** 2038 $93
Basket Pressed McLaren Vale Cabernet Sauvignon 2010 Bright crimson-purple; open-fermented, basket-pressed and matured for 14 months in French oak. It is a very stylish, medium- to full-bodied Cabernet with a long life ahead, the balance of the cassis/blackcurrant fruit, oak and tannins impeccable. Screwcap. 14% alc. **Rating** 96 **To** 2040 $51

Basket Pressed McLaren Vale Cabernet Sauvignon 2008 Deep crimson; this is a very classy, perfectly balanced Cabernet with a future far longer than mine. In the 18 months since first tasted (Mar '11), the wine has revealed more of its personality, with cedary oak enhancing the edge of austerity that great Cabernet should have, and which adds to its length. Screwcap. 14% alc. **Rating** 96 To 2030 $54

Rhythm Stick Wines ★★★★★

PO Box 270, Clare, SA 5453 **Region** Clare Valley
T (08) 8843 4325 **www**.rhythmstickwines.com.au **Open** By appt
Winemaker Tim Adams **Est.** 2007 **Dozens** 1000 **Vyds** 1.62ha
Rhythm Stick has come a long way in a short time, and with a small vineyard. It is owned by Ron and Jeanette Ely, who in 1997 purchased a 3.2ha property at Penwortham. The couple had already decided that in the future they would plant a vineyard, and simply to obtain experience they planted 135 cabernet sauvignon cuttings from Waninga Vineyards in four short rows. They have produced a few dozen bottles of Cabernet a year, sharing it with friends. In '02 they planted riesling, and the first harvest followed in '06, the grapes from this and the ensuing two vintages sold to Clare Valley winemakers. Prior to the '09 harvest they were advised that due to the GFC no grapes would be required, which advanced Ron's planned retirement after 40 years in electrical engineering consulting and management. The '09 vintage produced 20 tonnes of fruit, and the wines had what can only be described as spectacular success for a first-time producer.

ΨΨΨΨΨ **Red Robin Clare Valley Riesling 2012** Light straw-green; the fragrant, flowery bouquet leads into a lime and lemon citrus tango on the palate; the long, lingering finish is dry, though not shatteringly so, the acidity well balanced. Screwcap. 12.5% alc. **Rating** 94 To 2019 $20

Richard Hamilton ★★★★★

Cnr Main Road/Johnston Road, McLaren Vale, SA 5171 **Region** McLaren Vale
T (08) 8323 8830 **www**.leconfieldwines.com **Open** Mon–Fri 10–5, w'ends & public hols 11–5
Winemaker Paul Gordon, Tim Bailey **Est.** 1972 **Dozens** 25 000 **Vyds** 73.09ha
Richard Hamilton has outstanding estate vineyards, some of great age, all fully mature. An experienced and skilled winemaking team has allowed the full potential of those vineyards to be realised. The quality, style and consistency of both red and white wines have reached a new level; being able to keep only the best parcels for the Richard Hamilton brand is an enormous advantage. Exports to the UK, the US, Canada, Denmark, Sweden, Germany, Belgium, Malaysia, Vietnam, Hong Kong, Singapore, Japan, China and NZ.

ΨΨΨΨΨ **Centurion Old Vine McLaren Vale Shiraz 2011** The very old vines have produced the goods, the colour a deep and vibrant crimson-purple, the palate with a galaxy of black fruits, licorice, spice and dark chocolate flavours, the tannins ripe, oak limited to a custodian role. Screwcap. 14% alc. **Rating** 95 To 2031 $75

 McLaren Vale Shiraz 2011 Strong, full colour; the cool vintage provided benefits to those who kept disease at bay; these spicy dark berry aromas and flavours are normally restricted to cool regions. They work really well in the dark chocolate and blackberry fruit of this bargain basement wine. Screwcap. 14% alc. **Rating** 94 To 2026 $20

ΨΨΨΨΨ **Colton's McLaren Vale G.S.M 2011** Bright red fruits, with raspberry, licorice and fresh garden herbs, most notably thyme; the palate is medium-bodied, with crunchy acidity and chewy tannins in balance with the fruit. Screwcap. 14.5% alc. **Rating** 90 To 2018 $20 BE

ΨΨΨΨ **Almond Grove McLaren Vale Chardonnay 2011** Melon, white peach and a little charcuterie complexity on the bouquet; generous on entry and fleshy, fine acidity and well-handled oak all play a role in a seamless transition across the palate. Screwcap. 13% alc. **Rating** 89 To 2015 $16 BE

Richard Meyman Wines   ★★★★☆

PO Box 173, Franklin, Tas 7113 **Region** Southern Tasmania
T 0417 492 835 **www**.richardmeymanwines.com.au **Open** Not
Winemaker Winemaking Tasmania **Est.** 2010 **Dozens** 480
Richard Meyman had accumulated many years in the wine trade as grower, owner and
manager before returning to Tasmania to run and resurrect the important Nocton Park
vineyard in the Richmond/Coal River area. Few would dispute the primacy of pinot noir
as Tasmania's finest grape variety, and its multifaceted riesling is in the same quality league.
So it is that Richard has chosen those two varieties, and put them in the hands of Tasmania's
leading contract winemaker.

🍷🍷🍷🍷🍷 **Bersenbrück Pinot Noir 2011** Deep colour; Tasmania's answer to Central
Otago, with a deeply fruited bouquet inexorably feeding into the layered, full-
bodied (for pinot noir) palate swollen with plum and black cherry fruit, the
only question being over Bob Campbell MW's tag of a 'tadpole' structure – big
upfront then tailing away. Time will help answer the question. Screwcap. 13.5% alc.
Rating 93 **To** 2020 $35
Colebrook Road Pinot Noir 2012 Full crimson-purple, bright and clear; has
the effortless power that Tasmanian pinot can achieve in most vintages, power
that has the wine in a clenched fist now, but with the certainty of opening up,
softening, and showing all that is locked within it at the moment. Screwcap.
13.6% alc. **Rating** 92 **To** 2022 $28
Waseca Riesling 2012 Light straw-green; a powerful, no-compromise wine, its
muscular build based on a low pH, high natural acidity and just a touch of residual
sugar that is below the taste threshold; its best lies in the future. Screwcap. 12% alc.
Rating 91 **To** 2020 $24

🍷🍷🍷🍷 **Colebrook Road Pinot Noir 2011** Rating 89 To 2015 $25

Ridgemill Estate   ★★★★

218 Donges Road, Severnlea, Qld 4352 **Region** Granite Belt
T (07) 4683 5211 **www**.ridgemillestate.com **Open** Fri–Mon 10–5, Sun 10–3
Winemaker Martin Cooper, Peter McGlashan **Est.** 1998 **Dozens** 900 **Vyds** 2.1ha
Martin Cooper and Dianne Maddison acquired what was then known as Emerald Hill
Winery in 2004. In '05 they reshaped the vineyards, which now have plantings of chardonnay,
tempranillo, shiraz, merlot and cabernet sauvignon, saperavi, shiraz, verdelho and viognier,
setting a course down the alternative variety road.

🍷🍷🍷🍷🍷 **Granite Belt Cabernet Malbec Merlot 2010** Good blackcurrant fruit, with
a generous helping of oak to add complexity and overall flavour; time will see the
fruit assert itself. Screwcap. 13.5% alc. **Rating** 91 **To** 2025 $25
Granite Belt Verdelho 2012 Since when did three stars from *Winestate* merit
a round, gold sticker? Quartz-white, it's an interesting wine, with tangy citrus/
grapefruit/passionfruit suggesting a significantly lower alcohol level. For what it's
worth, I think it deserved more than the faint praise of three stars from *Winestate*.
Screwcap. 14% alc. **Rating** 90 **To** 2014 $20
Granite Belt Cabernet Malbec 2010 While (good-quality) oak is obvious,
it is well integrated and balanced with the blackcurrant and blackberry fruit of
the medium-bodied palate. Both this and the Cabernet Malbec Merlot are full of
potential. Screwcap. 13.5% alc. **Rating** 90 **To** 2025 $20

🍷🍷🍷🍷 **Granite Belt Rose 2012** Rating 89 To 2014 $18
Granite Belt Shiraz 2010 Rating 88 To 2015 $25

RidgeView Wines   ★★★★☆

273 Sweetwater Road, Pokolbin, NSW 2320 **Region** Hunter Valley
T (02) 6574 7332 **www**.ridgeview.com.au **Open** 7 days 10–5
Winemaker Darren Scott, Gary MacLean, Mark Woods **Est.** 2000 **Dozens** 3000 **Vyds** 9ha

Darren and Tracey Scott (plus their four children and extended family) have transformed a 40ha timbered farm into a vineyard, together with self-contained accommodation and cellar door. The lion's share of the plantings are 4.5ha of shiraz, with cabernet sauvignon, chambourcin, merlot, pinot gris, viognier and traminer making up a somewhat eclectic selection of varieties. In 2010 the family celebrated 10 years in business by opening a cellar door and restaurant. Exports to Japan.

ЙЙЙЙЙ Generations Reserve Semillon 2009 Vibrant green hue; showing a little toasty development on the bouquet alongside lemon sherbet and straw; the palate is linear and focused, with generosity now a feature, after some time in bottle; long and evenly balanced. Screwcap. 10.8% alc. **Rating** 94 **To** 2022 $30 BE

ЙЙЙЙЙ **Tipple's Gold Botrytis Semillon 2006 Rating** 93 **To** 2017 $25
Impressions Shiraz 2011 Rating 91 **To** 2022 $30 BE

Rieslingfreak   ★★★★☆
8 Roenfeldt Drive, Tanunda, SA 5352 (postal) **Region** Clare Valley
T (08) 8563 3963 **www**.rieslingfreak.com **Open** Not
Winemaker John Hughes **Est.** 2009 **Dozens** 1000 **Vyds** 20ha
The name of John Hughes' winery leaves no doubt about his long-term ambition: to explore every avenue of Riesling, whether bone-dry or quite sweet, coming from regions across the wine world, albeit with a strong focus on Australia. The first two wines come from his Clare Valley vineyard, and offer No. 3 (dry) and No. 5 (off-dry). Exports to Canada, Hong Kong and NZ.

ЙЙЙЙЙ No. 3 Riesling 2012 Sourced from the Clare Valley, the bouquet has a complex mix of spice, talc and floral blossom, the delicious palate with a mix of citrus (dominant) and of passionfruit (just a hint). Has excellent line, length and balance. Screwcap. 12.5% alc. **Rating** 94 **To** 2025 $23

ЙЙЙЙЙ No. 4 Riesling 2012 **Rating** 91 **To** 2022 $23

Rileys of Eden Valley   ★★★★★
PO Box 71, Eden Valley, SA 5235 **Region** Eden Valley
T (08) 8564 1029 **www**.rileysofedenvalley.com.au **Open** Not
Winemaker Jo Irvine (Contract) **Est.** 2006 **Dozens** 650 **Vyds** 7.7ha
Rileys of Eden Valley is owned by parents Terry and Jan with son Peter, who way back in 1982 purchased 32ha of a grazing property that they believed had potential for quality grape production. The first vines were planted in that year and over the next 16 years plantings extended to 7.2ha. Minimal planting has occurred since, but in '08 0.8ha of merlot was grafted to savagnin (in the belief that it was albarino). In '98 Terry retired from his position of Professor of Mechanical Engineering at the University of SA, allowing him to concentrate on the vineyard, and, more recently, winemaking activities, but the whole family (including granddaughter Maddy) have been involved in the development of the property. It had always been intended that the grapes would be sold, but when not all the grapes were contracted in '06, the Rileys decided to produce some wine (even though they ended up with buyers for all of the production that year).

ЙЙЙЙЙ Family Riesling 2012 Bright, light straw-green; a delicious mouthfeel (and mouthful) of skilfully made Riesling from a top vintage. The back label 'slide rule' of sweetness (or dryness) shows this to be past the halfway mark between dry and off-dry, meaning the small amount of residual sugar (and low alcohol) expresses itself more as intense lime juice than as sweetness per se. Screwcap. 11.5% alc. **Rating** 94 **To** 2025 $22

✪ Jump Ship Shiraz 2010 Good crimson-purple; a potent, full-bodied shiraz from a single estate block; it spent 15 months in new and used French oak, which is interwoven through the layers of black fruits of the bouquet and palate, along with notes of spice and licorice. Screwcap. 14.5% alc. **Rating** 94 **To** 2025 $24

ЙЙЙЙЙ Family Riesling 2011 **Rating** 90 **To** 2016 $22

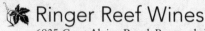 Ringer Reef Wines

6835 Great Alpine Road, Porepunkah, Vic 3740 **Region** Alpine Valleys
T (03) 5756 2805 **www.ringerreef.com.au Open** Fri–Mon, school & public hols 12–5
Winemaker Bruce Holm **Est.** 2001 **Dozens** 1000 **Vyds** 4.1ha

This is the venture of Bruce and Annie Holm, Bruce having been involved in large-scale commercial wine production in Griffith and Mildura for 30 years before getting itchy feet. In 1996 he and Annie began searching for an appropriate property, finding an ideal 35ha one at Porepunkah. The first vines were planted in '98, and, except during vintage, Bruce travelled from Mildura every weekend to maintain the property. In 2000 they moved to Porepunkah, Bruce working first at Gapsted Wines, then with Sam Miranda Wines before 'retiring' in '08. In the meantime a winery and cellar door sales had been built in '05, and they now have a Joseph's Coat of chardonnay, merlot, montepulciano, moscato giallo, nebbiolo, petit manseng, pinot noir, sangiovese and sauvignon blanc.

Alpine Valleys Chardonnay 2010 Medium green-yellow; barrel fermentation in French oak, then lees-stirred before being bottled in Dec '10; the wine has absorbed much of the oak, its stone fruit and melon flavours to the fore. Screwcap. 13.5% alc. **Rating** 90 **To** 2014 $22

Alpine Valleys Merlot 2008 Rating 88 **To** 2013 $24

Riposte

PO Box 256, Lobethal, SA 5241 **Region** Adelaide Hills
T (08) 8389 8149 **www.timknappstein.com.au Open** Not
Winemaker Tim Knappstein **Est.** 2006 **Dozens** 8500

It's never too late to teach an old dog new tricks when the old dog in question is Tim Knappstein. With 40 years of winemaking and more than 500 wine show awards under his belt, Tim started yet another new wine life with Riposte, a subtle response to the various vicissitudes he has suffered in recent years. While having no continuing financial interest in Lenswood Vineyards, established many years ago, Tim is able to source grapes from it and also from other prime sites in surrounding areas. The prices for almost all of the wines are astonishingly low. Exports to Denmark, Indonesia and China.

The Foil Adelaide Hills Sauvignon Blanc 2012 Bright greenish straw; vibrantly fresh and incisive, with kiwifruit, citrus and passionfruit on the bouquet, precisely replayed on the long, very well balanced palate. Outstanding value. Screwcap. 12.5% alc. **Rating** 94 **To** 2014 $20

The Stiletto Adelaide Hills Pinot Gris 2012 Pale straw-green; has a rarely encountered pungent and varietally expressive bouquet with nashi pear and clove aromas, the vibrant palate no less emphatic through to its long finish. Great value. Screwcap. 13% alc. **Rating** 94 **To** 2014 $20

The Dagger Adelaide Hills Pinot Noir 2012 Excellent crimson-purple; the bouquet offers red cherry and plum fruit which are the building blocks of the palate, cemented by spicy/savoury nuances on the back-palate. Exceptional low price. Screwcap. 13.5% alc. **Rating** 94 **To** 2019 $20

The Sabre Adelaide Hills Pinot Noir 2010 Fresh, light crimson; the fresh, fragrant bouquet leads into a well-structured and balanced palate, with an array of small-berry fruits and spices, the finish long and satisfying. Is even better than it was in Feb '12. Screwcap. 14% alc. **Rating** 94 **To** 2017 $29

The Scimitar Clare Valley Riesling 2012 Pale straw-green; a complex wine due to the richness and texture of the fruit, not winery wizardry; ready to go. Screwcap. 12.5% alc. **Rating** 91 **To** 2016 $20

The Halberd White Co-Ferment 2012 Rating 91 **To** 2016 $25

River Park   ★★★☆

River Park Road, Cowra, NSW 2794 **Region** Cowra
T (02) 6342 3596 **www**.riverparkwines.com.au **Open** By appt
Winemaker Hunter Wine Services **Est.** 1994 **Dozens** 960 **Vyds** 12ha
Bill and Chris Murphy established River Park with 6ha each of chardonnay and cabernet sauvignon on the banks of the Lachlan River, on the outskirts of Cowra. In a familiar pattern, the vineyard was expanded in the boom days, with wine being sold in bulk to larger producers, but has now returned to its original size, all wine being made and sold under the River Park label.

 Cowra Rose 2011 Vivid, light purple-crimson; apparently made from estate-grown cabernet, it has a fragrant cherry blossom bouquet, joined by some raspberry on the palate; while distinctly fruity, it is pleasantly dry and definitely food-friendly. Screwcap. 12.5% alc. **Rating** 90 **To** 2014 $18

Cowra Cabernet Sauvignon 2009 **Rating** 88 **To** 2014 $18

Rivergate Wines   ★★★★

580 Goornong Road, Axedale, Vic 3551 **Region** Bendigo
T (03) 5439 7367 **www**.rivergatewines.com.au **Open** By appt
Winemaker Greg Dedman, Geoff Kerr, Andrew Kutlarz **Est.** 1999 **Dozens** 550 **Vyds** 2.2ha
Rivergate Wines is the Kerr family business, producing intense-flavoured, full-bodied wines at Axedale, midway between Bendigo and Heathcote. They specialise in growing and producing Shiraz, from low-yielding, hand-tended, estate vines. The wines are matured in French and American oak barriques for 12 months. When seasonal conditions permit, a small amount of Reserve Shiraz, which spends two years in barrel, is made.

Bendigo Shiraz 2008 Has retained good colour given its age; matured for 12 months in a mix of new and used American and French oak barrels; its medium- to full-bodied palate has plenty of black fruits that have benefited from that maturation regime. Screwcap. 14.5% alc. **Rating** 92 **To** 2028 $25

Riversdale Estate   ★★★★★

222 Denholms Road, Cambridge, Tas 7170 **Region** Southern Tasmania
T (03) 6248 5666 **www**.riversdaleestate.com.au **Open** At Zero Cafe, Hobart
Winemaker Nick Badrice **Est.** 1991 **Dozens** 10000 **Vyds** 23ha
Ian Roberts purchased the Riversdale property in 1980 while a university student, and says he paid a record price for the district. The unique feature of the property is its frontage to the Pittwater waterfront, which acts as a buffer against frost, and also moderates the climate during the ripening phase. It is a large property, with over 20ha of vines, and one of the largest olive groves in Tasmania, producing 50 olive-based products. Five families live permanently on the estate, providing all the labour for the various operations, which also include four 5-star French Provincial cottages overlooking the vines. Wine quality is consistently good.

Crater Coal River Valley Chardonnay 2011 Light straw-green; a high-quality wine that is built on the foundation of Tasmanian acidity that ripples through the grapefruit and white peach fruit, helping sideline the French oak in which the wine was fermented; length, finish and aftertaste are wholly convincing. Screwcap. 13.5% alc. **Rating** 95 **To** 2020 $45
Centaurus Coal River Valley Pinot Noir 2011 Bright crimson-purple of impressive clarity and depth; a powerful, rich and densely packed Pinot, with dark plum, black cherry and spice on a structure of fine but persistent tannins, oak playing a support role. Will be long-lived, and deserves time in bottle. Screwcap. 14.5% alc. **Rating** 95 **To** 2023 $42

Cygnus Coal River Valley Riesling 2012 **Rating** 93 **To** 2022 $36
Coal River Valley Riesling 2012 **Rating** 93 **To** 2017 $23

Coal River Valley Pinot Noir 2011 Rating 93 To 2016 $26
Coal River Valley Pinot Gris 2012 Rating 90 To 2014 $26

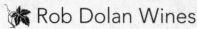 # Rob Dolan Wines   ★★★★★

21–23 Delaneys Road, South Warrandyte, Vic 3134 **Region** Yarra Valley
T (03) 9876 5885 **www**.robdolanwines.com.au **Open** By appt
Winemaker Rob Dolan, Peter Mackey **Est.** 2010 **Dozens** 5000
Rob Dolan has been making wine in the Yarra Valley for over 20 years, and knows every nook and cranny. In 2011 (having previously parted company with Sticks) he was able to purchase the Hardys Yarra Burn winery at an enticing price. It is singularly well equipped, and, as well as making the Rob Dolan wines, he will be able to carry on an extensive contract winemaking business.

🍷🍷🍷🍷🍷 Yarra Valley Chardonnay 2010 Still a light, bright straw-green; the wine
✪   has very good balance, texture and complexity; while the chardonnay fruit has
         some grapefruit zest, it is interwoven with white peach, and nutty/creamy/toasty
         nuances from well-handled barrel fermentation of whole or part; minerally acidity
         drives the finish. Screwcap. 13% alc. **Rating** 94 **To** 2017 $25
         Yarra Valley Pinot Noir 2010 Very good retention of crimson-purple hue; the
         bouquet of red and black cherry and plums tells you precisely what to expect
         from the layered fore- and mid-palate; foresty/spicy tannins add to the mouthfeel
         and length without attacking the varietal fruit. Impressive wine, with plenty to
         support further time in bottle. Screwcap. 13% alc. **Rating** 94 **To** 2020 $30

🍷🍷🍷🍷🍷 True Colours Yarra Valley Cabernet Shiraz Merlot 2012 Full purple-
✪   crimson; a rare, if not unique, blend in the Yarra Valley, and has taken full advantage
         of the '12 vintage; the blackcurrant and blackberry fruit is perfectly ripe, as are the
         tannins, the oak integrated. Screwcap. 13.5% alc. **Rating** 93 **To** 2020 $20
✪   True Colours Yarra Valley Sauvignon Blanc Semillon 2012 Water white
         after a 12-month gestation, a simple statement of fact, not a criticism; the wine has
         a fragrant bouquet and a very attractive array of lemon/citrus and peach/lychee
         fruit flavours woven through a web of minerally acidity. Excellent value. Screwcap.
         12% alc. **Rating** 92 **To** 2014 $20
         Yarra Valley Pinot Gris 2012 Rating 91 To 2014 $25
✪   True Colours Yarra Valley Dry Rose 2012 Salmon-pink; interesting rose, as it
         has a bubble of red berry fruit on the mid-palate before moving on to a textured
         back-palate, the finish striking a more savoury pose; nicely dry and firm. Screwcap.
         12.5% alc. **Rating** 91 **To** 2014 $20

Robert Channon Wines   ★★★☆

32 Bradley Lane, Amiens, Qld 4352 **Region** Granite Belt
T (07) 4683 3260 **www**.robertchannonwines.com **Open** Mon, Tues & Fri 11–4,
w'ends 10–5
Winemaker Stephen Oliver **Est.** 1998 **Dozens** 3000 **Vyds** 8ha
Peggy and Robert Channon have established verdelho, chardonnay, pinot gris, shiraz, cabernet sauvignon and pinot noir under permanent bird protection netting. The initial cost of installing permanent netting is high, but in the long term it is well worth it: it excludes birds and protects the grapes against hail damage. Also, there is no pressure to pick the grapes before they are fully ripe. The winery has established a particular reputation for its Verdelho. Exports to China.

🍷🍷🍷🍷🍷 Verdelho 2012 This takes the verdelho to another level of length and intensity
         altogether, with the flavours spreading through the length and breadth of the
         palate, the fruit salad notes tempered by a jab of citrus/lemon. Screwcap. 12.5% alc.
         Rating 93 **To** 2016 $28

🍷🍷🍷🍷 Chardonnay 2012 Light straw-green; a well-made wine with honeydew melon,
✪   stone fruit and fig flavours, together with a touch of toasty oak. As ready now as it
        will ever be. Screwcap. 13.9% alc. **Rating** 89 **To** 2015 $20

Pinot Gris 2012 Rating 89 To 2014 $20
Pinot Noir 2011 Rating 89 To 2016 $20
Singing Lake Verdelho 2012 Rating 88 To 2015 $20

Robert Oatley Vineyards   ★★★★★

Craigmoor Road, Mudgee, NSW 2850 **Region** Mudgee
T (02) 6372 2208 **www.**robertoatley.com.au **Open** 7 days 10–4
Winemaker Chris Hancock, Larry Cherubino, Derek Fitzgerald **Est.** 2006 **Dozens** NFP
Vyds 440ha

Robert Oatley Vineyards is the venture of the Oatley family, previously best known as the owners of Rosemount Estate until it was sold to Southcorp. The chairman is Bob Oatley; the new venture is run by son Sandy, with considerable hitting power added by deputy executive chairman Chris Hancock. Wild Oats, as anyone with the remotest interest in yachting and the Sydney–Hobart Yacht Race will know, has been the name of Bob's racing yachts. The family has long owned vineyards in Mudgee, but the business was rapidly expanded by the acquisition of the Montrose winery and the Craigmoor cellar door and restaurant. The family has completed a $10 million upgrade of the Montrose winery. The recruitment of Larry Cherubino as a winemaker has been a major factor in the radical reshaping of the overall business, with all of the best wines now coming coming from WA. While there is a plethora of wines, stripped to its essentials the portfolio is easy to understand: at the bottom, James Oatley Tic Tok; next Wild Oats; then Robert Oatley; and at the top, Robert Oatley limited releases. Exports to the UK, the US and other major markets.

ΨΨΨΨΨ **Robert Oatley Finisterre Margaret River Chardonnay 2010** The complex bouquet has an attractive touch of Burgundian funk before the vibrant and lively palate comes into play; with grapefruit, white peach and subtle French oak inputs. The finesse, length and attendant citrussy/minerally acidity of the wine is excellent. Screwcap. 12.8% alc. **Rating** 96 **To** 2022 $36

Robert Oatley The Pennant Margaret River Chardonnay 2010 Bright straw-green; a beautifully crafted and detailed wine, superfine in its impact on the palate, yet with extreme length. It has clearly been picked at exactly the right moment, and the overall balance is impeccable. Screwcap. 13% alc. **Rating** 96 **To** 2020 $70

Robert Oatley Finisterre Margaret River Cabernet Sauvignon 2009 The purity of this wine comes through with the utmost clarity on the bouquet, with fragrant blackcurrant/cassis aromas, the medium- to full-bodied palate a great example of Margaret River cabernet, the focused fruit supported by tannins that, while firm, are in no way out of balance. The contribution of French oak is obvious, but not over the top. Screwcap. 14% alc. **Rating** 96 **To** 2029 $39

Robert Oatley Finisterre Porongurup Riesling 2012 Pale quartz; a Riesling with all the precision and focus that Porongurup invests in the variety; the balance between the lime/green apple fruit and minerally acidity is perfect, as are the steely line and length. A lovely wine now, but how great will it be in 5–10 years down the track? Screwcap. 11% alc. **Rating** 95 **To** 2027 $33

Robert Oatley Finisterre Mudgee Chardonnay 2011 Pale straw-green; the most elegant Chardonnay I have encountered (over a 40-year period) from Mudgee. Early picking (and the consequent low alcohol) has resulted in finely detailed white peach and citrus aromas and flavours, the barrel fermentation/ oak influence cleverly restrained. Crisp acidity adds length to the finish. Screwcap. 12.6% alc. **Rating** 95 **To** 2018 $32

Robert Oatley Great Southern Riesling 2012 Rating 94 To 2020 $24

Robert Oatley Finisterre Pemberton Sauvignon Blanc 2012 Rating 94 To 2014 $33

Robert Oatley The Pennant Mudgee Chardonnay 2011 Rating 94 To 2018 $70

Robert Oatley Finisterre Denmark Pinot Noir 2011 Rating 94 To 2018 $37

Robert Oatley The Pennant Margaret River Cabernet Sauvignon 2010 Rating 94 To 2040 $80

⊗   **Craigmoor Estate Botrytis 2009** Very youthful colour for a wine of this style; a surprise packet, its sauvignon blanc semillon blend seldom achieving this level of flavour in Australia; packed with juicy mandarin and cumquat fruit flavours, the luscious sweetness perfectly balanced by acidity. It is so enjoyable now that it won't last long in the cellar, but has many years left. 500ml. Screwcap. 9.5% alc. Rating 94 To 2018 $20

ŸŸŸŸŸ   **Robert Oatley Margaret River Sauvignon Blanc 2012** Rating 93 To 2014 $25
Robert Oatley Margaret River Chardonnay 2012 Rating 92 To 2018 $25
Robert Oatley Mornington Peninsula Pinot Noir 2010 Rating 92 To 2016 $24
Robert Oatley Finisterre Mornington Peninsula Pinot Noir 2011 Rating 91 To 2014 $37
Robert Oatley McLaren Vale Shiraz 2011 Rating 91 To 2021 $25
Robert Oatley Margaret River Cabernet Sauvignon 2011 Rating 91 To 2021 $25

⊗   **Wild Oats Sauvignon Blanc 2012** Entirely sourced from the southern parts of WA, the bouquet and palate focus on the full spectrum of tropical fruits, but there is plenty of structure and bite from the grainy/minerally acidity on the long, faintly herbal finish. Screwcap. 12.8% alc. Rating 90 To 2014 $19

Robert Stein Vineyard   ★★★★★

Pipeclay Lane, Mudgee, NSW 2850 **Region** Mudgee
T (02) 6373 3991 **www**.robertstein.com.au **Open** 7 days 10–4.30
Winemaker Jacob Stein **Est.** 1976 **Dozens** 20 000 **Vyds** 18.67ha
While three generations of the family have been involved since Robert (Bob) Stein began the establishment of the vineyard, the chain stretches even further back, going to Bob's great-great-grandfather, Johann Stein, who was brought to Australia by the Macarthur family to supervise the planting of the Camden Park vineyard. Bob's grandson Jacob has now taken over winemaking responsibilities. Jacob worked vintages in Italy, Canada, Margaret River and Avoca, and, more particularly, in the Rheingau and Rheinhessen regions of Germany. Since his return to the winery one success has followed another, and Jacob was named Gourmet Traveller Young Winemaker of the Year '12. Exports to Germany, Hong Kong, Singapore and China.

ŸŸŸŸŸ   **Mudgee Riesling 2012** Won two trophies at the Mudgee Wine Show '12, including Best White Wine of Show. Fully dry, it nonetheless has a highly expressive floral bouquet and an even classier palate; here, lime juice and minerality engage in a courtly dance. Screwcap. 11% alc. Rating 95 To 2022 $40
Reserve Mudgee Shiraz 2011 Good purple-crimson; black fruits on the bouquet intensify on the palate, backed by a framework of potent tannins; the balance is there for cellaring. Screwcap. 13.5% alc. Rating 95 To 2026 $50

⊗   **Mudgee Saignee 2012** The pink colour has a hint of salmon; a true saignee made by bleeding juice from freshly crushed cabernet sauvignon and shiraz, the remainder fermented in the usual way. Spicy oak is obvious on the bouquet, less so on the lively red berry palate the fruit and acidity in perfect harmony. A seriously elegant Rose. Screwcap. 13.5% alc. Rating 94 To 2014 $20
Reserve Mudgee Cabernet Sauvignon 2011 The hue is good, although not particularly deep, but the wine in the glass – and in the mouth – lends credence to Jacob Stein's forecast of up to 20 years' improvement. I'm not totally convinced, for there are touches of leafy/minty/lemony notes to the back-palate and finish; the structure is an altogether different matter, for there is no doubt about its quality. Screwcap. 14% alc. Rating 94 To 2030 $50
Off Dry Mudgee Riesling RS 11 2012 Quartz-white; with only 11g/l of residual sugar, this wine must have been picked very early, and its entire life lies ahead; it is in no sense green, simply vibrant and minerally while allowing lime and apple to point the way for the future. It's a cheeky price, but if you don't ask, you don't get. Screwcap. 10% alc. Rating 94 To 2030 $35

Harvest Gold 2012 Bright gold; a great example of how a botrytised Semillon can have the intensity, focus and lightness of foot normally reserved for Rieslings; this really is a very good wine, given a farewell kiss by a brief sojourn in French oak. 375ml. Screwcap. 10% alc. **Rating** 94 **To** 2015 $25

ఇఇఇఇఇ Mudgee Shiraz Viognier 2011 **Rating** 92 **To** 2021 $25
✪ Mudgee Rose 2012 A 60/40% blend of cabernet sauvignon and merlot; the aim was to focus on the perfumed cherry/berry fruit, and has done just that; the fascinating aspect is the balance and mouthfeel, the touch of sweetness largely passing without notice. Screwcap. 11.5% alc. **Rating** 91 **To** 2014 $15
Mudgee Shiraz 2011 **Rating** 91 **To** 2017 $25

Robertson of Clare ★★★★

PO Box 149, Killara, NSW 2071 **Region** Clare Valley
T (02) 9499 6002 **www**.rocwines.com.au **Open** Not
Winemaker Simon Gilbert, Leigh Eldredge, Biagio Famularo **Est.** 2004 **Dozens** NFP
This is the highly unusual venture of Bryan Robertson, using the experience of Simon Gilbert and Leigh Eldredge to produce the single red wine made for the brand. The Bordeaux varieties that go to produce the MAX V wine are all grown in the Clare Valley, and individual varietal parcels are matured in 19 variations of 100% new French oak barrels. The primary fermentation takes place in barrel using what is called 'vinification integrale'. Exports to the UK, the US, Singapore, Hong Kong and China.

ఇఇఇఇఇ MAX V 2009 A wine that deserves its 'unique' epithet: a 57/22/7/7/7% blend of cabernet sauvignon, merlot, cabernet franc, malbec and petit verdot, each component hand-picked and sorted, each fermented separately with one-third in new French 400-litre vinification integrale barrels, the remainder in Mintaro slate fermenters, before 32 months in 100% new French barriques with 19 variations in cooper, forest, toast, etc. Is it flamboyantly OTT? Yes, of course, but its luscious oak-cased flavours and texture do have a certain mesmeric appeal for would-be heroes. Screwcap. 14.9% alc. **Rating** 91 **To** 2050 $75

Rochford Wines ★★★★★

878–880 Maroondah Highway, Coldstream, Vic 3770 **Region** Yarra Valley
T (03) 5962 2119 **www**.rochfordwines.com **Open** 7 days 9–5
Winemaker Marc Lunt **Est.** 1988 **Dozens** 13 000 **Vyds** 23.2ha
This Yarra Valley property was purchased by Helmut Konecsny in 2002; he had already established a reputation for producing pinot noir and chardonnay from the family-owned Romsey Park vineyard in the Macedon Ranges. Since '10, Helmut focused predominantly on his Yarra Valley wineries and vineyards, with some grapes still sourced from small parcel growers in the Macedon Ranges. Winemaker Marc Lunt had a stellar career as a Flying Winemaker in Bordeaux and Burgundy; in the latter region he worked at Armand Rousseau and Domaine de la Romanee-Conti. Rochford has a large restaurant and café, cellar door, retail shop, expansive natural amphitheatre and observation tower. It is a showpiece in the region, hosting a series of popular summer concerts. Exports to the UK, the US, Canada, Sweden, the Philippines, Singapore, Hong Kong and China.

ఇఇఇఇఇ Isabella's Vineyard Yarra Valley Chardonnay 2011 From Rochford's 30-year-old, steeply sloping, vineyard. A very elegant wine, with perfectly ripened varietal fruit, and the length for which the best Yarra Valley Chardonnays are known. Screwcap. 13% alc. **Rating** 95 **To** 2020 $40
Yarra Valley Chardonnay 2011 Bright, gleaming straw-green; it has precision, focus and drive to its mix of grapefruit and white peach flavours, crisp acidity lengthening the palate and finish. Screwcap. 12.5% alc. **Rating** 94 **To** 2018 $30
Yarra Valley Syrah 2010 Unfined and unfiltered, but is bright and clear crimson-purple; maceration pre- and post-fermentation have resulted in a strong texture and structure framing the red fruits at the core of the wine, 15 months on lees in French oak also playing a role. Impressive wine. Screwcap. 13.5% alc. **Rating** 94 **To** 2025 $30

Yarra Valley la Droite 2010 Cabernet franc and merlot, are often treated as poor cousins in the Yarra Valley, but this medium-bodied wine has both elegance and intensity to its red and black fruits esconced in a web of fine, savoury tannins. Screwcap. 13.5% alc. **Rating** 94 To 2023 $30

ΨΨΨΨΨ **Yarra Valley Sauvignon 2012 Rating** 93 To 2014 $27
Yarra Valley Chardonnay 2010 Rating 93 To 2018 $30
Yarra Valley Cabernet Franc 2011 Rating 93 To 2020 $30
Yarra Valley Sauvignon 2011 Rating 92 To 2014 $30
Yarra Valley Pinot Gris 2012 Rating 92 To 2014 $30
Isabella's Vineyard Cabernet Sauvignon 2010 Rating 92 To 2023 $57
Yarra Valley Sauvignon Blanc 2012 Rating 91 To 2013 $27
Yarra Valley Pinot Noir 2010 Rating 91 To 2017 $30
la Gauche Yarra Valley Cabernet 2010 Rating 91 To 2025 $30
Macedon Ranges Pinot Chardonnay 2009 Rating 91 To 2016 $34
Latitude Yarra Valley Chardonnay 2011 Rating 90 To 2016 $25
Macedon Ranges Pinot Noir 2010 Rating 90 To 2017 $33
la Gauche Yarra Valley Cabernet 2011 Rating 90 To 2017 $30

RockBare   ★★★★☆

102 Main St, Hahndorf, SA 5245 **Region** McLaren Vale
T (08) 8388 7155 **www**.rockbare.com.au **Open** 7 days 10.30–5
Winemaker Marty O'Flaherty **Est.** 2000 **Dozens** 50000 **Vyds** 47ha
A native of WA, Tim Burvill moved to SA in 1993 to do the winemaking course at Adelaide University's Roseworthy campus. Having completed an honours degree in oenology, he was recruited by Southcorp and quickly found himself in a senior winemaking position, responsible for super-premium whites including Penfolds Yattarna. He oversees the team that makes the RockBare wines under lend-lease arrangements with other wineries. Has moved to a new cellar door in the centre of Hahndorf. Exports to all major markets.

ΨΨΨΨΨ **Barossa Babe Shiraz 2009** Good red-purple; the cork had a major crease line down one side, with wine travelling over the top of the cork, but there is such of volume of rich, supple black fruits, the wine may well rise above this challenge. It spent 24 months in new French oak; the tannins are ripe and velvety, and the picture of Babe on the back label is a portrait of the wine, every bit as much as of Babe. 15% alc. **Rating** 94 To 2024 $40

ΨΨΨΨΨ **McLaren Vale Chardonnay 2012** McLaren Vale's record with chardonnay
✪ started with a bang 25 years ago, but it's been hard going since then. More wines like this might redress the balance, for all the right buttons have been pressed: picked early with good natural acidity, and only given a touch of oak, but lees-stirred and bottled while fresh. It is crisp and crunchy, and the finish is long and bright. Screwcap. 13% alc. **Rating** 92 To 2017 $20

✪ **Mojo Shiraz 2012** Deep red-purple; the lush black fruit aromas do not deceive, for the palate is so stacked with blackberry and black cherry fruit it borders on viscous, but instead is velvety. There is a feeling that the alcohol may be closer to 15%, but if you want yards of flavour at a bargain price, this is for you. Screwcap. 14.5% alc. **Rating** 92 To 2027 $20

✪ **Mojo Cabernet Sauvignon 2011** SA (front label) and Coonawarra (back label) explain the theme, with varieties coming from matching regions across the state. This is a well-constructed, medium- to full-bodied wine, showing the typical blackcurrant, earth and mint flavours of Coonawarra cabernet. Screwcap. 13.5% alc. **Rating** 90 To 2021 $20

Rockcliffe   ★★★★★

18 Hamilton Road, Denmark, WA 6333 **Region** Denmark
T (08) 9848 2622 **www**.matildasestate.com **Open** 7 days 11–5
Winemaker Coby Ladwig, Brenden Smith, Luke Eckersley **Est.** 1990 **Dozens** 6000
Vyds 10ha

The Rockcliffe winery and vineyard business, formerly known as Matilda's Estate, is owned by citizen of the world Steve Hall. The wine ranges echo local surf place names, headed by Rockcliffe itself, but extending to Third Reef, Forty Foot Drop and Quarram Rocks. Since building the onsite winery in 2007, and putting the winemaking team in charge, one success has followed another, culminating in the trophy for Best Winery Under 300 Tonnes at the Perth Wine Show '12. Exports to Malaysia, Singapore and Hong Kong.

Great Southern Chardonnay 2011 Light straw-green; an intense, stylish Chardonnay that has soaked up its barrel-ferment oak, throwing the emphasis of its bouquet and long palate onto its mix of grapefruit and white peach flavours, bolstered by crisp acidity. Screwcap. 13% alc. **Rating** 94 **To** 2018 $35

Third Reef Great Southern Shiraz 2009 Still has a deep crimson-purple colour; the complex bouquet of spice, licorice and bramble fruits leads into a supple, rich, medium- to full-bodied palate with an abundance of blackberry and plum fruit, the tannins on the finish particularly impressive. Screwcap. 14% alc. **Rating** 94 **To** 2029 $25

Great Southern Cabernet Sauvignon 2009 A blend of 86% cabernet sauvignon plus 9% merlot and 5% cabernet franc. A tightly structured, medium-bodied, vibrant Cabernet with cassis the driver, the other components adding to the vibrancy and not in any way blurring the message of the cabernet varietal character. Screwcap. 14% alc. **Rating** 94 **To** 2029 $35

Great Southern Pinot Noir 2011 **Rating** 93 **To** 2016 $35

Third Reef Great Southern Shiraz Cabernet 2009 Medium purple-crimson; the fragrant bouquet and medium-bodied palate offer spice, pepper, black and red fruits and modest oak (which is as it should be). Best of all is the juicy, fresh mouthfeel and flavours, making this a compelling wine in every respect, and terrific value. Screwcap. 14% alc. **Rating** 93 **To** 2019 $20

Third Reef Great Southern Chardonnay 2011 Barrel fermentation in used oak has allowed the impressive, and fresh, array of nectarine, peach and grapefruit aromas and flavours free rein to express themselves; the palate has excellent length and balance. Great value. Screwcap. 13.4% alc. **Rating** 92 **To** 2017 $20

Third Reef Sauvignon Blanc 2012 **Rating** 90 **To** 2014 $20

Quarram Rocks Sauvignon Blanc Semillon 2012 Counterintuitively, has a greater range to its fruit spectrum than Third Reef Sauvignon Blanc, with gooseberry, citrus and a flick of fresh-cut grass; good acidity also helps the mouthfeel. The value is obvious. Screwcap. 13% alc. **Rating** 90 **To** 2015 $16

Rockford ★★★★★

131 Krondorf Road, Tanunda, SA 5352 **Region** Barossa Valley
T (08) 8563 2720 **www.**rockfordwines.com.au **Open** 7 days 11–5
Winemaker Robert O'Callaghan, Ben Radford **Est.** 1984 **Dozens** NFP
Rockford can only be described as an icon, no matter how overused that word may be. It has a devoted band of customers who buy most of the wine through the cellar door or mail order (Rocky O'Callaghan's entrancing annual newsletter is like no other). Some wine is sold through restaurants, and there are two retailers in Sydney, and one each in Melbourne, Brisbane and Perth. Whether they will have the Basket Press Shiraz available is another matter; it is as scarce as Henschke Hill of Grace (and less expensive). Ben Radford, whom I first met in South Africa some years ago, has been entrenched as Rocky's right-hand man, and is destined to take over responsibility for winemaking when the time comes for Rocky to step back from an active role. Exports to the UK, Canada, Switzerland, Russia, Vietnam, South Korea, Singapore, Japan, Hong Kong, China and NZ.

Basket Press Barossa Shiraz 2010 Deep garnet with a purple hue; this benchmark wine is laden with vibrant purple and black fruits, floral notes, earthy complexity and well-executed oak handling; the palate is juicy, direct and layered, with fine-grained tannins providing an armchair ride for the vibrant and plush fruit that is on board. Cork. 14.5% alc. **Rating** 96 **To** 2030 $57 BE

Black Shiraz NV Deep garnet-red; this is the Aug '12 disgorgement, following 3 years in large old oak, and at least 1 year on lees in this bottle; it is a totally reliable, utterly seductive, and uniquely Australian style. It has long future on cork if that is what you want. 13.5% alc. **Rating** 96 **To** 2020 $58

SVS Flaxman Vineyard Shiraz 2004 This is a Barossa shiraz of the most monumental proportions, heaving with black plums, liquorice, tar, coal steam and a wall of firm, fine tannins. It finds its own sense of balance, holding impressive freshness at almost a decade of age. Screwcap. 15.5% alc. **Rating** 94 **To** 2019 $90 TS

Rod & Spur Barossa Valley Shiraz Cabernet 2009 Deep red-purple; retains the generosity expected of Rockford, but also has exemplary balance, even finesse, to its amalgam of blackberry, blackcurrant and plum fruit; the oak is subtle, the tannins fine. May well outlive its cork. 14.5% alc. **Rating** 94 **To** 2024 $31

Rifle Range Cabernet Sauvignon 2010 A bright and fragrant red bouquet, showing a little crushed leaf complexity and well-handled oak; the palate is focused and linear, with the tannins and acid working seamlessly together for a long and even finish. Cork. 14.5% alc. **Rating** 94 **To** 2025 $39 BE

ŸŸŸŸŸ **Moppa Springs Grenache Mataro Shiraz 2008 Rating** 91 **To** 2017 $25
Hand Picked Eden Valley Riesling 2010 Rating 90 **To** 2016 $21
Local Growers Barossa Semillon 2008 Rating 90 **To** 2016 $20 BE
Barossa Valley Alicante Bouchet 2012 Rating 90 **To** 2014 $18

Rockridge Estate   ★★★

PO Box 374, Kent Town, SA 5071 **Region** Clare Valley
T (08) 8376 9563 **www**.rockridgewines.com.au **Open** Not
Winemaker Justin Ardill (red), Peter Leske (white) **Est.** 2007 **Dozens** 7500 **Vyds** 40ha
In the Vine Pull Scheme of the 1980s, the 120ha Leasingham Wines vineyard in the hills immediately above the hamlet of Leasingham was removed. Partially replanted in '99, this precious block of terra rossa over deep limestone is producing outstanding grapes, sold to Tim Adams, Kilikanoon, Reilly's, Claymore, Old Station, Foster's and Yalumba. In 2007 owners Andrew Miller, Richard Yeend and Justin Ardill decided to retain a significant part of the crop to produce Riesling, Shiraz and Sparkling Riesling, purchasing sauvignon blanc from premium cool-climate regions. Rockridge Estate is a custom label exclusively sold through Cellarbrations, The Bottle-O and IGA plus Liquor.

ŸŸŸŸ   **Sauvignon Blanc 2012** Pale quartz; the climate/terroir of the Clare Valley doesn't suit sauvignon blanc, and in this hyper-competitive sector, the bland, inoffensive flavours of this wine can't compete on any criteria other than price, however well made it may be. Screwcap. 12.5% alc. **Rating** 87 **To** 2013 $15

Rocky Passes Estate   ★★★★★

1590 Highlands Road, Whiteheads Creek, Vic 3660 **Region** Upper Goulburn
T (03) 5796 9366 **www**.rockypasses.com.au **Open** Sun 11–5, or by appt
Winemaker Vitto Oles **Est.** 2000 **Dozens** 500 **Vyds** 2ha
Vitto Oles and Candi Westney run this tiny, cool-climate, carbon-neutral venture situated at the southern end of the Strathbogie Ranges, which in fact falls in the Upper Goulburn region. They have planted 1.6ha of shiraz and 0.4ha of viognier, growing the vines with minimal irrigation and preferring organic and biodynamic soil treatments. Vitto is also a fine furniture designer and maker, with a studio at Rocky Passes. No wine was made in 2011 due to vintage conditions; the '10 Syrah was still available at the time of going to print.

ŸŸŸŸŸ **Syrah 2010** Good colour; a wine that builds on the promise of the '09, with a
✪   complex bouquet of leather, spice and licorice over black fruits, the medium- to full-bodied palate providing a replay of the bouquet, but with greater intensity; excellent cellaring potential, and outstanding value. Diam. 14.5% alc. **Rating** 94 **To** 2025 $18

Rocland Estate

PO Box 679, Nuriootpa, SA 5355 **Region** Barossa Valley
T (08) 8562 2142 **www**.roclandestate.com **Open** By appt
Winemaker Sarah Siddons **Est.** 2000 **Dozens** 21 000 **Vyds** 6ha
Rocland Estate is primarily a bulk winemaking facility for contract work, but Frank Rocca
does have 6ha of shiraz to make the Rocland wines, supplemented by contract-grown grapes.
Largely destined for export markets but with retail distribution in Adelaide. Rocland releases
wines under the Lot 147, Kilroy Was Here, Duck Duck Goose, Chocolate Box and the
charmingly named Ass Kisser labels. Exports to the UK, the US, Singapore, China and NZ.

ŸŸŸŸŸ **Chocolate Box A Variety of Indulgence Shiraz 2010** Inky purple; a densely
packed wine achieved with super-ripe grapes; its a long way from my preferred
style, but the fruit is like a black hole in space, sucking any alcohol heat, dead fruit
and tannins from sight. Screwcap. 15.5% alc. **Rating** 90 **To** 2020 $25

ŸŸŸŸ **Chocolate Box A Variety of Indulgence GSM 2010** **Rating** 89
To 2017 $25
Chocolate Box A Variety of Indulgence Cabernet Sauvignon 2010
Rating 87 **To** 2015 $25

Rohrlach Family Wines

PO Box 864, Nuriootpa, SA 5355 **Region** Barossa Valley
T (08) 8562 4121 **www**.rohrlachfamilywines.com.au **Open** Not
Winemaker Peter Schell (Contract) **Est.** 2000 **Dozens** 1000 **Vyds** 160.6ha
Brothers Kevin, Graham and Wayne Rohrlach, with wives Lyn, Lynette and Kaylene, are
third-generation owners of prime vineyard land, the first plantings made back in 1930 by their
paternal grandfather. Until 2000 the grapes were sold to two leading Barossa wineries, but (in
a common story) in that year some of the grapes were retained to make the first vintage of
what became Rohrlach Family Wines. In '03 the family received the ultimate local accolade
when the Barons of the Barossa gave them the title of 'Vignerons of the Year'.

ŸŸŸŸŸ **Mum's Block Barossa Valley Shiraz 2010** Strong red-purple; while medium-
to full-bodied, all the components of blackberry, plum and licorice fruit, ripe
tannins and vanillin oak, are in balance, ensuring a long and prosperous life.
Screwcap. 14.5% alc. **Rating** 94 **To** 2040 $43

ŸŸŸŸ **Family Reserve Barossa Valley Merlot 2011** **Rating** 89 **To** 2015 $26
Family Reserve Barossa Valley Cabernet Sauvignon 2011 **Rating** 87
To 2014 $26

Rolf Binder Veritas Winery

Cnr Seppeltsfield Road/Stelzer Road, Tanunda, SA 5352 **Region** Barossa Valley
T (08) 8562 3300 **www**.rolfbinder.com **Open** Mon–Sat 10–4.30
Winemaker Rolf Binder, Christa Deans **Est.** 1955 **Dozens** 30 000 **Vyds** 36ha
The change of accent from Veritas to Rolf Binder came with the 50th anniversary of the
winery, established by the parents of Rolf and sister Christa Deans. The growth in production
and sales is due to the quality of the wines rather than the (hitherto) rather laid-back approach
to marketing. The winery produces a full range of all the main white and red wines sourced
from the Barossa and Eden Valleys. It has had conspicuous success with Semillon at the Barossa
Valley Wine Show, but the red wines are equally commendable. Exports to all major markets.

ŸŸŸŸŸ **Eden Valley Riesling 2012** A perfumed lime blossom bouquet leads into a very
❂ appealing juicy palate, with more lime juice on the finish than many from the
vintage. Bargain. Screwcap. 12.5% alc. **Rating** 94 **To** 2018 $18
JJ Hahn Western Ridge 1975 Planting Barossa Valley Shiraz 2010
Good purple-crimson; the bouquet is fragrant and rich, the medium-bodied palate
a mix of silk and velvet textures, the fruit a vibrant range of red and black berries
and spice; ultra fine-boned tannins on the finish underline the quality of the wine.
Screwcap. 14% alc. **Rating** 94 **To** 2030 $28

Hanisch Barossa Valley Shiraz 2010 While sitting at the big end of the Barossa spectrum, doesn't overstep on ripeness, and demands some time to fully integrate; the bouquet has a prominent splash of toasty oak sitting atop abundant black fruits, bitter chocolate and violets; the full-bodied palate is expressive, thickly textured, and long and unevolved with the oak once again coming to the fore on the finish. Cork. 14.5% alc. **Rating** 94 **To** 2025 $125 BE

✪ **JJ Hahn Reginald Barossa Valley Shiraz Cabernet Sauvignon 2010** Richly robed and layered with a cascade of black fruits and a touch of cassis from the splash of cabernet; cedar and mocha nuances are offset by gently savoury tannins. Screwcap. 13.5% alc. **Rating** 94 **To** 2030 $18

Heinrich Barossa Valley Shiraz Mataro Grenache 2010 Bright crimson-purple; what a pleasure to taste this blend at such a modest alcohol level, which has provided a vibrant and fresh display of plum, spice and fragrant red fruits variously contributed by the components, with some very old vines providing part of the wine. Screwcap. 13.5% alc. **Rating** 94 **To** 2025 $32

ҶҶҶҶҶ **JJ Hahn Homestead Barossa Valley Cabernet Sauvignon 2010**
✪ The colour is excellent, the cassis and redcurrant fruit vibrantly flavoured, the tannins ripe. How good would it have been without the American oak we will never know, but it's still great value. Screwcap. 13.5% alc. **Rating** 93 **To** 2030 $18

Heinrich Shiraz Mataro Grenache 2009 **Rating** 92 **To** 2024 $32

✪ **Barossa Valley Shiraz 2011** Medium red-purple; some of the best old vine shiraz has been used in this wine and it has paid dividends. It is a very attractive, juicy medium-bodied wine with red berry, licorice and a nicely judged touch of oak. Screwcap. 13.5% alc. **Rating** 91 **To** 2016 $18

Eden Valley Shiraz 2010 **Rating** 91 **To** 2018 $25

Rolf Binder's Bull's Blood Shiraz Mataro Pressings 2009 **Rating** 91 **To** 2018 $45 BE

✪ **Veritas Barossa Valley Mourvedre Grenache 2012** Bright and fresh with jubey red confectionery fruits offset by a fragrant lick of sage; light- to medium-bodied with lively acidity and an uncomplicated fruity conclusion. Screwcap. 13.5% alc. **Rating** 90 **To** 2018 $20 BE

ҶҶҶҶ **Veritas Tramino Frizzante 2012** This breaks the mould; a blend of
✪ gewurztraminer and white frontignac, it is crammed with sweet fruit flavours offset by just a touch of spritz; unambiguously dessert style. Screwcap. 9% alc. **Rating** 89 **To** 2016 $15

Romney Park Wines   ★★★★★

Lot 100 Johnson Road, Balhannah, SA 5242 **Region** Adelaide Hills
T (08) 8398 0698 **www.**romneyparkwines.com.au **Open** By appt
Winemaker Rod and Rachel Short **Est.** 1997 **Dozens** 1000 **Vyds** 3ha
Rod and Rachel Short began the planting of chardonnay, shiraz and pinot noir in 1997. The first vintage was in 2002, made from 100% estate-grown grapes. Yields are limited to 3.7–5 tonnes per hectare for the red wines, and 2–3 tonnes for the Chardonnay. The vineyard is managed organically, with guinea fowl cleaning up the insects, all vines hand-picked and hand-pruned. In every way (including the wines) has the beauty of a hand-painted miniature. Exports to China.

ҶҶҶҶҶ **Adelaide Hills Pinot Noir 2010** Estate-grown clones 777, 114, 115 and MV6 yielding 3.7 tonnes per hectare; 80% whole berries, 20% whole bunches; 10-day cold soak, then wild yeast fermentation; matured in used barriques. All this paid big dividends, with excellent colour, a complex, focused and balanced palate; long and stylish. Diam. 13.7% alc. **Rating** 96 **To** 2018 $45

Reserve Adelaide Hills Shiraz 2010 A row-by-row hand-picked selection of the best grapes; 100% cultured yeast for open fermentation in 50% new French barriques; this has another level of velvety fruit density, which absorbed the higher percentage of new oak without a murmur; the result is a luscious yet perfectly balanced wine. Diam. 13.7% alc. **Rating** 96 **To** 2035 $55

Adelaide Hills Sauvignon Blanc 2012 Hand-picked, whole bunch-pressed in a basket press (a challenging task), wild yeast barrel-fermented in 3-year-old French oak, partial mlf and 9 months in barrel followed; obviously a highly detailed and textured wine, with a precisely calibrated mix of citrus and tropical fruit flavours. Diam. 13% alc. **Rating** 94 **To** 2014 $35

Adelaide Hills Shiraz 2010 Good red-purple colour and clarity; has an abundance of black cherry, licorice and spice fruit; the tannin and oak contributions are notably symbiotic. Diam. 13.7% alc. **Rating** 94 **To** 2030 $45

Adelaide Hills Blanc de Blancs 2010 Brilliant straw-green; fermented in this bottle and hand-disgorged by Rod Short on 1 Aug '12, 2 years since tiraged in Aug '10. Barrel-fermented base wine with abundant white peach, honey/cream and brioche. Crown seal. 12.5% alc. **Rating** 94 **To** 2015 $42

Three Guineas Adelaide Hills Pinot Noir 2010 Clear, light, bright crimson; has bell-clear varietal expression; open-fermented with wild yeast, then matured for 18 months in older French oak barriques; spicy red fruits and silky tannins are the strong points of a very well-priced – and well-balanced – Pinot Noir. Diam. 13.5% alc. **Rating** 92 **To** 2015 $19

Ros Ritchie Wines ★★★★★

52 Crosby's Lane, Mansfield, Vic 3722 **Region** Upper Goulburn
T 0448 900 541 **www**.rosritchiewines.com **Open** By appt
Winemaker Ros Ritchie **Est.** 2008 **Dozens** 2000 **Vyds** 5ha
This is the new venture of Ros Ritchie and husband John. Ros was winemaker at the Ritchie family's Delatite winery from 1981 to 2006, but moved on to establish her own winery with John in '08. They lease a vineyard planted to merlot and cabernet sauvignon on a northeastern slope close to Mansfield. They source their white wines from growers who work in tandem with them to provide high-quality grapes. Foremost are Gumbleton's Vineyard, Retief's Vineyard and Baxendale's Vineyard, the last planted by the very experienced viticulturist Jim Baxendale (and wife Ruth) high on the Woodfield Plateau above the King River Valley. All the vineyards are managed with minimal spray regimes. Exports to Hong Kong and China.

Dead Man's Hill Vineyard Gewurztraminer 2012 Ros Ritchie has always been noted for her Gewurztraminers, the reputation gained at Delatite, and she has carried it on to her new winery. Here spice and rose petal aromas flow through to the vibrant palate, which finishes with cleansing acidity, not phenolics. Screwcap. 13% alc. **Rating** 94 **To** 2016 $25

Baxendale's Vineyard Cabernet Sauvignon 2010 Medium red-purple; juicy cassis fruit is the mainstay of the bouquet and palate, the length and carry of the varietal fruit growing each time you revisit the wine and also dwell on its aftertaste; considerable panache and elegance at work. Screwcap. 14% alc. **Rating** 94 **To** 2020 $27

Barwite Vineyard Riesling 2012 **Rating** 93 **To** 2020 $25
Cowan's Vineyard Tempranillo 2011 **Rating** 93 **To** 2018 $27
Timbertop Vineyard Nebbiolo 2010 **Rating** 90 **To** 2016 $27

Rosabrook Margaret River Wine ★★★★★

Yungarra Estate, Lot 68 Yungarra Drive, Quedjinup, WA 6281 **Region** Margaret River
T (08) 9368 4555 **www**.rosabrook.com.au **Open** Not
Winemaker Brian Fletcher **Est.** 1980 **Dozens** 8000 **Vyds** 10ha
Mike and Sally Calneggia have been at the forefront of vineyard development in Margaret River over the past decade, but also have various winemaking interests. The original Rosabrook Estate vineyards were established progressively between 1984 and '96. In 2007 Rosabrook relocated its estate vineyard to the northwestern end of the Margaret River wine region, overlooking Geographe Bay and the Indian Ocean. The warm days and cool nights, influenced by the ocean, result in slow, mild-ripening conditions. Exports to Dubai, Hong Kong and China.

ΨΨΨΨΨ **Single Vineyard Estate Chardonnay 2012** Light straw-green; different batches
are fermented separately and then blended before maturation in new French oak.
An unusual approach, but the quality of the fruit shines through like a beacon in
this elegant wine, with classic white peach and grapefruit flavours, the finish as fresh
and breezy as a spring day. Screwcap. 13.5% alc. **Rating** 95 **To** 2019 $40
Single Vineyard Estate Cabernet Sauvignon 2011 Deep crimson-purple;
classic Margaret River cabernet, flooded with blackcurrant/cassis and redcurrant
fruit, seamlessly folded into the new French oak in which it was matured; the
tannin management is exemplary. Screwcap. 14.5% alc. **Rating** 95 **To** 2026 $40

ΨΨΨΨΨ
✪ **Sauvignon Blanc Semillon 2012** A fresh and elegant 57/43% blend, the
complexity coming from the multi-vineyard sources and the varietal blend rather
than work in the winery; the flavours are finely strung between pea and tropical
fruits, the finish long. Screwcap. 13% alc. **Rating** 92 **To** 2014 $18
✪ **Cabernet Merlot 2011** Bright purple-crimson; vibrantly fresh and juicy cassis
fruit drives the medium-bodied palate through to a long, lingering conclusion.
Time in bottle will build the complexity it presently lacks (if that is what you
want). Screwcap. 14% alc. **Rating** 90 **To** 2018 $20

Rosby   ★★★★

122 Strikes Lane, Mudgee, NSW 2850 **Region** Mudgee
T (02) 6373 3856 **www**.rosby.com.au **Open** By appt
Winemaker Tim Stevens **Est.** 1996 **Dozens** 1000 **Vyds** 6ha
Gerald and Kaye Norton-Knight have 4ha of shiraz and 2ha of cabernet sauvignon established
on what is truly a unique site in Mudgee. Many vignerons like to think that their vineyard has
special qualities, but in this instance the belief is well based. It is situated in a small valley, with
unusual red basalt over a quartz gravel structure, encouraging deep root growth, and making
the use of water far less critical than normal. Tim Stevens of Huntington Estate has purchased
some of the ample production, as well as making the Rosby wines.

ΨΨΨΨΨ
✪ **Mudgee Shiraz 2010** Good hue and depth; this is a truly delicious medium-
bodied Shiraz, which has a strong sense of place to its core of plum and blackberry
fruit, tannins ripe and soft, the oak totally integrated. Good value. Screwcap.
14.1% alc. **Rating** 91 **To** 2025 $18
✪ **Mudgee Cabernet Sauvignon 2010** Good colour; an attractive Cabernet,
ticking all the boxes at this price; the blackcurrant fruit is strongly varietal, and the
tannins and oak are well balanced and equally well integrated. Screwcap. 13.4% alc.
Rating 91 **To** 2018 $18

Rosemount Estate   ★★★★★

114 Chaffeys Road, McLaren Vale, SA 5171 **Region** McLaren Vale
T (08) 8323 6220 **www**.rosemountestate.com.au **Open** Mon–Sat 10–5, Sun & public
hols 11–5
Winemaker Matt Koch, Andrew Locke, Randall Cummins **Est.** 1888 **Dozens** 3 million
Vyds 441ha
Rosemount Estate has vineyards in McLaren Vale, Fleurieu, Coonawarra and Robe that are
the anchor for its top-of-the-range wines. It also has access to other TWE estate-grown grapes,
but the major part of its intake for the Diamond Label wines is supplied by contract growers
across SA, NSW, Vic and WA. As the tasting notes show, the quality and range of the wines has
greatly improved over the past few years as Rosemount Estate endeavours to undo the damage
done to the brand around the new millennium. Abandoning the diamond-shaped bottle is but
one tangible signpost of the future. Exports to all major markets.

ΨΨΨΨΨ **Limited Release McLaren Vale Cabernet Sauvignon 2010** Another wine
in the Rosemount Estate portfolio to show the determination of TWE and its
winemakers to revive Rosemount's reputation. This is a classy cassis-accented,
medium-bodied Cabernet, with quality French oak in balanced support on the
long finish. Screwcap. 14% alc. **Rating** 95 **To** 2025 $30

Nursery Project Langhorne Creek Fiano 2012 One of the most interesting new/alternative varieties. It has a bracing and crisp texture with savoury pear and apple skin flavours, and well above average length. Full of interest and promise. Screwcap. 13% alc. **Rating** 94 **To** 2015 $25

McLaren Vale G.S.M 2011 No shrinking violet, this rendition of an Australian classic combines red and black fruits, sage, licorice and violets on the bouquet; the palate borders on full-bodied, revealing serious intent and layers of flavour and texture; long, luscious and poised, and extremely well executed. Screwcap. 14% alc. **Rating** 94 **To** 2018 $40 BE

Single Vineyard McLaren Vale Cabernet Sauvignon 2011 Vibrant purple hue; impressively concentrated, showing essency blackcurrant and cedar aromas, with just a suggestion of crushed leaf; the palate is full-bodied and thickly textured, with lashings of black fruit, well-handled fine oak and a long and succulent finish. Screwcap. 14% alc. **Rating** 94 **To** 2025 $50 BE

♀♀♀♀♀ Balmoral McLaren Vale Syrah 2011 **Rating** 93 **To** 2022 $75 BE

✪ District Release Robe Chardonnay 2012 Light straw-green; true to its region, this is an elegant, fresh and lively wine, the winemaking team wisely keeping oak to a minimum; white peach, grapefruit and apple all contribute to the fragrant bouquet and long palate. Screwcap. 13.5% alc. **Rating** 92 **To** 2015 $20

Nursery Project McLaren Vale Mataro 2011 **Rating** 92 **To** 2018 $30

✪ District Release McLaren Vale Traditional 2011 As always, a polished wine that exhibits the hallmarks of the varieties within (cabernet sauvignon, merlot and petit verdot), showing cassis, cedar, violets and a suggestion of brambly complexity; medium-bodied, vibrant and full of energy and verve, the fragrant finish is poised and precise; will age gracefully. Screwcap. 13.5% alc. **Rating** 91 **To** 2022 $20 BE

✪ Bright and Fresh Semillon Sauvignon Blanc 2012 Lives up to its name, bright and fresh, but this is not achieved at the expense of its tropical lime juice flavours, the low alcohol helping to keep the finish lively. Screwcap. 11.5% alc. **Rating** 90 **To** 2014 $12

✪ Diamond Label Shiraz 2012 Good purple-crimson; over-delivers on price, with aromatic red and black cherry fruit on its bouquet and medium-bodied palate; fine tannins and a touch of oak complete the picture. Screwcap. 13.5% alc. **Rating** 90 **To** 2020 $16

♀♀♀♀ Fruity and Fulsome Grenache Shiraz 2012 The message on the label is
✪ fulfilled with a vibrant and attractive, medium-bodied expression of this traditional blend; designed with immediate consumption in mind, and when made like this, why not? Screwcap. 13% alc. **Rating** 89 **To** 2015 $12 BE

Rosenthal Wines ★★★★☆

PO Box 1458, South Perth, WA 6951 **Region** Blackwood Valley
T 0407 773 966 **www**.rosenthalwines.com.au **Open** Not
Winemaker Matilda's Estate (Coby Ladwig) **Est.** 2001 **Dozens** 1000 **Vyds** 4ha
Perth medical specialist Dr John Rosenthal heads Rosenthal Wines, which is a small part of the much larger 180ha Springfield Park cattle stud situated between Bridgetown and Manjimup. He acquired the property from Gerald and Marjorie Richings, who in 1997 had planted a small vineyard as a minor diversification. The Rosenthals extended the vineyard, which is equally divided between shiraz and cabernet sauvignon. The wines have had significant show success, chiefly in WA-based shows.

♀♀♀♀♀ Richings Shiraz 2011 Medium to full red-purple; the bouquet and palate do show the new French oak first up, but then the concentrated, full-bodied black fruits, licorice and spice fruit come through with a swathe of ripe tannins. Will flourish over decades to come. Screwcap. 14% alc. **Rating** 93 **To** 2036 $25

The Naomi Cabernet Shiraz 2011 An estate-grown, 60/40% blend, matured in new French oak, elegant and poised, with a savoury/spicy cast to the fruit and its supporting tannins. The oak is certainly evident, but not excessive, and adds to the length of the palate. Screwcap. 14% alc. **Rating** 93 **To** 2026 $30

Rosenvale Wines   ★★★★★

Lot 385 Railway Terrace, Nuriootpa, SA 5355 **Region** Barossa Valley
T 0407 390 788 **www**.rosenvale.com.au **Open** By appt
Winemaker James Rosenzweig, Chris Taylor **Est.** 1999 **Dozens** 2000 **Vyds** 105ha
The Rosenzweig family vineyards, some old and some new, are planted to riesling, semillon, chardonnay, grenache, shiraz, merlot and cabernet sauvignon. Most of the grapes are sold to other producers, but since 2000 some have been retained and vinified for release under the Rosenvale label. A cellar door opened in 2012.

ŸŸŸŸŸ Old Vines Reserve Barossa Valley Shiraz 2010 Altogether superior to its '10 Estate sibling, with greater depth, intensity and focus to its black fruits; the tannin structure and oak are precisely balanced. Diam. 14.5% alc. **Rating** 94 **To** 2025 $39
Old Vines Reserve Barossa Valley Cabernet Sauvignon 2010 The vintage encouraged full varietal expression without elevated alcohol, as this wine handsomely shows; no more than medium-bodied, the tannins are fine and soft, the French oak in balance. Diam. 14.5% alc. **Rating** 94 **To** 2025 $39

ŸŸŸŸŸ Estate Barossa Cabernet Sauvignon 2010 **Rating** 91 **To** 2018 $24
Estate Barossa Valley Shiraz 2010 **Rating** 90 **To** 2020 $24

Rosily Vineyard   ★★★★★

871 Yelverton Road, Wilyabrup, WA 6284 **Region** Margaret River
T (08) 9755 6336 **www**.rosily.com.au **Open** 7 days Dec–Jan 11–5
Winemaker Mike Lemmes **Est.** 1994 **Dozens** 7000 **Vyds** 12.28ha
Partners Mike and Barb Scott, and Ken and Dot Allan acquired the Rosily Vineyard site in 1994, and planted to sauvignon blanc, semillon, chardonnay, cabernet sauvignon, merlot, shiraz, grenache and cabernet franc. The first crops were sold to other makers in the region, but by '99 Rosily had built a 120-tonne capacity winery. Since then it has gone from strength to strength, all of its estate-grown grapes being vinified under the Rosily Vineyard label. Exports to the UK, the Maldives, Singapore and China.

ŸŸŸŸŸ Margaret River Sauvignon Blanc 2012 Pale straw-green; creative winemaking
✪ (10% fermented in new French oak) and high-quality fruit have resulted in a vibrant wine, with very good mouthfeel to the intense flavours of lemongrass, gooseberry and stone fruit; a precisely pitched finish seals the deal. Exceptional value. Screwcap. 13% alc. **Rating** 94 **To** 2014 $19
✪ Margaret River Chardonnay 2011 A convincing example of Margaret River chardonnay, the depth of the fruit from a mix of the Mendoza clone (60%) and others, including the Dijon clones; barrel fermentation in 60% new French oak frames the assemblage of white peach, nectarine and grapefruit varietal flavours plus toasty cashew notes ex oak. Screwcap. 13.5% alc. **Rating** 94 **To** 2018 $23

ŸŸŸŸŸ Margaret River Semillon Sauvignon Blanc 2012 This wine has a tightly
✪ focused and structured palate with grass, herb and lemon zest to the fore, and the barest hint of toasty oak. It has considerable length, and will cellar well. Exceptional value. 520 dozen made. Screwcap. 13% alc. **Rating** 93 **To** 2016 $20
Margaret River Cabernet Sauvignon 2010 **Rating** 93 **To** 2025 $25
✪ Margaret River Merlot 2010 Light red-purple; while only light- to medium-bodied, and with oak obvious throughout, surprises with the way the plum and red berry flavours build progressively through the length of the palate and into the aftertaste, assisted by fine-grained tannins. Screwcap. 14% alc. **Rating** 90 **To** 2018 $20
Margaret River Cabernet Sauvignon 2011 **Rating** 90 **To** 2024 $25

Ross Hill Wines   ★★★★★

134 Wallace Lane, Orange, NSW 2800 **Region** Orange
T (02) 6365 3223 **www**.rosshillwines.com.au **Open** W'ends & public hols 10–4, or by appt
Winemaker Phil Kerney **Est.** 1994 **Dozens** 15 000 **Vyds** 18.2ha

Owned by the Robson and Jones families. Chardonnay, merlot, sauvignon blanc, cabernet franc, shiraz and pinot noir have been established on north-facing, gentle slopes at an elevation of 800m. No insecticides are used in the vineyard, the grapes are hand-picked and the vines are hand-pruned. The arrival of Phil Kerney from the Mornington Peninsula is significant, as is the increase from 12ha to just over 18ha of estate vineyards, production increasing from 300 dozen to its present level. The onsite winery, opened in time for the 2009 vintage, has also had a major impact. Exports to Singapore, the Maldives, Sri Lanka, Hong Kong and China.

🍷🍷🍷🍷 **Pinnacle Series Orange Sauvignon Blanc 2012** Whole bunch-pressed and wild-fermented; picked at a lower baume than Jessica & Lily, which gives it a stronger minerally base and more focus and power; the flavours of citrus and passionfruit are evident right from the first taste, continuing to build all the way to the finish and aftertaste. Screwcap. 11.5% alc. **Rating** 95 **To** 2014 $27
Pinnacle Series Orange Chardonnay 2012 Whole bunch-pressed and taken direct to French barrels for wild yeast fermentation. Intense white peach and nectarine fruit is accompanied by an attractive hint of the French oak. Screwcap. 12.1% alc. **Rating** 94 **To** 2020 $32
Orange Vintage Brut 2009 Pale green-straw; chardonnay and pinot noir, wild yeast-fermented, with 3 years on yeast lees; has considerable flavour, complexity, bordering on savoury. Diam. 12.5% alc. **Rating** 94 **To** 2018 $36

🍷🍷🍷🍷 **Jessica & Lily Orange Sauvignon Blanc 2012** Pale colour; has strength to
✪ the texture and structure that surround the tropical fruit. A prime example of the synergy between region and variety showing through in sauvignon blanc at this price. Screwcap. 12.2% alc. **Rating** 92 **To** 2014 $18
Pinnacle Series Orange Pinot Gris 2012 Rating 92 **To** 2014 $22

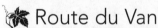 Route du Van ★★★★

PO Box 1465, Warrnambool, Vic 3280 **Region** Various
T (03) 5561 7422 **www**.routeduvan.com **Open** Not
Winemaker Tod Dexter **Est.** 2010 **Dozens** 3000
The Dexter (Todd and Debbie) and Bird (Ian and Ruth, David and Marie) families have been making or selling wine for 30 years. They were holidaying in the picturesque vineyards and ancient Bastide villages of southwest France when they decided to do something new that was all about fun: fun for them, and fun for the consumers who bought their wines, which would have a distinctive southern French feel to them. Thus the first two wines are a Viognier Chardonnay and a Dolcetto Shiraz. The prices are also friendly, at $17–20 a bottle, bistros one of the target markets. Exports to the UK and the US.

🍷🍷🍷🍷 **Yarra Valley Gioia Bianco 2011** A League of Nations blend of sauvignon blanc,
✪ pinot gris, viognier and chardonnay; the team played with fire in ending up with this alcohol level, but there are plenty of exuberant and ripe fruit flavours offset by zingy acidity. Screwcap. 11.8% alc. **Rating** 90 **To** 2014 $19
Geelong Pinot Noir 2011 Light, clear red showing the first stage of development; while light-bodied thanks to the vintage, there is good varietal expression to the spiced cherry aromas and flavours, and balanced texture/structure. Not forced to pretend there was more fruit to play with. Drink now. Screwcap. 13% alc. **Rating** 90 **To** 2014 $19

Rowanston on the Track ★★★☆

2710 Burke & Wills Track, Glenhope, Vic 3444 **Region** Macedon Ranges
T (03) 5425 5492 **www**.rowanston.com **Open** 7 days 10–5
Winemaker Laura Sparrow, John Frederiksen **Est.** 2003 **Dozens** 5000 **Vyds** 9.3ha
John and Marilyn Frederiksen are no strangers to grapegrowing and winemaking in the Macedon Ranges. They founded Metcalfe Valley Vineyard in 1995, planting 5.6ha of shiraz, going on to win gold medals at local wine shows. They sold the vineyard in early 2003 and moved to their new property, which now has over 9ha of vines (shiraz, riesling, sauvignon blanc, merlot and pinot noir). The heavy red soils and basalt ridges hold moisture, which

allows watering to be kept to a minimum. Rowanston has joined the Wine Export Initiative (WEXI), a co-operative of 35 small wineries across Australia that has recently opened two retail outlets in Singapore. Exports to the UK, Hong Kong and Singapore.

ŸŸŸŸŸ **Macedon Ranges Riesling 2012** Pale quartz-green; an interesting wine, early-picked, and with only the barest hint of sweetness on the aftertaste; attractive, juicy lime and apple flavours provide context and mouthfeel. Screwcap. 11% alc. **Rating** 92 **To** 2020 $20

Rudderless   ★★★★★

Victory Hotel, Main South Road, Sellicks Beach, SA 5174 **Region** McLaren Vale
T (08) 8556 3083 **www**.rudderlesswines.com.au **Open** 7 days
Winemaker Pete Fraser (Contract) **Est.** 2004 **Dozens** 450 **Vyds** 2ha
It's a long story how Doug Govan, owner of the Victory Hotel (circa 1858), came to choose the name Rudderless for his vineyard adjacent to the hotel. The vineyard, divided among shiraz, graciano, grenache, malbec, mataro and viognier, surrounds the hotel, which is situated in the foothills of the Southern Willunga Escarpment as it falls into the sea. The wines have had little attention outside SA; partly because Doug sells most of the wine through the Victory Hotel, and partly because of his laid-back attitude, which means he has kept a low profile.

ŸŸŸŸŸ **Sellicks Hill McLaren Vale Grenache 2010** Excellent colour for grenache, vibrant crimson-purple, and what follows doesn't disappoint; the bouquet is very fragrant, in tune with the bright red fruits of the palate, and the silky tannins running through its length. All this at 13.5% alcohol. Cellaring potential? Yes, but why stand by and wait for the wine to lose its vibrancy? Screwcap. **Rating** 96 **To** 2018 $35
Sellicks Hill McLaren Vale Shiraz Malbec 2010 Medium red-purple; even at its most southerly point, McLaren Vale still stamps its terroir on its wines with that dark chocolate character. This wine brings malbec's plummy fruit into play, joining with the shiraz to bring a juicy energy and supple flow to the wine, and to its lively finish. Screwcap. 13.5% alc. **Rating** 94 **To** 2025 $35

ŸŸŸŸŸ **Sellicks Hill McLaren Vale Malbec 2010 Rating** 92 **To** 2017 $35

🍂 Rusty Mutt   ★★★★★

26 Columbia Avenue, Clapham, SA 5062 (postal) **Region** McLaren Vale
T 0402 050 820 **www**.rustymutt.com.au **Open** Not
Winemaker Scott Heidrich **Est.** 2009 **Dozens** 500
Scott Heidrich has lived under the shadow of Geoff Merrill for 20 years, but has partially emerged into the sunlight with his virtual micro-winery. Back in 2006 close friends and family (Nicole and Alan Francis, Stuart Evans, David Lipman and Phil Cole) persuaded Scott to take advantage of the wonderful quality of the grapes that year and make a small batch of shiraz. They adroitly skipped the '07, '08 and '09 vintages given the climate and other issues of those years, and returned to the fray in '10. The wines are made at a friend's micro-winery in McLaren Flat. The name Rusty Mutt comes from Scott's interest in Chinese astrology, and Feng Shui; Scott was born in the year of the Dog, with the dominant element being metal, hence Rusty Mutt. What the ownership group doesn't drink is sold through fine wine retailers and selected restaurants, with a small amount exported to Singapore.

ŸŸŸŸŸ **Shiraz 2010** Hand-picked, open-fermented, hand-plunged, basket-pressed. Vivid purple-crimson, it has a juicy, supple palate with red and black fruits coated by McLaren Vale chocolate, the texture silky, the structure well balanced. Very attractive wine. Screwcap. 14.5% alc. **Rating** 94 **To** 2025 $28
Shiraz 2006 Shows the development expected of a 7-year-old Shiraz, but it has plenty of life left in it, and still has excellent regional typicity with its mix of black fruits and dark chocolate. Screwcap. 14% alc. **Rating** 94 **To** 2019 $25

Rutherglen Estates ★★★★

Cnr Great Northern Road/Murray Valley Highway, Rutherglen, Vic 3685 **Region** Rutherglen
T (02) 6032 7999 **www**.rutherglenestates.com.au **Open** At Tuileries Complex,
Rutherglen 7 days 10–6
Winemaker Marc Scalzo **Est.** 1997 **Dozens** 20 000 **Vyds** 26.5ha

Rutherglen Estates is one of the larger growers in the region. The focus of the business has
changed in recent times: it has slightly reduced its own fruit intake while maintaining its
contract processing. Production has turned to table wine made from parcels of fruit hand-
selected from the five Rutherglen vineyard sites. Rhône and Mediterranean varieties such
as durif, viognier, shiraz and sangiovese are a move away from traditional varieties, as are
alternative varieties including zinfandel, fiano and savagnin. Exports to the UK, the US and
other major markets.

ŸŸŸŸŸ **Renaissance Viognier Roussanne Marsanne 2010** Each variety contributes
its personality without treading on the toes of the others; there is peach, apricot
and a freshness from the marsanne. Another few years could see the wine build
even more. Screwcap. 13% alc. **Rating** 91 **To** 2016 $31

✪ **Single Vineyard Shiraz 2010** A remarkably, unexpectedly, elegant wine, the
answer lying in its modest alcohol. It allows the fragrant red berry fruits at its
heart free rein, and the winemaker has very sensibly backed off on oak and tannin
extraction. Screwcap. 13% alc. **Rating** 90 **To** 2016 $16

Single Vineyard Durif 2009 Deep purple-crimson (what else?); has the dark
fruit bouquet and full-bodied palate of tar, earth, blackberry and licorice; typically,
after all this thunder and lightning, the tannins are soft. Screwcap. 14.5% alc.
Rating 90 **To** 2020 $23

ŸŸŸŸ **Burgoyne's Block Grenache Shiraz Mourvedre 2009** A thoroughly
✪ enjoyable wine with no pretensions to complexity or longevity, its red fruits
sprinkled with spice and pepper, plus the ghost of French oak and tannins walking
the ramparts of the finish. Screwcap. 14% alc. **Rating** 89 **To** 2015 $16

✪ **Single Vineyard Pinot Grigio 2012** A very faint pink tinge to the colour
heralds some positive grigio fruit; pear and almond is a fair summation. Well
priced. Screwcap. 13% alc. **Rating** 88 **To** 2014 $14

Single Vineyard Arneis 2012 Rating 88 **To** 2014 $17
BdV Fortified Early Harvest Muscat 2012 Rating 88 **To** 2014 $21
Single Vineyard Savagnin 2012 Rating 87 **To** 2014 $17
Single Vineyard Tempranillo 2011 Rating 87 **To** 2015 $21

Rymill Coonawarra ★★★★★

Riddoch Highway, Coonawarra, SA 5263 **Region** Coonawarra
T (08) 8736 5001 **www**.rymill.com.au **Open** 7 days 10–5
Winemaker Sandrine Gimon **Est.** 1974 **Dozens** 35 000 **Vyds** 144ha

The Rymills are descendants of John Riddoch and have long owned some of the finest
Coonawarra soil, upon which they have grown grapes since 1970. The promotion of
Champagne-trained Sandrine Gimon to chief winemaker (after three years as winemaker
at Rymill) is interesting. Sandrine is a European version of a Flying Winemaker, having
managed a winery in Bordeaux, and made wine in Champagne, Languedoc, Romania and
WA. Sandrine became an Australian citizen in 2011. The winery building also houses the
cellar door and art exhibitions, which, together with viewing platforms of the winery, make
it a must-see destination for tourists. Exports to all major markets.

ŸŸŸŸŸ **Single Vineyard No. 8 Chardonnay 2012** An elegant Chardonnay from a
region often producing richer styles; the bouquet offers nectarine, wood spice and
toasty aromas; the palate is taut, dry and full of energy, with a subtle layering of
fruit and well-handled oak. Screwcap. 12% alc. **Rating** 94 **To** 2018 $27 BE

Cabernet Sauvignon 2010 Full crimson-purple; has more richness, texture
and weight than many of the prior vintages of this wine; fully ripened cassis and
savoury/earthy regional fruit is framed by plentiful ripe tannins and French oak.
Diam. 14.5% alc. **Rating** 94 **To** 2025 $34

Maturation Release Cabernet Sauvignon 2005 Deep garnet; the mature bouquet offers both dark fruits and cedary development, with violets and cassis; the palate is lively and full-bodied, delivering freshness and complexity and a very long, taut acid conclusion. Diam. 14% alc. **Rating** 94 **To** 2018 $45 BE

 The Yearling Sauvignon Blanc 2012 The vintage has lifted this wine above the usual pleasant but unremarkable level for Coonawarra sauvignon blanc, with a vibrant and seamless flow of tropical, citrus and herbal flavours, tropical the major component. Top value. Screwcap. 12.5% alc. **Rating** 92 **To** 2013 $16
Shiraz 2010 **Rating** 90 **To** 2018 $30 BE

 # Sabrina River Wines

695 Bents Road, Ballandean, Qld 4382 **Region** Granite Belt
T (07) 4684 1052 www.sabrinariverwines.com.au **Open** Not
Winemaker Jim Barnes **Est.** 2009 **Dozens** 400 **Vyds** 7.5ha

Kevin Tuckwell, who graduated from Roseworthy in 1957, was born at Angaston and was a champion vine pruner in his youth. He left the Barossa Valley to go to Qld, first owning a successful truck and tractor sales and service business, thereafter purchasing Barangarook sheep station at Inglewood, running 10 000 sheep. His aim was to turn it into the best property in the region, and he did just that, allowing him to sell the property and retire to the coast at Sanctuary Cove. However, in 2009 he fell to the temptation of buying a vineyard in the Granite Belt, largely planted to cabernet sauvignon and merlot. Ian Macrow entered the scene, having had the room next door to Kevin at Roseworthy, leading to a lifetime friendship. Ian became involved in agri-politics, and was at one stage a member of the Australian Wheat Board. He and his wife used to assist with work at Barangarook, and when Kevin acquired what came to be known as Sabrina River, Ian came on board as marketing and sales manager.

Granite Belt Cabernet Merlot 2009 Good colour; somewhat rustic, but has some redcurrant and blackcurrant fruit and controlled tannins on the medium-bodied palate; the finish is quite juicy. Screwcap. 13.8% alc. **Rating** 87 **To** 2015 $22
Limited Release Granite Belt Cabernet Sauvignon 2009 Good colour; a robust wine that spent over a year in new French oak, and might have been better with less oak in the mix, or more attention to fining the wine before it was bottled; there is some good-quality fruit waiting to express itself. Screwcap. 13.8% alc. **Rating** 87 **To** 2016 $29

Saddler's Creek ★★★★★

Marrowbone Road, Pokolbin, NSW 2320 **Region** Hunter Valley
T (02) 4991 1770 www.saddlerscreek.com **Open** 7 days 10–5
Winemaker Nick Flanagan, Brett Woodward **Est.** 1989 **Dozens** 6000 **Vyds** 10ha

Saddler's Creek is a boutique winery that is little known outside the Hunter Valley but has built a loyal following of dedicated supporters. Came onto the scene over 20 years ago with some rich, bold wines, and maintains this style today. Fruit is sourced from the Hunter Valley and Langhorne Creek, with occasional forays into McLaren Vale, Wrattonbully and other premium fruit-growing regions. Exports to Sweden, the Cook Islands and China.

Aged Release Classic Hunter Semillon 2004 Bright green-gold; has delicious lemon preserve and toast on both bouquet and palate; the finish is very long, with lemon sherbet acidity persisting into the aftertaste. Screwcap. 10.5% alc. **Rating** 94 **To** 2019 $32
Aged Release Classic Hunter Semillon 1998 Very good colour for age and closure; there is vitality and freshness to the citrus, honey and toast flavours, the acidity playing a crucial role. Cork. 11.5% alc. **Rating** 94 **To** 2015 $39
Reserve Chardonnay 2012 Light straw-green; hand-picked at dawn, and given only subtle French oak handling, an approach that works well. In the modern style, with flavours in the white flesh stone fruit/citrus/melon spectrum; the balance and length are impeccable. Screwcap. 13% alc. **Rating** 94 **To** 2017 $32

ŸŸŸŸŸ **Classic Hunter Semillon 2011** Rating 93 To 2021 $25
✪ **Saddler's Hunter Valley Chardonnay 2012** The approach to the winemaking of both this and the Reserve seems nigh-on identical, except for slightly earlier picking here, the flavours fractionally more towards citrus and apple, the oak even more subtle. Screwcap. 12.5% alc. **Rating** 93 To 2017 $26
Aged Release Classic Hunter Semillon 2000 Rating 92 To 2015 $39
Bluegrass Cabernet Sauvignon 2010 Rating 90 To 2018 $38

St Aidan   ★★★★

754 Ferguson Road, Dardanup, WA 6236 **Region** Geographe
T (08) 9728 3007 **www**.saintaidan.com.au **Open** Mon–Tues, Thurs–Fri 11–4, w'ends & public hols 11–5
Winemaker Mark Messenger (Contract) **Est.** 1996 **Dozens** 1500 **Vyds** 2.6ha
Phil and Mary Smith purchased their property at Dardanup in 1991, a 20min drive from the Bunbury hospital where Phil works. They first ventured into Red Globe table grapes, planting 1ha in 1994–2005, followed by 1ha of mandarins and oranges. With this experience, and with Mary completing a TAFE viticulture course, they extended their horizons by planting 1ha each of cabernet sauvignon and chardonnay in '97, 0.5ha of muscat in '01, and semillon and sauvignon blanc thereafter.

ŸŸŸŸŸ **Geographe Cabernet Merlot 2009** Gold and silver medals at two local derbies in '11 are not in the least surprising, for the wine has very attractive juicy red and blackcurrant fruits with fine, silky tannins on the long, well-balanced palate, and is travelling well. Screwcap. 14.5% alc. **Rating** 93 To 2019 $24
Geographe Chardonnay 2010 The wine spent 10 months on yeast lees in French oak, and has responded well; it has positive texture, complexity and length, with grapefruit to the fore, but white peach and creamy/nutty notes are also in the mix. Screwcap. 14% alc. **Rating** 92 To 2016 $24

ŸŸŸŸ **Geographe Sauvignon Blanc Semillon 2011** Rating 87 To 2013 $18

St Anne's Vineyards   ★★★☆

Cnr Perricoota Road/24 Lane, Moama, NSW 2731 **Region** Perricoota
T (03) 5480 0099 **www**.stanneswinery.com.au **Open** 7 days 9–5
Winemaker Richard McLean **Est.** 1972 **Dozens** 80 000 **Vyds** 182ha
The McLean family has a multi-pronged grapegrowing and winemaking business, with 182ha of vines on the Murray River in the Perricoota region. Here all of the mainstream varieties are grown, the lion's share chardonnay, shiraz, cabernet sauvignon and merlot, with lesser quantities of semillon, sauvignon blanc, durif and petit verdot. There is also a very small planting at Myrniong in the Pentland Hills, a 50min drive from the heart of Melbourne, where the main cellar door is situated. It specialises in weddings and similar events, and is open 7 days 9–5. There are then three other cellar doors: Moama (Perricoota Lane), Lorne (150 Mount Joy Parade) and Echuca (53 Murray Esplanade). Exports to China.

ŸŸŸŸŸ **Chardonnay 2011** Unsurprisingly, by some distance the best of St Anne's Murray River wines; white peach, melon, hazelnut and gently toasty French oak are all in symbiotic balance. Ready now. Screwcap. 13% alc. **Rating** 90 To 2014 $16

ŸŸŸŸ **Shinbone Alley Liqueur Tokay NV** Rating 89 To 2014 $25
✪ **Sauvignon Blanc 2012** Quartz-white; it's hard to imagine a more difficult climate for sauvignon blanc, but what I assume to be the specific sauvignon blanc cultured yeast has gone a long way to making a silk purse from a sow's ear; gentle tropical fruit flavours. Screwcap. 12% alc. **Rating** 88 To 2013 $16
Shiraz 2010 Rating 87 To 2015 $20
Foundry NV Rating 87 To 2014 $20
Liqueur Muscat NV Rating 87 To 2014 $25

St Brioc Wines

PO Box 867, McLaren Vale, SA 5171 **Region** McLaren Vale
T 0423 777 088 **www.**stbriocwines.com.au **Open** Not
Winemaker Contract **Est.** 2008 **Dozens** 250

St Brioc Wines is a collaboration between sisters Jo Madigan and Trish Wenk and their families. The name comes from the property where the girls spent their early years; the logo and label are inspired by the Celtic symbol dedicated to St Brioc, the Inchbrayok Cross.

ŢŢŢŢ   **The Cure McLaren Vale Shiraz 2009** Deep crimson; the bouquet offers aromas of cold tea, spiced plums and blackberry jam; the palate is lively and generous, forward and accessible; best consumed in the short to medium term. Screwcap. 15.1% alc. **Rating** 88 **To** 2018 $22 BE

St Hallett

St Hallett Road, Tanunda, SA 5352 **Region** Barossa Valley
T (08) 8563 7000 **www.**sthallett.com.au **Open** 7 days 10–5
Winemaker Stuart Blackwell, Toby Barlow **Est.** 1944 **Dozens** 210 000

St Hallett sources all grapes from within the Barossa GI, and is synonymous with the region's icon variety, shiraz. Old Block is the ultra-premium leader of the band (using old-vine grapes from Lyndoch and Eden Valley), supported by Blackwell (Greenock, Ebenezer and Seppeltsfield). Toby Barlow and Stuart Blackwell continue to explore the geographical, geological and climatic diversity of the Barossa, manifested through individual processing of all vineyards and single vineyard releases. St Hallett has also had conspicuous wine show success with its Eden Valley Riesling and Poacher's Semillon Sauvignon Blanc. Exports to all major markets.

ŢŢŢŢŢ   **Old Block Barossa Shiraz 2009** Fresh crimson-purple; the quality of the fruit filling the bouquet transposes directly to the medium- to full-bodied palate, in turn overflowing with luscious fruit. The finish is the high point of the wine, bringing all the best characters together; glorious, juicy fruit and touches of licorice and dark chocolate. WAK screwcap. 14.4% alc. **Rating** 96 **To** 2034 $100

ŢŢŢŢŢ
✪   **Sirens of Eden 2011** St Hallett is exploring new ground in the Barossa with this gewurztraminer/kerner/riesling assemblage. This may seem an unusual blend, but it is a consummately crafted and eminently drinkable blend with enticing mouthfeel. Understated nashi pear, subtle lychee, citrus zest and spice make this the perfect Asian fusion partner. Screwcap. 12.5% alc. **Rating** 93 **To** 2013 $19 TS

✪   **Western Front Barossa Shiraz 2010** Generous depth of Barossa character, is brimming with sweet black plums, spicy rhubarb and licorice, concluding with a distinctive black olive note and supple, softly supportive tannins. Dan Murphy exclusive. Screwcap. 14% alc. **Rating** 91 **To** 2015 $15 TS

The Reward Cabernet Sauvignon 2010 **Rating** 91 **To** 2022 $50 BE

✪   **Gamekeeper's Barossa Shiraz Cabernet 2010** Deep colour, revealing the ripe and opulent nature of the shiraz, with some leafy complexity from the cabernet; the palate combines generosity and firmness on the finish with aplomb. Exceptional value. Screwcap. 14% alc. **Rating** 90 **To** 2018 $14 BE

ŢŢŢŢ
✪   **Gamekeeper's Barossa Shiraz 2010** Deep crimson, red; the bouquet offers a vibrant array of red fruits, florals and some fruitcake spice; the palate is medium-bodied, soft and supple, looking to provide an accessible, user-friendly and quite frankly joyous wine; enjoy and be happy. Good value. Screwcap. 14% alc. **Rating** 89 **To** 2017 $14 BE

St Huberts

Cnr Maroondah Highway/St Huberts Road, Coldstream, Vic 3770 **Region** Yarra Valley
T (03) 5960 7096 **www.**sthuberts.com.au **Open** 7 days 10–5
Winemaker Greg Jarratt **Est.** 1966 **Dozens** NFP **Vyds** 20.49ha

A once-famous winery (in the context of the Yarra Valley) that is now part of TWE. The wines are now made at Coldstream Hills, and are on an upward trajectory. Winemaker Greg Jarratt has complete control of all winemaking decisions, and the grapes come from vineyards all owned by St Huberts at the time it was acquired (many years ago) from its founders; neither Coldstream Hills or any other part of TWE has access to those grapes.

♟♟♟♟♟ **Yarra Valley Chardonnay 2012** Pale straw-green; a sophisticated wine,
✪ managing to combine elegance with complexity; whole bunch-pressed into predominantly used French oak, it has some mlf influences adding nutty complexity to the mainframe of white peach and grapefruit flavours typical of Yarra Valley chardonnay. Screwcap. 12.5% alc. **Rating** 95 **To** 2020 $27

✪ **Yarra Valley Pinot Noir 2012** Very good colour; the fragrant bouquet has a mix of red and black fruits that flow into the supple and long palate; here notes of spice and oak join the red cherry and plum fruit, with fine-grained tannins and quality (but restrained) oak. Screwcap. 13.5% alc. **Rating** 95 **To** 2021 $33

Yarra Valley Roussanne 2012 Bright straw-green; hand-picked grapes, whole bunch-pressed, and fermented in French barriques. The combination of flinty minerality with pear, white peach and citrus flavours, allied with some spice, is particularly appealing. Screwcap. 12.5% alc. **Rating** 94 **To** 2020 $30

Yarra Valley Late Harvest Viognier 2012 Light, bright gold; very late harvest – a man versus bird war – ultimately hand-picked; the fermentation was stopped halfway through, leaving a very rich palate. The absence of botrytis may reduce complexity, but it means the retention of clear apricot and peach varietal character. 375ml. Screwcap. 9% alc. **Rating** 94 **To** 2016 $30

♟♟♟♟♟ **Hubert the Stag Yarra Valley Pinot Noir 2012** Bright, clear crimson-purple;
✪ a no-holds-barred, complex, medium- to full-bodied Pinot with an impressive tannin structure framing the plum and black cherry fruits. Whether or not made for early consumption, will in fact live for years to come. Screwcap. 13.5% alc. **Rating** 92 **To** 2020 $24

St John's Road ★★★★

PO Box 311, Greenock, SA 5360 **Region** Barossa Valley
T (08) 8423 0272 www.stjohnsroad.com **Open** Not
Winemaker Kim Jackson **Est.** 2002 **Dozens** 8000
Following the tragic death of founder Martin Rawlinson from motor neurone disease, there was a period of inactivity before Adelaide wine identity Alister Mibus and Dale Wyman purchased the St John's Road label. The policy of selecting the best possible parcels of fruit from the Barossa and Eden Valleys continues, even though the prices are decidedly modest. As the *2014 Wine Companion* was going to press, St John's Road was purchased by the Hesketh family. Exports to Canada and China.

♟♟♟♟♟ **Motley Bunch GSM 2010** Very good hue; full to the brim with bright and
✪ juicy red (predominantly) and black fruits, tannins present but compliant, the finish fresh and vibrant. An altogether delicious drink needing no cellaring. Screwcap. 14.5% alc. **Rating** 93 **To** 2016 $20

✪ **Pretty & Pure Adelaide Hills Sauvignon Blanc 2012** Has above-average depth to its tropical fruit flavours, with guava, stone fruit and passionfruit all contributing. Justifies its name. Screwcap. 12% alc. **Rating** 91 **To** 2013 $18

✪ **Peace of Eden Riesling 2012** Light straw-green; has the mix of ripe though fine lime and lemon that is the hallmark of Eden Valley; the depth of fruit will allow the wine to develop reasonably quickly; it is already accessible. Screwcap. 12% alc. **Rating** 90 **To** 2015 $20

Line & Length Barossa Valley Cabernet Sauvignon 2010 Bright crimson-purple; it takes a while for the length and line to capture the taster, and for the varietal character to develop, but it does on the second innings (or taste), with cassis to the fore. Screwcap. 14.5% alc. **Rating** 90 **To** 2018 $22

♟♟♟♟ **Lost Love Moscato 2012 Rating** 88 **To** 2013 $18

St Leonards Vineyard

St Leonards Road, Wahgunyah, Vic 3687 **Region** Rutherglen
T 1800 021 621 **www**.stleonardswine.com.au **Open** Thurs–Mon 10–5
Winemaker Dan Crane, Nick Brown **Est.** 1860 **Dozens** 25 000 **Vyds** 8ha
An old favourite, relaunched in late 1997 with a range of premium wines cleverly marketed through an attractive cellar door and bistro at the historic winery on the banks of the Murray. It is essentially a satellite operation of All Saints, under the same ownership and management. Exports to the UK and Hong Kong.

Cabernet Franc 2012 Very good crimson-purple; an unexpected burst of juicy red fruits on the medium-bodied palate; cool fermentation and a short maturation have preserved everything on offer; the hint of dried herb adds to the appeal. Screwcap. 13% alc. **Rating** 93 **To** 2018 $28

Semillon Sauvignon Blanc 2012 Rating 87 **To** 2014 $22

St Margaret's Vineyard

1654 Osmington Road, Margaret River, WA 6285 **Region** Margaret River
T 0439 574 599 **www**.stmargaretsvineyard.com.au **Open** By appt
Winemaker Alex Scott, Naturaliste Vintners **Est.** 1996 **Dozens** 400 **Vyds** 13.4ha
Alex Scott is owner and manager of the family business which, he says, 'is a unique poly-cultural venture with cattle, garlic, and assorted chooks, ducks, pets and pests all playing their part in the ecosystem of the property'. The major part, however, is 7ha of cabernet sauvignon, 3ha of chardonnay, 2.4ha of sauvignon blanc and 1ha of merlot. The whites are made at Naturaliste Vintners (Bruce Dukes), Alex makes the red wines with open fermenters, a basket press and old French oak barrels (in which the wines spend two years). Minimal sulphur additions are used.

Cabernet Sauvignon 2010 Purple-crimson of medium depth; speaks of both variety and region, although it is no more than light- to medium-bodied, and has a slightly green/minty finish. Screwcap. 13.2% alc. **Rating** 89 **To** 2016 $15
Sauvignon Blanc 2012 Pale quartz; decidedly odd labelling with the suggestion of an old church window on the front, and an abstract map on the back label. The flavours are varietal but weak. Young vines? Screwcap. 12.5% alc. **Rating** 87 **To** 2013 $13

St Regis

35 Princes Highway, Waurn Ponds, Vic 3216 **Region** Geelong
T (03) 5241 8406 **www**.stregis.com.au **Open** 7 days 11–5
Winemaker Peter Nicol **Est.** 1997 **Dozens** 500 **Vyds** 1ha
St Regis is a family-run boutique winery focusing on estate-grown shiraz, and locally sourced chardonnay and pinot noir. Each year the harvest is hand-picked by members of the family and friends, with Peter Nicol (assisted by wife Viv) the executive onsite winemaker. While Peter has a technical background in horticulture, he is a self-taught winemaker, and has taught himself well, also making wines for others.

Geelong Chardonnay 2011 Pale quartz; a testament to the cool vintage that allowed full flavour development at low alcohol levels, the peach and melon fruit perfectly balanced by acidity; the purity and balance of the wine (where did the oak go?) deserve 3-4 years to show what really lies within. Screwcap. 12% alc. **Rating** 91 **To** 2017 $20
The Reg Geelong Shiraz 2011 A handwritten note on the bottle reads 'Picked 15 May, too cold to entertain wild fermentation, but did receive two weeks maceration'. The light, bright colour suggested things might be better in the glass, and so it proved, for there is a delicious flavour spectrum around ripe cherry fruit and spice. Screwcap. 13.6% alc. **Rating** 90 **To** 2017 $25

Salet Wines

12 Peel Street, Currarong, NSW 2540 **Region** Various
T 0403 384 384 **www**.salet.com.au **Open** By appt
Winemaker Michael Salecich **Est.** 2002 **Dozens** 300
Michael Salecich hails from Croatia, where his family has made wine for many generations. His winemaking methods are strongly influenced by the practices of his Croatian family, whom he visits each year. He buys his grapes from SA, bringing them to his onsite winery in refrigerated trucks. Here the wines are crushed and fermented, and then matured in shaved hogsheads for three and a half years, in the style of Barolo made the traditional way.

ŸŸŸŸŸ **Basket Press Shiraz 2009** The colour is bright crimson-purple, but both the bouquet and palate are encased in a veneer of vanillin oak; there is varietal blackberry fruit under that veneer, and you cannot gainsay the overall volume of flavour. Screwcap. 14.5% alc. **Rating** 90 **To** 2020 $30

ŸŸŸŸ **Basket Press Shiraz 2007 Rating** 87 **To** 2014 $30
Basket Press Shiraz Cabernet Sauvignon 2009 Rating 87 **To** 2016 $30

Salitage

Vasse Highway, Pemberton, WA 6260 **Region** Pemberton
T (08) 9776 1771 **www**.salitage.com.au **Open** 7 days 10–4
Winemaker Patrick Coutts **Est.** 1989 **Dozens** 10 000 **Vyds** 21.4ha
Owned and operated by John and Jenny Horgan, Salitage is a showpiece of Pemberton. John had worked and studied under the guidance of Robert Mondavi in California, and also acquired a share in the famous Burgundy winery, La Pousse D'or (with other Aussie investors, all of whom have since sold out). Together with Bill and Sandra Pannell's Picardy, it is a bellwether for the reputation of the region. Exports to Europe, Indonesia, South Korea, Singapore, Taiwan and China.

ŸŸŸŸŸ **Pemberton Sauvignon Blanc 2012** Pale quartz-green; estate-grown, with fully mature vines; has abundant varietal expression on its bouquet and palate alike, with passionfruit, guava and lychee to the fore. Screwcap. 14% alc. **Rating** 90 **To** 2014 $22

✪ **Treehouse Sauvignon Blanc 2011** An attractive wine, with a bouquet of gently tropical fruits and a palate that delivers more of the same; it has good balance, length and overall presence. Screwcap. 13.5% alc. **Rating** 90 **To** 2013 $18

✪ **Pemberton Unwooded Chardonnay 2012** Very pale straw-green; has better length than many unwooded Chardonnays, suggesting there may have been some lees contact; whether or not, the creamy note adds a dimension to its stone fruit flavours. Screwcap. 14% alc. **Rating** 90 **To** 2015 $20

ŸŸŸŸ **Pemberton 2009 Rating** 89 **To** 2017 $33
Pemberton Chardonnay 2012 Rating 87 **To** 2014 $35
Pemberton Rose 2010 Rating 87 **To** 2012 $20

Salo Wines

28 Dorothy Street, Healesville, Vic 3777 (postal) **Region** Yarra Valley
T (03) 5962 5331 **www**.salowines.com.au **Open** Not
Winemaker Steve Flamsteed, Dave Mackintosh **Est.** 2008 **Dozens** 250
Business partners Steve Flamsteed and Dave Mackintosh say that Salo means dirty and a little uncouth, which, with the Australian sense of humour, means it can be used as a term of endearment. They wish to keep their wines a little dirty by using hands-off, minimal winemaking except for a few strange techniques to make more gritty, textured wines. Thus the 2010 Chardonnay, using grapes grown on the Gladysdale Vineyard in the Upper Yarra Valley, was made using 85% whole bunch-pressed grapes, the juice going direct to barrel with full solids for a wild yeast fermentation in puncheons, but the remaining 15% was fermented

on skins and stems. The whacky 'orange' ferment was stirred a few times and both portions were blended in early September, the mlf prevented. Then they looked across the ditch to Hawke's Bay, NZ, and found some outstanding shiraz. Quantities are unfortunately minuscule, with 150 dozen bottles of Chardonnay and 100 dozen of Syrah, both wonderful wines (tasting notes on www.winecompanion.com.au). Exports to Hong Kong.

Salomon Estate

PO Box 829, McLaren Vale, SA 5171 **Region** Southern Fleurieu
T 0417 470 590 **www.**salomonwines.com **Open** Not
Winemaker Bert Salomon, Mike Farmilo **Est.** 1997 **Dozens** 6500 **Vyds** 12.1ha
Bert Salomon is an Austrian winemaker with a long-established family winery in the Kremstal region, not far from Vienna. He became acquainted with Australia during his time with import company Schlumberger in Vienna; he was the first to import Australian wines (Penfolds) into Austria, in the mid 1980s, and later became head of the Austrian Wine Bureau. He was so taken by Adelaide that he moved his family there for the first few months each year, sending his young children to school and setting in place an Australian red winemaking venture. He retired from the Bureau and is now a full-time travelling winemaker, running the family winery in the northern hemisphere vintage, and overseeing the making of the Salomon Estate wines at Chapel Hill. Exports to the UK, the US, and other major markets.

ΥΥΥΥΥ **Finniss River Shiraz 2010** Good red-purple; the complex array of black fruits on the bouquet, together with some oak, is joined by dark chocolate on the medium- to full-bodied palate; the texture and structure are excellent, as is the length of the wine. Cork. 14.5% alc. **Rating** 94 **To** 2020 $35

Fleurieu Peninsula Syrah V 2011 A clever front label, signalling the presence of 4% viognier, spelled out on the back label (5% is the minimum for front label disclosure). The colour is bright crimson-purple, and the flavours are no less bright, with juicy red berry fruits and a touch of oak spice driving the bouquet and palate alike. Screwcap. 14.5% alc. **Rating** 94 **To** 2016 $26

Aestatis Grenache Shiraz Mourvedre 2010 The fragrant red fruit aromas of the bouquet partially set the scene, covering the grenache component, but not so much the darker berry fruits and structure contributed by the shiraz; a very good wine from a very good vintage. Screwcap. 14% alc. **Rating** 94 **To** 2020 $43

Finniss River Cabernet Sauvignon 2010 Bright crimson-purple; a high-quality evocation of perfectly ripened cabernet, with resplendent cassis fruit on the medium-bodied palate, the tannins fine, the oak subtle. A badly stained, pock-marked cork. 14.5% alc. **Rating** 94 **To** 2015 $32

ΥΥΥΥΥ ✪ **Norwood Shiraz Cabernet 2011** Good hue and depth; has achieved full flavour ripeness, and the decision to employ used oak for its 12 months in barrel was totally correct. The display of blackberry, plum and blackcurrant, with wisps of dark chocolate and licorice plus balanced tannins, makes a mockery of the price. Screwcap. 14.5% alc. **Rating** 92 **To** 2018 $21

Saltire Wines

247 Wilderness Road, Lovedale, NSW 2320 **Region** Hunter Valley
T (02) 4930 7594 **Open** 7 days 10–5
Winemaker Daniel Binet **Est.** 2008 **Dozens** 2000 **Vyds** 6ha
The Warraroong vineyard was planted in 1978, the name an Aboriginal word for 'hillside', reflecting the southwesterly aspect of the property, which looks back towards the Brokenback Range and Watagan Mountains. In 2007 Katrina and Russell Leslie moved to the Hunter Valley, buying existing wineries and/or brands, with the early stages under the Swish Wine umbrella. Tin Soldier came and went, and after protracted discussions, Wandin Estate also became part of the group. Warraroong Estate is now at the head of the businesses, with the highly talented and very experienced Daniel Binet chief winemaker.

ΨΨΨΨΨ **Alasdair Shiraz 2011** The dedication to the late Alasdair Sutherland is not explained on the back label, but no matter, he would have been mightily pleased with this wine. It has a strong varietal signature, and an earthy/brambly sense of place on the long finish. Screwcap. 14.5% alc. **Rating** 94 **To** 2026 $25

ΨΨΨΨΨ **Eden Valley Riesling 2012 Rating** 90 **To** 2016 $25

Saltram   ★★★★★

Nuriootpa Road, Angaston, SA 5353 **Region** Barossa Valley
T (08) 8561 0200 **www**.saltramwines.com.au **Open** 7 days 10–5
Winemaker Shavaughn Wells, Richard Mattner **Est.** 1859 **Dozens** 150 000
There is no doubt that Saltram has taken strides towards regaining the reputation it held 30 or so years ago. Grape sourcing has come back to the Barossa Valley for the flagship wines. The red wines, in particular, have enjoyed great show success over the past few years, with No. 1 Shiraz and Mamre Brook leading the charge. Exports to all major markets.

ΨΨΨΨΨ **Single Vineyard Collector's Vintage Moculta Rd Vineyard Barossa Shiraz 2010** Deep crimson-purple; the wine spent 24 months in used vats which has placed all the emphasis on the excellent black fruits, spice and licorice flavours, the fine, but persistent and savoury, tannins adding to the overall appeal of a remarkable wine. Screwcap. 14.5% alc. **Rating** 96 **To** 2035 $95

✪ **Mamre Brook Eden Valley Riesling 2012** Bright green; the fragrant, blossom-filled aromas promise that which the palate delivers in spades with its lissom array of lemon and lime flavours threaded through by refreshing acidity. Screwcap. 12.5% alc. **Rating** 95 **To** 2025 $20

The Journal Barossa Valley Shiraz 2009 Bright purple-crimson through to the rim; a rich, complex, medium- to full-bodied wine, with layer upon layer of flavour of ripe plum, black cherry and blackberry fruit in a womb of new oak and ripe tannins. Cork. 14.5% alc. **Rating** 95 **To** 2035 $125

ΨΨΨΨΨ **Metala Langhorne Creek Shiraz Cabernet 2010 Rating** 93 **To** 2025 $19
Mamre Brook Barossa Cabernet Sauvignon 2010 Rating 93 **To** 2030 $38
Mamre Brook Barossa Cabernet Sauvignon 2009 Rating 92 **To** 2029 $38
Limited Release Winemaker's Selection Barossa Valley Semillon 2012
Rating 91 **To** 2020 $25
Limited Release Winemaker's Selection Barossa Valley Fiano 2012
Rating 90 **To** 2014 $25

Sam Miranda of King Valley   ★★★★

1019 Snow Road, Oxley, Vic 3678 **Region** King Valley
T (03) 5727 3888 **www**.sammiranda.com.au **Open** 7 days 10–5
Winemaker Sam Miranda **Est.** 2004 **Dozens** 25 000 **Vyds** 15ha
Sam Miranda, grandson of Francesco Miranda, joined the family business in 1991, striking out on his own in 2004 after Miranda Wines was purchased by McGuigan Simeon. The High Plains Vineyard is in the Upper King Valley at an altitude of 450m; estate plantings are supplemented by some purchased grapes. In '05 Sam purchased Symphonia Wines, and has kept its identity intact and separate from the Sam Miranda brand. Exports to the UK and China.

ΨΨΨΨΨ **Cellar Door Release Riesling 2008** Still pale straw-green; the wine is
✪ developing so slowly it's not easy to work out where it may go in the future; indeed, there is a strong case for drinking it now, enjoying its lime, lemon and apple fruit. Screwcap. 12% alc. **Rating** 92 **To** 2015 $20

✪ **Cellar Door Release Arneis 2012** If lemon/lime zest and skin, plus an unsweetened sorbet on the finish, are reckoned to be the varietal markets for arneis, this wine has it in spades. Screwcap. 11.5% alc. **Rating** 92 **To** 2014 $20

Cellar Door Release Tannat 2009 The soft nature of the tannin structure of most King Valley red wines comes into its own with this wine, its dark berry fruits almost velvety, until tannins of moderate dimension take over on the finish. Screwcap. 13.9% alc. **Rating** 91 **To** 2030 $30

Cellar Door Release Super King Sangiovese Cabernet 2010 No. 3. Bright, clear purple-red; has excellent texture and supple mouthfeel to its array of red cherry, cassis and spice (there is also a dash of shiraz in the wine) supported by silky tannins and a whisper of oak. Screwcap. 13.5% alc. **Rating** 90 **To** 2020 $30
Cellar Door Release Tempranillo 2010 Medium purple-red; has the full range of varietal expression from dark cherry fruit, spice and a twist of lemon peel disputing primacy with tannins on the finish. Another Sam Miranda wine needing time in bottle. Screwcap. 13% alc. **Rating** 90 **To** 2025 $30

ŶŶŶŶ Cellar Door Release Pinot Noir 2010 Rating 89 To 2015 $25
Shiraz 2012 Rating 89 To 2016 $18
TNT Tempranillo Nebbiolo Tannat 2010 Rating 89 To 2025 $30
Chardonnay Pinot Noir 2010 Rating 89 To 2014 $30
Cellar Door Release Pinot Grigio 2012 Rating 88 To 2014 $20
Caterina 2011 Rating 88 To 2014 $30

Samuel's Gorge ★★★★★

193 Chaffeys Road, McLaren, SA 5171 **Region** McLaren Vale
T (08) 8323 8651 **www**.gorge.com.au **Open** 7 days 11–5
Winemaker Justin McNamee **Est.** 2003 **Dozens** 3000 **Vyds** 10ha
After a wandering winemaking career in various parts of the world, Justin McNamee became a winemaker at Tatachilla in 1996, where he remained until 2003, leaving to found Samuel's Gorge. He has established his winery in a barn built in 1853, part of the old Seaview Homestead. The historic property was owned by Sir Samuel Way, variously Chief Justice of the South Australian Supreme Court and Lieutenant Governor of the state. The grapes come from small contract growers spread across the ever-changing (unofficial) subregions of McLaren Vale, and are basket-pressed and fermented in old open slate fermenters lined with beeswax – with impressive results, even in the face of the wet '11 vintage. Exports to the UK, the US, Canada and Hong Kong.

ŶŶŶŶŶ Mosaic of Dreams Grenache Mourvedre Shiraz 2009 A 43/43/14% blend; a lengthy sojourn in oak has welded the varieties together, the blackberry, plum, spice and dark chocolate running in a continuous stream across the palate; the length is very good, the balance likewise. Bottle development since Mar '12 has added to the complexity of the wine. Cork. 14.5% alc. **Rating** 94 **To** 2019 $75
Kaleidoscope Horizons Tempranillo Grenache 2009 Dark crimson-purple; has developed since being tasted in Mar '12 immediately after being bottled, and only now released; it is full-bodied, but not aggressively so, with black and red cherry fruit, spice, licorice and a touch of tempranillo's tamarillo; the tannins are evident, but balanced, and should stand the wine in good stead over the years ahead. Cork. 14% alc. **Rating** 94 **To** 2024 $75
McLaren Vale Mourvedre 2011 A rich, layered and ripe wine coming from the clouds in more ways than one; has layers of black fruits, ripe tannins and that touch of regional chocolate; hard to do better than this in '11. Cork. 15% alc. Rating 94 To 2021 $35

ŶŶŶŶŶ McLaren Vale Tempranillo 2011 Rating 92 To 2018 $35
Comet Tail Sparkling Shiraz 2010 Rating 92 To 2025 $50

Sandalford

3210 West Swan Road, Caversham, WA 6055 **Region** Margaret River
T (08) 9374 9374 **www**.sandalford.com **Open** 7 days 9–5
Winemaker Hope Metcalf **Est.** 1840 **Dozens** 60000 **Vyds** 105ha
Sandalford is one of Australia's oldest and largest privately owned wineries. In 1970 it moved beyond its original Swan Valley base, purchasing a substantial property in Margaret River that is now the main source of its premium grapes. The wines are released at four levels, starting with Element, then the Margaret River range, next Estate Reserve and finally, Prendiville. Exports to all major markets.

ŦŦŦŦŦ Estate Reserve Margaret River Shiraz 2010 This wine finished its
fermentation in new and 1-year-old French oak barriques, a technique that gives
rise to the supple tannins and superior oak integration on the medium-bodied
palate; spices of all kinds are evident on the bouquet, but are only a seasoning for
its black cherry and plum fruit. Screwcap. 14% alc. **Rating** 95 **To** 2035 $34

Estate Reserve Margaret River Cabernet Sauvignon 2010 Clear crimson-
purple; a wine built for the long haul, its foundation high-quality Margaret River
cabernet with a central core of cassis complexed by 18 months in new and 1-year-
old French barriques and ripe, strong tannins. Patience needed, and will be repaid.
Screwcap. 14.5% alc. **Rating** 95 **To** 2040 $40

Estate Reserve Margaret River Chardonnay 2012 Pale straw, vibrant green
hue; the restrained bouquet offers grapefruit, nectarine and fresh cashew; the
palate is lively, fresh and taut, with a long, dry and mineral-laden finish. Screwcap.
14% alc. **Rating** 94 **To** 2018 $35 BE

Prendiville Reserve Margaret River Shiraz 2011 Deep crimson; the bouquet
offers a healthy dose of fine oak spices, red fruits, lavender and licorice; the palate
is medium- to full-bodied with ample fine-grained tannins and fresh acidity
providing line and length; the oak is dominant at this early stage, but time should
see integration. Screwcap. 14.5% alc. **Rating** 94 **To** 2025 $90 BE

ŦŦŦŦŦ
✪ Estate Reserve Margaret River Sauvignon Blanc Semillon 2012
Light straw-green; the fragrant bouquet has aromas of passionfruit and lemon, the
elegant palate adding gooseberry/kiwifruit to the mix; a touch more acidity on
the finish would have made a good wine better still. Screwcap. 13% alc. **Rating** 93
To 2014 $20

✪ Margaret River Rose 2012 Full crimson-purple; flooded with red and black
cherry fruit on the bouquet and palate; good tannins and faintly citrussy acidity;
a classic early-picked cabernet sauvignon rose style first used over 30 years ago by
Houghton. Screwcap. 13% alc. **Rating** 92 **To** 2014 $19

Sanguine Estate ★★★★★

77 Shurans Lane, Heathcote, Vic 3523 **Region** Heathcote
T (03) 5433 3111 **www**.sanguinewines.com.au **Open** W'ends & public hols 10–5, or by appt
Winemaker Mark Hunter **Est.** 1997 **Dozens** 3500 **Vyds** 21.57ha
The Hunter family – parents Linda and Tony at the head, and their children Mark and Jodi,
with their respective partners Melissa and Brett – began establishing the vineyard in 1997.
It has grown to 20.16ha of shiraz, with token plantings of chardonnay, viognier, merlot,
tempranillo, petit verdot, cabernet sauvignon and cabernet franc. Low-yielding vines and
the magic of the Heathcote region have produced Shiraz of exceptional intensity, which has
received rave reviews in the US, and led to the 'sold out' sign being posted almost immediately
upon release. With the ever-expanding vineyard, Mark has become full-time vigneron, and
Jodi part-time marketer and business developer. Exports to Singapore and China.

ŦŦŦŦŦ Music Festival Shiraz 2010 A full-bodied, rich and layered palate with
abundant black fruits, dark chocolate and licorice, plus velvety tannins and vanillin
oak all come together very well. Screwcap. 14.5% alc. **Rating** 94 **To** 2025 $30

Cabernet Sauvignon Cabernet Franc Petit Verdot 2011 A 70/15/15%
blend; the liberal levels of cassis, redcurrant, black olive and spice are standouts for
'11; while medium- to full-bodied, the wine has elegance, balance and length.
Screwcap. 14.5% alc. **Rating** 94 **To** 2026 $25

ŦŦŦŦ Heathcote Tempranillo 2011 **Rating** 89 **To** 2016 $30
Progeny Heathcote Shiraz 2011 **Rating** 88 **To** 2018 $20

❧ Santolin Wines ★★★★★

c/- 21–23 Delaneys Road, South Warrandyte, Vic 3136 **Region** Yarra Valley
T 0402 278 464 **www**.facebook.com/santolinwines **Open** Not
Winemaker Adrian Santolin **Est.** 2012 **Dozens** 450

Adrian Santolin grew up in Griffith, NSW, and has worked in the wine industry since he was 15. He moved to the Yarra Valley in '07 with wife Rebecca, who has worked in marketing roles at various wineries since '00. Adrian's love of pinot noir led him to work at wineries such as Wedgetail Estate, Rochford, De Bortoli, Sticks and Rob Dolan Wines. In 2012 his dream became true when he was able to buy 2 tonnes of pinot noir from the Thousand Candles Vineyard, increasing production in '13 to 4 tonnes, split between chardonnay and pinot noir, the chardonnay sourced from Yarraland Vineyard at Chirnside Park. 2012 was a very good vintage for pinot noir in the Yarra Valley, but '13 may well prove to be better still – it suggests you should seriously consider buying the wine sight unseen. Exports to the UK.

ᵧᵧᵧᵧᵧ Individual Vineyard Yarra Valley Pinot Noir 2012 Light to medium crimson-purple. This vintage produced exceptional pinot noir in the Yarra Valley, and the intensity of the red and dark cherry fruits has absorbed the stemmy notes that 100% whole bunches can impose. Screwcap. 13.5% alc. **Rating** 94 **To** 2018 $40

Saracen Estates

3517 Caves Road, Wilyabrup, WA 6280 **Region** Margaret River
T (08) 9755 6000 **www**.saracenestates.com.au **Open** 7 days 11–5
Winemaker Bob Cartwright (Consultant) **Est.** 1998 **Dozens** 6000 **Vyds** 16.94ha
Maree and Luke Saraceni's first foray into the wine industry came via a small import business. Saracen Estates is situated on a 40ha property in a striking building comprising a cellar door and a wine education centre. The visitor facility also incorporates a craft brewery, restaurant and beautifully landscaped gardens. The vineyard property on Caves Road has almost 17ha under vine, from which the high-quality wines are produced. Saracen Estates won the trophy for Most Successful Exhibitor Margaret River Wine Show '10.

ᵧᵧᵧᵧᵧ Reserve Margaret River Chardonnay 2010 This is a complex wine, in part reflecting its alcohol, in part its barrel fermentation in new French oak, and in part its extended lees contact. It has largely absorbed the oak, but it needed a touch more acidity for higher points still. Screwcap. 14.7% alc. **Rating** 94 **To** 2016 $60
Margaret River Shiraz 2010 Good purple-crimson; the attractive, berry-filled bouquet introduces a juicy wine, with supple red and black fruits supported by silky tannins and evident oak on the medium-bodied palate and the long, harmonious finish. Screwcap. 13.6% alc. **Rating** 94 **To** 2025 $35
Reserve Margaret River Shiraz 2010 Curiously, the colour is slightly more developed than that of its sibling from the same vintage; but the overall weight and mouthfeel provides more finesse and texture, in large part due to the skilled use of French oak. Screwcap. 13.5% alc. **Rating** 94 **To** 2025 $60

ᵧᵧᵧᵧᵧ Margaret River Chardonnay 2009 Rating 93 **To** 2015 $35

Sarsfield Estate

345 Duncan Road, Sarsfield, Vic 3875 **Region** Gippsland
T (03) 5156 8962 **www**.sarsfieldestate.com.au **Open** By appt
Winemaker Dr Suzanne Rutschmann **Est.** 1995 **Dozens** 1000 **Vyds** 2ha
Owned by Suzanne Rutschmann, who has a PhD in Chemistry, a Diploma in Horticulture and a BSc (Wine Science) from CSU, and Swiss-born Peter Albrecht, a civil and structural engineer who has also undertaken various courses in agriculture and viticulture. For a part-time occupation, these are exceptionally impressive credentials. Sarsfield Pinot Noir has enjoyed success in both domestic and international wine shows. No insecticides are used in the vineyard (pinot noir, cabernet, shiraz, cabernet franc and merlot), the winery runs on solar and wind energy and relies entirely on rain water.

ᵧᵧᵧᵧᵧ Pinot Noir 2010 The crimson-purple colour is bright and welcoming; the bouquet and palate are flush with red fruits, the texture and balance very good; oh for a screwcap. 13.8% alc. **Rating** 93 **To** 2015 $25

Cabernets Shiraz Merlot 2009 Relatively light colour, although the hue is good; a powerful, brooding, savoury style, blackcurrant fruit bedded down in persistent, albeit ripe, tannins and 18 months in French oak. Screwcap. 13.3% alc. **Rating** 91 **To** 2019 $22

♟♟♟♟ **Cabernets Shiraz Merlot 2010 Rating** 89 **To** 2018 $22 BE

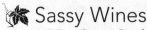 # Sassy Wines ★★★

469 Emu Swamp Road, Orange, NSW 2800 **Region** Orange
T 0409 311 395 **www.sassywines.com.au Open** By appt
Winemaker Peter Logan, Rob Coles **Est.** 2005 **Dozens** 400 **Vyds** 6.2ha
Rob and Fliss Coles may be new to Orange, but not to the business of grapegrowing. They first established a vineyard in the Cowra region in 1997, but moved to Orange to pursue cooler climate varieties in '05, with the establishment of 6.2ha of vines more or less equally split between sauvignon blanc, arneis, riesling, pinot gris, pinot noir and shiraz. Organic and biodynamic principles are used in the vineyard, always a challenge in the early years.

♟♟♟♟ **Orange Pinot Noir 2010** Estate-grown, open-fermented, hand-plunged and matured for 8 months in new and used French oak. Savoury, spicy, foresty fruit notes and a generous amount of oak are the drivers; the fruit may have been more prominent a year or two ago. Screwcap. 13.7% alc. **Rating** 88 **To** 2014 $30

The Ivor Orange Arneis 2012 Bright green-straw; early picking has helped the floral aromas, and the wine certainly meets the Coles' desire for a crisp style with natural acidity. Screwcap. 11.5% alc. **Rating** 87 **To** 2014 $20

SC Pannell ★★★★★

PO Box 1159, Unley BC, SA 5061 **Region** McLaren Vale ·
T (08) 8271 7118 **www.scpannell.com.au Open** Not
Winemaker Stephen Pannell **Est.** 2004 **Dozens** 15 000 **Vyds** 13ha
The only surprising piece of background is that it took (an admittedly still reasonably youthful) Stephen Pannell (and wife Fiona) so long to cut the painter from Constellation/Hardys and establish their own winemaking and consulting business. Steve radiates intensity, and extended experience has resulted in wines of the highest quality right from the first vintage. The Pannells purchased their first vineyard in McLaren Vale, planted in 1891, with a precious 3.57ha of shiraz; grenache, his most loved variety, will be one of the first varieties he plants. Stephen manages the vineyard, with the aim of generating full flavour ripeness as close to 13% as possible. The future for the Pannells is limitless, the icon status of the label already established. Exports to the UK, the US and Singapore.

♟♟♟♟♟ **McLaren Vale Grenache 2010** Made from 68-year-old vines, open-fermented and matured for 14 months in old French oak puncheons, deliberately throwing all the focus onto the fruit. This is McLaren Vale grenache at its best, with a satin texture and intense red fruits, tannins a filmy gauze providing perfectly calibrated support. Screwcap. 14.5% alc. **Rating** 97 **To** 2025 $60

Adelaide Hills Sauvignon Blanc 2012 The grapes come from a low-yielding (5 tonnes per hectare) vineyard, the cool fermentation initiated by cultured yeast (and a mystery element). Pale straw-green; a fragrant, notably flowery, bouquet leads into a remarkably layered and textured palate, with green and white fruit flavours, and grainy minerality coming through on the finish. At its prime over the '13 calendar year. Screwcap. 13% alc. **Rating** 96 **To** 2013 $27

✪ **Adelaide Hills Syrah 2010** The fragrant bouquet has a panoply of spice and pepper overtones to its black fruits; 16 months in French puncheons has imparted both flavour and texture to the medium-bodied, but very complex, palate, with a delicious savoury twist to the finish. Screwcap. 14% alc. **Rating** 96 **To** 2040 $27

McLaren Vale Grenache 2011 Deep crimson; a compelling and complex bouquet offering not only ripe red and black fruits, but also Provençale garrigue, ironstone and game; the palate offers layers of fruit, and the evenly balanced tannins and fresh acidity combine to create a long and expansive finish that is simply precise and pure. Screwcap. 14% alc. **Rating** 96 **To** 2025 $60 BE

McLaren Vale Grenache Shiraz 2010 Full purple-crimson. Says Steve Pannell, 'After 22 years of making wine in McLaren Vale, this blend continues to be my favourite wine to make and drink.' The fragrant bouquet of red and black fruits comes through strongly on the complex, medium-bodied palate, fine-grained tannins a feature on the long finish. Screwcap. 14% alc. **Rating** 96 **To** 2025 $43

McLaren Vale Shiraz 2011 Deep colour; dark and brooding black fruits, fresh bitumen, saltbush, anise and clove on the bouquet; the palate is medium-bodied and focused, with the abundant level of fruit in balance with the medium-grained tannins and a light seasoning of well-handled oak; all this at a lowly 13.5% alc. Bravo. Screwcap. **Rating** 95 **To** 2025 $60 BE

McLaren Vale Shiraz 2010 Good crimson-purple; the result of a long-range program devised by Steve Pannell and father and son grapegrowers Richard and Ian Leslie to produce grapes with full flavour development at 13° baume; it is very complex and full-flavoured, yet is only medium-bodied, and has a juicy brightness to its finish. Screwcap. 13.5% alc. **Rating** 95 **To** 2035 $60

Adelaide Hills Arido 2012 Rating 94 To 2014 $23
Adelaide Hills Nebbiolo 2009 Rating 94 To 2020 $50 BE

ŶŶŶŶŶ **Adelaide Hills Pinot Grigio 2012** Rating 93 To 2014 $27
Pronto 2010 Rating 93 To 2017 $23
McLaren Vale Tempranillo Touriga 2011 Rating 93 To 2018 $27 BE
Adelaide Hills Pronto Bianco 2012 Rating 91 To 2013 $23

Scarborough Wine Co ★★★★☆

179 Gillards Road, Pokolbin, NSW 2320 **Region** Hunter Valley
T (02) 4998 7563 **www.**scarboroughwine.com.au **Open** 7 days 9–5
Winemaker Ian and Jerome Scarborough **Est.** 1985 **Dozens** 25 000 **Vyds** 14ha
Ian Scarborough honed his white winemaking skills during his years as a consultant, and has brought all those skills to his own label. He makes three different styles of Chardonnay: the Blue Label is a light, elegant, Chablis style for the export market; a richer barrel-fermented wine (Yellow Label) is primarily directed to the Australian market; the third is the White Label, a cellar door-only wine made in the best vintages. The Scarborough family also acquired a portion of the old Lindemans Sunshine Vineyard (after it lay fallow for 30 years) and planted it with semillon and (quixotically) pinot noir. Scarborough has recently opened a second cellar door 'Scarborough on Hermitage' at 972 Hermitage Rd, Pokolbin NSW 2320 (open Thurs–Mon 10–5). Exports to the UK and the US.

ŶŶŶŶŶ **White Label Hunter Valley Shiraz 2011** Deep garnet-purple hue; restrained black cherry and fresh blood plum aromas are complemented by a healthy seasoning of spicy oak, with clove a feature; the medium-boded palate reveals tightly packed tannins and fresh acidity, playing foil to luscious fruits that linger seductively on the finish. Screwcap. 14.5% alc. **Rating** 94 **To** 2024 $60 BE

ŶŶŶŶŶ **Black Label Shiraz 2010** Rating 91 To 2020 $27 BE
White Label Hunter Valley Semillon 2011 Rating 90 To 2022 $27 BE

Scarpantoni Estate ★★★★☆

Scarpantoni Drive, McLaren Flat, SA 5171 **Region** McLaren Vale
T (08) 8383 0186 **www.**scarpantoniwines.com **Open** Mon–Fri 9–5, w'ends & public hols 11–5
Winemaker Michael and Filippo Scarpantoni, David Fleming **Est.** 1979 **Dozens** 37 000 **Vyds** 35ha
Scarpantoni has come a long way since Domenico Scarpantoni purchased his first vineyard in 1958. He worked for Thomas Hardy at its Tintara winery, then as vineyard manager for Seaview Wines, and soon became one of the largest private grapegrowers in the region. The winery was built in 1979 with help from sons Michael and Filippo, who continue to manage the company. Michael and Filippo grew up on part of Oxenberry Farm, originally settled in

1840, and in 1998 were able to purchase part of the property. The Oxenberry wines are made in a different style from those of Scarpantoni, and are available only from its cellar door at 24–26 Kangarilla Road. Exports to the UK and other major markets.

🍷🍷🍷🍷🍷 **Estate Reserve Shiraz Cabernet Sauvignon 2010** A 70/30% blend, the hue bright, although not deep; notwithstanding the dominance of the shiraz in percentage terms, the cabernet certainly makes its presence felt, adding blackcurrant/cassis notes to the more hearty blackberry fruits of the shiraz, and giving a juicy lift to the finish. Screwcap. 14.5% alc. **Rating** 94 **To** 2035 $40

🍷🍷🍷🍷🍷 **Block 3 McLaren Vale Shiraz 2010 Rating** 93 **To** 2020 $30
✪ **Oxenberry Two Tribes 2010** Good colour, bright and vibrant; this blend of shiraz and grenache works much better than The Bullocks, grenache taking the place of cabernet sauvignon, and thus sharply reducing the tannin load. Indeed, this is a lovely full-flavoured blend that McLaren Vale does so well. Screwcap. 14.5% alc. **Rating** 93 **To** 2018 $20
Brothers' Block Cabernet Sauvignon 2010 Rating 93 **To** 2025 $30
Oxenberry The Trailblazers 2010 Rating 91 **To** 2018 $30
Pinot Noir 2012 Rating 90 **To** 2018 $25
California Road Old Vine Shiraz 2010 Rating 90 **To** 2025 $25
Barbera 2010 Rating 90 **To** 2016 $25

Schindler Northway Downs   ★★★☆

437 Stumpy Gully Road, Balnarring, Vic 3926 **Region** Mornington Peninsula
T (03) 5983 1945 **www**.northwaydowns.com.au **Open** First w'end of month
Winemaker Sandro Mosele, Greg Ray (Contract) **Est.** 1996 **Dozens** 250 **Vyds** 6ha
The Schindler family planted the first 2ha of pinot noir and chardonnay in 1996. A further 4ha of pinot noir was planted on an ideal north-facing slope in 1999, and the first vintage followed in 2000. The cellar door offers traditional Austrian food and live Austrian music.

Schubert Estate   ★★★★★

Roennfeldt Road, Marananga, SA 5355 **Region** Barossa Valley
T (08) 8562 3375 **www**.schubertestate.com **Open** By appt
Winemaker Steve Schubert **Est.** 2000 **Dozens** 1100 **Vyds** 14ha
Steve and Cecilia Schubert are primarily grapegrowers, with 12ha of shiraz and 2ha of viognier. They purchased the 25ha property in 1986, when it was in such a derelict state that there was no point trying to save the old vines. Both were working in other areas, so it was some years before they began replanting, at a little under 2ha per year. Almost all the production is sold to Torbreck. In 2000 they decided to keep enough grapes to make a barrique of wine for their own (and friends') consumption. They were sufficiently encouraged by the outcome to venture into the dizzy heights of two hogsheads a year (since increased to four or so). The wine is made with wild yeast, open fermentation, basket-pressing and bottling without filtration. Exports to Germany and Hong Kong.

🍷🍷🍷🍷🍷 **Goose-yard Block Barossa Valley Shiraz 2010** The vineyard corners the century-old Schubert home, attesting to the use the land once had. An opulent, medium- to full-bodied wine with a cascade of black fruits and licorice, the tannins fine and – of course – ripe. Screwcap. 15% alc. **Rating** 96 **To** 2040 $55
The Sentinel Barossa Valley Shiraz 2009 Deep purple; open-fermented, basket-pressed into French and American oak; richer and more layered than the Gosling, with abundant plum fruit, gently chewy tannins and mocha oak. Screwcap. 14.5% alc. **Rating** 94 **To** 2024 $25
The Gander Reserve Barossa Valley Shiraz 2008 Has retained purple colour well; the highly expressive blackberry, licorice and plum bouquet is precisely reflected on the palate, except for a generous infusion of French oak. Diam. 15% alc. **Rating** 94 **To** 2028 $90

ΨΨΨΨ♀   **The Gosling Single Vineyard Barossa Valley Shiraz 2010** Striking deep
✪   purple; lives up to the promise of its colour, with masses of blackberry and plum
        fruit, dark cooking spice and ripe tannins. Compelling value for a wine to drink
        now or in 10 years. Screwcap. 14.5% alc. **Rating** 93 **To** 2020 $20

Schulz Vignerons   ★★★☆

PO Box 121, Nuriootpa, SA 5355 **Region** Barossa Valley
T (08) 8565 6257 **Open** By appt
Winemaker David Powell (Contract) **Est.** 2003 **Dozens** 500 **Vyds** 58.5ha

Marcus and Roslyn Schulz are the fifth generation of one of the best-known wine families
(or, rather, extended families) in the Barossa Valley. Four generations of grapegrowing and
winemaking precede them, but they went down a new path by initiating biological farming
in 2002. They have moved from irrigation and extensive spraying to a situation where the
vines are now virtually dry-grown, producing generous yields of high-quality grapes, using
natural nitrogen created by the active soil biology, and minimal chemical input. The vineyard is
planted to 12 varieties, shiraz, mourvedre, grenache and cabernet sauvignon leading the band.
They are also actively involved in a local co-operative campaign to protect blocks of native
vegetation to encourage biodiversity.

ΨΨΨΨ   **Benjamin Barossa Valley Shiraz 2009** Deep colour, with blackberry coulis,
       prune and mocha on display; sweet-fruited and unctuous on the palate, with
       plenty of concentration; ultimately a little simple. Screwcap. 14.5% alc. **Rating** 87
       To 2018 $25 BE
       Johann Barossa Valley Zinfandel 2008 Super-ripe and showing red-fruited
       and spicy jammy characters on the bouquet; the palate follows suit, with a sweet
       core of simple fruit, in keeping with the varietal expression. Screwcap. 14.5% alc.
       Rating 87 **To** 2015 $20 BE

Schwarz Wine Company

Biscay Road, Tanunda, SA 5352 **Region** Barossa Valley
T 0417 881 923 **www.**schwarzwineco.com.au **Open** At Artisans of Barossa
Winemaker Jason Schwarz **Est.** 2001 **Dozens** 3000

The economical name is appropriate for a business that started with 1 tonne of grapes making
two hogsheads of wine in 2001. The shiraz was purchased from Jason Schwarz's parents'
vineyard in Bethany, the vines planted 60 years ago; the following year half a tonne of grenache
was added, once again purchased from the parents. Production remained static until '05, when
the grape sale agreements to another (larger) winery were terminated, freeing up 1.8ha of
shiraz and 0.8ha of grenache. From this point on things moved more quickly: in '06 Jason,
while working with Peter Schell of Spinifex, formed a partnership (Biscay Road Vintners)
with Peter. Using grapes purchased from other growers, production has reached the target of
3000 dozen. Exports to the US, Canada, France, Singapore, Hong Kong and China.

ΨΨΨΨΨ   **The Schiller Barossa Valley Shiraz 2010** A precious eight rows of 400 vines
        planted 130 years ago were snatched from the jaws of the bulldozers, the reprieve
        now permanent. It takes full-bodied onto another level with the intensity and
        complexity of its flavours (not its alcohol), which encompass black fruits, tar, earth,
        licorice and bramble. Screwcap. 15% alc. **Rating** 96 **To** 2040 $70
        Nitschke Block Barossa Valley Shiraz 2010 Vivid purple-crimson; riotously
        full-bodied, with juicy blackberry nip, licorice and dark chocolate fruit flavours,
        yet the tannins are modest, the oak likewise with a small footprint. Lovely stuff.
        Screwcap. 14.5% alc. **Rating** 95 **To** 2035 $38
        The Dust Kicker Barossa Valley Shiraz 2010 The back label discloses
        the presence of mataro, necessarily less than 15%. The colour is a very healthy
        crimson-purple, the bouquet and palate with a spicy nuance that presumably
        reflects the mataro; the major play is the array of black fruits, licorice and dark
        chocolate powder with a truly appealing sombre/savoury finish. Screwcap.
        14.3% alc. **Rating** 94 **To** 2025 $28

�w�w�w�w♀ **The Dust Kicker Barossa Valley Rose 2012** Pale pink; a supple and smooth
✪ 60/40% blend of grenache and mataro with red berry and pink grapefruit aromas
and flavours; the relatively low alcohol works to perfection, the finish zesty and
bright. Very good value. Screwcap. 12.8% alc. **Rating** 92 **To** 2014 $20
Thiele Road Barossa Valley Grenache 2010 Rating 92 **To** 2020 $32
✪ **The Dust Kicker Barossa Valley GSM 2010** There is greater depth to
this grenache, shiraz, mataro blend than most, reflecting the vintage and Jason
Schwarz's commendable attitude to alcohol. Thus it has a full array of warm spices
to its primary red berry and plum aromas and flavours, the tannins in precisely
positioned support. Screwcap. 14.4% alc. **Rating** 91 **To** 2020 $20

Scion Vineyard & Winery ★★★☆

74 Slaughterhouse Road, Rutherglen, Vic 3685 **Region** Rutherglen
T (02) 6032 8844 **www**.scionvineyard.com **Open** 7 days 10–5
Winemaker Jan and Rowland Milhinch **Est.** 2002 **Dozens** 1400 **Vyds** 3.75ha
Scion Vineyard was established by retired audiologist Jan Milhinch, who is a great-great-
granddaughter of GF Morris, founder of the most famous Rutherglen wine family. She has
now handed the baton to son Rowland (Rowly), who will continue to manage the vineyard,
which is planted on a quartz-laden red clay slope to durif, viognier, brown muscat and
orange muscat.

♀♀♀♀♀ **Rose Muscat 2012** Bright pink; rose petal Turkish Delight dessert style; good
balance and acidity. Silver medal Melbourne Wine Show '12. 500ml. Screwcap.
12.8% alc. **Rating** 90 **To** 2014 $29

♀♀♀♀ **Rose 2012 Rating** 88 **To** 2014 $19
Affinity 2010 Rating 87 **To** 2014 $22
Fleur 2012 Rating 87 **To** 2014 $22

Scorpo Wines ★★★★★

23 Old Bittern-Dromana Road, Merricks North, Vic 3926 **Region** Mornington Peninsula
T (03) 5989 7697 **www**.scorpowines.com.au **Open** By appt
Winemaker Paul Scorpo, Sandro Mosele (Contract) **Est.** 1997 **Dozens** 3500
Vyds 9.64ha
Paul Scorpo has a background as a horticulturist/landscape architect, working on major
projects ranging from private gardens to golf courses in Australia, Europe and Asia. His family
has a love of food, wine and gardens, all of which led to them buying a derelict apple and
cherry orchard on gentle rolling hills between Port Phillip and Westernport Bays. Part of
a ridge system that climbs up to Red Hill, it offers north and northeast-facing slopes on
red-brown clay loam soils. They have established pinot gris (4.84ha), pinot noir (2.8ha),
chardonnay (1ha) and shiraz (1ha). Exports to Singapore and Hong Kong.

♀♀♀♀♀ **Mornington Peninsula Pinot Gris 2012** Whole bunch-pressed, cold-settled,
then wild yeast-fermented in used (4 years and older) French barriques; the
intention is to build structure akin to Alsace pinot gris, and it succeeds admirably;
this lovely mouthfeel does not strip the wine of fruit flavour. Screwcap. 13.5% alc.
Rating 95 To 2015 $35
Noirien Mornington Peninsula Pinot Noir 2012 Strong, clear crimson-
purple; a fleshy, but structured, pinot with an abundance of plum and black cherry
fruit on its bouquet and palate; very good spicy tannins run through the length of
the palate, guaranteeing a long and prosperous life. Noirien was a medieval name
for pinot. Screwcap. 14% alc. Rating 95 To 2022 $30
Aubaine Mornington Peninsula Chardonnay 2011 The wine was wild yeast
barrel-fermented and remained in barrel for 9 months. It has exceptional grainy
texture with its grapefruit pith/zest and green apple flavours, all bordering on
savoury, but compelling. Screwcap. 13% alc. **Rating** 94 **To** 2020 $30

Mornington Peninsula Pinot Noir 2011 Very good hue, although, inevitably, not deep; achieved full ripeness, no mean feat in '11, with the aromas and flavours grounded in plum fruit; the palate has very good tannin structure to support the fruit, and the wine has time to go. Screwcap. 13.5% alc. **Rating** 94 **To** 2020 $46

♥♥♥♥♡ Mornington Peninsula Chardonnay 2010 Rating 91 **To** 2020 $38

Scotchmans Hill   ★★★★★

190 Scotchmans Road, Drysdale, Vic 3222 **Region** Geelong
T (03) 5251 3176 **www**.scotchmans.com.au **Open** 7 days 10.30–5.30
Winemaker Robin Brockett, Marcus Holt **Est.** 1982 **Dozens** 70 000
In Oct 2012 Scotchmans Hill entered into a long-term lease arrangement for the use of the former Pettavel winery (The Hill). A group of private local investors had acquired the winery and restaurant from the receivers of the business, and have effectively split the business in two. The Pettavel brand will disappear, and Scotchmans Hill will use the winery facility for storage of bulk and bottled wine, dry goods storage and bottling, consolidating all of the winemaking operations at the existing Scotchmans Hill winery. The Hill will serve as the new home for concerts, events, weddings and functions. Exports to Asia and other major markets.

♥♥♥♥♥ Cornelius Single Vineyard Bellarine Peninsula Sauvignon 2011 Pale straw
✪ colour; a very complex and very intense wine with a Loire Valley, Didier Dageuneau, homage; it is almost (but not quite) painfully precise; minerally, citrus-driven, its barrel-ferment origins only a matter of academic interest. Screwcap. 13% alc. **Rating** 96 **To** 2015 $40

Cornelius Single Vineyard Bellarine Peninsula Syrah 2010 Bright crimson-purple; the bouquet ranges through blackberry, black cherry, spice, pepper and licorice, all of which come through on the vibrantly flavoured palate, proclaiming its cool climate; the tannins are perfectly pitched, the finish exceptionally long. Screwcap. 14.5% alc. **Rating** 96 **To** 2030 $65

Sutton Vineyard Bellarine Peninsula Chardonnay 2009 A high quality wine, with an inherent balance that sets it apart; highly attractive fig, melon, peach and grapefruit flavours are gently caressed by French oak, the finish long and balanced. Screwcap. 13% alc. **Rating** 95 **To** 2020 $55

✪ **Bellarine Peninsula Shiraz 2010** Hand-picked and destemmed into small fermenters for a 5-day pre-fermentation soak, then wild yeast-fermented before spending 15 months in French barriques; has a striking vibrancy of flavour to its red and black fruits, with spice and licorice also in play on the long, medium-bodied palate. Screwcap. 14.5% alc. **Rating** 95 **To** 2030 $27

Bellarine Peninsula Chardonnay 2011 Bright, light straw-green; an elegant and fluent wine, with a seamless union between the fruit and the oak; the fruit is in mainstream cool-climate style, with white peach and a splash of grapefruit. Screwcap. 13.5% alc. **Rating** 94 **To** 2017 $30

Cornelius Single Vineyard Bellarine Peninsula Chardonnay 2010 Pale, gleaming straw-green; has the iron fist in a velvet glove of the Cornelius range, although a little more iron wouldn't go astray. Has great focus, line and length, its pure varietal fruit merely caressed by the oak in which it was fermented and matured. Screwcap. 13.5% alc. **Rating** 94 **To** 2020 $55

Norfolk Vineyard Pinot Noir 2010 A powerful and complex wine with an array of blood plum and black cherry fruit; the contribution of French oak is obvious, but integrated and balanced, the surge of fruit on the finish and aftertaste attesting to that. Screwcap. 14% alc. **Rating** 94 **To** 2019 $55

Cornelius Single Vineyard Bellarine Peninsula Pinot Noir 2010 Bright red hue; a complex, indeed imperious, Pinot Noir with a strong, dark berry bouquet and palate, the latter with a generous serve of foresty tannins carried along by the power of the fruit. Screwcap. 14% alc. **Rating** 94 **To** 2020 $55

Norfolk Vineyard Bellarine Peninsula Pinot Noir 2009 Bright, purple hue; an elegant wine; the maritime terroir blunted the impact of the Feb heatwave, allowing the ideal growing conditions either side to shape the wine. Screwcap. 13% alc. **Rating** 94 **To** 2017 $55

Reserve Henry Frost Shiraz 2009 This has more elegance and brightness than most Clare Valley Shirazs, with attractive red berry fruits dominant, but some black fruits also evident in the mix; the tannins are fine, the oak fully integrated. Screwcap. 14.5% alc. **Rating** 94 **To** 2029 $55

ƤƤƤƤƤ **Sutton Vineyard Chardonnay 2010 Rating** 93 **To** 2019 $55
Bellarine Peninsula Pinot Noir 2011 Rating 93 **To** 2016 $32

✪ **Henry Frost Riesling 2012** From no less than six districts in the Clare Valley; conventionally made with cold fermentation of clear juice, the surge of flavour on the finish points to a low level of residual sugar balanced by crisp acidity. Compelling value. Screwcap. 12% alc. **Rating** 92 **To** 2020 $15

✪ **Swan Bay Sauvignon Blanc Semillon 2011** Exceptional drive and intensity on the palate, lemon, gooseberry and tropical flavours all in a single embrace, the finish fresh and zesty. Since first tasted it has kept excellent focus and structure, the fruit register very different from the '12s, with lemon zest, herb and capsicum supported by minerally acidity. Screwcap. 12.5% alc. **Rating** 92 **To** 2013 $15

✪ **Ferryman Mornington Peninsula Chardonnay 2011** A very elegant and fine wine with stone fruit and melon flavours that have absorbed all the oak, the finish clean and fresh. Screwcap. 13.5% alc. **Rating** 92 **To** 2017 $22
Cornelius Single Vineyard Pinot Gris 2011 Rating 92 **To** 2014 $40

✪ **Estella McLaren Vale Shiraz 2010** This wine delivers infinitely more than its price suggests; full of fragrant plum and blackberry fruit shot through with licorice and bitter chocolate; the tannins are fine, the French and American oak not the least obvious. In the 6 months since first tasted, its inherent finesse and elegance have bloomed. Screwcap. 14.5% alc. **Rating** 92 **To** 2020 $15

✪ **Henry Frost Clare Valley Cabernet Merlot 2010** Like the Henry Frost Shiraz, has a refreshing lightness of touch, and has made light of 18 months in French oak. This is a lively and delicious red berry wine, ready to drink whenever the mood takes you. Screwcap. 14.5% alc. **Rating** 92 **To** 2016 $20

✪ **Bellarine Peninsula Sauvignon Blanc 2012** Given 2 months' lees contact in tank post-fermentation, but otherwise clinical/traditional cool-ferment winemaking. Has above-average drive and length to the palate thanks to pronounced lemony acidity on the finish. Screwcap. 13% alc. **Rating** 91 **To** 2014 $20

✪ **Swan Bay Bellarine Peninsula Chardonnay 2012** Some oak has been introduced, says the back label. Well, it's not obvious, and not really needed, for the wine has pristine freshness, excellent varietal expression and is ludicrously good value with its grapefruit and melon fruit flying from the masthead. Screwcap. 13.5% alc. **Rating** 91 **To** 2015 $15

✪ **Henry Frost Clare Valley Sangiovese 2010** Destemmed and cold-soaked for 2–3 days, wild yeast-fermented for 7–9 days, 2 weeks' post-fermentation maceration, pressed to barrel for mlf, bottled Feb '12. It is a powerful Sangiovese, with black, as well as red, cherry fruit and firm tannins. Bring on the pasta. Screwcap. 14.5% alc. **Rating** 91 **To** 2024 $20
Estella McLaren Vale Cabernet Sauvignon 2010 Rating 90 **To** 2018 $20
Bellarine Peninsula Late Harvest Riesling 2012 Rating 90 **To** 2015 $20

ƤƤƤƤ
✪ **Hill Chardonnay 2012** From Adelaide Hills and Geelong. While apparently unoaked, the wine does have some grainy texture that is appealing, as are the subtle grapefruit add-ons to the primary stone fruit flavours. A wolf in sheep's clothing, and terrific value. Screwcap. 13.5% alc. **Rating** 89 **To** 2014 $12

Scott ★★★★★

Old Woollen Mill, Main Street, Lobethal, SA 5241 **Region** Adelaide Hills
T 0439 553 228 **www.**scottwinemaking.com.au **Open** By appt
Winemaker Sam Scott **Est.** 2009 **Dozens** 3000
Sam Scott's great-grandfather worked in the cellar for Max Schubert, and passed his knowledge to Sam's grandfather. It was he who gave Sam his early education. He enrolled in business at university, continuing the casual retailing he had started while at school with

Booze Brothers, picking up the trail with Baily & Baily. Next came wholesale experience with David Ridge, selling iconic Australian and Italian wines. This led to a job with Michael Fragos at Tatachilla in '00, and since then he has been the 'I've been everywhere man' model, working all over Australia, and in California. He moved to Bird in Hand winery at the end of '06, where Andrew Nugent indicated that it was about time he took the plunge on his own account. Sam is a star in the making. Like many, he was hard hit by the '11 vintage. Exports to the UK.

ΨΨΨΨΨ **Adelaide Hills Shiraz 2010** Immediately takes attention with its fragrant, spicy bouquet linked to a precise and firm, medium- to full-bodied palate. Here black fruits play tag with spice, pepper and licorice, the tannins fine but appropriately persistent. Screwcap. 14.5% alc. **Rating** 95 **To** 2030 $40

✪ **La Prova Adelaide Hills Aglianico Rosato 2012** Pale pink; aglianico is an Italian variety that has been around in Australia in isolated patches for several decades. This was picked very early, given 6 hours' skin contact in the press, then cool-fermented to protect the freshness but not cut back on the spicy, savoury fruit expression and its refreshingly bone-dry finish. A Rose with real attitude. Screwcap. 12.5% alc. **Rating** 94 **To** 2014 $23

ΨΨΨΨΨ **La Prova Adelaide Hills Pinot Grigio 2012 Rating** 91 **To** 2013 $23
Adelaide Hills Fiano 2012 Rating 90 **To** 2014 $26

Seabrook Wines   ★★★★★

Lot 350 Light Pass Road, Tanunda, SA 5352 **Region** Barossa Valley
T 0427 224 353 **www.**seabrookwines.com.au **Open** By appt
Winemaker Hamish Seabrook **Est.** 2004 **Dozens** 1500 **Vyds** 2ha
Hamish Seabrook is the youngest generation of a proud Melbourne wine family once involved in wholesale and retail distribution, and as leading show judges of their respective generations. Hamish, too, is a wine show judge, but was the first to venture into winemaking, working with Best's and Brown Brothers in Vic before moving to SA with wife Joanne. Hamish set up his own winery on the family property in Vine Vale. Here they have a small planting of shiraz, but also continue to source small amounts of shiraz from the Barossa and Pyrenees. Exports to Hong Kong and China.

ΨΨΨΨΨ **The Merchant Barossa Valley Shiraz 2010** Deep crimson-purple; in some ways seeks to change places with The Chairman; full of delicious blackberry, spice and licorice fruit, this is the more elegant of the two wines; the medium-bodied palate is beautifully weighted, fruit, oak and tannins seamlessly bound, the finish clear and uncluttered. Screwcap. 14.5% alc. **Rating** 95 **To** 2030 $35

The Chairman Great Western Shiraz 2010 Medium to full crimson-purple; the fragrant bouquet has a complex array of black fruits, licorice, pepper and mocha, the palate richly endowed with a plush array of plum cake, black fruits and quality oak, the tannins ripe and balanced. Screwcap. 14.5% alc. **Rating** 94 **To** 2030 $28

ΨΨΨΨΨ **The Judge Eden Valley Riesling 2012 Rating** 93 **To** 2020 $22

Sedona Estate   ★★★★☆

182 Shannons Road, Murrindindi, Vic 3717 **Region** Upper Goulburn
T (03) 9730 2883 **www.**sedonaestate.com.au **Open** Wed–Sun & public hols 11–5
Winemaker Paul Evans **Est.** 1998 **Dozens** 2500 **Vyds** 4ha
Sedona Estate, established by Paul Evans and Sonja Herges, is located in the picturesque Yea Valley, gateway to Victoria's high country. The unique combination of abundant sunshine, cool nights and low rainfall in this elevated wine region provides a true cool climate for growing premium-quality fruit. January 2011 saw the completion of the new winery, which has played its part in the increased production.

ŦŦŦŦŦ Yea Valley Sangiovese 2011 Bright red-purple; this is a pretty smart wine, period. It is wonderfully fine and supple, its pristine cherry fruit, not its tannins, defining the finish. Screwcap. 13% alc. **Rating** 94 **To** 2021 $25

ŦŦŦŦŦ **Yea Valley Riesling 2011 Rating** 93 **To** 2021 $22
Yea Valley Cabernet Merlot 2010 Rating 91 **To** 2020 $22

See Saw ★★★

PO Box 611, Manly, NSW 1655 **Region** Hunter Valley
T (02) 8966 9020 **www.**seesawwine.com **Open** Not
Winemaker Hamish MacGowan, Andrew Margan **Est.** 2006 **Dozens** 8000
This is another venture of Hamish MacGowan, the winemaker-cum-marketer who is responsible for Angus the Bull (see separate entry). Prior to setting out on his own, Hamish worked for Andrew Margan, who now has his own substantial winery and business in the Hunter Valley. The wine they make for the See Saw label is a blend of semillon from the Hunter Valley and sauvignon blanc from high-altitude vineyards in the Central Ranges. Exports to the UK, Singapore and Thailand.

ŦŦŦŦ **Semillon Sauvignon Blanc 2012** The straw-green colour introduces a wine largely driven by herbal/unsweetened lemon/citrus acidity, and a consequentially tart finish. Screwcap. 11.5% alc. **Rating** 88 **To** 2013 $19

Semprevino ★★★★

1 Waverly Drive, Willunga, SA 5171 **Region** McLaren Vale
T 0417 142 110 **www.**semprevino.com.au **Open** Not
Winemaker Russell Schroder **Est.** 2006 **Dozens** 400
Semprevino is the venture of three men who became close friends while studying at Monash University in early 1990s – Russell Schroder (mechanical engineering), Simon Doak and David Bruce (both science) – although all three branched out in different directions after graduating in 1993. The prime mover is Russell who, after working for CRA/Rio Tinto for five years, left on a four-month trip to Western Europe and became captivated with the life of a vigneron. Returning to Australia, he enrolled part-time in wine science at CSU, spending the next six years working for Bluescope Steel at Hastings on the Mornington Peninsula, obtaining his wine science degree in 2005. Between '03 and '06 he worked vintages in Italy and Vic, coming under the wing of Stephen Pannell at Tinlins (where the Semprevino wines are made) in '06.

ŦŦŦŦŦ **McLaren Vale Grenache Shiraz 2011** A 64/36% blend from old vines that
✪ has risen triumphantly above the challenges of the vintage. It has good depth, texture and structure to its spiced plum and cherry compote, with ripe tannins to conclude. Screwcap. 14.7% alc. **Rating** 93 **To** 2018 $24

ŦŦŦŦ **McLaren Vale Semillon 2012 Rating** 87 **To** 2016 $18

Seppelt ★★★★★

36 Cemetery Road, Great Western, Vic 3377 **Region** Grampians
T (03) 5361 2239 **www.**seppelt.com.au **Open** 7 days 10–5
Winemaker Adam Carnaby, Melanie Chester **Est.** 1865 **Dozens** NFP **Vyds** 500ha
Australia's best-known producer of sparkling wine, always immaculate in its given price range but also producing excellent Great Western-sourced table wines, especially long-lived Shiraz and Australia's best Sparkling Shirazs. The glitzy labels of the past have rightly been consigned to the rubbish bin, and the product range has been significantly rationalised and improved. Following the sale of Seppeltsfield to Kilikanoon, this is the sole operating arm of Seppelt under TWE ownership. Exports to the UK and Europe.

ŦŦŦŦŦ Chalambar Shiraz 2009 A label with a great heritage, and fulfils its birthright in every detail of the stylish bouquet and palate; black fruits, spice and black pepper enliven the long, medium-bodied palate; the tannin structure and oak are exemplary. Screwcap. 13.5% alc. **Rating** 96 **To** 2040 $27

Jaluka Henty Chardonnay 2011 The wine has considerable textural complexity, its vibrant fruit with a crosscut of creamy complexity, possibly with some mlf at work. Very well priced. Screwcap. 12.5% alc. **Rating** 94 **To** 2020 $27

Salinger Vintage Cuvee 2008 Complex, fine and elegant, without any diminution in fruit flavours; the brioche is there on the mid-palate and finish that sets it apart. Trophy Best Sparkling Wine Adelaide Wine Show '11. Cork. 12% alc. **Rating** 94 **To** 2015 $30

Grampians Riesling 2011 Pale straw-green; the floral bouquet introduces a cleverly made wine, setting the ripe citrus fruit and good natural acidity on an off-dry style, filling the mid- and back-palate with juicy fruit. Screwcap. 11.5% alc. **Rating** 94 **To** 2021 $27

Seppeltsfield ★★★★★

Seppeltsfield Road, Seppeltsfield via Nuriootpa, SA 5355 **Region** Barossa Valley
T (08) 8568 6200 **www.**seppeltsfield.com.au **Open** 7 days 10.30–5
Winemaker Fiona Donald **Est.** 1851 **Dozens** 10 000 **Vyds** 100ha
This historic Seppelt property and its treasure trove of fortified wines dating back to 1878 was purchased by Janet Holmes à Court, Greg Paramor and Kilikanoon Wines in 2007, from Foster's Wine Estates (now Treasury Wine Estates). Foster's kept the Seppelt brand for table and sparkling wines, mostly produced at Great Western, Vic. In 2009 Warren Randall (ex Sparkling winemaker for Seppelt at Great Western in the 1980s) acquired 50% of Seppeltsfield and became Managing Director. In February 2013, Randall increased his shareholding in Seppeltsfield to over 90%. The change will also mark a further commitment to the making of table wine as well as more focused marketing of the treasure trove of fortified wines.

♀♀♀♀♀ **100 Year Old Para Liqueur 1913** Procure the smallest capacity crystal glass to taste this wine; a micro-sip goes a very long way. The deepest burnt umber colour imaginable; so viscous it doesn't pour, just oozes out of the bottle, thickly coating the sides of the glass, slowly separating into slowly retreating separate streams, creating an effect like marble. The hyper-intense flavours of raisin, burnt toffee and plum pudding search out every nook and cranny of your mouth, the aftertaste lingering for an impossibly long time. Cork. 21.2% alc. **Rating** 100 **To** 2014 $330

Grand Rutherglen DP57 Tokay Solero NV Very hard to spit when tasting professionally! Superb balance, particularly to the fresh finish and aftertaste. My cup of tea here, more luscious than the Grand Muscat, possibly because demand is greater for the Muscat; filled with honey, butterscotch and tea leaf. Has an minimum average age of 10 years. Screwcap. 17% alc. **Rating** 96 **To** 2014 $32

Rich Rare Venerable Solero DP38 NV Light golden brown, with just a hint of olive; here the honeyed flavours are more persistent, accompanied by dried fruit and nut flavours. Has tremendous length; it is not until the aftertaste that the rancio demands another sip to start the process again. Average age 18 years, but fresh as a daisy. 500ml. Screwcap. 21.5% alc. **Rating** 95 **To** 2014 $32

Para 1992 Matured for 21 years, says the neck label. Bright golden-tawny, the last remnants of red disappearing; marvellously mouth-filling and luscious, has less of the fearsome acidity some of these very old blends can build up. Screwcap. 20.5% alc. **Rating** 95 **To** 2014 $80

Grand Rutherglen Muscat DP63 NV Brown-gold; ultra-complex texture and structure; essence of raisin and a hint of rosewater on the bouquet, with an unctuous mouthfeel to the spicy plum pudding flavours and raisin fruit; long, lingering finish. Screwcap. 17% alc. **Rating** 95 **To** 2014 $32

Barossa Shiraz 2011 Both the bouquet and medium- to full-bodied palate have a degree of generosity above the norm for the vintage, with spicy plum and blackberry fruit flavours; the strongest and best feature of the wine is its supple tannin structure. Screwcap. 14% alc. **Rating** 94 **To** 2021 $30

Shiraz Touriga Grenache 2011 The flavours and balance of this medium-bodied wine are harmonious. It was presumably these characters that led to its trophy at the Barossa Valley Wine Show '12 for Best Shiraz-Dominant Blend from '11. Maturation in used French oak puncheons has allowed the bright, spicy, red berry fruits free opportunity to express themselves, and the tannins have not been pushed by additives. Screwcap. 13.5% alc. **Rating** 94 **To** 2017 $30

DP116 Aged Flor Solero NV Yellow bronze-old gold; has nutty, dried fruit peel aromas, then a palate which plays hide and seek; one moment with sweet honeyed nuances, the next dry and nutty, with the crosscut of rancio driving the finish; has an average age of 15 years. Serve slightly chilled and keep in the fridge once opened. 500ml. Screwcap. 21.5% alc. **Rating** 94 **To** 2014 $32

Grand Para NV The average age is a minimum of 10 years; a very luscious and complex wine with intense spicy dried fruit/fruit peel/biscuit/Christmas cake; long, drying, spicy finish with gentle rancio. Screwcap. 20% alc. **Rating** 94 **To** 2014 $35

♟♟♟♟♟ **Estate Rose 2011** The 60–80-year-old bush-pruned vines have previously
✪ provided grapes for fortified wines, '11 a first for table wine. It is bursting with candied red fruit aromas and flavours that linger on the palate, with a faint prickle of spritz. Screwcap. 13.5% alc. **Rating** 90 **To** 2013 $19

Serafino Wines

Kangarilla Road, McLaren Vale, SA 5171 **Region** McLaren Vale
T (08) 8323 0157 **www.**serafinowines.com.au **Open** Mon–Fri 10–4.30, w'ends & public hols 10–4.30
Winemaker Charles Whish **Est.** 2000 **Dozens** 30 000 **Vyds** 100ha
After the sale of Maglieri Wines to Beringer Blass in 1998, Maglieri founder Serafino (Steve) Maglieri acquired the McLarens on the Lake complex originally established by Andrew Garrett. The operation draws upon 40ha each of shiraz and cabernet sauvignon, 7ha of chardonnay, 2ha each of merlot, semillon, barbera, nebbiolo and sangiovese, and 1ha of grenache. Part of the grape production is sold. Between 1997 and 2007, Serafino Wines won a succession of major trophies in Australia and the UK. The Cabernet Sauvignon has been particularly successful. Exports to the UK, the US, Canada, Hong Kong, Malaysia and NZ.

♟♟♟♟♟ **Terremoto Single Vineyard McLaren Vale Syrah 2010** Deep, dense purple-crimson; veteran McLaren Vale winemaker Charles Whish has used mainstream winemaking methods, recognising the innate power and concentration of the profound blackberry, licorice, plum and dark chocolate flavours of the full-bodied palate. It has excellent balance, line and length, and a very long lifespan. 300 dozen made. Diam. 14.5% alc. **Rating** 95 **To** 2040 $110

Sharktooth McLaren Vale Shiraz 2010 Deep crimson; dark and brooding on the bouquet, offering lashings of black fruits, with red fruit highlights, not to mention mocha and roasted meat; the full-bodied palate is lively and complex, with tangy acidity providing a counterpoint to the dark fruit and ample firm but fine tannins. Diam. 14.4% alc. **Rating** 94 **To** 2022 $70 BE

Sorrento McLaren Vale Grenache 2012 Mid garnet, bright; a bright and inviting bouquet of raspberry, blackberry, dried herbs and lavender; the palate is fresh and pure-fruited, with a backbone of refreshing tannin. Screwcap. 14% alc. **Rating** 94 **To** 2022 $22 BE

SGV Reserve McLaren Vale Sangiovese 2009 Excellent colour; this is a very serious Sangiovese, with potent spicy black cherry aromas; the full-bodied palate brings cherry, blackberry and tar together, and just when you think the savoury tannins may dominate, that varietal cherry kicks back. Screwcap. 14% alc. **Rating** 94 **To** 2025 $35

♟♟♟♟♟ **GSM McLaren Vale Grenache Shiraz Mataro 2011 Rating** 92 **To** 2020 $26
BDX McLaren Vale Cabernet Sauvignon Merlot Carmenere Cabernet Franc 2011 Rating 91 **To** 2018 $26

Seraph's Crossing ★★★★

PO Box 5753, Clare, SA 5453 **Region** Clare Valley
T 0412 132 549 **Open** Not
Winemaker Harry Dickinson **Est.** 2006 **Dozens** 450 **Vyds** 5ha
In a moment of enlightened madness, Harry Dickinson gave up his career as a lawyer in a major London law firm to work in the wine business. He helped run the International Wine Challenge for three years, followed by stints with various wine retailers, and some PR work for the German Wine Information Service. He worked his first vintage in Australia at Hardys Tintara winery in 1997 with Stephen Pannell and Larry Cherubino; their work with open fermenters, basket presses and winemaking philosophy made a huge impression. Following a period as a wine retailer in North Adelaide, he returned to winery work in 1999, in various wineries in the Clare Valley. During this time he and wife Chan bought a 75ha property. They restored the 1880s house on the property, and the vineyards have been extended from the original 1ha to shiraz (2ha), grenache, mourvedre and zinfandel (1ha each). The shiraz is hand-picked, destemmed, fermented with wild yeast, and, at the end of fermentation, is pressed directly to barrel, where it remains for 28 months (with no racking) prior to blending and bottling with no fining or filtration. Exports to the UK, the US and Ireland.

♀♀♀♀♀ **Eternal Watch Clare Valley Shiraz 2010** Sourced from a vineyard in Armagh. Deep crimson-purple; it is astonishingly deep and complex, so much so that it clings to the mouth like an old muscat from Rutherglen (without the sweetness, of course); it has some intriguing licorice/anise/dark chocolate flavours as well as layers of blackberry fruit. Screwcap. 14.9% alc. **Rating** 93 **To** 2040 $25
Clare Valley Shiraz 2009 Dense purple-crimson; a massive wine with more of everything than one might imagine possible. It has magimixed blackberry, liqueur-soaked plums, bitter chocolate, licorice and spices, all of which submerge the tannins. Screwcap. 16.3% alc. **Rating** 92 **To** 2040 $38
Venus and Mars Clare Valley Shiraz 2010 The colour is darker and slightly less vibrant than Eternal Watch; has some of the same thickly thatched texture; it has touches of aldehyde, and both wines desperately need biodynamically farmed beef to accompany them. Screwcap. 15.1% alc. **Rating** 91 **To** 2040 $32

Serrat ★★★★★

PO Box 478, Yarra Glen, Vic 3775 **Region** Yarra Valley
T (03) 9730 1439 **www**.serrat.com.au **Open** Not
Winemaker Tom Carson **Est.** 2001 **Dozens** 300 **Vyds** 2.04ha
Serrat is the family business of Tom Carson (after a 12-year reign at Yering Station, now running Yabby Lake and Heathcote Estate for the Kirby family) and wife Nadege Suné. They have close-planted (at 8800 vines per hectare) 0.8ha each of pinot noir and chardonnay, 0.42ha of shiraz, and a sprinkling of viognier. Serrat was devastated by the Black Saturday bushfires in February 2009, the entire vintage destroyed. The '13 vintage saw business as normal, with the quality of the grapes outstanding.

♀♀♀♀♀ **Yarra Valley Chardonnay 2011** Pale straw-green; a perfectly proportioned and sculptured wine, with white flowers on the bouquet, white peach and nectarine on the palate, the barrel fermentation in French oak a means to an end, not an end in itself, so perfect is the balance of all the inputs. A great example of top-end modern Australian Chardonnay. Screwcap. 13% alc. **Rating** 96 **To** 2019 $35
Yarra Valley Pinot Noir 2011 Excellent colour (and clarity) given the vintage; the bouquet is exquisitely fragrant and flowery, the palate with pure pinot red fruit flavours, the tannins silky. There will be few Yarra Valley Pinots from '11 to equal the quality and poise of this wine. Screwcap. 13% alc. **Rating** 95 **To** 2017 $35

Setanta Wines ★★★★★

Glen Ewin Estate, Lower Hermitage Road, SA 5131 **Region** Adelaide Hills
T 0419 850 932 **www**.setantawines.com.au **Open** Tues–Sun 11–4
Winemaker Briony Hoare **Est.** 1997 **Dozens** 5000 **Vyds** 26ha

Setanta is a family-owned operation involving Sheilagh Sullivan, her husband Tony, and brother Bernard; the latter is the viticulturist, while Tony and Sheilagh manage marketing, administration and so forth. Of Irish parentage (they are first-generation Australians), they chose Setanta, Ireland's most famous mythological hero, as the brand name. The beautiful and striking labels tell the individual stories that give rise to the names of the wines. No wines received for the *2014 Wine Companion*, but a five-star rating has been maintained. Exports to Ireland, of course; also to the UK, Singapore, Hong Kong and Japan.

Settlement Wines

Lot 101 Seaview Road, McLaren Vale, SA 5171 **Region** McLaren Vale
T (08) 8323 7344 **www**.settlementwines.com.au **Open** Mon–Fri 10–5, w'ends & public hols 11–5
Winemaker Vincenzo Berlingieri **Est.** 1992 **Dozens** 3500
Vincenzo Berlingieri is a larger than life graduate of Perugia University, Italy. He arrived in Melbourne with beard flowing and arms waving (his words) in 1964 as a research scientist to work in plant genetics. He subsequently moved to SA, and gained considerable publicity for the winery he then owned, and for his larger than life wines. There is nothing new in the reincarnated Settlement Wines; it still has big table wines, but with specialties in liqueurs and fortified wines.

 **Cellar Door Series Sparkling Shiraz NV** I have only ever seen this wine at cellar door over wood-fired pizzas, and its stylish craftsmanship and delicious price immediately ranked it at the top of the Settlement portfolio. It proclaims the unbridled joy of young shiraz in all its white pepper, spice, blackberry and black plum glory, with a chorus of support from attractively textured, finely structured tannins. Cork. 12% alc. **Rating** 92 **To** 2015 $15 TS

Seven Ochres Vineyard ★★★

PO Box 202, Dunsborough, WA 6281 **Region** Margaret River
T (08) 9755 2030 **www**.sevenochres.com.au **Open** Not
Winemaker Chris Harding **Est.** 1998 **Dozens** 500 **Vyds** 4ha
Chris and Alice Harding have taken a circuitous route to the Margaret River, Chris' interest in wine blossoming while working at the Royal Sydney Yacht Squadron in the late 1970s, before moving to Scotland. He and wife Alice returned to Australia in '94, settling in the Margaret River region with their young family. They established the Viticlone Supplies Grapevine Nursery, and now have 60 varieties and over 120 clones available. Some of the more exotic varieties in propagation are vermentino, fiano, mondeuse, lagrein, sagrantino, cilliegiolo and sangiovese brunello di montalcino. They have established 1ha of viognier, encouraged by the early results from this variety. They have also purchased cabernet sauvignon, petit verdot and merlot from a single vineyard site in the northern part of the Margaret River.

Seven Sundays ★★★

PO Box 925, Gladesville, NSW 1675 **Region** Various
T 0411 701 700 **www**.sevensundays.com.au **Open** Not
Winemaker Petersons, Michael Hudson **Est.** 2009 **Dozens** 17 000
This is the virtual winery of Les Hill, best known as a television actor in *Underbelly*, *Rescue Special Ops* and *Home and Away*, and grazier David Flowers, the latter with a large sheep and cattle farm located in Trunkey Creek. They purchase grapes from the Hunter Valley, Mudgee and Adelaide Hills, and have the wines made at Petersons Champagne House. There is a heavy focus on exports to China, with limited Australian distribution.

Hunter Valley Sauvignon Blanc Semillon 2011 The Hunter Valley is shown as the sole region on the front label, the back label suggesting the sauvignon blanc comes from the Adelaide Hills, which is consistent with the flavours of the wine, however modest. Screwcap. 12.5% alc. **Rating** 87 **To** 2013 $16

Sevenhill Cellars

College Road, Sevenhill, SA 5453 **Region** Clare Valley
T (08) 8843 4222 **www**.sevenhill.com.au **Open** Mon–Fri 9–5, w'ends & public hols 10–5
Winemaker Liz Heidenreich, Brother John May **Est.** 1851 **Dozens** 25 000 **Vyds** 102ha
One of the historical treasures of Australia; the oft-photographed stone wine cellars are the
oldest in the Clare Valley, and winemaking remains an enterprise within the Jesuit Province
of Australia. Value for money is excellent, particularly for the powerful Shiraz and Riesling;
all the wines reflect the estate-grown grapes from old vines. Notwithstanding the difficult
economic times, Sevenhill Cellars has increased its vineyard holdings from 74ha to 102ha,
and production has risen. Exports to the US, Ireland, Switzerland, Indonesia, Malaysia, Japan,
Vietnam and China.

Inigo Clare Valley Riesling 2012 Bottled and released in May '12, its scented,
floral bouquet and expressive palate are an early testament to the quality of the
vintage; it has a similarly evocative palate, with citrus fruit framed by slatey acidity
on a lingering finish. Great bargain. Screwcap. 12% alc. **Rating** 95 To 2022 $20
St Francis Xavier Single Vineyard 2012 Clare riesling at its best, deceptively
delicate and elegant, but with great length and hidden power that will take
it through decades to come. The floral bouquet leads into a palate with lime,
grapefruit, and fine acidity. Screwcap. 12% alc. **Rating** 95 To 2032 $35
St Ignatius 2010 Full crimson-purple; cabernet sauvignon, merlot, malbec and
cabernet franc were planted in 1991, always intended to make this wine. The
full-bodied palate has blackcurrant, plum, licorice, earth and tar set in a crown of
tannins and quality oak. The balance is there to justify long cellaring. Screwcap.
14.2% alc. **Rating** 95 To 2040 $40
St Aloysius 2010 Pale, but bright, straw-green; the bouquet has a mix of flowers
and talc, the deceptively elegant palate revealing its inner strength and length on
retasting several times. A slow-developing, classic Riesling. Screwcap. 11.5% alc.
Rating 94 To 2025 $35

Brother John May Reserve Shiraz 2009 Rating 92 To 2030 $85
Inigo Clare Valley Grenache 2010 Rating 90 To 2016 $25

Seville Estate

65 Linwood Road, Seville, Vic 3139 **Region** Yarra Valley
T (03) 5964 2622 **www**.sevilleestate.com.au **Open** 7 days 10–5
Winemaker Dylan McMahon **Est.** 1970 **Dozens** 6000 **Vyds** 8.08ha
Dr Peter McMahon and wife Margaret commenced planting Seville Estate in 1972, part of
the resurgence of the Yarra Valley. Peter and Margaret retired in '97, selling to Brokenwood.
Graham and Margaret Van Der Meulen acquired the property in 2005, bringing it back into
family ownership. Graham and Margaret are hands-on in the vineyard and winery, working
closely with winemaker Dylan McMahon, who is the grandson of Peter and Margaret. The
philosophy is to capture the fruit expression of the vineyard in styles that reflect the cool
climate. Exports to Fiji, Taiwan, South Korea, Hong Kong, Singapore and China.

Reserve Yarra Valley Chardonnay 2011 Pale quartz; in the Chablis spectrum,
with citrus and mineral characters running through the heart of the wine, and
reflecting the cool vintage; it scores for its pristine elegance and length. Top gold
Yarra Valley Wine Show '12. Screwcap. 12.5% alc. **Rating** 95 To 2017 $60
Yarra Valley Chardonnay 2011 As good an expression of Yarra Valley
chardonnay as you are likely to find: tightly framed and focused white peach,
grapefruit and creamy/nutty nuances have all the drive and energy you could
wish for, the aftertaste as potent as the first taste. Screwcap. 12.5% alc. **Rating** 95
To 2020 $33
Yarra Valley Riesling 2012 Pale, bright straw-green; it retains brightness and
focus to its lime and apple fruit, and while the texture is based on some phenolics,
it all comes together remarkably harmoniously. Screwcap. 12% alc. **Rating** 94
To 2020 $33

Yarra Valley Blanc de Blanc 2010 Bright straw-green; bottle-fermented Chardonnay was given 18 months on lees prior to disgorgement, but then given zero dosage; the result is a very fresh aperitif style of considerable appeal. Crown seal. 12.5% alc. **Rating** 94 **To** 2014 $45

¶¶¶¶¶ **The Barber Yarra Valley Chardonnay 2012** Sourced from small vineyards in
✪   the Upper Yarra Valley, and that origin is immediately apparent in the bracing, crisp and long palate, where citrus/grapefruit flavours outbid the stone fruit and melon for attention, the finish fresh and dry. Screwcap. 13% alc. **Rating** 91 **To** 2016 $22
The Barber Yarra Valley Fume Blanc 2012 Rating 90 **To** 2015 $25 BE
✪   **The Barber Yarra Valley Shiraz 2011** A medium-bodied and savoury expression of the vintage, with red fruits, sage and peppery spice all prominently on display; the palate is fine-boned and accessible, with fresh acidity providing insight into a healthy mid term life ahead. Screwcap. 13% alc. **Rating** 90 **To** 2020 $22 BE
Yarra Valley Shiraz 2011 Rating 90 **To** 2020 $33 BE

Seville Hill

8 Paynes Road, Seville, Vic 3139 **Region** Yarra Valley
T (03) 5964 3284 **www**.sevillehill.com.au **Open** 7 days 10–6
Winemaker Dominic Bucci, John D'Aloisio **Est.** 1991 **Dozens** 3000
John and Josie D'Aloisio have had a long-term involvement in the agricultural industry, which ultimately led to the establishment of the Seville Hill vineyard in 1991. There they have 2.4ha of cabernet sauvignon and 1.3ha each of merlot, shiraz and chardonnay. John makes the wines with Dominic Bucci, a long-time Yarra resident and winemaker.

¶¶¶¶¶ Yarra Valley Cabernet Sauvignon 2006 Has retained good hue and depth of colour, the cork having done its job well. There is a truly impressive display of cassis and redcurrant fruit, embraced by supple tannins and quality oak. Cellar door only. Cork. 14.8% alc. **Rating** 94 **To** 2020 $50

¶¶¶¶¶ **Reserve Yarra Valley Chardonnay 2008 Rating** 91 **To** 2017 $25
Reserve Yarra Valley Shiraz 2009 Rating 91 **To** 2020 $30

Shadowfax

★★★★★

K Road, Werribee, Vic 3030 **Region** Geelong
T (03) 9731 4420 **www**.shadowfax.com.au **Open** 7 days 11–5
Winemaker Matt Harrop **Est.** 2000 **Dozens** 15 000
Shadowfax is part of an awesome development at Werribee Park, a mere 20mins from Melbourne. The truly striking winery, designed by Wood Marsh Architects and built in 2000, is adjacent to the extraordinary private home built in the 1880s by the Chirnside family and known as The Mansion. It was then the centrepiece of a 40 000ha pastoral empire, and the appropriately magnificent gardens were part of the reason for the property being acquired by Parks Victoria in the early 1970s. The Mansion is now The Mansion Hotel, with 92 rooms and suites. Exports to the UK, Japan, NZ and Singapore.

¶¶¶¶¶ Geelong Chardonnay 2012 The hand-picked grapes come from vineyards
✪   across Geelong; barrel-fermented with wild yeast, it has fully capitalised on the vintage, with both length and depth to its layered white peach/nectarine/grapefruit flavours. Screwcap. 13% alc. **Rating** 95 **To** 2018 $32
Macedon Ranges Chardonnay 2011 Pale quartz; there has been a deliberate decision to employ only used oak to focus purely on the very fine flavour and structure of the fruit, with mineral strands woven through the white peach and grapefruit flavours. Screwcap. 13% alc. **Rating** 95 **To** 2021 $45
Geelong Pinot Noir 2012 Light, bright red; a relatively light-bodied Pinot, but with a turbocharged burst of power through the back-palate and finish, where red fruits merge first with spicy notes, then a savoury aftertaste adding to the length. Screwcap. 13% alc. **Rating** 94 **To** 2018 $32

ŶŶŶŶ♀ **Adelaide Hills Sauvignon Blanc 2012** Pale straw-green; wild fermentation
✪   and lees contact have led to a wine with texture, structure and particularly good
       acidity; apple, kiwifruit, guava and grapefruit all add to the flavour complexity of a
       very good Sauvignon Blanc. Screwcap. 12.5% alc. **Rating** 93 **To** 2014 $22
✪   **Geelong Riesling 2012** Straw-green; a complex bouquet and palate offer
       lemon, lime and apple aromas and flavours in a seamless, come-hither stream.
       Ready now, but will hold. Screwcap. 12.5% alc. **Rating** 92 **To** 2017 $22
       Chardonnay 2011 Rating 92 **To** 2018 $32
       Minnow 2012 Rating 91 **To** 2016 $26

Shaw + Smith   ★★★★★

136 Jones Road, Balhannah, SA 5242 **Region** Adelaide Hills
T (08) 8398 0500 **www**.shawandsmith.com **Open** 7 days 11–5
Winemaker Martin Shaw, Adam Wadewitz **Est.** 1989 **Dozens** NFP **Vyds** 62.9ha
Cousins Martin Shaw and Michael Hill-Smith MW already had unbeatable experience when
they founded Shaw + Smith as a virtual winery in 1989. The brand was firmly established as a
leading producer of Sauvignon Blanc by the time they acquired a 42ha property at Woodside
known as the M3 Vineyard, as it is owned by Michael and Matthew Hill-Smith and Martin
Shaw. It produces the grapes for the M3 Chardonnay, and the most important part of the
Sauvignon Blanc. In '99 Martin and Michael purchased the 36ha Balhannah property, building
the superbly designed winery in 2000 and planting more sauvignon blanc, shiraz, pinot noir
and riesling. Exports to all major markets.

ŶŶŶŶŶ **Adelaide Hills Sauvignon Blanc 2012** Pale straw-green; has the usual laser
✪   precision of this wine, amplified by the perfect growing season and low yields; the
       bouquet and palate hover between grapefruit and tropical aromas and flavours,
       the palate with excellent persistence and length. Australia's best Sauvignon Blanc.
       Screwcap. 12.5% alc. **Rating** 96 **To** 2014 $28
       M3 Adelaide Hills Chardonnay 2012 Pale straw-green; a very elegant and
       finely structured wine, with white stone fruit, melon and grapefruit flavours,
       the acidity perfectly balanced, the oak restrained. Screwcap. 13% alc. **Rating** 96
       To 2020 $42

ŶŶŶŶ♀ **Incognito Shiraz 2010** Incognito is in every way baby Shaw + Smith Shiraz –
✪   declassified, but it can't have been far off making the cut. A cool-climate shiraz
       of style and persistence, beautiful texture and elegant refinement. Complexity
       of charcuterie and game overlay a core of dark cherry and black plum fruit.
       Screwcap. 14% alc. **Rating** 93 **To** 2018 $19 TS
✪   **Incognito Pinot Noir 2010** Shaw + Smith Pinot Noir hit a crescendo when
       its vines reached 12 years of age in '10, and Incognito is the declassified portion.
       Refreshingly elegant and pure red cherries and dried herbs are woven together
       with silky tannins, creating one of the best bargain Pinots I've tasted in years.
       Screwcap. 13% alc. **Rating** 92 **To** 2013 $19 TS

Shaw Vineyard Estate

34 Isabel Drive, Murrumbateman, NSW 2582 **Region** Canberra District
T (02) 6227 5827 **www**.shawvineyards.com.au **Open** Wed–Sun & public hols 10–5
Winemaker Bryan Currie, Graeme Shaw **Est.** 1999 **Dozens** 14 000 **Vyds** 33ha
Graeme and Ann Shaw established their vineyard (cabernet sauvignon, merlot, shiraz, semillon
and riesling) in 1998 on a 280ha fine wool-producing property established in the mid 1800s
and known as Olleyville. It is one of the largest privately owned vineyard holdings in the
Canberra area, and one of the few to produce 100% estate-grown wines. Their children
are fully employed in the family business, Michael as viticulturist and Tanya as cellar door
manager. The cellar door offers a wide range of local produce, as well as handmade ceramics
from Deruta in Italy. Fifty dollars from each dozen sale from the Laughter Series range is
donated to Camp Quality. No wines were produced in 2012 due to poor vintage conditions.
Exports to Canada, The Netherlands, Vietnam, Singapore, Thailand, the Philippines and China.

ŶŶŶŶŶ **Premium Canberra Cabernet Sauvignon 2009** Deep crimson-purple;
✪ redcurrant and blackcurrant fruit make their mark instantly, but it is on the second
and third tastings that the quality of the balance, texture and structure become
apparent. This is a seriously good Cabernet at a great price. Screwcap. 14% alc.
Rating 94 **To** 2029 $22

ŶŶŶŶŶ **Winemakers Selection Cabernet Sauvignon 2009** I would not have
✪ imagined that Canberra could pull elegantly appealing Cabernet out of its bag of
sub-$15 tricks, but here it is, in all of its vibrant rose petal, lifted violet, crunchy
redcurrant and pure red cherry glory. A portion of barrel maturation provide
subtle oak support, reinforcing fine, supple tannins. Screwcap. 14% alc. **Rating** 90
To 2014 $14 TS

She-Oak Hill Vineyard ★★★★

82 Hope Street, South Yarra, Vic 3141 (postal) **Region** Heathcote
T (03) 9866 7890 **www.**sheoakhill.com.au **Open** Not
Winemaker Sanguine Estate (Mark Hunter) **Est.** 1995 **Dozens** 500 **Vyds** 5ha
This is the venture of Judith Firkin, Gordon and Julian Leckie, who between 1975 and '95
planted shiraz (4.25ha) and chardonnay (0.75ha). The vineyard is located on the southern and
eastern slopes of She Oak Hill, 6km north of Heathcote. It lies between Jasper Hill, Emily's
Paddock and Mt Ida vineyards, and thus has the same type of porous, deep red Cambrian soil.
The decision to opt for dry-grown vines has meant low yields. Lower than usual alcohol level
is a feature of the wines, which have won a number of wine show medals.

ŶŶŶŶŶ **Estate Heathcote Shiraz 2010** Estate-grown, wild yeast-fermented and
matured in French oak (30% new); this has resulted in a juicy, spicy red and
black-fruited wine, the oak just a little assertive at this stage. Screwcap. 14.5% alc.
Rating 90 **To** 2020 $25

Sheer Drop Wines ★★★★

208 Faraday-Sutton Grange Road, Faraday, Vic 3451 (postal) **Region** Bendigo
T (03) 5474 3077 **www.**sheerdropwines.com.au **Open** Not
Winemaker Sarah Squire **Est.** 1995 **Dozens** 15000 **Vyds** 103ha
This is quite a story. Jo Clifford and Garth Doolan ask the rhetorical question, 'So how does
a couple with four young children stay sane while juggling 2500 fine wool merinos, 120ha
of grapes, and 100000 litres of premium, cool-climate wine? In a town such as Castlemaine,
the answer is obvious: you just create your own circus troupe!' They might have added they
enlisted the talents of painter Katharina Rapp to design the striking labels.

ŶŶŶŶŶ **Shiraz 2008** Has retained good hue and depth to the colour; this wine has
undoubtedly benefited from the warm vintage and skilled winemaking; it
is medium- to full-bodied, with a juicy assemblage of black fruits, spices, an
(unexpected) touch of dark chocolate, licorice also present; the oak and tannins are
precisely balanced with the fruit. Screwcap. 14.7% alc. **Rating** 94 **To** 2023 $25

ŶŶŶŶ **Chardonnay Pinot Noir NV Rating** 89 **To** 2014 $25

Shelmerdine Vineyards ★★★★★

Merindoc Vineyard, Lancefield Road, Tooborac, Vic 3522 **Region** Heathcote
T (03) 5433 5188 **www.**shelmerdine.com.au **Open** 7 days 10–5
Winemaker De Bortoli (Yarra Valley) **Est.** 1989 **Dozens** 6500 **Vyds** 62ha
Stephen Shelmerdine has been a major figure in the wine industry for over 25 years, like
his family (who founded Mitchelton Winery) before him, and has been honoured for his
many services to the industry. The venture has vineyards spread over three sites: Lusatia Park
in the Yarra Valley, and Merindoc Vineyard and Willoughby Bridge in the Heathcote region.
Substantial quantities of the grapes produced are sold to others; a small amount of high-quality
wine is contract-made. Exports to China.

ŸŸŸŸŸ Yarra Valley Blanc de Noirs 2007 From 100% estate-grown Upper Yarra pinot
noir made using the traditional method, and spent 5 years on lees before being
disgorged in June '12; has a combination of spiced red berry fruits and distinct
nutty/bready notes on the finish. Very expensive to make, cheap (relatively) to buy.
Diam. 13.5% alc. **Rating** 94 To 2015 $38

ŸŸŸŸŸ Merindoc Heathcote Viognier 2012 **Rating** 93 To 2015 $29
Merindoc Heathcote Riesling 2012 **Rating** 90 To 2015 $24

Shenton Ridge ★★★☆

PO Box 37, Margaret River, WA 6285 **Region** Margaret River
T (08) 9726 1284 www.shentonridge.com.au **Open** Not
Winemaker Dave Johnson **Est.** 2002 **Dozens** 3000 **Vyds** 6.5ha
The Catalano family purchased the Shenton Ridge property in the Jindong area of Margaret
River in 2002. The choice lay between extracting the gravel-rich soils or planting a vineyard;
the coin came down on the side of a vineyard, and vines (predominantly shiraz, chardonnay
and merlot) were planted. Andrea Catalano is now the sole owner and manager of the vineyard.

ŸŸŸŸŸ Margaret River Semillon Sauvignon Blanc 2012 A 60/40% blend, with a
strong grassy/snow pea/asparagus opening, moving to an unexpectedly tropical
fruit-dominated finish and aftertaste. 650 dozen made. Screwcap. 12.3% alc.
Rating 90 To 2014 $19

ŸŸŸŸ Margaret River Rose 2012 **Rating** 89 To 2013 $19
Biaggio Rossario Shiraz Reserve 2009 **Rating** 89 To 2019 $25

Shepherd's Hut ★★★★☆

PO Box 194, Darlington, WA 6070 **Region** Porongurup
T (08) 9299 6700 www.shepherdshutwines.com **Open** Not
Winemaker Rob Diletti **Est.** 1996 **Dozens** 2000 **Vyds** 15.5ha
The shepherd's hut that appears on the wine label was one of four stone huts used in the
1850s to house shepherds tending large flocks of sheep. When WA pathologist Dr Michael
Wishart (and family) purchased the property in 1996, the hut was in a state of extreme
disrepair. It has since been restored, still featuring the honey-coloured Mount Barker stone.
Riesling, chardonnay, sauvignon blanc, shiraz and cabernet sauvignon have been established.
The business is now owned by son Philip and wife Cathy, who also run a large farm of mainly
cattle. Most of the grapes are sold to other makers in the region, but those retained make high-
quality wine at mouth-watering prices thanks to the skill of contract winemaker Rob Diletti.

ŸŸŸŸŸ Porongurup Shiraz 2009 Has retained bright, light crimson-purple hue;
✪ a fragrant, perfumed red berry and spice bouquet leads into a juicy, light- to
medium-bodied palate complexed by French oak and superfine tannins. Lovely
stuff. Screwcap. 14.5% alc. **Rating** 94 To 2020 $22

ŸŸŸŸŸ Porongurup Chardonnay 2010 Whole bunch-pressed and taken direct to
✪ barrel for wild yeast fermentation; very tightly focused and structured, fruit rather
than oak doing the talking; the flavours are of grapefruit and apple, the acidity the
key. Gold medal Sydney Wine Show. Screwcap. 12.7% alc. **Rating** 93 To 2017 $22
✪ Porongurup Cabernet Sauvignon 2009 Light, bright crimson-purple; the
fragrant red berry and spice bouquet leads into an elegant, light- to medium-
bodied palate with juicy redcurrant and cassis fruit framed by a subtle French oak
and superfine tannins that, together, prolong the finish and aftertaste. Screwcap.
13.5% alc. **Rating** 93 To 2019 $22

Shingleback ★★★★★

3 Stump Hill Road, McLaren Vale, SA 5171 **Region** McLaren Vale
T (08) 8323 7388 www.shingleback.com.au **Open** 7 days 10–5
Winemaker John Davey, Dan Hills **Est.** 1995 **Dozens** 100000 **Vyds** 100ha
Brothers Kym and John Davey planted and nurture their family-owned and sustainably
managed vineyard on land purchased by their grandfather in the 1950s. Shingleback has been

a success story since its establishment in 1995. Originally focused on export, as times have changed, so has its focus. Its 100ha of estate vineyards are one of the keys to that success, winning the Jimmy Watson Trophy '06 for its '05 D Block Cabernet Sauvignon another. The well-made wines are rich and full-flavoured, but not overripe (and, hence, not excessively alcoholic). Exceptional results with its '11 Shirazs. Exports to the UK, the US, Canada, Switzerland, Germany, Indonesia, China and NZ.

ŸŸŸŸŸ **The Gate McLaren Vale Shiraz 2011** How this depth of colour was achieved in '11 I don't know; even less the full-bodied palate. Maybe 15% of high-quality '12 shiraz was blended (entirely legal), but that is less important than the splendidly rich palate festooned with high-quality oak and good tannins. Cork. 14.5% alc. Rating 94 To 2026 $35

Unedited McLaren Vale Shiraz 2011 While the use of heavy bottles is frowned upon by many, this epic wine is housed in one. That being stated, the contents reveal a deeply complex and powerful bouquet, with heady aromas of blackberry, spiced plum, mocha and fresh earth; the palate is powerfully proportioned, yet maintains freshness and focus. Diam. 14.5% alc. Rating 94 To 2030 $70 BE

ŸŸŸŸŸ **The Davey Estate Shiraz 2011** Rating 92 To 2019 $25

The Davey Estate Reserve Cabernet Sauvignon 2011 Rating 92 To 2019 $25

D Block Reserve McLaren Vale Shiraz 2011 Rating 91 To 2025 $60 BE

✪ **Red Knot McLaren Vale Shiraz 2012** Deep, dense, purple-red; absolutely full of black fruits, dark chocolate, earth and licorice fruit, the tannins in proportion, French and American oak likewise. Screwcap. 14% alc. Rating 90 To 2017 $15

ŸŸŸŸ **Black Prince McLaren Vale Shiraz Cabernet Sauvignon 2011** Its
✪ extraordinary deep purple-crimson colour caused my tannin and extract antennae to go into overdrive, but the black berry (blackcurrant/plum) and dark chocolate aromas and flavours have absorbed much of the slightly rustic tannin impact. Screwcap. 14% alc. Rating 89 To 2016 $16

✪ **Red Knot Cabernet Sauvignon 2012** Clearly made with the intention of giving maximum value, with blackcurrant, black olive, earth and dark chocolate erected on a superstructure of tannins and oak. A wine worthy of a few years in the cellar. Screwcap. 14% alc. Rating 89 To 2018 $15

Shottesbrooke ★★★★★

Bagshaws Road, McLaren Flat, SA 5171 **Region** McLaren Vale
T (08) 8383 0002 **www**.shottesbrooke.com.au **Open** Mon–Fri 10–4.30, w'ends & public hols 11–5
Winemaker Hamish Maguire, Duncan Kennedy **Est.** 1984 **Dozens** 12 000 **Vyds** 30.64ha
Founded by Nick Holmes, who has since passed the winemaking baton to stepson Hamish Maguire, Shottesbrooke these days is a very different business from that of the 1980s and '90s. As well as the great advantage of over 30ha of mature vines in McLaren Vale, it has ongoing access to sauvignon blanc from the Adelaide Hills. Exports to all major markets.

ŸŸŸŸŸ **Blewitt Springs Shiraz 2010** Good colour; has the innate elegance of Blewitt Springs; a mix of predominantly black fruits, quality oak and ripe tannins coalesce on the medium-bodied palate, a gently savoury finish to the advantage of the wine. Screwcap. 14.5% alc. Rating 94 To 2025 $38

Eliza Reserve McLaren Vale Shiraz 2009 Light red-purple; has attractive red fruit aromas, moving more towards black, on the light- to medium-bodied palate; a decidedly elegant evocation of McLaren Vale shiraz; oak, tannins and alcohol all restrained. Screwcap. 14% alc. Rating 94 To 2020 $45

ŸŸŸŸŸ **Eliza Reserve McLaren Vale Shiraz 2010** Rating 91 To 2022 $50 BE
✪ **Merlot 2010** Has enough black olive and tarry/earthy characters to stamp its varietal origin on the bouquet and medium-bodied palate; the overall balance and length are also good. Screwcap. 14.5% alc. Rating 91 To 2020 $20

✪   **Adelaide Hills Sauvignon Blanc 2012** Light straw-green; the fragrant bouquet leads into a juicy, supple palate, the flavours ranging from gooseberry to citrus, the finish clean and fresh. Screwcap. 13% alc. **Rating** 90 **To** 2013 $20

♀♀♀♀   **Regional Series Shiraz 2012** A rather odd name for a South Eastern Australian
✪   wine, but it has vivid purple-crimson colour and lashings of sweet cherry and plum fruit, the finish dry; may not have seen any oak. Very good value nonetheless. Screwcap. 14% alc. **Rating** 88 **To** 2015 $14

🍇 ShowBlock Estate   ★★★★★

Flagstaff Hill Road, Currency Creek, SA 5214 **Region** Currency Creek
T (08) 7225 6059 **www**.showblock.com.au **Open** Tues–Sat 9.30–5
Winemaker John Adamopoulos **Est.** 2008 **Dozens** 6000 **Vyds** 12ha
This is the venture of John and Sarae Adamopoulos, who (in 2008) acquired 12ha of shiraz, cabernet sauvignon and merlot which had been planted in 1997. John's father and uncles have grown grapes in McLaren Vale since migrating to Australia from Greece in the '50s and '60s, and he has now followed in their footsteps. In a prior life John was an engineer and thereafter and engineering teacher, but he is now the full-time carer for ShowBlock Estate. It has made a spectacular debut in the *Wine Companion*, with high-quality wines at yesterday's prices.

♀♀♀♀♀   **Shiraz Cabernet Sauvignon 2010** Excellent purple-crimson; the palate
✪   overflows with exuberantly intense blackberry, blackcurrant and licorice fruit, the tannins fine and supple, the oak incidental, the finish very long. Some will love this wine now, others down the track, but it will always give pleasure. Screwcap. 14.5% alc. **Rating** 94 **To** 2020 $18

✪   **Cabernet Sauvignon 2010** Full purple-crimson; an impressive Cabernet in every way, especially at this price; it has a full array of blackcurrant, redcurrant and a whisper of dark chocolate on both the bouquet and medium- to full-bodied palate, the latter sustained by ripe tannins, and has considerable length. Outstanding bargain. Screwcap. 14.5% alc. **Rating** 94 **To** 2025 $18

♀♀♀♀♀   **Cabernet Shiraz Merlot 2010** Has the deep, bright fruit of the '10 ShowBlock
✪   red wines; the fruit on the palate likewise has depth and richness, the three-way blend working synergistically, its inherent lusciousness balanced by fine, savoury tannins. Screwcap. 14.5% alc. **Rating** 93 **To** 2030 $18
    The Manifester's Shiraz 2010 Rating 91 **To** 2025 $38
✪   **Marsanne Roussanne Viognier 2010** The three varieties all contribute to the complexity of the bouquet and palate, the viognier possibly disproportionate to its percentage; the wine has peach, apricot and honeysuckle, with nuances of spice and ginger, and is neither phenolic nor sweet. Screwcap. 14% alc. **Rating** 90 **To** 2015 $15

Sidewood Estate   ★★★★☆

2 Hunt Road, Hahndorf, SA 5245 (postal) **Region** Adelaide Hills
T (08) 8388 7084 **www**.sidewood.com.au **Open** Not
Winemaker Natasha Mooney **Est.** 2000 **Dozens** 12 000 **Vyds** 62.7ha
Sidewood Estate is part-vineyard and part-horse stables and racehorse training. Owned by Owen and Cassandra Inglis since 2004, both aspects of the business are flourishing. Sidewood Estate lies in the Onkaparinga Valley, with the westerly vines weathering the coldest climate in the Adelaide Hills. In recent times Sidewood Estate has undergone a substantial planting regeneration program, the vineyard growing to over 60ha, and extensive investment in modern viticulture equipment has resulted in improved yields. Wines are released under the Sidewood Estate, Stable Hill and Mappinga labels; Mappinga is the new premier range, named after the road on which Sidewood resides. A cellar door is planned. Exports to the UK, the US, Canada, Belgium, Malaysia, Hong Kong, Singapore, Thailand and China.

ỴỴỴỴỴ **Mappinga Adelaide Hills Chardonnay 2011** Light straw-green; has above-average intensity and focus, due as much to the region as the vintage; notes of flint and mineral run through the citrussy overtones to the stone fruit and melon, French oak playing a support role. Screwcap. 12% alc. **Rating** 93 **To** 2021 $35

✪ **Adelaide Hills Pinot Gris 2012** Bright straw-green; a vibrant, fresh and precise wine, nashi pear and apple in a lemony acid sauce; leaves the mouth tingling. Screwcap. 13.5% alc. **Rating** 93 **To** 2014 $20

✪ **Adelaide Hills Shiraz 2010** Hand-picked and said to be 'whole bunch pressed', a highly unusual approach for a red wine, likewise its maturation in 'St Alliers' barriques. Is an impressive medium-bodied wine with the slice of cool-grown shiraz to the fore. Screwcap. 14% alc. **Rating** 93 **To** 2020 $25

✪ **Adelaide Hills Sauvignon Blanc 2012** Pale straw-green; a bright, fresh and tangy wine, with a zesty citrus/lime/pineapple/tropical basket of flavours. Screwcap. 12.5% alc. **Rating** 92 **To** 2013 $20

Sieber Road Wines   ★★★★

Sieber Road, Tanunda, SA 5352 **Region** Barossa Valley
T (08) 8562 8038 **www.**sieberwines.com **Open** 7 days 11–4
Winemaker Tony Carapetis **Est.** 1999 **Dozens** 4500 **Vyds** 18ha
Richard and Val Sieber are the third generation to run Redlands, the family property, traditionally a cropping/grazing farm. They have diversified into viticulture with shiraz (14ha) the lion's share, the remainder viognier, grenache and mourvedre. Son Ben Sieber is the viticulturist. Exports to Canada and China.

ỴỴỴỴỴ **Special Release Barossa Valley Shiraz 2010** Vivid purple hue; the bouquet offers black fruits, spicy oak, tar, licorice and toffee; the palate is full-bodied and densely packed with fruit, tannin and oak, with time a needed ingredient to see full integration. Screwcap. 14.1% alc. **Rating** 92 **To** 2022 $28 BE

Ernest Barossa Valley Shiraz 2010 Deeply coloured, with ripe blackberry fruit aromas, prune, licorice, fruitcake and charry oak on the bouquet; the palate is generous and big-boned, with a long charry note wrestling for dominance over the powerful tannins. Screwcap. 14.7% alc. **Rating** 90 **To** 2018 $20 BE

ỴỴỴỴ **Barossa Valley Shiraz Viognier 2010** **Rating** 88 **To** 2017 $18 BE
Barossa Valley Rose 2012 **Rating** 87 **To** 2014 $18 BE

Silver Spoon   ★★★☆

503 Heathcote-Rochester Road, Heathcote, Mount Camel, Vic 3523 **Region** Heathcote
T 0412 868 236 **www.**silverspoonestate.com.au **Open** By appt
Winemaker Peter Young **Est.** 2008 **Dozens** 250 **Vyds** 2.7ha
When Peter and Tracie Young purchased an existing shiraz vineyard on the top of the Mt Camel range in 2008, they did not waste any time. They immediately planted a second vineyard on the east side, and constructed a small winery. The name comes from the Silver Spoon fault line that delineates the Cambrian volcanic rock, and the old silver mines on the property. Peter became familiar with vineyards when working as a geologist in the 1970s in the Hunter Valley, and more recently completed the Master of Wine Technology and Viticulture degree at Melbourne University. They practise sustainable viticulture.

ỴỴỴỴỴ **Heathcote Shiraz 2009** The same 92% shiraz/8% viognier as the '10. The colour is good, the bouquet and palate with an attractive array of spicy red fruits, and a slight lift to the finish; overall, not as much extract or structure as one might expect from the region. Screwcap. 12.9% alc. **Rating** 90 **To** 2016 $38

ỴỴỴỴ **Heathcote Shiraz 2010** **Rating** 87 **To** 2014 $28

Silverstream Wines   ★★★★

2365 Scotsdale Road, Denmark, WA 6333 **Region** Denmark
T (08) 9840 9119 **www**.silverstreamwines.com **Open** By appt
Winemaker James Kellie, Michael Garland **Est.** 1997 **Dozens** 3000 **Vyds** 9ha
Tony and Felicity Ruse have 9ha of chardonnay, merlot, cabernet franc, pinot noir, riesling
and viognier in their vineyard 23km from Denmark. The wines are contract-made, and after
some hesitation, the Ruses decided that their very pretty garden and orchard more than
justified opening a cellar door, a decision supported by the quality of the wines on offer at
very reasonable prices.

 Riesling 2012 A restrained bouquet, exhibiting fresh-cut lemon and lime; the
palate is bone dry, with pronounced acidity and drawing the finish to a long and
fresh conclusion. Screwcap. 12.3% alc. **Rating** 90 **To** 2017 $22 BE

Silverwood Wines   ★★★★

66 Bittern-Dromana Road, Balnarring, Vic 3926 **Region** Mornington Peninsula
T 0419 890 317 **www**.silverwoodwines.com.au **Open** Not
Winemaker Paul Dennis, Phillip Kittle **Est.** 1997 **Dozens** 900 **Vyds** 3.2ha
Paul and Denise Dennis were inspired to establish Silverwood after living in France for a year.
They, with members of their family, did much of the establishment work on the vineyard
(pinot noir, chardonnay and sauvignon blanc), which is meticulously maintained. All of the
grapes are now used for Silverwood (in earlier years some were sold). Exports to Hong Kong
and Singapore.

 Estate Mornington Peninsula Pinot Noir 2010 Spends 11 months in French
barriques, and is the result of a selection of the best of those barrels. While the
colour is relatively light, the hue is good, and the overall impression is freshness;
the one question is whether the oak is a little too obvious, but it's difficult to
gainsay the gently warm flavours it adds to the small red berry fruits of the palate.
Screwcap. 13.3% alc. **Rating** 91 **To** 2018 $27

The Reserve Pinot Noir 2008 Rating 89 **To** 2016 $40

Simon Whitlam & Co.   ★★★★

PO Box 1108, Woollahra, NSW 1350 **Region** Hunter Valley Zone
T (02) 9007 5331 **Open** Not
Winemaker Graeme Scott (Contract) **Est.** 1979 **Dozens** 2000
My association with the owners of Simon Whitlam – Andrew and Hady Simon, Nicholas
and Judy Whitlam, and Grant Breen – dates back to the late 1970s, at which time I was
a consultant to the Simons' leading wine retail shop in Sydney, Camperdown Cellars. The
association continued for a time after I moved to Melbourne in '83, but ceased altogether
in '87 when Camperdown Cellars was sold, thereafter being merged with Arrowfield Wines.
The Simon Whitlam label was part of the deal, and it passed through a number of corporate
owners until 20 years later, when the original partners regained control of the business. It is a
virtual winery, the grapes purchased and the wine contract-made. This reflects the combined
marketing and financial expertise of the partners. Exports to New Caledonia and China.

Reserve McLaren Vale Cabernet Sauvignon 2010 A more than useful
McLaren Vale Cabernet from an extremely useful vintage; the medium-bodied
palate has attractive cassis fruit with nuances of earth, chocolate and oak spice, the
tannins persistent but fine. Screwcap. 14.5% alc. **Rating** 93 **To** 2025 $35
McLaren Vale Shiraz 2009 Good retention of hue; the expressive black fruits,
licorice and dark chocolate aromas of the bouquet are precisely replicated on
the medium-bodied palate, cosseted by American oak and ripe tannins. Has the
balance to age very well. Screwcap. 14% alc. **Rating** 91 **To** 2024 $23

Hunter Valley Petit Verdot 2010 As ever, good colour; petit verdot does best in warmer climates, and it is no surprise that this medium- to full-bodied wine should have good dark berry fruits with a touch of savoury black olive on the finish. Screwcap. 13% alc. **Rating** 90 **To** 2017 $23

ȚȚȚȚ **Reserve Hunter Valley Shiraz 2010 Rating** 87 **To** 2014 $29

Sinapius Vineyard ★★★★

4232 Bridport Road, Pipers Brook, Tas 7254 **Region** Northern Tasmania
T 0417 341 764 **www.**sinapius.com.au **Open** Thur–Mon 11–4
Winemaker Vaughn Dell, Linda Morice **Est.** 2005 **Dozens** 800 **Vyds** 3ha
Vaughn Dell and Linda Morice purchased the former Golders Vineyard in 2005 (originally planted 1994). More recent vineyard plantings include 13 clones of pinot noir and eight clones of chardonnay, as well as small amounts of gruner veltliner and pinot gris. The new vineyard area is close-planted, ranging from 5100 vines per hectare for the gruner veltliner to 10250 vines per hectare for the pinot noir and chardonnay. The wines are made onsite with a minimalist approach: natural ferments, basket-pressing, extended lees ageing and minimal fining and filtration. Exports to The Netherlands.

ȚȚȚȚȚ **Pipers Brook Chardonnay 2010** A wine of linear focus and textural presence, it's tightly coiled, honed and restrained in its youth, projecting focused lemon and white peach fruit, which sit slightly disjoint from its cashew nut French oak themes. It promises to unravel impressively over the coming years. Screwcap. 13.5% alc. **Rating** 92 **To** 2018 $40 TS
Pipers Brook Pinot Noir 2011 Vibrant mid cherry red; lifted red fruits, clove and cinnamon provide the bouquet; the palate is light-bodied and precise, with taut acidity and fine-grained tannins; the finish offers a toasty note that is harmonious with the fruit on offer. Screwcap. 13.5% alc. **Rating** 90 **To** 2015 $45 BE
Pipers Brook Riesling 2012 Devoid of colour when 10 months old; it does, however, have bright lemon, lime and mineral flavours; the balance is good, and all the wine needs is a minimum of 3 years in bottle. Screwcap. 9% alc. **Rating** 90 **To** 2020 $28

ȚȚȚȚ **Pipers Brook Chardonnay 2011 Rating** 87 **To** 2016 $45 BE

Sinclair of Scotsburn ★★★☆

256 Wiggins Road, Scotsburn, Vic 3352 **Region** Ballarat
T (03) 5341 3936 **www.**sinclairofscotsburn.com.au **Open** W'ends 11–4, Mon–Fri by appt
Winemaker Scott Ireland **Est.** 1997 **Dozens** 140 **Vyds** 2ha
David and (the late) Barbara Sinclair purchased their property in 2001. At that time 1.2ha of chardonnay and 0.8ha of pinot noir had been planted, but had struggled, the pinot noir yielding less than 0.25 tonnes in '02. With the aid of limited drip irrigation, cane pruning, low crop levels and bird netting, limited quantities of high-quality chardonnay and pinot have since been produced. Two-thirds of the annual production is sold to Tomboy Hill and Provenance Wines, the remaining third made for the Sinclair of Scotsburn label.

ȚȚȚȚ **Wallijak Chardonnay 2010** Has the delicacy of the very cool climate, with crunchy grapefruit and peach flavours which have absorbed its oak, although not its acidity. Screwcap. 13.5% alc. **Rating** 89 **To** 2015 $21
Wallijak Chardonnay 2009 Light straw-green; has retained its youth thanks to the double-edged sword of its high acidity, which thins out the fruit to a degree – time won't fix this. Screwcap. 13.5% alc. **Rating** 88 **To** 2014 $21
Manor House Pinot Noir 2010 Light but bright colour; proclaims its cool-grown origins with unusual spicy/bitter nuances on the fore-palate, and a very savoury finish. Screwcap. 13.5% alc. **Rating** 87 **To** 2014 $21

Sinclair's Gully ★★★★

288 Colonial Drive, Norton Summit, SA 5136 **Region** Adelaide Hills
T (08) 8390 1995 **www**.sinclairsgully.com **Open** W'ends & public hols 12–4 (Aug–June),
Fri 5–9 (Jan–Mar), or by appt
Winemaker Contract **Est.** 1998 **Dozens** 800 **Vyds** 1ha

Sue and Sean Delaney purchased their property at Norton Summit in 1997. The property had a significant stand of remnant native vegetation, with a State Conservation Rating, and much energy has been spent in restoring 8ha of pristine bushland, home to 130 species of native plants and 66 species of native birds, some recorded as threatened or rare. The adoption of biodynamic viticulture has coincided with numerous awards for the protection of the natural environment and, more recently, eco-tourism; they operate the only eco-certified cellar door in the Adelaide Hills, and have won innumerable ecological and general tourism awards. Sparkling wine disgorgement demonstrations are a particular attraction.

ΨΨΨΨΩ **Rubida 2008** The base wine, a blend of pinot noir and chardonnay, was basket-pressed and barrel-fermented before being taken to bottle for the second fermentation. A complex and rich wine with considerable flavour; the dosage is a little high. Cork. 13% alc. **Rating** 93 **To** 2015 $55
Adelaide Hills Chardonnay 2011 Bright straw-green; a juicy, fresh and decidedly tangy wine, the fruit pushing some French oak maturation well into the background. Grapefruit, crunchy apple and white peach all sound the bell. Screwcap. 12.5% alc. **Rating** 91 **To** 2017 $28

ΨΨΨΨ **Talia 2009 Rating** 88 **To** 2014 $40
Adelaide Hills Pinot Noir 2011 Rating 87 **To** 2014 $28

Singlefile Wines ★★★★★

90 Walter Road, Denmark, WA 6333 **Region** Denmark
T 1300 885 807 **www**.singlefilewines.com **Open** 7 days 11–5
Winemaker Mike Garland, Coby Ladwig (Contract) **Est.** 2007 **Dozens** 6000 **Vyds** 3.75ha

In 1986 geologists Phil and Viv Snowden moved from South Africa to Perth, where they developed their their successful multinational mining and resource services company, Snowden Resources. Following the sale of their company in 2004, they decided to turn their attention to their long-held desire to make and enjoy fine wine. Their research of the principal wine regions of Australia confirmed their desire to settle where cool-climate wines of outstanding quality could be produced. In '07 they bought an established vineyard (planted '89) in the beautiful Denmark subregion. They pulled out the old shiraz and merlot vines, planted chardonnay, and retained Larry Cherubino to set up partnerships with established vineyards in Frankland River, Porongurup, Denmark, Pemberton and Margaret River to make the rest of the wines in the distinguished Singlefile portfolio. The cellar door, tasting room and restaurant are strongly recommended. Exports to the US and China.

ΨΨΨΨΨ **Family Reserve Denmark Chardonnay 2011** A wine that carries its complexity as if it were weightless; layered and long, it has great line and balance. Top gold medal James Halliday Chardonnay Challenge '12. Screwcap. 13.3% alc. **Rating** 96 **To** 2019 $45
Frankland River Shiraz 2011 Deep purple-crimson, it is an extremely rich and complex wine, its full-bodied, plush palate full of black fruits, licorice and spice; despite all this concentration and power, it is very well balanced, and has the base of ripe tannins to repay extended cellaring. Screwcap. 14.5% alc. **Rating** 95 **To** 2031 $37
Barossa Valley Shiraz 2010 Deep purple-crimson, it has been very well made, its registry of blackberry, black cherry and satsuma plum welded together by fine, savoury tannins and quality oak. Screwcap. 14.7% alc. **Rating** 95 **To** 2030 $70

✪ **Porongurup Riesling 2012** Pale quartz-green; the young rieslings of Porongurup share the same reticence as most young semillons, and you have to draw on the library of experience in watching them burst into a many-splendoured display with 3 or 4 years bottle age. Paradoxically, it is often the most reticent young wines that make the greatest transformation, and this is one such example. Screwcap. 11.5% alc. **Rating** 94 **To** 2027 $25
Denmark Chardonnay 2012 A Chardonnay with attitude, displaying strong white peach and citrus on both bouquet and palate, oak and crunchy acidity giving emphasis and length to the finish. Screwcap. 13.9% alc. **Rating** 94 **To** 2020 $30

🍷🍷🍷🍷🍷 **Denmark Pinot Noir 2011 Rating** 93 **To** 2017 $30
Margaret River Cabernet Sauvignon Merlot 2011 Rating 93 **To** 2021 $37
✪ **Run Free The Duo Great Southern Cabernet Merlot 2011** Bright, vivid red-purple, it has delicious juicy cassis, plum and redcurrant fruit supported by silky tannins and a light touch of French oak. Will hold, but will never be more easily enjoyed than it is now. Screwcap. 14.3% alc. **Rating** 93 **To** 2017 $25
✪ **Run Free The Sisters Great Southern Sauvignon Blanc Semillon 2012** Exceptionally fragrant, spanning all the way from green bean to passionfruit, and simply builds on those characters on the juicy, full-flavoured palate. Great value. Screwcap. 13.5% alc. **Rating** 92 **To** 2014 $20
✪ **Denmark Semillon Sauvignon Blanc 2012** The bouquet is clean and fresh, the action comes on the vibrant and energetic palate, with its lemon/lemongrass/mineral flavours. It is a wine that will definitely repay cellaring. Screwcap. 13.3% alc. **Rating** 92 **To** 2017 $25
✪ **Run Free Great Southern La vie en Rose 2012** Bright, light pink; a well above average Rose, the fragrant and red berry/flower-scented bouquet leading into a fresh red cherry palate; clear, fresh and uncluttered, it finishes crisp and dry. Good value. Screwcap. 13.5% alc. **Rating** 92 **To** 2014 $20
Run Free Sweet Tilly 2012 Rating 92 **To** 2015 $20
Pemberton Fume Blanc 2012 Rating 90 **To** 2015 $30

Sir Paz Estate   ★★★★

384 George Street, Fitzroy, Vic 3065 **Region** Yarra Valley
T (03) 9417 9337 **www.**sirpaz.com **Open** By appt
Winemaker Rob Dolan, Glen Olsen, John Zapris **Est.** 1997 **Dozens** 4500 **Vyds** 22ha
The Zapris family established Sir Paz Estate in 1997, planting just under 6ha of shiraz; the first release of 2001 scored an emphatic gold medal at the Victorian Wines Show '03 as the highest scored entry. The success led to the planting of additional merlot, chardonnay and sauvignon blanc. It is not hard to see the anagrammatic derivation of the name. Exports to the US, Canada, Mexico, Germany, United Arab Emirates and China.

🍷🍷🍷🍷🍷 **Yarra Valley Shiraz 2008** This is a full-bodied Yarra Valley Shiraz still in its infancy, and can be given the extra decade or so it needs with total confidence in good cellaring conditions; over this period the opulence of the fruit will gain more texture. Diam. 14.5% alc. **Rating** 93 **To** 2025 $68

Sirromet Wines

850–938 Mount Cotton Road, Mount Cotton, Qld 4165 **Region** Queensland Coastal
T (07) 3206 2999 **www.**sirromet.com **Open** 7 days 9–4.30
Winemaker Adam Chapman, Jessica Ferguson **Est.** 1998 **Dozens** 30 000 **Vyds** 85.6ha
This ambitious venture has succeeded in its aim of creating Qld's premier winery. The founding Morris family retained a leading architect to design the striking state-of-the-art winery; the state's foremost viticultural consultant to plant three major vineyards (in the Granite Belt); and the most skilled winemaker practising in Qld, Adam Chapman, to make the wine. It has a 200-seat restaurant and is firmly aimed at the tourist market, taking advantage

of its situation, halfway between Brisbane and the Gold Coast. In 2009 it mothballed part of its Granite Belt vineyards, thus reducing production in the face of the GFC. The blocks so treated were then flooded in '11, leaving the blocks in commission unharmed. Exports to Sweden, South Korea, Papua New Guinea, Hong Kong, China and Japan.

ŸŸŸŸŸ **LM Private Collection Granite Belt Cabernet Sauvignon Petit Verdot Merlot 2010** The colour is very good crimson-purple, bright and clear, and the medium-bodied palate has been crafted with a sure touch to showcase the pristine cassis and redcurrant fruit; cedary oak and nigh-on perfect tannins provide the structure for a top-flight wine. Screwcap. 14.2% alc. **Rating** 96 **To** 2030 $99
Wild Granite Belt Shiraz Viognier 2010 The shiraz and viognier were co-fermented with wild yeast after a pre-fermentation cold soak (6 days in all) followed by 14 months in oak. The fragrant, spicy bouquet is followed by a fresh, supple medium-bodied palate with more red than black fruits, and a long, finely detailed finish. Screwcap. 13.1% alc. **Rating** 94 **To** 2020 $55

ŸŸŸŸŸ **Seven Scenes Granite Belt Cabernet Sauvignon 2010** **Rating** 93 **To** 2020 $30
Seven Scenes Granite Belt Chardonnay 2011 **Rating** 92 **To** 2016 $35
Seven Scenes Granite Belt Viognier 2010 **Rating** 90 **To** 2015 $30

ŸŸŸŸ ✪ **820 Above Granite Belt Pinot Gris 2011** Has distinct touches of cinnamon/anise to go with the pear fruit. It adds interest to a well-balanced, well-made wine. Screwcap. 13.7% alc. **Rating** 89 **To** 2014 $19

Sisters Run

PO Box 382, Tanunda, SA 5352 **Region** Barossa
T (08) 8563 1400 **www**.sistersrun.com.au **Open** Not
Winemaker Elena Brooks **Est.** 2001 **Dozens** NFP
Sister's Run is owned by noted Barossa Valley vignerons Carl and Peggy Lindner (owners of Langmeil), directly employing the skills of Elena Brooks as winemaker, and, indirectly, the marketing know-how of husband Zar Brooks. The Stiletto and Boot are those of Elena, and the motto 'The truth is in the vineyard, but the proof is in the glass' is, I would guess, the work of Zar Brooks. The prices of the wines, and their quality in the face of the 2011 vintage, make this a brand to watch (and buy). Exports to all major markets.

ŸŸŸŸŸ ✪ **Bethlehem Block Gomersal Cabernet 2010** Good hue of modest depth; the fragrant cassis-accented bouquet is a bright start, and the finely structured, juicy red and black fruits of the medium-bodied palate are most appealing. Seriously good value. Screwcap. 14.5% alc. **Rating** 93 **To** 2020 $20

✪ **Babylon Block Lyndoch Riesling 2011** Pale straw; leaves no doubt about the cool growing conditions through the season, with slate/mineral/herb nuances on the mid-palate, leaving it until the last moment for lime/citrus to make its appearance on the finish and, in particular, the aftertaste. Could surprise with bottle age. Screwcap. 11.5% alc. **Rating** 91 **To** 2019 $20

✪ **Calvary Hill Lyndoch Shiraz 2010** Good hue, although not starry bright; as honest as the day is long, in the very heart of time-honoured Barossa Valley style; the flavours are rich and ripe, but not the least over the top; the oak is subtle, and the tannins ripe. It will wait for you if you wish, but don't keep a lady waiting too long. Screwcap. 14.5% alc. **Rating** 91 **To** 2016 $20

✪ **Barossa Valley Shiraz 2008** Bright, light red-purple; a deceptive wine, starting off quietly, but then building rapidly through the palate as fruit, tannins and obvious oak all take hold. Has an unusual frenetic Zar Brooks label. Screwcap. 14.5% alc. **Rating** 90 **To** 2020 $18

ŸŸŸŸ **Sunday Slippers Lyndoch Chardonnay 2011** **Rating** 89 **To** 2015 $20
Calvary Hill Lyndoch Shiraz 2009 **Rating** 88 **To** 2015 $20

Sittella Wines ★★★★★

100 Barrett Street, Herne Hill, WA 6056 **Region** Swan Valley
T (08) 9296 2600 **www**.sittella.com.au **Open** Tues–Sun & public hols 11–5
Winemaker Colby Quirk **Est.** 1998 **Dozens** 8000 **Vyds** 10ha
Perth couple Simon and Maaike Berns acquired a 7ha block (with 5ha of vines) at Herne Hill, making the first wine in 1998 and opening a most attractive cellar door facility later in the year. They also own the Wildberry Springs Estate vineyard in the Margaret River region. Consistent and significant wine show success has brought well-deserved recognition for the wines. A triumphant return to the *Wine Companion* after going AWOL from last year's edition.

ΨΨΨΨΨ **Margaret River Sauvignon Blanc Semillon 2011** The fragrant bouquet, and
✪ lively, juicy palate, are far more attractive than its '12 counterpart; citrus to the fore and snow pea and grassy/herbal notes in the background make oak utterly irrelevant; has excellent length. Screwcap. 12.6% alc. **Rating** 94 **To** 2016 $22
Reserve Swan Valley Shiraz 2011 Dense red-purple; the richness of the dark fruits on the bouquet continues on the full-bodied, although soft and velvety, palate; blackberry and dark chocolate are balanced by obvious but positive French oak. Needs time to lose its baby fat, but given the benefit of any doubt. Screwcap. 13.5% alc. **Rating** 94 **To** 2026 $38
Berns Reserve 2011 Bright crimson-purple; a very impressive wine, estate-grown Margaret River cabernet sauvignon having soaked up the 18 months spent in French oak; the balance between fruit, oak and tannins is nigh-on perfect. Screwcap. 13.5% alc. **Rating** 94 **To** 2026 $38
Berns Reserve 2009 Bright crimson; fractionally more luscious than the '10, but from the same family style; there are perfectly pitched, gently savoury tannins, backed by the right amount of French oak. Margaret River Cabernet Sauvignon. Screwcap. 13.9% alc. **Rating** 94 **To** 2029 $38

ΨΨΨΨΨ **Berns and Walsh Cane Cut Verdelho 2012** The cane cutting seems to have
✪ had limited effect, but stopping the fermentation with significant residual sugar has had more; has good balance, with heightened focus and flavour, citrussy acidity to the fore. 375ml. Screwcap. 10% alc. **Rating** 93 **To** 2015 $20
✪ **Margaret River Chardonnay 2011** Pale straw-green; produced from Sittella's estate vineyard in Margaret River, and in typical sotto voce Sittella style, stone fruit and melon fruit woven through subtle oak, the overall balance very good. Screwcap. 12.5% alc. **Rating** 92 **To** 2017 $23
✪ **Silk 2011** The interplay between the two vintages of all the Sittella whites is interesting, sometimes the younger, sometimes the older, wine gaining a slim supremacy. This traditional WA/Swan Valley blend of verdelho, chenin blanc and chardonnay performs very well in this instance, with positive fruit running through to a long finish. Screwcap. 13% alc. **Rating** 91 **To** 2015 $17
✪ **Swan Valley Shiraz 2011** Well made, and an interesting approach to early picking; the colour is bright, the dark fruits of the bouquet and medium-bodied palate with well-judged French oak and gentle, ripe tannins providing very good balance and length. Screwcap. 12.6% alc. **Rating** 91 **To** 2021 $21
Show Reserve Liqueur Verdelho NV Rating 91 **To** 2014 $38

Skillogalee ★★★★★

Trevarrick Road, Sevenhill via Clare, SA 5453 **Region** Clare Valley
T (08) 8843 4311 **www**.skillogalee.com.au **Open** 7 days 10–5
Winemaker Dave Palmer **Est.** 1970 **Dozens** 15 000 **Vyds** 50.3ha
David and Diana Palmer purchased the small hillside stone winery from the George family at the end of the 1980s and have fully capitalised on the exceptional fruit quality of the Skillogalee vineyards. All the wines are generous and full-flavoured, particularly the reds. In 2002 the Palmers purchased next-door neighbour Waninga Vineyards, with 30ha of 30-year-old vines, allowing an increase in production without any change in quality or style. Exports to the UK, Canada, Switzerland, Hong Kong, Malaysia, Singapore and NZ.

ŶŶŶŶŶ Clare Valley Riesling 2012 Bright, light straw-green; full to the brim on the bouquet and palate with fragrant lime and grapefruit aromas and flavours; the palate has very good length and persistence, the aftertaste fresh and clean. Screwcap. 12.5% alc. **Rating** 95 **To** 2027 $25

ŶŶŶŶŶ Basket Pressed Clare Valley Shiraz 2009 **Rating** 91 **To** 2019 $29
Clare Valley Gewurztraminer 2012 **Rating** 90 **To** 2016 $26

Skimstone

1307 Castlereagh Highway, Apple Tree Flat, Mudgee, NSW 2850 **Region** Mudgee
T (02) 6373 1220 **www**.skimstone.com.au **Open** Thurs–Mon & public hols 11–5
Winemaker Joshua Clementson **Est.** 2009 **Dozens** 3000 **Vyds** 15ha
This is a joint venture between Josh and Kate Clementson and Michael and Anne-Marie Horton; the Clementsons live on and run the estate and cellar door. Josh had previously worked for Orlando (one year), then Peter Logan (five years), and has been vineyard manager at Huntington Estate for the past three vintages. The partners were thus able to see the potential of the rundown Apple Tree Flat vineyard in 2007, and have since worked hard to bring the vineyard back to full health. They have particular faith in sangiovese and barbera (5ha) as varieties for the future.

ŶŶŶŶŶ Mudgee Sangiovese Rose 2012 Has a surprising amount of red cherry fruit,
✪   with an intriguing but very attractive citrus twist on the finish; dry yet fruity. Screwcap. 12.5% alc. **Rating** 92 **To** 2014 $22
Tre Onde Mudgee Sangiovese Barbera Cabernet 2011 The three components (60/20/20%) were blended during fermentation. Red and black cherries take the lead, but there are savoury/earthy/dark chocolate nuances to add flavour and texture complexity. Screwcap. 14% alc. **Rating** 91 **To** 2026 $40

Smallfry Wines

13 Murray Street, Angaston, SA 5353 **Region** Barossa Valley
T (08) 8564 2182 **www**.smallfrywines.com.au **Open** By appt (T 0412 153 243)
Winemaker Wayne Ahrens **Est.** 2005 **Dozens** 1000 **Vyds** 27ha
The engagingly named Smallfry Wines is the venture of Wayne Ahrens and partner Suzi Hilder. Wayne is from a fifth-generation Barossa family; Suzi is the daughter of well-known Upper Hunter viticulturist Richard Hilder and wife Del, partners in Pyramid Hill Wines. Both have degrees from CSU, and both have extensive experience – Suzi as a senior viticulturist for TWE, and Wayne with a track record that includes seven vintages as a cellar hand at Orlando Wyndham and other smaller Barossa wineries. They have a 10ha vineyard in the Eden Valley (led by cabernet sauvignon and riesling), and a long-established 17ha vineyard in the Vine Vale area of the Barossa Valley, which has no less than 16 varieties, led by shiraz, grenache, semillon, mourvedre, cabernet sauvignon and riesling. Exports to the UK, the Philippines, Indonesia, Singapore, Hong Kong and China.

ŶŶŶŶŶ Aged Release Eden Valley Riesling 2007 The colour is still bright and light; shows how well the delicate Smallfry style evolves; there is a greater range of apple/lime/honey/toast flavours, but the journey is still to be completed. Screwcap. 11% alc. **Rating** 94 **To** 2017 $25
Barossa Valley Shiraz Muscadelle 2009 Medium red-purple, some development; a complex wine with spicy/savoury nuances imparted in part by the muscadelle, in part by the oak; the medium-bodied palate has good line, length and balance. Screwcap. 15.1% alc. **Rating** 94 **To** 2024 $48
Barossa Valley Shiraz Muscadelle 2008 Only 30 dozen made, the muscadelle interplanted and co-fermented with the shiraz; picked before the heatwave, the flavours are complex, but with riper, plumper characters than those of the '09. Screwcap. 14% alc. **Rating** 94 **To** 2023 $48

ŶŶŶŶŶ **Eden Valley Riesling 2012** It is easy to pass by without paying enough
✪ attention to this wine, with its very good balance between fruit, acidity and
minerality; the lemongrass flavours will assume a honeyed sheen with bottle age.
Screwcap. 11% alc. **Rating** 93 **To** 2020 $18

✪ **Joven 2012** An exotic blend of tempranillo, garnacha, monastrel, carinena
and bastardo made without any addition of SO_2, and not producing any during
fermentation (usually around 5ppm); the brilliant purple hue is followed by a
wonderfully juicy red and blue fruit palate, tannins (like SO_2) more significant for
their absence than their presence. Screwcap. 14% alc. **Rating** 92 **To** 2013 $20
Barossa Valley Shiraz 2010 Rating 90 **To** 2018 $28
Barossa Valley Gilbert 2010 Rating 90 **To** 2014 $35

Smidge Wines ★★★★☆

62 Austral Terrace, Malvern, SA 5061 (postal) **Region** South Eastern Australia
T (08) 8272 0369 **www**.smidgewines.com **Open** Not
Winemaker Matt Wenk **Est.** 2004 **Dozens** 1000
Matt Wenk and Trish Callaghan have many things in common: joint ownership of Smidge
Wines, marriage, and their real day jobs. Matt has a distinguished record as a Flying Winemaker
and, in Australia, has worked with Tim Knappstein and then Peter Leske at Nepenthe. These
days he is the winemaker for Two Hands Wines (and Sandow's End). Trish holds a senior
position in one of the world's largest IT services companies. The Houdini label provides
entry-level wines, followed by the white label varietal wines (The Cellar-pod Viognier, Adam
Shiraz, The Tardy Zinfandel, The Donald Zinfandel and Le Grenouille Merlot), with flagship
S Smitch Shiraz at the top. All the Magic Dirt wines are made in precisely the same way, and
each is a best barrel selection (French oak) from selected areas of the Barossa Valley. At Smidge's
request, no prices are shown for the wines. Exports to the UK and the US.

ŶŶŶŶŶ **Magic Dirt Moppa Barossa Valley Shiraz 2010** Impenetrable colour; dark
and brooding on the bouquet with a lifted vine-sap complexity, licorice and
fruitcake spice on display; the palate is dense and dark-fruited, with ample chewy
tannins, yet lightness returns on the finish to provide a harmonious conclusion;
big-boned, but with finesse. Cork. 14.9% alc. **Rating** 94 **To** 2025 BE

ŶŶŶŶŶ **Magic Dirt Greenock Barossa Valley Shiraz 2010 Rating** 91 **To** 2018 BE
Pedra Branca Barossa Valley Mourvedre 2011 Rating 90 **To** 2020 BE

Smith & Hooper of Wrattonbully ★★★★☆

Caves Edward Road, Naracoorte, SA 5271 **Region** Wrattonbully
T 0412 847 383 **www**.smithandhooper.com **Open** By appt
Winemaker Peter Gambetta **Est.** 1994 **Dozens** 15 000 **Vyds** 62ha
On one view of the matter, Smith & Hooper is simply one of many brands within various of
the Hill-Smith family financial/corporate structures. However, it is estate-based, with cabernet
sauvignon and merlot planted on the Hooper Vineyard in 1994, and cabernet sauvignon and
merlot planted on the Smith Vineyard in '98. Spread across both vineyards are 9ha of trial
varieties. Exports to all major markets.

ŶŶŶŶŶ **Reserve Merlot 2010** Has retained good hue; an elegant but positively flavoured
wine with good varietal character from start to finish; plum, redcurrant and black
olive fruit flavours are supported by well-balanced and integrated tannins and oak.
Cork. 14% alc. **Rating** 94 **To** 2025 $30

ŶŶŶŶŶ **Cabernet Sauvignon Merlot 2009 Rating** 91 **To** 2019 $22

Snake + Herring ★★★★★

PO Box 918, Dunsborough, WA 6281 **Region** South West Australia Zone
T 0419 487 427 **www**.snakeandherring.com.au **Open** Not
Winemaker Tony Davis **Est.** 2010 **Dozens** 5000

This is the venture of Tony Davis (Snake) and Redmond Sweeny (Herring). Both started university degrees but then found that they were utterly unsuited to their respective courses. Having stumbled across Margaret River, Tony's life changed forever; he enrolled at Adelaide University's Roseworthy Campus, thereafter doing vintages in the Eden Valley, Oregon, Beaujolais and Tasmania, before three years at Plantagenet, next Brown Brothers, then a senior winemaking role at Yalumba, Millbrook winery in the Perth Hills, and finally four years with Howard Park in Margaret River. Redmond's circuitous course included a chartered accounting degree and employment with an international accounting firm in Busselton, and the subsequent establishment of Forester Estate in 2001 in partnership with Kevin McKay. Back on home turf he is the marketing and financial controller of Snake + Herring.

ŶŶŶŶŶ **Business Time Mount Barker Great Southern Shiraz 2011** Deep, bright purple-crimson; built to live and evolve over decades. It is unashamedly full-bodied, with layer upon layer of plum, licorice/anise and quality oak, the tannins ripe, but to the fore right now. Screwcap. 13.5% alc. **Rating** 96 **To** 2041 $35

High and Dry Porongurup Great Southern Riesling 2012 Light to medium straw-green; a wine in the mainstream of the tightly framed Porongurup style, but grabs attention with its mouth-watering citrussy acidity spearing through the length of the palate. Screwcap. 11.5% alc. **Rating** 94 **To** 2015 $28

Teardrop Mt Barker Great Southern Riesling 2012 Bright green-straw; generosity and harmony are the key words here, with ripe lime juice balanced by delicate but persistent acidity; there are even hints of tropical/passionfruit characters. Screwcap. 11% alc. **Rating** 94 **To** 2020 $28

✪ **Perfect Day Margaret River Sauvignon Blanc Semillon 2012** A 79/21% blend from Karridale, the southernmost and coolest part of Margaret River. A wine that strikes out on its own in the context of the region, with potent lemon zest/lemon pith characters on the bouquet and fore-palate that are reluctant to let anything other than barrel ageing grab attention. I like the wine; others may not. Screwcap. 12.5% alc. **Rating** 94 **To** 2017 $23

ŶŶŶŶŶ **The Distance Higher Ground Porongurup Cabernet Sauvignon 2011** **Rating** 92 **To** 2020 $60 BE
Wide Open Road Great Southern Pinot Noir 2012 **Rating** 91 **To** 2015 $23
Cannonball Margaret River Cabernet Sauvignon Merlot Petit Verdot 2011 **Rating** 91 **To** 2020 $38 BE

Snobs Creek Wines ★★★☆

486 Goulburn Valley Highway, via Alexandra, Vic 3714 **Region** Upper Goulburn
T (03) 9596 3043 **www.**snobscreekvineyard.com.au **Open** W'ends 11–5
Winemaker Marcus Gillon **Est.** 1996 **Dozens** 1500 **Vyds** 5ha
The vineyard is situated where Snobs Creek joins the Goulburn River, 5km below the Lake Eildon wall. The varieties grown are shiraz (2.5ha), sauvignon blanc (1.5ha) and chardonnay (1ha); all manage to produce no more then 7.4 tonnes per hectare. Is described as a cool-climate vineyard in a landscaped environment.

ŶŶŶŶŶ **Reserve Chardonnay 2010** The colour is still bright and pale, and the wine has lost none of the freshness and clarity of its youth; it has absorbed the new French oak component, leaving white peach and honeydew melon on the mid-palate, picking up touch of citrus on the long, well-balanced finish. Screwcap. 13.2% alc. **Rating** 93 **To** 2017 $30

ŶŶŶŶ **Reserve Pinot Noir 2010** **Rating** 87 **To** 2015 $30
V.S.P. Shiraz 2010 **Rating** 87 **To** 2015 $20

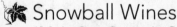 # Snowball Wines ★★★☆

11 Irvine Street, Peppermint Grove, WA 6011 (postal) **Region** Margaret River
T 0417 917 769 **www.**snowballwines.com **Open** Not
Winemaker Mike Edwards, Nav Singh, Bernie Stanlake **Est.** 2000 **Dozens** 200 **Vyds** 0.4ha

Snowball might seem an odd name for a Margaret River winery until you learn it was established by GP Phil Snowball and wife Louise. The original idea was to simply have a weekend escape from Phil's busy Cottesloe general practice, but within three years of the purchase of the property in 1996, the bug had bit. However, given that there was only 0.4ha available for planting, it was never going to get out of control, even though the pair decided to do all of the vineyard work themselves. They also retained Bernie Stanlake to make the wines, further limiting the margin for error.

🍷🍷🍷🍷🍷 **Merlot Cabernet Sauvignon Cabernet Franc 2009** This estate-grown 53/25/22% blend spending 16–18 months in 30–50% French oak, the precise choices vintage-dependent; the blend works exceptionally well, and skilled winemaking is also evident in the cherry, plum and cassis fruit that is the raison d'être of the wine. Screwcap. 13.5% alc. **Rating** 93 **To** 2020 $27

🍷🍷🍷🍷 **Merlot Cabernet Sauvignon Cabernet Franc 2010** **Rating** 88 **To** 2015 $23

Somerled

89 Main Street, Hahndorf, SA 5245 **Region** Adelaide Hills
T (08) 8388 7478 **www**.somerled.com.au **Open** Thurs–Sun 10–6
Winemaker Rob Moody **Est.** 2001 **Dozens** 2500
This is the venture of Robin and Heather Moody, and daughters Emma and Lucinda. The quietly spoken Robin (with a degree in oenology) joined Penfolds in 1969, and remained with Penfolds/Southcorp until 2001. In that year the Moodys commenced establishing a range of wines using contract-grown grapes, and now produce a sparkling wine, Sauvignon Blanc, Chardonnay, Fume Blanc and Picnic Races Red and Shiraz (from Kangaroo Island). The name comes from the bay gelding that Robin's grandfather raced to victory in the amateur steeplechase at the Oakbank Picnic Races in 1908, and which took its name from the Scottish king who defeated the Vikings in 1156. The other names, obviously enough, follow in the footsteps of Somerled. Exports to Hong Kong and China.

🍷🍷🍷🍷🍷 **McLaren Vale Shiraz 2007** While the wine spent over 2 years in mainly French oak, and emanates from the tough '07 vintage, it comes together very well, with good length and balance. If it were not for the cork, I would be more bullish about its lively longevity. 14.5% alc. **Rating** 91 **To** 2017 $34

Somerset Hill Wines ★★★☆

540 McLeod Road, Denmark, WA 6333 **Region** Denmark
T (08) 9840 9388 **www**.somersethillwines.com.au **Open** 7 days 11–5 summer, winter 11–4
Winemaker Graham Upson **Est.** 1995 **Dozens** 3500 **Vyds** 10.7ha
Graham Upson planted pinot noir, chardonnay, semillon, merlot, pinot meunier and sauvignon blanc in 1995 on one of the coolest and latest-ripening sites in WA. The limestone cellar door area has sweeping views out over the ocean and to the Stirling Ranges, and also sells Belgian chocolates. Exports to the UK, Denmark, Russia, Poland, China and Japan.

🍷🍷🍷🍷🍷 **Merlot 2012** Bright crimson-purple; even if I, as the winemaker, thought a Merlot tasted of 'ripe stewed fruit', I would not dream of describing it as such on the back label; what we have here is a mix of cassis, plum and a touch of black olive, with balanced oak and tannins. Screwcap. 14% alc. **Rating** 90 **To** 2019 $28

🍷🍷🍷🍷 **Pinot Noir 2012** **Rating** 89 **To** 2016 $28

Sons & Brothers Vineyard

Spring Terrace Road, Millthorpe, NSW 2798 **Region** Orange
T (02) 6366 5117 **www**.sonsandbrothers.com.au **Open** Not
Winemaker Dr Chris Bourke **Est.** 1978 **Dozens** 250 **Vyds** 2ha
Chris and Kathryn Bourke do not pull their punches when they say, 'Our vineyard has had a chequered history because in 1978 we were trying to establish ourselves in a non-existent wine region with no local knowledge and limited personal knowledge of grapegrowing and

winemaking. It took us about 15 years of hit and miss before we started producing regular supplies of appropriate grape varieties at appropriate ripeness levels for sales to other NSW wineries.' Chris has published two fascinating papers on the origins of savagnin in Europe, and also traced its movements in Australia after it was one of the varieties collected by James Busby – and moved just in time to save the last plantings in NSW of Busby's importation. The idea is that a percentage will be co-fermented with the Cabernet Shiraz blend which is the mainstay of the winery.

ΨΨΨΨΨ
✪
Cabernet Shiraz 2005 Has held remarkable hue and depth; a 60/40% blend given a year in barrel then 5 years in bottle under a stainless steel crown seal. The flavours of blackberry, blackcurrant and plum are very well balanced by fine tannins and the memory of oak. Given its age and quality, an exceptional bargain. 13.5% alc. **Rating** 94 **To** 2020 $25

ΨΨΨΨΩ
✪
Cabernet of Millthorpe 2010 A blend of cabernet sauvignon, shiraz and savagnin, the colour is light, although the hue is good. While only light- to medium-bodied, the wine has considerable length and overall freshness and fragrance; red berry fruits dominate, albeit with some blue and black fruit nuances, the tannins fine. Full of interest due to the old-vine savagnin. Crown seal. 13.4% alc. **Rating** 92 **To** 2020 $25

Sons of Eden   ★★★★★

Penrice Road, Angaston, SA 5353 **Region** Barossa Valley
T (08) 8564 2363 **www.**sonsofeden.com **Open** 7 days 10–6
Winemaker Corey Ryan, Simon Cowham **Est.** 2000 **Dozens** 7000 **Vyds** 60ha
Sons of Eden is the venture of winemaker Corey Ryan and viticulturist Simon Cowham, who both learnt and refined their skills in the vineyards and cellars of Eden Valley. Corey is a trained oenologist with over 20 vintages under his belt, having cut his teeth as a winemaker at Henschke. Thereafter he worked for Rouge Homme and Penfolds in Coonawarra, backed up with winemaking stints in the Rhône Valley; in 2002 he took the opportunity to work in NZ for Villa Maria Estates. Simon has a similarly international career, covering such diverse organisations as Oddbins, UK and the Winemakers' Federation of Australia. Switching from the business side to grapegrowing when he qualified as a viticulturist, he worked for Yalumba as technical manager of the Heggies and Pewsey Vale vineyards. With this background, it comes as no surprise that the estate-grown wines are of outstanding quality. Exports to the US, Hong Kong, the Philippines, Taiwan and China.

ΨΨΨΨΨ
✪
Freya Eden Valley Riesling 2012 This is classic Eden Valley at its best; the fragrant, flowery citrus blossom aromas lead into a laser-cut palate, at once juicy yet minerally, the flavours hitting the tip of the tongue as the wine enters the mouth, and then refusing to go away. Screwcap. 12% alc. **Rating** 96 **To** 2025 $25
Romulus Old Vine Barossa Valley Shiraz 2010 A deeper, more purple, and more dense, hue than Remus; the wine spent 20 months in American oak, which has combined with the opulent black fruits and licorice to provide a flamboyant wine that somehow cuts through its layers of flavour. These are two heroic Shirazs. Cork. 14.5% alc. **Rating** 96 **To** 2035 $70
Remus Old Vine Eden Valley Shiraz 2010 A complex, luscious wine that shows its 22-month maturation in mainly new French oak; the fruit flavours are in a black cherry and spice spectrum, the tannins plentiful but ripe, reflecting the minimal fining. Cork. 14.5% alc. **Rating** 95 **To** 2030 $70
Pumpa Eden Valley Cabernet Sauvignon Shiraz 2010 Full purple-crimson; a 47/24/9% blend of cabernet sauvignon, shiraz and tempranillo that is loaded with flavour and character; cassis, black cherry and blackberry all react synergistically, with a seductive bitter chocolate/earth character attached to the tannins. Great value. Screwcap. 14.5% alc. **Rating** 94 **To** 2025 $25

♥♥♥♥♡ **Zephyrus Barossa Valley Shiraz 2011** Rating 93 To 2026 $35
✪ **Kennedy Barossa Valley Grenache Shiraz Mourvedre 2011** Bright crimson-purple hue; a 30/37/24% blend; particularly attractive wine in the context of '11, with abundant sweet dark berry fruit without any Turkish Delight/confection flavours; there is a seamless flow of flavour from the first sip right the way through to the aftertaste. Screwcap. 14% alc. **Rating** 93 **To** 2021 $25

Soul Growers

PO Box 805, Tanunda, SA 5352 (postal) **Region** Barossa Valley
T 0439 026 727 **www**.soulgrowers.com **Open** By appt
Winemaker James Lindner, Paul Lindner, David Cruickshank **Est.** 1998 **Dozens** 4000
Vyds 6.8ha
Soul Growers has four owners, headed by Paul Heinicke (Managing Director/winemaker) and David Cruickshank (senior winemaker). Paul and James Lindners's main focus is Langmeil Wines, but they play a role as directors/winemakers. The estate vineyards are mainly on hillside country in the Seppeltsfield area, with shiraz, cabernet sauvignon, grenache and chardonnay the most important, and lesser plantings of mataro and black muscat; there are then pocket-handkerchief blocks of shiraz at Tanunda, mataro at Nuriootpa and a 1.2ha planting of grenache at Krondorf. Exports to the US, Canada, Singapore, Hong Kong and China.

♥♥♥♥♡ **Slow Grown Barossa Shiraz 2010** Pushing the boundaries of ripeness can be a tricky game to play; the bouquet offers spicy oak, red fruits and fruitcake aromas, and the palate is mid weighted on entry, warm on the finish and a little tough in the middle; a little more freshness would go a long way, yet there is still plenty to like. Cork. 15.5% alc. **Rating** 92 **To** 2018 $50 BE
Single Vineyard Barossa Malbec 2010 A big, rich and ripe rendition of the variety, displaying regional characters of bitter chocolate, prunes and a little blue fruit complexity; the palate is fleshy and fresh, with a briary freshness that is in harmony with the fruit. Screwcap. 15.5% alc. **Rating** 90 **To** 2018 $25 BE

♥♥♥♥ **Single Vineyard Eden Valley Riesling 2012** Rating 88 To 2017 $20 BE
Soul Sister Barossa Rose 2012 Rating 88 To 2014 $18 BE
Provident Barossa Valley Shiraz 2010 Rating 88 To 2018 $25 BE
Resurgence Barossa Shiraz Cabernet Sauvignon 2010 Rating 88 To 2017 $25 BE
Cellar Dweller Cabernet Sauvignon 2010 Rating 88 To 2017 $50 BE

Soumah

18 Hexham Road, Gruyere, Vic 3770 **Region** Yarra Valley
T (03) 5962 4716 **www**.soumah.com.au **Open** Mon, Thurs–Fri 11–4, w'ends & public hols 10–5
Winemaker Scott McCarthy **Est.** 1997 **Dozens** 6000 **Vyds** 19.5ha
Unravelling the story behind the exotically named Soumah and its strikingly labelled Savarro (reminiscent of 19th-century baroque design) was a voyage of discovery up and down a series of minor dead-end roads. This despite the fact that Soumah is within walking distance of my house at Coldstream Hills. Soumah is in fact an acronym meaning South of Maroondah (Highway), while Savarro is an alternative name for savagnin. It is a venture of the Butcher family, headed by patriarch Frank Wynyard Butcher, who was a horticultural scientist with the Victorian Department of Primary Industry for more than 30 years. Two of his sons, Greg and Brett, together with their families, own the Soumah project; Greg a retired electrical engineer, is revelling in the day-to-day management of Soumah, while non-executive director Brett has international experience in the hospitality industry as CEO of the Langham Group, and a long involvement in retailing wines to restaurants in many countries. Tim Brown is viticultural director. All of the many varieties planted have been clonally selected and grafted onto rootstock, with the long-term future in mind, although some of the sauvignon blanc is already being grafted over to bracchetto. Exports to Canada, Hong Kong, Japan and China.

ŶŶŶŶŶ **Single Vineyard Yarra Valley Chardonnay 2011** Brilliant green-straw; a very complex and intense wine, the mlf fully justified, for there is still abundant acidity in the backbone of the palate to sustain the rich stone fruit and citrus flavours. Screwcap. 12% alc. **Rating** 94 **To** 2019 $34

ŶŶŶŶ♀ **Single Vineyard Yarra Valley Pinot Noir 2011 Rating** 92 **To** 2016 $29
Skye Blox Yarra Valley Chardonnay 2012 Rating 91 **To** 2017 $20
Single Vineyard Yarra Valley Savarro 2012 Rating 91 **To** 2015 $26 BE
Single Vineyard Yarra Valley Pinot Grigio 2012 Rating 90 **To** 2014 $24

South Channel Wines   ★★★☆

485 Bittern-Dromana Road, Red Hill, Vic 3937 (postal) **Region** Mornington Peninsula
T 0412 361 531 **Open** Not
Winemaker Tony Lee (Contract) **Est.** 1997 **Dozens** 1100 **Vyds** 4.1ha
Leading Melbourne orthopaedic surgeon David Booth has planted just over 4ha of pinot noir, pinot gris and shiraz on a large property situated on warm, northern slopes overlooking Dromana and the busy South Channel leading to the port of Melbourne. 'At times,' says David Booth, 'the big ships seem to appear in the vineyard.' Other varieties are being trialled in a nursery section, and the range of wines may increase somewhere down the track.

ŶŶŶŶ♀ **Mornington Peninsula Shiraz 2006** First tasted almost 5 years ago by Ben
✪   Edwards, and given 90 points. Miraculously, it is still available, and – despite its light body – it still has fresh and lively spicy red berry fruits. But enjoy it now. Screwcap. 14.5% alc. **Rating** 90 **To** 2014 $15

ŶŶŶŶ **Mornington Peninsula Pinot Noir 2010** Light, bright red. This is a no-frills
✪   Pinot Noir, but it has clear varietal expression courtesy of red fruits with a subtle savoury/spicy overlay. Ready now. Screwcap. 13.5% alc. **Rating** 89 **To** 2014 $18
✪   **Mornington Peninsula Dry White 2012** A puppy dogs' tails blend of vermentino, viognier, roussanne and sauvignon blanc; has plenty of assorted fruit flavours, and a cleansing, bright finish. Screwcap. 12.5% alc. **Rating** 88 **To** 2014 $15

Spinifex   ★★★★★

PO Box 511, Nuriootpa, SA 5355 **Region** Barossa Valley
T (08) 8564 2059 **www**.spinifexwines.com.au **Open** At Artisans of Barossa
Winemaker Peter Schell **Est.** 2001 **Dozens** 4000
Peter Schell and Magali Gely are a husband and wife team from NZ who came to Australia in the early 1990s to study oenology and marketing at Roseworthy College. They have spent four vintages making wine in France, mainly in the south, where Magali's family were vignerons for generations near Montpellier. The focus at Spinifex is the red varieties that dominate in the south of France: mataro (more correctly mourvedre), grenache, shiraz and cinsaut. The wine is made in open fermenters, basket-pressed, given partial wild (indigenous) fermentations, and relatively long post-ferment maceration. This is a very old approach, but nowadays à la mode. As far as I am concerned Spinifex out-Torbrecks Torbreck. Exports to the UK, the US, Canada, Belgium, Taiwan, Singapore, Hong Kong and NZ.

ŶŶŶŶŶ **La Maline 2010** An effusive and supple array of juicy red and black fruits on the medium-bodied palate; there are ample oak and fluffy tannins to add texture, but it's the fruit that does the talking. The name is not a play on Guigal's La Mouline, but (minus the 'La') is French for crafty or cunning. Screwcap. 14.5% alc. **Rating** 95 **To** 2030 $60
Esprit 2010 Good hue, although not especially deep, or expected to be. A blend of mataro, shiraz, grenache and cinsaut that joyously reflects the '10 vintage with its cascade of red cherry, raspberry, strawberry – plus any other berry flavour you care to name – and a long finish that is at once silky and savoury. Screwcap. 14% alc. **Rating** 95 **To** 2020 $35

Bête Noir 2010 Medium crimson-purple; a very complex and potent wine, its medium- to full-bodied palate built on a structure of savoury, ripe tannins running from start to finish on the palate, and fusing the black fruit flavours into a single line. 'Bête noir' is the bane of one's existence. Screwcap. 14% alc. Rating 94 To 2030 $42

Indigene 2010 Medium purple-red; a blend of mataro (mouvredre) and shiraz that has a firmer structure than Esprit, its flavours with black cherry and plum to the fore; it needs a little more patience, but will repay it. Screwcap. 14.5% alc. Rating 94 To 2025 $60

ŸŸŸŸŸ Papillon 2011 Rating 92 To 2015 $26
D.R.S. Vineyard 2010 Rating 91 To 2017 $48

Spook Hill Wines ★★★

PO Box 335, Cadell, SA 5321 **Region** Riverland
T 0428 403 235 **www**.spookhillwines.com **Open** Not
Winemaker Jock Gordon **Est.** 1999 **Dozens** 1000 **Vyds** 10ha
Owner and winemaker Jock Gordon Jr's family have been grapegrowers for three generations, but in 1999 Jock took the plunge into commercial winemaking after a successful career as an amateur winemaker. He has 8ha of shiraz, 1ha of alicante bouschet and 1ha split between mourvedre and durif, supplemented by grapes from local growers. The Spook Hill vineyard is situated in the Cadell Valley, a former oxbow of the Murray River now bypassed by the river channel; silt soil deposited in the ancient river valley is especially suited to viticulture. The wines are open-fermented, basket-pressed and matured in the onsite winery.

ŸŸŸŸ
✪ The Apparition Cabernet Blend 2009 Good colour; a fresh, light- to medium-bodied wine with an array of red and black fruits, a touch of mint, and fine tannins; the American oak has worked surprisingly well, staying in the background. Screwcap. 12.3% alc. Rating 89 To 2015 $20

✪ Petty Criminal Petit Verdot 2010 Unsurprisingly, has the deepest colour of the Spook Hill reds. It is an exercise in naked power, the full-bodied palate with black fruits, a strong tannin backbone and vanillin American oak. A large T-bone over charcoal would meet its soulmate in this wine. Screwcap. 14.9% alc. Rating 89 To 2020 $19

Spring Vale Vineyards ★★★★☆

130 Spring Vale Road, Cranbrook, Tas 7190 **Region** East Coast Tasmania
T (03) 6257 8208 **www**.springvalewines.com **Open** 7 days 11–4
Winemaker Kristen and David Cush **Est.** 1986 **Dozens** 10 000 **Vyds** 12.1ha
Rodney Lyne has progressively established pinot noir (6.5ha), chardonnay (2ha), gewurztraminer (1.6ha), pinot gris and sauvignon blanc (1ha each). Spring Vale also owns the Melrose Vineyard, which is planted to pinot noir (3ha), sauvignon blanc and riesling (1ha each) and chardonnay (0.5ha). Exports to Singapore.

ŸŸŸŸŸ Pinot Noir 2010 Offers a savoury array of aromas, with dark cherry, cold tea, game and damp forest floor; light-bodied and finely detailed, the palate reveals taut acidity and fine tannins wrapped around silky red fruits; expansive, with lead pencil oak a feature on the finish. Screwcap. 13.5% alc. Rating 94 To 2017 $40 BE

ŸŸŸŸŸ Reserve Chardonnay 2011 Rating 91 To 2017 $40 BE
Gewurztraminer 2012 Rating 90 To 2015 $35 BE
Sauvignon Blanc 2012 Rating 90 To 2015 $25 BE

Springs Hill Vineyard ★★★☆

Schuller Road, Blewitt Springs, SA 5171 **Region** McLaren Vale
T (08) 8383 7001 **www**.springshill.com.au **Open** Sun & public hols
Winemaker Anthony and Gary Whaite **Est.** 1998 **Dozens** 1000 **Vyds** 17.1ha

Anthony and Gary Whaite began the planting of their vineyard in 1975 with cabernet sauvignon and shiraz and have slowly expanded it over the years with merlot, mourvedre and grenache. The vines are dry-grown, and the whole operation from vine to wine is carried out by the pair. They use traditional small-batch winemaking techniques of open fermenters, which are hand-plunged, basket-pressed, etc.

ΨΨΨΨΨ **Blewitt Springs Cabernet Sauvignon 2010** Full purple-crimson; its fruit
flavours are brooding and black, and the tannins, while ripe, need to soften.
Has the balance to repay a minimum of 5 years' cellaring. Screwcap. 14.5% alc.
Rating 91 **To** 2023 $29

ΨΨΨΨ **Blewitt Springs Merlot 2010 Rating** 89 **To** 2018 $29
Blewitt Springs Grenache 2010 Rating 87 **To** 2016 $29 BE

Squitchy Lane Vineyard   ★★★★

Medhurst Road, Coldstream, Vic 3770 **Region** Yarra Valley
T (03) 5964 9114 **www**.squitchylane.com.au **Open** W'ends 11–4
Winemaker Robert Paul **Est.** 1982 **Dozens** 2000 **Vyds** 5.75ha
Owner Mike Fitzpatrick acquired his taste for fine wine while a Rhodes scholar at Oxford University in the 1970s. Returning to Australia he guided Carlton Football Club to two premierships as captain, then established Melbourne-based finance company Squitchy Lane Holdings. The wines of Mount Mary inspired him to look for his own vineyard, and in '96 he found a vineyard of sauvignon blanc, chardonnay, pinot noir, merlot, cabernet franc and cabernet sauvignon planted in '82 just around the corner from Coldstream Hills and Yarra Yering. In '04 he put in place a team to take the venture through to the next stage, with wines under the Squitchy Lane label, launched in '07. Since '09 the wines have been made at Sticks.

ΨΨΨΨΨ **Yarra Valley Fume Blanc 2012** Barrel fermentation in French oak seems to
have enhanced the tropical fruit flavours, not what one might expect, given the
modest alcohol; perhaps the 30-year-old vines are the answer. Whatever, it's a rich
and complex wine. Screwcap. 12.5% alc. **Rating** 92 **To** 2014 $26
Yarra Valley Chardonnay 2011 Barrel-fermented in French oak and followed
by 10 months' lees contact. While clearly varietal, the palate doesn't have the
energy, acidity or length of the best Chardonnays of the vintage, but is a good
second. Screwcap. 12.5% alc. **Rating** 91 **To** 2017 $26
SQL Yarra Valley Red Square 2010 A thoroughly unusual blend of cabernet
sauvignon, cabernet franc, merlot and shiraz; the colour is bright but light, as are
the predominantly cassis/red fruit aromas and flavours, the finish dry and crisp.
Screwcap. 13% alc. **Rating** 90 **To** 2018 $22

Staniford Wine Co   ★★★★★

20 Jackson Street, Mount Barker, WA 6324 **Region** Great Southern
T 0405 157 687 **www**.stanifordwineco.com.au **Open** Not
Winemaker Michael Staniford **Est.** 2010 **Dozens** 500
Michael Staniford has been making wine in the Great Southern region since 1995, principally as senior winemaker for Alkoomi at Frankland River, with additional experience as a contract maker for other wineries. The business is built around single vineyard wines; the first two releases are a Chardonnay (Mendoza clone) from a 20-year-old vineyard in Albany, and a Cabernet Sauvignon from a 15-year-old vineyard at Denbarker in Mount Barker. The quality of these two wines is every bit as one would expect. Michael plans to introduce a Riesling and Shiraz with a similar individual vineyard origin, quality being the first requirement.

ΨΨΨΨΨ **Great Southern Reserve Cabernet Sauvignon 2011** A high-quality wine
✪ from top to toe, opening with deep, bright crimson-purple, moving to a bouquet
flooded with cassis and intriguing touches of spice, thence to a medium- to full-
bodied, but perfectly balanced, palate; here the juicy cassis fruit is invested with a
sense of gravitas by firm tannins and cedary oak. Bred to stay. Screwcap. 13.5% alc.
Rating 96 **To** 2041 $36

Great Southern Reserve Chardonnay 2011 Deep, glowing yellow-green; the grapes were grown in the Albany subregion from mature, low-yielding vines, the fruit of sufficient depth and intensity to justify the use of 100% new French oak; despite this power, and resultant complexity, the wine is so well balanced it retains elegance. The finish and aftertaste are especially impressive. Screwcap. 13.5% alc. Rating 94 To 2018 $36

Stanton & Killeen Wines

440 Jacks Road, Murray Valley Highway, Rutherglen, Vic 3685 **Region** Rutherglen
T (02) 6032 9457 **www**.stantonandkilleenwines.com.au **Open** Mon–Sat 9–5, Sun 10–5
Winemaker Brendan Heath, Simon Killeen **Est.** 1875 **Dozens** 20000 **Vyds** 38ha
Stanton & Killeen is a family-owned winery with over 100 years and seven generations of winemaking experience. Following the tragic death of Chris Killeen some years earlier, 2011 saw the return of Simon (ex wine science tertiary studies), Natasha (likewise with university studies) and mother Wendy Killeen. Simon and Natasha are working in various roles, including vineyard management, marketing and winemaking, while Wendy has taken on the role of CEO. Brendan Heath continues his role as long-term winemaker. Exports to the UK.

ΤΤΤΤΤ Rare Rutherglen Topaque NV Deep olive-brown; very complex, with strong rancio acting to cleave the burnt caramel/toffee, Christmas cake, honey and grilled nut flavours; the age is obvious from the viscosity of the wine. A new and impressive addition to the portfolio. 375ml. Screwcap. 18.5% alc. Rating 97 To 2014 $100

Rare Rutherglen Muscat NV All hints of red have gone, leaving a brown centre grading to hints of olive on the rim; this is the final step up the ladder of lusciousness, incredibly rich, the rancio sufficient to do its job of balancing the wine, but no more; there is a cornucopia of flavours and spices; it has huge length and intensity. 375ml. Screwcap. 18.5% alc. Rating 97 To 2014 $100

Grand Rutherglen Topaque NV Bright and clear orange-brown; a total contrast to Buller, Morris, Chambers et al., with all the emphasis on the fresh tea leaf, butterscotch and Christmas cake varietal fruit. Screwcap. 18.5% alc. Rating 96 To 2014 $80

Grand Rutherglen Muscat NV The rim of the colour is olive-brown; the bouquet is very complex and powerful, the palate with multiple layers of flavour and glorious texture; the art here has been to keep the wine fresh despite its age. Has a glorious finish, long and sustained. 500ml. Screwcap. 18.5% alc. Rating 96 To 2014 $80

Classic Rutherglen Topaque NV Golden brown; strong tea leaf, toffee and malt varietal aromas and flavours are indeed classic, with enough rancio to provide cut and freshness. The wine has an average age of 12 years, substantial for a Classic style. 500ml. Screwcap. 18% alc. Rating 95 To 2014 $34

Rutherglen Vintage Fortified 2007 Some colour development; as ever, has true vintage port characters from its blend of durif, touriga, tinta roriz, shiraz, tinta cao and tinta barroca; dark cherry and spice fruits; lively finish of high quality, the spirit not obvious. Cork. 18% alc. Rating 95 To 2030 $32

Classic Rutherglen Muscat NV Rating 94 To 2013 $34

ΤΤΤΤΥ Rutherglen Topaque NV Yellow-gold; classic toffee, caramel, shortbread biscuit
✪ and cold tea aromas and flavours, then a pleasingly fresh, almost dry, finish. 500ml. Screwcap. 17.5% alc. Rating 91 To 2014 $20

✪ Rutherglen Muscat NV Bright tawny colour; the high-toned spirit on the bouquet lifts rather than obscures the fruit; intense and raisiny, yet fresh. 500ml. Screwcap. 17.5% alc. Rating 90 To 2014 $20

Star Lane

51 Star Lane, Beechworth, Vic 3747 **Region** Beechworth
T (03) 5728 7268 **www**.starlanewinery.com.au **Open** By appt
Winemaker Liz Barnes **Est.** 1996 **Dozens** 1500 **Vyds** 8ha

Star Lane is the venture of Brett and Liz Barnes together with Kate and Rex Lucas. Both families have small vineyards, the Barnes's of merlot and shiraz, and the Lucas's with sangiovese and nebbiolo. Liz is the winemaker, and has received encouragement and assistance from Rick Kinzbrunner; Brett is overall vineyard manager.

♀♀♀♀♀ Beechworth Shiraz 2010 Light red-purple; despite its alcohol, is dominated by savoury/spicy characters, although red fruits do poke their nose through on the back-palate and finish. Diam. 14.2% alc. **Rating** 90 **To** 2017 $55
Beechworth Merlot 2010 Medium red-purple; an appropriately medium-bodied wine with a complex melange of fruit, spice and oak; the flavours are in a cassis/plum spectrum, and the superfine tannins are a feature of the palate. Diam. 14.2% alc. **Rating** 90 **To** 2017 $55
Beechworth Nebbiolo 2009 The colour is typically light, but has retained good hue; the wine also has more sour cherry fruit (relative to the inevitable tannins) than most. Indeed, I will pay it the ultimate compliment of admitting I could drink, and quite possibly enjoy, a glass. Diam. 14.2% alc. **Rating** 90 **To** 2018 $50

Steels Creek Estate

1 Sewell Road, Steels Creek, Vic 3775 **Region** Yarra Valley
T (03) 5965 2448 **www**.steelsckestate.com.au **Open** W'ends & public hols 10–6, or by appt
Winemaker Simon Peirce **Est.** 1981 **Dozens** 400 **Vyds** 1.7ha
The Steels Creek vineyard (chardonnay, shiraz, cabernet sauvignon, cabernet franc and colombard), family-operated since 1981, is located in the picturesque Steels Creek Valley, with views towards the Kinglake National Park. The wines are made onsite by winemaker owner Simon Peirce following renovations to the winery, which now includes a barrel room and cool-store facility. The five-star rating has been retained due to the exceptional response to the challenges of the 2011 vintage. Exports to China.

♀♀♀♀♀ Yarra Valley Cabernet Sauvignon 2011 Good hue; despite its modest alcohol, shows no green characters whatsoever, just juicy cassis and redcurrant fruit backed by fine tannins and subtle French oak; excellent length and balance. Great outcome for the vintage. Diam. 12.5% alc. **Rating** 93 **To** 2021 $35
Yarra Valley Shiraz 2011 Good crimson-purple; a very creditable outcome, with many good aspects to its red berry aroma and flavour; the only issue is a little sharpness of the fruit, and I simply don't know whether this will soften with bottle age. Diam. 13.5% alc. **Rating** 90 **To** 2018 $35

♀♀♀♀ Yarra Valley Colombard 2012 Rating 87 **To** 2015 $20

Steels Gate

227 Greenwoods Lane, Steels Creek, Vic 3775 **Region** Yarra Valley
T (03) 5988 6662 **www**.steelsgate.com.au **Open** Not
Winemaker Han Lau **Est.** 2010 **Dozens** 160 **Vyds** 2ha
Brad Atkins and Matthew Davis acquired a 2ha vineyard of 25–30-year-old dry-grown chardonnay and pinot noir in 2009. There is also 14+ha of natural bushland, which backs onto the national park. For reasons unexplained, the also have a particular love of gates, and as the property is at the end of Steels Creek, the choice of Steels Gate was obvious. The next step was to engage French designer Cecile Darcy to create what is known today as the Steels Gate logo.

♀♀♀♀♀ Yarra Valley Chardonnay 2011 Vibrant and incisive grapefruit to the fore, giving it energy and drive, in turn enhanced by early picking and high natural acidity; barrel fermentation in 20% new French oak has worked well, introducing as much texture as nutty flavour nuances. Screwcap. 12.4% alc. **Rating** 92 **To** 2017 $25

Stefani Estate

389 Heathcote-Rochester Road, Heathcote, Vic 3523 **Region** Heathcote
T (03) 9570 8750 **www**.stefaniestatewines.com.au **Open** By appt
Winemaker Mario Marson **Est.** 2002 **Dozens** 3200 **Vyds** 27.6ha

Stefano Stefani came to Australia in 1985. Business success has allowed Stefano and wife Rina to follow in the footsteps of Stefano's grandfather, who had a vineyard and was an avid wine collector. The first property they acquired was at Long Gully Road in the Yarra Valley, planted to pinot grigio, cabernet sauvignon, chardonnay and pinot noir. The next was in Heathcote, where they acquired a property adjoining that of Mario Marson (ex Mount Mary), built a winery and established 14.4ha of vineyard, planted to shiraz, cabernet sauvignon, merlot, cabernet franc, malbec and petit verdot. In 2003 a second Yarra Valley property, named The View, reflecting its high altitude, was acquired and Dijon clones of chardonnay and pinot noir were planted. In addition, 1.6ha of sangiovese, mammolo bianco, malvasia, aleatico, trebbiano and crepolino bianco have been established, using scion material from the original Stefani vineyard in Tuscany. Mario Marson oversees the operation of all the vineyards and is also the winemaker. He is also able to use the winery to make his own brand wines, completing the business link. Exports to Italy and China.

ɤɤɤɤɤ **The View Yarra Valley Pinot Noir 2010** Deep, full purple-crimson; this is a powerful Pinot, with black cherry and plum fruit still to build on the savoury/forest nuances within that fruit; could be very long-lived. Diam. 13.5% alc. **Rating** 94 **To** 2022 $45
Heathcote Vineyard Shiraz 2010 An elegant interpretation of Heathcote, but full of flavour; blackberry, spice, plum and distinct ground coffee are all to be found, yet there is a most appealing lightness of foot to the medium-bodied palate. Diam. 14.5% alc. **Rating** 94 **To** 2025 $45
The Gate Yarra Valley Shiraz 2010 The colour is slightly brighter than the Heathcote, and the fruit expression is centred around curry and spice; less expected is the amount of extract from the extended maceration, which seems to magnify the amount of oak rather than the tannins. Diam. 14% alc. **Rating** 94 **To** 2025 $45

ɤɤɤɤɤ **Heathcote Vineyard Viognier Blend 2011 Rating** 92 **To** 2016 $30
Boccalupo Yarra Valley Sangiovese 2010 Rating 90 **To** 2016 $35

Stefano de Pieri   ★★★★

27 Deakin Avenue, Mildura, Vic 3502 **Region** Murray Darling
T (03) 5021 3627 **www**.stefano.com.au **Open** Mon–Fri 8–6, w'ends 8–2
Winemaker Sally Blackwell, Stefano de Pieri **Est.** 2005 **Dozens** 25 000
Stefano de Pieri decided to have his own range of wines that reflect his Italian spirit and the region he lives in. Mostly hand-picked, the fruit comes from a variety of Mildura vineyards, including the highly respected Chalmers Nursery vineyard. They are intended to be fresh and zesty, deliberately aiming at lower alcohol, to retain as much natural acidity as possible, designed to go with food, and inexpensive and easy to enjoy, reflecting Stefano's philosophy of generosity and warmth. The emphasis is on the Italian varieties, from arneis to aglianico, including a frizzante pinot grigio and the innovative blend of moscato gialla, garganega and greco, while retaining some of the local workhorses such as cabernet and chardonnay.

ɤɤɤɤɤ **di qualita Fiano Arneis 2012** This blend of two Italian varieties, each with its
✪ acolytes in Australia, comes together well, with its citrus, pear and fresh ginger flavours backed by crisp acidity. Fiano hails from the warm to hot climate of southern Italy, arneis from the much cooler Piedmont. Screwcap. 11.5% alc. **Rating** 90 **To** 2014 $20

ɤɤɤɤ **L'Unico 2010 Rating** 89 **To** 2015 $25
di qualita Prosecco NV Rating 89 **To** 2013 $24
Pinot Grigio 2012 Rating 88 **To** 2013 $17
di qualita Arneis 2012 Rating 88 **To** 2014 $20
di qualita Rose 2012 Rating 88 **To** 2014 $20
Tre Viti 2012 Rating 87 **To** 2013 $16

Stefano Lubiana

60 Rowbottoms Road, Granton, Tas 7030 **Region** Southern Tasmania
T (03) 6263 7457 **www**.slw.com.au **Open** Sun–Thurs 11–3 (closed some public hols)
Winemaker Steve Lubiana **Est.** 1990 **Dozens** NFP **Vyds** 25ha

Monique and Steve Lubiana left Riverland grapegrowing and winemaking in 1990, and purchased a greenfield site at Granton. The first Pinot Chardonnay sparkling and Pinot Noir and Chardonnay table wines were made in '93. Five years later they began total organic vineyard management, evolving into a program of biodynamic management. The 2008 experiments with pinot noir were astonishing, although there were so many variables it made technical comparisons impossible; the only constant was May '09 bottling. Exports to the UK, Singapore, Japan, Indonesia and China.

Selection 2/3 Pinot Noir 2008 Bright red-purple, remarkable retention of hue; the freshest, best balanced and most expressive of the three Selection Pinots. Delicious cherry and plum fruit, with silky tannins and the longest finish. Screwcap. 14% alc. **Rating** 95 **To** 2020 $60

Primavera Chardonnay 2010 For a second label Chardonnay, there's nothing second rate here. Gunflint and charcuterie complexity meld magnificently with intricately defined grapefruit and lemon zest, finishing long, textural and stunning. Screwcap. 13.5% alc. **Rating** 94 **To** 2018 $28 TS

Primavera Pinot Noir 2011 Excellent clarity and depth to its crimson-purple colour; the bouquet has dark berry fruit with an exotic touch of fruit spice; the palate is supple, smooth and even, with black cherry, plum and a continuation of the spice of the bouquet. Screwcap. 13.5% alc. **Rating** 94 **To** 2020 $30

Selection 1/3 Pinot Noir 2008 The bouquet is very fragrant, with spicy/savoury characters to the fore on both the bouquet and palate. The least expressive of the Selection Pinot Noirs. Diam. 14% alc. **Rating** 94 **To** 2015 $60

Selection 3/3 Pinot Noir 2008 The deepest colour of the three wines; the palate is the fullest-bodied, thanks in no small measure to the new oak. Dark fruits manage to enter the auction, and this wine needs more time. Diam. 14% alc. **Rating** 94 **To** 2023 $60

Vintage Brut 2005 A 60/40% blend of chardonnay and pinot noir. The base wine did not have any oak maturation, but was taken through 100% mlf. It was taken to bottle in Nov '05, and disgorged in Oct '13. Bright, pale straw-green, excellent mousse; strong toasty/brioche aromas, layers of fruit flavour, with some pinot influence. Cork. 12.5% alc. **Rating** 94 **To** 2017 $53

Brut Reserve NV Rating 93 **To** 2016 $34
Primavera Chardonnay 2011 Rating 92 **To** 2021 $28
Sauvignon Blanc 2012 Rating 91 **To** 2014 $28

Stella Bella Wines ★★★★★

205 Rosabrook Road, Margaret River, WA 6285 **Region** Margaret River
T (08) 9758 8611 **www**.stellabella.com.au **Open** 7 days 10–5
Winemaker Stuart Pym, Luke Jolliffe **Est.** 1997 **Dozens** 50 000 **Vyds** 87.9ha

This enormously successful privately owned winemaking business produces wines of true regional expression, with fruit sourced from the central and southern parts of Margaret River. The company operates almost 90ha of vineyard and has its own winery in Karridale. Serie Luminosa Cabernet Sauvignon is an outstanding flagship for Stella Bella. Exports of Stella Bella, Suckfizzle and Skuttlebutt labels to the UK, the US and other major markets.

Suckfizzle Margaret River Sauvignon Blanc Semillon 2008 A blend that 'has a long maturation' over 18 months in French oak, all with a nod to White Bordeaux. Light straw-green, this is one of the best blends of this type in Margaret River, and hence, Australia; it is long, intense and distinctly savoury, powerful on the way in, elegant and long on the way out. Screwcap. 13% alc. **Rating** 96 **To** 2020 $45

Suckfizzle Margaret River Sauvignon Blanc Semillon 2010 This rendition shows plenty of sleek vanillin oak, but there is a range of exotic fruits also on display; the palate is deeply textured, long and complex. Screwcap. 13.5% alc. Rating 95 To 2020 $45 BE

Margaret River Chardonnay 2010 Bright straw-green; the aromatic flowery bouquet and delicate fruit on entry into the mouth is quickly changed by the intensity, grip and length of the back-palate and finish; the acidity is balanced, and of critical importance. A wine certain to age with majestic grace. Screwcap. 13% alc. Rating 95 To 2020 $32

Serie Luminosa Margaret River Cabernet Sauvignon 2009 From the very low-yielding '09 vintage, estate-grown and a selection of the best barrels; clear, bright red-purple, the wine is an exercise in harmony, with positive contributions from each of the black and red berry fruit, cedary oak, and positively silky tannins. Screwcap. 14% alc. Rating 95 To 2029 $75

✪ **Margaret River Sauvignon Blanc 2012** The first signs of richness are apparent from the colour; has the necessary texture and structure (ex 20% barrel ferment in new and used French oak, plus 6 months on yeast lees) to carry the potent gooseberry and passionfruit flavours without any cloying phenolics. Screwcap. 13.5% alc. Rating 94 To 2014 $24

Margaret River Cabernet Sauvignon 2010 The hue is good, although the colour is not deep; reflects the move towards more elegant styles in Margaret River, the emphasis on the blackcurrant/cassis and redcurrant fruit, French oak and tannins in pure support roles. Screwcap. 14% alc. Rating 94 To 2024 $32

Suckfizzle Margaret River Cabernet Sauvignon 2008 While the tannins are substantial, they have already started to soften and recede back into the berry fruit 18 months after first tasted in Mar '11. Screwcap. 14.5% alc. Rating 94 To 2028 $55

Margaret River Sangiovese Cabernet Sauvignon 2010 The light, clear red-purple is doubtless driven by the sangiovese, which has also provided the red cherry fruit component of the bouquet and palate; the tannins of the two varieties have not doubled up, leaving plenty of room for that cherry fruit, plus the cassis of the cabernet. Works well. Screwcap. 14% alc. Rating 94 To 2025 $30

♟♟♟♟♟ **Margaret River Viognier 2011** Rating 92 To 2015 $28

✪ **Skuttlebutt Margaret River Sauvignon Blanc Semillon 2012** This is a well-made example of a classic blend with a little winemaking twist for added complexity, as there is a struck match character that sits neatly among the stone and tropical fruits on offer; the palate is fleshy and lively, offering good drinking at a very reasonable price. Screwcap. 13.5% alc. Rating 91 To 2014 $18 BE

✪ **Skuttlebutt Otro Vino 2010** A blend of touriga nacional and tinta cao available from cellar door. Vivid crimson-purple, it has a beguiling mix of red and glacé cherries on the bouquet foretelling the spiced panforte flavours of the light- to medium-bodied palate. Bargain. Screwcap. 14.5% alc. Rating 91 To 2017 $18

✪ **Skuttlebutt Margaret River Shiraz Merlot Sangiovese Rose 2012** Pale pink, touches of salmon; spicy red fruits on the bouquet, and again on the even, well-balanced palate, with some sangiovese tannins adding interest. Screwcap. 13.5% alc. Rating 90 To 2014 $18

Step Rd Winery/Beresford Wines   ★★★☆

Davidson Road, Langhorne Creek, SA 5255 **Region** Langhorne Creek
T (08) 8300 0900 **www**.steprd.com **Open** Not
Winemaker Chris Dix **Est.** 1985 **Dozens** 40 000 **Vyds** 27.59ha

In April 2012 VOK Beverages acquired the brands of Step Rd and Beresford, the 5000-tonne winery built in Langhorne Creek, all stock, and 27.6ha of vines in the Blewitt Springs district of McLaren Vale. The business has operated on an environmentally aware basis, and nothing will change as far as that is concerned. The grapes coming from the Blewitt Springs vineyard are but a small part of the production, with grapes also sourced from the Adelaide Hills, Langhorne Creek and Riverland regions, plus additional purchases from McLaren Vale.

ㅜㅜㅜㅜ♀   **Step Rd Langhorne Creek Cabernet Sauvignon 2010** This is a rich,
✪   bordering on velvety, Cabernet overflowing with cassis fruit, touches of dark
chocolate and mocha, and the soft tannins for which Langhorne Creek is so well
known. Excellent value for a now or later wine. Cork. 14.5% alc. **Rating** 92
To 2020 $22

ㅜㅜㅜㅜ   **Beresford Highwood Sauvignon Blanc 2012 Rating** 89 To 2013 $15
Beresford Highwood Pinot Grigio 2012 Rating 87 To 2013 $15

Stephen John Wines   ★★★☆

Sollys Hill Road, Watervale, SA 5452 **Region** Clare Valley
T (08) 8843 0105 **www.**stephenjohnwines.com **Open** 7 days 11–5
Winemaker Stephen John **Est.** 1994 **Dozens** 5000 **Vyds** 5ha
The John family is one of the best known in the Barossa Valley, with branches running
Australia's best cooperage (AP John & Sons) and providing the former chief winemaker
of Lindemans (Philip John) and the former chief winemaker of Quelltaler (Stephen John).
Stephen and Rita John have now formed their own family business in the Clare Valley, based
on a vineyard (riesling and shiraz) overlooking Watervale, and supplemented by grapes from
local growers. The cellar door is a renovated 80-year-old stable full of rustic charm. Exports
to Canada, Malaysia, Thailand, the Maldives and Singapore.

ㅜㅜㅜㅜ♀   **Dry Grown Clare Valley Shiraz 2011** Deep colour, with essency blackberry
pastille aromas offset by mocha and lavender; the palate is juicy and fresh, and
despite the concentration, is medium-bodied and light on its feet. Screwcap.
14.5% alc. **Rating** 90 To 2018 $25 BE

ㅜㅜㅜㅜ   **Watervale Riesling 2012 Rating** 87 To 2015 $25 BE

Sticks Yarra Valley   ★★★★★

179 Glenview Road, Yarra Glen, Vic 3775 **Region** Yarra Valley
T (03) 9730 1022 **www.**sticks.com.au **Open** 7 days 10–5
Winemaker Travis Bush **Est.** 2000 **Dozens** 60 000 **Vyds** 24ha
In 2005 the former Yarra Ridge winery, with a 3000-tonne capacity and over 20ha of
vineyards planted mainly in 1983, was acquired by a partnership headed by Rob 'Sticks'
Dolan. The estate production is significantly supplemented by contract-grown grapes sourced
elsewhere in the Yarra Valley and surrounding regions. Sticks also provides substantial contract-
making facilities for wineries throughout the Yarra Valley. While remaining a shareholder,
Rob has ceased to have any management or winemaking role at Sticks, and has established
his own winemaking business (see separate entry). Exports to the UK, the US, Hong Kong
and China.

ㅜㅜㅜㅜ♀   **No. 29 Vineyard Select Chardonnay 2011** Similar straw colour to the
standard Chardonnay; the palate is fuller and rounder, with some oak in play, but
the fruit flavours traverse the same range of white peach, nectarine and nougat on
the long palate. Screwcap. 12.7% alc. **Rating** 93 To 2017 $35
✪   **Sauvignon Blanc 2012** Light, bright green-straw; the brave, very early picking
decision has paid off with this vibrantly fresh and juicy Sauvignon Blanc, with
passionfruit, citrus and lychee to the fore, lemony acidity driving the long finish.
Very good value. Screwcap. 11.5% alc. **Rating** 92 To 2014 $18
Botrytis Riesling 2010 Slightly unexpected from '10 (as opposed to '11), but
is opulently luscious, with lime marmalade, peach and cumquat fruit, the acid
balance spot on. Screwcap. 8% alc. **Rating** 92 To 2017 $25

ㅜㅜㅜㅜ   **Chardonnay 2011** Some colour development, most likely from extended lees
✪   contact; white peach, nectarine, melon and nougat come together on the balanced,
light- to medium-bodied palate. Screwcap. 12.5% alc. **Rating** 89 To 2016 $20
Pinot Grigio 2012 Rating 88 To 2014 $18

Stockman's Ridge Wines   ★★★☆

2160 Limekilns Road, Bathurst NSW 2795 **Region** Orange
T (02) 9972 3440 **www**.stockmansridge.com.au **Open** 1st Sun each month 10–5
Winemaker Jonathan Hambrook **Est.** 2004 **Dozens** 1000 **Vyds** 3ha
Jonathan Hambrook purchased what he aptly named Stockman's Ridge in 2002. Situated 20km north of Bathurst at 900m above sea level, it has spectacular views to the south. A cherry orchard was established, cattle grazing commenced, a 1 million litre dam completed, and sequential planting throughout '04 and '05, with shiraz, pinot gris, pinot noir and savagnin the varieties chosen. Jonathan has also leased two vineyards in Orange planted to merlot, shiraz, pinot gris and sauvignon blanc. While he has no formal winemaking qualifications, he is able to draw on advice from David Lowe (Lowe Family Wines), Mark Renzaglia (Winburndale Wines) and Phil Kerney (Ross Hill).

♀♀♀♀♀ **Rider Orange Sauvignon Blanc 2012** Light straw-green; a tangy, zesty
Sauvignon Blanc with grapefruit, guava and snow pea flavours to the fore; precisely what was 'the use of French oak' we are not told, but its impact is textural, rather than flavour-enhancing. Screwcap. 12.9% alc. **Rating** 90 **To** 2013 $23

♀♀♀♀ **Rider Bathurst Pinot Gris 2012 Rating** 89 **To** 2013 $23
Outlaw Orange Shiraz 2009 Rating 89 **To** 2015 $35
Outlaw Orange Cabernet Sauvignon 2009 Rating 89 **To** 2020 $35
Rider Orange Pinot Gris 2011 Rating 87 **To** 2013 $23

Stomp Wine   ★★★

1273 Milbrodale Road, Broke, NSW 2330 **Region** Hunter Valley
T (02) 6579 1400 **www**.stompwine.com.au **Open** W'ends 10.30–4.30, or by appt
Winemaker Michael McManus **Est.** 2004 **Dozens** 750
After a lifetime in the food and beverage industry, Michael and Meredith McManus made a decisive move to full-time occupation in all aspects of winemaking. They have set up Stomp Winemaking, a contract winemaker designed to keep small and larger parcels of grapes separate through the fermentation and maturation process, thus meeting the needs of boutique wine producers in the Hunter Valley. The addition of their own label, Stomp, is a small but important part of their business.

♀♀♀♀ **Limited Release Shiraz 2011** Deep garnet; the bouquet offers spiced plum
aromas with mocha, licorice and dried leather; the palate is medium-bodied, forward and accessible; should be consumed in the short to medium term. Screwcap. 13% alc. **Rating** 87 **To** 2016 $48 BE

Stone Bridge Wines   ★★★☆

Section 113 Gillentown Road, Clare, SA 5453 **Region** Clare Valley
T (08) 8843 4143 **www**.stonebridgewines.com.au **Open** Thurs–Mon 10–4
Winemaker Craig Thomson, Angela Meaney **Est.** 2005 **Dozens** 6000 **Vyds** 29ha
Stone Bridge Wines started out as a hobby but has turned into a commercial enterprise for its owners, Craig and Lisa Thomson. They say that Craig's 16 years as a baker have assisted in the art of winemaking: 'It's all about the mix.' Their own patch of shiraz provides only a small part of the annual crush; riesling, pinot gris, cabernet sauvignon and malbec are purchased from local growers. The cellar door is a rammed-earth and iron building with picturesque surrounds, where on Sundays Sept–May (weather permitting), visitors can relax and enjoy a gourmet wood-oven pizza. Exports to Canada and China.

♀♀♀♀♀ **Clare Valley Shiraz 2010** Solid crimson-purple; spent 19 months in a mix
of new and used oak, the origin not specified, but totally or partly American, as it gives a mocha/vanilla character to the fruit on the bouquet and full-bodied palate alike; the layers of black fruits earned it a gold medal at the Australian Small Winemakers Show '12. Screwcap. 14.5% alc. **Rating** 91 **To** 2025 $25

♀♀♀♀ **The Gardener Clare Valley Rose 2012 Rating** 88 **To** 2014 $18

Stonefish ★★★★

24 Kangarilla Road, McLaren Vale, SA 5171 **Region** Various
T (02) 9668 9930 **www**.stonefishwines.com.au **Open** Not
Winemaker Contract, Peter Papanikitas **Est.** 2000 **Dozens** 20 000

Founder and owner Peter Papanikitas has been involved in various facets of the wine industry for the past 30 years. Initially his contact was with companies that included Penfolds, Lindemans and Leo Buring, then he spent five years working for Cinzano, gaining experience in worldwide sales and marketing. In 2000 he established Stonefish, a virtual winery operation, with a de facto partnership between Peter and the various grapegrowers and winemakers who supply him with the finished wines. The wines include Brut Cuvee, Sauvignon Blanc, Chardonnay, Verdelho, Shiraz, Merlot and Cabernet Sauvignon, all at $15, and a Reserve Shiraz and Limited Edition Chardonnay at $20. Exports to China, Thailand, Vietnam, Hong Kong, Indonesia, the Philippines, Singapore and Fiji.

ΨΨΨΨ♀ **Reserve Margaret River Cabernet Sauvignon 2010** Medium red-purple;
✪   slightly left field, but I like the description of blackcurrant with a touch of bay leaf; it is medium-bodied, and all the fruit, oak and tannin components are in balance. Screwcap. 14% alc. **Rating** 91 **To** 2020 $20

✪   **Margaret River Sauvignon Blanc 2012** Pale straw; kiwi, gooseberry and tropical fruits are not intense, but have more than enough flavour to satisfy consumers at this price point. Screwcap. 13.5% alc. **Rating** 90 **To** 2014 $15

ΨΨΨΨ **Margaret River Chardonnay 2012** Bright, light straw-green; a smooth and
✪   supple Margaret River Chardonnay, with all the attention on the stone fruit, melon and fig fruit, citrus appearing as part of the acidity on the finish. Well priced. Screwcap. 14% alc. **Rating** 89 **To** 2015 $20

Reserve Barossa Valley Shiraz 2011 Rating 87 **To** 2015 $20

Stoney Rise ★★★★★

Hendersons Lane, Gravelly Beach, Tas 7276 **Region** Northern Tasmania
T (03) 6394 3678 **www**.stoneyrise.com **Open** Thurs–Mon 11–5
Winemaker Joe Holyman **Est.** 2000 **Dozens** 2000

This is the venture of Joe and Lou Holyman. The Holyman family has been involved in vineyards in Tasmania for 20 years, but Joe's career in the wine industry, first as a sales rep, then as a wine buyer, and more recently working in wineries in NZ, Portugal, France, Mout Benson and Coonawarra, gave him an exceptionally broad-based understanding of wine. In 2004 Joe and Lou purchased the former Rotherhythe vineyard, which had been established in 1986 but was in a somewhat rundown state, and set about restoring the vineyard to its former glory, with 3ha of pinot noir and 1ha of chardonnay. There are two ranges: the Stoney Rise wines, focusing on fruit and early drinkability, and the Holyman wines with more structure, more new oak and the best grapes, here the focus on length and potential longevity. Exports to the UK, The Netherlands and Japan.

ΨΨΨΨΨ **Holyman Pinot Noir 2011** Far deeper and more purple than the standard version; an altogether serious Pinot Noir with spicy/savoury nuances to its black cherry and plum manifesting themselves right from the outset, and persisting through to the long, complex finish. Screwcap. 14% alc. **Rating** 95 **To** 2021 $45

✪   **Pinot Noir 2012** Striking purple-crimson; the fragrant, almost flowery, bouquet leads into a delicious palate of morello and red cherries; the mouthfeel is positively juicy, bringing a touch of spice, and even pepper, into the finish. Great drinking now, but will hold. Screwcap. 13% alc. **Rating** 94 **To** 2019 $29

Holyman Project X Pinot Noir 2010 Has deeper, more vibrant colour than the varietal, not at all what one would expect from 100% whole-bunch fermentation; there is a pantechnicon of berry/forest/tannin aromas and flavours boding well for the long-term future, but those tannins need to soften before the fruit dries up. Screwcap. 13% alc. **Rating** 94 **To** 2025 $90

♀♀♀♀♀ **Chardonnay 2011** Proclaims its cool Tasmanian origin the second it enters the
✪　　mouth, with the flinty acidity that underpins all Tasmanian white wines. While
barrel-fermented, oak plays a subservient role in a wine barely out of its diapers;
a long life ahead for the grapefruit and apple flavours that drive the long palate.
Screwcap. 13% alc. **Rating** 93 **To** 2021 $29

✪　　**Pinot Noir 2011** Light colour by Tasmanian standards, but proves once again that
colour can deceive with pinot; it has abundant red and black cherry fruit, and a
touch of mint, cradled by perfectly weighted and supple tannins that play through
to the long finish. Screwcap. 13.5% alc. **Rating** 93 **To** 2018 $29

Stonier Wines ★★★★★

Cnr Thompson's Lane/Frankston-Flinders Road, Merricks, Vic 3916
Region Mornington Peninsula
T (03) 5989 8300 **www.**stonier.com.au **Open** 7 days 11–5
Winemaker Michael Symons **Est.** 1978 **Dozens** 25 000 **Vyds** 17.6ha
This may be one of the most senior wineries on the Mornington Peninsula, but that does
not stop it moving with the times. It has embarked on a serious sustainability program that
touches on all aspects of its operations. It is one of the few wineries in Australia to measure its
carbon footprint in detail, using the officially recognised system of WFA; it is steadily reducing
its consumption of electricity; it uses rainwater; it has created a balanced ecosystem in the
vineyard by strategic planting of cover crops and reduction of sprays; and has reduced its need
to irrigate. None of this has in any way affected (other than beneficially) the quality of its
wines. Exports to Europe, Canada, Malaysia, Vietnam, Hong Kong and China.

♀♀♀♀♀ **Lyncroft Vineyard Mornington Peninsula Chardonnay 2011** Made in the
same way as KBS, but only 60% mlf. A tangy, concise and focused palate, with
grapefruit and white peach fruit running through to the long finish. Screwcap.
13% alc. **Rating** 95 **To** 2021 $45
Lyncroft Vineyard Mornington Peninsula Pinot Noir 2010 With beguiling
definition and layered complexity, dried herbs and undergrowth overlap a core
of red cherry fruit, meshing effortlessly with seamlessly textured tannins. Hints
of pepper, woodsmoke and understated exoticism add subtle intrigue. Screwcap.
14% alc. **Rating** 95 **To** 2017 $55 TS
Mornington Peninsula Chardonnay 2012 Incredibly, comes from 14 different
vineyards 'with the centre of gravity near Merricks' says winemaker Mike Symons.
This is a vibrant and fresh wine, stone fruit, melon and creamy/nutty flavours
to the fore. I still wonder why so many Mornington Peninsula winemakers are
wedded to mlf. Screwcap. 13.5% alc. **Rating** 94 **To** 2018 $25
Reserve Mornington Peninsula Chardonnay 2011 A blend from KBS and
Lyncroft Vineyards, whole bunch-pressed, barrel-fermented (25% new oak), 80%
mlf, the components blended after 9 months, then returned to barrel for a further
5 months. A juicy palate, Lyncroft seeming to have more influence on the finish.
Screwcap. 13% alc. **Rating** 94 **To** 2020 $45
Mornington Peninsula Chardonnay Pinot Noir 2009 An 85/15% blend,
with well over 2 years on yeast lees and age on cork. It has good mousse, and the
low dosage highlights the freshness of the citrus/apple/grapefruit flavours on the
long finish. Diam. 11.5% alc. **Rating** 94 **To** 2016 $30

♀♀♀♀♀ **KBS Vineyard Chardonnay 2011 Rating** 93 **To** 2018 $55
KBS Vineyard Pinot Noir 2011 Rating 92 **To** 2019 $75
Mornington Peninsula Pinot Noir 2011 Rating 92 **To** 2018 $28 BE
Mornington Peninsula Chardonnay 2011 Rating 90 **To** 2015 $25 BE
Reserve Mornington Peninsula Pinot Noir 2011 Rating 90 **To** 2017 $55

Streicker ★★★★★

412 Abbeys Farm Road, Yallingup, WA 6282 (postal) **Region** Margaret River
T (08) 9755 2108 **www.**streickerwines.com.au **Open** Not
Winemaker Naturaliste Vintners (Bruce Dukes) **Est.** 2002 **Dozens** 2400 **Vyds** 146.09ha

This multifaceted business is owned by New York resident John Streicker. It began in 2002 when he purchased the Yallingup Protea Farm and Vineyards, and was followed by the purchase of the Ironstone Vineyard in '03, and finally the Bridgeland Vineyard, which has one of the largest dams in the region: 1km long and covering 18ha. The Ironstone Vineyard is one of the oldest vineyards in the Wilyabrup area, and required significant rehabilitation after its acquisition. Virtually all the grapes from the three vineyards are sold, and the proteas (from 12ha) are exported to the US and Hong Kong.

ŸŸŸŸŸ Ironstone Block Old Vine Margaret River Chardonnay 2010 Light but bright green-straw; the sheer intensity of the flavour of the wine puts it in a category all of its own, the foundation of juicy grapefruit and white peach flavours supported by strong minerality/acidity, in turn making the oak a lesser player. Has developed well since March '12. Screwcap. 13% alc. Rating 96 To 2020 $35

Stuart Wines ★★★★☆

105 Killara Road, Gruyere, Vic 3770 (postal) **Region** Yarra Valley
T (03) 5964 9000 **www**.stuartwinesco.com.au **Open** Not
Winemaker Peter Wilson, Stephen Phillips **Est.** 1999 **Dozens** 95 000 **Vyds** 128.9ha
Hendra Widjaja came to Australia from Indonesia to establish a vineyard and winery, and he initially chose the Yarra Valley for the first vineyard, thereafter establishing a larger one in Heathcote. The Yarra Valley vineyard has 62.4ha (pinot noir, shiraz, cabernet sauvignon, merlot, chardonnay, sangiovese, pinot gris, mataro, petit verdot and viognier), the Heathcote vineyard 66.5ha (shiraz, nebbiolo, tempranillo, merlot, viognier and cabernet sauvignon). The wines are made at the Heathcote winery. Wines are released under the Cahillton, White Box and Huma labels. Exports to Germany, The Netherlands, Indonesia, Malaysia, Macau, Taiwan, Hong Kong, China and NZ.

ŸŸŸŸŸ Whitebox Jeff Fenech Signature Yarra Valley Shiraz 2010 This big brother
✪ of the Huma has more of everything: colour, intensity, texture and length, yet the flavour spectrum is very similar – which, I suppose, is exactly what should be expected. Its length and balance are exemplary, reflecting the ideal vintage conditions. Screwcap. 14% alc. Rating 94 To 2020 $23

ŸŸŸŸŸ Cahillton Heathcote Shiraz 2009 There is a small problem with the labelling
✪ of this wine: while the front and back label specify (in large type) Heathcote as the origin, the back label also says 'This Cahillton wine is sourced from our vineyard in the Yarra Valley'. Vivid purple crimson colour; it is an elegant medium-bodied wine with very attractive red and black fruits, fine tannins and quality oak. Great value. Screwcap. 15% alc. Rating 93 To 2024 $23
Whitebox Jeff Fenech Signature Yarra Valley Sangiovese 2010
Rating 92 To 2016 $23
Whitebox Jeff Fenech Signature Yarra Valley Pinot Noir 2009 Rating 90
To 2015 $23

ŸŸŸŸ Huma Yarra Valley Shiraz 2010 An estate-grown shiraz with obvious French
✪ oak (however infused) at this price is astonishing. While the colour isn't deep, it is healthy, and the wine has abundant plum fruit and soft tannins; ready for immediate consumption. Screwcap. 14.5% alc. Rating 89 To 2015 $10

Stumpy Gully ★★★★★

1247 Stumpy Gully Road, Moorooduc, Vic 3933 **Region** Mornington Peninsula
T (03) 5978 8429 **www**.stumpygully.com.au **Open** W'ends 11–5
Winemaker Wendy, Frank and Michael Zantvoort **Est.** 1988 **Dozens** 10 000 **Vyds** 40ha
Frank and Wendy Zantvoort began planting their first vineyard in 1988; Wendy subsequently graduated with a Bachelor of Science (Oenology) from CSU. Together with son Michael, the Zantvoorts look after all aspects of grapegrowing and winemaking. In addition to the original vineyard, they have deliberately gone against prevailing thinking with their Moorooduc vineyard, planting it solely to red varieties, predominantly cabernet sauvignon, merlot and

shiraz. They believe they have one of the warmest sites on the Peninsula, and that ripening will present no problems. (Peninsula Panorama is their second label.) Exports to all major markets.

ᵱᵱᵱᵱᵱ **Crooked Post Mornington Peninsula Shiraz 2010** Very good colour; an eye-opener: served blind, I would never guess it came from the Mornington Peninsula, heading instead to Heathcote or Bendigo. It is a velvety, lush wine with warm fruit flavours and soft, plush tannins. All the more impressive is the flavour, not driven by alcohol. Diam. 13.5% alc. **Rating** 94 **To** 2030 $48
Mornington Peninsula Sangiovese 2012 Light red-purple; this is a seriously good – and enjoyable – Sangiovese, with bright cherry fruit given free rein by the use of used French barriques (1–5 years old). It sits there, quietly knowing you are going to go back for as many glasses as you can filch from your dinner partner. Screwcap. 13.7% alc. **Rating** 94 **To** 2016 $25

ᵱᵱᵱᵱᵱ **Shark Point Mornington Peninsula Pinot Gris 2011 Rating** 90 **To** 2014 $30
✪ **Peninsula Panorama Pinot Noir 2012** Light, clear red-purple; a more than useful Pinot Noir at this rare (for Mornington Peninsula) price point; red and black fruits are coupled with spices, and there is an almost creamy texture. Very good drink-soon style. Screwcap. 13.5% alc. **Rating** 90 **To** 2014 $15
Mornington Peninsula Merlot 2012 Rating 90 **To** 2017 $25

ᵱᵱᵱᵱ **Peninsula Panorama Chardonnay 2012** Mornington Peninsula is one of the
✪ regions in which unoaked Chardonnay can capture and hold the attention to whatever degree is needed (and that shouldn't be much). This has clear varietal definition, although it does fall off on the finish to a degree. Screwcap. 13.6% alc. **Rating** 89 **To** 2014 $15

Summerfield   ★★★★★

5967 Stawell-Avoca Road, Moonambel, Vic 3478 **Region** Pyrenees
T (03) 5467 2264 **www.**summerfieldwines.com **Open** 7 days 10–5
Winemaker Mark Summerfield **Est.** 1979 **Dozens** 10 000 **Vyds** 13.49ha
Founder Ian Summerfield has now handed over the winemaking reins to son Mark, who produces consistently outstanding and awesomely concentrated Shiraz and Cabernet Sauvignon, both in varietal and Reserve forms. The red wines are built for the long haul, for lovers of full-bodied styles, and will richly repay cellaring. Exports are now directed solely to China.

ᵱᵱᵱᵱᵱ **Reserve Shiraz 2011** An interesting wine, outside the usual Summerfield style, although none the worse for that; the dark fruits are interwoven with savoury black olive and bitter chocolate, the tannin and oak management impeccable. Screwcap. 13.5% alc. **Rating** 96 **To** 2036 $50
R2 Shiraz 2011 Dense purple-crimson; has found a way around the vintage challenge; while only medium-bodied, it has great drive to its display of black fruits, licorice, oak and ripe tannins. As each Summerfield Shiraz from this vintage is tasted, more is revealed. Cork. 14.5% alc. **Rating** 95 **To** 2036 $50
Saieh Shiraz 2011 The cool vintage has given Mark Summerfield an opportunity he has taken with both hands to craft wines of greater elegance than prior vintages, but with equal intensity; here spice and crushed pepper sit alongside very attractive black fruits and balanced tannins. Screwcap. 14% alc. **Rating** 95 **To** 2026 $35

ᵱᵱᵱᵱᵱ **Reserve Cabernet Sauvignon 2011 Rating** 91 **To** 2021 $50
Shiraz 2011 Rating 90 **To** 2021 $30

Surveyor's Hill Vineyards   ★★★★

215 Brooklands Road, Wallaroo, NSW 2618 **Region** Canberra District
T (02) 6230 2046 **www.**survhill.com.au **Open** W'ends & public hols, or by appt
Winemaker Brindabella Hills (Dr Roger Harris), Greg Gallagher (sparkling) **Est.** 1986
Dozens 1000 **Vyds** 10ha

Surveyor's Hill vineyard is on the slopes of the eponymous hill, at 550–680m above sea level. It is an ancient volcano, producing granite-derived, coarse-structured (and hence well-drained) sandy soils of low fertility. This has to be the ultimate patchwork-quilt winery, with 1ha each of chardonnay, shiraz and viognier; 0.5ha each of roussanne, marsanne, aglianico, nero d'avola, mourvedre, grenache, muscadelle, moscato giallo, cabernet franc and riesling; and lesser amounts of semillon, sauvignon blanc, touriga nacional and cabernet sauvignon.

ŸŸŸŸŸ **Hills of Hall Riesling 2012** Picked immediately after heavy rain to prevent the vines taking up the water into the berries, hence the low alcohol, and a balancing touch of residual sugar; astute winemaking. Screwcap. 10.5% alc. **Rating** 91 **To** 2017 $22

✪ **Hills of Hall Chardonnay 2012** Pale quartz-straw; a zesty, lively Chardonnay with grapefruit shaping both its bouquet and fresh palate. A good example of the unoaked style thanks to its inherent balance, this despite its very low alcohol. Screwcap. 11.6% alc. **Rating** 90 **To** 2015 $20

✪ **Hills of Hall Autumn Gold 2012** Said to be simply late-picked, but you have to wonder whether some cane cutting was also involved, for it is an extremely luscious blend of semillon and sauvignon blanc – but no botrytis; good acidity. 375ml. Screwcap. 8.8% alc. **Rating** 90 **To** 2015 $13

ŸŸŸŸ **Hills of Hall Semillon Sauvignon Blanc 2012 Rating** 88 **To** 2014 $20

Sutherland Estate   ★★★★★

2010 Melba Highway, Dixons Creek, Vic 3775 **Region** Yarra Valley
T 0402 052 287 **www**.sutherlandestate.com.au **Open** W'ends & public hols 10–5
Winemaker Phil Kelly (Contract), Cathy Phelan, Angus Ridley **Est.** 2000 **Dozens** 1500
Vyds 4ha
The Phelan family established Sutherland Estate in 2000 when they purchased a mature 2ha vineyard at Dixons Creek. Further plantings followed: the plantings now consist of 1ha each of chardonnay and pinot noir, and 0.5ha each of gewurztraminer, cabernet sauvignon, tempranillo and shiraz. Ron Phelan designed and built the cellar door, which enjoys stunning views over the Yarra Valley, while daughter Cathy studied wine science at CSU. The sparkling and white wines are made by Phil Kelly, the reds by Cathy and partner Angus Ridley (who has been at Coldstream Hills for the last eight years, and is the winemaker of the Tollana Mornington Pinot Noir).

ŸŸŸŸŸ **Daniel's Hill Vineyards Yarra Valley Pinot Noir 2012** Deep, but clear, purple-
✪ red; rich damson plum and cherry aromas lead the bouquet, the palate seamlessly picking up the theme with a juicy display of red and black cherries allied with superfine tannins; very good balance and length. Screwcap. 13.2% alc. **Rating** 94 **To** 2020 $28

Yarra Valley Pinot Noir Chardonnay 2009 Bottle-fermented, disgorged Aug '12 with a full 3 years on lees. A faint tinge of pink points to the dominant pinot noir, and to the touch of red fruits through the citrussy acidity and drive. Half was released under crown seal, half Diam. 11.9% alc. **Rating** 94 **To** 2017 $30

ŸŸŸŸŸ **Daniel's Hill Vineyards Chardonnay 2012 Rating** 93 **To** 2018 $28

Sutton Grange Winery   ★★★★

Carnochans Road, Sutton Grange, Vic 3448 **Region** Bendigo
T (03) 9261 9959 **www**.suttongrange.com.au **Open** First Sun each month 12–4
Winemaker Gilles Lapalus **Est.** 1998 **Dozens** 5000 **Vyds** 12ha
The 400ha Sutton Grange property is a horse training facility acquired in 1996 by Peter Sidwell, a Melbourne businessman with horse racing and breeding interests. A lunch visit to the property by long-term friends Alec Epis and Stuart Anderson led to the decision to plant syrah, merlot, cabernet sauvignon, viognier and sangiovese, and to the recruitment of French winemaker Gilles Lapalus, who just happens to be the partner of Stuart's daughter. Exports to the UK, Canada, Switzerland and Malaysia.

ŶŶŶŶỸ **Estate Ram's Horn Block Syrah 2008** Medium red-purple; a complex, medium- to full-bodied wine with savoury/spicy/peppery notes woven through the black fruits, yet not interfering with the lively finish, which is unexpectedly juicy. Screwcap. 14% alc. **Rating** 93 **To** 2023 $60

Fairbank Rouge 2010 Deep red-purple; a blend of shiraz, merlot and sangiovese that is certainly not light-bodied (Sutton Grange's description); medium-bodied at least. That said, doesn't have the usual Sutton Grange tannin signature, its spicy black and red fruits with soft, velvety mouthfeel. Has cruised through the last 3 years, and will not curl up its toes anytime soon. Screwcap. 12% alc. **Rating** 91 **To** 2015 $22

Estate Syrah 2008 Deep purple-red; has much in common with the Ram's Horn Block; while still built around savoury black fruits, is a little more fleshy and less structured. Screwcap. 14% alc. **Rating** 91 **To** 2018 $50

Estate Cabernet Merlot 2008 Hand-picked before the heatwave (but during the long drought). Medium- to full-bodied, it has varietal blackcurrant fruit on the fore-palate, merging with earthy/savoury tannins on the finish. Will appeal to lovers of Bordeaux. Screwcap. 13% alc. **Rating** 91 **To** 2023 $50

Estate Viognier 2011 Winemaker Gilles Lapalus has managed to persuade viognier to display some good texture and structure without any phenolic heaviness; just how much varietal fruit expression can be expected is another matter. Screwcap. 14.5% alc. **Rating** 90 **To** 2015 $45

Fairbank Viognier 2011 Bright straw-green; this has less texture and structure than the Estate, but displays more peach/apricot varietal fruit; it's a question which you value more highly. Screwcap. 14% alc. **Rating** 90 **To** 2015 $30

ŶŶŶŶ **Fairbank Rose 2012** **Rating** 89 **To** 2014 $22
Estate Rose 2011 **Rating** 89 **To** 2014 $32
Estate Giove 2009 **Rating** 89 **To** 2019 $60
Fairbank Cabernet Sauvignon Merlot 2006 **Rating** 88 **To** 2015 $25
Fairbank Syrah 2008 **Rating** 87 **To** 2016 $25

Swallows Welcome   ★★★

542 Wallis Road, Witchcliffe, WA 6286 **Region** Margaret River
T (08) 9757 6348 **Open** Tues–Sun 11–4.30
Winemaker Tim Negus **Est.** 1994 **Dozens** 300 **Vyds** 1.9ha
Swallows Welcome is Margaret River's smallest winery, located in a mudbrick chapel and owned by Tim and Patricia Negus. He is winemaker and vineyard worker, while Patricia is a well-known watercolour artist and book illustrator. The estate plantings of cabernet sauvignon, cabernet franc and merlot were established between 1994 and '96; until 2003 the grapes were sold, but in that year the purchase contract ended, and Tim's winemaking career commenced. The area under vine has been decreased from 3ha to just under 2ha, making the business more manageable.

ŶŶŶŶ **Pensioners Port NV** Unexpectedly dry and spicy, with true fortified dry red flavours; you can't legally use the word 'port' any more, but I doubt that will worry anyone. Zork. 17.5% alc. **Rating** 89 **To** 2014 $20

Margaret River Cabernet 2010 Good colour; a robust, rustic Cabernet with a truly curious label of two cows in the foreground, and the commentary including 'Hand picked, then basket pressed. Fermentation and matured in American oak barrels.' However all that may be, there is good varietal fruit. Twin top. 13.1% alc. **Rating** 87 **To** 2014 $14

Hair of the Dog Red Cabernet Franc Merlot 2009 Here the welcome is from a Jack Russell dog. Oh boy, is this an Irish label or is it not? In large type you have Cabernet Franc Merlot, but immediately under it Cabernet Sauvignon 70% Cabernet Franc 30% with no sign or overprint. Ironically, this is an enjoyable light- to medium-bodied wine, with fresh cassis fruit and fine tannins. Cork. 12.5% alc. **Rating** 87 **To** 2014 $14

Swan Valley Wines ★★★★

261 Haddrill Road, Baskerville, WA 6065 **Region** Swan Valley
T (08) 9296 1501 **www**.swanvalleywines.com.au **Open** Fri–Sun & public hols 10–5
Winemaker Paul Hoffman, Karen Holper **Est.** 1999 **Dozens** 3000 **Vyds** 6ha
Peter and Paula Hoffman, with sons Paul and Thomas, acquired their property in 1989. It had
a long history of grapegrowing, and the prior owner had registered the name Swan Valley
Wines back in '83. In '99 the family built a winery to handle the estate-grown chenin blanc,
grenache, semillon and cabernet sauvignon. The decision to release three Chenin Blancs from
2010 labelled Sec, Demi Sec and Moelleux respectively, was a precise (completely legitimate)
copy of some of the best Loire Valley producers of Chenin Blanc, the most notable being
Marc Bredif. Those wines have cellaring capacity of 70 years or more if kept in the cool chalk
caves on the banks of the Loire Valley. The Australian climate will not permit that, but it will
be interesting to see how the three wines develop.

ΨΨΨΨΩ **Extent Mourvedre Grenache Rose 2012** Wild yeast-fermented and aged on
lees; needs air when opened. The very pale salmon-pink hue does not foretell the
amount of red fruit flavours on the palate, nor the delicately savoury/spicy finish.
Very good value for a Rose. Screwcap. 12.8% alc. **Rating** 90 **To** 2014 $17
Tawny Port 2011 A blend of shiraz and grenache that has some real age and
rancio; biscuit, raisin, toffee and spice. Diam. 18% alc. **Rating** 90 **To** 2014 $30

ΨΨΨΨ **Extent Malbec Petit Verdot 2011** Light, although bright, colour; when the
wine enters the mouth, the softly sweet and fleshy fruit flavours suggest there may
be some residual sugar sweetness, but there isn't. Will appeal to almost all who cross
the threshold of the cellar door. Screwcap. 12% alc. **Rating** 89 **To** 2014 $18

Swinging Bridge ★★★★

33 Gaskill Street, Canowindra, NSW 2804 **Region** Central Ranges Zone
T 0409 246 609 **www**.swingingbridge.com.au **Open** Fri–Sun 11–6
Winemaker Tom Ward **Est.** 1995 **Dozens** 4000 **Vyds** 14ha
Swinging Bridge was founded by Mark Ward, who immigrated to Australia in 1965 from the
UK with an honours degree in agricultural science from Cambridge University. He has been
succeeded by Tom and Georgie Ward. The vineyard is part of a farming property, Gayton,
10km from Canowindra. The name comes from a suspension walking bridge that crosses the
Belubula River at the foot of the vineyard. Since the first wines were made in 1997, Swinging
Bridge has had considerable wine show success.

ΨΨΨΨΩ **Orange Sauvignon Blanc 2012** Estate-grown. Well made, with a small
proportion of barrel ferment, and the whole wine given lees contact. It has
attractive lime/lemon/passionfruit aromas and flavours, and the length is
impressive. Excellent value. Screwcap. 12.3% alc. **Rating** 91 **To** 2014 $19
Orange Pinot Gris 2012 Light straw-green; the aromas and flavours are in the
mainstream of spiced pear and apple, but there is also some creamy texture that is
not so usual, and gives the wine that little bit of extra interest. Screwcap. 13.5% alc.
Rating 90 **To** 2014 $19

Swings & Roundabouts ★★★★★

2807 Caves Road, Yallingup, WA 6232 **Region** Margaret River
T (08) 9756 6640 **www**.swings.com.au **Open** 7 days 10–5
Winemaker Brian Fletcher **Est.** 2004 **Dozens** 25 000 **Vyds** 5.86ha
The Swings & Roundabouts name comes from the expression used to encapsulate the eternal
balancing act between the various aspects of grape and wine production. Swings aims to
balance the serious side with a touch of fun. There are four ranges: Kiss Chasey, Life of Riley,
Swings & Roundabouts and the Backyard Stories. Exports to the US and China.

ΨΨΨΨΨ **Backyard Stories Margaret River Chardonnay 2012** Bright green-straw;
a very attractive wine, with white peach and grapefruit in an Indian arm wrestle
for dominance, and neither quitting, together putting the French oak in its place.
Screwcap. 13.5% alc. **Rating** 94 **To** 2020 $32

✪ **Margaret River Shiraz 2011** Vivd purple-red; a fragrant and juicy mix of red cherry, spice, licorice and pepper; there is a hint of oak (American) and fine, silky tannins on the finish. Top value. Screwcap. 14% alc. **Rating** 94 **To** 2021 $22

♀♀♀♀♀ **Margaret River Cabernet Merlot 2011** Fresh crimson-purple hue; has more
✪ presence, flavour and weight than most at this price point, certain to be discounted to $20 at retail; black and redcurrant fruit have a generous helping of oak and tannins to complete the picture. Screwcap. 14% alc. **Rating** 93 **To** 2026 $22

✪ **Margaret River Sauvignon Blanc Semillon 2012** Pale straw-green; scores for its length rather than depth, the flavours fresh and crisp, but more or less anchored to the tropical spectrum, finishing with good acidity. Screwcap. 12.5% alc. **Rating** 91 **To** 2014 $22

Backyard Stories Chenin Blanc 2011 Rating 90 **To** 2026 $29

✪ **Margaret River Rose 2012** Bright, light pink; a lively array of red fruits, tinged with spice, on the bouquet and palate; the finish is fresh, fruity and crisp. Well made. Screwcap. 12.5% alc. **Rating** 90 **To** 2013 $20

Symphonia Wines   ★★★★

1699 Boggy Creek Road, Myrrhee, Vic 3732 **Region** King Valley
T (02) 4952 5117 **Open** By appt
Winemaker Robert Paul (Consultant) **Est.** 1998 **Dozens** 1500 **Vyds** 15ha
Peter Read and his family were veterans of the King Valley, commencing the development of their vineyard in 1981. As a result of extensive trips to both Western and Eastern Europe, Peter embarked on an ambitious project to trial a series of grape varieties little known in this country, the vineyard going on to supply Brown Brothers, De Bortoli, William Downie and Pizzini. In 2005 Peter and Suzanne Evans purchased the business. They continue to work closely with alternative varieties including saperavi, savagnin, tannin and petit manseng, with consulting advice from Robert Paul.

♀♀♀♀♀ **Winemakers Reserve King Valley Savagnin 2008** Light straw-green; one of
✪ the early vintages of savagnin, barrel-fermented and kept on lees for 14 months. Peach (white and yellow) and citrus zest come through despite its barrel fermentation and time in bottle; further validation of the worth of the variety. Screwcap. 12.5% alc. **Rating** 91 **To** 2015 $20

King Valley Pinot Grigio 2012 A very lively, crisp and crunchy grigio with as much citrus and apple as pear and spice, but all up, with considerable attraction. Screwcap. 12.5% alc. **Rating** 90 **To** 2014 $20

King Valley Savagnin 2012 The back label is almost brutally frank: 'I thought it was albarino.' It has a savoury intensity to its stone fruit and pear fruit that will ensure the variety remains in production. Screwcap. 14.1% alc. **Rating** 90 **To** 2014 $20

La Solista King Valley Tempranillo 2011 An elegant, supple, light- to medium-bodied red and black cherry-filled palate. A very attractive drink-now, or soon, style. Screwcap. 12.5% alc. **Rating** 90 **To** 2015 $22

La Solista King Valley Tempranillo 2010 The far easier vintage (compared to '11) has resulted in more texture, and a slightly darker bias in the cherry fruit; it is strictly a case of six of one, half a dozen of the other between this and the '11. Screwcap. 13% alc. **Rating** 90 **To** 2014 $22

♀♀♀♀ **King Valley Pinot Grigio 2011 Rating** 89 **To** 2013 $20

Symphony Hill Wines   ★★★★★

2017 Eukey Road, Ballandean, Qld 4382 **Region** Granite Belt
T (07) 4684 1388 **www.**symphonyhill.com.au **Open** 7 days 10–4
Winemaker Mike Hayes **Est.** 1999 **Dozens** 5000 **Vyds** 3.5ha
Ewen Macpherson purchased what was then an old table grape and orchard property in 1996. In partnership with Ewen's parents, Bob and Jill Macpherson, they developed the vineyard, while Ewen completed his Bachelor of Applied Science in viticulture (2003). The vineyard

(now much expanded) has been established using state-of-the-art technology; vineyard manager and winemaker Mike Hayes is a third-generation viticulturist in the Granite Belt region. He also has impressive academic achievements, with a degree in viticulture, followed by a Masters in Professional Studies – Viticulture, and was awarded a Churchill Fellowship (in '12) to study alternative wine grape varieties in Europe. The vineyard is planted to verdelho, viognier, pinot noir, shiraz and cabernet sauvignon. Symphony Hill has firmly established its reputation as one of the Granite Belt's foremost wineries. Exports to China and Japan.

ŸŸŸŸŸ Gewurztraminer 2012 Captures the exotic musk and bath talc aromas typical of the variety; the palate is lively and fresh, with lovely detail and line, and a long, textured and dry finish. Screwcap. 12.6% alc. **Rating** 94 **To** 2016 $25 BE

✪ Reserve Sauvignon Blanc 2012 The grapes come from across the border in New England, and the quality of the wine is such that it sits comfortably in the company of Australia's best Sauvignon Blancs; the flavours of citrus, lychee and passionfruit have a structural web of citrus/mineral acidity on the long finish. Screwcap. 11.7% alc. **Rating** 94 **To** 2013 $25

Reserve Granite Belt Shiraz 2008 A quality wine with plenty to say, even if the breathless excitement of white pepper, spicy cinnamon, dark chocolate, licorice, vanilla, lifted red cherry, black olive, mocha, savoury fruit, coconut oak and anise described on the back label does cover the field. Gold medal Melbourne Wine Show '11. Screwcap. 13.8% alc. **Rating** 94 **To** 2023 $65

ŸŸŸŸŸ Pinot Gris 2012 **Rating** 92 **To** 2014 $30
Reserve Granite Belt Verdelho 2012 **Rating** 91 **To** 2016 $25 BE

Syrahmi   ★★★★☆
PO Box 438, Heathcote, Vic 3523 **Region** Heathcote
T 0407 057 471 **www.**syrahmi**.com.au Open** Not
Winemaker Adam Foster **Est.** 2004 **Dozens** 1000
Adam Foster worked as a chef in Vic and London before moving to the front of house and becoming increasingly interested in wine. He then worked as a cellar hand with a who's who in Australia and France, including Torbreck, Chapoutier, Mitchelton, Domaine Ogier, Heathcote Winery, Jasper Hill and Domaine Pierre Gaillard. He became convinced that the Cambrian soils of Heathcote could produce the best possible Shiraz, and since 2004 has purchased grapes from the region. Exports to the US and Japan.

ŸŸŸŸŸ La La Shiraz 2009 Light to medium red-purple; 100% whole bunch fermentation, followed by 36 months in 100% new French oak; I don't think Guigal should be too worried, nor that everyone will queue up to buy the wine (the amount of oak may worry some), but I think the brave approach deserves applause. Screwcap. 13.8% alc. **Rating** 94 **To** 2029 $120

ŸŸŸŸŸ Demi Heathcote Shiraz 2012 Medium purple-crimson; the bouquet is highly
✪ spiced, with plum and raspberry aromas; the palate is lively and fresh thanks to prominent acidity, and also to the stalky characters that please me, but not everyone. Just bottled when tasted, and will settle down. Screwcap. 13.5% alc. **Rating** 93 **To** 2020 $25
Finesse Heathcote Shiraz 2011 **Rating** 93 **To** 2020 $55
Siren Heathcote Shiraz 2010 **Rating** 93 **To** 2025 $55

T'Gallant   ★★★★☆
1385 Mornington-Flinders Road, Main Ridge, Vic 3928 **Region** Mornington Peninsula
T (03) 5931 1300 **www.**tgallant**.com.au Open** 7 days 9–5
Winemaker Kevin McCarthy **Est.** 1990 **Dozens** NFP **Vyds** 8ha
Husband-and-wife consultant winemakers Kevin McCarthy and Kathleen Quealy carved out such an important niche market for the T'Gallant label that in 2003, after protracted negotiations, it was acquired by Beringer Blass (now part of TWE). The acquisition of a 15ha

property and the planting of 8ha of pinot gris gives the business a firm geographic base, as well as providing increased resources for its signature wine. Exports to the US.

🍷🍷🍷🍷🍷 **Tribute Pinot Gris 2012** An unapologetically hedonistic version of pinot gris; ripe and exotic on the bouquet with poached pear, bath talc and lavender; richly textured, unctuous and, as the label points out on the PinotG Style Spectrum™, is indeed luscious. Screwcap. 15% alc. **Rating** 94 **To** 2016 $39 BE

🍷🍷🍷🍷🍷 **Grace Pinot Grigio 2012 Rating** 90 **To** 2015 $29 BE
Imogen Pinot Gris 2012 Rating 90 **To** 2015 $26 BE
Juliet Pinot Grigio 2011 Rating 90 **To** 2013 $20

✪ **Cape Schanck Pinot Grigio 2011** Straw colour; the wine has enough richness to take it towards pinot gris territory, with an even flow of apple and pear, concluding with citrussy acidity. Perhaps the vintage prevented a clearer demarcation from Juliet Pinot Gris. Screwcap. 12% alc. **Rating** 90 **To** 2013 $20

Tahbilk ★★★★★

Goulburn Valley Highway, Tabilk, Vic 3608 **Region** Nagambie Lakes
T (03) 5794 2555 **www**.tahbilk.com.au **Open** Mon–Sat 9–5, Sun 11–5
Winemaker Alister Purbrick, Neil Larson, Alan George **Est.** 1860 **Dozens** 100 000
Vyds 221.50ha
A winery steeped in tradition (with National Trust classification), which should be visited at least once by every wine-conscious Australian, and which makes wines – particularly red wines – utterly in keeping with that tradition. The essence of that heritage comes in the form of the tiny quantities of Shiraz made entirely from vines planted in 1860. Tahbilk has a wetlands project, with walks connected by short journeys on a small punt. Serendipitous, perhaps, but the current release wines are absolutely outstanding. Exports to all major markets.

🍷🍷🍷🍷🍷 **1860 Vines Shiraz 2007** Outstanding retention of crimson hue, bright and clear on the rim; the bouquet sets the scene for the intense and pure black and red berry fruits of the medium-bodied palate, its exceptional length drawn out by fine-grained tannins, oak an incidental extra. Cork. 14% alc. **Rating** 97 **To** 2030 $215

1927 Vines Marsanne 2003 Has six trophies to its credit, mainly from shows with user volume requirements for entry; its colour is still pale straw-green, and the wine has extraordinary freshness and vibrancy; lemon juice, honeysuckle and hints of toast and spice are all threaded through by a spine of acidity on the long, lingering palate. Screwcap. 11% alc. **Rating** 96 **To** 2028 $40

Eric Stevens Purbrick Cabernet Sauvignon 2007 Shares the exceptional hue of the 1860 Vines, and a significant element of the fruit profile of that wine, all this from an unfancied year; it has black fruits, touches of pepper, licorice and spice, and the medium- to full-bodied palate has ripe tannins to carry it through the decades ahead. Screwcap. 14.5% alc. **Rating** 95 **To** 2030 $60

Eric Stevens Purbrick Cabernet Sauvignon 2007 Made from estate-grown vines with an average age of over 40 years; is still in its early years of development, but the earthy/minty blackberry fruit has already asserted its dominance over the dusty tannins, and the wine has admirable length, the oak handling meticulous. Screwcap. 13.5% alc. **Rating** 95 **To** 2030 $60

✪ **Cabernet Sauvignon 2009** Positive red-purple, still youthful; blackcurrant, earth, spice and cedar run through the bouquet and medium- to full-bodied palate, which has considerable drive and length, tannins perfectly pitched. In its infancy, its future assured. Screwcap. 13.5% alc. **Rating** 94 **To** 2029 $20

🍷🍷🍷🍷🍷 **Sibling Rivalry King Valley Pinot Gris 2012 Rating** 93 **To** 2014 $24
✪ **Shiraz 2009** Bright, clear crimson-purple; positive oak embraces blackberry, black cherry and plum fruit, the tannins evident but soft – one of the most obvious hallmarks of the change. Screwcap. 13.5% alc. **Rating** 93 **To** 2029 $20

✪   **Marsanne 2012** Light straw-green. Lemon/citrus is dominant at this stage, but there is a hint of honey on the finish and aftertaste that will grow into full-on honey and honeysuckle in 5+ years. Screwcap. 12.5% alc. **Rating** 91 **To** 2017 $15
Sibling Rivalry Geelong Pinot Noir 2010 Rating 90 **To** 2015 $26

Talisman Wines   ★★★★

PO Box 354, Cottesloe, WA 6911 **Region** Geographe
T 0401 559 266 www.talismanwines.com.au **Open** Not
Winemaker Peter Stanlake **Est.** 2009 **Dozens** 1700 **Vyds** 9ha
Kim Robinson (and wife Jenny) began the development of their vineyard in 2000, and now have cabernet, shiraz, malbec, zinfandel, chardonnay, riesling and sauvignon blanc. Kim says that 'after eight frustrating years of selling grapes to Evans & Tate and Wolf Blass, we decided to optimise the vineyard and attempt to make quality wines'. The measure of their success was the award of at least one gold medal for each of the wines submitted up to and including the Geographe Wine Show '10. They say this could not have been achieved without the assistance of vineyard manager Victor Bertola, and winemaker Peter Stanlake.

♟♟♟♟♟ **Ferguson Valley Riesling 2012** Pale quartz; the low alcohol and light colour
✪   suggest the wine will have significant residual sugar – but it doesn't; instead it has delicate flavours of herb, crushed lime leaf, green apple and crunchy acidity on the dry finish. Deserves, and will repay, patience. Screwcap. 10.9% alc. **Rating** 90 **To** 2022 $20

✪   **Ferguson Valley Sauvignon Blanc Fume 2012** Pale straw, bright; a toned-down bouquet of citrus, coriander and tropical fruits; the palate is fresh and accessible and displays enough texture and depth to persist evenly on the finish. Screwcap. 11.1% alc. **Rating** 90 **To** 2015 $18 BE

♟♟♟♟ **Ferguson Valley Shiraz 2011 Rating** 88 **To** 2020 $30 BE
Ferguson Valley Cabernet Malbec 2010 Rating 88 **To** 2018 $20 BE
Ferguson Valley Malbec 2010 Rating 87 **To** 2017 $30 BE

Tallavera Grove/Carillion   ★★★★★

749 Mount View Road, Mount View, NSW 2325 **Region** Hunter Valley
T (02) 4990 7535 www.tallaveragrove.com.au **Open** Thurs–Mon 10–5
Winemaker Jim Chatto **Est.** 2000 **Dozens** 2500 **Vyds** 40ha
Tallavera Grove is one of the many wine interests of Dr John Davis and family. The family is a 50% owner of Briar Ridge, a 12ha vineyard in Coonawarra, a 100ha vineyard at Wrattonbully (Stonefields Vineyard) and a 36ha vineyard at Orange (the Carillion wines are sourced from this vineyard). The 40ha Hunter Valley vineyards are planted to chardonnay, shiraz, semillon, verdelho, cabernet sauvignon and viognier.

♟♟♟♟♟ **Fenestella Hunter Valley Shiraz 2011** Deep crimson-purple; waves of red cherry and blackberry fruit surge backwards and forwards over the intense and complex bouquet, gaining another dimension on the intensely focused, full-bodied palate, with high quality French oak and very fine tannins. Great wine from a top vintage. Screwcap. 13.7% alc. **Rating** 96 **To** 2041 $45
Tallavera Grove Hunter Valley Semillon 2012 Classic Hunter Valley semillon style; while the fruit/acid balance has already been written in stone, the lemon zest/lemongrass and mineral notes are as yet delicate compared to where they will be in 5+ years. Screwcap. 10.8% alc. **Rating** 94 **To** 2022 $25
Tallavera Grove Hunter Valley Shiraz 2011 Deep purple-red; a complex bouquet gives equal space to regional and varietal aromas, and not much changes on the medium-bodied palate; plum and blackberry fruits are neatly trimmed by savoury tannins, and appropriate oak influence. Screwcap. 13.5% alc. **Rating** 94 **To** 2031 $25

♟♟♟♟♟ **Tallavera Grove Semillon Verdelho 2005 Rating** 93 **To** 2020 $30
Tallavera Grove Friandise Dessert Pinot Gris 2012 Rating 92 **To** 2015 $25

✪ **Carillion Estate Grown Orange Verduzzo 2012** Verduzzo has had a foothold in the Yarra Valley for well over 20 years, but this is its first move into NSW on a commercial basis. Grippy texture and mouthfeel is the main varietal attribute in this wine, although there is some citrus on show. Well made, but a work in progress. Screwcap. 13.5% alc. **Rating** 90 **To** 2014 $22

Taltarni ★★★★☆

339 Taltarni Road, Moonambel, Vic 3478 **Region** Pyrenees
T (03) 5459 7900 **www**.taltarni.com.au **Open** 7 days 10–5
Winemaker Robert Heywood **Est.** 1972 **Dozens** 80 000 **Vyds** 78.5ha
In 2009 the American owner and founder of Clos du Val (Napa Valley), Taltarni and Clover Hill (see separate entry) brought the management of these three businesses and Domaine de Nizas (Languedoc) under one roof. The group is known as Goelet Wine Estates. Taltarni is the largest of the Australian ventures, its estate vineyards of great value and underpinning the substantial annual production. There is no question it makes good red wines, but given its region, the climate/terroir of its very large estate vineyards and the age of the vines, one has the constantly nagging feeling that it ought to do better. Exports to all major markets.

🍷🍷🍷🍷🍷 **Shiraz Mourvedre 2008** Deep colour, particularly given the age of the wine; complex and full-bodied, it has sombre black fruits, licorice and leather flavours, backed by ripe though chunky tannins, all suggesting it has time to go on a long journey. It has a serious cork. 14.5% alc. **Rating** 94 **To** 2028 $40

🍷🍷🍷🍷🍷 **Estate Pyrenees Shiraz 2010 Rating** 92 **To** 2025 $40 BE
Reserve Shiraz Cabernet Sauvignon 2005 Rating 92 **To** 2020 $65 BE
✪ **Chardonnay Pinot Noir Pinot Meunier Brut 2010** Made using the traditional method. The white fruits and citrus of chardonnay drive the cuvee, which has very good length and balance, some spicy notes coming through on the finish. Diam. 12.5% alc. **Rating** 92 **To** 2015 $26
✪ **Rose 2012** Pale pink and bright, the savoury nature of sangiovese shines through on the bouquet, offering red fruits, fennel and briary notes; the palate is bone dry and vibrant, almost crunchy in its definition, and thoroughly refreshing. Screwcap. 12.2% alc. **Rating** 90 **To** 2014 $17 BE
Sangiovese Cabernet Merlot 2009 Rating 90 **To** 2017 $25 BE

Tamar Ridge/Pirie ★★★★★

653 Auburn Road, Kayena, Tas 7270 **Region** Northern Tasmania
T (03) 6394 1114 **www**.brownbrothers.com.au **Open** 7 days 9–5
Winemaker Tom Ravech **Est.** 1994 **Dozens** 15 000 **Vyds** 200ha
In August 2010 Brown Brothers purchased Tamar Ridge from Gunns Limited for $32.5 million. While Dr Andrew Pirie has retired from his former position of CEO and chief winemaker, he has been at pains to point out that the end of his five-year tenure happened to coincide with the acquisition. Tasmania is the one region of Australia with demand for grapes and wine exceeding supply. Moreover, Tamar Ridge has been very well managed during the seven years it was owned by Gunns. Exports to all major markets.

🍷🍷🍷🍷🍷 **Tamar Ridge Kayena Vineyard Riesling 2012** Pale, bright straw-green; the
✪ style of this Riesling is unmistakably Tasmanian, with its framework of crunchy, drying acidity wrapped around a totally delicious mix of lime and passionfruit flavours. Screwcap. 12% alc. **Rating** 95 **To** 2022 $24
Tamar Ridge Riesling 2012 A 100% state-grown Tamar Valley wine. It has the lime and apple focus and minerality of young Tasmanian Rieslings, providing a guaranteed base for bottle development over the next decade before plateauing thereafter. Screwcap. 11.5% alc. **Rating** 94 **To** 2027 $24
✪ **Tamar Ridge Pinot Noir 2011** Deep colour; a powerful wine, the fruit anchored on ripe plum fruit, the structure on foresty tannins. Cellar this while enjoying the Devil's Corner and/or Tasmanian Hill. Screwcap. 13.6% alc. **Rating** 94 **To** 2020 $30

Pirie NV The base wine is chardonnay and pinot noir grown on the estate White Hills Vineyard in the Tamar Valley. Has a faint blush to the colour courtesy of the pinot noir; the bouquet is notably complex, with toasty brioche to the fore, the generous palate with ripe stone fruit and red berry notes; despite this generosity, the finish is fresh, clear and well balanced. Cork. 12% alc. **Rating** 94 **To** 2015 $33

Tamar Ridge Limited Release Botrytis Riesling 2011 Orange-gold; Tasmania produces these Botrytis Rieslings with nonchalant ease, supple and unctuous, yet with refreshing acidity on the finish to cumquat, honey, lime and marmalade. 375ml. Screwcap. 9.5% alc. **Rating** 94 **To** 2016 $25

ⵟⵟⵟⵟⵟ **Tamar Ridge Kayena Vineyard Pinot Gris 2011 Rating** 92 **To** 2014 $26
Tamar Ridge Chardonnay 2011 Rating 91 **To** 2017 $26

✪ **Tasmanian Hill Pinot Noir 2011** Bright, clear crimson; has a perfumed red cherry/berry bouquet, and a smooth, fruit-driven palate with ripe cherry, blood plum and spicy tannins. Totally delicious, and great value; the price/quality ratio must send a shiver down the spine of mainland producers of Pinot Noir. Screwcap. 13.5% alc. **Rating** 91 **To** 2018 $18

Tambo Estate

96 Pages Road, Tambo Upper, Vic 3885 **Region** Gippsland
T (03) 5156 4921 **Open** By appt
Winemaker Alastair Butt **Est.** 1994 **Dozens** 800 **Vyds** 5.11ha

Bill and Pam Williams returned to Australia in the early 1990s after seven years overseas, and began the search for a property which met the specific requirements for high quality table wines established by Dr John Gladstones in his masterwork *Viticulture and Environment*. They chose a property in the foothills of the Victorian Alps on the inland side of the Gippsland Lakes, with predominantly sheltered, north-facing slopes. They planted a little over 5ha of chardonnay (the lion's share of the plantings, with 3.4ha), sauvignon blanc, pinot noir, cabernet sauvignon and a splash of merlot. They are mightily pleased to have secured the services of Alastair Butt (one-time maker at Seville Estate), and no less pleased that the grapes they sold to Shadowfax have produced outstanding wines. Tambo's performance in '11 was remarkable, and the reason for the 5-star rating.

ⵟⵟⵟⵟⵟ **Gippsland Lakes Sauvignon Blanc 2012** Pale straw-green; the fragrant
✪ bouquet of citrus and white peach (intruding into early-picked chardonnay territory, but doing so with élan) leads into a beautifully juicy palate that transcends normal stainless steel cold-fermented Sauvignon Blanc. Great value. Screwcap. 12.2% alc. **Rating** 94 **To** 2014 $18

ⵟⵟⵟⵟⵟ **Gippsland Lakes Cabernet Sauvignon 2011** Bright crimson-purple; the
✪ fragrant cassis-accented bouquet has just a hint of spice, all pointing to the cool climate, but neither on the bouquet of juicy red fruits or the palate is there any sign of under-ripe fruit. A really enjoyable, uncomplicated, wine that may given even more pleasure down the track if you are tempted to leave some and drink some. Screwcap. 12.9% alc. **Rating** 93 **To** 2021 $18

✪ **Gippsland Lakes Cabernet Sauvignon 2010** Obviously the colour, while good, is more developed than that of the '11, and the wine is significantly richer, indeed verging on medium- to full-bodied, with grainy/savoury tannins threaded through the blackcurrant fruit; the oak, too, makes a positive contribution. Exceptional value. Screwcap. 13.2% alc. **Rating** 93 **To** 2025 $18

ⵟⵟⵟⵟ **Gippsland Lakes Chardonnay 2011** The bouquet is fresh and fragrant, the
✪ palate similarly fresh, but light-bodied; sensibly, there has not been any attempt to bulk it up with oak, leaving the citrus/stone fruit flavours intact. Screwcap. 12.7% alc. **Rating** 89 **To** 2015 $18

Tamburlaine

358 McDonalds Road, Pokolbin, NSW 2321 **Region** Hunter Valley
T (02) 4998 4200 **www**.mywinery.com **Open** 7 days 9.30–5
Winemaker Mark Davidson, Ashley Horner **Est.** 1966 **Dozens** 80000
A thriving business that until exports started to grow significantly sold over 90% of its wine through the cellar door and by mailing list (with an active tasting club members' cellar program offering wines held and matured at Tamburlaine). The maturing of the estate-owned Orange vineyard has led to a dramatic rise in quality across the range. Both the Hunter Valley and Orange vineyards are now certified organic. Exports to the UK, the US and other major markets.

🍷🍷🍷🍷🍷 **Reserve Hunter Valley Chardonnay 2012** Very much in the modern style of Hunter Valley chardonnay: partial wild yeast barrel fermentation, partial mlf and lees contact of early picked fruit, the oak unobtrusive; citrus and white peach are dominant, the finish fresh. Screwcap. 13.1% alc. **Rating** 94 **To** 2016 $30
Reserve Orange Chardonnay 2012 Despite the radically different climate of Orange and the Hunter Valley, the two '12 Reserve Tamburlaine wines have more in common than less; there is more grapefruit/citrus in this wine, and the finish lingers a little longer. Screwcap. 13.7% alc. **Rating** 94 **To** 2020 $30
Reserve Hunter Valley Syrah 2011 A very well made medium-bodied Shiraz/Syrah, with smooth, supple black cherry and plum fruit, the oak (American) integrated, the tannins fine. Screwcap. 13.5% alc. **Rating** 94 **To** 2035 $44
Reserve Orange Syrah 2011 A very different set of flavours and aromas, with red berry fruits, spices and French oak running through the lithe medium-bodied palate, the finish fine and silky. Exceptional outcome for the vintage. Screwcap. 13.3% alc. **Rating** 94 **To** 2030 $44
Reserve Orange Merlot 2011 Bright, clear purple-crimson; this does have true varietal character, with cassis and black olive/earth aromas and flavours; the palate is just into medium-bodied territory (a good thing) and is light on its feet, the tannins fine and lacy, the oak good. Screwcap. 13.5% alc. **Rating** 94 **To** 2020 $44

🍷🍷🍷🍷🍷 **Reserve Orange Riesling 2012 Rating** 93 **To** 2022 $30
Reserve Orange Cabernet Sauvignon 2011 Rating 93 **To** 2031 $44
Reserve Hunter Valley Semillon 2012 Rating 92 **To** 2022 $30
Reserve Orange Malbec 2011 Rating 91 **To** 2016 $44
Reserve Orange Sauvignon Blanc 2012 Rating 90 **To** 2014 $30
Wine Lovers Orange Sauvignon Blanc 2011 Rating 90 **To** 2013 $20
Wine Lovers Orange Marsanne 2012 Rating 90 **To** 2016 $28

🍷🍷🍷🍷
✪ **On the Grapevine Premium Chardonnay 2011** Pale straw-green; one of the more successful of the On the Grapevine series of wines; the light-bodied, fresh stone fruit and citrus flavours have the barest touch of oak, a sensible winemaking option. Screwcap. 12.5% alc. **Rating** 89 **To** 2014 $17

Taminick Cellars

339 Booth Road, Taminick via Glenrowan, Vic 3675 **Region** Glenrowan
T (03) 5766 2282 **www**.taminickcellars.com.au **Open** Mon–Sat 9–5, Sun 10–5
Winemaker James Booth **Est.** 1904 **Dozens** 2000 **Vyds** 19.7ha
Peter Booth is a third-generation member of the Booth family, who have owned this winery since Esca Booth purchased the property in 1904. James Booth, fourth-generation and current winemaker, completed his wine science degree at CSU in 2008. The red wines are massively flavoured and very long-lived, notably from the 9ha of shiraz planted in 1919. Trebbiano and alicante bouschet were also planted in '19, with much newer arrivals including nero d'Avola. The wines are sold through the cellar door, mail order and a selection of independent retailers in Melbourne and Sydney. Exports to Hong Kong.

ŶŶŶŶŶ **Generations IV Shiraz 2008** Was given 94 points when first tasted in Dec '09, and is still remarkably fresh, fragrant and elegant. Its purple-crimsons colour is excellent, its red berry fruits full of life, the tannins ripe and fine. How it's still available, I don't know. Screwcap. 14% alc. **Rating** 94 **To** 2020 $24

ŶŶŶŶŶ **Chardonnay 2012** Pale, bright straw-green; a remarkable achievement for estate-
✪ grown grapes. Early picking was a key decision, as was the barrel fermentation in predominantly used oak; the result is a lively, fresh wine with a mix of grapefruit, lemon curd, lemon juice and more smoky notes from the barrel ferment. The value is obvious. Screwcap. 12.5% alc. **Rating** 91 **To** 2016 $15
Generations IV Janus Shiraz Trebbiano 2012 Rating 91 **To** 2022 $24
✪ **1919 Series Shiraz 2010** Has good colour; plum and blackberry fruit on the bouquet and palate is flavoursome, but the decision not to fine the wine has left it with somewhat pervasive tannins. A very good curate's egg at a bargain price. Screwcap. 14.2% alc. **Rating** 90 **To** 2020 $16
✪ **Cabernet Sauvignon 2010** Light to medium red-purple; This light- to medium-bodied Cabernet is a prime example, with its cassis fruit offset by fine, savoury tannins. It shouldn't be possible in Glenrowan. Screwcap. 13.8% alc. **Rating** 90 **To** 2018 $16
Generations IV Nero d'Avola 2011 Rating 90 **To** 2018 $24

Tapanappa ★★★★★

PO Box 174, Crafers, SA 5152 **Region** South Australia
T 0419 843 751 www.tapanappawines.com.au **Open** Not
Winemaker Brian Croser **Est.** 2002 **Dozens** 3000 **Vyds** 16.7ha
The Tapanappa partners are Brian Croser (formerly of Petaluma), Jean-Charles Cazes of Chateau Lynch-Bages in Pauillac, and Société Jacques Bollinger, the parent company of Champagne Bollinger. The partnership has three vineyard sites in Australia: the Whalebone Vineyard at Wrattonbully (planted to cabernet sauvignon, shiraz and merlot over 30 years ago); the Tiers Vineyard (chardonnay) at Piccadilly in the Adelaide Hills (the remainder of the Tiers Vineyard chardonnay continues to be sold to Petaluma); and the Foggy Hill Vineyard on the southern tip of the Fleurieu Peninsula (pinot noir). Exports to all major markets.

ŶŶŶŶŶ **Whalebone Vineyard Wrattonbully Merlot Cabernet Franc 2008**
The 60/40% blend was given 20 months in French oak (30% new) before being bottled unfiltered. The colour is vivid purple-crimson, the medium-bodied palate exceptionally supple and smooth, the tannins silky and fine. A truly lovely wine. Cork. 14% alc. **Rating** 96 **To** 2033 $75
Parawa Fleurieu Peninsula Pinot Noir 2012 Strong, clear and deep colour; a thoroughly serious Pinot Noir, with a fragrant bouquet followed by a black cherry and plum palate with excellent texture and structure; tannins and oak are woven through the mid-palate and into the finish. Will repay cellaring. Screwcap. 14% alc. **Rating** 95 **To** 2021 $35
Foggy Hill Vineyard Fleurieu Peninsula Pinot Noir 2010 Light, but still bright primary colour; an elegant and polished wine, harmony its key word; fruit, oak (30% new), tannins and acidity have been precisely judged; the palate is only light- to medium-bodied, yet has great length and persistence to its red berry fruits. Screwcap. 13% alc. **Rating** 95 **To** 2019 $50
Whalebone Vineyard Wrattonbully Cabernet Shiraz 2008 The late Len Evans would doubtless have taken great delight in pointing out the quality of this 70/30% blend, used in the first Petaluma Coonawarra, but not thereafter. This has been made in the same way as the Merlot Cabernet Franc, but is fuller bodied, with more obvious texture, and will benefit from more time. 460 dozen made. Cork. 14.5% alc. **Rating** 95 **To** 2038 $55
Piccadilly Valley Chardonnay 2011 Bright green-yellow; a wine born of Brian Croser's long experience with the Piccadilly Valley and chardonnay; white peach and melon fruit is interwoven with finely judged oak, the mlf handled expertly. Screwcap. 12.8% alc. **Rating** 94 **To** 2017 $39

Tar & Roses/Trust ★★★★☆

61 Vickers Lane, Nagambie, Vic 3608 (postal) **Region** Central Victoria Zone
T (03) 5794 1811 **www**.tarandroses.com.au **Open** Not
Winemaker Don Lewis, Narelle King **Est.** 2004 **Dozens** 15 000 **Vyds** 5ha
Tar & Roses is one of the more interesting new arrivals on the Australian winemaking scene, even though the partners, Don Lewis and Narelle King, have been making wine together for many years at Mitchelton and – for the past three years – Priorat, Spain. Don came from a grapegrowing family in Red Cliffs, near Mildura, and in his youth was press-ganged into working in the vineyard. When he left home he swore never to be involved in vineyards again, but in 1973 he found himself accepting the position of assistant winemaker to Colin Preece at Mitchelton, where he remained until his retirement 32 years later. Narelle, having qualified as a chartered accountant, set off to travel, and while in South America met a young Australian winemaker who had just completed vintage in Argentina, and who lived in France. The lifestyle appealed greatly, so on her return to Australia she obtained her winemaking degree from CSU and was offered work by Mitchelton as a bookkeeper and cellar hand. Together they are making wines that are a mosaic of Australia, Italy and Spain in their inspiration.

🍷🍷🍷🍷🍷 **Trust Shiraz 2011** No region of origin specified; the colour is bright crimson-
✪ purple of moderate depth, the bouquet with red fruits and cinnamon spice that comes through strongly on the textured, medium-bodied palate, along with cherry and raspberry flavours. An altogether intriguing and enjoyable medium-bodied wine. Screwcap. 14% alc. **Rating** 93 **To** 2021 $27
✪ **Tar & Roses Heathcote Shiraz 2012** Deep purple-crimson; a particularly complex bouquet and palate, with allspice, pepper, licorice and tar (why not?); the tannins are fine, the medium-bodied palate long and even, the finish with a juicy farewell. Very good value. Screwcap. 14.2% alc. **Rating** 92 **To** 2018 $20
Tar & Roses Heathcote Sangiovese 2012 Very attractive, with red cherry and morello cherry woven with typical tannins, and a recurrent theme of spice and tannins. Screwcap. 13.7% alc. **Rating** 92 **To** 2018 $24
✪ **Tar & Roses Central Victoria Pinot Grigio 2012** Full-on pale pink, almost into rose territory; it may be autosuggestion, but there seem to be hints of wild strawberry along with pear and stone fruit; regardless, the finish is crisp and lively. Screwcap. 13.8% alc. **Rating** 90 **To** 2014 $18

Tarrawarra Estate ★★★★★

311 Healesville-Yarra Glen Road, Yarra Glen, Vic 3775 **Region** Yarra Valley
T (03) 5962 3311 **www**.tarrawarra.com.au **Open** Tues–Sun 11–5
Winemaker Clare Halloran **Est.** 1983 **Dozens** 15 000 **Vyds** 28.98ha
Tarrawarra is, and always has been, one of the top-tier wineries in the Yarra Valley. Founded by Marc Besen AO and wife Eva, it has operated on the basis that quality is paramount, cost a secondary concern. The creation of the Tarrawarra Museum of Art (twma.com.au) in a purpose-built building constitutes another reason to visit the winery; indeed, many visitors come specifically to look at the ever-changing displays in the Museum. On the wine front, Clare Halloran adopts a low profile while nonetheless being actively engaged in numerous winemaking events, be they Yarra Valley or Victorian (as in the case of the annual Pinot Noir Workshop). Changes in the vineyard include the planting of shiraz and merlot, and in the winery, the creation of a four-tier range: a deluxe MDB label made in tiny quantities and only when the vintage permits; a single vineyard duo (J-Block Shiraz and K-Block Merlot); a Reserve range of Chardonnay and Pinot Noir; and the 100% estate-grown varietal range. Exports to France, the Maldives and Singapore.

🍷🍷🍷🍷🍷 **Reserve Yarra Valley Chardonnay 2011** Shares the finesse and fragrance of its sibling, but has greater complexity and a little more new oak influence; its length and balance are particularly good. Screwcap. 13% alc. **Rating** 95 **To** 2020 $50
✪ **Yarra Valley Chardonnay 2011** Has all the fragrance and finesse the cool vintage gave to many of the top Yarra Valley chardonnays; white peach and some nectarine flavours have barrel-ferment oak influence, the latter neatly balanced so as not to threaten the fruit. Screwcap. 12.5% alc. **Rating** 94 **To** 2019 $25

Pinot Noir Rose 2011 Pale salmon-pink; one of very few Roses on the market with a bone dry, crisp and savoury/spicy finish. It has more than a passing resemblance to the roses of Provence, and will happily match any Mediterranean food. Screwcap. 12.5% alc. **Rating** 94 **To** 2013 $22

ŦŦŦŦŶ **Yarra Valley Viognier Roussanne Marsanne 2011 Rating** 91 **To** 2017 $30
K-Block Yarra Valley Merlot 2011 Rating 91 **To** 2018 $35

Tatachilla   ★★★★★

151 Main Road, McLaren Vale, SA 5171 **Region** McLaren Vale
T (08) 8323 8656 **www**.tatachillawines.com.au **Open** Not
Winemaker Fanchon Ferrandi **Est.** 1903 **Dozens** 43 000 **Vyds** 12.4ha
Tatachilla was reborn in 1995 but has had a tumultuous history going back to 1903. Between '03 and '61 the winery was owned by Penfolds; it was closed in '61 and reopened in '65 as the Southern Vales Co-operative. In the late '80s it was purchased and renamed The Vales but did not flourish; in '93 it was purchased by local grower Vic Zerella and former Kaiser Stuhl chief executive Keith Smith. After extensive renovations, the winery was officially reopened in '95 and won a number of tourist awards and accolades. It became part of Banksia Wines in 2001, in turn acquired by Lion Nathan in '02. Exports to all major markets.

ŦŦŦŦŦ **Foundation McLaren Vale Shiraz 2008** Has retained deep colour; while full-bodied and potent, seems to have escaped the clutches of the '08 heatwave, and unquestionably speaks loud about its McLaren Vale origin. Blackberry, spice, licorice, dark chocolate and more sombre notes are woven through a base of ripe tannins and integrated oak. Screwcap. 14.5% alc. **Rating** 94 **To** 2030 $55
McLaren Vale Cabernet Sauvignon 2010 Deep purple-crimson; a medium- to full-bodied wine reflecting both the vintage and the synergy between the region and the variety with its exuberant blackcurrant fruit and good tannins. Screwcap. 14.5% alc. **Rating** 94 **To** 2025 $24

ŦŦŦŦŶ **McLaren Vale Shiraz 2010 Rating** 93 **To** 2020 $24

Tatler Wines

477 Lovedale Road, Lovedale, NSW 2321 **Region** Hunter Valley
T (02) 4930 9139 **www**.tatlerwines.com **Open** 7 days 10–5
Winemaker Daniel Binet **Est.** 1998 **Dozens** 6000 **Vyds** 15ha
Tatler Wines is a family-owned company headed by Sydney hoteliers, brothers Theo and Spiro Isak (Isakidis). The name comes from the Tatler Hotel on George Street, Sydney, which was purchased by father James (Dimitri) Isak in 1974 and operated by the family until its closure in '86. In '98 the Tatler name was reborn with the purchase of a 40ha property in Lovedale. The vineyard is planted to 7ha of chardonnay and 4ha each of semillon and shiraz; the wines are made onsite in the recently renovated winery. Exports to the US.

ŦŦŦŦŦ **Museum Release Nigel's Hunter Valley Semillon 2007** Has that glorious incandescent green colour of Semillon reaching the first stage of its maturity; it still has the particular lemon butter/lemon juice flavours of the '07 vintage, and while it will not fade or broaden, it is unlikely to give more pleasure than it does now. Screwcap. 10.4% alc. **Rating** 94 **To** 2017 $35

ŦŦŦŦŶ **Dimitri's Paddock Hunter Valley Chardonnay 2011 Rating** 91 **To** 2016 $25

Taylor Ferguson

Level 1, 62 Albert Street, Preston, Vic 3072 (postal) **Region** South Eastern Australia
T (03) 9487 2599 **www**.alepat.com.au **Open** Not
Winemaker Norman Lever **Est.** 1996 **Dozens** 40 000
Taylor Ferguson is the much-altered descendant of a business of that name established in Melbourne in 1898. A connecting web joins it with Alexander & Paterson (1892) and the much more recent distribution business of Alepat Taylor. The development of the Taylor

Ferguson wines has been directed by winemaker Norman Lever, using grapes sourced from various regions, mainly Coonawarra, Langhorne Creek and the Riverina. The wines have a strong domestic and export focus including Germany, Iraq, Singapore, Malaysia, Vietnam, Taiwan and China.

ŸŸŸŸŸ **Directors Reserve Limited Release Hilltops Shiraz 2010** Medium red-
✪ purple; despite the front label specifying McLaren Vale as the region, the back label (correctly) denotes Hilltops as the source; it has a well-composed medium- to full-bodied palate, with black cherry, spice and licorice fruit, vanillin American oak and fine tannins all in the frame. Cork. 14.5% alc. **Rating** 92 **To** 2018 $20

ŸŸŸŸ **Premium Selection Willbriggie Estate Durif 2010** The colour is good,
✪ although not as inky as some Durifs; warm climates suit durif, softening its armour plate, and here introducing spice and earthy notes alongside the dark berry fruits; the tannins are in no way fearsome. Screwcap. 14% alc. **Rating** 89 **To** 2015 $15
Premium Selection Langhorne Creek Shiraz Cabernet 2010 Rating 88 **To** 2014 $15
✪ **Coonawarra Cabernet Sauvignon 2010** Medium red-purple; the palate opens with cassis and redcurrant fruit with a touch of Coonawarra earth and mint, closing with French oak, and dusty tannins that do tend to dry the palate – a small issue in the context of the price. Screwcap. 14% alc. **Rating** 88 **To** 2016 $12

Taylors ★★★★★

Taylors Road, Auburn, SA 5451 **Region** Clare Valley
T (08) 8849 1111 **www.**taylorswines.com.au **Open** Mon–Fri 9–5, Sat & public hols 10–5, Sun 10–4
Winemaker Adam Eggins, Ryan Waples, Chad Bowman **Est.** 1969 **Dozens** 250 000 **Vyds** 400ha
The family-founded and owned Taylors continues to flourish and expand – its vineyards now by far the largest holding in the Clare Valley. There have also been changes in terms of both the winemaking team and the wine style and quality, particularly through the outstanding St Andrews range. With each passing vintage, Taylors is managing to do the same for the Clare Valley as Peter Lehmann is doing for the Barossa Valley. Taylors celebrated its 40th vintage in fine style with the much anticipated 2012 vintage. Exports (under the Wakefield brand due to trademark reasons) to all major markets.

ŸŸŸŸŸ **St Andrews Single Vineyard Release Clare Valley Riesling 2012** A high-class Clare Riesling, fully reflecting the top vintage and a small selection of the best plots of the vineyard resulting in a wine of singular length and intensity to its palate, lemon zest and unsweetened lime married to crisp acidity. Screwcap. 12.5% alc. **Rating** 96 **To** 2025 $35
St Andrews Single Vineyard Release Clare Valley Shiraz 2010 Deep colour; displays essency blackberry fruit aromas with fine, spicy oak notes and a splash of vanilla; the palate is medium-bodied, with velvety texture, fine-grained tannins in abundance, and a long, luscious and poised finish. Screwcap. 14.5% alc. **Rating** 95 **To** 2025 $60 BE
✪ **Clare Valley Riesling 2012** A delicious Riesling; lime, lemon and a trace of ripe apple dance across the tongue and well into the finish and aftertaste. Taylors has been making very good Riesling for decades, but this still came as a (very pleasant) surprise. Screwcap. 13% alc. **Rating** 94 **To** 2022 $19
St Andrews Single Vineyard Release Clare Valley Cabernet Sauvignon 2010 Bright, full purple-crimson; the bouquet is fragrant, the medium-bodied palate with good varietal expression courtesy of redcurrant and cassis; excellently balanced and integrated tannins follow on the back-palate, French oak in its due place. Screwcap. 14% alc. **Rating** 94 **To** 2025 $60

ŸŸŸŸŸ **Jaraman Clare Valley Eden Valley Riesling 2012 Rating** 93 **To** 2019 $25
St Andrews Single Vineyard Release Clare Valley Chardonnay 2012 Rating 92 **To** 2017 $35 BE

❂   **Clare Valley Shiraz 2010** All but one of the four gold medals (and trophy) emblazoned on the front label are, well, curious, the one with unquestionable status the International Wine & Spirits Competition '12 (UK). It is a generous wine, with abundant red and black fruits, ripe tannins and come-hither oak that provided the floorboards for its show success. Great value. Screwcap. 14% alc. **Rating** 91 **To** 2018 $19

🍷🍷🍷🍷   **Clare Valley Merlot 2012** Good colour; a rich and round palate with abundant
❂   plum fruit; a tribute to the vintage rather than the variety. Screwcap. 14% alc. **Rating** 89 **To** 2016 $19

❂   **Clare Valley Cabernet Sauvignon 2010** Reassuring, bright crimson-purple; used French oak maturation, plus ripe, gentle tannins and blackcurrant fruit mean it is ready now, but will cruise through another 5+ years. Screwcap. 14% alc. **Rating** 89 **To** 2016 $19

TeAro Estate

20 Queen Street, Williamstown, SA 5351 **Region** Barossa Valley
T (08) 8524 6860 **www.**tearoestate.com **Open** Fri–Mon 10–5, or by appt
Winemaker Todd Rowett, Russell Johnson **Est.** 2001 **Dozens** 1500 **Vyds** 58.2ha
TeAro Estate is a family-owned and operated wine business located in the southern Barossa Valley. In 1919 great-grandfather Charlie Fromm married Minnie Kappler, who named their home block TeAro. They planted shiraz and semillon, their only equipment a single crowbar (and their bare hands). Under the guidance of second- and third-generation family members Ron and Trevor, the vineyard has grown to just over 58ha. Until 2001 the grapes were sold, but in that year Trevor decided to have a tonne of Shiraz made for the local football club. It has been the fourth generation, including vigneron Ryan Fromm and brother-in-law Todd Rowett, that has been responsible for the proliferation of varieties. The vineyards are planted (in descending size) to shiraz, cabernet sauvignon, semillon, chardonnay, pinot noir, riesling, viognier, sauvignon blanc, pinot gris, tempranillo, merlot, mourvedre and grenache. Exports to China.

🍷🍷🍷🍷🍷   **Two Charlies Barossa Valley G.S.M. 2011** Like the Iron Fist Grenache, has
❂   remarkable freshness and intensity to its display of red and black fruits on the medium- to full-bodied palate; even more surprising – and gratifying – are the tannins. Screwcap. 14.7% alc. **Rating** 93 **To** 2016 $22

The Charging Bull Barossa Valley Tempranillo 2010 Good colour; an unusually rich, full-bodied Tempranillo, with black cherry fruit spiked with oriental spices and complexed by ripe tannins. Might well develop into something special. Screwcap. 14.8% alc. **Rating** 92 **To** 2020 $30

The Charred Door Barossa Valley Shiraz 2010 Relatively light colour; a pleasant light- to medium bodied Shiraz, with black and red fruits, a sprinkle of spice, and several dabs of oak; the tannin and oak contributions have been held in restraint. Screwcap. 14.5% alc. **Rating** 90 **To** 2018 $28

❂   **Iron Fist Barossa Valley Grenache 2011** Light but bright colour; the bouquet is fragrant, and despite the alcohol, the palate has more spicy/savoury notes than usual, and the cool (wet) vintage has some bright red fruit notes in place of Turkish Delight. Screwcap. 14.8% alc. **Rating** 90 **To** 2014 $20

🍷🍷🍷🍷   **Barefooter Cellar Reserve Merlot 2008** Rating 87 To 2014 $35

Tellurian

408 Tranter Road, Toolleen, Vic 3551 **Region** Heathcote
T 0431 004 766 **www.**tellurianwines.com.au **Open** By appt
Winemaker Tobias Ansted **Est.** 2003 **Dozens** 3000 **Vyds** 21.87ha
The vineyard is situated on the western side of Mt Camel at Toolleen, on the red Cambrian soil that has made Heathcote one of the foremost regions in Australia for the production of Shiraz (Tellurian means 'of the earth'). Planning is underway for the construction of a winery

on the Toolleen vineyard site. Further Rhône red and white varieties were planted on the Tellurian property in 2011. Exports to China.

ΨΨΨΨ **Pastiche Heathcote Shiraz 2011** Deep garnet; showing a little savoury development of fresh leather, bay leaf and dark plum on the bouquet; medium-bodied and spicy on the palate, with red fruits and fine tannins lingering evenly on the finish. Screwcap. 13.9% alc. **Rating** 90 **To** 2017 $27 BE

ΨΨΨΨ **Heathcote Marsanne 2012** **Rating** 89 **To** 2016 $28 BE

Temple Bruer ★★★

Milang Road, Strathalbyn, SA 5255 **Region** Langhorne Creek
T (08) 8537 0203 **www.**templebruer.com.au **Open** Mon–Fri 9.30–4.30
Winemaker David Bruer, Vanessa Altmann, Verity Stanistreet **Est.** 1980 **Dozens** 10 000
Vyds 19.2ha
Temple Bruer was in the vanguard of the organic movement in Australia and was the focal point for the formation of Organic Vignerons Australia. Part of the production from its estate vineyards is used for its own label, part is sold. Winemaker-owner David Bruer also has a vine propagation nursery, likewise run on an organic basis. Exports to the UK, the US, Canada, Sweden and Japan.

ΨΨΨΨ **Organic Langhorne Creek Shiraz Malbec 2008** Showing developed leather and mocha notes on the dark-fruited bouquet; the palate is still fresh, with tangy acidity providing line to the savoury nature of the fruit. Screwcap. 14.5% alc. **Rating** 88 **To** 2016 $18 BE

Tempus Two Wines

Broke Road, Pokolbin, NSW 2321 **Region** Hunter Valley
T (02) 4993 3999 **www.**tempustwo.com.au **Open** 7 days 10–5
Winemaker Andrew Duff **Est.** 1997 **Dozens** 55 000
Tempus Two is the name for what was once Hermitage Road Wines. It is a mix of Latin (Tempus means time) and English; the change was forced on the winery by the EU Wine Agreement and the prohibition of the use of 'hermitage' on Australian wine labels. It has been a major success story, production growing from 6000 dozen in 1997 to over 50 000 dozen today. Its cellar door, restaurant complex (including the Oishii Japanese restaurant) and small convention facilities are situated in a striking building. The design polarises opinion; I like it. Exports to all major markets.

ΨΨΨΨ **Pewter Hunter Valley Semillon 2012** Quartz-white; a bottle shape and metallic label you either love or hate – at best a distraction from the purity and precision of the excellent young semillon, its future pre-ordained thanks to the balance, line and length of its citrus and mineral fruit. Screwcap. 11% alc. **Rating** 93 **To** 2022 $30
Pewter Pinot Noir Chardonnay 2010 Made from chardonnay, pinot noir and pinot meunier from cool vineyard sites throughout SA and Vic. It is light-bodied and fresh, with distinct passionfruit and white peach flavours from early-picked grapes. Diam. 11.5% alc. **Rating** 93 **To** 2015 $32
Copper Series Wilde Chardonnay 2011 A Hunter Valley/Adelaide Hills blend, wild yeast barrel-fermented, which has all the complexity one might hope for, the fruit flavours running from stone fruit into the first signs of tropical. Drink sooner rather than later. Screwcap. 13% alc. **Rating** 92 **To** 2015 $22
Pewter Barossa Shiraz 2011 Light, clear crimson-red; whether the wine will be given a fair trial is problematic, but it does have bright red fruit flavours on its light but fresh palate. Screwcap. 14% alc. **Rating** 90 **To** 2016 $32
Pewter Botrytis Semillon 2009 Green-gold; has plenty of sweet, honeyed fruit, but is not as intense or complex as the best wines of this type, and – given the bottle size – is not cheap. 250ml. Diam. 10% alc. **Rating** 90 **To** 2014 $20

♥♥♥♥
✿   **Semillon Sauvignon Blanc 2012** Pale straw-green; semillon dominates the
bouquet and palate to the extent that the wine is akin to semillon with a flourish.
I am happy with this outcome, but those looking for sauvignon blanc may be
disappointed. Screwcap. 11.5% alc. **Rating** 89 **To** 2014 $15
Copper Series Grenache Shiraz Mourvedre 2011 Rating 87 **To** 2014 $22

Ten Men

870 Maroondah Highway, Coldstream, Vic 3770 (postal) **Region** Yarra Valley
T 0409 767 838 **www**.tenmenwines.com **Open** Not
Winemaker Ben Portet **Est.** 2009 **Dozens** 250
Owner Ben Portet is the 10th-generation winemaker in the Portet family, father Dominique
(for many years in charge of Taltarni) and uncle Bernard (long-serving winemaker at
Clos Duval in the Napa Valley) members of the ninth generation. Ben has a winemaking
background second to none, building on his degree in oenology from Adelaide University
with four vintages at Petaluma (while completing his university studies), thereafter Bordeaux
(Chateau Beychevelle), Champagne (Louis Roederer), the Rhône Valley (M. Chapoutier),
Stellenbosch (Warwick Estate), and the Napa Valley (Vineyard 29). His 'day job' is assisting his
father at Dominique Portet (see separate entry). His skill in dealing with the 2011 vintage
makes a 5-star rating only a question of time.

♥♥♥♥♀   **Pyrenees Shiraz 2011** Bright hue, although not particularly deep; everything in
'11 pointed to a savoury, earthy style of shiraz, and that is what has emerged, the
antithesis of fruit bombs from other parts of South Eastern Australia. Ben Portet
has been content to allow the vintage to speak. Screwcap. 13% alc. **Rating** 92
To 2026 $40

Ten Miles East

8 Debneys Road, Norton Summit, SA 5136 **Region** Adelaide Hills
T (08) 8390 1723 **www**.tenmileseast.com **Open** Sun 11–5
Winemaker John Greenshields, Taiita and James Champniss **Est.** 2003 **Dozens** 500
Vyds 1.71ha
Ten Miles East takes its name from the fact that it is that distance and direction from the
Adelaide GPO. It is the venture of industry veteran John Greenshields, and Robin and Judith
Smallacombe and is, to put it mildly, an interesting one. Its home vineyard in the Adelaide
Hills is planted principally to riesling and sauvignon blanc, with smaller plantings of pinot
noir, shiraz, carmenere and saperavi, a Joseph's coat if ever there was one. Next, there is a
joint-venture vineyard on the Yorke Peninsula planted to shiraz (3000 vines) and carmenere
(1000 vines). Finally, Ten Miles East purchases 2–4 tonnes of shiraz per year from Wrattonbully
(where, many years ago, John founded Koppamurra, now Tapanappa). The winery and cellar
door are in what was the Auldwood Cider Factory, built in 1962.

♥♥♥♥♀
✿   **Adelaide Hills Shiraz 2010** Deep purple-crimson; its high alcohol might have
compromised the cool-climate characters of the wine, but it has, if anything,
intensified them; spice, pepper, star anise and licorice are all woven through the
black cherry base of the medium-bodied palate (and the fragrant bouquet).
Bargain basement. Screwcap. 14.8% alc. **Rating** 93 **To** 2020 $20
✿   **Adelaide Hills Arneis 2012** Arneis needs a cool climate like Adelaide Hills
to flourish as it does here; aromas of almond and pear on the bouquet translate
into citrus pith and almond on a decisive palate. Screwcap. 12.2% alc. **Rating** 90
To 2015 $16

♥♥♥♥
✿   **Adelaide Hills Sauvignon Blanc 2012** Has that particular Adelaide Hills
stamp on Sauvignon Blanc: more steel in the structure, and flavours equally poised
between herbal and tropical. No one can complain: it won't frighten the horses,
and the price is right. Screwcap. 12.6% alc. **Rating** 89 **To** 2014 $16
Adelaide Hills Saperavi 2010 Rating 87 **To** 2030 $30

Ten Minutes by Tractor

1333 Mornington-Flinders Road, Main Ridge, Vic 3928 **Region** Mornington Peninsula
T (03) 5989 6455 **www**.tenminutesbytractor.com.au **Open** 7 days 11–5
Winemaker Richard McIntyre, Martin Spedding **Est.** 1999 **Dozens** 6000 **Vyds** 34.4ha
The energy, drive and vision of Martin Spedding have transformed Ten Minutes by Tractor since he acquired the business in early 2004. In mid 2006 Ten Minutes By Tractor purchased the McCutcheon Vineyard; it also has long-term leases on the other two original home vineyards (Judd and Wallis), thus having complete control over grape production. Three new vineyards have been added in recent years: the one at the cellar door and restaurant site is organically certified and is used to trial organic viticultural practices that are progressively being employed across all the vineyards; the others are in the north of the Peninsula. There are now three labels: the first is Single Vineyard, from the home Judd, McCutcheon and Wallace Vineyards; next is Estate, the best blend of Pinot and of Chardonnay from the home vineyards; and, finally, 10X from the other estate-owned Mornington Peninsula vineyards. The winemaking partnership between Rick McIntyre and Martin continues to evolve, with a focus on traditional Burgundian and natural winemaking techniques. The restaurant has one of the best wine lists to be found at any winery. Exports to the UK, Canada, Sweden and Switzerland.

ᵀᵀᵀᵀᵀ **Wallis Mornington Peninsula Chardonnay 2011** Here there is a much riper mouthfeel, white peach, melon and fig all in a creamy web. Given that all three of the individual vineyard Chardonnays are made in the same way, a spectacular demonstration of terroir at work, and Montrachet at play. Screwcap. 13% alc. **Rating** 96 **To** 2021 $65
McCutcheon Mornington Peninsula Chardonnay 2011 Has another layer of intensity and complexity, white peach and nectarine edging their way towards centre stage, but still with grapefruit zest making a significant contribution. Screwcap. 13% alc. **Rating** 95 **To** 2020 $65
Estate Mornington Peninsula Chardonnay 2011 Focused, fine and tight, the citrus and stone fruit components woven together in a skein of minerality. All Ten Minutes by Tractor Chardonnays are made the same way every year: hand-picked, whole bunch-pressed, wild yeast-fermented and matured for 10 months in new and used French oak barriques. Screwcap. 13% alc. **Rating** 94 **To** 2019 $42

ᵀᵀᵀᵀᵠ **10X Mornington Peninsula Pinot Gris 2011** **Rating** 93 **To** 2014 $28
10X Mornington Peninsula Chardonnay 2011 **Rating** 92 **To** 2018 $30
McCutcheon Pinot Noir 2011 **Rating** 92 **To** 2017 $75
Estate Mornington Peninsula Pinot Noir 2011 **Rating** 90 **To** 2016 $46

Tenafeate Creek Wines

Lot 2 Gawler-One Tree Hill Road, One Tree Hill, SA 5114 **Region** Adelaide Zone
T (08) 8280 7715 **www**.tenafeatecreekwines.com.au **Open** Fri–Sun & public hols 11–5
Winemaker Larry and Michael Costa **Est.** 2002 **Dozens** 3000 **Vyds** 1ha
Long-term friends Larry Costa, a former hairdresser, and Dominic Rinaldi, an accountant, embarked on winemaking as a hobby in 2002. The property, with its 1ha of shiraz, cabernet sauvignon and merlot, is situated on the rolling countryside of One Tree Hill in the Mount Lofty Ranges. From a small beginning, the business has grown rapidly, with grenache, nebbiolo, sangiovese, petit verdot, chardonnay, semillon and sauvignon blanc purchased to supplement the estate-grown grapes. Michael Costa, Larry's son, has 12 vintages under his belt, mainly in the Barossa Valley, with Flying Winemaker stints to southern Italy and Provence. The red wines have won many medals over the years. Back vintages of Shiraz and Cabernet Sauvignon are available from the cellar door.

ᵀᵀᵀᵀᵀ
☆ **Basket Press Shiraz 2010** Deep purple-crimson; the quality of the fruit from this vintage was more than a match for the 22 months the wine spent in new and used French and American oak; the mouthfeel is vibrant and fresh, despite the depth of the black and red fruit flavours; the spicy, savoury tannins on the finish add a further dimension. Screwcap. 14.5% alc. **Rating** 95 **To** 2030 $25

🍷🍷🍷🍷🍷 **Sangiovese Rose 2012** The expressive bouquet has attractive notes of red
✪   berries and nougat, the light but juicy palate of red cherry and spice with
                  admirable length and balance. Lovely Rose; acidity and a hint of sweetness cleverly
                  poised. Screwcap. 12.5% alc. **Rating** 93 **To** 2014 $18
✪   **Limestone Coast Sauvignon Blanc 2012** Quartz-white; while the aromas and
           flavours are not intense, there is enough tropical fruit and vibrant, citrussy acidity
           to satisfy even the most critical palate. Screwcap. 12% alc. **Rating** 90 **To** 2014 $20
           Basket Press Nebbiolo 2010 Rating 90 **To** 2015 $35

Terindah Estate   ★★★★

90 McAdams Lane, Bellarine, Vic 3223 **Region** Geelong
T (03) 5251 5536 **www**.terindahestate.com **Open** 7 days 10–4
Winemaker Anthony Brain **Est.** 2003 **Dozens** 2000 **Vyds** 5.6ha
Retired quantity surveyor Peter Slattery bought the 48ha property in 2001, intending to plant
the vineyard, make wine and develop a restaurant. He has achieved all of this (with help from
others, of course), planting shiraz (0.5ha), pinot noir (1.8ha), pinot gris (1ha), picolit (0.6ha),
chardonnay (0.4ha) and zinfandel (0.3ha). Picolit is most interesting: it is a highly regarded
grape in northern Italy, where it makes small quantities of high-quality sweet wine. It has
proved to be very temperamental here, as in Italy, with very unreliable fruitset.

🍷🍷🍷🍷🍷 **Bellarine Peninsula Chardonnay 2011** Light yellow-green; think of a lemon
                  just picked from the tree, cut and given the smallest amount of sugar. How it
                  achieved this flavour against its sufficient alcohol, I'm not sure, but it has freshness
                  on its side. Screwcap. 13.2% alc. **Rating** 90 **To** 2016 $32

🍷🍷🍷🍷 **Bellarine Peninsula Pinot Gris 2011 Rating** 88 **To** 2014 $27
          Bellarine Peninsula Pinot Noir 2011 Rating 88 **To** 2015 $32

Terra Felix   ★★★☆

PO Box 2029, Wattletree Road, Malvern East, Vic 3134 **Region** Central Victoria Zone
T 0419 539 108 **www**.terrafelix.com.au **Open** Not
Winemaker Robert Paul **Est.** 2001 **Dozens** 14 000
Terra Felix was for many years a brand of Tallarook Wines, jointly owned by the Riebl family
and by Peter Simon, Stan Olszewski and John Nicholson. In 2005 it was decided to separate
the businesses, with Luis Riebl now solely concerned with the production of the Tallarook
wines. Peter and Stan had run the Stanley Wine Company in Clare over 20 years ago, leaving
it in the early 1980s, but always harboured a desire to be involved in the industry as owners.
Grapes continue to be sourced from Tallarook and are supplemented by some from other local
growers. They have worked hard to establish export markets as well as on-premise distribution
in Australia, with one-third of the production exported to India and China.

🍷🍷🍷🍷 **La Vie En Rose 2011** A bone-dry, savoury Rose made from 100% mourvedre
          grown in Central Victoria; it is in the food-friendly mainstream of the modern,
          dry style. Screwcap. 14% alc. **Rating** 88 **To** 2013 $18
          McLaren Vale Cabernet Sauvignon 2010 An earthy bouquet of dark fruits,
          spice and vine sap; the palate shows a distinct saline quality, is medium-bodied
          and finishes with a savoury bitter twist that is not altogether unpleasant. Cork.
          14.8% alc. **Rating** 87 **To** 2017 $30 BE
          Adelaide Hills Cabernet Sauvignon 2008 Mid garnet, browning; showing
          some leathery development; mulberry and earthy notes in abundance; medium-
          bodied and finishing with a bitter amaro 'European' feel. Cork. 14.1% alc.
          Rating 87 **To** 2015 $25 BE

Terramore Wines   ★★★★

Box 1, Coonawarra, SA 5263 **Region** Coonawarra
T (08) 8736 5139 **www**.terramorewines.com.au **Open** Not
Winemaker Ben Wurst **Est.** 2009 **Dozens** 3000 **Vyds** 38ha

The Gartner family (parents Phil and Mandy, and three children, Taylor, Abbi and Cooper) has been involved in grapegrowing in Coonawarra for 20 or so years, and also runs a company managing 300ha of vineyards in Coonawarra and Padthaway. With the downwards pressure on grape prices, in 2009 they decided to keep part of the crop from their estate vineyards (25ha of cabernet sauvignon, 10ha shiraz and 3ha of sauvignon blanc) and venture into the wine market. They chose Barbara Harkness, the Adelaide designer famous for creating the yellow tail label, to come up with a name and a label design. The name is doggerel Italian, 'terra' for earth and 'amore' for love, thus for the love of wine – and why not, with prices such as these.

Coonawarra Shiraz 2009 Has retained good hue and depth of colour, and is very different from the '10, with pugnacious blackberry fruit and savoury tannins in good balance. Drink the '10 and cellar this wine for another decade if you can. Great value. WAK screwcap. 13.9% alc. **Rating** 93 **To** 2029 $19

Coonawarra Shiraz 2010 Medium purple-red; a more than useful Shiraz at this price; the bouquet is pure and fragrant, and the medium-bodied palate, while not flashy, has attractive red and black fruits, well balanced by fine tannins and subtle oak. Top value. WAK screwcap. 14.1% alc. **Rating** 92 **To** 2018 $19

Coonawarra Cabernet Sauvignon 2010 Good colour; slightly rustic, but does have good regional fruit expression with its blackcurrant, earth, tar and mint aromas and flavours; the medium- to full-bodied palate will support cellaring. Very well priced. WAK screwcap. 14.1% alc. **Rating** 91 **To** 2025 $19

Terre à Terre   ★★★★★

PO Box 3128, Unley, SA 5061 **Region** Wrattonbully
T 0400 700 447 **www.**terroir-selections.com.au **Open** Not
Winemaker Xavier Bizot **Est.** 2008 **Dozens** 2000 **Vyds** 7ha
It would be hard to imagine two better-credentialled owners than Xavier Bizot (son of the late Christian Bizot of Bollinger fame) and wife Lucy Croser (daughter of Brian and Ann Croser). 'Terre à terre', incidentally, is a French expression meaning down-to-earth. The close-planted vineyard is on a limestone ridge, adjacent to Tapanappa's Whalebone Vineyard. The vineyard area has increased (3ha of cabernet sauvignon, 2ha of sauvignon blanc and 1ha each of cabernet franc and shiraz), with an additional 0.5ha of pinot noir leased. This has led to a doubling of production. Wines are released under the Terre à Terre, Down to Earth, Sacrebleu and Daosa labels.

Down to Earth Wrattonbully Sauvignon Blanc 2012 Pale straw-green; an intense, focused wine fermented in French oak barrels of various sizes and ages, purely a means of investing the wine with its extra structural dimensions and in now way inhibiting the display of lychee and ripe citrus/pineapple fruit. Top tier stuff. Screwcap. 13.9% alc. **Rating** 96 **To** 2014 $26

Wrattonbully Sauvignon Blanc 2012 Bright straw-green; continuing Terre à Terre's tradition of exceptionally complex Sauvignon Blanc in a white Bordeaux mould. Literally coats the mouth, but is not phenolic, just long and luscious. Screwcap. 13.5% alc. **Rating** 95 **To** 2014 $30

Wrattonbully Cabernet Sauvignon 2010 Bright, clear crimson-purple; it is decidedly French (Bordeaux) in style, with persistent and firm tannins running through the long cassis-accented palate. Will richly repay patience. 300 dozen made. Screwcap. 14.5% alc. **Rating** 94 **To** 2030 $35

Daosa Single Vineyard Piccadilly Valley Blanc de Blancs 2009 Pale straw-green, good mousse; after primary fermentation and 9 months' maturation in used French oak barriques, it was tiraged and kept on lees for 30 months. It is delicately structured, with a very low dosage of 5g/l; the flavours of citrus and apple are enhanced by the crisp, dry finish. Cork. 12.2% alc. **Rating** 94 **To** 2015 $51

Wrattonbully Late Harvest Pinot Gris 2012 Rating 92 **To** 2014 $30

Sacrebleu! Wrattonbully Cabernet Sauvignon 2011 Rating 88 **To** 2014 $19

Tertini Wines   ★★★★★

Kells Creek Road, Mittagong, NSW 2575 **Region** Southern Highlands
T (02) 4878 5213 **www.tertiniwines.com.au Open** Thurs–Mon 10–5, or by appt
Winemaker Jonathan Holgate **Est.** 2000 **Dozens** 4000 **Vyds** 7.9ha
When Julian Tertini began the development of Tertini Wines in 2000, he followed in the footsteps of Joseph Vogt 145 years earlier. History does not relate the degree of success that Joseph had, but the site he chose then was, as it is now, a good one. Tertini has pinot noir and riesling (1.8ha each), cabernet sauvignon and chardonnay (1ha each), arneis (0.9ha), pinot gris (0.8ha), merlot (0.4ha) and lagrein (0.2ha). Winemaker Jonathan Holgate, who is responsible for the outstanding results achieved at Tertini, presides over High Range Vintners, a contract winemaking business also owned by Julian Tertini. Exports to Asia.

♟♟♟♟♟ Limited Release Chardonnay 2011 Bright, pale straw-green; delicious, pure chardonnay varietal fruit, white peach, nectarine and citrus all intertwined in a single fluid stream, the barrel-ferment oak totally absorbed. Screwcap. 13% alc. Rating 95 To 2020 $40
Reserve Southern Highlands Pinot Noir 2009 Fully developed colour; a very savoury, spicy wine that won a gold medal and trophy at the NSW Wine Awards '12 and a gold medal at the Boutique Wine Awards '12. It has fully ripe, verging confit, plum fruit, the overall balance and length impressive. I would be careful about further cellaring. Screwcap. 13.5% alc. Rating 94 To 2016 $58

♟♟♟♟♀ Southern Highlands Semi-Dry Riesling 2012 Rating 92 To 2020 $33
Reserve Southern Highlands Arneis 2012 Rating 90 To 2014 $35

Teusner   ★★★★★

29 Jane Place, Tanunda, SA 5352 (postal) **Region** Barossa Valley
T (08) 8562 4147 **www.teusner.com.au Open** At Artisans of Barossa
Winemaker Kym Teusner, Phil Lehmann **Est.** 2001 **Dozens** 15 000
Teusner is a partnership between former Torbreck winemaker Kym Teusner and brother-in-law Michael Page, and is typical of the new wave of winemakers determined to protect very old, low-yielding, dry-grown Barossa vines. The winery approach is based on lees ageing, little racking, no fining or filtration, and no new American oak. As each year passes, the consistency, quality (and range) of the wines increases; there must be an end point, but it's not easy to guess when, or even if, it will be reached. Exports to the UK, the US and other major markets.

♟♟♟♟♟ Albert 2010 Bright crimson-purple; the aromatic spice and berry-filled bouquet leads into a medium-bodied palate where finely detailed dark cherry and plum fruit coalesces seamlessly with fine, ripe tannins and high-quality oak. Grenache/Shiraz/Mourvedre. Screwcap. 14.5% alc. Rating 96 To 2035 $48
✪ Woodside Adelaide Hills Sauvignon Blanc 2012 Bright straw-green; it seems Teusner can work the same magic with sauvignon blanc as he does with his better-known red wines; this is a positively juicy and joyous rendition of the variety, passionfruit to the fore, backed by kiwifruit and a touch of pineapple, and ripe citrussy acidity. Screwcap. 12.5% alc. Rating 94 To 2014 $18

♟♟♟♟♀ The Independent Shiraz Mataro 2011 Teusner pulled a rabbit (or a cat) out
✪ of the bag with this wine; it has abundant blackberry, licorice and even some dark chocolate nuances on the medium-bodied palate, the finish with a burst of fresh fruit and fine tannins. Screwcap. 14.5% alc. Rating 93 To 2021 $19
✪ Salsa 2012 Light, pale puce; a grenache, mataro, shiraz rose; a foreplay of waves of red fruits on the bouquet is consummated on the supple and seductive palate. Screwcap. 13% alc. Rating 92 To 2014 $22
✪ The Riebke Northern Barossa Shiraz 2011 Good hue; has more integrity to the expression of place and variety than any other '11 Barossa Valley Shiraz at this price, and needs no excuses; the bouquet is fragrant, the medium-bodied palate supple, with plum and blackberry fruit supported by ripe tannins. Screwcap. 14.5% alc. Rating 92 To 2018 $20

Joshua 2011 Rating 91 To 2020 $28
Joshua 2012 Rating 90 To 2017 $29

 # The Alchemists

PO Box 74, Cowaramup, WA 6284 **Region** Margaret River
T (08) 9755 5007 **www.**alchemistswines.com.au **Open** Not
Winemaker Dave Johnson **Est.** 2009 **Dozens** 3000 **Vyds** 13.6ha
Brad and Sarah Mitchell were metallurgists for 15 and 20 years respectively, working on gold and hydro-metallurgical plants, having studied metallurgy and chemistry at university. Now they see themselves as alchemists, changing grapes into wine. When they purchased the vineyard in 2007 it was already 11 years old, the prior owners having sold the grapes to various well-known Margaret River wineries. Since taking control of the vineyard, they have removed vines on unsuitable soil, and grafted others, moves that have paid dividends, and allowed contract winemaker Dave Johnson (at Credaro Family Winery) to make a series of wines that have been consistent medal winners at significant wine shows.

Margaret River Merlot 2010 Excellent colour for a 1-year-old wine, let alone 3 years, still a bright crimson-purple; it sets the scene for a succulently rich, velvety palate with layers of red and blue fruits, silky but persistent tannins, good oak, and a prodigiously long finish. Trophy for Best Merlot Qantas Wine Show WA '12. Screwcap. 14% alc. **Rating** 96 To 2020 $25

Reserve Elixir Margaret River Semillon Sauvignon Blanc 2012 A taut and finely structured wine with snap pea, grass and lemongrass intermingling on the bouquet and fore-palate, slowly unwinding into light tropical nuances on the fresh finish and aftertaste. Screwcap. 12.5% alc. **Rating** 95 To 2016 $25

Margaret River Cabernet Merlot 2010 Two gold (including Margaret River Wine Show) medals in '11. Curiously, the colour is not as bright as that of the Merlot, and the wine is altogether more savoury in flavour, albeit with very good structure and balance, the tannins more powerful, as befits a cabernet-dominant wine. Screwcap. 14% alc. **Rating** 94 To 2025 $25

The Carriages Vineyard

549 Kotta Road, Echuca, Vic 3564 **Region** Goulburn Valley
T (03) 5483 7767 **www.**thecarriagesvineyard.com.au **Open** By appt
Winemaker Greg Dedman, Australian Vintage Services **Est.** 1996 **Dozens** 400 **Vyds** 6ha
David and Lyndall Johnson began the development of The Carriages in 1996, and now have cabernet sauvignon (2.5ha), merlot (2ha), chardonnay (1ha) and semillon (0.5ha). The name and the innovative packaging stem from four old railway carriages which the Johnsons have painstakingly rehabilitated, and now live in. Each bottle is identified with a cardboard rail ticket that is strikingly similar to the tickets of bygone years. The ticket shows the brand name, the vintage, the variety, the number of standard drinks, the alcohol and the bottle number (which is in fact the ticket number, or vice versa). The ticket is fixed to the label with fine twine, so it can be either removed as a memento or used for further orders.

Echuca Cabernet Merlot 2011 Good colour for the region and vintage; like the Merlot, spent 12 months in new American oak, but the impact is not as great here, allowing some cassis fruit to make its appearance. Diam. 14% alc. **Rating** 88 To 2015 $25

Echuca Chardonnay 2012 There is no question that every effort is made in the vineyard to keep yields low, and allow picking at modest alcohol levels without reducing the profile of the varietal fruit, here unaided by oak. Screwcap. 12.5% alc. **Rating** 87 To 2014 $18

Echuca Merlot 2010 Light to medium red-purple; 12 months in new American oak was, quite simply, the wrong type of oak and 6 months too long; however, I can well imagine that cellar door visitors will have very different views, for the texture and tannin balance are good, and there is substantial all-up flavour. Diam. 14% alc. **Rating** 87 To 2015 $22

The Grapes of Ross

PO Box 14, Lyndoch, SA 5351 **Region** Barossa Valley
T (08) 8524 4214 **www**.grapesofross.com.au **Open** Not
Winemaker Ross Virgara **Est.** 2006 **Dozens** 2000

Ross Virgara spent much of his life in the broader food and wine industry, taking the plunge into commercial winemaking in 2006. The grapes come from a fourth-generation family property in the Lyndoch Valley, and the aim is to make fruit-driven styles of quality wine. His fondness for frontignac led to the first release of Moscato, followed in due course by Rose, Merlot Cabernet and Old Bush Vine Grenache. Exports to China.

ŸŸŸŸŸ **The Charmer Barossa Valley Sangiovese Merlot Cabernet Sauvignon 2010** Unusually, but successfully, the three varieties were co-fermented, and the wine spent 20 months in French oak. There is a little bit of alcohol heat, but also good fruit depth, and the tannins aren't excessive, leaving the red berry flavours free to express themselves. Screwcap. 15% alc. **Rating** 91 **To** 2016 $23

ŸŸŸŸ **Black Rose Single Vineyard Barossa Valley Shiraz 2010** Rating 88 To 2017 $33
Barossa Valley Moscato 2012 Rating 87 To 2013 $18

The Growers

1071 Wildwood Road, Yallingup, WA 6282 **Region** Margaret River
T (08) 9755 2121 **www**.thegrowers.com **Open** 7 days 10–5
Winemaker Philip May **Est.** 2002 **Dozens** 12000 **Vyds** 60ha

The Growers (once Abbey Vale) is a syndicate of 17 growers with vineyards spread across all six regions in South West Australia, and 400ha planted to all the major varieties. Five shareholders have key vineyards in the Margaret River region, where the group is based. The modestly priced wines are released under the Niche, Legs, Peppermint Grove, Jack Star, Reward and Dedication labels. Exports to Vietnam, South Korea, Thailand, Singapore, Taiwan, China and NZ.

The Hairy Arm

18 Plant Street, Northcote, Vic 3070 (postal) **Region** Sunbury
T 0409 110 462 **www**.hairyarm.com **Open** Not
Winemaker Steven Worley **Est.** 2004 **Dozens** 500

Steven graduated as an exploration geologist with a Master of Geology degree, followed by a postgraduate Diploma in Oenology and Viticulture. Until December 2009 he was general manager of Galli Estate Winery, The Hairy Arm Wine Company having started as a university project in '04. It has grown from a labour of love to a semi-commercial undertaking, focusing exclusively on shiraz grown variously in the Heathcote, Sunbury, Upper Goulburn Valley and Yarra Valley regions. The hairy arm, incidentally, is Steven's.

ŸŸŸŸŸ **Sunbury Shiraz 2011** Light crimson-purple; picked late in the season, open-fermented and spent 12 months in French (Remond) oak; not fined or filtered; spicy red fruits on the bouquet set the flavour spectrum for the palate, with the addition of some unobtrusive oak and fine tannins. A very good outcome for the vintage. Screwcap. 13.5% alc. **Rating** 92 **To** 2021 $30

ŸŸŸŸ **Heathcote Nebbiolo 2010** Rating 89 To 2015 $45

🍇 The Hunter Vineyard

PO Box 1254, Pokolbin, NSW 2320 **Region** Hunter Valley
T 0419 206 985 **www**.thehuntervineyard.com.au **Open** Not
Winemaker Nick Paterson **Est.** 1974 **Dozens** 500 **Vyds** 2.8ha

Hunter Vineyard's 2.8ha of gewurztraminer and cabernet sauvignon were originally planted in 1974 by Frank Brady, the vineyard known as Taliondal. The cabernet grapes were sold to Lake's Folly for some years, but the vineyard then fell into disuse. Neal and Marcia Flett purchased the property in 2008 and have nursed the vines back into production. The plantings are on one of the highest points in the Hunter Valley, situated on a limestone ridge.

🍷🍷🍷🍷 **Cabernet Sauvignon 2011** The wine has excellent crimson-purple colour, and there is crystal-clear varietal character on the long, medium-bodied, perfectly balanced palate. Winemaker Nick Paterson has pulled off a miracle. Screwcap. 13.6% alc. **Rating** 94 **To** 2026 $25

🍷🍷🍷🍷 **Reserve Press Gewurztraminer 2012 Rating** 92 **To** 2017 $22

The Islander Estate Vineyards ★★★★★

PO Box 868, Kingscote, SA 5223 **Region** Kangaroo Island
T (08) 8553 9008 **www**.iev.com.au **Open** By appt
Winemaker Jacques Lurton **Est.** 2000 **Dozens** 5500 **Vyds** 10ha
Established by one of the most famous Flying Winemakers in the world, Bordeaux-born and trained and part-time Australian resident Jacques Lurton. He has established a close-planted vineyard; the principal varieties are cabernet franc, shiraz and sangiovese, with lesser amounts of grenache, malbec, semillon and viognier. After several vintages experimenting with a blend of sangiovese and cabernet franc, Jacques has settled on a blend of cabernet franc and around 10% malbec as the varietal base of the signature wine, The Investigator. Exports to the UK, Canada, France, Denmark, The Netherlands, Finland, United Arab Emirates, Hong Kong, Macau, China and NZ.

🍷🍷🍷🍷 **The Investigator Cabernet Franc 2006** Like the prior vintage, has excellent colour retention of primary hues; the fragrant bouquet evolves over 30 minutes after pouring, and the palate has significantly greater depth of dark berry fruits than prior Islander red wines, ripe tannins in precisely judged support. Cork. 14% alc. **Rating** 95 **To** 2021 $70
Wally White Semillon 2010 Bright straw-green, very good for age; Jacques Lurton's family background with white Bordeaux shines through this French oak, barrel-fermented Semillon. The oak adds layers of flavour and texture, making it eminently drinkable now, but is certain to build opulence over the next 5 or so years. Screwcap. 13.5% alc. **Rating** 94 **To** 2018 $35

🍷🍷🍷🍷 **The White 2012** A 70/30% blend of semillon and viognier, given a touch of
✪ French oak; a complex wine that has not had any acid added, amplifying the round mouthfeel. How it will age is an open question. Screwcap. 13.5% alc. **Rating** 92 **To** 2014 $20
✪ **The Red 2010** I'm willing to bet this blend of malbec, cabernet franc, shiraz, viognier and grenache does deserve that overused wine 'unique'. Eighteen months in French oak has led to the seamless union of the gently spicy/savoury array of berry fruits, and helped provide the texture which might otherwise have been lacking. Screwcap. 14% alc. **Rating** 91 **To** 2020 $20

The Lake House Denmark ★★★★★

106 Turner Road, Denmark, WA 6333 **Region** Denmark
T (08) 9848 2444 **www**.lakehousedenmark.com.au **Open** 7 days 11–5
Winemaker Harewood Estate (James Kellie) **Est.** 1995 **Dozens** 6000 **Vyds** 5.2ha
Garry Capelli and Leanne Rogers purchased the property in 2005 and have since created the Lake House Denmark. They have restructured the vineyard to grow varieties suited to the climate – chardonnay, pinot noir, semillon and sauvignon blanc – incorporating biodynamic principles. They also control a couple of small family-owned vineyards in Frankland River and Mount Barker, with a similar ethos. Wines are released in three tiers: the flagship Premium Reserve range, the Postcard Series and the quirky He Said, She Said easy-drinking wines. The combined cellar door, restaurant and gourmet food emporium is a popular destination.

ᵠᵠᵠᵠᵠ **Premium Reserve Single Vineyard Semillon Sauvignon Blanc 2012**
Similar to the Premium Block Selection, except for more citrus – ranging from
lemon to lime to grapefruit – components that provide a zesty, lively platform
for the tropical fruits that it shares with the Premium Block Selection. Screwcap.
12.5% alc. **Rating** 95 **To** 2017 $32

Premium Reserve Single Vineyard Frankland Shiraz 2010 Deep purple-
crimson; here the emphasis is on satsuma plum, blackberry, licorice and oak
on both the bouquet and the medium- to full-bodied palate. Ripe tannins add
another layer to a complex wine with a long life ahead. Screwcap. 14.5% alc.
Rating 95 **To** 2040 $45

Premium Block Selection Semillon Sauvignon Blanc 2012 Has good,
bright straw-green colour; there is a lot going on with both the bouquet and
palate of this wine, but its panoply of aromas and flavours are not the least heavy
or extractive; instead citrus, passionfruit, guava and lychee float effortlessly from
start to finish. Screwcap. 12.5% alc. **Rating** 94 **To** 2016 $25

Premium Reserve Single Vineyard Chardonnay 2011 The colour is still
very pale; a super-elegant style, the one question, is it too elegant? The barrel-
ferment characters are not in doubt, but have been well controlled; the fruit
flavours are all in the stone fruit and melon spectrum, with some toasty/cashew
notes ex the oak. Screwcap. 13.5% alc. **Rating** 94 **To** 2017 $35

Premium Reserve Premium Shiraz 2010 Bright crimson-purple; the fragrant
bouquet exudes spice and pepper in conjunction with the small, black-berried
fruits of the medium-bodied palate, neatly sewn together by the gently savoury,
spicy tannins and well-integrated oak. Screwcap. 14.5% alc. **Rating** 94 **To** 2030 $35

Premium Reserve Single Vineyard Frankland Shiraz 2009 Light red-purple,
not 100% bright; the French oak is obvious, but it is the spice, black cherry and
blackberry fruit that drives the wine from the mid-palate through to the finish and
lingering aftertaste. A slightly lighter hand with the oak might have made an even
better wine. Screwcap. 14.5% alc. **Rating** 94 **To** 2024 $45

Methode Traditionnelle Brut Cuvee Chardonnay Pinot Noir 2008 The
pinot noir has bequeathed a pale pink-bronze colour; the primary fermentation
has introduced a touch of vanillin oak that adds to the overall richness of the
palate, while not compromising the balance of the finish; extended lees contact a
plus. Cork. 13% alc. **Rating** 94 **To** 2016 $35

ᵠᵠᵠᵠᵠ **He Said She Said Sauvignon Blanc Semillon 2012** The 60/40% blend of
✪ dominant sauvignon blanc is reflected in the effusive array of tropical fruits of
almost every description. Yet there are also grassy/green pea nuances that could
come from either variety, and that add further to a delicious blend. Great value.
Screwcap. 13% alc. **Rating** 93 **To** 2015 $17

Premium Block Selection Shiraz 2011 **Rating** 93 **To** 2025 $25

Single Vineyard Selection Semillon Sauvignon Blanc 2011 **Rating** 92
To 2015 $25

Premium Reserve Single Vineyard Pinot Noir 2011 **Rating** 91 **To** 2017 $45

Premium Block Selection Shiraz 2010 **Rating** 90 **To** 2020 $25

✪ **He Said She Said Shiraz Cabernet 2011** Full crimson-purple; the blend also
contains a small amount of merlot, and is appropriately complex, with blackberry,
blackcurrant and an unexpected contribution of dark chocolate; good tannins and
oak management are also distinct pluses. Very good value. Screwcap. 14.5% alc.
Rating 90 **To** 2018 $17

The Lane Vineyard   ★★★★★

Ravenswood Lane, Hahndorf, SA 5245 **Region** Adelaide Hills
T (08) 8388 1250 **www.thelane.com.au Open** 7 days 10–4.30
Winemaker Michael Schreurs, Hugh Guthrie **Est.** 1993 **Dozens** 25 000 **Vyds** 75ha
After 15 years at The Lane Vineyard, Helen and John Edwards, and sons Marty and Ben, took
an important step towards realising their long-held dream – to grow, make and sell estate-based
wines that have a true sense of place. In 2005, at the end of the (now discontinued) Starvedog

Lane joint venture with Hardys, they commissioned a state-of-the-art 500-tonne winery, bistro and cellar door overlooking their vineyards on picturesque Ravenswood Lane. Having previously invested in Delatite, and much earlier established Coombe Farm in the Yarra Valley, the Vestey Group (UK), headed by Lord Samuel Vestey and the Right Honourable Mark Vestey, have acquired a significant shareholding in the Lane Vineyard. Exports to the UK, the US, Canada, The Netherlands, Belgium, Hong Kong and China.

ΨΨΨΨΨ **John Crighton Adelaide Hills Shiraz Cabernet Sauvignon 2009** Medium red-purple; combines elegance with length, harmony, intense red and black fruits, and fine spicy/savoury tannins. A convincing tribute, and is fairly priced. WAK screwcap. 13.5% alc. **Rating** 96 **To** 2029 $110

Reginald Germein Adelaide Hills Chardonnay 2010 This has the extra dimension of texture and structure that the Beginning lacks, thanks largely to the strands of crunch/minerally acidity that weave their way through the multifaceted fruit. Seriously good Chardonnay. WAK screwcap. 13% alc. **Rating** 95 **To** 2020 $100

Reunion Adelaide Hills Shiraz 2010 Retains the elegance of the other Lane '10 Shirazs, yet is powerful and full-bodied, with multiple layers of black cherry, blackberry, spice and plentiful ripe tannins, the new oak totally integrated. WAK screwcap. 14% alc. **Rating** 95 **To** 2030 $65

Beginning Adelaide Hills Chardonnay 2010 A rich, layered and complex wine, with white peach, nectarine, fig and creamy cashew aromas and flavours, oak and fruit welded together. One suspects mlf has been used – if so, I might not have gone down that path. Screwcap. 13% alc. **Rating** 94 **To** 2017 $39

Block 14 Basket Press Adelaide Hills Shiraz 2010 Medium red-purple; the aromatic bouquet offers a burst of spice and red cherry fruit, the medium-bodied palate continuing with the same theme in an effortless and harmonious celebration of a first-class vintage (and winemaking). WAK screwcap. 14% alc. **Rating** 94 **To** 2025 $39

Block 1 Adelaide Hills Cabernet Merlot 2010 Medium to full red-purple; both the bouquet and palate are full of redcurrant and cassis fruit, tannins woven through the palate and aftertaste along with quality French oak. Impressive wine. Screwcap. 14% alc. **Rating** 94 **To** 2030 $39

ΨΨΨΨΨ **Block 10 Adelaide Hills Sauvignon Blanc 2012 Rating** 93 **To** 2013 $25

✪ **Block 1A Adelaide Hills Chardonnay 2012** Pale straw-green; the bouquet is complex, reflecting the wine's being composed of a number of different parcels from different fermentation vessels, the net result of which is that 60% of the blend had oak influence; this has in no way diminished the delicious melon, stone fruit and fig flavours, nor the citrussy acidity on the finish. WAK screwcap. 13% alc. **Rating** 93 **To** 2017 $20

19th Meeting Cabernet Sauvignon 2010 Rating 93 **To** 2025 $65

Block 3 Adelaide Hills Chardonnay 2010 Rating 92 **To** 2018 $25

Block 5 Adelaide Hills Shiraz 2010 Rating 92 **To** 2020 $30

The Ninth Mile   ★★★☆

PO Box 254, Beechworth, Vic 3747 **Region** Beechworth
T (03) 5728 3052 **www**.theninthmile.com **Open** Not
Winemaker Adrian Kearton **Est.** 2003 **Dozens** 200 **Vyds** 1ha
Adrian and Conna Kearton have established their vineyard in part on what was once the Mayday Hills 'lunatic asylum' vegetable garden, and in part in the township of Stanley, 9km southeast of Beechworth and at an elevation of 750m. It is hardly surprising that the Keartons say their wines are handmade.

ΨΨΨΨΨ **Beechworth Pinot Noir 2011** Light crimson-purple; there is a slight hint of confit fruit, but in all other respects this is a good Pinot Noir, the silky palate with good balance and length. In cooler vintages Beechworth pinot noir works. Screwcap. 13% alc. **Rating** 90 **To** 2016 $28

ΨΨΨΨ **Viognier 2012 Rating** 89 **To** 2014 $22

The Old Faithful Estate ★★★★★

281 Tatachilla Road, McLaren Vale, SA 5171 **Region** McLaren Vale
T 0419 383 907 **www**.adelaidewinemakers.com.au **Open** By appt
Winemaker Nick Haselgrove, Warren Randall **Est.** 2005 **Dozens** 1500 **Vyds** 5ha
This is a 50/50 joint venture between American John Larchet and Adelaide Winemakers (see separate entry). Larchet has long had a leading role as a specialist importer of Australian wines into the US, and guarantees the business whatever sales it needs there. Its shiraz, grenache and mourvedre come from old, single-site blocks in McLaren Vale. Exports to the US, Canada, Switzerland, Russia, Hong Kong and China.

🍷🍷🍷🍷 **Top of the Hill McLaren Vale Shiraz 2010** Dense, deep purple-crimson; the bouquet leaves absolutely no doubt about the region of origin of this full-bodied wine, even less doubt of its variety. It is absolutely crammed with black fruits and tannins, yet is not the least extractive. This has a virtually unlimited life. Diam. 14.5% alc. **Rating** 96 **To** 2060 $50
Northern Exposure McLaren Vale Grenache 2010 Very good hue for age; ultra-traditional McLaren Vale style made from a single 70-year-old vineyard plot; there are not only strong red fruits, but also that regional dark chocolate joining with life-sustaining tannins. Diam. 14.5% alc. **Rating** 95 **To** 2025 $50

The Roy Kidman Wine Co ★★★★

Comaum School Road, Coonawarra, SA 5263 **Region** Coonawarra
T 0417 878 933 **www**.roykidman.com.au **Open** Not
Winemaker Peter Douglas (Contract) **Est.** 2003 **Dozens** 5000 **Vyds** 55.9ha
Branches of the Kidman family have been part of Coonawarra viticulture since 1970, and long before that one of the great names in the Australian cattle industry. Tim, Philip and Mardi Kidman (brothers and sister) run a separate business from that of cousin Sid Kidman, with 40.2ha of cabernet sauvignon and 15.7ha of shiraz, planting the first 2ha of shiraz in 1970, and moving into wine production in 2003, albeit still selling the major part of the grape production. Roy the Cattleman (Cabernet Sauvignon) is a tribute to their paternal grandfather, who worked as a stockman for his uncle Sir Sidney Kidman. Exports to Sweden, Hong Kong, Singapore, Malaysia, Thailand and China.

🍷🍷🍷🍷 **Roy the Cattleman Coonawarra Cabernet Sauvignon 2005** Deep colour, and with a blackcurrant pastille bouquet; the palate is still fresh and vibrant, though showing plenty of development and cedary complexity; excellent value for a wine of that age. Screwcap. 14.7% alc. **Rating** 90 **To** 2018 $28 BE

The Story Wines ★★★★★

9/229 Balaclava Road, Caulfield North, Vic 3161 (postal) **Region** Grampians
T 0411 697 912 **www**.thestory.com.au **Open** Not
Winemaker Rory Lane **Est.** 2004 **Dozens** 1850
Over the years I have come across winemakers with degrees in atomic science, doctors with specialties spanning every human condition, town planners, sculptors and painters, and Rory Lane adds yet another to the list: a degree in ancient Greek literature. He says that after completing his degree, and 'desperately wanting to delay an entry into the real world, I stumbled across and enrolled in a postgraduate wine technology and marketing course at Monash University, where I soon became hooked on … the wondrous connection between land, human and liquid'. Vintages in Australia and Oregon germinated the seed, and he zeroed in on the Grampians, where he purchases small parcels of high-quality grapes, making the wines in a small factory where he has assembled a basket press, a few open fermenters, a mono pump and some decent French oak.

🍷🍷🍷🍷 **Westgate Vineyard Grampians Blanc Marsanne Roussanne Viognier 2012** Gleaming straw-green; picked and pressed together, then wild yeast-fermented in used French barriques; the wine has real gravitas, is complex and mouthfilling, and cries out for some years in bottle to show it really can do tricks. Screwcap. 13.5% alc. **Rating** 93 **To** 2017 $27

Garden Gully Vineyard Grampians Shiraz 2011 Light to medium red, looking as if it might develop quickly. There is a streak of earthy/spicy/pepper character that runs through the bouquet and palate, joining with the black cherry fruit and cedary oak. Screwcap. 13.5% alc. **Rating** 93 **To** 2020 $49

Tempest Grampians Shiraz 2011 Produced from the Westgate, Garden Gully and Jallukar Ridge vineyards, assembled after stringent declassification of lesser wines. Very different from Garden Gully, with sweeter/riper fruit, even though the alcohol is the same, and the oak is a little more obvious (also curious). Screwcap. 13.5% alc. **Rating** 92 **To** 2025 $25

The Trades

13/30 Peel Road, O'Connor, WA 6163 (postal) **Region** Margaret River
T (08) 9331 2188 **www**.terrawines.com.au **Open** Not
Winemaker Brad Wehr (Contract) **Est.** 2006 **Dozens** 1200
Thierry Ruault and Rachel Taylor have run a wholesale wine business in Perth since 1993, representing a group of top-end Australian and foreign producers. By definition, the wines they offered to their clientele were well above $20 per bottle, and they decided to fill the gap with a contract-made Shiraz from the Adelaide Hills, and a Sauvignon Blanc from Margaret River.

The Wanderer

2850 Launching Place Road, Gembrook, Vic 3783 **Region** Yarra Valley
T 0415 529 639 **www**.wandererwines.com **Open** By appt
Winemaker Andrew Marks **Est.** 2005 **Dozens** 500
Andrew Marks is the son of Ian and June Marks, owners of Gembrook Hill, and after graduating from Adelaide University with a degree in oenology he joined Southcorp, working for six years at Penfolds (Barossa Valley) and Seppelt (Great Western), as well as undertaking vintages in Coonawarra and France. He has since worked in the Hunter Valley, the Great Southern, Sonoma County in the US and Costa Brava in Spain – hence the name of his business.

ΨΨΨΨΨ **Yarra Valley Pinot Noir 2011** Very pale, but bright, hue; the wine is the product of the cool, wet vintage, not ideal for the red soils of the Upper Yarra Valley; it has pretty red cherry and strawberry flavours, but not enough drive on the finish. Best enjoyed sooner rather than later. Diam. 13.5% alc. **Rating** 90 **To** 2015 $55

The Willows Vineyard

Light Pass Road, Light Pass, Barossa Valley, SA 5355 **Region** Barossa Valley
T (08) 8562 1080 **www**.thewillowsvineyard.com.au **Open** Wed–Mon 10.30–4.30,
Tues by appt
Winemaker Peter and Michael Scholz **Est.** 1989 **Dozens** 6500 **Vyds** 42.74ha
The Scholz family have been grapegrowers for generations and have over 40ha of vineyards, selling part and retaining the remainder of the crop. Current-generation winemakers Peter and Michael Scholz make smooth, well-balanced and flavoursome wines under their own label, some marketed with some bottle age. Exports to the UK, Canada, Switzerland, China and NZ.

ΨΨΨΨΨ **Bonesetter Barossa Shiraz 2010** Dense, inky purple; the blackberry, spice and licorice fruit of the bouquet swells up even further on the palate, with dark chocolate nuances, vanillin oak and resplendently ripe tannins. The cork is of high quality and has been perfectly inserted, just as well for a wine of this potential longevity and that needs to slim down a bit. 14.7% alc. **Rating** 94 **To** 2040 $56

ΨΨΨΨΨ **Barossa Valley Shiraz 2010** Deep purple-crimson; an impressive wine at
✪   its price; its perfectly ripened fruit has a little spice to add further interest, the American and French oak doing precisely what was asked of it. Screwcap. 14.5% alc. **Rating** 93 **To** 2025 $26

Barossa Valley Cabernet Sauvignon 2010 **Rating** 92 **To** 2025 $26

✪ **Single Vineyard Barossa Valley Semillon 2012** From 76-year-old estate-grown (and carefully tended) vines; the Scholz brothers have observed the winemaking revolution inspired by Peter Lehmann in doing away with oak and picking earlier, and this wine ripples with juicy lemon/lemon curd flavours, making patience irrelevant. Screwcap. 11.5% alc. **Rating** 91 **To** 2016 $17

✪ **Barossa Valley Riesling 2012** Pale, bright straw-green; citrus blossom and peel aromas are soothsayers for the palate, which has the benison of good acidity, giving direction, length and balance. Certain to cellar well over the next 5 years. Screwcap. 11.5% alc. **Rating** 90 **To** 2018 $17

Thick as Thieves Wines ★★★★★

355 Healesville-Kooweerup Road, Badger Creek, Vic 3777 **Region** Yarra Valley
T 0417 184 690 **www**.tatwines.com.au **Open** By appt
Winemaker Syd Bradford **Est.** 2009 **Dozens** 1200 **Vyds** 1ha

Syd Bradford is living proof that small can be beautiful, and, equally, that an old dog can learn new tricks. A growing interest in good food and wine might have come to nothing had it not been for Pfeiffer Wines giving him a vintage job in '03. In that year he enrolled in the wine science course at CSU, moving to the Yarra Valley in '05. He gained experience at Coldstream Hills (vintage cellar hand), Rochford (assistant winemaker), Domaine Chandon (cellar hand) and Giant Steps/Innocent Bystander (assistant winemaker). In '06 Syd achieved the Dean's Award of Academic Excellence at CSU and in '07 was the sole recipient of the A&G Engineering Scholarship. Aged 35, he was desperate to have a go at crafting his own 'babies', and in '09 came across a small parcel of arneis from the Hoddles Creek area, and Thick as Thieves was born. In '10 he purchased small parcels of arneis, chardonnay, pinot noir and nebbiolo, making his wine in a home-away-from-home. The techniques used to make his babies could only come from someone who has spent a long time observing and thinking about what he might do if he were calling the shots. Exports to Japan and Singapore.

🍷🍷🍷🍷🍷 **Another Bloody Yarra Valley Chardonnay 2012** A very good example of Yarra Valley chardonnay, with intense grapefruit and stone fruit flavours on a palate of very good length. Screwcap. 12.9% alc. **Rating** 95 **To** 2020 $35

The Show Pony Yarra Valley Sauvignon Blanc 2012 Bright straw-green; wild yeast-fermented in used French barriques, then stirred until bottled in July '12. There has to be a good fruit base to allow this approach to work, and it was here. Initially strongly textured, the fruit claims the back-palate and long finish. Screwcap. 12.9% alc. **Rating** 94 **To** 2014 $25

Plump Yarra Valley Pinot Noir 2012 Excellent crimson-purple; clones MV6 and 114 were destemmed (90%) with a 4-day cold soak, 10% whole bunch carbonic maceration for 10 days; wild yeast fermentation that, in the context of the exceptional vintage, has resulted in a very complex wine. Screwcap. 13.2% alc. **Rating** 94 **To** 2020 $35

🍷🍷🍷🍷 **La Vie Rustique Yarra Valley Pinot Noir Rose 2012** **Rating** 91 **To** 2014 $23

Third Child ★★★★

134 Mt Rumney Road, Mt Rumney, Tas 7170 (postal) **Region** Southern Tasmania
T 0419 132 184 **www**.thirdchildvineyard.com.au **Open** Not
Winemaker John Skinner, Rob Drew **Est.** 2000 **Dozens** 350 **Vyds** 3ha

John and Marcia Skinner planted 2.5ha of pinot noir and 0.5ha of riesling in 2000. It is very much a hands-on operation, the only concession being the enlistment of Rob Drew (from an adjoining property) to help John with the winemaking. When the first vintage ('04) was reaching the stage of being bottled and labelled, the Skinners could not come up with a name and asked their daughter Claire. 'Easy,' she said. 'You've got two kids already; considering the care taken and time spent at the farm, it's your third child.'

🍷🍷🍷🍷 **Benjamin Daniel Pinot Noir 2011** Named after the first grandson and assembled from the best barrels, this cuvee is deeply coloured, and displaying a dark plum, spice and brambly bouquet; the palate has good weight and flesh, with a juicy and straightforward finish. Screwcap. 13.5% alc. **Rating** 90 **To** 2017 $25 BE

♥♥♥♥ Riesling 2012 Rating 88 To 2016 $20 BE
Thomas Nicholas Pinot Noir 2011 Rating 88 To 2017 $20 BE

Thomas Vineyard Estate   ★★★★☆

PO Box 490, McLaren Vale, SA 5171 **Region** McLaren Vale
T (08) 8557 8583 **www.thomasvineyard.com.au Open** Not
Winemaker Trevor Tucker **Est.** 1998 **Dozens** 1000 **Vyds** 5.26ha
Merv and Dawne Thomas thought long and hard before purchasing the property on which
they have established their vineyard. It is 3km from the coast of the Gulf of St Vincent on the
Fleurieu Peninsula, with a clay over limestone soil known locally as 'Bay of Biscay'. They had
a dream start to the business when the 2004 Shiraz won the trophy for Best Single Vineyard
Wine (red or white) at the McLaren Vale Wine Show '05, the Reserve Shiraz also winning a
gold medal. Exports to the US, Hong Kong and Singapore.

♥♥♥♥♥ Estate Reserve McLaren Vale Shiraz 2010 Full-bodied in every respect, thus
deserving the 'Big Red' self-description (also given to its sibling), but not in any
way departing from a region/variety symbiotic link; black fruits, dark chocolate
and French oak all contribute. Screwcap. 14.5% alc. **Rating** 94 **To** 2030 $45

♥♥♥♥♡ McLaren Vale Shiraz 2010 Full purple-red; it trenchantly proclaims its varietal
❂ and regional symbiosis, with black fruits and dark chocolate equally sharing the
stage, oak a largely incidental extra, savoury tannins providing the finish. Screwcap.
14% alc. **Rating** 91 **To** 2025 $20

Thomas Wines   ★★★★★

c/- The Small Winemakers Centre, McDonalds Road, Pokolbin, NSW 2321
Region Hunter Valley
T 0418 456 853 **www.thomaswines.com.au Open** 7 days 10–5
Winemaker Andrew Thomas, Phil Le Messurier **Est.** 1997 **Dozens** 7000 **Vyds** 3ha
Andrew Thomas came to the Hunter Valley from McLaren Vale to join the winemaking team
at Tyrrell's. After 13 years, he left to undertake contract work and to continue the development
of his own label. He makes individual vineyard wines, underlining the subtle differences
between the various subregions of the Hunter. Plans for the construction of an estate winery
have been abandoned for the time being, and for the foreseeable future he will continue
to lease the James Estate winery on Hermitage Road, while the cellar door will continue
at the Small Winemakers Centre. The major part of the production comes from long-term
arrangements with growers of semillon (15ha) and shiraz (25ha); an additional 3ha of shiraz is
leased. The quality of the wines and the reputation of Andrew Thomas have never been higher.

♥♥♥♥♥ Cellar Reserve Braemore Individual Vineyard Hunter Valley Semillon
❂ 2007 Glorious bright green-quartz; a perfect example of a wonderfully elegant
Hunter Semillon that even now is at the start of its life, its lemon/lemongrass
flavours woven around racy acidity. Screwcap. 10.5% alc. **Rating** 96 **To** 2020 $45
Kiss Limited Release Hunter Valley Shiraz 2011 A very sophisticated and
fragrant bouquet offering red fruits, violets, charcuterie and Asian spices; the palate
is racy, scintillating in its nervosity, with luscious levels of fruit, well-handled oak
and a long, expansive, compelling and completely unevolved palate; time will not
weary this wine. Screwcap. 13.5% alc. **Rating** 96 **To** 2035 $60 BE
Kiss Limited Release Hunter Valley Shiraz 2010 Outstanding colour and
clarity; pays equal homage to its variety and region, elegance and complexity
likewise having equal say, the red and black fruits woven through with fine, silky
tannins; has perfect length and balance to guarantee a very long life. Screwcap.
13.5% alc. **Rating** 96 **To** 2040 $60
Braemore Individual Vineyard Hunter Valley Semillon 2012 Pale quartz-
green; lemon and lime characters fill the bouquet and palate with juice, zest,
pith and crushed leaf all in the driving seat; the typical semillon acidity also has a
dressing of citrus. Screwcap. 10.5% alc. **Rating** 95 **To** 2027 $28

✪   **DJV Vineyard Selection Hunter Valley Shiraz 2011** Designed and made in a traditional 'Hunter River Burgundy' style, the bouquet offers an alluring array of red fruits, Asian spices, ironstone and floral highlights; the palate is medium-bodied and softly textured, with fine-grained tannins playing foil to the tightly wound fruit and lively acidity. Screwcap. 13% alc. **Rating** 95 **To** 2022 $30 BE

✪   **Two of a Kind Semillon Sauvignon Blanc 2012** A 52/48% blend of Hunter Valley semillon and Adelaide Hills sauvignon blanc; the aromatic bouquet leads into a citrus-driven opening on the palate; thereafter the flavours intensify and expand dramatically, with kiwifruit and sweet lime juice making their presence felt well into the finish and aftertaste. Screwcap. 12% alc. **Rating** 94 **To** 2015 $20
Elenay Shiraz 2011 Rating 94 **To** 2022 $45 BE

♟♟♟♟♟ **Two of a Kind Shiraz 2011 Rating** 93 **To** 2021 $24
Sweetwater Hunter Valley Shiraz 2011 Rating 92 **To** 2020 $35 BE

Thompson Estate   ★★★★★

299 Tom Cullity Drive, Wilyabrup, WA 6284 **Region** Margaret River
T (08) 9386 1751 **www**.thompsonestate.com **Open** 7 days 11–5
Winemaker Bob Cartwright **Est.** 1994 **Dozens** 10 000 **Vyds** 28.63ha
Cardiologist Peter Thompson planted the first vines at Thompson Estate in 1997, inspired by his and his family's shareholdings in the Pierro and Fire Gully vineyards, and by visits to many of the world's premium wine regions. The vineyard is planted to cabernet sauvignon, cabernet franc, merlot, chardonnay, sauvignon blanc, semillon, pinot noir and malbec. Thompson Estate wines have been made solely by Bob Cartwright (former Leeuwin Estate winemaker) since 2006 at its state-of-the-art winery. Exports to the UK, the US, Canada, India and Hong Kong.

♟♟♟♟♟ **Andrea 2010** An 80/10/10% blend of cabernet sauvignon, merlot and cabernet franc that spent 18 months in French barriques; the bouquet and medium-bodied palate show the impact of that oak, but there is ample red and blackcurrant fruit to sustain it, particularly on the finish and aftertaste, where it most counts; ripe tannins also come to the party. Screwcap. 14% alc. **Rating** 95 **To** 2030 $45
Margaret River Cabernet Sauvignon 2010 Deep crimson, bright; a restrained and elegant expression on the bouquet offering pure red and blackcurrant aromas, offset by cigar box and violets; the medium-bodied palate is lively, silky in texture with ample fine-grained tannins wound seamlessly together with fine well-handled oak lingering on the long finish. Screwcap. 14% alc. **Rating** 95 **To** 2025 $40 BE
Margaret River Chardonnay 2010 Bright green-gold; clonal selection and 8 months in French oak are two of the contributors to an impressive wine, its layers of ripe melon and stone fruit offset by citrussy/minerally acidity on the finish. Screwcap. 13.5% alc. **Rating** 94 **To** 2018 $40
Margaret River Cabernet Sauvignon 2009 Deep garnet; a distinctly mellow and accessible bouquet with dark fruits and crushed leaf on display; soft and generous on the palate, despite the ample level of fine-grained tannins, and complex, long and silky on the finish; the elegant nature of this wine is commendable and most alluring. Screwcap. 13.5% alc. **Rating** 94 **To** 2020 $40 BE

♟♟♟♟♟ **Margaret River Semillon Sauvignon Blanc 2012 Rating** 93 **To** 2015 $30 BE
Locum Margaret River Cabernet Merlot 2011 Rating 92 **To** 2020 $25 BE

Thorn-Clarke Wines   ★★★★★

Milton Park, Gawler Park Road, Angaston, SA 5353 **Region** Barossa Valley
T (08) 8564 3036 **www**.thornclarkewines.com.au **Open** Mon–Fri 9–5, Sat 11–4
Winemaker Helen McCarthy **Est.** 1987 **Dozens** 80 000 **Vyds** 268ha
Established by David and Cheryl Clarke (née Thorn), and son Sam, Thorn-Clarke is one of the largest family-owned estate-based businesses in the Barossa. Their winery is close to the border between the Barossa and Eden Valleys, and three of their four vineyards are in the Eden Valley: the Mt Crawford Vineyard is at the southern end, while the Milton Park and Sandpiper vineyards are further north. The fourth vineyard is at St Kitts, in the northern end of the

Barossa Ranges, established when no other vignerons had ventured onto what was hitherto considered unsuitable soil. In all four vineyards careful soil mapping has resulted in matching of variety and site, with all of the major varieties represented. The quality of grapes retained for the Thorn-Clarke label has resulted in a succession of trophy and gold medal-winning wines at very competitive prices. The arrival of the highly credentialled Helen McCarthy as winemaker in 2011 means wine quality continues in safe hands. Exports to all major markets.

ŸŸŸŸŸ **William Randell Barossa Shiraz 2010** Inky purple-crimson; as the colour promises, a wine saturated with every manner of black fruits and bitter chocolate; despite this, it has an open-weave texture keeping it light on its feet, and allowing a farewell of juicy fruit to find its way through the high-quality oak and fine tannins. An exceptional Shiraz. Screwcap. 14.5% alc. **Rating** 97 **To** 2050 $60
William Randell Eden Valley Cabernet Sauvignon 2010 Full crimson-purple; while quite soft overall, both in fruit and tannin terms, the wine is full-bodied and fleshy, with dark chocolate and licorice joining the blackcurrant fruit and cedary oak. Screwcap. 14% alc. **Rating** 94 **To** 2025 $60

✪ **Shotfire Quartage Barossa Cabernet Sauvignon Cabernet Franc Merlot Petit Verdot 2010** Good purple-crimson; as is so often the case, defies commonly accepted views about the Barossa's (ie including the Eden Valley) ability to produce high-quality examples of a Bordeaux blend; there is an invigorating freshness and lightness of touch to this berry-fruited wine that draws it through to a long, lingering finish. Screwcap. 14% alc. **Rating** 94 **To** 2020 $20

ŸŸŸŸŸ **Sandpiper Eden Valley Riesling 2012** A spicy dryness runs right through
✪ the palate, bolstered by persistent, although balanced, acidity. A wine begging for time in bottle, its long future laid out for all to see. Screwcap. 13% alc. **Rating** 91 **To** 2025 $16
St Kitts Vineyard on Truro Volcanic Soil Barossa Valley Malbec 2010 **Rating** 90 **To** 2018 $35 BE

Thousand Candles ★★★★★
PO Box 148, Seville, Vic 3139 **Region** Yarra Valley
T 0400 654 512 **Open** Not
Winemaker William Downie **Est.** 2010 **Dozens** 1000 **Vyds** 37ha
What is now called the Thousand Candles vineyard was originally known as Killara Estate, which had been planted in 1997. The Thousand Candles name comes from a 19th century account harking back to its Indigenous occupiers. A ceremony granting free passage to the lands around the property was witnessed by a European who, referring to the tribesmen dramatically holding aloft their firesticks, remarked, 'It's as if the twilight of the evening had been interrupted by a thousand candles.' And indeed the property is a dramatic one, plunging from a height of several hundred metres above the Yarra River down to its flood plains. It is the east-facing upper level flat land and the upper part of the slopes that was planted to 91ha of vines. Another level of drama was added with the first wine release under the new ownership (itself shrouded in mystery) at a mind-bending $100.

ŸŸŸŸŸ **Yarra Valley Shiraz 2011** One of the most daring releases of recent times, not so much for its blend of shiraz, pinot noir and sauvignon blanc as its bold shot at 100% whole bunch fermentation in the cold, wet '11, from a vineyard so rundown it almost didn't crop at all. Bill Downie has worked his magic to create a hauntingly ethereal wine of internal harmony, silky structure and captivating exoticism. Diam. 12.5% alc. **Rating** 95 **To** 2026 $100 TS

Three Dark Horses ★★★★
49 Fraser Avenue, Happy Valley, SA 5159 **Region** McLaren Vale
T 0405 294 500 **www.**3dhcom.au **Open** Not
Winemaker Matt Broomhead **Est.** 2009 **Dozens** 1200
Three Dark Horses is the new project for former Coriole winemaker Matt Broomhead. After vintages in southern Italy and the Rhône Valley he returned to McLaren Vale in 2009 and,

with his father Alan, runs this small business buying quality grapes. The third dark horse is Matt's 87-year-old grandfather, a vintage regular.

ŦŦŦŦŶ **McLaren Vale Grenache Rose 2012** Vivid crimson-purple; a very attractive
✪ style, picked at exactly the right moment to provide a burst of raspberry and strawberry fruit on a precise and dry palate, the finish and aftertaste fresh and invigorating. Screwcap. 13.5% alc. **Rating** 93 **To** 2014 $20

✪ **McLaren Vale Shiraz Grenache Touriga 2009** Its declaration of its terroir booms loud with its strong overlay of dark chocolate to the cherry and raspberry fruit; it is medium-bodied, and has very good texture and structure. Screwcap. 14.5% alc. **Rating** 92 **To** 2029 $20
McLaren Vale Shiraz 2011 McLaren Vale produced some seriously good shiraz grapes in '11; this is a medium- to full-bodied wine, the black fruits and bitter chocolate cradled by French oak and ample tannins; just a little furry around the edges. Screwcap. 14% alc. **Rating** 90 **To** 2021 $25

ŦŦŦŦ **McLaren Vale Grenache 2011** **Rating** 88 **To** 2014 $25

3 Drops   ★★★★★

PO Box 1828, Applecross, WA 6953 **Region** Mount Barker
T (08) 9315 4721 **www.**3drops.com **Open** Not
Winemaker Robert Diletti (Contract) **Est.** 1998 **Dozens** 5000 **Vyds** 21.5ha
The three drops are not the three founders (John Bradbury, Joanne Bradbury and, formerly, Nicola Wallich), but wine, olive oil and water, all of which come from the substantial property at Mt Barker. The plantings are riesling, sauvignon blanc, semillon, chardonnay, cabernet sauvignon, merlot, shiraz and cabernet franc, irrigated – like the olive trees – by a large wetland on the property. The business expanded significantly in 2007 with the purchase of the 14.7ha Patterson's Vineyard. Exports to Canada, Hong Kong and China.

ŦŦŦŦŦ **Mount Barker Riesling 2012** The floral, fragrant bouquet announces a wine with intense lime and lemon fruit underscored by minerally acidity; lovely now, better still in a decade. Screwcap. 12.5% alc. **Rating** 95 **To** 2022 $26
Mount Barker Chardonnay 2011 Bright straw-green; has the classic cool-climate mix of grapefruit and white peach on the bouquet and palate, augmented by a controlled infusion of French oak; masterful winemaking enhances the length of the wine. Screwcap. 13.5% alc. **Rating** 94 **To** 2018 $26
✪ **Mount Barker Cabernets 2011** Crimson-purple; a blend of cabernet sauvignon and cabernet franc, with a fragrant bouquet leading into a gently luscious, medium-bodied palate overflowing with cassis and redcurrant fruit backed by precisely measured oak and tannin support. Screwcap. 14.5% alc. **Rating** 94 **To** 2026 $24

ŦŦŦŦŶ **Mount Barker Shiraz 2011** **Rating** 93 **To** 2018 $26 BE
Mount Barker Shiraz 2010 **Rating** 91 **To** 2020 $25
Mount Barker Sauvignon Blanc 2012 **Rating** 90 **To** 2013 $22
Mount Barker Pinot Noir 2011 **Rating** 90 **To** 2016 $29
Mount Barker Merlot 2011 **Rating** 90 **To** 2014 $25

3 Oceans Wine Company   ★★★★☆

Cnr Boundary Road/Bussell Highway, Cowaramup, WA 6284 **Region** Margaret River
T (08) 9756 5656 **www.**palandri.com.au **Open** 7 days 10–5
Winemaker Ben Roodhouse, Jonathan Mettam **Est.** 1999 **Dozens** 160 000
After a period of spectacular growth and marketing activity, Palandri went into voluntary administration in February 2008. In June of that year the Ma family, through their 3 Oceans Wine Company Pty Ltd, acquired the Margaret River winery, the 30-year-old Margaret River vineyard and 347ha of Frankland River vineyards. In October '08 it also acquired the Palandri and Baldivis Estate brands. There is a strong focus on the emerging markets of the Asia–Pacific region, without neglecting the domestic market. Continuing investment in Margaret River

and Frankland River was rewarded with the Trophy for Best Shiraz at the Qantas Wine Show of WA '12. Exports to the UK and Asia

♥♥♥♥♥ **Vita Novus Frankland River Shiraz 2009** Medium red-purple; the wine spent 16 months in French and American oak, but the fragrant red and black cherry fruit makes light of the oak on the bouquet and medium-bodied palate alike; spice, pepper and fruit are seamlessly joined, the finish long and balanced. Screwcap. 14% alc. **Rating** 94 **To** 2029 $35

♥♥♥♥♀ **Vita Novus Sauvignon Blanc Semillon 2010** **Rating** 93 **To** 2014 $29
Vita Novus Cabernet Sauvignon 2009 **Rating** 91 **To** 2020 $35
Vita Novus Chardonnay 2011 **Rating** 90 **To** 2017 $29

Three Willows Vineyard   ★★★☆

46 Montana Road, Red Hills, Tas 7304 **Region** Northern Tasmania
T 0438 507 069 **www.**threewillowsvineyard.com.au **Open** Most days 10.30–5 (summer), 11–4.30 (winter)
Winemaker Philip Parés **Est.** 2002 **Dozens** 200 **Vyds** 1.8ha
Philip Parés and Lyn Prove have planted a micro-vineyard with pinot noir, pinot gris and baco noir (a hybrid). It is 50km west of Launceston, near Deloraine, on a gentle north-facing slope at an elevation of 220–250m. The present tiny production will peak at around 250 dozen.

♥♥♥♥♀ **Pinot Gris 2011** This is an 'orange wine' colour and concept, utilising skin contact to add complexity before fermentation; the result here provides aromas of potato skin, glazed pear and cinnamon; texturally speaking the wine has a very dry and grippy finish, with a prickle of alcohol noticeable. An interesting wine indeed. Screwcap. 14% alc. **Rating** 90 **To** 2015 $25 BE

♥♥♥♥ **Home Block Pinot Noir 2010** **Rating** 87 **To** 2016 $27 BE

Three Wishes Vineyard   ★★★★

655 Craigburn Road, Hillwood, Tas 7252 **Region** Northern Tasmania
T 0488 948 330 **www.**threewishesvineyard.com.au **Open** W'ends & public hols Dec–Apr, or by appt
Winemaker Holm Oak (Rebecca Wilson), Delamere (Fran Austin) **Est.** 1998
Dozens 600 **Vyds** 2.5ha
Peter and Natalie Whish-Wilson began the establishment of their vineyard in 1998 while they were working in Hong Kong, delegating the management tasks to parents Rosemary and Tony until 2003. Peter and Natalie took a year's sabbatical to do the first vintage, with their children, aged six and four, also involved in tending the vines. The seachange became permanent, Peter completing his winemaking degree from CSU in '96. The original vineyard has been extended, and now comprises 1ha each of pinot noir, chardonnay and riesling. Exports to Sweden.

♥♥♥♥♀ **Pinot Noir 2010** Clear, bright crimson-purple, virtually identical to that of the '11; both the bouquet and the palate have greater weight and complexity to the red and dark berry fruits; the overall mouthfeel is more supple and satisfying. Screwcap. 13.5% alc. **Rating** 93 **To** 2018 $35

✪ **Riesling 2010** Pale straw-green; the fragrant, lime-infused bouquet leads into an elegant and well-balanced, light- to medium-bodied palate, the flavours ranging through citrus and green apple. Screwcap. 12% alc. **Rating** 90 **To** 2017 $22
Pinot Noir 2011 Clear, bright crimson-purple; the fragrant red fruit bouquet leads into a fresh, light- to medium-bodied palate, finely boned tannins giving sufficient texture and structure to carry it through for up to 5 years. Screwcap. 13% alc. **Rating** 90 **To** 2018 $35

♥♥♥♥ **Chardonnay 2009** **Rating** 89 **To** 2015 $25
Chardonnay 2010 **Rating** 88 **To** 2016 $25

Tidswell Wines

14 Sydenham Road, Norwood, SA 5067 **Region** Limestone Coast Zone
T (08) 8363 5800 **www**.tidswellwines.com.au **Open** By appt
Winemaker Ben Tidswell, Wine Wise Consultancy **Est.** 1994 **Dozens** 3000 **Vyds** 136.4ha
The Tidswell family (now in the shape of Andrea and Ben Tidswell) has two large vineyards in
the Limestone Coast Zone near Bool Lagoon; the lion's share is planted to cabernet sauvignon
and shiraz, with smaller plantings of merlot, sauvignon blanc, petit verdot, vermentino and
pinot gris. Fifty per cent of the vineyards are organically certified, and more will be converted
in due course. Wines are released under the Jennifer, Heathfield Ridge and Caves Road labels.
Exports to Canada, Denmark, Germany, Singapore, Japan and China.

ŸŸŸŸŸ **Jennifer Limited Release Cabernet Sauvignon 2010** Has layered cassis
and redcurrant fruit, the oak well integrated, the balance good. Surprising it has
only won three bronze medals, albeit in the best wine shows. Cork. 14.5% alc.
Rating 93 **To** 2025 $45

✪ **Heathfield Ridge Shiraz 2010** Deep colour; a supple and smooth medium- to
full-bodied single vineyard shiraz matured for 18 months in half American, half
French oak, 38% new; the spicy fruit has soaked up that oak, and the tannins are
ripe and well integrated. Screwcap. 14.5% alc. **Rating** 92 **To** 2020 $23

✪ **Heathfield Ridge Sauvignon Blanc 2012** Lime/citrus and tropical/
passionfruit on the bouquet and palate grabs attention, and extends the length of
the palate. Screwcap. 12.5% alc. **Rating** 90 **To** 2014 $19

✪ **Heathfield Ridge Cabernet Rose 2012** Bright, light crimson; early-picked
cabernet has been made in mainstream Australian fashion, cold-fermented in tank
and bottled asap thereafter. The bouquet and palate focus on cassis and raspberry,
the finish extended by a skilfully handled 6.8g/l of residual sugar and 6.9g/l of
acidity. Screwcap. 13% alc. **Rating** 90 **To** 2013 $19

Tilbrook Estate

17/1 Adelaide-Lobethal Road, Lobethal, SA 5241 **Region** Adelaide Hills
T (08) 8389 5318 **www**.tilbrookestate.com.au **Open** Fri–Mon & public hols 11–5, or
by appt
Winemaker James Tilbrook **Est.** 1998 **Dozens** 1500 **Vyds** 4.98ha
James and Annabelle Tilbrook have almost 5ha of multi-clone chardonnay and pinot noir,
plus sauvignon blanc and pinot gris, at Lenswood. The winery and cellar door are in the
old Onkaparinga Woollen Mills building in Lobethal; this not only provides an atmospheric
home, but also helps meet the very strict environmental requirements of the Adelaide Hills
in dealing with winery waste water. English-born James came to Australia in 1986, aged 22,
but a car accident led to his return to England. Working for Oddbins and passing the WSET
diploma set his future course. He returned to Australia, met Annabelle, purchased the vineyard
and began planting it in '99. The close-planted pinot noir block, with a row width of 1.25m,
is being converted to 2.5m by the simple expedient of pulling out every second row.

ŸŸŸŸŸ **Adelaide Hills Sauvignon Blanc 2012** Fermented in stainless steel, but kept
on lees for six months; has well above-average intensity of flavour, with gooseberry,
lime, guava and passionfruit all rolled up together, the intensity continuing through
to the finish and aftertaste. Screwcap. 13% alc. **Rating** 94 **To** 2014 $22

ŸŸŸŸŸ **Adelaide Hills Pinot Gris 2012** Estate-grown, whole bunch-pressed, cool-
✪ fermented in tank with 7 months' ageing on lees; the wine has good varietal
expression in true gris style, with pear and peach flavours; mimics Alsace with the
lees contact and high alcohol. Screwcap. 14% alc. **Rating** 90 **To** 2014 $22

Tilly Devine

82a Northgate Street, Unley Park, SA 5061 (postal) **Region** McLaren Vale
T (08) 8271 4546 **www**.tillydevine.com.au **Open** Not
Winemaker Matthew Rechner **Est.** 2008 **Dozens** 900

Tilly Devine (formerly Antipodean Vintners) started in 2008 as a venture between five friends – Mark and Simone Perks, Jamie Craig, Sarah Matthews and Angelo Tsirbas – who were all self-confessed wine enthusiasts. Their goal is to produce small batches of wine that best represent the location and vintage where the grapes are sourced. They buy the grapes for their wine from 80- to 90-year-old vines in McLaren Vale. The first release, from '08, was an outstanding wine. 'Tilly Devine' is rhyming slang for 'wine'.

ΨΨΨΨΨ **McLaren Vale Shiraz 2008** Deep crimson-purple, there is more than enough blackberry, plum and licorice fruit to accommodate the French oak; the mouthfeel is velvety, the finish soft but very long; no issue whatsoever with the alcohol or the tannins; the region also comes through with clarion clarity. Vino-Lok. 14.9% alc. Rating 96 To 2028 $38

McLaren Vale Shiraz 2009 The grapes come from 90-year-old vines; cold-soaked, open-fermented and matured in French oak (30% new). The bouquet and palate are very complex, with black fruits, dark chocolate, licorice and oak aromas and flavours all coalescing. Vino-Lok. 14.9% alc. Rating 94 To 2024 $36

McLaren Vale Cabernet 2009 From 80-year-old vines, a rarity anywhere; cold-soaked and open-fermented, then matured in French oak; this is a full-bodied Cabernet, its cassis fruit nuanced by distinct touches of bitter chocolate and savoury tannins. Vino-Lok. 14.6% alc. Rating 94 To 2024 $28

Tim Adams ★★★★★

Warenda Road, Clare, SA 5453 **Region** Clare Valley
T (08) 8842 2429 **www.**timadamswines.com.au **Open** Mon–Fri 10.30–5, w'ends 11–5
Winemaker Tim Adams, Brett Schutz **Est.** 1986 **Dozens** 70000 **Vyds** 145ha

Tim Adams and partner Pam Goldsack preside over a highly successful business. New plantings give more than 10ha of tempranillo and pinot gris, and about 3.5ha of viognier, in each case with a very clear idea about the style of wine to be produced. In 2009 the business took a giant step forward with the acquisition of the 80ha Leasingham Rogers Vineyard from CWA for a reported price of $850000, followed in '11 by the purchase of the Leasingham winery and winemaking equipment (for less than replacement cost). The only asset retained by Accolade Wines (the new owner of CWA) is the Leasingham brand name. The winery will become a major contract winemaking facility for the region. Exports to the UK, The Netherlands, Sweden, Russia, Hong Kong and China.

ΨΨΨΨΨ **Reserve Clare Valley Cabernet Malbec 2008** Tim Adams learnt about the synergy these two varieties have while working at Leasingham many years ago, but I suspect the co-fermentation he used with this wine was his innovation; likewise, 24 months in 100% new French oak. If ever a wine was bred to stay it is this, which will continue to develop for at least 20 years, its forceful tannins softening as it does so, the black fruits remaining dominant. WAK screwcap. 14.5% alc. Rating 95 To 2040 $35

✪ **Clare Valley Cabernet Malbec 2008** The colour is still solid, and this celebrated regional blend (thanks to Wendouree and Leasingham) is living up to its reputation here, with its blackcurrant and plum fruit, ripe tannins and integrated oak. Screwcap. 14.5% alc. Rating 94 To 2028 $24

Clare Valley Cabernet Malbec 2007 Has held onto its youthful colour; it shows no sign of the toughness of the vintage, instead offering an array of black fruit flavours unique to Clare Valley cabernet malbec. Screwcap. 14.5% alc. Rating 94 To 2022 $25

ΨΨΨΨΨ **Clare Valley Riesling 2012** From three estate vineyards spread throughout the
✪ Clare Valley. An attractive, well-balanced wine from start to finish, with sweet citrus fruit, gentle acidity and good length. Screwcap. 11.5% alc. Rating 93 To 2018 $22

✪ **Clare Valley Semillon 2010** Counter to most approaches to semillon (especially the Hunter Valley and Peter Lehmann), given 12 hours' skin contact, then barrel-fermented in 100% new French oak, followed by 6 months in that oak. The result is, of course, far more complex than the vast majority of 2-year-old semillons, with layers of lemon-accented fruit. Good value if you like the style. Screwcap. 13% alc. Rating 93 To 2016 $22

Clare Valley Shiraz 2009 Rating 93 To 2024 $25
Clare Valley Shiraz 2010 Rating 90 To 2020 $24
The Aberfeldy 2009 Rating 90 To 2019 $55

Tim Gramp ★★★★☆

Mintaro/Leasingham Road, Watervale, SA 5452 **Region** Clare Valley
T (08) 8344 4079 **www.**timgrampwines.com.au **Open** W'ends 12–4
Winemaker Tim Gramp **Est.** 1990 **Dozens** 6000 **Vyds** 16ha
Tim Gramp has quietly built up a very successful business, and by keeping overheads to a minimum provides good wines at modest prices. Over the years the estate vineyards (shiraz, riesling, cabernet sauvignon and grenache) have been expanded significantly. Exports to the UK, Taiwan and Malaysia.

ΨΨΨΨΨ   **Gilbert Valley Mt Lofty Ranges Shiraz 2010** Deep, dense purple-crimson; the bouquet is filled with black fruits and dabs of spice, the juicy, medium- to full-bodied palate flooded with more of the same; it avoids over-extraction, the tannins ripe and soft, the oak evident, but well integrated. Screwcap. 14.5% alc. **Rating** 94 To 2025 $23

ΨΨΨΨΨ   **Basket Pressed Watervale Cabernet Sauvignon 2010** Bright, although not particularly deep, hue; a lively cabernet bounding with cassis/redcurrant fruit that belies its alcohol, and has more elegance than many Clare Valley Cabernets. Screwcap. 14.5% alc. **Rating** 92 To 2020 $22

Watervale Riesling 2012 Light straw-green; has striking minerally, slatey structure already evident, in turn allied with lemon rind, lime pith and apple skin flavours. Outside the norm for '12, but full of potential. Screwcap. 12% alc. **Rating** 90 To 2020 $20

Tim McNeil Wines ★★★★☆

Lot 31 Springvale Road, Watervale, SA 5452 **Region** Clare Valley
T (08) 8843 0040 **www.**timmcneilwines.com.au **Open** Fri–Sun & public hols 11–5
Winemaker Tim McNeil **Est.** 2004 **Dozens** 1500 **Vyds** 2ha
When Tim and Cass McNeil established Tim McNeil Wines, Tim had long since given up his teaching career, graduating with a degree in oenology from Adelaide University in 1999. During his university years he worked at Yalumba, then moved with Cass to the Clare Valley in 2001, spending four years as a winemaker at Jim Barry Wines followed by six vintages at Kilikanoon. In Aug '10 Tim McNeil Wines became his full-time job. The McNeils' 16ha property at Watervale includes mature, dry-grown riesling, and they intend to plant shiraz, currently purchasing that variety from the Barossa Valley. The cellar door overlooks the riesling vineyard, with panoramic views of Watervale and beyond. Exports to Canada.

ΨΨΨΨΨ   Clare Valley Shiraz 2010 Dense purple-crimson; it is densely packed with blackberry, black cherry, plum and licorice fruit framed by ripe tannins and integrated oak. It has the balance and richness to sustain a very long life. Screwcap. 14.5% alc. **Rating** 95 To 2050 $30

ΨΨΨΨ   **Watervale Riesling 2012 Rating** 89 To 2016 $22

Tim Smith Wines ★★★★★

PO Box 446, Tanunda, SA 5352 **Region** Barossa Valley
T 0416 396 730 **www.**timsmithwines.com.au **Open** Not
Winemaker Tim Smith **Est.** 2002 **Dozens** 3000 **Vyds** 1ha
With a talent for sourcing exceptional old vine fruit from the Barossa floor, Tim Smith has created a small but credible portfolio of wines, currently including Mataro, Grenache, Shiraz, Viognier and, more recently, Eden Valley Riesling. Tim left his full-time winemaking role with a large Barossa brand in 2011, allowing him to concentrate 100% of his energy on his own brand. In '12 Tim joined forces with the team from First Drop (see separate entry), and has

moved winemaking operations to a brand-new winery, fondly named 'Home of the Brave', in Nuriootpa. Exports to the UK, the US, Canada, Denmark, Taiwan and Singapore.

ΨΨΨΨΨ **Eden Valley Riesling 2012** Pale straw-green; a delicately elegant style, with citrus pith/rind interleaved with minerally acidity; early picking, and not retention of residual sugar, has resulted in the low alcohol. Needs more time to build flavour and character, but has the balance to do so. Screwcap. 11.5% alc. **Rating** 93 **To** 2020 $25

Eden Valley Viognier 2012 Mid gold; a highly expressive, fragrant and perfumed wine, full of exotic spiced apricots and musk; the thickly textured palate is spot on, as the richness is held in check by enough acidity to provide freshness and persistence. Screwcap. 13.5% alc. **Rating** 92 **To** 2016 $29 BE

Barossa Mataro Grenache Shiraz 2011 Has gone a fair way to make a silk purse out of a sow's ear, with a blend that faced particular challenges in '11; there are hints of mint alongside the red fruits, and a bracing finish to the palate. Drink sooner rather than later. Screwcap. 14% alc. **Rating** 90 **To** 2015 $28

Tinderbox Vineyard ★★★★

Tinderbox, Tas 7054 **Region** Southern Tasmania
T 0409 975 450 **Open** By appt
Winemaker Contract **Est.** 1994 **Dozens** 220 **Vyds** 2ha
Liz McGown may have retired from specialist nursing (some years ago), but is busier than ever, having taken on the running of the 400ha Tinderbox fat lamb and fine merino wool property after a lease (which had run for 22 years) terminated. Liz describes Tinderbox as a vineyard between the sun and the sea, and looking out over the vineyard towards Bruny Island in the distance, it is not hard to see why. The attractive label was designed by Barry Tucker, who was so charmed by Liz's request that he waived his usual (substantial) fee.

ΨΨΨΨΨ **Traditional Method Vintage Sparkling 2008** No varieties specified, but the pale pink colour says there is pinot noir present; the flavours underline that, with strawberry and citrus driving the fresh, long finish. Very good label design. Diam. 12.5% alc. **Rating** 90 **To** 2014 $50

Tinklers Vineyard ★★★★★

Pokolbin Mountains Road, Pokolbin, NSW 2320 **Region** Hunter Valley
T (02) 4998 7435 **www.**tinklers.com.au **Open** 7 days 10–5
Winemaker Usher Tinkler **Est.** 1997 **Dozens** 2000 **Vyds** 41ha
Three generations of the Tinkler family have been involved with the property since 1942. Originally a beef and dairy farm, vines have been both pulled out and replanted at various stages, and part of the adjoining 80-year-old Ben Ean Vineyard has been acquired. Plantings include semillon (14ha), shiraz (11.5ha), chardonnay (6.5ha) and smaller areas of merlot, muscat and viognier. In 2008 a new winery, adjoining the cellar door, was completed; all Tinklers wines are now vinified here (distinguished by a gold strip at the bottom of the label). The majority of the grape production continues to be sold to McWilliam's and Tyrrell's. Usher has resigned his role as chief winemaker at Poole's Rock and Cockfighter's Ghost to take on full-time responsibility at Tinklers, and plans are afoot to increase production to meet demand.

ΨΨΨΨΨ **U and I Shiraz 2011** Young Usher Tinkler is on the rise, and his '11 Shiraz might set a new high-water mark. A wine of wonderfully primary violets, pure and intense black cherries and juicy black plums, undergirded by fine-grained and seamlessly balanced tannins. Screwcap. 13.5% alc. **Rating** 95 **To** 2021 $35 TS

Old Vines Hunter Valley Shiraz 2011 Mid crimson; the bouquet offers fragrant red fruits with a splash of briary complexity; light- to medium-bodied, the fresh red fruits, vibrant acidity and fine-grained tannins speak of purity over complexity, as elegance and accessibility come to the fore. Screwcap. 13% alc. **Rating** 94 **To** 2020 $30 BE

ŦŦŦŦŶ School Block Hunter Valley Semillon 2011 Rating 92 To 2022 $22 BE
       School Block Hunter Valley Semillon 2007 Rating 92 To 2020 $25 BE
       School Block Hunter Valley Semillon 2006 Rating 92 To 2018 $25 BE
       Hunter Valley Shiraz Viognier 2011 Rating 91 To 2018 $25 BE
       PMR Merlot 2011 Rating 90 To 2018 $25 BE

Tintara   ★★★★☆

202 Main Road, McLaren Vale, SA 5171 **Region** McLaren Vale
T (08) 8329 4124 **www.tintara.com.au Open** 7 days 10–4.30
Winemaker Neville Rowe **Est.** 1863 **Dozens** NFP
Tintara was the third of the three substantial winery and vineyard enterprises in the early
days of McLaren Vale. It was established by Dr Alexander Kelly, who purchased 280ha of land
in 1861 and planted the first vines in 1863. It grew rapidly – indeed too rapidly, because it
ran into financial difficulties and was acquired by Thomas Hardy in 1876. He recovered his
purchase price by wine sales over the following year. Exports to the US, Canada, Europe and
Pacific Islands.

ŦŦŦŦŦ McLaren Vale Shiraz 2010 Deep crimson-purple; built in the fortress style of
       Tintara with fruit, oak and tannins all on display from the outset; it also announces
       its McLaren Vale region of origin in a booming voice, bitter chocolate merging
       with savoury cedar nuances on the finish. Screwcap. 14.5% alc. **Rating** 94
       To 2035 $27

ŦŦŦŦ   McLaren Vale Cabernet Sauvignon 2010 Rating 89 To 2025 $27

Tintilla Wines   ★★★★★

725 Hermitage Road, Pokolbin, NSW 2320 **Region** Hunter Valley
T (02) 6574 7093 **www.tintilla.com.au Open** 7 days 10.30–6
Winemaker James and Robert Lusby **Est.** 1993 **Dozens** 4000 **Vyds** 6.52ha
The Lusby family has established shiraz (2.2ha), sangiovese (1.6ha), merlot (1.32ha), semillon
(1.2ha) and cabernet sauvignon (0.2ha) on a northeast-facing slope with red clay and
limestone soil. Tintilla was the first winery to plant sangiovese in the Hunter Valley (1995).
The family has also planted an olive grove producing four different types of olives, which are
cured and sold from the estate. No wines received for the *2014 Wine Companion*, but a five-star
rating has been maintained.

Tisdall Wines   ★★★

19–29 Cornelia Creek Road, Echuca, Vic 3564 **Region** Goulburn Valley
T (03) 5482 1911 **www.ballande.com.au Open** 7 days 9.30–5 at Murray Esplanade Cellars
Winemaker Michael Clayden **Est.** 1971 **Dozens** 50 000 **Vyds** 56ha
Tisdall Wines is not so much a new winery as a reborn one. The vineyard, with most of
the mainstream varieties, has been in continuous production since 1971. It is planted to
chardonnay, merlot, sauvignon blanc, cabernet sauvignon, riesling, semillon and shiraz. Under
the ownership of the Ballande Group, which acquired the business in '99, the focus has been
international markets, with exports to France, China, Malaysia, Noumea and Taiwan.

ŦŦŦŦ   Hereford Central Victoria Heathcote Shiraz 2010 Medium red-purple;
       Tisdall has waxed and waned over the past 20+ years, now returning to Heathcote
       for this light- to medium-bodied Shiraz, branded by Central Victorian eucalypt
       mint. Screwcap. 13.8% alc. **Rating** 88 **To** 2015 $15

Tobin Wines   ★★★★

34 Ricca Road, Ballandean, Qld 4382 **Region** Granite Belt
T (07) 4684 1235 **www.tobinwines.com.au Open** 7 days 10–5
Winemaker Adrian Tobin **Est.** 1964 **Dozens** 1200 **Vyds** 5.9ha

In the early 1960s the Ricca family planted table grapes, followed by shiraz and semillon in '64–66; these are said to be the oldest vinifera vines in the Granite Belt region. The Tobin family (headed by Adrian and Frances) purchased the vineyard in 2000 and has increased plantings, which now consist of shiraz, cabernet sauvignon, merlot, tempranillo, semillon, verdelho, chardonnay, muscat sauvignon blanc, with some remaining rows of table grapes. The emphasis has moved towards quality bottled wines, with considerable success, as the tasting notes show.

ŸŸŸŸ♀ **Luella Plum Cabernet 2011** Very good crimson-purple; Luella is Adrian Tobin's fifth grandchild; it is an elegant, medium-bodied wine with classic cassis fruit flavours, fine, ripe tannins and integrated oak. Bottle 534 of 1800. Screwcap. 14.5% alc. **Rating** 93 **To** 2021 $45

Aged Release Isabella Semillon 2007 Deep straw, vivid green hue; showing the full effect and benefits of some time in bottle, the bouquet reveals fresh toast, lemon curd and straw aromas; the palate is fleshy and generous, with a long tail of acidity and toasted nut aromas a feature on the finish. Screwcap. 11.3% alc. **Rating** 92 **To** 2015 $50 BE

Max Aged Release Shiraz 2008 Very good colour retention; this was a very good wine (92 points) when tasted a little over 3 years ago, and has not disappointed. While only medium-bodied, it has spicy plum fruit supported by fine tannins, oak not competing for space on the palate. Bottle no. 1741 of 2500 on a snappy neck tag. Screwcap. 14.7% alc. **Rating** 92 **To** 2018 $55

Isabella Semillon 2011 Pale straw, bright; the bouquet offers exotic gun flint, guava and cut grass aromas; the palate is fleshy and forward, with nutty flavours lingering on the fresh finish; will be a versatile wine for food matching. Screwcap. 11.3% alc. **Rating** 91 **To** 2018 $28 BE

Gertie Semillon Sauvignon Blanc 2011 Pale straw, bright; a focused and restrained bouquet, offering cut grass, guava and straw; the palate is tense and vibrant, with a strong textural component drawing out the finish to an even and harmonious conclusion. Screwcap. 11.7% alc. **Rating** 91 **To** 2015 $28 BE

Jacob Tempranillo 2012 Bottle 380 of 900. An attractive light- to medium-bodied Tempranillo, with lively cherry fruit, fine tannins and minimal oak. Screwcap. 13% alc. **Rating** 91 **To** 2017 $45

ŸŸŸŸ Kate Sauvignon Blanc 2012 **Rating** 89 **To** 2014 $28 BE
Lily Chardonnay 2012 **Rating** 89 **To** 2015 $28 BE
Max Shiraz Block Two 2011 **Rating** 88 **To** 2015 $45
Elliot Aged Release Merlot 2008 **Rating** 88 **To** 2018 $55

Tokar Estate   ★★★★☆

6 Maddens Lane, Coldstream, Vic 3770 **Region** Yarra Valley
T (03) 5964 9585 **www**.tokarestate.com.au **Open** 7 days 10.30–5
Winemaker Martin Siebert **Est.** 1996 **Dozens** 4000 **Vyds** 14ha
Leon Tokar established 14ha of now mature chardonnay, pinot noir, shiraz, cabernet sauvignon and tempranillo at Tokar Estate, one of many vineyards on Maddens Lane. All the wines are from the estate, badged Single Vineyard (which they are), and have performed well in regional shows, with early success for the Tempranillo.

ŸŸŸŸ♀ **Yarra Valley Chardonnay 2012** Wild fermented in new French puncheons, and to be released in Oct '13. As complex as its vinification would suggest, and will benefit from the extra 6 months in bottle (tasted March '13), giving it time to break the shackles and open up more. Screwcap. 13.2% alc. **Rating** 92 **To** 2019 $30

✪   **Yarra Valley Tempra Rosa 2012** Estate-grown tempranillo was wild yeast barrel-fermented in used French oak and early-bottled to capture its freshness. Light magenta in colour, it has fresh red cherry fruit offset by a spicy/savoury texture and structure. Well conceived and well executed. Screwcap. 13.5% alc. **Rating** 91 **To** 2014 $22

Tomboy Hill

★★★★★

204 Sim Street, Ballarat, Vic 3350 (postal) **Region** Ballarat
T (03) 5331 3785 **Open** Not
Winemaker Scott Ireland (Contract) **Est.** 1984 **Dozens** 750 **Vyds** 3.6ha

Former schoolteacher Ian Watson seems to be following the same path as Lindsay McCall of Paringa Estate (also a former schoolteacher) in extracting greater quality and style than any other winemaker in his region, in this case Ballarat. Since 1984 Ian has slowly and patiently built up a patchwork quilt of small plantings of chardonnay and pinot noir. In the better years, single vineyard Chardonnay and/or Pinot Noir are released; Rebellion Chardonnay and Pinot Noir are multi-vineyard blends, but all 100% Ballarat. I have a particular fondness for the style, and was awed by the quality of the 2011 wines.

🍷🍷🍷🍷🍷 **Smythes Creek Ballarat Goldfields Pinot Noir 2011** Good colour, light but bright; the aromas and flavours are anchored to gently fruit-sweet plum and cherry, the mouthfeel supple and juicy; the mix of new and used French oak (as with Rebellion) has been judiciously handled. A truly attractive wine, from the vintage from hell. Screwcap. 13% alc. **Rating** 95 **To** 2018 $45
Rebellion Ballarat Goldfields Pinot Noir 2011 Light to medium red-purple, better than many '11s; the fragrant bouquet has an unusual array of cinnamon spice and charcuterie aromas, the palate following on with greater intensity than most from southern Vic in '11, its red and black small berry fruits showing no hint of unripeness, just that foresty/sauvage grip that is Tomboy Hill's mark. Screwcap. 13% alc. **Rating** 94 **To** 2017 $30

Tomich Wines

★★★★★

87 King William Road, Unley, SA 5061 **Region** Adelaide Hills
T (08) 8272 9388 **www.**tomichwines.com **Open** Mon–Fri 10–4, w'ends 11–4.30
Winemaker John and Randal Tomich, Peter Leske (Contract) **Est.** 2002 **Dozens** 15 000
Vyds 80ha

There is an element of irony in this family venture. Patriarch John Tomich was born on a vineyard near Mildura, where he learnt first-hand the skills and knowledge required for premium grapegrowing. He went on to become a well-known Adelaide ear, nose and throat specialist. Taking the wheel full circle, he completed postgraduate studies in winemaking at the University of Adelaide in 2002, and embarked on the Master of Wine revision course from the Institute of Masters of Wine. His son Randal is a cutting from the old vine (metaphorically speaking), having invented new equipment and techniques for tending the family's vineyard in the Adelaide Hills near Woodside, resulting in a 60% saving in time and fuel costs. Most of the grapes are sold, but the amount of wine made under the Tomich brand makes it far from a hobby. Exports to China, Hong Kong and Singapore.

🍷🍷🍷🍷🍷 **Tomich Hill Ice-Block E Adelaide Hills Riesling Gewurztraminer 2011** Full orange, with some burnished gold; the ice wine treatment (freezing the water to concentrate the juice) has been taken to a far extreme here, glace and dried apricots and cumquats reaching every corner of the mouth. Will conquer the sweetest dessert. 375ml. Screwcap. 12% alc. **Rating** 95 **To** 2015 $25
Family Reserve Adelaide Hills Gewurzt 2012 Bright, pale straw-green; the bouquet is very expressive, with authentic rose petal, lychee and spice aromas, the palate adding Turkish Delight and citrus to a distinguished gewurztraminer. A rare beast in Australia. Screwcap. 13.5% alc. **Rating** 94 **To** 2017 $40
Tomich Hill Adelaide Hills Vin Gris of Pinot Noir Rose 2012 This salmon-pink Rose was wild-fermented and aged for 6 months in French barriques; the bouquet offers a blend of strawberry and spice, raspberry joining in on the long and singularly intense palate, with a twist of citrussy acidity on the finish and aftertaste. Screwcap. 12.5% alc. **Rating** 94 **To** 2014 $25
 Tomich Hill Hilltop Adelaide Hills Pinot Noir 2012 Good hue, if a little light; a Pinot Noir with attitude, its red cherry and spice bouquet followed by a lithe palate built on red fruits and quality tannins, oak a given. I particularly like the purity of this wine. Screwcap. 13% alc. **Rating** 94 **To** 2018 $25

ŶŶŶŶŶ **Tomich Hill Single Vineyard Adelaide Hills Sauvignon Blanc 2012** Pale
✪ straw-green; an elegant and fragrant wine, fermented with just a passing waft
of oak threaded through the mix of lemon/citrus, gooseberry and snow pea.
Screwcap. 13% alc. **Rating** 93 **To** 2014 $20
Tomich Hill Adelaide Hills Pinot Noir 2010 Rating 93 **To** 2016 $30
Tomich Hill Shiraz 2010 Rating 93 **To** 2025 $25

✪ **Wing and a Prayer Adelaide Hills Sauvignon Blanc 2012** Light straw-
green; the bouquet is fragrant, with passionfruit, citrus and guava aromas that are
faithfully replayed on the bright, well-balanced palate. Exceptional value. Screwcap.
13% alc. **Rating** 92 **To** 2014 $15
**Tomich Hill Family Reserve Single Vineyard Adelaide Hills Chardonnay
2010 Rating** 92 **To** 2015 $40

✪ **Tomich Hill Single Vineyard Adelaide Hills Chardonnay 2012** Light
straw-green; assembled without a fanfare of trumpets, and despite some barrel
fermentation, and some battonage (lees stirring), leaves the emphasis on the white
peach fruit, and its creamy texture. Screwcap. 13% alc. **Rating** 90 **To** 2016 $20
Tomich Hill Adelaide Hills Vin Gris of Pinot Noir Rose 2011 Rating 90
To 2013 $25

✪ **M Adelaide Hills Chardonnay Pinot NV** A 65/35% blend of chardonnay and
pinot noir, utilising wines from the '09, '10 and '11 vintages, specifically designed
to be drunk young and fresh. Light straw-green, good mousse; a delicate and finely
balanced wine with crisp, fresh apple and citrus flavours, the finish long and well
balanced. The only thing it lacks is complexity, but that is not needed when it is to
be enjoyed as an aperitif. Cork. 12% alc. **Rating** 90 **To** 2014 $20

ŶŶŶŶ **Rhyme and Reason Adelaide Hills Pinot Gris 2012** The pink colour is
✪ marked, almost to the point of rose; poached pear, apple and melon flavours are all
in play in this very well priced wine; the dry, albeit fruity, finish is a plus. Screwcap.
12.5% alc. **Rating** 89 **To** 2014 $15

Toolangi Vineyards ★★★★★

PO Box 9431, South Yarra, Vic 3141 **Region** Yarra Valley
T (03) 9827 9977 **www**.toolangi.com **Open** By appt
Winemaker Various contract **Est.** 1995 **Dozens** 8000 **Vyds** 12.2ha
Garry and Julie Hounsell acquired their property in the Dixons Creek area of the Yarra
Valley, adjoining the Toolangi State Forest, in 1995. The primary accent is on pinot noir and
chardonnay; they account for all but 2.7ha, which is predominantly shiraz and a little viognier.
Winemaking is by Yering Station (Willy Lunn), Giaconda (Rick Kinzbrunner), Hoddles
Creek Estate (Franco D'Anna) and Oakridge (David Bicknell), as impressive a quartet of
winemakers as one could wish for. Exports to the UK, Hong Kong and Singapore.

ŶŶŶŶŶ **Block F Yarra Valley Chardonnay 2011** This is the classic iron fist in a
velvet glove, the sheer power and intensity on the back-palate and finish striking
without warning on the finish and aftertaste; the flavours are three-dimensional,
encompassing every flavour and nuance of perfectly ripened chardonnay fruit,
which has eaten 11 months in oak. Screwcap. 13% alc. **Rating** 97 **To** 2024 $55
Reserve Yarra Valley Chardonnay 2010 Made by Rick Kinzbrunner of
Giaconda fame, who is able to craft Chardonnay with exceptional texture and
flavour complexity. He is happy to walk a later-picking highwire, bringing
grapefruit zest and juice, white peach and cashew bound together by strong
minerally acidity. It shares the length with other Yarra Valley Chardonnays, but was
far less easy to recognise. Screwcap. 14% alc. **Rating** 97 **To** 2020 $80
Pauls Lane Yarra Valley Chardonnay 2011 Pauls Lane abuts Toolangi's
vineyards on one side, the Toolangi state forest on another. A single block was
hand-picked and made at Hoddles Creek Estate by Franco D'Anna in his usual
restrained style, except for a surge of stone fruit on the back-palate and finish,
11 months in French oak hardly breaking the water. First-class wine. Screwcap.
13.5% alc. **Rating** 96 **To** 2021 $42

Reserve Yarra Valley Shiraz 2010 Made at Oakridge, and spent 10 months in French oak. A powerful and complex wine, showing just how much varietal expression can be achieved at this alcohol level, for it is medium-bodied, not full-bodied; the black cherry/blackberry fruits are framed by quality French oak, the tannins judged to perfection. Screwcap. 13% alc. **Rating** 96 **To** 2030 $65

✪ Yarra Valley Chardonnay 2011 Estate-grown from low-yielding vineyards; barrel-fermented at Yering Station and Oakridge Estate; blended at Yering Station, and bottled there after 11 months in oak. It is a very elegant wine with melon and white peach in the driver's seat, the oak subtle. Screwcap. 13% alc. **Rating** 94 **To** 2020 $25

Estate Yarra Valley Chardonnay 2011 **Rating** 94 **To** 2020 $42
Block E Yarra Valley Pinot Noir 2011 **Rating** 94 **To** 2017 $75
Yarra Valley Shiraz 2012 **Rating** 94 **To** 2027 $25

♟♟♟♟♟ Pauls Lane Yarra Valley Pinot Noir 2011 **Rating** 93 **To** 2018 $42
Yarra Valley Shiraz 2010 **Rating** 93 **To** 2020 $23
Estate Yarra Valley Pinot Noir 2011 **Rating** 92 **To** 2017 $42

✪ Emanai 2012 An unoaked blend of chardonnay and viognier made for Toolangi by Franco d'Anna, whose gentle touch makes this often clumsy blend an unqualified success; white peach, apricot and ripe citrus fruit neatly combined. Screwcap. 12.5% alc. **Rating** 91 **To** 2014 $20

Yarra Valley Pinot Noir 2011 **Rating** 90 **To** 2016 $25

🌿 Toolern Vale Hills Vineyard   ★★★★

53–103 McPhersons Road, Toolern Vale, Vic 3337 **Region** Sunbury
T 0422 727 529 **www.**toolernvalehillswinery.com.au **Open** W'ends 11–4.30, or by appt
Winemaker Owen Latta **Est.** 1994 **Dozens** 3000 **Vyds** 20.2ha

John Travassaros remembers helping his grandfather make wine in Kithra, Greece when he (John) was a young boy. When he came to Australia, John planted 50 vines on the hills of Toolern Vale, hoping one day to create a fully functional vineyard and winery. His dream is now a reality, as he had established a little over 20ha of vines (in descending order of size: merlot, cabernet sauvignon, shiraz, sauvignon blanc, chardonnay and pinot noir). The winery that enabled the next step to be taken was constructed in 2005; the pricing of the wines is the icing on the cake (for his clientele).

♟♟♟♟♟ 50 Vines Cabernet Sauvignon 2009 The ferment was initiated by wild yeast
✪ and completed with cultured yeasts in open fermenters; the wine was matured in French oak (20% new) and was neither fined nor filtered; low yield resulted in a full-flavoured, luscious palate, with cassis and plum fruit, the oak integrated, the tannin balance good. Screwcap. 13% alc. **Rating** 93 **To** 2024 $25

✪ 50 Vines Sauvignon Blanc 2011 An elegant and highly focused wine, with a mix of citrus and tropical fruits, especially passionfruit. A very attractive cool-grown Sauvignon Blanc. Screwcap. 13.4% alc. **Rating** 92 **To** 2014 $15

✪ 50 Vines Chardonnay 2011 Hand-picked, whole bunch-pressed, 100% barrel-fermented in French oak (15% new), 50% wild, 50% cultured yeast, 70% mlf. The fruit intensity is moderate, so the nutty/creamy oak influence does show, but is not over the top, leaving the citrus, melon and stone fruit varietal characters room to express themselves. Screwcap. 13.4% alc. **Rating** 91 **To** 2017 $19

✪ 50 Vines Fume Sauvignon Blanc 2011 Light straw-green; whole bunch-pressed; 100% barrel-fermented in French oak (15% new) with wild yeast, 50% cultured yeast; 70% mlf; 10 months on lees with minimal stirring. This complex array of inputs has not overridden the lemony/citrus fruit, and natural acidity is still very evident. Screwcap. 13.1% alc. **Rating** 90 **To** 2014 $15

50 Vines Merlot 2010 Medium red-purple; open-fermented, wild yeasts to commence, cultured to complete fermentation; then 12 months in French oak (15% new) on full lees. The flavours are fully ripe in warm-climate style (rather than cool-grown), with plum and cassis flavours. Neither fined nor filtered. Screwcap. 13.6% alc. **Rating** 90 **To** 2017 $25

50 Vines Merlot 2009 Made in identical fashion to the '10; the extra year has seen the fruit slim down fractionally, and the cedary oak to become a little more obvious. Both are interesting Merlots given their origin. Screwcap. 13.2% alc. Rating 90 To 2016 $25

♀♀♀♀   **50 Vines Shiraz 2010** Rating 88 To 2016 $25
50 Vines Shiraz 2009 Rating 88 To 2015 $25

Toorak Winery

Vineyard 279 Toorak Road, Leeton, NSW 2705 **Region** Riverina
T (02) 6953 2333 **www**.toorakwines.com.au **Open** Mon–Fri 10–5, Sat by appt
Winemaker Robert Bruno **Est.** 1965 **Dozens** 200000 **Vyds** 145ha
A traditional, long-established Riverina producer with a strong Italian-based clientele around Australia. Production has increased significantly, utilising substantial estate plantings and grapes purchased from other growers in the Riverina and elsewhere. Wines are released under the Toorak Estate, Willandra Estate, Bondi Blue and Amesbury Estate labels. While, in absolute terms, the quality is not great, the low-priced wines in fact over-deliver in many instances. Exports to the US, Norway, Russia, Nigeria, India, Singapore and China.

♀♀♀♀   **Willandra Estate Leeton Selection Shiraz 2012** Bright colour, with a red fruit and spicy bouquet; toasty oak comes through on the palate; while fresh and fragrant, is deisgned for early consumption. Screwcap. 12.5% alc. Rating 87 To 2015 $12 BE

Topers Wines

PO Box 253, Bowral, NSW 2576 **Region** Central Ranges Zone
T (02) 4887 1215 **Open** Not
Winemaker Madrez Wine Services (Chris Derrez, Lucy Maddox) **Est.** 2010
Dozens 400 **Vyds** 8ha
Jonathan (Ding) Bell was a contemporary of mine at Sydney University Law School in the latter part of the 1950s and early '60s. He went on to practise in Queanbeyan/Canberra, while I remained in Sydney. He and wife Elizabeth run a mixed farming and grazing enterprise at Chase Farm in the Southern Highlands of NSW, but as part of a family business restructure, Liz took over the running of an 8ha vineyard at Kelvin Grove, near Canowindra. They plan to sell a proportion of the grape production, while slowly increasing the amount made, and introducing a sparkling Chardonnay.

♀♀♀♀   **Central Ranges Chardonnay 2012** Early picked, and barrel-fermented in used oak with lees stirring; it is well balanced, the only issue being a lack of intensity. The vintage was a very difficult one, with significant rainfall issues. In the circumstances, a very creditable result. Screwcap. 12.8% alc. Rating 88 To 2015 $23

Topper's Mountain Wines ★★★★

5km Guyra Road, Tingha, NSW 2369 **Region** New England
T 0411 880 580 **www**.toppers.com.au **Open** By appt
Winemaker Mike Hayes **Est.** 2000 **Dozens** 1200 **Vyds** 9.79ha
Following a partnership dissolution, Topper's Mountain is now solely owned by Mark Kirkby. Planting began in the spring of 2000, with the ultimate fruit salad trial of 15 rows each of innumerable varieties and clones. The total area planted was made up of 28 separate plantings, many of these with only 200 vines in a block. As varieties proved unsuited, they were grafted to those that held the most promise. Thus far, Gewurztraminer and Sauvignon Blanc hold most promise among the white wines, the Mediterranean reds doing better than their French cousins. The original 28 varieties are now down to 16; chardonnay, gewurztraminer, sauvignon blanc, tempranillo, shiraz and merlot are the commercial varieties, the remainder in the fruit salad block still under evaluation. Integrated Pest Management has been successfully adopted throughout the vineyard. Champion Winery of Show, New England Wine Show '11.

ŸŸŸŸŸ **New England Gewurztraminer 2012** Pale colour, and restrained in character, with musk, bath talc and a hint of fresh lychee; the palate is lively, taut and chalky in texture, providing freshness and missing out on any oiliness the variety can provide. Screwcap. 12.6% alc. **Rating** 92 **To** 2016 $35 BE

New England Sauvignon Blanc 2012 Pale colour, with a pungent gooseberry, cut grass and passionfruit bouquet; the palate is taut, racy and finishes with a dry chalky and refreshing texture. Screwcap. 11.7% alc. **Rating** 90 **To** 2014 $30 BE

Torbreck Vintners   ★★★★★

Roennfeldt Road, Marananga, SA 5352 **Region** Barossa Valley
T (08) 8562 4155 **www**.torbreck.com **Open** 7 days 10–6
Winemaker David Powell **Est.** 1994 **Dozens** 70 000 **Vyds** 86ha
Of all the Barossa Valley wineries to grab the headlines in the US, with demand pulling prices up to undreamt-of levels, Torbreck stands supreme. David Powell has not let success go to his head, or subvert the individuality and sheer quality of his wines, all created around very old, dry-grown, bush-pruned vineyards. The top quartet is led by The Laird (single vineyard Shiraz), RunRig (Shiraz/Viognier), The Factor (Shiraz) and Descendant (Shiraz/Viognier); next The Struie (Shiraz) and The Steading (Grenache/Mataro/Shiraz). Notwithstanding the depth and richness of the wines, they have a remarkable degree of finesse. In 2008 the ownership was restructured, Californian vintner Peter Kight (of Quivira Vineyards) acquiring shares. The Laird is a cool $700 a bottle. Exports to all major markets.

ŸŸŸŸŸ **The Factor 2009** Deep purple-crimson; this Shiraz achieves its full-bodied weight with ease, indeed outright nonchalance; its bouquet heralds the blackberry and dark chocolate fruit to come on the textured palate, the ripe tannin and oak contributions in immaculate balance. Cork. 14.5% alc. **Rating** 96 **To** 2034 $125

RunRig 2010 Deep purple-crimson; alcohol analysis can confuse, for the alcohol evident here seems little different from that of Descendant (15%), and the contribution of the viognier to the shiraz no less evident; the full-bodied palate is immensely rich and yet supple, the black and red fruits flowing through the length of the palate and into the aftertaste; oak and tannins are seamlessly welded into the fruit. Cork. 16% alc. **Rating** 96 **To** 2035 $225

Descendant 2009 Deep purple-red; here the lower alcohol does speak, along with more light and shade in the bouquet and the medium- to full-bodied palate; there are notes of spice and savoury licorice coupled with some red fruit nuances, even though blackberry and satsuma plum provide the mainframe for a distinguished wine. Cork. 14.5% alc. **Rating** 96 **To** 2035 $125

Descendant 2010 Dark purple-crimson; the grapes come from vines established from cuttings from the old vines that make RunRig. The complex black fruits and licorice of the bouquet are precisely replayed on the full-bodied palate, with added mocha/dark chocolate; the tannins are full and round, giving the wine balance and length. Cork. 15% alc. **Rating** 95 **To** 2030 $125

The Steading 2010 A blend of grenache, shiraz and mataro that has greater weight and complexity than the colour would suggest, even to the extent of touches of spice and chocolate; the overall balance between fruit, oak and tannins is good, and merits medium-term cellaring. Screwcap. 15% alc. **Rating** 94 **To** 2020 $38

ŸŸŸŸŸ **Les Amis 2010 Rating** 93 **To** 2020 $188
The Steading Blanc 2012 Rating 92 **To** 2017 $38
The Struie 2011 Rating 92 **To** 2026 $49
Kyloe 2010 Rating 92 **To** 2018 $49

Torzi Matthews Vintners   ★★★★

Cnr Eden Valley Road/Sugarloaf Hill Road, Mount McKenzie, SA5353 **Region** Eden Valley
T 0412 323 486 **www**.torzimatthews.com.au **Open** At Taste Eden Valley, Angaston
Winemaker Domenic Torzi **Est.** 1996 **Dozens** 4000 **Vyds** 13ha

Domenic Torzi and Tracy Matthews, former Adelaide Plains residents, searched for a number of years before finding a block at Mt McKenzie in the Eden Valley. The block they chose is in a hollow; the soil is meagre, and they were in no way deterred by the knowledge that it would be frost-prone. The result is predictably low yields, concentrated further by drying the grapes on racks and reducing the weight by around 30% (the Appassimento method is used in Italy to produce Amarone-style wines). Newer plantings of sangiovese and negro amaro, and an extension of the original plantings of shiraz and riesling, has seen the wine range increase. Exports to the US, Denmark, Singapore, Hong Kong and China.

🍷🍷🍷🍷🍷 **Vigna Cantina Barossa Valley Trebbiano 2011** This wine captures the straw, fennel and distinctly savoury nature of the variety made in an Italian style; the palate reveals a little amaro bitterness at the finish, providing freshness and contrast; food please. Screwcap. 12.5% alc. **Rating** 90 To 2015 $22 BE

✪ **Schist Rock Eden Valley Shiraz 2011** Deep garnet; the bouquet offers a spicy array of black fruits and wet slate, no doubt due to the schist the vineyard is planted on (the power of suggestion?); the palate is medium-bodied and thickly textured with plump sweet fruits making way for a finish of bony tannins. Screwcap. 14% alc. **Rating** 90 To 2016 $18 BE

🍷🍷🍷🍷 **Frost Dodger Eden Valley Shiraz 2010 Rating** 88 To 2016 $30 BE
Vigna Cantina Negro Amaro 2012 Rating 88 To 2015 $22 BE

Totino Estate ★★★★☆

982 Port Road, Albert Park, SA 5014 (postal) **Region** Adelaide Hills
T (08) 8349 1200 **www**.totinowines.com.au **Open** Not
Winemaker Damien Harris, Greg Clack **Est.** 1992 **Dozens** 15 000 **Vyds** 29ha
Don Totino migrated from Italy in 1968, and at the age of 18 became the youngest barber in Australia. He soon moved on, into general food and importing and distribution. Festival City, as the business is known, has been highly successful, recognised by a recent significant award from the Italian government. In '98 he purchased a rundown vineyard at Paracombe in the Adelaide Hills, since extending the plantings to 29ha of chardonnay, pinot grigio, sauvignon blanc, sangiovese and shiraz. Various family members, including daughter Linda, are involved in the business. Exports to Canada, Italy and China.

🍷🍷🍷🍷🍷 **Adelaide Hills Sauvignon Blanc 2012** Quartz-white; has vivid passionfruit and snow pea flavours, an unusual conjunction in a wine with the focus, intensity and freshness this has; minerally acidity provides the finishing touch. Screwcap. 13% alc. Rating 94 To 2014 $18

🍷🍷🍷🍷🍷 **Adelaide Hills Sauvignon Blanc 2011** While retaining the freshness of its
✪ youth, the wine has a core of grapefruit and lychee fruit bolstered by crisp acidity driving through on the finish. Screwcap. 12.5% alc. **Rating** 91 To 2013 $18

✪ **Adelaide Hills Pinot Grigio 2012** Estate-grown grapes give a lively and crisp wine, with a mainstream varietal flow of nashi pear, apple and citrus on a long, well-balanced palate. Screwcap. 13.5% alc. **Rating** 90 To 2014 $18
Adelaide Hills Sangiovese Rose 2011 Rating 90 To 2014 $18

Tower Estate

Cnr Broke Road/Hall Road, Pokolbin, NSW 2320 **Region** Hunter Valley
T (02) 4998 7989 **www**.towerestatewines.com **Open** 7 days 10–5
Winemaker Andrew Leembruggen, Usher Tinkler **Est.** 1999 **Dozens** 10 000 **Vyds** 12.6ha
Tower Estate was founded by the late Len Evans, with the award-winning 5-star Tower Lodge accommodation and convention centre a part of the development. Tower Estate continues to draw upon varieties and regions that have a particular synergy, the aim being to make the best possible wines in the top sector of the wine market. In Nov '12 Andrew Leembruggen and Usher Tinkler were appointed as winemakers; both grew up in the Hunter Valley, and cut their winemaking teeth there before becoming Flying Winemakers, but always returning home to roost in the valley. They have stellar records. Exports to the UK.

🍷🍷🍷🍷🍷 **Hunter Valley Chardonnay 2011** Bright straw-green; unsurprisingly, a different display of fruit flavours than the Bowyer Ridge Chardonnay, even though the wild ferment approach has been the same; here nectarine and melon come to the fore, with citrus manifesting itself on the finish; the oak level, too, has been deliberately tuned down. Screwcap. 12.5% alc. **Rating** 94 **To** 2017 $30

Tasmania Pinot Noir 2011 Very good colour; is a blend from two vineyards, Panorama, on the Huon River, and Meadowbank, on the Derwent; a delicious Pinot, with red cherry and wild strawberry leading the way, some spice and gossamer tannins on the finish. Screwcap. 13.5% alc. **Rating** 94 **To** 2017 $30

Hunter Valley Shiraz 2011 Bright purple-red; a barrel selection was made after 16 months in French oak; it is a beautifully modulated and structured example of Hunter Valley shiraz; plum, black cherry and a hint of spice; the oak is not the least intrusive. Screwcap. 13.5% alc. **Rating** 94 **To** 2031 $32

🍷🍷🍷🍷🍷 **Bowyer Ridge Adelaide Hills Chardonnay 2011 Rating** 93 **To** 2018 $30
Hunter Valley Semillon 2012 Rating 90 **To** 2018 $22 BE

Train Trak   ★★★★

957 Healesville-Yarra Glen Road, Yarra Glen, Vic 3775 **Region** Yarra Valley
T (03) 9730 1314 **www**.traintrak.com.au **Open** Wed–Sun 10–5
Winemaker Robert Paul (Contract) **Est.** 1995 **Dozens** 2400 **Vyds** 16ha
The unusual name comes from the Yarra Glen to Healesville railway, which was built in 1889 and abandoned in 1980 – part of it passes by the Train Trak vineyard. The vineyard is planted to pinot noir, cabernet sauvignon, chardonnay and shiraz. Exports to Canada, Pacific Islands, China and Japan.

🍷🍷🍷🍷🍷 **Yarra Valley Chardonnay 2011** Picked from the two best blocks on the estate, part tank- and part barrel-fermented, then aged on lees for 8 months prior to bottling. The approach has worked well, with white peach and honeydew melon, rather than oak, dominating the long, well-balanced palate. Screwcap. 12% alc. **Rating** 92 **To** 2017 $25

🍷🍷🍷🍷 **Yarra Valley Pinot Rose 2011 Rating** 89 **To** 2014 $18
Yarra Valley Pinot Chardonnay 2008 Rating 88 **To** 2014 $25
Yarra Valley Pinot Rose 2012 Rating 87 **To** 2014 $18

🍇 Travertine Wines   ★★★☆

110 Old North Road, Pokolbin, NSW 2320 **Region** Hunter Valley
T (02) 6574 7329 **www**.travertinewines.com.au **Open** Fri–Sun 10–4
Winemaker Damien Stevens **Est.** 1988 **Dozens** 3000 **Vyds** 12.85ha
This is the reincarnation of Pendarves Estate, originally planted by medico-cum-wine historian-cum wine health activist Dr Phillip Norrie. It was purchased by Graham Burns in January 2008, and vineyard manager Chris Dibley, who had previously worked in the vineyard, was brought back to 'get the place back up to scratch'. There is a Joseph's coat of plantings, including verdelho (2.66ha), pinot noir (2.37ha), shiraz (2.1ha), chardonnay (1.83ha) and chambourcin (1.7ha), and lesser plantings of tannat, semillon and merlot. Wine quality is a little variable, but there are some nice wines currently available.

🍷🍷🍷🍷🍷 **Hunter Valley Verdelho 2011** Light straw-green; has clear-cut varietal
✪ character, with fruit salad and a drizzle of citrus; there is considerable drive and length to a superior example of the variety, and time to go. Screwcap. 13.2% alc. **Rating** 93 **To** 2015 $20

🍷🍷🍷🍷 **Hunter Valley Chardonnay 2009 Rating** 89 **To** 2014 $18
Hunter Valley Merlot 2009 Rating 87 **To** 2014 $20

Treasury Wine Estates   ★★★★★

The Atrium, 58 Queensbridge Street, Southbank, Vic 3006 **Region** Various
T 1300 651 650 **www**.tweglobal.com **Open** Not
Winemaker Mark Robertson **Est.** 2005 **Dozens** NFP **Vyds** 11ha
Treasury Wine Estates (TWE), the renamed wine division of Foster's Group Limited, was fully separated from Foster's via a separate listing on the Australian Securities Exchange in May 2011. It has the full range of wine businesses: from those with a dedicated winery or wineries, household brand names and long-term grape supply from owned vineyards or contract arrangements, through to brands that have been stripped of their wineries and vineyards, but continue to have a significant brand presence in the marketplace. Those who fall into the dedicated winery/estate vineyards pattern are Penfolds, Wynns Coonawarra Estate, Seppelt, Baileys of Glenrowan, Devil's Lair, St Huberts and Coldstream Hills. Other brands include Annie's Lane, Heemskerk, Ingoldby, Jamiesons Run, Leo Buring, Lindemans, Rosemount Estate, Saltram, T'Gallant, Tollana, Wolf Blass and Yellowglen. Exports to all major markets.

Treeton Estate   ★★★

163 North Treeton Road, Cowaramup, WA 6284 **Region** Margaret River
T (08) 9755 5481 **www**.treetonestate.com.au **Open** 7 days 10–6
Winemaker David McGowan **Est.** 1982 **Dozens** 3000 **Vyds** 7.5ha
In 1982 David McGowan and wife Corinne purchased the 30ha property upon which Treeton Estate is established, planting the vineyard two years later (shiraz, sauvignon blanc, chenin blanc, cabernet sauvignon and chardonnay). The wines are light and fresh, sometimes rather too much so. Exports to Southeast Asia and China.

Trellis   ★★★★★

Valley Farm Road, Healesville, Vic 3777 **Region** Yarra Valley
T (03) 5962 5723 **www**.trelliswines.com.au **Open** By appt
Winemaker Luke Houlihan **Est.** 2007 **Dozens** 535 **Vyds** 3.2ha
This is the venture of winemaker Luke Houlihan and viticulturist Greg Dunnett. Luke was formerly winemaker at Yarra Ridge and Long Gully Estate, and Greg owns Valley Farm Vineyard. The pinot noir has had several distinguished purchasers over the years, and there has never been any doubt about the quality of the fruit, which is from the dry-grown vines. The partners have put the problems of the 2007 and '09 vintages behind them, with lovely '08s and '10s from the Yarra Valley neatly stitched in with an '07 and '09 Syrah from Heathcote. No wines received for the *2014 Wine Companion*, but a five-star rating has been maintained.

Trentham Estate   ★★★★☆

Sturt Highway, Trentham Cliffs, NSW 2738 **Region** Murray Darling
T (03) 5024 8888 **www**.trenthamestate.com.au **Open** 7 days 9.30–5
Winemaker Anthony Murphy, Shane Kerr **Est.** 1988 **Dozens** 60 000 **Vyds** 50.65ha
Remarkably consistent tasting notes across all wine styles from all vintages attest to the expertise of ex-Mildara winemaker Tony Murphy, a well-known and highly regarded producer, with estate vineyards on the Murray Darling. With an eye to the future, but also to broadening the range of the wines on offer, Trentham Estate is selectively buying grapes from other regions with a track record for the chosen varieties. The value for money is unfailingly excellent. Exports to the UK and other major markets.

♥♥♥♥♥ **Heathcote Shiraz 2009** Clear red-purple; the depth of fruit on the bouquet and medium-bodied palate belies the colour; ripe satsuma plum and spice/pepper nuances drive the bouquet and palate alike, oak a means to an end, not an end in itself. Screwcap. 14% alc. **Rating** 94 **To** 2024 $30

♥♥♥♥♀ **La Famiglia Sangiovese Rose 2012** Bright crimson-red; loaded with tangy,
✪ juicy fruit flavours in a sour cherry/red cherry spectrum; has considerable intensity and length, with a drizzle of lemon on the finish and aftertaste. Screwcap. 12% alc. **Rating** 92 **To** 2014 $14

ŸŸŸŸ **La Famiglia Vermentino 2011** The variety has established a home away from
✪ home along the Murray River, its lemon/lemon zest flavours making a refreshing
summer white wine. This is a very good, well-priced, example. Screwcap. 12% alc.
Rating 89 **To** 2013 $16

✪ **Cabernet Sauvignon Merlot 2010** Time and again Tony Murphy shows what
can be achieved with Riverland grapes when the vintage is good; this medium-
bodied wine has ample varietal black and redcurrant fruit with a savoury lift to the
finish. Great value. Screwcap. 14.5% alc. **Rating** 89 **To** 2016 $14

✪ **Murphy's Lore Chardonnay 2012** A well-made, no frills, no oak Chardonnay
that has plenty of varietal flavour and just a touch of sweetness on the finish. Good
value. Screwcap. 13.5% alc. **Rating** 87 **To** 2013 $10

Trevelen Farm ★★★★★

506 Weir Road, Cranbrook, WA 6321 **Region** Great Southern
T (08) 9826 1052 **www.**trevelenfarm.com.au **Open** Fri–Mon 10.30–4.30, or by appt
Winemaker Harewood Estate (James Kellie) **Est.** 1993 **Dozens** 3000 **Vyds** 6.5ha
In 2008 John and Katie Sprigg decided to pass ownership of their 1300ha wool, meat and
grain-producing farm to son Ben and wife Louise. However, they have kept control of the
6.5ha of sauvignon blanc, riesling, chardonnay, cabernet sauvignon and merlot planted in
1993. Each wine is made as a 100% varietal, and when demand requires, they will increase
production by purchasing grapes from growers in the Frankland River subregion. Riesling
will remain the centrepiece of the range. Enticing prices. Exports to Japan, Macau and China.

ŸŸŸŸŸ **Riesling 2012** Remarkably brilliant quartz-green; while the scale on the back
✪ label accurately indicates a wine near the extreme of the dry range, the wine
is so loaded with lime and lemon sherbet fruit you might think it to be a little
sugar-sweet, but this is simply the fruit calling in angelic song. Screwcap. 11% alc.
Rating 96 **To** 2025 $25
Frankland Reserve Shiraz 2010 Medium to full red-purple; the bouquet and
light- to medium-bodied palate present a flowing bowl of red and black cherry,
spice, licorice, mocha/chocolate and fine-grained tannins before a juicy aftertaste.
It all works very well. Screwcap. 14.5% alc. **Rating** 94 **To** 2020 $25

ŸŸŸŸŸ **Reserve Frankland Merlot 2010 Rating** 92 **To** 2017 $23
✪ **Katie's Kiss Riesling 2012** Light straw-green; it's curious how young Rieslings
with substantial residual sugar are often closed on the bouquet, yet full of vitality
on the palate, even though typically they are made from the pressings unsuited for
dry wine use. This is a bargain. Screwcap. 9% alc. **Rating** 91 **To** 2020 $14

✪ **The Maritime Pinot Noir 2011** Bright, light crimson-purple; an elegant wine
reflecting its maturation in predominantly new French puncheons; it has distinct
savoury/briary nuances, and needed greater depth of fruit to carry the oak; that
said, it has its appeal, particularly at this price, and is ready to drink now. Screwcap.
14% alc. **Rating** 90 **To** 2015 $20

Trevor Jones Fine Wines ★★★★★

123 Jollytown Road, Lyndoch, SA 5351 **Region** Barossa Valley
T 0417 869 981 **www.**trevorjonesfinewines.com.au **Open** By appt
Winemaker Trevor Jones **Est.** 1998 **Dozens** 4000 **Vyds** 5ha
The Trevor Jones and Kellermeister brands were for many years linked by family ties. Up to
2010 Trevor Jones (the person) was winemaker and production manager for Kellermeister, but
he has left to concentrate on the eponymous business owned by himself and wife Mandy. He
now makes his wines at Torbreck, but plans to have his own winery operational in time for the
2014 vintage. With 34 years' winemaking experience, he is also providing consultancy advice
to wineries in the Barossa. No wines received for the *2014 Wine Companion*, but a five-star
rating has been maintained. Exports to the US, Switzerland and Japan.

Trifon Estate Wines

PO Box 258, Murchison, Vic 3610 **Region** Central Victoria Zone
T (03) 9432 9811 **Open** Not
Winemaker Jurie Germishuys **Est.** 1998 **Dozens** 170 000 **Vyds** 232ha
Trifon Estate has flown under the radar since it was establish by Commodity Traders Australia
in 1998. Since that time 232ha of vines have been planted to 15 varieties, the lion's share to
shiraz (54ha), chardonnay (39ha), cabernet sauvignon (34ha) and merlot (28ha). It is a tribute
to the management of the operation that the decision was taken to completely declassify the
2011 vintage. I tasted without being aware of the bottling dates, most of the wines reviewed
being in fact bottled in Dec '12 to Jan '13, with up to eight years in tank. Exports to China.

Sangiovese 2012 Bright red; the fragrant bouquet of red berries/cherries is
followed by a palate with more of the same, plus fine, spicy tannins on the long,
balanced finish. Excellent value. Screwcap. 13.9% alc. **Rating** 91 **To** 2015 $20

Marsanne 2008 Bright straw-green; has not suffered from its near-5 years in
tank, and bottling under screwcap will protect it for the future; there is attractive
varietal honeysuckle fruit, and the acidity is well balanced. Good now, but will
hold, and possible improve. 13% alc. **Rating** 90 **To** 2017 $20

Shiraz 2005 Rating 87 **To** 2015 $37
Shiraz 2004 Rating 87 **To** 2015 $37
Cabernet Sauvignon 2010 Rating 87 **To** 2015 $20

Truffle Hill Wines

Seven Day Road, Manjimup, WA 6248 **Region** Pemberton
T (08) 9777 2474 **www.**wineandtruffle.com.au **Open** 7 days 10–4.30
Winemaker Mark Aitken **Est.** 1997 **Dozens** 4500 **Vyds** 10.5ha
Owned by a group of investors from various parts of Australia who have successfully
achieved their vision of producing fine wines and black truffles. The winemaking side is
under the care of Mark Aitken, who, having graduated as dux of his class in applied science
at Curtin University in 2000, joined Chestnut Grove as winemaker in '02. The truffle side
of the business is run under the direction of Harry Eslick, with 13 000 truffle-inoculated
hazelnut and oak trees on the property, which have now produced truffles, some of
prodigious size. Exports to Japan.

Reserve Series Manjimup Shiraz 2009 Medium red-purple; the fragrant and
complex bouquet has nuances of tar and licorice underpinning its black fruits, the
flavours on the juicy medium-bodied palate also taking in plum, mocha and cedar.
Screwcap. 14.3% alc. **Rating** 94 **To** 2024 $35

Pemberton Merlot 2011 There is no question that Pemberton can produce
Merlot with good varietal character, weight and texture, and this wine is a prime
example; it has bright colour, and the fragrant bouquet and light- to medium-
bodied palate offers a lively mix of cassis and mulberry fruit, a hint of olive, and
fine, ripe tannins. Screwcap. 14% alc. **Rating** 93 **To** 2016 $22
Reserve Series Pemberton Cane-cut Riesling 2011 Rating 93 **To** 2016 $28
Manjimup Shiraz 2011 Healthy purple-crimson; a fragrant bouquet of
predominantly plum and blackberry fruit, with nuances of spice, leads into a juicy,
medium-bodied palate, which brings a splash of French oak and fine tannins into
play. Screwcap. 14.5% alc. **Rating** 91 **To** 2021 $22

Tscharke

376 Seppeltsfield Road, Marananga, SA 5360 **Region** Barossa Valley
T 0438 628 178 **www.**tscharke.com.au **Open** Thurs–Mon 10–5
Winemaker Damien Tscharke **Est.** 2001 **Dozens** 5000 **Vyds** 28ha
Damien Tscharke grew up in the Barossa Valley among the vineyards at Seppeltsfield and
Marananga. In 2001 he began the production of Glaymond, four estate-grown wines based

on what he calls the classic varieties (following the trend of having catchy, snappy names), followed by wines under the Tscharke brand using the alternative varieties of tempranillo, graciano, zinfandel, montepulciano and savagnin. Like the Glaymond wines, these are estate-grown, albeit in very limited quantities. Exports to the US, Canada, Denmark, Belgium, Germany, Israel, Indonesia, Singapore and China.

ΨΨΨΨΨ **MGA Fortune Shiraz 2007** Amazing deep purple hue for a 6-year-old wine, the grapes from the Marananga district, hence the name. The bouquet and palate are exceptionally intense, indeed demanding; liqueur-soaked plums, blackberries, dark chocolate, spice and licorice are all to be found. There is none of the toughness of most '07s, and it has a very long life ahead. Released Jul '13. Screwcap. 14.8% alc. **Rating** 95 **To** 2037 $120

ΨΨΨΨΨ **Tscharke The Master Marananga Montepulciano 2011** Very good colour,
✪ bright, deep purple-crimson; the opposite approach to Only Son Tempranillo, with a 40-day sojourn on skins before being pressed; here it all makes sense, the plum/red fruit flavours nicely balanced by tannins. Exceptional effort for the year. Screwcap. 14% alc. **Rating** 93 **To** 2019 $24
Barossa Grounds Collection Marananga Gnaedenfrei Vineyard Shiraz 2010 Rating 91 **To** 2023 $32
Barossa Grounds Collection Marananga Stonewell Vineyard Mataro 2010 Rating 91 **To** 2020 $32
Glaymond Distinction Barossa Valley Shiraz 2008 Rating 90 **To** 2030 $90
Barossa Grounds Collection Marananga Stonewell Vineyard Cabernet Sauvignon 2010 Rating 90 **To** 2020 $32
Tcharke Only Son Marananga Tempranillo 2011 Rating 90 **To** 2018 $24

Tuck's Ridge   ★★★★★

37 Shoreham Road, Red Hill South, Vic 3937 **Region** Mornington Peninsula
T (03) 5989 8660 **www.**tucksridge.com.au **Open** 7 days 11–5
Winemaker Michael Kyberd, Matthew Bisogni **Est.** 1985 **Dozens** 6500 **Vyds** 3.4ha
Tuck's Ridge has changed focus significantly since selling its large Red Hill vineyard. It retained the Buckle Vineyards of chardonnay and pinot noir that consistently provide outstanding grapes (and wine). The major part of the production is purchased from the Turramurra Vineyard. Exports to the US and Hong Kong.

ΨΨΨΨΨ **Buckle Pinot Noir 2010** Bright, clear crimson; as ever, a wine of great purity and supreme elegance from a 25-year-old, low-yielding vineyard; plum and cherry intermingle on the bouquet and intense, lively palate, French oak totally integrated, the tannins superfine but persistent. Produced from a single block of MV6 yielding 3 tonnes per hectare, the wine matured in 30% new French oak. 211 dozen made. Screwcap. 13.7% alc. **Rating** 97 **To** 2022 $100
Mornington Peninsula Chardonnay 2011 Fragrant, citrus-tinged bouquet leads into a bracingly fresh palate, with white peach and grapefruit the major players in the fruit orchestra; the French oak is totally integrated, the finish long and vibrant. Screwcap. 12.9% alc. **Rating** 94 **To** 2018 $29
Turramurra Chardonnay 2011 Light straw-green; has the difficult-to-describe, but unmistakable, Mornington Peninsula imprint on the fruit, with a firm core yet soft and delicate exterior, the flavours of nectarine, citrus and creamy cashew before a crisp acid finish. Screwcap. 13.4% alc. **Rating** 94 **To** 2019 $35

ΨΨΨΨΨ **Buckle Chardonnay 2011 Rating** 93 **To** 2017 $50
Mornington Peninsula Savagnin 2012 Rating 93 **To** 2016 $30
Mornington Peninsula Sauvignon Blanc 2012 Rating 90 **To** 2013 $24

Tulloch ★★★★★

'Glen Elgin', 638 De Beyers Road, Pokolbin, NSW 2321 **Region** Hunter Valley
T (02) 4998 7580 **www.**tullochwines.com.au **Open** 7 days 10–5
Winemaker Jay Tulloch, First Creek Winemaking Services **Est.** 1895 **Dozens** 35 000
Vyds 80ha
The Tulloch brand continues to build success on success. Its primary grape source is estate vines owned by part shareholder Inglewood Vineyard in the Upper Hunter Valley. It also owns the JYT Vineyard established by Jay Tulloch in the mid 1980s at the foot of the Brokenback Range in the heart of Pokolbin. The third source is contract-grown fruit from other growers in the Hunter Valley and further afield. Skilled winemaking by First Creek Winemaking Services has put the icing on the winemaking cake, and Christina Tulloch is a livewire marketer. By way of postscript, 2013 marked Jay Tulloch's 50th Hunter Valley vintage. Exports to Belgium, the Philippines, Singapore, Hong Kong, Malaysia, Thailand, Japan and China.

♟♟♟♟♟ **Vineyard Selection Hunter Valley Semillon 2012** Pale quartz; a strikingly
✪ vibrant and juicy palate, with lemon drop and green apple flavours, the acidity like a spear running through the wine, guaranteeing a long and prosperous life. Screwcap. 11% alc. Rating 94 To 2025 $20
Private Bin Pokolbin Dry Red Shiraz 2011 Celebrates the lifelong links between the Walker and Tulloch families. The hue is very good, although not dense; while only medium-bodied, has intense berry fruit flavours girdled by fine, ripe tannins and positive oak. Will nonchalantly cruise past its 30th birthday. Screwcap. 13.5% alc. **Rating** 94 **To** 2041 $50

♟♟♟♟♟ **JYT Selection Semillon 2012** Rating 93 To 2022 $25 BE
JYT Selection 2011 Rating 93 To 2026 $40
EM Limited Release Chardonnay 2012 Rating 92 To 2018 $28 BE
Hector of Glen Elgin Limited Release Shiraz 2010 Rating 92 To 2030 $60
Vineyard Selection Hunter Valley Verdelho 2012 Rating 90 To 2013 $20
✪ **Hunter Valley Verdelho 2012** Both viticultural and winemaking skills have given this wine far more intensity and length than the norm, the citrus flavours bordering on savoury, so powerful are they. Screwcap. 12.6% alc. **Rating** 90 **To** 2015 $16
✪ **Vineyard Selection Hunter Valley Shiraz 2011** A pleasant, light- to medium-bodied Shiraz, picked at the right moment, and underlining the fact that the Hunter Valley did not suffer the way much of the rest of South Eastern Australia did; there are juicy red and black fruit flavours supported by fine, persistent tannins on the medium-bodied palate, giving balance and length. Screwcap. 13.4% alc. **Rating** 90 **To** 2017 $20
Pokolbin Dry Red Shiraz 2011 Rating 90 To 2019 $25
Cellar Door Release Mudgee Sangiovese 2011 Rating 90 To 2016 $25
Cellar Door Release Hunter Valley Late Picked Verdelho 2012 Rating 90 To 2016 $20 BE

♟♟♟♟ **Hunter Valley Semillon Sauvignon Blanc 2012** Unusually, both components
✪ come from the Hunter Valley. The ripe citrus fruit on the fore-palate is attractive enough, but it is the finish that defines the wine, with its urgent drive of unsweetened lemon and lime juice. Full of interest, and good value. Screwcap. 11.2% alc. **Rating** 89 **To** 2014 $16

Turkey Flat ★★★★★

Bethany Road, Tanunda, SA 5352 **Region** Barossa Valley
T (08) 8563 2851 **www.**turkeyflat.com.au **Open** 7 days 11–5
Winemaker Mark Bulman **Est.** 1990 **Dozens** 20 000 **Vyds** 47.83ha
The establishment date of Turkey Flat is given as 1990 but it might equally well have been 1870 (or thereabouts), when the Schulz family purchased the Turkey Flat vineyard, or 1847, when the vineyard was first planted to the very old shiraz that still grows there today alongside 8ha of equally old grenache. Plantings have since expanded significantly, now comprising

shiraz (24.04ha), grenache (10.5ha), cabernet sauvignon (5.89ha), mourvedre (3.7ha), and smaller plantings of marsanne, viognier and dolcetto. Following the dissolution of Peter and Christie's marriage, Peter sold his share of the business to Christie, and ceased to have any involvement after Jan 2013. The only comfort for Peter was the continued involvement of the Schulz family through fifth-generation sons William, Alex and Oliver. Exports to the UK, the US and other major markets.

ΨΨΨΨΨ Barossa Valley Shiraz 2010 Strong crimson-purple; one of the best Turkey Flat Shirazs to date; the palate is exceedingly complex and very intense, yet ends with a burst of red and black fruits to accompany all that has gone before. It could be mistaken for a wine from a cooler climate, such is its length and balance, the finish full of joy. Screwcap. 14.5% alc. **Rating** 97 **To** 2030 $40

Single Vineyard The Twist Barossa Valley Shiraz 2010 A decidedly lifted and aromatic bouquet, showing floral and dried herb notes, alongside essency and ripe red fruits; the palate is a little tannic, yet extremely persistent on the finish. A sleeper, with time in the cellar an absolute must. Screwcap. 14% alc. **Rating** 95 **To** 2025 $80 BE

Barossa Valley Sparkling Shiraz NV Blend no. 7, released Nov '12. One of very few sparkling Shirazs made from top-quality shiraz, given time in cask before tiraging, then extended time on lees, and usually some reserve wines. A minimum dosage is the icing on the cake; will benefit from further time in bottle, but it's not essential. Crown seal. 14% alc. **Rating** 95 **To** 2020 $40

✪ **Barossa Valley Rose 2012** Bright puce; both the fragrant, perfumed bouquet and lively palate express red fruits to the exclusion of all else: strawberry, raspberry and red cherries; the flavours are remarkably persistent, extending well into the aftertaste. Lovely rose. Screwcap. 13% alc. **Rating** 94 **To** 2013 $20

Single Vineyard The Conqueror Barossa Valley Shiraz 2010 Impenetrable colour; a dark and brooding bouquet of black fruits, saltbush, ironstone and fruitcake spices; the palate is muscular and deeply fruited, with chewy tannins a feature alongside ample layers of sweet fruit; long, luscious and intense, this is simply more of everything. Screwcap. 14.5% alc. **Rating** 94 **To** 2022 $80 BE

Butchers Block Red 2010 Has held its colour very well, with no change since tasted in February. The tasting note remains the same, as does its long future, so I adopt it here. Part of the grapes come from the home vineyard that has some of the oldest vines in the Barossa. The wine has the drive, focus and intensity often missing from this Barossa blend; that said, there are both black and distinctly red fruit components, and the tannins are firm. Give it 10 years, then line it up with a top Rhone Valley example. Outrageous value. Screwcap. 14.5% alc. **Rating** 94 **To** 2030 $20

ΨΨΨΨΫ Barossa Valley Shiraz 2011 Rating 92 **To** 2020 $42 BE

Single Vineyard The Great Barossa Valley Shiraz 2010 Rating 92 **To** 2020 $80 BE

Barossa Valley Cabernet Sauvignon 2011 Rating 90 **To** 2018 $40 BE

Barossa Valley Mourvedre 2011 Rating 90 **To** 2020 $32 BE

Turner's Crossing Vineyard ★★★★★

747 Old Bridgewater-Serpentine Road, Serpentine, Vic 3517 **Region** Bendigo
T 0427 843 528 **www**.turnerscrossing.com **Open** Not
Winemaker Sergio Carlei **Est.** 1998 **Dozens** 6000 **Vyds** 42ha

The name of this outstanding vineyard comes from local farmers crossing the Loddon River in the mid to late 1800s on their way to the nearest town. The vineyard was planted in 1999 by former corporate executive and lecturer in the business school at La Trobe University, Paul Jenkins. However, Paul's experience as a self-taught viticulturist dates back to '85, when he established his first vineyard at Prospect Hill, planting all the vines himself. The grapes from both vineyards have gone to a who's who of winemakers in Central Victoria, but an increasing amount is being made under the Turner's Crossing label, not surprising given the exceptional quality of the wines. Phil Bennett and winemaker Sergio Carlei have joined Paul as co-owners of the vineyard, with Sergio putting his money where his winemaking mouth is. Exports to the UK, the US, Canada, Taiwan, Singapore and China.

🍷🍷🍷🍷🍷 The Cut Shiraz 2010 Medium to full red-purple; a full-bodied Shiraz with a panoply of predominantly black fruits (blackberry to the fore) together with spiced plum and licorice; the tannins are ripe and plentiful, the oak well balanced. Diam. 14.9% alc. **Rating** 95 **To** 2030 $90
Bendigo Cabernet Shiraz 2010 The colour is an excellent purple-crimson, deep but bright, and there is an extremely attractive meeting of minds between the blend components, each playing off the other, pure fruits all to the fore. Screwcap. 14.5% alc. **Rating** 95 **To** 2030 $69

🍷🍷🍷🍷🍷 Bendigo Cabernet Sauvignon 2008 **Rating** 91 **To** 2023 $30

Twisted Gum Wines

2271 Eukey Road, Ballandean, Qld 4382 **Region** Granite Belt
T (07) 4684 1282 **www.**twistedgum.com.au **Open** W'ends & public hols 10–4, or by appt
Winemaker Andy Williams (Contract) **Est.** 2007 **Dozens** 600 **Vyds** 2.8ha
Tim and Michelle Coelli bring diverse and interesting backgrounds to this venture. During his university days in the early 1980s Tim began reading weekly wine columns of a certain journalist and bought recommended red wines from Wynns and Peter Lehmann, liked the wines, and with wife Michelle 'bought dozens and dozens ...'. Tim became a research economist, and during periods of living and working in Europe, he and Michelle became well acquainted with the wines of France, Spain and Italy. She has a degree in agricultural science which, she says, 'has not been well utilised because four children came along (currently aged 5 to 16)'. When they found a beautiful 40ha bush property on a ridge near Ballandean (at an altitude of 900m) with vines already planted, they did not hesitate. The vineyard was in need of TLC, and this has been provided in various ways, including the spreading of mulch under the vines to retain moisture, suppress weeds and improve soil structure.

🍷🍷🍷🍷🍷 Granite Belt Shiraz 2010 Deep purple-red; a superior vintage, with abundant black fruits on its bouquet and medium- to full-bodied palate, where plum, blackberry and black cherry all have free rein, positive tannins securing the future. Screwcap. 14% alc. **Rating** 91 **To** 2018 $25
Granite Belt Shiraz Cabernet Sauvignon 2010 Good crimson-purple; shiraz appears to be the dominant partner in the blend, with the signposts of blackberry and black cherry, and also the soft, fleshy palate, with its ripe tannins. Screwcap. 14% alc. **Rating** 91 **To** 2020 $25

🍷🍷🍷🍷 Granite Belt Chardonnay 2011 **Rating** 87 **To** 2013 $20
Granite Belt Shiraz 2011 **Rating** 87 **To** 2016 $25

Two Bud Spur

1033 Woodbridge Hill Road, Gardners Bay, Tas 7112 **Region** Southern Tasmania
T (03) 6234 4252 **www.**twobudspur.com.au **Open** Not
Winemaker Winstead (Neil Snare) **Est.** 1996 **Dozens** 300 **Vyds** 2.2ha
Marine scientists Craig Mundy and Karen Miller purchased Two Bud Spur vineyard in 2006 as a stress release from their day jobs (they still work full-time, managing the vineyard in their spare time). Their viticultural expertise came from voracious reading of books and scientific literature, and the management of a nearby 0.5 pinot vineyard in the lead-up to the '06 vintage, an experience that led directly to their purchase of Two Bud Spur. This vineyard has had a chequered history, with its present name between 1996 and '03, then Grandview Vineyard '04 to '06, and from '07 onwards back to its original name. The vineyard had been run organically, but with disastrous results: disease, weeds, nutrients, canopy management and pruning all required attention, as did the boundary fences and not-quite-complete trellis. Craig and Karen were emboldened by the fact that, as they say, 'it couldn't get much worse, so there was not much risk of ruining anything'. They depict a two-bud spur, the base architecture for all spur-pruned vineyards, on their label.

ŶŶŶŶ♀ **Nouveau 2012** A cuckoo in the nest, made from 100% gamay using the
✪   Beaujolais technique of carbonic maceration for a week or so, followed by a wild
         yeast fermentation. Light crimson-purple, its Nouveau name signalling a wine
         designed for early drinking, with savoury wild cherry and raspberry fruit; there
         are no tannins or oak to get in the way, and the wine is very well made. Screwcap.
         11.8% alc. **Rating** 92 **To** 2014 $22

ŶŶŶŶ **Pinot Noir 2010 Rating** 88 **To** 2014 $30

Two Dorks Estate   ★★★★

PO Box 24032, Melbourne, Vic 3001 **Region** Heathcote
T 0409 134 332 **Open** Not
Winemaker Mark Bladon **Est.** 2001 **Dozens** 50 **Vyds** 2ha
Owners Mark Bladon and wife Nektaria Achimastos (described by Mark as 'Vineyard
Goddess') have an exceptionally keen sense of humour. Having chosen a site in the southern
end of Heathcote off the Cambrian soil ('In truth, the land in the area is not the best,' Mark
admits), they planted 2ha of dry-grown vines in 2001. The ensuing seven years of drought
meant that development of the vines has been painstakingly slow, and simultaneously
demanding of much TLC and that sense of humour. The vineyard is predominantly shiraz,
with a patch of viognier and 0.5ha of cabernet sauvignon and merlot. The frost, drought, fire
and brimstone of '09 meant no estate-grown wine from that year, and all replacement vines
will be shiraz. Mark has given the Vineyard Goddess a yellow card, but acknowledges that 'to
be fair, even Jesus – an acknowledged miracle worker, wine-wise – needed water to make
the stuff!'

ŶŶŶŶ♀ **Heathcote Shiraz 2011** Light to medium red-purple; unusually, no '10 was
         released ('not good enough'), yet this wine has made light of the challenges of the
         vintage. There is an abundance of juicy red and black fruits and warm spices; has
         excellent length, line and balance. Screwcap. 13.2% alc. **Rating** 92 **To** 2025 $27

Two Hands Wines   ★★★★★

Neldner Road, Marananga, SA 5355 **Region** Barossa Valley
T (08) 8562 4566 **www.**twohandswines.com **Open** 7 days 10–5
Winemaker Matthew Wenk **Est.** 2000 **Dozens** 50 000 **Vyds** 15ha
The 'hands' in question are those of SA businessmen Michael Twelftree and Richard Mintz,
Michael in particular having extensive experience in marketing Australian wine in the US
(for other producers). On the principle that if big is good, bigger is better, the style of the
wines has been aimed squarely at the palate of Robert Parker Jr and *Wine Spectator*'s Harvey
Steiman. Grapes are sourced from the Barossa Valley (where the business has 15ha of shiraz),
McLaren Vale, Clare Valley, Langhorne Creek and Padthaway. The retention of cork closures,
the emphasis on sweet fruit, and the soft tannin structure all signify the precise marketing
strategy of what is a very successful business. Exports to the US and other major markets.

ŶŶŶŶŶ **The Wolf Clare Valley Riesling 2012** Quartz-green; a wine that already reflects
         the outstanding vintage in the Clare and Eden Valleys, brimful of luscious lemon
         and lime fruit wrapped around an inner core of mineral/slate. Screwcap. 12.5% alc.
         Rating 94 **To** 2027 $25
         Lily's Garden McLaren Vale Shiraz 2011 Deeply coloured, and offering an
         array of ripe black fruits, licorice, bitter chocolate and some sappy complexity; the
         palate is medium to full-bodied, fleshy, and showing fresh acidity, and is ultimately
         in complete harmony and balance. Cork. 14.8% alc. **Rating** 94 **To** 2022 $60 BE
         Harry & Edward's Garden Langhorne Creek Shiraz 2010 Bright crimson-
         purple; bravely tries to make light of its alcohol burden, and almost succeeds;
         certainly, there is more light and shade than in the Bella's Garden, and the tannins
         are nicely balanced, leaving room for the blackberry and plum fruit to express
         itself. Cork. 15.5% alc. **Rating** 94 **To** 2025 $60

Samantha's Garden Clare Valley Shiraz 2010 Unashamedly full-bodied, but has good balance, texture and structure to its bedrock of blackberry/blackcurrant fruit; well-handled tannins and oak also add to a wine destined for a long life, cork permitting. 14.8% alc. **Rating** 94 **To** 2030 $60

Twelftree Blewitt Springs McLaren Vale Grenache 2010 Some colour development, although bright and clear. A very elegant and truly refined Grenache with red berry/cherry fruits, and a sprinkle of spice. Screwcap. 14.5% alc. **Rating** 94 **To** 2020 $45

Twelftree Greenock Barossa Valley Grenache 2010 I am a simple chap, and read in wonderment Michael Twelftree's description of the bouquet, thus I see plums, spiced if you prefer, and a palate that is, as suggested, full and even, with a long finish. Most of all, it doesn't have the confection character of many Barossa Valley Grenaches. Screwcap. 15% alc. **Rating** 94 **To** 2020 $45

ΨΨΨΨΨ **The Boy Eden Valley Riesling 2012** The virtual absence of any colour suggests
✪ whole bunch pressing and free-run juice, talismans for the future of the wine; it is so perfectly balanced it will likely be drunk well before it reaches adulthood. Screwcap. 11.5% alc. **Rating** 93 **To** 2032 $25

Lily's Garden McLaren Vale Shiraz 2010 **Rating** 93 **To** 2030 $60

Sophie's Garden Padthaway Shiraz 2010 **Rating** 93 **To** 2020 $60

Twelftree barr Eden Barossa Shiraz Mataro 2012 **Rating** 93 **To** 2022 $35

✪ **Brave Faces Barossa Valley Grenache Shiraz Mataro 2011** Light, clear crimson; the fragrant red berry bouquet leads into a light- to medium-bodied palate with better fruit expression than most such blends from this vintage; supple mouthfeel to a light- to medium-bodied wine makes for enjoyable early drinking. Screwcap. 14.3% alc. **Rating** 92 **To** 2018 $27

Bella's Garden Barossa Valley Shiraz 2010 **Rating** 91 **To** 2025 $60

Max's Garden Heathcote Shiraz 2010 **Rating** 91 **To** 2025 $60

Twelftree Gomersal Grenache 2010 **Rating** 91 **To** 2017 $45

Twelftree Greenock Grenache Mataro 2010 **Rating** 91 **To** 2017 $35

✪ **Sexy Beast McLaren Vale Cabernet Sauvignon 2011** It's not easy to see how McLaren Vale cabernet could achieve this ripeness in '11, but it obviously has, with awesome viticulture and winemaking providing the answer; blackcurrant, dark chocolate fruit and tannins are in plentiful supply on the palate and finish. Screwcap. 14.8% alc. **Rating** 91 **To** 2018 $27

✪ **Angels' Share McLaren Vale Shiraz 2011** Full purple-red; some clever footwork in the vineyard and winery alike has produced a medium- to full-bodied wine with no shortage of fruit flavour or extract; just a little chunky, perhaps. Screwcap. 14.5% alc. **Rating** 90 **To** 2020 $27

Twelftree Blewitt Springs Shiraz 2010 **Rating** 90 **To** 2030 $60

2 Mates
★★★★☆

Cnr Kangarilla Road/Foggo Road, McLaren Vale, SA 5171 **Region** McLaren Vale
T 0411 111 198 **www.2mates.com.au Open** 7 days 11–5
Winemaker Matt Rechner, Mark Venable, David Minear **Est.** 2003 **Dozens** 500
The two mates are Mark Venable and David Minear, who say, 'Over a big drink in a small bar in Italy a few years back, we talked about making "our perfect Australian Shiraz". When we got back, we decided to have a go.' The wine ('05) was duly made, and won a silver medal at the *Decanter Magazine* World Wine Awards in London, in some exalted company.

ΨΨΨΨΨ **McLaren Vale Shiraz 2010** Part of the grapes came from 140-year-old vines, the other from much younger vines; the wine is an undeniably full-bodied and powerful blend of black fruits, regional dark chocolate, savoury tannins and oak – but is not alcoholic. Screwcap. 15% alc. **Rating** 94 **To** 2025 $30

ΨΨΨΨΨ **McLaren Vale Sparkling Shiraz NV** **Rating** 90 **To** 2016 $19

ΨΨΨΨ
✪
Adelaide Hills Sauvignon Blanc 2012 Straw-green; shelters at the grassy end of the sauvignon blanc spectrum, with snow pea, capsicum and herb aromas and flavours, but surprises with the length of its palate and finish. Well priced. Screwcap. 12% alc. **Rating** 89 **To** 2014 $15

201 ★★★★

PO Box 731, Caringbah, NSW 1495 **Region** Hunter Valley
T 0420 905 608 **www**.201.com.au **Open** Not
Winemaker Scott Stephens **Est.** 1998 **Dozens** 750 **Vyds** 4ha

Yet another winery with a numeric name giving book indexers and sommeliers nightmares, but better than the unpronounceable GPS co-ordinates used by another winery. Owners and partners Barbara Smith and Geoff Schippers purchased the 4ha former Rothbury Ridge vineyard in 2006. At that stage it had a quixotic planting of 1.6ha of durif and 1.2ha of chambourcin dating back to the early 1990s, when both varieties were uncommon, and the new owners sensibly decided to plant an additional 0.6ha each of semillon and barbera. It is a weekend retreat for Barbara and Geoff, who have busy lives in Sydney.

ΨΨΨΨΩ
Semi Semi 2012 Quartz-white; accurately described on the back label as off-dry Semillon, even if the front label is out of the *Times* crossword; attractive sweet lemon juice fruit flavours perfectly cut by acidity; leaves the mouth fresh. Screwcap. 8.8% alc. **Rating** 90 **To** 2020 $18

Two Rivers ★★★★☆

2 Yarrawa Road, Denman, NSW 2328 **Region** Hunter Valley
T (02) 6547 2556 **www**.tworiverswines.com.au **Open** 7 days 11–4
Winemaker First Creek Winemaking Services **Est.** 1988 **Dozens** 9000 **Vyds** 68.43ha

A significant part of the viticultural scene in the Upper Hunter Valley, with almost 70ha of vineyards, involving a total investment of around $7 million. Part of the fruit is sold under long-term contracts, and part is made for the expanding winemaking and marketing operations of Two Rivers, the chief brand of Inglewood Vineyards. The emphasis is on Chardonnay and Semillon, and the wines have been medal winners at the Hunter Valley Wine Show. It is also a partner in the Tulloch business, together with the Tulloch and Angove families, and supplies much of the grapes for the Tulloch label. A contemporary cellar door adds significantly to the appeal of the Upper Hunter Valley as a wine-tourist destination.

ΨΨΨΨΨ
✪
Stones Throw Hunter Valley Semillon 2012 Pale straw-green; fully mature vines and skilled contract winemaking provide a zesty, tangy lemon zest, lemon juice and lemongrass trifecta of flavours wrapped around a core of crisp acidity. Exceptional value. Screwcap. 10.5% alc. **Rating** 94 **To** 2027 $16

ΨΨΨΨΩ
✪
Reserve Hunter Valley Chardonnay 2012 Early picking and some fast, skilled, footwork in the winery has produced a startlingly incisive Chardonnay with some of the indicia expected of very cool-grown wine; lemon, lime and grapefruit flavours have absorbed the oak, leaving room for a last-gasp touch of white peach to come through. Screwcap. 12.8% alc. **Rating** 93 **To** 2017 $24

✪
Semillon Sauvignon Blanc 2012 An 85/15% blend of Hunter Valley semillon and Adelaide Hills sauvignon blanc. Light straw-green; a wholly logical fusion of varietal and regional contributions, with a seamless river of lemongrass, citrus and passionfruit aromas and flavours; the palate has excellent length, and all up this is a great outcome from a difficult vintage in both regions. Screwcap. 11.5% alc. **Rating** 90 **To** 2014 $16

ΨΨΨΨ
✪
Hidden Hive Hunter Valley Verdelho 2012 At the lemon juice end of the spectrum, which intensified the flavours and draws out the finish, making an ideal summer seafood, fish and chips wine. Screwcap. 12.5% alc. **Rating** 89 **To** 2014 $16

✪
Rocky Crossing Hunter Valley Cabernet Sauvignon 2011 Good hue; matured in French and American oak; the bouquet is impressive, the palate with cassis and earth flavours, the tannins just a little edgy. Good value. Screwcap. 13.3% alc. **Rating** 89 **To** 2016 $16

Twofold ★★★★★

142 Beulah Road, Norwood, SA 5067 (postal) **Region** Various
T (02) 9572 7285 **Open** Not
Winemaker Tim Stock, Nick Stock, Neil Pike (Contract) **Est.** 2002 **Dozens** 800
This is the venture of brothers Nick and Tim Stock, both of whom have had a varied background in the wine industry (primarily at the marketing end, whether as sommeliers or in wholesale) and both of whom have excellent palates. Their contacts have allowed them to source single vineyard Rieslings from Sevenhill in the Clare and Eden valleys, a single vineyard Shiraz from Heathcote, and an Eden Vineyard Riesling. As one might expect, the quality of the wines is excellent. No wines received for the *2014 Wine Companion*, but a five-star rating has been maintained.

Tynan Wines ★★★★

PO Box 652, Torquay, Vic 3228 **Region** Various
T 0402 442 614 **www.**tynanwines.com **Open** Not
Winemaker Mark Tynan **Est.** 2009 **Dozens** 400
This is the virtual winery business of Mark Tynan. He sources grapes from regions particularly suited to the variety in question, including chardonnay and pinot noir from Orange for the very successful traditional method sparkling wines, the table wines being Hunter Valley Verdelho, Canberra District Pinot Noir and Mudgee Cabernet Sauvignon. Mark has been making the wines in conjunction with Peter Wendt at Pierre's Wines in the Hunter Valley, and hopes to continue the journey with Scott Ireland at Provenance Wines in Geelong in the future.

🍷🍷🍷🍷 **Methode Traditionelle Hunter Valley Sparkling Shiraz 2009** Youthful colour; there is no clue how long the wine spent on yeast lees, and the fruit flavours are fresh; the balance of the wine, and its low dosage, are commendable. Would richly repay further time in bottle. Crown seal. 13.5% alc. **Rating** 92 **To** 2016 $40
Orange Brut 2010 A 60/40% chardonnay/pinot noir blend from grapes grown at the Mayfield Vineyard, made in the traditional method; the flavours are fresh, with just a touch of bready complexity, the overall impact quite delicate and seductive. Surprise packet. Crown seal. 12% alc. **Rating** 91 **To** 2014 $40
Orange Sparkling Rose 2010 Despite its fully pink colour, is a 50/50% chardonnay/pinot noir blend from the Mayfield Vineyard, made using the traditional method; the flowery, fragrant red fruit bouquet is essentially replayed on the gently sweet palate; will have many admirers. Crown seal. 12% alc. **Rating** 91 **To** 2015 $40

🍷🍷🍷 **Hunter Valley Verdelho 2012** Rating 89 To 2014 $25
Mudgee Cabernet Sauvignon 2011 Rating 89 To 2017 $30
Canberra Pinot Noir 2011 Rating 88 To 2015 $20

Tyrrell's ★★★★★

Broke Road, Pokolbin, NSW 2321 **Region** Hunter Valley
T (02) 4993 7000 **www.**tyrrells.com.au **Open** Mon–Sat 8.30–5, Sun 10–4
Winemaker Andrew Spinaze, Mark Richardson **Est.** 1858 **Dozens** 400 000
Vyds 158.22ha
One of the most successful family wineries, a humble operation for the first 110 years of its life that has grown out of all recognition over the past 40 years. In 2003 it cleared the decks by selling its Long Flat range of wines for an eight-figure sum, allowing it to focus on its premium, super-premium and ultra-premium wines: Vat 1 Semillon is one of the most dominant wines in the Australian show system, and Vat 47 Chardonnay is one of the pacesetters for this variety. It has an awesome portfolio of single vineyard Semillons released when 5–6 years old. Its estate plantings are over 116ha in the Hunter Valley, 15ha in the Limestone Coast and 26ha in Heathcote. Exports to all major markets.

πππππ **Vat 1 Hunter Semillon 2006** The display of 14 gold medals and seven trophies on the bottle borders on the vulgar, however richly it deserves this haul. The lemon/mineral flavours are exceptionally fresh and vibrant, lingering for minutes on the finish and aftertaste; a freak wine that will live as long as any red wine of similar age. Screwcap. 10.5% alc. **Rating** 97 **To** 2046 $55

Vat 9 Hunter Shiraz 2011 Bright, clear crimson-purple; from the oldest and best blocks on the estate Ashmans Vineyard, with its striking red volcanic clay soils; hand-picked and fermented in open vats before maturation for 16 months in new and used 2700-litre French casks. However good Johnno's Shiraz may be, this wine has greater intensity, drive and length, with persistent fine tannins and positive but balanced oak. Screwcap. 12.9% alc. **Rating** 97 **To** 2036 $75

Johnno's Basket Pressed Semillon 2012 Pale quartz in colour, the winemaking techniques are a deliberate throwback to yesterday, with basket-pressing, only partial juice clarification, and 'traditional fermentation' (not cold) techniques, all contributing to its special texture. Screwcap. 10.5% alc. **Rating** 96 **To** 2040 $35

Johnno's Shiraz 2011 Its bright, clear crimson-purple colour is striking, and doesn't mislead; the flavours on the light- to medium-bodied palate are juicy and pure, with red and black cherry, and the tannins are fine. Oak is evident, but not the least extractive. Screwcap. 12.5% alc. **Rating** 96 **To** 2031 $49

Vat 1 Hunter Semillon 2012 Sold through the Private Bin Wine Club only as a young wine, the main commercial release 6 years later; lemon juice and lemon curd flavours follow logically from the bouquet, lemony acidity lingering long in the mouth after the wine is swallowed. Screwcap. 10.5% alc. **Rating** 95 **To** 2020 $35

Single Vineyard Stevens Hunter Semillon 2008 Gleaming green-yellow; a classic and wonderfully expressive Hunter bouquet, with lemon curd, toast and straw; the palate is very lively, and while at face value this appears forward, the tension on the finish provides length and complexity, pointing to a healthy future. Already on the march to maturity with a distinct honeyed overlay to the fruit flavours. Screwcap. 11.3% alc. **Rating** 95 **To** 2020 $35

Lunatiq Heathcote Shiraz 2010 Very attractive, gently spiced red and black fruits immediately spring from the bouquet, then lead the energetic and highly focused medium-bodied palate with great fruit purity; the tannins are fine, the finish very long. Screwcap. 14% alc. **Rating** 95 **To** 2030 $35

Winemaker's Selection 4 Acres Shiraz 2011 Rating 94 To 2026 $49

ππππ̣ **Vat 8 Hunter Valley Shiraz Cabernet 2011** Rating 93 To 2026 $70

✪ **Brookdale Hunter Valley Semillon 2012** One of the first Semillons of the vintage to hit the ground, it's true to the season in its predictably taut and razor-sharp style of firm acid, cut grass, lemon and lime. A zesty lunchtime aperitif, or give it a few years to flesh out. Screwcap. 11% alc. **Rating** 91 **To** 2015 $20 TS

✪ **Old Winery Hunter Valley Chardonnay 2012** The varietal fruit is vibrant and clear, with white-flesh stone fruit and citrus to the fore; there is the faintest suggestion of oak that has been carefully kept in check. The best Hunter Valley Chardonnay in its price group. Screwcap. 12.5% alc. **Rating** 90 **To** 2014 $12

Lost Block McLaren Vale Rose 2012 Rating 90 To 2014 $17

Ulithorne   ★★★★★

The Mill at Middleton, 29 Mill Terrace, Middleton, SA 5213 **Region** McLaren Vale
T (08) 8554 2411 **www**.ulithorne.com.au **Open** W'ends & public hols 10–4
Winemaker Rose Kentish, Brian Light **Est.** 1971 **Dozens** 1800
Ulithorne produces small quantities of red wines from selected parcels of grapes from a vineyard in McLaren Vale planted by Rose Kentish's father-in-law, Frank Harrison, over 40 years ago. Rose's dream of making small-batch, high-quality wines from exceptional grapegrowing regions around the world has taken her to France, where she has made a Vermentinu on the island of Corsica and a Rose in Provence under the Ulithorne label.

The cellar door is located in a converted flour mill in Middleton. Exports to the UK, Canada, The Netherlands, Malaysia and China.

ŸŸŸŸŸ Frux Frugis McLaren Vale Shiraz 2010 Proclaims its region of origin with a generous helping of chocolate; the oak, too, has not been spared, and the ripe tannins provide the third leg of the tripod; on repeated retastings the black cherry and plum fruit finally asserts itself. Screwcap. 14.5% alc. Rating 94 To 2025 $45
Chi McLaren Vale Grenache Shiraz 2010 Medium red-purple; every bit as attractive as its bloodlines would suggest, with bright red berry fruits ex the grenache given structure from the shiraz; the two components are at once synergistic and seamless. Screwcap. 14.5% alc. Rating 94 To 2025 $38

ŸŸŸŸ Paternus McLaren Vale Cabernet Shiraz 2010 Rating 88 To 2017 $45

Umamu Estate ★★★★★

PO Box 1269, Margaret River, WA 6285 **Region** Margaret River
T (08) 9757 5058 **www**.umamuestate.com **Open** Not
Winemaker Bruce Dukes (Contract) **Est.** 2005 **Dozens** 4000 **Vyds** 16.3ha
Chief executive Charmaine Saw explains, 'My life has been a journey towards Umamu. An upbringing in both eastern and western cultures, graduating in natural science, training as a chef, combined with a passion for the arts and experience as a management consultant have all contributed to my building the business creatively yet professionally.' The palindrome Umamu, says Charmaine, is inspired by balance and contentment. In practical terms this means an organic approach to viticulture and a deep respect for the terroir. In 1997, Charmaine's parents fell in love with the property and its plantings, dating back to 1978, of cabernet sauvignon (6ha), chardonnay (3.5ha), shiraz (1.7ha), semillon (2.2ha), sauvignon blanc (1.5ha), merlot (0.9ha) and cabernet franc (0.7ha); the maiden vintage under the Umamu label followed in '05. Exports to the UK, Hong Kong, Malaysia and Singapore.

ŸŸŸŸŸ Margaret River Cabernet Sauvignon 2010 Strong purple-crimson; a high-quality, classic Cabernet, with blackcurrant fruit on the one hand, fine-grained, ripe tannins and quality French oak on the other. A faultless, perfectly balanced, wine. Screwcap. 13.3% alc. Rating 96 To 2035 $58

✪ Mac's Chardonnay 2010 Bright green-straw; the bouquet is good, but does not prepare you for the intensity and purity of the palate, where white-flesh stone fruit and grapefruit draw saliva from every corner of the mouth. Great value for a classic wine. Screwcap. 13.5% alc. Rating 95 To 2023 $28
Margaret River Shiraz 2010 Fragrant spice and pepper nuances to the red and black cherry fruit of the bouquet foreshadow a superb, medium-bodied palate, with a long and lingering display of satin-smooth fruit, oak largely a bystander. Screwcap. 13.5% alc. Rating 95 To 2030 $32

✪ Margaret River Sauvignon Blanc Semillon 2010 Light straw-green; a prime example of the way the best of these blends – even where sauvignon blanc is the dominant partner – can age with intense grace. Here ripe citrus and guava fruit has a subtext of spicy oak, which plays little role on the cleansing, bright finish. Screwcap. 13% alc. Rating 94 To 2015 $23

ŸŸŸŸŸ Margaret River Cabernet Merlot 2010 Rating 92 To 2025 $32

Upper Reach ★★★★

77 Memorial Avenue, Baskerville, WA 6056 **Region** Swan Valley
T (08) 9296 0078 **www**.upperreach.com.au **Open** 7 days 11–5
Winemaker Derek Pearse **Est.** 1996 **Dozens** 4000 **Vyds** 8.45ha
This 10ha property on the banks of the upper reaches of the Swan River was purchased by Laura Rowe and Derek Pearse in 1996. The original 4ha vineyard has been expanded, and plantings now include chardonnay, shiraz, cabernet sauvignon, verdelho, semillon, merlot, petit verdot and muscat. All wines are estate-grown. The fish on the label, incidentally, is black bream, which can be found in the pools of the Swan River during the summer months. Upper Reach has won numerous wine show awards in recent years.

ettttt The Gig Shiraz Grenache 2011 Deep, vibrant garnet; the bouquet reveals
confectionery raspberry, blackberry pastille, sage and licorice; medium-bodied
and lively on the palate, with a spicy black pepper note an intriguing element to
conclude. Screwcap. 14% alc. **Rating** 91 **To** 2018 $22 BE
Verdelho 2012 Pale straw, vivid green hue; a fragrant and perfumed bouquet of
mandarin, lime and bath talc; the palate is racy, dry and chalky, fresh and focused,
and ready now. Screwcap. 13% alc. **Rating** 90 **To** 2015 $20 BE
Reserve Swan Valley Shiraz 2010 Concentrated aromas of blackberry pastille,
tar, licorice and leather on the bouquet; the full-bodied palate is thickly textured
and rich, dense and chewy, with light returning on the finish thanks to tangy
acidity. Screwcap. 14% alc. **Rating** 90 **To** 2020 $32 BE

ettt **Reserve Swan Valley Chardonnay 2012** Rating 89 To 2016 $28 BE
Swan Valley Cabernet Sauvignon 2011 Rating 88 To 2016 $30 BE
Swan Valley Petit Verdot 2011 Rating 88 To 2016 $35 BE
Tempranillo 2011 Rating 88 To 2016 $25 BE

Vale Wines

2914 Frankston-Flinders Road, Balnarring, Vic 3926 **Region** Mornington Peninsula
T (03) 5983 1521 **www**.valewines.com.au **Open** 7 days 11–5
Winemaker John and Caroline Vale **Est.** 1991 **Dozens** 400 **Vyds** 1.7ha
After a lifetime in the retail liquor industry, John and Susan Vale took a busman's retirement
by purchasing a grazing property at Balnarring in 1991. After some trial and error the estate
plantings are now riesling, gewurztraminer, tempranillo and durif, the intake supplemented
by the purchase of chardonnay and pinot gris from local growers. The Vales have a continuing
business, Winemaking Supplies & Services Pty Ltd, a winery supply wholesaler. Daughter
Caroline, with a science degree from Melbourne University and a winemaking degree from
CSU, has had a varied international and Australian winemaking career. In 2009 she formally
opened a contract sparkling wine production facility – Mousse and Bead – utilising clients'
estate-grown grapes, estate-grown base wines, or wines sourced from other growers in
the region.

ettttt **Petite Syrah 2010** Dense colour; stacked with dense black fruit aromas and
flavours, and some exotic herbs and spices (including cinnamon) on the palate.
Interesting climate for petite syrah. Screwcap. 13.4% alc. **Rating** 90 **To** 2020 $20

Valhalla Wines

163 All Saints Road, Wahgunyah, Vic 3687 **Region** Rutherglen
T (02) 6033 1438 **www**.valhallawines.com.au **Open** 7 days 10–4
Winemaker Anton Therkildsen **Est.** 2001 **Dozens** 1400 **Vyds** 2.5ha
This is the venture of Anton Therkildsen and wife Antoinette Del Popolo. They acquired
the property in 2001, and in '02 began the planting of shiraz (1.6ha) and durif (0.9ha). They
intend to expand the vineyard with marsanne, viognier, grenache, mourvedre and riesling,
reflecting their primary interest in the wines of the Rhône Valley. For the time being, they
are relying on contract-grown grapes to develop these wine styles. The straw-bale winery was
built in '07, underlining their desire for sustainable viticulture and biodiversity, with minimal
use of sprays and annual planting of cover crops between the rows. A worm farm and the
composting of grape skins and stalks complete the picture.

ettttt **Rutherglen Shiraz 2010** Medium red-purple; a neatly constructed wine, all
about restraint and balance; red fruits drive the bouquet and light- to medium-
bodied palate, will of the wisp tannins and oak doing their job without threatening
the fruit. Nothing to be gained by cellaring the wine, nor is it needed. Screwcap.
13.2% alc. **Rating** 90 **To** 2015 $26

ettt **Rutherglen Marsanne 2011** Rating 89 To 2020 $22
Rutherglen Durif 2010 Rating 87 To 2020 $30

Vasarelli Wines

164 Main Road, McLaren Vale, SA 5171 **Region** McLaren Vale
T (08) 8323 7980 **Open** 7 days 8–5
Winemaker Hamish Seabrook (Contract) **Est.** 1995 **Dozens** 25 000 **Vyds** 33ha
Pasquale (Pat) and Vittoria (Vicky) Vasarelli moved with their parents from Melbourne to McLaren Vale in 1976. They began the establishment of their vineyard, and over the succeeding years increased the area under vine to its present size, planted to semillon, sauvignon blanc, chardonnay, pinot gris, vermentino, shiraz, cabernet sauvignon and merlot. Until '95 the grapes were sold to other producers, but in that year they joined Cellarmaster Wines and the Vasarelli label was born. In a reverse play to the usual pattern, they opened a cellar door in 2009 on a small property they had purchased in '92.

Pasquale's Selection 2010 A blend of cabernet sauvignon, cabernet franc and merlot, not at all common in McLaren Vale, but works well here; how much the high-quality vintage is responsible is anyone's guess, but the bright cassis fruit gives a juicy mouthfeel, augmented by cedary oak and fine tannins. Screwcap. 14% alc. **Rating** 92 **To** 2020 $29

Currency Creek Vermentino 2012 A polished and supple version of vermentino in terms of its structure, but with similar complex citrus zest and skin flavours; ever so faintly dilute. Screwcap. 12.5% alc. **Rating** 89 **To** 2014 $17
Family Reserve McLaren Vale Shiraz 2010 Rating 89 **To** 2018 $25

Vasse Felix

Cnr Tom Cullitty Drive/Caves Road, Cowaramup, WA 6284 **Region** Margaret River
T (08) 9756 5000 **www.vassefelix.com.au Open** 7 days 10–5
Winemaker Virginia Willcock **Est.** 1967 **Dozens** 150 000 **Vyds** 232ha
Vasse Felix was the first winery to be built in Margaret River. Owned and operated by the Holmes à Court family since 1987, Vasse Felix has undergone extensive changes and expansion. In recent years chief winemaker Virginia Willcock has energised the winemaking and viticultural team with her no-nonsense and fierce commitment to quality. The estate vineyards contribute all but a small part of the annual production, and are scrupulously managed, quality the sole driver. There are four ranges of wines: Heytesbury (a Cabernet blend) and Heytesbury Chardonnay; the Estate range of varietal wines; Classic Dry White and Dry Red; then Theatre White and Red. Limited quantities of specialty wines include Cane Cut Semillon, Viognier, Tempranillo and Silver Knight. Exports to all major markets.

Heytesbury Margaret River Chardonnay 2010 Has swept all before it in the wine shows in '11. Multiple small batches were wild-fermented with cloudy juice in 71% new French oak, 29% older, and were lees-stirred for 12 months. Fruit selection was the building block, with a number of high-performing clones. The tactile sensation in the mouth is awe-inspiring, as is the latent power and intensity. State of the art in Australia. Screwcap. 13% alc. **Rating** 97 **To** 2025 $60
Heytesbury Margaret River Chardonnay 2011 Bright straw-green; has the poised elegance that has become the hallmark of Vasse Felix Heytesbury Chardonnay, every component finely detailed and in balance with every other component; it is driven by its stone fruit in the first instance, but with oak and acidity also contributing to the texture and complexity of the wine. Screwcap. 13% alc. **Rating** 96 **To** 2021 $60
Heytesbury 2010 A powerhouse of concentration, wrapped seamlessly together with layers of cassis, red fruits, cedar, crushed leaf and violets; the palate is expansive yet precise, with an impressively long and persistent thread of elegant tannins and balanced acidity; this blend of cabernet sauvignon, petit verdot and malbec is sure to age gracefully. Screwcap. 14.5% alc. **Rating** 96 **To** 2045 $90 BE
Heytesbury 2009 A 69/16/15% blend of cabernet sauvignon, petit verdot and malbec that spent 18 months in 62% new French oak. The tannins resulting from the 30 days' post-fermentation maceration of 60% of the blend are in perfect harmony with the dominant blackcurrant fruit on the long palate. A very good example of a great style. Screwcap. 14.5% alc. **Rating** 96 **To** 2040 $90

✪ **Margaret River Sauvignon Blanc Semillon 2012** Pale straw, vibrant hue; a layered bouquet of straw, citrus, tropical fruits and fresh-crushed nettle aromas; the palate is understated and fine-boned, with delicacy a feature; ultimately finely detailed, harmonious and surprisingly long on the finish; excellent winemaking on display. Screwcap. 12.5% alc. **Rating** 94 **To** 2015 $26 BE

✪ **Margaret River Chardonnay 2011** At once elegant and intense, with a minerally edge to the structure that bodes well for the future, the fruit flavours of nectarine, lemon and peach. Screwcap. 12.5% alc. **Rating** 94 **To** 2019 $29

✪ **Classic Dry Red Margaret River Shiraz Cabernet Sauvignon 2010** Stylish and immaculately balanced, with a vibrancy to sustain the medium- to full-bodied palate over many years to come, a vibrancy promised by the perfumed bouquet, spice, black and red cherry fruit, hints of licorice and pepper accompanying the (French) oak. Screwcap. 14.5% alc. **Rating** 94 **To** 2025 $20

✪ **Margaret River Cabernet Sauvignon Merlot 2010** Clear crimson-purple; Heystesbury may be in another league, but this is a serious, high-quality wine, with intense blackcurrant fruit and persistent savoury tannins running through the palate providing texture and structure for medium- to long-term cellaring. Screwcap. 14.5% alc. **Rating** 94 **To** 2025 $26

Margaret River Cabernet Sauvignon 2010 Rating 94 To 2025 $40 BE

ΨΨΨΨΨ **Classic Dry White Margaret River Semillon Sauvignon Blanc 2012** Light
✪ straw-green; the wine is stacked with lemon/citrus, passionfruit and white-flesh stone fruit, bright and crisp acidity providing both balance and length. Screwcap. 12% alc. **Rating** 91 **To** 2014 $20

✪ **Classic Dry Red Margaret River Shiraz Cabernet Sauvignon 2011**
A bright and effusive offering of this classic Aussie blend, showing the red fruits of shiraz in the region, offset by a little leafy cabernet and cassis; medium-bodied and precise, and ultimately excellent value. Screwcap. 14.5% alc. **Rating** 90 **To** 2017 $19 BE

Cabernet Sauvignon Merlot 2011 Rating 90 To 2018 $26 BE

Verdun Park Wines ★★★

PO Box 41, Verdun, SA 5245 **Region** Adelaide Hills
T (08) 8388 7357 **www.verdunparkwines.com.au Open** Not
Winemaker Michael Sykes **Est.** 2009 **Dozens** 700 **Vyds** 2ha
Verdun Park is owned by Sandy and Bob Voumard (with backgrounds in education and accountancy) and run with the assistance of their daughter Danielle and son-in-law Shaun (viticulturist). The initial release, 2009 Lyla Sauvignon Blanc, was made from specifically selected contract-grown grapes, and went on to win a gold medal at the fiercely contested (for sauvignon blanc) Adelaide Hills Wine Show '09.

ΨΨΨΨ **Adelaide Hills Ruby Rose 2012** Made from 10-year-old shiraz vines, its colour is bright crimson-purple, its mid-palate flavour is rich and ripe – despite the lowish alcohol – and its finish is fruity but dry. Screwcap. 12.5% alc. **Rating** 89 **To** 2013 $20

Veronique ★★★★

PO Box 599, Angaston, SA 5353 **Region** Barossa Valley
T (08) 8565 3214 **www.veroniquewines.com.au Open** Not
Winemaker Domenic Torzi, Peter Manning **Est.** 2004 **Dozens** 1500
Peter Manning, general manager of Angas Park Fruits, and wife Vicki moved to Mt McKenzie in the 1990s. His wine consumption soon focused on Barossa Shiraz, and he quickly became a close drinking partner with Domenic Torzi of all things shiraz. By 2004 the Mannings decided it was high time to produce a Barossa Shiraz of their own, and, with the help of Torzi, sourced grapes from three outstanding blocks. The vineyards also include mataro and grenache (thoroughly excusable in the context) and sauvignon blanc.

ⓎⓎⓎⓎⓎ   **Foundation Barossa Shiraz 2009** Sourced from Veronique's estate vineyards in
✪   Greenock and the Eden Valley, and matured for 30 months in a mix of French and
      American oak. The colour is a vivid, deep purple-crimson, the wine is full-bodied,
      with luscious black fruits in a cocoon of cedary oak, the tannins controlled.
      Compelling value. Screwcap. 14.7% alc. **Rating** 93 **To** 2029 $20

Victory Point Wines ★★★★★

4 Holben Road, Cowaramup, WA 6284 **Region** Margaret River
T 0417 954 6555 **www.**victorypointwines.com **Open** By appt
Winemaker Mark Messenger (Contract) **Est.** 1997 **Dozens** 2500 **Vyds** 14.8ha
Judith and Gary Berson (the latter a partner in the Perth office of a national law firm) have
set their aims high. They have established their vineyard without irrigation, emulating those of
Margaret River pioneers (including Moss Wood). The plantings comprise 2ha chardonnay, the
remainder the Bordeaux varieties, with cabernet sauvignon (6ha), merlot (2ha), cabernet franc
(1.5ha), malbec (0.3ha) and petit verdot (0.3ha). In some vintages, a Petit Verdot and Malbec
Cabernet Franc are made in limited quantities.

ⓎⓎⓎⓎⓎ   Margaret River Chardonnay 2010 Made from the four Dijon Burgundy
      clones plus the Mendoza clone; the quality of the grapes shines through like a
      beacon, the multiple fruit (and oak) flavours welded seamlessly into a coherent
      whole, the palate long and beautifully balanced, the flavours still fresh and
      succulent. Screwcap. 13% alc. Rating 96 To 2023 $40
      The Mallee Root Margaret River Cabernet Sauvignon Malbec Petit
      Verdot 2008 A 33/33/25/9% blend of cabernet sauvignon, malbec, petit verdot
      and merlot. The colour is still bright, and the complex, full-bodied palate has
      abundant black fruits, tannins and oak all in measured support. Will be very long-
      lived. Screwcap. 14% alc. **Rating** 94 **To** 2033 $26

🍇 View Road Wines ★★★

Peacocks Road, Lenswood, SA 5240 **Region** Adelaide Hills
T 0402 180 383 **Open** Not
Winemaker Josh Tuckfield **Est.** 2011 **Dozens** 50
This is the venture of son Josh and father Brian Tuckfield. While working as a sommelier in
Maximillian's restaurant in the Adelaide Hills, Josh came to know many winemakers well.
He was fascinated by the wines made by Tom Shobbrook, and worked as an unpaid cellar
hand before taking the plunge and venturing into micro-commerical winemaking in the
challenging 2011 vintage. Largely following the Shobbrook approach of natural winemaking,
the grapes were wild-fermented in a blue poly picking bin, and left on skins for nine
weeks before being pressed and gravity-fed into an old French oak barrique. No additions
of any kind were made other than minimal SO_2. All things considered, the outcome was
sufficiently good to encourage Josh to increase his winemaking to include Chardonnay from
Piccadilly Valley, Sagrantino from McLaren Vale and Shiraz from Blewitt Springs; he will build
production up to 500 dozen over the next few years. (For the record, I knew nothing of the
background when I tasted the wine.)

ⓎⓎⓎⓎ   **Picked by my Wife Langhorne Creek Sangiovese 2011** 'Made with love
      and a little frustration', says the label, but with no further explanation. Light red-
      purple, little more than rose, the wine is predictably light-bodied, but does have
      authentic red cherry/raspberry fruit nuances, the tannins fine. Cork. 12.6% alc.
      Rating 88 **To** 2014 $16

Vigna Bottin ★★★☆

14 Clifton Court, McLaren Vale, SA 5171 (postal) **Region** McLaren Vale
T 0414 562 956 **www.**vignabottin.com.au **Open** Not
Winemaker Paolo Bottin **Est.** 2004 **Dozens** 650 **Vyds** 16ha

The Bottin family migrated to Australia in 1954 from Treviso in northern Italy, where they were grapegrowers. The family began growing grapes in McLaren Vale in 1970, focusing on mainstream varieties for sale to wineries in the region. When son Paolo and wife Maria made a trip back to Italy in '98, they were inspired to do more, and, says Paolo, 'My love for barbera and sangiovese was sealed during a vintage in Pavia. I came straight home to plant both varieties in our family plot. My father was finally happy!' They now trade under the catchy phrase 'Italian Vines, Australian Wines'.

♥♥♥♥♡ McLaren Vale Shiraz 2010 Dense, dark purple; nicknamed BJ in the winery, standing for Bone Juice (an expression I've never heard before), and coming with an instruction 'drink it with meat'; having tasted the wine, with its full-bodied whirlpool of black fruits, bitter chocolate and ripe tannins, I understand BJ and agree with the instruction. Screwcap. 14.5% alc. **Rating** 91 **To** 2030 $30

♥♥♥♥ McLaren Vale Sangiovese 2010 Rating 89 **To** 2015 $26
McLaren Vale Vermentino 2011 Rating 88 **To** 2014 $22

Viking Wines   ★★★☆

4 Coswell Court, Torquay, Qld 4655 (postal) **Region** Barossa Valley
T (07) 4125 4368 **www.**vikingwines.com **Open** Not
Winemaker Kym Teusner (Contract) **Est.** 1994 **Dozens** 1500 **Vyds** 10ha
With 50-year-old, dry-grown and near-organic vineyards yielding 1–1.5 tonnes per acre in Marananga, Viking Wines was 'discovered' by Robert Parker Jr with inevitable consequences for the price of its top Shiraz. There are 5ha of shiraz and 3ha of cabernet sauvignon. The Odin's Honour wines (made by sister company Tord-Viking Wines) also come from old (20–100 years) dry-grown vines around Marananga and Greenock. Exports to Denmark, Sweden, Singapore and Hong Kong.

♥♥♥♥♡ Grand Barossa Valley Shiraz 2010 Dense, deep purple-crimson; has a similar array of black fruits, licorice, dark chocolate and mocha to the '11, but is of brighter character thanks to the '10 vintage; it has also reacted well to its 18 months in French and American oak, all the fruit, oak and tannins in balance on the medium-bodied palate, the alcohol no issue. Screwcap. 15% alc. **Rating** 91 **To** 2025 $25

♥♥♥♥ Barossa Valley Shiraz Cabernet 2010 Rating 89 **To** 2025 $25
Grand Barossa Valley Shiraz 2011 Rating 87 **To** 2015 $25

Vinaceous   ★★★★☆

49 Bennett Street, East Perth, WA 6004 (postal) **Region** Various
T (08) 9221 4666 **www.**vinaceous.com.au **Open** Not
Winemaker Gavin Berry, Michael Kerrigan, Elena Brooks (Contract) **Est.** 2007
Dozens 16 000
This is the somewhat quirky venture of wine marketer Nick Stacy (West Cape Howe), Michael Kerrigan (winemaker/partner Hay Shed Hill) and Gavin Berry (winemaker/partner West Cape Howe). The brand is primarily directed at the US market, which took 90% of the four wines in the first release, the remaining 10% shared among all other markets. The wines are not primarily sourced from WA, as one might expect, but variously from McLaren Vale, Barossa Valley and the Limestone Coast, with a Verdelho, and the possibility of a Reserve Shiraz, from WA. The wines are coupled with an ornate, turn-of-the-19th-century label. Exports to the US, Canada, Denmark, the Philippines, Thailand, Singapore and Hong Kong.

♥♥♥♥♥ Raconteur Barossa Valley Cabernet Sauvignon 2010 From 80-year-old
✪   vines (a rarity in the Barossa Valley), hand-picked, open-fermented and matured in used French barriques; throws all the focus on the elegant, medium-bodied palate with its clear cassis varietal expression. A tribute to the vintage (or vice versa). Screwcap. 14.5% alc. **Rating** 94 **To** 2020 $25

ΨΨΨΨΨ **Snake Charmer McLaren Vale Shiraz 2010** Deep crimson-purple; west meets
✪ east with this archetypal McLaren Vale Shiraz; its medium-bodied black and red
fruits have absorbed the 12 months in French and American oak, and the tannins
provide finely pitched support in the long palate. A serious wine with a fun label.
Screwcap. 14.5% alc. **Rating** 93 **To** 2020 $25

✪ **Divine Light Margaret River Sauvignon Blanc 2012** Pale quartz-green;
oak has played no part in shaping this wine, allowing the varietal expression of
sauvignon blanc free rein, with gentle tropical/lychee on the fore-palate, citrus on
the back-palate and finish. Screwcap. 12% alc. **Rating** 90 **To** 2014 $21

Vinden Estate ★★★☆

17 Gillards Road, Pokolbin, NSW 2320 **Region** Hunter Valley
T (02) 4998 7410 **www**.vindenestate.com.au **Open** Wed–Sun 10–5
Winemaker Guy Vinden, John Baruzzi (Consultant) **Est.** 1998 **Dozens** 4500 **Vyds** 6.5ha
Sandra and Guy Vinden have a beautiful home and cellar door, landscaped gardens and
a vineyard that includes shiraz (2.5ha), merlot and alicante bouschet (2ha each), with the
Brokenback mountain range in the distance. The wines are made onsite, using estate-grown
red grapes; semillon and chardonnay are purchased from other growers. The reds are open-
fermented, hand-plunged and basket-pressed.

ΨΨΨΨΨ **Hunter Valley Semillon 2012** Quartz-green; charged with lemon/lemongrass/
✪ lime fruit, with as much fruit as a '12 Riesling; delicious now, but has the acidity
to cruise through the next 5–10 years, adding further lustre (and higher points).
Screwcap. 10.5% alc. **Rating** 93 **To** 2022 $20

ΨΨΨΨ **Hunter Valley Semillon Sauvignon Blanc 2012 Rating** 89 **To** 2014 $23
Estate Reserve Hunter Valley Verdelho 2012 Rating 89 **To** 2014 $23
Basket Press Hunter Valley Shiraz 2011 Rating 89 **To** 2019 $30

Vinea Marson ★★★★★

411 Heathcote-Rochester Road, Heathcote, Vic 3523 **Region** Heathcote
T (03) 5433 2768 **www**.vineamarson.com **Open** By appt
Winemaker Mario Marson **Est.** 2000 **Dozens** 2000 **Vyds** 7.12ha
Owner-winemaker Mario Marson spent many years as the winemaker viticulturist with
the late Dr John Middleton at the celebrated Mount Mary. He purchased the Vinea Marson
property in 1999, on the eastern slopes of the Mt Camel Range, and has planted shiraz and
viognier, plus Italian varieties sangiovese, nebbiolo, barbera and refosco dal peduncolo rosso.
Since leaving Mount Mary, he has undertaken vintage work at Isole e Olena in Tuscany,
worked as winemaker at Jasper Hill vineyard, and as consultant and winemaker for Stefani
Estate. Exports to Sweden and China.

ΨΨΨΨΨ **Grazia 2011** A 40/40/10/10% blend of pinot bianco, sauvignon blanc, friulano
✪ and malvasia d'Istria, this tribute to the textural whites of Friuli in Italy offers
savoury aromas of lemon curd, sage, crushed chalk and hazelnut; deeply textured
and with an attractive marzipan note running through its core, there is a softness
and suppleness that is beguiling, though thoroughly different on many levels.
Diam. 12.5% alc. **Rating** 94 **To** 2017 $24 BE

Rose 2011 Made absolutely bone dry in the style of Southern France or
Northern Spain; despite that dryness and colour, there is a pure line of spicy fruit
which runs the length of the palate. Screwcap. 13.5% alc. **Rating** 94 **To** 2014 $24

ΨΨΨΨΨ **Viognier 2011** Pale green-straw; apparently barrel-fermented in used oak; it has
✪ complex aromas and – in particular – flavours, with spicy/savoury nuances to the
apricot and peach fruit; good length and balance. Diam. 13.5% alc. **Rating** 92
To 2014 $24

Syrah 2010 Rating 92 **To** 2018 $44 BE
Syrah 2009 Rating 92 **To** 2018 $44 BE

Sangiovese 2009 Rating 92 To 2016 $38 BE
Nebbiolo 2009 Rating 91 To 2016 $44 BE
Sangiovese 2010 Rating 90 To 2016 $38 BE

Vinifera Wines

194 Henry Lawson Drive, Mudgee, NSW 2850 **Region** Mudgee
T (02) 6372 2461 **www.**viniferawines.com.au **Open** Mon–Sat 10–5, Sun 10–4
Winemaker Jacob Stein **Est.** 1997 **Dozens** 1200 **Vyds** 12ha
Having lived in Mudgee for 15 years, Tony McKendry (a regional medical superintendent) and wife Debbie succumbed to the lure; they planted their small (1.5ha) vineyard in 1995. In Debbie's words, 'Tony, in his spare two minutes per day, also decided to start Wine Science at CSU in 1992.' She continues, 'His trying to live 27 hours per day (plus our four kids!) fell to pieces when he was involved in a severe car smash in 1997. Two months in hospital stopped full-time medical work, and the winery dreams became inevitable.' Financial compensation finally came through and the small winery was built. The now-expanded vineyard includes chardonnay, cabernet sauvignon (3ha each), semillon, tempranillo, grenache (1.5ha each) and smaller plantings of graciano and monastrell.

ŸŸŸŸŸ **Chardonnay 2012** Pale, bright straw-green; a lively and crisp chardonnay picked at the exact moment to protect natural acidity, yet develop varietal character; it is not intense, but there is good balance between the white peach and citrus components, and the finish is clean. Screwcap. 12.9% alc. **Rating** 90 **To** 2014 $19
Mudgee Fortified Cabernet Liqueur NV Something different, but not something great; to achieve that, you need years in barrel; that said, does have some spicy notes and texture. 375ml. Screwcap. 17.5% alc. **Rating** 90 **To** 2014 $28

ŸŸŸŸ **Easter Semillon 2012 Rating** 89 **To** 2016 $28
Dry Rose 2012 Rating 88 **To** 2014 $16

Vinrock

23 George Street, Thebarton, SA 5031 (postal) **Region** McLaren Vale
T (08) 8408 8900 **www.**vinrock.com **Open** Not
Winemaker Michael Fragos (Consultant) **Est.** 1998 **Dozens** 10 500 **Vyds** 30ha
Owners Don Luca, Marco Iannetti and Anthony De Pizzol all have backgrounds in the wine industry, none more than Don, a former board member of Tatachilla. He also planted the Luca Vineyard in 1998 (20ha of shiraz, 5ha each of grenache and cabernet sauvignon). The majority of the grapes are sold, but steadily increasing quantities of wine have been made from the best blocks in the vineyard. Made better 2011 wines than most, the prices right. Exports to Canada, Hong Kong, China and NZ.

ŸŸŸŸŸ **McLaren Vale Grenache Shiraz Mataro 2012** Full purple-red; largely estate-grown, this is a quintessential regional wine, generous and rich, with a velvety mouthful of red and black fruits, dark chocolate, quality oak and ripe tannins. It will live for decades, improving for at least the first 10 years. Screwcap. 14.5% alc. **Rating** 93 **To** 2037 $24

Bayliss Road Hillside Block McLaren Vale Shiraz 2010 Deep purple-red; a decidedly appealing medium- to full-bodied Shiraz at this price point; black and blue fruits coalesce with dark chocolate and ripe tannins on the palate, marginalising the influence of oak. Screwcap. 14.5% alc. **Rating** 91 **To** 2020 $17
McLaren Vale Cabernet Sauvignon 2011 Medium purple-red; careful viticulture and winemaking have combined to produce a clearly articulated, medium-bodied Cabernet with good balance and mouthfeel, the tannins ripe and well integrated, oak likewise. Screwcap. 14.5% alc. **Rating** 90 **To** 2017 $22

ŸŸŸŸ **McLaren Vale Shiraz 2011 Rating** 89 **To** 2018 $24
Terra Mia McLaren Vale Shiraz 2011 Good colour, similar to its '11 McLaren Vale sibling; this has slightly less weight, being medium- to full-bodied at best, and while the oak is obvious, it has better structural balance. Screwcap. 14.5% alc. **Rating** 89 **To** 2017 $17

McLaren Vale Grenache Shiraz Mataro 2011 Rating 89 To 2016 $23
Terra Mia McLaren Vale Cabernet Sauvignon 2011 Rating 87 To 2015 $17

Vintners Ridge Estate ★★★★

Lot 18 Veraison Place, Yallingup, Margaret River, WA 6285 **Region** Margaret River
T 0417 956 943 **www.**vintnersridge.com.au **Open** By appt
Winemaker Flying Fish Cove (Simon Ding) **Est.** 2001 **Dozens** 650 **Vyds** 2.1ha
When Maree and Robin Adair purchased the Vintners Ridge vineyard in 2006 (cabernet sauvignon), it had already produced three crops, having been planted in Nov '01 (which is a perfectly permissible establishment date). The vineyard overlooks the picturesque Geographe Bay. The Adairs have had great wine show success with their Cabernet Sauvignons.

🍷🍷🍷🍷🍷 **Margaret River Cabernet Sauvignon 2011** Mid garnet; red fruits, earth and a little spice are evident on the bouquet; the palate is medium-bodied and has good length, with strong tannins on the finish. Screwcap. 14.7% alc. **Rating** 90 To 2020 $30 BE

Voyager Estate

Lot 1 Stevens Road, Margaret River, WA 6285 **Region** Margaret River
T (08) 9757 6354 **www.**voyagerestate.com.au **Open** 7 days 10–5
Winemaker Steve James, Travis Lemm **Est.** 1978 **Dozens** 40 000 **Vyds** 110ha
Michael Wright, son of Peter Wright, who was a founding member of the Hancock & Wright Group at the forefront of mining in WA, pursued several avenues of business and agriculture before setting his sights on owning a vineyard and winery. It was thus an easy decision when he was able to buy what was then called Freycinet Estate from founder and leading viticulturist Peter Gherardi in 1991. Peter had established the vineyard in '78, and it has been significantly expanded by Michael over the ensuing years. Apart from the Cape Dutch-style tasting room and vast rose garden, the signpost for the estate is the massive Australian flag pole – after Parliament House in Canberra, the second largest flag pole in Australia. Michael has never done things by halves, and has had the financial resources to turn Voyager Estate into one of the best vineyards and wineries in the region. Exports to Asia and other major markets.

🍷🍷🍷🍷🍷 **Margaret River Cabernet Sauvignon Merlot 2009** The attention to detail in this wine is obvious from the beginning, and while the level of new oak is a feature on the bouquet, the depth, complexity and layers of dark fruits, cedar, black olive and graphite minerality is astounding; the mouthfeel further enhances the picture, with a seamless transition across the palate, powerful on entry and then tightening up for maximum restraint and fine-grained tannin persistence on the finish. Screwcap. 14% alc. **Rating** 97 To 2040 $75 BE
Margaret River Chardonnay 2010 Pale gold, vibrant green hue; the highly expressive and complex bouquet of grapefruit, cashew and fresh charcuterie is in complete harmony; the palate follows suit, with power and depth held in check by taut acidity and a little grip on the finish; long, even, unevolved and while will age with grace, is totally beguiling and ready today. Screwcap. 13% alc. **Rating** 96 To 2020 $45 BE
Project 95 Margaret River Chardonnay 2009 Only 100 dozen bottles were made of this wine, all to be sold through restaurants. An immensely attractive wine, fruit-driven, and very long in the mouth, grapefruit, mineral/slate and crisp acidity not at all blunted by the mlf. Screwcap. 12.9% alc. **Rating** 96 To 2024 $55
Margaret River Shiraz 2011 Vibrant purple hue; an extravagant array of aromas from redcurrant, blackberry, plum, clove and violets; medium-bodied and layered with well-handled oak, fine-grained tannins and a plush core of fruit that opens up with a pinot-like peacock's tail of flavour; the development of this wine should be enthralling, but giving it the opportunity to do so may prove a challenge. Screwcap. 13.8% alc. **Rating** 96 To 2025 $40 BE

Margaret River Shiraz 2010 The winemaking was (relatively) conventional, with destemmed grapes fermented in open and closed vessels, pressed and matured for 12 months in a mix of French (80%) and American (20%) barrels (26% new) for 11 months. The wild card was 1% co-fermented viognier, which helped its superb purple-crimson colour, its fragrant bouquet and brightly flavoured palate. Intense and long, it has immaculate balance, rounded off with fine, savoury tannins. Screwcap. 13.5% alc. **Rating** 96 **To** 2034 $38

ҮҮҮҮҮ **Girt by Sea Cabernet Merlot 2011 Rating** 93 **To** 2022 $27 BE

✪ **Margaret River Sauvignon Blanc Semillon 2012** Light straw-green; has the complexity and richness of flavour expected of Voyager, the flavours in the tropical spectrum of passionfruit, guava and gooseberry, balanced by gently lemony acidity. Screwcap. 13% alc. **Rating** 92 **To** 2014 $24

Vue on Halcyon   ★★★★☆

19 Uplands Road, Chirnside Park, Vic 3116 **Region** Yarra Valley
T (03) 9726 7111 **www**.vueonhalcyon.com.au **Open** W'ends 10–2
Winemaker Richard Rackley **Est.** 1982 **Dozens** 840 **Vyds** 6ha
This is the reincarnation (although under the same family ownership) of Halcyon Daze. Founded by Richard and Cheryl Rackley in 1982, it is now owned and run by Dean and Rennae Rackley. The new name comes from the newly built wedding and function venue. The wines made are Riesling, Chardonnay, Pinot Noir, Close-Planted Pinot Noir, Cabernet Sauvignon and a Cabernet Sauvignon/Merlot/Cabernet Franc blend.

ҮҮҮҮҮ **Yarra Valley Chardonnay 2010** Light straw-green; has excellent varietal expression, with juicy stone fruit, grapefruit and citrus aromas and flavours; oak has been absorbed by this lovely display of varietal fruit. Screwcap. 12.8% alc. **Rating** 94 **To** 2029 $32

ҮҮҮҮҮ **Yarra Valley Cabernet Sauvignon Merlot Franc 2009 Rating** 93 **To** 2019 $36

Close Planted Yarra Valley Pinot Noir 2009 Rating 90 **To** 2015 $54
Yarra Valley Noble Riesling 2011 Rating 90 **To** 2016 $28

Walter Clappis Wine Co.   ★★★★★

Rifle Range Road, McLaren Vale, SA 5171 **Region** McLaren Vale
T (08) 8323 8818 **www**.hedonistwines.com.au **Open** Not
Winemaker Walter Clappis, Kimberly Clappis **Est.** 1982 **Dozens** 10 000 **Vyds** 35ha
Walter Clappis (once known as Bill) has been a stalwart of the McLaren Vale wine scene for decades. The estate plantings of shiraz (14ha), cabernet sauvignon (10ha), merlot (9ha) and tempranillo (2ha) are the cornerstone of his new business, which also provides the home for the Amicus wines. Exports to the UK, the US, Canada, Belgium, The Netherlands, Malaysia, Singapore, China and Japan.

ҮҮҮҮҮ **Amicus Reserve Shiraz 2008** Almost as densely packed as the '10 Hedonist Reserve, but does allow some juicy fruit to come through on the finish and aftertaste, while still proclaiming its regional origin in stentorian vinous speech, black fruits wrapped in dark chocolate. Cork. 14.5% alc. **Rating** 95 **To** 2028 $55

The Hedonist Reserve Shiraz 2010 Even denser colour than its junior brother, and multiplies the density of the body and flavour, the mouthfeel suggesting there may have been some juice run-off before fermentation commenced. Whether or not that is correct is of purely academic interest; it is the end result that matters, but I don't think this is a better wine (nor less meritorious) than its sibling. Screwcap. 14% alc. **Rating** 94 **To** 2035 $65

✪ **The Hedonist McLaren Vale Shiraz 2010** Deep purple-crimson; the grapes were biodynamically grown, and the wine is of such intensity that it has absorbed the new American oak in which it was matured; it is classic McLaren Vale, its blackberry fruit suffused with dark chocolate and ripe, but savoury, tannins. Great value. Screwcap. 14% alc. **Rating** 94 **To** 2030 $25

ΨΨΨΨΨ **The Hedonist McLaren Vale Sangiovese Rose 2012** Pale, bright pink;
✪   light-bodied, but has juicy red cherry fruit and good length. Screwcap. 13% alc.
     Rating 90 **To** 2014 $19

Walter Wines   ★★★

179 Tinja Lane, Mudgee, NSW 2850 **Region** Mudgee
T (02) 6372 9143 **www.**walterwines.com.au **Open** Thurs–Tues 10.30–4.30
Winemaker David Lowe, Frank Newman (Contract) **Est.** 2005 **Dozens** 500 **Vyds** 17ha
Lynn and Paul Walter had been keen observers of Mudgee and its wines for 15 years before
deciding to take the plunge and plant a 17ha vineyard. It was the mid 1990s, and all the
portents were good. As competition increased, and prices for grapes decreased, they realised
that their original business plan of simply being growers for local producers was not going to
be financially viable, even though they thought the downturn would prove to be a temporary
one. In 2005 they had an opportunity to export bulk wine to Germany, and this triggered a
decision to also have wine contract-made for sale under their own label.

ΨΨΨΨ **Federation Hill Mudgee Sparkling Shiraz 2010** Light, bright red-purple;
     a pleasant, well-balanced wine disgorged Mar '12 after almost 2 years on yeast
     lees; in a sweeter style, which has wide appeal. Diam. 13.5% alc. **Rating** 89
     To 2016 $32

Wandin Hunter Valley   ★★★★★

12 Wilderness Road, Lovedale, NSW 2320 **Region** Hunter Valley
T (02) 4930 9888 **www.**wandinhuntervalley.com.au **Open** 7 days 10–5
Winemaker Daniel Binet **Est.** 1973 **Dozens** 8000 **Vyds** 8ha
After some uncertainty, and changes of heart, Wandin Hunter Valley is now owned by
Warraroong Estate (which in turn was formerly known as Swish Wine), and is part of an
impressive portfolio of vineyards and brands. The cards have been thoroughly shuffled, and it
will be interesting to see how they play out. Exports to China.

ΨΨΨΨΨ **Estate Shiraz 2011** Medium purple-crimson; matured in a mix of new, 1- and
✪   2-year-old French barriques and hogsheads; has beautifully sweet cherry and plum
     fruit framed by the perfectly judged oak and fine, ripe tannins; the more I taste
     these '11 Hunter Valley Shirazs, the more I am entranced by them – and in this
     instance, by the price. Screwcap. 14% alc. **Rating** 95 **To** 2036 $25
     Reserve Semillon 2009 Still has youthful, vibrant colour, the bouquet is
     unevolved and reveals pure lime sherbet, straw and a mere suggestion of toasty
     development; the palate is focused, pure-fruited and linear and ageing slowly and
     gracefully. Screwcap. 10.5% alc. **Rating** 94 **To** 2022 $30 BE
     Reserve Hunter Valley Chardonnay 2007 This Chardonnay has held on
     to the quality it showed when 1 year old in a convincing fashion, the colour
     a remarkable light straw-green, the palate with vibrant white peach and citrus
     flavours complexed by fine quality oak. The points remain as they were when the
     wine was tasted in Jul '08. Screwcap. 14% alc. **Rating** 94 **To** 2017 $40
     Bridie's Reserve Shiraz 2011 Mid crimson, purple hue; a fragrant and
     expressive bouquet of satsuma plum, mocha and licorice; the palate is focused
     and evenly balanced; lingering mocha notes from the generous levels of oak will
     diminish quickly, and the end result will be attractive indeed. Screwcap. 14% alc.
     Rating 94 **To** 2025 $40 BE
     Estate Shiraz 2010 Remarkable retention of vivid crimson-purple hue; it has a
     splendidly fragrant bouquet of red berry fruits ranging across cherry to raspberry,
     the sense of place yet to emerge – but it is certain to do so with 5+ years in bottle.
     A totally seductive wine. Screwcap. 13.5% alc. **Rating** 94 **To** 2030 $25

ΨΨΨΨΨ **Reserve Semillon 2012** Pale quartz; here the low-alcohol envelope is pushed to
✪   (but not over) its limit, the flavours all circling around the central pole of lemon,
     lemongrass, lemon curd, lemon sherbet and lemony minerality. Not for the faint-
     hearted, and needs time. Screwcap. 9.5% alc. **Rating** 93 **To** 2025 $25

Reserve Hunter Valley Chardonnay 2009 Rating 92 To 2016 $40 BE
Aggie's Reserve Chardonnay 2011 Rating 91 To 2018 $25

Wanted Man   ★★★★☆

School House Lane, Heathcote, Vic 3523 **Region** Heathcote
T (03) 9654 4664 **www.**wantedman.com.au **Open** Not
Winemaker Matt Harrop, Simon Osicka **Est.** 1996 **Dozens** 2000 **Vyds** 9.3ha
The Wanted Man vineyard was planted in 1996, and has been managed by Andrew Clarke
since 2000, producing Jinks Creek's Heathcote Shiraz. That wine was sufficiently impressive
to lead Andrew and partner Peter Bartholomew (a Melbourne restaurateur) to purchase the
vineyard in '06, and give it its own identity. The vineyard is planted to shiraz (4ha), marsanne,
viognier, grenache, roussanne and mourvedre. The potent winemaking duo, and the quality
of the wines they crafted in '11, suggests that even better wines will appear next. The quirky
Ned Kelly label is the work of Mark Knight, cartoonist for the *Herald Sun*. Exports to the UK,
Canada, Denmark, France and Hong Kong.

ΨΨΨΨΨ Single Vineyard Heathcote Shiraz 2010 The gently spicy, faintly earthy
aromas of the bouquet are replayed on the medium-bodied palate, but just when
you think you have nailed it, the complexity and length of the back-palate, finish
and aftertaste hit you. Screwcap. 13.5% alc. Rating 94 To 2025 $35

ΨΨΨΨΨ Single Vineyard Heathcote Marsanne Viognier 2011 Rating 92
To 2015 $35
Single Vineyard Heathcote Marsanne Viognier 2010 Rating 91
To 2014 $35

Wantirna Estate   ★★★★★

10 Bushy Park Lane, Wantirna South, Vic 3152 **Region** Yarra Valley
T (03) 9801 2367 **www.**wantirnaestate.com.au **Open** Not
Winemaker Maryann and Reg Egan **Est.** 1963 **Dozens** 830 **Vyds** 4.2ha
Reg and Bertina (Tina) Egan were among the early movers in the rebirth of the Yarra Valley.
The vineyard surrounds the house in which they live, which also incorporates the winery.
These days Reg describes himself as the interfering winemaker, but in the early years he did
everything, dashing from his legal practice to the winery to check on the ferments. Today much
of the winemaking responsibility has been transferred to daughter Maryann, who has a degree
in wine science from CSU. Both have honed their practical skills among the small domaines
and châteaux of Burgundy and Bordeaux, where the single vineyard, terroir-driven wines have
inspired them. Maryann was also a winemaker for many years in Domaine Chandon's infancy.
Tina keeps the mailing list and accounts under control, as well as having that all-important
role of looking after the pickers during vintage. Like all small wineries, it is a family affair, with
everyone involved in some way. Exports to Hong Kong, Singapore and Japan.

ΨΨΨΨΨ Amelia Yarra Valley Cabernet Sauvignon Merlot 2010 Deep crimson,
vibrant hue; a highly perfumed and complex bouquet, revealing red and black
fruits, briar and a mere suggestion of cedary complexity; the palate is fine-boned
and pure-fruited, with silky tannins, fresh acidity and a long and expansive finish;
a benchmark example from one of the original stalwarts of the Yarra Valley. Diam.
13.5% alc. Rating 95 To 2025 $65 BE

ΨΨΨΨΨ Isabella Yarra Valley Chardonnay 2011 Rating 91 To 2018 $60 BE
Lily Yarra Valley Pinot Noir 2011 Rating 90 To 2018 $65 BE

Warner Glen Estate   ★★★★★

PO Box 218, Melville, WA 6956 **Region** Margaret River
T (08) 9337 4601 **www.**warnerglenestate.com.au **Open** Not
Winemaker Bruce Dukes, Amanda Kramer (Contract) **Est.** 1993 **Dozens** 15 000
Vyds 30.8ha

Father John and son Travis French purchased a 100ha property abutting the Chapman Brook and Blackwood National Park in Margaret River in 1992. Says Travis, 'We then realised that we had to do something with it, so the thing at the time was to plant vines, and so we did.' Sauvignon blanc and semillon constitute the lion's share, but there are significant plantings of chardonnay, cabernet sauvignon, shiraz and merlot. Until 2006 they were content to sell their grapes to Cape Mentelle, but in that year decided to have wine contract-made by the highly experienced Bruce Dukes and Amanda Kramer. Given the maturity of the vineyards, it is not surprising that the wines are of such high quality. Warner Glen and Frog Belly are the main labels, Smokin' Gun and The Pick outliers; all are good value. Exports to China.

ŸŸŸŸŸ **Frog Belly Margaret River Sauvignon Blanc 2012** Light straw-green; the
✪ bouquet immediately signals sauvignon blanc with an intense array of grapefruit, tropical fruit and stone fruit that play through the equally intense and focused palate. Screwcap. 12.9% alc. **Rating** 94 **To** 2014 $18
Margaret River Sauvignon Blanc Semillon Sur Lie 2012 Pale straw-green; sophisticated winemaking has produced a compelling outcome; has distinct nettle and citrus pith aromas and flavours, the finish long and bracing. Screwcap. 13% alc. **Rating** 94 **To** 2016 $30

ŸŸŸŸŸ **Margaret River Chardonnay 2011 Rating** 93 **To** 2018 $30

Warrabilla ★★★★★

6152 Murray Valley Highway, Rutherglen, Vic 3685 **Region** Rutherglen
T (02) 6035 7242 **www.**warrabillawines.com.au **Open** 7 days 10–5
Winemaker Andrew Sutherland Smith **Est.** 1990 **Dozens** 10 000 **Vyds** 21ha
Andrew Sutherland Smith and wife Carol have built a formidable reputation for their wines, headed by the Reserve trio of Durif, Cabernet Sauvignon and Shiraz, quintessential examples of Rutherglen red table wine at its most opulent. Their vineyard has been extended with the planting of riesling and zinfandel. Andrew spent 15 years with All Saints, McWilliam's, Yellowglen, Fairfield and Chambers before setting up Warrabilla, and his accumulated experience shines through in the wines. No wines were released from the 2011 vintage.

ŸŸŸŸŸ **Reserve Muscat NV** Deeply coloured and luscious and inviting in style, with layers of fruitcake, marzipan, raisins and toffee all on display; the palate is warm, long and inviting, with a strong spiced biscuit personality an attractive conclusion. Screwcap. 18.5% alc. **Rating** 94 **To** 2014 $36 BE

ŸŸŸŸ **Archers Old Tawny NV** The bouquet offers toffee, raisins and burnt caramel; the palate follows with fresh toasty oak a dominant feature, and the acidity fairly assertive, showing plenty of drive; a spirit burn is a discordant note to conclude. Screwcap. 18% alc. **Rating** 89 **To** 2014 $19 BE
Reserve Riesling 2012 Rating 87 **To** 2015 $19 BE

Warramate ★★★★★

27 Maddens Lane, Gruyere, Vic 3770 **Region** Yarra Valley
T (03) 5964 9219 **www.**warramatewines.com.au **Open** 7 days 10–5
Winemaker Paul Bridgeman **Est.** 1970 **Dozens** 4000 **Vyds** 6.6ha
A long-established and perfectly situated winery reaping the full benefits of its 40-year-old vines; recent plantings have increased production. All the wines are well made, the Shiraz providing further proof (if such be needed) of the suitability of the variety to the region. In 2011 was purchased by the partnership that owns the adjoining Yarra Yering; the Warramate Vineyard and brand have been kept as a separate operation, using its existing vineyards for the brand. Paul Bridgeman made some very impressive wines in '11 despite incessant rain in the growing season.

ŸŸŸŸŸ **Black Label Yarra Valley Cabernet Sauvignon 2010** In 2000 Warramate
✪ significantly extended its vineyard area by converting a horse paddock, planting the cabernet (inter alia) from which this wine is made. It is full of gloriously juicy cassis fruit, and the oak has been judged to perfection. Screwcap. 13.5% alc. **Rating** 95 **To** 2025 $25

✪   **Black Label Yarra Valley Shiraz 2010** Bright, full red-purple; from the new vines planted with four clones in '00; a testament to the vintage and to skilled winemaking, the spicy fruit, tannins and oak in a seamless stream running the length of the medium-bodied palate. Screwcap. 13.5% alc. **Rating** 94 To 2025 $25

White Label Yarra Valley Cabernet Merlot 2011 Medium red-purple; the blend also includes some cabernet franc. This is an unqualified success in the teeth of the challenging vintage; it has cassis/blackcurrant and redcurrant supported by ample tannins and quality oak. Screwcap. 13.5% alc. **Rating** 94 To 2026 $40

♇♇♇♇♇   **White Label Yarra Valley Riesling 2012 Rating** 90 To 2016 $28
White Label Yarra Valley Pinot Noir 2011 Rating 90 To 2016 $25

Warrenmang Vineyard & Resort   ★★★★★

Mountain Creek Road, Moonambel, Vic 3478 **Region** Pyrenees
T (03) 5467 2233 **www**.warrenmang.com.au **Open** 7 days 10–5
Winemaker Sean Schwager **Est.** 1974 **Dozens** 15000 **Vyds** 32.1ha
Luigi and Athalie Bazzani continue to watch over Warrenmang; a new, partially underground barrel room with earthen walls has been completed, wine quality remains high, and the accommodation for over 80 guests, plus a restaurant, underpin the business. Over the 34 years that Luigi and Athalie have been at Warrenmang, a very loyal clientele has been built up. The business is quietly on the market, Luigi and Athalie having long since earned their retirement. They have taken one step to reduce their workload by employing (in 2012) the highly experienced Christine and Craig Roeger to manage the resort. Exports to Denmark, The Netherlands, Poland, Taiwan, Singapore, Malaysia and China.

♇♇♇♇♇
✪   **Bazzani Pyrenees Shiraz Cabernet 2010** Vibrant purple-crimson; has an attractive dark berry bouquet, red berries joining in on the medium-bodied palate; the tannins are positive, oak largely incidental, with the balance to justify long-term cellaring. Screwcap. 13.5% alc. **Rating** 95 To 2022 $15

Grand Pyrenees 2008 A blend of cabernet sauvignon, merlot, cabernet franc and shiraz, each fermented separately, and matured for up to 24 months in French or American oak. The colour is still healthy and deep, and the rich blackcurrant, blackberry and plum fruit carries both the oak and the tannins with comparative (and impressive) ease. Screwcap. 13.5% alc. **Rating** 94 To 2023 $35

♇♇♇♇♇   **Pyrenees Sauvignon Blanc 2011 Rating** 92 To 2014 $25

Warwick Billings   ★★★★★

c/- Post Office, Lenswood, SA 5240 (postal) **Region** Adelaide Hills
T 0405 437 864 **www**.wowique.com.au **Open** Not
Winemaker Warwick Billings **Est.** 2009 **Dozens** 250
This is the venture of Warwick Billings and partner Rose Kemp. Warwick was a cider maker in the UK who came to study at Roseworthy, and got diverted into the wine world. He completed postgraduate oenology at Adelaide University in 1995, and worked for Miranda Wine, Orlando and Angove Family Winemakers from 2002 to '08, along the way moonlighting in France and Spain for 12 vintages. Warwick's approach to his eponymous label is self-deprecating, beginning with the name Wowique, and saying, 'Occasionally a vineyard sings to the winemaker. [We] have taken one of these songs and out it into a bottle.' The vineyard in question is an unusual clone of chardonnay nurtured on a sloping hilltop site in Mt Torrens. The self-deprecation continues with the wine simply being labelled Wowique Blanc, which presumably sells because it is so good, not because of the name. Warwick's final word on all of this is, 'The winemaking is unashamedly inspired by Burgundy, but care is take to acknowledge that the soil is different, the clones are often different, the climate is definitely different, and the end consumer is usually different.'

▼▼▼▼▼ **Wowique Chardonnay 2011** Light straw-green; hand-picked and whole bunch-pressed; there are penetrating barrel ferment oak aromas on the bouquet, with the influence of 100% mlf obvious. The palate has complex white peach, nectarine and fig flavours, and a long, lingering finish where ripe citrus makes a belated appearance. Screwcap. 12.1% alc. **Rating** 94 **To** 2017 $30

Water Wheel ★★★★

Bridgewater-on-Loddon, Bridgewater, Vic 3516 **Region** Bendigo
T (03) 5437 3060 **www.**waterwheelwine.com **Open** Mon–Fri 9–5, w'ends & public hols 12–4
Winemaker Peter Cumming, Bill Trevaskis **Est.** 1972 **Dozens** 35 000 **Vyds** 136ha
Peter Cumming, with more than two decades of winemaking under his belt, has quietly built on the reputation of Water Wheel year by year. The winery is owned by the Cumming family, which has farmed in the Bendigo region for 50+ years, with horticulture and viticulture special areas of interest. Over half the vineyard area is planted to shiraz (75ha), followed by chardonnay, sauvignon blanc (15ha each), cabernet sauvignon, malbec (10ha each), and smaller plantings of petit verdot, semillon, roussanne and grenache. Despite the ravages of drought affecting the 2008, '09 and '10 vintages, then the rain-drenched '11, followed by record floods at the end of that year, Water Wheel continues to produce wines that over-deliver on their modest prices. Exports to the UK, the US, Canada, Switzerland, Denmark, Singapore, Thailand, China and NZ.

▼▼▼▼♀ **Memsie Homestead Bendigo Shiraz 2012** Vivid purple-crimson; we all ✪ know what a great vintage '12 was for South Eastern Australia and the southern half of Vic, Bendigo on the dividing line; well, there are no half measures about this beautiful wine, the best from Water Wheel for many years, and outstanding value – indeed unbelievably good. Screwcap. 14.5% alc. **Rating** 91 **To** 2020 $10
✪ **Bendigo Sauvignon Blanc 2012** Pale straw-green; in the long tradition of Water Wheel style, with a mix of citrus and tropical fruit, fleshed out on the finish by a hint of sweetness balanced by acidity. Screwcap. 12.5% alc. **Rating** 90 **To** 2013 $14

Watershed Premium Wines ★★★★★

Cnr Bussell Highway/Darch Road, Margaret River, WA 6285 **Region** Margaret River
T (08) 9758 8633 **www.**watershedwines.com.au **Open** 7 days 10–5
Winemaker Severine Logan **Est.** 2002 **Dozens** 130 000 **Vyds** 187ha
Watershed Wines has been established by a syndicate of investors, and no expense has been spared in establishing the substantial vineyard and building a striking cellar door, with a 200-seat café and restaurant. Situated towards the southern end of the Margaret River region, its neighbours include Voyager Estate and Leeuwin Estate. Exports to Germany, Indonesia, Fiji, Thailand, Papua New Guinea, Singapore, Hong Kong and China.

▼▼▼▼▼ **Senses Margaret River Sauvignon Blanc 2012** Offers citrus and tropical fruits offset by a splash of bath talc; the palate is lively, focused, dry and thoroughly refreshing, not to mention surprisingly long; executed with aplomb. Screwcap. 12.5% alc. **Rating** 94 **To** 2015 $27 BE
Awakening Single Vineyard Margaret River Chardonnay 2011 A truly restrained style of chardonnay, with grapefruit, nectarine and bath talc complexity on display; the palate is racy and finely detailed with a long finish and an expansive array of flavours. Screwcap. 13.5% alc. **Rating** 94 **To** 2022 $45 BE
Awakening Margaret River Cabernet Sauvignon 2010 Deep colour and displaying the very essence of cassis on the bouquet, with layers of aromas and full-bodied flavours from cedar to black olive; a ripe, juicy and well-heeled wine, showing accessibility today, and the form to go a long way into the future. Screwcap. 14% alc. **Rating** 94 **To** 2025 $100 BE

ŸŸŸŸ♀ **Shades Margaret River Sauvignon Blanc Semillon 2012** A clean, fresh,
✪   vibrant and punchy drink-early example of this classic blend, showing vitality and
         energy. Screwcap. 12% alc. **Rating** 90 **To** 2014 $17 BE
         Senses Margaret River Shiraz 2010 Rating 90 **To** 2020 $27 BE

Waterton Vineyards   ★★★★☆

PO Box 125, Beaconsfield, Tas 7270 **Region** Northern Tasmania
T (03) 6394 7214 **www**.watertonhall.com.au **Open** Not
Winemaker Winemaking Tasmania (Julian Alcorso) **Est.** 2006 **Dozens** 450 **Vyds** 2ha
Jennifer Baird and Peter Cameron purchased this remarkable property in 2002. Waterton
Hall was built in the 1850s and modified extensively by well-known neo-gothic architect
Alexander North in 1910. The property was owned by the Catholic church from '49–96,
variously used as a school, a boys' home and a retreat. Following its sale the new owners
planted 1ha of riesling at the end of the '90s. Jennifer and Peter extended the vineyard
with 1ha of shiraz, electing to sell the riesling until 2006, when part was first made under
the Waterton label. The plans are to use the existing buildings to provide a restaurant,
accommodation and function facilities.

ŸŸŸŸŸ **Riesling 2012** Bright straw-green; has all the intensity that Tasmania provides
         without effort, and few mainland regions can match; the inbuilt acidity and low
         pH provide the structure; it is on the finish and aftertaste that the power of the
         citrus fruit shines through. Screwcap. 11.9% alc. **Rating** 94 **To** 2022 $30

ŸŸŸŸ **Shiraz 2008 Rating** 89 **To** 2015 $35

WayWood Wines   ★★★★★

PO Box 746, Willunga, SA 5172 **Region** McLaren Vale
T (08) 8556 4536 **www**.waywoodwines.com **Open** By appt
Winemaker Andrew Wood **Est.** 2005 **Dozens** 1000
This is the venture of Andrew Wood and Lisa Robertson, the culmination of their wayward
odyssey. Andrew left his career as a sommelier in London, and retrained as a winemaker,
working in Portugal, the UK, Italy and the Granite Belt (an eclectic selection if ever there was
one), and settling in McLaren Vale in early 2004. Working with Kangarilla Road winery for
the next six years, while making small quantities of Shiraz, Cabernets and Tempranillo from
purchased grapes, led them to Nebbiolo and Shiraz, the first vintage of those varieties made
in '12. The wines are made in small batches, utilising cold soaking and extended maceration.

ŸŸŸŸŸ **McLaren Vale Shiraz 2010** Dense purple-crimson; a blend of grapes from
✪   the diverse terroirs of Clarendon, Willunga and Sellicks Hill, the end result a
         quintessential McLaren Vale shiraz. It is crammed with supple black fruits in
         a shroud of dark chocolate, tannins and oak precisely weighted. Great value.
         Screwcap. 14.7% alc. **Rating** 95 **To** 2030 $24
✪   **McLaren Vale Cabernet Sauvignon 2010** Medium red-purple; utterly belies
         its 14.8% alcohol because of the vibrancy, length and finesse of its medium-bodied
         palate, where blackcurrant, black olive, cedar and just a touch of bitter chocolate
         coalesce, knitted together by the fine savoury tannins. Screwcap. 14.8% alc.
         Rating 95 **To** 2025 $28
         McLaren Vale Cabernet Sangiovese 2010 The two varieties were
         co-fermented, which may explain the good colour, the rich dark berry bouquet,
         and the velvety, spicy palate. Impressive winemaking, and some quality grapes to
         start with. Screwcap. 14.9% alc. **Rating** 94 **To** 2020 $35

ŸŸŸŸ♀ **Adelaide Hills Pinot Grigio 2012 Rating** 93 **To** 2014 $24
✪   **McLaren Vale Nebbiolo 2010** Remarkable hue for a nebbiolo; the maritime
         climate of McLaren Vale is far removed from the fog-shrouded hills of Piedmont,
         but this wine goes some way to pulling the hemispheres together, the black
         cherry/sour cherry and persistent savoury tannins strongly varietal. Screwcap.
         14.5% alc. **Rating** 93 **To** 2025 $28
         McLaren Vale Tempranillo 2011 Rating 91 **To** 2017 $35

Wedgetail Estate

40 Hildebrand Road, Cottles Bridge, Vic 3099 **Region** Yarra Valley
T (03) 9714 8661 **www**.wedgetailestate.com.au **Open** Last w'end each month, or by appt
Winemaker Guy Lamothe **Est.** 1994 **Dozens** 1500 **Vyds** 5.5ha
Canadian-born photographer Guy Lamothe and partner Dena Ashbolt started making wine
in the basement of their Carlton home in the 1980s. The idea of their own vineyard started
to take hold, and the search for a property began. Then, in their words, 'one Sunday, when we
were "just out for a drive", we drove past our current home. The slopes are amazing, true goat
terrain, and it is on these steep slopes that in 1994 we planted our first block of pinot noir.'
While the vines were growing Lamothe enrolled in the winemaking course at CSU, having
already gained practical experience working in the Yarra Valley (Tarrawarra), the Mornington
Peninsula and Meursault (Burgundy). Exports to the UK, Canada, Singapore, Hong Kong
and China.

ŸŸŸŸŸ **Single Vineyard Yarra Valley Pinot Noir 2012** Bright, full red-purple; open-
fermented, wild yeast, then 10 months in French oak. A delicious, fragrant, pinot
full of velvety, plummy fruit, the tannins plentiful but soft, the oak subdued, the
finish long and supple. Screwcap. 13% alc. **Rating** 94 **To** 2020 $42
Single Vineyard Yarra Valley Shiraz 2012 Vivid purple-crimson; a textured
and rich wine that abounds with blackberry, plum, spice, pepper and ripe but
balanced tannins; 10 months in French oak has put the finishing touches on the
wine. Screwcap. 13% alc. **Rating** 94 **To** 2027 $38

ŸŸŸŸŸ **Special Release Yarra Valley Merlot 2012** **Rating** 92 **To** 2022 $48

Wellbush Vineyard

659 Huntly-Fosterville Road, Bagshot, Vic 3551 **Region** Bendigo
T (03) 5448 8515 **www**.thewellbushvineyard.com.au **Open** W'ends 11–4, Mon–Fri by appt
Winemaker Wes Vine, Greg Dedman **Est.** 2006 **Dozens** 450 **Vyds** 1.44ha
David and Lynn Wallace purchased the 10ha property in 2006; it brought with it a long history.
In the early years of the last century it was a Chinese market garden, the hand-built ponds
remaining today. In 1975 the first chardonnay, shiraz, cabernet sauvignon and merlot vines
were planted, with further plantings of shiraz in '98; an addition to the cabernet sauvignon the
following year brought the vineyard to its present level. The Wallaces (David having studied for
his Bachelor of Applied Science (wine science) at CSU) say, 'Our aims and aspirations are to
produce the best-quality grapes we possibly can and eventually produce our own handcrafted
wines, give up our day jobs and grow old ungracefully in our beautiful vineyard.'

ŸŸŸŸŸ **Bendigo Chardonnay 2012** Pale straw-green hue; the gentle bouquet offers
✪ aromas of melon, nectarine, struck flint and fennel; the palate reveals racy acidity, a
dry chalky texture and an expansive fresh cashew conclusion. Screwcap. 14% alc.
Rating 90 **To** 2018 $18 BE

Wendouree

Wendouree Road, Clare, SA 5453 **Region** Clare Valley
T (08) 8842 2896 **Open** Not
Winemaker Tony Brady **Est.** 1895 **Dozens** 1800 **Vyds** 12ha
An iron fist in a velvet glove best describes these extraordinary wines. They are fashioned
with passion and precision from the very old vineyard (shiraz, cabernet sauvignon, malbec,
mataro and muscat of alexandria), with its unique terroir, by Tony and Lita Brady, who rightly
see themselves as custodians of a priceless treasure. The 100-year-old stone winery is virtually
unchanged from the day it was built; this is in every sense a treasure beyond price. I should
explain, I buy three wines from Wendouree every year, always including the Shiraz. This is the
only way I am able to provide tasting notes, and it's almost inevitably a last-minute exercise
as I suddenly realise there are no notes in place. Moreover, Wendouree has never made any
comment about its wines, and I realise that the change in style, away from full-bodied to
medium-bodied, seems a permanent fixture of the landscape, not a one-off result of a given

vintage. The best news of all is that I may actually get to drink some of the Wendourees I have bought over the past 10 years before I die, and not have to rely on my few remaining bottles from the 1970s (and rather more from the '80s and '90s).

♟♟♟♟♟ Cabernet Sauvignon 2009 Wendouree occupies a truly unique site that sets its wines apart from all others in the Clare Valley, none more so than its cabernet, which has all the attributes of high-quality, cool-grown cabernet. This is a very convincing wine, with great precision, length and balance. WAK screwcap. 13.6% alc. **Rating** 96 **To** 2040 $55

Shiraz 2009 Bright, clear crimson; a super-elegant and refined Shiraz, with black cherry, blood plum and blackberry fruit to the fore; the tannins do make their presence felt on the finish, as does a touch of French oak, but neither threatens the balance of the wine. WAK screwcap. 13.8% alc. **Rating** 95 **To** 2029 $55

Cabernet Malbec 2009 Clear, bright colour; true to the blend, the malbec introduces some plummy nuances to the mid-palate, its only opportunity in a cabernet that is so perfectly balanced. Another wonderfully elegant wine. WAK screwcap. 13.8% alc. **Rating** 95 **To** 2035 $50

Shiraz Mataro 2009 Light, bright and clear crimson-purple; an immaculately balanced and structured blend, no more than medium-bodied, but with intense cherry and plum fruit wrapped in a veil of silky tannins. Don't be fooled; this wine will live for decades. WAK screwcap. 13.8% alc. **Rating** 94 **To** 2030 $50

West Cape Howe Wines   ★★★★★

Lot 14923 Muir Highway, Mount Barker, WA 6324 **Region** Mount Barker
T (08) 9892 1444 **www.**westcapehowewines.com.au **Open** 7 days 10–5
Winemaker Gavin Berry, Dave Cleary, Andrew Siddell **Est.** 1997 **Dozens** 75 000
After a highly successful seven years, West Cape Howe founders Brenden and Kylie Smith moved on, selling the business to a partnership including Gavin Berry (until 2004, senior winemaker at Plantagenet) and viticulturist Rob Quenby. As well as existing fruit sources, West Cape Howe now has the 80ha Lansdale Vineyard, planted in 1989, as its primary fruit source. In March '09 it purchased the 7700 tonne capacity Goundrey winery and 237ha Goundrey estate vineyards from CWA; the grapes from these plantings will be purchased by Accolade Wines (the new owner of CWA) for years to come. The move vastly increases West Cape Howe's business base, and facilitates contract winemaking to generate cash flow. So should the exemplary quality and very modest prices of the wines. Exports to the UK, the US, Denmark, Germany, Singapore and Hong Kong.

♟♟♟♟♟
✪ Mount Barker Riesling 2012 A glorious array of citrus and passionfruit flavours build progressively through the length of the palate and into the finish and aftertaste, in the manner of great pinot noir. Trophy Perth Wine Show '12. Ridiculously good value. Screwcap. 12.5% alc. **Rating** 96 **To** 2032 $22

✪ Two Peeps Albany Sauvignon Blanc Semillon 2012 Partial barrel fermentation and lees contact have given the wine an excellent spicy/creamy texture that marries with the supple lemony/stone fruit flavours. Gold medal Qantas Wine Show of WA '12. Screwcap. 13.2% alc. **Rating** 95 **To** 2016 $22

✪ Hannah's Hill Frankland Cabernet Merlot 2011 From the Russell Road Vineyard, and named for the tireless worker who was central to its development many years ago. Has multiple layers to its medium- to full-bodied palate, blackcurrant, plum, tannins and French oak all contributing to a complex wine with a long life ahead. Screwcap. 14% alc. **Rating** 95 **To** 2031 $22

✪ Book Ends Great Southern Cabernet Sauvignon 2010 Vivid crimson-purple; fresh as a daisy, with vibrant redcurrant and cherry fruit; the cedary oak is, of course, evident, as are silky tannins; the wine can be enjoyed tonight or in 20 years. Screwcap. 14% alc. **Rating** 95 **To** 2020 $27

✪ Two Peeps Sauvignon Blanc Semillon 2012 A 52/48% barrel-fermented blend of sauvignon blanc and semillon. Originally produced for the personal consumption of the winemakers, it came into public prominence when awarded a top gold medal at the Mount Barker Wine Show '12. Screwcap. 13.2% alc. **Rating** 94 **To** 2016 $19

✪ **Shiraz 2011** Full purple-crimson; only the southwest of WA could produce a juicy wine of this quality at this price. It counterposes juicy red berry fruits with savoury black fruits and fine, persistent tannins. Good now, even better in 10 years (or any time in between). Screwcap. 14.5% alc. **Rating** 94 **To** 2026 $17

✪ **Two Steps Great Southern Shiraz 2010** Good purple-crimson; while using the Great Southern region on the label, it is in fact from the Mount Barker subregion, its spicy/savoury medium-bodied black fruits lingering long on the finish and aftertaste; the role of oak and tannins has been finely scripted. Screwcap. 14% alc. **Rating** 94 **To** 2025 $27

♙♙♙♙♙ **Cabernet Merlot 2011** Convincing purple-crimson colour; 12 months' ✪ maturation in used French oak has resulted in the best possible outcome for this juicy, supple, joyously red berry-fruited wine; terrific value for drinking today or in 5 years or whenever you wish. Screwcap. 14.5% alc. **Rating** 92 **To** 2017 $17

✪ **Rose 2012** Vivid light crimson; made from early-picked cabernet franc; very good balance and texture underlie the fresh cherry and spice characters of the bouquet and the long, dry palate. Good with tapas. Screwcap. 13% alc. **Rating** 91 **To** 2014 $17

Mount Barker Sauvignon Blanc 2012 Rating 90 **To** 2014 $22

✪ **Chardonnay 2012** Pale straw-green; picked at the exact moment (or moments for multiple pickings) for the unwooded style, avoiding a crossover into sauvignon blanc, but not losing natural acidity; white peach, citrus and some tropical notes do the trick. Screwcap. 13% alc. **Rating** 90 **To** 2014 $17

Westend Estate Wines ★★★★☆

1283 Brayne Road, Griffith, NSW 2680 **Region** Riverina
T (02) 6969 0800 **www**.westendestate.com **Open** Mon–Fri 8.30–5, w'ends 10–4
Winemaker William Calabria, Bryan Currie, Emma Norbiato **Est.** 1945
Dozens 300 000 **Vyds** 64ha

Along with a number of Riverina producers, Westend Estate has successfully lifted both the quality and the packaging of its wines. Its leading 3 Bridges range, which has an impressive array of gold medals to its credit, is anchored in part on estate vineyards. Bill Calabria has been involved in the Australian wine industry for more than 40 years, and is understandably proud of the achievements of both Westend and the Riverina wine industry as a whole. Westend is moving with the times, increasing its plantings of durif, and introducing aglianico, nero d'Avola, and st macaire (on the verge of extinction, once grown in Bordeaux, Westend's 2ha now the largest planting in the world). Equally importantly, it is casting its net over the Canberra District, Hilltops and King Valley, premium regions, taking this one step further by acquiring a 12ha vineyard in the Barossa Valley. A producer that consistently delivers exceptional value for money across the entire range. Exports to the UK, the US, Canada, Brazil, Russia, India, Malaysia, Thailand, Singapore, Japan and China.

♙♙♙♙♙ **3 Bridges Cabernet Sauvignon 2011** Good purple-crimson; the wet vintage ✪ led to a blend of Hilltops and Riverina (normally 3 Bridges is 100% Riverina), which went on to win the Stodart Trophy at the Queensland Wine Show '12. It has been remarkably well made, with excellent varietal expression from its cassis fruit, ripe tannins and quality oak. Screwcap. 14% alc. **Rating** 95 **To** 2036 $25

♙♙♙♙♙ **Richland Pinot Grigio 2012** Won a gold medal at the Melbourne Wine Show ✪ '12, then a Blue-Gold (Top 100) at the Sydney International Wine Show '13. Its special character is the laser precision of the stream of pear and green apple flavours running through its long palate; its balance and aftertaste are also excellent. And the value! Screwcap. 12.5% alc. **Rating** 93 **To** 2014 $11

3 Bridges Limited Release Durif 2009 Rating 93 **To** 2029 $55
Francesco Show Reserve Grand Liqueur Muscat NV Rating 93 **To** 2025 $35 BE

✪ **Cool Climate Eden Valley Riesling 2012** Pale straw-green; a floral/flowery lime and lemon blossom bouquet leads into a palate with unusual depth to its range of citrus flavours and emphatic finish; from a single vineyard in the Eden Valley, and is excellent value for a style that will not need extended cellaring. Screwcap. 13% alc. **Rating** 92 **To** 2016 $15

✪   **Cool Climate Series King Valley Sauvignon Blanc Semillon 2012** Pale quartz-green; the wine has far more presence and character than most in the price group (sub-$15); both the bouquet and palate bring sweet lemon, passionfruit and gooseberry together with some snow pea and fresh-cut grass flavours on the bright finish. Screwcap. 12% alc. **Rating** 92 **To** 2014 $15

✪   **Richland Shiraz 2012** Deep crimson, bright; lifted and pure black fruit aromas are offset by a little smoked meat complexity from well-handled oak; the palate is fresh, generous and lively, poised and with enough stuffing to linger pleasantly on the fairly long conclusion. Screwcap. 14.5% alc. **Rating** 92 **To** 2018 $16 BE

Francesco Show Reserve Grand Tawny NV Rating 92 **To** 2025 $35 BE

✪   **Cool Climate Series Tumbarumba Pinot Noir 2012** Light but bright colour; has to be right up near the top of pinot noirs hovering around $15; the bouquet is fragrant, with red fruits to the fore, and the palate, although somewhat light in fruit, has a savoury texture and fine, persistent tannins. A pinot for nebbiolo lovers. Screwcap. 13% alc. **Rating** 90 **To** 2017 $16

✪   **3 Bridges Cabernet Sauvignon 2010** Cassis/blackcurrant and mocha/cedar oak join together on the bouquet and medium-bodied palate alike, the tannins ripe and soft; there is also an appealing juicy streak to the wine running through to the finish and aftertaste. Screwcap. 14.5% alc. **Rating** 90 **To** 2016 $20

✪   **Cool Climate Series Hilltops Tempranillo 2011** Deep crimson; the bouquet offers cola aromas with toasty oak prominent, and a little sage complexity lying beneath; medium-bodied, fresh and focused, the lively palate offers plenty of visceral pleasure for early drinking. Value plus. Screwcap. 13.5% alc. **Rating** 90 **To** 2016 $16 BE

3 Bridges Durif 2010 Rating 90 **To** 2015 $25

🍷🍷🍷🍷
✪   **Poker Face Chardonnay 2012** Here again, Poker Face shows that extra touch of varietal expression above and beyond the norm for the Riverina, with a distinct grapefruit touch alongside its stone fruit persona. I prefer the crisp, open finish of this wine to its Richland sibling. Screwcap. 13% alc. **Rating** 89 **To** 2014 $8

✪   **Poker Face Shiraz 2012** Bright colour, and bright in character, with clever winemaking enhancing the fresh red and black fruits on display; the palate is juicy, lively and evenly balanced despite finishing with a little prick of alcohol heat; excellent value for the price. Screwcap. 14.5% alc. **Rating** 89 **To** 2016 $8 BE

✪   **Calabria Private Bin Nero d'Avola 2010** Light red-purple; an unexpectedly elegant wine with spicy red cherry fruits, fine tannins and supple, juicy mouthfeel. Very good casual drinking, and no need for cellaring. Screwcap. 13.5% alc. **Rating** 89 **To** 2014 $16

Western Range Wines   ★★★★

1995 Chittering Road, Lower Chittering, WA 6084 **Region** Perth Hills
T (08) 9571 8800 **www.**westernrangewines.com.au **Open** 7 days 10–5
Winemaker Israel De Brito **Est.** 2001 **Dozens** 25 000 **Vyds** 125ha
The business that was established in 2001 by a small syndicate of investors, including Marilyn Corderory, Malcolm McCusker, and Terry and Kevin Prindiville, was acquired by Palinda Wines in late 2012; at the same time Palinda acquired Woodside Valley Estate. Palinda Wines is based in Hong Kong, and is the private family company of Chinese businessman Jacky Wong. He has 150 stores in Hong Kong and mainland China selling beer, wine and spirits, and will thus act both as importer and retailer. Exports to Canada, Poland, Russia, China and Japan.

🍷🍷🍷🍷🍷 **Single Vineyard Series Maryville Shiraz 2010** While having many things in common with Asset, the colour is a little deeper, the bouquet and palate a touch more intense, with plum joining the black cherry fruit; overall, well balanced and made. Screwcap. 14% alc. **Rating** 91 **To** 2018 $35

Single Vineyard Series Aset Shiraz 2010 Medium red-purple; 350 dozen produced from a single vineyard block in the Chittering Valley; while the fruit density is only moderate, the tannin and oak contributions have not overwhelmed the black cherry fruit of the palate. Screwcap. 14% alc. **Rating** 90 **To** 2017 $35

ṬṬṬṬ Lot 88 Chardonnay 2010 Rating 88 To 2014 $18
Lot 88 Shiraz 2010 Rating 88 To 2015 $18
Baroque Series Blanco 2012 Rating 87 To 2013 $22
Lot 88 Cabernet Sauvignon 2009 Rating 87 To 2015 $18

Westlake Vineyards   ★★★★★

Diagonal Road, Koonunga, SA 5355 **Region** Barossa Valley
T 0428 656 208 **www**.westlakevineyards.com.au **Open** By appt
Winemaker Darren Westlake **Est.** 1999 **Dozens** 400 **Vyds** 36.2ha
Darren and Suzanne Westlake tend 22ha of shiraz, 6.5ha of cabernet sauvignon, 2ha of viognier, and smaller plantings of petit verdot, durif, mataro, grenache and graciano planted on two properties in the Koonunga area of the Barossa Valley. They do all the vineyard work personally, and have a long list of high-profile winemakers queued up to buy the grapes, leaving only a small amount for production under the Westlake label. Suzanne is a sixth-generation descendant of Johann George Kalleske, who came to SA from Prussia in 1838, while the 717 Convicts label draws on the history of Darren's ancestor Edward Westlake, who was transported to Australia in 1788.

ṬṬṬṬṬ Eleazar Barossa Valley Shiraz 2010 Bursting at the seams with the richness and intensity of its Aladdin's Cave of black fruits and everything you could imagine associated with it. The unique feature of the Westlakes's '10 shirazs is the savoury, almost bitter underlay that has affinities with the greatest wines of the northern Rhône Valley. Cork. 14.9% alc. **Rating** 97 To 2040 $55
717 Convicts The Warden Barossa Valley Shiraz 2010 Deep, inky crimson-purple; has many similarities to Albert's Block, capturing all of the multitude of flavours of that wine, here with a slightly smoother mouthfeel. These wines are clearly a reflection of exceptional viticultural care and expertise. Cork. 14.7% alc. **Rating** 96 To 2035 $35
Albert's Block Barossa Valley Shiraz 2010 Deep purple-crimson; crammed to the rafters with black fruits, bitter chocolate and tar, oak somewhere in the background. These characters are simultaneously symbiotic and synergistic, and defy you to unravel them. Cork. 14.8% alc. **Rating** 96 To 2035 $30

WH Sweetland   ★★★★★

146 Parker Road, Bannockburn, Vic 3331 (postal) **Region** Geelong
T (03) 5281 1651 **www**.sweetland.com.au **Open** Not
Winemaker Lethbridge Wines (Ray Nadeson) **Est.** 2001 **Dozens** 70 **Vyds** 2.5ha
Bill Sweetland's family crest depicts ears of wheat and bunches of grapes, and the family first settled in the Hunter Valley in the 1820s. Bill says it was thus inevitable he should start a vineyard, and he has done so with pinot noir, with the skill of Ray Nadeson making the most of the exceptional grapes produced in 2010.

ṬṬṬṬ Bannockburn Pinot Noir 2010 Good hue and depth; shares some of the characters of its illustrious neighbours, with strongly foresty/spicy characters underlying the cornucopia of red and black plum and cherry fruit; it has excellent structure, texture and length to the finish. Screwcap. 13.5% alc. **Rating** 94 To 2020 $35

Whinstone Estate   ★★★☆

295 Dunns Creek Road, Red Hill, Vic 3937 **Region** Mornington Peninsula
T (03) 5989 7217 **www**.whinstone.com.au **Open** W'ends, or by appt
Winemaker Montalto Estate (Simon Black) **Est.** 1994 **Dozens** 1000 **Vyds** 3ha
Whinstone Estate has developed a reputation for growing fine fruit which has been sold to several of the larger premium winemakers on the Mornington Peninsula, while retaining a small amount for wines under the Whinstone Estate label. The vineyard includes pinot noir, pinot gris, chardonnay and sauvignon blanc. In late 2011 Guoing and Diana He purchased

Whinstone Estate. The aim is to continue to grow quality fruit and produce single vineyard wines for the Australian market. Exports to China under The Elms label.

♀♀♀♀♀ **Mornington Peninsula Shiraz 2011** Good colour; has fared well in the face of '11, with spicy red and black cherry fruit on the bouquet and medium-bodied palate; oak and tannins play a good support role. Cork. 13.5% alc. **Rating** 90 To 2018 $25

♀♀♀♀ **Mornington Peninsula Sauvignon Blanc 2012** Rating 89 To 2013 $21
Mornington Peninsula Pinot Grigio 2012 Rating 87 To 2013 $23
Mornington Peninsula Pinot Noir 2011 Rating 87 To 2014 $25

Whispering Hills

580 Warburton Highway, Seville, Vic 3139 **Region** Yarra Valley
T (03) 5964 2822 **www**.whisperinghills.com.au **Open** 7 days 10–6
Winemaker Murray and Darcy Lyons **Est.** 1985 **Dozens** 1000 **Vyds** 5ha
Whispering Hills is owned and operated by the Lyons family (Audrey and Darcy Lyons). Darcy is responsible for the winemaking, while Audrey takes care of the cellar door and distribution. The vineyard was established in 1985 with further plantings in '96 and some grafting in 2003, and now consists of cabernet sauvignon (2ha), riesling, chardonnay and pinot noir (1ha each). Exports to Sweden and Japan.

♀♀♀♀ **Hoddles Creek Yarra Valley Pinot Noir 2012** Deep garnet; showing developed notes of spiced plums, the palate is soft, forward and fleshy, with fresh acidity cleaning up the finish. Screwcap. 13% alc. **Rating** 87 To 2015 $28 BE

Whistler Wines

Seppeltsfield Road, Marananga, SA 5355 **Region** Barossa Valley
T (08) 8562 4942 **www**.whistlerwines.com **Open** 7 days 10.30–5
Winemaker Troy Kalleske, Christa Deans **Est.** 1999 **Dozens** 8000 **Vyds** 14ha
Brothers Martin and Chris Pfeiffer and their families have created one of the Barossa's hidden secrets: the vines and the cellar door are tucked away from the view of those travelling along Seppeltsfield Road. Martin has over 25 years' viticultural experience with Southcorp, and Chris brings marketing skills from many years as a publisher. The wines are from estate-grown shiraz (6ha), merlot (2ha), cabernet sauvignon, riesling (1.3ha each), mourvedre, grenache (1.2ha each) and semillon (1ha). Exports to Canada, Denmark, Taiwan, Hong Kong and China.

♀♀♀♀♀ **The Reserve Barossa Shiraz 2009** Good colour, healthy and deep; from a small block of estate dry-grown, severely pruned low-yielding vines, the black fruits intensely focused on the mid-palate, and spearing upwards on the finish, where the alcohol makes its mark. Screwcap. 15.5% alc. **Rating** 93 To 2025 $66
The Reserve Barossa Semillon 2010 Gleaming yellow-green; a full-bodied, luscious Semillon with citrus, honey and toast aromas and flavours all on parade. Is now at or close to its best, but will hold for a few years. Screwcap. 12.5% alc. **Rating** 90 To 2015 $23

♀♀♀♀ **Barossa Mourvedre 2009** Rating 89 To 2016 $27
Barossa Riesling 2012 Rating 88 To 2015 $23

Whitfield Estate ★★★☆

198 McIntyre Road, Scotsdale, Denmark, WA 6333 **Region** Great Southern
T (08) 9840 9016 **www**.whitfieldestate.com.au **Open** Thurs–Mon 10–5, 7 days during school hols
Winemaker Dave Cleary, James Kellie **Est.** 1994 **Dozens** 2500 **Vyds** 4.8ha
Graham and Kelly Howard acquired the Whitfield Estate vineyard (planted in 1994) in 2005. The estate is planted to chardonnay (2.5ha) and shiraz (2.3ha), the majority of which is sold to West Cape Howe, who contract-make the remaining grapes for Whitfield Estate. Other

varieties are also purchased from growers in the region. The Picnic in the Paddock Café offers fresh, locally produced, seasonal dishes.

♀♀♀♀♀ **Shiraz 2011** Bright mid garnet; a fragrant and attractively perfumed bouquet
✪ of red fruits, thyme and ironstone; medium-bodied, fleshy and accessible, this is
the embodiment of an easygoing, spicy red; a wine to enjoy. Screwcap. 13.5% alc.
Rating 90 **To** 2018 $18 BE

Wicks Estate Wines ★★★★

21 Franklin Street, Adelaide, SA 5000 (postal) **Region** Adelaide Hills
T (08) 8212 0004 **www**.wicksestate.com.au **Open** Not
Winemaker Tim Knappstein, Leigh Ratzmer **Est.** 2000 **Dozens** 20 000 **Vyds** 38.1ha
Tim and Simon Wicks had a long-term involvement with orchard and nursery operations at Highbury in the Adelaide Hills prior to purchasing the 54ha property at Woodside in 1999. They planted fractionally less than 40ha of chardonnay, riesling, sauvignon blanc, shiraz, merlot and cabernet sauvignon, following this with the construction of a winery in 2004. Wicks Estate has won more than its fair share of wine show medals over the years, the wines priced well below their full worth. Exports to The Netherlands and China.

♀♀♀♀♀ **Adelaide Hills Sauvignon Blanc 2012** Light straw-green; a no-frills style, with
✪ all the emphasis on varietal fruit expression that straddles fresh-mown grass, citrus
and tropical fruit notes, the finish fresh and lively. Trophy Adelaide Hills Wine
Show '12. Screwcap. 13% alc. **Rating** 93 **To** 2013 $18
✪ **Adelaide Hills Pinot Noir 2012** Spectacular deep, but bright, crimson-purple; a
Pinot that is all about red (mainly) and black cherry, its bouquet and palate utterly
consistent; there are some spicy/savoury notes hiding behind the fruit that will
emerge in a few years' time, making this an even greater bargain than it is now.
Screwcap. 13.5% alc. **Rating** 93 **To** 2020 $20
✪ **Adelaide Hills Riesling 2012** The gently floral bouquet has citrus blossom
aromas flowing through to the finely built palate, lime and lemon fruit promptly
announcing their presence; good acidity provides a flourish on the finish.
Screwcap. 13% alc. **Rating** 91 **To** 2017 $18

♀♀♀♀ **Adelaide Hills Chardonnay 2012** **Rating** 88 **To** 2014 $18

Wignalls Wines ★★★★

448 Chester Pass Road (Highway 1), Albany, WA 6330 **Region** Albany
T (08) 9841 2848 **www**.wignallswines.com.au **Open** 7 days 11–4
Winemaker Rob Wignall, Michael Perkins **Est.** 1982 **Dozens** 10 000 **Vyds** 18.5ha
While the estate vineyards have a diverse range of sauvignon blanc, semillon, chardonnay, pinot noir, merlot, shiraz, cabernet franc and cabernet sauvignon, founder Bill Wignall was one of the early movers with pinot noir, producing wines that, by the standards of their time, were well in front of anything else coming out of WA (and up with the then limited amounts being made in Vic and Tas). The star dimmed, problems in the vineyard and with contract winemaking both playing a role. The establishment of an onsite winery, and the assumption of the winemaking role by son Rob, with significant input by Michael Perkins, has seen the range of wines increase. Exports to Denmark, Japan, Singapore and China.

♀♀♀♀♀ **Albany Sauvignon Blanc 2012** The bouquet is relatively reserved, the palate
altogether more expressive, with lots of lees work highlighting the mix of cut grass,
herb and ripe fruits, including gooseberry; a supple finish. Screwcap. 14.3% alc.
Rating 93 **To** 2014 $19
Albany Pinot Noir 2011 Light colour; spice, cherry and plum aromas continue
onto the palate, which has above-average structure thanks to well-managed tannins
and a touch of savoury forest floor. Screwcap. 14% alc. **Rating** 92 **To** 2017 $31
Albany Chardonnay 2011 Bright straw-green; estate-grown, fermented with a
mix of wild and cultured yeast in part new, part used French oak. The wine has
a range of citrus, honeydew melon and peach fruit, the oak restrained, the length
good rather than great. Screwcap. 14% alc. **Rating** 91 **To** 2017 $35

Wild Dog Winery

Warragul-Korrumburra Road, Warragul, Vic 3820 **Region** Gippsland
T (03) 5623 1117 **www**.wilddogwinery.com **Open** 7 days 11–5
Winemaker Folkert Janssen **Est.** 1982 **Dozens** 3000 **Vyds** 10.1ha
Wild Dog is a family-owned business operated by Gary and Judy Surman. Since acquiring the business in 2005 much work has been done in the vineyard (planted in 1982) with grafting, replanting and retrellising, and through winery expansion (all wines are now made onsite). They have also built a restaurant overlooking the vineyard. Now one of the larger wineries in Gippsland, having won four trophies at the Gippsland Wine Show '08 and Most Successful Exhibitor in '09, it would seem there is much to be confident about. Exports to China and Japan.

ŶŶŶŶŶ **Gippsland Pinot Noir 2010** Bright, clear red-purple; the fragrant red berry and spice aromas on the bouquet lead into a palate of considerable length and intensity, with intriguing notes of spice and anise moving more to centre stage, allied with oak. Don't be concerned, it all comes together well. Screwcap. 13.5% alc. Rating 92 To 2018 $24

ŶŶŶŶ **Gippsland Semillon 2006** Bright straw-green; very different from Hunter Valley Semillon, with more herbal characters allied with grainy acidity; first tasted over 6 years ago, and still shows similar flavours. No need to cellar it longer, but it won't fall apart anytime soon. Screwcap. 13% alc. **Rating** 89 **To** 2016 $17
Gippsland Wild Rose 2012 Rating 88 To 2014 $21

Wild Fox Organic Wines

PO Box 343, Prospect SA 5082 **Region** Adelaide Plains
T (08) 8342 5321 **www**.wildfoxwines.com **Open** Not
Winemaker Mark Jamieson **Est.** 1998 **Dozens** 12000 **Vyds** 17ha
Prior generations of the Markou family lived in the village of Agrelopo (meaning wild fox) on the Greek island of Chios. Now in Australia, the family has continued its involvement with growing grapes and making wine, with managing director Petros Markou acknowledging that it was his brother Terry who originally purchased the vineyard as a hobby farm, having the vision to move to certified organic status in 1998. The vineyard is planted to shiraz, merlot, sauvignon blanc and cabernet sauvignon. Tasting notes for their Marlborough Sauvignon Blanc can be seen on www.winecompanion.com.au. Exports to the US, The Netherlands, Hong Kong and Singapore.

ŶŶŶŶ **Pinot Gris 2012** Pale pink-blush; carries both organic and biodynamic certification logos. It has a full load of flavour and phenolics in the style of Alsace, and is certainly in the gris mould, if a little rough and ready. Screwcap. 12.8% alc. Rating 87 To 2014 $20
Merlot 2008 Not preservative free, the back label talking of certified organic and biodynamic practices, the front label simply saying 'made with organic grapes', the origin simply SA. It is a well-balanced wine, with plum fruit and mocha/fruitcake oak-derived characters. Screwcap. 14.5% alc. **Rating** 87 **To** 2015 $20

Willespie

555 Harmans Mill Road, Wilyabrup via Cowaramup, WA 6284 **Region** Margaret River
T (08) 9755 6248 **www**.willespie.com.au **Open** 7 days 10.30–5
Winemaker Anthony Neilson **Est.** 1976 **Dozens** 5000 **Vyds** 17.53ha
Willespie has produced many attractive white wines over the years, typically in brisk, herbaceous Margaret River style; all are fruit- rather than oak-driven. The business has been on the market for some time, and part of the vineyards have been sold. Exports to the UK, Malaysia and Japan.

 PPPPP **Shiraz 2008** Has retained both depth of colour and hue; this medium- to full-
✪   bodied wine has multiple layers of black fruits and oak on the bouquet, tannins
      joining the party on the palate; nuances of dark chocolate also chime in, and the
      wine has a long future ahead. Diam. 15% alc. **Rating** 93 **To** 2033 $25
      Old School Margaret River Cabernet Sauvignon 2007 Very good colour
      for age. It has abundant blackcurrant fruit and firm cabernet tannins, oak in
      restraint, although not the alcohol. Diam. 15.1% alc. **Rating** 91 **To** 2027 $65
✪   **Margaret River Red 2009** Medium purple-red; a cabernet sauvignon/merlot
      blend with unexpectedly luscious blackcurrant and plum fruit, gentle oak allied
      with a touch of mocha and soft tannins. Ready now. Screwcap. 14% alc. **Rating** 90
      To 2015 $20

PPPP **Margaret River Verdelho 2010** Rating 87 To 2014 $20

Willoughby Park   ★★★★★
678 South Coast Highway, Denmark, WA 6333 **Region** Great Southern
T (08) 9848 1555 **www**.willoughbypark.com.au **Open** 7 days 10–5
Winemaker Andries Mostert **Est.** 2010 **Dozens** 18000 **Vyds** 18.2ha
Bob Fowler, who comes from a rural background and has always hankered after a farming life,
stumbled across the opportunity to achieve this in early 2010. Together with wife Marilyn,
he purchased the former West Cape Howe winery and surrounding vineyard that had
become available when West Cape Howe moved into the far larger Goundrey winery. In '11
Willoughby Park purchased the Kalgan River vineyard and business name, and winemaking
operations have been transferred to Willoughby Park. There are now three labels: Willoughby
Park, the Great Southern premium brand for estate and purchased grapes; Kalgan River, a
single vineyard range; and Jamie & Charli, a sub-$20 Great Southern range of wines. Exports
to Norway and China.

PPPPP **Great Southern Sauvignon Blanc 2012** Quartz-white; the aromatic bouquet
      introduces a lively palate opening with fleeting grass/herb characters before
      moving on smartly to passionfruit and gooseberry on the juicy palate. Screwcap.
      13% alc. **Rating** 94 **To** 2014 $26
      Kalgan River Albany Chardonnay 2011 Barrel fermentation in French
      oak has imparted some smoky bacon characters to the bouquet, turning more
      to cashew on the palate as the intense white peach, pear and grapefruit flavours
      impose themselves and drive the long, well-balanced palate. Screwcap. 13.5% alc.
      Rating 94 To 2019 $40

PPPPP **Denmark Riesling 2012** Rating 93 To 2022 $26
      Kalgan River Albany Riesling 2011 Rating 93 To 2021 $35
      Blackwood Valley Tempranillo Rose 2012 Rating 92 To 2014 $26

Willow Bridge Estate   ★★★★★
Gardin Court Drive, Dardanup, WA 6236 **Region** Geographe
T (08) 9728 0055 **www**.willowbridge.com.au **Open** 7 days 11–5
Winemaker Simon Burnell, Jane Dunkley **Est.** 1997 **Dozens** 20000 **Vyds** 59ha
Jeff and Vicky Dewar have followed a fast track in developing Willow Bridge Estate since
acquiring the spectacular 180ha hillside property in the Ferguson Valley: chardonnay, semillon,
sauvignon blanc, shiraz and cabernet sauvignon were planted, with merlot, tempranillo, chenin
blanc and viognier following. Willow Bridge won three Most Successful Western Australian
Exhibitor trophies at the Perth Wine Show in recent years. Many of its wines offer exceptional
value for money. Exports to the UK, the US and other major markets.

PPPPP **Black Dog Geographe Shiraz 2011** Deep, bright crimson-purple; a very
      distinguished Shiraz, with exuberant black fruits and spices on the bouquet and
      gloriously supple, long, medium-bodied palate; the oak is perfectly balanced and
      integrated, the tannins likewise. Screwcap. 14% alc. **Rating** 96 **To** 2036 $60

✪   **Geographe Fume 2012** A 65/35% blend of sauvignon blanc and semillon, hand-picked, whole bunch-pressed and wild-fermented in French oak (20% new); partial mlf, and 9 months on lees. The wine has repaid the extra time and expense involved, still with delicious tropical fruit on the mid-palate, surrounded by nutty/creamy nuances; overall balance and mouthfeel are equally good. Screwcap. 12.5% alc. **Rating** 95 **To** 2015 $25

G1-10 Geographe Chardonnay 2012 A single vineyard, single block chardonnay (Gingin clone), hand-picked, whole bunch-pressed, wild yeast fermentation in French oak (35% new), partial mlf and 9 months on lees. The Gingin clone is particularly obvious on the bouquet, less so on the very fine, long and intense palate, tangy acidity drawing out the finish and aftertaste. Screwcap. 13% alc. **Rating** 95 **To** 2020 $30

✪   **Solana Geographe Tempranillo 2011** Medium purple-crimson; has more density and weight than most Australian Tempranillos, but still retains clear varietal characters and a degree of elegance; red and black cherries abound, used French oak was cleverly chosen, and the tannins are ripe and balanced. Remarkable wine. Screwcap. 13% alc. **Rating** 95 **To** 2021 $25

G1-10 Geographe Chardonnay 2011 A special basket-pressed, wild yeast barrel-fermented and matured selection, given partial mlf and 10 months' lees contact; these were the final winemaking inputs to a vibrantly complex palate, easily absorbing those inputs into the integrity of the white peach and nectarine fruit. The name is a delphic reference to the biblical book of Genesis chapter 1, verse 10. Screwcap. 13% alc. **Rating** 94 **To** 2017 $30

✪   **Dragonfly Geographe Rose 2012** Light but vivid puce; a fragrant and elegant wine, with aromas of rose petal and small red fruits, the palate with exemplary definition and focus. Screwcap. 12.5% alc. **Rating** 94 **To** 2014 $17

Gravel Pit Geographe Shiraz 2011 Dense purple-crimson; this is the full-bodied big brother of Dragonfly, the impact of more extraction and more oak quite evident, and demanding patience. Screwcap. 13.8% alc. **Rating** 94 **To** 2026 $30

✪   **Dragonfly Geographe Shiraz 2011** Strong purple-crimson; has exemplary cool-grown shiraz varietal character, with plum, blackberry, licorice and spice all on parade; the balance and texture are admirable, as is the contribution of French oak. Outstanding bargain. Screwcap. 13.5% alc. **Rating** 94 **To** 2021 $17

♟♟♟♟♟ **Pemberton Fume Sauvignon Blanc 2011 Rating** 93 **To** 2014 $25
✪   **Dragonfly Geographe Sauvignon Blanc Semillon 2012** Light straw-green; the intense aromas and flavours of a cascade of tropical fruits intermingling with lime, grapefruit and lemon citrus have been given a touch of texture by a small portion of barrel-fermented wine. Clever winemaking. Screwcap. 12% alc. **Rating** 93 **To** 2014 $17

✪   **Dragonfly Geographe Chenin Blanc 2012** Light straw-green; if you were going to drink Chenin Blanc, this is a very good start, overflowing with delicious fruit-sweet fruit salad flavours, and with perfect citrussy/crunchy acidity on the finish. Screwcap. 12.5% alc. **Rating** 92 **To** 2014 $17

Willow Creek Vineyard ★★★★★

166 Balnarring Road, Merricks North, Vic 3926 **Region** Mornington Peninsula
T (03) 5989 7448 **www**.willow-creek.com.au **Open** 7 days 11–5
Winemaker Geraldine McFaul **Est.** 1989 **Dozens** 5000 **Vyds** 11.15ha
Willow Creek Vineyard is a significant presence in the Mornington Peninsula, with the mature vineyard planted to pinot noir, chardonnay, cabernet sauvignon, sauvignon blanc and pinot gris. The grape intake is supplemented by small, quality parcels purchased from local growers. The Willow Creek wines rank with the best from the Peninsula, the arrival of Geraldine McFaul as winemaker promising a continuation in the quality of the wines.

🍷🍷🍷🍷🍷 Mornington Peninsula Sauvignon Blanc 2012 Estate-grown, hand-picked, whole bunch-pressed and barrel-fermented; an expensive exercise, but justified by the quality of the wine, with a deliciously juicy stream of passionfruit, guava and ripe citrus, the last inhabiting the balanced acidity; the oak has added to the texture and structure of the wine without in any way diminishing the fruit. Screwcap. 12.5% alc. **Rating** 95 **To** 2015 $35

Mornington Peninsula Pinot Gris 2012 Barrel fermentation has transformed the wine, giving it both texture and structure, but leaving plenty of room for spiced pear and apple fruit. Screwcap. 13.5% alc. **Rating** 94 **To** 2014 $35

🍷🍷🍷🍷🍷 Mornington Peninsula Pinot Noir 2011 **Rating** 92 **To** 2015 $40

Mornington Peninsula Rose 2012 **Rating** 91 **To** 2014 $25

Wills Domain

Cnr Brash Road/Abbey Farm Road, Yallingup, WA 6281 **Region** Margaret River
T (08) 9755 2327 **www.**willsdomain.com.au **Open** 7 days 10–5
Winemaker Naturaliste Vintners (Bruce Dukes) **Est.** 1985 **Dozens** 12500 **Vyds** 20.8ha
When the Haunold family purchased the original Wills Domain vineyard in 2000, they were adding another chapter to a family history of winemaking stretching back to 1383 in what is now Austria. Remarkable though that may be, more remarkable is that 37-year-old Darren, who lost the use of his legs in an accident in 1989, runs the estate (including part of the pruning) from his wheelchair. The vineyard is planted to shiraz, semillon, cabernet sauvignon, sauvignon blanc, chardonnay, merlot, petit verdot, malbec, cabernet franc and viognier. Exports to the UK, the US, Singapore, Malaysia, Indonesia, South Korea and Hong Kong.

🍷🍷🍷🍷🍷 Margaret River Chardonnay 2011 Bright green-straw; the instantly complex and fragrant bouquet signals the purity of the white peach and grapefruit flavours, which have been delicately framed by quality French oak. Will continue to develop well. Screwcap. 14% alc. **Rating** 95 **To** 2019 $35

Reserve Margaret River Shiraz 2010 Emphasises the ability of Margaret River to produce shiraz of the excellent quality in a medium-bodied frame, here with a dash of viognier to tie up the parcel. It has a seamless blend of red and black cherry/berry fruit, quality French oak, and gently spicy/savoury tannins. Screwcap. 13.5% alc. **Rating** 95 **To** 2030 $45

Reserve Margaret River Cabernet Sauvignon 2010 Purple-crimson of medium depth; the fragrant bouquet verges on the flowery, and signals the seductive lightness of touch of the wine on the palate, which finishes with a cassis/berry lift rather than tannins; that said, there is plenty of structure, and great length. Screwcap. 14% alc. **Rating** 95 **To** 2030 $55

Aged Release Margaret River Semillon 2007 Bright straw-green, light for age; has aged with the surety of Hunter Valley semillon, but gone down its own distinctive pathway, building texture, structure and line; the flavours range from herb, snow pea and lemongrass to honey and vanilla, the acidity providing a lifeline stretching well into the future. Screwcap. 13.5% alc. **Rating** 94 **To** 2027 $45

Margaret River Reserve Bitza 2010 Strong purple-crimson; a blend of merlot, petit verdot, malbec, cabernet franc and cabernet sauvignon; cassis, black olive and cedar ripple through to the finish on a bed of superfine-grained tannins. Screwcap. 14% alc. **Rating** 94 **To** 2025 $35

Margaret River Reserve Bitza 2009 A blend of merlot, petit verdot, malbec, cabernet franc and cabernet sauvignon; the fragrant and expressive bouquet sets the scene for the redcurrant and blackcurrant flavours of the long, well-balanced palate, quality oak and fine-grained tannins completing the picture. Re-tasted Nov '12. Screwcap. 14% alc. **Rating** 94 **To** 2029 $40

Reserve Margaret River Cabernet Sauvignon 2009 An elegant, medium-bodied wine, with purity of varietal fruit expression on both the fragrant bouquet and palate; the control of both tannins and oak has given free play to that fruit. Screwcap. 14% alc. **Rating** 94 **To** 2025 $45

ＹＹＹＹＹ **Margaret River Semillon Sauvignon Blanc 2012** Pale straw-green; the
✪ fragrant, flowery bouquet is followed by a deceptively delicate palate with an array
of passionfruit and gooseberry flavours tied up with a bow of citrussy acidity.
Screwcap. 12.5% alc. **Rating** 93 **To** 2014 $20

✪ **Margaret River Shiraz 2011** Deep but bright purple-crimson; a pleasing,
medium-bodied palate follows a gently spicy bouquet; a small amount of viognier
was added, though seemingly not co-fermented; has milky tannins and spiced
cherry fruitcake flavours. Screwcap. 14% alc. **Rating** 90 **To** 2016 $20

Willunga Creek Wines   ★★★☆

230 Delabole Road, Willunga, SA 5172 **Region** McLaren Vale
T (08) 8556 2244 **www**.willungacreekwines.com.au **Open** W'ends 10–5, or by appt
Winemaker Goe De Fabio, Phil Christiansen **Est.** 2002 **Dozens** 4000 **Vyds** 7.2ha
David and Julie Cheesley purchased the property in the early 1990s, and embarked on a
vineyard development program that has established 3.2ha each of cabernet sauvignon and
shiraz and 0.4 each of grenache and merlot. The vines are planted on terraced sloping hills,
the wind exposure helping the Cheesleys' organic management of the vineyard. The Willunga
name and the Black Duck brand come from the Aboriginal word 'willangga', which means
black duck. The cellar door is a refurbished circa 1850 building in the town of Willunga.
Exports to the UK and Hong Kong.

ＹＹＹＹＹ **Black Duck McLaren Vale Shiraz 2008** Has retained good hue; a juicy, vibrant
✪ wine that was surely picked before the heatwave, with blackberry, black cherry, a
touch of dark chocolate, and a final surge of flavour on the finish that is fresh, not
heavy. Diam. 14.5% alc. **Rating** 93 **To** 2028 $25

ＹＹＹＹ **Black Duck McLaren Vale Merlot 2011** **Rating** 88 **To** 2019 $25
Out for a Duck Cabernet Shiraz 2007 **Rating** 87 **To** 2015 $25

Willunga 100 Wines   ★★★★★

c/- Haselgrove, Sand Road, McLaren Vale, SA 5171 **Region** McLaren Vale
T 0427 271 280 **www**.willunga100.com **Open** By appt
Winemaker Tim James, Kate Day **Est.** 2005 **Dozens** 20 000
This venture is now solely owned by Liberty Wines UK, sourcing its grapes from McLaren
Vale and from Adelaide Hills (pinot gris and a portion of its viognier). Tim James has come
on board as consultant winemaker, Kate Day continuing in the executive role. The business
has export links to many parts of the world in addition to the UK.

ＹＹＹＹＹ **McLaren Vale Shiraz Viognier 2010** Intense purple-crimson; a come-hither
✪ palate of satsuma plum, spice and licorice has the freshness more common in
cool regions, the tannins fine and supple, oak balanced and integrated. Screwcap.
14% alc. **Rating** 94 **To** 2020 $25
The Tithing Grenache 2010 Medium red-purple; typical McLaren Vale
grenache, with more colour, more flavour and more structure than those from the
Barossa or Clare Valleys; there is a sweetness to the red and black fruits (in no way
linked to sugar) that seduces the palate, even though oak and tannins are both in
play. Screwcap. 14.5% alc. **Rating** 94 **To** 2020 $45

✪ **McLaren Vale Tempranillo 2012** Intense purple-crimson; a very convincing
and attractive Tempranillo, flooded with black cherry and raspberry fruits offset by
fine-grained, but persistent, tannins that add to both flavour and texture. Screwcap.
14% alc. **Rating** 94 **To** 2022 $25

ＹＹＹＹＹ **Adelaide Hills Viognier 2012** Pale straw-green; has more vitality and
freshness – attitude, if you will – than most, even if there seems to be more citrus
than apricot in its make-up. May reward a couple of years in bottle, and given the
benefit of the doubt. Screwcap. 14% alc. **Rating** 90 **To** 2015 $25

Wilson Vineyard

Polish Hill River, Sevenhill via Clare, SA 5453 **Region** Clare Valley
T (08) 8843 4310 **www**.wilsonvineyard.com.au **Open** W'ends 10–4
Winemaker Daniel Wilson **Est.** 1974 **Dozens** 3000 **Vyds** 11.9ha
In 2009 the winery and general operations were passed on to son Daniel Wilson, the second generation. Daniel, a graduate of CSU, spent three years in the Barossa with some of Australia's largest winemakers before returning to Clare in 2003. Parents John and Pat Wilson still contribute in a limited capacity, content to watch developments in the business they created. Daniel continues to follow John's beliefs about keeping quality high, often at the expense of volume, and rather than talk about it, believes the proof is in the bottle. At Daniel's side are wife Tamara and daughters Poppy and Isabelle, who help keep the wheels turning behind the scenes.

ŶŶŶŶŶ
✪　**Watervale Riesling 2012** Bright quartz-green; the highly aromatic bouquet leads into a precisely framed palate, where citrus, a touch of passionfruit and cleansing acidity coalesce to provide a Riesling of considerable distinction and exceptional value. Screwcap. 12% alc. **Rating** 95 **To** 2022 $18
　Polish Hill River Riesling 2012 Bright straw-green; while having family similarity to the DJW, this wine has greater focus and intensity, and more lime juice flavours at its core, balanced by crisp, lingering acidity. Screwcap. 12.5% alc. **Rating** 95 **To** 2027 $28

ŶŶŶŶŶ
✪　**DJW Clare Valley Riesling 2012** Bright straw-green; this is a finely articulated and polished (no puns in tasting notes) wine, gentle citrus fruit and slatey acidity in harmonious balance. Screwcap. 12.5% alc. **Rating** 93 **To** 2020 $23
　Hand Plunge Clare Valley Shiraz 2008 Rating 93 **To** 2028 $38
✪　**DJW Clare Valley Riesling 2011** Bright, light straw-green; a rich, fleshy Riesling, with lime juice the primary driver, and some tropical nuances adding somewhat atypical fruit sweetness. Screwcap. 12% alc. **Rating** 92 **To** 2021 $22
　Clare Valley Tempranillo 2009 Rating 90 **To** 2016 $26

Wily Trout

Marakei-Nanima Road, via Hall, NSW 2618 **Region** Canberra District
T (02) 6230 2487 **www**.poacherspantry.com.au **Open** 7 days 10–5
Winemaker Dr Roger Harris, Nick Spencer (Contract) **Est.** 1998 **Dozens** 8000
Vyds 20ha
The Wily Trout vineyard, owned by Robert and Susan Bruce, shares its home with the Poachers Pantry, a renowned gourmet smokehouse. The quality of the wines is very good, and a testament to the skills of the contract winemakers. The northeast-facing slopes, at an elevation of 720m, provide some air drainage and hence protection against spring frosts. The production increase (from 3000 dozen) speaks for itself.

ŶŶŶŶŶ
　Canberra District Sauvignon Blanc 2012 Pale green-quartz; has excellent intensity and focus, the palate bringing grass, herb, citrus, passionfruit and mineral acidity in a seamless stream across the palate and into the lingering finish and aftertaste. Screwcap. 12.6% alc. **Rating** 94 **To** 2014 $30

ŶŶŶŶ
　Canberra District Shiraz 2006 Rating 89 **To** 2015 $34

Wimbaliri Wines

3180 Barton Highway, Murrumbateman, NSW 2582 **Region** Canberra District
T (02) 6227 5921 **www**.wimbaliri.com.au **Open** W'ends 10–5, or by appt
Winemaker Scott Gledhill **Est.** 1988 **Dozens** 800 **Vyds** 2.2ha
John and Margaret Andersen moved to the Canberra District in 1987 and began establishing their vineyard at Murrumbateman in '88; the property borders highly regarded Canberra producer Clonakilla. The vineyard is close-planted with chardonnay, pinot noir, shiraz, cabernet sauvignon and merlot (plus a few vines of cabernet franc). Prior to the 2009 vintage the winery was purchased by Scott and Sarah Gledhill. Scott, born in Wallsend (NSW), is a

sixth-generation descendant of German vine dressers who emigrated to the Hunter Valley in the 1850s; Sarah draws upon her science background to assist in the vineyard and winemaking.

ΨΨΨΨΨ **Special Release First Vines Murrumbateman Cabernet Merlot 2009** Like the '10, co-fermented, and spent over 2 years in barrel; here the inclusion of used American oak, and significantly higher alcohol, have resulted in a richer wine, also with a heavily stained Diam. 14.5% alc. **Rating** 90 **To** 2016 $25

ΨΨΨΨ **Murrumbateman Rose 2012 Rating** 89 To 2014 $18
First Vines Murrumbateman Cabernet Merlot 2010 Rating 89
To 2015 $25

Windance Wines

2764 Caves Road, Yallingup, WA 6282 **Region** Margaret River
T (08) 9755 2293 **www**.windance.com.au **Open** 7 days 10–5
Winemaker Simon Ding, Michael (Tyke) Wheatley **Est.** 1998 **Dozens** 3500 **Vyds** 7.25ha
Drew and Rosemary Brent-White own this family business, situated 5km south of Yallingup. Cabernet sauvignon, shiraz, sauvignon blanc, semillon and merlot have been established, incorporating sustainable land management and organic farming practices where possible. The wines are exclusively estate-grown.

ΨΨΨΨΨ **Margaret River Sauvignon Blanc Semillon 2012** A delicious wine, on the
✪   cusp between sweet citrus and tropical fruit aromas and flavours. It flows across the tongue, refreshing and not demanding, the aftertaste a spring day. Trophy Best White Blend, Qantas Wine Show of WA '12. Screwcap. 12% alc. **Rating** 95 To 2014 $20

ΨΨΨΨΨ **Margaret River Shiraz 2011** While only medium-bodied at best, has plenty of
✪   shape and texture to its red and black fruits courtesy of persistent, but very fine, tannins and moderate French oak. Screwcap. 14.5% alc. **Rating** 90 **To** 2017 $22
✪   **Margaret River Cabernet Merlot 2011** Strong red-purple; a generously endowed medium- to full-bodied wine with red- and blackcurrant fruit. It has time on its side, with enough tannins to help steer its course over the years ahead. Screwcap. 14.5% alc. **Rating** 90 **To** 2021 $22

Windowrie Estate

Windowrie Road, Canowindra, NSW 2804 **Region** Cowra
T (02) 6344 3234 **www**.windowrie.com.au **Open** At the Mill, Cowra
Winemaker Antonio D'Onise **Est.** 1988 **Dozens** 30 000 **Vyds** 240ha
Windowrie Estate was established by the O'Dea family in 1988 on a substantial grazing property at Canowindra, 30km north of Cowra and in the same viticultural region. A portion of the grapes from the substantial vineyard is sold to other makers, but increasing quantities are being made for the Windowrie Estate and The Mill labels; the Chardonnays have enjoyed show success. The cellar door is in a flour mill built in 1861 from local granite; it ceased operations in 1905 and lay unoccupied for 91 years until restored by the O'Dea family. Exports to Canada, China, Japan and Singapore

ΨΨΨΨΨ **Family Reserve Orange Pinot Gris 2012** Light straw-green; an extended period of lees contact post-fermentation in stainless steel has helped build a palate with a more creamy texture than many, but not detracting from its intense citrus/white peach/pear flavours. Screwcap. 12% alc. **Rating** 92 **To** 2014 $25
Family Reserve Cowra Chardonnay 2012 The use of new and used French oak maturation for 8 months has paid dividends for a very well balanced wine with flavours of stone fruit and citrus to the fore, oak playing a secondary role. Screwcap. 13% alc. **Rating** 91 **To** 2017 $25

Windows Estate

4 Quininup Road, Yallingup, WA 6282 **Region** Margaret River
T (08) 9755 2719 **www**.windowsestate.com **Open** 7 days 10–5
Winemaker Mick Scott, Chris Davies **Est.** 1996 **Dozens** 4500 **Vyds** 6.3ha
Len and Barbara Davies progressively established their vineyard (cabernet sauvignon, shiraz, chenin blanc, chardonnay, semillon, sauvignon blanc and merlot), initially selling the grapes. In 2006 the decision was taken to move to winemaking. It has been rewarded with considerable show success for its consistently good wines. Exports to Germany, Malaysia, Singapore, Taiwan and China.

 Single Vineyard Margaret River Sauvignon Blanc 2012 Quartz-white; has
❂   a delicacy that is achieved despite an array of varietal flavours ranging from snow pea and citrus to gooseberry and passionfruit; very likely whole bunch-pressed. Finishes with good acidity. Screwcap. 12% alc. **Rating** 94 **To** 2013 $22
❂   **Single Vineyard Margaret River Semillon Sauvignon Blanc 2012** Pale quartz-green; a worthy successor to the '11 blend, the fragrant bouquet and palate offering a pristine, juicy blend of citrus, lemongrass, gooseberry and passionfruit. Screwcap. 12% alc. **Rating** 94 **To** 2014 $22
Single Vineyard Margaret River Chardonnay 2011 A wine of depth and complexity on both bouquet and palate; nectarine and white peach fruit are folded into a creamy/nutty sauce ex the oak and barrel fermentation, but balanced by acidity on the finish. Screwcap. 13.5% alc. **Rating** 94 **To** 2017 $35
Limited Release Margaret River Petit Verdot Malbec 2010 The first Limited Release from Windows Estate; open-fermented and matured for 18 months in French oak barriques; it has plush/lush dark berry fruits, the tannins fine and ripe. Screwcap. 14.5% alc. **Rating** 94 **To** 2030 $40

Basket Pressed Cabernet Sauvignon 2011 **Rating** 93 **To** 2022 $35 BE
Basket Pressed Cabernet Merlot 2011 **Rating** 91 **To** 2018 $28 BE

WindshakeR ★★★

PO Box 8706, Perth BC, WA 6849 **Region** Swan District
T (08) 9393 2885 **www**.windshaker.com.au **Open** Not
Winemaker Ryan Sudano **Est.** 2003 **Dozens** NFP **Vyds** 20.1ha
The Moltoni family has owned a 2000ha farming property for three generations. Robert Moltoni is the driving force, establishing WindshakeR in 2003. The vineyard (carnelian, semillon, shiraz and verdelho) is 9km north of Gingin, and looks out over the hills to the sea. Moltoni is an accomplished poet, and I cannot help but quote one of his poems: 'Easterlies whistle through the gums/Crashing over silent ridges/Bathing vines in Namatjira Crimson/WindshakeR, WindshakeR, WindshakeR/The ghost winds whisper down/Off the red plains to the sea.' Exports to the US and China.

Reserve Shiraz 2010 Deeply coloured, and showing some development, as the lifted bouquet shows prune, black fruits and fruitcake; the palate is warm and rich on entry, just falling a little short on the finish. Diam. 14.9% alc. **Rating** 87 **To** 2015 $20 BE
Reserve Carnelian 2010 Deep garnet; a ripe and essency bouquet of blackberry pastille and ironstone; the medium-bodied palate is soft, fleshy and forward, ultimately one-dimensional, but with a bit of character. Diam. 14.2% alc. **Rating** 87 **To** 2016 $20 BE

wine by brad

PO Box 475, Margaret River, WA 6285 **Region** Margaret River
T 0409 572 957 **www**.winebybrad.com.au **Open** Not
Winemaker Brad Wehr, Contract **Est.** 2003 **Dozens** 5000
Brad Wehr says that wine by brad 'is the result of a couple of influential winemakers and shadowy ruffians deciding there was something to be gained by putting together some pretty

neat parcels of wine from the region, creating their own label, and releasing it with minimal fuss'. The premium Mantra range is made from separately sourced grapes. Exports to Ireland, Canada, South Korea and Singapore.

ΥΥΥΥΥ
✪
Mantra Journey Margaret River Shiraz 2010 Light to medium red-purple; a fragrant and juicy medium-bodied wine, strongly influenced by its potpourri of a multitude of spices, ground red and black pepper, red cherry relegating blackberry to second place on the light- to medium-bodied palate, fine tannins completing the journey. Screwcap. 13.5% alc. **Rating** 94 **To** 2020 $25

ΥΥΥΥΥ
✪
Mantra Affirmation Margaret River Semillon Sauvignon Blanc 2012 Light straw-green; paradoxically, the use of some French oak seems to have lifted, rather than subdued, the varietal fruit interplays, as well as providing structure; passionfruit and guava are the pacemakers, lemon/citrus courtesy of the semillon component. Screwcap. 13% alc. **Rating** 93 **To** 2014 $20

✪
Mantra Abundance Margaret River Cabernet Sauvignon 2010 An attractive medium-bodied Cabernet, bringing blackcurrant, touches of olive and briar, and gently ripe tannins into play, framed by French oak. So well balanced it can be enjoyed now or in a decade. Screwcap. 13% alc. **Rating** 93 **To** 2020 $25

✪
Mantra Revelation Margaret River Sauvignon Blanc 2012 Spicy passionfruit, citrus, lemon and lime, fleshy stone fruit, gooseberry, grapefruit, banana, passionfruit, sweet pineapple – all this, and a touch of vanillin oak per the back label. The surprising thing is that the wine is not schizophrenic; rather it is well structured, the oak subtle, but of structural importance. Screwcap. 13% alc. **Rating** 92 **To** 2014 $20

✪
Margaret River Cabernet Merlot 2010 Medium red-purple; a savoury blend with a passing nod to Bordeaux; cassis, touches of capsicum and herb, cedary oak and persistent, fine-grained tannins allow it to punch well above its price point. Screwcap. 13.5% alc. **Rating** 92 **To** 2018 $18

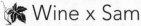 Wine x Sam   NR

1896 Tarcombe Road, Avenel, Vic 3664 (postal) **Region** Strathbogie Ranges
T 0408 587 702 **www**.winebysam.com.au **Open** Not
Winemaker Sam Plunkett, Arran Murphy **Est. Dozens** 30 000 **Vyds** 10.2ha
There are more twists and turns behind the story of Wine x Sam than an episode of *Australian Story*. Fully detailed, they extend to two tightly typed A4 pages, so I will have to content myself with milepost explanations. In 1991 Sam Plunkett returned home to the family farm with an economics degree and a Melbourne rock band experience. Grapes were planted, and the family made the mudbrick winery using materials from the site. They made a manual 1-tonne rotofermenter, the first crusher and the tanks. A decade or so later they set up a new winery in the township of Avenel, and once again did it all themselves on a very much larger scale. In 2004 they were able to buy a large neighbouring winery (Dominion Wines), and this brought forth a partnership with the Fowles family. Then, in '11, Fowles bought the Plunkett family's shareholding, leaving part of the vineyard (7ha of shiraz with 3.2ha of chardonnay). Whatever temptation there was to build a third winery (and equipment) by hand was dispelled when the opportunity came to set up winemaking at the Taresch family's Elgo Estate winery. Less than two years later the Plunkett interests had leased the entire Elgo winery, and now have the responsibility for making the Elgo wines as well as their own brands, The Butterfly Effect and The Victorian. A large contract make for Naked Wines will see 20 000 dozen go to this destination alone, but with plenty of flesh left on the bone for the Wine x Sam wines. Exports to the UK, the US and China.

Wines by KT   ★★★★★

Main North Road, Watervale, SA 5452 **Region** Clare Valley
T 0419 855 500 **www**.winesbykt.com **Open** By appt
Winemaker Kerri Thompson **Est.** 2006 **Dozens** 1400

KT is winemaker Kerri Thompson. Kerri graduated with a degree in oenology from Roseworthy Agricultural College in 1993, and thereafter made wine in McLaren Vale, Tuscany, Beaujolais and the Clare Valley, becoming well known as the Leasingham winemaker in the Clare Valley. She resigned from Leasingham in 2006 after seven years at the helm, and after a short break became winemaker at Crabtree. Here she is also able to make Wines by KT, sourcing the grapes from two local vineyards, one biodynamic, the other farmed with sulphur and copper sprays only. Exports to the UK.

ŸŸŸŸŸ **Churinga Vineyard Watervale Shiraz 2010** Deep, bright crimson-purple. Elegance is not normally associated with Clare Valley shiraz, but this beautifully poised wine has it in spades. The perfectly ripened black fruits are cosseted by integrated French oak, and the tannins are immaculate. Screwcap. 14% alc. **Rating** 96 **To** 2035 $44

Melva Wild Fermented Riesling 2012 Brilliant, light straw-green; satin smooth, ripe citrus flavours caress the mouth from start to finish, the beguiling sweetness refusing to take no for an answer. Very seductive. Screwcap. 12.5% alc. **Rating** 95 **To** 2025 $29

Churinga Vineyard Watervale Riesling 2012 Bright, pale green-straw, it is startling in its tightly wound intensity and length, lime and green apple fighting for space. Screwcap. 13% alc. **Rating** 95 **To** 2032 $34

✪ **5452 Riesling 2012** In case you wondered, 5452 is the postcode for Watervale. Light, gleaming green, the bouquet immediately sets the parameters for a wine of utmost varietal purity, translating into balance and length on the palate. Screwcap. 12.5% alc. **Rating** 94 **To** 2027 $21

Peglidis Vineyard Watervale Riesling 2012 There is an arresting mineral barb to the bouquet, quickly obscured by the flowing, supple citrus and apple flavours of the palate and of its lingering aftertaste. Will develop with classy, effortless style. Screwcap. 12% alc. **Rating** 94 **To** 2032 $34

Churinga Vineyard Watervale Cabernet Sauvignon 2010 Medium red-purple; the highly fragrant bouquet introduces a wine that effortlessly achieves layers of ripe fruit at a significantly lower alcohol than most of its peers. It is approachable right now, but will be even better in 10 years when the impact of the oak will have diminished. Screwcap. 13.5% alc. **Rating** 94 **To** 2025 $44

Winetrust Estates ★★★★

PO Box 541, Balgowlah, NSW 2093 **Region** South Eastern Australia
T (02) 9949 9250 **www.**winetrustestates.com **Open** Not
Winemaker Rob Moody and various consultants **Est.** 1999 **Dozens** 57 000 **Vyds** 88.9ha
Mark Arnold is the man behind Winetrust Estates, drawing on a lifetime of experience in all aspects of the wine industry. It does not own a winery, drawing grapes from three states and five regions, and using contract winemakers according to the origin of the grapes (either self-grown, contract-grown or produced under a joint venture). The top-of-the-range Picarus red wines come from the Limestone Coast; the other ranges are Ocean Grove and Firebox Ridge Wines, covering all the major varietal wines plus a few newcomers. To add another string to its bow, it also makes wines for several other businesses. Exports to the US, Canada, China, Japan, Singapore, Hong Kong and Thailand.

ŸŸŸŸŸ **Picarus Wrattonbully Cabernet Sauvignon 2010** Good colour; a very
✪ enjoyable and expressive Cabernet, matured in French and Hungarian oak for 12 months, then redcurrant and cassis fruit in full bloom, the tannins fine and well-balanced, the oak not overt. Screwcap. 14.5% alc. **Rating** 93 **To** 2020 $24

Picarus Wrattonbully Shiraz 2010 One of the best Picarus Shirazs for some time; it is fresh and elegant, the light- to medium-bodied palate with small berry fruits, spices and oak nuances from the league of nations oak selection. Screwcap. 14.5% alc. **Rating** 90 **To** 2020 $24

ŸŸŸŸ **Picarus Wrattonbully Pinot Gris 2012 Rating** 89 **To** 2014 $18
Ocean Grove Cellar Reserve Eighteen Merlot 2012 Rating 87 **To** 2014 $14

Argon Bay Vineyards Reserve Margaret River Cabernet Merlot 2012
Rating 87 To 2014 $18
Firebox Ridge Swan Hill Tempranillo 2012 Rating 87 To 2014 $17

Winstead

75 Winstead Road, Bagdad, Tas 7030 **Region** Southern Tasmania
T (03) 6268 6417 **Open** By appt
Winemaker Neil Snare **Est.** 1989 **Dozens** 350
The good news about Winstead is the outstanding quality of its extremely generous and rich
Pinot Noirs, rivalling those of Freycinet for the abundance of their fruit flavour without
any sacrifice of varietal character. The bad news is that production is so limited, with only
0.8ha of pinot noir and 0.4ha riesling being tended by fly fishing devotee Neil Snare and
wife Julieanne.

Ensnared Sparkling Pinot Noir 2004 Pale pink-straw; a gold medal back in
'10 at the Tas Wine Show, this bottle from its fourth disgorgement, with 7 years on
lees. A very classy late-disgorged Pinot Noir with delicious, fine, forest strawberry
and red berry fruit, plus spicy notes. Diam. 11.4% alc. **Rating** 95 To 2015 $35

Riesling 2012 Light straw-green; has considerable upfront aroma and flavour, in
a ripe, verging on tropical, citrus spectrum, so much so that the normal Tasmanian
acidity is almost hidden. Will drink best over the next few years. Screwcap. 12% alc.
Rating 90 To 2015 $20

Estate Sauvignon 2011 The enigma of Tasmanian sauvignon blanc continues,
however, for the flavours are of ripe/tropical fruits, grassy notes and acidity not
evident. The question is how come at 12% alcohol? Putting this question into the
irrelevant box, it's a nice wine. Screwcap. 12% alc. **Rating** 90 To 2014 $20

Winter Creek Wine

Barossa Junction, Barossa Valley Way, Tanunda, SA 5352 **Region** Barossa Valley
T 0427 246 382 **www**.wintercreekwine.com.au **Open** Fri–Mon 10–5
Winemaker Pam Cross, Michael Sawyer **Est.** 2000 **Dozens** 300 **Vyds** 3ha
The Cross family established their small vineyard at Williamstown in the cooler foothills of
the southern Barossa Valley in 1993. There is 2ha of Smart Dyson trellised shiraz, and 1ha of
88-year-old grenache which was acquired in 2001. They also produce Sauvignon Blanc and
Pinot Gris from grapes purchased from the Adelaide Hills, and Riesling and Chardonnay
Pinot Noir from the Eden Valley.

Southern Barossa Shiraz 2010 Bright crimson-purple hue; an elegant, smooth
and supple medium-bodied palate is focused on red and black fruits which have
absorbed 24 months' maturation in French oak without turning a hair; the tannins,
too, are silky and gentle. Screwcap. 14% alc. **Rating** 93 To 2020 $25

Adelaide Hills Sauvignon Blanc 2012 Bright straw-green; the fragrant
bouquet tells of the mix of grass/herb, kiwifruit and passionfruit on the long, even
and well-balanced palate. Screwcap. 12.8% alc. **Rating** 91 To 2013 $18

The Barossa Bigwigs Shiraz Grenache NV A medium- to full-bodied wine,
its aromas and flavours in a black, rather than red, fruit spectrum. The real question
comes from the amount of French oak in which the shiraz spent up to 20 months.
Screwcap. 14% alc. **Rating** 89 To 2020 $20

Wirra Wirra

McMurtrie Road, McLaren Vale, SA 5171 **Region** McLaren Vale
T (08) 8323 8414 **www**.wirrawirra.com **Open** Mon–Sat 10–5, Sun & public hols 11–5
Winemaker Paul Smith, Paul Carpenter **Est.** 1894 **Dozens** 180 000 **Vyds** 51.31ha
Long respected for the consistency of its white wines, Wirra Wirra has now established an
equally formidable reputation for its reds. The wines are of exemplary character, quality and

style, The Angelus Cabernet Sauvignon and RWS Shiraz battling each other for supremacy, while the recently added The Absconder Grenache is one to watch. Long may the battle continue under the direction of managing director Andrew Kay and the winemaking team of Paul Smith and Paul Carpenter, who continue to forge along the path of excellence first trod by the late (and much loved) Greg Trott, the pioneering founder of the modern-day Wirra Wirra, who passed away in 2005. Exports to all major markets.

ΨΨΨΨΨ **RSW McLaren Vale Shiraz 2011** Deep crimson-purple, in marked contrast to the '11 Catapult; a dramatic exhibition of what could be achieved in the vintage with ultra-careful fruit sorting; it is profoundly fragrant and flavoured, with black fruits, bitter chocolate and spice spearing through the long palate. Screwcap. 14.5% alc. **Rating** 96 **To** 2031 $70

Chook Block Shiraz 2010 Highly expressive, both of flavours to come, and (unusually) of the plush, velvety texture of the deep black fruits, dark chocolate, licorice and oak tannins. It is the control of the alcohol that gives this wine its special qualities. Screwcap. 14% alc. **Rating** 96 **To** 2040 $130

The Angelus McLaren Vale Cabernet Sauvignon 2010 Deep purple-crimson; a reaffirmation of the ability of McLaren Vale to produce cabernet sauvignon of great authority and power; black fruits are the order of the day, the ripe tannins skilfully moulded, the oak integrated. The overall length and balance is impeccable. Screwcap. 14.5% alc. **Rating** 96 **To** 2030 $65

✪ **Hiding Champion Adelaide Hills Sauvignon Blanc 2012** Pale straw-green; elegantly encapsulates all the qualities of Adelaide Hills that make the region the best in Australia for sauvignon blanc, in no need of semillon or oak to push its credentials; totally delicious tropical fruit salad driven by the urgency of citrussy acidity. Exceptional value. Screwcap. 12.5% alc. **Rating** 95 **To** 2014 $23

The 12th Man Adelaide Hills Chardonnay 2012 Very pale colour; right in the swim of modern Australian chardonnay, with lower alcohol, wild yeast fermentation, lower new oak, and larger-format barrels. The result is an intense, long palate with a mix of savoury, citrus, white peach and cashew flavours on the very long palate. Screwcap. 12.5% alc. **Rating** 95 **To** 2019 $32

Patritti Single Vineyard Shiraz 2010 Part of the Scarce Earth series, only 50 dozen bottles made; from 4-year-old vines in Blewitt Springs, the wine brings together a distinguished vineyard and sensitive winemaking; it has outstanding length and presence, with juicy black fruits and some chocolate nuances cosseted by high-quality oak. Screwcap. 14.5% alc. **Rating** 95 **To** 2035 $132

✪ **The Lost Watch Adelaide Hills Riesling 2012** Pale quartz-green; has that extra touch of finesse that the Adelaide Hills confers on its rieslings, even if the flavour is not as marked as that of the Clare/Eden Valley; delicacy and balance the order of the day, plus the benison of the vintage. Screwcap. 12.5% alc. **Rating** 94 **To** 2020 $20

Woodhenge McLaren Vale Shiraz 2011 Rating 94 **To** 2021 $35

The Angelus McLaren Vale Cabernet Sauvignon 2011 Rating 94 **To** 2026 $70

ΨΨΨΨΨ **Mrs Wigley McLaren Vale Grenache Rose 2012** Vivid crimson-purple; ✪ manages to bring intensity and depth to its array of red fruit flavours, but with no hint of sweetness or inappropriate extract; the dry finish lingers long in the mouth, bringing back the red fruits of the mid-palate; food style. Screwcap. 13.5% alc. **Rating** 93 **To** 2014 $19

✪ **Scrubby Rise Adelaide Shiraz Cabernet Petit Verdot 2011** One assumes the small boat being rowed along the top of a vine row does not indicate a macabre sense of humour, for this is another success for the vintage, with sweet red and black fruits embedded in the chocolate running through the length of the palate. A delicious wine for early drinking. Screwcap. 14.5% alc. **Rating** 92 **To** 2016 $17

Church Block McLaren Vale Cabernet Sauvignon Shiraz Merlot 2011 Rating 92 **To** 2018 $24

Original Blend McLaren Vale Grenache Shiraz 2011 Rating 90
To 2015 $24
Esperanza McLaren Vale Monastrell 2010 Rating 90 To 2018 $35

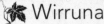 Wirruna ★★★★★

660 Wallington Road, Wallington, Vic 3222 **Region** Geelong
T 0411 333 377 **Open** By appt
Winemaker Banks Road (Will Derham) **Est.** 2012 **Dozens** 75 **Vyds** 0.8ha
Not to be confused with Wirruna Estate in Bethanga (North East Victoria Zone). Geelong surgeon Richard Rahdon, and Katharine (and three young children), purchased the 4.5ha property some years ago; it used to be the Wirruna Garden Nursery, and has a hectare of established traditional gardens. In 2009 they transplanted five-year-old pinot gris vines from Portarlington. This is not an easy task, but it succeeded, producing a small crop in '12. They plan to plant more pinot gris and pinot noir; in the meantime they have taken responsibility for a neighbour's vineyard, planted to pinot noir, the first vintage in '13.

🍷🍷🍷🍷🍷 Pinot Gris 2012 A faint touch of bronze-pink to the colour points to some skin contact; its richness and depth were no doubt the reason for its gold medal and trophy success at the Geelong Wine Show '12; it is most definitely in gris style, with overtones of Alsace. Screwcap. 13.6% alc. **Rating** 94 **To** 2014 $33

Wise Wine ★★★★★

Lot 4 Eagle Bay Road, Eagle Bay, WA 6281 **Region** Margaret River
T (08) 9756 8627 **www.**wisewine.com.au **Open** 7 days 10–5
Winemaker Jake Bacchus, Imogen Casely, Larry Cherubino (Consultant) **Est.** 1986
Dozens 15 000 **Vyds** 6ha
Wise Wine, headed by Perth entrepreneur Ron Wise, has been a remarkably consistent producer of high-quality wine. The vineyard adjacent to the winery in the Margaret River is supplemented by contract-grown grapes from Pemberton, Manjimup and Frankland River. The estate plantings are (in descending order of size) cabernet sauvignon, shiraz and zinfandel. The value for money of many of the wines is extraordinarily good. Exports to Sri Lanka, Vietnam, Malaysia, Hong Kong and Singapore.

🍷🍷🍷🍷🍷 Lot 80 Pemberton Sauvignon Blanc 2012 Bright green-straw; toasty French oak is evident on the bouquet, but yields to the succulent and intense array of tropical fruits on the palate, with enough acidity to cleanse and refresh the finish. Screwcap. 13.8% alc. **Rating** 94 **To** 2014 $35
Leaf Reserve Margaret River Chardonnay 2011 A civilised Chardonnay, with layers of easily peeled flavours, most running in the riper end of the spectrum (custard apple, the back label suggests, although I'm not convinced), with some creamy/nutty nuances to the ripe stone fruit at its core. Screwcap. 13% alc. **Rating** 94 **To** 2019 $28

🍷🍷🍷🍷🍷 Leaf Frankland River Riesling 2012 **Rating** 93 **To** 2022 $28
✪ Margaret River Shiraz 2011 Good hue, though light and slightly turbid; sweet red and black cherry, plum, spice and pepper combine to form an appealing, distinctly savoury, medium-bodied palate. Great value; drink now or in 10 years' time. Screwcap. 14% alc. **Rating** 93 **To** 2021 $20
✪ The Coat Door Wine Company Classic Red Grenache Shiraz Mataro 2011 Bright colour; French oak (largely old) maturation has added an extra dimension to this seductively juicy red berry, light- to medium-bodied wine; the tannins are largely hidden. The fruit range is significantly brighter than many of its eastern states counterparts. Utterly exceptional value. Screwcap. 13.5% alc. **Rating** 93 **To** 2016 $15
✪ The Coat Door Wine Company Classic White Sauvignon Blanc Semillon 2011 The attempt to phonetically link this wine to Burgundy's Cote d'Or is curious to say the least; this distraction to one side, the freshness and vibrancy of the palate, and its cornerstone of passionfruit, make this exceptional value. Screwcap. 13% alc. **Rating** 92 **To** 2014 $15

✪ **Margaret River Great Southern Chardonnay 2012** A wine that creeps up on you, with a cross web of flavours from the two regions, offering white peach, nectarine and cashew, with a substrate of citrus/grapefruit. Very good length and balance. Screwcap. 13.5% alc. **Rating** 92 **To** 2018 $20

Pemberton Pinot Grigio 2012 Rating 92 **To** 2013 $28

✪ **Sea Urchin Margaret River Cabernet Rose 2012** Very pale pink; the fragrant, tangy and zesty aromas lead into a fresh, cassis and redcurrant palate, finishing crisp and clean. In the style Houghton made famous many years ago. Screwcap. 13% alc. **Rating** 91 **To** 2013 $20

✪ **Frankland River Late Picked Voiginer (sic) 2012** Wine label collectors should delight in this (mis)spelling of viognier; there are some interesting orange/apricot/ marmalade flavours, and good acidity. Screwcap. 12% alc. **Rating** 90 **To** 2014 $20

Witches Falls Winery ★★★★★

79 Main Western Road, North Tamborine, Qld 4272 **Region** Queensland Coastal
T (07) 5545 2609 **www.**witchesfalls.com.au **Open** Mon–Fri 10–4, w'ends 10–5
Winemaker Jon Heslop **Est.** 2004 **Dozens** 12 000 **Vyds** 0.4ha
Witches Falls is the venture of Jon and Kim Heslop. Jon has a deep interest in experimenting with progressive vinification methods in order to achieve exceptional and interesting results. He has a degree in applied science (oenology) from CSU, and experience working in the Barossa and Hunter Valleys as well as at Domaine Chantel Lescure, Burgundy, and a Napa-based wine grower in California. Witches Falls grapes are sourced from the Granite Belt, and it is one of the consistently good performers in that context. Exports to Malaysia and China.

🍷🍷🍷🍷🍷 **Wild Ferment Granite Belt Sauvignon Blanc 2011** Wild yeast-fermented in new and used French oak, with 2 months' lees stirring and a further 8 months' maturation in barrel might have drowned the fruit, but it hasn't done so. The grass/herbal/capsicum flavours are drawn out by citrussy acidity to a very successful conclusion. Screwcap. 12.2% alc. **Rating** 94 **To** 2014 $30

Wild Ferment Granite Belt Chardonnay 2011 Sophisticated and skilled winemaking is very obvious, with cloudy juice taken straight to new and used French oak barriques for a wild ferment to self-initiate; the white peach and nectarine fruit sits very comfortably with the toasty/cashew oak. Screwcap. 13.6% alc. **Rating** 94 **To** 2017 $30

🍷🍷🍷🍷♀ **Granite Belt Chardonnay 2009 Rating** 90 **To** 2014 $22
Co-Inoculated Granite Belt Verdelho 2012 Rating 90 **To** 2014 $22

Witchmount Estate ★★★★☆

557 Leakes Road, Plumpton, Vic 3335 **Region** Sunbury
T (03) 9747 1055 **www.**witchmount.com.au **Open** Wed–Fri 11–4, w'ends 11–5
Winemaker Steve Goodwin **Est.** 1991 **Dozens** 8000 **Vyds** 25.5ha
Gaye and Matt Ramunno operate Witchmount Estate in conjunction with its Italian restaurant and function rooms. The vineyard is planted to shiraz (12ha), cabernet sauvignon (6ha) and chardonnay (2ha), with lesser amounts of sauvignon blanc, pinot gris, merlot, tempranillo and barbera. The quality of the wines has been consistent, the prices very modest. Exports to China.

🍷🍷🍷🍷🍷 **Cabernet Sauvignon 2009** Medium red-purple; open-fermented in small batches and matured in new French oak, it displays good varietal blackcurrant fruit on its medium-bodied palate, cigar box/cedar coming in unison with the fine tannins on the finish. Screwcap. 14% alc. **Rating** 94 **To** 2029 $35

🍷🍷🍷🍷♀ **Reserve Shiraz 2010 Rating** 93 **To** 2025 $45
Pinot Gris 2011 Rating 91 **To** 2014 $26
Shiraz 2010 Rating 90 **To** 2020 $35

Wobbly Tom Wines

PO Box 48, Stirling North, SA 5710 **Region** Southern Flinders Ranges
T 0427 442 634 **www.**bundaleercottage.com.au **Open** Not
Winemaker Angela Meaney **Est.** 2005 **Dozens** 450 **Vyds** 2.5ha

Justin and Donna Burman purchased their property in the beautiful Bundaleer Forest, in the Southern Flinders Ranges region. A second reason for purchasing the property was a 'tree change' for their young family in a renovated cottage on the site. They planted shiraz in 2000, and also 1700 olive trees. The name came from their young son Tom's vigilance when he saw a wallaby sheltering in the shade, and called out, 'There's a wobbly in the vines.'

ŶŶŶŶŶ **Southern Flinders Ranges Shiraz 2010** Deep colour; a rich, full-bodied
✪   Shiraz with a convincing display of multiple black fruits, spice, licorice and ripe
           tannins. Has taken full advantage of the vintage, and is exceptional value. Screwcap.
           14% alc. **Rating** 93 To 2025 $17

ŶŶŶŶ **Southern Flinders Ranges Rose 2012 Rating** 88 To 2013 $17

Wolf Blass

Bilyara Vineyards, 97 Sturt Highway, Nuriootpa, SA 5355 **Region** Barossa Valley
T (08) 8568 7311 **www.**wolfblasswines.com.au **Open** Mon–Fri 9–5, w'ends & public hols 10–5
Winemaker Chris Hatcher (Chief), Matt O'Leary, Marie Clay **Est.** 1966 **Dozens** NFP

Although merged with Mildara and now under the giant umbrella of TWE, the brands (as expected) have been left largely intact. The Wolf Blass wines are made at all price points, ranging through Red Label, Yellow Label, Gold Label, Brown Label, Grey Label, Black Label and Platinum Label, at one price point or another covering every one of the main varietals. The pre-eminent quality of the red wines over the white wines has reasserted itself, but without in any way diminishing the attraction the latter have. All of this has occurred under the leadership of Chris Hatcher, who has harnessed the talents of the winemaking team and encouraged the changes in style. Exports to all major markets.

ŶŶŶŶŶ **Grey Label McLaren Vale Shiraz 2011** Excellent crimson-purple; if ever
           proof were needed that the best vineyards in McLaren Vale fared remarkably well
           in '11, this wine provides it. The flavours are precise, reflecting perfectly ripened
           fruit, with some dark chocolate along with the generous French and American
           oak (what else?); the tannins have their usual glossy polish. Screwcap. 14.5% alc.
           Rating 94 To 2021 $45

           Platinum Label Barossa Shiraz 2010 Impenetrable colour; the headline act
           of the Wolf Blass stable is simply more of everything, displaying lavish levels of
           black fruits, smoky oak and bitter chocolate on the bouquet; staggering fruit
           concentration and plenty of chewy tannins, provide a long and hedonistic journey
           from start to finish. Screwcap. 14.8% alc. **Rating** 94 To 2035 $170 BE

           Gold Label Coonawarra Cabernet Sauvignon 2010 Deep purple-magenta
           hue; the restrained and elegant bouquet offers black fruits, dried herbs, lead pencil
           oak and a hint of violet; the tannins are moderate and fine-grained, with the
           tightly wound fruit and acidity drawing out the finish to a long, complex and even
           conclusion. Screwcap. 14% alc. **Rating** 94 To 2025 $28 BE

           Black Label Cabernet Sauvignon Shiraz Malbec 2009 As ever, this is no
           shrinking violet, as it is full throttle, pedal to the metal power, with super-ripe,
           black fruit melding with fine-grained toasty oak in abundance; the palate is
           densely packed, big-boned and hefty, yet remains relatively light on its feet; big is
           beautiful for some. Screwcap. 15.4% alc. **Rating** 94 To 2022 $130 BE

ŶŶŶŶŶ **Yellow Label Shiraz 2011** Deep crimson; the bouquet offers aromas of fresh
✪   blackberry, clove, mocha and fruitcake spice; medium-bodied, fleshy and full of
           juicy red and black fruits on the palate, the even finish is accessible and user-
           friendly in style. Gold medal Sydney Wine Show '13. Exceptional value. Screwcap.
           13.5% alc. **Rating** 93 To 2018 $18 BE

✪ **The Red Sash Shiraz Cabernet 2010** Rating 93 To 2025 $45 BE
✪ **Silver Label Langhorne Creek Cabernet Merlot 2010** Strong crimson-purple; the bouquet and medium-bodied palate have a complex array of blackcurrant, vanillin – almost creamy – oak, and a mix of spice and mint on the finish. Screwcap. 14.5% alc. Rating 93 To 2020 $20

Gold Label Adelaide Hills Shiraz Viognier 2010 Rating 92 To 2025 $28
Gold Label Botrytis Semillon 2011 Rating 91 To 2018 $25
Gold Label Adelaide Hills Sauvignon Blanc 2012 Rating 90 To 2015 $25 BE
White Label Specially Aged Release Adelaide Hills Chardonnay 2010 Rating 90 To 2017 $34 BE

✪ **Red Label Shiraz Grenache 2012** Vibrant purple hue; a lifted, fragrant and generally attractive red fruit and wood spice bouquet; the palate is juicy, fun-filled and lively, with simple generosity and freshness a welcoming aspect; enjoy and be happy. Screwcap. 13.5% alc. Rating 90 To 2018 $14 BE

✪ **Yellow Label Merlot 2012** Mid garnet, bright; fragrant and fresh with red fruits, leafy complexity and spiced plums on the bouquet; the palate is juicy on entry, with a backbone of tannins and black olive that delivers structure, and a tail of mocha oak. Screwcap. 13.5% alc. Rating 90 To 2018 $18 BE

✪ **Yellow Label Moscato 2012** A fragrant and grapey perfume, with a little pear and spice; the palate is lively, fresh, and while sweet, offers refreshing acidity to provide energy on the finish; very good execution of the style. Screwcap. 5% alc. Rating 90 To 2014 $18 BE

✪ **Yellow Label Reserve Australian Tawny NV** A fine and complex bouquet of raisin, toffee brittle, rancio nutty notes and a hint of floral complexity; the palate is unctuous on entry, drying out with warm alcohol from the spirit addition. Screwcap. 17.5% alc. Rating 90 To 2014 $18 BE

🍷🍷🍷🍷 **Red Label Shiraz Cabernet 2012** Mid garnet, vibrant hue; a fragrant blend
✪ of red and black fruits, spicy oak and a little sappy complexity; medium-bodied with plenty of presence, fine acidity and juicy, accessible fruits; freshness is the key. Screwcap. 13.5% alc. Rating 89 To 2018 $14 BE

Wolseley Wines   ★★★★

1790 Hendy Main Road, Paraparap, Vic 3240 **Region** Geelong
T 0412 990 638 **www**.wolseleywines.com **Open** W'ends 11–5, or by appt
Winemaker Will Wolseley **Est.** 1992 **Dozens** 2000
Will Wolseley grew up in Somerset, England, and from an early age made blackberry wine at home. He came to Australia in 1986 and enrolled in wine science at CSU, gathering vintage experience at various wineries over the next five years. A two-year search for an ideal vineyard site resulted in the acquisition of property on the gently sloping hills of Paraparap, inland from Bells Beach, Torquay. He established 6.5ha of pinot noir, cabernet sauvignon, chardonnay, shiraz, cabernet franc and semillon. Hail storms, frost and drought delayed the first commercial vintage until '98, but the solar-powered winery is now in full production.

🍷🍷🍷🍷🍷 **Geelong Botrytis Semillon 2010** Bright yellow-gold; exceptionally luscious, the low alcohol indicating several hundred g/l of sugar; cumquat, candied/glace fruits, honeycomb and vanilla. For the sweetest, richest desserts. 375ml. Screwcap. 9% alc. Rating 93 To 2015 $30

Geelong Pinot Noir 2009 Very turbid/cloudy; cried out for a cross-flow filter. This is a rich, full-blooded and -bodied pinot noir, with ripe (not overripe) plum and black cherry fruit supported by ripe tannins and some French oak. Screwcap. 13.5% alc. Rating 92 To 2017 $25

Geelong Botrytis Semillon 2009 Remarkable consistency of colour over this wine, the '09 and '11; this is neatly balanced, and has some nice nutty/oaky nuances. Good with mid weight desserts, cake in particular. 375ml. Screwcap. 11% alc. Rating 90 To 2015 $30

ΨΨΨΨ   Geelong Chardonnay 2011 Rating 89 To 2016 $30
Geelong Cabernet Sauvignon 2006 Rating 89 To 2015 $25
Geelong Shiraz 2010 Rating 87 To 2015 $25

Wombat Lodge   ★★★

PO Box 460, Cowaramup, WA 6284 **Region** Margaret River
T 0418 948 125 **www**.wombatlodgewines.com.au **Open** Not
Winemaker Jan McIntosh, Ian Bell **Est.** 1997 **Dozens** 600 **Vyds** 4ha
It pays to have a keenly developed sense of humour if you are a small winemaker committed
to producing the very best possible wine regardless of cost and market constraints. The short
version (and I quote) is: 'Warick (sic) Gerrard, owner/consumer; Jan McIntosh, winemaker
and life partner; Matt Lewis, viticulture and adopted son; 60ha of central Wilyabrup land, two
houses and 60 cows; 4ha of spoilt vines and 600 dozen of red wine.' There is a much longer
version, underlining Danny's freedom to organically grow the vines with limited irrigation
reducing yield and maximising quality, and Jan's freedom to buy as much French oak as she
wishes. The outcome is four clones of cabernet sauvignon, merlot, cabernet franc, malbec,
petit verdot and semillon, selling for the ludicrously low price of $140 per dozen plus postage.
Verging on surreal is the fact that the red wines mature for 14–16 months in 30% new and
70% used French oak barriques.

ΨΨΨΨ   **Reserve Margaret River Cabernet Sauvignon 2010** This is the first Reserve
release from Wombat Lodge. The colour is excellent, bright crimson-purple, and
the wine is striking – striking because of the tannins that so badly needed fining.
There is so much to the wine, one can pray that those tannins loosen their grip
over the next 2–3 years. Until then, I would treat it as a speculative investment.
Screwcap. 14.5% alc. **Rating** 89 To 2015 $20

✪   **Margaret River Cabernet Sauvignon Merlot 2011** Light to medium red-
purple; there are some savoury/minty/green nuances, but there is some overall
depth and varietal character, making this a good barbecue red at the right price.
Screwcap. 13.5% alc. **Rating** 87 To 2014 $12

Wood Park   ★★★★

263 Kneebones Gap Road, Markwood, Vic 3678 **Region** King Valley
T (03) 5727 3778 **www**.woodparkwines.com.au **Open** At Milawa Cheese Factory
7 days 10–5
Winemaker John Stokes, Richard Tevillian **Est.** 1989 **Dozens** 7000 **Vyds** 16ha
John Stokes planted the first vines at Wood Park in 1989 as part of a diversification program
for his property at Bobinawarrah, in the hills of the Lower King Valley, east of Milawa. The
vineyard is managed with minimal chemical use, winemaking a mix of modern and traditional
techniques. Some impressive wines have been made over the years. Exports to Taiwan,
Singapore, Hong Kong and China.

ΨΨΨΨΨ   **Reserve King Valley Cabernet Sauvignon 2009** Deep garnet; revealing
essency blackcurrant pastille on the bouquet, with olive and bay leaf; the palate is
medium to full-bodied, showing an integration of tannins due to bottle age, and a
long savoury conclusion. Screwcap. 13.7% alc. **Rating** 91 To 2018 $40 BE
Whitlands King Valley Pinot Gris 2012 Deep bronzing colour, and a stylish
example of gaining texture and complexity through skin contact; the acidity is
lively and the grippy texture provides length and interest; a style set to polarise.
Screwcap. 13% alc. **Rating** 90 To 2016 $22 BE

✪   **Wild's Gully King Valley Cabernet Merlot 2012** Deep magenta, vibrant hue;
fresh black fruits, thyme and black olive notes are evident on the bouquet; fleshy,
forward and firm yet supple, the juicy fruit and succulent acidity provides a well-
heeled, early-drinking, medium-bodied dry red. Screwcap. 13% alc. **Rating** 90
To 2018 $16 BE

ΨΨΨΨ   Meadow Creek Alpine Valleys Chardonnay 2011 Rating 88 To 2016 $26 BE

Woodgate Wines ★★★★

PO Box 71, Manjimup, WA 6258 **Region** Manjimup
T (08) 9772 4288 **www**.woodgatewines.com.au **Open** Not
Winemaker Mark Aitken **Est.** 2006 **Dozens** 3500 **Vyds** 5ha
This is the family owned business of Mark and wife Tracey Aitken, Tracey's mother, Jeannette Smith, and her brother Robert and his wife Linda Hatton. Mark became a mature-age student at Curtin University, obtaining his oenology degree in 2001 as Dux, earning a trip to Bordeaux to undertake vintage, returning to work at Manjimup's Chestnut Grove winery from '02. In '05 he and Tracey began their own contract winemaking business, as well as making wine for their Woodgate brand. Most of the grapes come from the estate plantings of cabernet sauvignon, chardonnay, sauvignon blanc, pinot noir and merlot, supplemented by some purchases. The name of the sparkling wine, Bojangles, reflects the family's musical heritage, which stretches back three generations and includes vocalists, guitarists, pianists, a trumpeter, a saxophonist, two drummers and a double bass player.

♟♟♟♟♟ **Reserve Manjimup Pinot Noir 2011** Bright, clear crimson-red; the complex bouquet has red berry/cherry fruit and intriguing almond/white chocolate nuances, the supple palate a replay of the bouquet, red fruits centre stage, spice and oak notes adding complexity. Well-made Pinot, with more to come. Screwcap. 14% alc. **Rating** 93 **To** 2020 $30

✪ **Shiraz Cabernet Merlot 2010** Good hue and clarity; shiraz contributes the major part to the blend with a fragrant red cherry and plum bouquet picked up by the medium-bodied palate, which has excellent texture and structure thanks to its fine tannins. Screwcap. 13.5% alc. **Rating** 93 **To** 2025 $17

Bojangles Blanc de Blanc 2008 Still has a bright, light straw-green colour; a crisp, firm wine despite, or perhaps thanks to, its 100% chardonnay base; lively citrus/lime flavours are well balanced, acidity just where it should be. Cork. 13% alc. **Rating** 93 **To** 2016 $30

✪ **Semillon Sauvignon Blanc 2011** Light straw-green; while having the same alcohol as the Sauvignon Blanc, has a somewhat riper and rounder mouthfeel from the start to the finish, where there are distinct touches of white peach, albeit underwritten by crisp acidity. Screwcap. 13% alc. **Rating** 91 **To** 2014 $17

Manjimup Semillon 2012 Bright straw-green; a complex, rich style with considerable weight and texture. 25% of the blend was barrel-fermented in 1-year-old French oak, followed by 6 months' maturation. Another 25% of the blend was tank-fermented then matured in new French oak for 3 months; the balance was tank-fermented. Screwcap. 13% alc. **Rating** 90 **To** 2017 $25

✪ **Sauvignon Blanc 2011** Light straw-green; an interesting wine, opening with ripe, tropical fruit notes, then tightening upon the mid-palate before minerally acidity provides thrust on the finish. Screwcap. 13% alc. **Rating** 90 **To** 2013 $17

Bojangles Pinot Noir Chardonnay 2009 Bottle-fermented. Straw colour, good mousse; a mix of rich fruits and more delicate nuances from the crisp acidity. Still coming to terms with itself. Cork. 13% alc. **Rating** 90 **To** 2015 $30

♟♟♟♟ **Manjimup Merlot 2011 Rating** 89 **To** 2020 $20

Woodlands ★★★★★

3948 Caves Road, Wilyabrup, WA 6284 **Region** Margaret River
T (08) 9755 6226 **www**.woodlandswines.com **Open** 7 days 10–5
Winemaker Stuart and Andrew Watson **Est.** 1973 **Dozens** 12500 **Vyds** 18.77ha
Founder David Watson had spectacular success with the Cabernets he made in 1979 and the early '80s. Commuting from Perth on weekends and holidays, as well as raising a family, became all too much, and for some years the grapes from Woodlands were sold to other Margaret River producers. With the arrival of grown sons Stuart and Andrew (Stuart primarily responsible for winemaking), the estate has bounced back to pre-eminence. The wines come in four price bands, the bulk of the production under the Chardonnay and Cabernet Merlot

varietals, then a series of Reserve and Special Reserves, then Reserve de la Cave, and finally Cabernet Sauvignon. The top-end wines primarily come from the original Woodlands Vineyard, where the vines are 40 years old. Exports to the UK, Indonesia, Malaysia, South Korea, Singapore, Japan and China.

🍷🍷🍷🍷🍷 **Margaret River Cabernet Sauvignon 2010** Heather Jean. Deep, bright crimson; restrained and complex on the bouquet, showing cedar, red fruits, violets and licorice; the medium- to full-bodied palate is pure-fruited, focused, displaying an abundance of fine-grained tannins, a fine acid line and a long and expansive conclusion. Screwcap. 13.5% alc. **Rating** 96 **To** 2030 $130 BE

✪ **Margaret River Cabernet Merlot 2011** As usual, Woodlands manages to combine elegance with intensity, length with finesse; there is a core of red berry fruits within a savoury, black olive outer skin; tannins and oak are balanced and totally integrated. Screwcap. 13.5% alc. **Rating** 95 **To** 2026 $23

Reserve de la Cave Margaret River Cabernet Franc 2011 Deep crimson colour, and effusive in blue and black fruit character, with a strong violet lift and a little cigar box complexity thrown in for good measure; the palate is full-bodied, concentrated and full of ample tannins; an expansive finish. Screwcap. 13.5% alc. **Rating** 95 **To** 2022 $75 BE

Chloe 2011 Mid gold; in every regard this is a savoury Chardonnay, showing mealy complexity, grilled cashew, fresh fig and lifted spicy oak; the fleshy and full-bodied palate is long, succulent and grapefruit-laden, with juicy acidity a fitting counterpoint to such intensity of fruit; big-boned and beautiful for it. Screwcap. 13.5% alc. **Rating** 94 **To** 2017 $75 BE

Reserve de la Cave Margaret River Malbec 2011 Only 300 bottle's made; the bouquet offers plump and fresh blueberry, blackberry and spiced plum, with a tidy seasoning of high-quality oak; the fleshy palate is fresh, focused, concentrated and amply endowed with fruit, gravelly tannins and acid in balance. Screwcap. 13.5% alc. **Rating** 94 **To** 2025 $75 BE

🍷🍷🍷🍷🍷 **Margaret 2011 Rating** 92 **To** 2020 $45 BE

✪ **Margaret River Cabernet Franc Merlot 2011** Bright, clear crimson-purple; the message of a fragrant, scented red berry bouquet changes tack smartly as the tannins of the otherwise medium-bodied palate take hold; needed fining or longer in barrel. Screwcap. 13.5% alc. **Rating** 91 **To** 2018 $23

Margaret River Chardonnay 2012 Rating 90 **To** 2017 $23 BE
Emily 2011 Rating 90 **To** 2020 $40 BE

🌿 Woods Crampton   ★★★★★

96 Princeton Avenue, Adamstown Heights, NSW 2208 **Region** South Australia
T 0417 670 655 **www.**fourthwavewine.com.au **Open** Not
Winemaker Nicholas Crampton, Aaron Woods **Est.** 2010 **Dozens** 1500
This is the most impressive new venture of Nicholas Crampton (now having reduced his association with McWilliam's to a consultancy role) and winemaking friend Aaron Woods. The two make the wines at the Sons of Eden winery with input advice from Igor Kucic. They have wisely steered clear of the 2011 vintage.

🍷🍷🍷🍷🍷 **High Eden Riesling 2012** Hand-picked and whole bunch-pressed, with only
✪   500 litres per tonne (normally up to 700 litres) extracted, and a mere 250 dozen made. Despite the gentle approach, is full of lime/lemon/lemongrass fruit that will develop a third dimension of lemon curd with 5 years in bottle. A truly lovely wine. Screwcap. 12.5% alc. **Rating** 95 **To** 2027 $25

✪ **Eden Valley Shiraz 2010** Three low-yielding 50- to 70-year-old vineyards; hand-picked with 10% whole bunch inclusion in the ferment, hand-plunged, then aged in used oak. Bright crimson-purple, it has a very complex, plushy textured mid-palate, with fine tannins and good acidity tightening up the finish to perfection. Screwcap. 14% alc. **Rating** 95 **To** 2030 $25

✪ **Old Vine Barossa Valley Mataro 2010** I suppose hand-plunged grapes from an 80-year-old vineyard matured in large-format oak vats for 18 months without racking, with minimal sulphur and no fining qualifies as natural wine, but it deserves far more than that epithet; wondrously juicy and supple red fruits soar above this usually hard-edged variety. Screwcap. 14.5% alc. **Rating** 94 **To** 2020 $25

♟♟♟♟♟ **Barossa Valley Mataro Rose 2012** The mataro also has a dash of grenache and
✪ shiraz, and was given 12 hours' skin contact before it was pressed direct to used oak puncheons for wild yeast fermentation, then 6 months on lees, some magic preventing mlf. The result is a deliciously fruity array of raspberry, cranberry and cherry fruit in a light-bodied red wine that goes well beyond the normal Rose template. 440 dozen made. Screwcap. 13.5% alc. **Rating** 92 **To** 2014 $19

Woodside Valley Estate

PO Box 332, Greenwood, WA 6924 **Region** Margaret River
T (08) 9345 4065 **www**.woodsidevalleyestate.com.au **Open** Not
Winemaker Kevin McKay, Tod Payne **Est.** 1998 **Dozens** 1800 **Vyds** 19.4ha
The business that was established in 1998 by a small syndicate of investors headed by Peter Woods was acquired by Palinda Wines in late 2012; at the same time Palinda acquired Western Range Wines. Palinda Wines is based in Hong Kong, and is the private family company of Chinese businessman Jacky Wong. He has 150 stores in Hong Kong and mainland China selling beer, wine and spirits, and will thus act both as importer and retailer. No wines received for the *2014 Wine Companion*, but a five-star rating has been maintained. Exports to the UK, the US, Singapore, China and Japan.

Woodstock ★★★★★

215 Douglas Gully Road, McLaren Flat, SA 5171 **Region** McLaren Vale
T (08) 8383 0156 **www**.woodstockwine.com.au **Open** 7 days 10–5
Winemaker Scott Collett, Ben Glaetzer **Est.** 1905 **Dozens** 28 000 **Vyds** 18.44ha
One of the stalwarts of McLaren Vale, owned by Scott Collett, who produces archetypal and invariably reliable full-bodied red wines, spectacular botrytis sweet whites and high quality (25-year-old) Tawny Port. Also offers a totally charming reception-cum-restaurant, which does a roaring trade with wedding receptions. Exports to most major markets.

♟♟♟♟♟ **The Stocks Single Vineyard McLaren Vale Shiraz 2010** The grapes for this wine come from 31 rows of low-yielding vines planted circa 1900, certainly more than 100 years ago. It is quintessentially McLaren Vale in style, with black and red fruits and dark chocolate supported by fine-grained and persistent tannins, and well-handled oak. Screwcap. 14.9% alc. **Rating** 95 **To** 2030 $65

♟♟♟♟♟ **Mary McTaggart McLaren Vale Riesling 2012** Rating 90 **To** 2017 $25
Pilot's View McLaren Vale Shiraz 2011 Rating 90 **To** 2016 $38
The Octogenarian Grenache Tempranillo 2011 Rating 90 **To** 2015 $32
McLaren Vale Muscat NV Rating 90 **To** 2014 $20 BE

Woody Nook ★★★★★

506 Metricup Road, Wilyabrup, WA 6280 **Region** Margaret River
T (08) 9755 7547 **www**.woodynook.com.au **Open** 7 days 10–4.30
Winemaker Neil Gallagher, Michael Brophy **Est.** 1982 **Dozens** 7500 **Vyds** 14.23ha
Woody Nook, with a backdrop of 18ha of majestic marri and jarrah forest, doesn't have the high profile of the biggest names in Margaret River, but has had major success in wine shows over the years. It was purchased by Peter and Jane Bailey in 2000, and major renovations and expansions in '02 and '04 have transformed Woody Nook, with a new winery, a gallery tasting room for larger groups and an alfresco dining area by the pond. A link with the past is Neil Gallagher's continuing role as winemaker, viticulturist and minority shareholder. Exports to the UK, the US, Canada, Bermuda, Hong Kong and China.

ŶŶŶŶŶ Kelly's Farewell Margaret River Semillon Sauvignon Blanc 2012 Has that
✪ extra dimension of complexity and fruit expression on both bouquet and palate
that Woody Nook can achieve, causing you to wonder whether oak has made a
contribution (it hasn't). Tropical lychee/passionfruit intermingles with grassy/citrus
counterpoints, the result emphatic. Screwcap. 13.5% alc. **Rating** 94 **To** 2014 $22
Single Vineyard Margaret River Cabernet Merlot 2011 An estate-grown
80/20% blend; a supple and instantly appealing blend of blackcurrant and red fruits
with quality French oak and a cross-weave of ripe, almost succulent, tannins. The
overall balance is faultless, and will sustain the wine for as long (or short) as your
patience allows. Diam. 14.5% alc. **Rating** 94 **To** 2026 $32
Gallagher's Choice Margaret River Cabernet Sauvignon 2011 Deep
purple-crimson; an intense and full-bodied wine, full of ripe cassis, gently offset by
nuances of black olive and cedary oak, the tannins framing all that has gone before.
Diam. 14.5% alc. **Rating** 94 **To** 2031 $45
✪ Killdog Creek Margaret River Tempranillo 2011 Strong crimson-purple;
the complex, dark cherry-filled bouquet is followed by a powerful palate; black
cherry, morello cherry and sour cherry are all in play, the tannin structure perfect.
Screwcap. 14% alc. **Rating** 94 **To** 2020 $22

ŶŶŶŶ♀ Margaret River Shiraz 2010 Rating 92 To 2030 $35

Writer's Block/Noonji Estate ★★★★☆

386 Wilderness Road, Lovedale, NSW 2321 **Region** Hunter Valley
T (02) 4998 6965 **www**.writersblockwines.com.au **Open** W'ends & public hols 10–4,
Mon–Fri by appt
Winemaker Nick Paterson **Est.** 2004 **Dozens** 250 **Vyds** 5.5ha
Self-described wine tragics Peter and Barbara Jensen chose to leave Sydney to pursue their
dream of owning a small vineyard in an idyllic setting in the Hunter Valley. In 2004 they found
a block of 40-year-old vines and began the long task of completely rejuvenating the vineyard,
securing the services of Nick Paterson (Chateau Pâto) as contract winemaker. The 2.5ha of
chardonnay included in the plantings are among the oldest in the Hunter Valley. Drew Gibson
acquired Noonji Estate several years ago, but still sells and stocks Noonji Estate-labelled wines,
while introducing Writer's Block in '11.

ŶŶŶŶŶ Writer's Block Old Vine Single Estate Hunter Valley Semillon 2011
The grapes come from vines nearing 50 years old. It borders on blasphemy to
drink it now; yes, the flavours surge through and around the mouth, but with an
intensity and length that is truly remarkable. This wine will be still unfolding as
I am pushing up daisies. Screwcap. 10.7% alc. **Rating** 96 **To** 2041 $24

ŶŶŶŶ♀ Writer's Block Hunter Valley Chardonnay 2011 Rating 93 To 2018 $25

Wykari Wines ★★★★☆

PO Box 905, Clare, SA 5453 **Region** Clare Valley
T (08) 8842 1841 **www**.wykariwines.com.au **Open** Not
Winemaker Neil Paulett **Est.** 2006 **Dozens** 1200 **Vyds** 20ha
This is the venture of two local Clare families, Rob and Mandy Knight, and Peter and Robyn
Shearer. Together they own two vineyards, one to the north, and the other to the south of
Clare. The vineyards were first planted in 1974, and are dry-grown and hand-pruned. In all
there is shiraz, riesling, cabernet sauvignon and chardonnay. Until 2009 much of the riesling
and shiraz was sold to Leasingham Wines, but since '06 Wykari has steadily increased its
production from 600 dozen to its present level. Excess grapes continue to be sold.

ŶŶŶŶŶ Single Vineyard Clare Valley Shiraz 2010 From dry-grown estate vines
planted in 1974. It has excellent, deep purple-crimson colour; as the colour
promises, this is a rich, velvety and succulent wine with a full range of black fruits,
tempered on the finish by a web of fine tannins, spice and cedary oak. Screwcap.
14.6% alc. **Rating** 94 **To** 2030 $26

ŢŢŢŢ♀ **Clare Valley Riesling 2012** This is absolutely classic Clare Riesling, with only
⊗ 2g/l of residual sugar (undetectable on the palate); the lemon, lime and apple
fruit is still in its primary phase, but will begin to open up in 3–4 years, and reach
a triumphant plateau from 10 years onwards. Screwcap. 12.1% alc. **Rating** 92
To 2025 $18
Clare Valley Cabernet Sauvignon 2010 Rating 90 **To** 2020 $22

Wyndham Estate ★★★

700 Dalwood Road, Dalwood, NSW 2335 **Region** Hunter Valley
T (02) 4938 3444 **www.**wyndhamestate.com **Open** 7 days 9.30–4.30 except public hols
Winemaker Ben Bryant **Est.** 1828 **Dozens** 800 000 **Vyds** 55ha
This historic property is now merely a shop front for the Wyndham Estate label. The Bin
wines often surprise with their quality, representing excellent value; the Show Reserve wines,
likewise, can be very good. The wines come from various parts of South Eastern Australia,
sometimes specified, sometimes not. It's easy to dismiss these wines with faint praise, which
does no justice whatsoever to their quality and their value for money. Exports to Canada,
Europe and Asia.

ŢŢŢŢ **Bin 555 Shiraz 2009** Predominantly sourced from Langhorne Creek, Padthaway
⊗ and the Barossa Valley. Its texture, structure and balance are very good considering
its price; black cherry, plum and some spice flavours all come together well.
Screwcap. 14% alc. **Rating** 89 **To** 2015 $16
Bin 555 Shiraz 2010 Good crimson-purple hue and clarity; has plenty of red
and black fruits, a dash of chocolate, and mocha on the finish. Screwcap. 14% alc.
Rating 88 **To** 2016 $16
Bin 444 Cabernet Sauvignon 2010 A blend of Padthaway, Langhorne Creek
and Barossa Valley grapes. Has good varietal presence in an amiable fashion, making
it as enjoyable now as it will be in 5 years. Honest value. Screwcap. 13.8% alc.
Rating 88 **To** 2016 $16

Wynns Coonawarra Estate ★★★★★

Memorial Drive, Coonawarra, SA 5263 **Region** Coonawarra
T (08) 8736 2225 **www.**wynns.com.au **Open** 7 days 10–5
Winemaker Sue Hodder, Luke Skeer, Sarah Pidgeon **Est.** 1897 **Dozens** NFP
Large-scale production has not prevented Wynns from producing excellent wines covering
the full price spectrum, from the bargain-basement Riesling and Shiraz through to the deluxe
John Riddoch Cabernet Sauvignon and Michael Shiraz. Even with steady price increases,
Wynns offers extraordinary value for money. The large investments made since 2000 in
rejuvenating and replanting key blocks under the direction of Allen Jenkins, and skilled
winemaking by Sue Hodder, have resulted in wines of far greater finesse and elegance than
most of their predecessors. Exports to the UK, the US, Canada and Asia.

ŢŢŢŢŢ **Black Label Shiraz 2010** Make no mistake, this aristocratic wine is far removed
from the standard varietal release. The complex, spicy black fruits of the bouquet
command immediate attention, and the textured layers of flavour on the palate
build on the bouquet, with black fruits, spice and oak all contributing to a very
impressive wine. Screwcap. 13.5% alc. **Rating** 96 **To** 2030 $40
V&A Lane Selected Vineyards Shiraz 2010 When first tasted in Mar '12 it
elicited the following tasting note: deep purple-crimson; this is a beautifully weighted
and constructed shiraz; the medium-bodied palate effortlessly displays blackberry,
sweet earth and classy oak, with fine tannins running through the very long finish
and aftertaste. Not bad, you might think. But 5 months later, and in the company
of all the Wynnsday releases, it was even better, its elegance shining through like a
beacon without diminishing its other numerous virtues. All of which caused me to
lift the points from 95 to 96. Screwcap. 13.5% alc. **Rating** 96 **To** 2035 $60

ŢŢŢŢ♀ **Shiraz 2011 Rating** 92 **To** 2021 $25
The Siding Cabernet Sauvignon 2011 Rating 92 **To** 2019 $25

Xabregas ★★★★★

1683 Porongurup Road, Porongurup, WA 6324 **Region** Mount Barker
T (08) 9321 2366 **www**.xabregas.com.au **Open** Not
Winemaker Martin Cooper **Est.** 1996 **Dozens** 10 000 **Vyds** 118ha
Owners of Xabregas, the Hogan family, have five generations of WA history and family interests in sheep grazing and forestry in the Great Southern, dating back to the 1860s. Terry Hogan, founding chairman, felt the Mount Barker region was 'far too good dirt to waste on blue gums', and vines were planted in 1996. The Hogan family concentrates on the region's strengths – Shiraz and Riesling. Exports to the US, Singapore, Japan, China and NZ.

ΨΨΨΨΨ **X by Xabregas Spencer Syrah 2010** Has the same massive bottle and minimalistic label as Figtree; the colour is slightly less bright, but the wine has significantly greater depth and complexity, with smoky/savoury/licorice/earth nuances all in play; unashamedly full-bodied, yet not the least clunky. WAK screwcap. 14.3% alc. **Rating** 95 **To** 2030 $40
X by Xabregas Spencer Riesling 2011 Despite the much lower alcohol than '11 Figtree, only part is due to the fermentation being stopped, and it is the shape of the palate, more than its weight, that leads me to prefer this wine. The acidity that is present from the word go, emphasising the lime juice fruit, provides another point of difference. Screwcap. 10.7% alc. **Rating** 94 **To** 2026 $40
X by Xabregas Figtree Syrah 2010 Vivid purple-crimson; despite the intensity and length of the strongly spiced black fruits, the balance of the wine is very impressive, as is its cellaring future. WAK screwcap. 13.8% alc. **Rating** 94 **To** 2025 $40

ΨΨΨΨΨ **X by Xabregas Figtree Riesling 2011 Rating** 92 **To** 2019 $40

Xanadu Wines ★★★★★

Boodjidup Road, Margaret River, WA 6285 **Region** Margaret River
T (08) 9758 9500 **www**.xanaduwines.com **Open** 7 days 10–5
Winemaker Glenn Goodall **Est.** 1977 **Dozens** 70 000 **Vyds** 109.5ha
Xanadu fell prey to over-ambitious expansion and to the increasingly tight trading conditions in 2005 as wine surpluses hit hard. The assets were acquired by the Rathbone Group, completing the Yering Station/Mount Langi Ghiran/Xanadu group. The prime assets were (and are) the 110ha of vineyards and winery. The increasing production has been matched by a major lift in quality. In '12 the Rathbone Group wine interests were placed on the market for sale either as a group or individually. Exports to most major markets.

ΨΨΨΨΨ **Reserve Margaret River Chardonnay 2010** Still light straw-green; it takes the elegance of its sister wine, Stevens Road, onto another level with its accompanying intensity and utterly exceptional length. There is a seamless union between the pink grapefruit and white peach fruit, quality French oak and citrussy/minerally acidity; it is that acidity that draws out the extreme length of the palate. Screwcap. 13.5% alc. **Rating** 97 **To** 2020 $85
Reserve Margaret River Chardonnay 2011 Produced from the lowest yielding vines on the estate; whole bunch-pressed, with wild yeast fermentation in French barriques; after 9 months' maturation, a barrel selection was made. It is even more intense and focused than the standard Chardonnay, and has exceptional length thanks to its natural acidity. Screwcap. 13.5% alc. **Rating** 96 **To** 2025 $85
✪ **Margaret River Shiraz 2010** Sophisticated winemaking; whole berries in static fermenters for the major part, another part wild-fermented in small open fermenters; another part co-fermented with viognier. Vibrant red and black fruits, spicy oak and impressive structure from fine-grained tannins. Screwcap. 14.5% alc. **Rating** 95 **To** 2035 $29
Margaret River Cabernet Sauvignon 2010 Fermented in small batches, some given extended maceration post-fermentation, then given 14 months in French oak (40% new). The colour is bright and clear, and there is a most appealing nature to the blackcurrant and redcurrant fruit; the oak and tannins are perfectly balanced. Screwcap. 14% alc. **Rating** 95 **To** 2025 $35

Reserve Margaret River Cabernet Sauvignon 2010 A 90/10% blend of cabernet sauvignon and petit verdot matured in French oak (65% new) for 16 months. The colour is no deeper than Stevens Road, but the hue is a brilliant crimson. It is a wine in two parts, but with a connecting bridge; initially it is filled with cassis, red fruits and plum, before savoury, lingering tannins arrive to extend the finish. Screwcap. 14% alc. **Rating** 95 To 2030 $85

✪ **Margaret River Chardonnay 2011** Hand-picked and whole bunch-pressed, the wild yeast fermentation in French oak. The wine is particularly intense, with very good structure and texture to its mix of white peach, almond and citrus flavours running through the long palate. Screwcap. 13.5% alc. **Rating** 94 To 2020 $29
Stevens Road Margaret River Cabernet Sauvignon 2010 Rating 94 To 2025 $65

♀♀♀♀♀ **Next of Kin Margaret River Cabernet Sauvignon 2010** Light to medium
✪ red-purple; it should come as no surprise to find clear and precise juicy blackcurrant and redcurrant cabernet varietal character on both the bouquet and palate of this medium-bodied wine, backed and complexed by cedary oak and tannins. Screwcap. 14% alc. **Rating** 93 To 2023 $18
Margaret River Sauvignon Blanc Semillon 2012 Rating 92 To 2015 $26
Margaret River Rose 2012 Rating 90 To 2014 $26

♀♀♀♀ **Next of Kin Margaret River Sauvignon Blanc Semillon 2012** Despite the
✪ modest alcohol (by Margaret River standards) and the semillon component, the wine has an array of tropical fruits ranging through guava, lychee and passionfruit. Drink asap. Well priced. Screwcap. 12.5% alc. **Rating** 89 To 2013 $18

Yabby Lake Vineyard ★★★★★

86–112 Tuerong Road, Tuerong, Vic 3937 **Region** Mornington Peninsula
T (03) 5974 3729 **www**.yabbylake.com **Open** 7 days 10–5
Winemaker Tom Carson, Chris Forge **Est.** 1998 **Dozens** 3350 **Vyds** 50.8ha
This high-profile wine business was established by Robert and Mem Kirby (of Village Roadshow), who had been landowners in the Mornington Peninsula for decades. In 1998 they established Yabby Lake Vineyard, under the direction of vineyard manager Keith Harris; the vineyard is on a north-facing slope, capturing maximum sunshine while also receiving sea breezes. The main focus is the 25.4ha of pinot noir, 14ha of chardonnay and 7.7ha of pinot gris; shiraz, merlot and sauvignon blanc take a back seat. The arrival of the hugely talented Tom Carson as Group Winemaker has added lustre to the winery and its wines. The initiative of opening cellar doors in five cities in China is without parallel, facilitated by the involvement of a Chinese partner. On the home front, after 10 years of planning, Robert and Mem handed control of the family's vineyards and brands to their children, Nina and Clark, in 2008. Exports to the US, the UK, Canada, Sweden, Singapore, Hong Kong and China.

♀♀♀♀♀ **Single Block Release Block 6 Mornington Peninsula Pinot Noir 2010** Crimson-purple; has a super-fragrant, floral bouquet with exotic spices, almost into forest floor; tight, intense and quite savoury, it has perfect balance and superb tannins. Yet it is the length and finesse of the red fruits at its core that is the key to this wine. Screwcap. 14% alc. **Rating** 97 To 2025 $80
Single Vineyard Mornington Peninsula Chardonnay 2011 Bright straw-green; all about intensity and purity, the fruit expression almost painful in its precision, drawing saliva from the mouth on the aftertaste. The utmost care has been taken not to allow oak to act as more than a medium. Screwcap. 12% alc. **Rating** 95 To 2021 $45
✪ **Red Claw Mornington Peninsula Chardonnay 2010** Light straw-green; has a complex, faintly funky (in the best sense) bouquet, and has all the ripe, white-fleshed stone fruit and melon you could wish for. Oak plays a minor role in the inherent freshness and length of a wine that (paradoxically) has intensified over the past 12 months. Screwcap. 12.5% alc. **Rating** 94 To 2016 $24

Single Vineyard Mornington Peninsula Pinot Gris 2012 Not only a single vineyard, but a single block, hand-picked, whole bunch-pressed and partially barrel-fermented. The process has added perfume and spice, but not cluttered the mouthfeel, which is like liquid silk, pear and apple the foremost flavours. Screwcap. 13% alc. **Rating** 94 **To** 2014 $30

Single Vineyard Mornington Peninsula Pinot Noir 2011 Deeper colour than the '11 Red Claw Pinot; the fragrant, perfumed cherry blossom bouquet is followed by an elegant, red-berried palate, the tannins silky but sustained, the French oak held in restraint; the key words here are length and finesse, spice to emerge down the track. Screwcap. 13.5% alc. **Rating** 94 **To** 2017 $60

✪ **Single Vineyard Mornington Peninsula Syrah 2009** Medium purple-red; a rich, supple, dark-berried, full-bodied wine that falls outside the usual parameters of the Mornington Peninsula (except for Paringa Estate); the stepped tannin structure is particularly impressive, echoing the slightly spicy notes of the bouquet; the oak has been deftly handled. Screwcap. 14.5% alc. **Rating** 94 **To** 2029 $30

🍷🍷🍷🍷🍷 **Red Claw Mornington Peninsula Chardonnay 2011** Light, bright straw-
✪ green; the citrus, stone fruit and lemon aromas and flavours have been given free rein on the very long and finely pitched palate; it fully reflects the cool growing season that endowed the grapes with high natural acidity and low pH. Screwcap. 12.5% alc. **Rating** 93 **To** 2020 $23

✪ **Red Claw Mornington Peninsula Pinot Noir 2010** Bright, clear crimson-purple; intense blood plum and dark berry fruit aromas with a waft of French oak flow through to the palate, where they back off a little on the mid-palate before coming through strongly on the finish. It has flourished in the 12 months since first tasted, its price (reduced) adding yet more appeal and complexity. Screwcap. 14% alc. **Rating** 93 **To** 2016 $24

✪ **Pink Claw Mornington Peninsula Pinot Noir Rose 2012** Pale pink; the pink capsule and the name give the same message: a portion (unspecified) of the profits will go to research into breast cancer. The wine has the extra dimension of flavour, texture and structure typical of Yabby Lake wines, Rose no exception. Screwcap. 13% alc. **Rating** 92 **To** 2014 $23

✪ **Red Claw Mornington Peninsula Pinot Noir 2011** Has distinctly more colour and depth than most Mornington Peninsula Pinots from '11, with crimson to the fore; the bouquet is fragrant, the palate with black and red cherry fruit sustained by quality tannins giving rise to a touch of forest on the finish. Screwcap. 13.5% alc. **Rating** 92 **To** 2016 $25

Red Claw Mornington Peninsula Sauvignon Blanc 2012 **Rating** 90 **To** 2014 $23

Yal Yal Estate
★★★★☆

2 Boyanda Road, Glen Iris, Vic 3146 (postal) **Region** Mornington Peninsula
T 0416 112 703 **www**.yalyal.com.au **Open** Not
Winemaker Sandro Mosele **Est.** 1997 **Dozens** 650 **Vyds** 2.63ha
In 2008 Liz and Simon Gillies acquired a vineyard planted in 1997 to 1.6ha of chardonnay and a little over 1ha of pinot noir. Since 2000 the wines have been made by Sandro Mosele (under the watchful eyes of the Gillies). The wines are available through mail order and specialist retail stores.

🍷🍷🍷🍷🍷 **Yal Yal Rd Mornington Peninsula Chardonnay 2011** Pale, bright straw-
✪ green; a vibrantly juicy and fresh palate, with intense grapefruit, white peach and nectarine flavours, cashew and French oak ghostly influences on the lingering finish. A major success. Screwcap. 13% alc. **Rating** 95 **To** 2019 $30

🍷🍷🍷🍷 **Yal Yal Rd Mornington Peninsula Pinot Noir 2011** **Rating** 87 **To** 2014 $35

Yalumba ★★★★★

Eden Valley Road, Angaston, SA 5353 **Region** Eden Valley
T (08) 8561 3200 **www**.yalumba.com **Open** 7 days 10–5
Winemaker Louisa Rose (chief), Peter Gambetta, Kevin Glastonbury **Est.** 1849
Dozens 930 000 **Vyds** 150ha

Family-owned and run by Robert Hill-Smith, Yalumba has a long commitment to quality and great vision in its selection of vineyard sites, new varieties and brands. It has always been a serious player at the top end of full-bodied (and full-blooded) Australian reds, and was a pioneer in the use of screwcaps. While its estate vineyards are largely planted to mainstream varieties, it has taken marketing ownership of viognier. However, these days its own brands revolve around the Y Series and a number of stand-alone brands across the length and breadth of SA. Yalumba has been very successful in building its export base. Exports to all major markets.

🍷🍷🍷🍷🍷 **The Virgilius Eden Valley Viognier 2009** First tasted over 2 years ago, and has coasted through the intervening time, the colour gleaming green, the palate elegant, the mouthfeel (often the Achilles heel of viognier) superb, with mandarin, peach and apricot in a silken web of citrussy acidity. Proves that if viognier is good enough, cellaring carries no fears. Screwcap. 13.5% alc. **Rating** 96 **To** 2017 $50

FSW8B Wrattonbully Botrytis Viognier 2012 Medium yellow-green; the amazing feature of this wine is not that it is exceedingly unctuous and rich, but the way it has retained, indeed magnified its varietal character, with apricot and peach essence. Screwcap. 10.5% alc. **Rating** 96 **To** 2018 $30

Paradox Northern Barossa Valley Shiraz 2010 This is a very good Shiraz, one (unintended) paradox a heavyweight bottle and a very ordinary short cork; the more important paradox is the delightful intensity of the savoury black fruits achieved with sub-13% alcohol; the length of the palate is also excellent. 12.9% alc. **Rating** 95 **To** 2025 $43

Eden Valley Shiraz + Viognier 2010 Vivid purple hue; the fresh and fragrant bouquet offers black fruits, violets and anise; the medium-bodied palate is fleshy and generous, with a backbone of fine tannins and a lingering charry toast note on the fine-boned finish. Cork. 13.5% alc. **Rating** 95 **To** 2020 $37 BE

✪ **The Strapper Barossa Grenache Shiraz Mataro 2011** Vivid red hue; highly perfumed and pure on the bouquet, showing red fruits, violets and dried herbs; the palate is medium-bodied, fleshy and fragrant, with a charmingly fresh finish; this is a wine to enjoy without thinking and not necessarily in moderation. Screwcap. 13.8% alc. **Rating** 94 **To** 2018 $22 BE

✪ **The Scribbler Cabernet Sauvignon Shiraz 2010** Bright colour; bright and pure cassis, redcurrant and fresh leather on display; the medium- to full-bodied palate is vibrant and complex, long and layered, with plenty of stuffing for the future, and enough fruit to enjoy in the short term. Screwcap. 13.5% alc. **Rating** 94 **To** 2020 $23 BE

🍷🍷🍷🍷♀ **Eden Valley Viognier 2011 Rating** 93 **To** 2014 $25

✪ **Patchwork Barossa Shiraz 2010** Full purple-crimson; a blend of material from higher altitude, cooler sites and warmer valley floor vineyards; the ambiguity lies in the use of the term 'Barossa', which covers both the Eden and Barossa Valleys; it is a generous wine, with sweet red and black fruits, mocha and fruitcake, the tannins soft and plump. Screwcap. 13.5% alc. **Rating** 93 **To** 2020 $22

✪ **Y Series Viognier 2012** Mid gold; highly perfumed and exotic on the bouquet, showing spiced apricot and cashew; the palate is fleshy, unctuous and reveals a backbone of vibrant acidity, finishing fresh and fine. Screwcap. 14% alc. **Rating** 91 **To** 2015 $15 BE

✪ **Y Series Sauvignon Blanc 2012** Pale straw, bright; a combination of freshly squeezed lemon juice and gooseberry; the palate is dry and very high in acid, with a seriously mouth-puckering finish; one for the die-hard sauvignon fans out there. Screwcap. 12% alc. **Rating** 90 **To** 2014 $15 BE

Y Series Shiraz Viognier 2011 Rating 90 **To** 2016 $15 BE
Bush Vine Barossa Grenache 2011 Rating 90 **To** 2014 $22

Yalumba The Menzies (Coonawarra) ★★★★☆

Riddoch Highway, Coonawarra, SA 5263 **Region** Coonawarra
T (08) 8737 3603 **www.**yalumba.com **Open** 7 days 10–4.30
Winemaker Peter Gambetta **Est.** 2002 **Dozens** 5000 **Vyds** 29ha
The Hill-Smith family had been buying grapes from Coonawarra and elsewhere in the
Limestone Coast Zone long before it became a landowner there. In 1993 it purchased the
20ha vineyard that had provided the grapes previously purchased, and a year later added a
nearby 16ha block. Together, these vineyards now have 22ha of cabernet sauvignon and 3.5ha
each of merlot and shiraz. The next step was the establishment of the 35ha Mawson's Vineyard
in the Wrattonbully region. The third step was to build The Menzies Wine Room on the
first property acquired – named Menzies Vineyard – and to offer the full range of Limestone
Coast wines through this striking rammed-earth tasting and function centre. Exports to all
major markets.

ΥΥΥΥΥ **The Cigar 2010** I sincerely doubt that Robert Hill-Smith's decision to use corks
(especially pockmarked examples as here) will win him many friends in Australia
at this price point. All of which is a pity, because this Cabernet Sauvignon has
vibrant cassis/mulberry/redcurrant fruit on its well-balanced, medium-bodied
palate. 13.5% alc. **Rating** 92 **To** 2020 $28

Yangarra Estate Vineyard ★★★★★

809 McLaren Flat Road, Kangarilla SA 5171 **Region** McLaren Vale
T (08) 8383 7459 **www.**yangarra.com **Open** 7 days 10–5
Winemaker Peter Fraser, Charlie Seppelt, Shelley Thompson **Est.** 2000 **Dozens** 15 000
Vyds 89.3ha
This is the Australian operation of Kendall-Jackson, one of the leading premium wine
producers in California. In 2000 Kendall-Jackson acquired the 172ha Eringa Park vineyard
from Normans Wines (the oldest vines dated back to 1923). The renamed Yangarra Estate
Vineyard is the estate base for the operation, which built a state-of-the-art premium red wine
facility in '10, and is moving to certified organic status with its vineyards. In '12 it purchased
the historic Clarendon Vineyard from the estate of the late Alan Hickinbotham – it had been
on the market for $10 million, but the actual price paid was not disclosed. Whatever it may
have been, it represents a major endorsement of the prospects for top-quality Australian wines.
Exports to the UK, the US and other major markets.

ΥΥΥΥΥ **Small Pot Whole Bunch McLaren Vale Shiraz 2010** Strong purple-crimson;
it's a technique more common in cool regions but it works very well here, with
regional bitter chocolate and savoury black fruit flavours lifted by the spicy notes
and extra texture from the use of whole bunches. Sophisticated winemaking.
Screwcap. 14% alc. **Rating** 95 **To** 2030 $45
Ironheart McLaren Vale Shiraz 2010 Deep colour, bright; an uncompromising
bouquet of essency red and dark fruits, with licorice and tar also on display; the
palate is finely poised as the fresh acidity plays the perfect foil to the ample and
chewy medium-grained tannins that simply roll around the mouth, and provide a
long and distinguished finish. Screwcap. 14.5% alc. **Rating** 94 **To** 2025 $100 BE

✪ **McLaren Vale Shiraz 2010** Berry sorting, 12% whole bunches, pre-fermentation
cold soak and some carbonic maceration, wild yeast-fermented, and kept on lees in
French oak (20% new) for over 12 months has produced the best Shiraz yet from
Yangarra (other than Small Pot). Medium- to full-bodied, it has multiple layers of
juicy black fruits, plus touches of licorice and dark chocolate supported by ripe
tannins on the long finish. Screwcap. 14.5% alc. **Rating** 94 **To** 2025 $25
Old Vine McLaren Vale Grenache 2011 Light but bright and clear crimson-
purple; some estate-owned vineyards were able to rise above the challenges of the
vintage, and the winemakers sorted the grapes berry by berry in the winery to
achieve results such as this – a highly aromatic and pure red-berried wine, with
supple mouthfeel and no hint of green fruit. Screwcap. 13.5% alc. **Rating** 94
To 2018 $32

High Sands Grenache 2010 Deeply coloured, bright purple hue; the bouquet reveals black fruits, prune, mocha and licorice; the palate is densely packed with tannins and ironstone minerality; this is about as muscular a rendition of grenache as can be achieved. Screwcap. 14.5% alc. **Rating** 94 **To** 2022 $100 BE

Grenache Shiraz Mourvedre 2011 Bright purple hue; an intoxicating and fragrant bouquet of spicy red fruits, earth tones and Provençale garrigue; the medium-bodied palate is juicy, meticulous, energetic and poised, offering harmony of all parts; concludes with a long and expansive finish. Screwcap. 14% alc. **Rating** 94 **To** 2022 $28 BE

 McLaren Vale Viognier 2011 Rating 92 **To** 2014 $25

Yarra Burn ★★★★☆

10 Beenak Road, Hoddles Creek, Vic 3139 **Region** Yarra Valley
T 1800 088 711 **www**.yarraburn.com.au **Open** Not
Winemaker Ed Carr **Est.** 1975 **Dozens** NFP **Vyds** 88ha
At least in terms of name, this is the focal point of Accolade's Yarra Valley operations. However, the winery has effectively been closed, and the wines are now made elsewhere. The 88ha of Upper Yarra vineyard remain. The lack of interest in the brand and its quality is as sad as it is obvious. Exports to the US, Indonesia, Malaysia, Pacific Islands, China and Japan.

 Pinot Noir Chardonnay Rose 2006 While pinot noir (74.4%) and chardonnay (23.8%) are the drivers, it also contains pinot meunier (1.5%) and petit verdot (0.3%). Bright salmon-pink; ironically, this Rose has dispensed with the pinot meunier in the '07 Pinot Noir Chardonnay Pinot Meunier; what is more, it is more savoury and focused, with rosehip flavours and a textured palate finishing with fine tannins (yes, they do exist in sparkling wines). Cork. 12.5% alc. **Rating** 94 **To** 2015 $26

Pinot Noir Chardonnay Pinot Meunier 2007 A 46.6/44.8/8.6% blend sourced from the Yarra Valley. First tasted in Feb '10, this wine disgorged 27 months later, in May '12. Pale straw-green, good mousse; has considerable elegance, finesse and length. The one query is the slightly elevated dosage, although I can't work out the rationale. Regardless, great value. Cork. 12.5% alc. **Rating** 93 **To** 2016 $26

Yarra Yarra ★★★★★

239 Hunts Lane, Steels Creek, Vic 3775 **Region** Yarra Valley
T (03) 5965 2380 **www**.yarrayarravineyard.com.au **Open** By appt
Winemaker Ian Maclean **Est.** 1979 **Dozens** NFP **Vyds** 9.3ha
Despite its small production, the wines of Yarra Yarra have found their way into a veritable who's who of Melbourne's best restaurants, encouraging Ian Maclean to increase the estate plantings from 2ha to over 7ha in 1996 and '97. Demand for the beautifully crafted wines continued to exceed supply, so the Macleans planted yet more vines and increased winery capacity. All this seemed to go up in flames as the terrible 2009 Black Saturday bushfires consumed the winery, irreplaceable museum stock from '83 to 2000, the then yet-to-be-bottled '08 Syrah and '06 and '08 Sauvignon Blanc Semillon (the '07 vintage had been destroyed by frost), and scorched or burnt 50% of the estate vineyards. Friends rallied to the cause, and Ian has embarked on the long job of repairing/replacing the vineyard trellis system, methodically replanting the half of the vineyard destroyed by fire and introducing the use of organic/biodynamic sprays. The new winery was finished at the end of April '10, too late for the vintage, which was made in one of the farm buildings not destroyed. When friends asked why he should do all this, having turned 65, his answer was simple: 'My greatest wines have yet to be made.' No wines received for the *2014 Wine Companion*, but a five-star rating has been maintained. Exports to Singapore, Malaysia, Taiwan and Hong Kong.

Yarra Yering   ★★★★★

Briarty Road, Coldstream, Vic 3770 **Region** Yarra Valley
T (03) 5964 9267 **www**.yarrayering.com **Open** 7 days 10–5
Winemaker Paul Bridgeman **Est.** 1969 **Dozens** 4000 **Vyds** 26.37ha

In September 2008, founder Bailey Carrodus died, and in April '09 Yarra Yering was on the market. It was Bailey Carrodus' clear wish and expectation that any purchaser would continue to manage the vineyard and winery, and hence the wine style, in much the same way as he had done for the previous 40 years. Its acquisition in June '09 by a small group of investment bankers seems certain to fulfil that wish. The low-yielding, unirrigated vineyards have always produced wines of extraordinary depth and intensity, and there is every reason to suppose that there will be no change in the years ahead. Dry Red No. 1 is a cabernet blend; Dry Red No. 2 is a shiraz blend; Dry Red No. 3 is a blend of touriga, tinta cao, tinta amarela, roriz and sousao; Pinot Noir and Chardonnay are not hidden behind delphic numbers; Underhill Shiraz is from an adjacent vineyard purchased by Yarra Yering over a decade ago; and Potsorts is an extraordinary vintage port style made from the same varieties as Dry Red No. 3. Achieved the near impossible in 2011. Exports to the UK, the US, Singapore and Hong Kong.

ŸŸŸŸŸ **Dry Red No. 2 2011** A blend of shiraz, mataro, viognier and marsanne, shiraz the major player. The hue is excellent, the bouquet is fragrant, and the medium-bodied palate positively sings; the red fruits are wreathed in a web of fine spices, mainly fruit-derived, but in part from French oak. A lovely, unforced wine. Drink now or in 20 years. Cork. 13% alc. **Rating** 96 **To** 2031 $89

Dry Red No. 1 2011 Cabernet sauvignon leads the blend, with smaller amounts of merlot, malbec and petit verdot. The hue is good, the fragrant, berry-filled bouquet faithfully reflected in the vibrant, medium-bodied palate, where fruit, oak and tannins coalesce into a triumphantly harmonious whole. Cork. 13.5% alc. **Rating** 96 **To** 2031 $89

Dry Red No. 1 2005 Mature re-release. Considerable colour development, but there is no sign of premature ageing on the medium-bodied palate, with its harmonious display of redcurrant and cassis fruit framed by cedary French oak. Cork. 13% alc. **Rating** 95 **To** 2020 $95

Dry Red No. 3 2011 The dry red version of Potsorts; a marvellously complex, savoury blend of dark/black fruits of every description, licorice, tar and pepper included for good measure, the tannins measured, oak already fully digested. Cork. 14% alc. **Rating** 95 **To** 2041 $85

Dry Red No. 3 2010 Good crimson-purple colour introduces a medium-bodied wine with a distinctive array of lively red fruits and exotic spices; the tannins and oak are neatly balanced and integrated. Cork. 13.5% alc. **Rating** 95 **To** 2025 $81

Chardonnay 2011 Rating 94 **To** 2016 $84
Pinot Noir 2011 Rating 94 **To** 2017 $84
Underhill Shiraz 2011 Rating 94 **To** 2021 $84
Agincourt Cabernet Malbec 2011 Rating 94 **To** 2026 $84

ŸŸŸŸ♀ **Barbiolo 2011 Rating** 93 **To** 2020 $85

Yarrabank   ★★★★★

38 Melba Highway, Yarra Glen, Vic 3775 **Region** Yarra Valley
T (03) 9730 0100 **www**.yering.com **Open** 7 days 10–5
Winemaker Michel Parisot, Willy Lunn, Darren Rathbone **Est.** 1993 **Dozens** 5000
Vyds 4ha

Yarrabank is a highly successful joint venture between the French Champagne house Devaux and Yering Station, established in 1993. Until '97 the Yarrabank Cuvee Brut was made under Claude Thibaut's direction at Domaine Chandon, but thereafter the entire operation has been conducted at Yarrabank. There are 4ha of dedicated 'estate' vineyards at Yering Station (planted to pinot noir and chardonnay); the balance of the intake comes from other growers in the Yarra Valley and southern Vic. Wine quality has consistently been outstanding, frequently with an unmatched finesse and delicacy. In '12 the Rathbone Group wine interests were placed on the market for sale either as a group or individually. Exports to all major markets.

♟♟♟♟♟ **Late Disgorged 2004** Vibrant straw-gold; still wonderfully youthful after more than 7 years on lees, citrus and nectarine flavours more powerful and focused than the bready/yeast characters that have slowly built during the time on lees, the length of the palate most impressive. It has gained even more vibrancy over the past 6 months, since first tasted; counterintuitive, perhaps, but that's how I see it. Cork. 12.5% alc. **Rating** 96 **To** 2015 $55

Cuvee 2008 Bright colour, and good mousse; the palate is rich and complex, with bready/brioche characters running through the fruit flavours of white peach and nectarine, amplified by 4 years on lees; the finish is as substantial as it is long, the dosage carefully controlled. Cork. 13% alc. **Rating** 95 **To** 2014 $38

♟♟♟♟♟ **Cuvee 2009 Rating** 93 **To** 2013 $38

YarraLoch   ★★★★★

Studio 308, 15–87 Gladstone Street, South Melbourne, Vic 3205 **Region** Yarra Valley
T (03) 9696 1604 **www.**yarraloch.com.au **Open** By appt
Winemaker David Bicknell **Est.** 1998 **Dozens** 3000 **Vyds** 12ha
This is the ambitious project of successful investment banker Stephen Wood. He has taken the best possible advice, and has not hesitated to provide appropriate financial resources to a venture that has no exact parallel in the Yarra Valley or anywhere else in Australia. Twelve hectares of vineyards may not seem so unusual, but in fact he has assembled three entirely different sites, 70km apart, each matched to the needs of the variety/varieties planted on that site. Pinot noir (4.4ha) is planted on the Steep Hill Vineyard, with a northeast orientation, and a shaley rock and ironstone soil. Cabernet sauvignon (4ha) has been planted at Kangaroo Ground, with a dry, steep northwest-facing site and abundant sun exposure in the warmest part of the day, ensuring full ripeness. Just over 3.5ha of merlot, shiraz, chardonnay and viognier are planted at the Upper Plenty Vineyard, 50km from Kangaroo Ground. This has an average temperature 2°C cooler and a ripening period 2–3 weeks later than the warmest parts of the Yarra Valley. Add skilled winemaking and some sophisticated (and beautiful) packaging, and you have a 5-star recipe for success. Exports to Hong Kong, Malaysia and China.

♟♟♟♟♟ **Single Vineyard Chardonnay 2011** Bright straw-green; a wine that sings the praises of the '11 vintage for Yarra chardonnay; marries intensity with finesse, precision with flavour, the last given by white peach, nectarine and grapefruit flavours undimmed by French oak, and driving the brilliantly long finish. Hasn't lost one iota of its freshness. Screwcap. 12.5% alc. **Rating** 96 **To** 2018 $32

Single Vineyard Chardonnay 2012 An elegant wine in all respects, and with a particular, creamy mouthfeel from its fruit/oak-engendered flavour profile, well described by YarraLoch as lemon/lemon curd. Screwcap. 12.5% alc. **Rating** 94 **To** 2019 $32

Stephanie's Dream Shiraz 2007 Has retained very good colour; fruit and oak spice are on display throughout, but do not threaten the plum and blackberry fruit; the medium-bodied palate is supple and smooth, the tannins and oak simply supporting that which has gone before. Diam. 14.5% alc. **Rating** 94 **To** 2025 $40

♟♟♟♟♟ **Stephanie's Dream Pinot Noir 2011 Rating** 91 **To** 2016 $59
Single Vineyard Arneis 2012 Rating 90 **To** 2015 $25

Yarrambat Estate

45 Laurie Street, Yarrambat, Vic 3091 (postal) **Region** Yarra Valley
T (03) 9717 3710 **www.**yarrambatestate.com.au **Open** By appt
Winemaker John Ellis (Contract) **Est.** 1995 **Dozens** 1500 **Vyds** 2.6ha
Ivan McQuilkin has chardonnay, pinot noir, cabernet sauvignon and merlot in his vineyard in the northwestern corner of the Yarra Valley, not far from the Plenty River. It is very much an alternative occupation for Ivan, whose principal activity is as an international taxation consultant to expatriate employees. While the decision to make wine was at least in part triggered by falling grape prices, hindsight proves it to have been a good one, because some of the wines are not only good, but offer exceptional value for money. Exports to Singapore and China.

ŢŢŢŢŢ **Cabernet Merlot 2010** Good crimson-purple hue, although not deep; the
✪   fragrant bouquet leads into an intensely flavoured and structured palate, with
       red fruits leading the charge, but backed up by good tannin and oak support.
       Screwcap. 13.7% alc. **Rating** 94 **To** 2025 $18

ŢŢŢŢŢ **Cabernet Merlot 2009** Excellent hue; here the fruit is principally blackcurrant,
✪   rather than the redcurrant of the '10; seemingly avoided the smoke taint issues of
       the vintage, and has a long life ahead. Screwcap. 13% alc. **Rating** 93 **To** 2019 $18
✪   **Pinot Noir 2011** Light, clear crimson-purple; the fragrant bouquet of cherry
       (dominant) and plum is followed by a most attractive palate with good structure,
       length and balance; no apology for the vintage is needed. Screwcap. 13.1% alc.
       Rating 92 **To** 2017 $18

ŢŢŢŢ   **Chardonnay 2011** The striking label brings together the Yarra Valley and its
✪   Aboriginal inhabitants; the estate-grown grapes are transported to Hanging Rock
       where John Ellis makes the wine; he does so with sensitivity and style. The flavours
       are not intense, but are so well balanced you would never think the alcohol is so
       low. Screwcap. 12.3% alc. **Rating** 89 **To** 2015 $16

Yarran Wines   ★★★★☆

178 Myall Park Road, Yenda, NSW 2681 **Region** Riverina
T (02) 6968 1125 **www**.yarranwines.com.au **Open** Mon–Sat 10–5
Winemaker Sam Brewer **Est.** 2000 **Dozens** 6000 **Vyds** 30ha
Lorraine Brewer (and late husband John) have been grapegrowers for over 30 years, and when
son Sam went to CSU to complete a degree in wine science, they celebrated his graduation
by crushing 1 tonne of shiraz, fermenting the grapes in a milk vat. The majority of the grapes
from the estate plantings are sold, but each year a little more has been made under the Yarran
banner; along the way a winery with a crush capacity of 150 tonnes has been built. Sam
worked for Southcorp and De Bortoli in Australia, and overseas (in the US and China), but
after 10 years decided, in 2009, to take the plunge and concentrate on the family winery,
together with his parents. The majority of the grapes come from the family vineyard, but some
parcels are sourced from growers, including Lake Cooper Estate in the Heathcote region. It is
intended that the portfolio of regions will be gradually increased, and Sam has demonstrated
his ability to make silk purses out of sow's ears, and sell them for the latter. Exports to China.

ŢŢŢŢŢ **Leopardwood Limited Release Heathcote Shiraz 2010** Full, clear red-
✪   purple; the highly expressive bouquet of ripe plum, berry and spice flows into
       a textured medium-bodied palate, where rounded tannins and oak provide a
       framework for the luscious, but not the least jammy, fruit. Has impeccable balance,
       and is as fresh as the day it was first tasted, 9 months ago. Screwcap. 14% alc.
       Rating 94 **To** 2025 $18

ŢŢŢŢŢ **Leopardwood Limited Release Heathcote Shiraz 2011** Medium purple-
✪   red; a pre-ferment cold soak, then a warm primary fermentation, and barrel to
       barrel racking have all been aimed to maximise and protect the varietal fruit
       expression. The outcome is far, far better than for many Heathcote reds at double
       the price; the flavours are of ripe, black fruits and spices, and the tannins provide
       excellent structure. Screwcap. 14% alc. **Rating** 93 **To** 2026 $19
✪   **Leopardwood Limited Release Yenda Petit Verdot 2011** Petit verdot
       carries the flag of its deep colour regardless of vintage; the colour is very good, and
       the tannin structure remarkable, distinctly European in its feel. As ever, excellent
       value. Screwcap. 14% alc. **Rating** 93 **To** 2017 $19
✪   **Sauvignon Blanc Semillon 2012** Bright straw-green; steps must have been
       taken to keep the yield below normal Riverina levels, for there is an abundance of
       sweet tropical and citrus flavours, the balance excellent, the finish fresh and clear.
       Screwcap. 11.5% alc. **Rating** 91 **To** 2013 $12
✪   **Chardonnay 2012** Pale quartz-green; fresh and flavourful, with stone fruit and
       citrus to the fore, and a hint of subliminal French oak on the finish. The usual
       exceptional value from Yarran. Screwcap. 12.5% alc. **Rating** 90 **To** 2014 $12

ŶŶŶŶ Pinot Grigio 2012 Hand-picked at night and whole bunch-pressed, a very
✪ expensive pathway for a wine at this price, but has paid a handsome dividend, with
a floral bouquet and a tropical edge to the pear of the palate; the mouthfeel and
balance are also impressive. Screwcap. 12% alc. **Rating** 89 **To** 2013 $12

✪ Cabernet Sauvignon 2011 Light, bright crimson-purple; a typical tour de force
of winemaking by Sam Brewer; open fermentation and a carefully controlled dose
of vanillin oak give the wine an extra dimension and – most particularly – length.
Screwcap. 13.5% alc. **Rating** 89 **To** 2014 $12

✪ Moscato NV Light straw-green; has above-average intensity of overall flavour and
good balance; particularly good value. Screwcap. 8.5% alc. **Rating** 88 **To** 2013 $13

Yarrawood Estate

1275 Melba Highway, Yarra Glen, Vic 3775 **Region** Yarra Valley
T (03) 9730 2003 **www**.yarrawood.com.au **Open** Mon–Fri 10–5, w'ends 8–5
Winemaker Contract **Est.** 1996 **Dozens** 15000 **Vyds** 40.6ha
Yarrawood Estate has pinot noir (10.6ha), cabernet sauvignon (7.9ha), chardonnay (7.2ha),
merlot (5.3ha), shiraz (4.5ha) and lesser amounts of sauvignon blanc, riesling and verdelho. The
Tall Tales wines are contract-made from the estate-grown grapes. The cellar door and café are
located on the Melba Highway, 3km north of Yarra Glen, overlooking the vineyard. Exports
to Papua New Guinea, Japan, Singapore and China.

ŶŶŶŶŶ Tall Tales Sauvignon Blanc 2012 An attractive fruit-driven Sauvignon Blanc,
✪ the full array of tropical fruits on display: kiwifruit, passionfruit, lychee and guava,
tempered by citrus-accented acidity on the finish. Great value. Screwcap. 13% alc.
Rating 92 **To** 2014 $19

✪ Yarra Valley Chardonnay 2011 Light green-yellow; has focus and intensity
to its mix of grapefruit, white peach and nectarine fruit; neatly chiselled grainy
acidity is as important as the barrel-ferment oak in giving the wine texture and
shape. Good value. Screwcap. 13% alc. **Rating** 91 **To** 2017 $18

✪ Yarra Valley Pinot Noir 2012 Bright purple-crimson; the perfumed bouquet
leads into an elegant palate, with cherry and plum firmly in the driver's seat; as yet
it is firm and one-dimensional, but will gain complexity with a few more years
in bottle, the only caveat the level of acidity. Good value even with that caveat.
Screwcap. 13% alc. **Rating** 91 **To** 2017 $18

Tall Tales Cabernet Sauvignon 2010 Good red-purple; a light- to medium-
bodied Cabernet, with good structure and mouthfeel to the blackcurrant and
redcurrant fruit; the tannins are fine, and the oak well integrated. Has capitalised
on the good vintage. Screwcap. 14% alc. **Rating** 90 **To** 2019 $24

Yarrh Wines

440 Greenwood Road, Murrumbateman, NSW 2582 **Region** Canberra District
T (02) 6227 1474 **www**.yarrhwines.com.au **Open** Thurs–Mon & public hols 11–5
Winemaker Fiona Wholohan **Est.** 1997 **Dozens** 3000 **Vyds** 6ha
It is probably best to quickly say that Yarrh is Aboriginal for 'running water', and is neither
onomatopoeic nor letters taken from the partners' names, the partners being Fiona Wholohan,
Neil McGregor and Peta and Christopher Mackenzie Davey. The vineyard was planted in
three stages between 1997 and 2000, and there are now cabernet sauvignon, shiraz, sauvignon
blanc, riesling, pinot noir and sangiovese (in descending order). All of the wines are estate-
grown, and competently made by Fiona.

ŶŶŶŶŶ Canberra District Riesling 2011 Still quartz-white; classic Canberra District
✪ riesling, its low alcohol and early picking not in any way reducing its varietal
expression on either the bouquet or palate; the perfumed bouquet leads into
brilliantly focused lime, lemon and crystalline acidity on the palate and aftertaste.
Screwcap. 11.5% alc. **Rating** 94 **To** 2021 $25

ŶŶŶŶŶ Canberra District Shiraz 2011 **Rating** 90 **To** 2016 $25

Yass Valley Wines   ★★★☆

5 Crisps Lane, Murrumbateman, NSW 2582 **Region** Canberra District
T (02) 6227 5592 **www**.yassvalleywines.com.au **Open** Wed–Sun & public hols 10–5,
or by appt
Winemaker Declan Brown **Est.** 1978 **Dozens** 700 **Vyds** 2.87ha
Anne Hillier and late husband Michael (Mick) Withers purchased Yass Valley Wines in 1991,
and subsequently rehabilitated the then rundown vineyards and extended the plantings
(merlot, shiraz, barbera, chardonnay, verdelho, gewurztraminer and semillon). Declan Brown
was employed to make the wines in 2012, and it is these wines (and a small quantity previously
made by Mick) that are being sold.

ŶŶŶŶŶ **Riesling 2011** Pale quartz-green; the flowery bouquet leads into early-picked
flavours on the citrussy palate, where some residual sugar plays rounders with
acidity; brave winemaking. Screwcap. 10.5% alc. **Rating** 90 **To** 2016 $25

Yaxley Estate

31 Dransfield Road, Copping, Tas 7174 **Region** Southern Tasmania
T (03) 6253 5222 **www**.yaxleyestate.com **Open** At Copping Museum, Arthur Highway
Winemaker Frogmore Creek, Kilbowie Wines (Peter Shields) **Est.** 1991 **Dozens** 100
Vyds 1.5ha
While Yaxley Estate was established back in 1991, it was not until '98 that it offered each of
the four wines from its vineyard plantings. Once again, it is the small batch-handling skills (and
patience) of Frogmore Creek that have made the venture possible. The vineyard (pinot gris,
sauvignon blanc, pinot noir and chardonnay) was certified organic in 2010. In the '13 bushfires
in Tasmania, Yaxley was the only vineyard to be destroyed by fire, a cruel fate. Owner John
Yaxley, himself a country firefighter, had the choice of using the vineyard sprinkler system to
save the vineyard or a shed that housed $60000 worth of wine. He chose the latter, but also
lost the grand Pentagon-shaped hilltop house.

ŶŶŶŶŶ **Pinot Gris 2012** Pale straw-green; a crisp and crunchy, organically grown,
gris with as much green apple as pear; I don't know about the gris (as opposed
to grigio) name, but it's what is in the glass that matters. Screwcap. 13.8% alc.
Rating 92 **To** 2014 $35

Yelland & Papps

Lot 501 Nuraip Road, Nuriootpa, SA 5355 **Region** Barossa Valley
T (08) 8562 3510 **www**.yellandandpapps.com **Open** Mon, Wed–Sat 10–4, Tues & Sun
by appt
Winemaker Michael Papps **Est.** 2005 **Dozens** 3000 **Vyds** 1ha
Michael and Susan Papps (née Yelland) set up this venture after their marriage in 2005. Susan
decided she did not want to give up her surname entirely, and thus has been able to keep
her family name in the business. Michael has the technical background, having lived in the
Barossa Valley for more than 20 years, working at local wineries, bottling facilities and wine
technology businesses. Susan, who grew up on the Yorke Peninsula, headed to New York for a
year, working and studying at the Windows of the World Wine School. The quantity of wine
made is limited by the scarcity of the high-quality grapes they manage to secure from the
Greenock area for their wines.

ŶŶŶŶŶ **Divine Barossa Valley Shiraz 2010** Full purple-crimson; the bouquet exudes
blackberry, black cherry and plum fruit, the flavours of the intense, medium- to
full-bodied palate precisely tracking those characters, adding some new oak and
ripe tannins. An object lesson in achieving intense Shiraz of high quality at a
controlled alcohol level. Screwcap. 14% alc. **Rating** 96 **To** 2040 $75
Second Take Shiraz 2012 The deeply-fruited bouquet leads into an
immaculately balanced and structured medium- to full-bodied palate, with plum,
black cherry and blackberry to the fore, quality oak and fine-grained tannins
bringing up the finish. Screwcap. 13.5% alc. **Rating** 95 **To** 2027 $40

Divine Barossa Valley Grenache 2010 Yelland & Papps clearly have access to some exceptional grapes, and then protect the fruit flavour they provide, here bright and juicy red cherry and satsuma plum, oak and tannins precisely calibrated and balanced. Delicious. Screwcap. 14.5% alc. **Rating** 95 **To** 2020 $75

☻ **Delight Barossa Valley Vermentino 2012** Pale straw; a highly perfumed, striking bouquet leads into a no less emphatic palate, with tangy, mouth-watering lemon and mandarin flavours to the fore, the finish clean, crisp and breezy. Totally delicious summer wine. Screwcap. 12% alc. **Rating** 94 **To** 2014 $20

Devote Greenock Barossa Valley Shiraz 2011 Medium purple-red; the medium-bodied palate offers a juicy mix of red and black fruits, a sheen of new oak, and fine, spicy tannins. Has not been fed steroids. Screwcap. 13.5% alc. **Rating** 94 **To** 2021 $35

Second Take Grenache 2012 Excellent colour; rich raspberry, red cherry and damson plum fruit aromas and flavours; impressive handling of grenache, particularly in the Barossa Valley context. Screwcap. 14% alc. **Rating** 94 **To** 2020 $40

 Devote Barossa Valley Shiraz Roussanne 2011 Rating 93 To 2020 $35
Devote Barossa Valley Roussanne 2012 Rating 90 To 2025 $35

Yellowglen   ★★★★☆

The Atrium, 58 Queensbridge Street, Southbank, Vic 3006 **Region** South Eastern Australia **T** 1300 651 650 **www.**yellowglen.com **Open** Not
Winemaker Charles Hargrave, Trina Smith **Est.** 1971 **Dozens** NFP
Yellowglen is not only the leading producer of sparkling wine in the TWE group, but the largest producer of sparkling wine in Australia. In 2012 it announced a major restructuring of its product range, adding single vineyard traditional method wines under the Exceptional Vintage XV label. Moreover, Trina Smith is a highly accomplished winemaker with much of the day to day (and, of course, vintage) responsibilities for the wines. Exports to the UK, the US and NZ.

Exceptional Vintage XV Piccadilly 2002 Pale, bright straw-gold; the complex bouquet with notes of bread, cashew and citrus leads into an equally complex palate. Here intense citrus and green apple fruit has a subtext of cashew, the overall outcome a wine of singular purity and length. Gold medal National Wine Show '12. Cork. 12% alc. **Rating** 95 **To** 2015 $50

Exceptional Vintage XV Piccadilly 2004 Rating 93 To 2017 $50
Vintage Perle Rose 2006 Rating 93 To 2016 $30

Yeowarra Hill   ★★★★

152 Drapers Road, Colac, Vic 3250 **Region** Geelong
T (03) 5232 1507 **www.**yeowarrahill.com.au **Open** By appt
Winemaker Dinny Goonan **Est.** 1998 **Dozens** 140 **Vyds** 1ha
Bronwyn and Keith Thomas planted pinot noir (two-thirds) and chardonnay over 1998 and '99. They say the early vintages were consumed by family and friends, and as the vines have gained maturity and moved to full-cropping, part of the production has been sold to other wineries in the region. The business is part of a function venue, which has expansive views of Colac, with the vineyard in the foreground.

Limited Release Pinot Noir 2012 Has excellent colour, and both the bouquet
☻ and palate are charged with red and black cherry fruit wreathed with a garland of spice; in pinot terms is medium- to full-bodied, but not overworked, and will repay 5+ years in the cellar. Excellent value. Screwcap. 13.5% alc. **Rating** 93 **To** 2022 $20

Yering Station

★★★★★

38 Melba Highway, Yarra Glen, Vic 3775 **Region** Yarra Valley
T (03) 9730 0100 **www**.yering.com **Open** 7 days 10–5
Winemaker Willy Lunn, Darren Rathbone **Est.** 1988 **Dozens** 60 000 **Vyds** 112ha

The historic Yering Station (or at least the portion of the property on which the cellar door sales and vineyard are established) was purchased by the Rathbone family in 1996 and is also the site of the Yarrabank joint venture with French Champagne house Devaux (see separate entry). A spectacular and very large winery was built, immediately becoming, one of the focal points of the Yarra Valley, particularly as the historic Chateau Yering, where luxury accommodation and fine dining are available, is next door. Yering Station's own restaurant is open every day for lunch, providing the best lunchtime cuisine in the Valley. William (Willy) Lunn, a graduate of Adelaide University has more than 24 years' cool-climate winemaking experience around the world, including at Petaluma, Shaw + Smith and Argyle Winery (Oregon). Exports to all major markets.

🍷🍷🍷🍷🍷 **Reserve Yarra Valley Shiraz Viognier 2010** Light, bright hue; the bouquet is highly fragrant, clearly a function of the viognier; the medium-bodied palate is full to the brim with vibrant black and red cherry fruit, leaving just enough space for the French oak and fine-grained tannins to add their contribution. Will be very long-lived. Screwcap. 14.5% alc. **Rating** 96 **To** 2030 $90

Yarra Valley Cabernet Sauvignon 2010 Strong but clear purple-crimson; a distinguished Cabernet with deep and satisfying blackcurrant/cassis fruit aromas and flavours; the medium- to full-bodied palate has exemplary balance and structure, both ripe tannins and quality oak adding complexity. A minimum 20-year life ahead. Satisfying elegance. Screwcap. 14% alc. **Rating** 96 **To** 2030 $38

Yarra Valley Chardonnay 2011 Barrel-fermented and matured in a mix of new and used French oak for 11 months. It has excellent balance, and the nectarine/white peach fruit intensifies on the back-palate and long finish. Screwcap. 12% alc. **Rating** 95 **To** 2019 $38

Reserve Yarra Valley Pinot Noir 2010 Light crimson; the fragrant, red berry aromas lead into an intense, elegant and very long palate, juicy red berry fruit interwoven with satin tannins. A seriously lovely Pinot that has benefited greatly from the extra 12 months since first tasted. Screwcap. 13.8% alc. **Rating** 95 **To** 2018 $90

Reserve Yarra Valley Chardonnay 2012 Pale straw-green; an ultimate exercise in finesse and delicacy; everything is in balance, and the future of the wine is assured; the only question is whether there is enough substance to the fruit to take it to the highest level. Screwcap. 12.5% alc. **Rating** 94 **To** 2020 $90

Yarra Valley Shiraz Viognier 2011 Co-fermented with viognier and matured in a mix of new and used French barriques, the colour bright and clear; it is an unqualified success, with vibrant red cherry and plum fruit, fine tannins and integrated oak. Screwcap. 14% alc. **Rating** 94 **To** 2026 $38

🍷🍷🍷🍷🍷 **Yarra Valley Pinot Noir 2011 Rating** 91 **To** 2016 $38
✪ **Little Yering Cabernet Shiraz 2010** The purple-crimson colour is good, and the two varieties both contribute, cabernet the tannin structure, shiraz the plum and blackberry fruit of the mid-palate. Will repay medium-term cellaring. Screwcap. 14.5% alc. **Rating** 91 **To** 2020 $18

✪ **Little Yering Yarra Valley Chardonnay 2012** Very pale straw-green; attractive Yarra Valley Chardonnay aromas and flavours with white peach and melon to the fore, plus just a hint of oak; overall, well balanced. Screwcap. 13% alc. **Rating** 90 **To** 2016 $18

Village Yarra Valley Chardonnay 2011 Rating 90 **To** 2016 $24
Village Yarra Valley Marsanne Viognier 2011 Rating 90 **To** 2016 $24
Village Yarra Valley Pinot Noir 2011 Rating 90 **To** 2016 $24

🍷🍷🍷🍷 **Little Yering Yarra Valley Pinot Noir 2012** Good purple-crimson; matured
✪ in used French oak for 12 months; an honest, what you see is what you get style, with cherry/raspberry fruit, tannins (plenty) and oak. Good value; may surprise with a few years in bottle. Screwcap. 13.5% alc. **Rating** 89 **To** 2016 $18

Yeringberg

Maroondah Highway, Coldstream, Vic 3770 **Region** Yarra Valley
T (03) 9739 1453 **www.**yeringberg.com **Open** By appt
Winemaker Guill and Sandra de Pury **Est.** 1863 **Dozens** 1500 **Vyds** 2.65ha
Guill de Pury and daughter Sandra, with Guill's wife Katherine in the background, make wines for the new millennium from the low-yielding vines re-established in the heart of what was one of the most famous (and infinitely larger) vineyards of the 19th century. In the riper years, the red wines have a velvety generosity of flavour rarely encountered, yet never lose varietal character, while the long-lived Marsanne Roussanne takes students of history back to Yeringberg's fame in the 19th century. Exports to the US, Switzerland, Japan, Hong Kong and China.

♀♀♀♀♀ **Yarra Valley Shiraz 2010** Bright purple-red hue; elegance is the key word for this medium-bodied wine, elegance expressed by its fusion of red and black fruits, licorice, multi-spice, and superbly silky but continuous tannins. Diam. 14% alc. **Rating** 97 **To** 2025 $60
Yarra Valley Pinot Noir 2010 Clear, bright red-purple; a seriously good pinot noir, with detail and balance immediately obvious; gently savoury/foresty tannins and integrated French oak frame the dark cherry fruit at the heart of the wine. Diam. 13.5% alc. **Rating** 96 **To** 2019 $75
Yeringberg 2010 The full Bordeaux blend of cabernet sauvignon, cabernet franc, merlot, malbec and petit verdot; a quite lovely display of black and redcurrant fruit supported by silky tannins and quality oak; it has achieved all this with only 13% alc., and the wine will live for decades. Diam. **Rating** 96 **To** 2050 $75
Yarra Valley Viognier 2011 Bright, light straw-green; very skilled winemaking – and the advantages of the vineyard – have combined to invest the wine with very clear varietal flavours of apricot allied with a richly textured finish. Diam. 12.5% alc. **Rating** 94 **To** 2015 $35
Yarra Valley Marsanne Roussanne 2011 Pale straw-green; at the dawn of its life, apple peel, citrus, spice and chalky acidity all waiting quietly for their time to come out. Has a proud pedigree. Diam. 12.5% alc. **Rating** 94 **To** 2015 $50

♀♀♀♀♀ **Yarra Valley Chardonnay 2011** **Rating** 93 **To** 2021 $50

Yilgarnia

1847 Redmond West Road, Redmond, WA 6327 **Region** Denmark
T (08) 9845 3031 **www.**yilgarnia.com.au **Open** Fri–Mon, school & public hols 11–5 (closed May–Sept)
Winemaker Contract **Est.** 1997 **Dozens** 3000 **Vyds** 13ha
Melbourne-educated Peter Buxton travelled across the Nullarbor over 40 years ago and settled on a bush block of 405 acres on the Hay River, 6km north of Wilson Inlet. For the first 10 years Peter worked for the Department of Agriculture in Albany, surveying several of the early vineyards in WA, and recognised the potential of his family's property. The vineyard (chardonnay, sauvignon blanc, shiraz, cabernet sauvignon, shiraz and semillon) is planted on north-facing blocks, the geological history of which stretches back 2 billion years. Exports to Singapore.

♀♀♀♀♀ **Denmark Semillon Sauvignon Blanc 2012** Vibrant hue; the bouquet offers
✪ citrus, straw and struck match complexity; the palate is dry and chalky, with true presence and a surprisingly long and harmonious conclusion. Great value. Screwcap. 13.5% alc. **Rating** 91 **To** 2015 $17 BE

♀♀♀♀ **Denmark Sauvignon Blanc 2012** **Rating** 87 **To** 2014 $19 BE
Denmark Shiraz 2010 **Rating** 87 **To** 2018 $24 BE

Z4 Wines

PO Box 57, Campbell, ACT 2612 **Region** Canberra District
T (02) 6248 6445 **www.Z4wines.com.au Open** Not
Winemaker Canberra Winemakers **Est.** 2007 **Dozens** 1200
Z4 Wines is the venture of the very energetic Bill Mason and wife Maria. The name derives
from the Masons' four children, each having a Christian name starting with 'Z'. Bill has been
distributing wine in Canberra since 2004, with a small but distinguished list of wineries, which
he represents with considerable marketing flair. The Z4 wines are listed on many Canberra
restaurant wine lists, and are stocked by leading independent wine retailers. Exports to China.

Zarephath Wines ★★★★☆

424 Moorialup Road, East Porongurup, WA 6324 **Region** Porongurup
T (08) 9853 1152 **www.zarephathwines.com Open** Mon–Sat 10–5, Sun 12–4
Winemaker Robert Diletti **Est.** 1994 **Dozens** 1500 **Vyds** 8.9ha
The Zarephath vineyard is owned and operated by Brothers and Sisters of The Christ Circle,
a Benedictine community. They say the most outstanding feature of the location is the feeling
of peace and tranquillity that permeates the site, something I can well believe on the basis of
numerous visits to the Porongurups. Plantings include chardonnay, cabernet sauvignon, pinot
noir, shiraz, riesling and merlot.

♉♉♉♉♉ **Porongurup Chardonnay 2011** Light straw-green; a precisely detailed and
elegant wine, with equal contributions of white peach and grapefruit flavours, soft
and subtle French oak running alongside the fruit on the lingering, zesty finish.
First-class winemaking of quality fruit. Screwcap. 13% alc. **Rating** 94 **To** 2019 $30

♉♉♉♉♉ **Porongurup Pinot Noir 2011 Rating** 91 **To** 2017 $30
Porongurup Shiraz Cabernet 2011 Rating 90 **To** 2020 $25

Zema Estate ★★★★★

Riddoch Highway, Coonawarra, SA 5263 **Region** Coonawarra
T (08) 8736 3219 **www.zema.com.au Open** 7 days 9–5
Winemaker Greg Clayfield **Est.** 1982 **Dozens** 20 000 **Vyds** 61ha
Zema is one of the last outposts of hand-pruning in Coonawarra, with members of the Zema
family tending the vineyard in the heart of Coonawarra's terra rossa soil. Winemaking
practices are straightforward; if ever there was an example of great wines being made in the
vineyard, this is it. The extremely popular and equally talented former Lindemans winemaker
Greg Clayfield has joined the team, replacing long-term winemaker Tom Simons. Exports to
the UK, Vietnam, Hong Kong, Japan and Singapore.

♉♉♉♉♉ **Family Selection Coonawarra Cabernet Sauvignon 2008** Deep crimson,
bright; a dark, compelling and concentrated black fruit offering, with cassis
and violets the prominent theme; the palate is juicy on entry, laden with sweet
fruit, and then the structure comes along to draw out the long, full-bodied and
harmonious finish. Screwcap. 14.5% alc. **Rating** 95 **To** 2025 $45 BE
Saluti Coonawarra Cabernet Shiraz 2006 Strong colour; an extremely rich
55/45% blend, the fruit luscious and supple, the flavours of ripe black fruits, the
tannins ripe and the oak positive. Has a storehouse of flavour for a long life ahead.
Screwcap. 15% alc. **Rating** 95 **To** 2030 $75
Family Selection Coonawarra Shiraz 2008 Deep garnet, bright; a fresh and
vibrant spice-laden bouquet with mulberry, fine oak and black olive on display; the
palate is focused and lively with firm tannins and zesty acidity in equal proportion
to the dark fruits on offer; long and layered, with a healthy future ahead. Screwcap.
14.5% alc. **Rating** 94 **To** 2025 $45 BE
✪ **Coonawarra Cabernet Sauvignon 2010** Good hue; the elegant, medium-
bodied palate has a classic Coonawarra cabernet sense of place, with fresh and
lively plum, mulberry and cherry fruit, backed by perfectly balanced and integrated
oak and tannins. Screwcap. 14% alc. **Rating** 94 **To** 2025 $29

♉♉♉♉♉ **Coonawarra Shiraz 2009 Rating** 92 **To** 2018 $25 BE

Zig Zag Road ★★★☆

201 Zig Zag Road, Drummond, Vic 3446 **Region** Macedon Ranges
T (03) 5423 9390 **www**.zigzagwines.com.au **Open** Thurs–Mon 10–5
Winemaker Eric Bellchambers, Llew Knight **Est.** 1972 **Dozens** 500 **Vyds** 4.5ha
Zig Zag Road's dry-grown vines produce relatively low yields, and until 1996 the grapes were sold to Hanging Rock Winery. In 1996 the decision was taken to manage the property on a full-time basis, and to make the wine onsite. In 2002 Eric and Anne Bellchambers became the third owners of this vineyard, planted by Roger Aldridge in 1972. The Bellchambers have extended the plantings with riesling and merlot, supplementing the older plantings of shiraz, cabernet sauvignon and pinot noir.

🍷🍷🍷🍷 **Macedon Ranges Riesling 2012** Bright colour, with fresh-cut nectarine and lavender on the perfumed bouquet; the palate is dry and angular, finishing with a steely, ironstone and slightly bitter, yet not unpleasant, conclusion. Screwcap. 12.5% alc. **Rating** 89 **To** 2017 $22 BE

Zilzie Wines ★★★★

544 Kulkyne Way, Karadoc, Vic 3496 **Region** Murray Darling
T (03) 5025 8100 **www**.zilziewines.com **Open** Not
Winemaker Mark Zeppel **Est.** 1999 **Dozens** 200 000 **Vyds** 572ha
The Forbes family has been farming Zilzie Estate since the early 1990s; it is currently run by Ian and Ros Forbes, with sons Steven and Andrew. A diverse range of farming activities now includes grapegrowing from substantial vineyards. Having established a dominant position as a supplier of grapes to Southcorp, Zilzie formed a wine company in '99, and built a winery in 2000, expanding it in '06 to its current capacity of 35 000 tonnes. The wines consistently far exceed expectations, given their prices, that consistency driving the production volume to 200 000 dozen – this in an extremely competitive market. The business includes contract processing, winemaking and storage, and its own wines, enticingly priced. Exports to the UK, Canada, Hong Kong and China.

🍷🍷🍷🍷½ ✪ **Regional Collection Yarra Valley Chardonnay 2012** Bright straw-green; Zilzie had a stroke of fortune in being able to purchase Yarra Valley grapes of the quality evident in this stylish wine. White peach, grapefruit and minerally acidity have just a touch of creamy complexity, possibly oak-derived. Screwcap. 13% alc. **Rating** 92 **To** 2017 $18

✪ **Regional Collection Adelaide Hills Pinot Gris 2012** Quartz-green; a Pinot Gris with undoubted presence and character, with a blossom-filled bouquet and pear and honeysuckle flavours on the well-balanced palate. Part of an impressive Regional Collection series. Screwcap. 13% alc. **Rating** 90 **To** 2014 $18

✪ **Estate Shiraz 2012** Bright crimson-purple; a fresh, well-balanced Shiraz with juicy plum and spice fruit on the medium-bodied palate, and a clever infusion of oak. This comprehensively over-delivers, a joint tribute to the winemaker and the vintage. Screwcap. 14% alc. **Rating** 90 **To** 2015 $12

✪ **Regional Collection Barossa Shiraz 2011** Good hue, though relatively light; how the back label could describe the wine as full-bodied is beyond me; it is in fact light-bodied, but with elegance and harmony, its red berry fruits with a whisker of oak spice and fine tannins. Screwcap. 13% alc. **Rating** 90 **To** 2016 $18

🍷🍷🍷🍷 ✪ **Estate Cabernet Sauvignon 2012** Strong crimson-purple; this isn't a champion heavyweight fighter, rather a relatively light-bodied Cabernet that can land a few punches well above its weight, simply because it is light on its feet, with clear cassis fruit, burdened neither by oak chips nor added tannins. Just great value. Screwcap. 13.5% alc. **Rating** 89 **To** 2014 $12

✪ **Selection 23 Sauvignon Blanc 2012** Pale straw-green; despite its early picking and overall freshness, has some appealing tropical/passionfruit flavours; great bargain at this price. Screwcap. 11.5% alc. **Rating** 88 **To** 2013 $11

✪   **Selection 23 Chardonnay 2012** Pale but bright green; another impressive Selection 23 from Zilzie; there is a touch of sweetness, but there is sufficient acidity to balance the pleasing stone fruit flavours. Screwcap. 13.5% alc. **Rating** 88 To 2013 $11

✪   **Selection 23 Rose 2012** Full bright pink; the wine is made from a blend of shiraz and sangiovese; the fresh and juicy palate has a foundation of red berry fruits, with a twist of lemon zest. Very well made, and equally well priced. Screwcap. 12.5% alc. **Rating** 88 To 2013 $11

✪   **Bulloak Cabernet Merlot 2012** If this is representative of a wine surplus, consumers should say their daily prayers for its continuance. It has excellent purple-crimson colour, and is flush with cassis fruit, needing neither oak nor tannins to compete. Exceptional value. Screwcap. 14% alc. **Rating** 88 To 2014 $9
Bulloak Sauvignon Blanc 2012 Rating 87 To 2013 $9
Estate Pinot Grigio 2012 Rating 87 To 2013 $12
Selection 23 Cabernet Merlot 2012 Rating 87 To 2014 $11
Selection 23 Moscato 2012 Rating 87 To 2013 $11
Bulloak Moscato 2012 Rating 87 To 2013 $9

Zitta Wines   ★★★☆

3 Union Street, Dulwich, SA 5065 (postal) **Region** Barossa Valley
T 0419 819 414 **www**.zitta.com.au **Open** Not
Winemaker Angelo De Fazio **Est.** 2004 **Dozens** 20 000 **Vyds** 26.3ha
Owner Angelo De Fazio says that all he knows about viticulture and winemaking came from his father (and generations before him). It is partly this influence that has shaped the label and brand name: Zitta is Italian for 'quiet' and the seeming reflection of the letters of the name Zitta is in fact nothing of the kind; turn the bottle upside down, and you will see it is the word Quiet. The Zitta vineyard dates back to 1864, with a few vines remaining from that time, and a block planted with cuttings taken from those vines. Shiraz dominates the plantings (22ha), the balance made up of chardonnay, grenache and a few mourvedre vines; only a small amount of the production is retained for the Zitta label. Tradition there may be, but there is also some highly sophisticated writing and marketing in the background material and their website. Exports to China.

🍷🍷🍷🍷🍷   **Single Vineyard Greenock Barossa Valley Shiraz 2010** Having first tasted the '10 Bernado Shiraz, I approached this wine with a certain degree of fear and trepidation. However, despite its higher alcohol, it has more focus to its intense, dark fruits, the palate ending with a savoury flourish. Screwcap. 15.5% alc. **Rating** 93 To 2030 $45

🍷🍷🍷🍷   **Single Vineyard Bernardo Shiraz 2010** Rating 89 To 2025 $30

Zonte's Footstep

Main Road, McLaren Vale, SA 5171 **Region** McLaren Vale
T (08) 8556 2457 **www**.zontesfootstep.com.au **Open** Not
Winemaker Ben Riggs **Est.** 1997 **Dozens** 50 000 **Vyds** 214.72ha
Zonte's Footstep has been very successful since a group of long-standing friends, collectively with deep knowledge of every aspect of the wine business, decided it was time to do something together. Along the way, there has been some shuffling of the deck chairs, all achieved without any ill feelings from those who moved sideways or backwards. The major change has been a broadening of the regions (Langhorne Creek, McLaren Vale, the Barossa and Clare Valleys and elsewhere) from which the grapes are sourced. Even here, however, most of the vineyards supplying grapes are owned by members of the Zonte's Footstep partnership. The wine quality is as good as the prices are modest. Exports to all major markets.

ҰҰҰҰҰ **Lake Doctor Single Site Langhorne Creek Shiraz 2010** The touch of viognier (less than 5%) has added a degree of freshness and elegance to the multitude of flavours of this medium-bodied wine, the fragrance of the bouquet sending the first signals of the red and black fruits, spice and controlled oak flavours; fine, ripe tannins lengthen the finish. Screwcap. 14.5% alc. **Rating** 94 To 2020 $20

✪ **Baron Von Nemesis Single Site Barossa Valley Shiraz 2010** Deep crimson, bright; a vibrant perfume of blackberry, sage and charry oak aromas; the palate is medium-bodied, fleshy and accessible, with tightly wound tannins and lively acidity working seamlessly together on the long and even finish. Screwcap. 14.5% alc. **Rating** 94 To 2020 $22 BE

Z-Force 2010 An 85/15% blend of shiraz and petite syrah (aka durif) from McLaren Vale; a full-blooded and full-bodied wine that manages to retain some lightness of touch despite its alcohol and its varietal blend, dark chocolate coming through on the finish. Screwcap. 15% alc. **Rating** 94 To 2025 $50

ҰҰҰҰҰ **Chocolate Factory Single Site McLaren Vale Shiraz 2010** Good colour and
✪ depth; the long back label might have inspired a 21st century Shakespeare to write Much Ado About Nothing; it must have been tempting to write at least a sonnet about the depth and typicity of the plush plum, blackberry and dark chocolate wine, embroidered with oak and soft tannins. Screwcap. 14.5% alc. **Rating** 93 To 2025 $20

Lake Doctor Shiraz 2012 Rating 92 To 2018 $22 BE

✪ **Excalibur Single Site Adelaide Hills Sauvignon Blanc 2012** Lifted and fragrant with nectarine, citrus blossom and a splash of passionfruit; the palate is lively, fresh and full of juicy fruit; best consumed now Screwcap. 13% alc. **Rating** 90 To 2014 $18 BE

Scarlet Ladybird Rose 2012 Rating 90 To 2014 $18 BE

Chocolate Factory Shiraz 2011 Rating 90 To 2018 $22 BE

Canto di Lago Sangiovese Barbera 2011 Rating 90 To 2016 $20

Index

♀	**Cellar door sales**
⚍	**Food:** lunch platters to à la carte restaurants
⊢	**Accommodation:** B&B cottages to luxury vineyard apartments
⚱	**Music events:** monthly jazz in the vineyard to spectacular yearly concerts

Kangaroo Island (SA)

King Valley (Vic)

Mornington Peninsula (Vic)

The following wineries appear on www.winecompanion.com.au: